Human Trafficking and Modern Slavery Law and Practice

Third Edition

Human Trafficking and Modern Slavery Law and Practice

Third Edition

Philippa Southwell
Solicitor Advocate, Southwell & Partners

Michelle L Brewer
Judge of the Upper Tribunal

Ben Douglas-Jones KC
5 Paper Buildings Chambers and St Philips Chambers

Contributors

Paramjit Ahluwalia, *Barrister, One Pump Court Chambers*
Steven Bird, *Consultant, Hodge Jones & Allen Solicitors*
Phil Brewer, *Advisor, Human Trafficking Foundation*
Daniel Bunting, *Barrister, 2 Dr Johnson's Buildings Chambers*
Lindsay Cundall, *Solicitor, ATLEU (Anti-Trafficking and Labour Exploitation Unit)*
Emma Fitzsimons, *Barrister, Garden Court Chambers*
Silvia Nicolaou Garcia, *Solicitor, Bindmans*
Zoe Harper, *Barrister, Doughty Street Chambers*
Steve Harvey, *Independent Law Enforcement Advisor and Human Trafficking Expert*
Caroline Haughey OBE, KC, *Furnival Chambers*
His Honour Judge Andrew Johnson
Kalvir Kaur, *Solicitor, Freedom from Torture*
Geeta Koska, *Barrister, One Pump Court Chambers*
Catherine Meredith, *Barrister, Doughty Street Chambers*
Krishnendu Mukherjee, *Barrister and Indian Advocate, Doughty Street Chambers*
Amelia Nice, *Barrister, Doughty Street Chambers*
Louise Price, *Barrister, Doughty Street Chambers*
Hina Rai, *District Judge, Westminster Magistrates' Court*
Jonathan Elystan Rees KC, *5 Paper Buildings Chambers, Apex Chambers, Cardiff*
James Robottom, *Barrister, Matrix Chambers*
His Honour Judge Nathanial Rudolf KC, *Circuit Judge, Inner London Crown Court*
Basmah Sahib, *Solicitor Bindmans*
Katy Sheridan, *Barrister, Matrix Chambers*
Maya Sikand KC, *Doughty Street Chambers*
Dame Sara Thornton DBE QPM, *Professor of Modern Slavery, University of Nottingham*
Jennifer Twite, *Barrister, Garden Court Chambers*
Anthony Vaughan KC, *Associate Tenant, Doughty Street Chambers*
Dr Eileen Walsh, *Helen Bamber Foundation*
Louise Willocx, *Barrister, Doughty Street Chambers*
Rachel Witkin, *International Anti-Trafficking Consultant*
Her Honour Judge Lynette Woodrow, *Circuit Judge, Snaresbrook Crown Court*
Zubier Yazdani, *Partner, Deighton Pierce Glynn*

Bloomsbury Professional

LONDON • DUBLIN • EDINBURGH • NEW YORK • NEW DELHI • SYDNEY

BLOOMSBURY PROFESSIONAL

Bloomsbury Publishing Plc
50 Bedford Square, London, WC1B 3DP, UK
1385 Broadway, New York, 10018, USA

Bloomsbury Publishing Ireland Ltd
29 Earlsfort Terrace, Dublin 2, D02 AY28, Ireland

First published in Great Britain 2026

1

British Library Cataloguing-in-Publication Data
A catalogue record for this book is available from the British Library.

ISBN:	PB:	978 1 52652 914 5
	Epdf:	978 1 52652 916 9
	Epub:	978 1 52652 915 2

Typeset by Evolution Design and Digital Ltd (Kent)
Printed and bound by CPI Group (UK) Ltd, Croydon CR0 4YY

MIX
Paper | Supporting responsible forestry
FSC® C013056
FSC
www.fsc.org

For product safety related questions contact productsafety@bloomsbury.com

To find out more about our authors and books visit www.bloomsburyprofessional.com. Here you will find extracts, author information, details of forthcoming events and the option to sign up for our newsletters

Foreword to third edition

Since the publication of the first two editions of this highly regarded volume the trafficking in human beings has continued. The law has expanded and developed. This third edition introduces several new topics and updates others with characteristic scholarship, rigorous analysis and practical guidance. It is the essential text book for all working in this developing area.

Slavery, servitude, forced or compulsory labour are defined by reference to domestic and international law, with helpful additional reference to cases in this jurisdiction and in the ECtHR. With commendable clarity the legal foundations, domestic and international, of the approach to these cases are set out in **Chapter 1**. The authors are to be congratulated for incorporating into that chapter their analysis and comment upon the recent decision of the Court of Appeal in *R v Webb and Somerset How* [2025] EWCA Crim 1491.

The new chapter on prosecuting in the International Criminal Court examines its jurisdiction, the scope and range of offences including war crimes and crimes against humanity and the practicalities of dealing with cases. The authors analyse a recent policy document from the Office of the Prosecutor on Slavery Crimes, the first of its kind in the world 'to help discharge the Office's responsibility to fully and effectively investigate and prosecute slavery crimes' within the jurisdiction of the ICC, to present 'the principles underlying the Office's approach to slavery crimes', and to outline 'relevant aspects of its practice. This chapter, like almost every other in this book repays re reading for the novice and experienced practitioner alike.

The examination and codification of forms of exploitation is timely, as are the explanations of how reforms, including the Modern Slavery Act 2015, Nationality and Borders Act 2022, and Illegal Migration Act 2023, have reshaped domestic law and its relationship with international standards, including decisions of the ICC. This edition also explains how positive obligations under Article 4 ECHR apply, with expert analysis of key developments such as *VCL v UK*, *Begum v SSHD*, and *World Uyghur Congress v NCA*. Away from the detail of cases it explains the links between organised crime, terrorism and the trafficking of human beings and provides an instructive history of the origins of SIAC, the nature of its work and the complexity of dealing with secret evidence.

The new chapters on supply chain accountability, transnational corporate remedies, and trauma-informed practice will be welcomed by all. Of enormous value are the practical tools for practitioners and judges managing cases involving victims of exploitation, whether as victims or defendants (or both), the latter category often posing difficult questions which require a balancing exercise between the status of the defendant as victim and his or her status as defendant. Step-by-step guidance includes jury directions, routes to verdict, and identifying trafficking victims, a process (or its absence) that is often the subject of criticism in the appellate courts.

In his introduction to the first edition of this book Lord Thomas expressed the hope that it would make an important contribution to the protection of victims and the prosecution of the perpetrators of these heinous crimes. That it has fulfilled that hope is not in doubt. I warmly welcome this superb third edition.

Kate Thirlwall

The Rt Hon Lady Justice Thirlwall DBE

September 2026

Foreword to second edition

As was acknowledged in the introduction to the Report of the Modern Slavery Bill Evidence Review (Frank Field MP (now Baron Field of Birkenhead), Baroness Butler-Sloss and Sir John Randall MP (now Baron Randall of Uxbridge)) in 2013:

> 'Slavery flourishes to this day, although unlike two hundred years ago, it is now invisible. It continues behind front doors, in factories and on farms, in brothels and on the streets of our towns and cities. To give just a few examples, across the country today there are Vietnamese boys forced to work on cannabis farms, Nigerian women held in domestic servitude, Polish and British men controlled by criminals as forced labourers, and British and Eastern European girls trafficked into prostitution. This, however, is by no means a comprehensive list of either the forms of modern slavery taking place in Britain or of the primary nationalities that are being exploited. Victims of modern slavery are hidden in plain sight, often trapped by forces more subtle than lock and key.'

The Modern Slavery Act 2015 (effective as of 31 July 2015) placed on a statutory footing provisions relating to slavery and human trafficking. It contains provisions for the protection of victims. Criminal offences were created which included holding another person in slavery or requiring another person to perform forced or compulsory labour. The 2015 Act, together with a number of International Conventions which had been agreed in order to address the issue of modern slavery, has provided the legal foundation for proceedings instituted in the courts of England and Wales.

This book provides a detailed and practical guide to the legal regimes. The guidance is not confined to the courtroom. It realistically encompasses matters outside of a court hearing, relating to victims and those charged with a criminal offence. It is guidance which can properly form the basis of advice to be given by practitioners. It is necessary and welcome.

The Rt Hon Lady Justice Nicola Davies DBE

October 2020

Foreword to first edition

Until recently, most would have thought that, even though it had taken well into the twentieth century to abolish slavery, it was a scourge and heinous crime that no longer afflicted us. However, slavery had gone underground. As was said in the introduction to the Report of the Review Panel (Frank Field MP, Baroness Butler-Sloss and Sir John Randall MP) in 2013:

> 'Slavery flourishes to this day, although unlike two hundred years ago, it is now invisible. It continues behind front doors, in factories and on farms, in brothels and on the streets of our towns and cities. To give just a few examples, across the country today there are Vietnamese boys forced to work on cannabis farms, Nigerian women held in domestic servitude, Polish and British men controlled by criminals as forced labourers, and British and Eastern European girls trafficked into prostitution. This, however, is by no means a comprehensive list of either the forms of modern slavery taking place in Britain or of the primary nationalities that are being exploited. Victims of modern slavery are hidden in plain sight, often trapped by forces more subtle than lock and key.'

From 2000 International Conventions were agreed to deal with this scourge. Although in 2009 the UK government established a National Referral Mechanism to determine whether those who claimed to have been trafficked had in fact been trafficked, it was left to the judiciary (utilising the flexible nature of the common law in a series of decisions in 2011–2013) and to the Crown Prosecution Service (through the exercise of their independent prosecutorial discretion) to develop a legal regime for England and Wales in which the international obligations as they successively developed were given effect in the domestic law of England and Wales. In 2015 the Modern Slavery Act was passed, putting the law on a statutory footing with the additional benefits of strengthening the protection given to the victims of modern slavery and of making it easier to prosecute those who engage in trafficking. The Act generally came into effect on 31 July 2015, but was not retrospective.

Thus, in a relatively short period of time, a non-statutory and then a statutory regime were created to deal with the complex issues to which modern slavery gives rise. What was plainly needed was a practitioner's book that clearly described and explained the legal regimes and gave practical guidance to lawyers which would enable them to identify whether a person was a victim of modern slavery and how best to protect that person.

This book gives a very comprehensive guide to the legal regimes and much practical assistance. For example Chapter 6 gives a very comprehensive account about what should happen on arrest at the police station and the matters that the lawyer should consider; this is reinforced by clear guidance on ethics in Chapter 16. Another example of the practical guidance given, drawn from the experience of the authors, is Chapter 15, which provides a clear summary of ways in which victims are trafficked and exploited.

I therefore warmly welcome this book and very much hope it will make a real contribution to the protection of victims of trafficking and modern slavery and to the prosecution of those who perpetrate this most heinous of crime.

John Thomas

Lord Thomas of Cwmgiedd

January 2018

Preface

This work re-examines the legal definitions of human trafficking and modern slavery through in-depth, novel scholarship. It also weaves through each chapter a clear account of the positive obligations imposed by Article 4 ECHR, and how those obligations both frame the duties of public authorities and guide the interpretation of domestic law. The analysis is intentionally crossdisciplinary within the law itself: it traverses criminal, civil, human rights, public, refugee, extradition, and international criminal law, engaging with community care frameworks and procedural justice. These domains are interwoven, not examined in isolation, to reflect the realities of practice and to avoid the siloed approaches that have too often impeded protection for survivors. It approaches issues from the perspective of practitioners working in investigation, policing, defence, prosecution, civil, immigration, extradition, international and human rights law, drawing equally on judicial guidance reflected in jurisprudence, professional standards, and the insights of those involved in policy and advisory roles.

This edition overlays those domestic frameworks with principles from public international law and traumainformed practice, ensuring that legal interpretation is grounded in doctrinal rigour and sensitivity to survivors' lived experience.

Our approach is informed by global jurisprudence and the work of leading jurists and commentators whose analyses continue to shape, challenge, and advance this rapidly developing field. We have aimed not merely to consolidate established principles but to identify and interrogate areas that remain unsettled in the senior courts. We have examined past approaches and identified continuing lacunae in the legislative and policy architecture that hinder survivors' access to justice, protection, and reparation, while also recognising that some frameworks or practices may risk constraining fair and effective enforcement. We set out the legal principles governing when the duties of public authorities are engaged and consider, where relevant, whether the actions taken met the standard of reasonable and proportionate response required by the individual circumstances of the case.

Above all, this remains a practitionerled work, designed to equip those across multiple areas of law with the insight and analytical depth required to translate rights into effective remedies.

Since the publication of the second edition in 2020, the legal landscape surrounding human trafficking and modern slavery has evolved from an emerging area of practice into a complex, multijurisdictional discipline. Our objective for this third edition has been to move beyond a simple update, providing a fundamental reexamination of the legal and conceptual foundations of the field to prepare practitioners for an increasingly interlinked legal environment

Philippa Southwell

Michelle Brewer

Ben Douglas-Jones KC

September 2026

Contents

Editors' biographies

Philippa Southwell is Managing Director of Southwell & Partners, a leading law firm specialising in criminal, modern slavery and regulatory law. She was called to the Bar in 2009 as a barrister, and having cross-qualified, she practises as a Solicitor Advocate. Prior to founding Southwell and Partners, she founded the Human Trafficking & Modern Slavery Expert Directory. She is an internationally recognised expert in modern slavery law, she has acted in most leading forced criminality modern slavery cases, including *VCL v UK*, at all levels up to the European Court of Human Rights. She lectures extensively both domestically and throughout the Middle East and Europe. Philippa advises companies on modern slavery and human rights compliance. She was called to give evidence as a legal expert in the Home Affairs Select Committee Modern Slavery Inquiry. Philippa has acted on several hundred modern slavery cases and was one of the first lawyers in the country to advance a s 45 modern slavery defence. She has acted in most of the significant and leading forced criminality modern slavery appellant cases representing the victims of modern slavery at all levels, including the Court of Appeal, Supreme Court and European Court of Human Rights. She has been highly commended by the Law Society who have described her as 'a fierce criminal defence solicitor, who specialises in defending and representing victims of human trafficking who have been prosecuted for criminal offences. She is a leading criminal solicitor in this field'.

Michelle Brewer is a judge and former barrister whose advocacy and scholarship have shaped the jurisprudence on modern slavery and human trafficking. Her recognised expertise is grounded in decades of practice in senior courts, leading landmark cases that advanced the interpretation of states' obligations under Article 4 of the ECHR. She acted successfully as lead counsel in *VCL v UK* (2021), the first ECtHR case addressing prosecution of trafficking victims within Articles 4 and 6, and in *OGO v United Kingdom* (2014), securing a Rule 39 injunction preventing the trafficking victim's removal. She represented VCL in *R v Joseph & Others* (2017), was counsel in leading appellate and Supreme Court cases, including *R v LM* (2010), *R v L* (2013), and *Hounga v Allen* (2014). Her scholarship informs this edition, defining modern slavery and States' positive obligations under Article 4 ECHR.

Called to the Bar in 1998, Michelle specialised in public law, refugee and immigration law, civil liberties, and criminal appellate work. She advised statutory bodies, gave evidence to inquiries, and engaged UN mechanisms. As a judge, she co-authored Judicial College guidance on trafficking and modern slavery, contributes to the Crown Court Compendium, and trains judges nationally and internationally, including for the UN, Council of Europe, and OSCE. She delivered keynote addresses at global judicial conferences on slavery and related harms, including an OSCE international conference for Supreme Court Justices on the judiciary's role in combating slavery, trafficking and related harms reflecting her standing as a leading authority in this complex and evolving field.

Ben Douglas-Jones KC is a barrister at 5 Paper Buildings, London and St Philips Chambers, Birmingham. He is also a Deputy High Court Judge, a Crown Court Recorder, a Bencher (Gray's Inn) and an attorney-at-law in Grenada. He specialises in human rights, human trafficking and modern slavery, complex fraud, homicide, serious crime, regulatory and consumer law. He has appeared in dozens of leading appeals, in particular concerning human trafficking, refugees, human rights and financial crime, including before four successive Lords Chief Justices. Shortlisted for Crime Silk of the Year 2025 (*Legal 500*), Ben is described as 'an extremely talented barrister with exceptionally broad knowledge of the law, who can juggle the preparation of multiple complex cases concurrently' (*Chambers and Partners*). Ben is the editor/author of many leading publications including *Human Rights in Criminal Law* (Bloomsbury Professional); *AI in Criminal Law* (Bloomsbury Professional); *Archbold Criminal Pleading Evidence and Practice* (Sweet & Maxwell); *Rook and Ward on Sexual Offences Law & Practice* (Sweet & Maxwell); *Blackstone's Guide to the Consumer Rights Act 2015* (OUP); and human trafficking and immigration crime guidance for the Crown Prosecution Service, Law Society and Judicial College. He provides domestic and international modern slavery training to judges, legal practitioners and for regulatory compliance. Ben has provided evidence to governmental committees on trafficking and transparency of supply chains and has spoken in the Hague on international law, and its impact on national legal systems.

Contributors' biographies

Paramjit Ahluwalia is a barrister (called 2002, BA Oxon) at 1 Pump Court chambers. She is a contributing author to *Blackstone's Criminal Practice* (OUP), on the chapter 'Modern Slavery, Trafficking and Immigration Offences'.

Steven Bird qualified as a solicitor in 1990, and since then has been working in the criminal justice system dealing with serious fraud, regulatory and criminal cases. He founded Birds Solicitors in October 2000 which was merged into Hodge Jones and Allen (incorporating Birds Solicitors) in June 2025. He is a consultant at the merged practice. As part of its extensive appeal practice, Birds Solicitors was one of the first firms to take a case to the Court of Appeal raising issues of non-prosecution of trafficking victims. Steven is rated as a Senior Statesperson in the *Chambers and Partners* directory and is in the Hall of Fame category in the *Legal 500*. In 2016, he was admitted to the List of Counsel at the International Criminal Court. Steven is also a Director of Southwell & Partners, a specialist firm dealing with human trafficking cases which was formed in 2020. Steven is a Committee member of the London Criminal Courts Solicitors Association and the Criminal Appeal Lawyers Association where he is also the Chair. He is a member of the Fraud Lawyers Association and the Proceeds of Crime Lawyers Association. Steven is the co-author of the Police Station Advisers Index and has contributed chapters to *Taylor on Criminal Appeals* (OUP), *The Drugs Offences Handbook* (Bloomsbury Professional), *The Confiscation Law Handbook* (Bloomsbury Professional) and *The Criminal Cases Review Commission: Hope for the Innocent?* (Palgrave Macmillan UK).

Phil Brewer is a lecturer in law and criminology at St Mary's University, London as well as a specialist advisor on modern slavery at the Human Trafficking Foundation (HTF). His professional background is in law enforcement, having served 30 years with the London Metropolitan Police before retiring in 2019. His final posting was as head of the Modern Slavery and Kidnap Unit and the lead responsible officer for combatting modern slavery. Phil also regularly represented UK Policing at the Europol Trafficking Human Beings Expert Group. He has contributed to several exploitation-related publications, including The Truth about Modern Slavery by Emily Kenway and Stolen Lives by Louise Hulland. Phil is a trustee at Bucks SafeStep Foundation, a community-based charity built on a foundation of lived experience, supporting victims, survivors and their families in Buckinghamshire. He is also a member of the advisory board of The Daddyless Daughters Project CIC, a not-for-profit organisation supporting girls and young women affected by family breakdown, abuse and adversity.

Daniel Bunting is a barrister at 2 Dr Johnson's Buildings practising in criminal, immigration and public law. He has particular expertise in the cross-over of criminal and immigration law, and in appeals concerning the prosecution of victims of trafficking, where he has appeared in many of the leading cases in the area in the last fifteen years in the Court of Appeal. He is the author of *Immigration Offences – a Practitioner's Guide* (Bloomsbury Professional, 2023) and contributing editor to *Human Rights in Criminal Law* (Bloomsbury Professional, 2023). He sits as a Recorder of the Crown Court and as an Immigration Judge in the First-tier Tribunal.

Lindsay Cundall is the Public Law Supervisor, Strategic Litigation Lead and Housing and Support Unit Lead at ATLEU (Anti-Trafficking and Labour Exploitation Unit). She is a solicitor and Senior Immigration and Asylum Scheme Accredited Caseworker. She qualified with Wilson Solicitors LLP; her training was based in the immigration and public law departments. Lindsay previously worked at Refugee and Migrant Justice, Brighton Housing Trust and the UNHCR, Ecuador. Lindsay has extensive experience of preparing applications and appeals at all levels as well as complex judicial review applications. Lindsay was previously the Training Lead at ATLEU and has trained many support professionals and lawyers on supporting and representing survivors of modern slavery in the UK. She has a particular interest in representing victims of human trafficking/modern slavery, clients in detention/prisons and representing unaccompanied minors/young people. Lindsay is a member of the lawyers' network run by the Council of Europe's Group of Experts against Trafficking in Human Beings.

Emma Fitzsimons is a barrister at Garden Court Chambers. She practises in immigration and public law, with a focus on asylum, human rights and trafficking. She regularly represents victims of trafficking in statutory appeals, judicial review claims and civil claims for damages. She was part of the legal team instructed in the landmark case, *VCL and AN v UK* (2021) 73 EHRR 9. She is a contributing author to *Macdonald's Immigration Law and Practice* (11th edn, LexisNexis) and *LAG Migrant Support Handbook* (LAG).

Silvia Nicolaou Garcia is a solicitor at Bindmans. She specialises in bringing judicial review challenges against public authorities on behalf of victims of trafficking, children, detained individuals and NGOs. She has developed a particular interest and expertise in acting for victims of trafficking, particularly children and young adults who are at risk of being re-trafficked and are not receiving sufficient protection and financial support. Silvia also acts on behalf of individuals seeking recognition and protection by the State as victims of trafficking and modern slavery.

Zoe Harper is a barrister at Doughty Street Chambers. She practises in immigration, human rights and public law, specialising in complex cases involving trafficking, gender-based violence and refugee protection. She is ranked in both *Chambers and Partners* and the *Legal 500* directories where her expertise and experience in trafficking cases are recognised. She represents victims of trafficking before the Asylum and Immigration Chambers of both the First Tier and Upper Tribunals and in judicial review proceedings and is well-regarded for her sensitive and effective work with vulnerable clients. Zoe has an active and parallel practice in the Court of Protection giving rise to a further specialism in cases involving mental capacity, mental health and disability concerns. She has an extensive background in research, policy and advocacy across academic and NGO settings. She is a laureate of the René Cassin Foundation International Institute of Human Rights in Strasbourg and, since 2019, has regularly taught there on international and comparative human rights law and practice.

Steve Harvey was an operational police officer for 25 years, including five years with the National Criminal Intelligence Service, supporting the UK's first investigations into human trafficking and the smuggling of migrants. He was the first British police officer to be recruited to EUROPOL, and between 2003 and 2013, coordinated international investigations into human trafficking. He set up Europol's first dedicated response to this crime and was Head of Unit for Organised Crime in South East Europe, the Balkans and Turkey. Steve was one of the European Commission's Group of Experts on Trafficking in Human Beings. He is the only British police officer to have been appointed to this role and was the law enforcement lead in the drafting of the 2011 EU Directive on preventing and combating the trafficking of human beings. Since 2013, Steve has worked as an independent consultant supporting counter human trafficking initiatives throughout the world. He has reviewed human trafficking legislation, law enforcement working practices and developed counter-trafficking strategies and training programmes in Afghanistan, Albania, Federated States of Micronesia, Iraq, Pakistan, Papua New Guinea, the Solomon Islands, Türkiye and Vanuatu. More recently he has trained law enforcement and NGO personnel in Hungary and Slovakia on behalf of UNICEF and supported the development of UNICEF's Practical Guide for Frontline Responders on identifying victims and persons at risk of human trafficking. Steve is also a recognised expert witness. His human trafficking assessment in the case of Shamima Begum, was presented as evidence to the Special Immigration Appeals Commission and his conclusion that Shamima Begun was trafficked to Syria was accepted by the SIAC as credible.

Caroline Haughey OBE, KC is a criminal barrister at Furnival Chambers, specialising in modern slavery and human trafficking cases. Having prosecuted the first modern slavery case in Britain (*R v K (S)* [2011] 2 Cr App R 34), she was subsequently involved in advising the All Parliamentary group on the proposal for an Act, gave evidence before the Committee and subsequently advised on the drafting of the Modern Slavery Act 2015. Caroline has prosecuted a number of firsts under the Act, for example, child labour exploitation, child sex trafficking and 'victimless' (*R v Nguyen, Tran and Nguyen* [2019] EWCA Crim 670), as well as the largest trafficking and labour exploitation case in Europe, Operation Fort (*Brzezinski and others*). She lectures domestically and internationally including to the UNODC, Interpol and RUSI on the investigation and prosecution of modern slavery and trafficking cases. Caroline gave evidence to the Parliamentary Inquiry into whether Australia should have a Modern Slavery Act, as well as contributing to the Commonwealth Parliamentary

Group publications and lectures on modern slavery. Caroline was author of the first Independent Modern Slavery Act Review 2016, was joint legal advisor on the second Independent Modern Slavery Act Review, was the independent member of the Prime Minister's Modern Slavery Task Force and Special Advisor to the House of Lords Modern Slavery Act Committee. She has given evidence on a number of occasions before the Home Affairs Select Committee. She is a trustee of the Anti-Slavery Collective, a member of the McCain Institute Anti Trafficking advisory committee, a specialist advisor to Justice and Care and the founder of the Prosecutors Consortium, a group of specialist anti trafficking/modern slavery prosecutors from across the world.

His Honour Judge Andrew Johnson is a Circuit Judge, who sits at the Crown Court at St Albans. Prior to his appointment to the Circuit Bench in 2024, he was a barrister in practice at 5 Paper Buildings, who spent a number of years responding for the CPS Appeals and Review Unit to out-of-time applications and appeals by individuals who claimed they were victims of modern slavery who should not have been prosecuted. Amongst the leading cases he appeared in are *AAD*, *AFU* and *Henkoma*.

Kalvir Kaur is a solicitor at Freedom from Torture. Having qualified in 2002, she has extensive strategic and legal expertise in advocating for children, victims of trafficking and survivors of torture. She is an experienced national and international trainer having trained professional from a wide range of disciplines in the UK, France, Cyprus, Greece and The Netherlands. Kalvir has been awarded the Legal Aid Lawyer of the Year in the Immigration and Asylum category for her work with vulnerable clients, is the recipient of End Child Prostitution, Child Pornography and Trafficking of Children for Sexual Purposes (ECPAT UK) Children's Champion award and is a Vital Voices Fellow as child trafficking world leader. Kalvir has edited, authored and contributed to academic texts, the *Encyclopaedia of Trafficking*, best practice guides, research reports and campaigning literature.

Geeta Koska practises as a barrister at One Pump Court Chambers. She has a claimed-focused practice across private and public law, and represents clients in the county court, High Court and Court of Appeal. Geeta has been working on business and human rights issues for almost ten years, with organisations across Europe and India. Her work is focused on realising economic, social and cultural rights for workers and communities and developing innovative strategies to pursue accountability for business-related violations. She is an experienced trainer, having delivered training on the topic of business and human rights to legal representatives and government.

Dominic Lewis is a barrister at 5 Paper Buildings, from where he has practised since he was called in 2000. His primary specialism is in criminal law. Since 2011 he has been on the AG's panel of special advocates, in which capacity he regularly appears in immigration appeals (both in SIAC and the High Court) within the national security/serious organised crime context.

Catherine Meredith is a barrister at Doughty Street Chambers. She is recognised as a leading anti-trafficking and human rights specialist. Her broad practice covers public law and private law claims, domestic and international law, with a strong focus on asylum and immigration, anti-discrimination, and women's and children's rights. Catherine has been involved in ground-breaking trafficking cases at all levels of the domestic courts to the Supreme Court and international courts, including the ECtHR (eg *VCL and AN v the UK* (for Anti-Slavery International), and currently *Begum v UK* (for the UN Special Rapporteur on Trafficking in Persons (UNSR TIP) and the Inter-American Commission (*Siti Aisah v the USA*, also for the UNSR TIP). Catherine has advised NGOs on domestic legislation and policies affecting victims of trafficking, and Council of Europe and UN institutions (eg GRETA, UNODC, UNHCR, UNICEF and CEDAW) and UN Special Procedures on international anti-trafficking and human rights standards.

Krishnendu Mukherjee is a barrister and Indian advocate at Doughty Street Chambers, where he jointly leads the business and human rights (BHR) group. For 30 years he has practised in immigration law, including representing victims of trafficking and modern slavery. Since 2008 he has been practising in BHR in both India and in the UK, where he has represented individuals and communities against corporations before courts, filed OECD complaints, and advised communities, NGOs, trade unions and companies on BHR. This has led him to be called as an expert in the United Nations Office for the High Commissioner for Human Rights Accountability and Remedy Project and he is currently listed in *Chambers and Partners* Global Guide on BHR law. He regularly teaches BHR in universities, and in 2018 began the BHR roundtable at Doughty Street Chambers to bring together lawyers, civil society and business to promote this nascent but fast-moving area of law.

Amelia Nice is an extradition and human rights barrister at Doughty Street Chambers. In extradition, she works almost exclusively defending extradition requests and has successfully represented many particularly vulnerable clients, including victims of trafficking, domestic violence and/or those suffering from post-traumatic stress disorder. She has a track record running complex extradition cases involving concurrent child abuse, Care, Child Abduction and Trafficking proceedings. She appears frequently before the High Court as well as the Supreme Court. Amelia advises judicial authorities and private clients nationally and internationally on securing extradition requests to this country or pre-emptive action resisting extradition. Her international advisory practice involves challenges to Interpol, Mutual Legal Assistance, scenarios involving competing international obligations and training or advice on the associated risks. Amelia also works in the fields of Public Inquiries and Court of Protection. In both fields, her work has a particular focus on children's rights, mental capacity and trauma.

Louise Price (called to the Bar in 2007) is a barrister at Doughty Street Chambers. Her practice focuses on human rights and anti-discrimination law, in particular within the field of employment. She has represented victims of trafficking before both the employment tribunal and the employment appeal tribunal seeking compensation or enforcing labour rights on their behalf.

Hina Rai is a District Judge at Westminster Magistrates' Court and sits in the Immigration and Asylum Chamber. A former Crown Prosecutor, she has expertise in criminal law, extradition, terrorism, asylum, and human rights. Hina has represented the UK judiciary internationally, delivering training on human trafficking at an UNODC conference in Bangladesh, contributed to leading legal texts and is currently reviewing chapters on Modern Slavery, Trafficking and Immigration Offences for Blackstone's Criminal Practice. She also serves as a Diversity and Community Relations Judge.

Jonathan Elystan Rees KC is a senior criminal barrister based at 5 Paper Buildings, London and Apex Chambers, Cardiff, specialising in homicide, terrorism, serious fraud and international crime. In England & Wales, Jonathan regularly appears in serious organised crime related prosecutions, involving allegations of human trafficking and modern slavery. Since 2020, Jonathan has regularly appeared in The Hague, appearing for accused in a range of prosecutions and appeals before the Kosovo Specialist Chambers. Jonathan is the Chair of the Legal Wales Foundation, and Co-Chair, alongside Professor Yvonne McDermott-Rees, of the Legal Affairs Committee of the Welsh Centre for International Affairs based at the Temple of Peace, King Edward VII Ave, Cardiff. In 2023, Jonathan chaired the 'Support For Ukraine – Wales Conference' organised by the Welsh Government, UK Counter Terrorism Policing, CPS Cymru, and Children and Families Across Borders. In June 2024, Jonathan appeared as presenting counsel before the CCW Tribunal on Human Rights Abuses in Taiwan, Xinjiang and in the South Seas, based in The Hague. Jonathan also sits as a Recorder of the Crown Court and is a Bencher of the Inner Temple.

James Robottom is a barrister at Matrix chambers who specialises in the law of modern slavery across criminal, civil, human rights and public law. In 2025 he completed his PhD on the constitutional prohibition of slavery in England and Wales at King's College London.

His Honour Judge Nathaniel Rudolf KC is a Circuit Judge sitting a Southwark Crown Court. He has tried a number of cases where the defence has been one of modern slavery. He was a barrister for 25 years specialising in financial crime and proceeds of crime. He has co-authored a number of texts including Fraud: A Practitioner's Handbook the second edition of which is due.

Basmah Sahib is an accredited member of the Law Society's mental health panel scheme. She conducts her own advocacy in the First-tier Tribunal (Mental Health) and the Coroner's court. Basmah's mental health practice focuses on detained clients, including those who have been transferred to psychiatric hospital from immigration detention centres. She has also advised detained clients on repatriation to their country of origin, so they may receive mental health care and treatment in a more familiar environment with their families and loved ones nearby. Building on her niche mental health specialty, Basmah supports migrants with mental health difficulties – like PTSD from experiences like torture, slavery or childhood sexual abuse – with age disputes, accessing mental health care and treatment and accessing appropriate asylum accommodation. Basmah has advised and represented the students of a college for adults with learning disabilities in a judicial review challenge against the closure of the college without prior consultation with them, and with their families and carers. Basmah also represents vulnerable clients in Human Rights Act claims for unlawful detention arising from a failure to use, or misuse of, the authorisations in the Mental Health Act 1983 and Mental Capacity Act 2005. Outside her legal career, Basmah is a trustee for the charity Bail for Immigration Detainees.

Katy Sheridan is a barrister at Matrix Chambers, specialising in public and human rights law, education and discrimination law, and employment law. Within her public and human rights practice, Katy has acted in various matters concerning human trafficking and modern slavery (for example the lead claims against the Public Order Disqualification policy (2023/24), and AS and BXR (concerning the need for 'objective evidence' at the reasonable grounds stage)). Katy is ranked as a leading junior and/or rising star in administrative law and education in the directories, and is a member of the Equality and Human Rights Commission's Panel of Counsel.

Maya Sikand KC is a public law barrister at Doughty Street Chambers. Her specialist areas include human rights and tortious damages claims against public bodies, as well as statutory compensation claims, in particular in relation to victims of trafficking and modern slavery. Over the years, she has successfully represented numerous trafficked victims wrongfully convicted of crimes in the Court of Appeal. She is a contributing editor of the seminal criminal textbook *Archbold Criminal Pleading, Evidence & Practice* (Sweet & Maxwell).

Dame Sara Thornton DBE QPM is a Professor of Modern Slavery Policy at the Rights Lab in the University of Nottingham where her focus is on research in the area of prevention, business responses, supply chains, and the role of the financial sector in tackling modern slavery. She is particularly focussed on the important role of investors and works as a modern slavery consultant for CCLA Investment Management. Dame Sara completed a three-year term as the UK Independent Anti-Slavery Commissioner in April 2022, a role in which she spearheaded the UK's fight against human trafficking and modern slavery. Prior to that she spent 33 years in policing serving as Chief Constable of Thames Valley Police from 2007 until 2015 and was the first Chair of the National Police Chiefs' Council from 2015 to 2019. She was awarded the Queen's Police Medal in 2006, made a Commander of the Order of the British Empire in 2011 and a Dame Commander of the Order of the British Empire in 2019. She is an Honorary Air Commodore in the Royal Air Force supporting the work of the auxiliary police squadron, Chair of the Advisory Board for the

Leadership College of Government and the Chair of the Police Foundation. In 2022 she was awarded the Human Trafficking Foundation Trustee Award for Outstanding Contribution in the Fight against Modern Slavery.

Jennifer Twite is a barrister at Garden Court Chambers (2006 call). Her practice involves both public and private law claims, with a specialism in Children's Rights. She has particular expertise in areas involving youth justice, where issues concerning children being trafficked and/or criminally exploited are frequently engaged. She regularly represents children, age-disputed individuals and young adults in a wide range of judicial review proceedings and civil actions, many of whom are victims of trafficking. She has acted in a number of age-disputed cases in both the Upper Tribunal and also the criminal courts. She was Head of Strategic Litigation at Just for Kids Law where she led a number of high-profile campaigns about the rights of children in the criminal justice system, was a LALY finalist in the category of Children's Rights, also sits as a Deputy District Judge in the magistrates' courts and co-authors *Youth Justice Law and Practice* (LAG). She has been a regular contributor to the biannual Youth Justice Update in LAG for a number of years.

Anthony Vaughan KC is a leading barrister specialising in public law, human rights and equality law, and has particular expertise in immigration, deprivation of liberty and human trafficking law. His clients have included victims whose exploitation was linked to organised crime and terrorism, and he has successfully challenged decisions that wrongly treat trafficked persons as offenders rather than victims – both in the civil and criminal contexts. He is an Associate Tenant at Doughty Street Chambers in London, is ranked by the major legal directories, and is currently a Member of Parliament.

Dr Eileen Walsh is a clinical psychologist, working at Traumatic Stress Clinic, North London Foundation Trust (an NHS specialist trauma service) and at the Helen Bamber Foundation. She has specialised in working with people with a history of complex trauma, including victims of trafficking and modern slavery. She has 20 years' experience of psychological assessment and treatment, working at specialist psychological trauma clinics in the NHS and the charity sector. She has extensive experience of preparing independent psychological medico-legal reports focusing on mental health problems related to human rights abuses, including trafficking, and has a strong interest in the contribution of psychological research to legal processes.

Louise Willocx is a junior barrister at Doughty Street Chambers. She combines her busy criminal practice with extradition law and international law. Louise specialises in young vulnerable clients and therefore often represents victims of modern slavery. She also teaches human rights law at her alma mater, KU Leuven (Belgium). Further, Louise forms part of the Standing Group on Atrocity Crimes, an independent initiative dedicated to strengthening the UK's prevention and response to atrocity crimes, which include modern slavery. Prior to coming to the Bar, Louise worked as a judicial assistant at Colombia's transitional justice tribunal advising on international criminal law in high-profile cases against the FARC leadership. In this role, she advised the Court on the controversial slavery charges against the FARC leadership.

Rachel Witkin is an international Anti-Trafficking Consultant, and Affiliate and former Director at the Helen Bamber Foundation where she devised and ran a specialist Counter-Trafficking Programme for survivors (2011–2023). As lead author for the OSCE/ODIHR National Referral Mechanisms Handbook and related guidances, she works with ODIHR delegations on NRM country assessments and multi-agency training. She is Director of the Modern Slavery Community of Practice (affiliated with the Kings College London MSCOS project) which is centred in survivor leadership and curates inter-disciplinary forums for professionals to share working methods and perspectives, and link practice. She is an Honorary Fellow at St Mary's University where she teaches the Trauma Informed Code of Conduct (Witkin/Robjant, 2022). She previously worked for Amnesty International and for human rights law firms including Winstanley-Burgess. In 2015, she received the national Marsh Trust national Award for 'Outstanding Contribution to the Fight Against Modern Slavery'.

Her Honour Judge Lynette Woodrow is a Circuit Judge sitting at Snaresbrook Crown Court. Previously, Lynette was a Deputy Chief Crown Prosecutor at the CPS where she was the national lead for prosecuting modern slavery and a member of the Global Consortium of Experts in Prosecuting Human Trafficking. In that capacity, Lynette gave evidence on modern slavery and trafficking to the Women and Equalities Committee, the Home Affairs Select Committee and the House of Lords Modern Slavery Committee.

Zubier Yazdani is a partner at Deighton Pierce Glynn, a leading public law and civil liberties firm in the UK. He is an expert in administrative law, civil liberties and human rights law. He has litigated in courts at all levels and deals with cutting edge litigation for vulnerable clients who have suffered violations of their rights, particularly by the State. Zubier has a long-standing commitment to social justice with over 20 years' experience as a solicitor in relevant public law and civil claims with a focus on claims for victims of trafficking. He is recognised by peers for his work for this client group on remedies for abuses by the state and corporate bodies. He has worked on complex cases which push the boundaries of the law on cases concerning rights for victims of trafficking both under domestic and international law. Zubier provides training to his peers and has contributed to relevant publications.

Acknowledgements

The Editors wish to thank all authors of the third edition for being willing to share their expertise and knowledge and for their industry in bringing this work to completion. They also wish to thank the authors who contributed to the first and second editions, without whose work, this edition would not exist: Christine Beddoe, Pam Bowen CBE, Felicity Gerry KC, Bernie Gravett, Louise Hooper, Wayne Jordash KC, Gemma Loughran, Shu Shin Luh, Mary Westcott, and Hossein Zahir KC. Further thanks go all at Bloomsbury Professional for their support of this important work, as well as special thanks to Anna Douglas-Jones for her work in getting the publication of this work over the line.

Table of Statutes

[*All references are to paragraph number*]

Table of Statutory Instruments

[*All references are to paragraph number*]

Table of European and International Legislation

[*All references are to paragraph number*]

Table of Cases

[All references are to paragraph number]

D

N

Q

R

1 Legal foundations: defining slavery, servitude, forced or compulsory labour, and human trafficking

Michelle Brewer

Introduction

1.1

Justice for victims demands a clear appreciation of the separate legal character and scope of slavery, servitude, forced or compulsory labour, and human trafficking, together with an understanding where their boundaries may overlap. As the Court of Appeal in *SK*[1] stated:

> 'We have concluded that the judge's summing-up did not reflect with sufficient clarity the core elements of Article 4 of the Human Rights Convention – namely "slavery", "servitude" and "forced or compulsory labour" – which are integral to the offence provided for in section 4 of the 2004 Act. Those core elements are crisply defined in the judgment of the European Court of Human Rights in Siliadin.'

1.2

These offences now provided in ss 1 to 4 of the Modern Slavery Act 2015 (MSA 2015), correspond to the conduct proscribed under Art 4 of the European Convention on Human Rights (ECHR)[2]. It is essential to understand these as distinct yet interrelated offences, forming a hierarchy of the denial of personal autonomy, with slavery representing the most egregious and severe violation[3].

---

1 *R v SK* [2011] EWCA Crim 1691, [2012] Crim LR 63, at [39].

2 Art 4 does not expressly mention trafficking, however the ECtHR confirmed that human trafficking falls within its scope and is therefore prohibited (*Rantsev v Cyprus and Russia* App no 25965/04, ECtHR, 7 January 2010). It includes both domestic and cross-border cases, whether or not linked to organised crime (*SM v Croatia* App no 60561/14 (ECtHR, 25 June 2020) [296 and 303]; see also *Zoletic and Others v Azerbaijan* App no 20116/12 (ECtHR, 7 October 2021), at [155].

3 *R v SK* [2011] EWCA Crim 1691, [2012] Crim LR 63 at [24].

1.3

Slavery is a non-derogable rule of international law, enforceable against all states by the international community as a whole and is recognised as a crime against humanity under the Rome Statute of the International Criminal Court (1998)[4], warranting the most severe penal consequences[5]. The offending needs to be understood within this context. Chief Justice Gleeson of the High Court of Australia observed in *The Queen v Tang*[6], when considering an appeal against conviction for slavery:

> 'It is important not to debase the currency of the language, or to banalise crimes against humanity, by giving slavery a meaning that extends beyond the limits set by the text, context, and purpose of the 1926 Slavery Convention.'

1.4

Following the analysis of the constituent elements of these offences, this chapter next examines a series of judgments of the Court of Appeal (Criminal Division). In several cases, offences prosecuted as forced labour were, on the Crown's own case, more accurately characterised as servitude. In others, such as *R v Rooney*[7], the facts arguably constituted slavery. The Court of Appeal's analysis in *Webb* and *Somerset-How*[8] now reinforces that conclusion.

Purpose and structure of the chapter

1.5

Understanding the legal character and seriousness of these offences is only part of the picture. The United Kingdom's obligations under Art 4 ECHR extend beyond criminalisation and punishment; they encompass a broader framework of victim protection and state accountability.

1.6

Identifying the legal sources of slavery and related offences is therefore only the starting point. The greater challenge lies in interpreting these sources, both through the jurisprudence of the European Court of Human Rights (ECtHR) and under UK statute. This chapter analyses each of the concepts in a

4 Rome Statute (1998), Art 7.
5 *Attorney-General's Reference Nos 2, 3, 4 and 5 of 2013 (R v William Connors and Ors)* [2013] 2 Cr App R (S) 71 at [8].
6 [2008] HCA 39 (Australia).
7 [2019] EWCA Crim 681, at [75].
8 [2025] EWCA Crim 1491 at [92]-[93].

hierarchical order from slavery, servitude and forced or compulsory labour and concludes with human trafficking.

1.7

This chapter engages with a well-developed and influential body of legal scholarship on slavery and human trafficking.[9] Academic work in this field has significantly shaped how international and European human rights law define and apply these concepts. Senior appellate courts are experienced in this kind of interpretative task[10], and further clarification of key definitions is likely to follow. Against that background, this chapter addresses two core issues.

1.8

First, the ECtHR[11] adopts the definition of human trafficking set out in Art 4 of the Council of Europe Convention on Action against Trafficking in Human Beings (ECAT)[12] and it gives considerable weight[13] to GRETA's[14] evaluations when determining the scope of protection under Art 4 ECHR in trafficking cases. Although domestic offences of slavery, servitude, and forced or compulsory labour must be interpreted consistently with Art 4 ECHR, the definition of human trafficking both in criminal law and for the purposes of victim identification and support derives from domestic legislation. That definition does not mirror ECAT's and is rooted in an earlier criminal offence that pre-dates the Convention. In its Third Evaluation Report[15], GRETA expressed concern that the UK's definition diverges from international standards. The differing formulations are examined below. ECAT's definition therefore provides the baseline against which domestic trafficking offences and victim-identification frameworks are assessed throughout this book, even where the domestic wording departs from it.

9 See Jean Allain, *Slavery in International Law: Of Human Exploitation and Trafficking* (Martinus Nijhoff Publishers 2013); Jean Allain (ed), *The Legal Understanding of Slavery: From the Historical to the Contemporary* (OUP 2012). See also Vladislava Stoyanova, *Human Trafficking and Slavery Reconsidered: Conceptual Limits and States' Positive Obligations in European Law* (CUP 2017); and Anne Gallagher, *The International Law of Human Trafficking* (CUP 2010). These works and their subsequent publications represent leading scholarship in the legal definition of slavery and cognate offences and human trafficking and have significantly shaped contemporary understanding and application within international and European human rights law.

10 See *Public International Law in the Supreme Court of the United Kingdom* (2nd edn, UK Supreme Court, London 2024).

11 *VCL and AN v UK* at [149] and *FM v* Russia at [240], [295].

12 Council of Europe Convention on Action against Trafficking in Human Beings (opened for signature 16 May 2005, entered into force 1 February 2008) ETS No 197.

13 See *Chowdhury and Others v Greece*, App no 21884/15 (ECtHR, 30 March 2017), at [104].

14 The Council of Europe expert body that monitors how countries implement the Council of Europe Convention on Action against Trafficking in Human Beings (opened for signature 16 May 2005, entered into force 1 February 2008) ETS No 197.

15 GRETA, *Third Evaluation Round: Evaluation Report United Kingdom* GRETA (2021)12 (15 October 2021) paras 19–24 and 247 onwards.

1.9

Second, Art 4 itself does not define the acts it prohibits. To give content to these prohibitions, the ECtHR relies on definitions in foundational international instruments. While the Court adopts an evolutionary interpretive approach that allows the meaning of Art 4 to develop in line with evolving international norms, it has also emphasised that it lacks jurisdiction to interpret the substantive provisions of those instruments directly. This limitation has produced a degree of definitional uncertainty. As Judge Koskelo observed in *SM v Croatia*[16], even at Grand Chamber level the Court has struggled to delineate consistently the scope of the acts proscribed by Art 4. Consequently, ECtHR jurisprudence does not yet provide comprehensive or definitive guidance on the boundaries of these concepts.

Art 4 ECHR: bridging international and domestic law in the UK's dualist system

1.10

The United Kingdom is required to criminalise and interpret slavery and related acts consistently with Art 4 of the ECHR, owing to its positive obligations under that provision. These positive obligations, domestically incorporated through Schedule 1 to the Human Rights Act 1998, impose duties not only to prohibit, criminalise, and prosecute slavery, servitude, forced or compulsory labour, and human trafficking, but also to identify victims, protect and support them, ensure access to compensation, and investigate these crimes effectively so that offenders are held to account.

1.11

These positive obligations are examined in detail in **Chapters 4, 8, 10, 14** and **16**, which address both the operational and procedural dimensions of State responsibility. Throughout this book, it is assumed that such obligations arise, at the latest, once a positive reasonable-grounds decision has been made, and earlier where clear indicators of slavery, servitude, forced or compulsory labour or trafficking are present.

1.12

Interpreting and applying the domestic offences of slavery, servitude, forced or compulsory labour, and human trafficking requires these provisions to be construed in a manner consistent with Art 4 of the ECHR. Art 4, in turn, draws its substantive content from international law, which defines the acts it prohibits. Accordingly, any analysis of the United Kingdom's obligations must begin with

16 *SM v Croatia* App no 60561/14 (ECtHR, 25 June 2020).

the international legal framework that informs the meaning of Art 4 and the domestic offences.

The international legal foundations of slavery, servitude, forced labour and human trafficking

1.13

The legal definitions of slavery, servitude, and forced or compulsory labour emerge from an intersecting body of international law developed throughout the 20th century. The ECtHR has consistently interpreted Art 4 by reference to treaties that define these concepts, most notably the 1926 Slavery Convention[17], Supplementary Convention on the Abolition of Slavery, the Slave Trade, and Institutions and Practices Similar to Slavery ('the 1956 Supplementary Slavery Convention')[18], ILO Conventions Nos 29[19] and 105[20], the Palermo Protocol[21], and ECAT.

1.14

These instruments not only shape the scope of the rights protected under Art 4 ECHR but also inform the United Kingdom's positive obligations to prevent, protect against, and punish conduct contrary to Art 4.

The 1926 Slavery Convention and the ILO

1.15

The 1926 Slavery Convention, adopted under the League of Nations, provided the first international definition of slavery in Art 1 and obliged parties to 'take all necessary measures to prevent compulsory or forced labour from developing into conditions analogous to slavery.' In tandem with the 1926 Slavery Convention, responsibility was delegated to the International Labour Organisation ('ILO') for codifying forced labour standards. The Forced Labour Convention established both the definition and regulatory framework for forced labour.

17 Slavery Convention (signed 25 September 1926, entered into force 9 March 1927) 60 LNTS 254.

18 Supplementary Convention on the Abolition of Slavery, the Slave Trade, and Institutions and Practices Similar to Slavery (adopted 7 September 1956, entered into force 30 April 1957) 266 UNTS 3.

19 Convention concerning Forced or Compulsory Labour (Forced Labour Convention, 1930 (No. 29)) (adopted 28 June 1930, entered into force 1 May 1932).

20 Convention concerning the Abolition of Forced Labour (Abolition of Forced Labour Convention, 1957 (No 105)) (adopted 25 June 1957, entered into force 17 January 1959).

21 Protocol to Prevent, Suppress and Punish Trafficking in Persons, Especially Women and Children, supplementing the United Nations Convention against Transnational Organized Crime (adopted 15 November 2000, entered into force 25 December 2003) UNGA Res 55/25, annex II.

The 1956 Supplementary Slavery Convention

1.16

When the United Nations ('UN') assumed responsibility for both the ILO (from 1946) and the 1926 Slavery Convention (from 1949), it initiated a review process through an *Ad Hoc* Committee on Slavery to assess whether additional protections were needed. The review culminated in the 1956 Supplementary Slavery Convention, which in Art 1 identified four conventional practices of servitude. It retained the original 1926 definition of slavery in Art 7, underscoring the symbiotic relationship between the two instruments.

The Palermo Protocol

1.17

The UN Palermo Protocol (2000), supplementing the Convention against Transnational Organised Crime, provided the first internationally agreed definition of human trafficking and established a framework for prevention, prosecution, and victim protection.

ECAT

1.18

For human trafficking specifically, the ECtHR adopts the definition from the Council of Europe Convention Against Trafficking in Human Beings (2005) ('ECAT'), which itself references international conventions[22] when defining the minimum types of exploitation. ECAT adopted the same definition as provided by the Palermo Protocol, but crucially expanded its scope to include trafficking, whether national or transnational, and regardless of any connection to organised crime.

The contribution of International Criminal Tribunals and the International Criminal Court to the definition of slavery

1.19

The International Criminal Court (ICC) exercises its jurisdiction over persons charged with the most serious crimes of international concern, namely: crimes of genocide, crimes against humanity, war crimes and the crime of aggression.

22 Explanatory Report to the Council of Europe Convention on Action against Trafficking in Human Beings (CETS No 197, 16 May 2005) at [8], [88] and [93].

These crimes are codified in the Rome Statute[23]. Enslavement is a crime against humanity (Art 7(1)(c)); and the language of the crime of enslavement mirrors Art 1 of the 1926 Slavery Convention[24].

Consent in modern slavery offences: legal relevance and evidential implications

1.20

Before examining the individual offences under the Modern Slavery Act 2015 (MSA 2015) and their grounding in international penal law, it is necessary to address two distinct but related issues that cut across all provisions. First, while lack of consent is often assumed to be central to exploitation, it is *not* a required legal element of the offences under ss 1–4 of the MSA 2015. Second, where consent is said to have been given, its evidential significance, particularly in assessing whether an offence has been committed, must be carefully considered. These are conceptually distinct issues, as recognised by the Appeal Chamber in *Kunarac*[25], and must be analysed separately.

1.21

This foundational analysis is addressed at the outset to avoid repetition and to provide a coherent framework for examining each offence. The discussion below draws on principles articulated by the International Criminal Court (ICC), other international criminal tribunals, the European Court of Human Rights (ECtHR), and domestic case law.

Lack of consent is not an element of offences under ss 1–4 of the MSA 2015

1.22

For s 1 offences, s 1(5) provides:

> The consent of a person (whether an adult or a child) to any of the acts alleged to constitute holding the person in slavery or servitude, or requiring the person to perform forced or compulsory labour, does

23 Rome Statute (1998).

24 Art 7(2)(c) defines enslavement adopting the language of Art 1 of 1926 Slavery Convention. The reference to trafficking in persons is not additional to the slavery definition, rather it provides that trafficking in persons can constitute slavery but only if the exercise of powers attaching to ownership arise during trafficking.

25 *Prosecutor v Dragoljub Kunarac, Radomir Kovac and Zoran Vukovic* (Judgment) IT-96-23 & IT-96-23/1 (ICTY, Appeals Chamber, 12 June 2002).

not preclude a determination that the person is being held in slavery or servitude, or required to perform forced or compulsory labour.

Evidential value of consent in MSA 2015 offences

1.23

Where a putative victim's consent is relied on to defend allegations under ss 1–4 of the MSA 2015, or to justify a negative identification decision under the National Referral Mechanism (NRM)[26], its evidential weight must be assessed against the principles underlying these offences. In this context, an adult's consent may be vitiated by coercion, deception, or the exploitation of vulnerability, and its significance must be scrutinised carefully rather than taken at face value.

1.24

First, minors (ie children below 18 years old), cannot provide informed consent to slavery or related acts in ss 1–4 offences, as articulated by Lady Justice Hallett VP in *R v K, W, A*[27] at [60]–[61]:

> 'The prosecution does not need to prove a lack of consent on the part of the young courier or any element of coercion. Any such suggestion must be defeated by (i) the agreed position of all defendants that consent is no defence (as now made express in section 2(3) the Modern Slavery Act 2015); (ii) the protective purpose of the legislation; and (iii) the fact that the concept of 'choice' assumes the willingness of the chosen. Indeed, standing back, when the provision is viewed as a whole it is clear that the mischief it seeks to address is the very fact that a vulnerable person has consented; the Act is seeking to protect the young and the vulnerable from their own decision making.
>
> It follows that a prosecution under section 4 does not depend on the ability to call the individual said to have been exploited or the target of exploitation.'

1.25

The Court went on to conclude that the trial judge had wrongly construed the young person as a 'willing volunteer', which was material to whether there was a case to answer that could be put to the jury.

26 See **Chapter 4**.
27 *R v K, W, A* [2018] EWCA Crim 1432.

1.26

For adults where any of the means identified below, at **1.302, 1.306–3.11**, are used to achieve their consent to slavery or related acts, it is deemed irrelevant to whether they were held in slavery, servitude or subjected to forced or compulsory labour or trafficking. Moreover, consent is not established in law, if it is not voluntary.

1.27

In circumstances where there has been prior consent that is the product of the free will of a victim, this is not sufficient to exclude the characterisation of the work as slavery or related acts where the conditions of work or treatment change (see *Chowdhury and Others v Greece*[28] *and R v Rooney)*[29].

Slavery

Art 1 of the 1926 Slavery Convention

The status or condition of a person over whom any or all of the powers attaching to the right of ownership are exercised.

Slavery *de jure*: a person was formally recognised by law as property. The owner's rights, including the ability to buy, sell, inherit, or transfer the enslaved person, are legally defined and protected. Historical chattel slavery is the classic example. *Slavery, in its de jure form has been universally prohibited under international law, and no state currently recognises by law the right to own another human being.*

Slavery *de facto:* a person is subjected to ownership-like powers without legal recognition. Although the law prohibits slavery, the person is held in conditions that replicate ownership in practice. This involves exercising control equivalent to legal slavery, but without formal legal sanction.

The essence of slavery is the domination of another person's life so that they are deprived of any real personal autonomy. They are deprived of important freedoms by the coercion and controlling behaviour of another person.

R v Webb and Somerset-How [2025] EWCA Crim 1491 at [92]

28 App no 21884/15 (ECtHR, 30 March 2017), at [96].
29 *R v Rooney* [2019] EWCA Crim 681 at [75].

From International Treaty to Domestic Law

1.28

The definition in the 1926 Slavery Convention underpins the section 1 offence in the Modern Slavery Act 2015, but domestic interpretation reflects a clear conceptual shift. The focus has moved from the Convention's formulation of 'ownership as if a person were an object' to an emphasis on the practical reality of domination[30], the exercise of control over another person to a degree that substantially diminishes their personal autonomy. On this modern understanding, slavery is defined not by legal title but by the extent of control exerted in practice. This conception aligns with the international law notion of 'powers attaching to the right of ownership' in Art 1 of the 1926 Convention, re-expressed for contemporary forms of slavery.

Slavery and the courts: interpreting the 1926 Slavery Convention

From Chattel Ownership to the Exercise of Powers: The UK Courts' Approach to Slavery

1.29

In the Court of Appeal (Criminal Division) decision *R v SK*[31], Mr Justice Lindblom said:

> 'The essence of the concept of "slavery" is treating someone as belonging to oneself, by exercising some power over that person as one might over an animal or an object.'

1.30

Lord Briggs, in the Supreme Court's judgment in *Basfar v Wong*[32], observed that traditional chattel slavery, where an individual is legally owned as property, has effectively disappeared as a matter of contemporary law. He emphasised that the definition contained in the 1926 Slavery Convention, which refers to the exercise of 'any or all of the powers attaching to the right of ownership,' accommodates a broader conceptualisation of slavery that focuses on the substantive powers exercised over a person rather than on formal legal title. This interpretive development has been articulated with greater explicitness by the Vice President of the Court of Appeal (Criminal Division), Lord Justice Edis, giving judgment in *R v Webb and Somerset-How*[33].

---

30 *R v Webb and Somerset-How* [2025] EWCA Crim 1491.
31 *R v SK* [2011] EWCA Crim 1691, [2012] Crim LR 63 at [39].
32 [2022] UKSC 20, [2023] AC 33.
33 [2025] EWCA Crim 1491.

Enslavement as a crime against humanity: factual condition

1.31

The recognition of enslavement as a crime against humanity in the statutes of international tribunals, and later in the Rome Statute, expanded the legal understanding of slavery in three important ways: it clarified the substantive content of the offence; it generated the first comprehensive and contemporary judicial analysis of Art 1 of the 1926 Slavery Convention; and it developed practical indicators for identifying slavery based on the exercise of ownership-like powers rather than the existence of formal legal title.

1.32

By 2001-2002, the International Criminal Tribunal for the Former Yugoslavia ('ICTY') in *Prosecutor v Kunarac*[34] had concluded that Art 1 extends to *de facto* slavery (ie the 'condition of'), with the Appeals Chamber noting:

> 'The law does not know of a 'right of ownership over a person.' Art 1(1) of the 1926 Slavery Convention speaks more guardedly 'of a person over whom any or all of the powers attaching to the right of ownership are exercised.' That language is to be preferred.'

1.33

This interpretation established that slavery could exist without legal ownership if practical powers of ownership were exercised. The crime of enslavement was later incorporated into Art 7(1)(c) of the Rome Statute, and the ICC has adopted the ICTY interpretation of slavery, concluding that Art 1 of the 1926 Slavery Convention, properly interpreted, includes both *de facto* and *de jure* slavery.

1.34

'The Appeals Chamber in *Prosecutor v Kunarac*[35] explained that the old notion of *chattel slavery* has broadened to include modern forms of slavery where any of the powers associated with ownership are exercised. These forms do not involve the most extreme rights of ownership associated with *chattel slavery*, but they still involve some destruction of the victim's juridical personality; the difference is one of degree. The Appeals Chamber concluded that these contemporary forms were part of enslavement as a crime against humanity under customary international law.'

34 *Kunarac* (Appeals Chamber) Case No IT-96-23 and IT-96-23/I-A (12 June 2002) (Judgment) [118].
35 Ibid, [117].

Judicial interpretation of the 1926 Slavery Convention by the High Court of Australia

1.35

In *Queen v Tang*[36], the High Court of Australia undertook a detailed examination of Art 1 of the 1926 Slavery Convention to determine its correct interpretation, for the purpose of defining the domestic criminal offence of slavery, which incorporated the Art 1 1926 definition into Australian criminal law. This marked the first time a common law jurisdiction interpreted Art 1 of the Convention at the highest judicial level.

1.36

The Court noted the ECtHR's limited analysis of slavery in *Siliadin v France*[37]. Gleeson CJ observing that the absence of 'a genuine right of legal ownership' was self-evident, remarking of the ECtHR's analysis that the reasoning in *Siliadin* would not have sufficed had the case involved a serious issue of slavery[38]. Gleeson CJ observed that the Court's reasoning in *Siliadin* failed to address key elements of the slavery definition in Art 1 of the 1926 Slavery Convention, noting:

> '… the Court did not refer to the definition's reference to condition in the alternative to status, or to powers as well as rights, or to words "any or at all". It may be assumed that there is, in France, no such thing as "a genuine right of legal ownership" of a person.'[39]

1.37

Gleeson CJ provided a three-part rationale for interpreting Art 1 of the 1926 Slavery Convention as encompassing *de facto* slavery.

1.38

First, by the time many states, including Australia, became parties to the Convention, slavery as a legal status (*de jure*) had already been abolished in their domestic law.

1.39

Second, the Convention's purpose was to achieve the universal abolition of slavery, which necessarily includes its contemporary manifestations.

36 *Queen v Tang* [2008] HCA 39 (28 August 2008) (High Court of Australia).
37 App no 73316/01 (ECtHR, 26 July 2005).
38 Ibid, 31.
39 *Queen v Tang* [2008] HCA 39 (28 August 2008) (High Court of Australia).

1.40

Third, the use of the phrase 'status or condition' in Art 1 distinguishes between slavery as a legal status (*de jure*) and slavery as a factual condition (*de facto*). On this basis, the High Court of Australia concluded that the term 'condition' in Art 1 refers to *de facto* slavery.

Slavery in law: status, condition, and powers of ownership

'Status or condition' of a person

1.41

The phrase 'status or condition' encompasses both slavery as a legal status (*de jure*) and slavery existing in fact, ie the condition (*de facto*).

1.42

The central issue therefore in the determination of whether someone is held in slavery is whether someone exercises ownership-like powers over that person, not whether those powers are formally recognised by law.

Powers of ownership

1.43

The essence of slavery lies in the powers attached to the rights of ownership, such that they strip away a person's autonomy and agency; an erasure of their legal, 'juridical'[40], personality. In the French version of the 1926 Act, the term used is 'attributes' rather than 'powers'[41].

1.44

Allain describes ownership as implying a background relationship of control that we recognise as possession. This foundational power is central to the legal definition of slavery, where it is the owner, not the enslaved person, who determines when the status or condition of slavery comes to an end. In any given case of alleged slavery, the focus should be on possession manifesting as control.

40 Historically under slavery systems, particularly in the Americas, slave codes were based on the concept that enslaved persons were property, not persons. This legal framework fundamentally denied enslaved people their juridical personality.

41 Jean Allain, *Slavery in International Law*, Queen's University Belfast (2012) chs 3 and 6 https://www.researchgate.net/publication/3016713406 *Enslavement in International Criminal Law* from Slavery in International Law (accessed 16 October 2025) p.15.

1.45

Reflecting on Antony Honoré's seminal work on ownership published over 60 years ago, Allain notes that Honoré emphasised possession as 'the foundation on which the whole superstructure of ownership rests.'

1.46

As the High Court of Australia illustrated in *Queen v Tang*, while the *indicia* (set out below) assist the fact-finder in reaching a conclusion, they must not distract from the essence of slavery which is grounded in a condition defined by the fundamental nature of control which operates in substance like ownership.

1.47

In the *Brima*[42] case before the Special Court for Sierra Leone, the Trial Chamber accepted that 'a person may be enslaved for a short period of time provided that in that time the perpetrator intentionally exercised a degree of control over the person sufficient to constitute the *actus reus* of the crime [ie the exercise of those powers attaching to the right of ownership].'

1.48

As noted in the Bellagio-Harvard Guidelines on the Legal Parameters of Slavery (2012)[43] (the Bellagio-Harvard Guidelines), 'while the exact form of possession might vary, in essence it supposes control over a person by another such as a person might control a thing'. Such control may be physical but [...] more abstract manifestations of control of a person may be evident in [...] attempts to forge a new identity through compelling a new religion, language, place of residence, or forcing marriage'[44].

1.49

Gleeson CJ, in *Queen v Tang* (above), considered the 1953 United Nations Secretary General's report[45], which outlined the six traits of powers connoting ownership:

1. The person in servile status may be treated as a commodity, including being subject to purchase or exchange.

---

42 *The Prosecutor vs Alex Tamba Brima, Brima Bazzy Kamara and Santigie Borbor Kanu (the AFRC Accused)* SCSL-04-16-T, Special Court for Sierra Leone, 20 June 2007.

43 Bellagio-Harvard Guidelines on the Legal Parameters of Slavery (2012), Castan Centre for Human Rights Law. Australia.

44 Guideline 3 – Possession is Foundational to Slavery, Bellagio-Harvard Guidelines on the Legal Parameters of Slavery, 2012.

45 United Nations, Economic and Social Council, Slavery, the Slave Trade, and other forms of Servitude (Report of the Secretary-General), UN Doc, E/2357, 27 January 1953, p.28.

2. The person may be used by another with unrestricted control over their labour and personal autonomy, except where limited by law.
3. The products of the person's labour are appropriated by another without fair or proportionate compensation.
4. Control over the person may be transferred to another individual, as though they were property.
5. The servile condition is enduring and cannot be ended at the will of the person subjected to it.
6. Servile status is automatically passed on to the person's descendants.

1.50

The Court had to decide whether women subjected to debt bondage and required to perform sex work were held in slavery. The Court found that these women had been purchased, subjected to strict control, and exploited in ways that went beyond harsh or unlawful employment. The fact that they were treated as commodities, bought, had their movements restricted, and forced to work off artificially inflated debts, led the Court to conclude that the conditions amounted to slavery.

De facto *ownership*

1.51

A person may possess something, or someone, in a *de facto* sense without holding legal title. This distinction is particularly evident in cases involving illegal commodities such as drugs or firearms. Although individuals cannot claim lawful ownership of contraband, courts may nonetheless recognise *de facto* ownership based on the individual's control and intent to possess. This illustrates how ownership-like powers can exist independently of formal legal title, and helps conceptualise how domination over a person may amount to slavery in law[46].

Powers of ownership: slavery from birth and hereditary enslavement

1.52

Slavery can exist from birth.

46 Jean Allain, *Slavery in International Law*, Queen's University Belfast (2012) chs 3 and 6 <https://www.researchgate.net/publication/301671340_6_-*Enslavement_in_International_Criminal_Law*-_from_Slavery_in_International_Law> accessed [16 October 2024].

1.53

Under Roman law, the principle *partus sequitur ventrem* ('the child follows the womb') established that a child born to an enslaved woman was automatically enslaved from birth. This rule operated within a legal system in which human beings could be owned as property, and the child's status followed that of the mother irrespective of any further act of exploitation. Mere birth to an enslaved woman was sufficient to confer enslaved status. It was a principle that functioned in a context where *slavery de jure,* the lawful ownership of a person, was permissible.

1.54

De facto hereditary slavery has contemporary relevance, as seen in the indictment of Joseph Kony before the International Criminal Court (ICC). Joseph Kony has been charged with the enslavement of children born to enslaved women and girls in the Lord's Resistance Army. These charges reflect the ICC Office of the Prosecutor's Policy on Slavery Crimes (2024) recognising that enslavement can occur from birth[47]. Similar issues arise for children born to Yazidi women enslaved by ISIS. In *FM v Russia*[48], the factual matrix included the victims of Art 4 violations giving birth to children conceived through rape; the perpetrators then used the removal and abuse of the victims' children as an additional means of coercion and control over their mothers.

1.55

The ICC's approach to children born to enslaved mothers will confront the question of whether such infants can meaningfully possess juridical personality, the legal capacity to hold rights and obligations, when their mothers are themselves systematically denied that status.

1.56

Where a child is born to a mother held in slavery, the child's status may be inextricably linked to the mother's own lack of personal autonomy. In such circumstances, the child's rights, though acknowledged in principle under international law, may be incapable of practical realisation. The perpetrator's domination over the mother's environment which extends to the child, places the child within the same framework of domination and dependency.

1.57

The capacity of the perpetrator to separate mother and child, a hallmark of historical and contemporary systems of enslavement, treats the child in a way

47 Office of the Prosecutor, *Policy on Slavery Crimes* (International Criminal Court, 2 December 2024) <https://www.icc-cpi.int/sites/default/files/2024-12/policy-slavery-web-eng.pdf> accessed 24 March 2026.

48 *Case of FM and Others v Russia*, Apps Nos 71671/16 and 40190/18 (ECtHR, 10 December 2024).

that strips them of their basic legal standing, amounting to a contemporary form of slavery in the *Kunarac* sense, particularly when no mechanism exists to protect their rights.

1.58

While international law affirms that children possess legal personality from birth, the above illustrates how these rights may be rendered illusionary where all potential protectors: the mother, the State, and third parties are unable or prevented from enabling children to realise them.

1.59

In such settings, the child's experience of slavery from birth reflects a form of intergenerational invisibility and domination. It is strongly arguable, and increasingly recognised in international criminal practice, that the sustained subjugation of both mother and child meets the threshold set by the Rome Statute for the exercise of ownership-like powers, thereby establishing a condition of enslavement from the child's birth.

Children and slavery: worst forms of child labour, legal invisibility, and ownership powers

The Worst Forms of Child Labour Convention, 1999 (No 182)

1.60

The Worst Forms of Child Labour Convention, 1999 (No 182)[49], one of the ILO's fundamental human rights instruments, expressly includes, among the worst forms of child labour, in Art 1(a):

> 'all forms of slavery or practices similar to slavery, such as the sale and trafficking of children, debt bondage and serfdom and forced or compulsory labour, including forced or compulsory recruitment of children for use in armed conflict.'

1.61

While earlier instruments, such as Recommendation No 70, listed forced or compulsory labour separately from slavery, the accompanying the Worst Forms of Child Labour Recommendation[50] integrates it within the broader category of slavery and practices similar to slavery. This reflected the ILO's evolving

49 Convention concerning the Prohibition and Immediate Action for the Elimination of the Worst Forms of Child Labour (Worst Forms of Child Labour Convention, 1999 (No 182)) (adopted 17 June 1999, entered into force 19 November 2000), Art 3(a).

50 Worst Forms of Child Labour Recommendation, 1999 (No 190) (adopted 17 June 1999).

understanding of these converging concepts within the ILO framework over time, underscoring the increasing recognition that forced or compulsory labour, particularly involving children, could constitute slavery[51].

Erosion of juridical personality in unaccompanied and undocumented migrant children

1.62

Unaccompanied, stateless, or displaced children, who are often undocumented and lack lawful status or caregiver support, face serious risks to their legal recognition as persons entitled to rights. Their juridical personality, the legal acknowledgment of a person's capacity to hold and exercise rights, may be severely weakened by these circumstances. Without legal status or adult advocacy, such children can become functionally invisible within legal systems.

1.63

They often face significant barriers to asserting legal claims, accessing remedies, or benefiting from protections guaranteed under domestic or international law. In practice, the rights they possess in theory may be unattainable, leaving their legal personality largely symbolic.

1.64

In practical terms, control over these children may be exercised through relationships of dependency that create ownership-like dynamics. The position is not dissimilar to that of children born to enslaved mothers. In both situations, the child is placed under a degree of domination that diminishes their personal autonomy to a degree that makes any rights they hold effectively inaccessible. Circumstances of this kind can meet the substantive threshold of *de facto* slavery.

1.65

When assessing whether a child is held in slavery, servitude, or forced labour, it is crucial to examine their full context. Factors such as legal invisibility, dependency, control, and inherited vulnerability may, depending on their intensity and interaction, combine to create conditions that satisfy the definition of slavery under both international and domestic law, understood as domination that significantly diminishes personal autonomy.

51 Lee Swepston, *Forced or compulsory labour in International Human Rights Law* (ILO Working Paper, presented at the Conference "Shaping the Definition of Human Trafficking", Dickson Poon School of Law, King's College London, May 2014) at 1.

Powers of ownership: transfer of a child for remuneration or consideration

1.66

The ICC's Office for the Prosecutor recognises that transferring a child for remuneration or other consideration can also amount to exercising ownership-like control, even without explicit exploitation and would constitute the crime of enslavement under Art 7(1)(c) of the Rome Statute. This explicitly includes illegal adoption practices, where renumeration or other consideration arises.[52]

Modern Slavery Statutory Guidance: Illegal Adoption

1.67

At this juncture, it is important to note that the Modern Slavery Statutory Guidance identifies illegal adoption as a potentially ambiguous case of child trafficking. While it is listed as an indicator, its classification remains uncertain. At 2.69, the Statutory Guidance provides:

> 'Unclear cases: illegal adoption
>
> 2.69 Not every illegal adoption would be considered exploitation. A child might, for example, be sold or adopted illegally but not exploited. The purposes of baby-selling and human trafficking/modern slavery are not necessarily the same.
>
> 2.70 Some people assume that baby-selling for adoption is a form of human trafficking because it results in a profit by selling another person. However, illegally selling a child for adoption would not constitute trafficking where the child itself is not to be exploited. Baby-selling generally results in a situation that is non exploitative with respect to the child. Where the 'parents' are looking to adopt the child and give it a loving home it should be considered as an illegal adoption case but not a case of trafficking or modern slavery.'

1.68

The position advanced in the Statutory Guidance appears to sit uneasily with the conception of illegal adoption in international criminal law as articulated by the ICC Prosecutor. The Modern Slavery Statutory Guidance arguably mischaracterises the core element of slavery by treating *exploitation* as definitional, rather than as one possible *indicium* of slavery. Properly understood, the defining feature of slavery is the exercise of domination, manifested through control; exploitation may follow, but it is not a necessary constituent element.

52 Ibid.

It is therefore striking that conduct potentially prosecutable as a crime against humanity under international law might nevertheless fail to satisfy the threshold for an offence under s 1 of the MSA 2015.

Sexual slavery: a distinct legal category of enslavement under international criminal law

1.69

Sexual slavery is recognised under the Rome Statute as both a crime against humanity (Art 7(1)(g)) and as a war crime (Arts 8(2)(b)(xxii) and 8(2)(e)(vi)). The ICC has confirmed that sexual slavery constitutes a specific form of enslavement, qualified by the additional requirement that the victim is compelled to engage in acts of a sexual nature[53]. These acts include control over sexuality, reproductive autonomy (ie forced pregnancy or termination), and forced consummation of a marriage. The ICC Office of the Prosecutor Policy on Slavery Crimes identifies forced marriage as an indicium of enslavement, 'conjugal slavery'. The ICC Elements of Crimes for the crime against humanity of sexual slavery require that the perpetrator exercised powers attaching to ownership and caused the victim to engage in acts of a sexual nature by force, coercion, or abuse of a coercive environment, and that 'the perpetrator or another person obtained or expected to obtain pecuniary or other advantage in exchange for or in connection with the acts of a sexual nature.' The International Criminal Court Act 2001 (Elements of Crimes) Regulations[54] replicate this formulation, using the broad phrase 'pecuniary or other advantage' rather than 'financial advantage.'

1.70

Submissions provided to the Appeal Chamber in *Prosecutor v Dominic Ongwen*[55] on behalf of one of the *amici curiae*[56] make the important point:

> '43. Recognising that enslavement can come in different forms, one must turn to the substance of the relationship in question, rather than what a person may name it. In the *Ongwen* case what is required is a disassociation or unmasking of the form of what *Ongwen* and others in the LRA termed their so-called 'wives' from the substance of that

53 *Prosecutor v Dominic Ongwen* (Judgment) ICC-02/04-01/15 (International Criminal Court, 4 February 2021) [3051], 1050.

54 International Criminal Court Act 2001 (Elements of Crime) (No 2) Regulations 2004, SI 2004/3239.

55 *Prosecutor v Dominic Ongwen (Judgment on the appeal of Mr Dominic Ongwen against the decision of Trial Chamber IX of 6 May 2021 entitled 'Sentence')* ICC-02/04-01/15-2023 (ICC, Appeals Chamber, 15 December 2022).

56 Jean Allain, 'Request for Leave to Submit Observations on the Issue of Sexual and Gender-based Crimes' (International Criminal Court, Appeals Chamber, *Prosecutor v Dominic Ongwen*, ICC-02/04-01/15-1895, 14 November 2021).

> relationship. In so doing, it becomes evident that not only in substance did enslavement take place, but that such enslavement was initiated by a sexual element: through sexual violence, including rape, which placed the imprimatur of overwhelming control, of a type tantamount to possession, on these girls and women and, in so doing, vitiated their freedom and autonomy; that is: deprived them of their liberty. In this manner, Element 2 of the crime of Sexual Slavery, is met and is far from being incidental.'

1.71

Acts of a sexual nature were considered by the International Criminal Tribunal for Rwanda (ICTR) in *Prosecutor v Akayesu*[57]:

> 'considers sexual violence, which includes rape, as any act of a sexual nature which is committed on a person under circumstances which are coercive. **Sexual violence is not limited to physical invasion of the human body and may include acts which do not involve penetration or even physical contact**. The incident described by Witness KK in which the Accused ordered the Interahamwe [a Hutu paramilitary organization active in the Democratic Republic of the Congo and Uganda] to undress a student and force her to do gymnastics naked in the public courtyard of the bureau communal, in front of a crowd, constitutes sexual violence.' [emphasis added]

Modern Slavery Statutory Guidance: Sexual Exploitation

1.72

Notably, the Modern Slavery Statutory Guidance suggests that trafficking for sexual exploitation is less likely to arise where there is little or no evidence that the offender gained financially, socially, or politically from the conduct (para **2.28**). However, as the case law above shows, sexual slavery does not depend on proof of profit. The proper focus is on the substance of the relationship: whether domination akin to ownership is exercised, such that the perpetrator can use or dispose of a person at will. As in the *Ongwen* case it was necessary to look beyond the label of 'wife' to the reality of the relationship. Once the form was stripped away, it became clear that the women and girls concerned were held in conditions amounting to enslavement, initiated and maintained through sexual violence that imposed overwhelming control, tantamount to possession, and thereby extinguished their freedom and autonomy. It is this exercise of ownership-like power, not the presence or absence of profit, that defines the essence of sexual slavery.

57 *Prosecutor v Akayesu* (Trial Judgment) ICTR-96-4-T (2 September 1998) para 688.

1.73

A single incident of rape, intended by the perpetrator to be isolated, will rarely amount to sexual slavery. However, where the incident forms part of a broader pattern of control and domination that significantly reduces the victim's personal autonomy, the conduct may still constitute slavery. The touchstone remains whether the domination exercised is such that the perpetrator can use the person as they wish, reflecting powers akin to ownership. Even where that threshold is not reached, the conduct may nonetheless amount to servitude or forced labour, as examined below.

Characterising slavery: legal elements and evidentiary focus

1.74

In establishing the crime of slavery, the legal analysis centres on the mental state and conduct of the perpetrator, including acts or omissions. The presence of force, threat, compulsion, or lack of consent is not a required element, although such features may frequently accompany the offence (see **Chapter 18**).

1.75

In *Kunarac*[58], the ICTY held that slavery is defined by the exercise of ownership powers, not by the absence of consent, this has subsequently been confirmed in ICC's Elements of Crimes for enslavement. The crime's core lies in the perpetrator's domination of the victim, tantamount to ownership.

1.76

Three principles arise from the International Tribunals and ICC jurisprudence: (1) consent to slavery does not preclude the offence of slavery; (2) lack of consent need not be proven; (3) in coercive environments, true consent is impossible and renders any consent nugatory.

1.77

The existence of work, labour, sexual violence, reproductive harm, or other forms of exploitation is not required to establish slavery, even though such harms are frequently present in practice. A person may be well fed, clothed, and housed yet still be enslaved if their personal autonomy has been significantly

---

58 *Prosecutor v Kunarac, Kovać and Vuković*, Case Nos IT-96-23-T and IT-96-23/1-T (ICTY, Trial Chamber, 22 February 2001) and *Kunarac* (Appeals Chamber) Case No IT-96-23 and IT-96-23/I-A (12 June 2002) (Judgment).

reduced through domination. The appeal chamber in *Kunarac*[59] adopting the reasoning in *Pohl*[60], observed,

> 'Slavery may exist even without torture. Slaves may be well fed, well clothed, and comfortably housed, but they are still slaves if without lawful process they are deprived of their freedom by forceful restraint… **There is no such thing as benevolent slavery.** Involuntary servitude, even if tempered by humane treatment, is still slavery.'

1.78

The defining legal feature of slavery is the exercise of powers attaching to the right of ownership over another person. It is control and domination that constitutes the core of the offence.The legal characterisation of slavery does not depend on the victim's circumstances or apparent acquiescence, but rather on the perpetrator's conduct and the nature of the control exercised.

1.79

Indicia of slavery, as extrapolated from ICC jurisprudence, include:

- Restriction of autonomy
- Absence of free will
- Psychological oppression or mental coercion
- Use or threat of force
- Exploitation of vulnerability
- Control of sexuality
- Forced marriage or pregnancy
- Cruel treatment and abuse
- Assertion of exclusivity
- Duration of control (even if temporary)
- Power to purchase, sell or trade individuals
- Treatment as transferable property
- Disposal, mistreatment or neglect of a person
- Using, managing or profiting from the use of a person
- Reduction to servitude

59 *Prosecutor v Kunarac* (Appeal Judgment) IT-96-23 and IT-96-23/1-A (12 June 2002) [117].
60 *United States of America v Oswald Pohl and others* (Judgment) (1947) 5 Trials of War Criminals before the Nuremberg Military Tribunals under Control Council Law No 10 958.

- Forced labour
- Human trafficking
- Sexual gratification

1.80

Servitude, forced or compulsory labour, and human trafficking are *indicia* of, but not synonymous with, slavery. These practices only constitute slavery when they involve the exercise of ownership powers. The ICC in *Prosecutor v Dominic Ongwen* clarified that enslavement does not require physical confinement; inability to leave due to fear or vulnerability suffices. Temporary ownership-like control also meets the threshold for enslavement. The Trial Chamber in *Prosecution v Ntaganda*[61] observed that the exercise of the right of ownership over someone does not require a commercial transaction[62]. Physical abuse or torture is not required, as observed by the Appeal Chamber in *Prosecutor v Kunarac*[63], referencing the *Pohl*[64] case:

> 'There is no such thing as benevolent slavery. Involuntary servitude, even if tempered by humane treatment is still slavery.'

De facto slavery and the ECtHR: the jurisprudential shift from Siliadin to Rantsev

1.81

In *Siliadin v France*[65] (2005), the ECtHR, while primarily concerned with servitude and forced labour, narrowly interpreted slavery as requiring 'a genuine right of legal ownership,' effectively limiting the definition to *de jure* slavery (ie lawful ownership of a person), failing to address *de facto* slavery (ie ownership of a person in fact, but not law). The Court's analysis of slavery was cursory and failed to engage with the contemporaneous jurisprudence in *Prosecutor v Kunarac*[66].

1.82

The ECtHR in *Rantsev v Cyprus and Russia*[67] (2010) adopted a more expansive interpretative approach to Art 4 of the Convention. The Court acknowledged

61 *Prosecutor v Bosco Ntaganda* (Judgment) ICC-01/04-02/06-2359 (ICC, Trial Chamber VI, 8 July 2019).
62 Ibid.
63 *Kunarac* (Appeals Chamber) Case No IT-96-23 and IT-96-23/I-A (12 June 2002) (Judgment).
64 *United States v Pohl et al.*, Military Tribunal II, Nuremberg, Case No.4 (8 April 1947-3 November 1947; supplemental judgment, 11 August 1948).
65 *Siliadin v France*, App No 73316/01, ECtHR, 26 July 2005, at para 122.
66 *Kunarac* (Appeals Chamber) Case No IT-96-23 and IT-96-23/I-A (12 June 2002) (Judgment).
67 *Rantsev v Cyprus and Russia*, App no 25965/04, ECtHR, 7 January 2010 at [279]-[282].

that 'trafficking itself… falls within the scope of Art 4,' and notably, cited the Appeals Chamber in *Prosecutor v Kunarac,*[68] which had concluded that the traditional concept of slavery had evolved to encompass slavery based on the exercise of any or all powers attaching to the right of ownership (see above).

1.83

Significantly, *Rantsev* marks a shift in the Court's definitional approach to slavery. When extrapolating from its reasoning in *Siliadin*, the ECtHR omitted the qualifier '*legal*' in its definition of slavery, instead referring to the exercise of a 'genuine right of ownership' rather than a 'genuine right of *legal* ownership'[69]. From *Rantsev* onwards, the Court has consistently omitted the 'legal' qualifier, signalling a broader conceptualisation of slavery that focuses on the substance of control rather than its formal legal status[70].

1.84

This shift aligns with the evolutionary interpretative principles set out in the Vienna Convention on the Law of Treaties[71], which permit treaty terms to be interpreted in light of evolving human rights practices among Contracting Parties, developments in relevant international law, and the ordinary meaning of the terms within their contemporary context[72]. Formal legal slavery (*slavery de jure*) has been abolished across all Council of Europe member states, the ECHR must interpret Art 4 to address contemporary forms of slavery that persist in practice. This approach ensures that Art 4 remains aligned with the principles of the Universal Declaration of Human Rights[73] and other international instruments prohibiting slavery. This reflects the ECHR's role as a living instrument, capable of evolving to safeguard human rights in modern contexts.

68 Ibid.

69 Jean Allain, 'The European Court of Human Rights and Trafficking as Slavery: *Rantsev v Cyprus and Russia*' (2010) 10 *HRLR* 486.

70 'legal' was omitted from the following Art 4 ECtHR caselaw: *CN and V v France*, App no 67724/09 (ECtHR, 11 October 2012); *CN v United Kingdom*, App no 4239/08 (ECtHR, 13 November 2012); *M and Others v Italy and Bulgaria,* App no 40020/03 (ECtHR, 31 July 2012); *LE v Greece*, App no 71545/12 (ECtHR, 21 January 2016); *Chowdury and Others v Greece*, App no 21884/15 (ECtHR, 30 March 2017); *SM v Croatia*, App no 60561/14 (ECtHR, 25 June 2020); *FM and Others v Russia*, Apps nos 71671/16 and 40190/18 (ECtHR, 10 December 2024).

71 Vienna Convention on the Law of Treaties (adopted 23 May 1969, entered into force 27 January 1980) 1155 UNTS 331 (VCLT).

72 For a detailed analysis and critique of the ECtHR interpretative principles see: Steven Wheatley, 'Interpreting the ECHR in Light of the Increasingly High Standards Being Required by Human Rights: Insights from Social Ontology' (2024) 24 *Human Rights Law Review 1* https://doi.org/10.1093/hrlr/ngad031 and Vladislava Stoyanova, 'United Nations Against Slavery: Unravelling Concepts, Institutions and Obligations' (2017) 38 *Michigan Journal of International Law* 359 https://repository.law.umich.edu/mjil/vol38/iss3/2.

73 Universal Declaration of Human Rights (adopted 10 December 1948) UNGA Res 217 A(III) (UDHR).

1.85

Such interpretation is now consistent with the jurisprudence of international criminal tribunals and the International Criminal Court, which have consistently applied the 1926 Slavery Convention since the seminal judgment in *Kunarac,* by focusing on the exercise of ownership-like powers over individuals, irrespective of formal legal recognition.

De facto slavery as an offence under s 1 of the Modern Slavery Act 2015

1.86

The evolution from international law to domestic criminal law establishes that *de facto* slavery, slavery in fact, without formal legal ownership, constitutes the offence of slavery under s 1 of the Modern Slavery Act 2015. This has now been confirmed by the Court of Appeal in *R v Webb and Somerset-How*[74].

1.87

The Court of Appeal's judgment in *Webb* reflects the UK Supreme Court's observations in *Basfar v Wong*[75] and is consistent with the observations of Mr Justice Lindblom (as he then was) in *R v SK*[76] at [29]:

> 'Nor should the concepts be seen as archaic. To dismiss "slavery" as being merely reminiscent of an era remote from contemporary life in the United Kingdom is wrong.'

1.88

Together, these authorities establish that the exercise of domination over a person, to a sufficient degree, falls within the definition of slavery under both international and domestic law, whether or not any legal title exists.

1.89

To be clear, and consistent with the Court's analysis in *Webb*, it is both logical and legally necessary to conclude that *de facto* slavery constitutes slavery in s 1 of the MSA 2015, for two principal reasons.

74 [2025] EWCA Crim 1491.
75 [2022] UKSC 20, [2023] AC 33.
76 [2011] EWCA Crim 1691, [2012] Crim LR 63.

1.90

First, *de jure* slavery (chattel slavery), where individuals were legally recognised as property, has been a legal impossibility in the United Kingdom since the enactment of the Slavery Abolition Act 1833. Moreover, it has been universally outlawed under international law, with all states having formally abolished legal slavery.

1.91

Second, legislation must be read to give effect to its purpose. Section 1 of the MSA 2015 creates the offence of slavery. *De jure* (chattel) slavery is not that offence: to read it so would lead to absurdity, because no UK court recognises slavery as a lawful status, either when the Act was passed or now[77]. Section 1 can therefore only be understood as criminalising *de facto* slavery: situations in which domination is exercised over a person to a degree that significantly diminishes their personal autonomy, notwithstanding the absence of any legal title.

1.92

As the preceding analysis illustrates, there should now be no ambiguity that *de facto* slavery is slavery within the scope of the criminal offence under s 1 of the MSA 2015. Lord Justice Edis in *Webb* emphasised that s 1 must be interpreted 'in accordance with' Art 4 ECHR and compatibly with it, but that the Strasbourg decision in *Siliadin,* which defines slavery by reference to the exercise of powers attaching to a non-existent legal right of ownership, cannot be determinative for the purposes of domestic criminal law. He held that the classic 'chattel slavery' definition cannot sensibly delimit the scope of the 2015 Act. The legislation itself, including the broader conception of slavery in s 45, indicates that Parliament intended a wider, more practical definition capturing situations with the characteristics of ownership-like control, even though actual legal ownership cannot occur. He observed that while conduct resembling buying or selling a person would plainly fall within the offence, the statutory concept must extend beyond that, using concrete, contemporary language to identify circumstances where an offender exerts domination equivalent in substance, though not in law, to owning another human being.

1.93

What ultimately emerges from the Court of Appeal's analysis is a consolidated perspective, one shared by the ICC and the High Court of Australia, that moves us away from the archaic picture of a person being treated as property in the literal, object-like sense. Instead, it invites us to look closely at the lived reality of the victim: the way their autonomy is eroded, their choices narrowed, and

77 *R (PACCAR Inc) v Competition Appeal Tribunal* [2023] UKSC 28, [43].

their freedom extinguished through control. It is in that lived experience, rather than in the language of ownership, that the offence of slavery now resides.

Servitude

The Four Conventional Servitudes as defined under Art 1 of the 1956 Supplementary Convention

Debt Bonded Labour	(Art 1(a))
Serfdom	(Art 1(b)) or in its contemporary form Domestic Servitude
Servile Marriage	(Art 1(c)(i)–(iii))
Child Exploitation	(Art 1(d))

Servitude: from international conception to domestic criminal offence

1.94

Unlike slavery, the concept of servitude under Art 4 of the ECHR has diverged from its foundations in international law. As examined below, the 1956 Supplementary Slavery Convention on the Abolition of Slavery, specifically defines four categories of servitude, which have become largely overlooked by the ECtHR. Early jurisprudence, such as the European Commission's decision in *Van Droogenbroeck v Belgium*[78], correctly linked servitude to the proscribed acts in Art 1 of the 1956 Supplementary Slavery Convention, however, the context of the Commission's decision, later adopted by the Court in *Van Droogenbroeck*[79], has largely been forgotten.

1.95

In that case, Mr Van Droogenbroeck argued that he was in a state of servitude, having been tied to a penal settlement. It was in this context that the Commission observed:

> 'The distinction between "servitude" and "forced labour" is not explicitly stated. It may be considered, however, that in addition to the obligation to perform services for others, the notion of *servitude embraces the obligation for the "serf" to live on another person's property and the*

78 *Van Droogenbroeck v Belgium*, App no 7906/77, (Commission decision, 5 July 1979) DR 17 236.
79 (1982) 4 EHRR 443.

impossibility of altering his condition. Here the Commission is chiefly guided by Art 1 of the Supplementary Convention on the abolition of slavery, the slave trade and institutions and practices similar to slavery of 30 April 1956.' [Emphasis added]

1.96

Van *Droogenbroeck* is not authority for the proposition that the *impossibility of altering one's condition* is a determinative requirement of all forms of servitude in international law. The Commission was extrapolating from only one of the four categories of servitude to inform its decision on servitude where the work in that case was tied to a penal settlement.

1.97

Although the ECtHR has cited *Van Droogenbroeck* in subsequent Art 4 judgments as authority for concluding that the impossibility of altering one's condition is the defining feature of servitude, it has not substantively engaged with all the institutional forms of servitude set out in the 1956 Supplementary Slavery Convention. As examined below this limited judicial attention has left the definition of servitude under Art 4 ECHR increasingly detached from its treaty origins and framed more narrowly.

1.98

A question remains to be resolved by the senior courts whether the domestic offence of servitude under s 1 of the MSA 2015 extends to all four categories of servitude under international law, as identified in the 1956 Supplementary Slavery Convention, consistent with the European Commission's early approach.

1.99

This section traces how the 1956 Supplementary Slavery Convention gradually slipped to the margins of legal analysis, despite its clear conceptual framework. It revisits the early interpretive promise signalled in *Van Droogenbroeck* and considers how that opportunity was left under-developed. It then examines the consequences of the ECtHR's reluctance to build a coherent body of jurisprudence around the 1956 Supplementary Slavery Convention's expressly defined categories of servitude. The section concludes by assessing the implications of that gap for the scope and interpretation of the domestic offence of servitude.

The legal character of servitude: no singular definition

1.100

There is no single, composite legal definition of servitude in international law. Rather, servitude encompasses a range of conditions or practices that operate to dominate and control a victim. Whether various practices amount to servitude is dependent on their specific characteristics, as well as the severity and impact experienced by the victim.

Sources of legal meaning

1.101

Certain forms of servitude have been expressly defined in international law, while others have been clarified through judicial interpretation, particularly by the ECtHR. However, to date, the ECtHR has addressed only a narrow range of servitude practices, with its jurisprudence primarily focused on domestic servitude.

Historical Forms of Servitude and their Transformation into 'Practices Similar to Slavery' under the 1956 Supplementary Slavery Convention

1.102

During the drafting of the 1926 Slavery Convention, the Temporary Slavery Commission identified several categories of servitude practices that should be progressively abolished, even where they did not constitute slavery[80]. This led to the development of the 1956 Supplementary Slavery Convention. Notably, the opening paragraph of Art 1 of the Supplementary Convention acknowledges that the identified practices could also constitute slavery. The 1956 Supplementary Slavery Convention provided a legally binding framework for addressing the following practices of servitude: debt bondage, serfdom, servile marriage, and exploitation of children[81].

1.103

Until the penultimate draft, Art 1 of the 1956 Supplementary Slavery Convention described the listed practices as 'servitudes'[82]. To secure wider political agreement, the drafters later changed this wording to 'practices and institutions similar to slavery.' As the drafting history makes clear, this was a

80 Jean Allain, 'The International Legal Regime of Slavery and Human Exploitation and its Obfuscation by the Term of Art: "Slavery-Like Practice"' (2012) 10 *Cahiers de la recherche sur les droits fondamentaux* 27, 31 http://www.unicaen.fr/puc/html/spip0308.html?article947.

81 Art 1 of the 1956 Supplementary Slavery Convention.

82 Jean Allain, 'On the Curious Disappearance of Human Servitude from General International Law' (2009) *Journal of the History of International Law* 303 and Jean Allain, 'Servitude or Institutions or Practices Similar to Slavery' in *The Legal Classification of Contemporary Forms of Slavery under International Law* (Springer 2017).

change in terminology, not substance. The language shifted, but the scope and the specific practices identified for progressive abolition remained the same.

1.104

Behind the change in terminology lay an effort to avoid drawing attention to the inconsistency between the Supplementary Convention's gradual abolition of the entrenched practices and the immediate prohibition of servitude as provided under Art 4 of the Universal Declaration of Human Rights, adopted in 1948[83]. Although the UDHR was not legally binding, its moral authority was significant. States were prepared to sign a binding treaty that phased out the named practices, many of which were still embedded in colonial systems, but were unwilling to commit to the UDHR's standard of immediate and absolute prohibition of servitude[84].

1.105

Had the drafters retained the term 'servitudes' in the 1956 Supplementary Slavery Convention, it would not only have underscored the tension with the UDHR's requirement of immediate abolition but also drawn attention to entrenched servile practices in colonial territories, practices that continued to generate economic benefit for the colonising countries. Maintaining the term would likely have intensified pressure on those countries to eradicate such systems without delay. The terminology shift in the 1956 Supplementary Slavery Convention from 'practices of servitude' was therefore a deliberate drafting strategy, designed both to avoid a direct normative clash with the UDHR and to deflect scrutiny from practices whose continuation served colonial economic interests.

The four conventional practices of servitude

1.106

The four practices of servitude identified in the 1956 Supplementary Slavery Convention provide a structured and authoritative basis for understanding the differing forms that servitude may take. Although the ECtHR has not yet undertaken a systematic analysis of each practice under the rubric of 'servitude', their form and protective purpose, read alongside Art 4 ECHR, strongly support treating them as conventional exemplifications of servitude within contemporary international law.

83 Jean Allain, 'Servitude or Institutions or Practices Similar to Slavery' in *Slavery in International Law: Of Human Exploitation and Trafficking* (Martinus Nijhoff 2013) 143–202 https://doi.org/10.1163/9789004235731_006.

84 The same pressure did not arise in respect of Slavery, because bar Saudi Arabia and Yemen, slavery recognised by law no longer existed when the 1956 Supplementary Convention was ratified.

1.107

However, where a practice of servitude, on the facts of the case, has the character of exercising any or all powers of ownership, it will constitute slavery[85].

Debt bondage

1.108

Art 1(a) the 1956 Supplementary Slavery Convention defines debt bondage as:

> 'Debt bondage, that is to say, the status or condition arising from a pledge by a debtor of his personal services or of those of a person under his control as security for a debt, if the value of those services as reasonably assessed is not applied towards the liquidation of the debt or the length and nature of those services are not respectively limited and defined;'

1.109

In practice, debt-bonded labour often involves workers exploited through inflated or fraudulent debts, where costs such as food, housing, or recruitment fees are added to their loans. Their wages rarely reduce the debt, and repayment can extend across months, years or even generations, effectively depriving them of freedom and control over their labour. Debt bonded labour, may be evidenced by the absence of some or all these safeguards which emerged during the drafting of the 1956 Supplementary Slavery Convention[86]:

(a) Any agreement where someone works to pay off a debt should only be legal if contained within a written agreement.

(b) A procedure should exist by which an official can check and confirm the amount of the debt and the value of the work to be done. This should be included in the written agreement.

(c) It should be clear how much of the work's value goes to paying off the debt.

(d) The person who owes the debt should in no circumstances be required to work for the lender for more than a set maximum number of days.

(e) The value of the work agreed upon should not be less than the usual amount paid for such work in that area.

(f) The responsibility to do the work to pay off the debt should not be transferable to someone else.

85 See *Queen v Tang* [2008] HCA 39 237 CLR 1 (High Court of Australia, 28 August 2008) and the analysis of debt bonded labour.

86 *Ad Hoc* Committee on Slavery, 1951 recommendations of safeguards to prevent debt bonded labour.

(g) The agreement should not bind the debtor's heirs to work for the creditor.

1.110

Notably, the UN Special Rapporteur observed[87]:

> 'Debt bondage is a type of servitude but also can be characterised as slavery if the characteristics denoting ownership are present … It can also be classified as forced labour under the International Labour Organisation (ILO) Forced Labour Convention 1930 (No.29). This is "a pledge of service for the repayment of a debt. …it has sometimes been termed "peonage"'.

1.111

The High Court of Australia's reasoning in *Queen v Tang*[88] offers a valuable framework for understanding how debt bondage can constitute slavery.

Serfdom

1.112

Art 1(b) of the 1956 Supplementary Slavery Convention defines serfdom as:

> 'Serfdom, that is to say, the condition or status of a tenant who is by law, custom or agreement bound to live and labour on land belonging to another person and to render some determinate service to such other person, whether for reward or not, and is not free to change his status.'

1.113

Historically serfdom was a form of unfree rural labour, found in various regions around the world, in which peasants were legally or socially bound to the land and obliged to provide labour and other dues to those exercising control over that land. When assessed against the six ownership powers identified by the UN Secretary-General in 1953, it corresponds closely to several of these indicators of slavery. Scholars have argued that, in practice, serfdom is often indistinguishable from *de facto* slavery[89], a view that accords with the observations of the Court of Appeal in *Webb*[90].

87 Report of the Special Rapporteur on contemporary forms of slavery, including its causes and consequences – Note by the Secretariat, 'Debt bondage as a key form of contemporary slavery', UN Human Rights Council, 33rd session, A/HRC/33/46 (2016).

88 [2008] HCA 39.

89 Jean Allain, 'Servitude or Institutions or Practices Similar to Slavery' in Slavery in *International Law: Of Human Exploitation and Trafficking* (Martinus Nijhoff, 2013) 143–202 https://doi.org/10.1163/9789004235731_006.

90 *R v Webb and Somerset-How* [2025] EWCA Crim 1491 at [79].

1.114

The ECtHR has recognised that servitude is closely linked to slavery and constitutes a particularly grave denial of liberty, though not necessarily in the sense of physical confinement or restriction of movement. The Court has identified the following characteristics of servitude, or modern-day serfdom, in contemporary contexts:

1. Obligation to provide certain services to another;
2. The use of coercion to force compliance;
3. The obligation of the 'serf' to live on another's property; and
4. The perception of the 'serf' is that their condition is permanent and is unlikely to change.[91]

1.115

The ECtHR has confirmed that domestic servitude is a specific offence, distinct from trafficking and involves a complex set of dynamics, involving both overt and more subtle forms of coercion to force compliance[92]. This recognition is significant, as it reflects the psychological dimensions of coercion that may not involve physical restraint but nonetheless deprive the individual of autonomy.

1.116

The ECtHR considered the concept of serfdom in a contemporary context in *Siliadin v France*[93]. The applicant, a vulnerable minor without legal status or financial resources, was found to have been held in servitude. She was forced to work long hours as a domestic servant without pay, entirely dependent on her employers, and unable to leave or enjoy any free time. Her fear of arrest and complete isolation reinforced her lack of autonomy. The Court held that these cumulative vulnerabilities and circumstances amounted to servitude, referencing the definition of 'serfdom' under Art 1(b) of the 1956 Supplementary Slavery Convention. It distinguished the situation from forced labour, noting that the applicant believed her condition to be permanent and unchangeable.

1.117

In *FM v Russia*[94], where women were taken from their home countries and exploited in convenience stores in Moscow for periods ranging from six months

91 Ibid at [123]; *CN v United Kingdom* App no 4239/08 (ECtHR, 13 November 2012), at [91].
92 *CN v United Kingdom* App no 4239/08 (ECtHR, 13 November 2012), at [80].
93 *Siliadin v France*, App no 73316/01 (ECtHR, 26 July 2005) at [123].
94 *Case of FM and others v Russia*, Apps Nos 71671/16 and 40190/18 (ECtHR, 10 December 2024).

to ten years, the Court defined the treatment to which the applicants had been subjected as servitude.

1.118

A key indicator of enslavement, recognised in ICC jurisprudence, is the victim's perception that their condition is both permanent and inescapable. Significantly, the ECtHR failed to recognise that the facts in *Siliadin* and *FM v Russia*[95] were consistent with the six ownership-like powers underpinning slavery identified by the UN Secretary-General in 1953.

1.119

Unlike the detailed analysis undertaken by the High Court of Australia in *Queen v Tang*[96], the ECtHR has yet to explicitly make the connection between attributes it associates with servitude to the six ownership-like powers that underpin slavery in international law. This disconnect reveals a gap in the ECtHR's jurisprudence and underscores the need for a more integrated understanding of the conceptual overlap between servitude and slavery. This is examined further below.

Domestic jurisprudence on servitude

1.120

There is limited case law from the Court of Appeal Criminal Division specifically addressing servitude as a criminal offence. The leading authority before the enactment of the MSA 2015 was *R v SK*[97]. In *SK*, the Court focused on the core element of servitude: the compelled provision of services through coercion. This decision continues to inform the interpretation of servitude under the current statutory framework as discussed below (see analysis of *Webb* at 1.166).

Servile marriage

1.121

Art 1(c) of the 1956 Supplementary Slavery Convention identifies three practices which constitute servile marriage[98].

---

95 Ibid.
96 *Queen v Tang* [2008] HCA 39.
97 [2011] EWCA Crim 1691, [2012] Crim LR 63 at [24].
98 For a detailed analysis of the history of this form of servitude see Jean Allain, 'Servitude or Institutions or Practices Similar to Slavery' in *Slavery in International Law: Of Human Exploitation and Trafficking* (Martinus Nijhoff 2013) 143–202 https://doi.org/10.1163/9789004235731_006.

Bride purchase

1.122

The practice of bride purchase is defined at Art 1(c)(i) of the 1956 Supplementary Slavery Convention as:

> 'A woman, without the right to refuse, is given in marriage on payment or consideration in money or in kind to her parents, guardian, family or clan.'

1.123

Crucially, such arrangements may constitute bride purchase only where the woman is denied the right to refuse the marriage, that is, where her consent is not full, free, and informed. Under international human rights law[99], *full, free, and informed consent* requires that the individual:

- has the legal capacity to marry (including being above the minimum age),
- is free from coercion, pressure, deception, or manipulation,
- has adequate understanding of the nature, consequences, and obligations of marriage, and
- is able to express her will voluntarily, without fear or undue influence.

1.124

Where full, free, and informed consent is absent, a marriage may amount to servitude or slavery, particularly where the woman is treated as property or exchanged as consideration. If the criteria for servile marriage under Art 1(c) of the 1956 Supplementary Slavery Convention are met, the practice is likely indistinguishable from *de facto* slavery.

1.125

The second key requirement of bride purchase, as a form of servitude is that a payment, whether monetary or in kind, is made to her family or kin. In *Hadijatou Mani Koraou v La République du Niger*[100], the ECOWAS Court of Justice (the judicial body of the Economic Community of West African States)

99 See Universal Declaration of Human Rights (adopted 10 December 1948 UNGA Res 217 A(III)) art 16(2); Convention on the Elimination of All Forms of Discrimination Against Women (adopted 18 December 1979, entered into force 3 September 1981) 1249 UNTS 13, art 16(1)(b); Convention on the Rights of the Child (adopted 20 November 1989, entered into force 2 September 1990) 1577 UNTS 3, art 24(3); Human Rights Committee, 'General Comment No 28: Equality of Rights Between Men and Women (Art 3)' (29 March 2000) UN Doc CCPR/C/21/Rev.1/Add.10; Convention on Consent to Marriage, Minimum Age for Marriage and Registration of Marriages (adopted 7 November 1962, entered into force 9 December 1964) 521 UNTS 231.

100 Judgment No. ECW/CCJ/JUD/06/08 of 27 October 2008.

found that the applicant's purchase and subsequent servile marriage were not merely indicative of servitude but constituted slavery. The payment for her acquisition was treated as an *indicium* of ownership, placing her situation squarely within the legal definition of slavery.

1.126

Contemporary practices carried out without free, full, or informed consent may amount to servitude or slavery. These include temporary marriage arrangements, such as *mut'ah* or *zawaj al-misy⊠r* ('tourist marriage'), entered into between tourists and the families of young girls in exchange for a bride price. Although prohibited under Islamic law, such arrangements persist in some impoverished communities[101]. Other examples include *badal* marriage in Afghanistan. In this arrangement, one family gives a daughter in marriage to another family and, in return, receives that family's daughter to marry their own son. This reciprocal exchange avoids the payment of a dowry, with the daughter herself serving as the 'in-kind' consideration. The bride kidnapping practice may constitute bride purchase if there is payment or payment in kind. Even where those criteria are not satisfied, such arrangements may still constitute sexual slavery.

1.127

The Modern Slavery Statutory Guidance has identified forced marriage cases as 'unclear' and that 'they would not necessarily mean that a person is a victim of modern slavery'[102]. No rationale is provided for this statement; it is plain from international law, including international criminal law that forced marriage would very likely constitute slavery, and if not, it is a recognised practice of servitude.

Wife transfer

1.128

This practice is defined at Art 1(c)(ii) of the 1956 Supplementary Slavery Convention as:

> 'The husband of a woman, his family, or his clan, has the right to transfer her to another person for value received or otherwise.'

101 United Nations Office on Drugs and Crime, *Interlinkages between Trafficking in Persons and Marriage* (2020) https://www.unodc.org/documents/human-trafficking/2020/UNODC_Interlinkages_Trafficking_in_Persons_and_Marriage.pdf accessed 20 September 2025.

102 Home Office, Modern Slavery: Statutory Guidance for England and Wales (under s 49 of the Modern Slavery Act 2015) and Non-Statutory Guidance for Scotland and Northern Ireland (accessible version), version 4.4 (17 March 2026) <https://www.gov.uk/government/publications/modern-slavery-how-to-identify-and-support-victims> accessed 24 March 2026, at [2.75].

1.129

The negotiation history of this provision reveals that money is not the only means of '*value*' received.[103] It is likely where this definition is met, that it will also constitute *de facto* slavery.

1.130

A contemporary example of wife transfer has emerged among North Korean girls and women who have fled to China. Many were married to Chinese men for the sole purpose of bearing children. After giving birth, these women were frequently transferred or sold to another man to repeat the process, with the cycle sometimes continuing multiple times[104]. This practice became especially prevalent in rural areas during China's one-child policy, which had created a significant gender imbalance. Given the repeated commodification, lack of autonomy, and reproductive exploitation, this practice is likely to constitute slavery.

Widow inheritance

1.131

This practice is defined at Art 1(c)(iii) of the 1956 Supplementary Slavery Convention as:

> A woman on the death of her husband is liable to be inherited by another person.

1.132

This practice is often described as a form of levirate marriage, although it does not require that inheritance be limited to the heirs of the deceased husband. In many cases, it reflects a broader custom in which widows are treated as part of their late husband's estate, with no independent inheritance rights. Faced with exclusion from inheritance, widows may face the invidious choice of either being 'inherited' by a male relative or left destitute. Where such practices arise on the facts, they are likely to constitute slavery.

Child exploitation

1.133

Child exploitation as defined in Art 1(d) of the 1956 Supplementary Slavery Convention is:

103 United Nations, Economic and Social Council, Committee on the Drafting of a Supplementary Convention on Slavery and Servitude, Summary Record of the Eleventh Meeting, 20 January 1956, UN Doc. E/AC/SR.11, 24 February 1956, p.12.

104 Committee for Human Rights in North Korea, *Lives for Sale: Personal Accounts of Women Fleeing North Korea to China*, 2009, p.53.

> 'Any institution or practice whereby a child or young person under the age of 18 years is delivered by either or both of his natural parents or by his guardian to another person, whether for reward or not, with a view to the exploitation of the child or young person or of his labour.'

1.134

Art 1(d) requires that a child is delivered by a person (parent or guardian) to another person with a view to the exploitation of that child. This definition does not accommodate the situation of a child being exploited for their labour where they have no adult or guardian (ie orphaned, abandoned or separated children). Nor does it capture situations where a child is being exploited alongside their parents or guardians.

1.135

The Ad Hoc Slavery Committee's report[105] provides insight into the specific practices targeted by Art 1(d) of the 1956 Supplementary Slavery Convention. It identified a practice particularly prevalent in parts of the Far East, locally known as *mui tsei*, which typically involved the transfer of a young child, usually a girl, into domestic service through an adoption procedure, sometimes fraudulent. This arrangement effectively commodified the child's labour capacity. The Committee observed that not all such transfers amounted to servitude, and that in many cases parents acted in what they believed to be the child's best interests; it concluded that a status or condition of servitude therefore arose where the terms of the transfer enabled the child's exploitation without regard for their welfare.

1.136

The ECtHR in *Siliadin v France*[106], concerned with an applicant who had been a child domestic worker held in exploitative conditions, did not consider the intentions of the child's parents material to the question of servitude. The Court focused on the conditions of her labour and the employer's control over her, which deprived her of autonomy and dignity. This approach aligns with the Worst Forms of Child Labour Convention, which prohibits the worst forms of child labour irrespective of parental consent or the child's own consent. This is a principle embedded in anti-trafficking law and is central to the interpretation of child exploitation as a practice of servitude criminalised under s 1 of the MSA 2015. The correct approach is to assess the exploitative reality of the child's circumstances; there is no such thing as benign child exploitation, nor can a child be deemed to have consented to their own exploitation.

105 Report of the Ad Hoc Committee on Slavery (2nd session), 1951 recommendations of safeguards to prevent debt bonded labour, [Geneva]: UN, 4 May 1951, page 10.

106 *Siliadin v France*, App No 73316/01, ECtHR, 26 July 2005.

Child labour in international law: historical foundations and contemporary norms

1.137

The development of international law concerning child labour had been marked by significant cooperation between the League of Nations, the International Labour Organisation, and, subsequently, the United Nations Economic and Social Council. The drafting of foundational instruments, including the 1926 Slavery Convention, its 1956 Supplementary Slavery Convention, and the Forced Labour Convention, were characterised by a shared commitment to the abolition of slavery, the prevention of forced and exploitative labour, and the recognition of the particular vulnerability of children. These principles were conceived as interconnected rights, forming a coherent framework across the relevant regimes. Subsequent instruments, notably the United Nations Convention on the Rights of the Child (1989) (the UNCRC)[107] and the Worst Forms of Child Labour Convention, have built upon this foundation, further refining the international legal framework and placing increased emphasis on the protection of children from the worst forms of labour and exploitation.

1.138

The UNCRC (1989) obliges states to protect children from all forms of exploitation, including trafficking. While the UNCRC does not explicitly refer to slavery or related practices, its provisions are broad in scope.

1.139

The International Labour Organisation (ILO) defines child labour as work undertaken by individuals below the minimum age for employment: 13 years for light work, 15 years for general employment, and 18 years for hazardous work. Under Art 3(d) of the Worst Forms of Child Labour Convention, 1999 (No182), hazardous work performed by anyone under the age of 18 is classified as one of the worst forms of child labour (see below). Whether a particular form of work qualifies as child labour depends on several factors, including whether it is below the minimum age of employment (see above), the nature and conditions of the work, and the number of hours worked. More broadly, the ILO characterises child labour as work that deprives children of their childhood, potential, and dignity, and that is harmful to their physical or mental development. This includes work that is dangerous, interferes with education, or places excessive demands on children alongside their schooling[108].

---

107 Convention on the Rights of the Child (adopted 20 November 1989, entered into force 2 September 1990) 1577 UNTS 3 (CRC).

108 International Labour Organisation, *What is child labour* (ILO) https://www.ilo.org/topics/child-labour/what-child-labour accessed 20 September 2025.

ILO Convention No 182: Defining the Proscribed Worst Forms of Child Labour

1.140

Worst Forms of Child Labour Convention[109], ratified by all 187 ILO member states, defines a child as anyone under 18.

1.141

Art 3 states:

> 'For the purposes of this Convention, the term **the worst forms of child labour** comprises:
>
> (a) all forms of slavery or practices similar to slavery, such as the sale and trafficking of children, debt bondage and serfdom and forced or compulsory labour, including forced or compulsory recruitment of children for use in armed conflict;
>
> (b) the use, procuring or offering of a child for prostitution, for the production of pornography or for pornographic performances;
>
> (c) the use, procuring or offering of a child for illicit activities, in particular for the production and trafficking of drugs as defined in the relevant international treaties;
>
> (d) work which, by its nature or the circumstances in which it is carried out, is likely to harm the health, safety or morals of children.'

Debt bonded labour under Art 3(a) of Worst Forms of Child Labour Convention

1.142

Debt-bonded labour is a recognised worst form of child labour and a foundational servile practice proscribed by Art 1 of the 1956 Supplementary Slavery Convention. The High Court of Australia has confirmed that debt bondage can amount to slavery, reflecting the ownership-like control that such arrangements can entail. Debt bondage is a distinct, well-established form of servitude characterised by labour extracted under the pretext of repaying a debt. Where a debt bond is imposed on a child, particularly an unaccompanied or displaced child, careful consideration must be given to whether the circumstances amount to slavery, given their heightened vulnerability and the

109 Worst Forms of Child Labour Convention 1999 (182).

potential for domination that significantly reduces personal autonomy (see analysis at **1.62** above).

Hazardous child labour under Art 3(d) of Worst Forms of Child Labour Convention

1.143

Art 3(d) of Worst Forms of Child Labour Convention proscribes as a worst form of child labour 'hazardous work.' Art 4 requires states to define hazardous work through national legislation, guided by international standards, particularly, paragraphs 3 and 4 of the Worst Forms of Child Labour Recommendation. Paragraph 3 describes hazardous work as tasks that expose children to physical, psychological, or sexual abuse; work performed underground, underwater, at dangerous heights, or in confined spaces; work involving dangerous machinery or heavy loads; and work carried out in unhealthy environments or under especially difficult conditions, such as long hours, heavy workloads, or night shifts. Paragraph 4 calls for heightened protection of vulnerable groups, including younger children, girls, and those engaged in hidden or informal work, where girls may face increased risks of exploitation and harm.

Servitude, Child Labour, and the ECtHR: A Jurisprudential Disconnect

1.144

In *CN and V v France*[110], the ECtHR found that V, unlike her sister CN, had not been subjected to forced labour or servitude. Both sisters were brought to France by their aunt and required to perform domestic tasks. CN, who arrived at age 16, was made to carry out all household chores, care for a disabled child, and do gardening, without pay, rest days, or access to education or training. These conditions led to her social isolation and formed the basis for the Court's finding of forced labour and servitude.

1.145

V, who arrived at age 10, was permitted to attend school, had time for homework, and experienced less isolation. She was also able to alert a nurse to her situation. Although she assisted with housework after school, the Court concluded that her domestic duties did not impose an excessive or disproportionate burden. Her access to education and some degree of autonomy distinguished her circumstances from those of CN. While V did experience ill-treatment, the Court found that it was not connected to her domestic work and therefore

110 Application no 67724/09 (ECtHR, 11 October 2012).

did not amount to a 'menace of penalty' sufficient to establish forced labour. Moreover, V was unable to demonstrate that she perceived her situation as unchangeable, which precluded a finding of servitude.

1.146

The ECtHR's analysis contains two significant shortcomings. First, CN exhibited multiple indicators of control and domination characteristic of slavery, properly analysed against the 1926 indicators and ICC jurisprudence, CN's situation is best seen as *de facto* slavery rather than mere servitude. On the facts accepted by the Court, CN's aunt exercised control over every aspect of her life to a degree that left her without real personal autonomy or agency (see further analysis at **1.49**).

1.147

Second, the Court's reasoning in relation to V, that she had not been held in servitude or subjected to forced labour, lacked engagement with the broader framework of international child labour law, including ILO Conventions and the UNCRC. Crucially, the ECtHR did not examine French labour laws applicable to minors. Before V started school on her arrival in France, V, then aged 10, was required to perform all housework alongside her sister, without pay or rest. This contravened ILO Minimum Age Convention, 1973 (No 138)[111], which sets the minimum age for even light work at 13 years old or above. At the time of the police investigation, V was approximately 13 years old and had been providing domestic labour in the home from her arrival. According to the Court's accepted facts, both sisters were orphaned, lived in deplorable conditions (a converted, unheated cellar), and were subjected to threats, beatings, social isolation, and deprivation of food and medical care. V's aunt was convicted of aggravated assault against V. Despite attending school, V was still required to perform domestic work after school, and only she and CN were tasked with these duties.

1.148

The Court separated the violence V experienced at the hands of her aunt, from the domestic labour she performed, concluding that violence was not used with the explicit purpose of compelling work. This analysis was flawed in the following ways.

1.149

From the standpoint of international child labour law, by assessing V's circumstances age-blind through the limited framework of 'serfdom' and referencing only the definition of forced labour in the Forced Labour

111 Convention concerning Minimum Age for Admission to Employment (Minimum Age Convention, 1973 (No 138)) (adopted 26 June 1973, entered into force 19 June 1976).

Convention, the Court failed to engage with the more nuanced and protective standards established in international law for child labour. The Court overlooked the prohibition of hazardous child labour under Art 3(d) of Worst Forms of Child Labour Convention, and disregarded the Minimum Age Convention on the minimum age requirements, both of which demand vigilance in cases of child domestic work. The Court gave no consideration to the hours V worked, including on school days, weekends, and school holidays, or to her labour before the commencement of her schooling in France, all of which, clearly fell within the internationally recognised definition of child labour. The Court neglected to assess French labour law as it applied to V's employment from the ages of 10 to 13.

1.150

V's exposure to physical abuse was inseparable from her employment in the home, as her working and living conditions were indistinguishable; yet the Court did not assess whether these circumstances amounted to hazardous child labour prohibited by international law. Had the Court approached the facts on the basis that she was subjected to a proscribed worst form of child labour, it could only have concluded that this constituted child exploitation. Had the Court adopted an evolutionary interpretation of what constitutes child servitude, it is difficult to avoid the conclusion that V was also a victim of servitude, and the ECtHR's reasoning falls markedly short of coherence with international legal principles governing child labour.

1.151

On this analysis, the Court's reliance on a narrow conception of forced labour and on historical doctrines of serfdom resulted in a missed opportunity to capture the full gravity of both CN's and V's situations. In short, the approach adopted by the Court was the antithesis of an evolutionary interpretation of slavery and servitude within the contemporary international legal framework for protecting children from exploitative labour.

Child exploitation as servitude and the living instrument doctrine: realising the protective purpose of the ECHR

1.152

In *Siliadin*[112] *v France*, the Court explicitly linked the definition of child exploitation under the 1956 Supplementary Slavery Convention to servitude, affirming its place within the Art 4 framework; on this issue, this approach is welcomed.

112 App no 73316/01 (ECtHR, 26 July 2005).

1.153

As the Court made clear in *Al-Adsani v United Kingdom*[113], the Convention must be interpreted in accordance with the Vienna Convention on the Law of Treaties, taking account of, rather than in isolation of, relevant international law. This interpretative approach recognises the ECHR's object and purpose as a Convention for the collective enforcement of rights stated in the Universal Declaration of Human Rights (UDHR: see the preamble to the ECHR).

1.154

The Court acknowledged in *SM v Croatia*[114] the significance of ILO Conventions in shaping the scope of Art 4 protections. From this standpoint, Art 4 must evolve to recognise the categorical nature of servitude, moving beyond traditional serfdom or domestic servitude to encompass practices such as debt-bonded labour, servile marriage, and, critically, child exploitation. Interpretation of child exploitation in this context should be guided by Worst Forms of Child Labour Convention, a foundational ILO Convention which has universal ratification. These practices, depending on the circumstances, may also constitute slavery, but at a minimum, and consistent with international law, should be recognised as forms of servitude under Art 4.

1.155

Where the Court failed to engage with these universally accepted international standards, as in CN and V, it not only departs from its stated interpretative methodology but also adopts an approach more restrictive than the protections laid down in the core international conventions. This in turn weakens Art 4's ability to address contemporary forms of servitude and to recognise slavery where it arises.

Restricting servitude to serfdom: ECtHR's restrictive interpretation

1.156

The 1956 Supplementary Slavery Convention is the principal international instrument which has informed the ECtHR's interpretation of servitude under Art 4 of the ECHR.[115] However, the Court has consistently characterised

113 *Al-Adsani v United Kingdom*, App no 35763/97 (ECtHR, 21 November 2001).

114 *SM v Croatia* App no 60561/14 (ECtHR, 25 June 2020).

115 *Van Droogenbroeck v Belgium*, App no. 7906/77, (Commission decision, 5 July 1979) DR 17 236: 'The distinction between 'servitude' and 'forced labour' is not explicitly stated. It may be considered, however, that in addition to the obligation to perform services for others, the notion of servitude embraces the obligation for the 'serf' to live on another person's property and the impossibility of altering his condition. **Here the Commission is chiefly guided by Art 1 of the Supplementary Convention on the abolition of slavery, the slave trade and institutions and practices similar to slavery of 30 April 1956.** [Emphasis added].

servitude by the victim's perception of being unable to change their condition, using this as the key distinguishing feature from a person being subjected to forced labour. This may be a useful litmus test when considering contemporary examples of serfdom such as domestic servitude, but to restrict servitude to only contemporary forms of serfdom create two issues of significance and marks a divergence from international law.

1.157

First, this reflects an unduly narrow and rigid understanding of servitude, one that diverges from broader international legal standards. The ECtHR derives its interpretation from the definition of *serfdom* in Article 1(b) of the 1956 Supplementary Slavery Convention, which requires that the condition be perceived as unalterable. Yet among the four internationally recognised forms of servitude, serfdom, debt bondage, servile marriage, and child exploitation, only *serfdom* carries this perception of immutability. The remaining forms do not require the victim to believe their situation is permanent; such a belief may be present, but it is not a definitional element. Notably, debt bondage cases may give rise to a perception in the victim, that their labour is time-limited, ceasing when the debt is paid off.

1.158

The Court's current approach therefore fails to capture the full scope of servitude as understood in international law. Even if the ECtHR were to reject the relevance of these four conventional categories in interpreting Art 4, it does not explain why servitude, acknowledged by the Court to be closely linked to slavery, should be construed so narrowly. This is especially difficult to reconcile with the evolution of international law following the 1926 Slavery Convention, which culminated in the broader framework of the 1956 Supplementary Slavery Convention.

1.159

If the practices listed in the 1956 Supplementary Slavery Convention are excluded from the Art 4 concept of servitude or are only admitted subject to an added requirement that the victim must believe their situation cannot be changed, this sits uneasily with the interpretive obligation to ensure harmony with international law[116] when construing Convention rights. A narrowly framed definition risks weakening the protective purpose of Art 4 and leaving practices identified as servitude, later described as practices similar to slavery, without adequate Convention-level scrutiny.

116 See Georg Nolte, 'The European Court of Human Rights and the Sources of International Law' (Seminar on *The Contribution of the ECtHR to the Development of Public International Law*, Ministry of Foreign Affairs of the Czech Republic, in connection with the 59th Meeting of CAHDI, Prague, 23 September 2020) and Demir and Baykara v Turkey [GC], no. 34503/97, 12 November 2008.

1.160

This conceptually restrictive focus on serfdom may be partly explained by the nature of the cases which come before the Court for consideration under Art 4, cases largely, albeit not exclusively, concerned with domestic servitude. Consequently, this provides limited opportunity for the Court to engage with the broader framework of servitude provided in the 1956 Supplementary Slavery Convention. It may also be explained by the way the cases are argued before the Court. However, as analysed above, where the opportunity to consider child exploitation as a practice of servitude does arise, the Court's approach lacks consistency, depth of analysis or direct engagement with foundational conventions, particularly in the case of debt bonded labour or child exploitation.

1.161

Second, the Court's narrow interpretation of servitude risks collapsing it into slavery, thereby eroding the legal distinctions that international law seeks to maintain. While both are recognised as *jus cogens* norms, only slavery operates *erga omnes*. This conflation stems from the Court's blanket application of the victim's perception of 'unalterable condition' as a defining element of servitude, a criterion that more accurately serves as an indicium of slavery.

1.162

The ECtHR has failed to acknowledge that where the definition of *serfdom* is satisfied, the situation will often amount to slavery due to the presence of ownership-like powers. These include the requirement to perform specific services, compulsion to reside in accommodation controlled by another, and the belief that one's condition cannot be changed. That these features are reflective of slavery is evident in the UN Secretary-General's 1953 report and supported by the jurisprudence of the International Criminal Court[117]. These operate as *indicia* of slavery as observed by the Court of Appeal in *Webb*.[118]

1.163

To date, the ECtHR's jurisprudence has not meaningfully engaged with this conceptual overlap, despite its relevance to the tiered structure of Art 4 ECHR, which distinguishes between slavery, servitude, and forced or compulsory labour.

1.164

This was particularly stark in *FM v Russia*[119], in that case the medical evidence confirmed the circumstances of the victims included the repetitive use of force,

---

117 Jean Allain, 'Servitude or Institutions or Practices Similar to Slavery' in Slavery in International Law: Of Human Exploitation and Trafficking (Martinus Nijhoff 2013), 28 https://doi.org/10.1163/9789004235731_006.

118 *R v Webb and Somerset-How* [2025] EWCA Crim 1491 at [94] and [116].

119 *FM and others v Russia,* Apps Nos 71671/16 and 40190/18 (ECtHR, 10 December 2024).

head trauma, and sustained physical and psychological abuse over a ten-year period. Diagnoses included post-traumatic stress disorder, and injuries were documented shortly after escape. Victims consistently reported systematic rape, forced abortion, and the birth of children conceived through sexual violence. The removal and abuse of victims' children were used as coercive tools, with medical evidence corroborating the harm inflicted.

1.165

Witnesses and NGOs described the applicants as 'enslaved' and subjected to 'slave labour,' with one applicant referring to her experience as a ten-year period of slavery. Yet the ECtHR ultimately classified the situation as servitude, emphasising the applicants' perception that their circumstances were permanent and unlikely to change. This narrow framing fails to reflect the gravity of the abuse; assessed against the 1953 Secretary-General's six powers and ICC enslavement jurisprudence, the domination exercised very likely constituted slavery. This case highlights the urgent need for a more coherent and internationally aligned interpretation of the proscribed acts in Art 4.

Servitude under s 1 of the MSA 2015

1.166

A harmonious interpretation of 'servitude' under s 1 of the MSA 2015 and Art 4 ECHR strongly suggests that decision makers should integrate the four practices of servitude reflected in the 1956 Supplementary Slavery Convention, as the ECtHR acknowledged in *Van Droogenbroeck v Belgium*[120]. This approach promotes legal certainty by providing clearly defined and internationally grounded parameters for the offence, consistent with Art 7 ECHR. Ignoring these foundational categories, and their close connection to slavery, risks narrowing the scope of protection and overlooking conduct which, on the facts, may amount to slavery itself. This argument has not yet been advanced before the Court of Appeal (Criminal Division). In *Webb*, however, the Court reaffirmed that servitude entails the compelled provision of work or services under coercion, together with conditions that amount to a serious and sustained erosion of personal freedom. Synthesising *Siliadin*, *K*, and *Rantsev*, the Court explained that servitude extends beyond forced labour: it captures situations where a victim's autonomy is effectively extinguished through enduring control, dependency, and limits on movement and choice. The features the Court identified as constituting servitude are, in substance, indistinguishable from those described in the jurisprudence as characteristic of slavery, as the Court itself recognised.

120 *Van Droogenbroeck v Belgium* (1982) 4 EHRR 443 (ECtHR, 24 June 1982).

Notably however, to say that servitude can, on certain facts, constitute slavery is one thing; to treat slavery and servitude as a single offence is quite another. The former statement recognises a continuum of severity within Art 4; the latter risks erasing the hierarchy altogether. If the two concepts are merged for criminal law purposes, the specific and exceptional gravity of slavery, as the most egregious form of domination recognised in international law, risks being attenuated.

Forced or compulsory labour

Forced labour under s 1 of the Modern Slavery Act 2015

All work or service which is exacted from any person under the menace of any penalty and for which the said person has not offered himself voluntarily. (Art 1 of Forced Labour Convention, 1930, (No 29))

The **elements** of the offence are:

1. The individual was required to provide work or service.
2. The individual did so under the menace of any penalty.
3. The individual did not offer this voluntarily.

> 'For forced or compulsory labour to arise, the Court has held that there must be some physical or mental constraint, as well as some overriding of the person's will.'
>
> (*Rantsev v Cyprus and Russia*[121] at [276])

The legal definition of forced or compulsory labour

Forced or Compulsory Labour and Discrimination: International Standards and ECHR Jurisprudence

1.167

The international legal framework on forced or compulsory labour has evolved through international labour law, human rights law, and criminal law[122]. Conduct amounting to 'forced or compulsory labour' within the meaning of Art 4(2) ECHR, when committed with the requisite mental element, falls

121 App no 25965/04, ECtHR, 7 January 2010 (finalised 10 May 2010).

122 For a detailed analysis see Vladislava Stoyanova, United Nations Against Slavery: Unravelling Concepts, Institutions and Obligations, 38 MICH. J. INT'L L. 359 (2017).

within the offence in s 1 MSA 2015. In other words, treatment that breaches Art 4(2) is, in principle, criminalised as forced or compulsory labour under domestic law.

1.168

Its core definition originates in the Forced Labour Convention, refined by the Abolition of Forced Labour Convention. Interpretation of these instruments, particularly the delimitation of the scope of forced or compulsory labour, has been shaped by the ILO Committee of Experts, whose legal analyses, though non-binding, are widely regarded as authoritative. The Committee clarifies the scope and implementation of ILO obligations in national law and practice, although its interpretations have attracted criticism from leading scholars[123].

1.169

Forced labour is a recognised indicium of slavery but will not constitute slavery unless any or all powers of ownership are exercised[124].

1.170

The provision applies to 'any person'. This refers to adults as well as children, regardless of their nationality, and it is considered irrelevant whether the person is a national of the country in which the forced labour case has been identified.

1.171

Notably, the EU Forced Labour Regulations[125] aligns the definition of 'forced labour' with the International Labour Organisation (ILO) conventions, encompassing a wide range of coercive labour practices and includes where coercion is used as a means of discipline or discrimination[126].

1.172

In *FM v Russia*[127], the ECtHR identified the discriminatory dimension of the harm suffered under Art 4. The Court recognised that the applicants, foreign women with irregular immigration status, were subjected to trafficking and

123 Jean Allain, 'Forced or Compulsory Labour' in Slavery in International Law: Of Human Exploitation and Trafficking (Martinus Nijhoff Publishers 2013) ch 5.

124 Home Office, Modern Slavery: Statutory Guidance for England and Wales (under s 49 of the Modern Slavery Act 2015) and Non-Statutory Guidance for Scotland and Northern Ireland (accessible version), version 4.4 (17 March 2026) <https://www.gov.uk/government/publications/modern-slavery-how-to-identify-and-support-victims> accessed 24 March 2026.

125 Regulation (EU) 2024/3015 of the European Parliament and of the Council of 27 November 2024 on prohibiting products made with forced labour on the Union market and amending Directive (EU) 2019/1937 OJ L 3015/1, art 2 (2).

126 Regulation (EU) 2024/3015 of the European Parliament and of the Council of 27 November 2024 on prohibiting products made with forced labour on the Union market and amending Directive (EU) 2019/1937 OJ L /, art 2(2).

127 Apps Nos 71671/16 and 40190/18 (ECtHR, 10 December 2024), at [340-345].

servitude, with gender-based violence used as a tool of coercion. Crucially, the Court found that the respondent State's failure to fulfil its positive obligations under Art 4 amounted to discriminatory treatment, and that the passivity of the authorities created a climate conducive to exploitation.

1.173

This analysis is particularly significant in recognising how discrimination operates within the context of Art 4 violations. The Court acknowledged that the applicants' status as migrant women without regular immigration status contributed to their vulnerability and the State's failure to act. Another disproportionately affected group the Court identified were migrants, especially those without close family, friends, or support networks, whose irregular status often makes them fearful or reluctant to engage with local authorities. The Court's recognition of this dynamic reflects an important step in understanding how structural discrimination facilitates and sustains exploitation.

1.174

By framing the State's inaction as discriminatory under Art 14, the Court affirmed that trafficking and servitude are not only violations of personal liberty, but also manifestations of systemic inequality. This approach strengthens the interpretative framework of Art 4 by acknowledging that vulnerability to exploitation is often shaped by intersecting factors such as gender, immigration status, and social isolation.

1.175

This judgment demonstrates the Court's capacity to address the intersectional nature of Art 4 violations, where coercive labour practices are intertwined with gender and immigration status. It recognises that discrimination operates as a structural driver of vulnerability and influences the severity and nature of the harm suffered, making it necessary to read Art 14 alongside Art 4 to reflect victims lived experience of Art 4 violation(s).

ECtHR's use of Forced Labour Convention as a definitional baseline

1.176

The ECtHR takes as its starting point the definition of forced labour from Forced Labour Convention (No 29)[128], observing that the ILO Conventions are binding on almost all the Council of Europe Member States[129].

128 *Van der Mussele v Belgium* App No 8919/80 (1983) 6 EHRR 163, [1983] ECHR 8919/80, at 32.
129 *Siliadin v France* App no 73316/01 (ECtHR, 26 July 2005), at 115.

1.177

The ECtHR has developed a nuanced interpretation of forced labour under Art 4 of the ECHR, drawing on both ILO standards and broader human rights principles. While it aligns with the ILO Forced Labour Convention's definition, 'all work or service exacted under the menace of a penalty and for which the person has not offered themselves voluntarily', the Court has expanded its analysis to reflect contemporary realities, including structural inequalities, psychological coercion, and systemic exploitation.

1.178

Crucially, ECtHR jurisprudence, for the most part, moves beyond the ILO's traditional focus on state-imposed labour, such as colonial-era practices, to address forced labour by private agents and identifying state mechanisms or state-condoned practices which are said to perpetuate Art 4 violations.

The definition

1.179

The definition comprises of three core elements: (1) work or service; (2) the menace of any penalty; and (3) involuntariness or the absence of free and informed consent.

Work or service

1.180

The scope of 'work or service' is broad, encompassing all forms of labour. The nature of the activity performed, its legality or illegality under national law, or its recognition as an 'economic activity', are immaterial. It can apply as much to factory work as to prostitution, forced criminality or forced begging[130].

Menace of penalty

1.181

During the drafting of the Forced Labour Convention, the Workers' Group proposed adding 'or the loss of any rights or privileges' after 'under the menace of any penalty'. The amendment was withdrawn on the acceptance that the

130 Joint UN Commentary on the EU Directive – A Human Rights-Based Approach (2011) p 102, citing ILO, The Cost of Coercion (2009).

existing phrase already encompassed such consequences. Accordingly, 'under menace of penalty' should be read to include the loss of rights or privileges[131].

1.182

Beyond Physical Coercion: The ECtHR recognises that threats need not be overtly violent. Psychological pressure, such as threats to be sent back to a migrant worker's homeland (*CN v UK; Chowdury and Others v Greece*) or fear of arrest (*Siliadin*), or exploitation of extreme vulnerability (eg, poverty, lack of documentation), can satisfy the 'menace of penalty' requirement. The threat of a penalty can be inferred from circumstances, as held in *Siliadin,* where even without direct threats, the fact that the victim was a minor, unlawfully present in France and feared arrest were sufficient.

1.183

The Court of Appeal in *R v Rooney (Martin Senior)*[132], noted that menace of penalty can also take subtler forms of a psychological nature, identifying pressures consistent with the ECtHR jurisprudence above. Both the CPS guidance[133] and the Modern Slavery Statutory Guidance[134] provide detailed indicators of coercion and forced labour, offering a framework for identifying such exploitation in various contexts. In *A-G's Reference (Nos 37, 38 and 65 of 2010) (Khan),*[135] the Court of Appeal observed that the offence was made out in the absence of actual violence, noting the threats of violence and intimidation used.

1.184

Totality of circumstances: The ECtHR assesses factors like:

- Restrictions on freedom of movement (eg, confiscation of passports)
- Withholding of wages or excessive deductions
- Isolation from legal/social support systems
- Deception about working conditions

1.185

In *Chowdury v Greece*, migrant strawberry pickers in Greece were subjected to armed supervision, deplorable living conditions, and non-payment of wages, which the Court deemed forced labour despite the absence of physical restraint.

131 Jean Allain, 'Forced or Compulsory Labour' in Slavery in International Law: Of Human Exploitation and Trafficking (Martinus Nijhoff Publishers 2013) ch 5 at 13.

132 *R v Rooney (Martin Senior)* [2019] EWCA Crim 681.

133 Crown Prosecution Service, *Modern Slavery and Human Trafficking: Offences and Defences (Including Section 45)* (22 July 2025) <https://www.cps.gov.uk/legal-guidance/modern-slavery-and-human-trafficking-offences-and-defences-including-section-45> accessed 19 October 2025.

134 Home Office, *Modern Slavery: Statutory Guidance for England and Wales under s 49 of the Modern Slavery Act 2015 and Non-Statutory Guidance for Scotland and Northern Ireland* (10 October 2025).

135 *A-G's Reference (Nos 37, 38 and 65 of 2010)(Khan)* [2010] EWCA Crim 2880, [2011] Crim LR 336.

1.186

In *R v Rooney*, the Court affirmed that the assessment of whether a service constitutes forced or compulsory labour must be made by considering all the circumstances of the case, considering the underlying objectives of Art 4 ECHR. Prosecutors were directed to take into account industry-standard terms and conditions as a relevant factor in this analysis. This approach aligns with the reasoning adopted by the High Court of Australia in *Queen v Tang* and reflects international standards, including those of the International Labour Organisation (ILO).

Has not offered himself voluntarily

1.187

The ILO Committee of Experts has made clear that a worker's right to freely choose and leave employment is fundamental.

1.188

Laws that prevent workers from ending indefinite or long-term contracts with reasonable notice, or that require them to work beyond the end of a fixed-term contract, amount to forced or compulsory labour. Such restrictions undermine the worker's consent and are incompatible with the Convention. This is why debt bonded labour, as well as an identified practice of servitude, also constitutes forced labour.

1.189

Consent: The absence of consent or the presence of vulnerability, such as undocumented status or dependency, can transform exploitative work into forced labour, even if the victim initially appeared to agree to the arrangement (*Chowdury and Others v Greece)*. Notably in *A-G's Reference (Nos 37, 38 and 65 of 2010) (Khan)*[136] the Court of Appeal upheld convictions for forced labour, despite the nine complainants (or at least some) initially consenting to work for the Khan family, but conditions of work promised materially changed on arrival to the UK; despite the changed working conditions the complainants returned to work for the Khan family after time spent in their home country. The Court found that the victims' vulnerability and economic dependency, exploited by the employers, indicated forced labour. The Court stated that the workers return to their employers did not show their conditions were acceptable, rather, it highlighted ongoing exploitation of their vulnerability by the offenders. This aligns with the ILO Committee of Experts' view that the 'voluntary offer of

136 Ibid.

labour' and the 'menace of any penalty' are closely linked; freedom to work cannot exist under threat.

1.190

Vulnerability as a catalyst: States must account for structural vulnerabilities (eg, irregular migration status, poverty, gender) that enable exploitation. In *SM v Croatia*[137], the ECtHR held that states fail in their obligations if they do not address systemic gaps allowing traffickers to exploit such vulnerabilities.

1.191

ILO Framework: While the ECtHR defers to ILO definitions, it integrates human rights principles to address gaps. For example, it has condemned States for tolerating exploitative practices in informal sectors (eg, agriculture) where ILO oversight is limited.

1.192

Context-sensitive evolution: The ECtHR jurisprudence moves beyond the ILO's traditional focus on state-imposed labour (eg, colonial-era practices) to address private agents or businesses exploitation of individuals.

Indicia of Forced Labour

1.193

In *Hounga v Allen*[138], the Supreme Court cited with approval the ILO's indicators of forced labour.[139] These indicators, developed by the ILO to assist in identifying exploitative practices, were described by the ECtHR in *C.N. v United Kingdom*[140] as 'a valuable benchmark in the identification of forced labour'[141]. As listed by the courts, the indicators include:

1 threats or actual physical harm to the worker.

2 restriction of movement and confinement to the workplace or to a limited area.

3 debt bondage: where the worker works to pay off a debt or loan and is not paid for his or her services. The employer may provide food and accommodation at such inflated prices that the worker cannot escape the debt.

137 *SM v Croatia* App no 60561/14 (ECtHR, 25 June 2020).
138 *Hounga v Allen* [2014] UKSC 47, [2014] 1 WLR 2889, [2014] IRLR 811.
139 at [49].
140 *CN v UK* App No 4239/08 [2012] ECHR 1911.
141 Ibid at 35.

4 withholding of wages or excessive wage reductions that violate previously made agreements.

5 retention of passports and identity documents, so that the worker cannot leave, or prove his/her identity and status.

6 threat of denunciation to the authorities, where the worker is in an irregular immigration status.[142]

1.194

In *Chowdury v Greece*[143] the ECtHR held that freedom of movement is not determinative of whether there is forced labour.

Attorney General's Reference (Nos 37, 38 and 65 of 2010) (Khan)

1.195

Before the publishing of the current sentencing guidelines for section 1 MSA 2015 offences, the Court of Appeal in *A-G's Reference (Nos 37, 38 and 65 of 2010)*[144] identified a number of factors that 'require consideration when assessing the seriousness of an offence' of trafficking for exploitation where the exploitation took the form of forced labour. Those factors must now be understood alongside, rather than as a substitute for, the unified sentencing framework for slavery, servitude, and forced or compulsory labour[145]. Nevertheless, they remain a helpful illustration of the way in which the senior courts have approached the particular harm represented by forced labour under Art 4. In doing so, they shed light on a conception of seriousness rooted in an economic-migration context, as distinct from the status-based domination that is more characteristic of servitude and slavery.

1 The relevant factor is the extent of the deception or coercion employed in relation to the incoming worker. In cases of economic exploitation, coercion will generally be an exceptional aggravating element; the principal misconduct typically lies in inducing economic migrants to travel based on deceitful assurances of favourable employment conditions.

2 The assessment concerns the nature and extent of the exploitation the worker encounters on arrival. This includes considering how far the promises made to the worker are denied in practice, and the degree to which conditions in the workplace fall below generally accepted standards in the United Kingdom.

---

142 Ibid at 35. An ILO publication, ILO Indicators of Forced Labour lists 11 indicators that are 'derived from the theoretical and practical experience of the ILO's Special Action Programme to Combat Forced Labour'.

143 App No 21884/15, at para 123.

144 [2010] EWCA Crim 2880, [2011] Crim LR 336.

145 See **Chapter 9** for a more detailed analysis of the Sentencing Council Framework.

3 The focus is on the extent and manner of control exercised over the worker to ensure that he remains economically trapped.

4 The level of vulnerability of the incoming worker, usually economic but also physical and psychological.

5 The degree of harm suffered by the worker, physical, psychological and financial.

6 The assessment includes the level of organisation and planning involved, the gain sought or obtained, and the offender's role and position within the scheme.

7 The numbers of those exploited.

8 Previous convictions for similar offences.

Many of these features now find more general expression in the Sentencing Council's guidelines, which applies a common set of culpability and harm factors across the offences of slavery, servitude, and forced or compulsory labour. While the pursuit of coherence is understandable, this aggregation gives rise to difficulty. It risks blurring the important distinctions between the different Art 4 harms and, in doing so, may obscure the internal hierarchy that the jurisprudence has long recognised. It also creates a practical danger: that conduct approaching servitude or even slavery may be prosecuted and sentenced under the rubric of forced labour, thereby diluting the gravity properly attaching to those more serious forms of Art 4 violations.

The *Khan* factors are therefore retained here not as a surrogate 'mini-guidelines', but as an illustration from the case law of a mode of reasoning specific to forced labour. They provide a useful point of comparison against which the current guideline's tendency to flatten the categories can be assessed, and they help to mark with greater precision the thresholds at which forced labour gives way to servitude and, beyond that, to slavery.

The ECtHR: sexual exploitation as a form of forced labour and servitude

1.196

The Grand Chamber in *SM v Croatia*[146] defined 'exploitation of the prostitution of others' and 'other forms of sexual exploitation' as conduct within the scope of Art 4 ECHR, even when not all elements of trafficking are present, provided there is abuse of vulnerability, coercion, or deception. The Court clarified that forced or compulsory labour under Art 4 of the ECHR is intended to protect individuals from serious exploitation, such as forced prostitution, regardless

146 *SM v Croatia*, App no 60561/14 (ECtHR, 25 June 2020).

of whether it occurs within a human-trafficking context. Such conduct may also constitute servitude or slavery or violate other Convention provisions. Importantly, 'force' includes not only overt coercion but also subtle forms of pressure, as recognised in both the Court's case-law and international standards[147].

1.197

The term 'other forms of sexual exploitation' has not been defined in international law. The United Nations Office on Drugs and Crime (UNODC) defines 'exploitation of prostitution of others' as the unlawful obtaining of financial or other material benefit from the prostitution of another person[148]. It also defined 'sexual exploitation' as the obtaining of financial or other benefits through the involvement of another person in prostitution, sexual servitude or other kinds of sexual services, including pornographic acts or the production of pornographic materials.

1.198

In the Joint UN Commentary on the EU Directive – A Human Rights-Based Approach (2011), issued by the relevant United Nations bodies[149] the following was noted:

> 'Exploitation of prostitution of others and sexual exploitation are not defined in international law. The terms have been intentionally left undefined in the Protocol in order to allow all States, independent of their domestic policies on prostitution, to ratify the Protocol. While the Protocol draws a distinction between exploitation for forced labour or services and sexual exploitation, this should not lead to the conclusion that coercive sexual exploitation does not amount to forced labour or services, particularly in the context of trafficking. Coercive sexual exploitation and forced prostitution fall within the scope of the definition of forced labour'[150].

Forced labour as a criminal offence under the Modern Slavery Act 2015

1.199

The CPS does not publish data identifying which offences under ss 1–4 of the MSA 2015 is most frequently charged or result in conviction. However,

147 *SM v Croatia* at para. 300.
148 The Model Law against Trafficking in Persons See pages 13-15 and 19
149 The Office of the High Commissioner for Human Rights (OHCHR); the UN Refugee Agency (UNHCR); UNICEF; UNODC; UN Women; and the International Labour Organisation.
150 p. 104.

appellate jurisprudence provides some indication of practice. Decisions of the Court of Appeal (Criminal Division) have predominantly concerned forced labour under s 1, with far fewer appeals addressing servitude or slavery, and comparatively limited consideration of human trafficking offences under ss 2 and 3.

1.200

Forced labour cases that have come before the Court of Appeal include *R v Rooney (Martin)*[151], *R v Josie Connors and Others*[152], *Joyce*[153], and the *Attorney General's Reference (R v Zielinski)*[154].

De facto slavery by domination: Rooney, Zielinski and Connors

1.201

Although *Rooney*, *Connors*, and *Zielinski* were each prosecuted as conspiracies to require others to perform forced or compulsory labour under s 1 of the MSA 2015, the facts found by the jury show treatment that, in substance, reached the level of slavery.

1.202

At the core of these cases is domination over individuals such that their personal autonomy was so diminished as to amount to *de facto* slavery. This is most clearly seen when the facts are viewed through the lens of the indicia identified by the High Court of Australia in *Queen v Tang*[155]:

1. **Treatment as commodities**

   In *Rooney*, workers were recruited off the streets and treated as disposable labour. In *Connors*, the workforce was degraded and intimidated to generate profit for the conspirators. In *Zielinski*, the complainant (IO) was earmarked for a sham marriage to yield financial gain, commodifying her person.

2. **Unrestricted control over labour and personal autonomy**

   Across all three cases, the offenders dictated work, controlled movements, and withheld identity documents. In *Zielinski*, victims were guarded by day and barred from going out at night. These features reflect domination that markedly curtailed personal autonomy.

151 *R v Rooney (Martin)* [2019] EWCA Crim 681.
152 [2013] EWCA 1165.
153 [2017] EWCA Crim 337.
154 [2017] EWCA Crim 758.
155 [2008] HCA 39 (Australia).

3. **Appropriation of labour without fair remuneration**

   Victims were paid little or nothing. In *Rooney*, alcohol and food were used in place of wages. In *Zielinski*, wages were confiscated and victims were denied access to their own bank accounts. This economic control entrenched dependence and deepened the domination.

4. **Transferability and displacement of control**

   While not formally transferred, victims were moved between properties and locations. In *Zielinski*, control over IO included plans for a forced marriage extending the reach of domination beyond labour into intimate life.

5. **Enduring servile condition**

   The exploitation persisted. In *Rooney*, the court observed that 'none were ever truly free to leave' [75]. In *Connors*, victims were demoralised and believed there was no better alternative outside. In *Zielinski*, threats and violence were ongoing. Duration and inescapability reinforced the servile condition.

1.203

Taken together, these facts demonstrate that the offenders exercised control and domination over the victims to the point that they could be used, moved, and exploited for profit, in ways that significantly diminished the victims' personal autonomy.

Indicia of slavery present

1.204

The following *indicia* of slavery, drawn from international standards, were present across all three cases:

- **Restriction of autonomy**
- **Absence of free will**
- **Psychological oppression or mental coercion**
- **Use or threat of force**
- **Exploitation of vulnerability**
- **Cruel treatment and abuse**
- **Duration of control (even if temporary)**
- **Disposal, mistreatment or neglect of a person**
- **Using, managing or profiting from the use of a person**

- **Reduction to servitude**
- **Forced labour**

1.205
In *Zielinski*, additional indicia were present:

- **Control of sexuality and forced marriage** (IO targeted for sham marriage)
- **Assertion of exclusivity** (victims guarded and isolated)

1.206

These *indicia* reinforce the conclusion that the treatment in each case amounted to *de facto* slavery, even if not formally charged as such.

Servitude as serfdom present

1.207
The concept of serfdom, recognised as a form of servitude under Art 4 ECHR, involves:

1. Obligation to provide services to another
2. Obligation to live in accommodation provided by the exploiter
3. Use of coercion to force compliance
4. Perception that the condition is permanent or unlikely to change

1.208
Each case exhibited these features:

- **Bound to live in accommodation provided by the offender**
  In *Rooney*, workers lived on sites controlled by the family. In *Connors*, victims travelled and lived with the family. In *Zielinski*, victims were housed in guarded properties with strict rules.
- **Labour for the offender with little or no reward**

  In all cases, victims performed manual or domestic labour under coercion, receiving minimal or no pay. In *Rooney*, alcohol was used as a form of control and pseudo-payment.
- **Perception that the condition could not be changed**
  In *Rooney*, the court observed that 'none were ever truly free to leave' [75]. In *Connors*, the effect of the control exercised over the victims was

described in these terms: 'one manifestation of this level of control was that many of those exploited were effectively deprived of the will to leave; others were too demoralised to seek to leave; and yet others believed that the world outside had nothing better to offer them.' In *Zielinski*, victims were subjected to sustained threats and violence, restricted movement and under guard with no realistic means of escape.

1.209

These facts satisfy serfdom and thus servitude, and, taken together, constitute *de facto* slavery (see **1.203**), given the degree of control and domination exercised.

Servitude as debt bondage in R v Rooney

1.210

In *Rooney*, the Crown's case was that some of the complainants were held in debt-bondage, a recognised category of servitude under the 1956 Supplementary Slavery Convention (see above).

1.211

While *Rooney, Connors* and *Zielinski* were prosecuted as conspiracies to require forced labour, the facts accepted at trial disclose treatment that very strongly suggests the legal thresholds of servitude, serfdom, debt bondage and, in some cases, slavery, were met. The offenders exercised sustained control and domination over their victims, significantly reducing their personal autonomy and directing every aspect of their daily lives. The victims were moved, used, and put to work under coercive and abusive conditions in circumstances where meaningful choice was absent. Viewed through the lens articulated in *Webb*, the question is whether the patterns of control and domination in these cases reduced the victims' autonomy to such an extent, and for such a period, that they were effectively held in slavery. On the accepted evidence, many of the victims appear to have been subjected to precisely that degree of sustained domination. Even where the conduct fell short of slavery on the *Webb* test, the circumstances nonetheless amounted to servitude, serfdom, or debt-bonded labour.

1.212

These cases demonstrate the importance of appreciating the full legal and human-rights dimensions of treatment, and of ensuring that prosecutors and courts accurately differentiate between forced labour and the more serious offences of servitude and slavery.

Reframing legal understanding: slavery and servitude mischaracterised

1.213

Although *Rooney, Connors* and *Zielinski* were charged and convicted as conspiracies to require forced or compulsory labour, the accepted findings indicate conduct that, on proper analysis, may satisfy the higher thresholds of slavery or servitude rather than forced labour alone.

1.214

The difficulty, in part, reflects the legal context in which these prosecutions occurred. The relevant appellate jurisprudence largely pre-dated *Webb*, and there was limited domestic guidance on servitude or on how sustained control and domination should be assessed. In that landscape, it is unsurprising that conduct now understood to engage the higher thresholds of slavery or servitude was framed as forced labour.

1.215

This is not to suggest that prosecutorial decisions were wrong. Rather, the cases illustrate how, in the absence of clearer authority, caution, evidential complexity, and limited engagement with international standards contributed to under-classification. With the clarification provided in *Webb*, a more precise appraisal of domination and its impact on autonomy is now expected, making similar misalignment less likely in future.

1.216

Accurate classification matters for doctrinal clarity and for marking the gravity of the offending. Where sustained control and domination significantly diminish personal autonomy, the law should be willing to identify slavery or, at minimum, servitude. The Court of Appeal's approach in *Webb* sharpens that assessment and should inform future prosecutorial choices.

Delimitations under Art 4 ECHR[156]

1.217

Slavery and servitude are absolute; there can be no derogation from the absolute prohibition of slavery or servitude under Art 4(1)[157]. Art 4(2) states that 'no one shall be required to perform forced or compulsory labour,' this must be read

156 For a comprehensive analysis see: Virginia Mantouvalou, 'Work in prison: Reintegration or exclusion and exploitation?' (2024) 15(3) European Labour Law Journal 409.

157 *W., X., Y. and Z. v the United Kingdom*, Commission decision, 1968.

together with Art 4(3). The latter does not 'limit' the exercise of the right, but rather 'delimits' the very content of forced or compulsory labour.

1.218

As clarified by the Grand Chamber in *Stummer v Austria*[158], Art 4(3) specifies what is not to be regarded as 'forced or compulsory labour.'

> 'Art 4(3)(a) is 'any work required to be done in the ordinary course of detention imposed according to the provisions of Article 5' or during conditional release from such detention.
>
> Art 4(3)(b) is any service of a military character or, in case of conscientious objectors in where they are recognised, service exacted instead of compulsory military service.
>
> Art 4(3)(c) is any service exacted in case of an emergency or calamity threatening the life or wellbeing of the community.
>
> Art 4(3)(d) is any work or service which forms part of normal civic obligations.'

1.219

This follows but does not replicate Art 2.2 of Forced Labour Convention, which identifies work that does not constitute forced or compulsory labour.

'Art.3(b)' is examined in Chapter 16 (International Protection).

Delimitation Art 4(3)(a): prison work and compulsory labour

1.220

The Grand Chamber held that compulsory prison work falls within Art 4(3)(a), even when prisoners do not earn pension rights. In *Meier v Switzerland*[159], the Court confirmed that the principle of 'normalisation', the idea that prison life should resemble life outside as far as possible, is an important guide to prisoners' treatment but cannot override lawful requirements such as compulsory work. Thus, while normalisation promotes dignity and reduces the gap between custody and freedom, it does not prevent States from requiring prisoners to work, including beyond retirement age, where domestic law permits it. As for payment, the Court has recognised changing attitudes, reflected in the 1987 and 2006 European Prison Rules, which encourage fair remuneration for prison

158 *Stummer v Austria* (2011) 54 EHRR 11 at [120].
159 *Meier v Switzerland* App No 10109/14 ECHR, 9 May 2016.

work (*Zhelyazkov v Bulgaria*[160]; *Floroiu v Romania*[161]). However, the Court has also found no clear European consensus on the issue. The fact that a prisoner was not paid does not, on its own, prevent the work from being treated as 'work required in the ordinary course of detention'[162].

1.221

Art 4(3)(a) applies to work undertaken by anyone lawfully detained under Art 5, whether convicted or on remand. Notably, Art 5 lawful detention encompasses administrative detention (ie detention which is not court ordered, such as immigration detention) (Art 5(1)(f)); the detention of minors (Art 5(1)(d)) and the detention of those for 'the prevention of the spreading of infectious diseases, of persons of unsound mind, alcoholics or drug addicts or vagrants' (Art 5(1)(e)). As examined below the broad reach of 'detention' under Art 5 and the application of the delimitation under Art 4(3)(a) far exceeds that contained within the Forced Labour Convention.

1.222

The Divisional Court in *Government of Japan v Chappell and Wright*[163] applied the above principles in extradition proceedings, accepting Japan's compulsory prison work regime included limited choice, low pay, and strict discipline. In that case Mr Chappell and Mr Wright sought to resist extradition to Japan for the prosecution of an offence of robbery in Japan.

1.223

The Divisional Court did emphasise in its judgment that Art 4(3)(a) cannot excuse conduct amounting to slavery or servitude. The Supreme Court refused permission to appeal.

Conflicting international and regional standards on labour while detained

1.224

The approach adopted by the ECtHR on Art 4(3)(a) delimitation has faced significant criticism. Dissenting judges in *Stummer* and *Yakut Republican Trade-Union Federation v Russia*[164] held that blanket exclusion from labour rights contradicts evolving human dignity standards, particularly where compulsory work serves private profit without basic protections.

160 App no.11332/04, ECHR, 9 October 2012 at [36].
161 App no.15303/10, ECHR, 12 March 2013 at [34].
162 Ibid., [33].
163 *Government of Japan v Chappell and Wright* [2025] EWHC 166 (Admin).
164 *Yakut Republican Trade-Union Federation v Russia* App No 29582/09 ECHR, 7 Dec 2021.

1.225

Given the broad scope of what can constitute lawful detention under Art 5, such as prisoners on remand, children (including those in immigration detention), those subject to administrative non-court ordered detention (ie immigration detainees) and individuals detained on mental or other health grounds, it is perhaps understandable that concern has arisen over the ECtHR's significant departure from the restrictions imposed by the ILO Conventions on work performed while held in State-authorised detention.

1.226

The International Labour Organisation adopts a more stringent position under Forced Labour Convention.

1.227

Art 2(2) of the Forced Labour Convention excludes from the definition of forced or compulsory labour only work or service exacted from a ***person convicted of a crime by a court of law***. Where two conditions are met:

1. Any work or service imposed must be carried out under the supervision and control of a public authority (ie prison or probation authorities). This is a safeguarding measure to ensure working conditions remain within acceptable limits. This supervision and monitoring must be permanent and not limited to periodic inspections[165].
2. Compulsory work or services imposed on a convicted person are excluded from the definition of forced or compulsory labour only if the person 'is not hired to or placed at the disposal of private individuals, companies or associations.' Private employment is only permitted at the individual's own request, on a voluntary basis. This provision applies to work performed both within and outside prison premises.

1.228

The ILO has repeatedly criticised systems where prisoners work under compulsion for sub-minimum wages.

1.229

The Forced Labour Convention delimitation does not extend to any other category of detainees. Work or service performed by individuals who have not been convicted, such as those in pre-trial detention or held pending extradition where they face prosecution in the requested State would constitute forced labour under international law. The expression 'in a court of law' implies

165 ILO and NHRCM, Prison labour and employment conditions of convicts in Mongolia: an empirical study, 2016, page 6.

that guarantees, such as presumption of innocence, equality before the law, impartiality of proceedings, and independence and impartiality of courts, are observed. Therefore, under international law, remand prisoners can engage in voluntary work but cannot be made to undertake compulsory work.

1.230

Compulsory labour imposed while held in detention by administrative or non-judicial bodies or authorities is not compatible with Forced Labour Convention, compulsory labour in immigration detention or hospital facilities would violate Art.1 of the Convention.

1.231

A clear divergence exists between the ECtHR's approach and ILO international standards. The 'ordinary course of detention' delimitation, as interpreted by the ECtHR, provides less protection than ILO requirements regarding which detainees can come within the scope of the delimitation.

1.232

Article 4(3) ECHR does not mirror the structure or limits of Art 2(2) of Forced Labour Convention (No 29). The result is a doctrinal gap: conduct that is 'lawful' prison labour under Art 4(3)(a) may still fall short of ILO's authoritative standards. That tension remains unresolved in Strasbourg case law. The point matters in practice, including in extradition, where a person may face compulsory prison labour compliant with Art 4(3) but inconsistent with ILO norms. Internationally, the ILO regime operates as *lex specialis* in the labour field and is designed to complement, not conflict with, the wider UN human rights framework. The UDHR, though not a treaty, functions as an authoritative articulation of Charter rights and underpins the ECHR's purpose (see the Preamble). By the time the UDHR was adopted, Convention No 29 was already in force; the two have since been read together across the UN system. Against that backdrop, the dissonance lies not in the ILO or UDHR, but in the ECHR's construction of Art 4(3) and its subsequent interpretation.

Regulatory divergence and accession: the EU, ECtHR, and the future of UK prison labour exports

1.233

As stated above, the Forced Labour Regulation (EU) 2024/3015 (the Forced Labour Regulation) adopts the definition of forced labour wholesale from Forced Labour Convention, including Art 2.2, the delimitations[166]. It is

166 Regulation (EU) 2024/3015 of the European Parliament and of the Council of 27 November 2024 on prohibiting products made with forced labour on the Union market and amending Directive (EU) 2019/1937 [2024] OJ L, 12.12.2024, preamble (19) and Art.2(1).

divergence between EU law and the ECtHR, rather than the ECtHR and international law which may create a shift or support a wider consensus that the ECtHR said was lacking in *Strummer.*

1.234

Were the EU to accede to the ECHR, its institutions would come directly under the jurisdiction of the ECtHR[167]. A central tension lies in the potential mismatch between the Court's developing case law on Art 4(3) and the EU's Forced Labour Regulation. The EU regime reflects Art 2(2) of the Forced Labour Convention and therefore sets stricter standards than those currently derived from Art 4(3) ECHR. Accession would raise the question whether the ECtHR should adjust its interpretation of Art 4(3) to align with these higher EU standards, avoiding a divide between the two systems. If not, there is a risk of fragmentation, with EU law imposing more demanding obligations than those recognised by the Strasbourg Court, weakening the overall coherence of human rights protection in Europe.

1.235

While research highlights the rehabilitative and economic benefits of fair work in prison, the EU Forced Labour Regulation is specifically concerned with *compulsory* labour in prisons, as proscribed by Forced Labour Convention.

1.236

The Forced Labour Regulation has a broad reach across supply chains. Companies selling goods in the EU may face enforcement action even where forced labour occurred several tiers upstream, such as in the production of raw materials or components. Products produced or packaged using compulsory prison labour may fall within the scope of 'forced labour in the supply chain' under Art 3 of the Regulation and could therefore be prohibited from being placed on the EU market.

1.237

For exporting countries like the UK, compliance with ECtHR standards alone will no longer suffice to access the EU market. Despite the UK no longer being bound by EU law, goods or components produced or packaged in UK prisons and destined for export to the EU will need to comply with the EU Forced Labour Regulation once it comes into force[168].

167 For a detailed analysis of the implications of EU accession see: Vassilis P Tzevelekos, 'The EU's Accession to the ECHR: The Future of the Revised Draft Accession Agreement and a Call to End the *Bosphorus* Doctrine' (2025) 6 *European Convention on Human Rights Law Review* 1–14.

168 See Chapter 19.

1.238

Under Rule 31 of the Prison Rules 1999, convicted prisoners in the UK are required to undertake 'useful work' for up to ten hours per day as part of their sentence. This requirement does not apply to individuals held on remand. Although a full exploration of prisoners' labour rights in the UK is beyond the scope of this chapter, existing research shows that prison industries often involve low-skilled tasks such as assembly line work and packaging[169].

Human trafficking

Council of Europe Convention Against Trafficking In Human Beings (2005)

Trafficking as defined in Art 4 ECAT involves three core elements:

Action:	recruitment, transportation, transfer, harbouring or receipt of persons
Means ***(required for adult victims only)***	the threat or use of force or other forms of coercion, of abduction, of fraud, of deception, of the abuse of power or of a position of vulnerability or of the giving or receiving of payments or benefits to achieve the consent of a person having control over another person;
Purpose of Exploitation ***(as a minimum)***	the exploitation of the prostitution of others or other forms of sexual exploitation, forced labour or services, slavery or practices similar to slavery, servitude or the removal of organs.

Thresholds for Victims:

- **Adults:** All three elements: action, means, and for the purpose of must be established.
- **Children:** Only two elements: action and for the purpose of are required; the 'means' element is not necessary.

169 Ben Jarman and Helen Fair, *Working Prisoners in the UK: Laws, Policies and Practical Realities* (Briefing Paper, Institute for Crime & Justice Policy Research, July 2024); Virginia Mantouvalou, 'Human Rights for Working Prisoners' (8 September 2021) UK Labour Law Blog.

The legal definition of human trafficking

International definition of trafficking

1.239

The ECtHR adopts the definition of human trafficking in Art 4 of ECAT[170], which mirrors the core elements of the Palermo Protocol definition. The Court has made clear that victims must be identified and assessed, and human trafficking criminalised, in a manner consistent with the criteria set out in Art 4 ECAT. The ECAT definition is examined at **1.302**.

Domestic Regulations for Identification

1.240

As examined in Chapter 4, under the statutory framework created by the MSA 2015, as amended by the Nationality and Borders Act 2022 (NABA 2022), the Secretary of State is empowered to make regulations governing the identification and support of victims of modern slavery and human trafficking. These powers are conferred by s 50(2) MSA 2015 (as amended by s 60 NABA 2022) and by s 69(1) NABA 2022.

Domestic definitions of 'victim'

1.241

The principal regulations currently in force are the Slavery and Human Trafficking (Definition of Victim) Regulations 2022 ('the 2022 Regulations').

1.242

Regulation 2, read with regulation 1, defines a 'victim of slavery' as a person who has been subjected to slavery, servitude, or forced or compulsory labour, a definition to be interpreted in accordance with Art 4 ECHR.

1.243

Regulation 3 defines a 'victim of human trafficking' by drawing on selected elements of the s 2 MSA 2015 trafficking offence and combining them with aspects of the 'means' element in Art 4 of ECAT.

170 *Rantsev v Cyprus and Russia* (2010) 51 EHRR 1

Misalignment with ECAT

1.244

However, as examined below neither the statutory offence of human trafficking in ss 2 and 3 MSA 2015 nor the definition employed for the purposes of victim identification and support in the 2022 Regulations reproduces the ECAT definition. In consequence, three distinct definitional regimes operate in parallel: one for criminal liability, one for identification and support, and a further, non-aligned, treaty definition in ECAT.

State responsibility for private acts

1.245

Consistent with Art 1 of the ECHR, the ECtHR has clarified that where a human rights violation originates in unlawful acts of private individuals, the state may nonetheless incur responsibility under the Convention.

Positive obligations under Art 4

1.246

Art 4 ECHR imposes both negative and positive obligations. States must not themselves engage in slavery, servitude, forced or compulsory labour, or human trafficking, but consistent with Art 1 of the ECHR, they must also take operational measures to prevent, protect, investigate and punish such conduct, including by criminalising behaviour falling within Art 4 and establishing procedures for victim identification and support for those within their jurisdiction. An Art 4 breach can arise from the State's failure to exercise due diligence to prevent, protect and respond to the violation in accordance with its positive obligations.

Alignment with ECAT as a constitutional benchmark

1.247

The ECtHR has interpreted the positive obligations under Art 4 by drawing on the definitions of human trafficking in ECAT and the Palermo Protocol[171]. Academic analysis has similarly treated these instruments as setting the relevant international standards[172]. Where domestic definitions diverge from these international instruments, questions may arise as to whether the State has met its obligations under Art 4, particularly in relation to legal certainty and the

171 See *VCL and AN v United Kingdom; FM v Russia* [240], [273]-[277]; *SM v Croatia,* [289-90], [296-297] and [303].

172 See V Stoyanova, *Human Trafficking and Slavery Reconsidered. Conceptual Limits and States' Positive Obligations in European Law* (Cambridge University Press, 2017). *J v Austria,* App No. 58216/12, ECHR, Judgment on 17 January 2017 at [109], [111] and [115] and *VCL and AN v UK* at [160], [168] and [172].

effective protection of individuals who may have been trafficked. In the United Kingdom three parallel and materially different definitional regimes currently operate: one for criminal liability, one for NRM decision-making and support, and a separate treaty definition in ECAT. A further complexity arises from the Modern Slavery Statutory Guidance, which directs NRM decision-makers to the DfE Child Sexual Exploitation Guidance[173] when assessing child sexual exploitation. The DfE definition, however, diverges from the child-specific trafficking framework in three important respects. First, it requires an exchange or a financial advantage or increased status for the perpetrator conditions absent from ECAT and from the 2022 Regulations. Second, it requires coercion, manipulation or deception, thereby reintroducing means requirements that ECAT Art 4(c) and the Statutory Guidance itself expressly disapply for children. Third, it excludes cases where sexual gratification or power is the sole purpose and the child receives nothing, despite such conduct falling squarely within trafficking for sexual exploitation under international standards. The Statutory Guidance is therefore internally inconsistent: it states the ECAT-derived principle that no means element is required for child victims, while directing decision-makers to a definition that reintroduces such requirements. This creates a real risk of systematic under-identification of trafficked children in the child sexual exploitation context.

Divergence between the MSA 2015 trafficking offences and Art 4(a) ECAT

The evolution of the domestic trafficking offence and its departure from international standards

1.248

As observed by the Court of Appeal in *R v Ajay Stephens*[174], the predecessors to ss 2 and 3 of the Modern Slavery Act 2015 ('MSA 2015') were the offences of trafficking for sexual and non-sexual exploitation, including s 4 of the Asylum and Immigration (Treatment of Claimants, etc) Act 2004 ('the 2004 Act'). That provision, now repealed, was introduced specifically to address cross-border trafficking for labour exploitation[175].

1.249

The current trafficking offences in ss 2 and 3 MSA 2015 build on that earlier framework. While the MSA 2015 broadened the scope of the offence to

173 DfE Guidance Child sexual exploitation: definition and guide for practitioners 16 February 2017 https://www.gov.uk/government/publications/child-sexual-exploitationdefinition-and-guide-for-practitioners last accessed 24 July 2026.

174 *R v Ajay Stephens* [2022] EWCA Crim 410 at [18].

175 Home Office, *Secure Borders, Safe Haven: Integration with Diversity in Modern Britain* (Cm 5387, 2002) and Explanatory Note to the Act, [7].

encompass a wider range of exploitative conduct, its structure and terminology remain anchored in a legislative model developed before ECAT had taken shape.

1.250

This historical context matters. Section 4 of the 2004 Act was enacted before the adoption of ECAT in 2005 and long before the UK signed it[176]; it also pre-dated the ECtHR's landmark judgment in *Rantsev v Cyprus and Russia*[177], which first recognised that trafficking, as defined in Art 3(a) of the Palermo Protocol and Art 4(a) ECAT, falls within Art 4 ECHR and must be criminalised as a specific offence.

1.251

The offence previously found in s 4 of the 2004 Act was neither modelled on nor substantively aligned with the Palermo Protocol or ECAT, and nothing in its legislative history supports that Parliament intended alignment. Although the Explanatory Notes to the MSA 2015 later identified Palermo, ECAT, the EU Trafficking Directive and Art 4 ECHR as the relevant international framework, the Joint Committee on the Draft Modern Slavery Bill nonetheless expressed concern that the draft trafficking clause was narrower than those definitions, particularly because it did not clearly encompass 'harbouring or receiving'. The Government's response, set out in its Command Paper, rejected the suggestion of any material gap and emphasised the need for offences that were readily understood by practitioners[178]. This legislative trajectory, whereby ss 2 and 3 MSA 2015 adopt a structure and terminology that do not mirror the act–means–purpose model in Art 4 ECAT, raises the question whether, viewed through the lens of the ECtHR's reasoning in *CN v UK*[179], such divergence has implications for the scope of the United Kingdom's positive obligation under Art 4 to secure an effective criminal law framework addressing human trafficking.

Section 2 of the MSA 2015: structure of the trafficking offence

1.252

Section 2(1) of the MSA 2015 creates the offence of human trafficking by providing that a person commits the offence if they 'arrange or facilitate the travel' of another person with a view to that person being exploited. Section 2(3) explains that arranging or facilitating travel *may* include recruiting, transporting,

176 23 March 2007.

177 (2010) 51 EHRR 1.

178 Home Office, The Government Response to the Report from the Joint Committee on the Draft Modern Slavery Bill, Session 2013–14 HL Paper 166 / HC 1019: Draft Modern Slavery Bill (Cm 8889, June 2014).

179 App no. 4239/08, ECHR, Judgment on 13 November 2012.

transferring, harbouring, receiving the victim, or transferring or exchanging control over them.

1.253

This structure differs from the international definition of trafficking in ECAT and the Palermo Protocol, under which movement or 'travel' is not a required element of the offence. In those instruments, the listed acts: recruitment, transportation, transfer, harbouring, receipt, or exchange of control are stand-alone and disjunctive. By contrast, s 2 of the 2015 Act makes travel, or the arrangement or facilitation of travel, an essential ingredient, with s 2(3) operating only as illustrative ways in which travel may be arranged or facilitated.

1.254

As a result, the required nexus between the arrangement or facilitation of travel in s 2(1) and the acts listed in s 2(3) is uncertain. Certain acts recognised in ECAT and the Palermo Protocol, such as receiving, transferring, or exchanging control over a victim, may fall outside the natural wording of s 2 where they do not involve arranging or facilitating travel. If such conduct is not captured by the domestic offence of human trafficking, the legislation risks falling short of the State's positive obligations under Art 4 ECHR, given the ECtHR's emphasis that domestic trafficking offences and victim identification duties must reflect the criteria set out in ECAT and the Palermo Protocol[180].

Section 3 of the MSA 2015: Overview

1.255

Section 3 of the MSA 2015 defines 'exploitation' for the purposes of the trafficking offence in s 2. It does so, first, by cross-referring to slavery, servitude and forced or compulsory labour (s 3(2)), and to sexual exploitation (s3(3)) and removal of organs (s 3(4)), and secondly by creating additional, residual categories of exploitation in s 3(5)–(6), focused on securing services or benefits. These residual categories are therefore central where the conduct does not fall within s 1 or within sexual or organ-removal exploitation.

Section 3 of the MSA 2015: Sexual Exploitation

1.256

Section 3(3)(a) defines sexual exploitation for the purposes of the human trafficking offence where an offence has been committed under the Protection

180 *VCL and AN v UK* at [160] and [172].

of Children Act 1978, or Part 1 of the Sexual Offences Act 2003 (the 2003 Act). The narrow construction of sexual exploitation in the human trafficking offence reflects the issues identified at 1.251 above and may give rise to an Art.4 breach.

Sexual Exploitation: Section 3(3) and International/Art 4 ECHR Standards on Child Sexual Exploitation

1.257

The child sexual exploitation offences in ss 47–49 in the 2003 Act do not require proof of compulsion: they criminalise paying for the sexual services of a child, causing or inciting a child into sexual exploitation, and controlling a child in relation to such exploitation, based on the defendant's intentional conduct and the fact that the victim is under 18. These offences are established where the child is under 18 and the defendant does not reasonably believe the child to be 18 or over, or where the child is under 13, in which case belief as to age is irrelevant. Accordingly, where the child is aged 13 or above and the purchaser, controller or inciter holds an objectively reasonable belief that the child is 18 or over, no offence under ss 47–49 is made out.

1.258

Section 51 of the 2003 Act provides the statutory definition of *sexual exploitation* for the purposes of those offences. A person is treated as sexually exploited if, on at least one occasion and whether or not they were compelled, they offer or provide sexual services to another in return for payment or a promise of payment, whether the payment is to themselves or to a third party, or where an indecent image of them is recorded, streamed or otherwise transmitted. For these purposes:

> '"payment" means any financial advantage, including the discharge of an obligation to pay or the provision of goods or services (including sexual services) gratuitously or at a discount.'

1.259

The UK National Working Group for Sexually Exploited Children and Young People[181] describes child sexual exploitation as a type of child abuse that happens when a child is performing, and/or another or others are performing on them, sexual activities in exchange for something (eg food, accommodation, drugs, alcohol, cigarettes, affection, gifts, money). Referring to the situation of a child 'receiving' attention and affection from an adult who sexualises the

181 https://www.nspcc.org.uk/keeping-children-safe/types-of-abuse/child-sexual-exploitation/?utm_old=cse

relationship over time and then routinely sexually abuses the child (grooming). These definitions or descriptors are used in statutory guidance[182].

1.260

In its February 2022 report on child sexual exploitation, the Independent Inquiry into Child Sexual Abuse, led by Professor Alexis Jay OBE[183], observed that the English statutory definition of child sexual exploitation correctly recognises that an exchange may occur but is not an essential feature of exploitation.

1.261

As recorded at C.2 of the report, the panel said:

> '4. Abusers often use alcohol, drugs, actual or threatened violence, kindness and affection to develop a connection with a child they intend to exploit. The manipulation at the core of exploitation is often a result of an imbalance of power. While any child may be at risk of sexual exploitation, exploited children are often already vulnerable, with childhoods characterised by neglect, substance abuse and domestic violence. Many are in care or have a disability. Teenagers are particularly vulnerable to child sexual exploitation but younger children are increasingly exposed to such harm.
>
> 5. That some exploited children seem to cooperate with sexual activity should not be misinterpreted as consent. A child under the age of 13 can never legally give consent to sexual activity and such activity is a criminal offence. Too often, even today, children who are victims of these crimes are treated as if they were consenting when the reality is that they have been coerced or manipulated into sexual activity.'

1.262

However, the Panel criticised the accompanying requirement in the statutory guidance definition that, where no exchange is present, the perpetrator or facilitator must obtain a financial advantage or an increase in status. They concluded that this formulation is too restrictive, noting that child sexual exploitation can occur without either element. If such requirements were genuinely necessary to establish exploitation, the most serious cases, where children are violently coerced or brutalised into sexual activity, would fall outside the statutory definition.

182 Department for Education, Child Sexual Exploitation: Definition and a Guide for Practitioners, Local Leaders and Decision Makers Working to Protect Children from Child Sexual Exploitation (DfE February 2017).

183 Independent Inquiry into Child Sexual Abuse (Prof Alexis Jay OBE (chair)), *Child Sexual Exploitation by Organised Networks: Investigation Report* (HC 1059, February 2022).

1.263

As examined above at **1.69** and **1.198**, the ICC and other sources of interpretation of international law adopt a broader approach which underscores that 'sexual exploitation' should not be confined to situations where the exploiter receives a directly quantifiable financial gain. The UN has defined 'sexual exploitation' (not necessarily related to children) as follows: 'any actual or attempted abuse of a position of vulnerability, differential power, or trust, for sexual purposes, including, but not limited to, profiting monetarily, socially or politically from the sexual exploitation of another.'[184]

1.264

In respect of children, the UNODC recognises that, 'Child sexual exploitation involves child sexual abuse and/or other sexualised acts using children that involves an exchange of some kind (e.g., affection, food, drugs, and shelter).' Referring to 'pecuniary or other advantage' is deliberately open-textured. It encompasses not only monetary profit, debt-discharge or discounts, but also non-financial or in-kind benefits. The exploiter's 'advantage' is thus understood as any benefit derived from the victim's sexual exploitation.

1.265

Under the Worst Forms of Child Labour Convention, 1999 (No 182), the *use, procuring or offering of a child for prostitution, pornography or pornographic performances* is expressly and unequivocally identified as a worst form of child labour. The Convention imposes no requirement to establish that the child was compelled and does not make the child's protection contingent on the exploiter's knowledge or belief about age. The harm lies in the very act of using, procuring or offering a child for sexual purposes; the protections attach to the child's status as a child and the nature of the conduct, not to the perpetrator's *mens rea*.

1.266

This status-based approach is mirrored in Art 4 ECHR, which is absolute and permits no justification, balancing or limitation. The State's positive obligations include operational duties to protect where there are credible allegations of slavery, servitude, forced or compulsory labour or trafficking, and to maintain an effective legal and administrative framework against such practices. By defining sexual exploitation of children through the lens of the commission of a qualifying criminal offence in the 2003 Act, the domestic framework excludes cases in which the person procuring, inciting or controlling the child reasonably believed the child to be 18 or over. The absence of a domestic criminal offence cannot relieve the State of its obligation under Arts 1 and 4 ECHR to

184 UN Secretariat, "Secretary-General's Bulletin on Special Measures for Protection for Sexual Exploitation and Abuse."

identify, protect and effectively investigate circumstances that may amount to exploitation of a child; nor can it justify treating a child used for prostitution as falling outside the concept of 'exploitation' where, in international law, such use is already recognised as a worst form of child labour and, in most cases, as slavery, servitude or forced or compulsory labour regardless of the exploiter's belief as to age.

1.267

Taken together, these instruments and the inquiry point in the same direction: sexual exploitation arguably is not restricted to forms involving direct financial profit. The international framework, including ECAT, Recommendation No R (2000) 11 and the ICC's approach to sexual slavery, recognises that exploitation may arise wherever an exploiter derives a benefit, financial or otherwise, from the sexual use of another person.

Section 3 MSA 2015: the residual exploitation category

1.268

Section 3(5) provides that a person is exploited if they are used to provide services or benefits for another, but only where force, threats or deception are used to secure those services or benefits. The Explanatory Notes to the Modern Slavery Act 2015 indicate that this limb was aimed at practices such as forced begging or shoplifting[185]. It is not obvious why a separate residual category is needed. Where an adult is compelled to beg or to shoplift, the conduct will usually fall within forced or compulsory labour for the purposes of s 1; and, therefore in many cases, the same behaviour could be prosecuted under s 1 or would meet s 3(3), without recourse to the narrower residual limb in s 3(5). Against that background and given the well-documented harms of forced begging and forced criminality, the choice to impose a restrictive 'means' threshold in s 3(5), which omits the broader coercive and manipulative means recognised in ECAT (notably abuse of vulnerability), is hard to justify. The available legislative materials, including the Explanatory Notes, do not explain the purpose behind this provision.

1.269

Section 3(6) creates further categories of exploitation specifically for children and for 'vulnerable adults.' In each case the provision introduces a comparative and subjective test: the victim must have been selected because of a particular characteristic, and exploitation depends on how a hypothetical person without that characteristic would have behaved. These tests differ markedly from the

185 See the Explanatory Note to MSA 2015 at para 34.

ECAT model, which treats vulnerability in substantive terms and does not require comparator-based reasoning.

Section 3(6) as it applies to children

1.270

For children, section 3(6)(a) provides that a child is regarded as exploited only where they are used to provide services or benefits because they are a child, and where an adult, without the prescribed vulnerabilities[186], would likely have refused to be used for that purpose[187]. By contrast, under ECAT and the Palermo Protocol the question of whether a child has been exploited does not depend on the exploiter knowing, or being in a position where they ought to have known, that the victim was a child; the child's age and the nature of the conduct are sufficient to establish exploitation under those instruments.

1.271

This understanding is reinforced by international child-labour standards, in particular Worst Forms of Child Labour Convention (No 182), which the Explanatory Notes to the MSA 2015 identify as part of the relevant international framework on slavery, servitude and forced or compulsory labour. Convention No 182 requires States to prohibit and eliminate the worst forms of child labour for all under-18s. It includes the use of children for illicit activities or hazardous work. It does not make that classification depend on the exploiter's knowledge or motive. A child engaged in criminal, hazardous or otherwise exploitative work is within a worst form of child labour regardless of whether the perpetrator knew the child's age. On that basis, in the ILO child-labour regime the legal characterisation turns on objective facts: the child's age and the nature and conditions of the work. Lack of knowledge of age does not alter the exploitative character of using a child for services or benefits.

1.272

Section 3(6)(a) therefore imposes an additional evidential burden. It requires proof that the child's status as a child, and the belief that an adult would have refused, were factors in the offender's decision to target them[188]. This arguably significantly narrows protection by directing attention to hypothetical adult behaviour and the perpetrator's motivation, rather than to the inherent vulnerability of children and their exploitation. This risks creating a protection gap that is difficult to reconcile with the State's obligation under Art 1 ECHR to

186 Physical or mental illness, disability or family relationship.
187 *R v Ajay Stephens* [2022] EWCA Crim 410 at [18].
188 *R v Karamera* [2019] Cr App R 14.

secure, through effective criminal-law measures, the rights of children subjected to the worst forms of child labour within their jurisdiction.

Section 3(6) as it applies to vulnerable adults

1.273

For vulnerable adults, s 3(6)(b) provides that an adult is exploited if they are used, or someone attempts to use them, for services or benefits, and they are selected for that purpose because they are mentally or physically ill, disabled, or have a particular family relationship. It further requires that an adult without that illness, disability or family relationship would likely have refused to be used in this way. The provision thus recognises only certain forms of vulnerability and again ties exploitation to an 'ordinary adult' comparator.

1.274

This reflects, to some extent, the reality that traffickers often target people they perceive as less able to resist. However, the scope of the provision is narrow: vulnerabilities that are economic, migratory, social or emotional fall outside s 3(6)(b) unless the services or benefits were obtained through force, threats or deception, thereby reverting to the restrictive 'means' in s 3(5). This imposes a higher evidential bar than ECAT, which defines 'abuse of a position of vulnerability' broadly as exploiting any situation in which a person has no real or acceptable alternative but to submit to abuse, and lists physical, psychological, familial, social and economic vulnerabilities as examples.

1.275

Accordingly, forms of vulnerability frequently identified in trafficking cases, such as insecure immigration status, economic dependence or racialised targeting, are not expressly captured by s 3(6)(b). In *FM v Russia*, for example, immigration status was identified as the very reason the victims were targeted and was treated as engaging heightened Art 4 diligence; a domestic test that excludes such vulnerabilities or subjects them to an elevated 'means' threshold sits uncomfortably with that approach.

Consent, comparators and divergence from ECAT

1.276

Under Article 4(b) ECAT, the use of any of the identified means, such as abuse of a position of vulnerability, strips a person's apparent consent of legal effect, because those means are what induced the person to agree to provide services or benefits in the first place. Once improper means are used, the person's consent cannot legitimise the situation. This loss of valid consent is what can turn poor or precarious working conditions into exploitation. In ECAT's model, there is a clear sequence: the use of means invalidates consent, and the lack of valid consent may then render the extraction of services or benefits exploitative (see **1.195** above).

1.277

Section 3(6) adopts a materially different approach. For an adult to fall within this provision, it must be shown that the perpetrator targeted the individual because of one of the narrowly prescribed vulnerabilities (see 1.273 above) and, even then, that a hypothetical adult without those vulnerabilities would have likely refused to provide the same services or benefits. If this two-stage test is not met, the assessment reverts to whether force, threats or deception can be shown to have been used to obtain the services or benefits. The result is that, outside the tightly defined circumstances in s 3(6), the domestic framework requires demonstrable overt threats, force or deception before exploitation can be established, in contrast to the broader ECAT model in which the use of improper means vitiates consent and may thereby convert the provision of services or benefits into exploitation.

1.278

Read together, ss 3(5) and 3(6) therefore create a residual exploitation regime that is both conceptually and evidentially more restrictive than ECAT. Subtle or structural forms of abuse of vulnerability may not be captured unless they can be re-described as involving force, threats or deception, or as falling within one of the limited vulnerabilities listed in s 3(6). This produces a fundamental divergence from ECAT's broad understanding of vulnerability, its role in consent and how it can inform whether exploitation has arisen.

Re-characterising conduct under s 1 of the MSA 2015

1.279

Against this background, the conceptual breadth of slavery, servitude and forced or compulsory labour, as analysed above, and provided in ss 1 and 3(2) MSA 2015, assume particular significance. As a result, some of the situations that fit only awkwardly, or not at all, within ss 3(3), (5) and (6) may be more appropriately prosecuted under s 1 or ss 2 read with 3(2). Framing the offences in this way allows courts to draw on the wider, ECAT-consistent understanding of core concepts of sexual exploitation and vulnerability such as immigration or social status, gender, race or ethnicity, and economic dependence,[189] rather than relying on the narrower drafting in ss 3(3), (5) and (6) of MSA 2015.

189 Explanatory Report to ECAT at para. 77.

Divergence between the Slavery and Human Trafficking (Definition of Victim) Regulations 2022 and Art 4(a) of ECAT[190]

Regulation 3(5)(a) read with 3(6)(d): restriction of the 'means' element

1.280

The Slavery and Human Trafficking (Definition of Victim) Regulations 2022 adopt a two-stage structure for identifying a victim. That approach departs in several respects from the definition in Art 4(a) ECAT, including in its treatment of the 'means' element. No senior domestic court has yet determined whether the 2022 Regulations are compatible with ECAT. However, the narrowing of the 'means' limb sits uncomfortably with the Convention's broader understanding of abuse of a position of vulnerability and with the ECtHR's consistent reliance on the ECAT definition to inform Art 4 positive obligations arising in trafficking cases.

1.281

At the first stage, Regulation 3(5)(a) requires that an adult's travel has been arranged or facilitated through one of the recognised 'means' also reflected in ECAT, namely the threat or use of force, other forms of coercion, abduction, fraud, deception, abuse of power or of a position of vulnerability, or the giving or receiving of payments or benefits to obtain the consent of a person having control over another. This element broadly corresponds to Art 4(a)–(b) ECAT, which requires that one of these means be used at some point in the trafficking process for the purpose of exploitation.

1.282

The second stage, however, adopts a narrower approach. Regulation 3(6)(d) confines the means by which exploitation for the provision of services or benefits must be achieved to force, threats or deception, a threshold not found in ECAT. Because the regulation requires that the exploitation itself be secured through force, threats or deception, it excludes situations in which other means listed in Art 4(a) ECAT, such as other forms of coercion, abuse of a position of vulnerability or power, or the giving or receiving of benefits to obtain consent from a person in control, are used to obtain the individual's services or benefits. These means are examined further at **1.307–1.309**. Moreover, unlike s 3(5) MSA 2015, Regulation 3 contains no provision addressing vulnerable adults, even on the narrow basis provided in the Act.

190 For an in-depth analysis see Jason Haynes, 'Regressing from the Gold Standard: The UK's Slavery and Human Trafficking Regulations and the Narrowing of Victim Protection' (2024) 45 *Statute Law Review* mae059 <https://doi.org/10.1093/slr/mae059> accessed 20 October 2025.

1.283

This narrowing does not fully reflect the range of circumstances in which exploitation may occur, particularly where a person's decision-making is shaped by structural inequality, economic insecurity or social isolation rather than by overt force or threats. As discussed above in relation to the criminal offence of human trafficking and s 3(6), such vulnerabilities can undermine the validity of apparent consent in ways that are recognised within the broader ECAT framework.

1.284

The ECtHR emphasised in *VCL and AN v United Kingdom* that 'the assessment of whether a person is a victim of trafficking must be done consistently with the definition of trafficking as contained in the Palermo Protocol and the Council of Europe Anti-Trafficking Convention.' This underscores the importance of ensuring that domestic identification frameworks align with the standards set out in those instruments.

Regulation 3(5)(b) and the ambiguity of 'any method' in child trafficking cases

1.285

Regulation 3(5)(b) of the 2022 Regulations provides that:

> 'in a case where V is a child at the time the method is used, any method.'

1.286

Regulation 3(5)(a) of the 2022 Regulations defines the 'method' by which a person's travel must have been arranged or facilitated, using terms that mirror the 'means' in Art 4(a) ECAT: the threat or use of force, other forms of coercion, abduction, fraud, deception, abuse of power or of a position of vulnerability, or the giving or receiving of payments or benefits to obtain the consent of a person having control over another.

1.287

Art 4(c) of ECAT provides:

> 'The recruitment, transportation, transfer, harbouring or receipt of a child for the purpose of exploitation shall be considered "trafficking in human beings" even if this does not involve any of the means set forth in subparagraph (a).'

1.288

The ECAT provision reflects the principle that children cannot give valid consent to their own exploitation and, accordingly, that no 'means' requirement applies in their case. This sets a deliberately lower evidential threshold, recognising children's inherent vulnerability and the need for their protection to be independent of any inquiry into coercion, deception or other means. By contrast, the formulation 'any method' in Regulation 3(5)(b) introduces an implicit requirement that some form of method must still be identified, even if its nature is unrestricted. This creates ambiguity and departs from Art 4(c) ECAT, which expressly disapplies the means requirement entirely for children. The wording of the regulation therefore risks re-introducing an evidential hurdle, proof of a 'method', that ECAT intentionally removes in order to ensure that children are not required to demonstrate coercion or manipulation before being recognised as victims of trafficking.

Regulation 3(7): Definition of Sexual Exploitation

1.289

Under Regulation 3(6)(a) and (7), a person is regarded as 'prostituted by another person' where one individual (A) compels the victim to offer or provide sexual services to a different person in return for payment or a promise of payment. It does not matter whether the payment is made to A or to someone else. The focus of this definition is therefore on compulsion by A: it is the act of requiring the victim to provide sexual services to another person, for payment or the prospect of it, that brings the situation within the meaning of being 'prostituted by another person' for the purposes of the identification regulations.

1.290

Regulation 3(8) recognises additional forms of sexual exploitation, including where a child is the victim of an offence under Part 1 of the Sexual Offences Act 2003. This narrow definition of child sexual exploitation is analysed at **1.257–1.267** above. A criminal offence of sexual exploitation against a child under 18 years old is established if the person inciting, controlling or paying for the sexual services of a child 13 years old or over did not reasonably believe they were 18 years old or over. To adopt this requirement for the purposes of identifying a child who has been sexually exploited, is arguably misconceived where the child has been controlled, incited into sexual activities or paid for sexual services. In such circumstances, under the 2022 Regulations, the child can only be identified as a victim of sexual exploitation if they fall within Regulation 3(7), by demonstrating that they were compelled to offer or provide the sexual services.

Compulsion and Regulation 3's Misalignment with ECAT

1.291

Moreover, where a child cannot satisfy Regulation 3(8) and is required to rely on Regulation 3(7) to establish sexual exploitation, the introduction of 'compulsion' is both legally and conceptually problematic when analysed against the standards established under international law, particularly ECAT.

1.292

The 2022 Regulations do not define what 'compelled' means, either in Regulation 3(7) or in the general interpretive provisions. This creates uncertainty and increases the risk that the term will be applied inconsistently, especially because 'compulsion' is used differently across various areas of law.

1.293

In ECAT, compulsion appears only in relation to *the provision of non-punishment* (Art 26), which deals with criminal offending by victims. Similarly, under domestic law, s 45(3) of the MSA 2015 uses compulsion in the same way for adult victims. In both frameworks, compulsion is not part of the definition of trafficking or exploitation; it is only relevant to whether a victim should be criminally liable for offences linked to their exploitation (ie the offence was a direct consequence of their exploitation).

1.294

If compulsion were interpreted in line with ECAT and Art 26, it would need to be understood broadly. ECAT's Explanatory Report makes clear that compulsion includes *any* of the means listed in Art 4(a), such as deception, abuse of power, or abuse of vulnerability[191]. Accordingly, for adults, sexual exploitation under Regulation 7 arguably may be understood as occurring whenever any of the means listed in Art 4(a) ECAT are used for the purpose of sexual exploitation. This approach aligns with the ECtHR's observations on 'forced prostitution' in *SM v Croatia*[192].

1.295

However, Art 4(c) ECAT expressly removes the 'means' requirement for child victims, reflecting the principle that a child cannot consent to their own exploitation. The Modern Slavery Statutory Guidance adopts the same approach: a child does not need to be coerced or deceived to be recognised as a victim, because they cannot give informed consent to criminal or exploitative activity. Any child recruited, transported or transferred for the purpose of

191 Explanatory Report – CETS 197 – Action against Trafficking in Human Beings at [273].
192 *SM v Croatia* App no 60561/14 (ECtHR, 25 June 2020) at [301].

exploitation is therefore to be treated as a potential victim regardless of the presence or absence of 'means.'

1.296

Against that background, making 'compulsion' the decisive factor in determining whether sexual activity involving a child constitutes exploitation misconstrues ECAT. It effectively re-introduces a requirement for the child to show coercion or lack of consent before being recognised as a victim, contrary to the core principle that a child cannot consent to their own abuse. This mischaracterisation risks excluding trafficked children from protection where sexual exploitation occurs.

Kidnap for ransom as exploitation: regulation 3 of the Slavery and Human Trafficking (Definition of Victim) Regulations 2022

1.297

In *R (AAM) v Secretary of State for the Home Department*[193], the High Court examined whether the Claimant's experience of kidnap for ransom constituted exploitation within the meaning of Regulation 3 of the 2022 Regulations. The court concluded that the Secretary of State had misapplied the domestic legal framework by failing to engage with the broader definitions of 'means' and 'exploitation' set out in the Regulations.

1.298

Under Regulation 3(5)(ii), *kidnap* is expressly recognised as a means by which a person may be trafficked. The court highlighted that Parliament's inclusion of 'kidnap', defined in the Oxford English Dictionary as 'carry off (a person etc.) by illegal force or fraud esp. to obtain a ransom', was intentional and expansive. It was not confined to abduction for sexual or labour exploitation but extended to circumstances where the victim is kidnapped with a view to obtaining a benefit, such as ransom or extortion.

1.299

The court further clarified that Regulation 3(6) does not require that exploitation has occurred. It is sufficient that the individual was subjected to force, threats or deception designed to induce them to provide services or enable another person to acquire benefits. In the Claimant's case, the kidnap was undertaken with a view to securing a ransom, which the Court held fell squarely within the scope of exploitation as defined in the Regulations.

193 *R (AAM) v Secretary of State for the Home Department* [2025] EWHC 447 (Admin).

1.300

The Secretary of State sought to rely on Art 4 of ECAT, which refers only to 'abduction' and provides a narrower list of exploitation types. The Court however noted that the 2022 Regulations go beyond ECAT and the Palermo Protocol by including 'abduction, kidnap and false imprisonment' as recognised means, and by offering a more detailed and subdivided definition of exploitation. The domestic framework was designed to capture other forms of exploitation, including those not explicitly listed in ECAT.

1.301

The judgment confirms that kidnap for ransom, depending on the facts, may constitute exploitation for the purposes of identifying a victim of trafficking. The explanatory report to ECAT acknowledges that domestic legislation may target additional forms of exploitation beyond those enumerated in international instruments.

Council of Europe Convention against Trafficking in Human Beings (2005)

ECAT definition of Human Trafficking

1.302

Art.4 of ECAT provides:

'Art 4 – Definitions

For the purposes of this Convention:

a "Trafficking in human beings" shall mean the recruitment, transportation, transfer, harbouring or receipt of persons, by means of the threat or use of force or other forms of coercion, of abduction, of fraud, of deception, of the abuse of power or of a position of vulnerability or of the giving or receiving of payments or benefits to achieve the consent of a person having control over another person, for the purpose of exploitation. Exploitation shall include, at a minimum, the exploitation of the prostitution of others or other forms of sexual exploitation, forced labour or services, slavery or practices similar to slavery, servitude or the removal of organs;

b The consent of a victim of "trafficking in human beings" to the intended exploitation set forth in subparagraph (a) of this article shall be irrelevant where any of the means set forth in subparagraph (a) have been used;

c The recruitment, transportation, transfer, harbouring or receipt of a child for the purpose of exploitation shall be considered "trafficking in human beings" even if this does not involve any of the means set forth in subparagraph (a) of this article;

d "Child" shall mean any person under eighteen years of age;

e "Victim" shall mean any natural person who is subject to trafficking in human beings as defined in this article.'

1.303

Adults are required to satisfy all three components of the definition while children are only required to establish the action component and the purpose component.[194]

First component: The action of

1.304

The acts covered by the definition are broad and intended to criminalise all links in the trafficking chain. In the case of adults there needs to be a nexus between the act, achieved by the means (see below), for the purpose of exploitation. This definition is intended to create a criminal offence and therefore the intention of the person carrying out the act must be linked with the means and the purpose.

1.305

Recruitment includes any activity leading to exploitation, regardless of method of recruitment. As regards terminology, the Explanatory Report to ECAT clarifies that 'recruitment' includes recruitment by using new information technologies like the internet. Transportation does not require border crossing or illegal entry. Transfer involves handing over a person, even if the person is not accepted. Harbouring refers to accommodating victims at any stage[195]. Receipt includes receiving a person even if this is just meeting or instructing victims during their journey.

Second component: By means of

1.306

Means includes threat or use of force or other forms of physical or psychological coercion, deception, fraud, and the abuse of power or vulnerability. Coercion

194 *MS (Pakistan)* [2020] UKSC 9, [2020] 1 WLR 1373 at para 20.
195 R(BG) v Secretary of State for the Home Department [2016] EWHC 786 (Admin), para 49.

may be overt, such as violence, threats, or the withholding of identity documents, or more subtle, including manipulation or debt bondage. Psychological coercion can involve blackmail, intimidation, or the exploitation of economic hardship. For a helpful judicial analysis of coercion in the context of coercive and controlling behaviour, see the judgment of Mr Justice Hayden in *A County Council v LW & Anor*[196] and *F v M*[197].

1.307

Abuse of a position of vulnerability refers to the exploitation of any situation in which a person has no real or acceptable alternative but to submit to abuse. Vulnerability may be physical, psychological, emotional, familial, social, or economic in nature. Examples include insecurity or illegality of the victim's immigration status, economic dependence, or fragile health. In essence, any state of hardship that compels a person to accept exploitation may constitute such abuse[198].

1.308

The phrase 'giving or receiving of payments or benefits to achieve the consent of a person having control over another person' refers to situations where a third party, such as a parent, guardian, employer, or other authority figure, is offered money or benefits in exchange for allowing the victim to be exploited. This is an indicium of slavery.

1.309

ECAT Explanatory Report states:

> 'Thus, trafficking means much more than mere organised movement of persons for profit. The critical additional factors that distinguish trafficking from migrant smuggling are use of one of the means listed (force, deception, abuse of a situation of vulnerability and so on) throughout or at some stage in the process, and use of that means for the purpose of exploitation.'

Consent

1.310

The consent of a victim is irrelevant if any of the specified 'means' have been used to achieve the act. In other words, once it is established that improper means were employed, any apparent consent by the victim does not absolve

196 [2020] EWCOP 50 at para.21 and 22.
197 [2021] EWFC 4 at paras 103 to 109.
198 Explanatory Report to ECAT at para. 77.

the trafficker of criminal responsibility. For consent to be considered irrelevant based on abuse of position of vulnerability, the person to whom consent is given must have abused an existing or created vulnerability to secure an act intended to result in exploitation[199].

1.311

In cases involving children, ECAT dispenses with the 'means' element entirely: trafficking is established by the act and the exploitative purpose alone. This reflects the principle that children cannot legally give meaningful consent to their exploitation, regardless of any apparent agreement by the child or their guardians.

Third component: For the purpose of exploitation

Purpose

1.312

Exploitation does not need to occur for trafficking to be established; intent to exploit suffices to establish this component.

1.313

The Court of Appeal in *MN & IXU v Secretary of State for the Home Department*[200] emphasised that the concept of 'purpose' should be applied using ordinary language and common sense, with regard to the intended scope of ECAT. While the degree of proximity or closeness between the act and exploitation is relevant, the court warned against imposing tests of immediacy or a gloss which distracts from the language of Art 4(a) itself. The time interval between the act and future exploitation is relevant but not determinative, and the Court stressed a flexible, fact-specific approach focused on ordinary meaning rather than technical tests.

Exploitation

1.314

ECAT provides non-exhaustive forms of exploitation: the exploitation of the prostitution of others or other forms of sexual exploitation, forced labour or services, slavery or practices similar to slavery, servitude or the removal of organs.

199 UNODC, Issue Paper: Abuse of a Position of Vulnerability and other Means within the Definition of Trafficking in Persons (2012), pp. 90–91.
200 *MN & IXU v Secretary of State for the Home Department* [2020] EWCA Civ 1746; [2021] WLR 1956.

1.315

As academics have observed, 'exploitation' confirms the definitions of slavery, and the practices of servitude and forced or compulsory labour while allowing for the possibility of lesser or differing types of exploitation to fall within this definitional requirement[201].

1.316

New forms of exploitation continue to emerge, raising complex questions about whether they constitute slavery, related offences, or other exploitative practices. See for example reproductive exploitation[202] (see **1.320** below).

1.317

Most of the forms of exploitation have been considered above.

1.318

The UK courts and tribunals, and the ECtHR have recognised exploitation for criminal activities as a form of exploitation (eg, drug trafficking, forced begging). In the case of children, the use, offering or procuring a child for illicit activities is a proscribed worst form of child labour under ILO Convention 182 and will contravene Art 4 of the ECHR. As discussed above, this could constitute slavery, servitude or forced labour dependent on the facts (see sections on slavery, servitude and forced labour above).

From organ removal to reproductive exploitation: legal frameworks and emerging issues

1.319

ECAT expressly recognises organ removal as a form of exploitation. Neither the Palermo Protocol nor ECAT defines 'removal of organs,' leaving the term open to interpretation and national implementation. During the drafting of the Protocol, there was considerable debate within the Ad Hoc Committee about whether to include broader language such as 'trafficking in organs, tissues, or body parts.' Ultimately, only 'removal of organs' was adopted, to maintain the focus on offences against persons rather than their body parts.

201 Jean's Art – The International Legal Regime of Slavery and Human Exploitation and its Obfuscation by the Term of Art: "Slavery-like Practice".

202 European Network of Migrant Women and Coalition for the Abolition of Surrogate Motherhood, *Joint Investigation Migrant women and reproductive exploitation in the surrogacy industry,* October 2022.

1.320

Commentators have noted that the list of exploitative practices under ECAT is non-exhaustive, potentially allowing trafficking cases to encompass exploitation involving a person's tissues, cells, or other body parts. An emerging and growing form of exploitation is reproductive exploitation[203] which includes:

- forcing or coercing women to undergo egg harvesting for IVF;
- recruiting women as surrogate mothers where coercion or abuse of vulnerability is present;
- trafficking vulnerable pregnant women for illegal adoption; and/or
- grooming and recruiting girls or women as wives for foreign fighters (such as ISIS), not amounting to sexual slavery as defined in ICC case law, but involving coercive means.

While these forms of reproductive exploitation have not yet been squarely addressed in Art 4 or ECAT case law, they fall naturally within ECAT's non-exhaustive exploitation clause when assessed against the Convention's protective purpose and the broader understanding of enslavement and ownership-like domination in international criminal jurisprudence.

1.321

A notable case in Georgia involved over 100 Thai women who were promised paid surrogacy but were instead held captive, subjected to hormone treatments, and forced to undergo repeated egg retrieval procedures by a criminal network. The crimes were investigated and prosecuted under the domestic human trafficking laws. This case illustrates that while eggs are classified as gametes, not organs or tissues, the case was prosecuted as human trafficking and, on the facts, likely constituted slavery.

Trafficking for organ removal: the Obeta and Ekweremadu case

1.322

In *R v Obeta, Ekweremadu (Ike and Beatrice)*[204], the defendants were convicted of conspiracy to commit human trafficking, contrary to s 2 of the MSA 2015. The case concerned the trafficking of a young Nigerian man, anonymised as C, who

203 European Network of Migrant Women and Coalition for the Abolition of Surrogate Motherhood, Joint Investigation Migrant women and reproductive exploitation in the surrogacy industry, October 2022.

204 *R v Obeta and others* [2023] Sentencing Remarks (Johnson J, 5 May 2023) https://www.judiciary.uk/wp-content/uploads/2023/05/R-v-Obeta-and-others-sentencing-remarks.pdf accessed 20 September 2025.

was brought to the UK to donate a kidney to Sonia Ekweremadu, daughter of Ike and Beatrice. C was recruited under false pretences, with fabricated documents and promises of reward. Mr Justice Johnson observed in his sentencing remarks that the 'wealth and power inequality' between C and Ike Ekweremadu, noting the latter's political status, global property holdings, and substantial financial resources, in contrast to C's inability to afford basic transport. Obeta had previously undergone a transplant using similar deception and was found to have established a corrupt relationship with a hospital interpreter to coach C through any consultations with the NHS staff. On 3 May 2022, C escaped and reported to police, who recognised him as a potential trafficking victim and secured his protection. Although the transplant was ultimately refused, Johnson J criticised the failure of the clinicians at the Royal Free Hospital to refer the matter to the safeguarding team or the police, despite clear indicators of trafficking, including the tenuous claimed relationship, C's confusion, and lack of understanding of the process.

1.323

The Court found that the offence was complete upon the arrangement of travel for the purpose of exploitation and rejected the defence assertion that C had consented in any meaningful sense. On 5 May 2023, Obinna Obeta was sentenced to ten years' imprisonment; Ike Ekweremadu to nine years and eight months; and Beatrice Ekweremadu to four years and six months. All defendants were made subject to licence conditions and barred from working with vulnerable persons.

The Council of Europe Convention against Trafficking in Human Organs (CTHO)

1.324

The UNODC has published guidance emphasising that organ removal, unlike other forms of exploitation such as sexual exploitation or forced labour, may not always be inherently criminal, its legality depends on the context and the presence of coercion or lack of consent. A pivotal joint study by the Council of Europe (CoE) and the United Nations clarified the distinction between trafficking in organs, tissues, and cells (OTC) and trafficking in humans for organ removal. The study identified widespread confusion, noting trafficking in OTC focuses on illegal trade of organs/tissues, while the Palermo Protocol addresses cases where persons are trafficked specifically for organ extraction. The study recommended an international legal framework to combat OTC trafficking, prompting the Council of Europe Convention against Trafficking in Human Organs (CTHO). This instrument aims to close legal loopholes, enhance victim protection, and harmonise criminal justice responses, strengthening global efforts against both forms of trafficking.

1.325

The Council of Europe Convention against Trafficking in Human Organs (CTHO), also known as the Santiago de Compostela Convention (SCC), is the first binding regional instrument specifically targeting organ trafficking, and entered into force in 2018. The United Kingdom has signed but not ratified the CTHO. The Convention obliges states to criminalise all activities related to organ trafficking, with criminal offences set out in Arts 4 to 8. Art 4 criminalises the intentional removal of organs without the free, informed, and specific consent of the donor, or, in the case of deceased donors, without proper legal authorisation, where financial gain is involved. Legitimate compensation is expressly excluded from this prohibition. Art 5 criminalises the use of illicitly removed organs, while Art 6 encourages the criminalisation of implantations performed outside official systems. Art 7 addresses illicit solicitation, recruitment, and bribery in connection with organ removal or implantation, and Art 8 covers the entire chain of illicit organ handling.

1.326

The CTHO adopts the definition of 'human organ' from EU Directive 2010/45, and expressly excludes trafficking in tissues and cells, leaving these for future regulation. The Convention's consent requirements mirror those in the Convention on Human Rights and Biomedicine, mandating that consent be specific, written, fully informed, and overseen by an official body.

Lord Briggs and the academic debate in *Basfar v Wong*

Academic commentary

1.327

Lord Briggs, in *Basfar v Wong*, referred to a rich body of academic discourse on the scope and definition of human trafficking in international law. The debate centres on whether exploitation alone, absent a preceding process, can constitute trafficking under the Palermo Protocol.

1.328

Anne Gallagher, in *The International Law of Human Trafficking*[205], argued for a broad interpretation. She contended that the inclusion of terms such as 'harbouring' and 'receipt' in the definition extends its reach beyond the process of trafficking to encompass the end situation of exploitation. Gallagher writes:

205 Gallagher AT, *The International Law of Human Trafficking* (Cambridge University Press, 2010).

> 'The breadth of the action element has the effect of bringing, within potential reach of the definition, not just recruiters, brokers, and transporters but also owners and managers, supervisors, and controllers of any place of exploitation such as a brothel, farm, boat, factory, medical facility, or household.' (p. 33)

1.329

She further suggests that trafficking may occur even where there is no prior movement or recruitment, citing as an example a working environment that transitions from acceptable to coercively exploitative (p. 31).

1.330

This expansive view is challenged by Vladislava Stoyanova in *Human Trafficking and Slavery Reconsidered*[206]. Stoyanova argues that the five actions listed in the Palermo Protocol, recruitment, transportation, transfer, harbouring, and receipt, refer to a coercive or deceptive process leading to exploitation. She warns that Gallagher's interpretation risks collapsing the distinctions between trafficking and other forms of exploitation:

> 'If Gallagher's expanded vision of the definition of human trafficking is followed, then all the exploitative practices included in the 'purpose' element, including slavery, servitude and forced labour, have to be relabelled as human trafficking… The result would be complete convergence between the concepts of trafficking, and of slavery, servitude and forced labour, which would defeat the purpose for which these different concepts were introduced in international law.' (p. 38)

1.331

A process-focused interpretation is echoed by Professor Jean Allain, who characterises trafficking as a 'supply chain into exploitation'[207].

1.332

Previous editions of this chapter adopted Gallagher's analysis but now depart from it (see **1.335–1.336** below).

1.333

Lord Briggs while acknowledging the complexity of this debate ultimately declined to resolve it, because on the facts before the court, trafficking on either

206 Stoyanova V, *Human Trafficking and Slavery Reconsidered: Conceptual Limits and States' Positive Obligations in European Law* (Cambridge University Press, 2017).

207 *Slavery in International Law*, 2013, p. 355.

analysis was made out. He did however recite the observation of Gleeson CJ in *Queen v Tang*[208]:

> 'It is unnecessary and unhelpful… to seek to draw boundaries between and slavery cognate concepts such as servitude, peonage, forced labour, or debt bondage… Those who engage in the traffic in human beings are unlikely to be so obliging as to arrange their practices to conform to some convenient taxonomy.'

1.334

Gleeson CJ stressed that slavery is the most serious harm targeted by modern exploitation offences and should not be folded indiscriminately into trafficking or labour-abuse narratives. Scholars argue that servitude can 'morph' into slavery when domination reduces a person's personal autonomy to a significantly diminished level;Allain's gradualist model explains this by reference to increasing control over life and labour.

1.335

Against this backdrop, a number of legal scholars have criticised the ECtHR for a lack of conceptual discipline in its trafficking jurisprudence, in which 'human trafficking' is often treated as functionally equivalent to slavery, or the terminology is deployed interchangeably without sustained analysis of the relevant thresholds of the exploitation claimed. From the perspective advanced by Stoyanova, this risks eroding the distinct protective functions of each category by collapsing a process-based notion of trafficking into the status- or condition-based wrongs of slavery, servitude and forced labour, thereby undermining the very taxonomic differentiation that international law constructed.

1.336

The Court of Appeal's observation in *Webb* that criminal offences must be defined with a high degree of clarity is therefore of particular significance: where criminal liability and serious penal consequences attach, the elision of trafficking with slavery is not a matter of mere terminological looseness but of legality and foreseeability under the criminal law. On Stoyanova's reading, the concerns she and others articulate should thus be taken seriously not only as an exercise in doctrinal discipline but as a necessary corrective to safeguard both the integrity of the Art 4 taxonomy and the precision required of domestic and international criminal prohibitions.

208 [2008] HCA 39, at [29].

Choosing the appropriate legal framework: trafficking versus slavery, servitude or forced or compulsory labour

Current domestic definitional challenges with human trafficking

1.337

Given the definitional complexities surrounding human trafficking under domestic law, it may be more effective, where the facts permit, to pursue cases under the more clearly defined offences of slavery, servitude, or forced or compulsory labour. A renewed focus on these hierarchical concepts can help sharpen legal analysis and ensure that the most serious violations, such as slavery, are properly recognised and addressed.

1.338

This approach also presents an opportunity to develop jurisprudence around underutilised categories within the 1956 Supplementary Slavery Convention, including debt bondage, servile marriage, and child exploitation, areas that have received limited judicial attention in the UK.

1.339

Where the facts and evidence satisfy the legal definitions of slavery, servitude, or forced or compulsory labour, prosecution under these offences may be more straightforward than under the offence of human trafficking. This route can, depending on the circumstances, avoid the additional evidential burdens associated with proving trafficking under s 2 of the MSA 2015.

1.340

For example, consider a Vietnamese child found working as a gardener in a cannabis farm operated by an organised criminal network, or a child involved in county lines drug distribution. In both scenarios, the child is being used to cultivate or sell drugs, often in hazardous conditions. In the case of cannabis cultivation, there is extensive evidence of the dangers posed by illegal electricity extraction and exposure to toxic substances. In county lines operations, practices such as 'plugging' illustrate the severe physical and psychological harm inflicted on children.

1.341

These circumstances may constitute proscribed worst forms of child labour and, for the reasons examined above, amount to a recognised form of servitude. Depending on the facts, they may also meet the threshold for slavery. In the circumstances prosecution may be more straightforward under s 1 of the MSA 2015 rather than s 2 and 3(5) and (6).

1.342

Debt-bonded labour offers another illustration. A person held in debt bondage is, by definition, subjected to servitude and potentially slavery. Where the complainant has been held in debt bondage, prosecuting such cases under s 1 of the MSA 2015 allows the focus to remain on the core violation, whether the individual was subjected to slavery, servitude, or forced labour, without the need to establish the additional elements required for trafficking offences.

1.343

The legal tests for these offences are distinct. In cases of slavery, the essential question is whether the perpetrator's control and domination reduced the victim's personal autonomy to such an extent, and for such a period, that they were held in slavery. The focus is no longer on formal ownership-like powers, but on the *degree* and *duration* of domination and its effect on the victim's ability to exercise meaningful choice, as articulated in *Webb*. For servitude and forced or compulsory labour, the inquiry centres on whether the facts demonstrate one of the four recognised practices of servitude or meet the criteria for forced labour. Crucially, there is no requirement to prove that the perpetrator arranged or facilitated the movement of the victim, nor is it confined to the requirements of exploitation as defined in s 3 of the MSA 2015[209].

1.344

Accordingly, framing cases as slavery, servitude, or forced labour can ensure accountability for the gravest violations of Art 4 ECHR and provide robust victim protection, without the unnecessary burden of proving elements that are arguably not central to the core Art 4 ECHR violation.

1.345

However, framing a case as human trafficking, rather than relying on the distinct offences of slavery, servitude, or forced or compulsory labour, may be necessary in certain circumstances. This includes situations where the exploitation has not yet occurred, such as when a victim is intercepted prior to being exploited. It may also be appropriate where there is uncertainty as to whether the anticipated or observed exploitation meets the legal thresholds for slavery, servitude, or forced labour, particularly in cases involving emerging or novel forms of abuse.

1.346

In such instances, pursuing a prosecution for human trafficking may be more appropriate.

209 Section 1(1) of MSA 2015.

2 Trafficking operations and modus operandi

Dame Sara Thornton, Philippa Southwell, Ben Douglas-Jones KC, Phil Brewer and Steve Harvey

Introduction

2.1

The Global Estimates of Modern Slavery indicate that in 2021, 28 million people were in forced labour and 22 million were trapped in forced marriage. The number of people in modern slavery has risen significantly in the last five years. Ten million more people were in modern slavery in 2021 compared to 2016 global estimates[1]. The International Labour Organisation reported that forced labour in the private economy generates $236 billion in illegal profits per year. This is a 37% increase since 2014 and reflects both greater numbers in forced labour as well as the higher profits generated by exploitation[2].

2.2

There have been relatively low convictions of exploitation related offences, both pre- and post-enactment of the Modern Slavery Act 2015 ('MSA 2015')[3]. This crime is known by a few labels in the English language: modern slavery, trafficking in human beings, trafficking in persons, and human trafficking They are all directly linked to the text of the national legislation that guides the state's response in its prevention, investigation, prosecution, and victim support (see **Chapters 1** and **9**).

2.3

The common denominator in trafficking cases is exploitation and the criminal profit that is generated by an individual's exploitation. Some form of profit or gain is the reason why people are trafficked and it is a global, multi-billion-pound criminal industry. That is not to say trafficking cannot occur on a smaller

1 https://www.ilo.org/publications/major-publications/global-estimates-modern-slavery-forced-labour-and-forced-marriage (accessed 18 August 2025).

2 https://www.ilo.org/publications/major-publications/profits-and-poverty-economics-forced-labour

3 Her Majesty's Inspectorate of Constabulary and Fire & Rescue Services Report, 'Stolen Freedom: the policing response to modern slavery and human trafficking', October 2017; https://hmicfrs.justiceinspectorates.gov.uk/publications/stolen-freedom-the-policing-response-to-modern-slavery-and-human-trafficking/ (accessed 18 August 2025).

scale – it does. This type of trafficking is often seen in the overseas domestic workers cases, where workers, often with visas tied to their employers, have to work for little or no economic benefit, or in the trafficking of children for domestic labour or other small-scale labour exploitation.

2.4

The UK is a source, transit, and destination country for men, women, and children subjected to sex trafficking, forced criminality and forced labour, including domestic servitude. In 2024, a total of 19,125 potential victims of modern slavery were referred to the Home Office. This was the highest number since the NRM was introduced in 2009. The number of women referred was the highest on record, 4,937 (26%); the number of children was down from 7,432 (43%) in 2023 to 5,983 in 2024 (31%). The most common nationality referred was UK (23%) with Albanian at 13% and Vietnamese at 11%. Approximately 44% of victims referred into the NRM were exploited entirely outside the UK[4].

2.5

In the UK, human trafficking has existed in its 'modern' form for longer than it has been routinely investigated. Currently, the agencies with responsibility for investigating and collecting intelligence on human trafficking and modern slavery are the National Crime Agency ('NCA'), which has primacy on national investigations, all UK Police Forces, the UK Border Force, UK Immigration Enforcement and the Gangmasters and Labour Abuse Authority.

2.6

All identified victims are reported to the two Competent Authorities within the Home Office who oversee the NRM (the Single Competent Authority ('the SCA') and the Immigration Enforcement Competent Authority ('the IECA')). In April 2019, the Home Office took over responsibility as the UK's Single Competent Authority ('SCA') from the National Crime Agency ('NCA') and UK Visas and Immigration ('UKVI'). Then, on 8 November 2021 the Home Office created the IECA as a new body. The identification and protection of potential victims of modern slavery requires collaboration from many agencies and organisations. If one were to combine the law enforcement response with the support provided by international organisations, NGOs, charities and other civil society actors working in the field of preventing and combating human trafficking within and into the UK, the national response looks substantial.

4 Official Statistics; Modern slavery: National Referral Mechanism and Duty to Notify statistics UK, end of year summary 2024 Published 6 March 2025; https://www.gov.uk/government/statistics/modern-slavery-nrm-and-dtn-statistics-end-of-year-summary-2024/modern-slavery-national-referral-mechanism-and-duty-to-notify-statistics-uk-end-of-year-summary-2024 (accessed 25 January 2026).

2.7

These public authorities and a number of non-governmental organisations (for example the Salvation Army, Unseen UK and Barnardo's) are required by law to notify the Home Office if they have reasonable grounds to believe that a person may be a victim of slavery or human trafficking. Home Office competent authorities then determine whether a person is, on the balance of probabilities, a victim of slavery or trafficking. This process is conducted within the framework of the National Referral Mechanism. For those whose case receives a positive reasonable grounds decision, support is provided by the Modern Slavery Victim Care Contract and will include accommodation where necessary, financial support and access to a support worker. Recent changes in legislation, particularly the Nationality and Borders Act 2022, have restricted access to this support.

Exploitation typologies and common control methods

2.8

Victims of modern slavery are preyed upon due to a backdrop of complex issues. It is not possible to document all forms of exploitation in a short format, and there is no definitive list as human trafficking and associated exploitation is not static but evolves to meet demand. Common forms of exploitation in the UK are criminal exploitation, sexual exploitation, forced labour and domestic servitude. Traffickers are often professional criminals and will seek to exploit vulnerable people wherever they can. Just as exploitation can come in many forms, so does vulnerability. In this respect, and in all cases, an open mind is vital. Every jurisdiction has varying trafficking typologies; this can be seen both internationally and domestically. In 2017, the Polaris Project[5] recorded 25 typologies of trafficking throughout the USA. Each has its own business model, trafficker profiles, recruitment strategies, victim profiles and methods of control that facilitate human trafficking. In 2017, the Home Office published a paper entitled 'A Typology of Modern Slavery Offences'[6] which identified 17 different typologies. Until 2018, the NCA broke down referral statistics into four types only. These were domestic servitude, labour exploitation, sexual exploitation and unknown exploitation type as forms of exploitation in the UK. However, since 2019, the Home Office, qua SCA, has also included criminal exploitation (from the publication of the 2019 statistics onwards)[7]. The Crown Prosecution Service ('CPS') guidance 'Modern Slavery and human

5 See https://polarisproject.org/typology, last accessed 18 August 2025.

6 https://assets.publishing.service.gov.uk/government/uploads/system/uploads/attachment_data/file/652652/typology-modern-slavery-offences-horr93.pdf, last accessed 18 August 2025.

7 Available at https://www.gov.uk/government/statistics/national-referral-mechanism-statistics-uk-end-of-year-summary-2019, last accessed 18 August 2025.

trafficking: offences and defences, including the s 45 defence'[8] acknowledges that exploitation typologies, particularly involving children, are often varied, multimodal and can include:

- domestic servitude;
- labour exploitation;
- criminal activity (eg cannabis cultivation, drug supply including 'county lines', petty street crime, illegal street trade, drug mules etc);
- sexual exploitation (brothels, closed community, for child abuse images);
- application of residence;
- benefit fraud;
- forced begging;
- illegal adoption; and
- sham marriages.

2.9

Perpetrators use a variety of control methods to engage or coerce vulnerable individuals. The Home Office Guidance for Competent Authorities stipulates that an adult victim of human trafficking must have been subject to a 'means' – the threat or use of force or other form of coercion to achieve the consent of a person having control over another person. It is not necessary for there to have been 'means' for a child to be a victim, because children cannot give informed consent. Any child who is recruited, transported, or transferred for the purposes of exploitation is a potential victim, whether or not he has been forced or deceived[9] (see **Chapter 1**).

2.10

Adults and children can be controlled through subtle, sometimes invisible, forces that even the victims themselves might not be able to fully understand or be able to articulate. Understanding how perpetrators abuse and exploit a position of vulnerability is fundamental in the investigation of trafficking but the less obvious signs often get overlooked. Common control methods are discussed in the following paragraphs; these are often multimodal.

---

8 https://www.cps.gov.uk/legal-guidance/modern-slavery-and-human-trafficking-offences-and-defences-including-s-45, last accessed 18 August 2025.

9 Modern Slavery: statutory guidance for England and Wales (under s49 of the Modern Slavery Act 2015) updated 11 August 2025 § 2.11; https://www.gov.uk/government/publications/modern-slavery-how-to-identify-and-support-victims/modern-slavery-statutory-guidance-for-england-and-wales-under-s49-of-the-modern-slavery-act-2015-and-non-statutory-guidance-for-scotland-and-northe (last accessed 19 August 2025).

Physical and sexual violence

2.11

When physical abuse is used as a means of control, it can be single or repeated violent episodes of abuse. Alternatively, it can be manipulation of the victims by making them witness beatings given to someone else, combined with the threat that it will happen to them if they do not do what they are told. Sexual violence, including rape, is a form of control that often goes undetected and unreported in situations of labour exploitation, domestic servitude and criminal exploitation. Traffickers will sexually abuse for their own gratification, but also as a means to control, to intimidate and silence the victim. Sexual abuse can affect children, women and men but embarrassment, shame and stigma can prevent or delay disclosure. Non-consensual sex is exploitation even if there is no monetary gain.

Deception

2.12

The promise of a better life is a common form of deception used by traffickers. This is the point at which a web of deception traps victims into believing that the first steps they are taking will lead to a life better than the one they have now. This could be the promise of a job, or education, or to reunite with family or other promises that never materialise. The deception can be quite sophisticated, for example by using a fake job agency, advertising online, using family members as facilitators, or using other victims as recruiters. In other cases, the ongoing deception and manipulation associated with withholding of wages or illegitimate wage deductions acts as a further means of control. The deception can shift and evolve over time.

Debt

2.13

A close partner to deception is debt. Traffickers and their agents routinely use the accrual of debt and usury, where the rates of interest on loans are exorbitantly high, as a means to control victims. For example, what might appear as a genuine loan by an agent to finance travel arrangements traps the victim into a contract or agreement (verbal or otherwise) with the trafficker to pay back that debt. Debt bondage is a term often considered in situations where a victim is tied to one person or group for an unspecified amount of time and often for an unspecified amount. However, in human trafficking debt accrual as the means of control does not always have to conform to the strict notion of debt bondage. Victims can be sold or exchanged between traffickers and the debt rolls over. In some cultures, the stigma of not being able to pay back debt or the deep shame of asking family members to sell their assets to pay back the debt, is enough to hold victims bonded to the trafficker or their agents. The threat of being exposed for non-payment of debt is a common tactic when the abuser and abused come from the same culture, family or kinship group. The use of debt as a means to control can manifest in different ways. It can be used to control both adults and children and is a significant contributor to why some victims go missing and are later found to have been re-trafficked. It is common within Vietnamese trafficking models for an agent and/or trafficker to hold the property documents of a victim's family to ensure that the victim will pay back the debt. The property will be claimed if the debt is not paid off. The debt will often be inflated, variable and bear no relation to what the victim has been given (ie travel costs, accommodation, documents etc). See **Chapter 1** in respect of debt bondage.

Isolation

2.14

Keeping victims housed together, locking rooms and monitoring or removing any means of communication to the outside world are ways that traffickers keep control through isolating vulnerable people. Moving frequently from place to place reduces the likelihood of victims being identified by the public or police, and it also means that it is less likely the victim will be able to build trusting relationships with anyone or ask for help. Isolation can be both physical and emotional in nature. The circumstances can be just as controlling where the victim is not physically locked inside, because the terror of not knowing who to trust, whether the person with you is in similar circumstances or is an agent, can be debilitating. Isolation of a victim is often easy to achieve where the victim does not speak the language well, or at all, in the destination country and en route, and where a victim has irregular immigration status in these countries. A common tactic is for victims to be told that if they speak to outsiders including authorities they will be arrested and/or deported. Sometimes modes of communication are provided to victims (ie laptops and mobile phones) under the pretence of assisting them but are another means of controlling and monitoring the victim.

Dependency

2.15

Perpetrators knowingly and deliberately create a situation of dependency that increases the vulnerability of the victim and strengthens the control over them. Providing the only source of food and accommodation and taking away identification papers are common ways in which dependency is created. However, it can also involve the perpetrator deceiving, coercing or forcing the victim to take on a new identity by providing a different name on arrival, or the use of false documents and then subsequently threatening to report the victim to immigration officials. In other instances, it can involve the supply and withholding of drugs or alcohol or always being with the victim and speaking on his behalf, for example, when presenting at Accident and Emergency. In the case of children, a situation of dependency can be created quickly and with little effort due to their young age and immaturity. It is well known that a common ploy in respect of child victims of domestic servitude is that they are brought through British airports with a visa. Often this visa will be for an 'adult' rather than a child to avoid closer scrutiny and checks. Or the children are not detected because the accompanying adult, often masquerading as a family member, presents a passport and speaks to the Immigration Officer on the child's behalf. The child only later finds out the implications of entering the country on false documents and the trafficker threatens him with being handed over to immigration and police, something the child fears through his own knowledge of corrupt authorities in his home country.

Emotional control

2.16

Emotional control can take many different forms, and some of this is already covered in other parts of this chapter. Inducing fear by threatening to harm the victim's family is a corrosive means of controlling the victim. Even after the victim has been removed from the situation of exploitation, the paralysing fear of threats to family has long-term consequences, including refusal to disclose and the high risk of re-trafficking. Making victims collude in crimes and then threatening to expose them to police unless they acquiesce is another pernicious form of control that has consequences for safeguarding and in later immigration and legal proceedings. Threats or action taken to expose the victim's sexual history, including taking sexually explicit photographs or distributing images online, has a devastating impact on women and girls, but it can also affect boys and men in the same way, particularly, but not exclusively, in cultures or in faiths where homosexuality is considered taboo. Less obvious, but just as important, are signs of emotional control seen in situations described as 'Stockholm Syndrome', where through calculated manipulation by the perpetrator the victim forms a bond or strong emotional tie even though he may have suffered abuse. This is sometimes known as the 'Loverboy' model. Stockholm Syndrome can also be seen in cases of domestic servitude, where the victim has spent years living with the family in appalling conditions but has been responsible for every aspect of caring for the children and by developing a bond with them they do not want to be responsible for the parents being arrested and taken away from the children.

Culture and faith

2.17

There are several ceremonial practices linked to spirit possession that are used by human trafficking networks to control victims. It would be wrong to group all of them together as 'juju', as this is not the case. There are several quite different belief systems across the continent of Africa and around the world that traffickers have exploited. Many of them as means of control can be incomprehensible if you are not familiar with them; this can lead to victims not being believed or in some instances being derided for lacking credibility. Very subtle references to the oath or other aspects of control can be overlooked if you are unaware but can, if engaged with, assist in obtaining the victim's account in a way that reduces this risk of trauma or poor disclosure.

2.18

Juju, according to Andy Desmond, a former Metropolitan Police detective and trafficking consultant, is commonly used by human traffickers of Edo and Delta States of Nigeria. Traffickers have hijacked the cultural beliefs in juju to blackmail their victims. This often involves traditional priests paid to carry out the ceremonies, the strong belief in the spirits makes this a powerful weapon for traffickers. Once a potential victim has been put through and sworn an oath of obedience, he is often easy to control without the need for physical restraints. The bondage is in the beliefs: there is no requirement to lock up victims and have them watched. Juju has been used extensively to control Nigerian children trafficked to the UK and via the UK into other European countries for servitude and sexual exploitation. Practices such as Kindoki, from the Democratic Republic of the Congo, or Obi, Obeah, or Obia known in parts of Nigeria and the West Indies may also be methods of control and relate to spirit possession and mysticism.

2.19

A related area of abuse is the practice of denouncing children as practising witchcraft. This at times was 'proved' because bad luck has befallen the family, for instance illness or poverty. It is these children who are singled out, isolated and highly vulnerable to trafficking. Traffickers exploit their vulnerability and knowingly use the community condemnation of alleged witchcraft as a form of control. These children lose any sense of self-worth, feel rejected, blame themselves and are reluctant to speak out[10].

10 More detail on this subject is available at www.starsfoundation.org.uk/awards/organisations/stepping-stones-nigeria-child-empowerment-foundation, last accessed 17 December 2017.

2.20

Witchcraft and juju are not the only faith-based practices that have been linked to modern slavery and exploitation. In recent years, reports of various forms of exploitation, including the trafficking of human beings, have been connected to groups or cults that are considered to follow mainstream religions, such as Christianity. One example of this was within institutions known as the Magdalene or Magdalen Laundries, connected to the Catholic Church and often controlled by religious sisters. In Ireland alone, it is estimated over 10,000 women and girls were held in slave-like conditions within these institutions and forced to complete domestic-related tasks, such as laundry services, under the fear and threat of physical and psychological harm.

Family involvement

2.21

Human trafficking does happen with the knowledge, acquiescence and involvement of family members, husbands, boyfriends, or close acquaintances. Even after victims recognise and understand that they have been trafficked, the bonds of loyalty to the family or fear of the consequences of breaking free can be overwhelming. In cases of forced marriage, young females can be forced by families to enter an arrangement of marriage which is a cover for servitude in exchange for some form of benefit. This can also be an arranged marriage, agreed to by the victim, which on arrival becomes a servile marriage.

2.22

It would be naïve to think that some families do not know what will happen to their children when they send them away with local agents and facilitators even if the children themselves do not know all the arrangement details. Unaccompanied or separated children are especially vulnerable to trafficking and re-trafficking, in part because of the potential for risk if the child is reunited with family. In some cases, the family will have had complicit involvement, especially if a debt has to be repaid or where the stigma of sexual abuse makes the child an outcast. In other situations, filial piety, the deeply-entrenched cultural bond of loyalty to elders that exists in the Confucian beliefs found in Chinese and Vietnamese society, is part of a much more complex landscape of why children do not disclose abusive and exploitative relationships.

Human trafficking and modern slavery linked to foreign diasporas in the UK

2.23

The mono-ethnic exploitation by traffickers is a common occurrence within the UK, especially where an established or substantial diaspora exists. A common language, culture and knowledge of the environment provide leverage for an established migrant or a UK national in the UK over the newly arrived. The vulnerability of the migrant new to his or her surroundings leads to exploitation, and this is often found in the labour market which in many regions of the UK is dependent on a migrant labour force.

2.24

Other prevalent organised crime networks in the UK include Vietnamese, Chinese and, more recently, gangs from Latin America.

2.25

It is still the case that after recognising that the UK is and has been a country of origin, transit and destination for human trafficking and modern slavery for decades, the investigation of these crimes is still wholly reactive, usually the result of a complaint or report made by an escaped or rescued victim of trafficking.

2.26

Proactive investigation is the action taken by law enforcement to investigate suspected or potential incidents or sites of exploitation. There are numerous indicators of human trafficking and these 'clues' can be proactively investigated with a view to identifying human trafficking. The gathering of information which is believed to be connected to human trafficking can be developed into a 'profile' of what human trafficking 'looks like' in a certain location or environment. Profiling can be used to both target offenders and identify victims.

2.27

Traffickers have a profile, and a significant element of that profile will be the nationality of the trafficker, and this can often be established by identifying the nationality of victims of trafficking. Investigations in the UK indicate that victims are often trafficked by traffickers of their own nationality. The National Crime Agency (NCA) Strategic Assessment for 2024 identified based on referrals to the National Referral Mechanism (NRM) that 'UK nationals are the most commonly identified victims of modern slavery and human trafficking occurring in the UK, followed by Albanian, Vietnamese, Indian, and Romanian nationals. The 2025 NCA National Strategic Assessment of Serious and Organised Crime recorded, 'It is highly likely that, cumulatively, offenders linked to China currently pose the biggest non-British SOC threat to the UK' and that this threat included human trafficking and modern slavery[11].

2.28

Whilst every case of human trafficking needs to be investigated to establish the facts, it is highly likely that Albanian women and men will be trafficked

11 https://www.nationalcrimeagency.gov.uk/nsa-overview-of-soc-2025 (accessed 20 August 2025).

by Albanians, Romanian women and men will be trafficked by Romanians, Polish women and men will be trafficked by Poles, Nigerian women trafficked by Nigerian traffickers etc., etc. This is also the case in other countries where foreign nationals have settled and form significant communities.

2.29

It is therefore highly likely that foreign diaspora communities in the UK can be linked to human trafficking and modern slavery, primarily through the recruitment of fellow nationals and their transportation to the UK.

2.30

Paradigmatic Romanian community trafficking and slavery includes labour, sexual and criminal exploitation by family members and wider members of the community. Typically, victims are trafficked as children for sexual exploitation in Romania by a family member and later brought to the UK, where they are trafficked for labour exploitation, sexual exploitation and in acquisitive crime by Romanian nationals in the UK (often both family members and members of the community). The leverage applied to the victim in the UK includes the victim's inability to speak English which makes them dependent on others. The unfamiliar process of obtaining employment also makes such victims vulnerable, as do practices which include the false representation of UK immigration law to the victim and debt bondage built up through initial 'favours' to provide accommodation, food and clothing.

2.31

This methodology is mirrored in many cases of foreign national victims being exploited by traffickers of the same nationality.

2.32

An exemplar investigation is that of the Czech nationals, Ernest Drevenak and Veronika Bubencikova, who were found to have started exploiting men from the Czech Republic in 2015 – but were only captured in 2019. Drevenak ran the gang alongside his brother Zdenek. Their victims – who were homeless, unemployed or in very low-paid jobs in the Czech Republic – had been brought to the UK with the promise of a better life. Some were then put to work in Caxton, Cambridgeshire, at a branch of McDonald's – with the fast food chain now promising it had improved systems to spot 'potential risks'. Others were made to work for a factory providing bread for high street supermarkets and cramped into a property in Enfield, north London, where nine were living.[12]

12 https://www.dailymail.co.uk/news/article-13907461/moment-police-rescue-mcdonalds-slaves-from-london-home-victims-of-family-run-trafficking-gang-are-found-shivering-in-beds-as-photo-shows-ringleader-enjoying-beach-holiday.html; https://www.independent.co.uk/news/uk/crime/mcdonalds-slavery-uk-cambridge-gang-czech-b2621157.html (accessed 20 August 2025).

2.33

In Operation Fort, *R v Brzezinski et al.*[13], eight offenders, who were members and associates of two Polish crime families, were jailed after being convicted in two separate trials of crimes including trafficking, conspiracy to require another to perform forced labour and money laundering. Their sentences ranged from 3 to 11 years' imprisonment. The group of five men and three women targeted the most desperate from their homeland, including the homeless, ex-prisoners and alcoholics. The victims were transported to the UK by bus, but when they arrived they were housed in squalid homes around West Bromwich, Smethwick and Walsall, forced to sleep up to four in a room on filthy mattresses and had their wages 'farmed' from bank accounts on payday. The slaves were made to work long days at rubbish recycling centres, farms and turkey-gutting factories and given as little as £20 a week by their captors. But they were marched to banks and made to open accounts over which the gang had complete control. The gang also claimed benefits in the names of some of their victims, ranging in age from 17 to a man in his 60s[14].

Modus operandi of known modern slavery cases

2.34

In January 1998, West Sussex Police set up 'Operation Newbridge' to gather intelligence on children of West African origin and ethnicity who, having arrived in the UK at Gatwick Airport as unaccompanied minors, were routinely going missing after being placed in care. The suspicion was that they were being trafficked into the UK for sexual exploitation.

2.35

The investigation into the deaths of 23 Chinese nationals who drowned in Morecambe Bay on 5 February 2004 is probably the best example of a crime that had not yet registered on the law enforcement 'radar' until it came under significant public attention and was then scrutinised by criminal justice authorities. 'Trafficking in human beings' was not part of the UK law enforcement lexicon in 2004, yet there were clear indications almost four years earlier that the UK was being targeted by people smugglers and human traffickers.

2.36

On 18 June 2000, 58 Chinese illegal migrants were found suffocated in the back of a lorry that had arrived in Dover from Rotterdam via a channel ferry, driven by Perry Wacker, a Dutch national. Sentencing the driver at Maidstone

13 Birmingham Crown Court, July 2019.

14 https://www.bbc.co.uk/news/uk-england-birmingham-48881327 (accessed 20 August 2025).

Crown Court the following year, Mr Justice Moses (as he then was) said, 'human trafficking of this kind added to the climate of hostility against asylum seekers and encouraged government to take ever more draconian measures'.

2.37

Two months before the fatal shipment, Leo Nijveen, a close friend of Wacker's, was arrested by Kent Police after arriving at Dover with 50 Chinese migrants in his lorry. They had almost suffocated in transit and had been released by Nijveen on the crossing. Nijveen was released without charge by the UK authorities and returned to the Netherlands. Today, it is likely that he would have been investigated as a people smuggler and human trafficker.

2.38

It is highly likely that once the migrants had been smuggled into the UK they would have been trafficked within the UK to pay the costs of their facilitated illegal entry, the 'debt bondage' that is now so familiar in current human trafficking investigations. The Chinese nationals who died in Morecambe Bay in 2004 were victims of human trafficking. They were paying off the costs of their smuggling by collecting shellfish in hazardous conditions.

2.39

The Chinese migrants who died in Dover and in Morecambe Bay had been smuggled by Chinese 'Snakehead' gangs into the UK, and their internal trafficking would have been/was controlled by Chinese traffickers. The Gangmasters Licensing Authority (since replaced by the Gangmasters and Labour Abuse Authority) was established in 2005 as a direct result of this investigation and the facts established about the role of those persons managing the migrants as 'a workforce', so called gangmasters.

2.40

In 2007 'Operation Troy' led in the UK by SOCA and the UKHTC, working with police counterparts in Sweden, Denmark and Norway, investigated the trafficking of British males to Scandinavia by a 'traveller family'. The men, all homeless and vulnerable, were trafficked and forced to work laying tarmac at residential properties.

2.41

These widely-publicised cases emphasise that human trafficking is not a recent phenomenon. However, even today investigations, prosecutions and convictions for human trafficking, while far more common than they were, are not routine. The Modern Slavery and Human Rights Policy and Evidence Centre recorded in its May 2025 'Report outlining the reasons for low prosecution rates for modern slavery and recommendations to improve them':

'According to the Modern Slavery and Organised Immigration Crime Unit at the National Police Chiefs' Council (NPCC), as of June 2024, policing across the UK were dealing with at least 2,497 modern slavery and human trafficking investigations (including crimes committed against both adults and children). Yet in the year from July 2023 to June 2024, the Crown Prosecution Service (CPS) recorded 467 prosecutions for modern slavery-flagged crimes in England and Wales, of which 355 (76%) resulted in a conviction. In the same time frame (July 2023 to June 2024), Ministry of Justice statistics note that 114 defendants were proceeded against, 58 were convicted, and 58 sentenced for modern slavery offences in England and Wales. For comparison, in this same time frame of July 2023 to June 2024, there were 17,120 potential victims of modern slavery referred to the National Referral Mechanism across the UK.'[15]

2.42

The Council Framework Decision of 13 June 2002 provided the legal basis for EU Member States to operate in Joint Investigation Teams ('JITs'). It would take another six years before the first ever JIT against an organised human trafficking network was established.

2.43

In 2008, JIT Golf, led by the UK's Metropolitan Police Service in cooperation with the Romanian National Police, investigated an organised ethnic Roma child trafficking network operating across the EU. Romanian Roma children were trafficked to EU Member States and exploited for the purpose of 'street crime'. This coordinated two-year international investigation led to the first conviction for child trafficking, 10 years after West Sussex Police first investigated the phenomenon.

2.44

What the above-mentioned cases illustrate is that state authorities have been slow to respond effectively to an emerging criminal threat that was first recognised in the late 1990s and even now the number of prosecutions does not begin to reflect the scale of the trafficking and slavery crimes being committed.

Post Modern Slavery Act 2015

2.45

On 23 October 2019, 39 Vietnamese nationals were discovered dead inside a refrigerated lorry trailer in Grays, Essex. They had paid between £10,000 and

15 https://files.modernslaverypec.org/production/assets/downloads/Barriers-to-prosecutions-full-report.pdf?dm=1746710983 (accessed 20 August 2025).

£13,000 for the so called 'VIP route'. The trailer had travelled from Belgium to Purfleet and had been collected by an Irish registered lorry cab. The lengthy police investigation led to the identification of the smuggling ringleaders and their network of drivers willing to drive migrants from Europe to the UK. Eleven people were subsequently convicted in the UK. The CPS also pursued the assets of those involved and they were ordered to pay £284,000 in compensation to the 39 families[16].

2.46

There is a rising awareness of British victims of trafficking who are trafficked within the UK and also outside of the UK. Common forms of trafficking of British victims outside of the UK are for forced marriage and as drug mules. In respect of the latter, this is often trafficking within an organised criminal framework, with the organised criminal gangs operating over several jurisdictions.

2.47

In 2014, the Metropolitan Police identified several children being forced to transport and sell drugs on behalf of a London gang. This resulted in one of the first human trafficking prosecutions involving child criminal exploitation. As professional practice was shared across the UK, the possibility of using the Modern Slavery Act to prosecute exploiters has increased. Individuals under the age of 18 and involved in the supply of drugs are far more likely to be assessed by police and local authorities as potential victims alongside any decision to prosecute. Those individuals identified as controlling and exploiting children for a criminal purpose could be charged with modern slavery offences. This can be achieved using evidence such as financial and communications data, without always relying on the exploited child giving evidence (see **Chapter 17**).

Sexual exploitation

2.48

In May 2017, following a lengthy police investigation, Romelia Florentina Radu, Petre Niculescu and George Maracineanu were convicted of offences relating to human trafficking and sexual exploitation at Kingston Crown Court[17]. This was the first case prosecuted under the Modern Slavery Act 2015 involving a child victim. Radu and Niculescu had been trafficking Romanian women from their own Roma community to the UK for several years. The victims would

16 https://www.cps.gov.uk/cps/news/people-smugglers-ordered-pay-over-ps280000-criminal-profits-essex-lorry-deaths-case (accessed 20 August 2025).

17 https://www.theguardian.com/uk-news/2017/may/12/romanian-couple-jailed-trafficking-girl-prostitution-uk (accessed 20 August 2025).

be forced to work as sex workers in West London. Believing they were coming to the UK for a better life, many of the girls and women found themselves working 'on-street', meeting customers and then often using gardens or alleys in which to have sex. Failure to comply would result in violence being used against them. Despite their situation, none of the women sought help from the UK authorities. The threat of violence and the risk of rejection by their families were two significant contributing factors preventing them from doing so.

2.49

The group came to the notice of police in 2016. Maracineanu had been in contact with a Romanian woman via a dating website. He convinced her to travel to the UK on the promise of a relationship and helping her secure work as a waitress. When she arrived in London, Maracineanu handed her over to Radu and Niculescu. They forced her into work as a sex worker, threatening to tell her family if she refused to comply. The woman remained in this situation for three weeks until she found the courage to seek help from the Metropolitan Police.

2.50

This was the start of an investigation that lasted almost a year. In collaboration with Romanian law enforcement, the Metropolitan Police Modern Slavery and Kidnap Unit formed a Joint Investigation Team ('JIT') coordinated through Eurojust. Witnesses were located in Romania and the UK resulting in over 20 potential victims being identified. Evidence was gathered and an arrest phase instigated. During that phase a number of victims still being exploited were located and taken to safety. This included a 15-year-old girl whom Radu and Niculescu had trafficked when she was 14 years old.

2.51

Radu and Niculescu pleaded guilty to trafficking eight women and a child for the purpose of sexual exploitation. They received sentences of 14 years each in prison. Maracineanu was sentenced to two years and eight months' imprisonment for his role in this crime.

Labour exploitation

2.52

David Lupu, a Romanian National, was convicted of labour exploitation in 2018[18]. He recruited men from impoverished communities in Romania,

18 https://www.standard.co.uk/news/crime/jailed-gangmaster-who-forced-up-to-15-slaves-to-share-bunks-in-tiny-onebed-flat-a3799116.html (accessed 20 August 2025).

offering them £50 a day plus accommodation to work on construction sites. The accommodation Lupu provided was a one-bedroomed flat in Leyton, East London where up to 15 workers were housed in extremely poor conditions. He withheld their travel documents, controlled their movements, and assaulted them if they challenged him. He told the workers they would be arrested if they contacted the police.

2.53

Lupu arranged subcontract demolition work on large construction sites in London. Although he was paid in full for the work, he retained most of this, telling the workers the deductions were for outstanding debts they owed him. They also were made to work very long hours by Lupu.

2.54

The construction companies Lupu subcontracted from were unaware of the exploitation his victims faced daily. This was in part due to how he controlled them. Language barriers ensured there was little interaction with other construction workers on-site. It was not until two of his victims approached the police to complain they were being kept as slaves that the crime was uncovered. Lupu was sentenced to seven years' imprisonment.

2.55

Operation Fort (above at **2.33**) is one of the most egregious labour exploitation cases seen in England and Wales.

2.56

After a lengthy GLAA investigation a Carlisle man was convicted of keeping a vulnerable worker in a shed for 40 years and forcing him to work on the farm painting, slating and tarmacking. He was kept in an unheated shed which was only two metres long[19]. A similar case where a vulnerable man was held for 26 years resulted in a CICA pay out of £350,000. He was kept in squalor, beaten and forced to tarmac driveways. However the case had taken seven years to resolve[20].

2.57

The 2024 case of *Drevenak* and others (above at **2.32**) is another example of large-scale labour exploitation.

---

19 https://www.bbc.co.uk/news/uk-england-cumbria-60043132 (accessed 20 August 2025).

20 https://www.bbc.co.uk/news/articles/c724prnd489o#:~:text=%E2%80%9CCICA%20provides%20compensation%20to%20people,move%20on%20with%20their%20lives.%E2%80%9D (accessed 20 August 2025).

2.58

In recent years there has been growing concern about the exploitation of workers coming to the UK on Seasonal Worker Visas and Health and Social Care Visas. In response to shortages of UK workers in both sectors the government has introduced visas for overseas workers but in both cases there have been reports of exploitation. The charity Unseen UK which runs the Modern Slavery Helpline received reports of 140 cases in 2023 – the most of any sector. While the number of cases in agriculture has dropped in recent years there were still 49 reported in 2023[21]. While the majority of workers on these visas may experience good quality work, there is no doubt that the debt bondage in which many workers find themselves makes them extremely vulnerable to abuse.

Domestic Servitude

2.59

There is growing concern about domestic servitude where those employed by families have been exploited. In the significant case of *Basfar v Wong*[22] the Supreme Court ruled that diplomats who exploit domestic workers will not be able to claim immunity from actions in the UK courts. The media has also played an important role in raising awareness of this crime in a powerful documentary about the athlete Mo Farah who was trafficked into domestic servitude in the UK[23], and a Channel 4 investigation revealed the extent of the exploitation of women from the Philippines in the most affluent parts of London[24].

2.60

The March 2025 conviction of a Ugandan national and UK based PhD law student at Oxford University, who was also a United Nations judge, provides an insight into how domestic servitude is an accepted practice by some nationalities. It is often presented to a third-party observer as an act of kindness or generosity, and wholly compatible with individual offender's cultural upbringing and traditional custom[25].

---

21 https://www.unseenuk.org/wp-content/uploads/2024/05/Unseen-Helpline-Annual-Assessment_2023.pdf (accessed 20 August 2025).

22 [2022] UKSC 20; [2023] A.C. 33.

23 https://www.bbc.co.uk/news/uk-62123886 (accessed 20 August 2025).

24 https://www.channel4.com/news/the-domestic-slaves-rescued-from-londons-richest-streets (accessed 20 August 2025).

25 https://www.dailymail.co.uk/news/article-14500373/Family-Ugandan-judge-guilty-modern-slavery-forcing-young-woman-work-slave-blame-conviction-cultural-differences.html; https://www.theguardian.com/uk-news/2025/may/02/un-judge-lydia-mugambe-jailed-uk-exploitation-uganda (accessed 20 August 2025).

2.61

The experience of the authors of this chapter includes working in some African and Pacific Island countries which confirms how domestic servitude is accepted in some communities. Law enforcement officials and criminal justice practitioners often reveal in the course of training on human trafficking and modern slavery that they themselves employ a child, often a member of an impoverished arm of their extended family, as a domestic servant. Typically, they explain that the child is able to learn domestic skills and sometimes earn some money to provide for their own family. The servant child does not attend school and usually performs all domestic chores in the household, working long hours. When these circumstances are examined from the perspective of domestic and international exploitation law, officials and practitioners accept that the examples entail breaches of national and international law, but take the view that 'traditional law' and cultural practices take precedence. Typically, the parents and /or immediate family of the child concerned are complicit in the arrangement (see also Family Involvement at **2.21**, above). Therefore, it is highly unlikely that any complaints or reports would be made of these circumstances. Domestic servitude most clearly exposes the hidden nature of human trafficking/modern slavery.

Crime

2.62

Organised crime is involved in human trafficking, which is often referred to as 'an organised crime'. The following definition is helpful in explaining what that means:

> 'Organized criminal group' shall mean a structured group of three or more persons, existing for a period of time and acting in concert with the aim of committing one or more serious crimes or offences established in accordance with this Convention, in order to obtain, directly or indirectly, a financial or other material benefit'[26].

2.63

Most traffickers identified by state authorities, while investigating trafficking activity, worked in a group with at least two others, so in almost all cases, they were part of an organised crime group ('OCG'). That said, the dynamic or profile of an OCG will vary from case to case and its activity or operation will be driven or influenced by a range of factors, ie the push and pull factors which are the cause of an individual's vulnerability and susceptibility, the socio

26 UN Convention against Transnational Organized Crime 2000, Art 2a.

economic and environmental conditions or market forces and the ability or capacity of the criminals involved.

2.64

For example, ethnic Roma trafficking networks operating across the EU are solely engaged in the trafficking of ethnic Roma victims. These trafficking networks are often successful because of the significant discrimination suffered by the Roma across Europe. The structure of these trafficking groups is clan- and extended family-based. These networks often come to notice when there are investigations into the activities of children who are involved in organised street crime, such as pickpocketing and begging.

2.65

In a significant number of investigations where Roma children are exploited as street criminals, the traffickers are their parents or immediate family members. These networks operate in the capital cities of the EU's most wealthy countries, moving routinely and when necessary, swiftly from one country to another, taking advantage of the Schengen Free Travel Zone. For obvious reasons, a major challenge in an investigation involving ethnic Roma victims is obtaining a statement or testimony from the victim. The traffickers are aware of the challenges a child victim will present to the authorities and the 'use' of children has become a modus operandi, with the child victim being 'recycled' after initial detection.

2.66

Different trafficking groups active in the UK are also involved in defrauding 'the benefits system' using adults and children trafficked to the UK. The adults and children will be presented to the local authority as a newly arrived family, corroborated by good quality forged documents. Usually the fake family will be one parent and multiple children and will be entitled to a full range of benefits. Bank account details provided to the local authority will often be the traffickers' and any payment or debit cards will be handed to the traffickers. The fake family will be presented in another area to repeat the process or be returned to their country of origin. The traffickers will then maintain the pretence and receive all benefit payments.

2.67

The 'Loverboy' method is the term often used to describe the trafficking of a girl or young woman into forced prostitution where the recruitment involves a young, good looking man befriending the victim. The victim is in almost all cases a young woman who has no or limited experience of meeting or speaking with a boy or young man, who quickly becomes flattered by his attention, his conduct, and often apparent good financial circumstances. Very quickly the girl or young woman will be convinced she is in a loving and committed relationship with her new boyfriend, which she will inevitably keep secret from her family due to cultural and customary practices surrounding arranged relationships and marriage.

2.68

Early in the relationship the boyfriend will suggest that 'they' go to meet his parents (or something similar) in another city or even country with the intention of getting the girl to leave her home environment. On arrival in the new location the girl will then be forced into prostitution by her 'boyfriend' or be handed over to others to do the same. This methodology is often seen in the investigation of Albanian trafficking networks, where both traffickers and victims are ethnic Albanians, or belong to other Eastern European gangs.

2.69

In consideration of how traffickers may exploit social media and online communication platforms, the 'Loverboy' methodology described previously has now migrated to the online world. The 'analogue' Loverboy method required a physical meeting. The Loverboy recruiter had to identify and physically meet his intended target in order to begin the process of recruitment. A typical example from Albania would be a recruiter frequenting a university campus or a location frequented by students such as a cafe. The two persons would meet; often an unsolicited approach by the male recruiter would begin the entrapment of the female student. Often the target was a Muslim girl or woman who out of necessity would have to keep the meeting and contact secret from her family. As all further contact and meetings could only take place when it was possible for the intended victim to meet with the recruiter, this process could often play out over weeks and months and could fail with the intervention by family members.

2.70

With Instagram, TikTok, WhatsApp and Snapchat, backed up by the use of AI platforms such as ChatGPT, to enhance the false identity narrative, the necessary physical interaction of the Loverboy can now be replaced by a virtual identity, remote, highly secretive and operating in an environment with no risk. Popularly known as 'Catfishing', the NCA CEOP Education Team describes a 'catfish' as: 'someone who creates a fake profile online and pretends to be someone else' and 'with a view to starting a friendship or romantic relationship online'[27]. Traffickers are now catfishing to recruit girls and women for sexual exploitation.

27 https://www.ceopeducation.co.uk/11_18/lets-talk-about/relationships/catfishing/ (accessed 20 August 2025).

2.71

Recently, an employment platform created by the Swiss Agency for Development and Cooperation in Albania actively seeking the employment of a children's 'nanny' has provided a fertile environment for catfishing. In one instance, the platform fulfilled several objectives for a prospective applicant: leaving Albania to escape an arranged marriage; obtaining employment; and becoming independent. The site was being monitored by traffickers and a profile was created on Instagram to entrap the young woman. One of the key factors was that the man she began corresponding with said that he had business interest in Geneva and spent most of his time in Switzerland. Within days the young woman had been persuaded to fly at her own expense to Geneva. On arrival, she was taken to an AirBnB, raped and forced into prostitution. Objectively, the online process probably accelerated the usual Loverboy activity and outcome by weeks if not months.

2.72

A further objective of a catfish could be securing leverage over another person and using that leverage as a recruitment tactic: e.g. securing intimate images or videos, knowledge of personal background and habits, knowledge of family members.

2.73

Catfishing and the use of online communication channels has given human traffickers a level of anonymity and distance from two key elements of trafficking: the act and the means (see **Chapters 1** and **4**) – what is done and how it is done. It is conceivable that through catfishing, a trafficker now only has to meet the victim in person at the point of exploitation (the third element of trafficking), thus reducing even further the opportunities for law enforcement interdiction.

Criminal exploitation

2.74

Trafficking for criminal exploitation is often overlooked and misunderstood. Very little data has been recorded on the characterisation of criminal exploitation. Data collection systems are currently inadequate for a complete picture of the scale of criminal exploitation. Domestically we have seen the evolution of different types of criminal exploitation. This is manifesting in county lines drug running, and attached to this is possession of offensive weapons, targeted burglaries and robberies, and serious offences against a person.

2.75

The control mechanisms and grooming processes in many cases are similar, irrespective of the criminality. Routinely they will include physical and sexual violence, debt, dependency, isolation, culture and faith. In some cases, they are used to radicalise victims as well as to control or groom them. Victims are also groomed via social media and online.

2.76

Labour exploitation is the most common type of exploitation of adult victims in the UK, whilst criminal exploitation is the most common exploitation type for children[28]. It is of note that the highest number of referrals into the NRM for victim identification are British nationals. The second highest cohort are Albanian, Vietnamese and Chinese. The statistics reflect the rising issue of domestic child criminal exploitation of British nationals.

Criminal exploitation and 'county lines'

2.77

Over the last six years, the UK's approach to modern slavery and human trafficking has evolved and expanded. Prior to the introduction of the Modern Slavery Act in 2015, the majority of law enforcement activity focused on sexual exploitation. For example, specialist officers targeting vice activity in Central London began to focus more on addressing the exploitation of those working in the industry. This saw the London Metropolitan Police Clubs and Vice Unit become the Trafficking and Prostitution Unit. In 2012, it evolved again into a dedicated Human Trafficking Unit, investigating a much wider range of exploitation, although trafficking for sexual exploitation received most attention.

2.78

The term 'county lines' describes one modern slavery modus operandi that has received significant focus in recent years. As the UK's understanding of modern slavery evolves, how exploitation is recognised is also developing. The use of children by established gangs to run drugs is an example of that development. Historically, children's involvement in the transportation and dealing of drugs across the country would have resulted in their being convicted of serious offences. However, law enforcement agencies, along with local authorities and prosecutors, are now recognising the importance of identifying the underlying issues that may have caused a young person to commit such a serious criminal act in the first place. Recognising and investigating the coercion and control used by older gang members resulted in the first trafficking convictions for this particular modus operandi in 2019.

28 NRM referral statistics UK, Quarter 1, 2020 – January to March.

2.79

Professionals, particularly non-government organisations working within child safeguarding, had long been aware of how criminals had used control and coercion to manipulate and exploit children or the vulnerable. However, children caught transporting or dealing drugs on behalf of organised crime networks were until recently routinely arrested and charged with serious criminal offences.

2.80

There are many permutations as to how and why a child can become involved in criminal exploitation. There is not a single community, social standing or familial set-up that gives a clear vulnerability 'red flag' to help prevent the exploitation of children. There are, without doubt, certain situations that can make one child more vulnerable than another, but it would be extremely difficult to create a scenario that would remove all risk of a child becoming a victim, although child poverty plays a significant role.

2.81

The benefits for gangs and organised criminal networks targeting children are numerous. They can be easily coerced and controlled with tried and tested methods. Targeting and using children for the hands-on element of crimes offers senior gang members a cushion of protection from detection by law enforcement agencies and reduces the risk of prosecution. Coercion and control techniques are varied. They can include exerting or introducing the fear of violence, including sexual abuse. Creating a scenario of belonging to a particular group or gang can also be a draw factor. It offers a child a sense of security that may be lacking in his life. The promise of earning significant amounts of money or receiving expensive presents such as phones or designer clothing, particularly for those children with very little, can often be seen as a once in a lifetime opportunity. It is often this financial return for transporting or dealing drugs and carrying out other criminal acts on behalf of the gang that is the greatest draw. This can also be the greatest control tool for exploiters. It is not uncommon for exploiters to orchestrate a robbery or theft of drugs from the child. The child is then told he is indebted to the gang and must pay back the cost of the drugs he lost. Through fear of the consequences, a child can become even more tied to his exploiters and likely to take bigger risks on their behalf. Seeking help from the authorities to escape his situation is often not an option. No matter how exploited a child has become, being labelled an informant or 'snitch' by peers can place him and his family at even greater risk of harm. Many do not consider themselves a victim and they may believe their exploiters are their protectors. This means they are unlikely to seek help, disclose their circumstances when faced with prosecution or help bring their exploiters to justice.

2.82

Whilst the promise of making money, usually presented by the owner(s) of a phone line through displays of large quantities of cash, jewellery and high value cars, is a key tactic in recruiting boys and young men to work in a county lines drug operation, drug runners and those working in cuckoo houses very rarely accrue any tangible profit. It is also highly unlikely that any person found in premises or detained on the street is going to be a main 'player' in the drugs line, and often they are victims of trafficking.

2.83

Likewise, the boys and young men found locked inside residential cannabis 'grows', suburban houses converted to multi floor cannabis production enterprises, are often expendable or re-useable farmers- resources of the gangs that control the drug operation served by that location.

2.84

The typology of county lines drug operations and residential cannabis grows is known to the authorities. It is also known that many children and young people are exploited in these situations and therefore they should be presumed to be trafficked or victims of modern slavery. Whereas they might not consider themselves to be victims, law enforcement should recognise that it is highly likely that they are.

2.85

We are decades into investigating human trafficking but in many cases the response appears to be "because the coerced UK or foreign national child we arrested didn't declare their circumstances to us as we kicked the door down and placed them in handcuffs" and "they can't be victims".[29] Knowing what trafficking looks like and what the victims look like, the law enforcement response to dealing with children and young people detained in county lines and cannabis grow operations needs to be more informed and based on good practice. Even in May 2025, in *R v ADV,* the Court allowed an appeal against conviction in relation to a 2020 offence of being concerned in the production of cannabis. The case concerned a 15-year-old Vietnamese boy working as a cannabis gardener found in a warehouse which contained 2,230 cannabis plants in 32 rooms. Had the police investigated the possible exploitation of which there were many indicators, they would have seen that he was a victim of international trafficking, domestic trafficking, debt bondage and one of the worst forms of child labour in breach of ILO Convention 182. West Yorkshire police also stated that it had not referred any of the defendants *via* the NRM because, 'Although there is absolutely a responsibility to fairly investigate any

29 Court of Appeal Criminal Division (Jeremy Baker LJ, Cavanagh J; and HHJ Heather Norton sitting as a Judge of the CACD), 23 May 2025 (unreported).

defences raised; there is no obligation to refer into the NRM if the evidence points to the subject being a suspect.' The Court directed the Respondent to cause West Yorkshire Police to be told that officers should be trained in exploitation.

2.86

There should be no repeat offenders if a proper investigation is undertaken and, if a victim centred approach is employed, intelligence may be gathered which can be used as a platform for investigating more important and higher-level offenders. See also **2.87**, **2.89** and **2.91** below.

2.87

Repeat offending in county lines cases means many children and young adults involved in criminal exploitation, drug running and weapon running will routinely be repeat offenders and the criminality escalates in severity. This is often because victims come to owe larger and larger debts to their exploiter(s) each time they are arrested and drugs, money and criminal property are seized.

2.88

There is currently a fragmented approach in how British national victims are protected. It is difficult to break the exploitation cycle in such cases because the British national victim/offender will have family, community and geographic ties to a particular area. It is very difficult to relocate entire families to different areas of the UK to protect them from the organised criminal networks. It is far easier for safeguarding measures to be put in place for foreign national victims. On a practical level, for example, an unaccompanied foreign national minor can be transferred to a different authority within the UK and can be easily rehoused in a suitable and safe location. This is far more challenging when it involves a British national child.

2.89

Criminal exploitation remains a complex issue which requires a case-by-case assessment of the facts of the case. It is imperative that any 'county lines' investigation considers and actively investigates the potential exploitation of those involved.

2.90

Examples of criminal exploitation may not be immediately obvious and range from minor non-recordable offences to indictable only offences and those of the most serious nature. Organised criminal networks, and individuals who use human beings as commodities in this manner, continually evolve and adapt their modus operandi to evade the attention of the authorities and to increase profitability.

2.91

Often those who have been criminalised and prosecuted remain in a cycle of exploitation and will go on to be re-trafficked and re-criminalised several times. Criminalising victims in this way significantly reduces the possibility of the victims providing evidence or intelligence against their traffickers, so it is unsurprising that the UK continues to have low conviction rates of trafficking related offences.

2.92

The Law Society Practice Note on criminal prosecutions of victims of trafficking[30] lists common indicators of trafficking. Further non-exhaustive lists are provided by UN Office on Drugs and Crime[31] (see **Chapter 4**).

Trafficking and terrorism

An international perspective

2.93

The United Nations has documented a five-fold increase in the number of children detained in the context of armed conflict since 2012. This increase must be considered against many countries adopting much more aggressive counterterrorism measures.

2.94

In 2019, the UN Security Council Counter-Terrorism Committee Executive Directive ('CTED') published a report 'Identifying and exploring the nexus between human trafficking, terrorism and terrorism financing'[32].

2.95

In this report it recognised the following:

- Numerous studies have demonstrated a clear nexus between human trafficking and terrorism. Nonetheless, the two phenomena continue to be treated separately.
- Human trafficking has become increasingly attractive to non-State armed groups – most notably terrorist entities.

30 Updated 20 November 2023; www.lawsociety.org.uk/support-services/advice/practice-notes/criminal-prosecutions-of-victims-of-trafficking/ (accessed 20 August 2025).

31 See www.unodc.org/pdf/HT_indicators_E_LOWRES.pdf, last accessed 17 December 2017.

32 https://www.un.org/securitycouncil/ctc/sites/www.un.org.securitycouncil.ctc/files/files/documents/2021/Jan/ht-terrorism-nexus-cted-report.pdf (accessed 20 August 2025).

- Member states have little understanding of their vulnerability to the two phenomena and to the potential links between them.

2.96

Research into a nexus between trafficking and terrorism has revealed sophisticated recruiting methods used by terrorist groups:

- social media and with propaganda identifying and targeting individuals – intensive contact – moving to private communication where recruiters seek to influence and secure the trust of the individual. Common 'push/ pull' factors include:
  - limited employment opportunities;
  - family breakdown;
  - social isolation/disenfranchised from wider society/sense of being 'other';
  - behavioural issues, psychological problems or behaviours;
  - causing victims to feel that joining the 'cause' is necessary–building of a conviction; accompanied increasing isolation (micro-communities); and radicalisation strategies.

2.97

In the context of the Western foreign fighter recruited by IS, for example, there was a targeted recruitment strategy to recruit women and girls. This was to serve the following purposes:

(i) To promote the creation of a new generation of fighters.

(ii) The presence of 'wives' and 'sex slaves' was used as a means to encourage recruitment of foreign fighters and retention of those fighters.

(iii) Often foreign fighters and their intended wives would be deceived about their living conditions, their movement would be restricted, they would be required to produce multiple offspring and women and girls would be required to re-marry if their husband died.

(iv) Defection would be classified as apostasy carrying the death penalty.

(v) Isolation methods would be adopted.

2.98

In short, indicators of forced labour were identified in the recruitment and control of Western Foreign Fighters and their wives.

A domestic perspective

2.99

The definition of terrorism is very broad (Terrorism Act 2000, s 1) – by design. The spectrum of criminal conduct encompassed as such is diverse, for example, sending trainers to a 'brother' fighter in a war zone; circulating a video or publication; or carrying out an attack in the UK targeting civilians.

2.100

The domestic terrorism legislation does not distinguish between causes, ideologies and the merits of different organisations. Those engaged in an armed struggle fighting for democracy against an oppressive dictatorship can fall within the definition in the same way as it might apply to ISIS or far-right organisations.

2.101

Terrorism and the activities of those non-state actors engaged in violence for political, religious, or ideological reasons have, in recent years, garnered enormous attention and analysis.

2.102

There are various strands to the UK's response to acts of terrorism. Diversion is a significant limb of counter-terrorism strategy developed over the years. Whilst frequently controversial, the police and prosecuting authorities purport to engage in a multi-agency approach to identify those who are vulnerable to such recruitment or grooming approaches. There is a recognition that the recruitment strategies go far beyond the development and discussion of political or religious ideas and debates.

2.103

Running alongside this counter terrorism strategy are prosecutions for widely defined offences not generally used in other areas of criminal litigation. Upon conviction defendants face very lengthy and often uncertain sentences with an unparalleled degree of intrusion into their lives upon release.

Child soldiers and Western foreign fighters or supporters

2.104

As identified above, at least some groups/movements engaged in what is now defined as terrorism seek to target for recruitment those who are vulnerable and deploy various strategies to do so.

2.105

The attraction of idealistic young people to a cause, including one that engages the 'armed struggle' is not a modern phenomenon. This distinction becomes more nuanced in respect of children as evident in the county lines cases. Children recruited to fight in movements engaged in terrorist activities are children engaged in a proscribed worst form of child labour (ILO Convention 182). As dealt with in **Chapter 1**, such activities would amount to exploitation and children cannot consent to their own exploitation.

Mitigation

2.106

R v Boular[33] illustrates the limitations and difficulties of diversion as a strategy and provides an insight into the way traffickers can manipulate political and religious beliefs to achieve their ends.

2.107

Safaa Boular was a vulnerable 15-year-old girl targeted and radicalised by a female ISIS supporter and then by a much older man who purported to engage her in an online relationship. She was then directed to a male who was in his 30s and based in Syria (though originally from the UK). The groomer purported to be in love with Safaa and she in turn believed herself (despite the two never having met in person) to be married to him. He couched his approach in religious terminology but rapidly the exchanges became sexually explicit. The 'relationship' had the support and encouragement of Safaa's mother and sister who subscribed to the views of the groomer.

2.108

The initial intention of the groomer (who was targeting other vulnerable women at the same time) was to recruit Safaa to travel to Syria and join him. When unsuccessful due to the intervention of the authorities, it was alleged by the prosecution that he recruited her for a plot to attack targets in the UK. There were various attempts at diversion by the authorities, but none were successful as it was suggested she had been taught to anticipate the intervention and view it as a hostile act. Safaa was convicted by a jury of two counts of engaging in conduct preparatory to terrorism (contrary to the Terrorism Act 2006, s 5) relating to alleged plans to carry out attacks in Syria and/ or the UK in support of ISIS. She was sentenced to custody for life.

33 [2019] EWCA Crim 798.

2.109

On appeal, when considering the issue of grooming and exploitation, the Court observed that 'exploitation is a mitigating factor'[34] and that the question for the Court was the extent to which she was 'vulnerable to exploitation, influence and radicalisation'[35]. The appellate court concluded that the original trial judge had given insufficient weight to the twin key factors of Safaa's age and 'grooming (or indoctrination) taken in combination … it is necessary to take into account the fact that, throughout her adolescence, she had been in a home which was not only very dysfunctional, but which specifically exposed her to radicalisation … the effect was that she was all the more vulnerable when first the female ISIS recruiter and then Naweed Hussain turned their attentions to influencing her and directing her actions'. Her sentence was reduced by a reduction in her minimum term. She was sentenced to custody for life (a life sentence) with a minimum term of 11 years.

2.110

Safaa's case was one of the rare cases under the terrorism legislation to come before the courts where a defendant, in terms, advanced a defence based upon the agreed fact that she was groomed and exploited. The appeal court's judgment reflects the tension between protection of the public and the protection of the victim of grooming.

Organ trafficking

2.111

The World Health Organisation identifies that: '[Cell, tissues or organ transplantation] involves replacing non-functional cells, tissues or organs with healthy counterparts that are obtained from another individual through voluntary donation during their lifetime or after their death. Access to transplantation varies a lot between countries, as does the safety, quality, efficacy of donation and transplantation of human cells, tissues and organs. Growth and development of transplantation worldwide is highly unequal and faces many challenges including:

- lack of national strategies for transplantation;
- inadequate legislation, ethical frameworks and regulation, which may allow for practices such as organ trafficking;
- lack of donation, processing and transplantation infrastructure;
- deficient universal health coverage, meaning that access to transplantation is excluded; and

34 Judgment, at [53].
35 Judgment, at [55].

- low awareness and engagement amongst the public and healthcare professionals.

2.112

Ethical concerns are a major issue. The shortage of organs can lead to illegal activities, like trafficking in body parts for transplants'[36].

2.113

On 5 May 2023, Nigerian nationals Ike Ekweremadu, 60, Beatrice Ekweremadu, 56 and Dr Obinna Obeta, 51, were imprisoned for nine years and eight months, four years and six months, and ten years respectively at the Central Criminal Court for conspiring to arrange the travel of a man for the purpose of harvesting his organs. The daughter of Ike Ekweremadu, a senior Nigerian politician Sonia Ekweremadu, suffered from deteriorating kidneys and required regular dialysis. A 21-year-old street trader from Lagos was trafficked by the Ekweremadus to London as a potential kidney donor. He was falsely presented as a willing donor to a private renal unit at London's Royal Free Hospital with forged documents falsely claiming he was Sonia's cousin. When the proposed transplant was rejected, the victim reported to the Police in fear for his life because he believed he was being lined up for another transplant in Nigeria.

2.114

The kidney harvesting case highlighted vulnerabilities in the UK's vetting system for living transplant. Mr Justice Jeremy Johnson, in his sentencing remarks, echoed the prosecution's suggestion that 'a lesson to be learned from this case is that clinicians must be alive to the risk of trafficking and report cases like this when concerns arise'[37].

Common forms of forced criminality

2.115

Throughout England and Wales common offences committed by victims of modern slavery through criminal exploitation are as follows:

36 https://www.who.int/health-topics/transplantation#tab=tab_1 (accessed 20 August 2025).

37 https://www.theguardian.com/world/2023/may/05/met-police-investigate-more-organ-trafficking-cases-in-uk (accessed 20 August 2025).

Sex offences[38]	
Rape	Sexual Offences Act 2003, s 1
Assault by penetration	Sexual Offences Act 2003, s 2
Sexual assault	Sexual Offences Act 2003, s 3
Causing a person to engage in sexual activity without consent	Sexual Offences Act 2003, s 4
Rape of a child under 13	Sexual Offences Act 2003, s 5
Assault of a child under 13 by penetration	Sexual Offences Act 2003, s 6
Sexual assault of a child under 13	Sexual Offences Act 2003, s 7
Causing or Inciting a child under 13 to engage in sexual activity	Sexual Offences Act 2003, s 8
Sexual activity with a child	Sexual Offences Act 2003, s 9
Causing or Inciting a child to engage in sexual activity	Sexual Offences Act 2003, s 10
Engaging in sexual activity in the presence of a child	Sexual Offences Act 2003, s 11
Causing a child to watch a sex act	Sexual Offences Act 2003, s 12
Arranging or facilitating commission of a child sex offence	Sexual Offences Act 2003, s 14
Meeting a child following sexual grooming	Sexual Offences Act 2003, s 15
Sexual communication with a child	Sexual Offences Act 2003, s 15A
Sexual activity with a child family member	Sexual Offences Act 2003, s 25
Inciting a child family member to engage in sexual activity	Sexual Offences Act 2003, s 26
Sexual exploitation of children	Sexual Offences Act 2003, s 47
Causing or inciting sexual exploitation of a child	Sexual Offences Act 2003, s 48
Controlling a child in relation to sexual exploitation	Sexual Offences Act 2003, s 49

38 It is common that those trafficked for the purpose of sexual exploitation will graduate into senior roles within a sexual exploitation ring while still under the control of their trafficker. This is particularly common in females trafficked from countries such as Morocco, Nigeria and Eastern Europe. Many may incite sexual activity and have a role within a brothel, such as grooming others. Sex offences are also associated with other human trafficking and modern slavery offences, where victims will be forced into the trafficking of others. Such offences are, by Sch 4, offences to which the defence in s 45, MSA 2015 does not apply (see Chapter 10 for a full list of Sch 4 offences).

Arranging or facilitating sexual exploitation of a child	Sexual Offences Act 2003, s 50
Causing or inciting prostitution for gain	Sexual Offences Act 2003, s 52
Controlling prostitution for gain	Sexual Offences Act 2003, s 53
Paying for sexual services of a prostitute subjected to exploitative conduct	Sexual Offences Act 2003, s 53A
Trafficking people for sexual exploitation	Sexual Offences Act 2003, s 59A
Keeping a brothel	Sexual Offences Act 1956, s 33, s 33A
Soliciting	Street Offences Act 1959, s 1 and Sexual Offences Act 2003, s 51A
Theft offences[39]	
Theft	Theft Act 1968, s 1
Robbery	Theft Act 1968, s 8
Burglary	Theft Act 1968, s 9
Burglary with intent	Theft Act 1968, s 9(1)(a)
Aggravated burglary	Theft Act 1968, s 10
Abstracting electricity[40]	Theft Act 1968, s 13
Going equipped	Theft Act 1968, s 25
Handling stolen goods	Theft Act 1968, s 22
Begging[41]	Vagrancy Act 1824, s 3
Fraud offences[42]	
Fraud by false representation	Fraud Act 2006, s 2
Fraud by failing to disclose information	Fraud Act 2006, s 3

39 Victims are used to commit theft offences, ranging from pick pocketing to robberies and burglaries. Commonly children of Roma descent will be used to pick-pocket for organised gangs and by elder family members. There is a significant discrepancy between the number of children identified by authorities as victims of trafficking and the number who have been charged with dishonesty offences such as theft (pick-pocketing). It is also common for Eastern European victims who are trafficked for forced labour to also be forced to collect and provide fraudulent charity bag and money collections, and be involved in the theft of metals from industrial sites.

40 Commonly associated with cannabis production.

41 Commonly Roma organised crime networks will use younger family members, often minors, to beg. Such cases are often unrecorded, as individuals are not arrested.

42 Victims will often be charged with possession of false passports or identity documents or because they have come to the UK illegally. It is common that fraudulent identity documents will then be used to open bank accounts and to commit various forms of fraud, including benefit fraud. Traffickers will apply for benefits or arrange for a victim to take up legitimate work under a false identity. The bank account that their official salary will go into from a legitimate employer is commonly only accessible to the trafficker and the victim will receive minimal or no money for their work.

Possession or control of articles for use in fraud	Fraud Act 2006, s 6
Making or supplying articles for use in fraud	Fraud Act 2006, s 7
Obtaining services dishonestly	Fraud Act 2006, s 11
Making a false instrument (forgery)	Forgery and Counterfeiting Act 1981, s 1
Copying a false instrument	Forgery and Counterfeiting Act 1981, s 2
Using a false instrument	Forgery and Counterfeiting Act 1981, s 3
Using a copy of a false instrument	Forgery and Counterfeiting Act 1981, s 4
Having custody or control of specified kinds of false instruments	Forgery and Counterfeiting Act 1981, s 5(1)
Making or having custody etc of machines, paper etc for making false instruments of that kind	Forgery and Counterfeiting Act 1981, s 5(3)
Possession of false ID document	Identity Documents Act 2010, s 4
Possession of false ID document with intent	Identity Documents Act 2010, s 6
Counterfeiting notes or coins	Forgery and Counterfeiting Act 1981, s 14
Passing, tendering or delivering counterfeit notes or coins	Forgery and Counterfeiting Act 1981, s 15
Custody or control of counterfeit notes or coins	Forgery and Counterfeiting Act 1981, s 16
Making or having materials and implements for counterfeiting[43]	Forgery and Counterfeiting Act 1981, s 17
Importation and exporting of counterfeit notes or coins	Forgery and Counterfeiting Act 1981, s 20, s 21
Obtaining services dishonestly	Fraud Act 2006, s 11
Dishonest representations to obtain benefits	Social Security Administration Act 1992, s 111A, s 112

43 Victims may be forced to produce and sell counterfeit goods, such as coins, DVDs, counterfeit cosmetics and designer products. Frequently this offence involves Eastern European, Vietnamese and Chinese national victims.

Shoplifting	Magistrates' Court Act 1980, s 22A
Criminal damage[44]	
Criminal damage	Criminal Damage Act 1971, s 1(1)
Aggravated criminal damage	Criminal Damage Act 1971, s 1(2)
Threats to destroy or damage property	Criminal Damage Act 1971, s 2
Possession with intent to destroy or damage property	Criminal Damage Act 1971, s 3
Offensive weapons[45]	
Possession of a firearm or ammunition without certificate	Firearms Act 1968, s 1(1)
Possessing shot gun without certificate	Firearms Act 1968, s 2(1)
Possessing prohibited weapons or ammunition	Firearms Act 1968, s 5(1)(a), (ab), (aba), (ac), (ad), (ae), (af), (c)
Possessing prohibited weapons designed for discharge of noxious liquid etc	Firearms Act 1968, s 5(1)(b)
Possessing firearm disguised as other object	Firearms Act 1968, s 4(1A)(a)
Possessing other prohibited weapons	Firearms Act 1968, s 5(1A)(b), (c), (d), (e), (f), (g)
Possessing firearm with intent to cause fear of violence	Firearms Act 1968, s 16A
Carrying firearm or imitation in public place	Firearms Act 1968, s 19
Possession of offensive weapon	Prevention of Crime Act 1953, s 1
Possession of a bladed article	Criminal Justice Act 1988, s 139(1)
Minding a dangerous weapon	Violent Crime Reduction Act 2006, ss 28, 29

44 It is not uncommon for victims who have been re-trafficked to be prosecuted for criminal damage as a result of breaking electronic monitoring tags off, which they may be subject to whilst on bail and licence. Victims may also be charged with damaging property while trying to escape a trafficking situation. Such offences are listed in Sch 4 as offences to which the defence under MSA 2015, s 45 does not apply (see the Annex to **Chapter 10** for the full schedule).

45 It is common for victims, once they have arrived in the UK, to be used to transport weapons for their traffickers. This is commonly associated with running drugs and county lines cases.

Drugs offences[46]	
Possession of controlled drug	Misuse of Drugs Act 1971, s 5
Production or supply of controlled drug	Misuse of Drugs Act 1971, s 4
Being concerned in the supply of controlled drug	Misuse of Drugs Act 1971, s 4(3)(b)
Possession with intent to supply controlled drug	Misuse of Drugs Act 1971, s 5
Importing/exporting controlled drug	Misuse of Drugs Act 1971, s 3
Cultivation of cannabis	Misuse of Drugs Act 1971, s 6
Supplying articles for administering or preparing controlled drug	Misuse of Drugs Act 1971, s 9A
Producing psychoactive substance	Psychoactive Substances Act 2016, s 4
Supplying or offering to supply psychoactive substance	Psychoactive Substances Act 2016, s 5
Possession of psychoactive substance with intent to supply	Psychoactive Substances Act 2016, s 7
Money laundering offences[47]	
Concealing etc criminal property	Proceeds of Crime Act 2002, s 327
Money laundering	Proceeds of Crime Act 2002, s 328

46 It is common that victims will be put to work in domestic houses adapted for the purpose of drug production, commonly cannabis cultivation. This involves abstraction of electricity and use of hydroponic equipment to cultivate and grow cannabis plants. It is common for Chinese and Vietnamese nationals to be trafficked for this purpose. Other common drugs offences include drug importation. Many victims will be trafficked from their country of origin for the purpose of couriering drugs into the UK or be used as a mule or courier throughout their destination country. Domestic national victims, often minors, are used in this way to transport drugs and weapons throughout one jurisdiction. The CPS guidance on County Lines Offending (https://www.cps.gov.uk/legal-guidance/county-lines-offending (accessed 20 August 2025)) gives the following guidance: 'County lines operates by criminal networks from urban areas (in particular, London, the West Midlands and Merseyside) introducing a telephone number in a new area to sell drugs directly at street level. Potential buyers telephone a number which will have been used to send advertising texts and local runners are dispatched to make deliveries via a telephone 'relay or exchange' system. The 'runners' are invariably children, often boys aged 14 – 17 years, who are groomed with the promise of money and gifts and deployed or forced to carry out day to day dealing. Runaway and missing children are also used by the networks to expand inner city drugs operations into county towns. Children as young as 11 years of age have been reported as being recruited by these highly organised networks. …' Prosecutors are advised: 'There may be cases where, properly directed and evidenced, an offence under the Modern Slavery Act 2015 … can be considered. …'

47 Commonly associated with those who have been forced into prostitution and charged with trafficking and controlling prostitution offences, victims are often involved in money laundering offences in these circumstances.

Acquires, uses or has possession of criminal property	Proceeds of Crime Act 2002, s 329
Immigration offences[48]	
Entry without leave	Immigration Act 1971, s 24
Obtaining leave by deception	Immigration Act 1971, s 24A
Facilitating unlawful immigration	Immigration Act 1971, s 25
Failure to produce immigration documents	Asylum and Immigration (Treatment of Claimants) Act 2004, s 2
Failure to comply with requirement to provide information required to obtain travel documents	Asylum and Immigration (Treatment of Claimants) Act 2004, s 35
Illegal working	Immigration Act 1971, s 24B
Offences of human trafficking, slavery and forced labour	
Slavery	Modern Slavery Act 2015, s 1
Human trafficking	Modern Slavery Act 2015, s 2
Driving offences[49]	
Dangerous driving	Road Traffic Act 1988, s 2
Driving or being in charge when under the influence of drink or drugs	Road Traffic Act 1988, s 4
Using a vehicle in a dangerous condition	Road Traffic Act 1988, s 40A
Driving otherwise than in accordance with a licence	Road Traffic Act 1988, s 87
Driving while disqualified	Road Traffic Act 1988, s 103
Using vehicle without insurance	Road Traffic Act 1988, s 143
Forced and sham marriages[50]	
Forced marriage	Family Law Act 1996, s 63CA;
	Anti-Social Behaviour Crime and Policing Act 2014, s 121

48 Victims who are trafficked from outside the UK will frequently be charged with numerous immigration offences. If victims travel with an agent, they are likely to have possession of immigration documents for only a short period. Those who travel with legitimate documents commonly have their documents held by traffickers and then will over-stay visas or have their passports expire.

49 European national victims are commonly trafficked to the UK for forced labour exploitation and frequently have car insurance policies and vehicles registered in their names and/or with fraudulent documents. They may also be forced to drive vehicles without proper driving licences or insurance, and will commit numerous road traffic offences as a result.

50 These offences commonly involve EU nationals trafficked to marry non-EU nationals in order for the latter to gain residency; traffickers usually obtain the payment for the marriage.

Sham marriages	Criminal Law Act 1977, s 1(1)
	Conspiracy to facilitate breach of immigration law.
	Immigration Act 1971, s 25(1)
	Assisting unlawful immigration (facilitation)

3 Working with victims of trafficking and modern slavery: trauma-informed practice for legal professionals, public authorities, and support professionals

Rachel Witkin, Dr Eileen Walsh and Michelle Brewer

Introduction

Access to justice and professional conduct

3.1

Access to justice for victims of trafficking, slavery, and related harms ('victims') is significantly influenced by the quality of training and conduct of the professionals they encounter. A person-centred, trauma-informed approach is essential to ensure that legal processes do not compound trauma-related mental health issues or increase vulnerability. Victims must be able to access assistance, support, justice, and remedies, regardless of whether they choose to initiate criminal proceedings or cooperate with law enforcement or judicial authorities.

Purpose and structure of this chapter

3.2

This chapter provides practical guidance for professionals engaging with victims of trafficking, slavery, and related harms. It outlines key resources for victim care and support, offers an overview of common mental health conditions and relevant health-related challenges, and discusses the role of expert medical evidence and considerations around capacity. The chapter also introduces trauma-informed methods of working, including the recommended use of the *Trauma-Informed Code of Conduct for All Professionals Working with Survivors of Human Trafficking and Slavery*. These methods are applied to core tasks such as taking instructions and facilitating full disclosure of a victim's history.

Scope and cross-referencing

3.3

While this chapter outlines best practice and guidance on public authority interviews for identification and investigation, guidance is also provided in other chapters of the book. **Chapter 8** specifically addresses *special measures* and *participation directions* in court and tribunal proceedings, including in-hearing protections and procedural adaptations.

Terminology and scope of 'professionals', 'victims', and measures

3.4

In this chapter, 'professionals' refers to those securing accounts from victims of trafficking, slavery, or similar harm, encompassing legal practitioners, public officials (eg police, immigration, National Referral Mechanism First Responders), and third-sector workers involved in identification or legal proceedings. The guidance aims to foster trauma-informed practices across these roles and encourage responsible ethical engagement.

3.5

The term 'victim' is used instead of 'survivor' to align with statutory language and legal guidance relevant to professionals, although 'survivor' may be favoured in therapeutic or advocacy contexts.

3.6

'Reasonable adjustments'[1] or 'accommodations' are measures supporting victims' effective participation in pre-court or tribunal processes, such as interviews or legal instructions. In contrast, 'special measures' and 'participation directions'[2] refer to court or tribunal ordered steps enabling vulnerable or intimidated individuals to participate in hearings, including live links, screens, intermediaries, communication aids, or support persons. Decisions on these measures are made by judges, ensuring both procedural fairness and the protection of vulnerable parties in the justice process.

---

1 See **Chapter 8** on the discussion of 'reasonable adjustments' as provided by the Equality Act 2010.
2 This is a term adopted by the Family Courts.

Victim care and support: key sources of guidance

3.7

Effective responses to victim care and support before, throughout and beyond legal processes must be multi-agency, inter-disciplinary, pro-active and trauma-informed. All professionals working at any level with victims should ensure that they have an informed understanding of the National Referral Mechanism (NRM), the NRM victim care contract, the rights and entitlements of victims, including (where applicable) the right to apply for asylum and to pursue justice against the perpetrators. The following resources are recommended for use and reference:

3.8

The *Modern Slavery: Statutory Guidance for England and Wales*[3] is issued by the UK Government under s 49 of the Modern Slavery Act 2015 ('MSA 2015'). It sets out the framework for identifying, supporting, and safeguarding victims of modern slavery and human trafficking. Public authorities in England and Wales are legally required to have regard to this guidance and must act consistently with it unless they can demonstrate good reason not to. As such, it serves as a primary source of reference for professionals working with victims, particularly in relation to care, support, and the operation of the National Referral Mechanism (NRM). The guidance also includes non-statutory provisions applicable to Scotland and Northern Ireland.

3.9

The Solicitors Regulation Authority (SRA) has published two key documents: *Meeting the Needs of Vulnerable People* (2022)[4] and *Providing Services to People Who Are Vulnerable* (2016)[5]. These set out the professional duties of solicitors when working with individuals who may face barriers to participation in legal processes.

3.10

Solicitors must identify vulnerability early and take reasonable steps to meet the specific needs of clients and witnesses. Vulnerability may arise from personal

3 Home Office, *Modern Slavery: Statutory Guidance for England and Wales (under s49 of the Modern Slavery Act 2015) and non-statutory guidance for Scotland and Northern Ireland* (accessible version, updated 11 August 2025) https://www.gov.uk/government/publications/modern-slavery-how-to-identify-and-support-victims/modern-slavery-statutory-guidance-for-england-and-wales-under-s49-of-the-modern-slavery-act-2015-and-non-statutory-guidance-for-scotland-and-northern-ireland accessed 21 August 2025.

4 Solicitors Regulation Authority, *Meeting the Needs of Vulnerable People* (31 August 2022) https://www.sra.org.uk/solicitors/resources/meeting-needs-vulnerable-people. Accessed 16 August 2025.

5 Solicitors Regulation Authority, *Providing Services to People Who Are Vulnerable* (March 2016) https://www.sra.org.uk/risk/risk-resources/vulnerable-people. Accessed 16 August 2025.

characteristics, situational factors, or systemic barriers, and poor service or failure to make reasonable adjustments may itself create or exacerbate vulnerability. Core duties include adapting communication, making anticipatory adjustments, and supporting the court in identifying and implementing appropriate measures. Solicitors must also assess capacity where relevant and act in the best interests of clients who may lack capacity (see **Chapter 8**).

3.11

The SRA considers the exploitation of vulnerable individuals to be a serious aggravating factor in disciplinary proceedings. These duties should be embedded in daily practice and training, and treated as essential to the provision of competent, inclusive, and ethical legal services.

3.12

The Equal Treatment Bench Book (ETBB)[6] is a core judicial resource published by the Judicial College to support fair treatment and effective participation in legal proceedings. Written by judges for judges, it is used daily across courts and tribunals in England and Wales and is regularly cited in training and appellate decisions. While primarily aimed at judicial office holders, its practical guidance is widely relied upon by legal practitioners, litigants in person, and others involved in the justice system. The ETBB promotes awareness of the diverse circumstances of court and tribunal users and offers concrete steps to improve communication, participation, and procedural fairness. It is a living document, updated frequently to reflect legislative developments, case law, and evolving social contexts. The current edition includes a dedicated chapter on modern slavery, alongside guidance relevant to a wide range of protected characteristics and vulnerabilities.

3.13

The *OSCE/ODIHR NRM Handbook*[7] was produced by global anti-trafficking experts including survivor leaders working in all relevant fields. It provides a trauma-informed guidance model which all OSCE participating States and other nations can adapt and apply within their own national systems. The Handbook provides detailed guidance on the working methods, procedures and services that are required to provide adult and child victims with access to the four NRM 'pillars': (1) identification and protection; (2) individual support and access to services; (3) social inclusion; and (4) criminal justice and redress. It includes guidance on working with child victims of trafficking and detailed, practical guidance on victims' healthcare needs. It also contains adult and child risk assessment guides.

6 Judicial College, *Equal Treatment Bench Book* (July 2024, May 2025 update) https://www.judiciary.uk/guidance-and-resources/equal-treatment-bench-book/ accessed 8 January 2026.

7 OSCE Office of the Special Representative and Co-ordinator for Combating Trafficking in Human Beings, *NRM Handbook* (2nd edn, 2022).

3.14

The UK Slavery and Trafficking Survivor Care Standards[8] is a multi-agency consensus document which is published by the Human Trafficking Foundation (HTF). The Care Standards set out the minimum level of care adult survivors should expect across the UK. Now in their third iteration, they are the product of a year's collaboration by over 150 frontline practitioners, public officials, advisers and lived-experience experts. The Standards promote consistent, high-quality, survivor-centred care, with an annex addressing overlapping issues relating to children.

Awareness of mental health problems

3.15

It is important not to assume the presence or absence of mental health problems in victims, as these can only be diagnosed following a mental health assessment provided by qualified clinicians. However, OSCE/ODIHR *NRM Handbook*[9] contains useful guidance for all professionals on the mental health needs of victims. In order to work effectively on the cases of victims, legal practitioners should have a basic knowledge and awareness of psychological problems that may be experienced by this client group and understand how these may affect their mental health and their participation in legal proceedings.

3.16

Mental health problems that are prevalent amongst victims include depressive disorders, anxiety disorders, post-traumatic stress disorder ('PTSD')[10] and complex PTSD.[11] All mental health problems may impair functioning, and where symptoms are severe, guidance should always be sought from health professionals on how best to support that individual. Symptoms can be exacerbated when victims are required to go through court or tribunal proceedings, particularly in cases where they are asked to recount past traumatic events as part of this process.[12] Hence the need for lawyers, courts and tribunals to have awareness of such issues when preparing the case and when applying and/or considering applications for special measures in any legal proceedings.

---

8 Human Trafficking Foundation, *The Slavery and Trafficking Survivor Care Standards* (October 2025).

9 OSCE NRM Handbook (n 7) s 22.

10 S Oram, M Abas, D Bick et al, 'Human trafficking and health: A survey of male and female survivors in England' (2016) 106(6) *American Journal of Public Health* 1073–78.

11 Livia Ottisova, Patrick Smith, and Siân Oram, 'Psychological consequences of human trafficking: Complex posttraumatic stress disorder in trafficked children', 44 *Behavioral Medicine* 234–241.

12 Chaffelson, R., Smith, J. A., Katona, C., & Clements, H. (2022). The challenges faced during home office interview when seeking asylum in the United Kingdom: an interpretative phenomenological analysis. *Ethnic and Racial Studies*, *46*(7), 1269–1289. https://doi.org/10.1080/01419870.2022.2112255.

3.17

People who have Post-Traumatic Stress Disorder (PTSD)[13] and Complex PTSD[14] can have particular difficulties engaging in legal proceedings. These are memory disorders[15] that develop following traumatic events. They are more likely to develop after multiple traumatic events, and traumas involving deliberate harm from others that are often reported in the context of trafficking, slavery or related harms, including sexual violence and physical assault[16].

3.18

Traumatic memories are understood to be stored in a fragmented way in the brain, meaning that a victim who has PTSD or Complex PTSD may not be able to provide a coherent and chronological account of their history[17]. When a person with PTSD/CPTSD recalls a traumatic event, recollection may be experienced as if the event is happening again in the present moment. For example, if asked about an incident of rape, the victim may see images of this as if it is occurring again, hear sounds that were heard at the time, and feel the physical sensations felt during the rape. The victim may also feel the same emotions, think the same thoughts, and have the same bodily responses, that they experienced at the time of the trauma. Therefore, PTSD symptoms can have a marked impact on a person's ability to give a chronological account of the event, and the account provided may have gaps or inconsistencies[18]. For some people, giving an account of traumatic events can lead to a deterioration in mental health.

3.19

The meaning a victim gives to their history will have an impact on their provision of evidence. A person who has had traumatic experiences may re-experience intense negative emotions and thoughts when they recall the memory, such as fear, shame, guilt, anger, and self-blame. For example, if memories trigger feelings of shame[19], a person may not feel able to disclose an account of an event

13 American Psychiatric Association. (2022). Diagnostic and statistical manual of mental disorders (5th ed., text rev.). https://doi.org/10.1176/appi.books.9780890425787.

14 World Health Organization (2021). International statistical classification of diseases and related health problems (11th ed.). https://icd.who.int/.

15 For a helpful overview for the legal professional see Herlihy, J. & Turner, S. (2013). What do we know so far about emotion and refugee law? Northern Ireland Legal Quarterly, 64(1) 47–62.

16 Ottisova et al (2016). Prevalence and Risk ofViolence and the Mental, Physical and Sexual Health Problems Associated with Human Trafficking: An Updated Systematic Review. Epidemiology and Psychiatric Sciences.

17 Herlihy, J., Jobson, L. and Turner, S. (2012). Just Tell Us What Happened to You: Autobiographical Memory and Seeking Asylum. Applied Cognitive Psychology 26 661–676.

18 Herlihy J, Turner S. Should discrepant accounts given by asylum seekers be taken as proof of deceit? Torture. 2006;16(2):81-92. PMID: 17251640.

19 D Bogner, J Herlihy and C Brewin, 'Impact of Sexual Violence on Disclosure during Home Office Interviews' (2007) 191 British Journal of Psychiatry 75.

fully or disclose it at all. Shame-based memories are inclined to be particularly high when a person has a history of sexual abuse, rape and sexual exploitation.

3.20

The UNODC *Anti Trafficking Manual for Criminal Justice Practitioners* states:

> 'Levels of psychological trauma experienced by some victims (either before or during the trafficking process) may be so high that they are never going to be able to serve as witnesses in court or even give an account that can be used as the basis of intelligence. You should always be prepared to terminate an interview if necessary and seek immediate assistance for the individual. On the other hand, it is also possible that some individuals who initially present strong emotional reactions, may, with time and professional support or counselling, become perfectly capable witnesses'[20].

Additional considerations for children

3.21

Child victims commonly develop mental health problems such as depression and anxiety disorders, PTSD[21] and CPTSD[22]. They will often have been exposed to traumatic events and multiple forms of maltreatment which can include physical, emotional and sexual abuse. Additionally, it should be recognised that at crucial stages of their development they will have lacked appropriate caregivers or a stable home in which their needs are met. In cases where adults with a duty of care to a child (for example parents, family members, foster carers or pastoral figures) have become perpetrators who abuse and exploit them, children's ability to form trusting and healthy relationships will have been fundamentally damaged. This can make it extremely difficult for them to trust any adults, including those who are involved in their lives now, such as social care professionals, support workers and their legal representatives[23].

3.22

Disruption during children's crucial developmental years may mean that they lack the essential 'building blocks' of identity formation, which are necessary tools for effective psychological recovery. Children also have a narrower range

20 Module 3, at p 3.

21 L Kiss, NS Pocock, V Naisanguansri et al, 'Health of men, women, and children in post-trafficking services in Cambodia, Thailand, and Vietnam: an observational cross-sectional study' (2015) *The Lancet* 3, 3, e154–e161.

22 Livia Ottisova, Patrick Smith, and Siân Oram, 'Psychological consequences of human trafficking: Complex posttraumatic stress disorder in trafficked children', 44 *Behavioral Medicine* 234–241.

23 See also, OSCE NRM Handbook (n 7) s.17.3.

of previous life and learning experiences than adults, and therefore less capacity to make sense of, and deal with, the aftermath of their traumatic experiences. Childhood abuse, particularly sexual abuse and neglect, are risk factors for later commercial exploitation[24]. Those who have been exploited from an early age, or for a prolonged period, are highly likely to suffer complex, long-term mental health problems. A history of trafficking, slavery or related harms as a child is associated with longer duration of contact with mental health services[25].

Provision of treatment for mental health problems

3.23

Victims who are undergoing any legal proceedings should be able to access therapeutic care at any time that they wish to do so. Therapy for victims should be evidence-based and delivered by a qualified therapist who is registered with a recognised professional regulatory body. Therapists should have training and experience in the provision of evidence-based psychological treatments as defined in recognised guidelines such as those developed by the National Institute for Health and Care Excellence (NICE), which covers recommended treatment for children and adults[26]. It is important that therapy is understood by all parties to be a confidential and sensitive process.

3.24

Only qualified child/ adolescent specialist therapists should provide therapeutic care for children, and it should be evidence based. Crisis support interventions may also be required for the child's family members/ caregivers[27]. Pre-hearing therapy for children has been the subject of guidance[28]. The purpose of therapeutic support is to provide emotional

24 Karen Countryman-Roswurm and Brien Bolin, 'Domestic minor sex trafficking: Assessing and reducing risk' (2014) 31(6) *Child and Adolescent Social Work Journal* 521-538.

25 L Ottisova, P Smith, H Shetty, D Stahl, J Downs et al 'Psychological consequences of child trafficking: An historical cohort study of trafficked children in contact with secondary mental health services' (2018) *PLOS ONE* 13(3): e0192321. https://doi.org/10.1371/journal.pone.0192321.

26 OSCE/ODIHR NRM Handbook (2nd edn): Evidence-based models of therapy include Cognitive Behavioural Therapy (CBT) for PTSD, depression and anxiety disorders; Narrative Exposure Therapy (NET) and Eye Movement De-sensitisation and Reprocessing (EMDR) for PTSD. All of these evidence-based therapies involve a collaborative approach: the survivor and therapist agree goals and a plan for treatment together, including identifying problems that the survivor feels ready to address. Treatment aims to help each person to understand how their symptoms have developed, to build skills at managing these symptoms, and to find different ways of dealing with distressing thoughts and feelings.

27 Non-offending care-givers.

28 Multi-agency guidance, *Provision of Therapy to Child Witnesses Prior to a Criminal Trial*, available at: https://www.cps.gov.uk/legal-guidance/therapy-provision-therapy-child-witnesses-prior-criminal-trial, last accessed 11 February 2020 and *Child Exploitation: Definition and Guide for Practitioners* (2017), available at: https://www.gov.uk/government/publications/child-sexual-exploitation-definition-and-guide-for-practitioners, last accessed 11 February 2020.

support and counselling to decrease distress or psychological symptoms and behaviour or improve personal functioning. The provision of this is not a decision for the police or lawyers but a decision to be taken by those with parental responsibility for the child alongside the relevant professionals providing therapeutic assessment and support.

Other relevant health-related issues and difficulties

3.25

Professionals engaging or communicating with victims, including legal practitioners, public authorities, and third sector support organisations should bear in mind that victims may have undisclosed physical health conditions, injuries and difficulties which can affect their ability to manage basic tasks. These may never have been diagnosed, and they may result in victims experiencing feelings of embarrassment, shame or stigma. Victims may have cognitive difficulties for a range of reasons which can affect their understanding and/or remembering of information they are given. For example, some victims may have suffered head injuries which affect their cognitive function; in some cases, victims may be neurodivergent, including those with an intellectual disability, or other difficulties related to learning, communication, or cognition[29].

3.26

Victims often feel unable to ask for help, or they lack awareness that there may be treatment available for their specific health needs. This can mean they will not bring some of their problems to healthcare appointments, and in some cases healthcare professionals will not think to ask about the full range of potential problems. Healthcare records are rarely comprehensive, and significant health problems may have never been identified[30].

3.27

It is important that all professionals maintain awareness of the accommodations and reasonable adjustments required for all victims because of their vulnerability, fear and distress, regardless of any diagnosis. This should be considered at all points in the legal process, including when taking instructions, interviewing, giving legal advice and during court and tribunal proceedings[31].

29 Peterka-Benton, D., & Bowman, M. E. (2025). The Intersection of Human Trafficking and Disabilities: Editors' Introduction to the Special Issue. *Journal of Human Trafficking*, *11*(1), 1–3. https://doi.org/10.1080/23322705.2024.2430894.

30 C Ross, S Dimitrova, LM Howard et al, 'Human trafficking and health: a cross-sectional survey of NHS professionals contact with victims of human trafficking' (2015) *BMJ* 5, 8.

31 See Chapter 8 for special measures in court or tribunal proceedings.

Medico-legal reports: roles, responsibilities, and impact

Purpose and scope

3.28

A medico-legal report provides an expert clinical assessment[32] of an individual's mental and/or physical health in the context of legal proceedings or related processes, such as National Referral Mechanism (NRM) interviews or Home Office asylum interviews. Prepared by a qualified medical expert acting as an expert witness, the report typically includes a diagnosis, prognosis, and an evaluation of the individual's current health status. It also addresses the implications of that health status for legal engagement, including the person's ability to participate in proceedings, provide instructions, and give evidence. Where instructed, the report may comment on the consistency between the clinical findings and the individual's narrative of trauma[33], which can be particularly important in cases involving allegations of torture, trafficking, or modern slavery offences. The expert's opinion is informed by a clinical examination and responds to specific instructions from the legal representative. The report may provide recommendations for reasonable adjustments or special measures[34].

Responsibilities of legal practitioners

3.29

Legal practitioners have a duty to provide medical experts with clear, specific, and detailed instructions. These instructions, which are disclosable in legal proceedings, must include all relevant background information and procedural context. Practitioners should ensure that the expert is equipped to assess the likely impact of legal processes on the individual and to make clinical recommendations regarding reasonable adjustments and special measures that may support their participation. A medical expert should be provided with a full copy of the victim's medical records when preparing the medico-legal report[35].

32 Medical experts can sometimes be instructed to provide a clinical opinion based on medical records only, or to provide an opinion on another medico-legal report.

33 *KV (Sri Lanka) v Secretary of State for the Home Department* [2019] UKSC 10, [2019] 2 WLR 1. An assessment of consistency between clinical findings and the individual's account of trauma must remain within the boundaries of clinical expertise; it is not the role of the medical expert to assess credibility, which is a matter for the court or tribunal.

34 See Chapter 8 for Special Measures in tribunal or court proceedings and Judicial College, *Equal Treatment Bench Book* (July 2024, May 2025 update) https://www.judiciary.uk/guidance-and-resources/equal-treatment-bench-book/ accessed 8 January 2026.

35 See *HA (expert evidence, mental health) Sri Lanka [2022] UKUT 111 (IAC) (25 March 2022).*

3.30

Instructions should explicitly describe the legal procedures the individual will be involved in. Medical experts should not be expected to have detailed knowledge of victim identification protocols, law enforcement procedures, or the structure of court or tribunal hearings. Providing this context enables the expert to tailor their recommendations to the specific legal environment, ensuring that any proposed measures are relevant and practicable.

Standards for expert reports

3.31

To ensure that a medico-legal report carries appropriate weight in legal proceedings, it must comply with the procedural requirements of the relevant jurisdiction. These requirements, set out in court or tribunal practice directions, procedural rules, or guidance, should be clearly communicated to the expert in the instructions. Regardless of jurisdiction, experts owe an overriding duty to the court or tribunal to provide independent, objective, and unbiased opinion evidence. Reports must reflect the expert's own analysis, include a statement of qualifications, identify all material relied upon, and distinguish between facts known personally and those provided by others. Limitations, uncertainties, discrepancies and the range of professional opinion should be transparently addressed. The report must be clearly structured, reasoned, and include a summary of conclusions. It should be addressed to the court or tribunal, verified by a statement of truth, and formatted for clarity. If the expert's opinion changes materially after submission, this must be communicated promptly.

Clinical considerations and recommendations

3.32

The report should document any limitations on the individual's ability to provide an account, whether during instruction-taking, interviews, or while giving evidence. It must assess the person's capacity to consent to and engage in the assessment and recommend any necessary special measures[36] or adjustments to support their participation. This includes consideration of vulnerability, disability, and the psychological impact of recounting traumatic experiences, particularly where repetition is involved. Where communication difficulties are identified, the report should consider the need for an intermediary.

36 See **Chapter 8**.

3.33

The OSCE/ODIHR *National Referral Mechanism Handbook* notes that clinical documentation of physical and psychological injuries can reduce the risk of re-traumatisation during investigative questioning and help explain difficulties in providing coherent and consistent accounts[37]. Medico-legal reports should align with the UN *Istanbul Protocol*, which sets out authoritative guidelines for documenting torture and ill-treatment. The second edition offers expanded guidance on psychological harm, which is particularly relevant in cases involving trafficking or modern slavery[38].

Impact on public authorities and legal processes

3.34

Reasonable adjustments should be available as standard in interviews conducted by NRM First Responders, public authorities, and the use of special measures in court or tribunal proceedings involving vulnerable parties or witnesses. However, it is the responsibility of legal practitioners to make appropriate applications when representing victims. Independent medical evidence can significantly assist public authorities in identifying victims, planning support, conducting investigations, and ensuring fair legal processes.

3.35

While it is best practice to obtain a medico-legal report, such evidence may not be readily available, particularly evidence meeting the standard required for litigation. This must not result in unfair disadvantage. Legal practitioners should request special measures or reasonable adjustments in all cases involving potential or known victims, regardless of whether expert medical evidence is available. Any application must clearly explain its basis, and the guidance identified at the start of this chapter should help with this.

Capacity and engagement in legal processes

3.36

Legal practitioners are required to consider a client's attributes, needs and circumstances. This includes being satisfied that the client has the capacity

37 OSCE Office of the Special Representative and Co-ordinator for Combating Trafficking in Human Beings, *National Referral Mechanisms: Joining Efforts to Protect the Rights of Trafficked Persons: A Practical Handbook* (2nd edn, OSCE 2022) s 17.

38 Office of the United Nations High Commissioner for Human Rights, *Istanbul Protocol: Manual on the Effective Investigation and Documentation of Torture and Other Cruel, Inhuman or Degrading Treatment or Punishment* (2nd edn, UN 2022).

to instruct a solicitor[39] or barrister. As explained in **Chapter 8**, professional obligations arise for legal practitioners if there is any question concerning capacity. The assessment of capacity is both decision and activity specific[40] and adults are presumed to have capacity; specific evidence will be required to rebut this[41]. The legal principles of capacity to engage in legal proceedings are set out in **Chapter 8**. Medical experts can provide evidence on the capacity of an individual victim to give instructions, to be interviewed by public authorities, and participate in legal proceedings.

3.37

Capacity is a critical consideration at every stage of engagement with a potential or confirmed victim, including identification, investigation, securing instructions, providing legal advice, and participation in legal proceedings. Public authorities, such as the police, immigration officers, and the National Referral Mechanism's Single Competent Authority, must themselves assess whether an individual has the capacity to engage with the processes required of them. This includes evaluating whether the person has the capacity to participate in an interview. Such an assessment must consider how the interview will be conducted and how the individual is likely to respond. Importantly, capacity is not static; it can fluctuate, even within the course of a single interview. For instance, a person with PTSD may dissociate or experience other symptoms when recounting traumatic events, which can temporarily impair their capacity.

3.38

Where appropriate, adjustments to the interview format (or curtailing repeated interviews) should be considered to mitigate these effects. Any recommendations should be outlined in a medico-legal report and could include the presence of a trusted medical practitioner during the interview to monitor capacity. Guidance on adapting interview techniques and questioning styles is available in the *Equal Treatment Bench Book*[42] and the *20 Principles of Questioning*[43] produced by the Council of the Inns of Court. All interviews should be consistent with the *Principles on Effective Interviewing for Investigations and Information Gathering*[44]

39 Solicitors Regulation Authority Code of Conduct for Solicitors, RELs and RFLs at paragraph 34.

40 *Dunhill v Burgin (Nos 1 & 2)* [2014] UKSC 18.

41 *Royal Bank of Scotland Plc v AB15* [2020] UKEAT 0266/18/2702. The judgment relates to capacity to conduct proceedings before the Employment Tribunal, but the principles are of broader application.

42 Equal Treatment Bench Book (Judicial College, July 2024, updated May 2025) Chapter 2 https://www.judiciary.uk/about-the-judiciary/diversity/equal-treatment-bench-book/ accessed 21 August 2025.

43 Council of the Inns of Court, Advocacy for Vulnerable People and Children (Criminal Course): The 20 Principles of Questioning (2022) https://www.icca.ac.uk/wp-content/uploads/2023/03/20-Principles-of-Questioning.pdf accessed 21 August 2025.

44 *Principles on Effective Interviewing for Investigations and Information Gathering* (Steering Committee of Experts, May 2021) https://www.interviewingprinciples.com accessed 16 August 2025.

(2021), known as the Méndez Principles. These principles provide a globally recognised framework for ethical and trauma-informed interviewing[45].

Trauma-informed methods of working

3.39

Trauma-informed identification and interviewing are not simply matters of good practice; they form part of the State's positive obligations under Art 4 ECHR and Arts 10–13 ECAT to identify, protect, and assist victims effectively (**Chapter 4**). Any engagement with victims therefore requires professionals to apply practical, trauma-informed methods of working. These methods enable victims to participate meaningfully in legal and support processes, access their rights and entitlements, and pursue justice. Adopting a trauma-informed approach is integral to meeting the UK's duty to provide practical and effective protection for victims of trafficking and modern slavery, rather than an optional enhancement to existing procedures. In day-to-day practice, these methods give effect to the trauma-informed approach required by the Modern Slavery Statutory Guidance issued under s 49 MSA 2015.

3.40

As identified above, victims can suffer forms of psychological abuse and effects of physical violence which constitute torture or share the same fundamental components as torture, which underlines the need for non-coercive, trauma-informed interviewing methods[46]. The psychological consequences of these experiences are serious, and endure long after victims have left the direct control of their perpetrators. Victims should be understood to be vulnerable, with attendant risks that they may lose essential contact with services or fall victim to further crimes and harm if not appropriately advised and supported. Professionals should also maintain sensitivity to the gender and age of the victim, as well as other characteristics which exacerbate their vulnerability.

3.41

Acknowledging the psychological vulnerability of children and young people who have been trafficked or subjected to slavery or related harms is crucial to their well-being and ongoing protection. From a developmental point of view, it is useful to bear in mind that the maturity 'cut off' point between the 'minor' age of 17 and the 'majority' age of 18 is arbitrary, and it is not always possible to determine the exact age of some young people in any case. Young adult victims

45 The initiative was led by Juan E. Méndez during his tenure as United Nations Special Rapporteur on Torture, following his 2016 thematic report to the UN General Assembly which called for the development of international standards for non-coercive interviewing.

46 OSCE, Trafficking in Human Beings Amounting to Torture and other Forms of Ill-treatment, 2013.

can be vulnerable because of their youth as well as their trauma history and other factors[47]. Therefore, reasonable adjustments and special measures can be requested due to a victim's young age as well as any other reasons as to why they are vulnerable (see **Chapter 8**).

The Trauma-informed Code of Conduct for All Professionals (TiCC)[48]

3.42

The TiCC is a guidance document that provides insights for practice with survivors, relevant mental health information and simple, trauma-informed methods of working. It supports professionals' safe and effective working, both in person and online, enabling them to: (a) establish and maintain a mutual relationship of trust with victims in any working context or environment; (b) impart a consistent sense of calm, security and safety throughout the course of their work; (c) increase the confidence of victims and minimise the risks of causing distress and re-traumatisation; and (d) remain safe and well in the course of their work, avoiding secondary traumatisation and professional 'burnout'.

3.43

Professionals are encouraged to refer directly to the TiCC when conducting specific tasks relating to the case, including (but not limited to): preparation, meeting for the first time and at all subsequent times, taking detailed instructions, obtaining disclosure of a victim's personal information and history, applying for reasonable adjustments or special measures (see **Chapter 8**) and working remotely. It helps legal practitioners provide support and reassurance for victims through arduous legal processes and appearance at courts and tribunals. An outline summary of some key areas covered in the TiCC is provided below.

Preparation and approach to working with victims

3.44

The TiCC emphasises that communication awareness is central to everything we say and do, including both our words and our body language. It advises on the preparation and maintenance of a calm, consistent working environment;

47 N Stanley, S Oram, S Jakobowitz et al, 'The health needs and healthcare experiences of young people trafficked into the UK' (2016) 59 *Child Abuse and Neglect* 100–10.

48 Rachel Witkin and Katy Robjant, *The Trauma-Informed Code of Conduct for all Professionals Working with Survivors of Human Trafficking and Slavery* (2nd edn, Helen Bamber Foundation 2022).

how to work in a trauma-informed way with other professionals including interpreters; how to carefully assess, manage, and respond to the presence of other people who may accompany victims and how to work (if there is no other option) with parents in the presence of young children and babies. It advises on how to observe each person's presentation and gives basic guidance on mental health symptoms and responses which may arise during specific tasks.

Building a safe relationship to support disclosure

3.45

Regarding the challenging process of obtaining full disclosure of a person's history and account, the TiCC explains the effects of trauma on the brain in terms of its impact on chronological memory and provides guidance on how to respond if a victim experiences dissociation. It advises on how to help victims to access their calm mind and make informed decisions, including for example, by '*creating the illusion of time*.' It explains how gentle acknowledgement of memory intrusions or symptoms that victims may experience during engagement can be discussed in a simple, practical way to help them to feel comfortable, and avoid any pre-occupation with trying to conceal or suppress these. The process of disclosure requires that legal practitioners can appropriately acknowledge the information they are given, including that which is painful and personal. A helpful technique is to 'return to the here and now' when needed to minimise distress that can arise when victims discuss traumatic past events and uncertain futures.

Obtaining a victim's account in a trauma-informed way

3.46

The TiCC advises that all full accounts from victims 'begin at the beginning'. It is useful to begin with questions about birth and early childhood and proceed onward from there to build up an accurate picture of a victim's origins and circumstances. This is an effective way to capture details, because it assists victims' recall by working progressively and chronologically through a sequence of related events, enabling them to relate these events to each other. Where it is possible within role and remit, professionals can find the right question-answer format with each individual person; they can '*framework*' painful or sensitive topic areas that are forthcoming so that victims need not fear these suddenly arising. It provides words and phrasing, which can be more helpful than typically professional or legal language when eliciting an account, for example focusing simply on the words '*safe*' and '*safety*'. It also provides guidance on working with interpreters and other professionals who are present.

3.47

When victims disclose ritualised violence, this can be extremely distressing and may pose risks to their health and wellbeing. The TiCC explains how practices such as oath-taking ceremonies often have a deep and lasting impact on victims, including reinforcing fears and beliefs about perpetrators. These situations require professionals to consistently respond with particular care, sensitivity and balance.

3.48

The TiCC advises that, when seeking disclosure, it is essential to understand the individual's perception of others and of their wider environment, as this informs the proper interpretation of the circumstances in which exploitation may have occurred. This perspective can offer valuable insight into the nature of a victim's vulnerability to trafficking, slavery or related harms and may also assist in identifying the individuals or networks responsible. Legal practitioners and other professionals should avoid dismissing early accounts that appear inconsistent or incomplete. Victims often disclose their experiences gradually, and accounts may become more coherent over time as trust is established. Inconsistencies or apparent inaccuracies may be clarified through ongoing engagement, particularly where professionals work with survivors across multiple sessions[49].

A trauma-informed, rights-based approach to interviewing child victims[50]

3.49

International evidence increasingly supports the view that Multi-Disciplinary/Inter-Agency (MD/IA) models, such as Barnahus (Europe), Child Advocacy Centers (USA), and Child and Youth Advocacy Centres (Canada), offer a more effective and child-centred response to child victims and witnesses of abuse than traditional UK approaches. These models integrate child protection, justice, health, and therapeutic services, reducing the fragmentation that often characterises UK systems. Evidence from Iceland shows that Barnahus implementation led to increased prosecutions and convictions in child sexual abuse cases, attributed to structured forensic interviewing protocols that enhance evidentiary value while minimising trauma[51]. Similar protocols have

49 See *MN and IXU v Secretary of State for the Home Department* [2020] EWCA Civ 1746.

50 This section of the chapter was authored by Michelle Brewer, who also serves as the editor of *Human Trafficking and Modern Slavery: Law and Practice*.

51 M Vlachou, V Sebhelyi and A Adelaine, *Informing Bairns' Hoose Implementation in Scotland: A Literature Review* (Children and Young People's Centre for Justice 2025).

been adopted across European Barnahus centres and North American advocacy centres, with demonstrable improvements in investigative outcomes.

3.50

MD/IA models are underpinned by robust training and supervision frameworks. In Finland, for example, child interviewers undergo a one-year joint training programme, ensuring consistency and quality in forensic interviewing. In contrast, training across UK agencies remains variable and often insufficiently specialised[52].

3.51

The Barnahus model[53] is a child-centred, multidisciplinary and interagency approach to interviewing and supporting child victims and witnesses of violence, including trafficking and exploitation. Barnahus co-locates forensic interviewing, medical examination, therapeutic support, and legal processes in a single child-friendly setting. Its core aim is to prevent re-traumatisation, secure valid testimony, and uphold the child's rights to protection, participation, and support[54].

3.52

Barnahus has been successfully adapted across Europe, including in Sweden, Norway, and Denmark, and is endorsed by the PROMISE Barnahus Quality Standards as a model of best practice[55]. It has been piloted in some areas of the UK.

Why a trauma-informed approach is necessary

3.53

Children who have experienced trafficking, slavery or related harms often present with complex trauma, delayed disclosure, and heightened vulnerability to suggestibility[56]. Repeated interviews, unfamiliar environments, and adversarial questioning can compound trauma and undermine the reliability of their accounts. A trauma-informed approach recognises the psychological impact of abuse and prioritises the child's safety, dignity, and autonomy throughout the interview process[57].

52 Ibid.
53 Icelandic for 'Children's House'.
54 Children's Commissioner, *Barnahus Overview* (2015); PROMISE Project, *Barnahus Quality Standards* (2019).
55 PROMISE Project, *Barnahus Quality Standards*, Standards 1–10.
56 Korkman et al., *White Paper on Forensic Child Interviewing* (EAPL, 2024), pp. 6–8.
57 Ibid, pp. 13–15.

Key principles of best practice

3.54

Single Interview in a Child-Friendly Setting: Interviews should be conducted in a neutral, safe, and welcoming environment, ideally within a Barnahus or equivalent facility. The setting should be designed to reduce anxiety and avoid associations with punishment or illness[58].

3.55

Multidisciplinary Coordination: All relevant professionals, police, prosecutors, defence lawyers, other public authority officials and in non-criminal proceedings the child's lawyers, child protection, health and mental health services, as well as relevant public authority officials (ie, decision making immigration officer or case worker, Single Competent Authority designated case owner and Independent Child Trafficking Advocate) should collaborate in planning. An interview is then conducted by a specially trained paediatric psychotherapist interviewer in a child-friendly room which is video-linked to an observation room. The interview is witnessed by the child's advocate, social worker, the defence and prosecution teams, with a judge presiding. The interview is video recorded and may subsequently be used during a criminal trial or other legal proceedings[59]. In criminal proceedings, arrangements are in place which allow the defence to pose questions to the child victim/witness via a forensic interviewer. The accused is permitted to observe the child's testimony, via an audio-visual transmission to avoid potential contact between the accused and the child.

3.56

Evidence-Based Interview Protocols: Interviewers must use validated protocols such as the **NICHD**[60] or **Achieving Best Evidence (ABE)** guidelines. These protocols emphasise open-ended questioning, rapport-building, and phased interviewing (introduction, ground rules, practice recall, substantive interview, closure)[61].

3.57

Avoiding Suggestive Techniques: Interviewers must avoid leading questions, forced-choice formats, and suggestive props such as anatomically detailed dolls

58 Children's Commissioner Report, p. 4.

59 PROMISE Standards, Standard 6; Children's Commissioner Report, p. 6.

60 A NICHD interview is a structured, research-based forensic interview protocol designed for professionals conducting interviews with children who are suspected victims of sexual or physical abuse. Developed by the National Institute of Child Health and Human Development (NICHD), the protocol aims to improve the reliability and accuracy of children's accounts while minimising suggestive or leading questioning.

61 Korkman et al., pp. 11–12; Ministry of Justice, *Achieving Best Evidence* (2022).

or body diagrams. These methods have been shown to increase false reports and reduce accuracy[62].

Recording and use of testimony

3.58

Interviews should be electronically recorded and, where possible, used as the child's evidence in legal proceedings. This avoids the need for repeated testimony, and where this process is implemented, children are not subjected to cross-examination[63].

Cultural sensitivity and interpretation

3.59

Interviewers must consider cultural factors that may affect disclosure and communication. Where interpreters are needed, they should be trained in child interviewing and involved in pre-interview planning[64].

Support and therapeutic follow-up

3.60

Therapeutic support should be offered immediately after the interview, regardless of whether the case proceeds to a hearing[65]. The child's well-being must be prioritised throughout the process.

Application to cases of trafficking, slavery and related harms

3.61

As set out above, child victims may have experienced ritualised abuse, coercion, and instilled fears that inhibit disclosure[66]. A trauma-informed forensic interview can help elicit a coherent narrative while minimising distress. The Barnahus model's emphasis on early intervention, coordinated support, and child-friendly justice is particularly suited to these cases.

62 Korkman et al., pp. 22–23.
63 PROMISE Standards, Standard 6; Children's Commissioner Report, p. 6.
64 Korkman et al., pp. 21–22.
65 PROMISE Standards, Standard 8; Children's Commissioner Report, p. 7.
66 PROMISE Standards, Standard 3; Children's Commissioner Report, pp. 5–6.

4 The operative duty to identify victims of slavery, servitude, forced or compulsory labour, and human trafficking: the national referral mechanism and Art 4 ECHR

Michelle Brewer, Emma Fitzsimons and Katy Sheridan

The UK's framework for identifying victims and its relationship to Art 4 ECHR

4.1

This chapter examines how the UK identifies victims or potential victims of slavery, servitude, forced labour, and human trafficking under Art 4. An effective national system for identifying victims and for providing a recovery and reflection period, is central to the prevention of violations under Art 4 of the European Convention on Human Rights (ECHR). As Stoyanova observes, a robust national decision-making process for identification is instrumental to Art 4 compliance, because failures in identification allow serious abuses to remain unrecognised and unremedied[1]. The primary statutory mechanism for identification is the National Referral Mechanism (NRM). This mechanism is integral to the discharge of the United Kingdom's positive obligations under Art 4 of the ECHR, as given domestic effect by Schedule 1 to the Human Rights Act 1998. Where State mechanisms, most notably the NRM, fail to facilitate the identification of potential victims, the State risks breaching Art 4 and may be subject to legal challenge[2].

1 Vladislava Stoyanova, 'Human Trafficking and Slavery Reconsidered: Conceptual Limits and States' Positive Obligations in European Law' (Cambridge University Press 2017).

2 Findlay, J. (2025) 'Modern slavery, victim identification and the "victimized State"', *The British Journal of Criminology*, 65(3), pp. 504–520. doi: 10.1093/bjc/azae061. See submissions made to GRETA during the 4th Evaluation Round, currently ongoing at time of publication. GRETA is the Group of Experts on Action against Trafficking in Human Beings, the monitoring mechanism on human trafficking established by ECAT in Art. 36.

4.2

Article 1 of the ECHR requires all Contracting States to ensure effective respect for the Convention's substantive rights. The European Court of Human Rights (ECtHR) has held that Art 1 read with a substantive right, gives rise to both negative and positive obligations on the State. In the context of Art 4, the negative obligation requires the State to refrain from conduct that itself amounts to slavery, servitude, forced or compulsory labour, or human trafficking, or that constitutes unjustified interference with the rights protected by Art 4. As the Court made clear in *Siliadin v France*[3], mere non-interference by the State is insufficient. The positive obligations operate to require the State to take proactive measures to secure the practical and effective enjoyment of the right and are consequential to the substantive right. This requires States to take active steps to secure Convention rights, including through appropriate legislative, administrative and protective measures. Accordingly, a failure to discharge the positive obligations inherent in a substantive right may of itself constitute a violation of that right.

4.3

By identifying victims of Art 4 violations, National Referral Mechanism (NRM) decisions provide authoritative evidence of a credible suspicion which engages the State's operational positive obligations under Art 4 and informs the duties of other statutory agencies (see **4.4**). Those obligations may, however, arise earlier wherever competent authorities knew or ought to have known of facts which, objectively assessed, give rise to such a credible suspicion, irrespective of whether an NRM decision has yet been taken. Accurate identification is the gateway to those obligations, essential to securing victim protection by enabling recovery, reparation, investigation and prosecution. Identification must conform to the legal definitions of slavery and related acts under Art 4[4]. Accordingly, practitioners and public authorities must be familiar with these definitions to ensure compliance, particularly where the modern statutory guidance does not consistently align with international law interpretations (see **Chapter 1**).

4.4

In *MN and IXU v Secretary of State for the Home Department*[5], the Court of Appeal held that decisions under the National Referral Mechanism are gateway decisions to important rights. A failure to identify victims of trafficking or modern slavery may result in individuals being effectively and permanently denied access to the rights and protections to which they are legally entitled

3 *Siliadin v France* (2006) 43 EHRR 16 [148].
4 *VCL and AN v UK* (2021) 73 EHRR 9 at [149], [152], [160], [162] and [207].
5 [2020] EWCA Civ 1746 at [242].

under domestic and international law[6]. The NRM's positive reasonable grounds decision has been treated by the ECtHR as a determination made by a competent authority which is capable of triggering the State's positive obligations under the Convention.[7] A positive reasonable grounds decision will ordinarily evidence a credible suspicion that clearly engages those operational duties, but the existence and scope of the State's positive obligations under Art 4 do not depend on the timing or outcome of the NRM process. This is unsurprising. As the Court of Appeal explained in *R (TDT) v Secretary of State for the Home Department* [2018] 1 WLR 4922 at [35] and [38][8], the standard of proof at the 'reasonable grounds' stage aligns with the threshold required to engage the State's positive obligations under the Convention. Properly understood, that standard reflects a 'credible suspicion' threshold rather than a requirement for corroborative 'objective' evidence. As Underhill LJ further observed, such a credible suspicion may arise at the point of referral into the NRM or earlier, depending on the information available to the authorities. Conversely, a negative reasonable grounds decision cannot, of itself, extinguish the State's obligations under Art 4 where the surrounding material indicates a credible suspicion of slavery, servitude, forced or compulsory labour, or trafficking. Public authorities, courts and tribunals remain under a duty to assess the available evidence, and where appropriate to seek further information, rather than treating the absence of NRM recognition as determinative.

The role of positive obligations under Art 4 ECHR in victim identification and legal redress

4.5

Before turning to the operation of the NRM, it is necessary to identify the positive obligations that arise from the substantive right protected by Art 4 of the ECHR[9]. Such duties are a central part of the legal framework through which victims can access the rights and protections guaranteed by Art 4 and, where those rights are not respected, to seek redress before courts or tribunals.

4.6

The positive obligations arising under Art 4 of the ECHR also inform the interpretation and application of domestic legislation. By virtue of s 3 of the Human Rights Act 1998, courts are required, so far as possible, to read and

6 Anne T. Gallagher, *Human Rights and Human Trafficking* in A. Nollekamper and A. Plakokefalos (eds) The Practice of Shared Responsibility in International Law (Cambridge University Press, 2017) at p.11.

7 *VCL and AN v UK* (2021) 73 EHRR 9 at [162] and [152].

8 [2018] EWCA Civ 1395, [2018] 1 WLR 4922 at [31] (reciting *Hoang*), [35] and [38] (Underhill LJ's operative holding on the correspondence between credible suspicion and reasonable grounds).

9 See Marija Jovanovic, *State Responsibility for 'Modern Slavery' in Human Rights Law: A Right Not to Be Trafficked* (Oxford University Press 2023) 97.

give effect to legislation in a manner compatible with Convention rights. The ECtHR has recognised that specific measures within the Council of Europe Convention on Action against Trafficking in Human Beings 2005 (ECAT) inform the scope and content of the State's positive obligations under Art 4. Those same positive obligations have provided an important route by which the standards set out in ECAT have become justiciable in domestic law. Notably, a number of ECAT's substantive and procedural requirements have now been given domestic effect through statute, including the Modern Slavery Act 2015 (MSA 2015) and, more recently, the Nationality and Borders Act 2022 (NABA 2022). Domestic obligations in this area therefore derive both from Convention-compliant interpretation under the HRA 1998 and from express legislative incorporation of key elements of the ECAT framework. The interplay of ECAT and Art 4 of the ECHR is examined below.

Scope and structure of positive obligations under Art 4 ECHR

4.7

The development of positive obligations under Art 4 ECHR has been shaped through case law. As a result, these obligations continue to evolve, making it difficult to define their precise parameters at any given time.[10] Given that positive obligations are legal responsibilities imposed on public authorities, it is essential that those authorities have clarity and certainty about their scope and application.

4.8

Positive obligations which had crystallised in case law are outlined in *SM v Croatia*[11] and *Rantsev v Cyprus and Russia*[12]. The ECtHR affirmed that Art 4 ECHR imposes the following substantive and procedural positive obligations on states:

- Establish an effective legal and administrative framework to prohibit and penalise trafficking and related abuses (the *systems duty*).
- Take operational measures to prevent exploitation and protect potential victims (the *protective duty*).
- Conduct effective investigations capable of identifying and prosecuting the perpetrator(s) where there is a credible suspicion that there has been

10 For a detailed analysis, see V Stoyanova, *Human Trafficking and Slavery Reconsidered: Conceptual Limits and States' Positive Obligations in European Law* (CUP 2017), and see further her subsequent work on Art 4 positive obligations.

11 *S.M. v Croatia* [GC], (2021) 72 E.H.R.R. 1, [312–320].

12 *Rantsev v Cyprus and Russia,* (2010) 51 E.H.R.R. 1.

Art 4 violations or there is a real and immediate risk they may arise[13]. Further, there must be access to effective judicial remedies (the *procedural duties*).

- Secure restitution for victims in respect of the harm suffered (the *restitution duty*).

4.9

Other than the systems duty, the Court assesses compliance with positive obligations using a two-stage test:

1. Awareness of Risk: Whether the state knew, or ought to have known, of a credible suspicion that an individual was, or was at real and immediate risk of being, subjected to slavery, servitude, forced or compulsory labour, or trafficking.

2. State Response: Whether the state took appropriate and reasonable steps, within the scope of its powers, to prevent or respond where a credible suspicion arose.

4.10

These obligations are triggered where there is a credible suspicion that an individual may be a victim or is at real and immediate risk of becoming a victim of Art.4 abuse. The threshold is low, requiring only that the account or evidence is not inherently implausible[14], *prima facie* evidence known or ought to have been known to the authorities will trigger the positive obligations[15]. This threshold is examined at length in **Chapters 10, 14** and **16**. There is no requirement for the individual to self-identify or come forward; the duty to act is placed squarely on the State where a credible suspicion arises.

4.11

In *FM v Russia*[16] the ECtHR confirmed that the obligations under Art 4 ECHR: to protect victims, prevent trafficking, and prosecute perpetrators, do not operate in isolation but in synergy. Drawing on both the Palermo Protocol and ECAT, the Court emphasised that the State's positive obligations under Art 4 are inextricably linked and must be understood as forming a comprehensive and integrated framework. Consequently, a failure to comply with one or more of those obligations may significantly undermine the effectiveness of the framework as a whole, even where other obligations have nominally been met.

13 The nature and extent of the investigation was re-affirmed in *FM v Russia* (App Nos 71671/16 and 40190/18) ECtHR, 10 December 2024.

14 See *R (on the application of TDT) v Secretary of State for the Home Department* [2018] EWCA Civ 1395, [2018] 1 WLR 4922 for an analysis of what constitutes 'credible suspicion'.

15 *S.M. v Croatia* [GC], (2021) 72 E.H.R.R. 1.

16 *FM v Russia* (App nos 71671/16 and 40190/18) ECtHR, 10 December 2024 at [280].

4.12

The ECtHR has emphasised that positive obligations under Art 4 must not impose an unreasonable or disproportionate burden on public authorities. The assessment of what constitutes *reasonable* protective measures is context-specific and must consider all relevant circumstances, including the scope of the authorities' powers, the physical safety of the victim, and the rights of others. As the Court observed in *FM v Russia:*

> 'it is relevant to the consideration of the proportionality of any positive obligation arising in the present case that the Palermo Protocol requires States to endeavour to provide for their physical safety while in their territories.'[17]

4.13

As the Court held in *MC v Bulgaria*[18], children and other vulnerable individuals are owed special protection by the State. In such cases, the Court applies particularly strict scrutiny to the adequacy of the measures adopted to protect individuals from violence by non-state actors and affords the State a narrower margin of appreciation. In the context of Art 4 of the ECHR, the Court has recognised undocumented migrants and those without lawful status as a vulnerable group, requiring enhanced protection and vigilance by State authorities[19].

Legislative and administrative framework as a positive obligation under Art 4 ECHR

4.14

Article 4 of the ECHR imposes a duty on the State to establish an appropriate legislative and administrative framework to: (i) prevent trafficking or modern slavery; (ii) protect victims; and (iii) criminalise and punish Art 4 abuses. This framework must ensure the practical and effective protection of victims' rights. As discussed below, this systems duty requires having identification processes for victims that are both effective and fair.

4.15

It encompasses measures to regulate sectors commonly used as a cover for trafficking, slavery, or related exploitation. It also includes immigration rules

17 Ibid. The Court referring to see *Rantsev*, [286-287], and *S.M. v. Croatia*, [305].
18 *MC v Bulgaria* (2005) 40 E.H.R.R. 20 at [150], re-affirmed in *VCL and AN v UK* (2021) 73 E.H.R.R. 9 at [161].
19 *FM v Russia* (App nos 71671/16 and 40190/18) ECtHR, 10 December 2024 at [342].

aimed at preventing the facilitation or tolerance of such practices, alongside targeted training for law enforcement and immigration officials[20].

4.16

In *CN v United Kingdom*[21], the ECtHR found a violation of Art 4 due to the absence of a specific offence of domestic servitude in UK law at the relevant time. The Court held that the legislative framework was inadequate to provide practical and effective protection against treatment falling within the scope of Art 4.

4.17

In *IC v Republic of Moldova*[22], the Court held that the State's deinstitutionalisation framework failed to protect the applicant, a woman with intellectual disabilities, from trafficking and servitude after her discharge from State care. The regime lacked the safeguards necessary to protect individuals without capacity, rendering the protection required by Art 4 ineffective and giving rise to a substantive violation. The judgment confirms that the obligation to maintain an adequate legislative and administrative framework applies within specific policy settings.

Operational measures to protect victims: the state's protective duties under Art 4 ECHR

Underpinning purpose of protective measures

4.18

Operational measures to protect under Art 4 ECHR have two principal aims: to protect victims from further harm and to facilitate recovery. As the ECtHR has observed, steps which injure a victim or potential victim's physical, psychological or social recovery, impede access to support and services, or create obstacles to reintegration into society, leave the individual vulnerable to further harm under Art 4[23]. It is axiomatic that, without effective and fair processes to identify a potential victim, protection measures cannot be implemented.

The Systems Duty, Operational measures and the role of ECAT

4.19

Article 4 may impose positive, operational obligations on the State to take case-specific, proactive measures to safeguard identified or identifiable victims or

20 *Rantsev* at paras 284, 287.
21 *CN v United Kingdom* (2013) 56 EHRR 24.
22 *I.C. v Republic of Moldova* (2025) App no 36436/22 ECHR 152–157.
23 *VCL and AN v UK* (2021) 73 EHRR. 9 at [159].

potential victims. Without the fulfilment of operational duties, the protection and prevention measures required under Art 4 cannot be effectively implemented. Failure to give practical effect to these obligations in individual cases risks undermining the effectiveness of the system, particularly where such failures are systemic. As discussed below, these duties, though distinct from legislative or systemic obligations, operate within, and depend upon, those wider frameworks.

4.20

In determining the scope and content of operational obligations, particularly in cases of trafficking, slavery, servitude and forced labour, the ECtHR treats the standards set out in ECAT as relevant interpretive guidance for Art 4. ECAT requires States to adopt a broad range of measures to prevent, identify, protect, and assist victims of exploitation, extending beyond slavery, servitude, and forced or compulsory labour to human trafficking. As analysed below these ECAT-aligned measures reinforce and inform the State's Art 4 duty to ensure that victims are not further harmed by administrative or judicial processes, and that protection and recovery are delivered in practice, not merely guaranteed in law.

Identification

4.21

The Court in *R(ABW) v Secretary of State for the Home Department*[24] held that, as a matter of domestic law, Part 5 of the Nationality and Borders Act 2022 imposes a statutory obligation to complete the identification process and proceed to a conclusive grounds identification decision where a reasonable grounds decision has been made, an obligation grounded in the United Kingdom's treaty obligations under ECAT Art 10[25]. The domestic statutory architecture, as the Court recognised, is based on two stages: first, the making of a reasonable grounds decision, and secondly, a conclusive grounds decision, reflecting Parliament's intention to implement the two-stage process laid down in Art 10(2). However, the Court went on to consider the question whether a standalone duty to identify arises under Art 4 ECHR[26]. The Court held that, as matters presently stand, a positive obligation under Art 4 to identify victims or potential victims has been recognised by the ECtHR only where identification is linked to potential criminal proceedings or there exists a credible suspicion of a *future* risk of re-trafficking. Outside of those contexts the Court found no settled principle establishing a duty to facilitate identification of a potential victim under Art 4[27]. While the grounds in *ABW* succeeded, they did so on

24 [2025] EWHC 3280 (Admin) at [103]-[107].
25 Ibid, at [113]-[114].
26 [2025] EWHC 3280 (Admin) at [126]-[131].
27 *R(ABW)*, ibid, at [129]-[131].

statutory and ECAT grounds. Morris J did not uphold a direct breach of Art 4 ECHR, holding instead that Art 4 obligations and ECAT obligations 'need to be analysed separately' and that 'there is no automatic read across'. The question whether the systems duty under Article 4 extends to an independent obligation to complete the victim-identification process remains unresolved. The judgment in *ABW* did not engage with this issue, and the implications of that omission are examined below.

A recent development reinforces aspects of the analysis advanced in this chapter. In *AYA v Secretary of State for the Home Department*[28], Sheldon J accepted the framework articulated in *ABW*, that Art 4 contains no free-standing duty to identify victims of trafficking, yet his reasoning nonetheless underscores the central argument presented here: that effective identification is integral to the State's ability to discharge the positive obligations under Art 4. Sheldon J held that inadequate or inaccessible identification structures in the receiving State may place an individual at real risk of Art 4 breach, thereby demonstrating that identification functions as a necessary component of both the systems and operational duties, even in the absence of a standalone identification right. The editorial view is that identification is not ancillary to Art 4's positive obligations but a necessary ingredient of their practical fulfilment.

4.22

The starting point for the analysis which follows is that the identification of a victim of slavery, servitude, forced or compulsory labour or trafficking within Art 4 is not merely procedural but constitutive of protection. As the ECtHR has held protection encompasses facilitating the identification of victims by qualified persons[29]. Article 1 requires States to secure to everyone within their jurisdiction the rights and freedoms defined in Section 1 of the Convention, which in turn necessitates national operating systems that unlock those rights for victims[30]. The positive obligations framework under Art 4 operates at two levels: the systems level, requiring an effective legislative and administrative structure, and the operational level, requiring specific protective measures in individual cases. The systems dimension is grounded in Art 1. As the Supreme Court recognised in *DSD v Commissioner of Police of the Metropolis*[31], following *Assanidze v Georgia*, Art 1 'entails and requires the implementation of a national system capable of securing compliance with the Convention'.

4.23

The ECtHR has not yet addressed a specific systems duty to establish a domestic identification decision-making process, but the Court consistently holds that States' positive obligations under Art 4 'must be construed in the light of'

28 [2026] EWHC 552 (Admin).

29 *VCL and AN v UK* (2021) 73 EHRR 9 at [153].

30 Ibid at [121] and GRETA's submissions to the Court at [142].

31 *DSD v Commissioner of Police of the Metropolis* [2018] UKSC 11; [2018] 1 WLR 1967 at [27], [31]-[32].

ECAT[32]. Art 10(2) ECAT and its Explanatory Report describe identification as 'of paramount importance,' warning that failure to identify victims correctly risks continued denial of fundamental rights[33]. Identification is not contingent on criminal proceedings or a potential victim establishing a real and immediate risk of Art 4 harm: victims may be recognised even where perpetrators are not, and assistance under the Convention is not conditional on cooperation with law enforcement. GRETA's monitoring practice reflects this same protective logic, emphasising that identification should not depend on criminal proceedings[34]. Taken together, Art 4 obligations and the ECAT framework confirm that identification serves a protective, not primarily a criminal justice, function. It is the mechanism by which victims secure rights and assistance, and from which safeguards, including recovery, are calibrated to individual circumstances, regardless of whether prosecution is feasible. A fair and effective identification decision-making process is therefore integral to securing victim rights under Art 4. Read with Art 1, this obligation inherently entails a procedural guarantee requiring States to establish and operate a fair and effective decision-making process for victim identification. This guarantee is instrumental to making Convention rights practical and effective. The effectiveness of any such process would very likely be measured by whether it achieves its purpose: identifying victims and determining their status so that protection and recovery rights can be properly calibrated. In evaluating fairness of the process, the Court would consider whether the individual is involved in the process to an extent sufficient to safeguard their interests[35]. Both requirements presuppose a system that enables progression within the identification framework, with ECAT serving as a relevant interpretive benchmark for assessing effectiveness and fairness. An identification process which is inherently ineffective in identifying victims, or a specific cohort of victims, creates a risk of embedding and perpetuating the very abuses Art 4 prohibits[36]. This analysis does not treat the obligations arising under ECAT as coextensive with those imposed by Art 4; rather, it reflects the settled approach of treating ECAT as an external interpretive source that informs the scope and content of the State's positive obligations under the Convention.

4.24

As Lord Reed confirmed in *R (AB) v Secretary of State for the Home Department*[37], while domestic courts are not tasked with creating new principles of Convention

32 *VCL and AN v UK* (2021) 73 EHRR 9 at [150]; *Chowdury and Others v Greece* App no 21884/15 (ECtHR, 30 March 2017) at [104]; *SM v Croatia* [GC] App no 60561/14 (ECtHR, 25 June 2020) at [295].

33 Para. 127.

34 GRETA, Report concerning the implementation of the Council of Europe Convention on Action against Trafficking in Human Beings by Sweden (27 May 2014) GRETA (2014)11, para 134, 142.

35 *Tysiąc v Poland* App no 5410/03 (ECtHR, 20 March 2007) at [113]. See further Vladislava Stoyanova, *'Human Trafficking and Slavery Reconsidered'* (n 1) at p 397.

36 Vladislava Stoyanova, 'Human Trafficking and Slavery Reconsidered: Conceptual Limits and States' Positive Obligations in European Law' (Cambridge University Press 2017) at pp.394–400.

37 [2021] UKSC 28.

law, they are not precluded from developing the law on Convention rights beyond the current limits of Strasbourg jurisprudence. Where the ECtHR has not yet ruled on an issue, domestic courts may, and should, seek to anticipate how the Court would likely decide, drawing on established principles. This observation is particularly significant because, as legal scholars note, positive obligations under Art 4 have emerged through ECtHR case law, which remains limited and highly fact specific[38]. There is no single, codified framework for these obligations; rather, they have evolved incrementally and piecemeal through judicial interpretation. ECtHR jurisprudence however strongly indicates that where credible suspicion exists that a person may be an Art 4 victim, the State cannot meaningfully assess or discharge its obligations without determining whether the individual is in fact a victim and calibrating protection and recovery measures accordingly. To conclude otherwise would allow the State to acknowledge credible grounds yet abandon the very process through which victim status, and the protections contingent upon it, are established. As the Court of Appeal recognised in *R (MN and IXU) v Secretary of State for the Home Department*[39], the conclusive grounds decision is a 'gateway' decision that relates to important rights when victim status is finally established. The protective duties owed to victims may evolve and change throughout an identification process (see **Chapter 3**) and, as the ECtHR jurisprudence illustrates, the operational duties to protect extend to guaranteeing access to recovery and to compensation for pecuniary loss in trafficking/slavery cases[40].

4.25

The domestic courts have not yet determined whether Art 4 ECHR, read together with Art 1, gives rise to an autonomous systems duty to establish and operate a decision-making identification mechanism that is not contingent on criminal justice engagement or on proof of a real and immediate risk of Art 4 harm. This logically anterior question ought to have been resolved before the Court in *R (ABW)* could definitively decide whether the positive obligations under Art 4 require completion of the identification process in individual cases. The Court did not confront whether Art 4 itself obliges States to establish and maintain an effective identification system as a matter of systems duty. Instead, the Court moved directly to the operational level, holding that there is no settled principle requiring facilitation of identification outside criminal proceedings or in the absence of credible suspicion of future re-trafficking risk. That conclusion, however, addressed only whether existing ECtHR case law recognises such an operational duty; it did not engage with the prior question of whether recognition of a systems duty under Art 4 itself would generate

38 Vladislava Stoyanova, 'Human Trafficking and Slavery Reconsidered: Conceptual Limits and States' Positive Obligations in European Law' (Cambridge University Press 2017) at pp.394–400.

39 [2020] EWCA Civ 1746 at [242].

40 *VCL and AN v UK* (2021) 73 EHRR 9 at [153]; *Chowdury and Others v Greece* App no 21884/15 (ECtHR, 30 March 2017) at [110] and *Krachunova v Bulgaria* App No 18269/18 (ECtHR, 28 November 2023) at [169]–[173].

operational obligations to complete identification in individual cases. The protective logic underpinning Art 10 ECAT explicitly decouples identification from criminal justice responses. If, as is commonly accepted, ECAT functions as an interpretive benchmark for Art 4, the contention that Art 4 encompasses a corresponding systems duty to operationalise identification, and that such a duty, once acknowledged, would carry operational implications for completion of the process in individual cases has yet to be squarely addressed. The anterior systems question therefore remains unresolved, leaving open whether the operational obligations under Art 4 extend beyond the narrow contexts identified in *R (ABW)*.

4.26

Even if the anterior systems question under Art 4 remains unresolved, the operational consequences of credible suspicion are nonetheless engaged. Once a reasonable grounds decision has been made, Art 4 protective duties are triggered, and may already have been triggered at the point of referral (see **4.4** above). Those duties include obligations to secure the individual's social, psychological and physical recovery. The State must assess those recovery needs and take reasonable, proportionate steps to meet them, rather than impede them. Whether the individual is in fact a victim is central to that assessment; it determines the nature, intensity and duration of support required. Importantly, *R (ABW)* did not hold that such protective recovery duties arise only where there is a real and immediate risk of harm, nor that they are contingent on the existence of a criminal prosecution. Once credible suspicion exists, as it does following a positive reasonable grounds decision, the State cannot meaningfully discharge its obligations to assess and provide for recovery without determining victim status through the conclusive grounds process. Otherwise, the State could accept suspicion while ignoring the only process that determines victim status and point to no alternative mechanism. A scheme that purports to implement ECAT must therefore confront whether Art 4, read with Art 1, imposes a systems duty to secure effective identification. ECAT guides what Art 4 requires; and section 3 of the Human Rights Act requires legislation to be read, so far as possible, compatibly with those rights. The point is not yet settled domestically, and it was not analysed in R (ABW) as a systems duty arising under Art 4.

Measures under ECAT and Art 4

4.27

ECAT provides for a range of protective measures to both potential victims and victims, all of which are dependent on identification, including:

- **Non-removal during the identification process** (Art 10)
- **Assistance to aid recovery** (Art 12);
- **A recovery and reflection period** (Art 13);

- **A residence permit** in defined circumstances (Art 14);
- **Access to compensation procedures** (Art 15);
- **Safe and dignified return** to their country of origin (Art 16);
- **Protection from prosecution** for offences directly linked to their trafficking experience (Art 26).

4.28

As examined in **Chapters 5, 10, 14**, and **16**, the Nationality and Borders Act 2022 and the Modern Slavery Act 2015 (particularly ss 45 and 50A) have placed some of ECAT's protection measures identified above on a statutory footing.

Assessment of Risk

4.29

The obligation to take preventive operational measures to protect individuals at risk is most fully developed in the ECtHR's domestic violence jurisprudence. However, the parallels with human trafficking and other Art 4 harms are clear. Like domestic abuse, trafficking is rarely a single, isolated event; it is often a continuing pattern of exploitation, accompanied by a heightened risk of re-trafficking or subjection to other Art 4 harms.

4.30

The suite of positive obligations under ECAT, including victim identification and risk management, aims to enable victims to exit exploitative situations and prevent recurrence. These obligations support a more flexible application of the *Osman* standard, as developed in domestic violence cases. The ECtHR has clarified that the requirement of immediacy must be interpreted in light of the common trajectory of escalation in such cases. Harm may be ongoing or likely to recur, even if the precise time and place of an attack cannot be predicted. The Court recognises that the risk of harm may intensify over time, and that precise foreseeability is not required for the State's duty to act.

The duty to support, assist and recover

4.31

The recovery duty under Art 4 includes an obligation to assist victims in their physical, psychological, and social recovery, and to provide appropriate support for the consequences of past ill-treatment. In *Begum v Secretary of State*[41], Lady Carr LCJ observed that, to date, this duty has been recognised as arising where

41 *Begum v Secretary of State for the Home Department* [2021] EWCA Civ 765

the victim is present within the jurisdiction of the State. As with the duty to identify victims, the ECtHR has drawn upon ECAT obligations to inform the State's duty to assist victims in their physical, psychological, and social recovery[42].

4.32

In *J v Austria*[43], the ECtHR confirmed that treating someone as a potential victim of trafficking does not depend on prior confirmation that an offence has been proved. Support must be provided before any criminal finding is made, as withholding assistance until that point would defeat the protective purpose of Art 4[44]. As discussed above, those protective measures apply even when no criminal proceedings are underway (see **4.22**), and access to support must not be made contingent on such involvement. If recovery is compromised, the risk of further harm increases, the effectiveness of any investigation is diminished, and the principle of restitution, restoring victims, so far as possible, to their pre-exploitation position is weakened. The Court's approach to recovery was developed further in *Krachunova v Bulgaria*[45], which held for the first time that Art 4 requires States to enable victims to claim pecuniary compensation from traffickers for lost earnings. The Court identified four reasons: reducing the risk of re-trafficking; removing the financial incentive for traffickers; easing the strain on public resources used to support recovery; and encouraging victims to come forward and expose exploitation.

The recovery and reflection period under Art 13 ECAT

4.33

In *MN & IXU v Secretary of State for the Home Department*[46], Lord Justice Underhill explained that Art 13 ECAT provides a 'recovery and reflection period' where there are reasonable grounds to believe that a person is a victim of trafficking. This provision has two core elements: (1) the individual must not be removed from the territory during the period; and (2) they are entitled to support and protection under Art 12(1) and (2). These entitlements also arise under Art 10(2) in relation to identification.

4.34

The purpose of the recovery and reflection period is twofold: to allow the individual time to recover from trauma, and to provide an opportunity to consider cooperating with the investigation and prosecution of traffickers.

42 *Chowdury and Others v Greece* (App No 21884/15) ECtHR, 30 March 2017 at [110]; *VCL and AN v UK* [153].

43 *J. and Others v Austria* [2017] ECHR 150.

44 As reaffirmed by the ECtHR in *F.M. v Russia.*

45 App No 18269/18 (ECtHR, 28 November 2023) at [169]-[173].

46 *MN and IXU v Secretary of State for the Home Department* [2020] EWCA Civ 1746.

4.35

As examined below, Art 13 of ECAT has now been given statutory effect. In cases where public order considerations do not apply, it provides a statutory bar from removal[47] for individuals who have received a positive reasonable grounds decision.

Art. 13 ECAT and protective duty under Art. 4

4.36

In *MS (Pakistan),*[48] the Supreme Court noted that the ECtHR had found Greece in breach of its procedural obligation to investigate, in part because the public prosecutor had failed to provide the recovery and reflection period required under Art 13 ECAT[49]. Properly understood considering the ECtHR's interpretive approach and Lord Justice Underhill's analysis[50], Art 13 ECAT operates beyond the procedural duty to investigate and informs the protective obligations under Art 4. Article 13 sits within Chapter III of ECAT, which is concerned with the protection and assistance of victims and potential victims of trafficking. Some provisions apply to all victims; but Art 13 is directed to a particularly vulnerable group: potential victims who are present in a jurisdiction unlawfully or whose lawful status is precarious[51].

4.37

The Explanatory Report treats the aims of the recovery and reflection period as dual and distinct. The first purpose is to allow victims to begin recovering from the trauma they have suffered and to break free from the traffickers' influence. Recovery is understood to include the healing of physical injuries and the attainment of a basic level of psychological stability, without which victims remain vulnerable and unable to think or act independently[52]. The second purpose is to give victims the opportunity to reach an informed and unpressured decision about whether to cooperate with law enforcement authorities. This requires that they are no longer in shock, are aware of the assistance and protection available to them and understand the possible judicial proceedings. Only then can their account be reliable, and only then can any decision to assist an investigation or prosecution be truly informed.[53] Art 13 permits departure from the recovery and reflection period only on limited public-order grounds or where victim status is improperly claimed, a safeguard

47 Section 61(1) of the Nationality and Borders Act 2022.
48 *MS (Pakistan) v Secretary of State for the Home Department* [2020] UKSC 9.
49 *Chowdury v Greece* (App No 21884/15).
50 *R(TDT) v Secretary of State for the Home Department* [2018] EWCA Civ 1395, [2018] 1 WLR 4928
51 Council of Europe, Explanatory Report to the Council of Europe Convention on Action against Trafficking in Human Beings (CETS No 197, 2005) at [124] and [172].
52 Ibid at [173].
53 Ibid at [174].

designed to prevent abuse without undermining the protection owed to genuine victims. Its operation is considered further at **4.249** below and the drafting history of this provision is examined at length in **Chapter 14**.

Procedural obligations under Art 4 ECHR: scope, standards, and institutional responsibility

Distinct investigatory duties under Art 4

4.38

Where a person suffers harm prohibited under Art 4 of the ECHR, such as slavery, servitude, forced or compulsory labour, or human trafficking, committed by private individuals within the State's territory, the State bears a direct obligation to conduct an official investigation. This duty is not materially different from the investigative obligation that would arise if the perpetrator were a State agent[54]. The obligation to investigate is procedural in nature, but it is embedded within the substantive rights protected by Art 4 itself.

4.39

The ECtHR has drawn a clear distinction between two forms of investigatory obligations relevant to Art 4 ECHR:

1. Criminal Investigation: The obligation to initiate an official criminal investigation into credible allegations of exploitation or trafficking[55].
2. Judicial Fact-Finding: The requirement for a judicial mechanism capable of establishing the facts and sequence of events that allegedly led to the harm.

The rule of law and the autonomous duty to investigate under Art 4 ECHR

4.40

Article 4 of the Convention entails a procedural obligation to investigate where there is a credible suspicion that an individual's rights under that provision have been violated under Art 4. The scope and content of this obligation are informed by converging principles developed under Arts 2 and 3 ECHR[56],

---

54 *DSD v Commissioner of the Police of the Metropolis* [2018] UKSC 11, Lord Kerr (with whom Lady Hale agreed) at [24]; Lord Neuberger at [92]–[98]

55 In *Zoletic and Others v Azerbaijan* at [185], the ECtHR held that the duty to investigate entailed 'the domestic authorities' duty to apply in practice the relevant criminal law mechanisms put in place to prohibit and punish contrary to that provision.'

56 *MS (Pakistan) v Secretary of State for the Home Department* [2020] UKSC 9.

which similarly impose autonomous procedural duties on States to investigate serious violations of fundamental rights. A breach of the procedural obligation may be found even in the absence of a substantive violation, where the State fails to conduct an effective investigation into credible allegations[57].

4.41

First and foremost, this needs to be understood as a duty which is underpinned by the rule of law. The ECtHR has consistently affirmed that investigations into Art 4 abuses by non-state actors are essential to 'maintaining public confidence in state authorities' adherence to the rule of law and in preventing any appearance of collusion or tolerance of unlawful acts[58]. As stated by Lord Kerr in *DSD v Commissioner of Police of the Metropolis*[59] at [24] in the context of Art 3 duty to investigate:

> 'In order to be an effective deterrent, laws which prohibit conduct constituting a breach of article 3 must be rigorously enforced and complaints of such conduct must be properly investigated. There is a clear line of Strasbourg authority for the duty to properly investigate reported offences and allegations of ill-treatment, which is summarised with approval at para 172 of *O'Keeffe v Ireland* (35810/09):
>
> > 'The Court recalls the principles outlined in *CAS v Romania* (cited above, paras 68-70) to the effect that article 3 requires the authorities to conduct an effective official investigation into alleged ill-treatment inflicted by private individuals which investigation should, in principle, be capable of leading to the establishment of the facts of the case and to the identification and punishment of those responsible. That investigation should be conducted independently, promptly and with reasonable expedition. The victim should be able to participate effectively"

4.42

As the Court of Appeal made clear in *DSD*[60], a decision upheld by the Supreme Court, *serious* violent crime committed by non-state agents occupies a higher position on the scale of severity and, in such cases, a proper criminal investigation is required. While allegations of ill-treatment may meet the Art 3 threshold, not all require a full criminal investigation. Where the relevant facts are established,

---

57 See discussion on remedies in Marija Jovanovic, *State Responsibility for 'Modern Slavery' in Human Rights Law: A Right Not to Be Trafficked* (Oxford University Press 2023) 110-116.

58 *Nikolova and Velichkova v Bulgaria* no 7888/03, 20 December 2007 at [57], *Krachunova v. Bulgaria*, no. 18269/18, 28 November 2023 and *F.M. and Russia* (App nos 71671/16 and 40190/18) ECtHR, 10 December 2024 at [330].

59 [2018] UKSC 11.

60 *DSD v Commissioner of Police of the Metropolis; Korau v Chief Constable of Greater Manchester Police* [2015] EWCA Civ 646; [2016] QB 161.

the harm is the result of negligence, and no criminal act is involved, a full criminal inquiry may be unnecessary, inappropriate, or disproportionate[61].

4.43

The ECtHR has held that the investigative duty arising under Art 4 ECHR is binding on law enforcement and judicial authorities. Investigations must be carried out by those with the statutory powers and institutional competence to investigate and prosecute serious human rights violations, including all forms of Art 4 violations. Each authority is to act within its sphere of competence, applying the relevant criminal law to secure evidence, identify suspects, and bring prosecutions where appropriate. In short, the duty is one of criminal investigation by state agents equipped to enable the prosecution of such offences in the criminal courts[62].

4.44

This interpretation aligns with Lord Justice Burnett's conclusion in *Secretary of State for the Home Department v Hoang Anh Minh*[63], and was reaffirmed by the Supreme Court in *MS (Pakistan)*[64]. Furthermore, in *VCL and AN v United Kingdom*[65], the ECtHR confirmed that this duty extends to the Crown Prosecution Service, thereby encompassing prosecutorial authorities within the scope of the investigatory Art 4 obligation.

4.45

The duty to investigate arises irrespective of whether the alleged conduct involves State agents or private individuals. It is triggered once the authorities become aware or ought to have been aware of a credible suspicion of a violation and is not contingent on a formal complaint from the victim or their family. The ECtHR has held that 'any action or lack of action on the part of the victim cannot justify a lack of action on the part of the prosecuting authorities'[66]. As acknowledged in both ECtHR jurisprudence[67] and by Lord Justice Underhill in *R (TDT) v Secretary of State for the Home Department*[68], general evidence of a prevalence of Art 4 harms for a particularly vulnerable cohort is material and relevant to the question of whether there is an 'arguable claim'.

---

61 Ibid. at [43–46], [54], and [59–62].

62 *F.M. v Russia* (App nos 71671/16 and 40190/18) ECtHR, 10 December 2024 at [310].

63 *Secretary of State for the Home Department v Hoang Anh Minh* [2016] EWCA Civ 565; Imm AR 1272, [37].

64 [2020] UKSC 9.

65 *VCL and AN v UK* [195-200].

66 *SM v Croatia* at [336]. For an in-depth analysis see Marija Jovanovic, *State Responsibility for 'Modern Slavery' in Human Rights Law: A Right Not to Be Trafficked* (Oxford University Press 2023) 129-143.

67 See *Zoletic and Others v Azerbaijan* at [195] *and V.C.L and A.N. v UK* at [171]-[172] and [181].

68 [2018] EWCA Civ 1395, [2018] 1 WLR 4922.

Standards for an Effective Investigation

4.46

The obligation to investigate under Art 4 arises once the authorities become aware, or ought to have been aware, either through a formal complaint or other *prima facie* evidence, of circumstances that may engage the provision. At that point, the State is required to act of their own initiative, without waiting for the victim to initiate proceedings.

4.47

The investigatory duty under Art 4 ECHR is about the process, not the outcome. That means the state must take proper steps to investigate when there are signs someone may have been subjected to Art 4 harm. The duty is fulfilled by carrying out a serious and effective investigation, even if it doesn't lead to a prosecution or conviction. In *FM v Russia*[69], the Court for the first time found a violation of Art 14 in conjunction with Art 4 in a trafficking context, holding that the investigative inaction of the respondent State amounted to condoning trafficking, labour exploitation and gender-based violence and reflected a discriminatory attitude towards the applicants as women who were foreign workers with an irregular immigration status. The decision imports into Art 4 the duty to unmask discriminatory motives, previously established only under Arts 2 and 3.

4.48

Once triggered, the investigation must meet the following minimum standards:

- Independence and impartiality of the investigating body, particularly from those potentially implicated;
- Promptness and reasonable expedition[70], with urgency where there is a risk of ongoing harm;
- Effectiveness, meaning proactive evidence gathering, requiring authorities to take all reasonable steps to secure relevant evidence, including where appropriate medical evidence[71]. The investigation must be capable of leading to the establishment of the facts, identifying and punishing those responsible. The burden must not fall on the victim to initiate or sustain investigatory procedures. *This is a duty of means, not of result.*
- Victim participation, ensuring that victims or their families are involved to the extent necessary to safeguard their legitimate interests;

69 App Nos 71671/16 and 40190/18, 10 December 2024.
70 *Secic v Croatia* (2009) 49 E.H.R.R. 18.
71 *Beganović v Croatia* (Application No 46423/06) 25 June 2009.

- Proportionality, so that the obligation does not impose an impossible or disproportionate burden on the authorities.
- Where there is a suspicion that discriminatory attitudes may have motivated the Art.4 harm in respect of that victim (ie gender and/or unlawful migrant status), it is especially important that the official investigation is conducted with vigour and impartiality. This is essential not only to reaffirm society's condemnation of such conduct, but also to maintain the confidence of minority groups in the authorities' ability to protect them from discriminatory violence (see *FM v Russia* at [341]).
- Even where the trafficking or Art 4 harm occurred entirely outside the State's territory, the presence of a victim or potential victim within its jurisdiction engages the State's protective duties under Art 4. Those duties arise by virtue of the State's responsibility to the individual in its jurisdiction, not the location of the underlying harm. While the duty to conduct a domestic criminal investigation does not arise for jurisdictional reasons, as recognised in *J v Austria*, the State must still take protective measures. As part of the procedural duty that remains, the authorities are required to co-operate effectively with the competent authorities of the other State responsible for investigating the events abroad[72].

4.49

Only significant flaws in the investigative process will amount to a breach, those capable of undermining the investigation's ability to establish the circumstances of the case or identify those responsible. Minor errors or isolated omissions will not suffice.

The dual investigatory duty: pre-trial and judicial proceedings

4.50

The duty to investigate extends from the initial, pre-trial investigation through to, and including, the court proceedings[73]. It forms the essential foundation for the second strand of the obligation: the conduct of effective judicial proceedings. Judicial oversight cannot substitute for, or make good the absence of, a thorough investigation by law enforcement. Their roles are quite distinct. It is not for the judge to gather evidence, but to assess the evidence that has been lawfully obtained. A fact-finding judge must evaluate that material and

72 *Rantsev v Cyprus and Russia* [288] and *SM v Croatia* [313].

73 In *VCL and AN v UK*, the ECtHR examined pre-trial up to and including the Criminal Cases Review Commission reference as well as the Court of Appeal judgments both preceding and following that reference. In such cases the Court has adopted a 'particularly thorough scrutiny' (see *SM v Croatia* [315]-[317]).

reach reasoned conclusions on it. A trial judge must ensure that the evidence is presented clearly and fairly so that the jury can understand and assess it.

Institutional responsibility to investigate

4.51

Importantly as examined above, identification under the National Referral Mechanism (NRM) does not discharge the State's procedural duty under Art 4. As confirmed in *MS (Pakistan)*[74], this is a duty that rests primarily with the police, not the Competent Authority[75].

Failure to investigate bearing on other rights under the ECHR

4.52

This is examined in **Chapters 5, 10** and **14**.

The UK's framework for victim identification

4.53

Following the UK's ratification of ECAT in December 2008, the government established the National Referral Mechanism (NRM) to implement its identification obligations under Art 10[76]. Initially designed to identify and support victims of trafficking, the scope of the NRM was expanded on 31 July 2015 to include victims of modern slavery, encompassing slavery, servitude, and forced or compulsory labour as prohibited under Art 4 of the ECHR.

4.54

The NRM operates as the national framework for identifying and referring potential victims. It is the principal mechanism through which individuals are formally recognised as victims of Art 4 violations and thereby gain access to statutory support and protection. While administered by the Home Office, the NRM functions through a multi-agency approach, integrating law enforcement, local authorities, and specialist support organisations. This collaborative structure is essential not only for effective victim identification and safeguarding, but also for the broader aims of preventing trafficking, slavery, and related forms of exploitation.

---

74 *MS (Pakistan) v Secretary of State for the Home Department* [2020] UKSC 9.

75 *Secretary of State for the Home Department v Hoang Anh Minh* [2016] EWCA Civ 565; Imm AR 1272, [37].

76 ECAT was signed by the UK on 23 March 2007 and entered into force on 1 April 2009.

Statutory basis of the national referral mechanism

4.55

The NRM functions as the UK's framework for identifying and supporting victims of trafficking and modern slavery. The overarching statutory footing of the NRM is established through a combination of provisions in the Modern Slavery Act 2015 ('MSA 2015') and the Nationality and Borders Act 2022 ('NABA 2022'). Specifically:

- Section 50(2) of the MSA 2015, as amended by section 60 of NABA 2022, and s 69(1) of NABA, empower the Secretary of State for the Home Department to make regulations concerning the identification and support of victims of modern slavery and human trafficking.
- The relevant regulations made under these powers, which are currently in force, are the Slavery and Human Trafficking (Definition of Victim) Regulations 2022 ('the 2022 Regulations').
- These regulations may designate public authorities, defined in s 56(3) of the MSA 2015 as any public authority within the meaning of s 6 of the Human Rights Act 1998, excluding courts and tribunals, as responsible for determining whether there are reasonable grounds to believe that a person is a victim.
- A determination that such grounds exist is known as a 'positive reasonable grounds decision', as defined in s 61(1)(a) of the NABA 2022.
- Where a positive reasonable grounds decision has been made because here are reasonable grounds to believe that a person is a victim of slavery, servitude, forced or compulsory labour or human trafficking within the statutory framework outlined above, that person becomes an 'identified potential victim' pursuant to s 61(1) of the NABA 2022. This status triggers specific legal protections under s 61 of the NABA 2022, including a statutory bar to removal, where public order considerations do not apply. It also entitles the individual to assistance and support under s 50A of the MSA 2015.
- A conclusive grounds decision is a determination that there are conclusive grounds to believe a person is a victim of trafficking (s 61(3)(b)). It is made only after the individual has had the required recovery period (s 61(3)), and it is reached on the balance of probabilities[77].
- In addition, s 65 of the NABA 2022 provides that, where a person receives a positive conclusive grounds decision, they must be granted limited leave to remain, provided the criteria set out in s 65(2) are met.

77 Nationality and Borders Act 2022, section 60(4).

4.56

The identification framework mirrors the measure required by Art 10 of ECAT and as analysed above, it is strongly supported by the structure of Art 4 and the ECtHR's broader jurisprudence on systems duties that the ECHR requires a decision-making framework capable of identifying victims of Art 4 violations, even though the Court has not yet addressed this point expressly

4.57

Regulation 2 of the 2022 Regulations, read with Regulation 1, defines a 'victim of slavery' as a person who has been subjected to slavery, servitude, or forced or compulsory labour. This definition should be interpreted in accordance with Art 4 of the ECHR. These concepts are examined in detail in **Chapter 1**.

4.58

Regulation 3 sets out the definition of a victim of human trafficking. **Chapter 1** examines that definition and the tension it creates with Art 4 of the ECHR.

Operational Framework of the National Referral Mechanism

4.59

The operation of the NRM is operationally structured by the Modern Slavery Statutory Guidance[78], issued under s 49 of the MSA 2015, as amended by s 60 of the NABA 2022. The guidance structures how public authorities operationalise their duties, but it does not define the scope of those duties in law. Where its application would narrow the State's positive obligations under Art 4 or ECAT, it must be read compatibly, or if necessary, disapplied, by domestic decision-makers.

4.60

Under s 49, the Secretary of State is required to issue guidance to relevant public authorities and other appropriate persons. This guidance must cover:

- **Indicators** that a person may be a victim of slavery, servitude, forced or compulsory labour, or human trafficking;
- **Arrangements** for determining whether there are reasonable grounds to believe a person is a victim;
- **Arrangements** for providing assistance and support to such persons; and
- **Arrangements** for making a conclusive grounds decision, which must be determined on the balance of probabilities.

78 The iteration considered in this Chapter is: Home Office, Home Office, Modern Slavery: Statutory Guidance for England and Wales (under s 49 of the MSA 2015) and Non-Statutory Guidance for Scotland and Northern Ireland (Version 4.4, 13 February 2026) https://assets.publishing.service.gov.uk/media/6992efe075466636847f6b74/Version_for_gov.uk_-_Modern_Slavery_Guidance_v4.4.pdf.

4.61

The Secretary of State retains the power to review and revise the guidance periodically[79],and several iterations have been published[80]. Some iterations have been subject to successful legal challenge where they were applied in a manner inconsistent with the State's obligations under Art 4 and ECAT (see further below).

4.62

In addition, the definitions and procedures for identification are further detailed in the Modern Slavery (Identification of Victims) Regulations 2022; s 49(4) requires that the arrangements in the statutory guidance, include arrangements under these regulations.

Referral into the National Referral Mechanism

The role and responsibilities of first responders

4.63

Under the UK framework, the identification of potential victims of trafficking or modern slavery begins with a referral into the NRM by a designated First Responder Organisation. First Responders include public authorities, such as the police and local authorities, as well as approved non-public authority organisations. Only these bodies are authorised to make a referral to the Single Competent Authority, which is responsible for the identification decision. The list of authorised First Responder Organisations is set out in the Statutory Guidance, which distinguishes between public and non-public authority bodies.

Duties of public authority first responders

4.64

Public authorities acting as First Responders retain their own statutory duties and powers in relation to potential victims[81]. These responsibilities cannot be delegated to the Single Competent Authority. For example, local authorities and the police remain under a duty to investigate or to provide support to

79 Section 49(2) of the MSA 2015.

80 The Statutory Guidance has replaced the following guidance documents: 'Duty to notify the Home Office of potential victims of modern slavery'; 'Victims of modern slavery – frontline staff guidance'; 'Victims of modern slavery – Competent Authority guidance; Multi-Agency Assurance Panels – Process guidance'; and 'Modern slavery – duty to notify.'

81 Home Office, Modern Slavery: Statutory Guidance for England and Wales (under s 49 of the MSA 2015) and Non-Statutory Guidance for Scotland and Northern Ireland (Version 4.3, Updated December) [4.10] https://www.gov.uk/government/publications/modern-slavery-how-to-identify-and-support-victims accessed 26 January 2026.

children or vulnerable adults, as appropriate. These obligations are reflected in the Statutory Guidance. Moreover, under s 6 of the Human Rights Act 1998, public authorities must act compatibly with Art 4 ECHR.

The duty to notify

4.65

Under s 52 of the MSA 2015, specified public authorities in England and Wales are under a statutory Duty to Notify the Home Office when they encounter a potential victim of modern slavery[82]. This duty, in force since 1 November 2015, is reinforced by Home Office policy, which requires compliance by staff within UK Visas and Immigration (UKVI), Border Force, and Immigration Enforcement[83].

4.66

The Duty to Notify may be discharged in one of two ways:

- by referring the individual into the NRM (with the adult victim's consent); or
- where an adult does not consent, by submitting an anonymous notification to the Home Office.

4.67

The information required is set out in the Modern Slavery Act 2015 (Duty to Notify) Regulations 2015[84]. Both the NRM referral and Duty to Notify processes are completed online via the Modern Slavery Portal: www.modernslavery.gov.uk.

4.68

As explained below, the consent of a child is not required for referral into the NRM. Accordingly, where a public authority identifies a child as a potential victim, it is under a duty to make the referral into the NRM.

---

82 MSA 2015, s 52. The 'duty to notify' provision is set out in s 52, and applies to the following public authorities in England and Wales at the time of publication (additional public authorities may be added by regulations): (a) a chief officer of police for a police area, (b) the chief constable of the British Transport Police Force, (c) the National Crime Agency, (d) a county council, (e) a county borough council, (f) a district council, (g) a London borough council, (h) the Greater London Authority, (i) the Common Council of the City of London, (j) the Council of the Isles of Scilly, (k) the Gangmasters and Labour Abuse Authority.

83 See Home Office Duty to Notify Factsheet, available at: https://assets.publishing.service.gov.uk/media/5a7f259ce5274a2e87db4149/6.2286_HO_LL_factsheet_duty_to_notify_copy_V3.pdf (last accessed 20 August 2025).

84 SI 2015/1743.

Non-public authority first responders

4.69

There is, at present, no authority directly addressing the legal status, duties or potential liability of non-public authorities acting as First Responders within the NRM. While such organisations are formally recognised in this role and play a critical part in identifying and referring potential victims, it remains unsettled whether they exercise public functions for the purposes of the HRA 1998, or whether they owe a duty of care to individuals in the context of NRM referrals[85].

4.70

In considering whether a non-public authority is exercising public functions, the key question is whether the function it performs is closely connected to the exercise of governmental power[86].

Referrals shared with the police

4.71

All NRM referrals are passed to the police unless doing so would breach an obligation of confidence. The published guidance notes, however, that it is unlikely that any such obligation would prevent a First Responder from sharing with the police the information gathered for the referral[87].

4.72

The Competent Authority does not require the victim's consent to share information with the police and will do so in all cases referred into the NRM. This is particularly significant in circumstances where the potential victim is subject to criminal exploitation and has not yet come to the attention of law enforcement. While beyond the scope of this chapter, any such disclosure may raise complex issues on the privilege against self-incrimination, long-established in common law, particularly for those without legal representation at the time of the referral.

85 The relevant principles are set out in *YL v Birmingham City Council* [2007] UKHL 27 and *HXA (Respondent) v Surrey County Council (Appellant);YXA (a protected party by his litigation friend the Official Solicitor) (Respondent) v Wolverhampton City Council (Appellant)* [2023] UKSC 52.

86 *R(on the application of G) v The Governors of X School* [2011] UKSC 30, [2012] 1 AC 167.

87 Home Office, *National referral mechanism guidance: adult (England and Wales)* (updated 30 September 2025) [accessed 18 October 2025] at [9]-[10].

Professionals who are not first responders

4.73

Certain professionals, such as medical practitioners, legal representatives and prison officers, are not authorised First Responders and cannot make direct referrals into the NRM[88]. Where they have concerns that an individual may be a victim of trafficking or modern slavery, they should alert an authorised First Responder so that a referral can be made; failure to do so has been the subject of judicial criticism[89]. Concerns may also be reported through the Modern Slavery Helpline (0800 0121 700) or online[90].

4.74

For discussion of the role and responsibilities of legal representatives, see **Chapter 21** on Ethics.

4.75

In 2023, updated guidance was issued for prison staff in England and Wales on identifying and assisting potential or confirmed victims. It provides that, where modern slavery is suspected, prisons should facilitate First Responders in completing NRM referrals[91].

Mandatory child referrals and the role of the ICTG Service

Safeguarding children: referral duties and multi-agency coordination

4.76

Where there is any suspicion that a child is a victim of trafficking, slavery, servitude, or forced or compulsory labour, a referral to the NRM is mandatory. Consent of the child is not required. The paramount consideration is safeguarding (see **Chapter 5**), and referrals must be made without delay. Legal representatives acting for children should refer to **Chapter 21** (Ethics) for guidance on professional responsibilities.

88 Council of Europe, GRETA(2021)12, Third Evaluation Round, 'Access to justice and effective remedies for victims of trafficking in human beings – United Kingdom', paragraph 141.
89 *R v Obeta and others* [2023] Sentencing Remarks (Johnson J, 5 May 2023) https://www.judiciary.uk/wp-content/uploads/2023/05/R-v-Obeta-and-others-sentencing-remarks.pdf accessed 20 September 2025.
90 Available at: https://www.modernslavery.gov.uk/start (last accessed 20 August 2025).
91 HMPPS, Modern Slavery: Guidance for Prisons in England and Wales (Version 1.4, March 2023).

Role of other public authorities

4.77

Public authorities such as teachers must refer concerns to authorised First Responder Organisations and actively participate in multi-agency information sharing, in accordance with locally agreed Anti-Slavery Partnership strategies (See **Chapter 5**).

Independent Child Trafficking Guardians (ICTGs)

4.78

The UK has general duties to support victims of modern slavery, including child victims, arising from both domestic and international obligations. One way in which the Government meets these duties is through the Independent Child Trafficking Guardianship (ICTG) Service under section 48 of the Modern Slavery Act 2015. Although only partially commenced, once fully in force the Secretary of State must roll the service out across England and Wales within one month. Despite its name, the published ICTG material makes clear that the service is intended for child victims of modern slavery, including trafficking. In areas where the ICTG Service operates[92], ICTGs provide advocacy and specialist support, acting independently and in the child's best interests. They help the child navigate complex processes in the criminal justice, immigration and social care systems[93], ensuring that their voice is heard and that decision-making by public authorities properly reflects their best interests.

4.79

Statutory guidance is set out in the *Interim Guidance for Independent Child Trafficking Guardians* (May 2024), to which public authorities must give due regard as required by regulations made under section 48[94]. The Interim Guidance recognises child trafficking as a form of child abuse, and child protection procedures must be followed whenever trafficking or related exploitation is suspected[95]. The ICTG's involvement throughout the process is intended to protect the child from further harm, reduce the risk of repeat victimisation, re-trafficking or going missing, and support their recovery.

---

92 See Interim Guidance at [1] for the list of sites where ITCG are available.

93 Home Office, Modern Slavery: Statutory Guidance for England and Wales (under s 49 of the MSA 2015) and Non-Statutory Guidance for Scotland and Northern Ireland (Version 4.3, Updated December) [9] https://www.gov.uk/government/publications/modern-slavery-how-to-identify-and-support-victims accessed 26 January 2026.

94 Interim Guidance at §7.

95 Interim Guidance at §4–§5, §14, §19.

Referral process at ICTG sites

4.80

At sites where the ICTG Service operates, the First Responder must:[96]

- Refer the child through the Local Authority's safeguarding route;
- Refer the child into the ICTG Service;
- Complete the NRM referral form.

4.81

A dedicated ICTG Service online referral form is also available to alert the service to a potential child victim. Barnardo's, the current ICTG provider, is a designated First Responder and may submit NRM referrals where no other First Responder is available[97]. The same procedures apply when the ICTG Service itself acts as First Responder.

4.82

Referrals to the ICTG Service should be made as soon as possible, ideally on the same calendar day that information indicating potential victimhood is received[98].

Stage 1 of the National Referral Mechanism

Referral, documentation, and legal foundations for victim identification

4.83

The first stage of the National Referral Mechanism (NRM) involves referral by a designated First Responder to one of two Home Office bodies:

- The **Single Competent Authority (SCA)**, responsible for all children's cases and adult victims not subject to immigration enforcement.
- The **Immigration Enforcement Competent Authority (IECA)**, which primarily handles referrals involving individuals in immigration detention or facing deportation.

96 Interim Guidance at §22.
97 Interim Guidance at §24.
98 Interim Guidance at §26

4.84

Both authorities[99] apply a **two-stage decision-making process**: a **reasonable grounds decision**, followed by a **conclusive grounds decision**.

4.85

The referral process begins with the First Responder's completion of the digital NRM referral form, accessible via the Home Office's Modern Slavery Portal (www.modernslavery.gov.uk). The Statutory Guidance includes a hyperlink to the form, and First Responders are encouraged to consult the accompanying NRM prompt sheet, which outlines the questions asked and assists in preparing the referral.

4.86

The referral form is not intended to be a verbatim transcript of an interview. Rather, it is a structured mechanism for First Responders to present sufficient information, supported by documentary evidence where available, to enable the Competent Authority to make a reasonable grounds decision. Initial disclosures may be made when the individual is traumatised, distrustful, or unable to provide a full account. The guidance recognises this and permits supplementary evidence to be submitted at a later stage.

Documenting the account for NRM referral

4.87

Care must be taken when preparing the referral form to avoid re-traumatising the individual, particularly where they have not yet accessed support because they are not within the 'recovery and reflection period' provided for in s 61 of the NABA 2022, which gives effect to Art 13 of ECAT.

4.88

Requiring extensive evidence at this preliminary stage may conflict with the Slavery and Trafficking Survivor Care Standards and the Trauma-Informed Code of Conduct (see **Chapter 3**), as recognised in *MN and IXU v Secretary of State for the Home Department*[100].

99 Home Office, Modern Slavery: Statutory Guidance for England and Wales (under s 49 of the MSA 2015) and Non-Statutory Guidance for Scotland and Northern Ireland (Version 4.3, Updated December) [4.13-4.15] https://www.gov.uk/government/publications/modern-slavery-how-to-identify-and-support-victims accessed 26 January 2026.

100 [2020] EWCA Civ 1746; [2021] 1 WLR 1956 at para 253.

4.89

As set out below, the threshold at the reasonable grounds stage is whether there is *prima facie* evidence that the referred person is a victim of trafficking, slavery, or related exploitation (see Stage 2 below). Any representations made at the referral stage may benefit from reiterating the applicable threshold and then explain, with reference to the information provided, how that threshold is met.

4.90

An effective identification process is grounded in several core principles, which shape how referrals should be made and how victims should be supported from the outset.

1. **Legal Definitions Must Guide the Referral**

   Referring parties must understand the legal definitions of human trafficking, slavery, servitude, and forced or compulsory labour as set out in **Chapter 1** as proscribed by Art 4 ECHR. These definitions are *conceptually distinct* and inform the identification of relevant indicators and the assessment of disclosures. Without this legal foundation, referrals risk lacking coherence and evidential value.

2. **A Trauma-Informed Approach is Essential**

   As outlined in **Chapter 3**, victims may have experienced prolonged trauma, coercion, and deception, and may fear authorities due to past experiences or threats. Initial engagement affects trust, recovery, and the quality of information provided. First Responders and practitioners involved in the referral process must explain processes clearly, build trust, and remain sensitive to the victim's fears and beliefs.

3. **Purpose and Limitations of the NRM Referral Form**

   The NRM referral form is a structured tool, not an interview transcript, designed to present sufficient information, supported by documentary evidence where available, to enable a reasonable grounds decision. Initial disclosures may be incomplete because of trauma or distrust. The Government guidance recognises this and allows supplementary evidence to be provided later. Where a First Responder considers that trauma or lack of feeling safe has limited what the victim can disclose, this should be recorded to ensure the victim is not disadvantaged when further information emerges.

4. **Informed and Free Consent and Capacity for Adult Referrals**

   For adult referrals, First Responders must obtain informed consent and ensure the individual has capacity[101]. This includes explaining the

101 See **Chapters 3** and **8** concerning capacity.

purpose of the NRM, available support, and possible outcomes. If consent is withheld, and the First Responder is a public authority, a **Duty to Notify** referral must be submitted instead. While clear explanations may help overcome reluctance, no pressure should be applied.

Trauma-informed interview guidance for first responders

4.91

This section only provides an overview and should be read with Chapter 3.

- **Interview Necessity**: Assess whether a formal interview is required or whether credible indicators suffice. If an interview may cause harm, this must be noted in the referral.
- **Coordination with Authorities**: Where a public authority is investigating, consider whether a narrative from a non-public authority First Responder is necessary, taking into account timing, victim's condition, consent, and corroborating evidence.
- **Anticipated Legal Proceedings**: Assume future investigatory involvement. Interviews must meet high ethical standards, minimise re-traumatisation, and consider legal representation, support needs, and medical input.
- **Interpreter Protocols**: Use only accredited, trauma-informed interpreters. Community members must not be used. Note any limitations and avoid interpreters with ties to the victim's community.
- **Risk Management**: Protect victim identity and data. Avoid cultural shaming and re-traumatisation.
- **Evidence Threshold**: Early-stage evidence may be incomplete. Focus on identifying indicators rather than proving the case. Prioritise survivor welfare.
- **Non-Verbal Indicators**: Observe signs of control or distress. The absence of such signs does not negate victim status.
- **Legal Compliance**: Adherence to these principles supports the UK's obligations under Art 4 ECHR and ensures safe, reliable referrals.

Policy shift: removal of the objective evidence requirement

4.92

Until 30 January 2023, Home Office guidance was consistent with the Court of Appeal's judgment in *R (TDT) v SSHD*[102], which confirmed that the

102 [2018] EWCA 1395, [2018] 1 WLR 4922, at [35], [38].

reasonable grounds test was 'substantially the same' as the test for triggering the protection and investigation duties under Art 4 ECHR (ie credible suspicion threshold). Decision-makers were directed to establish credible suspicion where the putative victim's account was not inherently implausible and contained indicators of trafficking as defined in Art 4 of ECAT, namely, elements of action, means, and purpose.

4.93

In January 2023, revised Statutory Guidance issued by the then Home Secretary sought to raise the reasonable-grounds threshold by requiring "objective" evidence such as expert reports, witness statements or police records before a positive decision could be made. This led to refusals even where accounts were detailed and credible and drew sustained criticism for being inconsistent with Art 4 ECHR and ECAT, which require only *credible suspicion* at the initial stage. Following the judicial review in *AS and BXR v SSHD*[103], the Secretary of State conceded at the permission stage that the guidance was unlawful. The January 2023 wording was withdrawn and replaced on 10 July 2023 with guidance restoring the orthodox approach: indicators of trafficking and the person's own account will often suffice at the reasonable-grounds stage, particularly given the impact of trauma on early disclosure.

4.94

The claim in *AS and BXR* challenged the lawfulness of this "objective evidence" requirement. The claimants argued that it breached Art 4 by imposing a threshold higher than credible suspicion; that it was irrational, because the absence of objective evidence at referral tells nothing about whether someone is a victim; and that it was procedurally unfair, as it denied access to protection without a fair opportunity to present a case. The Secretary of State's concession, and the subsequent withdrawal of the guidance, reflected acceptance that the reasonable-grounds test must remain rooted in credible suspicion, informed by ECAT and by the realities of trauma, rather than in a front-loaded evidential standard appropriate only to a conclusive decision.

4.95

As a result of the challenge, the Secretary of State withdrew the policy and published revised guidance in July 2023.

103 *AS and BXR v Secretary of State for the Home Department*, High Court, judicial review proceedings issued May 2023 (unreported). The SSHD conceded at a permission hearing on 27–28 June 2023 that the January 2023 guidance was unlawful; revised guidance was published on 10 July 2023. <https://freemovement.org.uk/home-office-withdraws-objective-evidence-test-for-trafficking-decisions/> accessed 26 September 2025.

Current standard: contextual assessment of supporting evidence

4.96

Under the most recent iteration of the Statutory Guidance, the threshold for a reasonable grounds decision remains deliberately low and is aligned with the principle of credible suspicion under Art 4 ECHR. Decision-makers are no longer required to identify 'objective evidence' corroborating a potential victim's account to reach a positive reasonable grounds decision. Instead, the assessment must consider whether, in all the circumstances, it is reasonable to expect supporting evidence beyond the information provided by the First Responder. This includes evaluating the nature and timing of the referral, the type of exploitation alleged, and any contextual factors that may explain the absence of corroboration, such as trauma, fear, or distrust of authorities. The guidance explicitly recognises that the need for supporting evidence is relative to the content of the account, and that a detailed, internally consistent narrative may be sufficient to meet the threshold. Where indicators of trafficking, slavery, or related acts are present and the account is not inherently implausible, the reasonable grounds test may be satisfied without further corroboration.

General evidence supporting referral

4.97

Competent Authorities must assess both generic and specific evidence when considering a referral[104].

Country evidence

4.98

Assess whether public or government sources support the account of exploitation. Consider whether the type and location of exploitation align with known trends. Relevant sources include:

- UKVI Country Policy and Information Notes (CPINs)
- US Trafficking in Persons Report (annual)
- UN Special Rapporteur reports on trafficking and slavery
- UN Committee on the Rights of the Child reports and adjudications

104 Home Office, Modern Slavery: Statutory Guidance for England and Wales (under s 49 of the MSA 2015) and Non-Statutory Guidance for Scotland and Northern Ireland (Version 4.3, Updated December) [14] https://www.gov.uk/government/publications/modern-slavery-how-to-identify-and-support-victims accessed 26 January 2026.

- ILO Child Labour Monitoring reports
- NRM statistics and Anti-Slavery Commissioner reports
- Police intelligence (eg, CEOP, NCA reports)
- Historic guidance from the Association of Chief Police Officers (eg, cannabis farms)

4.99

Generic country evidence may support a referral even if the account is atypical. In *R (TDT)*, the Court of Appeal confirmed that reasonable grounds may be met where an individual belongs to a group known to be vulnerable to trafficking. The weight of such evidence depends on its reliability and relevance.

NGO Reports

4.100

Competent Authorities should also consider reports from specialist NGOs, including:

- ECPAT UK
- Anti-Slavery International
- The Children's Society
- Helen Bamber Foundation
- Freedom from Torture
- FLEX
- Kalayaan
- NSPCC

Specific evidence (as per statutory guidance)

4.101

Includes, but is not limited to:

- Indicators of modern slavery in the referral
- Expert reports supporting victim status
- Travel records confirming presence in relevant country
- Demographic vulnerability (eg, children, developmental delays)
- Reasonable adjustments required (see **Chapter 3**)

- Special measures required in litigation (see **Chapter 8**)
- Independent witness statements (eg, police officers)
- First Responder rationale and plausibility observations
- Missing information requested but not provided
- Prosecutorial evidence against alleged exploiter
- Views of trusted third parties (eg, safeguarding services, Independent Guardians)
- Referral context and rationale
- Timing of disclosure and any explanation for delay

Evidence from support providers

4.102

Support providers occupy a distinct role in the victim status determination process due to their expertise and sustained engagement with victims. Victims may distrust police or immigration authorities, whereas support organisations often build trust over time.

4.103

The Statutory Guidance[105] requires that evidence from support organisations be given due weight, though the Competent Authority is not obliged to accept it. Where such a report exists, the authority must seek to obtain it. Notably, under the Modern Slavery Victim Care Contract (MSVCC), support organisations providing care to potential or confirmed victims must conduct ongoing assessments of needs and risks (see **Chapter 5** – Safeguarding)[106].

4.104

While the Competent Authority is not under a legal obligation to treat the evidence provided by a support organisation as a 'trump card', its approach must be understood in light of the applicable legal threshold. The question is whether the evidence constitutes *prima facie* evidence that the individual may be a victim of trafficking, slavery, or related exploitation (see Stage 2 below).

105 Home Office, Modern Slavery: Statutory Guidance for England and Wales (under s 49 of the MSA 2015) and Non-Statutory Guidance for Scotland and Northern Ireland (Version 4.3, Updated December) [14] https://www.gov.uk/government/publications/modern-slavery-how-to-identify-and-support-victims accessed 26 January 2026.

106 *AB v Secretary of State for the Home Department* [2015] EWHC 1490 (Admin) at paras 40–41.

Expert evidence: medical reports and trauma assessment

4.105

Medical reports play a critical role in both the identification process and litigation. While admissibility in litigation is jurisdiction-specific, for the purposes of NRM identification, medical evidence put forward must be considered.

4.106

At the referral stage, such reports may enable victims to recount their experiences in a therapeutic setting, avoiding repeated disclosures, an approach consistent with the Barnahus model (see **Chapter 3**). However, it may not be possible at referral stage to secure a detailed account where there is evidence of trauma at point of referral. This must be made plain in the representations, even where a medical report is not available at present.

4.107

If a medical report is commissioned for the purposes of the referral, any medical assessment must be undertaken by a qualified practitioner and the evaluation of the individual's mental or physical health should meet the standards outlined in **Chapter 3**, and the report should be prepared accordingly.

4.108

For the purposes of an NRM referral, medical practitioners may express an opinion that their findings are consistent or inconsistent with the victim's account[107]. The weight given to the expert evidence may depend on whether alternative causes for the symptoms have been excluded. This applies equally to physical findings (eg, scarring) and psychological symptoms, as recognised in *MN and IXU*[108].

4.109

Where physical evidence is presented, it should be assessed by a qualified expert applying the Istanbul Protocol on the documentation of torture and ill-treatment[109] (see **Chapter 3**).

---

107 Home Office, Modern Slavery: Statutory Guidance for England and Wales (under s 49 of the MSA 2015) and Non-Statutory Guidance for Scotland and Northern Ireland (Version 4.3, Updated December) [14] https://www.gov.uk/government/publications/modern-slavery-how-to-identify-and-support-victims accessed 26 January 2026.

108 *R (on the application of MN and IXU) v Secretary of State for the Home Department* [2020] EWCA Civ 1746; [2021] 1 WLR 1956 at para 121(4).

109 *KV (Sri Lanka) v Secretary of State for the Home Department* [2019] UKSC 10; [2019] 1 WLR 1849.

4.110

When instructing mental health experts, it is essential to provide all relevant health records available (eg, GP, hospital, detention settings). The expert must address any inconsistencies between those records and their assessment. If no records exist, this must be explained in the report. Reports that fail to engage with available records may be afforded less weight.[110] The letter of instruction is disclosable.

4.111

The Statutory Guidance acknowledges that the expert may not have access to all information held by the Competent Authority[111]. Where the authority intends to rely on additional information to reject the expert's findings, procedural fairness requires that this be disclosed, and the expert given an opportunity to respond.

4.112

The Guidance also states that 'any evidence supplied must be capable of being verified by the Competent Authority where appropriate' [112]. Reports must therefore be properly sourced. Where the expert is the source of the information due to their expertise, this should be made explicit. Expert evidence is further addressed in **Chapters 3, 10** and **13**.

Historical victims and overseas exploitation

4.113

Victims who experienced trafficking, slavery or related acts historically, including prior to arrival in the UK or during their journey, remain entitled to identification and protection under the NRM[113].

4.114

Where trafficking, slavery etc occurred overseas, the Competent Authority must refer details of the alleged exploitation to the NRM Intelligence Hub, which may raise the matter with authorities in the country where the offence occurred. This ensures compliance with the UK's obligations under Art

110 *HA (expert evidence, mental health)* [2022] UKUT 00111.

111 Home Office, Modern Slavery: Statutory Guidance for England and Wales (under s 49 of the MSA 2015) and Non-Statutory Guidance for Scotland and Northern Ireland (Version 4.3, Updated December) [14] https://www.gov.uk/government/publications/modern-slavery-how-to-identify-and-support-victims accessed 26 January 2026.

112 Ibid. [14.36].

113 *R (on the application of Atamewan) v Secretary of State for the Home Department* [2013] EWHC 2727 (Admin), [2014] 1 WLR 1959 at paras 69–80.

27 ECAT, which requires international cooperation in combating trafficking[114], if this would give rise to any risks for the potential victim this should be made clear to the Competent Authority.

Stage Two: the reasonable grounds decision

Purpose and legal threshold of the reasonable grounds decision

4.115

Once a referral is received, the Competent Authority must make a reasonable grounds decision, ideally within five working days. This stage functions as an initial filter to identify potential victims and to enable access to support, including the recovery and reflection period under Art 13 ECAT. Recent pilot schemes devolving NRM decision-making for children to certain local authorities[115] further complicate this landscape. While intended to bring child protection and trafficking identification closer together, they risk introducing variability in thresholds and practice which must nevertheless remain anchored in Art 4 and ECAT obligations, not in local resource constraints or welfare paradigms that under-recognise exploitation.

4.116

The NABA 2022 has now placed support and assistance as well as the recovery and reflection period on a statutory footing[116] (examined at length in **Chapter 5**).

4.117

The legal threshold is deliberately low. The test is whether, taken in the round, the available evidence gives rise to reasonable grounds to believe that the individual is a victim of trafficking or slavery (s 61 of the NABA 2022). For children, the Art 4 threshold for credible suspicion must be interpreted considering their heightened vulnerability and the State's parallel obligations under the UN Convention on the Rights of the Child. In practice, this means that indicators of exploitation or control will often suffice to engage Art 4 operational duties and justify a positive reasonable grounds decision, without requiring the level of detail or coherence that might be expected from an adult.

114 Home Office, Modern Slavery: Statutory Guidance for England and Wales (under s 49 of the MSA 2015) and Non-Statutory Guidance for Scotland and Northern Ireland (Version 4.3, Updated December) [14] https://www.gov.uk/government/publications/modern-slavery-how-to-identify-and-support-victims accessed 26 January 2026.

115 Home Office, 'Decision making guidance for pilot sites in England and Wales' (child victims of modern slavery) (2025).

116 Sections 61 and 64 of NABA 2022 and s.50A of the MSA 2015.

4.118

Reasonable grounds to believe *is the same as* the ECtHR standard 'credible suspicion'[117].

4.119

As clarified in *SM v Croatia*[118], credible suspicion arises where there is *prima facie* evidence that the person is a victim of trafficking, slavery, or related exploitation. That is evidence as it appears without investigation, if not challenged or countered[119], would amount to trafficking, slavery or related acts.

4.120

This threshold, if met, will trigger a State's Art 4 positive protective obligations and procedural obligation to investigate[120].

Evaluation of evidence at the prima facie stage

4.121

At the *prima facie* stage, the Competent Authority is required to undertake a preliminary assessment of whether the available evidence, taken at its highest and without challenge, is sufficient to indicate that the individual may be a victim of trafficking, slavery, or related exploitation. This stage proceeds on the basis that no full investigation has yet been conducted. It does not require proof to a high standard, nor does it permit a detailed assessment of credibility.

4.122

The focus must remain on whether the individual has presented a *prima facie* case. Victims may not yet be able to provide a full or coherent account due to trauma, fear, shame, or a lack of trust[121]. Decision-makers must therefore consider whether it is reasonable, in the circumstances, to expect corroborative evidence beyond the victim's own account.

117 *R (on the application of TDT, by his litigation friend) v Secretary of State for the Home Department* [2018] EWCA Civ 1395; [2018] 1 WLR 4922 at [38].

118 *S.M. v Croatia* [GC], App no 60561/14 (ECtHR, 25 June 2020),

119 See *AM (Zimbabwe) v Secretary of State for the Home Department* [2020] UKSC 17, [2020] 1 WLR 1846, para 32.

120 *R (on the application of TDT, by his litigation friend) v Secretary of State for the Home Department* [2018] EWCA Civ 1395; [2018] 1 WLR 4922; *VCL v UK* (2021) 73 EHRR 9, [159] and *CN v UK* (2013) 56 EHRR 869, [71-72].

121 *MN and IXU v Secretary of State for the Home Department* [2020] EWCA Civ 1746; [2021] 1 WLR 1956.

4.123

Prima facie evidence is that which, if left unchallenged or uncontradicted, would be sufficient to establish a particular fact or proposition. A finding that the evidence does not meet this threshold should only be made where there is an obvious or inherent defect in the material relied upon, such as where the account is manifestly implausible, internally inconsistent to the point of incoherence, or incapable of belief on its own terms.

4.124

The assessment must be holistic. Evidence should not be considered in isolation but evaluated cumulatively, with due regard to the context in which it is provided. Only where the indicators, taken at face value, do not sufficiently support the narrative so as to give rise to a credible suspicion, will the threshold not be met.

Treatment of expert evidence

4.125

Expert evidence, where available, may assist in understanding why a potential victim's account may be delayed, inconsistent, or incomplete, particularly where such features are attributable to trauma, fear of reprisals, or psychological barriers to disclosure. It may also assist in identifying recognised indicators of exploitation and contextualising the presentation of the account.

4.126

Expert evidence must be evaluated with care. The Competent Authority is required to engage substantively with its conclusions and, if rejecting the evidence, must provide a clear and reasoned explanation. A failure to do so may amount to a failure to have due regard to applicable policy and may be irrational.

4.127

Rejection of expert evidence at the *prima facie* stage is only appropriate where there is a fundamental flaw, such as unreliable methodology that fundamentally undermines the assessment, manifest error, inherent and manifestly implausible opinion, or the expert report reveals internal inconsistencies to the point that the opinion given is incoherent. Absent such defects, expert evidence that is coherent, methodologically sound, and corroborates that indicators of trafficking or exploitation are present will ordinarily satisfy the *prima facie* threshold. It is difficult to conceive of circumstances in which properly presented expert evidence would not be sufficient at this stage, given the legal threshold.

4.128

If there are reasonable grounds for belief, the question of whether there are also reasonable grounds for disbelief is irrelevant at this stage.

Timing of the reasonable grounds decision

4.129

The reasonable grounds decision should be made within five working days of receipt of the referral to the Competent Authority. Delay in reaching a decision may result in unlawful detention or prevent the individual from accessing rights to which they are entitled.

4.130

A positive decision must be taken as soon as sufficient information is available, even if further evidence is anticipated. The same does not apply to a negative decision. Where a negative outcome is likely, the Competent Authority must engage with relevant agencies, such as the First Responder, support providers, police, and local authority, and offer an opportunity to provide any further information or evidence. This reflects the multi-agency, collaborative approach required under Art 10 of ECAT.

Relevance of criminal investigations

4.131

A victim of trafficking, slavery, or related exploitation is, first and foremost, a victim of crime. However, it is not necessary for there to be an ongoing criminal investigation in order to reach a positive reasonable grounds decision.

4.132

While the statutory guidance notes that the absence of evidence of a criminal offence, or delayed cooperation with law enforcement, may be relevant at this stage, allowing those factors to shape the decision risks diverting the process from its protective focus. As the ECtHR made clear in *Chowdury v Greece*[122], the authorities must not allow criminal-justice considerations to eclipse their protective duties under Art 4. The Court found a breach where the public prosecutor failed to investigate allegations from a group of workers despite factual indications that they had been employed under the same exploitative conditions as those whose cases proceeded and then rejected their request in

122 (App No 21884/15) ECtHR, 30 March 2017 at [120]–[121].

part because their complaint was 'belated'. That approach disregarded the anti-trafficking framework: Art 13 ECAT provides a recovery and reflection period precisely so that victims can regain stability and make an informed decision about cooperation. Conditioning protection or effective investigation on prompt engagement with the criminal process was therefore incompatible with Art 4, read in light of Art 13.

4.133

Requiring engagement with the criminal justice process as a precondition for recognition may place undue pressure on the individual and is inconsistent with the victim-centred approach enshrined in Art 1(b) of ECAT. That approach is difficult to reconcile with the positive obligations under Art 4, which are not contingent on the existence of, or cooperation with, a police investigation.

Positive reasonable grounds decision

4.134

Where a positive reasonable grounds decision is made, the individual must be notified, although reasons for the decision are not provided. The Competent Authority must also inform relevant agencies, including:

- the First Responder;
- the support provider and coordinating body (eg the Salvation Army, TARA, Migrant Help, or Women's Aid, depending on location);
- the local authority, in the case of children;
- the police, who should be notified promptly and asked to inform prosecutors where appropriate.

4.135

In the case of a child, the immediate priority is safeguarding and promoting welfare.

4.136

The decision minute which records the Competent Authority's reasons for reaching a positive decision is disclosable in legal proceedings[123].

123 Home Office, Modern Slavery: Statutory Guidance for England and Wales (under s 49 of the MSA 2015) and Non-Statutory Guidance for Scotland and Northern Ireland (Version 4.3, Updated December) [14.211-14.215] https://www.gov.uk/government/publications/modern-slavery-how-to-identify-and-support-victims accessed 26 January 2026.

Recovery and reflection period

4.137

A positive reasonable grounds decision triggers a minimum 30-day recovery and reflection period. During this time, the individual is entitled to support aimed at facilitating physical, psychological, and social recovery, in accordance with Art 12 of ECAT. The recovery and reflection period must be understood as integral to the positive protective duties owed to potential victims under Art 4 as outlined at the beginning of this chapter.

4.138

This support must include, at a minimum:

- appropriate and secure accommodation;
- psychological and material assistance;
- access to emergency medical treatment;
- translation and interpretation services, where needed;
- counselling and legal information in a language the individual understands;
- assistance in engaging with criminal proceedings;
- access to education for children.

4.139

The purpose of this period is to enable the individual to recover and to escape the influence of traffickers, and to make an informed decision about cooperating with the competent authorities. The duration must be sufficient to achieve these objectives.

4.140

Section 61 of the NABA 2022 provides that during this time, foreign nationals in receipt of a positive reasonable grounds decision are protected from expulsion, unless section 63(2) applies[124]. They are authorised to remain in the UK and ordinarily granted temporary admission or release where necessary.

Access to support

4.141

All potential victims of trafficking, slavery or related acts are entitled to the measures prescribed by Art 12 ECAT. This right is now embedded in domestic

124 At time of publication, decision making on Public Order Disqualification under the NRM had been paused (23 December 2025).

legislation (see below). The right to such support is not dependent on the victim reporting trafficking/slavery to the police, nor does it require there to be an active investigation. Many victims are extremely reluctant to report matters to the police because they are frightened of reprisals from their traffickers.

4.142

Decisions regarding the provision of support and assistance must take full account of the victim's safety and protection needs. For example, it may be necessary to accommodate the victim in a safe house located away from the area in which they were identified, to mitigate risk and ensure their security.

Support framework in Scotland and Northern Ireland

4.143

Statutory provision for the support and accommodation of victims is established in both Scotland[125] and Northern Ireland[126]. In each jurisdiction, legislation affirms that such support is not conditional on cooperation with criminal investigations, must be provided with the victim's consent, and must take account of their safety and protection needs[127]. Support must also be tailored to meet the assessed personal needs of the individual. The types of assistance set out in Art 12 of ECAT are explicitly referenced in both statutory frameworks[128].

4.144

In Scotland, the legislation mandates the provision of support and assistance from the date of a positive reasonable grounds decision until either the expiry of a period specified in regulations or the making of a negative conclusive grounds decision. It also confers discretion to provide support prior to the reasonable grounds decision and at other stages, including following a conclusive grounds decision[129].

4.145

In Northern Ireland, statutory provision guarantees support and accommodation for a minimum of 45 days, even where a negative decision is made within that period. Support may continue even if the individual leaves Northern Ireland or is ultimately determined not to be a victim on conclusive grounds. The

125 Human Trafficking and Exploitation (Scotland) Act 2015.

126 Human Trafficking and Exploitation (Criminal Justice and Support for Victims) Act (Northern Ireland) 2015.

127 Human Trafficking and Exploitation (Criminal Justice and Support for Victims) Act (Northern Ireland) 2015, s 18(5); Human Trafficking and Exploitation (Scotland) Act 2015, s 9(1) and (5).

128 Human Trafficking and Exploitation (Criminal Justice and Support for Victims) Act (Northern Ireland) 2015, s 18(7); Human Trafficking and Exploitation (Scotland) Act 2015, s 9(4).

129 Human Trafficking and Exploitation (Scotland) Act 2015 (Support for Victims) Regulations 2018, SSI 2018/90, s 9(1)–(3).

legislation also makes specific provision for assistance to support individuals exiting prostitution[130].

Support framework in England and Wales

4.146

The provision of support and assistance to victims in England and Wales is now governed by s 64 of the NABA 2022, which inserted s 50A into the MSA 2015. This legislative development is examined in detail in **Chapter 5**.

4.147

The mechanisms for delivering appropriate support include a Modern Slavery Victim Care Contract: see *R (ETX) v SSHD*[131]. The arrangements are commissioned by the Home Secretary and delivered by the Salvation Army as Prime Contractor. The duty to ensure support is provided remains with the Home Secretary[132].

4.148

Support under the MSVCC is intended to act as 'a bridge to life'[133], enabling adult victims to exit exploitation and begin rebuilding their lives. Following a positive reasonable grounds decision, and subject to the individual's consent, they will be supported under the MSVCC. During this Recovery Period, a risk-and needs-based assessment is undertaken to identify the appropriate support. This typically includes allocation of a dedicated NRM support worker to advocate on the victim's behalf[134].

4.149

Annex F to the Statutory Guidance sets out the categories of support available, which may include financial and material assistance, support for social recovery, interpretation and translation services, and access to counselling and psychological treatment[135].

---

130 Human Trafficking and Exploitation (Criminal Justice and Support for Victims) Act (Northern Ireland) 2015, s 18(3), (4), (8), (9), and (19).

131 [2025] EWHC 294 (Admin) at [38-40].

132 Ibid. [8.3-8.4] and *R (DMA) v Secretary of State for the Home Department* [2020] EWCA 3416 (Admin) at para 100.

133 Home Office, Modern Slavery: Statutory Guidance for England and Wales (under s 49 of the MSA 2015) and Non-Statutory Guidance for Scotland and Northern Ireland at [8.6] (Version 4.3, Updated December) [14.211-14.215] https://www.gov.uk/government/publications/modern-slavery-how-to-identify-and-support-victims accessed 26 January 2026.

134 Ibid [8.4-8.5].

135 Ibid. [8.7] and Annex F.

Access and challenges

4.150

It is beyond the scope of this chapter to provide a detailed analysis of all potential challenges arising under the MSVCC. However, issues may include delays in accessing payments, inadequate support provision, and premature termination of assistance. Practitioners encountering difficulties in securing tailored support for clients are advised to seek specialist legal or advocacy advice.

Negative Reasonable Grounds Decision

4.151

Where a negative reasonable grounds decision is made, the decision must be reviewed by a second, appropriately trained caseworker or manager[136]. If the individual has claimed asylum, the reviewing officer must not be directly involved in the asylum decision-making process[137].

4.152

The consequences of a negative reasonable grounds decision are serious. It may be that the individual's account is deemed so lacking in credibility that they are denied access to the limited protections of the recovery and reflection period, a short but critical window designed to provide a safe space in which victims may receive psychological, practical, and legal support. This support may be essential to enable fuller participation in the decision-making process prior to any conclusive grounds' determination.

4.153

In practice, a person accommodated by a support provider will be required to leave their accommodation following a negative decision. It is therefore imperative that potential victims obtain legal advice without delay to assess whether there are grounds to challenge the decision. The reasonable grounds decision is not an immigration decision; it does not attract a statutory right of appeal and can only be challenged by way of judicial review. In reviewing a reasonable grounds decision, the approach adopted by the court is summarised in *R (SM) v Secretary of State for the Home Department*[138].

---

136 Home Office, Modern Slavery: Statutory Guidance for England and Wales (under s 49 of the MSA 2015) and Non-Statutory Guidance for Scotland and Northern Ireland (Version 4.3, Updated December) [14.211-14.216] https://www.gov.uk/government/publications/modern-slavery-how-to-identify-and-support-victims accessed 26 January 2026.

137 Ibid. [7.20]. The Competent Authority may similarly review positive decisions but is not required to do so.

138 *R (SM) v Secretary of State for the Home Department* [2024] EWHC 1683 (Admin) at paragraphs [29]–[31].

Request to reconsider a negative reasonable grounds decision

4.154

The reconsideration policy operated by the Competent Authority is not embedded in statute and, at the time of writing, remains subject to legal challenge by way of judicial review. It is essential that legal representatives understand the policy basis for this process and the legal framework within which it operates.

4.155

It is important to note that the effect of paragraph 14.216 of version 4.4 of the Modern Slavery Statutory Guidance is that the reconsideration provisions will not apply to a person if the Secretary of State proposes to remove the putative victim to a country which is a signatory to ECAT.

4.156

In *R(CTK)*[139] the Secretary of State confirmed that any request for reconsideration would not be considered if an individual was removed.

4.157

The statutory guidance does make provision for a request for reconsideration where additional evidence is available that could demonstrate the individual is a victim of modern slavery, or where there are specific concerns that the original decision was not made in accordance with the statutory guidance. First Responders may request reconsideration, but legal representatives are equally entitled to do so[140].

4.158

Until late 2019, policy restricted reconsideration requests to First Responders only. This approach was found to be unlawful in *R (DS) v Secretary of State for the Home Department*[141], where the Court held that preventing victims from seeking reconsideration through legal advisers impaired the State's protective obligation to identify and support victims. The Court confirmed that the National Referral Mechanism (NRM) includes a discretionary power to reopen negative decisions, and that this discretion must be exercised in accordance with the continuing duty to identify victims. Relevant evidence casting doubt on the correctness of a prior decision must not be disregarded. To do so would dilute the protection afforded under Art 4 of the ECHR.

---

139 *R (CTK) v Secretary of State for the Home Department* [2025] EWCA 1264.

140 Home Office, Modern Slavery: Statutory Guidance for England and Wales (under s 49 of the MSA 2015) and Non-Statutory Guidance for Scotland and Northern Ireland (Version 4.3, Updated December) [14.211-14.217] https://www.gov.uk/government/publications/modern-slavery-how-to-identify-and-support-victims accessed 26 January 2026.

141 *R (on the application of DS) v Secretary of State for the Home Department* [2019] EWHC 3046 (Admin).

4.159

Legal representatives should be proactive in submitting reconsideration requests and providing any further evidence necessary to support the claim. Consideration should be given to the approach of the Competent Authority when evaluating the evidence and whether this was inconsistent with the legal threshold.

4.160

A refusal to consider such a request, particularly where credible indicators of trafficking, slavery or related acts are presented, may be incompatible with the State's duty to identify victims promptly upon receipt of a credible allegation (Art.4 ECHR).

4.161

Any refusal to reconsider the decision can be challenged by way of judicial review (see *R(Al Noor) v Secretary of State for the Home Department*)[142].

Restrictive timeframes and discretionary extensions: subject of ongoing legal challenge

Time limits for reconsideration requests

4.162

Since 12 February 2024, the Competent Authority has operated a policy requiring reconsideration requests to be submitted within 30 calendar days of the negative decision. Requests made outside this period must be accompanied by an application for an extension of time, setting out reasons why the evidence was not previously available and why additional time is required.

Discretion to extend time and the 'exceptional circumstances' test

4.163

The Statutory Guidance confirms that the Competent Authority retains discretion to accept late requests but will only do so in 'exceptional circumstances.' These are defined as situations where the individual was unable to obtain or provide information for reasons beyond their control, where safeguarding concerns are present, where the individual has recently exited an exploitative situation, or where other unforeseen barriers prevented timely submission.

142 *R(Al Noor) v Secretary of State for the Home Department* [2025] EWHC 922 (Admin).

Judicial interpretation: R (KM) v Secretary of State for the Home Department

4.164

In *R (KM) v Secretary of State for the Home Department*[143], the High Court held that an unlawfully withdrawn asylum claim could amount to 'exceptional circumstances' justifying an extension of time for reconsideration of a negative reasonable grounds decision. This illustrates the principle that procedural fairness and the protective obligations under Art 4 may require flexibility in applying time limits.

Ongoing legal challenge to the policy

4.165

This policy is currently the subject of a further judicial review, which remains ongoing at the time of publication. The claim, brought by the legal team representing the claimant, argues that the application of the 'exceptional circumstances' threshold is incompatible with the UK's obligations under Art 4 ECHR and Art 10 ECAT, both of which are said to require only a 'credible suspicion' for the identification and protection of victims (see above). The claimant's legal team also submits that the policy has a disproportionate impact on vulnerable individuals, citing the case of EO, whose reconsideration request was refused despite the submission of compelling evidence outside the 30-day timeframe[144].

Best practice in extension applications

4.166

In light of this legal challenge, it is advisable that any application for an extension of time should not only explain why the evidence could not be provided earlier but also address whether refusal to reconsider may breach the UK's positive obligations under Art 4 ECHR.

4.167

Several factors may impede timely preparation of reconsideration requests, including:

143 *R (on the application of KM) v Secretary of State for the Home Department* [2024] EWHC 2870 (Admin).

144 Georgina Fenton, 'Ongoing challenge to SSHD's policy regarding the identification of victims of trafficking' (Landmark Chambers, 22 April 2025) <https://www.landmarkchambers.co.uk/news-and-cases/blog/public-and-administrative-law/ongoing-challenge-to-sshds-policy-regarding-the-identification-of-victims-of-trafficking> accessed 26 September 2025.

- difficulties in obtaining instructions from individuals in detention or prison;
- delays in securing expert reports or prior authority for funding;
- the need to investigate vulnerabilities;
- the importance of adopting a trauma-informed approach to evidence gathering.

Common barriers to timely submission

4.168

These can be common challenges when working with vulnerable individuals and may render submission within the one-month timeframe impracticable. In such cases, it is essential to seek an extension in advance. Best practice is to support the extension request with a witness statement from the legal representative, setting out the outstanding steps required and explaining why procedural fairness necessitates additional time.

Evidence from civil society organisations

4.169

Further evidence of hardship concerning the current policy is provided by After Exploitation and the Anti-Trafficking Monitoring Group, who report that survivors often face abrupt loss of support, eviction, and psychological distress following a negative decision. They report that the shortened 30-day deadline is widely regarded as unworkable in the context of securing instructions from victims of trauma, language barriers, or limited access to legal aid. Only a small fraction of victims are reported as able to lodge reconsideration requests, and many are unaware of their right to do so due to poor communication and lack of translated materials[145].

Legal challenge to a negative reasonable grounds decision

4.170

The appropriate remedy for challenging a refusal to reconsider a negative reasonable grounds decision is by way of judicial review. The procedure for

145 After Exploitation and Anti-Trafficking Monitoring Group, *Modern Slavery Reconsiderations: Fact Sheet* (March 2025) <https://afterexploitation.com/wp-content/uploads/2025/03/briefing-modern-slavery-reconsiderations.-after-exploitation-atmg-20-03-2025.pdf> accessed 26 September 2025.

bringing such a challenge in relation to a negative NRM identification decision is set out in the following section (Stage 3).

Stage 3: conclusive grounds decision

Standard of proof and reasoning requirements

Standard of proof: balance of probabilities

4.171

The standard of proof for a conclusive grounds (CG) decision is the balance of probabilities. The test is whether, on the evidence available, it is more likely than not that the individual is a victim of human trafficking or modern slavery.

Legal elements of trafficking and modern slavery

4.172

The definitions of the Art 4 proscribed acts are analysed at length in **Chapter 1**.

Statutory Guidance and the duty to provide reasoned decisions

4.173

The Statutory Guidance imposes a high standard of reasoning on the Competent Authority. Where a decision turns on an assessment of credibility, the authority must undertake a careful and structured analysis of the relevant factors and provide a clear explanation of how credibility was assessed. This includes engaging with all material evidence and ensuring that adverse credibility findings are not made without proper justification. The reasoning must demonstrate that the authority has conscientiously applied the correct legal test and has considered the evidence in a trauma-informed and procedurally fair manner[146].

Evidential threshold and procedural safeguards

4.174

At the conclusive grounds stage, the Competent Authority is required to assess all available evidence and consider every factor that supports the identification of the individual as a victim of trafficking or modern slavery. The statutory

146 *R (on the application of M) v Secretary of State for the Home Department* [2015] EWHC 2467 (Admin) at para 55. See Chapter 3.

guidance requires that the authority must have before it all 'necessary information' before reaching a negative decision. Specifically, it states:

> 'Where it appears that the Conclusive Grounds decision may be negative on the balance of probabilities, the relevant competent authorities should contact the First Responder, support providers, police and Local Authority as appropriate (and ICTG where available, Northern Ireland Independent Guardian Service, or Scotland's Independent Child Trafficking Guardians service) to discuss their decision and give them the opportunity to provide any further information before taking the decision.'

Evidential assessment: indicators, credibility, and trauma-informed practice

4.175

The Competent Authority must weigh the strength of the indicators and evidence presented, including the credibility of the account. This requires a trauma-informed approach and a recognition that disclosure may be delayed or fragmented due to the psychological impact of exploitation.

Engagement with relevant agencies prior to negative decisions

4.176

Before making a negative decision, the individual should be given an opportunity to respond to any adverse inferences. As with the reasonable grounds decision, before the Competent Authority reaches a negative conclusion, it must first refer to the First Responder or other expert witnesses to clarify any inconsistencies in the claim[147]. See above regarding reasonable grounds decisions as this section applies equally to the making of conclusive grounds decisions.

Interview standards, child victims and multi-agency coordination

4.177

The Competent Authority may require an interview, but where an interview could have a detrimental impact, particularly in cases involving trauma, the Competent Authority should consider putting adverse points in writing. The decision to interview must balance the evidential value against the risk of re-traumatisation. Any interview conducted should adopt a trauma informed approach (see **Chapter 3**).

147 Home Office, Modern Slavery: Statutory Guidance for England and Wales (under s 49 of the MSA 2015) and Non-Statutory Guidance for Scotland and Northern Ireland at [14.13-14.14] (Version 4.3, Updated December 2025) *https://www.gov.uk/government/publications/modern-slavery-how-to-identify-and-support-victims* accessed 26 January 2026.

4.178

In the case of children, interviews should be conducted only if necessary, and only by trained child protection professionals (see **Chapter 3**). The Competent Authority should avoid interviewing a child for the purpose of reaching a decision under the NRM if:

- specialists in other agencies are available and capable of conducting the interview; or
- the relevant modern slavery issues have already been clarified during the asylum process;
- any interview of a child must conform with best practice (see **Chapter 3**).

Safeguards in criminal proceedings and the role of ABE protocols

4.179

Where the individual is a witness in an ongoing criminal prosecution, any interview should be conducted by an officer trained in Achieving Best Evidence (ABE) protocols to avoid undermining the credibility of the evidence and the integrity of the prosecution case. The Competent Authority must also avoid any appearance of offering inducements, which could compromise both the victim's testimony and the fairness of the criminal process.

Timing of the conclusive grounds decision

4.180

The statutory expectation is that a conclusive grounds decision should be made as soon as possible following the recovery and reflection period. However, in practice, the timescale depends on the circumstances of each case, and significant delays are common. Although delays have been subject to legal challenge, the High Court has held that they are not so widespread or severe as to render the system unlawful[148].

Prioritisation criteria

4.181

During litigation concerning delay, the Home Secretary disclosed that prioritisation criteria had been in operation since at least February 2023. These criteria allow decision-makers to prioritise certain conclusive grounds decisions,

148 *R (FH) v Secretary of State for the Home Department* EWHC 1327 (Admin).

including on a directly discriminatory basis for Albanian nationals, with the Stated aim of facilitating their removal from the UK. The High Court found this lawful, relying on a specific Ministerial arrangement under the Equality Act 2010[149].

Statutory Guidance: prioritisation categories

4.182

The Statutory Guidance now publicly sets out seven prioritisation categories for conclusive grounds decisions[150]:

1. Cases that are subject to a Ministerial Arrangement, direction or authorisation to prioritise from the Secretary of State for Home Department, or the Minister responsible for the National Referral Mechanism.

2. Cases linked to detained Foreign National Offenders where a specific prioritisation request has been received.

3. The following are considered equal priority:
   - Cases linked to the Criminal Justice System where the Competent Authorities have agreed to prioritise/expedite the decision, having been notified of a court hearing date or custody time limit.
   - Cases where a child is over the age of 17 but yet to turn 18 (age change cases).
   - Cases linked to a Judicial Review or Pre-Action Protocol and a decision timescale has been agreed or ordered as part of the litigation.

4. Cases with a specific safeguarding issue, unless there is an immediate or imminent risk to the individual where the case can be dealt with as higher priority.

5. Cases with an agreement to prioritise/expedite following a request from another Home Office team.

6. Cases involving the reconsideration of a previous Conclusive Grounds decision where a timescale has been agreed.

7. Cases being used to support Decision Maker training and development.

149 The Equality (Albanian Nationals) Arrangement 2023

150 Home Office, Modern Slavery: Statutory Guidance for England and Wales (under s 49 of the MSA 2015) and Non-Statutory Guidance for Scotland and Northern Ireland at [14.129] (Version 4.3, Updated December 2025) *https://www.gov.uk/government/publications/modern-slavery-how-to-identify-and-support-victims* accessed 26 January 2026.

Prioritisation and its impact on case preparation

4.183

Legal representatives should check whether a case falls within a prioritised category, as this may affect the timeframe for gathering evidence and making representations. Importantly, the guidance also allows for requests to delay a conclusive grounds decision, particularly where additional information is needed. Such requests should be supported by evidence, for example, delays in obtaining expert reports, legal aid, or instructions due to detention or vulnerability.

Interaction between NRM and asylum processes

4.184

In cases involving Albanian nationals, particular care may be required. It has been observed by third sector organisations and legal practitioners that conclusive grounds decisions may, in some instances, be prioritised and issued before all relevant evidence has been submitted.[151] This may occur alongside a certified refusal of an asylum or human rights claim, which can result in the individual being denied an in-country right of appeal to the First-tier Tribunal (Immigration and Asylum Chamber). While the NRM and asylum systems are formally distinct, their interaction may, in practice, lead to removal before trafficking or modern slavery claims have been fully identified or investigated. Such outcomes may raise concerns under Art 4 ECHR and Art 10 ECAT.

The importance of specialist legal representation

4.185

Given the complexity often associated with trafficking or modern slavery claims involving Albanian nationals, specialist legal representation is strongly recommended. These cases frequently involve multiple and overlapping forms of exploitation, including forced criminality[152] and sexual exploitation, and may require expert evidence to support the claim. There remains a body of

151 Helen Bamber Foundation, *Dismissing Risk: The Impact on Trafficking Survivors of Labelling Countries of Origin as 'Safe'* (April 2025) <https://www.helenbamber.org/sites/default/files/2025-04/Dismissing%20Risk_April%202025.pdf> accessed [26 January 2026]

152 Claudia Neale and Micah Anne Neale, *Trafficking and Organised Crime in Albania* (April 2025) <https://miclu.org/assets/uploads/Albania-trafficking-and-organised-crime-paper-April-2025.pdf> accessed [26 January 2026].

evidence[153] supporting the Upper Tribunal's established position that the risk of re-trafficking upon return to Albania can, in some cases, be real and ongoing[154].

Positive conclusive grounds decision: overview

4.186

Where a positive conclusive grounds decision is made, the individual is formally recognised as either:

- **a victim of modern slavery (human trafficking)**; or
- **a victim of modern slavery (slavery, servitude, or forced and compulsory labour)**.

4.187

For adults, the decision must be served on the individual or their legal representative[155].

4.188

For children, the decision must not be served directly on the child under any circumstances. Instead, it should be served on[156]:

- the child's legal representative;
- the First Responder;
- any relevant support provider;
- the relevant local authority; and
- the Independent Child Trafficking Guardian (ICTG), where one has been appointed.

153 *TD and AD (trafficked women) (CG)* [2016] UKUT 92 at official headnote para 1g. Much of the guidance is applicable to trafficked boys and men, which remains under recognised because of the interplay of gender, machismo and honour in Albania.

154 See for example, Mark Symes and Emma Fitzsimons, 'Albania: is it really a 'safe third country' for the purpose of certification?' 17 September 2024, for a critique of the Home Office's policy position in their Country Policy Information Notes on Albania. Available at: https://gardencourtchambers.co.uk/immigration-blog-albania-is-it-really-a-safe-country-for-the-purposes-of-certification/ (last accessed 26 January 2026).

155 Home Office, Modern Slavery: Statutory Guidance for England and Wales (under s 49 of the MSA 2015) and Non-Statutory Guidance for Scotland and Northern Ireland at [14.184] (Version 4.3, Updated December 2025) *https://www.gov.uk/government/publications/modern-slavery-how-to-identify-and-support-victims* accessed 26 January 2026.

156 Ibid. [14.185-14.186].

4.189

As with a reasonable grounds decision, the Competent Authority must also notify the police and request that they inform the Crown Prosecution Service (CPS) as soon as the decision is made.This ensures that any criminal proceedings or investigations involving the victim can be appropriately informed and supported[157].

Recovery support under the MSVCC framework

4.190

This is examined at length in **Chapter 5**.

4.191

Following a positive conclusive grounds decision, victims are entitled to a minimum of 45 days of continued support under the Modern Slavery Victim Care Contract (MSVCC)[158]. During this period, a *Recovery Needs Assessment* (RNA) is conducted to determine whether ongoing support remains necessary[159]. These arrangements reflect the recognition that recovery is not linear, and many victims may continue to require tailored support beyond formal identification.

4.192

Victims who have exited MSVCC support may request re-entry, but this must be initiated by the individual and assessed by the MSVCC Prime Contractor, currently the Salvation Army[160]. A refusal to re-admit a victim is a decision amenable to judicial review[161].

4.193

Access to support issues include difficulties accessing financial support, adequacy of care, or premature termination of services. Practitioners encountering such difficulties should seek specialist advice where support is not meeting the victim's assessed needs[162].

157 Ibid. [14.190–14.193].
158 Ibid. [7.12].
159 Ibid. [8.27] and see Home Office, *Recovery Needs Assessment (RNA): Guidance for Confirmed Victims of Modern Slavery* (Version 8.1) (accessed 26 January 2026).
160 Ibid. [8.34].
161 Ibid. [8.36–8.37].
162 Ibid. [8.38–8.46].

4.194

Although s 50 of the MSA 2015 empowers the Home Secretary to make regulations concerning victim support, this provision has not yet been brought into force at the time of writing.

Leave to remain for victims of trafficking: the legal framework pre- and post-30 January 2023

Discretionary leave prior to 30 January 2023

4.195

Before 30 January 2023, discretionary leave was granted to victims of modern slavery under executive policy, pursuant to the Home Secretary's general powers to grant leave to remain. The final version of the relevant policy was titled *Discretionary Leave Considerations for Victims of Modern Slavery* (v10, 16 March 2023) ('the DLR Policy').

4.196

Under this policy, leave was granted in three circumstances:

- Where leave was necessary owing to personal circumstances;
- Where leave was necessary to pursue compensation;
- Where the victim was assisting the police with their enquiries.

The legal challenges

4.197

In *R (PK (Ghana)) v Secretary of State for the Home Department*[163], the Court of Appeal held that an earlier version of the policy was unlawful for failing to reflect Art 14 of ECAT. The policy had imposed a 'compelling' threshold, whereas the correct test was whether leave was 'necessary' owing to the person's situation. The policy was subsequently amended.

4.198

In *R (EOG and KTT) v Secretary of State for the Home Department*[164], the Court of Appeal confirmed that challenges to Home Office policy because of non-ECAT compliance are justiciable where the policy purports to give effect to

163 *R (PK (Ghana)) v Secretary of State for the Home Department* [2018] EWCA Civ 98.
164 *R (SSA (Ethiopia)) v Secretary of State for the Home Department* JR-2021-LON-001894 (unreported) *https://tribunalsdecisions.service.gov.uk/utiac/jr-2021-lon-001894*.

ECAT. The Court held that Art 14 of ECAT requires that a confirmed victim of trafficking who is also an asylum seeker must be granted leave to remain while their asylum claim is pending. This form of leave became known as *KTT-leave.* The asylum claim need not be based solely on a fear of re-trafficking, provided that such fear forms part of the basis for fearing return.

4.199

In *R (XY) v Secretary of State for the Home Department*[165], the Court found that the Home Office had unlawfully paused decision-making, affecting at least 1,500 confirmed victims, and had breached its duty of candour, operating an undisclosed and unlawful policy until April 2023, which prevented confirmed victims from being granted *KTT-leave.* The Court also found breaches of Arts. 8 and 14 ECHR.

Statutory framework introduced on 30 January 2023

4.200

On 30 January 2023, s 65 of the NABA 2022 came into force, introducing a statutory basis for granting limited leave to confirmed victims of trafficking or modern slavery. On the same date, the Home Secretary inserted Appendix VTS (*Temporary Permission to Stay for Victims of Human Trafficking or Slavery*) into the Immigration Rules and published accompanying caseworker guidance[166].

4.201

The stated policy objective is to deliver a fair and effective permission to stay process by:

- Allowing victims to remain in the UK where they are cooperating with public authorities in investigations or prosecutions;
- Supporting a needs-based approach to victim support[167].

4.202

A confirmed victim must be automatically considered for permission to stay following a positive conclusive grounds decision[168].

165 *R (XY) v Secretary of State for the Home Department* [2024] EWHC 81 (Admin).
166 Home Office, *Temporary Permission to Stay Considerations for Victims of Human Trafficking or Slavery* (v 10, 3 December 2025).
167 Ibid. pp.8–9.
168 Ibid. p.15.

Statutory criteria for granting leave

4.203

Under s 65(2), the Home Secretary must grant leave where it is considered necessary for the purpose of:

- Assisting the person in recovering from physical or psychological harm arising from the exploitation (s 65(2)(a));
- Enabling the person to seek compensation (s 65(2)(b));
- Enabling cooperation with a public authority in connection with an investigation or prosecution (s 65(2)(c)).

4.204

These provisions are subject to disqualification under s 63(2), decision-making on disqualification was paused at time of publication.

4.205

Subsections 65(4) and (5) qualify the above duties. Leave is not considered necessary if:

- The person's recovery needs can be met in their country of origin or a third country to which they may be removed (s 65(4)(a));
- The person can reasonably seek compensation from abroad (s 65(4)(b)).

Transitional provisions and the R(KTT) cohort

4.206

The DLR Policy v.10 made transitional provision for victims with a positive conclusive grounds decision and a pending trafficking-related asylum claim as of 30 January 2023. These individuals were entitled to have their claims determined under the previous policy, unless they were subject to deportation orders or proceedings.

4.207

In *S and VLT*[169], the Court of Appeal upheld the exclusion of such individuals from the transitional provisions, concluding it was lawful on public policy grounds.

169 *S and VLT v Secretary of State for the Home Department* [2025] EWCA Civ 188.

Duration and nature of leave

4.208

The VTS Guidance[170] provides that:

- A 30-month grant is the norm for recovery or cooperation cases;
- A 12-month grant is typical for compensation cases.

4.209

The period of leave must reflect the individual facts of the case. There is no requirement to grant indefinite leave to remain (ILR) under this policy. The VTS route is not a route to settlement.

Risk of re-trafficking and evidential considerations

4.210

The VTS Policy expressly states that, for decisions made after 30 January 2023, there is no requirement to assess the risk of re-trafficking[171]. This marks a departure from the approach under the DLR Policy, where such assessments were routinely considered. However, the risk of re-trafficking may remain a live issue, particularly in cases involving ongoing psychological or physical recovery. Unresolved vulnerabilities, including interrupted treatment or support, are recognised risk factors for future exploitation and may warrant careful consideration in individual cases.

4.211

Expert evidence, particularly medical and country evidence, will be critical in supporting applications for further leave. Medical experts should address the impact of removal on recovery, including increased symptomology, vulnerability, and suicidal ideation. In compensation cases, barriers to justice from abroad should be clearly articulated, drawing on the jurisprudence addressing unfairness in exercising out-of-country appeals[172] and the issues identified in *R (HJK & Ors) v Director of Legal Aid Casework*[173]. Medical evidence should be consistent with the overarching duties owed by medical experts in litigation (see **Chapter 3**).

---

170 Home Office, *Temporary Permission to Stay Considerations for Victims of Human Trafficking or Slavery* (v 10, 3 December 2025) at pp.28-29.

171 Ibid. p.14.

172 *R (on the application of Kiarie and Byndloss) v Secretary of State of the Home Department* [2017] UKSC 42.

173 *R (HJK & Ors) v Director of Legal Aid Casework* [2025] EWHC 774 (Admin).

Judicial oversight on leave

4.212

Where the Competent Authority has mishandled a claim, this may be relevant to the period of leave granted[174]. Where expert evidence supports a specific period of leave for treatment, the decision-maker must engage with that evidence and afford it appropriate weight[175].

Negative conclusive grounds decision

4.213

Where a negative conclusive grounds decision is made, the Competent Authority must issue a reasoned decision to the individual and notify the First Responder, support provider, and local authority (where relevant)[176]. As with a reasonable grounds decision, the Competent Authority must also notify the police and request that they inform the Crown Prosecution Service (CPS)[177].

4.214

Following a negative conclusive grounds decision, any relevant immigration matters must be concluded.

4.215

Practitioners should note that the First-tier Tribunal(Immigration and Asylum Chamber) retains jurisdiction on appeal to reach its own findings of fact on whether an individual is a victim of trafficking or modern slavery, whether they require leave to remain to avoid a breach of human rights, and whether they qualify for refugee status or other forms of protection, Importantly, the Tribunal is not bound by the Competent Authority's negative conclusive grounds decision[178] (see **Chapter 16**).

4.216

An individual may request assisted voluntary return at any stage of the process. Following a negative conclusive grounds decision, the Home Office is required

174 *R (on the application of FT) v Secretary of State for the Home Department* [2017] UKUT 331 (IAC) at 74.

175 Ibid at [97], noting it was irrational to grant leave for the purpose of obtaining medical treatment for a shorter period than necessary to undertake that treatment.

176 Home Office, Modern Slavery: Statutory Guidance for England and Wales (under s 49 of the MSA 2015) and Non-Statutory Guidance for Scotland and Northern Ireland at [14.178] (Version 4.3, Updated December 2025) *https://www.gov.uk/government/publications/modern-slavery-how-to-identify-and-support-victims* accessed 26 January 2026.

177 Ibid. [14.192].

178 *MS (Pakistan) v Secretary of State for the Home Department* [2020] UKSC 9.

to inform the individual of this option and to provide information about any programmes specifically tailored for victims of modern slavery[179].

4.217

As previously noted, there remains a discretion to reconsider a negative identification decision. A reconsideration request does not need to originate from the First Responder and may be submitted by any party acting on the individual's behalf[180].

4.218

Legal challenges to negative reasonable or conclusive grounds decisions are brought by way of judicial review in the Administrative Court (see below). Any judicial review claim challenging a negative conclusive grounds decision must be filed promptly, and in any event within three months of the date of the decision. Practitioners should ensure that all procedural steps are taken within this timeframe, including pre-action correspondence and evidence gathering.

4.219

Where the legal challenge concerns a refusal to issue a residence permit, whether Discretionary Leave to Remain (DLR) or Victim of Trafficking Leave (VTS), the judicial review claim should be brought in the Upper Tribunal. An application for anonymity in the Administrative Court[181] or the Upper Tribunal[182] should be considered to protect the identity of the claimant (see Chapter 8).

Judicial review of NRM identification decisions: public law and Art 4 ECHR

4.220

Challenges to decisions made by the Competent Authority under the NRM may proceed on three legal fronts:

(i) public law principles,

179 Home Office, Modern Slavery: Statutory Guidance for England and Wales (under s 49 of the MSA 2015) and Non-Statutory Guidance for Scotland and Northern Ireland at [15.205],[15.207] (Version 4.3, Updated December 2025) *https://www.gov.uk/government/publications/modern-slavery-how-to-identify-and-support-victims* accessed 26 January 2026.

180 Ibid. [14.216–14.235].

181 Courts and Tribunals Judiciary, *The Administrative Court Judicial Review Guide 2025* (Judiciary of England and Wales, 2025) [7.12] https://www.judiciary.uk/publications/judicial-review-guide-2025/> accessed 26 September 2025.

182 Upper Tribunal Immigration and Asylum Chamber, *Guidance Note 2022 No 2: Anonymity Orders and Hearings in Private* (Judiciary of England and Wales, 2022) <https://www.judiciary.uk/publications/guidance-note-2022-no-2-anonymity-orders-and-hearings-in-private/> accessed 26 September 2025.

(ii) decision is contrary to statutory duties, and

(iii) alleged breaches of the United Kingdom's obligations under s 6(1) of the Human Rights Act 1998, specifically Art 4 ECHR.

Grounds of judicial review in Art 4 ECHR cases

4.221

In trafficking and modern slavery identification decisions, particularly those involving the refusal to reconsider negative identification outcomes, a range of public law grounds may be relied upon in judicial review proceedings. These grounds reflect both procedural and substantive defects in decision-making and are especially relevant where the consequences of the decision are serious and engage protective obligations under Art 4 ECHR.

4.222

The most common grounds of review include:

- **Breach of positive obligations** arising under Art 4 ECHR.
- **The decision gives rise to a significant risk of a substantive Art 4 ECHR violation** (ie risk of re-trafficking).
- **Errors of law or fact** – such as misapplication of the legal test for victim identification or incorrect factual findings.
- **Failure to give adequate reasons** – where the decision lacks adequate explanation or fails to address key evidence.
- **Substantive unfairness** – including decisions that are unjust in their outcome due to procedural or evidential deficiencies.
- **Failure to take into account material considerations / taking into account immaterial considerations** – such as ignoring relevant medical or safeguarding evidence or relying on irrelevant factors.
- **Irrationality** – where the decision is so unreasonable that no reasonable decision-maker could have reached it.
- **Breach of published policy** – including failure to follow the reconsideration guidance or apply the criteria for 'exceptional circumstances' properly.
- **Breaches of other human rights** – most commonly under **Art 3**, (inhuman, or degrading treatment and torture) and **Art 8** (private and family life) of the ECHR.

Heightened judicial scrutiny of NRM Decisions engaging Art 4 ECHR

4.223

In cases of trafficking, slavery and related exploitation, the consequences of a negative identification decision: loss of protection, risk of re-trafficking and withdrawal of support, are sufficiently grave to warrant heightened scrutiny. The Competent Authority must therefore show, by clear and conscientious reasoning, that it has considered all relevant matters, including any fresh evidence and the protective obligations under Art 4.

4.224

The standard of review, on judicial review, is substantive, not merely procedural, and requires the authority to show that it has applied the correct legal test in practice, not just in form.

4.225

Mr Justice Chamberlain's analysis in *KP v Secretary of State for Foreign, Commonwealth and Development Affairs*[183] provides the appropriate framework for the court's role in assessing the rationality of NRM decisions in this context. He observed that the intensity of substantive judicial review varies according to the significance of the interests affected and the seriousness of the potential consequences. Where a decision threatens interests of substantial moral or legal weight, such as the safety, dignity, or welfare of vulnerable individuals, a more rigorous standard of scrutiny is required, even if no formal legal right is engaged. It is not contingent upon the existence of a formal legal right, but rather on the seriousness of what is threatened by the impugned decision.

4.226

Where a heightened standard of review applies, as it does in decisions that determine the identification and protection of victims under Art 4 ECHR, it affects the court's approach to both procedural and substantive irrationality. In cases of procedural irrationality, the court will examine the decision-making process with greater care to ensure it is free from material flaws. That includes considering whether relevant evidence was properly taken into account and whether the decision-maker followed fair and lawful procedures.

4.227

In cases of outcome irrationality, where the substance of the decision is challenged, the court will look for a correspondingly stronger justification[184].

---

183 *KP v Secretary of State for Foreign, Commonwealth and Development Affairs* [2025] EWHC 370.
184 *R v Ministry of Defence, ex parte Smith* [1996] QB 517, 554.

The more serious the interests at stake, such as the risk of re-trafficking or the loss of protective support, the narrower the range of lawful outcomes open to the decision-maker[185]. In some situations, the gravity of the consequences may mean that only one rational decision is legally available.

Procedural safeguards in the NRM: a legal analysis of Art 6 ECHR

4.228

The determination of status as a victim of trafficking or slavery or related harms under the NRM may not automatically constitute a 'civil right' engaging Art 6 ECHR. However, recent jurisprudence and evolving legal analysis suggest that Art 6 guarantees may be engaged where the decision directly impacts: (i) access to remedies, such as compensation; (ii) support entitlements, social assistance and accommodation; and (iii) the fairness of related criminal proceedings, particularly where victim status influences prosecutorial decisions or sentencing and/or gives rise to a risk of self-incrimination.

Art.6 and access to legal aid for NRM referral

4.229

The High Court's decision in *R (HJK & Ors) v Director of Legal Aid Casework*[186] confirmed that the denial of legal aid to trafficking victims seeking access to the Criminal Injuries Compensation Scheme breached Art 6. This precedent may support a broader re-characterisation of NRM determinations as decisions concerning civil rights and obligations, particularly where they determine access to statutory support such as accommodation, healthcare, and financial assistance.

4.230

Unlike immigration control decisions excluded from Art 6 under *Maaouia v France*[187], NRM determinations apply to domestic and foreign nationals alike and trigger entitlements provided by Part 5 of the NABA 2022 and s 50A of the MSA 2015. As such, they align more closely with the reasoning in *Schuler-Zgraggen v Switzerland*, *Feldbrugge v Netherlands* and *Salesi v Italy*[188] where the

185 *Pham v Secretary of State for the Home Department* [2015] UKSC 19, [107]; *Mark Elliott, 'KP v Foreign Secretary*: A primer on rationality review' (Public Law for Everyone, 10 March 2025) <https://publiclawforeveryone.com/2025/03/10/kp-v-foreign-secretary-a-primer-on-rationality-review/> accessed 26 September 2025.

186 *R (HJK & Ors) v Director of Legal Aid Casework* [2025] EWHC 774 (Admin).

187 *Maaouia v France,* App no 39652/98, ECtHR, 5 October 2000.

188 *Schuler-Zgraggen v Switzerland* App no 14518/89, ECtHR, 24 June 1993.

ECtHR held that determinations affecting subsistence and welfare benefits fall within the scope of Art 6.

4.231

In this context, restrictions on legal aid funding for NRM referrals may also raise Art 6 concerns. Victims often face significant barriers: trauma, language difficulties, cognitive impairments, that prevent effective engagement with the process. If NRM determinations are properly characterised as determination of civil rights, then victims may be entitled to Exceptional Case Funding from the point of referral, ensuring access to legal representation and procedural fairness.

Arts 4 and 6 adequate judicial remedy

4.232

Judicial review may not constitute an effective remedy in cases involving contested decisions under the National Referral Mechanism (NRM), particularly where the central issue concerns factual determinations of victim status. This limitation reflects concerns identified by the ECtHR in *Tsfayo v United Kingdom*[189], where the Court found that judicial review was insufficient to meet the requirements of Art 6 of the Convention.

4.233

In *R (Talpada) v Secretary of State for the Home Department*[190] Lady Justice Hallett observed

> 'If there is a dispute of fact, and it is relevant to the legal issues which arise in a claim for judicial review, the court usually proceeds on written evidence. Since the burden of proof is usually on the person who asserts a fact to be true, if that burden is not discharged, the court will proceed on the basis that the fact has not been proved.'

4.234

In *Tsfayo*[191], the Court concluded that the domestic process did not provide an independent and impartial tribunal equipped to resolve the disputed issues of fact. The Court underscored that where the outcome of a dispute turns on the determination of primary facts, particularly matters of credibility, an effective remedy must encompass a procedure capable of receiving evidence and making its own factual findings. As already noted, judicial review operates within a far narrower constitutional frontier, directed to questions of legality, rationality, and procedural fairness. It is therefore not generally designed to undertake the

189 [2006] ECHR 543.
190 *R (Talpada) v Secretary of State for the Home Department* [2018] EWCA Civ 841 at [2].
191 [2006] ECHR 543.

kind of evaluative fact-finding, or reassessment of credibility, that the Strasbourg Court considered essential in that context.

Missing victims: procedural duties and legal considerations

Operational duty to protect under Art 4 ECHR

4.235

The operational duty under Art 4 ECHR includes a positive obligation to protect individual victims and potential victims from ill-treatment where there is credible suspicion that the person has been, or is at real and immediate risk of being, trafficked or subjected to slavery or related exploitation. This duty is engaged in circumstances where the risk is specific and identifiable, and it requires proactive protective measures by the State.

4.236

This obligation must be read alongside the procedural duty to investigate credible suspicion of trafficking, slavery or related acts. The protocols and policies concerning missing victims is also examined at length in **Chapter 5**.

Practitioner challenges and good practice

4.237

Victims who go missing present practical and legal challenges, particularly in relation to Legal Aid and the ability to obtain instructions. As a matter of good practice, Practitioners should seek a retainer and clear instructions from the client on how to proceed should they go missing,[192] this should be done in a trauma informed way (**Chapter 3**).

Competent Authority duties where victims are missing

4.238

Where a victim goes missing before a reasonable or conclusive grounds decision is made, and:

192 There is no requirement to obtain fresh instructions at each stage of proceedings (see e.g. *Donsland Ltd v Hoogstraten* [2002] EWCA Civ 253, [2002] PNLR 28 at para 19, per Tuckey LJ). However, there may be specific issues on which specific instructions are required. In general, it is likely that a judicial review relating to an historic decision (e.g. a reasonable or conclusive grounds decision) could be concluded, but any associated damages claim would have to be stayed.

- the available evidence is insufficient to meet the relevant threshold; and
- further evidence cannot be obtained due to the victim's absence,

4.239

The Competent Authority must take the following steps[193]:

Reporting and safeguarding

4.240

Report the individual as a vulnerable missing person to the police and ensure a marker is placed on the Police National Computer. Safeguarding services, children's or adult, as appropriate, must be notified.

Case suspension notifications

4.241

Notify relevant parties that the case has been suspended, including:

- the First Responder;
- the support provider (and the Salvation Army, where applicable);
- the local authority (in child cases);
- the Independent Child Trafficking Guardian (if appointed);
- the Home Office immigration casework team.

Criminal proceedings

4.242

If the individual is involved in criminal proceedings, the Competent Authority must notify the police (or the National Human Trafficking Unit in Scotland), and request that prosecutors are informed of the suspension[194].

---

193 Home Office, Modern Slavery: Statutory Guidance for England and Wales (under s 49 of the MSA 2015) and Non-Statutory Guidance for Scotland and Northern Ireland at [9.13, 9.17, 9.21, 12.28, 13.53, 14.197–14.201] (Version 4.3, updated December 2025) *https://www.gov.uk/government/publications/modern-slavery-how-to-identify-and-support-victims* accessed 26 January 2026.

194 Home Office, Modern Slavery: Statutory Guidance for England and Wales (under s 49 of the MSA 2015) and Non-Statutory Guidance for Scotland and Northern Ireland at [14.199] (Version 4.3, updated December 2025) *https://www.gov.uk/government/publications/modern-slavery-how-to-identify-and-support-victims* accessed 26 January 2026.

Internal record-keeping

4.243

Record the case as suspended and ensure immigration teams are aware of the individual's potential victim status should they be re-encountered.

4.244

The guidance makes clear that if sufficient information is available, a decision should be made. In practice, this means only positive decisions are likely where the victim is missing and further evidence cannot be obtained.

Risk of re-trafficking and judicial oversight

4.245

Where the reason for disappearance is unknown, re-trafficking must be considered a real possibility. Victims may reappear months later in exploitative settings such as cannabis farms or brothels.

4.246

In R(*TDT) v SSHD*[195], the Court of Appeal found a breach of Art 4 ECHR where a suspected Vietnamese child victim went missing after being released to a temple rather than safe accommodation. Similarly, in *CP (Vietnam) v SSHD*[196], the Administrative Court criticised the Home Secretary's failure to identify and protect a missing Vietnamese national.

4.247

In criminal appeals, the Court of Appeal has adopted a precautionary approach in cases involving missing victims[197]. Practitioners should seek protective orders where appropriate, including minimum safeguards in the event an appellant goes missing, such as:

- recognition of the individual as a potential trafficking or modern slavery victim;
- notification of their legal representative and support provider upon re-encounter;
- a temporary bar on removal.

---

195 *R (on the application of TDT) v SSHD* [2018] EWCA Civ 1395, [2018] 1 WLR.

196 *CP (Vietnam) v SSHD* [2018] EWHC 2122 (Admin).

197 *R v Okedare* [2014] EWCA Crim 228, [2014] 1 WLR 4071 at paras 23–34. The Administrative Court has taken a similar approach in judicial review proceedings – however, those cases are unreported.

4.248

Effective multi-agency coordination is essential to ensure that all relevant public authorities are promptly notified when an individual is reported missing and there are concerns about trafficking or re-trafficking.

Disqualification from protection: public order and bad faith under the NABA 2022

4.249

Part 5 of the NABA 2022 introduced a range of measures affecting the UK's modern slavery framework. These include changes to leave to remain provisions and the introduction of a disqualification regime, which excludes certain individuals from the protections of the National Referral Mechanism ('NRM') on grounds such as public order or bad faith. These provisions have attracted commentary and concern from some stakeholders and legal commentators, who argue that they may risk weakening protections for victims of modern slavery and trafficking.

Statutory criteria for disqualification

4.250

Since 30 January 2023, s 63 of the NABA 2022 has vested the Secretary of State with a discretionary power to disqualify an individual from recognition as a victim within the NRM and from the support ordinarily flowing from that status[198]. This power may be exercised even after a positive reasonable grounds decision, where the individual is assessed to be either a 'threat to public order' or to have advanced their claim 'in bad faith'; it is this mechanism that has become known as the Public Order Disqualification ('POD').

4.251

Where a POD is applied, the statutory bar on removal under sections 61 and 62 ceases to operate, as does the duty under section 65 to grant leave to remain. Section 63(3) provides a non-exhaustive list of circumstances in which a person may be treated as a threat to public order, including convictions for terrorism or serious criminal offences, the imposition of measures such as TPIMs or exclusion orders, and other indicators of national security risk. The threshold is notably low and may be satisfied by a custodial sentence of 12 months. Amendments

198 Section 50A(5) of the MSA 2015 provides that support and assistance arising under sections 50A(1) and (4) cease to apply where someone is subject to a Public Disqualification Order.

introduced by s 29 of the Illegal Migration Act 2023, if brought into force, would lower this threshold further to include individuals subject to conducive deportation (ie those with sentences under 12 months). They would also convert the Secretary of State's discretion into a duty to disqualify, save where 'compelling circumstances' justify an exception. At present, no commencement date has been announced for these amendments.

4.252

The operation of s 63 fell for detailed consideration in *R (ABW) v Secretary of State for the Home Department*[199]. In the context of a challenge to the POD decision in that case, Mr Justice Morris held, in a judgment handed down on 17 December 2025, that both the decision itself and certain passages of the Secretary of State's Modern Slavery Act Guidance were unlawful. He found that the Secretary of State was under a continuing obligation, arising under NABA and the Guidance, to progress to a Conclusive Grounds decision for as long as the individual remained in the United Kingdom, and that the failure to do so in the claimant's case constituted a breach of that duty.

4.253

Morris J further concluded that the discretion in s 63 must be exercised compatibly with Art 13(3) of ECAT. He held that those parts of the Guidance which imposed a presumption in favour of making a POD amounted to a misdirection of the statutory scheme and an unlawful fetter on the discretion conferred by Parliament, rendering the claimant's POD decision unlawful to the extent that it relied upon them. The Court's conclusions on whether the operation of section 63 breached the protective obligations arising under Art 4 of the ECHR are analysed at **4.21–4.26** above. As subsequently confirmed in the updated statutory guidance issued in December 2025, the Home Office has paused decision-making on PODs.

Positive obligations triggered under Art 4 and Statutory responsibilities of other public authorities

Law enforcement duty to investigate

4.254

The Modern Slavery Statutory Guidance provides that, following both a NRM referral and a positive reasonable grounds decision, the police must be notified and provided with information concerning these.

199 [2025] EWHC 3280 (Admin) at [103]-[107].

4.255

Once a positive reasonable grounds decision comes to the attention of the authorities, this alone triggers an obligation under Art 4 of the ECHR to conduct an effective criminal investigation[200]. The procedural obligation to investigate is grounded in the principles of effectiveness and accountability. As emphasised by the ECtHR, such investigations are essential to maintaining public confidence in the State's adherence to the rule of law and to preventing any perception of collusion or tolerance of unlawful acts[201].

Prior offending and the risk of disqualification

4.256

Irrespective of any Public Order Disqualification made under s 63 of the NABA 2022, the State's positive obligations under Art 4 ECHR remain engaged where there is a credible suspicion that an individual is a victim of trafficking, slavery or forced labour. Those obligations may require public authorities other than the Single Competent Authority to act so that statutory, protective and procedural duties are preserved and performed. In practice, most potential grounds for a POD arise in cases involving previous offending. This presents a particular difficulty because there is a well-recognised overlap between criminal behaviour and criminal exploitation. As the Court of Appeal (Criminal Division) has noted in appeals since 2008 (see **Chapter 13**), exploited individuals may be prosecuted without their victimhood being properly identified. Offending may be closely connected to entrenched vulnerabilities, mental illness, cognitive impairment, substance misuse, or histories of abuse and destitution, which both increase the risk of exploitation and obscure its early signs.

4.257

As the Court explained in *VCL and AN v United Kingdom* at [195]–[196]:

> "The fairness of proceedings requires that an accused should be able to obtain the whole range of services specifically associated with legal assistance. In this regard, counsel has to be able to secure without restriction the fundamental aspects of that person's defence: discussion of the case, organisation of the defence, collection of evidence favourable to the accused, preparation for questioning, support for an accused in distress and checking of the conditions of detention (see *Dvorski*, cited above, § 108).

200 *Nicolae Virgiliu Tanase v Romania* [GC] no 41720/13, 25 June 2019 [115].
201 *Nikolova and Velichkova v Bulgaria* App no 7888/03 (ECtHR, 20 December 2007) [57].

'Although victims of trafficking are not immune from prosecution, an individual's status as a victim of trafficking may affect whether there is sufficient evidence to prosecute and whether it is in the public interest to do so (see paragraph 161 above). **Evidence concerning an accused's status as a victim of trafficking is therefore a "fundamental aspect" of the defence which he or she should be able to secure without restriction**."'

4.258

Moreover, as Burnett LJ made clear in *Secretary of State for the Home Department v Hoang Anh Minh*[202], it is the police and the Crown Prosecution Service, not the Single Competent Authority, who bear the criminal investigatory and prosecutorial responsibilities.

4.259

As the ECtHR observed in *YG v Russia*[203], grave acts that engage fundamental values require effective criminal-law provisions and their application through an effective investigation and prosecution. Where the police receive a referral and a positive reasonable-grounds decision from a qualified person, the duty to investigate is engaged. The operation of a POD does not discharge that duty; nothing in the NABA 2022 cuts across the autonomous investigatory obligations imposed by Art 4 ECHR.

4.260

Where the Single Competent Authority declines to discharge protective functions by reason of s 63, other statutory agencies may be required to step in to address the resulting gap. This may be necessary to avoid a breach of the State's positive obligations under Article 4 of the Convention (see above).

Protective duties

4.261

As set out at the start of this chapter, the protective and procedural obligations arising under Art 4 ECHR including identification, support and assistance, the recovery and reflection period, and the duty to investigate, are interdependent and must be treated as a coherent whole. They are not contingent on a victim's willingness to cooperate with law enforcement; rather, they are designed to place individuals in a position where such cooperation is possible, while also facilitating recovery and preventing further breaches of Art 4. The ECtHR has made clear that where failures in protection occur in the context of

202 [2015] EWCA Civ 565.
203 *YG v Russia* (App No 8647/12), 30 August 2022 at [43].

investigatory duties, those deficiencies may amount to a violation of the State's positive obligations under Art 4[204].

4.262

Alongside the Home Office, other public authorities may hold safeguarding responsibilities towards potential victims of modern slavery, including duties of identification, support and assistance (see **Chapter 5**). These responsibilities are arguably engaged once a positive reasonable grounds decision has been made, consistent with the observations of Burnett LJ in *Secretary of State for the Home Department v Hoang Anh Minh*[205] and Underhill LJ in *R (TDT) v Secretary of State for the Home Department*[206].

4.263

It remains uncertain whether s 50A of the MSA 2015, read with ss 61 and 64 of the NABA 2022, was intended to displace the statutory functions of other public authorities responsible for providing care and assistance to victims, including potential victims. This question is especially relevant when considering s 50A alongside s 49(1)(b) of the MSA 2015. However, such an interpretation appears unlikely in the absence of express statutory wording removing the duties under, for example, s 42 of the Care Act 2014 or s 188(1) of the Housing Act 1996[207] in relation to individuals subject to a Public Order Disqualification (see Chapter 5).

Effective judicial consideration

4.264

A Public Order Disqualification (POD) does not, in itself, remove the jurisdiction of courts or tribunals to consider matters of trafficking or modern slavery where there is credible suspicion or *prima facie* evidence, provided there is no other statutory bar to jurisdiction.

4.265

As analysed at the beginning of this chapter, the protective and procedural elements, identification, support and assistance, the recovery and reflection period and investigatory duty, are interdependent and must be understood as operating in concert rather than in isolation. Protective obligations are not

204 *Chowdury and Others v Greece* App no 21884/15 (ECtHR, 30 March 2017 and *V.C.L and A.N. v UK* (2021) 73 EHRR 9.

205 *Secretary of State for the Home Department v Hoang Anh Minh* EWCA Civ 565; Imm AR 1272, [39].

206 *R(TDT) v Secretary of State for the Home Department* [2018] EWCA Civ 1395, [2018] 1 WLR at [35].

207 Ministry of Housing, Communities and Local Government, *Homelessness Code of Guidance for Local Authorities* (22 February 2018, updated 18 July 2025) ch 25. https://www.gov.uk/guidance/homelessness-code-of-guidance-for-local-authorities/chapter-25-modern-slavery-and-trafficking> accessed 13 October 2025.

contingent on cooperation with law enforcement; rather, they are designed, in part, to enable and support a putative victim who may choose to assist in a criminal investigation as well as to assist in recovery and prevent further Art.4 abuses. Where protective obligations have been breached in the context of investigatory duties, the ECtHR has found that such failures may constitute a violation of the State's positive obligations under Art 4 of the Convention.

Other potential grounds for legal challenge to Public Order Disqualification: procedural and substantive irregularities

4.266

Other common grounds of challenge include:

- Procedural unfairness: For example, where additional time is needed to obtain evidence or make representations, this may be relevant in cases involving detention or a change in legal representation.
- Failure to make lawful inquiries: Where relevant material, such as risk or needs assessments under the Victim Care Contract, has not been considered.
- Irrational or unlawful assessment: Where the decision maker fails to consider relevant factors or reaches conclusions that are unreasonable in law, particularly in relation to public order risk or the need for modern slavery-specific support.
- Breach of statutory guidance: Where the decision departs from the framework without justification.
- Unlawful re-trafficking assessment: In breach of Art 4 ECHR, for example, where key risk factors are overlooked or the assessment is flawed.

The Illegal Migration Act 2023 and Border Security, Asylum and Immigration Act 2025

4.267

Since 2022, aspects of the identification and support of potential trafficking victims have been incorporated into primary legislation. The Illegal Migration Act 2023 ('IMA 2023') introduced a duty on the Secretary of State to arrange removal from the UK under s 2, where specified conditions are met.

4.268

It also made significant changes to the entitlements of both potential and confirmed victims under ss 22–29. The effect of those provisions was suspended following the enactment of the Illegal Migration Act 2023 (Amendment) Regulations 2024 and has since been superseded by the Border Security, Asylum and Immigration Act 2025 (BSAIA 2025), which received Royal Assent on 2 December 2025.

Section 29 of the Illegal Migration Act 2023

4.269

Section 29 of the IMA 2023 amends s 63 of the Nationality and Borders Act 2022 so that competent authorities must, rather than may, disqualify certain potential victims of slavery or trafficking from protection on 'public order' or 'bad faith' grounds, and it expands the category of those who can be disqualified to include any non-British person convicted and sentenced to a term of imprisonment of any length, or liable to deportation. This provision has been retained but is not yet in force. Specialist bodies and NGOs have raised serious concerns that retaining s 29 under the new Border Security, Asylum and Immigration Act 2025 will convert an already controversial discretionary power into a mandatory exclusion regime, stripping a broad and loosely defined group of victims of recognition, support and assistance, in a way that conflicts with the non-punishment principle and the UK's obligations under ECAT and Art 4 ECHR.

4.270

Article 13(3) of ECAT does permit the withholding of the recovery and reflection period on grounds of public order or where victim status is improperly claimed, but both the Strasbourg case law and GRETA's 2024 Guidance Note emphasise that this exception must be construed narrowly. In *Chowdury v Greece*[208], the Court treated the protective architecture of ECAT as construed by GRETA, including the recovery and reflection period, as a significant interpretative aid when defining the State's positive obligations under Art 4 ECHR. It reiterated that identification, protection and assistance must be practical and effective rather than merely formal.

4.271

Read alongside *VCL and AN v United Kingdom*, where the Court emphasised the need for early and accurate identification of victims, the avoidance of penalising individuals for offending bound up with their exploitation, and the duty to secure effective protection, the direction of travel is clear. Public-order derogations which operate in a blanket or automatic way, without close attention to the individual circumstances, may breach the State's positive obligations under Art 4.

208 *Chowdury and Others v Greece* App no 21884/15 (ECtHR), 30 March 2017.

4.272

Against that background, the approach under s 29, which requires automatic disqualification from the protections of NABA s 63 on public-order or 'bad-faith' grounds and allows no real evaluative discretion to reflect the nexus between the offending and the trafficking experience, risks turning a narrowly framed treaty exception into a broad rule of exclusion. That is where the tension with *Chowdury*, with *VCL and AN*, and with the non-punishment principle is at its sharpest. A regime that excludes from recovery and residence those whose criminality arises from their exploitation sits uncomfortably with Art 4's requirement that anti-trafficking protections, informed by the Arts 13, 14 and 26 ECAT framework, operate in a practical and effective way for those who are most at risk.

Ongoing Significance of Re JR295 and the Windsor Framework

4.273

In *Re JR295's Application for Judicial Review*[209], the High Court in Northern Ireland disapplied several provisions of the Illegal Migration Act 2023 (IMA 2023) in Northern Ireland, including those bearing on modern-slavery and trafficking-related removals. The Court held that these provisions were incompatible with Art 2 of the Windsor Framework (Ireland/Northern Ireland Protocol), as implemented by s 7A of the European Union (Withdrawal) Act 2018, which requires the UK to ensure that there is no diminution of rights under the Belfast/Good Friday Agreement as a consequence of EU withdrawal. In particular, the Court found that certain IMA provisions operated to diminish protections that had previously derived from EU law and underpinned the human-rights and equality guarantees in the Agreement, and it therefore disapplied them in Northern Ireland.

4.274

The Court issued declarations of incompatibility under s 4 of the Human Rights Act 1998 in respect of ss 2(1), 5, 6, and 22 of the IMA 2023, insofar as they applied to potential victims of trafficking or modern slavery, finding those provisions incompatible with Arts 3, 4, and 8 of the ECHR. Although *JR295* did not address section 29 of the IMA 2023, which was not then in force and was not among the provisions challenged, the Court's reasoning on non-diminution and effective protection for victims of trafficking and modern slavery is likely to assume increased significance if section 29 is subsequently commenced and its compatibility with those obligations is tested.

209 [2024] NIKB 35.

4.275

The Secretary of State sought a stay of the High Court's orders pending appeal, but that application was refused on the ground that the appeal would not be rendered academic or nugatory in the absence of a stay, and that the issues raised were of sufficient importance to warrant continued enforcement of the declarations and disapplication orders while the appeal proceeded.

4.276

Before the Court of Appeal in Northern Ireland could hear the Secretary of State's appeal on the Art 2 Windsor Framework issues, two significant developments occurred:

1. The Court of Appeal delivered judgment in *Re Dillon* NICA 59, which also concerned the interpretation and enforceability of Art 2 of the Windsor Framework and the scope of the "no diminution" commitment. That decision clarified, among other things, that Art 2(1) is to be given a generous and purposive construction and that it can, in appropriate cases, require disapplication of primary legislation that would otherwise diminish rights protected by the Belfast/Good Friday Agreement.
2. On 30 January 2025, the Border Security, Asylum and Immigration Bill was introduced in Parliament. That Bill has since been enacted as the Border Security, Asylum and Immigration Act 2025, receiving Royal Assent on 2 December 2025 and now largely in force. The Act repeals the key impugned provisions of the IMA 2023, including the duty-to-remove regime and associated sections (such as ss 22–28), thereby removing the central statutory mechanism that underpinned the High Court's findings of incompatibility.

4.277

In light of these developments, the applicants in *Re JR295* (the Northern Ireland Human Rights Commission and **the** asylum-seeking child) applied to the Court of Appeal for a stay of the Secretary of State's appeal, arguing that it had become academic or, at least, that it should be stayed pending determination of the *Dillon* appeal. The Court of Appeal granted that stay, effectively suspending the appeal on the merits of the Art 2 issues.

4.278

The Secretary of State appealed to the Supreme Court against the Court of Appeal's grant of the stay, contending that the Court of Appeal had erred in treating the appeal as academic or otherwise in ordering a stay. The Supreme Court case (UKSC/2025/0084, with a linked NIHRC case UKSC/2025/0085) is framed as a challenge to the propriety of the stay itself, not to the underlying declarations of incompatibility or disapplication orders. Permission to appeal on the merits of the substantive Windsor Framework issues in the NIHRC case was refused by the Supreme Court on 28 July 2025, but the stay-appeal in *JR295* remains live and is distinct from any merits-based review.

4.279

At the time of writing (January 2026), the substantive appeal in *Re JR295* remains stayed; the Supreme Court proceedings concern whether the Court of Appeal was correct to grant that stay, rather than the underlying compatibility of the IMA provisions with Art 2 of the Windsor Framework or the ECHR.

5 Safeguarding in immigration and criminal detention – children and adults at risk

Silvia Nicolaou Garcia, Jim Robottom and Michelle Brewer

Introduction

5.1

This chapter[1] addresses the legal and policy frameworks governing the safeguarding of children and adults who are subject to immigration control and may be detained. It focuses particularly on those who are victims or potential victims of trafficking, modern slavery, or other forms of exploitation, and who may be at heightened risk due to their age, vulnerability, or circumstances of detention. (Since this chapter was finalised, the Border Security, Asylum and Immigration Act 2025 received royal assent on 2 December 2025, repealing the majority of the Illegal Migration Act 2023. See fn 64 at para **5.96**.)

5.2

This chapter should be read alongside the following:

Chapter 1:	Legal foundations: defining slavery, servitude, forced or compulsory labour and human trafficking
Chapter 3:	A trauma-informed approach
Chapter 4:	Identification of victims of human trafficking and modern slavery: the national referral mechanism and Art 4 ECHR
Chapter 6:	Age disputes in immigration and criminal proceedings
Chapter 8:	Special measures for victims of human trafficking and slavery
Chapter 10:	Criminal defences

1 Previous editions of this Chapter were authored by Shu Shin Luh and Christine Beddoe.

Structure of the chapter

5.3

This chapter is divided into three parts, reflecting the distinct statutory duties, procedural safeguards, and practical considerations that arise in relation to safeguarding obligations under Article 4 ECHR, the protection of children in immigration and criminal detention, and the safeguarding of adults who may be vulnerable or at risk in immigration detention.

5.4

Part 1 examines Art 4 of the European Convention on Human Rights (ECHR) and positive obligations arising specific to safeguarding and detention.

5.5

Part 2 examines the safeguarding of children within immigration and criminal detention contexts. It begins by outlining the legal foundations of child protection, including the Children Act 2004, the Modern Slavery Act 2015 ('MSA 2015'), and the UN Convention on the Rights of the Child. It then considers how vulnerability is assessed and the statutory duty to notify and to refer children into the National Referral Mechanism (NRM). The risks associated with detention are explored in depth, including the potential for children to go missing or be re-trafficked. The role of Independent Child Trafficking Guardians (ICTGs) is highlighted as a key protective measure. The analysis also addresses the impact of immigration control on children's welfare and the legal constraints governing the detention of children and families.

5.6

Part 3 focuses on safeguarding adults in immigration detention. It outlines the statutory powers of detention and the evolution of policy concerning vulnerable adults, including victims of torture and trafficking. The chapter reviews the Detention Centre Rules 2001, the Rule 35 mechanism, and the findings of the Shaw Review. It then sets out the Adults at Risk framework introduced by the Immigration Act 2016, including the evidentiary thresholds and decision-making guidance. The final sections address safeguarding considerations for victims of modern slavery and the legal duties of local authorities under the Care Act 2014 when planning for release and support in the community.

5.7

Throughout, the chapter highlights the intersection between safeguarding duties and immigration enforcement, and the importance of multi-agency cooperation, early identification, and trauma-informed practice. It aims to equip practitioners with a clear understanding of the legal obligations and practical tools necessary to protect vulnerable individuals in detention settings.

Part I: Art 4 ECHR – positive and substantive rights

5.8

The statutory duties and policy frameworks governing the safeguarding of children and vulnerable adults, including in contexts of immigration detention and victim protection, must be interpreted in accordance with Art 4 of the ECHR. Where there is a credible suspicion that a child or vulnerable adult has been subjected to harm within the scope of Art 4, the State is under a positive obligation to take protective and procedural action. These obligations are examined in detail in **Chapters 4** and **10**.

5.9

The statutory framework governing these groups must therefore be interpreted and applied through the lens of Art 4's positive obligations. In consequence, all statutory duties must operate, where engaged, in a manner that gives practical effect to those obligations and aligns with the protective and procedural requirements they impose.

5.10

A failure to do so may not only constitute a breach of the positive obligations under Art 4 but may also give rise to further substantive violations, including under Arts 3 and 4 of the ECHR.

The hierarchical status of Art 4 ECHR

5.11

Art 4 of the ECHR, alongside Arts 2 and 3, enshrines one of the Convention's core values: the absolute prohibition of slavery, servitude, forced or compulsory labour and human trafficking. Unlike qualified rights such as Art 8 ECHR, which are subject to proportionality and justification, Art 4(1) declares unequivocally that 'no one shall be held in slavery or servitude.' This prohibition admits no exceptions and is non-derogable under Art 15(2) of the Convention, even in times of public emergency.

Art 4 ECHR in the hierarchy of international norms

5.12

The prohibitions contained in Art 4 form part of customary international law and are recognised as *jus cogens* norms, peremptory principles from which no derogation is permitted. They also give rise to *erga omnes* obligations, binding all states irrespective of specific treaty commitments (see **Chapter 1**). Slavery is expressly categorised as a crime against humanity under Art 7 of the Rome Statute of the International Criminal Court, placing it within the same tier of international concern as torture and other forms of inhuman or degrading treatment prohibited under Art 3 ECHR.

5.13

The definitional scope of slavery, servitude, forced or compulsory labour, and human trafficking is examined in detail in **Chapter 1**.

Positive obligations under Art 4 ECHR

5.14

In addition to its negative obligations, Art 4 of the ECHR imposes both substantive and procedural positive duties on Contracting States. These obligations are designed to ensure the practical and effective protection of individuals, adults and children alike, from slavery, servitude, forced or compulsory labour, and human trafficking.

5.15

The positive obligations under Art 4 ECHR have been progressively shaped through the jurisprudence of the European Court of Human Rights (ECtHR). The Court interprets Art 4 in close alignment with Arts 2 and 3, recognising that the duties to prevent and respond to violations under these provisions share a common normative foundation. These Articles reflect what the Court has described as 'basic values' of democratic societies, a characterisation affirmed in *SM v Croatia*[2] and further supported in *Rantsev v Cyprus and Russia.*[3] Accordingly, the positive obligations developed under Arts 2 and 3, concerning the right to life and the prohibition of torture and inhuman or degrading treatment, are directly relevant to the interpretation and application of positive obligations arising in Art 4.

5.16

Substantively, states must take proactive operational measures to prevent and respond to exploitation. Procedurally, they are required to investigate and act where there is a credible suspicion that a person is a victim or at real risk of becoming one. In *BB v Slovakia*[4], the European Court of Human Rights (ECtHR) clarified that such suspicion is triggered by *prima facie* evidence of trafficking, evidence which, unchallenged, could establish a violation of Art 4.

2 *SM v Croatia* App no 60561/14, 25 June 2020.
3 *Rantsev v Cyprus and Russia,* App no 25965/04, 7 January 2010.
4 *BB v Slovakia* (2022) App no 48587/21, 24 October 2024.

Two-stage framework for assessing breach of Art 4 ECHR

5.17

The ECtHR assesses potential breaches of Art 4 ECHR through a two-stage framework, focusing first on the state's awareness of risk and then on the scope of its obligations.

Stage One: awareness of risk

5.18

The initial question is whether the State authorities knew or ought to have known of circumstances giving rise to a credible suspicion that an individual had been trafficked, held in slavery or servitude, subjected to forced or compulsory labour, or was at real and immediate risk of such treatment. This threshold is fact-sensitive and may be met by *prima facie* evidence or indicators of Art 4 harms.

Stage Two: scope of the state's positive obligations

5.19

Once credible suspicion arises, the state is required to discharge a range of positive obligations under Art 4, which include:

- **Legislative Duty**: Establishing a legal and administrative framework that prohibits and prevents trafficking and related Art 4 harms (*Prevention Duty*).
- **Operational Duty**: In individual cases taking protective measures to prevent trafficking and safeguard potential or recognised victims (*Protection and Recovery Duties*).
- **Investigative Duty**: Conducting an effective investigation into credible allegations of trafficking or other Art 4 violations (*Investigatory Duty*).
- **Restorative Duty**: Providing restitution or redress for harm suffered as a result of trafficking or related abuses under Art 4 (*Restorative Duty*).

5.20

This structured approach reflects the Court's emphasis on ensuring that the rights guaranteed under Art 4 are not merely theoretical but practical and effective.

Dual aims

5.21

In *VCL* and *AN v United Kingdom*[5], the ECtHR held that the duty to take operational measures under Art 4 has two principal aims:

- Protective Duty: to protect the victim from further harm; and
- Recovery Duty: to facilitate his or her recovery.

5.22

The scope and content of the above duties will be informed by the international framework concerning children such as the UN Convention on the Rights of the Child (UNCRC) and ILO Convention No 182 (the Convention concerning the Prohibition and Immediate Action for the Elimination of the Worst Forms of Child Labour, 1999) (see **Chapter 1**). Those duties will require a child specific analysis.

Interrelationship between Arts 3 and 4 ECHR in the protection of children and vulnerable adults

5.23

While Art 4 of the ECHR is central to cases involving trafficking, slavery, and related practices, it must not be considered in isolation from Art 3, particularly in contexts involving detention, recovery and assistance, or removal. The ECtHR has consistently recognised that Art 3 may be violated not only by direct acts of ill-treatment but also by omissions, especially where vulnerable individuals are under the control or care of the authorities.

5.24

In *Pretty v United Kingdom*[6], the Court held that suffering arising from naturally occurring illness may fall within the scope of Art 3 where such suffering is, or risks being, aggravated by conditions or treatment attributable to the State, including through detention or expulsion. This principle is of relevance in cases involving children or vulnerable adults who may be subject to immigration detention or removal without adequate safeguards.

5 *VCL and AN v United Kingdom,* App nos 77587/12 and 74603/12, 16 February 2021.
6 *Pretty v United Kingdom,* App no 2346/02, 29 April 2002.

5.25

Further, in *Keenan v United Kingdom*[7], the Court illustrated that the distinction between negative and positive obligations under Art 3 is not always clear-cut. Where a person with mental health vulnerabilities is in custody, a breach may arise from a combination of acts and omissions by the State.

5.26

This reinforces the principle that State responsibility under Art 3 extends not only to direct harm but also to failures to protect individuals from foreseeable risks.

5.27

In the context of children and vulnerable adults who may be victims of trafficking or other Art 4 violations, these jurisprudential developments underscore the need for safeguarding frameworks to operate in a manner that is consistent with both Arts 3 and 4. The failure to do so may result in breaches of the Convention, not only in respect of the positive obligations under Art 4 but also under the substantive protections afforded by Art 3.

Part II: safeguarding children

5.28

An assessment of whether a child is being exploited or is at risk of exploitation, including where there is reason to believe a child is a victim of trafficking, slavery, servitude, forced or compulsory labour (slavery or related harms), is first and foremost a child protection decision. These harms are serious criminal offences under ss 1-4 of the MSA 2015 and are child abuse.

5.29

The Children Act 2004, s 11(2) requires specified public authorities in England, including children's services, police, youth offending teams, schools and health authorities to exercise their functions having due regard to the need to safeguard and promote the welfare of children, and s 10 requires all authorities to cooperate with each other in doing so. In Wales, ss 5–7 of the Social Services and Well-being (Wales) Act 2014 impose duties to promote the well-being of children who require care and support, and to do so with specific regard to the United Kingdom's obligations under the UN Convention on the Rights of the Child.

7 *Keenan v United Kingdom*, App no 27229/95, 3 April 2001.

Integrated legal and policy framework for safeguarding children: general protections and responses to trafficking and modern slavery

The Children Act 2004

5.30

The Children and Social Work Act 2017 replaced Local Safeguarding Children Boards (LSCBs) with multi-agency safeguarding arrangements, inserting ss 16E–16G into the Children Act 2004. The three statutory safeguarding partners: the local authority, the chief officer of police, and the integrated care board (formerly the clinical commissioning group) are responsible for making arrangements for themselves and relevant agencies to work together for the purpose of safeguarding and promoting the welfare of children in their area. Working Together to Safeguard Children (December 2023)[8] requires these safeguarding partners to develop and publish their local arrangements, including localised policies and guidance on trafficking and exploitation. These arrangements should be publicly available via the safeguarding partnership website. The equivalent in Wales is made under the Social Services and Well-Being Act 2014, s 134.

Working together to safeguard children: multi-agency statutory and policy guidance on protecting children from trafficking, slavery, and exploitation

5.31

Working Together to Safeguard Children[9] remains the primary multi-agency guidance in England and sits alongside local arrangements and devolved frameworks in Wales, Scotland and Northern Ireland. It is updated periodically; the current edition at the time of writing (December 2023) consolidates earlier versions and continues to set the statutory expectations on how agencies should work together to identify and respond to children at risk of trafficking, slavery, servitude and forced or compulsory labour. This chapter proceeds based on that edition while recognising that practitioners must always refer to the most recent iteration of the guidance in force in their jurisdiction.

8 Department for Education, *Working Together to Safeguard Children: A guide to multi-agency working to help, protect and promote the welfare of children* (Statutory guidance, December 2023) https://www.gov.uk/government/publications/working-together-to-safeguard-children--2 accessed [23 August 2025]. The preceding guidance was published in 2011 by the Department for Education and the Home Office jointly published the practice guidance. See Department for Education/Home Office, *Safeguarding children who may have been trafficked* (October 2011), available at: www.gov.uk/government/publications/safeguarding-children-who-may-have-been-trafficked-practice-guidance, last accessed 29 March 2025.

9 Ibid.

5.32

The guidance applies to organisations and agencies who have functions relating to children and specifically to all local authorities, integrated care boards (ICBs) and the Chief Constable of Police within the local authority area[10]. It covers the broader responsibilities of all authorities who may have first contact with children suspected to be trafficked or exploited. Similar multi-agency guidance exists in Scotland and Northern Ireland.

5.33

The guidance is published alongside *Working together to safeguard children guidance on the statutory framework*[11] which brings together the key legislation relevant to safeguarding and promoting the welfare of children. The guidance has developed to better equip those agencies working with children at risk or have been trafficked or subjected to slavery or related harms[12].

5.34

The NSPCC[13] has collated published guidance by all four governments in the UK to help professionals identify and respond to a child who may have been trafficked (or a victim of slavery and related harms).

5.35

Published guidance is supplemented by *Care of Unaccompanied Migrant Children and Child Victims of Modern Slavery: Statutory Guidance for Local Authorities*, issued under s 7 of the Local Authority Social Services Act 1970. This provision requires local authorities, when exercising their social services functions, to act under the general guidance of the Secretary of State[14]. Although the statutory guidance is formally addressed to Chief Executives, Directors of Children's Services, and Lead Members for Children's Services, it is also relevant to the police and the Home Office, given their joint responsibility to cooperate with local authorities in safeguarding children. This guidance applies exclusively to England.

---

10 Previously these were the clinical commissioning group, a clinically led NHS organisation responsible for planning and commissioning most hospital and community health services in their area and were dissolved in July 2022.

11 Department for Education, *Working Together to Safeguard Children: Statutory Framework – Legislation Relevant to Safeguarding and Promoting the Welfare of Children* (December 2023) <https://assets.publishing.service.gov.uk/media/65797f1e0467eb000d55f689/Working_together_to_safeguard_children_2023_-_statutory_framework.pdf> accessed 6 October 2025.

12 Servitude, forced or compulsory labour (see Chapter 1 of this book).

13 NSPCC Learning, *Child trafficking and modern slavery* (NSPCC, updated 2023) https://learning.nspcc.org.uk/child-abuse-and-neglect/child-trafficking-and-modern-slavery accessed [accessed 23 August 2025].

14 Department for Education, *Care of unaccompanied migrant children and child victims of modern slavery Statutory guidance for local authorities* (November 2017), available at: https://www.gov.uk/government/publications/care-of-unaccompanied-and-trafficked-children, last accessed 23 August 2025.

5.36

Separate guidance applies in Wales, notably the *Child Trafficking: Operational Handbook*[15], which is intended to be used alongside the *All Wales Child Practice Guide: Safeguarding Children Who May Be Trafficked*[16] and the *Wales Safeguarding Procedures*[17].

5.37

In September 2008, the UK announced that it would lift its reservation to the 1989 UN Convention on the Rights of the Child (UNCRC) in respect of immigration matters concerning children. That announcement marked a significant step towards bringing the Home Office's obligations to safeguard and promote children's welfare closer into line with the framework in s 11 of the Children Act 2004, which had already required a wide range of public authorities in England and Wales (including local authorities, the police, youth offending teams, NHS bodies, schools and others)[18] to discharge their functions having regard to the need to safeguard and promote the welfare of children. In Scotland, broadly comparable duties to safeguard and promote children's welfare have long existed under the Children (Scotland) Act 1995, and, more recently, the UNCRC (Incorporation) (Scotland) Act 2024 has gone further by requiring devolved public authorities not to act incompatibly with the 'UNCRC requirements', thus giving the Convention direct effect in Scots law within devolved competence.

Section 17 support for NRPF families receiving MSVCC Assistance: R (GW) v Dudley MBC

5.38

The High Court's decision in *R (GW) v Dudley Metropolitan Borough Council*[19] provided important clarification on the scope of s 17 of the Children Act 1989 ('CA 1989') in cases involving families with no recourse to public funds (NRPF), particularly where a parent is a potential victim of trafficking or modern slavery receiving support under the Modern Slavery Victim Care Contract (MSVCC). The judgment addresses the interaction between MSVCC support and local

15 Welsh Government, *Child Trafficking: Operational Handbook* (September 2014), available at: https://gov.wales/sites/default/files/publications/2019-05/operational-handbook-child-trafficking.pdf, last accessed 29 March 2025.

16 Wales Safeguarding Procedures, *Responding to concerns about child trafficking* (Safeguarding Wales, updated 2023) https://safeguarding.wales/en/chi-i/chi-i-c6/c6-p3/ accessed [23 August 2025].

17 Wales Safeguarding Procedures, *Child safeguarding procedures* (Safeguarding Wales, updated 2023) https://safeguarding.wales/en/chi-i/ accessed [23 August 2025].

18 See the Children Act 2004, s 11(1) for the full list.

19 *R (GW) v Dudley Metropolitan Borough Council* [2025] EWHC 2140 (Admin).

authority duties under s 17, the correct legal threshold for assessing need, and the relevance of immigration status and returnability in determining eligibility.

5.39

The Court affirmed that s 17 support remains available to NRPF families, even where other forms of support such as MSVCC are in place. The judgment reinforces the need for lawful, holistic, and forward-looking assessments that focus on the child's welfare, rather than applying inappropriate thresholds or making assumptions about immigration outcomes. It also underscores the importance of respecting the statutory framework governing victims and the limits of local authority discretion in such cases.

MSVCC support does not preclude s 17 assistance

5.40

The Court held that receipt of MSVCC support does not exclude eligibility for s 17 support. There is no statutory provision preventing a local authority from providing s 17 assistance to a family receiving MSVCC support. The Essential Living Rate and Child Dependent Rate are subsistence-level provisions and do not necessarily meet broader welfare needs. The Recovery Rate, aimed at the adult potential victim's recovery, is not intended to meet the needs of dependent children.

5.41

Local authorities must conduct a holistic assessment of the child's needs, considering all sources of support. MSVCC support may be relevant to the assessment but cannot be treated as determinative or sufficient in itself.

Immigration status and returnability must be lawfully considered

5.42

The Court held that a local authority would act unlawfully if it concluded a child of an adult potential victim of trafficking or modern slavery was excluded from s 17 CA 1989 support because the family could return to their home country (or only offered support for them to do so), if that would force them to leave the UK.

5.43

It was observed that such an approach would, in substance, amount to requiring a potential victim of trafficking to leave the United Kingdom, in breach of s 61 of the Nationality and Borders Act 2022, as explained in *R (AM) v Secretary of State for the Home Department*[20]. Section 61 is, the Court held, even clearer than the well-established principle that a local authority may not pre-empt a pending and arguable application for leave to remain on ECHR grounds by withholding support in a manner that would force the applicant to depart the UK. By definition, a potential victim of trafficking has received a positive reasonable grounds decision; their claim cannot, therefore, be characterised as "obviously abusive or hopeless". In any event, whether a trafficking claim lacks merit is a matter for the National Referral Mechanism, not for the local authority, as *R (Clue)*[21] and *R (AM)* confirm.

5.44

A pending National Referral Mechanism decision[22] should constitute a barrier to removal, and local authorities cannot lawfully refuse support on the basis of anticipated departure from the UK. Immigration status must be considered in accordance with statutory and public law principles, and authorities must not pre-empt decisions by the Home Office.

5.45

The Court also noted that where a child is a potential victim of trafficking (or modern slavery), support may be implemented under s 17 of the CA 1989, as confirmed in *R (AM) v Secretary of State for the Home Department*[23], which recognised the applicability of s 17 duties in safeguarding and promoting the welfare of trafficked children.

Summary of approach to needs assessments for NPRF children

5.46

(i) Section 17 of the CA 1989 is the principal, and often sole, statutory mechanism through which local authorities provide support to children in families with no recourse to public funds (NRPF). While not all NRPF children will automatically qualify as 'in need,' the duty under s 17 and Schedule 2 is clear: authorities must assess whether a child's health or development is likely to be impaired without intervention. As established in *R (G) v Barnet*[24], this is a duty to assess, not an absolute duty to provide services. However, as affirmed in *R (AM) v SSHD*, the duty is not a hollow one, failure to conduct a lawful assessment is itself unlawful and amenable to judicial review. Crucially, under s 17(10), the legal focus is not merely on identifying need in the abstract, but on determining whether

20 *R (AM) v Secretary of State for the Home Department* [2024] 4 WLR 5 (HC) at [234].
21 *R (Clue) v Birmingham City Council* [2010] PTSR 2051.
22 See Chapter 4.
23 [2024] 4 WLR 5 (HC) at [234].
24 [2005] EWHC 1946 (Admin).

the child's needs would not be adequately met without the provision of services under Part III of the Act. This principle, drawn from *R (P)*[25] and *R (VC)*[26], underscores the importance of a holistic, forward-looking assessment that considers both the child's welfare and the adequacy of existing support[27].

(ii) This means the assessment can look at alternative (potential) support, from family or others, or authority provision outside Part III CA, like 'Early Help' (*R(BC)*)[28]. However, except for Asylum Support (under s 122(5) IAA), eligibility under s 17 CA 1989 is not excluded by support under another scheme, eg PVoT payments (*R(AM)*), still less eligibility under it (*R(VC)*). Authorities should be wary of anticipating a family's eligibility for Home Office support and should not require them to leave the UK if they have an arguable application for leave to stay: *R(Clue)*.

(iii) Similarly, the legal threshold for being 'in need' under s 17(10) CA 1989 is not the same as 'destitution' or 'homelessness' under other statutory schemes (*R(C) / R(DF)*[29]). However, just because a family may be 'destitute' or 'homeless' under another statutory scheme, that does not necessarily mean a child is 'in need' under s 17 CA 1989 (R(*VC*)).

(iv) Whether (i) a child is 'in need' and (ii) that need is for services under s 17/ Part III CA 1989, are evaluative questions for the professional judgement of social workers (*R(A)*).[30] The Court will not substitute its own judgement, but it will scrutinise the assessment on the usual judicial review grounds: (*R(G)*[31], *R(A)*) (albeit not with the same 'anxious scrutiny' as it will with an authority failing to meet an assessed need: *R(VC)*). These usual grounds include illegality (eg application of the wrong legal threshold like 'destitution', or superimposing a wrong legal exclusion, like receipt or eligibility of other support, save Asylum Support as in *R(VC)); or* because the family could leave the UK, when there is an arguable pending claim for leave (*R(Clue)); or* failing to take a forward-looking' approach: *R(TW)*)[32]. Alternatively, the ground may be procedural unfairness (eg not following Working Together guidance about the assessment process without good reason (R(DF)); unfairly rejecting credibility (R(O)); or relying on important new third-party information without giving the parents/ child a chance to respond (as alleged but rejected in *R (Ireneschild)*[33]). Or the ground for challenge could be irrationality, which is a 'high hurdle' (*R(BC))* but one which may be met if the assessment did not pay 'due

25 *R (P) v SSHD* [2001] 1 WLR 2002.
26 *R (VC) v Newcastle CC* [2012] PTSR 546.
27 Ibid.
28 *R (BC) v Surrey CC* [2025] EWCA Civ 719.
29 *R (C) v Southwark LBC* [2016] HLR 36 (CA); *R (DF) v Essex CC* [2025] PTSR 806.
30 *R (A) v Croydon LBC* [2009] 1 WLR 2557 (SC).
31 *R (G) v Barnet LBC* [2004] 2 AC 208 (HL).
32 *R (TW)) v Essex CC* [2025] EWCA Civ 4.
33 *R (Ireneschild) v Lambeth LBC* [2007] HLR 34 (CA)

regard' to the child's best interests and the need to safeguard and actively promote their welfare (*R(C)*).

(v) Whilst social workers' assessments must be 'diligent', appropriate respect must be given to their professional judgment, operating under pressure in financially straightened times with competing demands on resources (*R(O)*[34]). In particular, the assessment should be read by the Court fairly and realistically against its factual background in a practical way to discover its true meaning as the articulation of a social work judgement, not a legal one (McDonald / R(O)).

Section 55 safeguarding duty under the Borders, Citizenship and Immigration Act 2009

5.47

Section 55 of the Borders, Citizenship and Immigration Act 2009 imposes a statutory duty on immigration officers, when exercising functions on behalf of the Secretary of State under the Immigration Acts, to have regard to the need to safeguard and promote the welfare of children (s 55(2)(b)). In addition, officers must have regard to any guidance issued by the Secretary of State under s 55(3).

5.48

While the Act itself does not define the term 'welfare,' the statutory guidance *Every Child Matters*[35], issued under the Act, provides further clarification. At paragraph 1.4, the guidance states:

- protecting children from maltreatment;
- preventing impairment of children's health and development (where health means 'physical or mental health' and development means 'physical, intellectual, emotional, social or behavioural development');
- ensuring that children are growing up in circumstances consistent with the provision of safe and effective care;
- undertaking that role to enable those children to have optimum life chances and to enter adulthood successfully.

34 *R (O) v Lambeth* LBC [2016] EWHC 937 (Admin) and *McDonald v Kensington & Chelsea LBC* [2011] UKSC 33.

35 Every Child Matters Statutory guidance to the UK Border Agency on making arrangements to safeguard and promote the welfare of children, November 2009, available at: https://assets.publishing.service.gov.uk/media/5a7b9db0e5274a7318b8fd0b/change-for-children.pdf (accessed 23 August 2025).

5.49

This duty is closely aligned with the safeguarding obligations set out in the mirror provision of s 11 of the Children Act 2004. Although s 55 of the Borders, Citizenship and Immigration Act 2009 does not define 'welfare,' the courts have made clear that the duty to safeguard and promote welfare must be interpreted in a manner consistent with the spirit, if not the precise language, of the United Nations Convention on the Rights of the Child (UNCRC). Art 3(1) of the UNCRC requires that 'in all actions concerning children … the best interests of the child shall be a primary consideration.'

5.50

While the best interests of the child are not an overriding or absolute consideration, the Supreme Court in *ZH (Tanzania) v Secretary of State for the Home Department*[36] affirmed that they are a factor of the highest importance. The Court held that the child's best interests may only be outweighed by very strong countervailing factors[37].

5.51

The Every Child Matters Statutory Guidance, to which any person exercising any of the Secretary of State's immigration powers must have regard under s 55(3), provides expanded guidance governed by the following principles:

- the Home Office must maintain 'clear arrangements' and 'operation and policy instructions' to ensure the effectiveness of arrangements for safeguarding and promoting the child's welfare: paras 2.12 and 2.13;
- the duty is not limited to a requirement by the Home Office to put in place policies and a system for safeguarding children. It applies to individual decision-making across all areas of immigration law and is underpinned by a recognition that 'children cannot put on hold their growth or personal development until a potentially lengthy application process is resolved': para 2.20. See also *AAM v Secretary of State for the Home Department*[38];
- work with the child should be child-centred, take account of the child's views, informed by evidence, and have regard to the professional views and information available from other agencies involved with the child: paras 1.16 and 2.27;
- the onus is on the Home Office to demonstrate how a decision was made in compliance with the Borders Citizenship and Immigration Act 2009,

36 *ZH (Tanzania) v Secretary of State for the Home Department* [2011] UKSC 4, [2011] 2 AC 166 per Lady Hale at [23].
37 Ibid. Lady Hale at [25]–[27] and [33], Lord Hope at [44], and Lord Kerr at [46].
38 [2012] EWHC 2567 (QB) at [119].

s 55 both by the implementation of an operational policy and/or on an individual basis.

5.52

Further published guidance[39] records that the statutory duty must demonstrate:

- Fair treatment which meets the same standard a British child would receive;
- The child's interests being made a primary, although not the only consideration;
- No discrimination of any kind;
- Asylum applications are dealt with in a timely fashion;
- Identification of those that might be at risk from harm.

5.53

In *Nzolameso v Westminster City Council*[40], the Supreme Court held (at [24]–[27]) that the s 11 Children Act 2004 duty, which is analogous to that under s 55, applies not only to the formulation of general policies and practices, but also to their application in an individual case. This entails identifying 'the principal needs of the children, both individually and collectively, and having regard to the need to safeguard and promote them when making the decision': per Baroness Hale at [27].

5.54

In *R (CAO) v Secretary of State for the Home Department*, the Supreme Court held that, contrary to the obiter statement by Baroness Hale in *ZH (Tanzania)*[41], on an appeal against a negative asylum decision which engages the interests of a child (and therefore Art 8 ECHR), the First Tier Tribunal does not itself have to comply with the specific statutory duties under s 55(1) and (3), which are imposed on Home Office officials only. The First Tier Tribunal's role on appeal is to decide for itself whether removal is lawful in accordance with its duties under the Human Rights Act 1998 and Art 8 ECHR. A failure by Home Office officials to refer to the s 55(3) Guidance in making individual decisions will not in itself render such decisions unlawful, but in substance they must comply with the s 55(1) duty[42]. However, the Supreme Court made clear that:

39 Home Office, *Statutory Guidance: Children Act 1989 – Section 55 Guidance on the Duty to Refer* (2018) https://assets.publishing.service.gov.uk/media/5a81985ee5274a2e87dbe787/Section_55_v12.pdf accessed 23 August 2025.

40 *Nzolameso v Westminster City Council* [2015] UKSC 22, [2015] 2 All ER 942.

41 At [24].

42 [70]-[82].

'it is good practice for the decision-maker to refer to the duty and the matters to which it calls attention in terms, in order to demonstrate that the duty has indeed been complied with and put the question beyond doubt[43].

5.55

The limitations of assessing the best interests of the child solely through the framework of Art 8 ECHR have been the subject of sustained academic critique'[44].

The Modern Slavery Act 2015

Section 45: defence for slavery or trafficking victims who commit an offence

5.56

This is examined in detail in **Chapter 10**, where the defence available to children is distinguished from that applicable to adults.

Section 48: independent child trafficking advocates

5.57

This provision requires the Secretary of State to make arrangements for independent child trafficking advocates to be available to support and represent children where there are reasonable grounds to believe they may be victims of human trafficking. These advocates must act in the child's best interests and promote their well-being, including assisting with access to legal and other support services where appropriate.

5.58

The arrangements must, as far as practicable, ensure that the advocate is independent of those responsible for making decisions about the child. Provision may also be made for payments to those carrying out these functions.

43 At [82].

44 Jonathan Collinson, 'Making the Best Interests of the Child a Substantive Human Right at the Centre of National Level Expulsion Decisions' (2020) 38(3) *Netherlands Quarterly of Human Rights* 169; Jonathan Collinson, 'Beyond Decisions About a Child and Decisions Affecting a Child in Deportation Cases' (University of Huddersfield).

5.59

The Secretary of State is required to make regulations governing the operation of the advocacy scheme, including the conditions under which advocates may act, the process for their appointment, the timing of appointments, and the duties of public authorities to cooperate with advocates and provide access to relevant information.

5.60

Although section 48 of the Act provides a statutory basis for the Independent Child Trafficking Guardianship (ICTG) service, the full regulatory framework envisaged by the legislation has not yet been implemented. Specifically, the Secretary of State has not made the regulations required under section 48(6), which would formally define the scope, appointment process, and functions of independent child trafficking advocates, as well as the obligations of public authorities to cooperate with them.

The Interim Independent Child Trafficking Guardianship (ICTG) Service: legal basis, statutory guidance, scope and impact

5.61

The ICTG service operates under interim arrangements commissioned by the Home Office and delivered by Barnardo's. These arrangements are supported by statutory guidance and internal procedural tools, but they do not yet reflect the comprehensive regulatory scheme contemplated by the Act. As a result, while the service has developed a robust and responsive model of support, its reach remains limited and its legal footing incomplete.

5.62

The absence of regulations means that certain statutory duties, such as the requirement for public authorities to recognise and facilitate the advocate's role, are only enforceable in areas where the ICTG service is operational and under the terms of existing guidance. This has led to inconsistencies in access and implementation across local authorities and has prompted calls from practitioners and advocacy groups for the regulations to be brought forward and the service expanded nationally.

5.63

Initially focused on children without a parental figure in the UK, the service has evolved to include indirect support via Regional Practice Coordinators (RPCs) for children with parental responsibility, and more recently, piloted roles for Regional Practitioners and Post-18 Guardians to support young people with exceptional needs or those transitioning into adulthood[45].

5.64

The Home Office has developed interim guidance[46] and an RP flowchart (Appendix C)[47] to assist in identifying individual children who may benefit from Receiving Person (RP) support, and to outline the procedural steps necessary for such support to be provided. Referrals to RP support were frequently made through the child's Receiving Person Coordinator (RPC), which staff reported facilitated a smoother transition of care, as the children were already known to the Independent Child Trafficking Guardian (ICTG) service. In addition, frontline workers supporting children could initiate RP support requests directly, although these were typically preceded by consultation with other services involved in the child's care.

5.65

To determine whether a child met the threshold for exceptional need, an RP or RPC would complete a standardised RP template prior to discussion with an ICTG manager. This template incorporated a set of criteria used to assess exceptional need, including:

- concerns regarding familial exploitation;
- mental health or domestic abuse issues within the family;
- imminent transition to adult services;
- a history of limited engagement with local authority social services;
- pending legal proceedings;
- children from asylum-seeking families where those with parental responsibility require additional support[48].

---

45 Anna Skeels, Katy Huxley and Hannah Stott, *Outcomes for Children and Young People Affected by Modern Slavery: An Analysis of Independent Child Trafficking Guardianship Service Support in England and Wales* (Modern Slavery and Human Rights Policy and Evidence Centre, March 2024) https://modernslaverypec.org/resources/guardianship-service-outcomes accessed 23 August 2025, p 9-10.

46 Home Office, *Interim guidance for independent child trafficking guardians (accessible version)* (Statutory guidance, updated 14 May 2024) <https://www.gov.uk/government/publications/child-trafficking-advocates-early-adopter-sites/interim-guidance-for-independent-child-trafficking-guardians-accessible-version> accessed 7 October 2025.

47 https://assets.publishing.service.gov.uk/media/64b011c9fe36e000146fa92c/appendix-c-ictg-msa-evaluation.pdf.

48 Independent Child Trafficking Guardian (ICTG) Modern Slavery Act Evaluation, Home Office (2023) https://www.gov.uk/government/publications/independent-child-trafficking-guardian-ictg-msa-evaluation/independent-child-trafficking-guardian-ictg-msa-evaluation accessed 23 August 2025.

5.66

The ICTG service operates in only two-thirds[49] of local authorities in England and Wales[50]. Children who are within 100 days of turning 18 or whose age is disputed are excluded from the service[51]. Advocate groups have raised concerns that this limits the reach at critical points of vulnerability.

5.67

In areas where Independent Child Trafficking Guardians (ICTGs) are available, public authorities, including Immigration Enforcement, Border Force, and UK Visas and Immigration, who make decisions about or provide services to children must recognise, pay due regard to, and share relevant information with the ICTG. This obligation arises under regulations made pursuant to s 48(6)(e)(i) and (ii) of the MSA 2015.

5.68

There may be instances where a child first indicates that they have been trafficked during an asylum or police interview. In such cases, a referral to the ICTG Service should be made as soon as possible, and ideally on the same calendar day the information is disclosed. A 24/7 support line is available for advice[52], and referrals may also be submitted by authorised first responders via secure email[53].

5.69

Independent evaluations have found the ICTG Service to be flexible, trauma-informed, and responsive to the varied needs of children affected by modern slavery. The service operates a multi-layered support model, conceptualised as a 'pyramid', which includes safety, system navigation, advocacy, rights awareness, engagement in activities, and preparation for independence and transition[54].

---

49 Early Adopter Sites – Greater Manchester, Wales and Hampshire. The government extended the roll out of ICTGs to the West Midlands (October 2018); East Midlands (January 2019); and the London Borough of Croydon (April 2019) and in July 2019 and May 2024 published updated guidance. ICTG's now operate in: Greater London, Surrey, Essex, West Yorkshire, Merseyside, Kent, Warwickshire, North Yorkshire, Gloucestershire and Bristol, Lancashire, Bedfordshire, West Midlands, East Midlands, London Borough of Croydon, Great Manchester, Hampshire and Isle of Wight and Wales.

50 Ibid, p 10.

51 Ibid, p 10; see also Home Office, *Interim Guidance for Independent Child Trafficking Guardians: Accessible Version* (23 October 2018) https://www.gov.uk/government/publications/child-trafficking-advocates-early-adopter-sites/interim-guidance-for-independent-child-trafficking-guardians-accessible-version accessed 23 August 2025.

52 Tel: 0800 043 4303.

53 Email: trafficking.referrals@bypmk.cjsm.net.

54 ICTGs analysis full report (March 2024), p 31.

5.70

Children and young people consistently report positive outcomes, including feeling safer, more supported, and better understood. The ICTG practitioner's role as a 'trusted adult' is central to the service's effectiveness, particularly in promoting participation and safeguarding. The service also acts as a coordinating hub, supporting multi-agency collaboration and continuity of care[55].

5.71

Nonetheless, certain limitations have been observed and reported. The service does not currently have a mandate to provide post-18 support or to track long-term outcomes. Recommendations include expanding the service nationally, revising eligibility criteria, and developing participatory tools for outcome measurement. Legal practitioners should be aware of the ICTG Service as a key safeguarding partner in proceedings involving trafficked children and consider advocating for its broader implementation and integration into statutory frameworks.

Section 49: The Modern Slavery Act Statutory Guidance

5.72

The first iteration of the government's statutory guidance under s 49(1) of the MSA 2015 was published in March 2020[56]. For the first time, this guidance addressed child-specific aspects of trafficking and modern slavery. At the time of writing, the most recent iteration was updated in December 2025, with s 9 specifically addressing child victims of trafficking and modern slavery[57].

5.73

A welcome development in the statutory guidance is the inclusion of explanatory detail and definitions relating to child criminal exploitation, including county lines, as well as child sexual exploitation and an expanded list of risk indicators.

5.74

Notably, the guidance recognises the multi-nodal exploitation of children, including that victims of criminal exploitation may also be victims of sexual

55 Ibid, p 43–46.

56 Home Office, *Modern Slavery Act 2015 – Statutory Guidance for England and Wales (Version 1.00)* (March 2020) ('Statutory Guidance'), available at: https://www.gov.uk/government/publications/modern-slavery-how-to-identify-and-support-victims, last accessed 5 August 2020.

57 Home Office, *Modern slavery: statutory guidance for England and Wales (under s49 of the Modern Slavery Act 2015) and non-statutory guidance for Scotland and Northern Ireland* (GOV.UK, updated December 2025) accessed 31 January 2026.

exploitation. It strives to adopt a child-specific approach to defining the concepts of human trafficking, slavery, servitude, and forced or compulsory labour.

5.75

Advocacy groups consider that gaps remain in both policy and practice guidance concerning the protection of particularly vulnerable groups of children and young adults.

Section 50A (as inserted by the Nationality and Borders Act 2022)

5.76

Section 50A of the Act, inserted by s 64 of the NABA 2022, reinforces the statutory framework by imposing a duty on the Secretary of State to secure 'necessary assistance and support' for potential victims during the recovery period defined in s 61. While this provision applies to all victims, commentary from the House of Lords Library (2022) and ECPAT UK (2023) suggests that the evidential requirements may narrow access to protection, including for children.

5.77

As examined in **Chapters 4** and **14**, Art 13 of ECAT has directly informed the protective and procedural obligations under Art 4 ECHR (see *Chowdhury v Greece* discussed in Part 3 of **Chapter 14**). Read together, the MSA 2015 and the NABA 2022 have placed several ECAT provisions on a statutory footing.

Section 52: duty to notify

5.78

From 1 November 2015, specified public authorities in England and Wales have a statutory duty to notify the Secretary of State when they encounter an individual whom they have reasonable grounds to believe is a victim of modern slavery or human trafficking. This duty may be fulfilled in one of two ways[58]:

- **For children**, the duty is discharged by referring the potential victim into the National Referral Mechanism (NRM). Unlike adults, a child's consent is not required for the referral.

58 MSA 2015, s 52, Home Office, *Modern slavery: statutory guidance for England and Wales (under s49 of the Modern Slavery Act 2015) and non-statutory guidance for Scotland and Northern Ireland* (GOV.UK, updated December 2025) [4.2-4.4] accessed January 2026.

- **For adults**, where consent to enter the NRM is not given, the duty to notify is met by submitting a notification to the Home Office.

5.79

Schedule 2 of the Modern Slavery Act (Duty to Notify) Regulations 2015 sets out additional information that must be included in a notification where the potential victim is under the age of 18, or where the victim has provided consent. This includes the victim's name and date of birth, the names of individuals believed to have perpetrated the exploitation, and the names of any other persons suspected to be victims of the same perpetrators.

National Referral Mechanism

5.80

The NRM process is examined at length in **Chapter 4**.

5.81

Similar provisions arise in Scotland under s 38 of the Human Trafficking and Exploitation (Scotland) Act 2015. In Northern Ireland, these provisions are in s 13 of the Human Trafficking and Exploitation (Criminal Justice and Support for Victims) Act (Northern Ireland) 2015. All authorities, including UK Visas and Immigration, Border Force and Immigration Enforcement must comply with the duty[59].

5.82

Following an NRM referral, the Single Competent Authority ('SCA') must make the police aware of all modern slavery cases involving a child victim. In addition, the SCA must also contact the local authority (and independent child trafficked guardian where available).

5.83

In cases involving children, information is shared in accordance with the Principle of Information Sharing[60]. Upon receiving a referral from the NRM, the police must record it as a notifiable incident without delay. The Single Competent Authority (SCA) will subsequently inform the relevant police force of the outcome of the reasonable grounds' decision.

---

59 MSA 2015, s 52, Home Office, *Modern slavery: statutory guidance for England and Wales (under s49 of the Modern Slavery Act 2015) and non-statutory guidance for Scotland and Northern Ireland* (GOV.UK, updated December 2025) 31 January 2026.

60 Ibid. para 9.44.

5.84

If the decision is positive, the case must be recorded and counted as a crime. Where the decision is negative, or where the alleged criminality occurred entirely outside the UK, the case should be retained for intelligence purposes and recorded as a crime-related incident. In such instances, forces are not required to record the matter as a crime, although they may do so at their discretion.

5.85

Where a crime is recorded, the corresponding crime reference number must be shared with the SCA for inclusion in the case record. When providing this number, police should, where possible, indicate whether an investigation is underway or likely to be initiated[61].

Nationality and Borders Act 2022: child-relevant provisions and impacts

Statutory framework and amendments to the Modern Slavery Act 2015

5.86

Part 5 of the NABA introduced substantive amendments to the MSA 2015, several of which directly affect children who may be victims of trafficking or modern slavery.

5.87

Sections 58–64 place the identification and support of victims, including child victims, on a statutory footing for the first time. Section 61 establishes a statutory recovery period, during which removal or deportation is prohibited. This is particularly relevant to unaccompanied children and child asylum seekers, whose experiences of exploitation may only emerge after arrival in the UK.

5.88

As set out above s 64 inserts s 50A into the MSA 2015, imposing a duty on the Secretary of State to secure 'necessary assistance and support' during the recovery period.

61 Ibid. para 11.22.

5.89

Sections 58 and 59 introduce slavery and trafficking information notices, requiring individuals in immigration proceedings to disclose relevant evidence within specified timeframes.

5.90

Section 68 disapplies aspects of EU Directive 2011/36/EU (the Trafficking Directive) deemed incompatible with NABA 2022.

Consequential impact of Nationality and Borders Act 2022 on child victims

5.91

Although not all provisions of the NABA 2022 explicitly refer to children, their practical impact is significant. **Chapter 4** outlines legal challenges to the Public Order Disqualification provisions in the NABA 2022 which led to a pause in decision-making[62].

5.92

The following summarises key concerns identified by the Independent Anti-Slavery Commissioner and ECPAT UK in their joint report[63].

Alarming Increase in child trafficking

5.93

Between 2018 and 2023, referrals of children to the National Referral Mechanism (NRM) rose by 138%, with 7,432 children identified as potential victims in 2023 alone. This sharp escalation marks a crisis of unprecedented scale. Notably, children accounted for 44% of all NRM referrals, the highest proportion recorded to date, and 78% of those referred were British nationals. These figures challenge the prevailing assumption that trafficking is primarily an immigration issue. Instead, they highlight the domestic nature of exploitation,

62 In *R (ABW) v Secretary of State for the Home Department* [2025] EWHC 3280 (Admin), Morris J held on 17 December 2025 that the Secretary of State's Modern Slavery Statutory Guidance created an unlawful presumption in favour of making public order disqualification decisions under s 63 of the NABA 2022, and that s 63 must be construed compatibly with Art 13(3) ECAT as a narrow exception requiring case-by-case assessment. The court further held that the SSHD remains obliged to make conclusive grounds NRM decisions for potential victims of trafficking who have received reasonable grounds decisions, even where a POD has been applied. Permission to appeal was refused on 9 February 2026.

63 ECPAT UK and Independent Anti-Slavery Commissioner, 'Child Trafficking in the UK 2024: A Snapshot' (2024).

particularly through County Lines operations, where organised criminal networks systematically target and manipulate vulnerable British children. The resulting harm is profound, with long-term impacts including post-traumatic stress disorder, depression, and disrupted education, factors that entrench cycles of vulnerability within affected communities.

Legislative barriers to protection

5.94

The Nationality and Borders Act 2022 introduced evidentiary thresholds that many traumatised children are unable to meet, contributing to a significant increase in negative reasonable grounds decisions: from 10% in 2022 to 26% in 2023. The Act also contains disqualification provisions that exclude children with criminal records from protection, despite evidence indicating that 65% of those disqualified were victims of criminal exploitation. This framework risks penalising children for offences committed while under coercion or control and subsequently denies them access to safeguarding support.

5.95

The Illegal Migration Act 2023, when enacted, was reported to compound these concerns by disqualifying unaccompanied children from asylum consideration, mandating their removal upon turning 18, and permitting indefinite detention.

5.96

Notably, the provisions of the Illegal Migration Act relating to children have now been repealed[64]. However, the inadmissibility framework under the Nationality and Borders Act remains in force. The Home Office's current policy position reflects the statutory duty in s 55 of the Borders, Citizenship and Immigration Act 2009 to have regard to the need to safeguard and promote the welfare of children. Officers must consider the principles in the statutory guidance *Every Child Matters*, including fair treatment, the child's interests as a primary consideration, non-discrimination, timely processing, and identifying any risk of harm. Unaccompanied asylum-seeking children are not suitable for the inadmissibility processes, save that a child may be invited to withdraw their asylum claim where all the conditions for safe family reunification in a third country are met, and withdrawal is in the child's best interests. Families with

64 The Border Security, Asylum and Immigration Act 2025 received royal assent on 2 December 2025. Section 38 of the 2025 Act repeals the majority of the Illegal Migration Act 2023, including the duty to remove (ss 1–6), the provisions on unaccompanied children (ss 16–28), and certain modern slavery provisions (ss 21–28), but retains six clauses, notably s 12 (powers of detention) and s 59 (safe country list). The 2025 Act also introduces new provisions on border security and immigration enforcement. Practitioners should note that some IMA provisions discussed in this chapter have now been repealed by the 2025 Act, while others remain in force.

children under 18 remain subject to the family returns process, which may support removal on inadmissibility grounds[65].

Systemic challenges in child protection

5.97

Concerns have been raised regarding the accommodation of unaccompanied children by the Home Office, particularly in relation to the use of hotels. According to data reported by advocacy organisations and parliamentary sources, over 5,400 unaccompanied children were placed in non-statutory accommodation, with 467 recorded incidents of children going missing. Of these, 147 children were not located, and 90 remained missing as of October 2024.

5.98

This situation has been cited by commentators as indicative of wider systemic pressures within the child protection framework. Reports suggest that 81% of increased local authority spending is directed toward crisis intervention rather than preventative services, while residential care costs have risen by 66.2%. In some cases, children have reportedly been placed in unsuitable accommodation, including caravans, boats, and tents.

5.99

Further concerns have been expressed about the development of a two-tier care system for 16–17-year-olds, and research indicates that trafficked children are 1.2 times more likely to go missing from care. Organisations such as ECPAT UK and the Children's Commissioner have argued that these factors may contribute to increased vulnerability and risk of re-trafficking, underscoring the need for stable, secure, and child-centred care arrangements.

Inadequate prevention efforts

5.100

Despite data indicating that 78% of child trafficking victims are British nationals, concerns have been raised by organisations such as ECPAT UK and the Children's Society that domestic prevention efforts remain underfunded, while overseas anti-trafficking initiatives continue to receive priority investment.

5.101

This imbalance, they argue, risks missing critical opportunities for early intervention. In England alone, 1.4 million children are persistently absent from school, and school exclusions rose by over 20% in a single year. These trends

65 Home Office, *Inadmissibility: safe third country cases* (updated 27 June 2025) accessed 31 January 2026.

have prompted warnings that the education system is failing to identify and support children at risk of exploitation. The absence of statutory definitions for Child Criminal Exploitation (CCE) and Child Sexual Exploitation (CSE) has also been highlighted by practitioners as contributing to conceptual uncertainty, which may hinder effective recognition and response.

5.102

Additionally, fragmented multi-agency approaches across education, health, and social care are said to result in missed opportunities for early intervention when children first present with indicators of vulnerability.

Protection system gaps

5.103

Concerns have been raised about the consistency and effectiveness of the UK's child trafficking protection framework. Independent Child Trafficking Guardians (ICTGs) are currently available in only two-thirds of local authorities in England and Wales. Between 2020 and 2022, while 5,266 children were confirmed as victims of trafficking, fewer than 21 were granted discretionary leave to remain on trafficking grounds, a success rate of approximately 0.4% (ECPAT UK, 2023).

5.104

Transition into adulthood presents further challenges. Data indicates that 70% of children either withdraw from the National Referral Mechanism (NRM) or have their cases suspended before resolution. Only 13% are referred for adult support services, and just 6% receive such support (Children's Society, 2023). These figures suggest significant gaps in continuity of care.

5.105

Additional concerns include delays in accessing legal representation due to pressures on the legal aid system, and instances where child victims have been criminalised. Reports indicate that 18 children were wrongly charged with immigration offences, with 14 spending time in adult custodial settings (Refugee Council, 2024). These outcomes have led commentators to argue that the protection system may, in some cases, contribute to further harm rather than safeguarding vulnerable children.

Prosecution rates

5.106

Prosecution of child trafficking offences remains low. According to publicly available data, prosecutions declined from 32 in 2021 to 19 in 2023. The

Crown Prosecution Service does not routinely publish disaggregated data on child trafficking cases, which has prompted calls for greater transparency and accountability (Anti-Trafficking Monitoring Group, 2023).

5.107

Independent reviews have highlighted concerns about the criminal justice system's response. Survivors have reported negative experiences with law enforcement, including being treated as offenders rather than victims. Half of investigations were assessed as inadequate, often due to a lack of specialist training and awareness among officers (Children's Commissioner, 2023). These factors are said to contribute to a low-risk, high-reward environment for perpetrators, with limited deterrence and ongoing harm to victims.

Research and data gaps

5.108

The absence of comprehensive and consistent data collection has been identified as a barrier to effective policy development. For example, Department for Education figures recorded 2,710 trafficking cases, while the NRM reported 7,432 child referrals in the same period, highlighting discrepancies in how cases are identified and recorded across agencies (ECPAT UK, 2023).

5.109

There is currently no UK-wide published data on children considered under non-punishment provisions, making it difficult to assess the extent of victim criminalisation. Delays and limitations in responses to data requests from government departments have also been noted, raising concerns about institutional transparency.

5.110

Without systematic research into the effectiveness of prevention strategies or robust data-sharing mechanisms between safeguarding partners, policy decisions risk being made without a sufficient evidence base. This may result in resources being directed toward interventions of uncertain efficacy, while children remain exposed to exploitation.

Child-specific implications of proposed ss 58 and 59 of the NABA 2022

5.111

The Nottingham Rights Lab has identified several child-specific concerns in relation to ss 58 and 59 of the NABA 2022. If brought into force, these provisions would introduce Slavery and Trafficking Information Notices (STINs), which require individuals involved in immigration proceedings to disclose evidence relevant to their trafficking or slavery status within prescribed timeframes. Section 59 further stipulates that late compliance with a STIN may negatively affect the individual's credibility, unless there are 'good reasons' for the delay.

5.112

Although these provisions are not currently in force, the following concerns have been identified in anticipation of their potential application, particularly in cases involving children.

Lack of statutory distinction between adults and children

5.113

The legislation does not establish a clear statutory distinction between adult and child victims of trafficking, resulting in reliance on guidance rather than primary legislation for the protection of children. While the government has stated that children, defined as those under 18, are exempt from credibility assessments, it is unclear where this safeguard will be set out, if in guidance or secondary legislation this may be amended without any or minimal parliamentary oversight. This creates legal uncertainty and potential vulnerability, particularly in age assessment disputes. Research cited in the report indicates that 53% of individuals whose age was disputed were ultimately found to be children, underscoring the risk of subjecting minors to adult procedures.

Failure to account for trauma and child development

5.114

According to analysis by the Nottingham Rights Lab, Sections 58 and 59 do not adequately reflect the impact of trauma on victims' capacity or readiness to self-identify or disclose experiences within prescribed timeframes. This concern is particularly pronounced in relation to children, who may face additional developmental challenges that inhibit timely disclosure. The provisions do not sufficiently acknowledge that traumatic experiences can affect memory and recall, often resulting in delayed, fragmented, or initially inconsistent accounts. These patterns are especially common among children, who may lack the cognitive maturity to fully comprehend or articulate their experiences at the time they occur.

Contradiction of evidence-based understanding of child disclosure

5.115

The report highlighted that the provisions in Ss 58 and 59 appear inconsistent with the government's previously stated recognition that victims may not be able to disclose their experiences immediately or even identify themselves as victims. Academic research supports the view that disclosure is a complex and multi-dimensional process, which may unfold over an indeterminate period, even in environments characterised by trust and support. For children, this process is further complicated by developmental factors, coercive control or manipulation by traffickers, and fear or mistrust of authority figures.

Discriminatory application creating inequality

5.116

The Nottingham Rights Lab has raised concerns that the provisions in Ss 58 and 59 may give rise to discriminatory outcomes, potentially contravening Art 14 of the European Convention on Human Rights and Art 3 of the Council of Europe Convention on Action against Trafficking in Human Beings (ECAT). The framework appears to impose credibility penalties for delayed disclosure solely on victims with immigration claims, thereby creating unequal treatment among trafficking victims. This approach may disproportionately affect trafficked children, who frequently have complex immigration statuses and are at risk of being misidentified as adults, further compounding their vulnerability.

Conflict with Art 4 ECHR positive obligations

5.117

The analysis implicitly recognises that these provisions conflict with established jurisprudence that victims of trafficking cannot be required to identify themselves. Legal cases have affirmed that 'it can take victims a long time to come forward after their trafficking experience', and penalising delayed disclosure contradicts the state's positive obligations under Art 4 ECHR to identify and protect trafficking victims, particularly vulnerable children.

Guidance on safeguarding children vulnerable to trafficking and modern slavery: separated children, county lines, and missing persons

5.118

As with adults, children may be unaware that their situation is exploitative, harmful, or unusual. An enhanced list of child specific indicators is now included in the MSA 2015 statutory guidance[66] and both the general and child specific indicators should be consulted, and concerns recorded.

---

66 Home Office, *Modern slavery: statutory guidance for England and Wales (under s49 of the Modern Slavery Act 2015) and non-statutory guidance for Scotland and Northern Ireland* (GOV.UK, updated December2025) 31 January 2026], Annex A.

5.119

The College of Policing guidance on modern slavery directs that:

> 'Child victims of modern slavery are amongst the most vulnerable, the easiest to control and the least likely to admit to their situation. They may not show obvious signs of distress, as they may not realise that they have been enslaved or see themselves as being at risk of harm and in danger. Parents and relatives may also be involved in the exploitation of the child. Children are likely to be extremely loyal to their parents or carers so it is not likely that they will, of their own initiative, seek protection against such people.
>
> It is also possible that a child's experiences of modern slavery perpetrated by adults, and experience of corruption and abuse by police, officials and/or authorities in their home countries, may make them wary of all adults, including police officers. They may, therefore, be reluctant to disclose any information in an interview until they have built a trusting relationship with those interviewing. Interviews should take place in a child-friendly environment.
>
> During the interview, the child should be asked what measures would make them feel safe, how they perceive authority figures and people in uniform, and the police should clearly explain their role to the child. The child should be provided with emergency contact numbers, including 999, and know that these are free of charge. If a child is housed and goes missing before or after the interview, and is suspected of being enslaved or exploited, they should be treated as a missing person. A suitably trained person should conduct a debrief'[67].

Missing children, trafficking and slavery

5.120

In November 2016, ECPAT UK and Missing People published a report into unaccompanied and trafficked children who went missing from care. It was reported that more than a quarter of all trafficked children and over 500 unaccompanied asylum-seeking children went missing at least once in the year to September 2015, 207 of whom have not been found[68].

---

67 College of Policing, *Modern Slavery: First Response and National Referral Mechanism* (College of Policing, updated 2023) https://www.college.police.uk/app/major-investigation-and-public-protection/modern-slavery/first-response-and-national-referral-mechanism accessed 23 August 2025.

68 ECPAT UK and Missing People, *Heading back to Harm* (November 2016), available at: www.ecpat.org.uk/heading-back-to-harm-a-study-on-trafficked-and-unaccompanied-children-going-missing-from-care-in-the-uk, last accessed 29 March 2025.

5.121

In April 2022, ECPAT UK and Missing People published a further report into unaccompanied and trafficked children who went missing from care. The report found that the number of identified and suspected children who have gone missing from local authority care has increased, from 284 in 2018 to 378 in 2020: a 24.9% increase. It also found that 33% of trafficked children go missing from local authority care, in comparison to 1 in 10 looked after children and 1 in 100 children in the UK[69].

5.122

Certain groups of children are at particularly high risk of going missing. This may be due to coercion or control by traffickers, prior grooming, or fear of repercussions for themselves or their families if they do not return to those who exploit them. Some children may also struggle to trust authority figures, further increasing their vulnerability.

5.123

For example, children subjected to debt bondage, who owe a debt, or whose family members owe a debt for their journey, may feel compelled to return to traffickers.

5.124

Similarly, children who have been arrested for criminal offences may be especially vulnerable, both as potential witnesses to organised crime and due to fear of retaliation from those who exert control over them.

Statutory Guidance on missing children and trafficking risk

5.125

The *Statutory Guidance on Children Who Run Away or Go Missing from Home or Care* (2014), together with its accompanying flowchart, sets out procedural expectations for responding to children who go missing and are suspected of being victims of trafficking[70]. Paragraphs 73 to 79 of the guidance emphasise the shared responsibility of statutory agencies, including local authorities, police forces, the Home Office, and other relevant bodies, to collect, record, and share information to monitor and assess ongoing risk to the child.

69 ECPAT UK and Missing People, *When Harm Remains* (April 2022), available at: https://www.ecpat.org.uk/Handlers/Download.ashx?IDMF=bb993f93-9445-4f75-bc1e-d051d76ab668

70 Department for Education, *Statutory Guidance on Children Who Run Away or Go Missing from Home or Care* (2014) https://assets.publishing.service.gov.uk/media/5a7e089340f0b62302688bd0/Statutory_Guidance_-_Missing_from_care__3_.pdf accessed 23 August 2025.

5.126

The guidance recognises that risk is not static and may escalate rapidly, particularly in circumstances where the child is under stress. For example, risk may intensify following receipt of a phone call from a known associate or in anticipation of a court appearance. In such cases, the child may be more vulnerable to coercion, manipulation, or re-trafficking.

5.127

Importantly, the guidance stipulates that children who meet the profile of a trafficking victim and have gone missing, regardless of whether they have yet been referred to the National Referral Mechanism (NRM), should be treated by police as high-risk missing persons[71].

5.128

A child is considered high-risk where one or more of the following criteria apply:

- There are substantial grounds to believe that the child is in immediate danger due to their vulnerability;
- The child may have been the victim of a serious criminal offence;
- There are substantial grounds to believe that the public is at immediate risk.

5.129

These criteria are intended to ensure that safeguarding responses are proportionate to the level of risk and that appropriate protective measures are implemented without delay.

Criminal exploitation and county lines

5.130

A distinct cohort of children who go missing are those subject to criminal exploitation through county lines activity. This type of exploitation extends to all children and not just separated migrant children. For the s 45 MSA 2015 defence and its application to child victims of criminal exploitation, see Chapter 10 at **10.179**.

5.131

However, research does identify children with specific types of vulnerability who are particularly susceptible to this type of exploitation (learning differences, school exclusion, disabilities, care experienced, domestic violence or difficult domestic circumstances, living in areas with established gang presence and

71 See *R(TDT) v Secretary of State for the Home Department* [2018] EWCA Civ 1395, [2018] 1 WLR 4922.

influence or risks arising from minority ethnic background such as those in the Gypsy, Roma or Traveller communities or asylum seeking children or those without regularised immigration status[72]

5.132

The *Serious Violence Strategy* defines county lines as:

> 'Gangs and organised criminal networks involved in exporting illegal drugs into one or more importing areas [within the UK], using dedicated mobile phone lines or other forms of 'deal line'. They are likely to exploit children and vulnerable adults to move and store the drugs and money and they will often use coercion, intimidation, violence (including sexual violence) and weapons'[73].

5.133

Children exploited in this way may go missing from care placements or family homes, often reappearing in locations far from their usual residence. Their movements are typically controlled by criminal networks, and they may be coached, threatened, or otherwise manipulated to avoid detection or disclosure.

5.134

Detailed guidance on county lines exploitation is provided in the Home Office's *Criminal Exploitation of Children and Vulnerable Adults: County Lines Guidance*[74], the Crown Prosecution Service's *County Lines Offending: Legal Guidance* (2023)[75], and the statutory guidance issued under the Modern Slavery Act 2015.

Recognition of inherent vulnerability of separated children and trafficking, slavery or related harms

5.135

The Home Office acknowledges the general vulnerabilities of separated children. Within this cohort of children, it is important to recognise the distinct

72 Children's Rights Alliance for England, *Written Evidence to the Human Rights Committee for its Examination of the Eighth Periodic Report of the United Kingdom under the International Covenant on Civil and Political Rights* (February 2024) <https://crae.org.uk/sites/default/files/fields/download/FINAL%20CRAE%20Submission%20to%20ICCPR%20UK%20examination%205%20Feb%202024.pdf> accessed [31 January 2026].

73 *Serious Violence Strategy* (April 2018), available https://www.gov.uk/government/publications/serious-violence-strategy.

74 Home Office, *Criminal Exploitation of Children and Vulnerable Adults: County Lines Guidance* (2023) https://www.gov.uk/government/publications/criminal-exploitation-of-children-and-vulnerable-adults-county-lines/criminal-exploitation-of-children-and-vulnerable-adults-county-lines accessed 23 August 2025.

75 Crown Prosecution Service, *County Lines Offending: Legal Guidance* (2023) https://www.cps.gov.uk/legal-guidance/county-lines-offending accessed 23 August 2025.

and often heightened needs of those who have experienced trafficking or exploitation through modern slavery. These children represent a particularly vulnerable subgroup and require safeguarding responses that are specifically tailored to their experiences, beyond the standard provisions applicable to separated children more generally.

5.136

All children and young people are inherently vulnerable due to their age and developmental stage. However, assessing vulnerability requires professionals to look beyond verbal disclosures and to identify emotional, behavioural, and presentational indicators of risk. Timely action is essential, and appropriate protection measures should be implemented even in the absence of a direct disclosure from the child.

5.137

Guidance issued by the Association of Directors of Children's Services (ADCS) on trafficked children emphasises this approach, stating:

> '… Aside from the physical, sexual, or emotional abuse they may have suffered, many trafficked children have been forced by their traffickers to learn a story to tell if they are questioned. Many children and young people are under threat directly themselves or may have family members elsewhere who are under threat, or perceived threat. Children and young people may not know who they can trust. As a result, they may give information that is later contradictory to information provided initially. This is not necessarily an indication that a child or young person is trying to deceive social workers and should not be considered as such'[76]…

5.138

On discovery, children who are victims of human trafficking or modern slavery may not show any obvious signs of distress or imminent harm. PTSD and trauma responses in children at different developmental stages may vary significantly from adult presentations (see **Chapter 3**).

Operation Innerste and separated migrant children

5.139

Operation Innerste is a national, multi-agency safeguarding protocol in the UK, established in 2016 to address the specific risks faced by unaccompanied

76 ADCS, *Age Assessment Guidance* (October 2015), available at: http://adcs.org.uk/assets/documentation/Age_Assessment_Guidance_2015_Final.pdf, last accessed 29 March 2025.

migrant children, including those who are trafficked or seeking asylum, who go missing following arrival or initial contact with authorities. The protocol remains active and has undergone updates, most recently in October 2023[77], which included revised process guidance and broader implementation across police forces and local authorities.

5.140

By 2024, 38 to 39 out of 43 police forces in England and Wales had adopted Operation Innerste, reflecting its growing role in safeguarding practice. The key measures include:

Early rapport building

5.141

Operation Innerste brings together police, children's services, Independent Child Trafficking Guardians, Immigration Enforcement, and NGOs under a unified protocol. This multi-agency approach aims to reduce fragmented support and minimise trauma from repeated questioning. The protocol prioritises building trust and rapport with the child within the first 72 hours of contact. In one update, 98% of children remained in their placement at the 72-hour mark, suggesting early intervention may contribute to placement stability.

Immediate safeguarding focus

5.142

The protocol mandates partnership with Children's Social Care. Where delays occur in social worker attendance, the process may proceed to avoid compromising the child's safety. The protocol explicitly avoids questions about asylum or immigration status, focusing solely on safeguarding. Engagement is guided by the child's needs and rights, in line with domestic and international obligations under the UNCRC and ECHR Art 4.

Biometric identification

5.143

Police may take fingerprints and photographs to assist in identifying children at risk of going missing or being trafficked. This is framed as a safeguarding measure and should be explained in an age-appropriate manner.

77 National Police Chiefs' Council, *Operation Innerste: National Guidance for the Identification and Immediate Safeguarding of Unaccompanied Migrant Children* (Home Office, October 2023) https://assets.publishing.service.gov.uk/media/65393f23d10f3500139a696b/Op+Innerste.pdf accessed 23 August 2025.

5.144

The statutory basis for fingerprinting children is S 141 of the Immigration and Asylum Act 1999[78], which permits the taking of fingerprints from individuals aged 5 to 16 only if a responsible adult is present. However, this provision does not require a responsible adult for children aged 16–17, creating a statutory gap that has been widely criticised by differing groups[79].

5.145

The Scottish Biometrics Commissioner[80], in his 2023 Assurance Review, identified this gap as inconsistent with modern safeguarding standards and contrary to judicial developments, including the principles established in *R HC (a child, by his litigation friend CC) v The Secretary of State for the Home Department (1st Defendant) The Commissioner of Police of the Metropolis (2nd Defendant)*[81]. The Commissioner recommended that:

- Section 141 be amended to require a responsible adult for all children under 18.
- Biometric collection from children be authorised on a case-by-case basis by a senior officer (not below Inspector rank), considering the best interests of the child and the gravity of the offence.
- Blanket biometric collection policies be discontinued.

Standardised practice

5.146

Operation Innerste replaces inconsistent local practices with a national protocol, aiming to ensure all children receive comparable safeguarding responses regardless of where they present in the UK.

---

78 S141(3) of the Immigration and Asylum Act 1999 states that a 'responsible adult' is not required when taking fingerprints of anyone 16 years and over. However, the guidance provides that when dealing with a vulnerable unaccompanied migrant child (between the ages of 16 and 18), particularly where age cannot be verified and age requires assessment, best practice is to take fingerprints with a 'responsible adult' in attendance.

79 Emma Snaith, '*Deportation fears after police collect asylum-seeking children's biometric data*' (Liberty Investigates, 6 November 2023) https://libertyinvestigates.org.uk/Arts/deportation-fears-after-police-collect-asylum-seeking-childrens-biometric-data/ accessed 23 August 2025. Holly Maclean and Julia Swann, *Thematic Review of Biometric Data – Children and Young People's Perspectives* (Children and Young People's Centre for Justice, February 2023) https://www.cycj.org.uk.

80 *R (HC) (a child, by his litigation friend CC) v The Secretary of State for the Home Department (1st Defendant) The Commissioner of Police of the Metropolis (2nd Defendant)* [2013] EWHC 982 (Admin).

81 Scottish Biometrics Commissioner and Scottish Police Authority, *Joint Assurance Review of the Acquisition of Biometric Data from Children Arrested in Scotland* (Scottish Biometrics Commissioner, March 2023) Available at: https://www.biometricscommissioner.scot.

Information sharing and data protection

5.147

Agencies share information under strict data protection protocols to ensure rapid response if a child goes missing or is at risk. A 72-hour safeguarding check is required, using a standard email to the assigned social worker to confirm the child remains in safe accommodation.

5.148

However, the Commissioner's review found that Police Scotland's guidance fails to meet transparency standards under UK GDPR and the Scottish Biometrics Commissioner Act 2020. Specifically:

- Children are not adequately informed of the reasons for biometric collection, how their data will be used, or their rights to appeal.
- There is no clear policy on retention periods, and biometric data may be retained longer than legally permitted.

Referral to guardianship services

5.149

Children are referred to Independent Child Trafficking Guardians as soon as trafficking concerns arise, supporting early identification and protection.

Identified concerns and challenges in implementation of Operation Innerste

Dual use of biometric data

5.150

While biometric collection is intended for safeguarding, there is unease that data may be repurposed for immigration enforcement. This dual use risks undermining the protective intent of the protocol and may conflict with the child's best interests.

Informed consent and transparency

5.151

Children, often traumatised and without legal representation, may not fully understand the implications of biometric data collection. The absence of clear procedural safeguards and independent oversight increases the risk of misuse and erodes trust.

Role confusion between safeguarding and enforcement

5.152

The conflation of police roles, as both safeguarding agents and immigration enforcers, may deter disclosure, particularly among trafficked children fearing removal. This dynamic is incompatible with protective obligations under the UNCRC and ECHR.

Data retention and oversight

5.153

There is limited clarity on how long biometric data is retained and under what conditions it is deleted. The Commissioner's review found that retention periods for children's data often mirror adult standards, despite the heightened vulnerability of children. Recommendations include:

- Presumption in favour of deletion where lawful retention no longer applies.
- Improved management information to assess the utility and outcomes of biometric data collection.
- Public transparency on fingerprint and image metrics, not just DNA.

Lack of child-centred safeguards

5.154

Children and young people consulted in the thematic review expressed that biometric collection should only occur when necessary, proportionate, and justified. They emphasised the need for:

- Child-friendly environments.
- Trained officers.
- Trusted adults present during biometric procedures.
- Clear, accessible information about their rights.

Other prevention measures

Safeguarding children under trafficker control

5.155

The policy framework acknowledges that children may remain under the control of traffickers even after being placed in local authority care, detention, or custody. Without adequate support, such control can persist for extended periods, with serious implications for the child's safety and welfare.

5.156

To mitigate the risks associated with ongoing control by traffickers, safeguarding measures, although potentially intrusive in other contexts, may be necessary and proportionate when applied in the child's best interests. However, the implementation of such measures must be consistent with a trauma-informed approach (see **Chapter 3**) and informed by an understanding of the specific mechanisms of control used by traffickers, such as threats directed at the child or their family and friends. Failure to account for these dynamics when imposing safeguarding interventions may inadvertently exacerbate the child's trauma and increase the likelihood of the child attempting to return to their trafficker(s).

5.157

These measures may include:

- Monitoring contact with others and phone calls
- Identifying and tracing phone numbers found in clothing or possessions
- Examining SIM cards and tracking internet use
- Temporarily removing mobile phone and internet access
- Photographing the child and recording their clothing upon entry into care
- Escorting the child outside the home
- Placing children in specialist foster care out of area
- Conducting a multi-agency risk assessment to inform decisions about safe accommodation and the level of security required

5.158

Additional safeguarding precautions are necessary when children are held in immigration detention[82] or police custody, especially where co-defendants may pose a threat or influence the child's account[83].

82 See *R (TDT) v Secretary of State for the Home Department* [2018] EWCA Civ 1395, [2018] 1 WLR 4922.

83 Department for Education, *Statutory Guidance on Children Who Run Away or Go Missing from Home or Care* (2014) https://assets.publishing.service.gov.uk/media/5a7e089340f0b62302688bd0/Statutory_Guidance_-_Missing_from_care__3_.pdf accessed 23 August 2025.

Identification and safeguarding of trafficked children in the criminal justice system

5.159

This section should be read in conjunction with **Chapter 3** (Trauma-Informed Approach), **Chapter 6** (Age Disputes), and **Chapter 10** (Criminal Defences Available to Victims of Trafficking and Modern Slavery).

5.160

For any child or young person, where there is *prima facie* evidence that they have been trafficked or suffered slavery or related harms, then the protective and positive obligations under Art 4 are triggered[84]. That is evidence capable, if not challenged or countered[85], that they have been trafficked, held in slavery or related harms. This does not require the child or young person to cooperate with the authorities or self-identify as a victim. The case law is clear, the circumstances in which a child or young person is found can be sufficient to establish a credible suspicion that they are a victim of an Art4 abuse[86]. This is explicitly recognised in CPS published guidance[87].

5.161

CPS policy[88] has recognised that children are especially vulnerable to trafficking and exploitation and often require additional support. The policy confirms that the CPS treats child trafficking primarily as a child protection issue, recognising that child victims typically need welfare services and safeguarding. Their policy acknowledged that since trafficked children may be subject to criminal exploitation, their first contact is often with law enforcement. That prosecutors must work closely with police and child support organisations to ensure all relevant information is gathered and appropriate assessments are conducted.

5.162

When the first 24–48 hours of contact focus only on addressing the child or young person as an offender, the result is that the specific statutory safeguarding

84 *B.B. v Slovakia* App no 48587/21 (ECtHR, 24 October 2024) [79] and *S.M. v Croatia* App no 60561/14 (ECtHR, 25 June 2020) [113]–[114], [303].

85 See Chapter 14 which examines the 'credible suspicion' threshold.

86 *R (TDT) v Secretary of State for the Home Department* [2018] EWCA Civ 1395, [2018] 1 WLR 4922 and *VCL and AN v United Kingdom* (2021) ECHR 132.

87 Crown Prosecution Service, *Modern Slavery and Human Trafficking: Offences and Defences Including Section 45* (CPS, updated 2023) https://www.cps.gov.uk/legal-guidance/modern-slavery-and-human-trafficking-offences-and-defences-including-section-45 accessed 23 August 2025.

88 Crown Prosecution Service, *Policy for Prosecuting Cases of Human Trafficking* (CPS, 2011) https://www.cps.gov.uk/sites/default/files/documents/publications/policy_for_prosecuting_cases_of_human_trafficking.pdf accessed 23 August 2025.

and identification procedures for children who may be trafficked, experienced slavery or related harms are less likely to be triggered. Early indicators of trafficking, slavery or related harms, including behavioural and psychological indicators, are thus not observed, or recorded, and this has implications for subsequent immigration, criminal or care proceedings. If a child is subsequently released on police bail into the community or into local authority care without a robust risk assessment, then special protection measures will not be put into place and the risk of harm to the child escalates. The policy framework for safeguarding children and the MSA 2015 should prevent this from happening, but there are still significant gaps in training and management practices across the country.

Bail in criminal proceedings: children

5.163

Where the age of a young person charged with an offence is in dispute, the relevant legal considerations are addressed in **Chapter 6**.

5.164

See analysis below in respect of the interconnection between Arts 4 and 5 ECHR.

5.165

The UN Special Rapporteur on Trafficking in Persons, Siobhán Mullally, has reinforced the importance of protection principles in the context of detention[89]. Recommending that victims of trafficking should not be detained or placed in alternatives to detention. Instead, they should be promptly identified and referred to appropriate support services. She also advocates for secure residence status, not based on short-term or conditional permits, as recognised in her report (*A/75/169*, para 22). However, not all the Special Rapporteur's analysis has been accepted by the Senior Courts as presently reflective of the current scope of positive obligations as recognised by the ECtHR[90].

89 Siobhán Mullally, *Comments by the Special Rapporteur on trafficking in persons, especially women and children, on Draft General Comment No. 5 (2020) on migrants' rights to liberty and freedom from arbitrary detention* (Office of the United Nations High Commissioner for Human Rights, 2020) https://www.ohchr.org/Documents/Issues/Trafficking/Non-Punishment-Paper.pdf accessed 23 August 2025.

90 See consideration of the non-punishment principle in *Shamima Begum v Secretary of State for the Home Department* [2024] EWCA Civ 152.

5.166

The College of Policing accepts that all potential victims are vulnerable and should, therefore, be interviewed in compliance with guidance[91] (see **Chapter 3**). The Youth Justice Legal Centre has produced a guide for criminal practitioners representing child victims who are charged with offences connected to their trafficking, slavery or related harms[92].

5.167

As set out above, if there is *prima facie* evidence of trafficking, slavery or related harms, Art 4 positive and protective obligations will be triggered for all public authorities engaged or who should be engaging with the child.

5.168

Where a child victim of trafficking or exploitation is involved in criminal proceedings and has been charged with offences linked to their exploitation, the imposition of protective bail conditions should be actively considered when making an application for bail (see section above on missing children). As a minimum, it must be recognised that a conclusive grounds decision under the National Referral Mechanism (NRM) will not be made for at least 45 days, the statutory recovery and reflection period. In practice, this period may be significantly longer.

5.169

However, the existence of this delay does not alter the statutory safeguarding obligations owed to children at risk. All public authorities with safeguarding responsibilities must continue to discharge those duties in accordance with their legal obligations. The fact that a child is subject to criminal proceedings does not diminish the requirement to assess and respond to indicators of trafficking or exploitation, nor does it relieve authorities of their duty to ensure appropriate protection measures are in place (see *V.C.L and A.N. v UK*)[93].

5.170

When preparing and presenting any bail application on behalf of a child victim, consideration should be given to protective conditions such as no unsupervised use of phones or electronic equipment (see Safeguarding Children Under Trafficker Control above). It is common for victims who are being controlled by their traffickers or in debt bondage to contact either traffickers or those

91 College of Policing, *Modern Slavery: Risk and Identification* (College of Policing, updated 2023) https://www.college.police.uk/app/major-investigation-and-public-protection/modern-slavery/risk-and-identification accessed 23 August 2025.

92 Youth Justice Legal Centre, *Guide to Child Criminal Exploitation* (May 2022) https://yjlc.uk/sites/default/files/attachments/2022-05/YJLC-Guide-CCEMAY22.pdf accessed 23 August 2025.

93 *V.C.L. and A.N. v The United Kingdom*, App nos 77587/12 and 74603/12 (ECtHR, 16 February 2021).

who are involved in the organised criminal network. Proposed bail addresses or local authority accommodation should be suitable and not in an area where the victim's exploitation has taken place and where the traffickers operate.

Safeguarding children subject to immigration detention

Statutory powers to detain unaccompanied children subject to immigration control

5.171

Issues relating to the assessment of age in immigration detention contexts are addressed in detail in **Chapter 6**.

Immigration detention of children: legislative developments and human rights considerations

5.172

On 30 January 2025, the UK Government repealed provisions introduced by the *Illegal Migration Act 2023* that would have permitted the indefinite detention of children. Although those provisions had been enacted, they were never brought into force. Nonetheless, statutory provisions remain which allow for the detention of unaccompanied children in exceptional circumstances. These provisions are predicated on the assumption that a decision to remove the child from the United Kingdom can be made within 24 hours, where the child has not sought international protection.

5.173

Concerns have been raised regarding the potential impact of expedited procedures on the timely identification of child victims of trafficking. The evidence base, including material referenced in **Chapters 3** and **4**, indicates that disclosure by traumatised children is frequently delayed. In this context, the 2023 report by HM Chief Inspector of Prisons is of particular relevance. The report identified instances in which potential child victims of trafficking held in short-term holding facilities were not being recognised as such. The risks associated with delayed identification were also considered in *VCL and AN v United Kingdom*, where the European Court of Human Rights examined the consequences of failing to identify and protect child victims at an early stage.

5.174

The current statutory framework must be understood with reference to the United Kingdom's positive obligations under Art 4 of the ECHR, which require the implementation of effective operational measures to identify and protect victims of trafficking (see **Chapter 4**). In addition, Art 37 of the United Nations Convention on the Rights of the Child (UNCRC) provides that the detention of children shall be used only as a measure of last resort and for the shortest appropriate period.

5.175

Further consideration may be required when assessing the compatibility of the current statutory framework with the United Kingdom's obligations under the ECHR, in particular Art s 3 and 5. The jurisprudence of the ECtHR has emphasised that any deprivation of liberty, especially in the case of children or individuals with specific vulnerabilities, must be necessary, proportionate, and accompanied by appropriate safeguards. The Court has also recognised the importance of individualised assessments and the need to consider less restrictive alternatives to detention, considering the specific circumstances of each case.

Domestic legislation and policy framework

5.176

In the exercise of the statutory powers set out below, the starting position is as stated in the Home Office Detention General Instructions[94]:

> 'As a general principle, even where one of the statutory powers to detain is available in a particular case, unaccompanied children (that is persons under the age of 18) must not be detained other than in very exceptional circumstances. If unaccompanied children are detained, it must be for the shortest possible time, with appropriate care. This may include detention overnight, but a person detained as an unaccompanied child must not be held in an immigration removal centre in any circumstances. This includes age dispute cases where the person concerned has been given the benefit of the doubt and is being treated as a child. The very exceptional circumstances in which it might be appropriate to detain unaccompanied children are set out below…
>
> This exceptional measure is intended solely to deal with unexpected situations where it is necessary to detain unaccompanied children very briefly for their care and safety pending alternative arrangements being made. For example, collection by parents or relatives, by appropriate adult carers or friends, or by local authority children's services. It must not be used for other purposes. Efforts to secure alternative care arrangements in such cases must be made expeditiously.'

94 Home Office, *Detention: General Instructions* (Version 6, 22 January 2026) accessed 31 January 2026.

5.177

Under paragraph 16(2) of Schedule 2 to the Immigration Act 1971, an immigration officer may detain a person where there are reasonable grounds to suspect that the individual is liable to removal under specified immigration provisions.

5.178

Detention may occur pending either:

(a) a decision on whether to issue removal directions; or

(b) the execution of such directions once issued[95].

5.179

Where the person detained is an unaccompanied child, defined as someone under 18 who is not accompanied by a parent or carer, paragraph 18B introduces specific safeguards to limit and regulate detention.

Permissible location of detention

5.180

An unaccompanied child may only be detained in a short-term holding facility, unless:

(a) the child is being transferred to or from such a facility; or

(b) exceptional circumstances under paragraph 18(3) apply[96].

5.181

Paragraph 18(3) allows detention elsewhere only if the Secretary of State certifies that, by reason of exceptional circumstances and for the purpose of maintaining order or securing the safety of any person, it is not reasonably practicable to detain the child in a short-term holding facility[97]. This provision is intended to be used sparingly and only where necessary to protect safety or maintain operational order.

5.182

Detaining to interview a newly arrived unaccompanied child at port would *not* fall within the ambit of 'very exceptional circumstances'.

95 Immigration Act 1971, Sch 2, para 16(2).
96 Ibid, para 18B(1).
97 Ibid, para 18(3).

5.183

The Court of Appeal held in *R (AN and FA) v Secretary of State for the Home Department*[98] that once basic information has been obtained at port of entry from a newly arrived unaccompanied child, the Home Office must immediately refer the child to a relevant local authority children's services. Vulnerable children at risk of going missing should not be detained as a *de facto* way to stop them absconding. At this early stage, the Home Office should not be asking a child questions relating to why they have come to the UK. That is a question that should be asked in the presence of an appropriate adult. In accordance with the duty under s 55 of the Borders, Citizenship and Immigration Act 2009, the priority is to safeguard and promote the child's immediate welfare, including prompt referral to a local authority children's services department for safe accommodation and appropriate support.

Time

5.184

Detention of a unaccompanied child in a short-term holding facility is subject to a strict 24-hour limit and is only permissible while two conditions are met:

1. **Removal directions**: Either removal directions are already in force requiring removal within the 24-hour period, or a decision is likely to result in such directions[99].

2. **Reasonable belief**: The immigration officer must reasonably believe that the child will be removed within that period in accordance with those directions[100].

5.185

If the child is removed from the facility and detained elsewhere, they may be returned to the facility only if the original 24-hour period has not expired[101]. A child who has been released may also be detained again, but still subject to the same time and location constraints[102].

5.186

Where this statutory power is exercised, Home Office policy states that, in line with s 55 duties, officials must first take safeguarding steps when an unaccompanied child arrives without lawful status and has not claimed asylum and then assess removability and the availability of suitable reception arrangements in the destination country.

98 [2012] EWCA Civ 1636.
99 Ibid, para 18B(3).
100 Ibid, para 18B(4).
101 Ibid, para 18B(5
102 Ibid, para 18B(6).

5.187

The policy identifies three considerations with outcomes, which may follow:

1. **Removal**: If the child is removable and safe reception arrangements can be made, a notice of liability to remove may be served, and removal may proceed, subject to a full assessment of the circumstances.
2. **Immigration bail**: If the child is not removable and no safe reception arrangements can be made, immigration bail may be granted until the child turns 18, at which point the case should be reconsidered.
3. **Leave to remain**: In some cases, it may be appropriate to grant leave to remain, for example on Art 8 ECHR grounds, depending on the facts, including the duration of the child's residence in the UK.

Safeguarding in practice: gaps and risks identified

5.188

In January 2023, HM Chief Inspector of Prisons reported that unaccompanied children continued to be held for extended periods in short-term holding facilities at five airports and ten seaports[103]. The report raised ongoing concerns regarding procedural fairness and child welfare. **Chapter 6** specifically highlighted persistent issues in the handling of age disputes, noting the risk that vulnerable children may be incorrectly categorised and thereby denied appropriate safeguards.

5.189

The use of statutory powers permitting the detention and removal of unaccompanied children within a 24-hour timeframe should be considered in the context of these recurring safeguarding concerns, as documented by the inspectorate. These concerns are further reflected in findings from the Children's Commissioner and other third-sector investigations into the treatment of unaccompanied migrant children at UK border entry points.

Delayed local authority contact

5.190

Concerns regarding delayed initial contact with local authority children's services for unaccompanied children arriving in Dover were highlighted in the Children's Commissioner's report *Landing in Dover*[104].

---

103 HM Chief Inspector of Prisons (2023) 'Report on an unannounced inspection of short-term holding facilities managed by Border Force' available at: https://www.justiceinspectorates.gov.uk/hmiprisons/wpcontent/uploads/sites/4/2023/05/Border-Force-STHF-web-2023.pdf

104 Children's Commissioner for England, 'Landing in Dover' (January 2012) **https://www.childrenscommissioner.gov.uk/resource/landing-in-dover/** (accessed 9 October 2025), pp 7, 41–43, paras 0.3, 0.11, 0.14, 0.16, 7.9–7.11.

5.191

The report observed that engagement by social services frequently occurred only shortly before substantive interviews, raising safeguarding risks for vulnerable children.

5.192

Despite previous recommendations, the Children's Commissioner's 2023[105] follow-up report continues to criticise the lack of timely referral and support. It documents ongoing delays resulting in children waiting extended periods before receiving statutory care or oversight from qualified professionals. These systemic issues contribute to missed opportunities for safeguarding, appropriate screening, and early trauma support, and risk non-compliance with statutory duties owed to children under UK law.

Absence of an independent Responsible Adult

5.193

The *Landing in Dover* report[106] by the Children's Commissioner identified the absence of a suitably independent Responsible Adult during immigration interviews and initial processing as a significant safeguarding concern, particularly in relation to screening interviews and early questioning. The report noted that this absence may inhibit children's ability to communicate openly and compromises the protection of their rights and interests.

5.194

This concern is echoed in the Helen Bamber Foundation's 2025 report[107] and the Children's Commissioner's 2023 follow-up analysis[108], both of which confirm that the issue persists. According to these sources, children, especially those subject to age assessments, are frequently unrepresented during key procedural stages, including initial screening. This lack of advocacy and oversight may contribute to inappropriate treatment and procedural misunderstandings.

105 Children's Commissioner for England, 'Unaccompanied children in need of care' (November 2023) **https://assets.childrenscommissioner.gov.uk/wpuploads/2023/11/Unaccompanied-children-in-need-of-care-PDF.pdf** (accessed 9 October 2025), pp 6–8, 12, section 2.

106 Children's Commissioner for England, 'Landing in Dover' (January 2012) **https://www.childrenscommissioner.gov.uk/resource/landing-in-dover/** (accessed 9 October 2025), pp 7, 29, 37–38, 41–42, 53, paras 0.9, 0.11, 5.36, 6.1, 7.12–7.13, 8.28.

107 Helen Bamber Foundation, 'Serious safeguarding scandal: new data shows that hundreds of child refugees continue to be wrongly treated as adults' (July 2025) **https://www.helenbamber.org/resources/reportsbriefings/serious-safeguarding-scandal-new-data-shows-hundreds-child-refugees** (accessed 9 October 2025), paras 2–4.

108 Children's Commissioner for England, 'Unaccompanied children in need of care' (November 2023) **https://assets.childrenscommissioner.gov.uk/wpuploads/2023/11/Unaccompanied-children-in-need-of-care-PDF.pdf** (accessed 9 October 2025), pp 6–10, section 2, 1.2.

The cumulative effect, as described in both reports, is heightened vulnerability and increased risk of exploitation or miscommunication.

Deficiencies in interpreter provision

5.195

The *Landing in Dover* report[109] found chronic problems with the use of telephone interpreters for children: dialect differences, communication breakdowns, and resulting inaccuracies in recorded information during interviews and screening. These failures continue to be widely reported, with the Children's Commissioner's 2023[110] follow-up and charities[111] documenting cases where children's statements are misunderstood or mistranslated, leading to errors that can have lasting consequences for asylum and safeguarding assessments. The persistent lack of high-quality, face-to-face interpreter provision constitutes ongoing non-compliance with best practice and continues to undermine children's rights and welfare at the border.

Signing interview records without review

5.196

The *Landing in Dover* report[112] identified the practice of requiring children to sign screening or interview records without those records being read back to them for verification as a continuing safeguarding concern. This issue remains unresolved and, according to recent data, continues to occur with regularity. The result is that children may inadvertently confirm inaccurate or incomplete information.

5.197

The Children's Commissioner's subsequent findings[113] support this concern, noting that poor documentation practices continue to impede the fair and

109 Children's Commissioner for England, 'Landing in Dover' (January 2012) **https://www.childrenscommissioner.gov.uk/resource/landing-in-dover/** (accessed 9 October 2025), pp 7, 42–43, 53, paras 0.11, 7.12–7.16, 8.26.

110 Children's Commissioner for England, 'Unaccompanied children in need of care' (November 2023) **https://assets.childrenscommissioner.gov.uk/wpuploads/2023/11/Unaccompanied-children-in-need-of-care-PDF.pdf** (accessed 9 October 2025), p 8, 1.2, section 2.

111 Helen Bamber Foundation, 'Serious safeguarding scandal: new data shows that hundreds of child refugees continue to be wrongly treated as adults' (July 2025) **https://www.helenbamber.org/resources/reportsbriefings/serious-safeguarding-scandal-new-data-shows-hundreds-child-refugees** (accessed 9 October 2025), paras 2–5.

112 Children's Commissioner for England, 'Landing in Dover' (January 2012) **https://www.childrenscommissioner.gov.uk/resource/landing-in-dover/** (accessed 9 October 2025), pp 8, 44, 53, paras 0.11, 0.13, 7.19–7.20, 8.29–8.30.

113 Children's Commissioner for England, 'Unaccompanied children in need of care' (November 2023) **https://assets.childrenscommissioner.gov.uk/wpuploads/2023/11/Unaccompanied-children-in-need-of-care-PDF.pdf** (accessed 9 October 2025), pp 8–10, 12, 1.2, section 2.

lawful determination of children's status and needs. These practices fall short of statutory guidance and established best practice protocols, raising questions about procedural integrity and the adequacy of safeguards in place.

Questioning fear of return without a responsible adult

5.198

The *Landing in Dover* report[114] raised concerns about the practice of questioning unaccompanied children about their fear of return or substantive reasons for seeking asylum in the absence of a Responsible Adult. This issue remains prominent in more recent assessments.

5.199

Both the Helen Bamber Foundation[115] and the Children's Commissioner[116] have reported that children continue to be asked highly sensitive questions relating to potential threats or traumatic experiences without the presence of appropriate support or advocacy. These practices risk compounding trauma and may undermine procedural fairness, particularly where children are expected to disclose complex or distressing information without adequate safeguards.

Lack of clear policy guidance

5.200

Lack of clarity and consistency in policy guidance for front-line staff dealing with unaccompanied children was raised as a persistent concern by the Children's Commissioner in the *Landing in Dover* report[117] and is identified as an ongoing flaw in several recent reports. The Children's Commissioner's 2023 analysis[118]

114 Children's Commissioner for England, 'Landing in Dover' (January 2012) **https://www.childrenscommissioner.gov.uk/resource/landing-in-dover/** (accessed 9 October 2025), pp 8, 37–38, 45, 53, paras 0.12, 6.1, 7.25, 8.28.

115 Helen Bamber Foundation, 'Serious safeguarding scandal: new data shows that hundreds of child refugees continue to be wrongly treated as adults' (July 2025) **https://www.helenbamber.org/resources/reportsbriefings/serious-safeguarding-scandal-new-data-shows-hundreds-child-refugees** (accessed 9 October 2025), paras 2–6.

116 Children's Commissioner for England, 'Unaccompanied children in need of care' (November 2023) **https://assets.childrenscommissioner.gov.uk/wpuploads/2023/11/Unaccompanied-children-in-need-of-care-PDF.pdf** (accessed 9 October 2025), p 10, section 2, 1.2.

117 Children's Commissioner for England, 'Landing in Dover' (January 2012) **https://www.childrenscommissioner.gov.uk/resource/landing-in-dover/** (accessed 9 October 2025), pp 8, 45, 53, paras 0.12, 7.25, 8.27–8.30.

118 Children's Commissioner for England, 'Unaccompanied children in need of care' (November 2023) **https://assets.childrenscommissioner.gov.uk/wpuploads/2023/11/Unaccompanied-children-in-need-of-care-PDF.pdf** (accessed 9 October 2025), pp 9–12, section 2, 1.2.

and Helen Bamber Foundation's[119] interventions both confirm the continuing absence of robust, child-centred policy protocols, resulting in confusion and harmful practice across all major border locations.

Impact of immigration detention on children

5.201

Research conducted in the United Kingdom has consistently demonstrated the long-term harm caused by immigration detention to children, whether unaccompanied or detained with their families. Documented effects on physical and mental health include weight loss, sleep disturbances, nightmares, skin conditions, self-harm, attempted suicide, depression, and symptoms consistent with post-traumatic stress disorder[120].

International evidence of harm

5.202

International findings reinforce these concerns. Médecins Sans Frontières has reported serious medical and psychological consequences for refugee children detained in Greece and on Nauru Island, including trauma-related symptoms, developmental regression, and self-harm.[121] Similarly, recent studies examining Australia's immigration detention policies highlight the detrimental impact on children's health and wellbeing, as well as the negative effect on parental capacity[122]. Children in detention also face barriers to accessing healthcare and treatment, further compounding their vulnerability.

Safeguarding gaps for child victims of trafficking or modern slavery

5.203

Despite statutory duties under the Children Act 1989, the Modern Slavery Act 2015, and s 55 of the Borders, Citizenship and Immigration Act 2009,

119 Helen Bamber Foundation, 'Serious safeguarding scandal: new data shows that hundreds of child refugees continue to be wrongly treated as adults' (July 2025) **https://www.helenbamber.org/resources/reportsbriefings/serious-safeguarding-scandal-new-data-shows-hundreds-child-refugees** (accessed 9 October 2025), paras 6–7.

120 Refugee Council and others, *Joint Briefing: Immigration Detention of Children* (27 June 2023) https://www-media.refugeecouncil.org.uk/media/documents/Joint-child-detention-briefing-HoL-Report-27.06.2023.pdf accessed 23 August 2025.

121 Médecins Sans Frontières, *Invisible Suffering: The Mental Health Impact of Detention on Refugee Children* (2017).

122 Australian Human Rights Commission, *The Forgotten Children: National Inquiry into Children in Immigration Detention* (2014).

significant gaps remain in safeguarding arrangements for child victims of trafficking or modern slavery identified while in immigration detention in the UK. Although referral to the National Referral Mechanism (NRM) is intended to initiate community-based care and local authority involvement, there is no consistently coordinated process between the Home Office and local authority children's services to conduct risk assessments or convene multi-agency safeguarding meetings prior to a child's release. This gap is particularly acute in cases involving age disputes and children at risk of re-trafficking.

Legal findings on safeguarding failures

5.204

In *R (TDT) v Secretary of State for the Home Department*[123], the claimant went missing following release from detention due to the absence of safeguarding measures. The court found that the Home Office had failed to establish adequate systems to protect a potential child victim of trafficking, resulting in a breach of Art 4 of the European Convention on Human Rights.

Pilot initiatives and remaining challenges

5.205

Guidance and pilot initiatives, such as the Devolving Child Decision Making Programme[124], have introduced multi-agency decision-making structures in some regions. However, these do not yet constitute a nationwide procedural norm. The absence of a systematic approach to convening safeguarding meetings and conducting pre-release risk assessments continues to place child victims at increased risk of harm, including re-trafficking.

Family separation in immigration detention: s 55 and Art 8 ECHR

Statutory duty to safeguard children in immigration contexts

5.206

Section 55 of the Borders, Citizenship and Immigration Act 2009 requires the Home Office to carry out its immigration, asylum, and detention functions with regard to the need to safeguard and promote the welfare of children. Where the detention of a parent or primary carer results in separation from their child,

123 *R (TDT) v Secretary of State for the Home Department* [2018] EWHC 68 (Admin).

124 Home Office, *Devolving Child Decision-Making Pilot Programme: General Guidance* (2023) https://www.gov.uk/government/publications/piloting-devolving-decision-making-for-child-victims-of-modern-slavery/devolving-child-decision-making-pilot-programme-general-guidance-accessible-version accessed 23 August 2025.

this duty must be considered alongside Art 8 of the European Convention on Human Rights (ECHR), which protects the right to respect for private and family life.

Application in deportation and family separation cases

5.207

In deportation cases involving parents or primary carers, the potential separation from British citizen children engages both Art 8 ECHR and broader child welfare considerations. While the Supreme Court in *ZH (Tanzania)*[125] affirmed that a child's best interests must be treated as a 'primary consideration' under Art 3(1) UNCRC, it is now clear from *R (CAO)*[126] that the statutory duty under s 55 of the 2009 Act applies to Home Office officials, not to the First-tier Tribunal. Nonetheless, the underlying principles remain highly relevant. Where removal or detention risks severing family ties, decision-makers must give substantial weight to the child's welfare, recognising that administrative convenience cannot override the obligation to assess and protect the child's interests. The limitations of relying solely on Art 8 ECHR in such assessments have been the subject of sustained academic critique, particularly where the procedural safeguards of child-specific statutory duties are absent.

Relevant UNCRC provisions

5.208

Art 3(2) of the UNCRC requires States to ensure such protection and care as is necessary for the child's wellbeing, while Art 9(1) prohibits separation from parents against their will except where necessary and judicially authorised in the child's best interests. Although these provisions refer to 'parents,' they apply equally to primary carers. Art 12 further requires that children capable of forming their own views be given the opportunity to be heard in any proceedings affecting them, with their views given due weight in accordance with age and maturity.

Balancing welfare and enforcement considerations

5.209

In decisions involving detention, the Home Office must balance enforcement considerations, such as risks of absconding, harm, or reoffending, against the

125 [2011] UKSC 4, [2011] 2 AC 166.
126 *R (CAO) v Secretary of State for the Home Department* [2023] UKSC 30.

child's welfare. As confirmed in *R (NXT) v Secretary of State for the Home Department*[127], the child's best interests must be treated as a central, though not necessarily decisive, factor. They cannot be overridden by general administrative concerns.

Relevant ECtHR principles on immigration detention of children

5.210

The ECtHR has developed a robust body of jurisprudence concerning the immigration detention of children, both accompanied and unaccompanied, under Arts 3, 5, and 13 of the ECHR. The following principles are particularly pertinent:

Necessity and last resort

5.211

Detention must be strictly necessary to achieve a legitimate aim, such as removal, and must only be used when no less restrictive alternatives are available. This principle applies with force to children, whose detention must be a measure of last resort and for the shortest appropriate period[128].

Vulnerability and individual assessment

5.212

Authorities must assess the specific vulnerabilities of children, including age, trauma, health, and personal history, before authorising detention. The Court has found violations where such vulnerabilities were not adequately considered[129].

Conditions and duration

5.213

Detention must be for the shortest possible time and in conditions appropriate for children. The Court has identified three key factors in assessing compliance with Art 3:

127 *R (NXT) v Secretary of State for the Home Department* [2023] EWHC 969 (Admin).

128 *Rahimi v Greece* App no 8687/08 (ECtHR, 5 April 2011).

129 *Thimothawes v Belgium* App no 39061/11 (ECtHR, 4 April 2017); *Muskhadzhiyeva and Others v Belgium* App no 41442/07 (ECtHR, 19 January 2010); *Kanagaratnam and Others v Belgium* App no 15297/09 (ECtHR, 13 December 2011); *M.H. and Others v Croatia* App no 15670/18 (ECtHR, 18 November 2021).

- the child's age;
- the duration of detention; and
- the suitability of the premises for children's needs.

See *AB and Others v France* and *M.D. and AD v France.*[130]

5.214

Even short periods of detention in poor conditions have led to findings of violations (*SF and Others v Bulgaria).*[131] Where conditions are adequate, the duration remains a decisive factor (*RM and Others v France*; *NB and Others v France*, 2022).[132]

Unaccompanied children

5.215

The Court has emphasised the heightened vulnerability of unaccompanied children. Violations of Art 3 have been found in cases involving prolonged or inappropriate detention, including:

- *Rahimi v Greece*[133]: extremely vulnerable minor held in poor conditions.
- *HA and Others v Greece*[134]: minors aged 14 and 17 held in police custody for 21–33 days.
- *Abdullahi Elmi and Aweys Abubakar v Malta*[135]: minors detained for eight months pending age assessment.
- *Mubilanzila Mayeka and Kaniki Mitunga v Belgium*[136]: five-year-old child detained in an adult facility for two months.

Accompanied children and parental vulnerability

5.216

The presence of parents in detention does not absolve authorities of their duty to protect children. The Court has found violations of Art 3 in respect

130 *AB and Others v France* App no 11593/12 (ECtHR, 12 July 2016) [109]; *M.D. and A.D. v France* App no 57035/18 (ECtHR, 22 July 2021) at [63].
131 *S.F. and Others v Bulgaria* App no 8138/16 (ECtHR, 7 December 2017).
132 *R.M. and Others v France* App no 33201/11 (ECtHR, 12 July 2016); *NB and Others v France* App no 49775/20 (ECtHR, 10 November 2022).
133 *Rahimi v Greece* App no 8687/08 (ECtHR, 5 April 2011) [81-86].
134 *H.A. and Others v Greece* App no 19951/16 (ECtHR, 28 February 2019) [166-170].
135 *Abdullahi Elmi and Aweys Abubakar v Malta* App no 25794/13 (ECtHR, 22 November 2016) [105-115].
136 *Mubilanzila Mayeka and Kaniki Mitunga v Belgium* App no 13178/03 (ECtHR, 12 October 2006) [50-59].

of children, and in some cases, also in respect of accompanying parents where the parent was particularly vulnerable (eg breastfeeding or pregnant women)[137]. Immigration detention has been shown to cause marked deterioration in parental mental health. One review reported very high rates of psychopathology among detained parents, including mixed anxiety, depression and increased suicidal ideation, and found that many who had coped adequately beforehand were no longer able to care for or support their children in detention. The detention environment was described as undermining adequate parenting, leaving parents feeling disempowered, and impeding the support necessary for healthy child development, thereby placing children at heightened risk of adverse mental-health outcomes[138]. A subsequent systematic review of caregiver trauma and hardship reported that caregiver internalising symptoms and post-traumatic stress disorder impair parenting through emotion dysregulation, with downstream effects on children's mental health and wellbeing[139].

5.217

Studies on the intergenerational effects of parental incarceration similarly show that the trauma of parental imprisonment is independently associated with later depressive symptoms, rule-breaking behaviour, and poorer life outcomes in children. A recent systematic review of 21 studies involving 9,620 children in immigration detention found an extremely high prevalence of mental distress among detained children and concluded that any period of detention is associated with poor mental-health outcomes, with prolonged or harsher detention regimes being especially harmful[140].

Access to asylum procedures

5.218

Protection obligations may arise even where asylum has not been formally requested. Authorities must ensure access to interpretation, legal advice, and the ability to express protection needs[141].

---

137 *Muskhadzhiyeva and Others v Belgium* App no 41442/07 (ECtHR, 19 January 2010); *Popov v France* App nos 39472/07 and 39474/07 (ECtHR, 19 January 2012); *M.D. and A.D. v France* App no 57035/18 (ECtHR, 22 July 2021); *R.R. and Others v Hungary* App no 36037/17 (ECtHR, 2 March 2021); *H.M. and Others v Hungary* App no 38967/19 (ECtHR, 22 November 2022).

138 M von Werthern and others, 'The impact of immigration detention on mental health: a systematic review' (2018) 18 *BMC Psychiatry* 382 <https://doi.org/10.1186/s12888-018-1945-y>.

139 SKG Jensen and others, 'Intergenerational impacts of trauma and hardship through parenting' (2021) 62 *Journal of Child Psychology and Psychiatry* 989 <https://doi.org/10.1111/jcpp.13359>.

140 Isabella Priestley and others, 'The impact of immigration detention on children's mental health: systematic review' (2025) 227 *British Journal of Psychiatry* 870 <https://doi.org/10.1192/bjp.2025.29>.

141 *Hirsi Jamaa and Others v Italy* [GC] App no 27765/09 (ECtHR, 23 February 2012); *D v Bulgaria* App no 29447/17 (ECtHR, 17 June 2021).

Presumption of minority

5.219

A person claiming to be a minor must be treated as such unless the claim is clearly unfounded. Until a final age assessment is completed, the individual must benefit from safeguards applicable to children[142].

Positive obligations under Art 4 ECHR and procedural safeguards under Art 5 ECHR in the context of criminal and administrative detention

5.220

This section examines how failures to discharge positive obligations under Art 4 ECHR, specifically the duties to identify and investigate credible indicators of trafficking or modern slavery, can result in breaches of Art 5 ECHR, including its procedural safeguards under Art 5(4). These obligations apply to both criminal detention (Arts 5(1)(c), 5(3)) and administrative detention (Art 5(1)(f)).

Criminal detention: Zenati v Commissioner of Police of the Metropolis & CPS[143]

5.221

In *Zenati*, the Court of Appeal held that:

- Art 5(1)(c) applies beyond the initial court appearance. Continued detention must be justified by a reasonable suspicion, and authorities must promptly inform the court when such suspicion ceases [15–21].
- Art 5(3) requires special diligence in progressing investigations and proceedings. Delays or failures to disclose material information may render detention unlawful [43–44].

5.222

These principles underscore the procedural dimension of Art 5, requiring active and timely engagement by authorities to ensure detention remains lawful.

142 *AD v Malta* App no 29758/20 (ECtHR, 21 February 2023).
143 *Zenati* [2015] EWCA Civ 80; [2015] 2 WLR 1563.

Administrative detention: cross-application of Zenati principles

5.223

While *Zenati* concerned criminal detention, its reasoning is instructive for administrative detention under Article 5(1)(f). This provision permits detention for immigration control purposes, but only where removal is being pursued with due diligence.

- Continued detention becomes arbitrary if authorities fail to act on new information, such as credible indicators of trafficking or modern slavery.
- The failure to identify or investigate such indicators, as required under Art 4, may vitiate the lawfulness of detention under Art 5(1)(f).

Positive obligations under Art 4 ECHR: VCL and AN v UK

5.224

In *VCL and AN v UK*[144], the ECtHR reaffirmed that:

- States must identify and investigate potential trafficking victims where there is *prima facie* evidence.
- Failure to do so may result in breaches of Art 4 and undermine the protective framework of Art 5.

5.225

Where such failures occur, detention may breach Art 5(1)(f) (administrative) or Art 5(1)(c) (criminal), particularly if the individual should have been diverted from detention and provided with protection.

Procedural safeguards under Article 5(4): effective review of detention

5.226

Art 5(4) guarantees the right to challenge the lawfulness of detention before a court. The ECtHR has found violations where:

- Detainees were not informed of the reasons for their deprivation of liberty, depriving their right to appeal of all effective substance[145].

144 (2021) 73 EHRR 9.

145 *Khlaifia and Others v Italy* [GC] App no 16483/12 (ECtHR, 15 December 2016) [132].

- Detainees were informed of available remedies in a language they did not understand and were unable to contact a lawyer[146].
- No individual detention order was issued for children, preventing them from challenging their detention[147].
- Appeals were rendered ineffective due to procedural delays or replacement detention orders[148].
- Proceedings lacked an adversarial structure or equality of arms[149].
- Detention review was not conducted 'speedily'[150].

5.227

In immigration contexts, particularly where children and families are detained, national courts must examine the lawfulness of detention with particular expedition and diligence[151]. However, where an automatic review is not conducted within the time-limits set by domestic law but is nonetheless carried out speedily from an objective standpoint, there is no breach of Art 5(4)[152].

5.228

In *Bah v the Netherlands*[153], the ECtHR accepted exceptional circumstances (COVID-19 restrictions) where the applicant was not heard in person, but the lawyer's participation ensured compliance with Article 5(4).

Vulnerabilities and detention of children

5.229

The ECtHR has consistently held that immigration detention must account for the specific vulnerabilities of children, including age, health, and trauma. Detention may be inappropriate where these factors are not properly assessed[154]. The absence of individualised review or failure to consider protective obligations under Art 4 may render detention unlawful under Art 5(4).

146 *Rahimi v Greece* App no 8687/08 (ECtHR, 5 April 2011) [120].
147 *Minasian and Others v Moldova* App no. 26879/17, 17 January 2023 [49-54].
148 *Muhammad Saqawat v Belgium* App no 54962/18 (ECtHR, 30 June 2020); *Moustahi v France* App no 9347/14 (ECtHR, 25 June 2020).
149 *A and Others v United Kingdom* [GC] App no 3455/05 (ECtHR, 19 February 2009) [203]; *Al Husin v. Bosnia and Herzegovina* (No 2), App no 10112/16, 25 June 2019.
150 *Khlaifia and Others v Italy* [GC] App no 16483/12 (ECtHR, 15 December 2016) [131]; *B.A. v Cyprus,* no. 24607/20, 2 July 2024 [72-75]; *Khudyakova v Russia* App no 13476/04 (ECtHR, 8 January 2009) [92-100]; *Abdulkhakov v Russia* App no 14743/11 (ECtHR, 2 October 2012) [214]; *M.M. v Bulgaria,* no. 75832/13, 8 June 2017.
151 *GB and Others v Turkey,* no. 4633/15, 17 October 2019 [167,186].
152 *Aboya Boa Jean v Malta* App no 62676/16, 2 April 2019.
153 *Bah v the Netherlands,* no. 35751/20, 22 June 2021.
154 *Thimothawes v Belgium* App no 39061/11 (ECtHR, 4 April 2017).

5.230

The convergence of jurisprudence under Arts 4 and 5 ECHR establishes that:

- Failure to identify and investigate trafficking or modern slavery indicators may breach Art 4 and render detention unlawful under Arts 5(1)(c), 5(1)(f), 5(3) and 5(4).
- Procedural safeguards under Art 5(4) require timely, informed, and effective judicial review, particularly for vulnerable individuals.
- Authorities must act with diligence, transparency, and responsiveness once protective obligations are triggered.

PART III – Adult Safeguarding and the Legal Framework for Immigration Detention

5.231

The statutory powers governing immigration detention are broad. Once the basic conditions, such as liability to removal or deportation, and in some cases, service of a removal decision, are satisfied, there are no express statutory limits on the exercise of detention powers. That power is subject to several implied limitations, the *Hardial Singh* principles[155], detention for immigration purposes remains lawful only if removal is realistically achievable within a reasonable timeframe, and every effort is made to progress the removal. Any breach of these principles renders immigration detention unlawful. Consideration should also be given to the convergence of Arts 4 and 5 ECHR in the context of victims of modern slavery or trafficking held in administrative detention (see above).

5.232

The Secretary of State's detention policy is articulated principally through Detention: general instructions[156]. That refers to the 2001 Rules[157]. They were made pursuant to s 153 of the Immigration and Asylum Act 1999. The rules are concerned with 'the regulation and management of Detention Centres' and may, amongst other things, 'make provision for the safety, care, activities, discipline and care of detained persons'. The policy relating to detention is further explained in the Detention Rule 35 and Short-term Holding Facility rule 32 Process Guidance[158] and Detention Service Orders.

155 *R v Secretary of State for the Home Department ex parte Hardial Singh* [1984] 1WLR 704.

156 Home Office, *Detention General Instructions* (Gov.uk, last updated 22 January 2026) https://www.gov.uk/government/publications/offender-management/detention-general-instructions-accessible accessed 1 February 2026.

157 The Detention Centre Rules 2001, SI 2001/238.

158 Home Office, *Detention Centre Rule 35 Process and Short-Term Holding Facility rule 32 process* (Gov.uk, last updated 3 July 2025) https://www.gov.uk/government/publications/detention-rule-35-process/detention-centre-rule-35-process-accessible-version accessed 1 February 2026.

5.233

The Adults at Risk in Immigration Detention guidance[159] applies to all individuals being considered for immigration detention, including those already detained[160]. It reinforces the existing presumption against detention in immigration policy, particularly for vulnerable individuals. In *R (AH and IS) v Secretary of State for the Home Department*[161], the High Court clarified that the SSHD's Tameside duty of inquiry in immigration detention decisions extends, where there is prima facie evidence of severe mental health issues, to engaging with the individual's past medical assessments and current presentation as part of the 'context and background' of the detention decision. The court held that the SSHD had failed to comply with the Adults at Risk policy by not reconsidering detention after the claimants' displayed symptoms of severe mental illness during their second period of detention at Brook House IRC. Under the policy, detention may only be justified where the immigration-related factors outweigh the risks associated with the individual's vulnerability. There is a specific Adults at risk: detention of potential or confirmed victims of modern slavery guidance[162].

Detention centre rules: Rule 34 and Rule 35

Rule 34

5.234

Rule 34 of the 2001 Rules is designed to ensure that new arrivals are medically examined. That medical examination is in addition to a medical screening which is routinely conducted on admission by nursing staff. The Rule 34 examination need not be conducted by the appointed medical practitioner but can be done by a doctor chosen and paid for by the detainee. It is necessary for new arrivals to have a medical screening and examination to ensure that their medical needs are catered for in detention.

159 Home Office, *Adults at Risk in Immigration Detention* (Gov.uk, May 2024) https://assets.publishing.service.gov.uk/media/664b61e0993111924d9d3844/Adults+at+risk+in+immigration+detention.pdf accessed 1 February 2026. See also Home Office, *Management of adults at risk in immigration detention* (updated 10 January 2025) https://www.gov.uk/government/publications/adults-at-risk-in-immigration-detention, accessed 1 February 2026.

160 The lawfulness of aspects of the Adults at Risk framework remains under active judicial scrutiny. In *Medical Justice v Secretary of State for the Home Department* [2025] EWCA Civ 251, the Court of Appeal upheld the finding that Medical Justice had a legitimate expectation to be consulted on Adults at Risk policies, including the Second Opinion Policy for medico-legal reports. The SSHD has been granted permission to appeal to the Supreme Court (UKSC/2025/0065, 22 April 2025); the appeal had not been heard at the date of publication.

161 [2025] EWHC 3269 (Admin).

162 Home Office, *Adults at risk: detention of potential or confirmed victims of modern slavery* (updated 22 January 2026) https://www.gov.uk/government/publications/offender-management/adults-at-risk-detention-of-potential-or-confirmed-victims-of-modern-slavery-accessible-version accessed 1 February 2026.

5.235

If an immigration detainee, in the absence of good reason, is not medically examined within 24 hours of his arrival at a detention centre, his detention thereafter will be unlawful[163].

5.236

The Rule 34 examination is, in the context of a decision to detain, a stepping stone to a Rule 35 report.

Rule 35

5.237

Rule 35 is concerned with mental illness and other conditions which might make detention inappropriate. The Rule imposes an obligation upon the medical practitioner to 'report …on the case of any detained person, where the medical practitioner considers the detainee's:

- health is likely to be injuriously affected by continued detention or any conditions of detention.
- Is suspected of having suicidal intentions.
- may have been the victim of torture.

5.238

There is a standard pro forma available for submitting such reports. It enables the medical practitioner to identify which paragraph of Rule 35 is engaged and to provide any further information they consider relevant. The Rule does not prescribe the specific content of a report; rather, it requires the practitioner to report on any individual about whom they have concerns falling within paragraphs (1) to (3) of Rule 35. It is for the practitioner to determine the nature and extent of supporting information to accompany those concerns. In many cases, the concern may arise solely from the detainee's allegation of torture. The Secretary of State's policy anticipates that officials will receive the report and take appropriate steps in response.

5.239

In *R (on the application of EO) v Secretary of State for the Home Department*[164] it was held that torture, within the Secretary of State's detention policy, meant:

163 *R (on the application of EO) v Secretary of State for the Home Department* [2013] EWHC 1236 (Admin).
164 [2013] EWHC 1236 (Admin).

any act by which severe pain or suffering, whether physical or mental, is intentionally inflicted on a person for such purposes as obtaining from him or a third person information or a confession, punishing him for an act he or a third person has committed, or intimidating or coercing him or a third person, or for any reason based upon discrimination of any kind.

5.240

Rule 35 reports have played a critical role in identifying detainees as potential victims of trafficking or modern slavery. This underscores the importance of consistent compliance with both Rule 34 and Rule 35 of the Detention Centre Rules[165], which are designed to safeguard vulnerable individuals in immigration detention.

Adults at Risk framework

5.241

The Adults at Risk statutory guidance is not intended to alter the strong presumption in favour of liberty in respect of vulnerable detainees. There remains a clear presumption that detention will not be appropriate if a person is 'at risk'. The intention is that fewer people with a confirmed vulnerability will be detained in fewer instances and that where detention becomes necessary, it will be for the shortest period necessary.

5.242

However, the determination of who is at risk, and what weight to be placed on the evidence of'at risk' is more prescriptive under the Adults at Risk framework. At s 7, the Adults at Risk statutory guidance regards an individual as an adult at risk if:

- The individual declares that they are suffering from a condition, or have experienced a traumatic event (such as trafficking, torture, or sexual violence), that would be likely to render them particularly vulnerable to harm if placed in detention or if detention continues.
- Those considering or reviewing detention are aware of medical, professional, or observational evidence indicating that an individual is suffering from a condition, or has experienced a traumatic event (such as trafficking, torture, or sexual violence), that would be likely to render

165 Detention Action, *Response to the Call for Evidence: Adults at Risk in Immigration Detention* (25 February 2019) https://detentionaction.org.uk/wp-content/uploads/2019/03/2019_02_25_Detention-Action-Response-to-the-Call-for-Evidence_-%E2%80%98Adults-at-Risk-in-immigration-detention.pdf accessed 23 August 2025.

them particularly vulnerable to harm in detention, regardless of whether the individual has personally disclosed this.

5.243

Indicators that a person may be at risk include (but are not limited to) those identified at s 13, such as a person:

- suffering from a mental health condition or impairment (this may include more serious learning difficulties, psychiatric illness or clinical depression, depending on the nature and seriousness of the condition);
- having been a victim of torture;
- having been a victim of sexual or gender-based violence, including female genital mutilation;
- having been a victim of human trafficking or modern slavery;
- suffering from post-traumatic stress disorder (which may or may not be related to one of the above experiences);
- being pregnant (pregnant women will automatically be regarded as meeting level 3 evidence);
- suffering from a serious physical disability;
- suffering from other serious physical health conditions or illnesses;
- being aged 70 or over;
- being a transgender or intersex person.

5.244

The Adults at Risk statutory guidance, s 9, considers the weight to be placed on indicators that a person is an adult at risk:

- self-declaration of being at risk should be afforded limited weight and be regarded as 'Level 1 evidence';
- professional evidence (eg from a social worker, medical practitioner, or NGO), or official documentary evidence, which indicates that the individual is an adult at risk, should be afforded greater weight than a self-declaration. Individuals in these circumstances will be regarded as being at evidence level 2;
- professional evidence (eg from a social worker, medical practitioner or NGO) stating that the individual is at risk and that a period of detention would be likely to cause harm, for example, increase the severity of the symptoms or condition that have led to the individual being regarded as an adult at risk, should be afforded significant weight. Individuals in these circumstances will be regarded as being at evidence level 3.

5.245

The Adults at Risk in Immigration Detention caseworker guidance supplements the statutory framework by detailing how to assess the balance between evidence of vulnerability and immigration factors that may justify detention. The stronger the evidence of risk, the more serious the immigration factors must be to override the presumption in favour of liberty. For example, where a person is assessed as an adult at risk with Level 3 evidence, the highest level, the guidance recognises that detention is likely to cause harm. In such cases, detention should only be considered in limited circumstances, such as when removal is imminent, there are no barriers to removal, and appropriate arrangements are in place. Alternatively, detention may be justified if the individual poses a significant public protection concern, has received a custodial sentence of four years or more, or presents a serious national security risk.

5.246

The guidance further provides that, in Level 3 cases, decision-makers may need to seek a second professional opinion to ensure a fully informed assessment. According to the Home Office's online guidance, external medical reports should generally be referred for a second opinion, subject to limited exceptions.

5.247

This policy was challenged in *R (Medical Justice) v Secretary of State for the Home Department*[166]. The Administrative Court held that delaying a detention decision beyond a minimal period to await second opinion evidence was unlawful, given the statutory presumption against detention. However, the Court of Appeal overturned this finding, holding that the statutory guidance implicitly allowed caseworkers a reasonable period to seek independent evidence of vulnerability[167]. While the Court declined to define the limits of that period, it emphasised that it must be short and sufficient to allow meaningful inquiry. The Court of Appeal upheld the finding that the Home Secretary had acted unlawfully by failing to consult the charity Medical Justice when developing the second opinion policy.

Adults at Risk and modern slavery

5.248

The *Adults at Risk: Detention of Potential or Confirmed Victims of Modern Slavery* guidance[168] now provides a structured framework for assessing the

166 *Medical Justice v Secretary of State for the Home Department* [2024] EWHC 38 (Admin).
167 *Medical Justice v Secretary of State for the Home Department* [2025] EWCA Civ 251.
168 Home Office, *Adults at risk: detention of potential or confirmed victims of modern slavery* (updated 22 January 2026) https://www.gov.uk/government/publications/offender-management/adults-at-risk-detention-of-potential-or-confirmed-victims-of-modern-slavery-accessible-version accessed 1 February 2026.

appropriateness of detaining individuals identified as potential or confirmed victims of modern slavery.

5.249

Earlier unlawful-detention cases,[169] which held that individuals with reasonable grounds to be considered victims of trafficking should be released absent public-order concerns, relied on statutory guidance that is no longer in force. Those decisions therefore do not reflect the current legal position. Under the updated guidance, there is no presumption of release in such cases.

5.250

The guidance acknowledges that victims of modern slavery are at heightened risk of harm in detention. It therefore requires a case-by-case assessment of vulnerability, balancing the risk of harm to the individual against immigration control considerations, such as the risk of absconding or public protection concerns. A level-based evidential framework is applied, categorising the strength of evidence regarding an individual's vulnerability and informing the weight to be given to that evidence in detention decisions. The system comprises three levels:

- **Level 1** involves self-declaration by the individual, such as a personal claim of being a victim of modern slavery. While this may initiate further inquiry or referral to the National Referral Mechanism (NRM), it is not treated as strong evidence in isolation.
- **Level 2** consists of professional evidence from qualified individuals, such as medical practitioners, social workers, or support organisations, indicating that the person is at risk of harm if detained. This level carries moderate evidential weight and must be considered alongside other relevant factors.
  - A reasonable grounds competent authority decision will automatically be regarded as amounting to level 2 evidence. This is so even in cases in which the competent authority applies a public order disqualification or decides not to grant an addition to the 30-day recovery period, although it does not apply in cases in which the competent authority decides to disqualify an individual on bad faith grounds.
  - A positive Conclusive Grounds decision alone will automatically be regarded as amounting to level 2 evidence unless the decision is revoked on bad faith grounds. Where temporary permission to stay is granted after a positive conclusive grounds decision, the individual should be released.

169 *R (SW) v Secretary of state for the Home Department* [2018] EWHC 2684 (Admin), [2019] 1 WLR 2193; *R (XYL) v Secretary of state for the Home Department* [2017] EWHC 773 (Admin).

- **Level 3** represents the highest threshold of evidence. It includes either a positive reasonable or conclusive grounds decision from the NRM, or expert medical evidence confirming that detention would likely result in significant harm. This level strongly supports release from detention unless compelling public interest grounds justify continued detention.

5.251

The guidance underscores the importance of timely and accurate communication between agencies and the integration of NRM decisions into the detention review process. Where someone already detained receives a positive Reasonable Grounds decision, the Home Office must initiate a structured review process under the *Adults at Risk in Immigration Detention* policy. The caseworker must first conduct an ad-hoc detention and case progression review, automatically elevating the individual's vulnerability status to at least Level 2. All available indicators of risk, including professional evidence from social workers or medical practitioners, must be considered to determine whether continued detention is appropriate.

5.252

When considering public protection and compliance issues, caseworkers must be aware that the immigration history of the individual concerned may have been influenced by their trafficking or history of modern slavery.

5.253

The guidance states that, during the recovery period, the Home Office must consider the outcome of the Modern Slavery Needs Assessment. Where a potential victim is already detained and the required recovery services cannot be provided in the IRC or prison, the individual's vulnerability level must be raised to Level 3[170].

5.254

If detention is to continue and no extended recovery period has been granted, the case must be referred, subject to the individual's consent, to the Detention Engagement Team (DET) for a Modern Slavery Needs Interview within five working days. DET will also refer the individual to healthcare to assess whether their physical and mental health needs can be met in detention.

170 In *R (EM) v Secretary of State for the Home Department* [2018] 1 WLR 4386, the Court of Appeal held that Art 12 of ECAT does not require that the assistance and support provided to a victim of trafficking in detention be identical in form to that available in the community. It should be noted, however, that the case did not raise or consider the protective positive obligations arising under Art 4 of the ECHR, as discussed above.

5.255

Following these assessments, a senior caseworker (SEO or above) must decide whether the person's recovery needs can be supported in detention. If they cannot, the vulnerability level must be raised to Level 3 and recorded on form AAR MS 002 in Atlas. A further detention and case-progression review must then be completed and signed off by the responsible SEO, balancing immigration control considerations against the individual's vulnerabilities.

5.256

The outcome of the Modern Slavery Needs Assessment must be communicated to the individual using form AAR MS 003. Where detention is maintained, caseworkers must ensure that all identified support needs are met, including any arising from DET referrals. If a public order disqualification request is pending, the competent authority must be notified of the assessment outcome.

5.257

If there is any indication, from the individual, IRC staff, or the caseworker, that recovery needs have changed, a further Modern Slavery Needs Assessment should be arranged. The guidance also notes that potential victims of modern slavery may have overlapping vulnerabilities falling under the Adults at Risk in Immigration Detention policy and must be assessed accordingly.

Safeguarding and release from detention

5.258

Home Office guidance requires caseworkers, where release is authorised, to plan for the safe discharge of a potential or confirmed victim of modern slavery. This includes, subject to the individual's consent, referring them to The Salvation Army for assessment of recovery needs and for possible support under the Modern Slavery Victim Care Contract (MSVCC). However, evidence from NGOs and practitioners[171] indicates that this does not occur consistently in immigration detention: potential victims are not always promptly referred into, or adequately supported within, the NRM, and some remain detained or are released without appropriate NRM support or accommodation, contributing to prolonged detention and continued insecurity for trafficked individuals.

171 Detention Action, *Illegal Migration Bill and the Expansion of Immigration Detention: Briefing* (21 March 2023) <https://detentionaction.org.uk/wp-content/uploads/2023/03/Detention-Action-Briefing-Illegal-Migration-Bill-and-the-Expansion-of-Immigration-Detention-21.03.2023.pdf> accessed 1 February 2026. See also Detention Taskforce, *The Taskforce on Survivors of Trafficking in Immigration Detention (Detention Taskforce) IECA Briefing* (2024) <https://lawrs.org.uk/wp-content/uploads/2024/07/Detention-Taskforce-IECA-briefing-2.pdf> accessed 1 February 2026.

5.259

Safeguarding arrangements, including risk assessments and transition planning, must be coordinated to prevent re-exposure to trafficking or modern slavery risks. If consent is withheld, alternative release procedures must be followed in accordance with Detention Services Orders DSO 08/2016 and DSO 01/2018. Where IRC or healthcare staff have significant concerns about releasing a detainee considered to be at risk, a multi-disciplinary meeting (or teleconference if a physical meeting is not possible due to time constraints), should be held to agree a plan to safely release the individual. This should be expedited to avoid any impact on release timings as the Home Office will use the outcome of the meeting to inform implementation of the release decision. In cases where the detainee requires support or accommodation from the local authority, a referral should be made for a needs assessment prior to release.

Statutory support framework for victims of modern slavery

5.260

The statutory framework governing support for victims of modern slavery has been significantly expanded through recent legislative reforms. Part 5 of the NABA 2022 places the recovery and reflection period, and the broader support and assistance process for potential victims, on a statutory footing. This marks a shift away from reliance on contractual arrangements, establishing a legal obligation to provide support.

5.261

Section 65 of the NABA 2022 and s 50A of the MSA 2015 set out the eligibility criteria, minimum periods of support, and the nature of assistance to be delivered under the *Modern Slavery Victim Care Contract* (MSVCC). Upon a positive reasonable grounds decision within the NRM, support must be provided in accordance with statutory guidance. This includes emergency accommodation prior to a decision and comprehensive support thereafter, with providers under a legal duty to conduct regular needs and risk assessments.

5.262

While these provisions increase legal certainty and impose clearer obligations on support organisations, they have also attracted criticism. Concerns have been raised about the adequacy and accessibility of support in practice, and whether the statutory framework sufficiently reflects the protective obligations owed to victims under international and human rights law.

Eligibility and support under the Modern Slavery Victim Care Contract (MSVCC)

5.263

As above, a safe discharge under the Adults at Risk Modern Slavery Guidance will include a referral for assessment of MSVCC support. The MSVCC process is outside the scope of this chapter, however it was examined by the court in *R (ETX) v SSHD*[172].

5.264

In summary, the MSVCC provides support to individuals referred into the National Referral Mechanism (NRM) who may be victims of modern slavery. Eligibility and the nature of support depend on the stage of the identification process, specifically whether a reasonable grounds decision has been made.

5.265

The stages are as follows:

Pre-reasonable grounds decision

5.266

Before a formal reasonable grounds decision is issued, emergency support and assessment may be provided to address immediate risks:

Emergency support

5.267

Emergency accommodation and financial assistance may be offered to prevent destitution or further exploitation. This support is available immediately upon referral into the NRM.

Initial needs-based assessment

5.268

Where emergency accommodation is required, an initial assessment is conducted by The Salvation Army (the MSVCC prime contractor) or its subcontractors. This assessment identifies urgent welfare needs and risks, particularly relating to re-exploitation and homelessness.

172 *R (ETX) v SSHD* [2025] EWHC 294 (Admin) at [38-40].

Risk assessment

5.269

Provision of emergency accommodation is contingent on a risk assessment confirming that the individual has no safe alternative and would be at risk without support.

Post-reasonable grounds decision

5.270

Once a positive reasonable grounds decision is made, the individual is formally recognised as a potential victim of modern slavery and becomes eligible for the full MSVCC support package.

Comprehensive support

5.271

This includes secure accommodation, subsistence payments, and a dedicated support worker.

Recovery and reflection plan

5.272

A detailed needs-based assessment is undertaken to develop a tailored recovery and reflection plan, addressing the individual's specific circumstances.

Ongoing assessment

5.273

Support providers are required to conduct regular reviews of the individual's needs and risks throughout the support period.

Statutory framework for adult social care assessments

5.274

MSVCC support constitutes limited, recovery-focused assistance and does not displace or exhaust local authorities' independent safeguarding and care-and-support duties under the Care Act 2014 where the statutory thresholds are met. Local authorities must therefore still assess an adult's needs and, where appropriate, assume responsibility under the Care Act 2014, even where the individual is receiving MSVCC support. Part 1 of the Care Act 2014 sets out the framework within which local authority adult social care services should act where there appears to be a vulnerable adult in its area.

5.275

By the Care Act 2014, s 9(1), the local authority is required to undertake an assessment where it appears there is an adult who may have needs for care and support. The threshold for a request for an assessment is low. Questions about whether a person will require services at the end of the assessment process should form a part of the assessment process rather than be used as a barrier to the assessment process commencing.

5.276

Section 42 of the Care Act 2014 imposes a mandatory duty on local authorities to initiate a safeguarding enquiry where there is reasonable cause to suspect that an adult in its area, irrespective of their ordinary residence, meets the statutory criteria.

5.277

The duty arises where the following three conditions are satisfied:

1. The adult has needs for care and support, whether or not those needs are currently being met by the authority;
2. The adult is experiencing, or is at risk of, abuse or neglect; and
3. As a result of those care and support needs, the adult is unable to protect themselves from the risk of, or the experience of, such abuse or neglect.

5.278

The statutory threshold is deliberately broad, reflecting the preventative and protective purpose of the safeguarding framework. The duty to enquire is not contingent upon the adult being in receipt of services, nor does it require conclusive evidence of abuse or neglect, only a reasonable cause to suspect. The enquiry must be proportionate to the presenting concerns and may range from a simple conversation to a more formal multi-agency investigation, depending on the circumstances.

5.279

The *Care and Support Statutory Guidance*[173] issued under the Care Act 2014 explicitly recognises modern slavery as a form of abuse for the purposes of

173 Department of Health and Social Care, *Care and Support Statutory Guidance* (updated 22 July 2025) https://www.gov.uk/government/publications/care-act-statutory-guidance/care-and-support-statutory-guidance accessed 1 February 2026.

safeguarding. Paragraph 14.17 advises that local authorities should adopt a broad and flexible understanding of abuse and neglect, tailored to the circumstances of each individual case. While the statutory criteria under s 42 must be met before a safeguarding enquiry is triggered, exploitation is identified as a recurring theme across various abuse categories.

5.280

The *Care and Support Statutory Guidance* defines 'Modern slavery' as:

- Slavery;
- Human trafficking;
- Forced labour; and
- Domestic servitude.

Servitude is not however confined to domestic servitude (see **Chapter 1**).

5.281

The guidance highlights that traffickers and slave masters may use coercion, deception, and force to subject individuals to abuse, servitude, and inhumane treatment. This places modern slavery firmly within the scope of safeguarding responsibilities under the Care Act, requiring local authorities to respond appropriately where such concerns arise.

Purpose and conduct of the needs assessment

5.282

The Care Act assessment is to determine what needs, if any, the adult has; what impact the needs have on the adult's well-being; and what support is required. Regulation 3 of the Care and Support (Assessment) Regulations 2014 set down further requirements of the needs assessment, notably a requirement that the adult can participate in the process as effectively as possible, and the assessment is conducted in a proportionate way.

Consideration of wishes, preferences, and expertise

5.283

It is important for the local authority to have regard to the wishes and preferences of the adult, the outcome the adult seeks from assessment and the severity and overall extent of the adult's needs.

5.284

By regulation 5 of the Care and Support (Assessment) Regulations 2014, the local authority is obliged to ensure that anyone carrying out an assessment has the relevant skills, knowledge and competence and is appropriately trained. The local authority must also consult a person who has 'expertise in relation to the condition or other circumstances of the individual whose needs are being assessed in any case where it considers that the needs of the individual concerned require it to do so'. This should be done before or during the assessment process.

5.285

The need to draw on appropriate expertise, particularly where there are complex needs and specific clinical conditions, is reiterated in the statutory guidance to the Care Act 2014[174].

Determining eligibility for support

5.286

Where an assessment identifies needs, the local authority must decide if any of the needs are sufficient to meet the eligibility criteria and, if so, consider with the individual how to meet those needs. To be eligible, the individual must satisfy three requirements under the Care Act (Eligibility Criteria) Regulations 2015, reg 2.

5.287

The test is:

- needs must be the result of a physical or mental impairment or illness;
- as a result, the person assessed must be unable to achieve two or more specified outcomes (under reg 2(2));
- as a consequence, there is (or there is likely to be) a significant impact on the person's well-being.

Specified outcomes and the meaning of 'unable to achieve'

5.288

'Outcomes' is specified in the Care Act (Eligibility Criteria) Regulations 2015, reg 2(2). These are broadly drawn and cover: managing and maintaining

174 Department of Health and Social Care, *Care and Support Statutory Guidance* (updated 24 June 2022) https://www.gov.uk/government/publications/care-act-statutory-guidance/care-and-support-statutory-guidance accessed 24 August 2025 at paras 6.7, 6.86 and 6.88.

nutrition; maintaining personal hygiene; managing toilet needs; being appropriately clothed; being able to make use of the home safely; maintaining a habitable home environment; developing and maintaining family or other personal relationships; accessing and engaging in work, training, education or volunteering; making use of necessary facilities or services in the local community including public transport, and recreational facilities or services.

5.289

'Significant impact' carries its 'everyday meaning' and includes 'whether the adult's needs and their consequent inability to achieve the relevant outcomes will have an important consequential effect on their daily lives, their independence and their wellbeing'.

5.290

Paragraph 6.105 of the statutory guidance elaborates on what is meant by 'unable to achieve' an outcome under reg 2(3) and includes the following circumstances, where the adult:

- is unable to achieve the outcome without assistance: including where the adult may need prompting: for example, some adults may be physically able to wash but need reminding of the importance of personal hygiene;
- is able to achieve the outcome without assistance but doing so causes the adult significant pain, distress or anxiety: for example, an adult may be able to prepare a meal, but this would leave him in pain and unable to eat the meal;
- is able to achieve the outcome without assistance, but doing so endangers or is likely to endanger the health or safety of the adult, or of others: for example, if the health or safety of others could be endangered when an adult attempts to complete a task or an activity without relevant support;
- is able to achieve the outcome without assistance but takes significantly longer than would normally be expected: for example, an adult with a physical disability is able to dress himself in the morning, but it takes him a long time to do this, leaves him exhausted and prevents him from achieving other outcomes.

Accommodation as a component of eligible needs

5.291

Eligible needs can, in principle, be met by the provision of accommodation, particularly if the care and support would be rendered ineffective if accommodation is not provided. The Care Act 2014 is not directed at meeting a bare need for accommodation for those subject to immigration control because of destitution. However, where an individual subject to immigration control has accommodation related needs, they are to be provided by the local authority, without considering any support which may in the future be offered by the Home Secretary to avoid destitution. The Home Secretary has a free-standing residual duty to support a person subject to immigration control where it appears to her such a person is destitute or likely to become destitute.

Interim support pending assessment

5.292

Pending an assessment, the local authority has a power to provide interim care and support under the Care Act 2014, s 19. This would apply to vulnerable adults referred by the Home Office for assessment and who can be released into the community pending assessment. There is no reason in law for there to be delay in release simply because the assessment has not been completed, particularly where the criteria for detention are no longer met.

6 The legal significance of age: assessments, disputes, and their consequences in immigration, social welfare and criminal contexts

Jennifer Twite and Michelle Brewer

Introduction[1]

6.1

Refugee and migrant children who arrive in the United Kingdom unaccompanied, whether they are seeking asylum, are victims of modern slavery, or have been trafficked for the purposes of exploitation[2], are among the most vulnerable individuals encountered within the justice and welfare systems. **Chapter 1** examines the legal definitions of modern slavery and human trafficking. Age disputes frequently arise in these contexts, particularly where children are separated from caregivers and lack reliable identity documentation. Some children arrive without any identifying papers; others may carry documents that are false or misleading, having been instructed to misrepresent their age to avoid detection[3]. In some cases, traffickers or agents provide fabricated personal histories, including false dates of birth, to facilitate travel and the creation of fraudulent identity documents. Even where documentary evidence exists to support a claimed age, it may require translation or verification, and its provenance must be carefully assessed.

1 This chapter was authored by Shu Shin Luh in both the first and second editions.
2 See for example, the first three appellants in the linked appeals in *R v L* [2013] EWCA Crim 991, [2014] 1 All ER 113.
3 See Home Office and Department for Education: 'Safeguarding children who may have been trafficked: practice guidance' (18 October 2011), available at: https://www.gov.uk/government/publications/safeguarding-children-who-may-have-been-trafficked-practice-guidance last accessed 16 December 2025, and report: 'Heading back to Harm', ECPAT UK and Missing People (November 2016).

6.2

Determining a person's age is a critical step in ensuring that children receive the protections and entitlements afforded to them under domestic and international law. Age is not a mere administrative detail; it is central to how an individual is treated within the justice system, shaping the procedural safeguards available and the support to which they are entitled. When a child is wrongly assessed as an adult, the consequences are serious and wide-ranging. Misidentification may result in the denial of access to welfare services, education, legal representation, and guardianship. In the asylum and immigration process, it can lead to detention alongside adults and the risk of removal rather than protection. In criminal proceedings, it may expose children to adult custodial environments and sentencing regimes, depriving them of the special measures and protections that underpin youth justice.

6.3

For child victims of trafficking and modern slavery, misidentification of age significantly increases the risk that they will not be identified as victims; it also heightens the likelihood of children going missing and of being trafficked, subjected to slavery, or exposed to related harms within the UK.

6.4

This chapter will examine:

- the significance of age in International Law
- the significance of age in domestic law: Social Welfare, Immigration and Criminal considered
- the legal and policy frameworks that guide how public authorities assess age; and
- the procedures and approaches used to resolve age disputes in both immigration and criminal jurisdictions.

International law

The United Nations Convention on the Rights of the Child 1989

6.5

The United Nations Declaration on the Rights of the Child 1959 and the UN Convention on the Rights of the Child 1989 ('UNCRC') both require that a child enjoy special protection[4]. The guiding principle for safeguarding and promoting the welfare of children is contained in UNCRC, Art 3:

4 For discussion, see *R (on the application of HC) v Secretary of State for the Home Department* [2013] EWHC 982 (Admin), [2014] 1 WLR 1234.

'In all actions concerning children, whether undertaken by public or private social welfare institutions, courts of law, administrative authorities or legislative bodies, the best interests of the child should be of primary consideration.'

6.6

The principle of 'best interests' appears repeatedly throughout the UNCRC, for example in Arts 9, 18, 20 and 21. Whilst the UNCRC is not directly incorporated into the domestic law in England and Wales[5], the aims of the UNCRC and the best interests approach to affording children special protection are recognised across the different areas of law, including social welfare, education, immigration and crime[6]. In England and Wales, a breach of an article under the UNCRC cannot be litigated, as it does not apply directly in domestic law, but it may be relevant to the application of rights under the European Convention on Human Rights ('ECHR'), and in particular when assessing whether differential treatment is justifiable under Art 14 together with Art 8 in a matter concerning a child[7].

6.7

The special protection afforded under the UNCRC and in domestic law is predicated on an individual being in fact a child.

6.8

Article 1 of the UNCRC defines a child as a human being who is under the age of 18. The UK's domestic law adopts the same definition in almost all circumstances.

International law: child victims of slavery, servitude, forced or compulsory labour or trafficking

6.9

As detailed extensively in **Chapter 1**, both international and domestic law draw a clear distinction between adult and child victims, recognising the unique vulnerabilities of children. Where the victim is a child, the elements of criminal

5 The United Nations Convention on the Rights of the Child is now incorporated into Scots law through the United Nations Convention on the Rights of the Child (Incorporation) (Scotland) Act 2024.

6 See *ZH (Tanzania) v Secretary of State for the Home Department* [2011] UKSC 4, [2011] 2 AC 166; *R (on the application of HC) v Secretary of State for the Home Department* [2013] EWHC 982 (Admin), [2014] 1 WLR 1234; *R (on the application of Mathieson) v Secretary of State for Work and Pensions* [2015] UKSC 47, [2015] 1 WLR 3250; *R (on the application of SG) v Secretary of State for Work and Pensions* [2015] UKSC 16, [2015] 1 WLR 1449.

7 *R(on the application of SC) v Secretary of State for Work and Pensions* [2021] UKSC 26, [2022] AC 223.

offences[8], as well as the processes of identification and investigation, are adapted to reflect their specific needs and circumstances. The protections afforded to victims also differ for children, including the application of non-punishment provisions[9], which are tailored to safeguard child victims from being penalised for unlawful acts committed because of their exploitation.

Importance and relevance of age in the context of social welfare law

6.10

The Supreme Court has held in *R (on the application of A) v Croydon London Borough Council*[10] that a person's age is an objective fact which admits only a right or a wrong answer[11]. It is not a matter of subjective evaluation by an individual decision-maker, and certainly not a summary one without proper inquiries. The precedent fact of age is a gateway decision that unlocks access to the child of child-centred accommodation, support, and special protection in the immigration and youth justice context.

6.11

The *A v Croydon* case concerned a local authority children's services department, which was obliged to provide an unaccompanied asylum-seeking child with accommodation and support under the Children Act 1989, s 20[12] because there was no-one with parental responsibility and no family or friend able to take care of the child. Where a child falls under the criteria of s 20 the local authority must provide accommodation and has *no discretion* to do otherwise[13]. Section 105 of the Children Act 1989 defines a child objectively as someone under 18. If a person is a child, it unlocks a host of special protections that adult asylum-seekers cannot access.

6.12

Children who are taken into 'voluntary care', as s 20 accommodation is often described, are entitled to a suite of further special protection measures from the local authority (see **6.16–6.17** below). The authority is obliged to:

- arrange accommodation suitable to the child's needs and age;
- make educational provision for the child, whether the child is of statutory school age or beyond;

---

8 See **Chapters 1** and **9**.
9 See **Chapter 10**.
10 [2009] UKSC 8, [2009] 1 WLR 2557.
11 Per Lady Hale at [27] and [33], Lord Hope at [52]–[54].
12 See *Williams v London Borough of Hackney* [2018] UKSC 37 for the importance of s 20.
13 *R (G) v Southwark LBC* [2009] UKHL 26.

- support the child to access legal representation for immigration advice; and
- care for the child generally as a reasonable parent would do.

6.13

Once accommodated, the child is considered 'looked after' by the local authority under the Children Act 1989, s 22. The duty to promote and safeguard all aspects of the child's welfare is engaged and requires a best interest's approach to care planning for the child. The Judicial College Best Practice Guidance on ss 20 and 76 of the Children's Act 1989[14] is an important resource to practitioners and local authorities. This guidance outlines best practices for the use of voluntary accommodation under s 20 of the Children Act 1989 (England) and s 76 of the Social Services and Well-being (Wales) Act 2014. It aims to ensure lawful, informed, and child-focused decision-making by local authorities and practitioners. The Transparency Project[15] also provide a guidance note which is updated on Section 20: for both parents and professionals.

6.14

Accommodation arrangements are often highly dependent on the child's age. Whilst there are no hard and fast rules; arrangements should be made in accordance with the child's needs. Children aged 15 and under tend to be placed in foster care, whereas some 16- and 17-year-olds will be placed in semi-independent accommodation depending on their circumstances. Placements must be tailored to the individual child's needs.

6.15

Educational placements are also determined by the precise age of the child. For example, children under 16 are of statutory school age, and all children are obliged to be in education or training until the age of 18. The local authority, acting as corporate parent, is obliged in law to enrol the looked after child in education, whether in a school or otherwise in an alternative facility. There are continuing duties to promote the child's educational achievement beyond statutory school age if the child is looked after by the local authority.

6.16

The duties owed to 'looked after' children who are in voluntary care continue beyond the child's 18th birthday. When they turn 18, if they have

14 Judicial College, *Section 20 and Section 76 of the Children Act 1989: Best Practice Guidance* (March 2021) https://www.judiciary.uk/wp-content/uploads/2021/03/S-20-s-76-BPG-report_clickable.pdf accessed at 16 December 2025.

15 The Transparency Project, *Guidance on the Use of Section 20 of the Children Act 1989* (version 4, 19 January 2022) https://www.transparencyproject.org.uk/wp-content/uploads/Section-20-Guidance-v4-19-jan-2022.pdf accessed at 16 December 2025.

been looked after by the local authority, whether under a care order or under s 20 accommodation arrangements for 13 weeks or more, with at least one day being when the child is over the age of 16, they acquire status as former relevant children (defined under the Children Act 1989, s 23C(1)). Where they have been looked after for a shorter time so that they do not acquire the former relevant child status, they become a 'Qualifying Young Person' under the Children Act 1989, s 24.

6.17

Former relevant children under s 23C(4) of the Act continue to receive assistance from the local authority, which can include continued suitable accommodation arrangements in accordance with the former relevant child's needs, support to access education and vocational training and general advice and assistance. The local authority also has a duty to advise and befriend those qualifying young people who needs help of the kind provided under the Act[16]. This can also amount to help in kind or help with accommodation. In both cases the support should be akin to what a reasonable parent would provide for a child transitioning into adulthood. See paras 1.8 and 1.10 of the *Children Act 1989 Guidance and Regulations: Transition to Adulthood for care leavers*[17]. These leaving care duties continue until at least the former relevant child or qualifying young persons' 21st birthday and, in circumstances where they remain in education or are returning to education, the duties can continue up to that person's 25th birthday.

Importance and relevance of age in the context of asylum and immigration law

6.18

The objective fact of age is a material consideration in the exercise of immigration powers by the Home Office, both in decisions concerning the grant or refusal of leave to remain in respect of children, and in decisions relating to detention.

6.19

In all decisions concerning children, the Home Office is obliged to have due regard to the need to safeguard and promote the welfare of the child pursuant to the Borders, Citizenship and Immigration Act 2009, s 55. Section 55(6) defines children as those under the age of 18.

16 Section 24A Children Act 1989.
17 Department for Education (revised February 2022).

6.20

Section 55 was introduced following the United Kingdom's withdrawal of its reservation to the United Nations Convention on the Rights of the Child (UNCRC) in relation to immigration matters affecting children. Its language closely reflects the statutory duty imposed on public bodies, including local authorities, health services, police, and youth offending teams, under s 11 of the Children Act 2004.

6.21

As the Supreme Court stated in *CAO v Secretary of State for the Home Department*[18] at [97]

> 'As explained above, where a measure is adopted by a public authority which affects the private life or family life interests of a child, it is required under article 8 that the best interests of the child feature as a primary consideration in the decision-making process. As a public authority, the Secretary of State (and his or her officials) are obliged pursuant to section 6(1) of the HRA to act compatibly with the child's Convention rights, including by treating the child's best interests as a primary consideration. That obligation applies regardless of the operation of section 55. The FTT, which is also a public authority, is itself subject to the same obligation in relation to its own decision-making on an appeal.'

6.22

Specific immigration rules recognise and afford the special protection status required by children. For example, para 350 of the Immigration Rules[19] requires that in the case of unaccompanied children, priority and care is given to the handling of their cases. Paragraphs 352 and 352ZA set out the requirements for undertaking asylum interviews with children, including the requirement that the child be given an opportunity to have an appropriate adult present for the interview. Only decision-makers who have received specialist training can make decisions in asylum claims from children, and they must also observe a wealth of guidance on the different approach to be taken to assessing the credibility of child asylum seekers, having regard to the child's age and maturity and recognising that more weight may need to be given to objective evidence than to the child's subjective fears.

6.23

More importantly, in the context of immigration detention, by an amendment to the detention powers, the Immigration Act 1971, Sch 2, para 18B now

18 [2024] WLR(D) 454, [2024] 3 WLR 847, [2024] UKSC 32.
19 Published 29 February 2016, updated 26 November 2024.

prohibits the detention of an individual who is objectively and in fact a child, other than for 24 hours in a short-term holding facility when the circumstances as prescribed by para 18(3) are met.

6.24

Deprivation of a child's liberty would constitute a false imprisonment whether the Home Office reasonably believed or suspected him to be an adult at the time[20] (see **Chapter 5**). Where a dispute about age arises, the Home Office's policy is to presume that the person is a child (albeit age disputed) pending inquiries unless, and only unless the person's physical appearance *very strongly* suggests that he is significantly over 18. 'The term 'significantly over 18' was not clearly defined in the Home Office's age assessment policy, and this lack of clarity was challenged in *R (BF) v Secretary of State for the Home Department*[21]. The Court of Appeal criticised the ambiguity and emphasised that the policy should only be applied in cases where it is obvious that the individual is well above 18. However, the Supreme Court ultimately upheld the lawfulness of the Secretary of State's policy, finding that while the guidance could be improved, it did not render the policy itself unlawful[22].

Importance and relevance of age in the context of youth justice

6.25

The importance of establishing the right answer as to the objective fact of age is self-evident in the youth justice context. Children are treated fundamentally differently in all aspects of the Criminal Justice System as compared to adults. The principles that underpin this are enshrined in both international and domestic law.

6.26

In General Comment No 10 (2007) on *Children's Rights in Juvenile Justice*, the Committee on the Rights of the Child stated that children differ from adults in their physical and psychological development, and their emotional and educational needs. Such differences constitute the basis for the lesser culpability of children in conflict with the law. These and other differences are the reasons for a separate juvenile justice system and 'require a different treatment for children'. The protection of the best interests of the child is one reason why the

20 *R (on the application of AA) (Sudan) v Secretary of State for the Home Department* [2017] EWCA Civ 138, [2017] 1 WLR 2894.

21 [2019] EWCA Civ 872, [2020] 4 WLR 38.

22 *R(BF Eritrea) v Secretary of State for the Home Department* [2021] UKSC 38; 1 WLR 3967.

traditional objectives of criminal justice, such as retribution, must give way to rehabilitation and restorative justice objectives in dealing with child offenders[23].

6.27

If the court gets the answer to age wrong this may result in a putative child, wrongly deemed to be an adult, being denied the safeguards fundamental to the youth justice system, including the decision as to whether it was in the interests of justice to charge him with the offence. The fact that he was a child, if subsequently discovered will not automatically invalidate the conviction or proceedings[24], although it may give rise to an argument for an appeal.

Principles of youth justice

6.28

Articles 37 and 40 of the UNCRC are of importance in this context, as the former deals with detention and the latter with juvenile justice[25]:

> '17.1 Article 37(a) provides that 'no child shall be deprived of his or her liberty unlawfully or arbitrarily. The arrest, detention or imprisonment of a child shall be in conformity with the law and shall be used only as a measure of last resort and for the shortest appropriate period of time'. Article 37(c) provides that, 'every child deprived of liberty shall be treated with humanity and respect for the inherent dignity of the human person, and in a manner which takes into account the needs of persons of his or her age'.
>
> 17.2 This is echoed in Article 40 which in essence provides that any child of under 18 accused of, or guilty of, breaking the law must be treated with dignity and respect, and they have a range of minimum procedural rights which must be provided in a manner which takes account of their age and situation. Article 40(2)(b) describes the seven bare minimum requirements ('at least the following guarantees'),

23 The Supreme Court has held that the General Comments of the CRC provide 'authoritative guidance' on the effect of the provisions of the CRC: *R (on the application of Mathieson) v Secretary of State for Work and Pensions* [2015] UKSC 47, [2015] 1 WLR 3250 at [39], endorsing *R (on the application of SG) v Secretary of State for Work and Pensions* [2015] UKSC 16, [2015] 1 WLR 1449 at [105]–[106].

24 *R v Steed* [1990] 5 WLUK 7.

25 The essential safeguards in the UNCRC concerning children in conflict with the law are supplemented by many other specific instruments. See eg The United Nations Standard Minimum Rules for the Administration of Juvenile Justice ('the Beijing Rules' 1985); the United Nations Guidelines for the Prevention of Juvenile Delinquency ('the Riyadh Guidelines'); the United Nations Rules for the Protection of Juveniles Deprived of their Liberty ('the Havana Rules'); the UN Guidelines for Action on Children in the Criminal Justice System ('the Vienna Guidelines', 1997); and the UN Model Strategies and Practical Measures on the Elimination of Violence against Children in the Field of Crime Prevention and Criminal Justice (2014).

including the right to have the matter determined by a competent, independent and impartial authority or judicial body in a fair hearing according to the law, bearing in mind the best interests of the child, taking into account his or her age or situation; and the right to have his or her privacy fully respected at all stages of the proceedings.

17.3 Article 40(3) requires that State parties shall seek to promote the establishment of laws, procedures, authorities and institutions specifically applicable to children, rather than treating them in the same manner and through the same mechanisms as adult suspects or adult offenders.'

6.29

Domestic law concerning youth justice has also long recognised the need to have regard to a child's welfare, and the special position of children who offend, who are afforded special protections that emphasise rehabilitation and reintegration[26]. The principal aim of the youth justice system is to prevent offending by young people, as enshrined in the Crime and Disorder Act 1998, s 37(1). Thus, the approach to child defendants is necessarily different. The age of criminal responsibility is 10 years old[27]. Sentencing guidelines and sentencing powers are guided by age. The fact of age is significant for how the criminal justice system deals with a person.

The Youth Justice Charter

6.30

On 15 July 2025, the Ministry of Justice published the *Youth Justice Charter*[28], a consolidated document outlining the rights and entitlements of children aged 10 to 17 who come into contact with the youth justice system.

6.31

The Charter does not create new legal protections but brings together existing statutory standards and best practices to provide clarity and consistency across the system. Structured around five key stages: from initial police contact through to post-custody support. It sets out what children should expect from professionals including police officers, lawyers, youth justice workers, judges, and custody staff. It affirms every child's right to be treated with dignity, fairness,

26 *R v G* [2003] UKHL 50, [2004] 1 AC 1034.
27 CYPA 1933, s 50.
28 Ministry of Justice, *Youth Justice Charter* (15 July 2025) https://youthjusticecharter.campaign.gov.uk/ accessed 16 December 2025.

and respect, to receive legal support and clear information, to be heard, kept safe, and given opportunities for development.

6.32

Agencies across the youth justice system have committed to upholding these standards, and the Charter provides mechanisms for children to raise concerns where they believe these standards have not been met. It is intended as a practical tool to help children navigate the system and reinforce a rights-based approach to youth justice.

Decision to prosecute

6.33

The Crown Prosecution Service has detailed guidance (*The CPS: Children as Suspects and Defendants*[29]) on prosecuting child defendants. The public interest test for prosecution demands different considerations than in the context of an adult, requiring the CPS to consider the age and maturity of any suspect[30] when deciding whether to prosecute, and requires the prosecutor to consider the best interests and welfare of both the accused and the victim (if the latter is also a child).

Court venue

Youth Court

6.34

Most child defendants will have their cases heard in the Youth Court: a specialist court of summary jurisdiction[31], where the magistrates or district judges are required to undergo specialist training and where both the layout and the procedures of the court are different and are guided by the Youth Court Bench Book[32]. There is an assumption that the Youth Court is the most appropriate forum to try child defendants, having regard to the best interests and welfare of the child, the importance of a child's effective participation and a fair trial. This manifests in the material difference in trial environment and process in the Youth Court as compared to adult courts, including a less formal layout,

29 Crown Prosecution Service, *Children as Suspects and Defendants: Legal Guidance* https://www.cps.gov.uk/legal-guidance/children-suspects-and-defendants accessed 16 December 2025.

30 Para 4.14(d) Code for Crown Prosecutors, 26 October 2018.

31 CYPA 1933, s49.

32 Judicial College, *Youth Court Bench Book* (September 2025) https://www.judiciary.uk/about-the-judiciary/who-are-the-judiciary/magistrates/youth-court-bench-book/ accessed 16 December 2025.

private hearings where there is no public gallery[33] and automatic reporting restrictions[34] (see **Chapter 8** for Special Measures). The September 2025 *Youth Court Bench Book* explicitly notes that it now refers to all defendants under 18 as 'child' or 'children', replacing earlier references to 'child or young person', and explains that this change is to align terminology and encourage the distinct approach required when dealing with under-18s. CPS guidance similarly states that, for its purposes, 'the terms 'child' and 'children' will be used to refer to all young people below the age of 18.

6.35

The child's first court appearance in respect of an offence will be in the Youth Court unless he has an adult as a co-defendant.

6.36

Most children will remain in the Youth Court for their trial. This is significantly different to adult defendants who will be sent to the Crown Court if they are charged with an offence that is 'indictable only' or where the Magistrates' Court consider that they will receive a sentence of longer than 12 months' imprisonment.

6.37

Adults also have the right to elect trial by jury if they are charged with an 'either-way' offence. A child defendant does not have the right to elect a Crown Court trial.

6.38

They will only be sent to the Crown Court in cases where they have an adult co-defendant who has been sent to the Crown Court, and it is considered in the interests of justice for them to be tried together[35], or where they are charged with a serious offence[36]. Serious offences include certain offences such as murder, which must be sent to the Crown Court, and other 'grave crimes', where the Youth Court has a discretion to commit the case.

6.39

In the latter category, the case will only be sent to the Crown Court if there is a real prospect that the child would receive a custodial sentence exceeding two years[37]. The Youth Court has greater sentencing powers than the Magistrates' Court and can sentence a child to a custodial sentence of up to two years. Even

33 CYPA 1933, 47.
34 CYPA 1933, ss 47 and 49.
35 Crime and Disorder Act 1998, s 51(7).
36 Crime and Disorder Act 1998, s 51A.
37 Sentencing Council: *Sentencing Children and Young People, Overarching Principles,* 1 June 2017 para 2.8.

in cases where the sentence is likely to be significant the Youth Court will often retain the case and commit the child to the Crown Court for sentence, if found guilty after trial.

Crown Court

6.40

When a child does have a trial in the Crown Court special modifications and safeguards should be put in place to ensure that the child can effectively participate and to ensure that their welfare is considered. All criminal courts have a statutory duty to consider the welfare of any child before them, including the defendant[38]. These modifications should be considered at a Ground Rules Hearing and can include but are not limited to, allowing for less formal court set-up including the removal of wigs and gowns, the exclusion of the public, reporting restrictions and the attendance of parent or guardian and/or supporting adult[39]. See Chapter 8: Special Measures and the Child Defendants in the Crown Court Bench Book[40]. The latter is written by judges and commended by the Senior Courts as an essential guide.

Bail

6.41

Although the criteria for granting bail under the Bail Act 1976 are virtually the same for adults and children, there are several important differences which put the primacy of protection of the welfare of the child at their heart. For example, the court has a discretion to refuse bail where this is necessary for a child's welfare or protection[41]. A parent or guardian may be asked to act as surety as a condition of bail[42].

6.42

The local authority through the youth justice service has a statutory duty to support children on bail[43], this entails presenting the court with 'bail packages' in more serious cases where a child is supported by the youth justice service

38 CYPA 1933, s 44.

39 Lord Chief Justice, Criminal Practice Directions 2023 [2023] EWCA Crim 1, as amended November 2025: https://www.judiciary.uk/wp-content/uploads/2025/11/Criminal-Practice-Directions-2023-as-amended-Nov-2025.pdf accessed at 16 December 2025.

40 Judicial College, *Child Defendants in the Crown Court* (June 2025) https://www.judiciary.uk/wp-content/uploads/2025/06/Child-Defendants-in-the-Crown-Court-June-2025.pdf accessed 16 December 2025.

41 Bail Act 1976, Sch 1, para 1.

42 Bail Act 1976, s 3(7).

43 Crime and Disorder Act 1998 s38(4)(c).

throughout his time on bail. These support packages, along with the different approach to children and duty to consider their welfare mean that children are far more likely to be released on bail than an adult in a similar position. Further children without a suitable place to live where they can safely be bailed to will necessarily meet the criteria for local authority accommodation under the Children Act 1989, s 20.

6.43

Where bail is refused, the court adopts a markedly different approach to remand in the case of children compared to adults. The default position, where bail is withheld from a child, is that the child is remanded to local authority accommodation. This accommodation is typically non-secure and is often subject to specified conditions. A child may only be remanded to youth detention accommodation where stringent statutory criteria are met, reflecting the heightened protections afforded to children within the criminal justice system[44].

6.44

A child erroneously treated as an adult, is self-evidently excluded from the precautionary and protective measures afforded to children. Where an unaccompanied minor is incorrectly charged as an adult and lacks access to a suitable bail address, typically provided through local authority assistance, the consequence may be that they are remanded to an adult prison rather than placed in appropriate accommodation. This issue arose in *R (M) v Hammersmith Magistrates' Court*[45], where the High Court quashed the Magistrates' Court's decision and directed that the putative child be remanded to local authority accommodation under s 92 of the Legal Aid, Sentencing and Punishment of Offenders Act 2012 (LASPO), pending the outcome of an age assessment.'

Assessing age

Local authority age assessment, Merton Guidelines and the Nationality and Borders Act 2022

6.45

As early as 2003, local authority children's services developed a pro forma to support a more holistic approach to age assessment. This framework, adapted from the child development needs assessment model, identifies key domains of inquiry beyond physical appearance. It recognises that relying solely on physical appearance and demeanour is both risky and unreliable, particularly in

44 LASPO 2012, ss 91–107.
45 [2017] EWHC 1359 (Admin); [2017] 5 WLUK 130.

borderline cases involving individuals aged between 16 and 20. Ethnic, cultural, and situational factors can significantly influence how old a person presents[46], often leading to misjudgements. The guidance notes accompanying the pro forma explicitly caution that physical appearance and demeanour should be treated only as initial indicators, not as determinative factors. They are intended to prompt further inquiry, not determinative of the assessment process.

6.46

In *R (on the application of M) v The London Borough of Waltham Forest*[47] the Administrative Court confirmed that 'physical methods' of calculating age such as dental records or changes in height needed to be considered with considerable caution. There is no proven scientific process by which age can be precisely determined. Dental and wrist x-rays have long been criticised for the wide margin of error both by courts and by the Royal College of Paediatrics and Child Health in 1999 and in 2023[48].

6.47

Local authority guidance on age assessment has been progressively shaped and refined by case law, leading to the development of a set of core principles for conducting a fair and thorough factual inquiry into age. These principles extend well beyond superficial judgments based on physical appearance and demeanour.

6.48

Often referred to as the *Merton Guidelines*[49], these standards were summarised in *MVN v London Borough of Greenwich*[50], where the court outlined a list of factors at paragraph 30 that are essential to ensuring procedural fairness in age assessments. A similar set of procedural requirements was identified in *VS v Home Office*[51], and these were further refined and expanded upon in *R (AB) v Kent County Council*[52], which clarified and strengthened the expectations placed on public authorities when conducting age assessments.

---

46 *R (on the application of CJ) v Cardiff County Council* [2011] EWHC 23 (Admin), [2011] LGR 301 at [129]. In *R (on the application of HBH) v Secretary of State for the Home Department* [2009] EWHC 928 (Admin), the Administrative Court held that the methodology used to assess HBH's age was flawed because the court relied on an assessment limited to his appearance and demeanour.

47 [2021] EWHC 2241 (Admin); [2022] P.T.S.R. 150 at para 40.

48 Royal College of Paediatrics and Child Health, 'RCPCH Responds to UK Government Plans to Authorise Use of X-rays in Age Assessments of Children' (RCPCH, 10 January 2022) https://www.rcpch.ac.uk/news-events/news/rcpch-responds-uk-government-plans-authorise-use-x-rays-age-assessments-children accessed 16 December 2025.

49 From the case of *R (on the application of B) v Merton London Borough Council* [2003] EWHC 1689 (Admin).

50 [2015] EWHC 1942 (Admin).

51 [2014] EWHC 2483 (QB).

52 [2020] PTSR 746.

6.49

In *R(HAM)v London Borough of Brent*[53],Mr Justice Swift emphasised the need for the procedure to be fair, and that an age assessment may be quashed on that ground alone entirely independent of its substantive merit[54].

6.50

He stated that there were four principles that applied in these cases:

1. There is no burden of proof in determining the age of an individual (§10).
2. The local authority must make a determination based on reasonable enquiry and therefore take reasonable steps to obtain the information needed to decide (§10).
3. Where the age of an individual is not obvious such that it merits further enquiry or interview of that individual, any such procedure must be conducted fairly which should include an opportunity for an individual whose credibility is in doubt to respond to any suggestions that he is not telling the truth, often referred to as a 'minded to' interview (§11).
4. Finally, the requirement of fair procedure is one of substance not form and cannot be determined by adherence to a checklist. Whilst the 'lists' compiled in previous case law of what was required to make an assessment procedurally fair may be advisable, what was in fact required would be fact-specific to the individual case (§§12-14).

6.51

The lists of procedural requirements set out in the case law above continue to represent best practice and remain highly relevant in assessing whether an age determination has been properly conducted. However, failure to meet one of the criteria does not automatically render an assessment procedurally unfair. Any challenge must demonstrate how the specific omission or failure resulted in unfairness in the circumstances of the case.

6.52

These well-established principles have since been formally adopted in a comprehensive set of practice guidance published by the Association of Directors of Children's Services (ADCS) in April 2015[55]. The guidance was the product of over three years of consultation with a wide range of stakeholders, including the Home Office, children's rights organisations, the Children's Commissioner,

53 [2022] EWHC 1924 (Admin); [2022] PTSR 1779.

54 At [6].

55 Association of Directors of Children's Services, *Age Assessment Guidance* (April 2015) https://www.adcs.org.uk/age-assessment-guidance/ accessed 16 December 2025.

social workers, and legal representatives acting for individuals involved in age disputes. This guidance is cited in the Home Office guidance[56] on the National Age Assessment Board, discussed below, which states that it is Home Office policy that the NAAB must have regard to that best practice guidance.

6.53

Age assessments for unaccompanied asylum-seeking children whose age is in dispute were traditionally carried out by social workers within local authorities, usually in the area where the young person was living. The Nationality and Borders Act 2022 and the Illegal Migration Act 2023 have introduced significant changes by giving the Home Office new powers to establish the National Age Assessment Board (NAAB). The NAAB is authorised to conduct age assessments on behalf of the Home Office and has recruited its own social workers to carry out this function.

Statutory framework for age assessments under the Nationality and Borders Act 2022

6.54

Part 4 of the Nationality and Borders Act 2022 (NABA 2022) introduced a new statutory framework governing age assessments in the immigration context. Sections 49 to 57 of the Act mark a significant departure from the previous system, which relied primarily on Merton-compliant assessments conducted by local authorities, subject to judicial review.

6.55

The Act established the National Age Assessment Board (NAAB), to which local authorities may refer individuals where there is a dispute regarding age. Local authorities retain the discretion to conduct age assessments themselves. Separately, the Home Office may refer an individual to the NAAB either where the local authority is not involved in the age determination process, or where the Secretary of State has reason to question the local authority's conclusion[57]. Where a local authority undertakes an age assessment or accepts the individual's claimed age without conducting one, it is required to notify the Secretary of State of its decision[58] and to provide any supporting evidence that the Secretary of State reasonably requires[59].

56 The Operation of the National Age Assessment Board and section 50 and 51 of the NABA 2022, updated 2 July 2025 at p.20.
57 Section 51 NABA 2022.
58 Section 50(3) NABA 2022.
59 Section 50(4) NABA 2022.

6.56

Section 53 of the Act allows the Secretary of State to make regulations stipulating how age assessments under ss 50 and 51 must be conducted. The published guidance states that the Home Office policy, in the absence of such regulations, is that the NAAB should take into account the best practice guidance relevant for the country the individual resides in. For England this is the ADCS guidance cited above, and for Wales: the Unaccompanied Asylum Seeking Children Age assessment toolkit[60].

Policy Guidance on age assessment

6.57

Joint Working Guidance[61]: Following the enactment of the Nationality and Borders Act 2022 (NABA), in March 2023, the ADCS and Home Office replaced the original Joint Working Guidance setting out the agreed arrangements between the Home Office and Local Authority, where either disputes the age of a person identifying as a child. The provisions in NABA specific to age assessments are set out below. The guidance records that where the Home Office on receiving a local authority age assessment has concerns this should be discussed with the local authority[62].

6.58

National Age Assessment Board: Casework Guidance[63]: This sets out the policies and procedures for the operation of the National Age Assessment Board (NAAB).

6.59

Home Office: Assessing Age[64]: This guidance is intended for Home Office staff where they are dealing with an individual whose age is in doubt.

60 Published 29 June 2021, accessed on 16 December 2025 at: https://www.gov.wales/unaccompanied-asylum-seeking-children-age-assessment-toolkit.

61 Home Office and Department for Education, *Age Assessment: Joint Working Guidance* (March 2023) https://assets.publishing.service.gov.uk/media/642552272fa848000cec0f77/Age_Assessment_Joint_Working_Guidance.pdf accessed 24 August 2025.

62 Ibid. p.11.

63 Home Office, *The Operation of the National Age Assessment Board and Sections 50 and 51 of the NABA 2022* (Guidance, updated 2 July 2025) https://www.gov.uk/government/publications/national-age-assessment-board-caseworker-guidance/the-operation-of-the-national-age-assessment-board-and-sections-50-and-51-of-the-nationality-and-borders-act-2022-accessible accessed 16 December 2025.

64 Home Office, *Assessing Age: Guidance* (19 December 2025) https://assets.publishing.service.gov.uk/media/694954b81a2e540ccd8a5481/Assessing_age.pdf accessed 1 February 2026.

Procedural safeguards under ECHR

Art 8 ECHR

6.60

The European Court of Human Rights (ECtHR) has established that the age assessment process falls under the scope of Art 8 European Convention on Human Rights, engaging as it does a fundamental principle of a person's private life: the determination of their age.

6.61

The ECtHR first addressed procedural safeguards in age assessment under Art 8 in *Darboe and Camara v Italy*[65], holding that the reception conditions and age-assessment procedures applied to the applicant fell within the scope of Art 8 and that Italy's failure to provide adequate safeguards during the assessment process violated the right to private life. Recent cases of *AC v France*[66] and *FB v Belgium*[67] have further established that the Court will consider a determination of age that fails to adhere to adequate procedural safeguards will constitute a violation of Art 8. It is insufficient to demonstrate that there are safeguards within the national legal framework if the authorities fail to take reasonable measures to effectively guarantee them in the individual case.

6.62

The Court considered what was required by both national and international law in determining which safeguards were necessary, allowing for the individual State a margin of appreciation in deciding an individual's age, particularly in light of the best interests of the child, 'which should prevail in all decisions concerning the child'[68].Those must include allowing the individual to access the finding of his own age assessment, ensuring that the medical reports explicitly indicate a margin of error and where a decision rebutting the presumption of minority it contains clear individualised reasoning.

Art 4 ECHR

6.63

Chapters 4, 5, 10 and **16** examine at length the positive obligations arising under Art 4 ECHR.

65 App no 5765/20, 22 July 2021.
66 *A.C. v France* (Application no. 15457/20), 16 January 2025.
67 *FB v Belgium* (Application no. 47836/21), 6 March 2025.
68 *AC v France* (Application no. 15457/20), 16 January 2025 [154].

6.64

Unlike Art 8 ECHR, Art 4 is an absolute right, the following principles therefore need to be considered when considering whether an age disputed putative victim of trafficking or modern slavery has been provided adequate safeguards in the determination of their age.

6.65

The ECtHR has consistently affirmed that Art 4 of the Convention, which prohibits slavery, servitude, forced or compulsory labour and trafficking, imposes both preventive and protective obligations on States. These obligations are multifaceted and extend beyond mere prohibition of Art 4 harm.

6.66

Protection measures require States to facilitate the identification of victims by qualified professionals and to support their physical, psychological, and social recovery (see **Chapter 4**). As recognised in *Chowdury and Others v. Greece*[69], these measures are essential to ensuring that victims are not only identified but also meaningfully supported.

6.67

Art 4 also entails a procedural obligation to investigate situations where Art 4 abuse is suspected. Crucially, this duty to investigate is not contingent upon a formal complaint from the victim or their relatives (see **Chapter 10**). Once the matter comes to the attention of the authorities, they are required to act on their own initiative (*Chowdury)*[70].

6.68

The Court has made clear that the operational duties under Art 4 serve two principal aims: first, to protect the victim from further harm; and second, to facilitate their recovery.

6.69

Children are recognised by the courts as especially vulnerable. The protective measures applied by the State must therefore be effective and must include protective measures where there is a credible suspicion that an individual is a victim of Art 4 treatment or are at real and immediate risk of such harm, and mechanisms that provide effective deterrence against serious violations of personal integrity[71]. These obligations are grounded in the approach of the ECtHR to Arts 3 and 8 of the Convention and have been affirmed in cases

69 *Chowdury and Others v Greece* App no 21884/15 (ECtHR, 30 March 2017) at [10].
70 Ibid. [288].
71 *VCL and AN v UK* (Applications nos. 77587/12 and 74603/12), ECtHR, 16 February 2021.

such as *Söderman v Sweden*[72]; *MC and Others v. Bulgaria*[73]; and *Z and Others v the United Kingdom*[74]. The measures adopted must be directed towards safeguarding human dignity and promoting the best interests of the child.

6.70

Given that trafficking undermines the human dignity and fundamental freedoms of its victims, the same protective principles apply to the measures required under Art 4. As the Court observed in *Rantsev v. Cyprus and Russia*[75], trafficking represents a grave violation of these core values, and the State's response must reflect the seriousness of the harm involved.

6.71

The criticisms levelled against the National Age Assessment Board (NAAB), outlined below, may give rise to arguable breaches of the State's positive obligations under Art 4 of the ECHR, where there is *prima facie* evidence that the individual concerned is a potential victim of trafficking or modern slavery.

Establishment and role of the National Age Assessment Board (NAAB)

6.72

Sections 50 and 51 of NABA 2022 establish the National Age Assessment Board (NAAB), which has been operational since 31 March 2023. The NAAB is situated in the Home Office and provides a centralised mechanism for conducting age assessments on behalf of local authorities and reviewing those carried out by local authorities.

6.73

The intention is that responsibility for age assessments will gradually move from local authorities to the Home Office, and specifically to the NAAB.

Criticism

6.74

The quality and reliability of age assessments conducted by the National Age Assessment Board (NAAB) have been subject to challenge in criminal

72 (Application no. 5786/08), 12 November 2013 (Grand Chamber) at [81].
73 (Application no. 39272/98), 4 December 2003 at [108].
74 (Application no. 29392/95),10 May 2001 (Grand Chamber) at [73].
75 (Application no. 25965/04), 7 January 2010 at [282].

proceedings before the Youth Court[76]. These concerns have been echoed by both the Children's Commissioner[77] and the British Association of Social Workers (BASW)[78], particularly in the context of age-disputed asylum cases.

6.75

While BASW acknowledges the importance of consistency, lawfulness, and safeguarding in age assessment procedures, it has also highlighted the tension between the NAAB's role, and the broader statutory duties owed to children under the Children Act 1989. Local authorities, through their social work professionals, are under a legal duty pursuant to s 17 of the Act to assess the needs of children and to safeguard and promote their welfare. Age assessments conducted by social workers are therefore undertaken within a statutory framework that prioritises child welfare and operates independently of immigration control objectives.

6.76

The centralisation of age assessments within the NAAB, an entity situated within the Home Office, has raised concerns about the potential displacement of this statutory role. The Children's Commissioner and BASW have both expressed apprehension that such a shift may undermine the independence and child-centred focus that is fundamental to the integrity of the age assessment process.

6.77

As reported by Independent Chief Inspector of Borders and Immigration[79] few of the NAAB social workers were experienced in conducting age assessments before joining the NAAB. The Chief Inspector's report identified gaps in training, poor record keeping and decision-making which failed to provide adequate reasons or evidence the benefit of the doubt had been properly considered.

---

76 Garden Court Chambers, *Home Office Concedes Age Dispute Challenge and Accepts Child Refugee Wrongly Assessed to Be Adult Following Determination by District Judge in Criminal Court* (18 August 2025) https://gardencourtchambers.co.uk/home-office-concedes-age-dispute-challenge-and-accepts-child-refugee-wrongly-assessed-to-be-adult-following-determination-by-district-judge-in-criminal-court/ accessed 16 December 2025.

77 Children's Commissioner for England, *Briefing for Peers on the Illegal Migration Bill* (May 2023) https://assets.childrenscommissioner.gov.uk/wpuploads/2023/05/Briefing-for-Peers-on-Illegal-Migration-Bill-May-2023.pdf
accessed 16 December 2025.

78 National Age Assessment Board, *NAAB Statement – March 2023* https://basw.co.uk/sites/default/files/resources/naab_statement_-_march_2023.pdf accessed 16 December 2025 and https://basw.co.uk/policy-and-practice/resources/join-basw-demanding-uk-government-scraps-naab accessed 16 December 2025.

79 Independent Chief Inspector of Borders and Immigration, *An Inspection of the Home Office's Use of Age Assessments (July 2024 – February 2025)* (August 2025) https://assets.publishing.service.gov.uk/media/687f6f9dfdc190fb6b84685e/An_inspection_of_the_Home_Office_s_use_of_age_assessments__July_2024___February_2025_.pdf accessed at 16 December 2025.

6.78

It is essential to recognise that age assessment is not a mere administrative step within immigration decision-making. It is a substantive welfare determination with profound implications for the rights and protections afforded to children. Grounded in the principle of the child's best interests, the process must be approached with independence, rigour, and sensitivity to vulnerability. Centralising this function within a Home Office-led body arguably risks compromising these safeguards. Such a shift may expose the process to political or operational pressures that are fundamentally at odds with the statutory framework designed to protect children. Where the integrity of the assessment is diminished, so too is the ability of the system to uphold the rights and welfare of those it is intended to serve.

Definition of 'age-disputed person'

6.79

Section 49(1) provides:

> 'In this Part, "age-disputed person" means a person—
>
> (a) who requires leave to enter or remain in the United Kingdom (whether or not such leave has been given), and
>
> (b) in relation to whom—
>
> (i) a local authority,
>
> (ii) a public authority specified in regulations under section 50(1)(b), or
>
> (iii) the Secretary of State,
>
> has insufficient evidence to be sure of their age.'

6.80

It is arguable that the definition of an age-disputed individual, particularly the suggestion that a person falls within this category where there is insufficient evidence to 'be sure of their age', is incompatible with the presumption of minority.

6.81

The definition sets a problematically low threshold for triggering formal age assessment procedures. This formulation risks undermining the presumption of minority, a principle firmly established in ECHR jurisprudence, including

AC v France[80] where the ECtHR reaffirmed that national authorities must respect this presumption unless there are reasonable grounds to doubt the claimed age. The phrase 'insufficient evidence to be sure' is materially weaker than the standard of 'reasonable grounds to doubt,' which is endorsed in Council of Europe guidance and implicit in the *Merton* principles. By treating the absence of certainty as sufficient to initiate formal assessment, s 49(1) effectively shifts the practical burden onto the individual to prove their age, rather than maintaining the presumption of minority unless there is a positive basis to question it.

6.82

Advocacy groups have warned that, in practice, this definition could result in nearly all undocumented children being subjected to age assessments. As the Refugee and Migrant Children's Consortium observed, between 2019 and 2023, well over half (58%) of individuals subjected to age assessments were subsequently found to be children[81]. This suggests a pattern of systematic over-referral, raising concerns about the proportionality and fairness of the current threshold.

6.83

This presumption is particularly significant in the context of trafficking or modern slavery, where the vulnerability of potential child victims demands heightened procedural safeguards. Art 10 of the Council of Europe Convention on Action against Trafficking in Human Beings (ECAT) provides that any person claiming to be a child victim of trafficking must be presumed to be the age they claim, pending verification.

6.84

This principle is reflected in domestic law through s 51 of the Modern Slavery Act 2015, which requires that any individual for whom there are reasonable grounds to believe both that they may be a victim of trafficking and that they may be under 18 must be treated as a child unless and until their age is formally assessed or otherwise determined. This statutory presumption of minority is a critical safeguard, ensuring that potentially trafficked children are afforded the protections to which they are entitled during the period of uncertainty surrounding their age.

80 16 January 2025; application number 15457/20
81 Refugee and Migrant Children's Consortium, Age Disputes, September 2024, accessed on 16 December 2025 at https://refugeechildrensconsortium.org.uk/wp-content/uploads/2024/09/RMCC-Briefing-Age-Disputes-September-2024.pdf.

Burden of proof

6.85

It is well established that there is no burden of proof in age assessments carried out by local authorities, or in court decisions where such assessments were challenged[82], there is no burden on the individual to prove their age. This remains the case for assessments carried out by the NAAB, with no legislative changes to the burden of proof, and the Home Office guidance[83] provides that 'there is no burden of proof imposed on the young person to prove their age.'

Where age is determined by the Upper Tribunal there is no burden of proof, the court takes an inquisitorial approach[84]. The court determines the young person's age based on the balance of probabilities, taking into account the need to give the benefit of the doubt to the young person[85].

The standard of proof

6.86

The standard of proof for age assessments when conducted by either by the NAAB or the local authority is now 'the balance of probabilities'[86].

6.87

Further the Home Office guidance states[87] that: 'where, having considered the evidence, the decision maker concludes there is doubt as to whether an individual is over 18 or not, then in those circumstances, the decision-maker should give the young person the benefit of the doubt and conclude that they are under 18.'

6.88

The importance of giving the benefit of the doubt to the young person has been established in the case law[88] and is reaffirmed by the Strasbourg case law that confirms the importance of presumption of minority[89].

82 ADCS Guidance page 62; *R(CD) v Cardiff City Council* [2011] EWCA Civ 1590, *R(HAM) v London Borough of Brent* [2022] EWHC 1924 (Admin).
83 The Operation of the National Age Assessment Board and section 50 and 51 of the NABA 2022, updated 2 July 2025, p.23.
84 *R(on the application of AI) v West Berkshire Council* [2025] EWCA Civ 136.
85 *R(F and Ors) v London Borough of Lewisham* [2009] EWHC 3542 (Admin)
86 Sections 50(6) and 51(4).
87 The Operation of the National Age Assessment Board and section 50 and 51 of the NABA 2022, updated 2 July 2025, p.23.
88 *R(AB) v Kent* [2020] PTSR 746.at [30].
89 *AC v France,* (Application no. 15457/20), 16 January 2025.

Local authority referral

6.89

Where a local authority is required to determine the age of an individual whose age is disputed, whether to decide whether or how to exercise its functions under the children's legislation, or because the Secretary of State has given written notice that the claimed age is in doubt, it is under a statutory duty to respond in one of three ways.

6.90

It must either

(a) refer the individual to a NAAB for a formal age assessment; or

(b) conduct its own age assessment and notify the Secretary of State in writing of the outcome; or

(c) confirm in writing to the Secretary of State that it is satisfied the individual is the age they claim (or are claimed) to be, without undertaking a formal assessment.

6.91

Section 50(7)(b) of NABA 2022 provides that where the Local Authority has referred the person to NAAB to conduct the age assessment, the NAAB assessment will be 'binding on a local authority that has exercised or may exercise functions under relevant children's legislation in relation to the young person whose age has been assessed and where the local authority is aware of the assessment'[90]. It is also binding on the Home Office[91].

Local authority accept claimed age

6.92

Where the Local Authority has accepted the claimed age of the individual, but the Home Office 'believes there is doubt that the person is the age they claim to be', NAAB will conduct a Merton compliant age assessment[92]. The NAAB decision will not be binding on the local authority (s 51(3) of NABA 2022) in this instance.

---

90 Home Office and Department for Education, *Age Assessment: Joint Working Guidance* (March 2023) https://assets.publishing.service.gov.uk/media/642552272fa848000cec0f77/Age_Assessment_Joint_Working_Guidance.pdf accessed 24 August 2025 P.11.

91 Section 50(7)(a).

92 Ibid. P.11 and s.50(7)(b) of NABA 2022.

6.93

Where a local authority makes a decision on age that differs from the NAAB decision, it must then provide the relevant evidence and full age assessment report, where applicable to NAAB, who will treat it as new information under s 4 or 5 of the Nationality and Borders Act 2022 (Commencement No.5 And Transitional Provisions) Regulations 2023[93].

Home Office referral to NAAB

6.94

The Home Office may refer an individual to the NAAB for a designated person to conduct an age assessment in one of three situations. These are set out in s 51 NABA 2022.

6.95

First, there are cases in which the local authority has no duty under s 50 to consider an individual's age. That may arise, for example, where the local authority is not involved at all, such as with accompanied children. This is described as 'Scenario 1' in the Home Office guidance at page 28 and in the *Assessing Age* guidance[94]. In such situations, the guidance makes clear that the Home Office should notify the local authority that it is disputing the individual's age. The local authority must then decide whether it needs to know the young person's age. If it does, it must proceed under s 50, and s 51(2)(a) is not the correct route. If it does not, it may be appropriate for the Home Office to refer the case to the NAAB under s 51.

6.96

Second, there are cases in which the local authority has not yet referred the individual, has not told the Secretary of State that it will carry out its own age assessment, and has not said that no assessment is needed[95]. This is 'Scenario 3' in the guidance[96]. It normally arises where the local authority has failed to take the required steps within a reasonable time and has not offered a reasonable explanation for that failure. In such situations, the Home Office must first try to resolve the disagreement with the local authority before making a referral itself.

---

93 The Operation of the National Age Assessment Board and section 50 and 51 of the NABA 2022, updated 2 July 2025, p. 70.
94 Ibid. at p 41.
95 Section 51(2)(b)(i) NABA 2022.
96 At page 30.

6.97

Third in circumstances where the Secretary of State has reason to doubt the local authority's decision to accept the age of the individual, whether following its own assessment or otherwise[97]. This is set out as 'Scenario 2' in the guidance and will occur when the Home Office 'has legitimate reasons to disagree with the local authority's decision'[98]. The guidance provides that concerns must first be raised with the local authority before referring to the NAAB.

6.98

In such circumstances the outcome of a NAAB assessment is binding on the Secretary of State, but not the local authority[99].

Initial decisions on age: outcomes for those who present as children

6.99

The Assessing Age[100] guidance allows for three outcomes for those who present as children on arrival to the United Kingdom:

Outcome 1: A person who claims to be a child may only be treated as an adult if one of the following conditions is satisfied:

6.100

- **A Merton-compliant age assessment has been conducted by the National Age Assessment Board (NAAB),** concluding that the claimant is 18 or over. Under ss 50(7) and 51(3) of the Nationality and Borders Act 2022, such decisions are binding on the Secretary of State and immigration officers when exercising immigration functions. However, this binding effect may be displaced if the assessment is overturned by judicial review or revised in light of significant new evidence. It would also be binding on the Local Authority if the local authority had referred to the NAAB.
- **A Merton-compliant age assessment has been conducted by a local authority**, assessing the claimant to be 18 or over, and this has been accepted by the Home Office after:
  - giving significant weight to the assessment, and
  - taking into account all other reliable evidence.

97 Section 51(2)(b)(ii) NABA 2022.
98 The Operation of the National Age Assessment Board and section 50 and 51 of the NABA 2022, updated 2 July 2025, at page 29, and page 42 of the Assessing Age guidance, *supra*.
99 Section 51(3) NABA 2022.
100 Assessing Age, Home Office, version 11, *supra*.

- **Two Home Office officials,** one of whom must be of Chief Immigration Officer or Higher Executive Officer grade, have independently assessed that the claimant's physical appearance and demeanour very strongly suggest they are significantly over 18, and there is little or no supporting evidence for the claimed age. (see reference to *R (BF) v Secretary of State for the Home Department* above at **6.24**).
- **There is credible and clear documentary evidence** that they are 18 years of age or over.

Outcome 2: Decision to treat the claimant as a child

6.101

A claimant should be treated as a child where one of the following applies:

- **A Merton-compliant age assessment has been conducted by the National Age Assessment Board (NAAB),** concluding the claimant is under 18.
  - Under ss 50(7) and 51(3) of the Nationality and Borders Act 2022, such assessments are binding on the Secretary of State and immigration officers.
  - The assessment ceases to be binding if:
    - It is overturned by judicial review, or
    - A new assessment is made following significant new evidence.
- **A Merton-compliant age assessment has been conducted by a local authority, concluding the claimant is under 18,** and the Home Office has accepted the assessment after:
  - Giving significant weight to the findings, and
  - Considering all reliable evidence.
- **The claimant's age is doubted, but after careful consideration of the case specifics,** the benefit of the doubt is applied, and the claimed age is accepted.
- **There is credible and clear documentary evidence supporting the claimant's claimed age.**

Outcome 3: Decision to treat claimant as a child until further assessment of their age is completed

6.102

Where the claimant's age is not accepted, and the criteria for treating them as an adult are not met, they should be provisionally treated as a child until further assessment is completed. This applies where:

- The decision-maker cannot be sure the individual is an adult (as per Outcome 1), and
- The claimed age has not been accepted (as per Outcome 2).

6.103

Further assessment may include:

- Seeking the view of the local authority, and/or
- Requesting a Merton-compliant age assessment by the local authority or a referral to the NAAB.

6.104

The Joint Working Guidance confirms that where the Home Office disagrees with a local authority's age assessment, it must first raise its concerns directly with the authority, identifying: (i) any conflicting evidence, (ii) the Home Office considers the assessment is inadequately reasoned, (iii) the Home Office disagrees with the local authority's evaluation of the weight of the evidence before it[101].

6.105

If agreement cannot be reached, the matter is escalated to senior officials, an Assistant Director in the Home Office and the Head of Service in the local authority, for formal resolution, with the Home Office also notifying its safeguarding lead.

6.106

If disagreement persists, the Home Office may seek advice from the National Age Assessment Board (NAAB), which may liaise with both parties. If the NAAB is unable to assist, the case is escalated to the Director of Children's Services and the NAAB's Assistant Director, with further escalation to the Deputy Director of UASC Operations if necessary.

6.107

In certain cases, the Home Office may commission a NAAB age assessment under s 51 of the Nationality and Borders Act 2022. These assessments are binding on the Home Office, including immigration officers, but not on local authorities. Where a local authority has previously conducted an assessment, the NAAB's findings must be treated as new information and considered accordingly. The local authority is responsible for notifying the individual of the final decision.

101 Page 51 of Home Office, *Assessing Age: Guidance* (June 2025) *supra*.

6.108

The guidance states that while resolution is pending, the individual must be supported in accordance with the local authority's assessment, provided it aligns with case law, and safeguarding must be prioritised.

Procedural safeguards and the right to participate

6.109

The current guidance does not address whether the individual is informed of the Home Office's communication with the local authority, nor does it provide any mechanism for the individual to make representations in relation to conflicting evidence or the decision to commission a second age assessment. These omissions raise concerns under s 55 of the Borders, Citizenship and Immigration Act 2009, which requires the Secretary of State to have regard to the need to safeguard and promote the welfare of children in immigration, asylum, and nationality functions.

6.110

More broadly, the absence of a clear statutory power or policy framework enabling the individual's participation in this process engages fundamental principles of procedural fairness. The right to be heard in decisions affecting one's status and welfare is a core component of fair process. Recent decisions of the ECtHR, including *AC v France* and *FB v Belgium*, illustrate how procedural deficiencies in age determination may amount to breaches of Art 8 ECHR, and potentially Art 6 where the outcome affects access to social welfare entitlements. In this context, the lack of transparency and opportunity for meaningful engagement in the age assessment process may fall short of the procedural safeguards required under both domestic and international human rights standards.

Assessing age: scientific methods

6.111

The provisions in the NABA 2022 authorising the use of scientific methods in age assessments have now come into force. The Independent Chief Inspector of Borders and Immigration's 2025 inspection report made a number of criticisms of the Home Office's age assessment processes. On 22 July 2025, in a written ministerial statement, the Government confirmed that it would not proceed with rolling out intrusive scientific methods such as X-rays and MRI scans for age assessment, and instead announced further work to test and trial Artificial

Intelligence-based Facial Age Estimation with a view to deployment from 2026, subject to the outcome of those trials[102].

6.112

The statutory framework under the NABA 2022 nonetheless remains in place. Section 52 empowers the Secretary of State, by regulations, to specify scientific techniques, including imaging and other methods, for the purpose of assessing age, and was commenced on 20 November 2023. The Immigration (Age Assessments) Regulations 2024, which came into force on 10 January 2024, establish the framework under which designated authorities may request the use of such scientific methods in age assessments, and provide that an individual's unjustified refusal to undergo a specified method may be treated as damaging to their credibility.

6.113

Further powers were introduced by the Illegal Migration Act 2023, most notably section 58, which would have enabled the Secretary of State to make regulations providing that an individual could be treated as an adult if they refused, without good reason, to undergo a scientific age assessment. Section 58 was enacted but never commenced. It has now been repealed by the Border Security, Asylum and Immigration Act 2025, and therefore can no longer be brought into force.

6.114

These statutory powers had attracted significant criticism from professional and child-rights bodies, including the Children's Commissioner for England[103] and the Royal College of Paediatrics and Child Health[104], which have raised concerns about the ethics, reliability and impact of scientific methods in this context.The Chief Inspector's report[105] similarly noted the substantial body of academic, professional and practitioner material indicating that neither visual assessment of appearance and demeanour nor scientific and medical examinations (for example of bones and teeth) can reliably determine chronological age, because development is so heavily influenced by environment, life experiences and

102 Accessed on 16 December 2025 at https://questions-statements.parliament.uk/written-statements/detail/2025-07-22/hcws885.

103 Children's Commissioner for England, *Briefing for Peers on the Illegal Migration Bill* (May 2023) https://assets.childrenscommissioner.gov.uk/wpuploads/2023/05/Briefing-for-Peers-on-Illegal-Migration-Bill-May-2023.pdf accessed 16 December 2025.

104 Royal College of Paediatrics and Child Health,'RCPCH Responds to UK Government Plans to Authorise Use of X-rays in Age Assessments of Children' (RCPCH, 10 January 2022) https://www.rcpch.ac.uk/news-events/news/rcpch-responds-uk-government-plans-authorise-use-x-rays-age-assessments-children accessed 16 December 2025.

105 Independent Chief Inspector of Borders and Immigration, *An Inspection of the Home Office's Use of Age Assessments (July 2024 – February 2025)* (August 2025) https://assets.publishing.service.gov.uk/media/687f6f9dfdc190fb6b84685e/An_inspection_of_the_Home_Office_s_use_of_age_assessments__July_2024___February_2025_.pdf accessed 24 August 2025.

ethnicity that even careful application of such tests cannot establish with precision whether a person is 18 or older.

Assessing age: criminal justice agencies

6.115

The only comparable equivalent guidance in the criminal justice context is the Crown Prosecution Service's Legal Guidance on Children as Suspects and Defendants[106] and the CPS Guidance on Modern Slavery and human trafficking: offences and defences, including the s 45 defence[107]. The CPS Child Guidance states as follows:

> '*Determining the age of the offender*
>
> Section 99 Children and Young Persons Act 1933 and section 150 Magistrates' Courts Act 1980 sets out that where a person, whether charged with an offence or not, is brought before any court other than for the purpose of giving evidence, and it appears to the court that they are a child or young person, the court shall make enquiries as to their age, and the age presumed or declared by the court is deemed to be their true age. Section 405 Sentencing Act 2020 states that where the age of the offender must be determined by the court, or the Secretary of State, the person is deemed to be whatever age they appear to be after consideration of any available evidence by the court or the Secretary of State. Where the court has taken into account the available evidence and reached a determination, even if it is subsequently shown to be wrong, the original sentence remains valid, even if it was a sentence they could not have received had their true age been known: *Brown* [1989] 5 WLUK 246 and *Steed* [1990] 5 WLUK 72, which also emphasise that where there is a dispute as to the offenders' age, it is appropriate to adjourn to obtain any available evidence.
>
> Any dispute as to age should be raised at the first hearing. Where it is known that the age of the offender may be in dispute, prosecutors should ask the police to obtain documentary evidence of the offender's age such as their birth certificate, passport or identity cards. Other records such as custody records, PNC printouts and antecedents are more likely to have been based on inaccurate information given to the police.

106 Available at www.cps.gov.uk/legal-guidance/children-suspects-and-defendants, updated 4 August 2025 (last accessed 16 December 2025).

107 Available at https://www.cps.gov.uk/legal-guidance/modern-slavery-and-human-trafficking-offences-and-defences-including-section-45, updated 22 July 2025 (last accessed 16 December 2025).

> Difficulties can arise when the offender is a refugee or asylum seeker, as the documentary evidence listed in the paragraph above may well have been lost in transit. Guidance as to the assessments to be conducted in these circumstances is contained in the case of R (on the application of B) v Merton LBC [2003] EWHC 1689 (Admin). Despite the age of the case, this approach has been endorsed and re-stated in the 14 January 2022 Home Office guidance Assessing Age, which refers to Merton-compliant age assessments. Evidence put before the court by the offender which is inconsistent with other evidence should be challenged by way of cross examination.'

6.116

The CPS guidance on prosecuting victims of trafficking and modern slavery refers to the importance of determining age 'for the purposes of both modern slavery offences and non-prosecution principles including the s 45 defence'[108]. It specifically highlights the need for due inquiries to be made under the CYPA 1933, s 99, stating that any dispute of age ought to be addressed at the first court appearance or Plea and Trial Preparation Hearing.

6.117

Further that:

> 'Time may be required for the court to determine the issue and for proper enquiries to be made. The prosecutor should consider the question of age and only proceed on the basis that the person is not a child if they conclude that a court would more likely than not be satisfied of this fact. This is important, because those with responsibilities for victims may apply the presumption in section 51 of the 2015 Act pending the outcome of the inquiry, and the court may approach the inquiry asking itself if the person appears to have attained the age of 18 (see section 99) – but this does not preclude the defendant from raising this as an issue at trial and the prosecutor must remain focused on the standard and burden of proof throughout.'

6.118

No equivalent guidance has been issued specifically for Youth Justice Services, despite their statutory placement within local authority children's services. Given this structural alignment, it is arguable that the guidance issued by the Association of Directors of Children's Services (ADCS), which local authority

108 Crown Prosecution Service, *Modern Slavery and Human Trafficking: Offences and Defences, Including the Section 45 Defence* (Legal Guidance, International and Organised Crime, updated 22 July 2025) <https://www.cps.gov.uk/legal-guidance/modern-slavery-and-human-trafficking-offences-and-defences-including-section-45-defence> accessed 16 December 2025.

children's services are obliged to follow, ought also to be applied to Youth Justice Service teams to ensure consistency in safeguarding and welfare standards.

6.119

The Judicial College's 'Child Defendants in the Crown Court' Bench Book (September 2025) contains guidance on determining and deeming age for child defendants. Although the Youth Court Bench Book does not have a dedicated section on age determination, the same statutory deeming principles (for example, under s 99 of the Children and Young Persons Act 1933, s 150 of the Magistrates' Courts Act 1980 and s 405 of the Sentencing Act 2020) apply equally in the youth court.

6.120

The Benchbook confirms that the age of a child defendant is a very important matter. It provides the following principles:

- The court is under a duty to determine the age of the defendant.
- There is no onus of proof on the defendant themselves.
- Where there is any real doubt, it is usually right for the matter to be adjourned.
- It confirms *Merton* as the leading authority on assessing age, referring also to the judgments in *R v L and Ors*[109] and *R v Mohammed*[110].

6.121

In terms of the 'deeming hearing' the Bench Book provides that:

> '49. The 'deeming hearing':
>
> For the purposes of determining age, the court 'shall take such evidence as may be forthcoming', which may include:
>
> (1) oral evidence from the defendant, their family or friends concerning their stated age and details of their history
>
> (2) domestic documentation (birth certificate, passport etc.) including the PNC
>
> (3) foreign documentation (birth certificate, passport, ID card etc)
>
> (4) the physical appearance of the defendant
>
> (5) input from the YOT/YJS

109 [2013] EWCA Crim 991.
110 [2021] EWCA Crim 1375.

(6) input from any other agency which may have involvement with the defendant or their family.

50. The YOT/YJS will have a wide experience of dealing with children and will have a valuable part to play in assisting the court.

51. At the end of any hearing, the court will deem the defendant to be of a particular age, or within a certain age group. That decision should be recorded on the court record. The assessment of age is always a matter for the court; the judge is not bound by any position adopted by or agreed between the parties.'

Legal challenges against age assessments

6.122

Section 54 NABA 2022, when commenced, will provide a new statutory right of appeal to the First Tier Tribunal against an age assessment. Section 54 has not yet been brought into force, and according to the Home Office guidance from July 2025 'the Home Office continues to keep commencement of s 54 under review'[111]. The Assessing Age guidance at pages 71–73 deals with these appeals but provides that the guidance will be updated once the appeal process is brought into force. This guidance emphasises the importance of the FTT being provided with all relevant material as to age by both parties, including any age assessments that have been undertaken, and points to the case of *R(M and A) v London Borough of Lambeth and London Borough of Croydon*[112], where the Claimant was criticised for not drawing the tribunal's attention to the existence of an age assessment carried out by a local authority, and therefore known to the Claimant, but not known to the Home Office.

6.123

Currently therefore any age assessment decision made by either NAAB or a local authority may only be challenged by way of judicial review.

6.124

In *R (on the application of A) v Croydon London Borough Council,* the Supreme Court held in relation to 'the question whether a person is a 'child' that:

'there is a right or a wrong answer. It may be difficult to determine what the answer is. The decision-makers may have to do their best on

111 The Operation of the National Age Assessment Board and section 50 and 51 of the NABA 2022, updated 2 July 2025, p. 71.

112 [2008] EWHC 1364 (Admin).

the basis of less than perfect or conclusive evidence. But that is true of many questions of fact which regularly come before the courts. That does not prevent them from being questions for the courts rather than for other kinds of decision-makers'[113].

6.125

The public authority, whether the local authority or the Home Office, must make its own determination of age in the first instance. Judicial intervention is only required where that determination is disputed. As Lady Hale observed in *A v Croydon*, 'the better the quality of the initial decision-making, the less likely it is that the court will come to any different decision upon the evidence'[114]. It follows therefore that on a determination of age the court is not restricted to binary decision making between the age put forward by the Claimant, and the age put forward by the Respondent. It takes an inquisitorial rather than adversarial role and comes to its own conclusion as to age[115]. However, in an appeal where the correct approach will be fact specific and focusing on the two ages put forward will not necessarily be an error of law if appropriate in the circumstances[116].

6.126

At present, there is no statutory procedure for determining age in either the social welfare or immigration context. The significance of *A v Croydon* lies in the Supreme Court's confirmation that, in such cases, the Administrative Court has jurisdiction, via judicial review where there is disagreement over the factual conclusion reached by the authority, to determine the objective fact of a person's age where local authority duties or immigration powers are engaged. However the First Tier Tribunal will often make a decision as to age as part of a decision on asylum, as it is a relevant factual matter that the tribunal will need to determine if it remains in dispute. This is dealt with below.

6.127

As the claim is brought by way of judicial review, the child applicant still needs to satisfy that the case is arguable to obtain permission to proceed to trial. The test for permission is as formulated by the Court of Appeal in *R (on the application of FZ) v Croydon London Borough Council*[117]:

'whether the material before the court raises a factual case which, taken at its highest, could not properly succeed in a contested factual hearing.

113 [2009] UKSC 8, [2009] 1 WLR 2557 per Lady Hale at [27].
114 Ibid per Lady Hale at [33].
115 *R (F and Ors) v London Borough of Lewisham* [2009] EWHC 3542 (Admin); [2010] 1 FLR 1463, at [9].
116 *AI, R (on the application of) v West Berkshire Council* [2025] EWCA Civ 136.
117 [2011] EWCA Civ 59, [2011] PTSR 748.

If so, permission should be refused. If not, permission should normally be granted, subject to other discretionary factors, such as delay.'

6.128

A judicial review challenging an age assessment is usually transferred to the Upper Tribunal (Immigration and Asylum Chamber) for determination once permission has been granted. There is then a fact-finding hearing, pursuant to s 31A(3) of the Senior Courts Act 1981 and Art 11(c)(ii) of the First-tier Tribunal and Upper Tribunal (Chambers) Order[118].

6.129

The case is transferred if 'it appears to the High Court to be just and convenient' to make the transfer. The Upper Tribunal is more experienced in the age assessment of children and conducting fact-finding hearings. The law and the procedure are the same regardless of whether the case is heard in the Upper Tribunal or the Administrative Court.

6.130

The task of the Court or Upper Tribunal is not to determine whether the local authority's or the Home Office's assessment of age is right or wrong but, rather, the more fundamental question, the age of the child[119].

6.131

This requires a fact-finding exercise based on all the evidence made available to the court or tribunal. There is no burden on either the child or the public authority to prove the correctness of their assertion on age[120].

6.132

Many cases challenging an age assessment include an application for interim relief to ensure that the putative child is afforded the relevant protections under the Children Act pending the full hearing.

6.133

The test for interim relief in age assessment judicial reviews was considered by Mr Justice Fordham in *R (KRA) v Cheshire East Council*[121] who crystallised the matter into two questions for the court to consider:

---

118 *R(S) v London Borough of Croydon* [2011] EWHC 2091

119 *R (on the application of F) v Lewisham London Borough Council* [2009] EWHC 3542 (Admin), [2010] 1 FLR 1463.

120 *R (on the application of CJ) v Cardiff County Council* [2011] EWHC 23 (Admin), [2011] LGR 301, above.

121 [2024] EWHC 575 (Admin).

1. Whether the material before the court raises a factual case, which, taken at its highest, could properly succeed at a contested factual hearing, and
2. Where the balance of justice and injustice lies. Further 'an interim order may be more warranted in cases of evidenced vulnerability'[122].

6.134

It is rarely the case that the fact of age can be determined by documentary evidence, the Court or Tribunal at trial will receive a range of evidence, much of which will be opinion evidence from professionals as well as lay persons who have had contact over time with the putative child. This includes, for example, key workers, foster carers, volunteers at charitable organisations, counsellors, social workers, and medical professionals. The putative child would normally give evidence unless they are unable to do so.

6.135

In *R (MVN) v Greenwich LBC*[123] the judge held that an age assessment of a putative child was unlawful, inter alia, because the local authority had failed to consider the Home Office Guidance[124] to competent authorities on victims of human trafficking.

Determining age in asylum appeals: procedural and evidential standards in the First-tier Tribunal

6.136

Where age is disputed in the context of an asylum appeal, the position now depends on the role age plays in the refugee analysis. Section 32(2) of the NABA 2022 requires the decision-maker to determine, on the balance of probabilities, whether the claimant has a Convention characteristic (including membership of a particular social group) and whether they in fact fear persecution for that reason. Where age itself is advanced as the relevant Convention characteristic (for example as part of a particular social group defined by age), that provision requires age to be determined on the civil standard for the purposes of s 32(2)[125]. By contrast, where age is not itself the Convention ground but is one of the underlying factual issues feeding into credibility or future risk, the Tribunal has treated age, consistently with *Rawofi*

122 Ibid., [15] and following.
123 [2015] EWHC 1942 (Admin).
124 This guidance has been replaced by the Home Office, *Modern Slavery Act 2015: Statutory Guidance for England and Wales* (March 2020). However, the principles set out in previous guidance are repeated in this Statutory Guidance (see Annexes D and E).
125 Confirmed by *JCK v Secretary of State for the Home Department (Botswana)* [2024] UKUT 100 (IAC).

(age assessment – standard of proof)[126], as part of the overall assessment of risk to which the lower asylum standard of a 'reasonable degree of likelihood' applies, rather than the balance-of-probabilities standard used in local authority age-assessment judicial review in cases such as *R(CJ) v Cardiff*[127].

Approach of criminal court to a defendant whose age is disputed

6.137

The Court of Appeal dealt with the question of age where defendants may be victims of human trafficking: *R v L (C); R v N (HV); R v T (HD)*[128], Judge CJ, in giving judgment of the Court, observed:

> '[22] When the issue arises, we agree that compliance with these provisions in contemporary society requires much more than superficial observation of the defendant in court or in the dock to enable the judge to make an appropriate age assessment. The facial features of the defendant may provide a clue or two, but experience has shown that this is very soft evidence indeed and sometimes leave them with a misleading appearance. We also appreciate that young people from an ethnic group with which the court is unfamiliar may seem older, or indeed younger, than those from ethnic groups with which the court has greater experience. Therefore, when an age issue arises, the court must be provided with all the relevant evidence which bears on it. Although the court may adjourn proceedings for further investigations to be conducted, these have to be undertaken by one or other or both sides, or by the relevant social services. The court is not vested with any jurisdiction, and is not provided with the resources, to conduct its own investigations into the age of a potential defendant until after the investigation has completed its course and the individual in question is brought before the court'.

6.138

This is endorsed in the Child Defendants in the Crown Court Benchbook, which sets out the key principles for deeming age in the criminal courts.

6.139

The main provision on determining age is CYPA 1933, s 99(1), which states:

---

126 [2012] UKUT 00197 (IAC).

127 [2011] EWCA Civ 1590.

128 [2013] EWCA Crim 991; [2013] 2 Cr.App.R. 23 as referred to in Judicial College, *Child Defendants in the Crown Court* (June 2025) *supra*.

> 'Where a person, whether charged with an offence or not, is brought before *any court* otherwise than for the purpose of giving evidence, and it appears to the court that he is a child or young person, the court *shall make due inquiry* as to the age of that person and *for that purpose shall take such evidence as may be forthcoming at the hearing of the case*, but an order or judgment of the court shall not be invalidated by any subsequent proof that the age of that person has not been correctly stated to the court, and the age presumed or declared by the court to be the age of the person so brought before it shall, for the purposes of this Act, be deemed to be the true age of that person, and where it appears to the court that the person so brought before it has attained the [age of eighteen] years, that person shall for the purposes of this Act be deemed not to be a child or young person.'

6.140

There are similar provisions for the criminal court to deem the age of an individual in front of it, such as s 150 Magistrates' Courts Act 1980 and s 405 Sentencing Act 2020.

6.141

In the context of the youth justice system, this and other associated provisions place the responsibility for reaching a defendant's age on the magistrate or court before which the defendant is appearing. This approach conforms with the Supreme Court's decision in *A v Croydon* (above) as to there being a right or wrong answer to the question of age.

6.142

When an issue arises, the Court should ordinarily adjourn to allow further inquiries to be made into a defendant's age[129] Where a local authority have conducted a lawful age assessment the court should give that significant weight, but are not bound by it[130]. The plain meaning of the phrase 'due inquiry' in CYPA 1933, s 99(1) obliges the magistrate or a court to undertake a fact-finding exercise as to the objective fact of the defendant's age if a dispute still exists following any adjournment.

6.143

When the principles for assessing age, established over more than a decade in the local authority context, are considered in the round, the inquiry necessary to inform the criminal court of the right decision on age (insofar as this is possible) is one that requires a process of rigorous scrutiny. Such an approach

129 *R v L, HVN, THN, T* [2013] EWCA Crim 99; *R v Steed* [1990] 12 Cr App R (S) 230, *R(M) v Hammersmith Magistrates' Court [*2017] EWHC 1359 (Admin).

130 *N v Staines Magistrates Court [*2009] EWHC 3081 (Admin).

requires decisions on age to 'show by their reasoning that every factor which might tell in favour of the claimed age has been properly taken into account'[131]. This is 'axiomatic' in decisions which if made incorrectly may fundamentally and adversely impact on a putative child's ability to participate effectively in the trial process. It is also relevant to the application of the public interest test and some relevant to several defences, such as those under s 45 Modern Slavery Act 2015.

6.144

A necessary corollary of a rigorous approach to age assessment is the obligation to ensure that all relevant parties to the proceedings, most notably the putative child at the centre of the inquiry, are afforded a fair and meaningful opportunity to present such evidence as is available and relevant. This procedural safeguard is essential to securing, insofar as possible, an accurate and just determination of age.

6.145

Although, it could arguably be fuller, the advice provided in the CPS *Legal Guidance on Children as Suspects and Defendants*[132] as to the role of the CPS in this process does seek to conform to this approach:

> 'Any dispute as to age should be raised at the first hearing. Where it is known that the age of the offender may be in dispute, prosecutors should ask the police to obtain documentary evidence of the offender's age such as their birth certificate, passport or identity cards.

Effective participation and procedural fairness in age determination

6.146

It is important in any case that the putative child has a right to give evidence concerning a decision as to their age. This conforms with a core principle underpinning the youth justice system, ie the right of the child to be heard in any court proceedings to which he is a party, and to participate effectively[133]. See also para [34] of *ZH (Tanzania) v Secretary of State for the Home Department*[134], where Baroness Hale said:

> 'acknowledging that the best interests of the child must be a primary consideration … immediately raises the question of how these are to

131 *R (on the application of YH) v Secretary of State for the Home Department* [2010] EWCA Civ 116 at [24].
132 Available at https://www.cps.gov.uk/legal-guidance/children-suspects-and-defendants(last accessed 16 December 2025).
133 UN CRC, Arts 12 and 40.
134 [2011] UKSC 4, [2011] 2 AC 166.

be discovered. An important part of this is discovering the child's own view'.

6.147

Effective participation by the putative child is essential to a proper and lawful inquiry into age. It is a cornerstone of the fair trial guarantees protected under domestic and international law. It is unrealistic to expect that all relevant evidence concerning age will be available at the child's first appearance before the court, particularly where the child has only recently arrived in the UK or has been brought before the court following events such as immigration enforcement action or arrest during a police operation, for example at a suspected cannabis cultivation site.

6.148

The first appearance often involves critical decisions, such as bail, remand, venue, jurisdiction, and mode of trial, that are contingent on the court's view of the individual's age. To ensure that the child can effectively participate in this foundational stage of the proceedings, it is of paramount importance that the parties, and especially the putative child, are afforded a reasonable opportunity to adduce relevant evidence. This may include documentary material, expert reports, or other corroborative sources to assist the court in its inquiry.

6.149

In most cases, this will necessitate an adjournment to allow time for the evidence to be gathered and presented[135]. Such an approach is supported by established criminal case law and reflects the procedural fairness required in cases involving vulnerable individuals. A refusal to adjourn for these purposes should be the exception rather than the norm.

The role of social work expertise in age assessment

6.150

In the absence of verifiable documentary evidence of age, other sources of evidence, particularly from social work professionals with expertise in age assessment, can play a critical role. The Youth Court, recognising its duty to conduct a fair and informed inquiry, should invite the Youth Justice Service to refer the putative child defendant to the local authority for an opinion on age. This opinion should be provided by a qualified social worker with appropriate training and experience in age assessment.

135 See *R v Steed* [1990] 12 Cr App Rep (S) 230 and *R v Farmer* [2002] EWCA Crim 2128.

6.151

It is equally open to the Crown Prosecution Service or the defence to initiate such a referral. Courts have acknowledged that local authority social workers possess developed expertise in conducting holistic assessments of age, which consider not only physical appearance but also behaviour, developmental indicators, and background information.

6.152

Further, the criminal courts are empowered under s 9(2) of the Children and Young Persons Act 1969 to require the local authority to investigate matters relating to the 'home surroundings, school record, health and character' of the individual before the court. It is arguable that this power extends to requiring the local authority to investigate the individual's age, particularly where it is central to the proceedings.

Limits of mandatory age assessment and the precautionary approach

6.153

Local authority age assessments should not become a mandatory component of the criminal court's inquiry into age. The guidance issued by the Association of Directors of Children's Services (ADCS) cautions against conducting age assessments in all cases where a putative child lacks verified documentation. Instead, an assessment should only be undertaken where there is 'significant doubt' about the claimed age. This approach aligns with the Committee on the Rights of the Child's position in General Comment No 10, which advocates for a precautionary and protective stance.

6.154

The ADCS guidance allows a local authority to decline to undertake an age assessment if, upon consideration, it does not have significant doubt about the individual's claimed age. Where such a decision is reasoned and documented, it ought to carry substantial evidential weight in favour of accepting the individual as a child, or at least as under 18. This reinforces the principle that age assessments should be reserved for cases where there is a genuine and substantiated basis for dispute.

6.155

Pending the completion of the inquiry, the presumption in favour of childhood ought to be afforded to the putative child in accordance with the precautionary approach advocated for in General Comments Nos 6 and 10 and the ADCS guidance on age. Even if a local authority bail package is not immediately available, this would at least ensure that the putative youth defendant is remanded under LASPO 2012 to local authority accommodation unless the rigorous threshold for a Youth Detention Accommodation is met. All this serves to preserve the status quo in a precautionary manner having due regard to the putative child's best interests as a primary consideration.

6.156

Where a child is inadvertently prosecuted as an adult, this will ordinarily lead to a successful appeal against conviction, or sentence. In *R v O*[136] the Court of Appeal criticised the lower court, the defence and the prosecution for failing to recognise that O was a child and a victim of trafficking, noting that both the prosecution and defence had reason to believe she was younger, and questioning whether, given the failure to consider her age, there had been jurisdiction to hear the matter in the Crown Court.[137]

Section 99 Children and Young Persons Act 1933

6.157

The language of s 99 CYPA 1933 makes it clear that any sentence or order passed shall not be invalid if the age of the individual later turns out to be incorrect. This was the approach taken in the cases of *R v Steed*[138] and *R v Brown*[139], both cases where it later transpired that the respective defendants were 20 at the time of their convictions, and not 21 as the sentencing court had deemed them to be. However, notably these cases did not concern children.

6.158

In the light of the decision of the ECtHR in *VCL and AN v UK*[140], where the Court held there to be interlocking breaches of Arts 4 and 6, specifically breaches of the protective obligations to a potential victim of trafficking who is a putative child, the legislative provision may require further interpretation applying common law principles or s 3(1) of the HRA 1998. Particularly, where the age assessment determination of the court was itself in breach of positive obligations under Art.4 and in breach of Art 6 ECHR.

136 [2008] EWCA Crim 2835.
137 At para 18.
138 1990 5 WLUK 72.
139 (1989) 11 Cr App R (S) 263.
140 (2021) 73 EHRR 9.

Charging decisions and the presumption of minority in age-disputed cases

6.159

The correct approach of the Crown Prosecution Service when dealing with age-disputed individuals arrested for criminal offences was the subject of judicial review proceedings in *R (AB and Others) v Secretary of State for the Home Department and the Director of Public Prosecutions*, brought by four claimants who had been charged as adults with immigration-related offences, but were later accepted to be children. The claimants challenged the Home Office's decision to refer them for prosecution on the basis of a cursory and inadequate assessment of their age, a practice previously held unlawful in *R (H) v Secretary of State for the Home Department*, and also challenged the CPS's decision to prosecute them as adults without first ensuring that proper inquiries into their age had been undertaken or, alternatively, without affording them the benefit of the doubt that they might be children when applying the Full Code Test.

6.160

Those proceedings were compromised and there is no reported judgment, so no binding guidance emerged from the case itself. Since that settlement, however, the CPS has updated and consolidated its guidance on "Children as suspects and defendants", as well as internal guidance (disclosed under the Freedom of Information Act) on ss 24 and 25 of the Immigration Act 1971 where age is disputed, emphasising that any age dispute should be raised at the first hearing, that documentary and assessment evidence should be obtained promptly, and that the CPS policy is not to prosecute children for certain immigration offences.

6.161

This litigation raised important questions about procedural fairness, the presumption of minority, and the safeguarding obligations owed to children within the criminal justice system.

7 Investigating trafficking and exploitation offences

Caroline Haughey OBE, KC, Phil Brewer, Michelle Brewer and Ben Douglas-Jones KC

7.1

By their very nature modern slavery, exploitation and trafficking offences are complex and challenging. Often the complainant is reluctant to engage. This may be through fear, shame, denial or because the victims are themselves involved in criminality. Allegations may span long periods. Identification of victims and recovery of evidence may be difficult. A central principle within the European Convention on Action against Trafficking in Human Beings ('ECAT'), the EU Trafficking Directive and ECHR, Art 4, is that self-identification by a victim is not a pre-requisite to an investigation into their trafficking[1]. Where there is a credible suspicion[2] of trafficking, there should be an ECHR, Art 4 compliant criminal investigation (see below). All those involved in, or affected by, the investigation of exploitation need to be familiar with the operative duty to identify victims of slavery, servitude, forced or compulsory labour, and human trafficking: the national referral mechanism and Art 4 ECHR (see **Chapters 4** and **10**).

The complainant

7.2

The allegation can come to police attention in a variety of ways, including:

- through the complainant themselves – upon recovery from their situation or as an accused who discloses that their alleged criminality derived from being a victim of exploitation or criminality;
- through intelligence gathering;
- through a proactive and/or reactive operation;
- through a safeguarding report; or
- through a member of the public reporting a matter to the police.

1 See EU Trafficking Directive at preamble (15) and *Rantsev v Cyprus and Russia* (App No 25965/04).

2 See *R (on the application of TDT, by his litigation friend) v Secretary of State for the Home Department & Equality and Human Rights Commissioner intervening* [2018] EWCA Civ 1395 for a judicial analysis of 'credible suspicion'.

7.3

Complainant care is covered to a large degree by the statutory guidance to the Modern Slavery Act 2015 ('MSA 2015' and 'MSA guidance') for England and Wales published by the Home Office[3]. The MSA guidance also provides clear definitions and examples of the relevant terms and should be the starting point for all practitioners.

7.4

The MSA guidance also reminds stakeholders of the statutory obligation to notify the Home Office when a potential victim of modern slavery/human trafficking has been identified. This can be achieved either by reference to the National Referral Mechanism ('NRM') or if the potential victim refuses to engage with the NRM by direct notification to the Home Office via the Modern Slavery Portal[4].

Investigatory interviews[5]

7.5

Complainants can be reluctant to engage with the authorities, ashamed to admit that they are[6] the victims of exploitation. They may not recognise, through their vulnerabilities such as their cultural or social background, mental health, alcoholism, etc, that their conditions are exploitative or that they have been trafficked, or they may consent to the conditions in which they are trafficked or enslaved, eg sex workers being exploited in brothels[7] or drug dealers at the county end of a county line. As set out in **Chapter 8**, the psychological impact of trafficking can:

- result in PTSD/depression/anxiety disorders;
- stem from multiple forms of maltreatment such as physical, emotional, and sexual abuse;
- result in victims finding it extremely difficult to trust adults (children) or individuals in authority,

3 Home Office, *Modern Slavery Act 2015 – Statutory Guidance for England and Wales* https://www.gov.uk/government/publications/modern-slavery-how-to-identify-and-support-victims (v. 11 August 2025).

4 See https://www.modernslavery.gov.uk/start, accessed 11 August 2025.

5 In the writing of this section we are grateful for the assistance of Kalvir Kaur, Legal Advisor at Freedom from Torture.

6 Or perceive that they have allowed themselves to be.

7 Consent in sex trafficking is irrelevant, however, note the 'consent' issue in labour exploitation cases – freely given consent as opposed to least worst option consent is explored further in *R v Nguyen, Tran and Nguyen* [2019] EWCA Crim 670; *R v Rooney* [2019] EWCA Crim 681; and *R v K, W, A* [2018] EWCA Crim 1432. – county lines/consent.

- stem from exploitation from an early age or for a prolonged period likely to result in victims suffering complex, long-term mental health problems;
- stem from the effect of trauma on the brain.

7.6

Complainants may also consent as it is 'the least worst option' but this is not considered true consent[8].

7.7

The primary focus of any investigation should be on obtaining an account from the complainant by the most appropriate route for them. Complainants in MSA 2015 cases are 'vulnerable' for the purposes of special measures[9] and accounts can be obtained by means of pre-recorded Achieving Best Evidence ('ABE') interviews or s 9, Criminal Justice Act 1967 statements. It is vital to ensure that when such accounts are being obtained, and particularly when there are multiple accounts, that complainants are separated from each other to prevent allegations of witness contamination.

7.8

It is also vital to ensure that the complainant is empowered to choose the best means by which they want to give their account whether that be through a s 9 statement and or through an ABE interview.

7.9

In larger operations, when dealing with multiple complainants of the same nationality, care should be taken in selecting interpreters who speak the correct dialect and to ensure that interpreters are otherwise independent of the investigation. Foreign nationals may originate from small or close-knit communities, where social networks are strong, often intrafamilial and extensive. As a result, it is not uncommon for individuals to have direct or indirect associations with persons under investigation for offences that may align with culturally embedded and or socially acceptable patterns of behaviour.

7.10

Cultural humility, awareness and understanding are vital: isolated foreign national complainants will often return to the very people they accuse of exploiting them as they are considered the closest thing to continuity, support or family in the jurisdiction. Investigating officers should initiate the involvement with appropriate charities and organisations to ensure that the complainant does not feel isolated – this is particularly important with adolescent complainants in

8 *R -v- Nguyen, Tran and Nguyen* [2019] EWCA Crim 670.
9 Youth Justice and Criminal Evidence Act 1999, s 33(6)(d).

any form of exploitation who may view their perpetrators as the closest thing they have to a family. Effective working relationships between other agencies ensures that the number of accounts that complainants are required to give is reduced; the trauma of their experience is also lessened; and the complainant is subsequently more likely to commit to participating in the criminal justice system. Victim navigators[10] as led by Justice and Care are individuals trained to act as an independent go between for complainants and the criminal justice system and have been recommended for national implementation in the House of Lords Modern Slavery Act 2015 committee report of 2024[11].

7.11

The 2025 Standard Crime Contract (effective 1 October 2025) introduced heightened competency standards. Legal advice concerning modern slavery offences at the police station must now be overseen by a supervisor meeting specific 'serious crime' accreditation. This is designed to ensure that the s 45 defence is identified and raised at the earliest possible stage of the investigation (see **Chapter 10**).

7.12

Obtaining the account itself provides its own challenges. Often complainants are recruited and/or targeted because of their vulnerabilities – alcoholism, mental health issues, financial desperation- the same vulnerabilities which may impact on recollection and understanding of what has occurred. Deploying the recommendations made in the Advocacy Gateway guidelines is a prudent approach[12]. Experience has shown that, when obtaining such accounts, following a chronological approach has been most successful. Questions should be short, simple, tailored to a complainant's demeanour and educational needs and 'memory coat hangers' – birthdays, significant family events, significant public events eg Christmas, etc – should be used as memory hooks.

7.13

As a matter of course, those who allege they are victims of modern slavery should be referred via the NRM (adults must consent). Any notes made of the account upon which the Single Competent Authority makes its finding should be obtained by the prosecutor for the purposes of potential disclosure should the matter progress to trial. The same approach should be adopted with any of the NGOs or other agencies involved, as any account provided may be disclosable or otherwise become relevant, particularly, if the credibility of the complainant is a matter in issue.

10 https://justiceandcare.org/app/uploads/2023/01/JC-Victim-Navigator-Programme-Overview.pdf.
11 https://publications.parliament.uk/pa/ld5901/ldselect/ldmodslav/8/8.pdf.
12 https://www.theadvocatesgateway.org/toolkits-1-1-1.

Children

7.14

For children,

> '... aside from the physical, sexual or emotional abuse they may have suffered, many trafficked children have been forced by their traffickers to learn a story to tell if they are questioned. Many children and young people are under threat directly themselves, or may have family members elsewhere who are under threat, or perceived threat. Children and young people may not know at this stage who they can trust. As a result, they may give information that is later contradictory to information provided initially. This is not necessarily an indication that a child or young person is trying to deceive social workers, and should not be considered as such'[13].

7.15

The College of Policing guidance on modern slavery directed:

> 'Child victims of modern slavery are amongst the most vulnerable, the easiest to control and the least likely to admit to their situation. They may not show obvious signs of distress ... Parents and relatives may also be involved in their exploitation. Children are extremely loyal to their parents. So, it is unlikely they will seek protection against such people ... [They] may [be] wary of all adults, including police officers ... [and] may therefore be reluctant to disclose any information in an interview until they have built a trusting relationship ...'[14].

PEACE model of investigatory interviewing

7.16

The PEACE Model of investigative interviewing was developed in the early 1990s as a collaborative effort between law enforcement and psychologists in England and Wales. The model takes a conversational, non-confrontational approach to getting information from an investigation interview subject. With trafficking investigations, it is necessary to consider adapting the PEACE framework.

13 ADCS, *Age Assessment Guidance* (October 2015).
14 College of Policing Authorised Professional Practice: https://www.college.police.uk/app/major-investigation-and-public-protection/modern-slavery/first-response-and-national-referral-mechanism (accessed 12 August 2025).

Planning and preparation

7.17

A pre-interview plan is vital in identifying the areas that need to be covered (see below).

7.18

An interviewer needs to understand the following matters prior to embarking on the interview:

- likely 'push and pull' factors that led to the complainant being a target of trafficking (individual vulnerability, familial vulnerability, socio-economic vulnerability, structural vulnerability, and situational vulnerability);
- if a service provider is supporting the complainant, investigators should gather information to understand any triggers for the complainant that may impede any interview (eg colours, clothing, the layout of the room etc);
- the victim's mental health as this will have an impact on recollection (see **Chapter 8**);
- what, if any, special measures may be needed before the interview begins (eg an intermediary etc);
- the process of interviewing the victim, collecting corroborating evidence and investigating perpetrators will be more effective when the victim has continued presence in the country (if a foreign national) and the importance of accessing care and protection from a service provider as early in the process as possible;
- the importance of avoiding multiple interviews, as this risks re-traumatising the victim, which can result in conflicting accounts;
- gender issues can significantly affect the interviewer's capacity to obtain information and they need to be considered in advance of the interview. This is irrespective of the gender of the complainant (ie some male victims of trafficking who have been raped may find it difficult to make disclosure to a male interviewer);
- the background to the trafficker's modus operandi and the dynamics of the trafficking (eg if the complainant is Nigerian and the trafficker(s) are Nigerian or from another west African country, consider whether juju was used to maintain silence; or if the complainant is Vietnamese, consider whether he is in a current debt bond and whether there is a risk of the family in Vietnam being targeted if evidence is given against the traffickers).

7.19

Other pre-interview considerations, which are primarily relevant to children but could also be relevant to adults, should include:

- the physical location and layout of the interviewing room;
- positioning of parties;
- making the environment free from distracting noises (eg a ticking clock) and smells;
- avoiding distracting or blinding light;
- ensuring refreshments are available;
- the presence of others;
- the use of an interpreter.

7.20

It is also important to be culturally aware of the individual being interviewed ie understanding the nuance of their socio-economic background, family dynamic, religion, cultural heritage.

Engage and explain

7.21

The goals of the interview should be explained.

7.22

It is advisable to begin with topics designed to set the complainant/witness at ease. It is also important to personalise the interview.

7.23

In particular, in respect of children (and in some cases, adults), the following points should be considered as good practices:

- introducing oneself by name and greeting the child by name;
- wearing informal clothes;
- beginning with a brief conversation on a totally unrelated issue;
- adapting the communication level to that of the witness/interviewee;
- emphasising that the witness/interviewee should describe everything that comes into his or her mind;

- explaining that the appointment will require concentration;
- discouraging the child from guessing or inventing things when he does not remember or does not know;
- transferring control;
- avoiding filtering; and
- explaining that the witness/interviewee will be asked details of the event.

7.24

Consider the language used:

- ask short, simple questions and avoid 'front-loading', eg 'I suggest to you that …'; 'I put it to you …'; 'I believe you told us …';
- avoid phrases such as 'Do you follow?' at the end of questions;
- who/what/where/when questions are usually most easily understood;
- in respect of children, or those with poor mental health and or neurological divergence, complex questions are likely to result in incorrect or 'I don't know' responses, even though the individual does know the answer and could respond if the question were phrased simply;
- present one topic at a time;
- avoid closed questions (requiring or suggesting yes or no answers);
- avoid questions suggesting the answer;
- avoid 'Do you remember …' questions; and
- avoid forced choice questions.

7.25

In respect of children, the following concepts are important:

- it is necessary to probe into the child's understanding and use of words;
- children may struggle to locate the correct words to describe their experiences;
- without probing, the possibility will remain that an accurate account has not been elicited; and
- if the child understands the purpose of the questions, they are more likely to be engaged.

7.26

For both children and adults, it is important to be culturally aware. Specifically, in respect of children it should be understood that:

- a child's status in his home and in wider society varies; and
- cultural differences may be misinterpreted, such as:
  - lack of eye contact;
  - deference to adults; and
  - not referring to adults by their name and or using a term of respect eg auntie to refer to an older female individual who is not necessarily a family member.

Account and challenge

7.27

The account sought should be an open narrative at the outset. This can be then reviewed, and matters may be clarified with the victim.

7.28

The fine grain detail for exploration will include:

- *Travel*: how the traffickers were recruited; by whom? what was understood to be the offer vis-à-vis travel? what route was to be taken? what means of travel was to be used? what route was subsequently taken? who arranged the journey? how was it arranged? who controlled the journey? when did they leave? from where did they depart? what travel documents did they have when they left? what happened to those documents? who controlled the documents during the travel? when did they arrive? what was their point of arrival? who met them? how did they get to their final destination? who controlled that address? were they moved at any point after arrival? if so, for what purpose? by whom? how? and who arranged it?
- *Exploitation*: what did the traffickers do? who arranged the travel? how were they paid? by whom? how much? how much of it did they keep? where did they live? in what conditions did they live? was this what they were offered when they were recruited? was this voluntary? did they consent to the control/exploitation/employment, etc? what alternatives were there? how easy was it for them to remove themselves from their situation? was it possible for them to change the circumstances which caused the exploitation? were any threats made? were identity documents controlled? were bank accounts obtained or controlled? were their bank accounts and or personal details used in furtherance of other criminal activity (eg claiming of benefits in their name by someone else, wage diversion, fraud or money laundering)?
- *Intelligence to assist in financial investigations*: other businesses: who held the money? who was renting the property(ies)? etc (see below).

7.29

Interviewers/questioners should be aware that when a child is activating imaginative pictures of events:

- every single act of evoking a new "representation" (a discrete mental visualisation of a specific part of an event) interrupts the process of memory scanning and requires some mental effort;
- hopping from representation to representation may seriously reduce the amount of information recalled by the child; so
- it follows that the interviewer should exhaust one mental picture (eg get all the details concerning the classroom) before asking the child to switch to a different one (the playground), to avoid draining the child's mental energy.

Closure

7.30

Bringing the interview to a close should encompass the following:

- briefly summarising what the complainant/witness has said;
- explicitly telling the witness to correct the interviewer if they have missed anything out or have got something wrong;
- thanking the complainant/witness for their time and effort and asking if there is anything more they wish to communicate;
- explaining the next steps.

Investigations beyond the complainant's account

7.31

Investigations and subsequent prosecutions do not rest exclusively on the reliability or indeed the existence of an account from the complainant. The fact of someone being found in specific circumstances (even to which he consents) may be sufficient to amount to trafficking and/or exploitation[15]. Vital to any investigation and prosecution is corroborative evidence – caveated with the absence of some evidence, being equally compelling. Taking an investigative decision to focus on corroborative evidence capable of proving the case has significant benefits. It offsets the total reliability on individuals, who may be hostile to the prosecution or who may be in fear of the repercussions of having

15 *R v Nguyen, Tran and Nguyen* [2019] EWCA Crim 670; *R v K, W, A* [2018] EWCA Crim 1432.

to give evidence in court. It will also reduce the risk of a trial collapsing if victims or witnesses can no longer be located.

Other lines of enquiry

7.32

Most members of society in the UK have a social or electronic footprint. For a child this may be their NHS records, education, Department for Work and Pensions ('DWP') or local authority records – the absence of the existence of these can be as compelling as the existence of them – raising the question if it does not exist why not?

7.33

The same test can be applied to adults – an absence of social media or absence from an otherwise active social media account can lend support to the proposition that someone is in a non-consenting/controlled/exploitative environment. Absence of medical, social services, employment, DWP, financial records, etc[16] or a pause in activity gives rise to the same question – if not, why not?

7.34

Corroborative evidence can be found in a variety of forms and 'best evidence' is usually found from objective sources such as banks, utility providers, phone records and so forth, eg:

- **Travel records** – who travelled and when? who made the booking? in what name and how was it paid for? This together with any other information regarding the journeys of any of the complainants – this is of course applicable to any form of transport used, eg flight records etc. Checks should also be done at each port of entry and with the ferry companies to ascertain what other material of which they are in possession, eg the manifest. It is particularly helpful to have booking payment details as often this will show an element of involvement required under the trafficking legislation.

- **Banking** – This should include all account opening documents and the transaction history. This is relevant to demonstrate who was accessing which account and when. It also assists in demonstrating which account was being used to funnel the monies for other fraudulent activity being undertaken on the account(s). It is not unusual that some form of fraud is perpetuated as a means of control, eg wage diversion, loan fraud, money laundering, DWP fraud etc – and it is when such financial analysis is

16 Similar lines of investigation are explored in 'proof of life enquiries'.

undertaken that further linked criminality is often disclosed. Statements from the DWP and local authority confirming what benefits each of the complainants were in receipt of, who completed the forms to obtain those benefits and which accounts were in receipt of those benefits is also useful corroborative material, particularly when the same phone number is used to claim benefits for multiple apparently unrelated individuals. It is also suggested that Experian/credit score checks should be conducted on each complainant as often the perpetrators open accounts and register with utilities companies in complainants' names in order to conduct further fraudulent activity and/or exert control over the account. Conducting the Experian check may be a means of identifying what, if any, loans have been taken out in complainants' names and for what other purposes their identities have been used, as well as revealing other connected addresses, email accounts and phone numbers.

- **CCTV from banks** – Where possible CCTV footage should be obtained to cover the account opening as well as the use of ATM, cash deposit or counter services. This can be strong corroborative evidence of account control.
- **NI numbers** – These are often obtained under the direction of the perpetrators and the contact details provided can either corroborate the complainant's account based on dates and addresses or disclose further addresses.
- **Housing** – Information pertaining to control of an address can be compelling – who rents the address; who pays rent; and how; is the address a multiple occupancy address? Tenancy agreements are often taken out in complainants' names but not verified with their identity documents and with other people paying the rent; the names on tenancy agreements are frequently at odds with who is listed as paying for utilities and/or council tax. Such enquiries should also be cross-referenced with DWP records of who is claiming benefits at the address. For each address an enquiry into what, if any, police attendance has been made to the address, is a useful means of identifying who was at an address and when, as is any information held in respect of the address by the local authority, eg data collection records.
- **Employment records** – Often legitimate employment is used, be it through agencies or other means, which will generate a paper trail. This should be obtained to demonstrate which bank accounts wages were going into and which addresses employees/complainants were living at. Next of kin details and phone numbers provided can also be useful sources of further evidential enquiry.
- **GLAA** – A particularly useful agency when dealing with labour exploitation allegations, the Gangmasters' and Labour Abuse Authority should be asked to confirm that none of the alleged perpetrators are

known to them as having applied for a licence and if they have any further information on them.

- **NHS** – Complainants may refer to attending hospital/medical centres. The hospital/medical notes should be obtained, as they are capable of corroborating not only accounts of the complainants but also the contact details provided. They may also include confirmatory evidence of further separate instances of violence.
- **Local authority** – Local authority records range from data collection records to council tax information. Often local authorities will conduct brothel checks or other address checks recording persons present.
- **Utilities companies** – These will show whose name was registered at what address and when and often contain details of bank accounts and/or phone numbers provided as part of payment information.
- **Communications data evidence** – Often complainants will have no phone or if they do have one it will have limited contacts on it. The absence of contacts may be as compelling as being able to demonstrate links to particular contacts and can be evidence of control being exerted. Communications data also comprise snapshots of an individual's life. Data downloads can evidence caller identity and times and durations of calls that may corroborate allegations of control and coercion against named or traceable individuals. Cell site or Wi-Fi data can place handsets at specific locations or areas at certain times. Subscriber checks may show where a SIM or handset originated, who paid for them, details of the SIM contract or payments for, or top ups of, any pay as you go plan.
- **Social media** – This is often how recruitment has occurred (eg Facebook adverts etc) and a subsequently active account becoming disused can be corroborative evidence of control. It is often challenging to access social media accounts but publicly available pages may comprise useful evidence.
- **NRM support services** – Potential victims referred into the NRM receive care and support through the government's contractor. Care professionals work with victims throughout their recovery. It is important for the investigation team to remain in regular contact with both the victim and support providers as it provides invaluable reassurance, particularly if a victim is likely to be called to give evidence at trial. Through the recovery period, the victim may remember or disclose additional facts linked to his case to a support worker. This can often be additional information that will help the prosecution case.

7.35

Sections 22–29 of the Border Security, Asylum and Immigration Act 2025 grant law enforcement authorities significant powers to search and seize electronic devices from those suspected of immigration offences. In trafficking cases, these devices often contain critical evidence of coercion, such as debt ledgers or threatening messages. Investigators must exercise these powers in accordance with the Code of Practice for Victim Information Requests (January 2026), which mandates that such requests meet a "substantial probative value" test to protect the privacy of potential victims who are often initially treated as suspects.

International material

7.36

This includes:

- **International letters of request** – Often material will need to be obtained from foreign jurisdictions: the early identification of this line of enquiry is vital. Letters of request will be required which will need to specify in some detail the exact material required – and note that statements obtained in foreign jurisdictions will be in the form appropriate for that jurisdiction's procedural code.
- **Joint Investigation Teams** – A Joint Investigation Team ('JIT') 'is an international cooperation tool based on an agreement between competent authorities – both judicial (judges, prosecutors, investigative judges …) and law enforcement – of two or more states, established for a limited duration and for a specific purpose, to carry out criminal investigations in one or more of the involved states'[17]. One of the particular benefits of a JIT is that evidence properly obtained in the parallel jurisdiction, admissible in the courts of that jurisdiction and compliant with the European Convention on Human Rights, is admissible in the courts of the other parties to the agreement – eg, phone intercept material obtained in Hungary could then be admissible in a trial in England and Wales.

The accused

7.37

Enquiries into the accused and particularly their financial background can be informative. Often the motive for the alleged offending is greed and a careful review of bank accounts, international money transfers, fx transfers, crypto currency wallets and the like can either confirm or undermine the complainant's account and/or raise questions that require an explanation.

17 See https://www.europol.europa.eu/activities-services/joint-investigation-teams, accessed 12 August 2025.

7.38

As with complainants, similar enquiries should be made of the accused about:

- **Travel records** – This includes vehicle ownership and how vehicles were purchased.
- **Banking** – Financial evidence offers significant benefits to a modern slavery investigation. As offending is often money-driven, case officers should always consider a parallel financial investigation. Not only is it likely to support the modern slavery case, it can also offer other alternative prosecution opportunities, such as money laundering, where a trafficking case cannot be proved. As with complainants, enquiries should include all account opening documents and the transaction history together with DWP material detailing what benefits individuals are receiving; whether the accused is living beyond his means; and, if so, how. When dealing with foreign nationals, enquiries about their property ownership and financial background in their country of origin are useful, as this is often where profit from the criminal enterprise is directed.
- **Money transfers** – Inevitably, there is a need for the criminal property to be concealed or removed from the jurisdiction. When dealing with foreign national offenders an analysis of cash transfers abroad through money transfer organisations will often shed light on the hierarchy of, and control within, a criminal structure, the information provided on money transfer forms in order to send and or receive the monies can also be a rich seam of information: names, addresses, phone numbers.
- **Housing** – What addresses are rented, by whom, who is a party to the lease, how long have they been there, how is rent paid and by whom are all matters of possible relevance to an investigation.
- **Local authority** – Council tax returns and other data providing information as to who was living at what address and when is likely to be of relevance to an investigation.
- **Utility companies** – Whose name was registered at what address and when may be important.
- **Communications data evidence** – This type of evidence will very frequently show who was exerting control over whom, and when: it will be of particular importance in a conspiracy or joint enterprise as it may be that the agreement can be demonstrated from the data. Contact with complainants and/or employees together with the length of contact (both date parameters of contact and call length) may be relevant. The use of communications data may also provide evidence of the user's lifestyle. Analysing cell site information may evidence the location of a handset. Used alongside other information, such as Automatic Number Plate Reader ('ANPR') data, it may also confirm vehicles used by suspects in the context of offences or certain acts which may be pinpointed to

specific times. Another source of information can be found in the satellite navigation system in a vehicle which can disclose frequently used addresses and time of driving to those addresses.

- **Websites** – This evidence is particularly relevant in sexual exploitation cases. Sex sale platforms are now the most used means by which prostitution occurs in the UK. Although obtaining evidence from, or in relation to, some of these websites can be fraught with difficulty[18], open source material may be admissible. Use of the same postcode and/or contact number on image pages of sex workers can be deployed as evidence of control for the purposes of sexual exploitation (whether consenting or not). Likewise, payments from accounts of such websites can show who controlled the sex worker(s) advertising sites or pages. Service providers, in some circumstances, can detail locations of where accounts were accessed from or the type of device used when an account was set up.

7.39

Prosecutors, investigators and defence representatives must all be alive to the possibility that an accused in an exploitation/trafficking case may themselves have been the victim of trafficking and/or compelled to commit the alleged criminal act(s) at the direction of others[19]. The appropriate procedures should therefore be followed (see **Chapter 10**).

Charging

7.40

Exploitation and trafficking cases can be historical, complex, and multifaceted insofar as the criminality that is exposed is concerned. It is not uncommon for offending to predate MSA 2015 and or indeed traverse the MSA. In such circumstances charges should be split to reflect the appropriate legislation in force at the time. Examples of offences to consider can include the following: Offences of trafficking into/within the UK, contrary to s 4 of the Asylum and Immigration (Treatment of Claimants, etc.) Act 2004; acting as a gangmaster, of being in possession of false documents, or of entering into arrangements with gangmasters, contrary to ss 13 and 14 of the Gangmasters Licensing Act 2004, and of slavery, servitude and forced or compulsory labour, contrary to s 71 of the Coroners and Justice Act 2009 can be considered. With effect from 6 April 2013, two further offences of trafficking people, set out in ss 109 and 110 of the Protection of Freedoms Act 2012, trafficking people for sexual exploitation and

18 Many are registered/based abroad and reluctant to engage with UK or indeed any authorities and/or provide information in forms that are not compliant with court procedures.

19 MSA 2015, s 45. See **Chapter 7**.

trafficking people for labour and other exploitation, respectively, were brought into force, before being repealed when s 2 of MSA 2015 came into force. The first of these offences substituted a new s 59A in the Sexual Offences Act 2003, directed at covering the trafficking of individuals within and outside the UK with a view to sexual exploitation, and the second substituted a new s 4(1A) into the Asylum and Immigration (Treatment of Claimants, etc.) Act 2004; an offence to cover trafficking within and outside the UK with a view to non-sexual exploitation, largely directed at exploitation through labour (s 4(11)). Sections 1 to 4 of MSA 2015 came into force on 31 July 2015 (see **Chapter 9** for further detail of offences under MSA 2015).

7.41

Notably in trafficking and exploitation offending, it is not uncommon for there to be linked offending. This can range from the obvious associated acquisitive offence, such as money laundering, benefit fraud, wage diversion, account cloning etc which derives from the exploitation, to drug trafficking, sham marriages, excessive violence used as a form of control, and sexual violence. Where appropriate, separate charges should be preferred[20].

7.42

When indicting counts of slavery and trafficking, consideration should be given to *R v Webb and Somerset-How*[21] and *R v K (S)*[22]. *R v Webb and Somerset-How* makes it clear that slavery and servitude may be indicted together. *K* suggests in the context of s 4 Asylum and Immigration (Treatment of Claimants, etc.) Act 2004 counts, that specificity in particularising elements of an offence is likely to be necessary where a charge needs to encompass different ways of committing the offence (see **Chapter 9**). Those considering an indictment involving trafficking and/or slavery offences need to weigh up the criminality which may be encapsulated in any identified charge and balance that against the principle of totality in sentencing, with the permutations of possible convictions in mind. Simplifying these often complex cases for the jury is crucial, both to aid their understanding and to ensure the trial judge can, in due course, deliver a legally sound and accurate summing-up.

---

20 In some cases, violence should properly be subsumed within the facts of trafficking or slavery allegations as part of the general nature of the offending. It can then be considered as comprising aggravating features of offending for sentence. Offending that is connected specifically to the exploitation can often properly be approached in this way. On the other hand, sexual offences (e.g. sexual assault, rape etc) should invariably be separately charged, due to the serious nature of the offences, the different gravamen of the offending entailed in those charges and to assist courts with appropriate sentencing powers and ancillary orders available post-conviction.

21 [2023] EWCA Crim 1491.

22 [2011] 2 Cr App R 34, paras 44 and following.

7.43

The CPS updated its guidance in January 2026 to reflect a hierarchy of charging. Prosecutors are now encouraged to select the most readily provable offence. Where evidence of 'exploitation' for a s 2 MSA 2015 charge is complex, they may instead favour charging a s 21 Border Security, Asylum and Immigration Act 2025 offence (endangering life at sea) or s 25 Immigration Act 1971 (facilitation of illegal entry or arrival). The current Four-Stage Assessment for potential victims remains the mandatory framework for charging decisions in this context (see **Chapter 10**).

Risk orders

7.44

Part 2 MSA 2015 (ss 23 to 29) has brought into force the ability to use slavery and trafficking risk orders ('STROs'). An STRO is a civil order which may be made by a court in respect of an individual who has not been convicted of a slavery or trafficking offence. The court must be satisfied that there is a risk that a person (referred to as 'defendant' in s23 of MSA 2015) may commit a slavery or human trafficking offence and that the STRO is necessary to protect against the risk of harm from the defendant committing the offence. STROs enable action to be taken where this is necessary to prevent serious harm to the public notwithstanding the absence of a conviction. The standard of proof which applies is the enhanced civil standard.

7.45

These orders are invaluable, particularly when dealing with larger organised crime groups or where there is evidence of ongoing conduct despite police intervention. Maintaining complainant confidence in the criminal justice system is vital and orders such as STROs are vital in achieving this.

Disclosure

7.46

In most cases, the credibility of complainants' accounts of events in evidence will be in issue. Thus, any account provided by them to any agency will be potentially relevant and potentially disclosable. Obtaining this material early in the investigation enables a pragmatic evaluation of the weaknesses in accounts to be conducted. Investigators and prosecutors should be alive to elements of dishonesty that may appear in accounts. These are often not fatal to a case but merely symptomatic of the complainant's vulnerabilities and associated shame and fear.

7.47

International material may be required as it may show or comprise complainants' and defendants' bad character. It may also include psychiatric, state agency or other material that is relevant to a defence. This may need to be obtained via a letter of request. Early interaction with defence teams is often desirable or necessary.

7.48

Where credibility is in issue, the first account to the Single Competent Authority is also material that should fall to be considered as potentially disclosable. It is extremely unlikely that an NRM finding concerning an adult could be used as corroborative support that a complainant is a victim of trafficking or exploitation in a criminal trial. This position may alter when the appellate courts have determined the status of a Competent Authority decision in the context of defendant's defence at trial (see **Chapter 10**).

7.49

It is not unusual for complainants to have criminal backgrounds and issues which render their accounts susceptible to being challenged on credibility grounds. Such backgrounds and issues are often the cause or product of their vulnerability and subsequent exploitation. A sensitive approach to non-defendant bad character is commended. It may be appropriate for the court to give a balanced direction as to how exploitation may lead to the commission of offences or the giving of different accounts. Where ostensibly reprehensible behaviour is unproven, care should be taken to ensure that, before reliance is placed on it as bad character, consideration is given as to whether the alleged perpetrator acted criminally or whether, notwithstanding that it was a *prima facie* criminal activity, his criminality was expunged by the dominant force of compulsion of traffickers; see *R v L(C) and others*[23], *R v S(G)*[24], *R v AFU*[25] and the in-depth analysis of the law in **Chapter 10**.

7.50

Given the transnational nature of modern slavery, significant quantities of documents or exhibits may require interpreting before they can be properly assessed by the disclosure officer. This can be extremely costly and time consuming. Early consultation with prosecutors to agree a review policy – with the input of the defence and the court where necessary and appropriate – is critical where bulk data exists.

23 [2013] EWCA Crim 991; [2013] 2 Cr App R 23.
24 [2018] EWCA Crim 1824; [2019] 1 Cr App R 7.
25 [2023] EWCA Crim 23; [2023] 1 Cr App R 16.

Trial

7.51

The presentation of a complainant's account may be fraught with difficulty. Often lengthy periods of time are covered, complainants may be reluctant to detail the extent of what has occurred to them through fear or shame, and engaging the complainant with the court process should be a priority.

7.52

Complainants are by their nature vulnerable. How that vulnerability manifests itself must be something that the court, advocates and investigation officers consider, to enable best evidence to be given (see **Chapter 8**).

7.53

The vulnerable witness training course provided by the Inns of Court should be the starting point for any advocate. Consideration of specific needs such as an intermediary, interpreter, screens, video link and the giving of evidence from overseas[26] should also be key considerations, as should the location from where the complainant gives evidence (see **Chapter 8**).

7.54

The use of graphics packs as an aid to telling the story of the case is becoming increasingly accepted by courts generally. It has particular value in exploitation/trafficking cases, where it allows complainants to be asked about the source of documents relevant to them. Many documents may contain personal information irrelevant to the case but relevant to the complainant, such as family phone numbers, etc, which they would not want to be shown in open court. This should be borne in mind when displaying any such material.

7.55

Graphics bundles should also allow for the centralisation of evidence in a single place and allow evidence to be easily contextualised, theoretically reducing court time. As with many forms of criminality, breaking down matters chronologically and/or into specific areas of evidence, eg phones, accommodation, etc leads to an easier presentation of the case.

7.56

In cases with larger numbers of complainants, their specific accounts may become lost in the accounts of others and their exploitation diluted, so careful thought should be given to presentational aids. Consideration must be given to each account and to how that individual complainant was trafficked/exploited.

---

26 See *R v Kadir* [2022] EWCA Crim 1244; [2023] 1 WLR 532.

7.57

Special measures applications should be made for those complainants who request them. Supporting witness statements must detail what special measures are requested and why. Many complainants wish to see their perpetrator(s) in open court as a means of reclaiming ownership of their account (see **Chapter 8**).

7.58

There are no hard and fast rules for prosecuting such cases; however, the needs of the complainant to understand, participate in and engage with the criminal justice process are vital. Early understanding by them of what is to take place coupled with committed and culturally aware engagement by the investigating and prosecuting team will lead to a more effective, cogent and concise presentation of the case.

7.59

Foreign complainants who have returned to their home country are often reluctant to return to the UK to give evidence. Giving sufficient time for video link evidence as well as ensuring the appropriate documents are with the venue from which the evidence is to be given via the correct channels is vital. The following guidance provides an overview of how prosecutors can obtain evidence from overseas for use in criminal investigations or proceedings in England and Wales:

- CPS guidance, 'International Enquiries'[27];
- Joint Investigation Teams, Proceeds of Crime Legal Guidance[28];
- Extradition Legal Guidance.

7.60

The CPS Guidance helpfully provides:

> 'Evidence can be obtained from abroad in a variety of ways. The UK's domestic legislation regarding obtaining evidence from overseas is widely drafted. Section 7 Crime (International Cooperation) Act 2003 (CICA) permits an application to be made by ILOR but does not require it. The method you will need to use in a particular case will depend on the type of evidence/assistance you are requesting (see below) as well as the country you are seeking evidence from.

27 See https://www.cps.gov.uk/legal-guidance/international-enquiries, updated 24 July 2023; accessed 12 August 2025.

28 See http://www.eurojust.europa.eu/Practitioners/JITs/Pages/JITs-sitemap.aspx, accessed 12 August 2025.

Wherever possible, police to police channels should be used to obtain the assistance sought. A prosecutor should make the request where the evidence can only be obtained from the country concerned through MLA (using an ILOR) or, for participating EU Member States, through the EIO. Where the requested country is unable to provide the assistance via police to police channels, an ILOR or EIO should be considered and, as long as the material (whether intelligence or evidence) is being sought in relation to an ongoing criminal investigation and represents a reasonable line of enquiry, the prosecutor should issue an ILOR or EIO. Where a request from a prosecutor is not necessary, cooperation between domestic police and an overseas police authority can and should be used.'

8 Access to justice for victims of modern slavery and human trafficking: special measures in court and tribunal proceedings

Michelle Brewer, Paramjit Ahluwalia, Philippa Southwell and Kalvir Kaur

Introduction

8.1

In this chapter, we examine the legal and policy frameworks, along with published guidance, that protect access to justice for victims of human trafficking, slavery, and related offences.

8.2

As set out in **Chapter 3**, such victims will often have vulnerabilities, including disabling conditions, that require accommodations when they take part in litigation, whatever their role. The central focus here is on what measures can be taken to enable such individuals, whether appearing as witnesses, defendants, or parties, to participate fully in legal proceedings in both tribunals and courts. **Chapter 3** is an essential read when considering special measures in legal proceedings.

8.3

At the outset, it is important to highlight a key reference regularly used by the judiciary of England and Wales and endorsed by the appellate courts: the Equal Treatment Bench Book[1]. Written by judges for judges, this publication is not jurisdiction-specific and offers practical guidance on a wide range of vulnerabilities that may call for adaptations during litigation to ensure effective participation, and signposts differing adaptations and accommodations available for vulnerable people giving evidence. It is designed to complement, rather than replace, the legislative and policy frameworks governing special measures.

1 This is on the Courts and Tribunals Judiciary website and is regularly updated.

8.4

Other practical guidance includes the following:

- **The Advocate's Gateway**: these guides provide important assistance to practitioners in identifying and managing vulnerability and steps to be taken to ensure effective participation in litigation.
- **The Family Justice Council Guidelines in relation to children giving evidence in family proceedings**[2]: these guidelines can be adapted to non-family proceedings and are a useful tool.
- **The Inns of Court College of Advocacy, *20 Principles of Questioning Vulnerable Witnesses*** (March 2023)[3].
- **Presidential Guidance: Vulnerable parties and witnesses in Employment Tribunal proceedings (April 2020):** this draws on the criminal, family and civil frameworks to set out how adjustments could be made in the Employment Tribunal.
- **Joint Presidential Guidance No.1 of 2024: Appointment of litigation friends in the Upper Tribunal (Immigration and Asylum Chamber) and First-tier Tribunal (Immigration and Asylum Chamber).**
- **Senior President of Tribunals Child, Vulnerable Adult and Sensitive Witnesses Practice Direction (2008).**
- **Assessment of Mental Capacity: Guidance for Doctors and Lawyers,** published jointly by the Law Society and British Medical Association (BMA) (5th edition, published July 2022).

Understanding vulnerability, special measures and ground rules hearings

Vulnerability and special measures in legal proceedings

8.5

The term 'special measures' is not applied uniformly across courts and tribunals. In the family courts, for example, equivalent provisions are referred to as 'participation directions'. Conceptually, however, both terms refer to the same principle: a range of adjustments designed to support vulnerable or intimidated

2 'Guidelines in relation to children giving evidence in family proceedings': Working Party of the Family Justice Council (Dec 2011). See also 'Guidelines for Judges Meeting Children who are Subject to Family Proceedings': Family Justice Council (April 2010).

3 Inns of Court College of Advocacy, *20 Principles of Questioning Vulnerable Witnesses* (March 2023) https://www.icca.ac.uk/wp-content/uploads/2023/03/20-Principles-of-Questioning.pdf accessed [21 August 2025].

individuals in participating effectively in legal proceedings. These measures aim to reduce stress, anxiety, and other barriers that may inhibit a person from giving their best evidence or engaging fully in the justice process. For consistency, this book adopts the term 'special measures' throughout.

8.6

The use of special measures is not limited to individuals with disabilities. Vulnerability may arise from a variety of circumstances and is not always linked to immaturity or a diagnosed medical or mental condition. When assessing vulnerability in legal proceedings, courts and tribunals must consider a range of factors that may affect a party's or witness's ability to participate effectively. These include any actual or perceived intimidation, mental or physical health conditions, cognitive impairments, and the impact of ongoing medical treatment. The nature and extent of the information before the court or tribunal, the complexity of the issues in dispute, and the presence of abuse, whether domestic, sexual, physical, emotional, racial, cultural, or related to gender, sexual orientation, or human trafficking, slavery or related harms are also relevant.

8.7

Age, maturity, and understanding are critical considerations, alongside social and cultural background, ethnic origin, domestic circumstances, and religious beliefs. The court or tribunal must also consider any communication needs, including the use of aids or intermediaries, and whether the individual is subject to questioning. Special measures should reflect any characteristic that may affect the individual's ability to engage with the proceedings, ensuring that the process is fair and adapted to their needs.

8.8

For example, individuals who have experienced trafficking, slavery, or related harms may suffer emotional trauma and fear when asked to recount their experiences in a public hearing. This can lead to re-traumatisation and impair the quality of the evidence they are able to provide. For such individuals, prolonged periods of giving evidence, particularly when subjected to repetitive or oppressive questioning, can be counterproductive and may significantly hinder their ability to assist the court or tribunal.

8.9

Special measures can be adopted to mitigate these effects and may include:

- Use of screens or video links;
- Anonymity for the witness or party;
- Adjustments to the manner and duration of questioning;
- Scheduling of appropriate breaks during evidence;

- Restrictions on certain topics or types of questions;
- Use of signposting and simplified language during questioning;
- Submission of questions in writing prior to the hearing to avoid oral examination;
- Use of visual aids such as models, plans, or body maps to facilitate communication;
- Requirement for a parent or guardian to attend with a child or young person;
- Requirement for a support person to attend with an adult;
- Implementation of relevant reporting restrictions.

Ground rules hearings

8.10

The senior courts have deprecated the practice of identifying the need for special measures for vulnerable witnesses, parties or defendants only late in the proceedings. In *AM (Afghanistan) v Secretary of State for the Home Department (Lord Chancellor intervening)*[4], the Court of Appeal stressed that early identification of vulnerability is essential to minimise harm and ensure access to justice. This is best served by courts and tribunals holding a ground rules hearing where it becomes apparent a vulnerable witness, party or defendant will be participating in the proceedings.

8.11

Ground rules hearings are a procedural safeguard designed to facilitate the effective participation of vulnerable witnesses, parties or defendants in legal proceedings. They provide an opportunity for the court or tribunal, legal representatives, and if appointed, the intermediary to agree on necessary adaptations to the conduct of the hearing, particularly the manner and structure of questioning.

8.12

These hearings are mandatory in all cases involving intermediaries and are considered best practice in cases involving young or vulnerable witnesses, parties or defendants with communication needs.

---

4 *AM(Afghanistan) v Secretary of State for the Home Department (Lord Chancellor intervening)* [2017] EWCA Civ 1123.

8.13

The hearing typically addresses matters such as the use of communication aids, the duration and pacing of questioning, the need for breaks, and the formulation of developmentally appropriate questions. Where an intermediary is involved, the hearing establishes how they will assist the witness and alert the court or tribunal to any difficulties in understanding or participation.

8.14

In cases involving pre-recorded cross-examination (Youth Justice and Criminal Evidence Act 1999, s 28), a standardised ground rules hearing form is used to ensure consistency and thorough planning.

8.15

To support compliance, it is recommended that a ground rules hearing practice note be prepared, setting out agreed boundaries and expectations for questioning and conduct. This note may include details of the witness's vulnerabilities, communication needs, and any specific arrangements for the giving of evidence.

8.16

Ground rules hearings are essential to ensuring that vulnerable individuals can participate fully and fairly in the justice process.

8.17

In *Ajayi v Abu*[5] the court considered appropriate procedural modifications. It confirmed that if such steps were not taken where there is a risk of failing to adjust to court procedure for the trial, it would amount to a disproportionate interference with the claimant's Art 6 rights. The facts of this case, as set out in the judgment, help illustrate how this can work in practice; however, despite the practical difficulties, the court's reasons emphasised the importance of ensuring such measures are taken.

> 'By a letter dated 23 February 2017 the Claimant's representatives (ATLEU) requested special hearing arrangements for this trial in view of the allegations of trafficking, the alleged vulnerability of the Claimant and the risk that a failure to adjust court procedure for the trial would interfere disproportionately with Ms Ajayi's Article 6 rights to a fair hearing.
>
> I take note that Art. 11(4)(b) read with Art. 12 of the Directive on Preventing and Combating Trafficking in Human Beings and Protecting

5 [2017] EWHC 1946.

its Victim, 2011/36/EU, recognises that Member States must ensure that victims of trafficking receive specific treatment aimed at preventing as far as possible (consistent with national law and judicial discretion) that visual contact between victims and defendants including during the giving of evidence, so as to avoid secondary victimisation…

Whilst this is not a criminal trial I considered that it was appropriate consistent with the Overriding Objective, and with Art. 6 of the Convention to direct that the trial take place in a courtroom at the Royal Courts of Justice which provided (i) separate entrances and exits from the court for the Claimant and Defendant sides, (ii) screening so that during the giving of evidence the Claimant could be cross examined by counsel but would not be in the line of sight of the Defendants themselves and (iii) that there should be separate waiting areas for the two sides.

In the event the Court system struggled to meet those requirements and the trial started late. Only certain court rooms are suitable, and the appropriate court had been arranged and listed but it was nonetheless found to be in use for a different case and judge, which delayed matters. Witness screens had not been arranged by the Court Service and there was initial refusal by the relevant office to do so on the day (this was later resolved), and the room adjacent to the court affording direct access to the witness box, which had been set aside for use by the Claimant and legal team separately from the Defendants had been occupied by staff from a public inquiry, and could not be used. I commend the Masters' court staff assisting me 'on the ground' on morning of trial for having gone to great lengths to enable the trial to go ahead on the day. It is essential that the court fulfils its obligations in respect of proper measures to allow witnesses to give their testimony freely…' [3-8].

Communicating directions, orders and judgments in cases involving vulnerable parties and witnesses

8.18

In proceedings involving vulnerable individuals, the clarity and accessibility of judicial reasoning are of particular importance. While all judgments must be clear and well-reasoned, additional care should be taken in the language and structure used when the parties or witnesses include children, individuals with learning disabilities, or those with low literacy.

8.19

Judges are encouraged to include a plain-language summary of the decision, either within the judgment or as a separate document, to assist understanding.

This approach has been endorsed in several cases. For example, in *Re A: Letter to a Young Person*, Sir Peter Jackson included a direct letter to the child explaining the outcome in accessible terms[6]. Similarly, in *Lancashire County Council v Mr A, Mr B, The Children*[7], Jackson J deliberately kept the judgment concise so that the mother and older children could follow it.

8.20

In *A Council v Jack's Mother, Jack's Dad and Jack*[8], the judgment exemplified clarity in explaining the decision to a parent with a learning disability. In *Oxfordshire County Council v A Mother*[9], the judge appended a sympathetic explanatory letter to the judgment to support a parent with learning difficulties.

8.21

Tools such as online readability tests[10] can assist judges in simplifying written language for parties with low literacy. The Equal Treatment Bench Book also recommends the use of accessible summaries at the outset of judgments, particularly where the decision affects vulnerable individuals.

8.22

These practices ensure that all parties, regardless of vulnerability, can understand the outcome and reasoning of the court or tribunal.

Legal framework: disability and the Equality Act 2010

8.23

Under the Equality Act 2010, service providers are required to take reasonable steps, known as reasonable adjustments, to prevent disabled service users from experiencing disadvantage, so far as possible enabling them to access services on the same basis as those without a disability. Section 20 of the Equality Act sets out the legislative framework for the duty to make reasonable adjustments. For the purposes of the Act, a disability is defined as a physical or mental impairment that has a 'substantial'[11] and 'long-term'[12] adverse effect on a person's ability to carry out normal daily activities.

---

6 *Re A: Letter to a Young Person* [2017] EWFC 48.
7 *Lancashire County Council v Mr A, Mr B, The Children* [2016] EWFC 9.
8 *A Council v Jack's Mother, Jack's Dad and Jack*, Case No: SN17C00073 (27 March 2018).
9 *Oxfordshire County Council v A Mother (by her litigation friend, the Official Solicitor) and G* [2020] EWFC B40.
10 WebFX, 'Readability Test Tool' https://www.webfx.com/tools/read-able/ accessed 21 August 2025.
11 Means more than minor or trivial.
12 Means 12 months or more.

8.24

Courts and tribunals, however, are exempt from the prohibition in section 29 of the Equality Act 2010 against discrimination, meaning that a claim cannot be brought against a tribunal or court for failing to make reasonable adjustments under the Equality Act to accommodate a disability.

8.25

Nonetheless, tribunals and courts are under a duty to secure the effective participation of disabled individuals in proceedings; failure to do so may constitute an error of law. As Underhill LJ affirmed in *J v K*[13], judicial discretion must always take account of all relevant factors, including mental health or other disabilities, where these arise. Notably, Art 14 of the European Convention on Human Rights (ECHR) prohibits discrimination and contains no exception for courts and tribunals. However, Art 14 is not a standalone right and is dependent on another Convention right being in scope ie Art 6 (the right to a fair trial) or Art 8 (the right to respect for private and family life). Once disability is established, tribunals and courts must ensure that reasonable adjustments or special measures are in place to guarantee effective participation in proceedings.

8.26

Where the disabled individual is a party to proceedings, or a defendant, the question is whether the adjustment is necessary to achieve genuine equality of arms for someone with a relevant disability. Langstaff J (as he then was) in *Rackham v NHS Professionals Ltd*[14] likewise emphasised that the necessity and reasonableness of adjustments must be determined by reference to the needs of the individual, to secure proper participation.

Scope and jurisdictional focus of this chapter

8.27

This chapter is limited in scope and does not cover every jurisdiction within England and Wales. The focus is primarily on proceedings in tribunals and criminal courts. However, when discussing tribunals, relevant references to certain aspects of civil and criminal proceedings are included where appropriate.

8.28

There is much to learn from the practices of different courts and tribunals[15], and it is important to consider the range of approaches and practices when

13 *J v K* [2019] ICR 815 at [33].

14 UKEAT/0110/15/LA.

15 There are well developed principles and practices in the family courts, court of protection, mental health and SEND tribunals.

identifying special measures or reasonable adjustments to support an individual's effective participation in legal proceedings.

8.29

Legislative provisions for special measures vary according to the type of legal proceedings involved. Despite these differences, a consistent principle underpins all frameworks: every potential victim of trafficking, slavery or related acts must have a genuine opportunity to be heard and to present their case effectively. Special measures, such as the use of screens, live video links, intermediaries, and communication aids, are designed to support victims in giving their best evidence, tailored to the specific context of the proceedings.

8.30

For a comprehensive understanding, readers are encouraged to consult related chapters:

- **Chapter 1**: Defines the legal concepts of slavery, servitude, forced or compulsory labour, and human trafficking.
- **Chapter 3**: Explores the physical and mental health impacts of these offences on victims and identifies useful guidance on how to identify specific vulnerabilities of victims of trafficking and related acts.
- **Chapter 4**: Details the identification and protective obligations arising under Art 4 of the ECHR, where there is reasonable suspicion that an individual is a victim of trafficking, slavery, or related acts.

8.31

Together, these chapters provide a holistic view of the legal protections and support mechanisms available to victims, ensuring their rights and needs are addressed throughout the justice process irrespective of their role in those proceedings.

Safeguarding victims in judicial proceedings

Art 30 of the Council of Europe Convention on Action against Trafficking in Human Beings

8.32

Article 30 of the Council of Europe Convention on Action against Trafficking in Human Beings (ECAT) recognises the potential harm that judicial proceedings can cause to victims of trafficking. It requires States Parties to adopt legislative or other measures to ensure, in accordance with their internal law and the European Convention on Human Rights (particularly Art 6), that:

- Victims' private life and, where appropriate, identity are protected;
- Victims are safeguarded from intimidation and threats, with special attention given to the needs of child victims, including their right to special protection measures.

8.33

The Convention acknowledges that victims who testify against traffickers or seek compensation may face intimidation or threats from criminal networks. Media coverage can exacerbate this risk, compromising victims' privacy and impeding their social reintegration.

8.34

The explanatory report to the Convention clarifies that the measures under Art 30 are procedural in nature, distinct from the extrajudicial protections outlined in Art 28. These procedural safeguards must balance the rights of the defence with the rights and safety of victims and witnesses. Given the diversity of legal systems across Europe, the Convention sets out binding objectives but allows States discretion in how they achieve them.

8.35

In *Doorson v the Netherlands*[16], the European Court of Human Rights affirmed that while Art 6 does not explicitly require consideration of victims' interests, their safety and privacy fall within the scope of Art 8 and must be protected. The Court held that fair trial principles require a balance between the rights of the defence and those of victims and witnesses.

8.36

Further guidance is provided in Recommendation No R (97) 13 of the Committee of Ministers, which addresses witness intimidation and the rights of the defence. The Convention encourages States to draw on ECHR case law to implement protective measures such as:

- Non-public hearings, where exclusion of the press and public may be justified to protect the private life of victims or the interests of justice.
- Anonymity orders, ensuring that victims' names are not disclosed in court documents or proceedings.
- Procedural adaptations, such as allowing breaks during testimony or enabling victims to be accompanied by support persons.

16 (1996) 22 EHRR 330.

8.37

These measures are essential to ensuring that victims of trafficking can participate in judicial proceedings without fear, and with dignity and respect. They reflect a trauma-informed approach that recognises the vulnerability of victims and the need for judicial systems to respond with sensitivity and care.

Trauma-informed judicial practice: practical measures[17]

8.38

Many victims experience significant fear when engaging with the court or tribunal system, particularly those with prior experiences of prosecution, detention, or imprisonment, or those who have fled countries where authorities were a source of harm. For such individuals, the formal atmosphere of a courtroom can be intimidating. Measures such as informal dress for court professionals and holding hearings in less formal venues can help to reduce anxiety. Early preparation using photographs and diagrams of the hearing venue can familiarise victims with the layout and help them feel more at ease. Knowing practical details, such as the location of bathrooms or windows, can also provide comfort, allowing victims to orient themselves and focus on natural light or views during proceedings.

8.39

The physical positioning of professionals in the courtroom or tribunal can significantly affect a victim's ability to participate. Arrangements should avoid replicating settings where the victim may have previously been interrogated or subjected to distressing interviews. It may be beneficial for victims to meet the judge and opposing counsel or representative prior to the hearing. Such meetings can help victims, particularly involved in court proceedings, to understand the adversarial nature of the process and reduce the trauma of cross-examination.

8.40

Victims should be accompanied before, during, and after the hearing by independent advocates from trafficking-specialist NGOs. This support is particularly vital when victims are required to give evidence.

---

17 Useful resources for trauma informed judicial practice include: Center for Justice Innovation, *Trauma-Informed Practices for Criminal Courts: Implementation Opportunities* (May 2024), developed with support from the State Justice Institute, available at: https://www.innovatingjustice.org (accessed August 2025). Substance Abuse and Mental Health Services Administration (SAMHSA), *Essential Components of Trauma-Informed Judicial Practice* (2013), prepared by the National Association of State Mental Health Program Directors, available at: https://store.samhsa.gov.

8.41

Low self-esteem may inhibit victims from responding to questions with clarity or confidence. It is helpful to prepare them by explaining the questioning process in advance of the hearing beginning. Victims should be reassured that they can respond at their own pace and are not required to match the pace of the questioner. They should also be encouraged to ask for clarification if they do not understand a question. In some cultures, the perceived status of the questioner may make such requests seem inappropriate or even impossible, so this reassurance is essential.

8.42

Predictability in all aspects of the court or tribunal process is crucial. Victims who have experienced control and abuse in unpredictable ways are particularly vulnerable to anxiety when faced with unexpected events. They may fear being blamed or criticised. Providing opportunities for victims to ask questions and understand procedures helps prevent misinterpretation and reduces the risk of fear, intimidation, or re-traumatisation.

Special measures in tribunal proceedings

Tribunal structure and procedural flexibility

8.43

Under the Tribunals, Courts and Enforcement Act 2007 (TCEA 2007), the modern tribunal system comprises two principal structures: the First-tier Tribunal and the Upper Tribunal, each divided into specialist chambers. Employment Tribunals remain distinct (Employment Tribunals Act 1996).

8.44

Section 3(5) of the TCEA 2007 confers on the Upper Tribunal the status of a superior court of record, while s 25 grants it the same powers, rights, privileges, and authority as the High Court in relation to the attendance and examination of witnesses, the production and inspection of documents, and other matters incidental to its functions.

8.45

The practice and procedure of the First-tier Tribunal and Upper Tribunal are governed by:

- TCEA 2007,
- The relevant Tribunal Procedure Rules,
- Delegated legislation,

- Practice directions and practice statements,
- Case-specific directions, and
- The tribunal's inherent authority to manage its own proceedings.

8.46

In the Court of Appeal in *AM (Afghanistan) v Secretary of State for the Home Department (Lord Chancellor intervening)*[18], the Court emphasised the distinctive features of tribunal procedure. It noted that tribunals may admit and consider evidence that would not be admissible in civil or criminal courts. The Tribunal Procedure Rules promote flexibility and informality, and tribunals benefit from a wide range of specialist expertise. These features are particularly valuable in supporting the effective participation of vulnerable individuals.

8.47

Tribunals, in exercising their inquisitorial function, may raise issues of vulnerability on their own initiative. They are also empowered to take proactive steps to ensure that the necessary evidence is available to implement appropriate measures that enable effective participation.

8.48

Finally, in *Heal v The Chancellor, Master and Scholars of the University of Oxford & Ors*[19], Choudhury J provided authoritative guidance on both the procedural handling and substantive assessment of requests for reasonable adjustments.

AM (Afghanistan) *and recommended special measures*

8.49

The accommodations recommended in *AM (Afghanistan)*, which were considered appropriate by the Court of Appeal, illustrate the types of recommendations that can be sought.

8.50

In that appeal, a psychiatrist recommended a series of adjustments to enable a young person with learning difficulties to give evidence. The recommended measures included:

a. Informal court dress for advocates and judge

b. Informal venue for the hearing

18 *AM(Afghanistan) v Secretary of State for the Home Department (Lord Chancellor intervening)* [2017] EWCA Civ 1123.

19 *Heal v The Chancellor, Master and Scholars of the University of Oxford & Ors* [2020] ICR 1294.

c. Non-confrontational seating arrangements (eg round tables)

d. Exclusion of the public during the appellant's evidence

e. Restriction of courtroom attendees to essential personnel and a nominated support person

f. Use of open-ended, simplified questions

g. Judicial identification of points to be raised during cross-examination

8.51

The judge hearing the appeal gave these recommendations insufficient attention. The Court of Appeal held that the failure to implement the proposed special measures undermined the judge's findings on credibility.

8.52

Other measures adopted in tribunal proceedings have included permitting a carer for an autistic person to support the claimant in answering questions, taking breaks during the hearing, and making efforts to avoid repeated questions[20]. Having a support worker or carer sitting next to a vulnerable party or witness is an appropriate special measure to request, particularly if it assists the individual in staying calm[21].

Special measures for victims of human trafficking and modern slavery

Legislative protections in criminal proceedings applied in a tribunals context

8.53

In the criminal courts, victims of human trafficking and modern slavery who give evidence about their experiences benefit from specific legislative protections. Under s 17(4) of the Youth Justice and Criminal Evidence Act 1999, a complainant in respect of an offence under s 1 (Modern Slavery) or s 2 (Human Trafficking) is eligible for special measures when giving evidence, which will apply unless the witness explicitly informs the court that they do not wish to receive such assistance. Section 17(4) recognises that victims will experience fear and distress giving evidence of their experiences. The range of special measures are provided for in ss 23 to 30 of the Youth Justice and Criminal Evidence Act 1999 (see criminal section of this chapter)[22].

20 *M v SSWP (PIP)* [2018] UKUT 108 (AAC).

21 See: https://www.theadvocatesgateway.org/_files/ugd/1074f0_bc65d21318414ba8a622a99723fdb2a0.pdf last accessed 02 February 2026.

22 The Courts and Tribunals Bill, introduced on 25 February 2026, includes provisions intended to make special measures easier for victims to access and for practitioners to navigate, and guarantees jury trials for the most serious offences including people trafficking. The Bill was at an early stage at the time of writing.

8.54

The protections outlined above are legislated for criminal proceedings. The purpose of these provisions should inform tribunal practice when considering the use of special measures in cases concerning victims of human trafficking and modern slavery. Joint Presidential Guidance[23] has identified certain groups as inherently vulnerable, including children and victims of human trafficking[24].

8.55

Victims' experience of fear and distress when giving evidence of their experience will not be unique or isolated to criminal proceedings. Many perpetrators operate within organised criminal networks, and almost all tribunal hearings are, by default, held in public. Importantly, these individuals may remain at large and may not be subject to any criminal investigation or proceedings when a victim is required to give an account of their experience in tribunal proceedings.

8.56

These factors underscore the need for tribunals to give careful and proactive consideration to protective measures that ensure victims can participate safely and effectively. A recurring issue in such cases is the late disclosure of traumatic experiences, often compounded by a deep-seated fear of public authorities. It is therefore essential that those supporting victims identify and communicate any disclosures that may affect their ability to engage meaningfully in litigation to the tribunal at the earliest possible stage.

Protecting victims' identity and privacy

Anonymity orders

8.57

Disclosure of the identity of a victim of human trafficking or modern slavery and their account of trafficking or modern slavery could place a victim at significant risk. As set out in the explanatory report to the European Convention Against Trafficking in Human Beings ('ECAT') at 138:

> 'Article 11 protects trafficking victims' private life. Protection is essential for victims' physical safety, given the danger from their traffickers, but also (on account of the feelings of shame and the stigmatisation risk

23 Joint Presidential Guidance Note No 2 of 2010: Child, vulnerable adult and sensitive appellant guidance (Immigration and Asylum Chamber). Some of this guidance has been superseded by *AM(Afghanistan)* (5.2(iv)). In *Khan v Secretary of State for the Home Department* [2026] EWCA Civ 148, the Court of Appeal confirmed that the Guidance Note does not impose free-standing legal obligations; non-compliance is an error of law only where it produces material procedural unfairness or a materially flawed assessment of evidence. The court read AM (Afghanistan)'s 'most likely' formulation as indicating a fairness-based threshold rather than a rule of automatic invalidity.

24 Ibid, ftn.2 in the Guidance Note.

that attach to the trafficking, both for the victim and family, to preserve their chances of social reintegration in the country of origin or the receiving country.'

8.58

All tribunal procedure rules include provisions enabling a tribunal to issue orders that prohibit the disclosure or publication of specified documents or information related to proceedings. These orders may also restrict the publication of any material likely to lead to the identification of individuals involved in a case. Although such orders depart from the principle of open justice[25], the law recognises that anonymity must be preserved in certain circumstances.

8.59

Under s 2(1)(db) of the Sexual Offences (Amendment) Act 1992, individuals who allege that they have been trafficked in contravention of s 2 of the Modern Slavery Act 2015 (MSA 2015) are entitled to lifelong anonymity, equivalent to that afforded to complainants in sexual offence cases. It is important to note that offences under s 2 of the MSA 2015 have broad extra-territorial scope.

8.60

Section 2 of the MSA 2015 must be read alongside s 3, which defines 'exploitation' for the purposes of the s 2 offence. Exploitation includes conduct falling under s 1 of the Act, namely slavery, servitude, and forced or compulsory labour. Accordingly, s 2(1)(db) extends anonymity protections to victims of offences under s 1 of the MSA 2015.

8.61

Courts have refused to provide anonymity orders in trafficking and modern slavery cases. Consideration should be given to the rationale of the courts in the decisions of *R v Lurdita Baniulyte*[26] and *R (on the application of Al Noor)*[27].

Private hearings and reporting restrictions

8.62

All Upper Tribunal hearings are held in public, as required by rule 37(1)[28], unless the Tribunal directs otherwise. Most Chambers of the First-tier Tribunal also

25 Some tribunals have published guidance notes on the making of anonymity orders and the underlying principles to be considered. These notes provide a useful framework for both making and determining such applications.

26 *R v Lurdita Baniulyte* [2025] EWCA Crim 1205.

27 *R (on the application of Al Noor)* [2025] EWHC 922 (Admin).

28 The Tribunal Procedure (Upper Tribunal) Rules 2008.

conduct hearings in public. Whether a hearing is held in person or remotely, media representatives and members of the public are generally permitted to attend.

8.63

However, both the First-tier Tribunal and the Upper Tribunal have the power under their respective procedure rules to direct that all or part of a hearing be held in private and order reporting restrictions. Further, such orders can be made applying common law principles or pursuant to Art 6 of the European Convention on Human Rights (ECHR), where:

- it is necessary in the interests of justice, for example, to prevent frustration of the proceedings or to ensure a fair trial; or
- it is necessary to protect other legitimate interests, such as a party's right to respect for private and family life under Art 8 of the ECHR, or to safeguard the welfare of a child.

8.64

As observed by Lord Donaldson MR in *H v Ministry of Defence*[29]:

> 'In order that the citizens be not deterred from seeking access to justice through courts it is occasionally necessary to protect them from the consequences of public scrutiny of evidence, and in particular medical evidence, of a nature that such scrutiny would prove not only embarrassing but positively damaging to them.'

8.65

The fact that a hearing is held in private, or that an order or decision is issued only to the parties and not published online, does not in itself prevent the hearing, order, or decision from being reported publicly. Section 12 of the Administration of Justice Act 1960 provides that, except in cases concerning the maintenance or upbringing of children, the publication of reports of private proceedings is not, in itself, a contempt of court.

8.66

If it is considered necessary in a particular case to prohibit reporting of a private hearing, decision, or order, a specific order to that effect must be sought and made.

29 [1991] 2 All ER 834.

Litigation capacity and the role of litigation friends

8.67

Capacity issues may arise across all tribunal jurisdictions.

8.68

As the Court of Appeal in Northern Ireland[30] observed, the affordability of justice, access to legal representation, and the availability of support measures, such as the appointment of a litigation friend, are closely interconnected. Each is fundamentally linked to a litigant's right of access to a court and to a fair hearing. The determination that a litigant is entitled to the support of a litigation friend is of profound significance and must not be underestimated. There is an incontestable need for a framework that is simple, accessible, expeditious, and affordable to give effect to such determinations. Without this, and the necessary public funding, our legal system risks paying mere lip service to the long-established common law right to a fair hearing.

8.69

It is now settled law that any party lacking capacity must have a litigation friend in tribunal proceedings, mirroring the requirement found in the civil courts under Part 21 of the Civil Procedure Rules (CPR). As confirmed by the Court of Appeal in *AM (Afghanistan)*, tribunals have the authority to appoint a litigation friend for an appellant who lacks capacity to bring or conduct proceedings, even in the absence of an express provision within the relevant procedural rules.

8.70

A person who has been trafficked or subjected to slavery or related exploitation may lack capacity for a range of reasons, including disability, intellectual impairment, temporary or permanent neurological injury, or mental health difficulties (see Chapter 3). However, the presence of any such factor does not automatically mean that the individual lacks capacity to conduct the proceedings. Each case must be assessed on its own facts.

Understanding capacity: the legal framework

8.71

Litigation capacity refers specifically to a litigant's ability to conduct the specific legal proceedings in which they are involved. This includes the ability to understand, participate in, and follow the process of those proceedings. Any

30 *Galo v Bombardier Aerospace UK* [2023] NICA 50 at [59].

assessment of capacity must be both decision-specific and proceedings-specific, recognising that a litigant may regain capacity or that their capacity may be transient.

8.72

Lady Hale explained in *Dunhill v Burgin*[31]:

> 'The general approach of the common law, now confirmed in the Mental Capacity Act 2005, is that capacity is to be judged in relation to the decision or activity in question and not globally. Hence it was concluded in *Masterman-Lister (see below)*, that capacity for this purpose meant capacity to conduct the proceedings (which might be different from capacity to administer a large award resulting from the proceedings)'.

8.73

Sections 2 and 3 of the Mental Capacity Act 2005 (MCA 2005) set out the legal framework for determining whether an adult lacks capacity. Although statutory powers under the MCA 2005 may only be exercised by the Court of Protection and, in some cases, the High Court under its inherent jurisdiction, the Act provides a useful framework for assessing capacity in tribunal proceedings.

8.74

Section 1(2) of the MCA 2005 establishes a presumption of capacity in adults, which applies unless there is evidence to the contrary. However, where there is legitimate doubt or concern about a person's capacity to litigate, this presumption cannot be relied upon to avoid a proper assessment. The responsibility remains to assess and determine capacity where appropriate[32].

8.75

Useful guidance for tribunals can be found in the Joint Presidential Guidance No.1 of 2024: Appointment of litigation friends in the Upper Tribunal (Immigration and Asylum Chamber) and First-tier Tribunal (Immigration and Asylum Chamber)[33].

8.76

Importantly, the availability of legal advice or representation should not influence the assessment of capacity. The correct approach is to determine

31 *Dunhill v Burgin (Nos 1 & 2)* [2014] UKSC 18.

32 *Royal Bank of Scotland PLC v ABI* UKEAT/0266/18; Equal Treatment Bench Book, Chapter 5 para 43.

33 Joint Presidential Guidance No.1 of 2024: Appointment of litigation friends in the Upper Tribunal (Immigration and Asylum Chamber) and First-tier Tribunal (Immigration and Asylum Chamber): Courts and Tribunals Judiciary (2024).

whether the individual, adult or child, can understand, make, and communicate decisions about the proceedings. This assessment must be independent of the resources available to them.

8.77

Under the Civil Procedure Rules, a person who lacks capacity within the meaning of the MCA 2005 is defined as a 'protected party'. This designation ensures that appropriate safeguards, such as the appointment of a litigation friend, are in place to support their effective participation in legal proceedings.

Determining capacity: judicial role and expert evidence

8.78

The question of who determines whether a person lacks capacity to litigate in the specific proceedings they are involved in is a crucial one. While expert input can be invaluable, the ultimate responsibility lies with the judge in determining capacity as an issue of fact, bearing in mind that the Procedure Rules for the civil and family courts as well as the court of protection rules do not require medical evidence. Recognising that capacity can fluctuate, judges should, wherever possible, take steps to obtain the best available evidence to assist in assessing capacity, particularly where the individual is unrepresented, this is not confined to medical evidence but can be evidence from those who know the individual (ie friends, family, those supporting the individual).

8.79

Unless the issue of capacity is beyond doubt, the person alleged to lack capacity should be given an opportunity to make representations on the issue. The consequences of a finding that a person lacks capacity are of such significance (see below) that the judge should be cautious to reach this finding without the benefit of external expertise[34].

8.80

To determine whether a party lacks litigation capacity, the judge must consider two key questions:

1. Does the individual have difficulty understanding, retaining, using or weighing relevant information, or communicating decisions?
2. If such difficulties exist, are they caused by an impairment of, or disturbance in, the functioning of the person's mind or brain?

34 *Baker Tilly v Makar* [2013] EWHC 759 (QB).

8.81

The Supreme Court's decision in *A Local Authority v JB*[35] offers detailed guidance on the assessment of legal capacity under ss 2 and 3 of the Mental Capacity Act 2005 (MCA 2005), and serves as a valuable reference for judges and practitioners.

8.82

In tribunals although medical or expert evidence is not always required, a judge may find it necessary to seek such evidence to assist in determining capacity. The Tribunal Procedure Rules for both the First-tier Tribunal and the Upper Tribunal contain provisions enabling the tribunal to summon witnesses and/or order individuals to answer questions or produce documents relevant to any issue in the proceedings. This power may, for example, be used to direct a treating clinician to provide evidence regarding the individual's capacity to litigate. However, any professional or ethical considerations arising from such requests must be carefully weighed.

8.83

In summary, the assessment of litigation capacity is a judicial function, informed where appropriate by expert or medical evidence.

Children and capacity

8.84

The approach to capacity for children differs. In *JS v Secretary of State for the Home Department*[36], the Upper Tribunal provided guidance on when a litigation friend should be appointed for a child. There is no automatic requirement for a litigation friend for litigants under the age of 18. Generally:

- Children aged 16 or 17 are presumed to have capacity unless there are specific needs or vulnerabilities.
- Children under 12 will usually require a litigation friend.
- Children aged 12 to 15 should be assessed on a case-by-case basis.

8.85

For children, the common law *Gillick*[37] test applies. This test asks whether the child has 'sufficient understanding and intelligence to enable him or her to understand fully what is proposed.' It is a question of fact in each case whether

35 [2021] UKSC 52.
36 [2019] UKUT 00064 (IAC) at [79]–[83].
37 *Gillick v West Norfolk and Wisbech AHA* [1986] AC 112.

the child has the requisite understanding. The Gillick test is less structured than the MCA 2005 framework for adults, which may result in inconsistency and uncertainty in its application.

Consequences of a finding of lack of capacity

8.86

A determination that a person lacks capacity to litigate in the proceedings they are involved in carries significant and far-reaching consequences for both the individual and the conduct of the case. As has been observed[38], the defining feature of capacity cases is that, by definition, a person who lacks capacity is not validly participating in the proceedings. Without a properly appointed litigation friend acting in their best interests, the individual's fair trial rights, both under the common law and the European Convention on Human Rights (ECHR), are compromised.

8.87

Under Civil Procedure Rules (CPR) Part 21.3(4), any step taken in civil proceedings while a party lacked capacity and did not have a litigation friend is automatically invalid, unless the court orders otherwise. This strict rule is designed to protect vulnerable parties and uphold the integrity of the legal process. However, this principle of automatic invalidity does not apply in the same way in tribunal proceedings, as noted in cases such as *AB v RBS*[39] and *JS v Secretary of State for the Home Department.*

8.88

For legal representatives, the loss of capacity by a client has immediate practical implications. A solicitor cannot continue to act for a client who lacks capacity to litigate unless instructions are received from a litigation friend, attorney, or court-appointed deputy. In effect, the retainer between solicitor and client is terminated upon the client's loss of capacity, unless and until a litigation friend is appointed to provide instructions on the client's behalf[40].

8.89

The appointment of a litigation friend is therefore not a mere procedural formality; it is fundamental to safeguarding the individual's right of access to justice.

38 'Capacity for capacity': A review of the current position and considerations for the future, Part one of two), Upper Tribunal Judge Stout, Tribunals Journal – 3rd Edition (2023), Judicial College (accessed 14 July 2025).

39 (UKEAT/0187 and 0266/18/DA)).

40 *Blankley v Central Manchester and Manchester Children's University Hospital NHS Trust* [2015] 1 WLR 4307.

Appointment of a litigation friend

8.90

Where a person lacks capacity to conduct litigation in the proceedings they are involved in, the tribunal may appoint a litigation friend under its general case management powers[41]. A litigation friend is appointed to assist the individual in conducting the proceedings and to act in their best interests. This role may be fulfilled by a friend, relative, or where no suitable person is available, the Official Solicitor. However, a legal representative of the protected party cannot act as their litigation friend.

8.91

The Upper Tribunal (Immigration and Asylum Chamber) and the First-tier Tribunal (Immigration and Asylum Chamber) have issued Joint Presidential Guidance[42] specifically addressing the appointment of litigation friends. In proceedings before the Special Educational Needs and Disability (SEND) Tribunal, there are distinct legislative provisions governing the appointment of a representative.

8.92

The role of a litigation friend is not to act as a legal representative or to present the litigant's case in a professional capacity. Rather, the litigation friend acts in the individual's best interests and may give instructions and make decisions on their behalf, either with or without the involvement of a solicitor.

8.93

Before appointing a litigation friend, the tribunal must be satisfied that the proposed individual:

- is over 18 years of age;
- can act fairly and competently on behalf of the protected party; and
- does not have any interests in the proceedings that conflict with those of the protected party.

8.94

As Underhill LJ observed in *AM (Afghanistan)*, the appointment of a litigation friend involves granting 'wide authority to dispose of a party's legal rights,

41 See *AM(Afghanistan) v Secretary of State for the Home Department (Lord Chancellor intervening)* [2017] EWCA Civ 1123 at para. 44.

42 Joint Presidential Guidance No. 1 of 2024: Appointment of litigation friends in the Upper Tribunal (Immigration and Asylum Chamber) and First-tier Tribunal (Immigration and Asylum Chamber), in force from 2 December 2024.

either directly by bringing and/or compromising proceedings, or indirectly by the way in which he or she conducts those proceedings.'

When no-one suitable is available

8.95

The Official Solicitor, an officer of the Supreme Court appointed by the Lord Chancellor, may act as litigation friend as a measure of last resort. The Official Solicitor will only consent to act where:

- the party (or intended party) is a protected party;
- satisfactory arrangements have been made to secure the costs of legal representation; and
- no other person is able or willing to act.

Intermediaries and communication support

8.96

An intermediary is distinct from a litigation friend and serves a different function in legal proceedings. An intermediary is a communication specialist, often a speech and language therapist, whose role is to facilitate effective communication between the individual and public authorities (such as the police, local authorities, or the Home Office), legal representatives, and the court or tribunal.

8.97

Intermediaries are impartial and neutral, and their duty is to the tribunal or court, not to any party. They are not expert witnesses, nor do they give evidence in proceedings.

8.98

Tribunals' flexible case management powers and overriding objective enables the appointment of an intermediary to be made. In *Re M (A Child: Intermediaries*[43]*)*, the Court of Appeal (in the context of family proceedings) confirmed that the sole test for appointing an intermediary is whether it is necessary to achieve a fair hearing. This is a fact-specific assessment.

43 [2025] EWCA Civ 440.

8.99

Intermediaries can assist throughout legal proceedings, including when an individual is giving evidence. Their purpose is to ensure that communication is as complete, coherent, and accurate as possible. The President of the Family Division has issued helpful Practice Guidance on the use of intermediaries.

8.100

His Majesty's Courts and Tribunals Service (HMCTS) operates an intermediary service, and applications can be made online for an individual, whether a party or a witness, to be assessed for intermediary support at case conferences or hearings. Following assessment, the intermediary will make specific recommendations regarding the person's communication needs and outline steps to ensure those needs are met.

8.101

If the individual is not legally represented, the tribunal or court will determine whether intermediary support is necessary and, if so, arrange an assessment. Where the individual is legally represented, it is the legal representative who must make the application through the HMCTS service.

Adapting questioning, including cross-examination for vulnerable witnesses or parties in tribunals

8.102

Tribunals, like courts, have a duty to ensure that vulnerable witnesses and parties are questioned in a manner that enables them to participate effectively and give their best evidence. This duty, grounded in the overriding objective and supported by case law and procedural rules, requires judicial decision-makers to actively control the nature, tone, and duration of questioning.

8.103

Traditional cross-examination techniques may need to be modified or abandoned altogether. The Court of Appeal has emphasised that justice for both the vulnerable witness and the accused may require a 'radical departure' from conventional advocacy styles, with advocates adapting to the needs of the witness rather than expecting the witness to conform to standard legal practice[44].

44 *R v Wills* [2011] EWCA Crim 1938; *R v YGM* [2018] EWCA Crim 2458.

8.104

Key principles include:

- **Clarity and Simplicity**: Questions should be short, simple, and address only one issue at a time. Compound questions and complex syntax should be avoided[45].
- **Avoiding Pronouns**: Names should be used consistently to avoid confusion, particularly for witnesses with cognitive or developmental challenges.
- **Chronological or Thematic Structure**: Questions should follow a logical order, either chronologically or by topic, as advised by any intermediary.
- **Avoiding Directive and Tag Questions**: Coercive formats such as 'You're lying, aren't you?' should be replaced with open-ended alternatives like 'Did Jim touch you?' followed by 'How did Jim touch you?'. Tag questions are particularly problematic for children and adults with communication needs and should be avoided[46].
- **Avoiding Figurative Language and Present Tense**: Questions should be literal and clear, avoiding idioms or ambiguous phrasing.
- **Managing Challenges to Credibility**: Challenges to the witness's truthfulness should be developmentally appropriate and, where necessary, addressed simply and respectfully at the end of cross-examination. Repeated assertions that a vulnerable witness is lying are likely to cause distress and serve no proper evidential purpose[47].
- **Avoiding Forced Choice and Repetition**: Forced-choice questions may omit the correct answer, and repeated questioning can lead witnesses to change correct answers under pressure.
- **Avoiding Series of Leading Questions**: Repetitive 'yes' or 'no' formats can cue acquiescent responses and undermine the reliability of evidence.

8.105

Judges and tribunal members may impose time limits on cross-examination to protect the witness's wellbeing, with two hours generally considered the upper limit, subject to the witness's capacity[48]. In multi-party cases, cross-examination should be led by one advocate, with others contributing only supplementary points.

45 Louise Ellison and Rebecca Wheatcroft, 'Exploring the influence of courtroom questioning and pre-trial preparation on adult witness accuracy' (2010).
46 Lord Judge, 'Half a Century of Change: The Evidence of Child Victims', Toulmin Lecture, King's College London (2013).
47 Equal Treatment Bench Book (Judicial College, July 2024, updated February 2026) 56–57.
48 Ibid 57.

8.106

Where limitations are imposed, they must be clearly defined and explained to the parties. Judges must ensure compliance and intervene where necessary. The use of a ground rules hearing practice note, as recommended by the Inns of Court College of Advocacy, can help formalise these boundaries and ensure consistency throughout the proceedings[49]. These principles are supported by training materials such as the Inns of Court College of Advocacy's *20 Principles of Questioning* (2022)[50], and research demonstrating the risks of traditional questioning techniques for vulnerable witnesses[51].

Special measures in criminal proceedings

8.107

Special Measures are available equally to both prosecution and defence witnesses (s 19(1) Youth Justice Criminal Evidence Act 1999). The definition of a witness for the purposes of s 16 and s 17 YJCEA 1999 does not include an accused/defendant however. Groups eligible for special measures include:

i. Complainant/s who are witnesses in proceedings relating to the offences under s 1 or s 2 of the Modern Slavery Act 2015 (see s 17 (4A) YJCEA 1999). This is unless the witness informs the court of their wish not to be so eligible.

ii. Child witnesses – those under 18 at the time of hearing or the special measures order (s 16(1)a YJCEA 1999).

iii. For complainants of 'relevant' offences (which includes s.1 or s.2 of the Modern Slavery Act 2015, sexual offences, offences under s.1 Protection of Children Act 1978 and s.160 Criminal Justice Act 1988) – if the age of the complainant is uncertain and there are reasons to believe that the witness is under the age of 18, that witness is presumed to be under the age of 18 (see s 33(5) YJCEA 1999).

iv. Complainants in respect of sexual offences (s 17(4A) YJCEA 1999).

v. Complainants in respect of an offence where the behaviour of the accused amounted to domestic abuse, as per the meaning of the Domestic Abuse Act 2021 (s 17(4A) YJCEA 1999). Under s 1 Domestic Abuse Act 2021, behaviour includes physical or sexual abuse; violent

49 Inns of Court College of Advocacy, *Advocacy for Vulnerable People and Children (Criminal Course): National Training Programme* (2022).

50 Inns of Court College of Advocacy, *20 Principles of Questioning Vulnerable Witnesses* (March 2023) https://www.icca.ac.uk/wp-content/uploads/2023/03/20-Principles-of-Questioning.pdf accessed 21 August 2025.

51 Wheatcroft et al, 'Rethinking leading: the directive/non-directive divide' (University of Gloucestershire, 2015).

or threatening behaviour; controlling or coercive behaviour; economic abuse; psychological, emotional or other abuse.

vi. A witness to a relevant offence – relating to offences involving knives or guns under s 99 CAJA 2009.

vii. If the court considers the quality of evidence given by the witness is likely to be diminished by reason (s 16(2) YJCEA 1999) that the witness (a) suffers from mental disorder within the meaning of the Mental Health Act 1983; or (b) otherwise has a significant impairment of intelligence and social functioning; (c) that the witness has a physical disability or is suffering from a physical disorder. Quality of evidence relates to the completeness, coherence and accuracy of a witness's evidence (see s 16(5) YJCEA 1999).

viii. If the court is satisfied that the quality of evidence given by the witness is likely to be diminished by reason of fear or distress on the part of the witness in connection with testifying in proceedings (s 17(1) YJCEA 1999). In determining if a witness falls into s 17(1), a court *must* take into account in particular the nature and alleged circumstances of the offence to which the circumstances relate; the age of the witness; the social and cultural background and ethnic origins of the witness; the domestic and employment circumstances of the witness; any religious beliefs or political opinions of the witness. The court must also take into account any behaviour towards the witness by the accused; members of the family or associates of the accused; or any other person who is likely to be an accused or witness in the proceedings. In determining that question the court must in addition consider any views expressed by the witness.

8.108

In relation to witnesses found to be in fear or distress about giving evidence and those giving evidence in relation to offences under the MSA 2015, ss 1 and 2, orders can be made for them to give evidence in private[52] with associated restrictions on reporting[53]. Other statutory special measures available under the YJCEA 1999 for eligible witnesses are pre-recorded video evidence in chief[54], pre-recorded cross examination[55], restrictions on cross examination by the accused appearing in person[56], screens[57], live link[58], removal of wigs and gowns[59],

52 YJCEA 1999, s 25 as amended by the MSA 2015, s 46.
53 YJCEA 1999, s 46.
54 YJCEA 1999, s 27.
55 YJCEA 1999, s 28.
56 YJCEA 1999, ss 34–38.
57 YJCEA 1999, s 23.
58 YJCEA 1999, s 24.
59 YJCEA 1999, s 26.

assistance of an intermediary[60] and the use of aids to communication for young or incapacitated witnesses[61].

Applications for special measures for witnesses

8.109

Applications for any special measures, direction or order must be made (under the Criminal Procedure Rules 2025[62] (Crim PR), r 18.4) in writing as soon as reasonably practicable, and in any event not more than: (i) 20 business days after the defendant pleads not guilty, in a magistrates' court, or (ii) 10 business days after the defendant pleads not guilty, in the Crown Court. The relevant party must explain how the witness is eligible for assistance; explain why special measures would be likely to improve the quality of the witness's evidence; propose the measures that in the applicant's opinion would be likely to maximise the quality of evidence and detail views the witness has expressed. Further, if the applicant seeks a hearing, explain why this is needed (Crim PR, r 18.10). See Crim PR, r 18.9 for special measures directions where no application is required – this includes where a witness is eligible under s 16 or s 17 YJCEA 1999; notice is given at a preparation for trial hearing at the magistrates' court or PTPH at the Crown Court; and no other party opposes the giving of a direction for the benefit of that witness.

8.110

In a summary or youth court trial, judges who have ruled on a special measures application do not need to recuse themselves from hearing the substantive matter[63].

Child witnesses (other than accused)

8.111

Child witnesses are deemed eligible for numerous types of special measures as set out in the Youth Justice and Criminal Evidence Act 1999, ss 23–28, including pre-recorded evidence, an intermediary to assist with communication and/or aids to communication[64]. Legal Guidance has been issued by the CPS on 'Safeguarding Children as Victims and Witnesses' (updated at 24 May 2024). Of

60 YJCEA 1999, s 29.
61 YJCEA 1999, s 30.
62 SI 2025/909.
63 KL and *LK v DPP* (2002) 166 JP 369.
64 YJCEA 1999, s 19(1).

paramount importance are the principles of expedition, sensitivity and fairness and examples within the guidance include:

- expediting cases and dealing with them with fairness and sensitivity;
- where children have been sexually exploited, treating them as victims of abuse;
- consideration of the use of children as witnesses, witness care and of special measures to enable them to give evidence in the best way possible in terms of quality of their evidence and reducing trauma to them;
- engaging with other authorities and agencies to safeguard children.

8.112

In relation to child witnesses attending court, the courts in England and Wales have a much greater understanding than previously of vulnerability. Careful consideration should be given to the Criminal Procedure Rules. In addition, case-law and guidance in this area is regularly updated within the Crown Court Compendium and by The Advocate's Gateway[65].

8.113

The YJCEA 1999 introduced a number of 'special measures' which can be used to facilitate the giving of evidence by child witnesses. For child witnesses, special measures include the removal of wigs and gowns; live or remote link; use of a registered intermediary and s.28 visually recorded cross-examination.

8.114

Where s 28 YJCEA 1999 is applicable, a prosecutor must notify the court and defence at the first hearing and in addition:

i. Child witnesses under 18 are automatically eligible for special measures under s 16 of the Youth Justice and Criminal Evidence Act 1999.

ii. The primary rule in the case of a child witness (s 21 YJCEA 1999) is that the court must give a special measures direction which provides for any relevant recording to be admitted under s 27 (video recorded evidence-in-chief) and must provide for any evidence given by the witness in the proceedings (if not given by video recording) to be given by means of a live link in accordance with s 24.

iii. This primary rule has now been modified through s 100 of CAJA 2009 and the court can disapply the above, in circumstances where the child witness informs them if their wish is for the rules not to apply/should apply only in part and if the court is satisfied that not complying with the

65 Available at: https://www.theadvocatesgateway.org/toolkits, last accessed 25 September 2025.

rule would not diminish the quality of the witness's evidence. In making such a decision, the court will take into account the age and maturity of the witness; the ability of the witness to understand the consequences of giving evidence other than in accordance with the requirements under s 21(3) YJCEA 1999; the relationship between the witness and the accused; the witness's social and cultural background and ethnic origin and the nature and alleged circumstances of the offence to which the proceedings relate.

iv. Section 28 YJCEA 1999 allows for the cross-examination and re-examination of a child witness to be by video recording and for this to be admitted as evidence of the witness.

8.115

Under s 53(1) YJCEA 1999, all persons (whatever their age) at every stage in criminal proceedings are competent to give evidence. However, if it appears to the court that an individual is unable to understand questions put to them as a witness and unable to give answers which can be understood, then a person can be deemed as not competent by the court (see s 53(3) YJCEA 1999). The question of competence of a witness can be raised by a party to the proceedings, or by the court itself. If it is raised, then the party seeking to call the witness will need to satisfy the court on the balance of probabilities that the witness is competent.

8.116

Guidance has been provided on the appropriate style of cross examination of vulnerable witnesses in Wills (Practice Note)[66].In *R v YGM*[67] at [21] the court highlighted the following as best practice in a case involving cross-examination of a vulnerable witness:

i. The identification of any limitations on cross examination should take place at an early stage. This would normally occur at the ground rules hearing where the judge will discuss with the advocates the nature and extent of the limitations imposed and whether they are simply as to style or also relate to content.

ii. Before the witness is cross examined, it is best practice, that as well as giving the standard special measures direction, the trial judge also directs the jury in general terms that limitations have been placed on the defence advocate.

iii. If any specific issues of content have been identified that the cross examiner cannot explore, the judge may wish to direct the jury about them after the

66 Wills (Practice Note) [2011] EWCA Crim 1938.
67 *R v YGM* [2018] EWCA Crim 2458.

cross examination is completed. The judge should certainly direct the jury about them in the summing-up.

iv. Every advocate (and trial judge) is expected to ensure that they are up to date with current best practice in the treatment of vulnerable witnesses.

8.117

Trial process must cater for the needs of child witnesses and forensic techniques and cross-examination has to be adapted, to ensure a child witness can give the best evidence they are capable of (see *R v Barker*[68] and Crown Court Compendium at 10-5).

8.118

It is permissible in multi-handed trials to divide up topics between counsel so that a witness is not asked repeated questions on the same topics (see Crim PR 2025, r 3.13 (d) in relation to the courts being entitled to limit the examination, cross-examination or re-examination of a witness). Advocates will find the Advocates Gateway Toolkits of great assistance in this area.

Ground rules hearings

8.119

A Ground Rules hearing should be held in every case where there is a young or vulnerable witness. The Crown Court Compendium at 10-5 indicates that before the Ground Rules hearing, a defence advocate must serve on the court and on the prosecution a copy of the list of proposed questions to be put to the young or vulnerable witness, together with a copy of the defence statement. Further the Ground Rules hearing must, save in exceptional circumstances, take place before the day of trial. Trial advocates and any intermediary should be present. Issues to be addressed at a Ground Rules hearing include:

i. How the witness/defendant is to be addressed

ii. Whether a witness will have a 'witness companion' (see Crim PR, r 3.8(6))

iii. Breaks

iv. Ground Rules for the questioning of witness/defendants

v. Any additional questions to be asked by the prosecution in examination-in-chief

vi. Length of cross-examination

68 *R v Barker* [2010] EWCA Crim 4.

vii. Consideration in multi-handed cases, of who will conduct the cross-examination

viii. Aids to communication, if any

ix. Questions or topics submitted by advocates that can be put to the witness/defendant

x. What the jury are to be told about the limitations.

8.120

Ground Rules hearings are now used by judges to make directions for the fair treatment and effective participation of vulnerable defendants and vulnerable witnesses. Courts must take reasonable steps to ensure the effective participation of vulnerable defendants and witnesses[69]. This might include removing wigs and gowns, screening, and advance notice of questions the advocates plan to ask. The requirements for a Ground Rules hearing apply to vulnerable defendants in the same way that they do to vulnerable witnesses.

8.121

Where the defendant is a victim of trafficking, there are likely to be vulnerabilities which ought to be brought to the attention of the court at a Ground Rules hearing so that any necessary trial adaptations can be considered (see the discussion of the psychological impact of human trafficking at paras **8.2–8.7** above). Where practitioners obtain Psychiatric or Psychological evidence in relation to a defendant, the independent expert should be asked to advise upon trial adaptations (eg breaks, language usage with the accused) so that the court can take that into account at a Ground Rules hearing. In addition, measures can be adopted when evidence is given by witnesses so that a vulnerable defendant can follow the proceedings[70].

8.122

CPS Guidance now sets out specific criteria in relation to pre-trial visually recorded cross-examination (YJCEA 1999, s 28).

8.123

In the course of trial, the court would normally consider the following:

i. If for any reason, a Ground Rules hearing has not yet taken place before trial, or if there were changes/developments since then, the judge should discuss with advocates how any limitations on questioning will

---

69 See The Advocates Gateway Toolkits 1 and 1a, available at: https://www.theadvocatesgateway.org/toolkits, last accessed 25 September 2025.

70 *R v Cox* [2012] EWCA Crim 549, [2012] 2 Cr App Rep 63.

be explained to the jury before any recording of cross examination of a witness is played.

ii. The judge can give the jury the standard direction on special measures with a direction on the limitations that the judge has imposed on cross-examination and the reasons for them before the cross examination is played.

iii. The judge should consider if it is necessary to have a further discussion with the advocates before their closing submissions and the summing-up, on the limitations imposed and any areas where those limitations have had a material effect. In this way the advocates will know the areas upon which they can address the jury.

iv. In the summing-up, the judge should remind the jury of the limitations imposed and any areas identified where they have had a material effect upon the questions asked.

v. If any written directions are provided to the jury the judge should include with the standard special measures direction a direction in relation to limitations that have been imposed on the cross-examination.

8.124

Best practice was further clarified in the case of *R v YGM*[71], where the judge agreed to give a direction pointing out to the jury that counsel was not allowed to cross-examine the witness in the same way as he would cross examine another witness, but counsel was not allowed to make further comment in his closing speech:

> 'We believe that the following is best practice in a case involving cross examination of a vulnerable witness. First, the identification of any limitations on cross-examination should take place at an early stage. We assume that this will occur at the ground rules hearing where the judge will discuss with the advocates the nature and extent of the limitations imposed and whether they are simply as to style or also relate to content. Before the witness is cross examined, it is best practice, (as recommended by the Judicial College) that as well as giving the standard special measures direction, the trial judge also directs the jury in general terms that limitations have been placed on the defence advocate. If any specific issues of content have been identified that the cross examiner cannot explore, the judge may wish to direct the jury about them after the cross examination is completed. On any view, the judge should direct the jury about them in the summing-up. Finally, we should add that every advocate (and trial judge) is expected to ensure

71 *R v YGM* [2018] EWCA Crim 2458.

that they are up to date with current best practice in the treatment of vulnerable witnesses.'

Trial adaptations for accused persons/defendants who are trafficked persons

8.125

In cases involving accused persons who are also victims of trafficking, case preparation requires attention to how the accused person's vulnerability is relevant. This raises issues in relation to the prosecution allegation, any defence raised and the procedure to deal with the accused's presentation in court[72]. The statutory framework for witnesses expressly excludes defendants from the assistance of special measures, save for that of live link directions under s 33A YJCEA 1999. A live link direction allows for any oral evidence by an accused to be given through a live link. If an accused is under 18 at the time of any application, it would require their ability to participate effectively as a witness giving evidence orally to be compromised by their level of intellectual ability or social functioning and the use of a live link would enable them to participate more effectively in proceedings eg through improving the quality of their evidence. If an accused is over 18 at the time, then the requirements include that they suffer from a mental disorder under Mental Health Act 1983, or otherwise has a significant impairment of intelligence and social function; and for that reason is unable to participate effectively in the proceedings as a witness giving oral evidence and the use of a live link would enable them to participate more effectively in proceedings as a witness, by improving the quality of their evidence or otherwise.

8.126

Over the last two decades there has been a growing recognition that young defendants should have access to effective communication arrangements to enable them to fully participate in order to receive a fair trial[73]. The Criminal Procedure Rules 2023 (amended November 2025), PD 6 identifies the correct approach to children and vulnerable adult defendants appearing in the Crown Court. This requires the particular vulnerability to be recognised and is intended to enable the accused person effectively to participate in the proceedings. This exercise ought to consider the age, maturity, identified conditions and development of the accused person concerned and all other circumstances of the case[74].

72 *R v S* [2008] EWCA Crim 6; *R v Braham* [2013] EWCA Crim 3, [2013] 1 Cr App Rep 481; *R v Thompson* [2014] EWCA Crim 836.
73 *R (on the application of D) v Camberwell Youth Court* [2005] UKHL 4, [2005] 1 All ER 999.
74 *R v H* [2006] EWCA Crim 853.

8.127

The approach to be taken by criminal courts and the advocates is to ensure that the welfare of the child or otherwise vulnerable defendant is considered[75]. The process should be adapted to ensure the defendant can comprehend the proceedings and engage fully in his defence[76].

8.128

In relation to suspects and defendants, case law has developed in England and Wales as follows[77]:

1. In rare circumstances, an intermediary may be used for a vulnerable defendant to assist with effective participation, but it would be 'very rare' for an intermediary to be present for the whole trial[78].
2. The judge must make an assessment on the basis that the advocate will have undergone specific training and can conduct the case competently.
3. Where an intermediary is not available, special arrangements should be adopted and the judge is entitled to be more interventionist than usual.
4. It is the advocate's duty to do what is needed for the defendant to be able fully to participate in the trial.
5. Vulnerable defendants need not be asked questions about complex expert evidence.

8.129

It should be noted that a post-conviction diagnosis of autism may not give grounds to appeal so advocates should ensure they understand how to identify potential vulnerabilities[79].

8.130

In relation to a defendant's evidence, the procedural expectation is that an application should be made pursuant to the Crim PR, r 18 for a 'defendant's evidence direction'. Directions will be given to ensure the appropriate court adaptations are made and that the treatment and questioning of the defendant is approached in a suitable way to facilitate effective participation.The presumption

75 Children and Young Persons Act 1933, s 44.

76 *R (on the application of P) v West London Youth Court* [2005] EWHC 2583 (Admin), [2006] 1 All ER 477; *SC v UK* (2005) 40 EHRR 10.

77 *R v Anthony Cox* [2012] EWCA Crim 549; *R v Rashid* [2017] EWCA Crim 2; *R v Friend* [2004] EWCA Crim 2661; *R v Gareth Jones* [2018] EWCA Crim 2816.

78 See Chapter 20 on funding for defence intermediaries. See *TI v Bromley Youth Court* [2020] EWHC 1204 at para 39. Albeit the appointment of an intermediary is rare, it does not follow there is a 'high hurdle' to overcome if an intermediary is necessary for effective participation of defendant in trial process.

79 *R v Roddis* [2020] EWCA Crim 396.

is that adult defendants will be in court and, if they choose to give evidence, will do so in person but measures such as clearing the public gallery or regular breaks, the presence of a supporting person or the use of communication aids can be considered. Courts have inherent powers to ensure that a defendant receives a fair trial. These have been successfully deployed in the context of facilitating the participation of a vulnerable defendant by measures including directing that defendants have the assistance of an intermediary (see Crim PR, r.18.19)[80].

8.131

If a defendant is a victim of trafficking and has other vulnerabilities, the work of an intermediary can be invaluable in case preparation (see below). A Ground Rules hearing will be an opportunity to apply for the directions to include the use of an intermediary, where the supporting evidence is sufficient to demonstrate the need. The burden falls on the defence team to ensure that the defendant's needs have been properly identified and assessed.

Child defendants

8.132

Specific regard is to be had to the welfare of a young defendant, as required under s 44 of the Children and Young Persons Act 1933, together with Pts 1 and 3 of the Crim PR and Crim PR PD 6.2.8. Part 1 of the Crim PR sets out that part of the overriding objective of the Code is to ensure criminal cases are dealt with justly, and recognising the rights of a defendant in relation to ECHR, Art 6 (as incorporated by the Human Rights Act 1998). Article 6(3) provides that:

> 'Everyone charged with a criminal offence has the following minimum rights –
>
> (a) To be informed promptly, in a language which he understands and in detail, of the nature and cause of the accusation against him.
>
> (b) To have adequate time and facilities for the preparation of his defence.
>
> (c) To defend himself in person or through legal assistance of his own choosing, or if he has not sufficient means to pay for legal assistance to be given it free when the interests of justice so require.'

80 *R (on the application of C) v Sevenoaks Youth Court* [2009] EWHC 3088 (Admin), [2010] 1 All ER 735; *R (on the application of P) v West London Youth Court* [2005] EWHC 2583 (Admin), [2006] 1 All ER 477.

8.133

Article 3 of the United Nations Convention on the Rights of the Child sets out that the best interests of the child must be a top priority in all decisions and actions that affect children.

8.134

Crim PR, PD 6.2.8 highlights that communication needs (such as short attention span, suggestibility and reticence in relation to authority figures) are common to many witnesses and defendants under 18. Consideration must be given to the communication needs of all children and young people and to adapting the trial process to address any such needs. Assessment by an intermediary should be considered for witnesses and defendants under 18 years of age who seem liable to misunderstand questions or to experience difficulty expressing answers, including those who seem unlikely to recognise a problematic question and those who may be reluctant to tell a questioner in a position of authority if they do not understand (see Crim PD 6.2.9).

Attendance with parent/guardian at court

8.135

There is a requirement under s 34A of the Children and Young Persons Act 1933 that a parent or guardian shall be required to attend with a defendant under the age of 16 appearing before a court. Attendance may be required where a child is over the age of 16.

8.136

Where a child or young person is appearing in court it is usually appropriate for them to be produced in person at court. This ensures the court can properly engage with the youth and that the necessary level of engagement can be facilitated with the Youth Offending Team worker, defence representative and/ or appropriate adult.

Other matters to be considered in light of Crim PD

8.137

Consideration should be given as to whether robes and wigs should be worn (CPD 6.4.2.g):

8.138

It is generally desirable for those responsible for security of a vulnerable defendant in custody, especially if he is young, to not wear uniform and for there to be no recognisable police presence in the court room save for good reason (CPD 6.4.2.h).

8.139

Representatives should ensure that a reporting restriction under s 39 of CYPA 1933 is sought.

Vulnerable adult defendants

8.140

Accommodating a vulnerable person's needs is required under the Equality Act 2010, the European Convention on Human Rights, the UN Convention on the Rights of the Child and the UN Convention on the Right of Persons with Disabilities. Consideration should be given to the guidance within chapter 2 and 7 of the Equal Treatment Bench Book ('ETBB') (Judicial College, July 2024, updated February 2026).

8.141

There is no general definition of 'vulnerability' under the law[81].

8.142

Adult defendants who can be considered vulnerable include individuals who have experienced trauma, those with autism spectrum disorder, attention deficit (hyperactivity) disorder, mental health needs or learning disabilities, as well as those who are elderly and those with physical disabilities or health conditions (such as deafness) which may negatively affect their ability to effectively participate in the trial process. Parties should in addition be alert to potential 'hidden' vulnerabilities that may not be immediately apparent (Toolkit 1a Advocates Toolkit).

8.143

The ETBB highlights potential vulnerability and thus adjustments may be needed for individuals who have been subjected to modern slavery, as well as individuals who have been subjected to domestic abuse or sexual abuse.

8.144

Chapter 7 of the ETBB considers the position for victims of modern slavery. This ought to be of application to VOTs who are defendants as well. The ETBB notes that victims of modern slavery are likely to be 'vulnerable witnesses, considerably damaged by their experiences and wary of authority figures.' Further, at p134 that witnesses may be particularly susceptible to overbearing cross-examination, which risks both unnecessary distress and humiliation of

81 Equal Treatment Bench Book, Ch.2 – Judicial College, July 2024, updated February 2026.

the witness and worthless answers or silence. The ETBB notes that protected questioning techniques may be appropriate such as:

i. No repeated questions

ii. Short single-strand questions, ie one matter raised in the question at a time

iii. Giving structure to the questions

iv. Focused questions on the matters in dispute

v. Reduction in the use of leading questions

vi. Reduction in the use of tag questions.

Examples of adjustments and monitoring in trial

8.145

Criminal Practice Direction 6.4 details the case management powers that exist in relation to vulnerable Defendants. Relevant applications by representatives should be sought as early as possible.

i. CPD 6.4.1 – A Ground Rules hearing must always be considered in a case involving a young or otherwise vulnerable defendant.

ii. CPD 6.4.2.b – It may be appropriate to arrange for a vulnerable defendant to visit, during out of court hours and before the hearing so they can familiarise themselves with the courtroom.

iii. CPD 6.4.2.c – If the use of live link is being considered for a defendant, they should have an opportunity for a practice session. Any application for a live link in accordance with s 33A YJCEA 1999 is to be in compliance with Crim PR, r 3.36.

iv. CPD 6.4.2.g – In the Crown Court, the judge should consider whether robes and wigs should be worn and should take account of wishes of the vulnerable defendant.

v. CPD 6.4.5 – Access to the court room can be restricted, for example, limiting members of the public to those with an immediate and direct interest in the outcome.

Intermediaries

8.146

The primary function of an intermediary is to improve the quality of evidence and aid understanding between the court, the advocates and the witnesses or defendant. Intermediaries are independent of parties and owe their duty to the court.

8.147

Crim PR, r 18.3 defines an intermediary as 'a person

(i) Approved by the court for the purposes of s 29 YJCEA 1999

(ii) Asked to assess a defendant's communication needs, or

(iii) Appointed by the court to facilitate a defendant's effective participation in the trial, when the defendant gives evidence or at any other time, where otherwise that defendant's communication needs would impede such participation.'

8.148

In *R (on the application of OP) v The Secretary of State for Justice and Cheltenham Magistrates Court and Crown Prosecution Service. Just for Kids Law as Intervener*[82] it was held that there are two roles in a trial for which an intermediary is fitted:

1. general support, reassurance and calm interpretation of unfolding events;
2. skilled support and interpretation with the potential for intervention and on occasion suggestion to the Bench associated with the giving of evidence.

8.149

Intermediaries for witnesses or defendants have expertise but they are not expert witnesses. Case law has developed in England and Wales as follows[83]:

1. Ground Rules hearings should include the general care of the witness, including the length of questioning and frequency of breaks and the nature of the questions to be asked.
2. A young person in the Crown Court does not necessarily have to sit outside the dock during the trial.
3. It is not necessary to tailor legal directions by a judge because of a defendant's age, maturity, cognitive ability, etc.
4. It is the task of an intermediary to provide a report and to assist as directed by the judge. The judge decides measures necessary for effective

82 *R (on the application of OP) v The Secretary of State for Justice and Cheltenham Magistrates Court and Crown Prosecution Service. Just for Kids Law as Intervener* [2014] EWHC 1944 (Admin).

83 *R v Roddis* [2020] EWCA Crim 396; *R v Grant-Murray and others* [2017] EWCA Crim 1228; *R v Grant-Murray and Henry; R v McGill and Hewitt* [2017] EWCA Crim 1228; *R v Biddle* [2019] EWCA Crim 86; *R v Boxer* [2015] EWCA Crim 1684.

participation of the vulnerable person. At a trial a judge is not bound by rulings on these issues made by a previous judge.

5. The expectation is that advocates will have undertaken specific training.

6. Experts must obtain a full history of the defendant, consider it and analyse it for the benefit of the court.

Appointment of intermediary to facilitate a defendant's participation

8.150

It is for a court to determine whether to direct the appointment of an intermediary to assist a defendant; and if this should be for the whole duration or part of trial.

8.151

Under Crim PR, Part 18.19(1), a Court must exercise its power to appoint an intermediary to facilitate a defendant's effective participation in trial where

(a) The defendant's ability to participate is likely to be diminished by reason of –

  (i) Age, if the defendant is under 18, or;

  (ii) Mental disorder (as defined under s.1(2) of the Mental Health Act 1983), a significant impairment of intelligence and social functioning, or a physical disability or disorder; and

  (iii) The appointment is necessary for that purpose.

8.152

In considering if the appointment of an intermediary is necessary, as well who to appoint and the duration or purpose of appointment, the court must have regard to the following factors under Crim PR, Part 18.19 (2):

- Defendant's communication needs as reported to the court;
- Recommendations in any intermediary's report received by the court;
- Any views the defendant has expressed about receiving assistance of an intermediary or other measures or arrangements to facilitate the defendant's effective participation in trial;
- Likely impact of Defendant's age, if under 18, level of intellectual ability or social functioning on the ability to give evidence and to understand what is said and done by the court and other participants;

- Likely impact on such participation and on such understanding of any mental disorder or other significant impairment of intelligence or social functioning;
- Adequacy of arrangements for questioning defendant in absence of an intermediary;
- Any assistance defendant has received in past whilst giving evidence in legal proceedings, while being questioned during investigation, or as a defendant in a criminal case.
- Any assessment of the defendant's health by a mental health practitioner acting independently of the parties to assist the court;
- Any expert medical opinion that the court may have received; and
- Any other matter the court thinks relevant.

8.153

Unless the court otherwise directs, the appointment of an intermediary extends to facilitate a defendant's communication with that defendant's legal representatives for the duration and purpose of the appointment.

Witness anonymity

Sexual offences

8.154

By the Sexual Offences (Amendment) Act 1992, s 1, orders are automatic to protect the identity of complainants in alleged sexual offences listed in s 2.

8.155

Section 1 provides that:

> '(1) Where an allegation has been made that an offence to which this Act applies has been committed against a person, no matter relating to that person shall during that person's lifetime be included in any publication if it is likely to lead members of the public to identify that person as the person against whom the offence has been committed.
>
> (2) Where a person is accused of an offence to which this Act applies, no matter likely to lead members of the public to identify a person as the person against whom the offence is alleged to have been committed ('the complainant') shall during the complainant's lifetime be included in any publication.'

8.156

Section 2 of the Modern Slavery Act, namely human trafficking is an offence to which the provisions of s 1 Sexual Offences (Amendment) Act 1992 apply.

(Note that the provisions under s 1 Sexual Offences (Amendment) Act 1992 do not automatically apply to a defendant in the course of their trial who alleges that they are the victim of an offence of sexual offences or for example s 2 MSA 2015).

8.157

The prohibition can be lifted in limited circumstances:

- publicity is required by the accused to encourage witnesses to come forward, and the defence case would be seriously prejudiced otherwise; or
- the prohibition imposes a substantial restriction on reporting, and it is in the interests of justice to order otherwise.

8.158

It is worth noting that the common expression used that a witness has 'waived' anonymity is a misnomer. A witness cannot unilaterally waive a court order, although if a complainant does reveal his identity, this would be a powerful factor in lifting any order protecting identification.

Serious gang related crime

8.159

Investigation anonymity orders can be made in relation to specified witnesses pursuant to the Coroners and Justice Act 2009, ss 74–85, where the allegation is murder or manslaughter and the death was caused by shooting with a firearm or use of a knife. The police can apply for such an order to a Justice of the Peace, who must be satisfied that there are reasonable grounds for believing that a qualifying offence has been committed, the relevant person is aged between 11 and 30 and is likely to have been a member of a criminal group who is willing to assist but is fearing intimidation or harm and it is more likely than not that he will provide information that would assist the criminal investigation.

Necessity

8.160

Otherwise, witness anonymity is governed by the Coroners and Justice Act 2009, ss 86–90 and the Criminal Procedure Rules 2025, rr 18.14–18.18. It is a special measure of 'last practicable resort'[84]. The measure must be applied for in writing in advance and must satisfy three conditions:

(i) the anonymity order must be in the interests of justice where the witness would not otherwise give evidence and there would be no real harm to the public interest[85]; and

(ii) it must be necessary to protect the safety of the witness, another person, or to prevent serious damage to property[86]; and

(iii) it must be consistent with receiving a fair trial[87].

8.161

Withholding the name and address of a witness may be accompanied with necessary redacting from documents, use of a pseudonym, screens and voice alteration. Section 89(2) of the Coroners and Justice Act 2009 sets out a non-exhaustive list of factors for the court to consider, which is summarised below[88]. It is up to the court what weight to give to each factor, depending on the case in hand and dependent on what judicial directions are possible to maintain the safety of the trial[89]:

- the defendant's right to know the identity of the witness;
- the extent to which the credit of the witness is subject to challenge;
- any evidence of dishonesty;
- whether the witness's evidence is the sole or decisive evidence in the case[90];
- whether the evidence can be properly challenged without the witness being identified[91];
- other reasonably practicable means to protect the witness.

8.162

If a witness gives evidence anonymously, a judicial direction must be given to ensure there is no prejudice to the accused. This has in some cases gone beyond

84 *R v Donovan* [2012] EWCA Crim 2749.
85 *R v Mayers* [2008] EWCA Crim 2989, [2009] 2 All ER 145.
86 *R v Powar [2009] EWCA Crim 594*, [2009] 2 Cr App Rep 120; *R v Khan* [2010] EWCA Crim 1692.
87 *R v Ford* [2010] EWCA Crim 2250, [2011] Crim LR 475; *R v Fox* [2010] EWCA Crim 1280; *Pesukic v Switzerland* [2012] ECHR 2031; *Horncastle v UK* [2014] ECHR 1394.
88 *R v Taylor* [2010] EWCA Crim 830.
89 *R v Nazir* [2009] EWCA Crim 213; *R v Willett* [2011] EWCA Crim 2710, [2012] 2 Cr App Rep (S) 76; *R v Okuwa* [2010] EWCA Crim 832.
90 *R v Davis* [2008] UKHL 36, [2008] 1 AC 1128; *Al Khawaja v UK* (2012) 54 EHRR 807.
91 *R v Donovan* [2012] EWCA Crim 2749.

warning against speculation, specifically to direct that it has nothing to do with the accused[92].

Reporting identity of child witnesses and child defendants

8.163

For persons under the age of 18, in the youth court, reporting restrictions are automatic[93]. However, in trials on indictment, the power is discretionary. The Crown Court may make an order protecting the identification of children pursuant to the YJCEA 1999, s 45. The onus is on the court, but advocates should ensure an order is sought where the above anonymity restrictions do not apply. A s 45 order can only apply until the child is 18 unless the court makes a lifetime order pursuant to the YJCEA 1999, s 45A. The expectation is that a defendant will be named, but the rights of the child have been said to 'trump' the rights of the public to know[94]. In relation to trafficked children there is a powerful argument against publicity, particularly where that identification could lead to re-trafficking.

Adult defendant / Appellant anonymity

8.164

The general rule is that the name of a defendant will be made public in hearings in open court, both at first instance and appeal; as well as within decisions and orders made by a Court. Any derogation from or restriction upon open justice is exceptional and has to be based on strict necessity.

8.165

Practitioners should consider Crim PR, r 6.4 in relation to reporting restrictions and note that any application for discretionary reporting restriction orders should be notified not merely to other parties, but also to reporters (email distribution lists held by magistrates' and Crown Courts, see Crim PR, r 6.4(b)(ii).

8.166

If a Court is being asked to consider competing rights, such as those under Art 8 and Art 10 of the ECHR, then the Court will need to consider whether there

92 *R v Nazir* [2009] EWCA Crim 213; *R v Willett* [2011] EWCA Crim 2710, [2012] 2 Cr App Rep (S) 76 and see Crown Court Compendium, chs 3–8.

93 CYPA 1933, s 49.

94 *R v Lee* [1993] 2 All ER 170, [1993] 1 WLR 103; *R v Cormick* [2015] EWCA Crim 110, [2015] 1 Cr App Rep (S) 483.

is an interference with a right prescribed by law; secondly, if the interference pursues a legitimate aim; and thirdly whether the interference is necessary in a democratic society (applying decision of Supreme Court in *Abbasi v Newcastle upon Tyne Hospitals NHS Foundation Trust*[95]).

8.167

In terms of anonymity, there is a distinction between a withholding order (which permits or directs the withholding of the name of an accused and replacing it with a cipher) and a reporting restriction order, which prohibits publication of the withheld name or any other information that would be likely to identify the person who the court has directed should be anonymized (see *R v Baniulyte* at [97]).

8.168

A fact specific approach has been taken by the Court of Appeal in determining these cases. For example, where a trafficked person is suffering fear of reprisals from traffickers if identified, in *R v L; R v N*, the Court of Appeal recognised the following[96]:

> 'Article 28 of the CE Convention requires effective and appropriate protection from potential retaliation or intimidation, during and after investigation and prosecution of perpetrators, for victims and others who assist in the investigation and prosecution of crimes committed by traffickers. Disclosing names and details of victims and the accounts of their exploitation, which might involve disclosing the names of their traffickers in criminal or civil proceedings, may well hinder any future investigation of traffickers or a victim's willingness to co-operate with that investigation'.

8.169

The Court of Appeal also observed in *R v L; R v N*[97] that 'the need for consistency and the UK's obligations generally, we accept that it would, in principle, be desirable for the Court of Appeal Criminal Division to follow the practice adopted by the Civil Division and the Tribunals of anonymising the applicant in cases raising asylum and international protection issues.' The Court of Appeal have since summarised in *R v Baniulyte*[98] the approach practitioners should take when an accused person who is or may be a VOT appeals to the Court of Appeal and seeks anonymization.

95 [2025] UKSC 15.
96 [2017] EWCA Crim 2129, at [10].
97 Ibid, at [15].
98 *R v Baniulyte* [2025] EWCA Crim 1205.

'i) Although issues as to anonymity arise more frequently in such cases than in other applications and appeals, a VOT/VMS has no automatic right to anonymity, and no statutory provision imposes automatic reporting restrictions in favour of an adult accused who puts forward a defence under s45 of the MSA 2015. An order derogating from open justice should therefore not be made on a routine basis. As in any other case, a person seeking anonymity bears the burden of demonstrating by cogent evidence why a derogation is strictly necessary.

ii) Any application for anonymity must be made when the application for leave to appeal is lodged. The Criminal Appeal Office can then arrange for the applicant's name to be replaced by a cipher for listing and other purposes: that will be a convenient safeguard, but does not imply that the court will necessarily grant the application.

iii) The application must set out the order that is sought, the jurisdiction under which it can be made, and why it is strictly necessary for the order to be granted. With effect from 6 October 2025, a revised Criminal Procedure Rule 6.4 will apply to applications for reporting restrictions and other applications to derogate from open justice. It sets out what is required of an applicant.

iv) Any application for an anonymity order (and reporting restrictions) must be supported by evidence which establishes convincingly the need for the derogation(s) sought. Where it is contended that, if anonymity is not granted, there is a credible risk of physical harm or death, the nature of the threat and why an order for anonymity would avoid or reduce that risk must be explained.

v) If anonymity is sought on the grounds that the applicant has been anonymised in other proceedings, full details of those proceedings, and a copy of the order granting anonymity, must be provided. If it is contended that there is a risk of 'jigsaw identification' if an anonymity order is not granted, the nature of that risk and how it arises must be explained and demonstrated.

vi) The evidence submitted in support of the application must explain the extent to which there has been reporting of the identity of the person seeking anonymity and reporting restrictions as a result of the proceedings at first instance. Such evidence is necessary to assist this court to decide whether it is too late to impose an anonymity order.

vii) When the case comes before this court for hearing, it will generally be appropriate to address the issue of anonymisation at the outset.

The court may often think it right to make a withholding order and a reporting restriction order on a temporary basis, pending judgment or further order.

viii) The court must make a fact-specific assessment of the competing rights which are in issue, and determine whether the applicant has established that it is strictly necessary to derogate from open justice.

ix) The court should ensure that any withholding order and/or reporting restrictions are clearly stated in the orders made, and explained (at least briefly) in the judgment. When approving its judgment for publication, the court should similarly ensure that the frontispiece is endorsed with a clear warning as to any relevant order which has been made.'

8.170

The qualified right to privacy has some influence on restricting positive publication of ongoing investigations: current police guidance on releasing details and images of suspects requires balancing the risk to the public and the legitimate purpose, necessity and proportionality[99].

8.171

Regulation of publicity to ensure a fair trial is governed by the Contempt of Court Act 1981, which can include postponing reporting of proceedings until the conclusion of the trial or related proceedings and restricting publicity of the defendant's identity where naming would lead to the complainant being identified (note that this is almost invariably achieved by not naming the complainant himself).

8.172

The Judicial College's guide, Reporting Restrictions in the Criminal Courts[100], is aimed at assisting the lower courts in reaching decisions as to whether they can or must depart from the open justice principle and, if so, to what extent. The Guide sets out the statutory exceptions to the open justice principles, both automatic and discretionary. It does not provide any specific guidance for cases in the Court of Appeal Criminal Division[101].

8.173

Post *R v L, R v N* there have been further instances where the name of adult defendants have been anonymised in the Court of Appeal. In *R v O*[102] threats

99 ACPO, *Guidance on releasing images of suspects or defendants*, (available at library.college.police.uk).
100 April 2015 (revised July 2023).
101 See Chapter 13 for anonymity for applicants in the Court of Appeal Criminal Division.
102 *R v O* [2019] EWCA Crim 1389 at [2-3].

to kill had been made against the applicant who had experienced sexual exploitation and the Court was satisfied that her Art 3 rights were engaged. One reason why the name of the Applicant was anonymised in *R v AAC*[103] was due to her having been a victim of forced prostitution and the publication of her name would have been a significant interference with her right to respect for her private and family life.

Applications to move proceedings

8.174

Where an accused person raises human trafficking/modern slavery as a defence, he is required to attend a court local to where he has offended or been apprehended. It should be borne in mind that this may require travel to a 'danger or high-risk area', where his traffickers may still operate. Not only does this raise safeguarding issues, but it also causes additional anxiety for the trafficking victim defendant. Such issues can provide a basis for an application to move proceedings to a different court centre.

8.175

Further consideration should be had to the means of the trafficking victim defendant, if the proceedings are being held in a court that is a considerable distance from his address. Victims of modern slavery should be accommodated in locations that are secure and safe. Many are housed a considerable distance away and will have insufficient funds to travel to court. In such circumstances, consideration must be given to an application to move the proceedings if this will not place the individual in further danger. Section 75 of the Senior Courts Act 1981 regulates the place of trial. Variation of venue is governed by s 76. The defendant or the prosecutor, if dissatisfied with the place of trial as fixed by the magistrates' court, or by the Crown Court, may apply to the Crown Court for a direction, or further direction, varying the place of trial; and the court shall take the matter into consideration and may endorse or refuse the application, or give a direction not in compliance with the terms of the direction sought, as the court thinks fit. Either party may apply for a change of venue. Reasons may include possible prejudice to a defendant, or where the nature of the case has provoked particular public hostility, but the reasons cannot include securing a multiracial jury[104]. Whilst witness or victim intimidation is not a specific criterion, it should be a factor the court can take into account in order to comply with the protective procedural requirements.

103 *R v AAC* [2023] EWCA Crim 15.
104 *R v Ford* [1989] QB 868, [1989] 3 All ER 445; *R v Bansall* [1985] Crim LR 151.

Applications to hold a Crown Court hearing in camera

8.176

Under s 25 YJCEA 1999[105], there is a discretion for evidence to be given in private and to exclude individuals such as the general public, from the court during the giving of a witness's evidence (but allowance potentially to one named press representative under s 25(3), the accused, legal representatives in the proceedings and any interpreter/person appointed to assist the witness to remain). Such Special Measures direction under s 25 may only provide for exclusion where the proceedings relate to an offence under s 1 or s 2 MSA 2015 (or to a sexual offence or an offence under s 17(4A), or if it appears to the court there are reasonable grounds for believing that any person other than the accused has sought or will seek, to intimidate the witness in connection with testifying in the proceedings. See Crim PR, r.6.4 in relation to access restrictions to courts and Crim PR, r 6.6 in relation to applications seeking for trial to be conducted in private.

105 A special measure direction is available to exclude persons from the court during the giving of a witness's evidence, if proceedings relate to offence under s1 or 2 of MSA 2015; see s 25 ofYJCEA as amended post s 46(3) of MSA 2015.

9 Criminal offences of Modern Slavery and Human Trafficking

Ben Douglas-Jones KC, Daniel Bunting, Lynette Woodrow and Nathaniel Rudolf KC

Introduction

9.1

The Modern Slavery Act 2015 ('MSA 2015') includes substantive offences, at s 1, of slavery, servitude or forced and compulsory labour and, at s 2, human trafficking. These offences are a consolidation of existing offences from earlier statutes[1], as well as an attempt to address a lacuna identified in *CN v United Kingdom*[2], with the aim of simplifying enforcement[3]. Section 4 of the MSA 2015 also creates an offence of committing any offence with intent to commit an offence of human trafficking under s 2.

9.2

While the MSA 2015 requires s 1 offences to be construed in accordance with Art 4 European Convention on Human Rights (ECHR), the Convention itself merely states that 'no one shall be held in slavery or servitude' and 'no one shall be required to perform forced or compulsory labour' without defining what these terms mean. Consequently, the European Court of Human Rights (ECtHR) adopts an evolutionary interpretative approach, relying heavily on foundational international legal instruments, particularly the 1926 Slavery Convention and subsequent treaties, to provide the definitional backbone that gives substance to Art 4's prohibitions. This interpretative method reflects the ECHR's origins in the Universal Declaration of Human Rights and allows its meaning to develop alongside evolving international legal standards.

1 This came into force on 31 July 2015. For offences spanning that date, the MSA 2015 (Commencement No 1, Saving and Transitional Provisions) Regulations 2015 provides that 'it shall be conclusively presumed that the offence was committed wholly or partly before 31st July 2015.'
2 App No 4239/08 (13 February 2013).
3 584 HC Official Report (6th series) col 197, 8 July 2014 (Tracey Crouch).

9.3

The ECtHR's limited jurisprudence on Art 4, combined with judicial acknowledgments that the Court has struggled to define these concepts consistently even after Grand Chamber scrutiny, necessitates that domestic Courts and Tribunals fill the gaps and provide legal certainty. Therefore, any comprehensive analysis of modern slavery offences must begin with the foundational international conventions, as they provide the substantive legal framework that transforms Art 4's bare prohibitions into enforceable criminal law with clearly defined elements, a critical requirement for maintaining the principles of legal certainty and accessibility demanded by Art 7 ECHR.

9.4

This chapter outlines the legal elements of offences under ss 1 and 2 of the MSA 2015, while the substantive examination and detailed legal analysis of the individual offences of slavery, servitude, forced labour, compulsory labour, and human trafficking, as informed by international law conventions, is reserved for **Chapter 1**. This includes the recent case of *Webb* and *Somerset-How*[4] decided by the Court of Appeal (Criminal Division) directly considering both slavery and servitude.

Offences under the MSA 2015

Slavery, servitude and forced or compulsory labour: MSA 2015, s 1

9.5

Section 1 of the MSA 2015 provides as follows:

> '(1) A person commits an offence if –
>
> (a) the person holds another person in slavery or servitude and the circumstances are such that the person knows or ought to know that the other person is held in slavery or servitude, or
>
> (b) the person requires another person to perform forced or compulsory labour and the circumstances are such that the person knows or ought to know that the other person is being required to perform forced or compulsory labour.
>
> (2) In subsection (1) the references to holding a person in slavery or servitude or requiring a person to perform forced or compulsory labour are to be construed in accordance with Article 4 of the Human Rights Convention.

4 [2023] EWCA Crim 1491.

(3) In determining whether a person is being held in slavery or servitude or required to perform forced or compulsory labour, regard may be had to all the circumstances.

(4) For example, regard may be had –

(a) to any of the person's personal circumstances (such as the person being a child, the person's family relationships, and any mental or physical illness) which may make the person more vulnerable than other persons;

(b) to any work or services provided by the person, including work or services provided in circumstances which constitute exploitation within section 3(3) to (6).

(5) The consent of a person (whether an adult or a child) to any of the acts alleged to constitute holding the person in slavery or servitude, or requiring the person to perform forced or compulsory labour, does not preclude a determination that the person is being held in slavery or servitude, or required to perform forced or compulsory labour.'

Elements of the offence

Section 1(1)

9.6

For an offence to have been committed under this provision a person must have been held in slavery, servitude or required to perform forced or compulsory labour. This is materially different from the offence of human trafficking in the MSA 2015, s 2, which can be committed 'with a view' to exploitation even where that exploitation has not taken place.

9.7

The Court of Appeal in *R v SK*[5] stated the offences of slavery, servitude and forced or compulsory labour are hierarchical, with slavery representing the most serious form of exploitation. However, this was qualified in *Webb*[6] where the Court of Appeal said:

> 'We agree with the court in [S]*K* that the two ways of committing an offence under section 1(1)(a) of the 2015 are not mutually exclusive ….We would suggest that just as the expression "forced or compulsory labour" involves the use of two expressions whose meaning is very close to each other, so "slavery" and "servitude" do not mean that same thing, but the conditions they describe are so similar that in many cases

5 [2011] EWCA Crim 1691.
6 [2023] EWCA Crim 1491 at [79].

> both words will be apt to describe the condition to which the victim was reduced by the conduct of the perpetrator. That qualifies the conclusion in the same case that there is a hierarchy, in descending order of seriousness, from holding in slavery, through holding in servitude to requiring the performance of forced or compulsory labour. We would prefer to describe section 1(1)(a) as creating one offence involving conduct of a kind which involves slavery or servitude which are closely related concepts. Both will usually involve the domination of a person to induce them to provide work or services, and to constitute servitude, as we have held, that element must be present. We are about to consider the definition of slavery to show what additional conduct the inclusion of that word might capture. There is no purpose to be achieved by interpreting this statutory provision so that it creates two offences where the distinction between the different ingredients is so fine and where in very many cases both will be present. In our judgment it should be approached in the same way as the offence of "controlling or coercive behaviour", namely one offence which may be committed in two very similar and often indistinguishable ways.'

Two key principles follow from this.

9.8

First, as analysed in **Chapter 1**, the offences under s 1(a) and 1(b) are conceptually distinct. Where the conduct alleged meets the threshold for the more serious offences, such as slavery, it should be charged accordingly but slavery and servitude can be charged within the same count. When indicting the other offences, they should be separately indicted and not considered as being lesser included offences.

9.9

Secondly, where the conduct is most appropriately characterised as a s 1(a) or 1(b) or s 2 offence, the slavery, servitude, forced or compulsory labour or trafficking offence should be charged as such, even if other offences are also made out on the facts, and even if those offences carry the same maximum penalty. The Code for Crown Prosecutors requires prosecutors to select charges that allow the case to be presented clearly and simply[7], and that provide the Court with sufficient sentencing powers, including the ability to impose relevant ancillary orders.

9.10

In 2021, the Sentencing Council Guideline on *Slavery, Servitude and Forced or Compulsory Labour / Human Trafficking* (effective from 1 October 2021)[8]

---

7 See para 6.1.

8 This applies to all offenders aged 18 and older, who are sentenced on or after the effective date of this guideline, regardless of the date of the offence.

introduced a unified framework for sentencing these offences. While each offence is serious in its own right, this does not detract from their hierarchical structure, even with the qualification imposed by *Webb*[9], which remains central to both charging decisions and sentencing considerations. Slavery represents the most severe form of denial of autonomy within the hierarchy of offences that includes servitude and forced or compulsory labour.

Section 1(2)

Slavery

9.11

The criminal offence of slavery in England and Wales should be understood as arising where there is the exercise of any or all powers of ownership over another person. As analysed in **Chapter 1**, this concept is rooted in the 1926 Slavery Convention and developed through ICC jurisprudence, which defines slavery as the status or condition of a person over whom such powers are exercised; see **1.13–1.54**.

9.12

Importantly, the offence does not require formal legal ownership, which has been abolished in the UK since the Slavery Abolition Act 1833. It does include circumstances where a person is treated as property, and their autonomy and agency are effectively extinguished.

9.13

The legal test centres on whether the accused exercised powers typically associated with ownership, such as control over movement, labour, or decision-making. Contemporary slavery is necessarily *de facto*, as legal ownership of persons has been abolished globally. In *Webb*[10], the Court of Appeal offered the following definition of slavery:

> 'We consider that the essence of slavery is the domination of another person's life so that they are deprived of any real personal autonomy. They are deprived of important freedoms by the coercion and controlling behaviour of another person. This may involve a form of imprisonment, forced work, demands for sexual and other "services", or forced compliance with demands for obedience. They may have no freedom to decide where to live, or with whom.'

---

9 [2023] EWCA Crim 1491 at [79].
10 [2023] EWCA Crim 1491 at [92].

Servitude

9.14

The ECtHR's case law on Art 4 ECHR provides limited guidance on the offence of servitude, as its jurisprudence has primarily focused on domestic servitude, typically involving migrant women and girls working in private households. This narrow focus reflects findings by the Parliamentary Assembly of the Council of Europe and aligns with the ILO's Domestic Workers Convention, which highlights the vulnerability of domestic workers to exploitation. While the Court has identified indicators of servitude, such as unpaid labour, lack of freedom of movement, and psychological coercion, it has largely examined these through the lens of domestic work, as seen in *Siliadin v France*[11] and *CN and V v France*[12]. In these cases, the Court emphasised the victim's perceived inability to change their condition as a defining feature of servitude. However, as analysed in **Chapter 1**, this is a characteristic specific to serfdom, one of the four recognised practices of servitude under international law, and is not a necessary element of the others.

9.15

International law treats servitude as a categorical concept, encompassing four conventional practices: debt bondage, serfdom, servile marriage, and child exploitation. Each of these may give rise to the offence of servitude, and where any involve the exercise of powers attaching to ownership, they cross the threshold into slavery. The ECtHR's limited engagement with this broader framework restricts its utility in clarifying the legal boundaries of servitude under Art 4.

9.16

The criminal offence of servitude in England and Wales should be understood as arising in the circumstances explained in **Chapter 1**: see **1.55–1.102**. As *Webb*[13] reinforced, there remains a requirement for the provision of work or services under coercion.

Forced or compulsory labour

9.17

The definition comprises three core elements: (1) work or service; (2) the menace of any penalty; and (3) involuntariness or the absence of free and informed consent; see the extensive analysis and discussion of forced or

11 App No 73316/01 (2005) 43 EHRR 287, 20 BHRC 654.
12 App No 67724/09 (11 October 2012).
13 [2023] EWCA Crim 1491 at [73].

compulsory labour in **Chapter 1** at **1.103–1.226**. Sexual exploitation as forced or compulsory labour (or servitude) is dealt with at **1.115–1.117**.

Section 1(3) and (4)

9.18

In considering 'all of the circumstances', as required by the MSA 2015, s 1(3), one is first directed to questions of the victim's vulnerability. It is important to make clear that 'abuse of a position of vulnerability' is one of the possible 'means' by which a trafficking offence may be committed, but as the above cases illustrate 'abuse of position of vulnerability' is also a feature of servitude, forced and compulsory labour.

9.19

The ECtHR has repeatedly emphasised the wide array of circumstances which may be relevant, finding breaches of the Convention where states have taken too narrow a view. In *CN v United Kingdom*[14], the subtle means of coercion which might be employed were highlighted, including the taking of identity documents, retention of wages, and threat of denunciation (both implicit and explicit)[15]. Other factors which may be relevant would include working conditions, standard of accommodation if provided, and the passage of time: work which may have been voluntary initially may be seen to be forced or compulsory labour after wages have been retained for a lengthy period[16].

Section 1(5)

9.20

Section 1(5) makes clear that consent given by a complainant may not preclude a finding of slavery, servitude, or forced or compulsory labour.

Directing a jury on s 1 offences

9.21

Slavery, servitude and forced or compulsory labour are not defined in the MSA 2015. They are to be construed in accordance with Art 4, ECHR; see s 1(2), MSA 2015, above. Defining such terms for jury directions is a minefield. It is complex. The editors suggest that the following bases for directions – which

14 App No 4239/08 (13 February 2013).
15 *CN v United Kingdom* (App No 4239/08) (13 November 2012) at [80].
16 *Chowdury v Greece* (App No 21884/15) (30 March 2017) at [94] and [97].

will need to be refined in any individual case – are a helpful starting point[17]. As the Court of Appeal made clear in *Webb*[18] the directions must be tailored to the facts of the case:

> 'In our judgment the best way to direct a jury about the meaning of slavery is to produce a legal direction which is tailored to the facts of the case, rather as our paragraph [92] begins with a general statement of principle but then brings it to the facts of TSH's life during the period of the slavery. It will always be helpful to identify the conduct of the defendant which is said to amount to holding the person in slavery, and to direct the jury that they must decide whether that conduct had the effect of reducing the person's personal autonomy to such an extent and for such a period that it amounted to holding them in slavery.'

The Court continued[19] that the direction would have begun as follows:

'[T]he essence of slavery is the domination of another person's life so that they are deprived of any real personal autonomy. They are deprived of important freedoms by the coercion and controlling behaviour of another person. This may involve a form of imprisonment, forced work, demands for sexual and other "services", or forced compliance with demands for obedience. They may have no freedom to decide where to live, or with whom. In this case, TSH was denied the freedom to choose who would provide intimate personal care for him, the purpose of which was to preserve as much personal autonomy as possible, given the constraints of his physical disability. He could not decide when to go to the lavatory, when to go out of the house or whether to see his family. He reached the stage, according to the messages, when he wanted to die because it was his only escape from these miserable and squalid conditions. Counsel for the appellants have pointed to some things which he was able to do, and the resolution of the question of whether the restrictions imposed by the behaviour of the appellants amounted to a sufficient removal of his freedom was an issue for the jury to resolve on the evidence.'

Jury direction: adult slavery (non-sexual)

9.22

To find D guilty of slavery, the prosecution must make you sure of the following:

1. That D held V in slavery; and
2. That D knew or ought to have known that V was being held in slavery.

17 They are set out as directions which might be apposite in a particular case. They do not purport to be fit for all possible scenarios.

18 [2023] EWCA Crim 1491 at [95].

19 [2023] EWCA Crim 1491 at [92].

Slavery

9.23

The essence of slavery is the domination of another person's life so that they are deprived of any real personal autonomy. Autonomy is the ability to engage in behaviour by choice. A person who is subjected to slavery is deprived of important freedoms by the coercion and controlling behaviour of another person. In this case, the prosecution rely on the following features as demonstrating slavery.

A jury could be directed in the following terms:

> 'Lawyers sometimes describe this as exercising powers over a person as if they were owned, but what you must decide is whether, in reality, V's autonomy was removed in that way, through that level of control.'

In deciding whether the level of control exercised by D amounted to domination and removed V's real personal autonomy, you should look at the whole picture. The prosecution say that D's conduct amounted to domination because [set out the main features relied on by the prosecution]. The defence say that V retained real autonomy because [set out the main features relied on by the defence]. It is for you to decide, on all the evidence, whether you are sure that D's control went as far as domination of that kind, depriving V of real personal autonomy in important aspects of their life.

9.24

Depending on the particular facts of the case, the appropriate question for a jury to decide in any route to verdict might be in the following terms:

> 'Are you sure that the level of control exercised by D amounted to domination over V, depriving V of any real personal autonomy in important aspects of their life?'[20].

9.25

'Domination' means that the defendant's control over the complainant was so great that, in reality, the complainant could no longer live as a person with their own freedom to make real choices. It is **not** enough that the defendant was unpleasant, bossy or demanding. You need to consider whether the defendant's control was so strong that the complainant had no real choice about important parts of their everyday life.

20 This represents the authors' and editors' suggested approach to ensure that the threshold for slavery is set at the right level. It is not something which derives directly from the judgment.

9.26

Real personal autonomy means having a genuine ability to make your own decisions about important things, and to carry those decisions out in everyday life. Someone might still be able to make small or trivial choices, but that does not mean they have real autonomy if, in the things that matter, their life is effectively controlled by someone else.

9.27

Coercion may arise by [include as appropriate: the threat or use of force or other forms of coercion, of abduction, of fraud, of deception, of the abuse of power or of a position of vulnerability or of the giving or receiving of payments or benefits to achieve the consent of a person having control over another person][21].

All the circumstances

9.28

In determining whether D held V in slavery, you should have regard to 'all the circumstances'.

9.29

'All the circumstances' includes the personal circumstances of V and, in particular, V's vulnerability [indicia of vulnerability arising on the prosecution's case, if any] and the nature and circumstances of the work or services provided by V.

9.30

For s.1 offences, the prosecution is not confined to any predefined or prescriptive notion of 'vulnerability' in the way that ss 2 and 3 trafficking require. Jury directions must be tailored to assist the jury without narrowing the concept of vulnerability; see **Chapter 1**, which shows how vulnerability in this context can arise from almost any circumstance that, in reality, weakens a person's ability to resist domination or exploitation. *FM v Russia*[22] and the ECtHR jurisprudence show the range of factors which may give rise to vulnerability; eg: irregular or insecure immigration status, poverty, social isolation, inability to speak the local language, economic dependence, or any combination of disadvantages. ECAT's Explanatory Report[23] (para. 83) makes the same point – that vulnerability 'may be of any kind… physical, psychological, emotional, family-related, social or economic', including illegality of status or fragile health, and extends to 'any state of hardship' enabling the person to be controlled and dominated to a degree which significantly diminishes their personal autonomy.

---

21 As s 1 offences are to be construed by reference to Art 4 ECHR, these examples of coercion are taken from the means of trafficking in human beings under the international and regional instruments.

22 (Applications nos. 71671/16 and 40190/18).

23 https://rm.coe.int/16800d3812 (last accessed 5 February 2026).

9.31

Judges should not attempt any prescriptive approach when directing the jury on vulnerability.

The jury should be told that vulnerabilities, of whatever kind, may explain why a person is unable to avoid or resist dominating control.

In a particular case a jury could be directed:

> 'When considering whether V was vulnerable you need to consider all the circumstances of the case, all factors that in your common sense view might cause V to be vulnerable. In this case, you have in particular heard that V:
>
> [was a child aged [insert age] when they worked for D]
>
> [is related to D]
>
> [was suffering from [insert illness] at the time]
>
> [etc.]
>
> Those are matters you should consider when considering all the circumstances of the case when assessing whether V might have been more vulnerable than other persons.'

9.32

If the work or the conditions of work itself was exploitative [for example, if it was criminal activity, sexually degrading, or involved the removal of organs] that is a relevant and important part of the overall picture.

9.33

A person's vulnerability and the circumstances of the work are important because they can help you understand whether, and to what extent, D's conduct amounted to domination and control over V's life. In considering that overall picture, you may take into account any exploitation of V (for example, the nature of the work or services, and how V was treated), but you should remember that exploitation is not, by itself, a separate legal ingredient of the offence of slavery. These matters may also help explain why V did not escape, seek help, or object to their treatment.

Consent

9.34

Consent is not an element of the offence of slavery and is not, in itself, a defence. The law recognises slavery where domination and control reduce an individual's personal autonomy to a significantly diminished level, regardless of any agreement or apparent willingness.

9.35

The prosecution therefore does not have to prove that V did not consent to being held in slavery, and it is no answer to the charge that V may, at some point, have agreed to work for or live with D.

9.36

Evidence that V appeared to consent to carrying out work or services may still be relevant to the factual question of whether control was exercised over them to the extent they had no real personal autonomy.

However, you should consider whether, looking at all the circumstances, any consent was truly free, informed, and given with a real choice, or whether it was obtained or maintained through coercion, deception, force, exploitation of that person's vulnerability or other means.

Even where V initially agreed to work or to the living arrangements, that does not prevent the situation later becoming slavery if the V was unable to exercise their personal autonomy and leave that situation because of D's conduct.

Apparent consent which is not free and informed, or which is given in a coercive environment, or by abusing the individual's vulnerabilities, does not detract from a finding of slavery if you are sure that D's level of domination and control over V otherwise meets the legal test.

Jury direction: servitude by debt bonded labour

9.37

D is charged with servitude through debt bonded labour.

Servitude

9.38

'Servitude' means an obligation to provide services that is imposed by the use of force or coercion. Servitude may arise in different situations. One of those is debt bonded labour.

9.39

The prosecution must make you sure that

1. V owes a debt to D [or associates of D]; and

   [In this context, debt is not limited to money owed. It can arise from any transaction or benefit that places a person under an obligation, something they feel they must repay or make up for. This could include being given: drugs, especially to feed an addiction; accommodation, such as a place to stay; food, clothing, or transport or protection or assistance.]

2. V [or the persons under V's control] is forced or coerced to work for D [or his associates]; and
3. V does so in order to pay off what V [or persons under V's control] owes D [or associates of D]; and
4. either:

   (a) the fair value of V's work [or persons under V's control] is not used to reduce or pay off what V owes; or

   (b) there are no clear limits on how long V must work, and the specific type of work V must do is not clearly laid out[24]; and
5. D knew or ought to have known that V was being held in servitude through debt bonded labour.

9.40

Coercion may arise by [include as appropriate: the threat or use of force or other forms of coercion, of abduction, of fraud, of deception, of the abuse of power or of a position of vulnerability][25]. Because debt bondage amounts to deception, no additional coercion may be necessary[26].

All the circumstances and consent

9.41

See the commentary in the direction concerning slavery (above).

Jury direction: servitude by serfdom

9.42

D is charged with servitude through serfdom.

Servitude

9.43

'Servitude' means an obligation to provide services that is imposed by the use of force or coercion. Servitude may arise in different situations. One of those is serfdom.

24 See chapter 1 for the language from which this suggested direction derives.

25 These are non-exhaustive examples.

26 As s 1 offences are to be construed by reference to Art 4 ECHR, these examples of coercion are taken from the means of trafficking in human beings under the international and regional instruments.

9.44

Serfdom is where V lives on land owned by D (or their associates), is required by law, tradition, or an agreement to both live on that land and to work on it whether paid or not and is not free to change their status.

9.45

To find D guilty of servitude by serfdom, the prosecution must make you sure of the following:

1. that V lived on land owned by D (or D's associates);
2. that V was required [specify on the evidence whether by law, tradition, or an agreement] both to live on that land and to work on it;
3. that V was forced or coerced to work for D (or his associates) so that V was or believed they were unable to change their situation; and
4. that D knew or ought to have known that V was being held in servitude through serfdom.

9.46

Coercion may arise by (include as appropriate: the threat or use of force or other forms of coercion, of abduction, of fraud, of deception, of the abuse of power or of a position of vulnerability)[27].

All the circumstances and consent

9.47

See the commentary in the direction concerning slavery (above).

Direction for jury: forced or compulsory labour

9.48

D is accused of requiring another person, V, to perform forced or compulsory labour.

9.49

For you to find the defendant guilty of this offence, the prosecution must make you sure of two things:

- First, that V was in fact required to perform forced or compulsory labour by D (or D's associates).
- Second, that D knew, or ought to have known, that this was the case.

27 These are non-exhaustive examples.

9.50

First Question: Was it Forced or Compulsory Labour?

9.51

'Forced or compulsory labour' has three essential ingredients. The prosecution must make you sure of all of them.

1. Work or service

9.52

First, that V performed 'work or service'. This is a very broad term. It includes any kind of labour or any type of service. It does not matter whether the work was legal or illegal, or whether you would consider it a proper 'job'. It can cover anything from factory work to domestic chores, or even being made to beg or commit crimes.

2. Under the menace of a penalty

9.53

Second, that the work was performed under the 'menace of a penalty'. This expression comes from a 1930 legal convention. This phrase should not be used when directing a jury.[28]

9.54

A 'penalty' can be any harm or disadvantage, whether involving physical harm or not, that V was led to believe would happen if they did not do the work. The pressure can be psychological, which could include, for example, the threat of being reported to immigration authorities, the fear of being arrested, or the threat that they might lose certain rights or privileges.

9.55

The threat does not have to be spoken out loud. You can conclude that there was a 'menace of a penalty' by looking at all the circumstances of V's situation. For example, if V was particularly vulnerable because of their poverty, age, or immigration status, and that fear was exploited, that can be enough to satisfy this element.

3. The work was involuntary

9.56

Third, that V had not offered voluntarily to do the work. This means that V did not give their free and informed consent.

---

28 *R v Finch* [2026] EWCA Crim 477 at [32].

9.57

Even if a person initially agrees to do a job, that consent can be cancelled out by the circumstances that follow. Consent must be ongoing. A person must be genuinely free to stop working and to leave their employment without fearing that they will face a penalty for doing so. If they are not free to leave, the work is not voluntary.

9.58

(You might have heard evidence that V returned to work for D after a period away. This does not automatically mean the work was voluntary. You must consider *why* they returned. Was it because they were genuinely free and the conditions were acceptable, or was it because of ongoing pressure, vulnerability, or economic dependence which was being exploited?)

D's state of mind

9.59

After considering those three questions, you must ask whether the Prosecution has made you sure that D knew, or ought to have known, that V was being made to perform forced or compulsory labour.

All the circumstances

9.60

See the commentary in the direction concerning slavery (above).

Directing the jury where slavery and servitude are alleged

9.61

It follows from *Webb*, and the fact that s1(1)(a) creates one offence of holding someone in 'slavery or servitude', that in many cases a compendious direction should be given:

To find D guilty, the prosecution must make you sure of the following:

1. That D held V in slavery or servitude; and
2. That D knew or ought to have known that V was being held in slavery or servitude.

Before then giving the case specific directions on slavery and servitude as set out above.

Human trafficking: MSA 2015, s 2

9.62

This offence is created by the MSA 2015, s 2:

'2 Human trafficking

(1) A person commits an offence if the person arranges or facilitates the travel of another person ('V') with a view to V being exploited.

(2) It is irrelevant whether V consents to the travel (whether V is an adult or a child).

(3) A person may in particular arrange or facilitate V's travel by recruiting V, transporting or transferring V, harbouring or receiving V, or transferring or exchanging control over V.

(4) A person arranges or facilitates V's travel with a view to V being exploited only if—

(a) the person intends to exploit V (in any part of the world) during or after the travel, or

(b) the person knows or ought to know that another person is likely to exploit V (in any part of the world) during or after the travel.

(5) 'Travel' means—

(a) arriving in, or entering, any country,

(b) departing from any country,

(c) travelling within any country.

(6) A person who is a UK national commits an offence under this section regardless of—

(a) where the arranging or facilitating takes place, or

(b) where the travel takes place.

(7) A person who is not a UK national commits an offence under this section if—

(a) any part of the arranging or facilitating takes place in the United Kingdom, or

(b) the travel consists of arrival in or entry into, departure from, or travel within, the United Kingdom'.

Elements of the offence

9.63

Section 2 provides for a single offence of human trafficking. It includes sexual and non-sexual exploitation.

Arranging or facilitating travel for exploitation

9.64

Section 2(1) makes it a criminal offence to arrange or facilitate the travel of another person with a view to his being exploited. Travel is defined in s 2(5) as arriving in, entering, departing, or travelling within any country. It can immediately be seen that the scope of s 2, in this respect, is very broad. There is no minimum distance required for a journey to count as 'travel', although journeys involving truly minimal distances (such as walking between rooms) may well be excluded[29]. It therefore appears that, for example: (i) an occupier who accepts a person into his house (ie harbours or receives them) after a journey of a few miles, with a view to exploiting them, would be guilty of this offence; (ii) the principal operator of a county line drug supply operation (typically based in a city) who arranges for a street dealer (based in a county town) to walk from one part of the town to another with a view to exploiting them by causing them to sell drugs, would be guilty of this offence.

9.65

It was held in *R v Karemera*[30] in the context of the Asylum and Immigration (Treatment of Claimants, etc) Act 2004, s 4, ('the s 4, 2004 Act offence'), that the interpretation afforded to s 4 should be one that accorded with the statutory purpose of protecting the vulnerable from trafficking with a view to exploitation. The words 'arranging' and 'facilitating' should be given a broad construction. Thus 'arranging' the travel of a person would include such matters as transporting that person, procuring a third person to transport that person, or buying a ticket for that person. 'Facilitating' travel would include making such travel easier; and that it was possible in some circumstances simply instructing a person to travel to a particular place would amount to 'arranging or facilitating' that person's travel, although it would depend on the facts of the case[31]. It was held that 'arranging' was a common word which needed no further explanation to the jury and would include transporting B, procuring a third person to

---

29 *R v Ali* [2015] EWCA Crim 1279, [2015] 2 Cr App Rep 457 at [80] where it was said 'It is self-evident that walking, for instance, between adjacent rooms, or other journey involving truly minimal distances (for instances of a few feet or yards) may well be outside the ambit of this provision'. This was a case concerning the Sexual Offences Act (SOA) 2003, s 58 (trafficking within the UK for sexual exploitation), one of the precursors to the MSA 2015, s 2.

30 [2018] EWCA Crim 1432; [2019] 1 WLR 4761; [2019] 2 Cr App R 14.

31 Paras 44–47, 60–61.

transport B, or buying a ticket for B. 'Facilitating' was intended to be different from 'arranging' and would include 'making easier'. It was not sensible to lay down precise definitions of those terms and there was no fixed list of the conduct which could amount to either arranging or facilitating.

9.66

Section 2 of the MSA 2015 derived from s 4 of the 2004 Act and the statutory purpose of s 2 of the MSA 2015 is identical to s 4 of the 2004 Act. Both sections include the words 'facilitating' and 'arranging'. Therefore, *R v Karemera*[32] shows how these provisions should be interpreted in the context of the s 2 offence. It is not necessary to prove that the travel was arranged or facilitated by the specific 'means' listed in ECAT, Art 4.[33]

Consent irrelevant

9.67

Section 2(2) makes it clear that with a human trafficking offence the victim's consent to his travel (whether an adult or a child) is irrelevant. As held in *R v Karemera*[34], part of the statutory purpose of s 4 was to protect the vulnerable and that this should include protecting them from their own decision-making. In the context of s 4(1A) of the 2004 Act, accordingly the Crown did not have to prove a lack of consent on the part of the victim or any element of coercion.

Mens rea

9.68

Section 2(4) provides that the arranging or facilitating is done with a view to the exploitation of the victim if the perpetrator either:

- intends to exploit the victim; or
- knows or ought to know that any other person is likely to exploit the victim.

It is irrelevant where in the world that exploitation might take place.

9.69

The court had held in *R v Karemera* that the mens rea required was the carrying out of the arranging or facilitating 'with a view to the exploitation' of the victim (in that case a 'courier'). The arranger or facilitator must have either intended to exploit the victim or believed that someone else was likely to carry out some

32 [2019] 2 Cr App R 14.
33 *R v How* [2026] EWCA Crim 476.
34 Ibid.

undefined acts of exploitation; proof of actual exploitation was unnecessary. The Crown did not have to prove that the victim was an unwilling, coerced, or non-consenting participant, and a successful prosecution did not depend on the victim giving evidence. As set out above, consent was no defence: a vulnerable person might well consent to carrying drugs, and s 4(1A) sought to protect them from their own poor decision-making.

9.70

In *R v Karemera* (above; in the context of the s 4, 2004 Act offence) it was held that with a 'view to exploitation' required the prosecution to prove that the defendant intended to exploit a person, 'B', or believed that another person was likely to exploit B during or after the journey. It followed that it was not necessary to prove that the person arranging or facilitating travel was also the person who at some point would do or intended to exploit person 'B'. It was also not necessary for the prosecution to establish that the defendant (and/or another person) had gone on to exploit B in any of the ways defined in s 4(4)[35].

9.71

The phrase 'with a view to the exploitation' means either that the defendant intends to exploit the victim during or after travel or knows or ought to know someone else is likely to do so. Because the international law is arguably not reflected properly in s 2 (see below), what may not be captured by this phrase is exploitation of a victim in situ or a 'with a view to the exploitation' of a victim in situ where there has been no travel (ie an individual is harbouring a person B with a view to exploitation).

Harbouring

9.72

The s 2(3) examples of arranging or facilitating travel will have their ordinary English meaning; however, 'harbouring' can cause confusion. Harbouring is linked to providing or arranging accommodation for receipt of VOTs. Recruiters and those transferring the victim, harbouring or receiving the victim may have no involvement in the arranging or facilitation of the travel of the victim but do intend to exploit the victim, or know or ought to know that the victim will be exploited. These individuals may not be caught by the human trafficking offence because of the requirement for movement inherent in s 2 which is underscored by the inclusion of the word 'may' in s 2(3). Depending on the evidence, consideration should be given to charging all involved in the trafficking and exploitation with conspiracy to commit an offence of human trafficking or aiding and abetting an offence of human trafficking. This enables the prosecution of the perpetrators for their specific role in achieving the common purpose; ie the exploitation.

35 Paras [44]–[49], [51].

Concerns about the narrow scope of the offence under section 2

9.73

In the regional instruments, Council of Europe Convention on Action against Trafficking in Human Beings 2005 ('ECAT') and the EU Trafficking Directive (see **Chapter 1**), movement is not a necessary element of the trafficking definition. The language of s 2(3) derives from the s 4, 2004 Act offence and, whereas movement is not a necessary component of trafficking in regional law, travel or the arrangement or facilitation of travel is a necessary component of the s 2 human trafficking offence. The interplay between s 2(1) and s 2(3) does not reflect the way in which the 'acts' or 'actions' of trafficking operate in the regional instruments. It is unclear what, if any, nexus is required between arranging or facilitating 'travel' and the 'recruitment, transportation or transferring, harbouring, receiving or exchanging control over the victim'.

9.74

The scope of s 2 is narrower than the human trafficking offences defined in the ECAT and the EU Directive. Consequently, it remains unresolved whether a person could be found guilty of a section 2 offence for harbouring a victim if they had no role in the victim's travel to that place or their subsequent onward journey. Likewise, receiving and transferring or exchanging control of a victim may not be caught by the natural wording of s 2 of the MSA 2015. If those acts are not caught by the subsection, it will not be compliant with ECHR, Art 4 (see *CN v United Kingdom*). It may be possible to indict conspiracy to commit human trafficking to include conduct which would fall outside the section[36].

Extra territorial effect

9.75

Section 2(6) makes the offence extra-territorial in relation to UK nationals. It does not matter where in the world a UK national arranges or facilitates the travel. It does not matter what the country of arrival, entry, travel or departure is. In the Explanatory Notes to the MSA 2015, the example given is that if a

36 This may also have consequences for the s 45 defence for someone who is, for example, found running a cannabis factory and states that they were exploited and detained, but that this only started after their arrival there. However, the problem is more illusory in the context of the statutory defence – see **Chapter 10** more generally. By s 45(1)(c) (for adults) and s 45(4)(b) (children) the reference to 'slavery' is a reference to offences under s 1, MSA 2015. S 1 offences comprise slavery, servitude and forced or compulsory labour. By s 1(2), those concepts must be construed in accordance with Art 4, ECHR. As Art 4 offences include trafficking in human beings as defined in Art 4, ECAT, it is unnecessary to show movement in the context of the defence.

UK national trafficked a person from Spain to France, he could be prosecuted in England and Wales for this offence[37].

9.76

Section 2(7) provides for a more limited territorial reach in relation to non-UK nationals. If any part of the arranging or facilitating takes place in the UK, non-UK nationals will commit an offence. Likewise, if the UK is the country of arrival, entry, travel or departure, a non-UK national will commit an offence.

9.77

Travel can be caught by this offence whether it is cross border or within any country[38].

Exploitation: MSA 2015, s 3

9.78

'Exploitation' for the purposes of s 2 is defined exhaustively in MSA 2015, s 3. It includes exploitation arising only in the following circumstances:

(i) offences under the MSA 2015, s 1, sexual offences under the Sexual Offences Act 2003 ('SOA 2003'), Pt 1 or the Protection of Children Act 1978, s 1(1)(a) (indecent photographs), and organ harvesting and related activities under the Human Tissue Act 2004, ss 32 and 33 (MSA 2015, s 3(3) and (4));

(ii) activities that would amount to such offences if committed in England and Wales;

(iii) the use of force, threats or deception designed to induce the victim to provide services or benefits (MSA 2015, s 3(5));

(iv) the use or attempted use of a person to obtain services or benefits when that person has been chosen because he is a child or vulnerable adult and would otherwise be likely to refuse (MSA 2015, s 3(6)).

9.79

Subsection (5) of s 3 allows a wider degree of what can be exploitation (provided that there is use of threats, force or deception).

---

37 See case of *R v Iyamu* [2018] EWCA Crim 2166 where the defendant of dual nationality (British/Nigerian) trafficked victims from Nigeria to Germany. No elements of the offence were committed in the UK. The trial took place in the UK but the complainants gave evidence via live-link from Nigeria and Germany.

38 MSA 2015, s 2(5).

9.80

'Exploitation' is defined in s 3 to cover a broad range of circumstances. The definition is, with minor variations, an amalgamation of the definitions of exploitation in the two predecessor offences (trafficking for sexual exploitation under the SOA 2003, s 59A, and trafficking for exploitation under the Asylum and Immigration (Treatment of Claimants, etc) Act 2004 ('the 2004 Act'), s 4). In the case of adults, the scope of s 3(5) is particularly broad if force, threats or deception is involved. In the case of people 'chosen' for exploitation because they are under 18, ill, disabled or in a family relationship (when, but for those qualities, they would be likely to refuse to act), as with s 3(6), exploitation includes a very broad range of circumstances. 'Chosen', as with the Act 2004, s 4(4)(d), should not be replaced by the words 'initially recruited' and it should be given its 'natural and broad meaning'[39].

9.81

The effect of s 3(2) is that if a person is the victim of behaviour which involves the commission of an offence under s 1, MSA 2015 (or conduct which would amount to such an offence if committed in England and Wales) that person will be exploited for the purposes of s 2. In the context of trafficking, this makes ss 1 to 3 somewhat circular. By s 1(2), slavery, servitude and forced or compulsory labour are to be construed in accordance with Art 4, ECHR. Conduct amounting to the trafficking in human beings under Art 4, ECAT will amount to an offence under s 1 (see *Rantsev v Cyprus and Russia)*[40]. Therefore, the domestic offence of human trafficking, contrary to ss 2 and 3, construes 'exploitation' by reference to conduct including human trafficking within the international and regional instruments' meaning. The international meaning of trafficking does not require the victim's movement. The domestic definition of trafficking *prima facie* does.

9.82

The effect of sub-ss (3) and (4) is that if (i) something is done to or in respect of a person which involves the commission of a relevant indecent photographs or sexual offence or (ii) a person is encouraged, required or expected to do anything which involves the commission of relevant organ harvesting offence (or the conduct would involve the commission of such an offence if committed in England and Wales), then that person is exploited without more. Therefore, for example, in the case of a person who controls a sex worker in the context of prostitution for gain, an offence is committed under Part 1 of the Sexual Offences Act 2003 (s 53), the sex worker is exploited. There is no need to show any use of force, threats or deception designed to induce the sex worker to provide services or benefits (because sub-ss (3) and (4) are to be read disjunctively

39 *R v Karemera* [2018] EWCA Crim 1432, [2019] 2 Cr App R. 14 at [60]–[62].
40 (2010) BHRC 313.

from sub-s (5). It follows that if the sex worker is directed to an outcall, because that would involve the arrangement of travel, it would constitute an offence of human trafficking under s 2, MSA 2015.

9.83

In a case where sub-ss (3), (4) and (6) (see below) do not apply, for there to be 'exploitation' within the meaning of s 3, the use of force, threats or deception designed to induce the victim to provide services or benefits needs to be present (sub-s (5)). Each element of sub-s (5) comprises a separate way in which exploitation may be fulfilled.

9.84

Section 3(6) incorporates an element of causation into the language concerning choice. The two grounds identified in s 3(6) for the choice or future choice of the young (or disabled, etc) courier – that he is young and that a person without youth would be likely to refuse to be used for that purpose – has to be established. The question of causation is not one determined by an overly literal reading of the statutory language. In the present context, the prosecution need only establish that the age of the VOT and the likelihood of an adult refusing were two factors, possibly amongst many others, which form a part of the defendant's thinking. Each ground has to be 'a' factor but need not be the 'main' or 'principal' factor. It suffices to achieve Parliament's objective of protecting the vulnerable that the issue of the intended or likely choice on the grounds of age is a factor in the *mens rea*, and one which is more than *de minimis*. Such a formulation also provides adequate protection to defendants[41].

9.85

The wording of the MSA 2015, s 3(6) does not include the issue of 'consent'. With exploitation deriving from s 3(6), the prosecution does not need to prove a lack of consent on the part of the young, disabled, etc courier or any element of coercion. Indeed, the mischief the provision (in s 4(4)(d) of the 2004 Act from which s 3(6) derives) sought to address was that a vulnerable person had consented; the Act was seeking to protect the young and the vulnerable from their own decision-making.

9.86

Section 3(6) does not address the position in law (as per the EU Trafficking Directive, Art 2 or ECAT, Art 4) that the question of consent is entirely irrelevant to determining whether a child has been exploited. Further, s 3(6) conflates the position of two distinct (although at times overlapping) groups of trafficked victims: children and those who are in a position of vulnerability.

41 See *R v Karemera* (above), ibid, paras [52]–[55] and [59], where the court commented on s 4(4)(d) of the 2004 Act, from which the wording of s 3(6) derived.

Under Art 2(4) and para 11 of the Preamble to the EU Trafficking Directive, and Art 4, ECAT consent is irrelevant when considering whether a child is a VOT. Consent is also irrelevant in respect of adults where the 'means' of exploitation entails the use of force, threats, deception, coercion, abduction, abuse of power or a position of vulnerability, giving/receiving payments or benefits to achieve the consent of a person having control over another. Whilst s 2(2) of the MSA 2015 makes it clear that the victim's consent to the travel is irrelevant, some argue that s 3(6) of the MSA 2015 does not reflect the true position on the (ir)relevance of consent in these circumstances[42].

9.87

Further, s 3(6)(b) establishes a subjective test, importing a measure of evaluative judgement. ECAT and the EU Trafficking Directive do not require an evaluative judgement. Where the victim is a child, and he is subjected to an action which amounts to exploitation, objectively, that child has been trafficked. The test is an entirely *objective* test where children are concerned. It is irrelevant whether a reasonable adult may or may not have consented to the exploitation 'services' in the assessment of whether that child is an exploited child.

9.88

A prosecution under s 2, MSA 2015 relying on s 3(6) exploitation, does not depend on the ability to call as a witness the individual said to have been exploited or the target of exploitation[43]. This principle is underscored by the Court of Appeal decision of *R v Karemera*. It significantly helps to protect the VOTs and to ensure that traffickers are prosecuted. The case involved the terminating ruling of a Crown Court judge who determined that without the VOTs as witnesses the case should be withdrawn from the jury. The Court of Appeal overturned that decision.

9.89

This offence has a broad territorial scope: a UK national will be guilty of it regardless of where the travel, or the arranging or facilitating of it, takes place; a non-UK national will be guilty of it if any part of the travel, or its arranging or facilitation, takes place in the UK[44].

9.90

Three independent parliamentary inquiries, which called for evidence from a wide variety of sources, have found the offences in MSA 2015 to be sufficiently

42 *R v K, W, A* [2018] EWCA Crim 1432; *R v Nguyen, Tran and Nguyen* [2019] EWCA Crim 670; *R v Rooney and others* [2019] EWCA Crim 681.

43 *R v Karemera* (above), paras [60]–[62].

44 MSA 2015, s 2(6) and (7).

broad reaching and flexible to respond to different and emerging forms of exploitation.

9.91

As the Strasbourg Court made clear in *Chowdury v Greece*[45], to fulfil the positive obligation to criminalise and effectively punish any act referred to in ECHR, Art 4, States must establish a legislative and administrative framework that prohibits and punishes forced labour or compulsory labour, servitude and slavery. The court re-affirmed that trafficking falls within the scope of the ECHR, Art 4 and a legislative and administrative framework must be in place to punish any act of trafficking[46]. In *Rantsev v Cyprus and Russia*[47] the court held that human trafficking, within the meaning of the Palermo Protocol, Art 3(a) and ECAT, Art 4(a), fell within the scope of the ECHR, Art 4[48].

9.92

The EU Trafficking Directive, Art 2(1) requires Member States to take the necessary measures to ensure that the following intentional acts are punishable:

> 'The recruitment, transportation, transfer, harbouring or reception of persons, including the exchange or transfer of control over those persons, by means of the threat or use of force or other forms of coercion, of abduction, of fraud, of deception, of the abuse of position of power or of a position of vulnerability or of the giving or receiving of payments or benefits to achieve the consent of a person having control over another person, for the purpose of exploitation'[49].

9.93

This provision is dealt with in **Chapters 1** and **10**. The statutory language on the meaning of exploitation (MSA 2015, s 3) in s 3(4)–(6) does not mirror and/or reflect all the 'means' envisaged under the EU Trafficking Directive, Art 2(1) and/or ECAT, Art 4. Whereas the language of the EU Trafficking Directive, Art 2(1) and ECAT, Art 4 envisages that the 'means' by which exploitation is committed can apply across *all forms* of exploitation, the MSA 2015, s 3(4)–(6) suggests that different means apply depending on what the form of exploitation is. This is an approach that is at odds with the approach of the regional

45 App No 21884/15 (30 March 2017) at 105.
46 Ibid at para 86 and 87.
47 (2010) BHRC 313.
48 Para 282.
49 Following EU exit, the EU Directive has no retained application in England and Wales in criminal law. However, the ECtHR is likely to rely on the expanded definitions in the EU Directive, Art 2 to inform its approach to ECAT, Art 4; see **Chapter 10**. It is therefore important to understand the significance of expanded definitions in EU Directive, Art 2.

instruments defining trafficking and thus non-compliant with ECAT, Art 4 or the EU Trafficking Directive[50].

9.94

There has also been criticism of the failure of the MSA 2015 to provide a standalone offence of exploitation: exploitation within s 3 is a necessary condition for a trafficking offence under s 2, and comprises relevant evidence when determining whether a s 1 offence has been committed, but does not amount to an offence in itself[51]. The joint select committee on the Modern Slavery Bill proposed a standalone offence of exploitation[52]. However, having been considered in an independent parliamentary inquiry into the Act in 2019, it was again rejected[53]. A further parliamentary inquiry into the Act in 2024 did not make any recommendations for further offences to be introduced[54].

9.95

It could be argued that such a standalone 'exploitation' offence is unnecessary. Given the definition of exploitation in s 3, behaviour caught by it would in many cases amount to one or more other criminal offences (including offences under the MSA 2015, s 1, various sexual offences, and secondary participation in Human Tissue Act 2004 offences). Such offences, however, may not always carry appropriate maximum penalties: sentences for Human Tissue Act offences vary up to a maximum of three years' imprisonment, which may not adequately reflect the gravity of controlling organ harvesting or egg harvesting, for example.

9.96

In addition, whilst behaviour that amounts to exploitation under the MSA 2015, s 3 may *often* amount to another offence as well, it would not always. This is particularly true of the exploitation of children or vulnerable persons, as provided for by s 3(6). Any use or attempted use of such a person to obtain services or benefits amounts to exploitation, if he has been chosen because of his vulnerability and because he would otherwise be likely to refuse. This kind of exploitation would be unlikely to amount to another offence in most cases, unless the victim could be shown to have been forced to act as he did. Nor will it amount to trafficking unless there has been movement of the victim, or amount to forced or compulsory labour unless there is a menace of penalty[55].

---

50 *CN v United Kingdom* and *CN and V v France* (App No 67724/09) (11 October 2012).

51 See P Rook and R Ward, *Rook and Ward on Sexual Offences Law and Practice* (5th edn, Thomson Reuters, 2016).

52 Joint Committee on the Draft Modern Slavery Bill, *Draft Modern Slavery Bill Report* (2013–14, HL166, HC1019).

53 Independent review of the Modern Slavery Act: final report; 22 May 2019.

54 MSA 2015 Committee, 'The Modern Slavery Act 2015: becoming world-leading again', Report published 16 October 2024.

55 Joint Committee on the Draft Modern Slavery Bill, *Draft Modern Slavery Bill Report* (2013–14, HL166, HC1019) at [13]–[16].

9.97

Because of the permutations of ways in which an offence contrary to s 2 may be committed, while we have included a specimen jury direction, it will need to be adapted depending on the elements of both s 2 and s 3 relied on by the prosecution in any given case.

Direction for the jury: human trafficking (arranging travel with a view to exploitation by threat)

9.98

To find the defendant guilty of this offence, the prosecution must make you sure of two key elements:

1. That the defendant **arranged the travel** of another person, V.
2. That he did so **with a view to V being exploited**.

Element 1: did the defendant 'arrange travel'?

9.99

First, you must be sure that D arranged V's travel.

- **'Arranges'** should be given its ordinary meaning.[56] It includes organising, planning, or directing the travel. If you are sure that D directed or planned where V was to go, then you would be sure that he 'arranged' V's travel.
- **'Travel'** in law is not limited to long journeys or crossing borders. It simply means moving from one place to another, including within a town or between different towns. In this case, if you were sure that V's movement to various locations across a particular town to supply drugs was arranged, you would be sure that 'travel' was arranged.

Element 2: was it 'with a view to exploitation'?

9.100

This second element has two parts to it. The first is about D's state of mind. The second is about the nature of the intended exploitation.

56 This example is an 'arrangement' example. In a 'facilitation' case, the jury should be directed that 'facilitate' means 'make easier'.

The defendant's state of mind

9.101

The prosecution must make you sure that D arranged the travel **intending to exploit V** himself during or after the travel[57].

The nature of the intended exploitation

9.102

'Exploitation' has a specific legal meaning. For the purposes of this case, the prosecution must make you sure that the intended exploitation was: **the use of threats designed to induce V to provide services**[58].

- First, you must be sure there was the **use of threats**. 'Threats' is an ordinary English word which needs no explanation.
- Second, you must be sure that the threat was **designed to induce** V to provide services.

Transposition

Sentencing

Principles

9.103

The offences under MSA 2015, ss 1 and 2 both carry the same maximum sentence (life imprisonment) when tried on indictment and are also triable summarily with a maximum sentence of six months[59].

57 In the case of exploitation by someone other than D ('A'), the jury needs to be directed that they must be sure that D knew or ought to have known that A was likely to exploit P (in any part of the world) during or after the travel.

58 Exploitation here is based on s 3(5), MSA 2015. Where it is based on s 1 by virtue of s 3(3), see the General directions for the jury at **9.98** above and the direction for the relevant type of s 1 offence. Bear in mind that where 'exploitation' is based on s 1 by virtue of s 3(3), s 1 offences are hierarchical, so it is likely to be unnecessary to predicate exploitation on slavery or servitude, as it will be established by forced or compulsory labour.

59 MSA 2015, s 5(1). For offences committed after 2 May 2022, where the conviction was before 30 March 2023, the maximum was 12 months. From that point the maximum reverted to 6 months until 18 November 2024 when it was again increased to 12 months (The Sentencing Act 2020 (Magistrates' Court Sentencing Powers) (Amendment) Regulations 2024). The maximum has always been 12 months where the magistrates' court was sentencing two or more either way offences.

9.104

These are Sch 19, Sentencing Act 2020 ('Sentencing Code') offences for the purposes of sections 274 and 285, Sentencing Code (required life sentence for offence carrying life sentence). For offences committed on or after 3 December 2012, these are offences listed in Part 1 of Sch 15, Sentencing Code for the purposes of ss 273 and 283, Sentencing Code (life sentence for second listed offence). These are specified offences for the purposes of ss 266 and 279 (extended sentence for certain violent, sexual or terrorism offences) of the Sentencing Code.

9.105

The Sentencing Council Guideline for slavery, servitude and forced or compulsory labour/ human trafficking ('the Sentencing Council Guideline for slavery and trafficking') is effective for all offenders aged 18 and older, who are sentenced on or after 1 October 2021, regardless of the date of the offence.

9.106

There are nine stages or 'steps' involved in the sentencing of offenders for trafficking and slavery offences: (1) determining the offence category (by reference to culpability and harm); (2) reaching a starting point and category range of sentence from the assessment of culpability and harm at step 1 and then adjusting upwards for aggravating and downwards for mitigating factors; (3) considering any factors which indicate a reduction for assistance to the prosecution; (4) reducing the sentence to reflect the effect of guilty pleas; (5) considering the 'dangerousness' provisions under ss 274 and 285 (required life sentences for offence carrying life imprisonment) or 273 and 283 (custody for life for second listed offence) or 266 and 279 of the Sentencing Code (extended sentences for certain offences); (6) considering the totality principle; (7) considering ancillary orders; (8) giving reasons for the sentence imposed; and (9) considering whether to give credit for time spent on bail.

9.107

At step 1 the court first determines the offender's level of culpability, which is divided into three categories:

- **A – High Culpability:** This includes offenders who played a leading role, had a high degree of planning, and expected substantial financial or material gain. The use or threat of significant physical or sexual violence also falls into this category.
- **B – Medium Culpability:** Offenders in this category have a significant role, involve others through coercion or reward, and expect notable financial advantage. Some planning and the use or threat of some physical or sexual violence are also factors.

- **C – Lower Culpability:** This applies to offenders who were engaged through pressure or coercion, had a limited function under direction, and had little or no expectation of financial gain. This category also includes those who have been victims of slavery or trafficking themselves.

9.108

Next, the court assesses the level of harm caused to the victim(s), which is categorised into four levels:

- **Category 1:** This is the most serious level and involves exposure of the victim(s) to a high risk of death. A Category 2 offence can be elevated to this level due to the extreme nature of the harm or the combined impact of several factors.
- **Category 2:** This category includes serious physical or psychological harm with a substantial and/or long-term effect. It also covers cases where the victim's daily life is significantly impacted long-term, or where the victim was deceived or coerced into sexual activity.
- **Category 3:** This involves some physical or psychological harm, significant financial loss to the victim(s), or exposure to a risk of serious harm.
- **Category 4:** This is the lowest level of harm and includes limited physical or psychological harm and limited financial loss.

9.109

When assessing harm, the court considers that a loss of personal autonomy is an inherent feature of these offences. It is also noted that victims may not recognise themselves as such, which should be treated with caution by the sentencers.

9.110

Following the determination of the offender's culpability and the level of harm caused in step 1, the court proceeds to step 2 to establish a starting point and a sentencing range for the offence. An offence deemed to have the highest level of culpability (A) and the most severe harm (Category 1) has a starting point of 14 years' custody, with a sentencing range of 10 to 18 years' custody. At the other end of the scale, a case with the lowest culpability (C) and the least harm (Category 4) has a starting point of 26 weeks' custody and a range from a high-level community order to 18 months' custody.

9.111

This initial starting point applies to all offenders, regardless of whether they have previous convictions or have entered a guilty plea. The court then adjusts the sentence from this starting point. An upward or downward adjustment may be necessary to account for specific details of the case, such as the presence of multiple aggravating or mitigating factors within a single category or if the case falls on the borderline between two categories. This allows the court the flexibility to arrive at a sentence that accurately reflects the particular circumstances of the offence.

9.112

Factors that increase seriousness (aggravating factors) include those set out by law, such as having relevant previous convictions, committing the offence while on bail, or demonstrating hostility towards the victim based on their race, religion, sexual orientation, or other personal characteristics. Beyond these statutory factors, the court will also consider other circumstances that increase the seriousness of the crime. This includes offending that took place over a long period, was part of a large-scale and sophisticated commercial operation, or involved a deliberate targeting of particularly vulnerable individuals. The offender's actions towards the victim are also critical; the court will view the offence as more severe if there was gratuitous degradation of the victim, if their passport or identity documents were taken, if they were physically restrained, or if they were forced to commit other criminal acts. Furthermore, any steps taken to prevent the victim from reporting the offence or an abuse of a position of trust will also be treated as aggravating factors.

9.113

Mitigating factors include an offender having no recent or relevant convictions, showing genuine remorse, or demonstrating positive character, which may result in a lesser sentence. The court also considers the offender's personal situation, such as being the sole or primary carer for dependants, suffering from a mental disorder, learning disability, or a serious physical medical condition. An offender's youth and lack of maturity can be a mitigating factor, as can a difficult or deprived background. Significantly, if the offender has been a victim of slavery or trafficking themselves in a separate context, this will be taken into account[60]. Finally, the offender's conduct during the investigation is important; cooperation with the authorities, making early admissions, and having good prospects for rehabilitation through work or education can all contribute to a reduction in the sentence.

9.114

The Sentencing Council Guideline governs sentencing for all ss 1 and 2, MSA 2015 offences.

9.115

Attorney General's Reference (R v Zhang)[61] shows how important the Sentencing Council Guideline for slavery and trafficking is– and how serious such offences are to be treated for the purpose of sentencing. The sentencing judge fell into

60 **Chapter 10** should be read in this context.
61 [2025] EWCA Crim 376; [2025] 2 Cr App R (S) 16.

'gross error when he declined to apply the guideline in relation to the MSA 2015 offences'[62]. The case involved the controlling of sex workers in prostitution for gain and their trafficking, by being directed across London and the UK for outcalls. The judge said, 'I will pay more regard to [the guideline] that appl[ies] to count 2 [the sexual offences definitive guideline]'[63]. He proceeded to impose a grossly unduly lenient sentence.

9.116

Previous sentencing authorities will generally be of no assistance to a sentencing court once a Sentencing Council guideline has effect; *see R v Thelwall*[64].

9.117

The Sentencing Council Guideline underscores that, although slavery, servitude and forced or compulsory labour are hierarchical in terms of seriousness, the sentence for servitude will not necessarily be lower than that for slavery, etc.

9.118

This approach mirrors the effect of Lord Judge CJ's remarks concerning sentences under the Coroners and Justice Act 2009, s 71, the antecedent legislation creating the offence of holding someone in slavery or servitude, or requiring them to perform forced or compulsory labour. He noted, giving the judgment of the Court, that although the three forms of this offence do fall into a hierarchy, it does not necessarily follow that the maximum sentence for servitude must always be lower than that for slavery (and so on)[65]. There must be a deterrent element to sentences, given how hard it is for victims to complain, let alone bring their treatment to the attention of the authorities, and sentences 'must also emphasise that there is no victim so vulnerable to exploitation, that he or she somehow becomes invisible or unknown to or somehow beyond the protection of the law'[66]. Section 71 of the Coroners and Justice Act 2009 was in broadly the same terms as the MSA 2015, s 1, although it should be noted that the statutory maximum penalty for that offence was 14 years: the increased maximum penalty now applicable shows that Parliament's intention is that longer sentences should be imposed[67].

9.119

Notwithstanding *R v Thelwall* (above), *R v Zielinski*[68] may assist practitioners and judges in their approach to the assessment of culpability and harm as

---

62 At [33].
63 At [20].
64 [2016] EWCA Crim 1755; [2017] Crim LR 240.
65 *A-G's Reference (Nos 2-5 of 2013) (William Connors)* [2013] EWCA Crim 324, [2013] 2 Cr App Rep (S) 71 at [8].
66 Ibid at [10].
67 *R v Joyce* [2017] EWCA Crim 337 at [26].
68 [2017] EWCA Crim 758.

defined within the guideline. Z conspired with his family to deceive vulnerable Polish citizens with no command of English into coming to the UK under the false pretence that they would secure well paid employment. Once in the UK, the offender and his family subjected the victims to appalling living conditions, issued threats, assaulted them, and forced them to work in legitimate jobs while confiscating their wages.

9.120

Z was convicted of two counts of trafficking for exploitation, contrary to s 2, MSA 2015, and one count of conspiring to compel another person to perform forced or compulsory labour, in violation of s 1. His initial sentence was 12 months in prison for the trafficking charges and four years for the forced labour charge, to be served concurrently. Additionally, a slavery and trafficking prevention order (STPO) was imposed for a duration of ten years.

9.121

During sentencing, the judge remarked that contemporary events demonstrated a growing concern over this type of crime and highlighted the necessity for sentences to serve as a deterrent. The gravity of the offending was assessed with particular reference to the following nine factors:

(i) the extent of the scheme's organisation and planning;

(ii) the use of deception from the very beginning to persuade victims to travel to the UK;

(iii) the involvement of a comparatively large number of victims;

(iv) the long duration and persistent nature of the conspiracy;

(v) the substandard quality of the accommodation that was supplied;

(vi) the specific methods employed to maintain control over the victims;

(vii) the high degree of the victims' vulnerability;

(viii) the amount of harm the offending caused, including the lasting impact on the victims who gave evidence; and

(ix) the motivation of financial gain[69].

9.122

The Court of Appeal concluded that a four-year sentence following a trial was unduly lenient and needed to be substantially raised to match the gravity of what had transpired. Consequently, the sentences for the trafficking offences were

69 At [21].

increased to two and a half years, and the sentence for forced or compulsory labour was raised to seven years, with all terms to be served concurrently.

9.123

For other earlier sentencing authorities, see the 2nd Edition of this work.

9.124

Trafficking for sexual exploitation may, all other things being equal, attract a heavier sentence than trafficking for other exploitation[70]. The Sexual Offence guidelines published by the Sentencing Council in 2014 included a guideline for sentencing the offence of trafficking people for sexual exploitation ('the 2014 trafficking for sexual offences guideline'). This offence was created by s59A of the Sexual Offences Act 2003. The MSA 2015 repealed s 59A. However, by virtue of express wording within the Sentencing Council Guideline for slavery and trafficking the 2014 trafficking for sexual offences guideline may still be of use for sentencing cases of sexual exploitation prosecuted under s 2, MSA 2015.

9.125

The Council has added explanatory guidance to the existing sentencing guideline to assist parties wishing to use the guideline for this purpose[71]. In addition, Annex A of the Sexual Offences guideline provides a list of ancillary orders that can be made when sentencing a relevant sexual offence. This Annex has been amended to include relevant orders that can be made under the MSA 2015[72].

Committing any offence with intent to commit an offence under s 2

9.126

By s 4 of MSA 2015 'a person commits an offence … if [he] commits any offence with the intention of committing an offence under section 2 (including an offence committed by aiding, abetting, counselling or procuring an offence under that section)'. Section 4 creates an offence which mirrors s 62 of the Sexual Offences Act 2003: committing an offence with intent to commit a sexual offence (including an offence of aiding, abetting, counselling

70 *A-G's Reference (Nos 37, 38 and 65 of 2010) (Khan)* [2010] EWCA Crim 2880, [2011] 2 Cr App Rep (S) 31 at [16].

71 The link on the Sentencing Council website is no longer working. The following link is to its last iteration within the Internet Archive (Wayback Machine): https://web.archive.org/web/20221129173824/https://www.sentencingcouncil.org.uk/offences/magistrates-court/item/trafficking/ (accessed 18 August 2025).

72 The trafficking for sexual offences guideline appears at p 99 of the Archived Sexual Offences: Definitive Guideline, and the Annex is at p 153, of the Sexual Offences guideline: https://www.sentencingcouncil.org.uk/wp-content/uploads/Archived-Sexual-offences-Definitive-guideline.pdf (accessed 18 August 2025).

or procuring such an offence). Section 62 criminalises those who intend to commit a sexual offence or with intent to aid or abet the commission of a sexual offence. Section 4 was introduced to ensure parity for offences of non-sexual exploitation. Its purpose was to criminalise those who, for example, provided forged or false documents to enable the trafficking. Such behaviour could also amount to an inchoate offence of attempted human trafficking, or of aiding, abetting, counselling or procuring human trafficking, or of conspiring to commit a human trafficking offence. However, s 4 provides a means for enabling trafficking to be taken into consideration as an aggravating feature of another substantive offence. This section will have application for prosecution and defence practitioners alike in striving to ensure that the full criminality of any offending is properly encompassed within the charge.

9.127

Technically, s 4 creates two offences, since there are different maximum sentences applicable: in general, the maximum is ten years, but where the offence committed is kidnapping or false imprisonment, it is life imprisonment[73]. To date, prosecutions for an offence under s 4 have been predicated on kidnapping and false imprisonment, since they are frequently how victims have been recruited or exploited.

Unlawful restriction of liberty

9.128

Three offences that share the common feature of unlawful restriction of the victim's liberty are kidnapping, false imprisonment and child abduction. These offences may arise in a slavery, servitude, forced labour or compulsory labour or trafficking context. Where the criminal offence can properly be construed as either an MSA 2015, s 1 or s 2 offence then that would be the appropriate charge.

9.129

Prosecutors must apply the Code for Crown Prosecutors when deciding which charges to bring. When a range of different charges may cover the same conduct, prosecutors must apply paragraph 6.1 of the Code. This section explains that prosecutors should select charges which reflect the seriousness and extent of the offending; give the court adequate powers to sentence and impose appropriate post-conviction orders; allow a confiscation order to be made in appropriate cases; and enable the case to be presented in a clear and simple way. The offences of kidnap and false imprisonment carry the same maximum penalty as offences under MSA 2015.

73 MSA 2015, s 5(3).

Kidnapping and false imprisonment

9.130

These two common law offences, although separate offences with distinct elements, are often considered in the same cases.

Kidnapping – elements of the offence

9.131

The elements of kidnapping are as follows:

(i) deprivation of personal liberty;

(ii) the taking or carrying away of one person by another;

(iii) by force (or threat of force) or fraud;

(iv) without the consent of the person so taken or carried away;

(v) without lawful excuse[74].

9.132

The 'taking or carrying away' need not involve the victim being taken or carried very far: about 100 yards was sufficient in *R v Wellard*[75]. The victim himself can be the driver of the vehicle which carries him away, or indeed the victim can walk the relevant journey, if he does so as a result of force or fraud[76]. However, if the defendant merely induces the victim by fraud to take a journey on which the defendant does not accompany him, then this will not amount to 'taking and carrying away' or a deprivation of liberty[77].

9.133

A lack of consent may be inferred where (for example) the victim is too young to understand what it is he is consenting to. The consent of a parent in such a situation is not relevant to kidnapping (although if there is parental consent, it may give rise to a defence of lawful excuse)[78]. If the victim initially consents to

74 These elements are largely derived from the speech of Lord Brandon of Oakbrook, with which the rest of their Lordships materially agreed, in *R v D* [1984] AC 778 at 800. Although deprivation of liberty was not one of the elements enumerated in *D*, it was mentioned, and the Court of Appeal in *R v Hendy-Freegard* [2007] EWCA Crim 1236, [2008] QB 57 at [42] confirmed that this remained a necessary element of the offence. In respect of what is item (iii) on this list, Lord Brandon referred only to force or fraud, but it was clarified in *R v Archer* [2011] EWCA Crim 2252, [2012] Crim LR 292 at [27]–[30], that this includes a threat of force.

75 (1978) 67 Cr App Rep 364 at 367.

76 *R v Archer* [2011] EWCA Crim 2252, [2012] Crim LR 292 (victim drove himself and the defendant); *R v Wellard* (1978) 67 Cr App Rep 364 (victim walked with the defendant).

77 *R v Hendy-Freegard* [2007] EWCA Crim 1236, [2008] QB 57 at [58].

78 *R v D* [1984] AC 778 at 806.

the taking or carrying away, but that consent is later withdrawn, the offence is committed using force to maintain the kidnapping[79]. However, the requirement of force, threat of force, or fraud remains even where the victim is a child, and it is not hard to imagine cases in which force, threat or fraud may not be needed to induce a child (or an adult with impaired development) to go with the defendant[80]. In such cases the offence would not be made out, although a child abduction offence might be.

9.134

There is authority that a 'lawful excuse' must amount to necessity to be sufficient for a defence[81]. However, this decision has been rightly criticised as too restrictive (for example, criminalising the father who carries his child away after a visit to a grandmother's house)[82], and it seems unlikely it would be followed.

9.135

Both kidnapping and false imprisonment are described in the cases as offences of recklessness[83].

False imprisonment – elements of the offence

9.136

False imprisonment 'consists in the unlawful and intentional or reckless restraint of a victim's freedom of movement from a particular place. It is unlawful detention which stops the victim moving away as he would wish to move'[84]. This restraint may be physical but may also be by deliberate intimidation[85]. Intimidation may not be required, if the victim is compelled to remain[86].

9.137

The mens rea of false imprisonment is intention or reckless restraint of the victim's freedom of movement from a particular place[87]. The defendant's belief

79 *R v Lewis* (1993) 14 Cr App Rep (S) 744. This decision seems dubious – the different elements of the offence would appear not to coincide if the taking or carrying away occurs when there is consent. *R v Nnamdi* [2005] EWCA Crim 74 supports the view that they do need to coincide. In such circumstances it may be that false imprisonment is a more realistic charge.

80 *Re HM (vulnerable adult) (abduction)* [2010] EWHC 870 (Fam), [2010] 2 FLR 1057 at [60].

81 *R v Henman* [1987] Crim LR 333.

82 See the commentary in [1987] Crim LR 333.

83 *R v Hutchins* [1988] Crim LR 379.

84 *R v Rahman* (1985) 81 Cr App Rep 349 at 353–354.

85 *R v James* [1997] 34 LS Gaz R 27.

86 This would appear to be the effect of *Hunter v Johnson* (1884) 13 QBD 225, where it was unlawful for a school to detain a boy outside school hours, with no suggestion of violence or intimidation. Although it is not expressly described to be a case of false imprisonment, that is the logical inference. See also *R v Motroc (Ionut Viorel)*, WL 03083561 (2019) – false imprisonment need not be physical.

87 *R v Hutchins* [1988] Crim LR 379.

that he is acting in the victim's best interests does not amount to a defence, even if accepted[88].

Sentence

9.138

Both offences are triable only on indictment, and the maximum sentence is life imprisonment[89]. These are Schedule 19 offences for the purposes of sections 274 and 285 of the Sentencing Code (required life sentence for offence carrying life sentence). These are specified offences listed in part 1 of Schedule 18 for the purposes of ss 266 and 279 (extended sentence for certain violent, sexual or terrorism offences) of the Sentencing Code but automatic life sentences for second offences do not apply[90]. A Sentencing Council Guideline for kidnapping and false imprisonment came into effect for all offenders aged 18 and older, who are sentenced on or after 1 April 2025, regardless of the date of the offence ('the Sentencing Council kidnap guideline').

9.139

The Sentencing Council kidnap guideline requires the Crown Court to follow a clear, multi-step process to determine the appropriate sentence. Here is a summary of those steps:

Step 1: Determining the offence category

9.140

The first step is to assess the seriousness of the offence by considering the offender's culpability and the harm caused.

- Culpability is ranked as High (A), Medium (B), or Lower (C).
  - High culpability involves factors like prolonged detention, sophisticated planning, targeting of vulnerable victims, use of highly dangerous weapons, or torture.
  - Medium culpability includes the use of significant force or any weapon not in the high category and a planned offence.
  - Lower culpability involves limited force or planning, coercion of the offender, or substantially reduced responsibility due to a mental disorder.

88 Eg *R v Saker* [2011] EWCA Crim 1196, [2012] 1 Cr App Rep (S) 87.

89 Confirmed in respect of false imprisonment by *R v Szczerba* [2002] EWCA Crim 440, [2002] 2 Cr App Rep (S) 86 at [15]–[19].

90 False imprisonment and kidnapping do not feature in Sch 15, Sentencing Code.

- Harm is assessed in three categories.
  - Category 1 is for cases with very serious psychological harm or physical injury to the victim.
  - Category 2 involves serious psychological harm, distress, injury, or pain.
  - Category 3 covers all other cases.

9.141

The guideline acknowledges that a detrimental impact is inherent in all cases of kidnap and false imprisonment; therefore, the court's task is to assess the harm that arises *over and above* this inherent level. This assessment results in placing the offence into one of three harm categories.

Step 2: Starting point and category range

9.142

After determining the culpability and harm categories, the court uses a grid to find the sentencing starting point and range. For example, a high culpability (A) and high harm (Category 1) case has a starting point of 11 years' custody, within a range of 8 to 16 years. The court can then adjust the sentence within this range, considering any aggravating and mitigating factors.

9.143

Aggravating factors include statutory aggravating factors: any previous convictions, where the court must consider not just their existence, but their nature, relevance to the current offence, and the time that has elapsed since; whether the offence was committed whilst on bail; whether (for kidnap only)[91] the offence was committed against an emergency worker acting in their capacity as such (this is a significant aggravating factor, reflecting a clear public policy interest in protecting public servants); and other aggravating factors: offence committed in a domestic abuse context, particularly where there is a history of violence or abuse towards the victim; the presence of children during the offence; particularly vulnerable victim (and this vulnerability was not already accounted for at step 1); holding a victim in an isolated location; humiliation or degrading treatment; the commission of the offence for financial gain; part of a group action; committed in the context of other criminal activity; abuse of a position of trust or a dominant position over the victim; being under the influence of alcohol or drugs; committing the offence while on licence or while subject to a court order; and any attempt wrongly to place blame on others.

91 See s 67 of the Sentencing Code.

9.144

Mitigating factors include the offender being in a lesser or subordinate role or acting under the direction of others; co-operation with the investigation or early admissions; a demonstration of remorse; an absence of previous convictions (or none that are recent or relevant); evidence of positive character or exemplary conduct; a difficult or deprived background; specific life events like pregnancy, childbirth, and post-natal care; whether the offender is a sole or primary carer for dependent relatives; the offender's age and/or lack of maturity, particularly for those in the 18–25 age bracket; presence of a mental disorder or learning disability (where not already a determinative factor in step 1); a physical disability or serious medical condition; prospects of or engagement in work, training, or education; a demonstrated determination to address addiction or offending behaviour.

Step 3: Reduction for assistance to the prosecution

9.145

The court considers if a sentence reduction is warranted for any assistance the offender has given to the police or prosecutors.

Step 4: Reduction for guilty pleas

9.146

The sentence can be reduced to reflect the stage at which a guilty plea was entered.

Step 5: Dangerousness

9.147

The court must assess whether the offender is 'dangerous,' which could lead to a life sentence or an extended sentence to protect the public.

Step 6: Totality principle

9.148

If the offender is being sentenced for multiple crimes, the court must ensure the total sentence is just and proportionate to the overall offending.

Step 7: Compensation and ancillary orders

9.149

The court must consider making additional orders, such as a compensation order for the victim or a sexual harm prevention order.

Step 8: Reasons

9.150

The court is required to give reasons for the sentence it imposes and explain its effect.

Step 9: Consideration for time spent on bail

9.151

Finally, the court must consider giving credit for any time the offender has spent on bail under a tagged curfew.

9.152

As set out above, previous sentencing authorities will generally be of no assistance to a sentencing court once a Sentencing Council guideline has effect; *see R v Thelwall.*

Child abduction

9.153

As mentioned above, an offence under the Child Abduction Act 1984, s 2 might be used in place of a kidnapping charge, especially where the element of force, threat or fraud is absent. Section 2(1) is in the following terms:

> 'Subject to subsection (3) below, a person, other than one mentioned in subsection (2) below commits an offence if, without lawful authority or reasonable excuse, he takes or detains a child under the age of sixteen—
>
> (a) so as to remove him from the lawful control of any person having lawful control of the child; or
>
> (b) so as to keep him out of the lawful control of any person entitled to lawful control of the child.'

9.154

Broadly speaking, the persons mentioned in s 2(2), who cannot be guilty of this offence, are parents and guardians. Section 2(3) provides defences which are discussed below.

9.155

There are two ways of committing the offence, as set out in s 2(1)(a) and (b), and an offence under subsection (1)(a) is not committed by an unlawful taking or detention after the victim has already been removed from the lawful control of, for example, his parents[92].

9.156

In s 3(a) of the Child Abduction Act 1984, 'taking' is defined broadly: 'a person shall be regarded as taking a child if he causes or induces the child to accompany him or any other person or causes the child to be taken'. Section 3(c) provides a similarly broad definition of 'detaining'. The consent of the child is irrelevant to the offence – even if one cause of the child being removed from or kept out of the lawful control of the relevant person is the child's own free choice, the offence will still be committed if the defendant's actions are an effective cause of the child accompanying him[93].

9.157

The taking or detention of the child must be intentional or reckless – but it is not part of the offence to prove that the defendant knew that by doing so he was removing or keeping the child from the lawful control of someone else. However, in some cases, a lack of such knowledge might be linked to a reasonable excuse[94]. The burden of proving that there was no lawful authority or reasonable excuse is on the Crown[95]. What can amount to a 'reasonable excuse' is not defined by statute. At present there is no restriction imposed on the defence by case law. Case law concerning 'reasonable excuse' in other contexts is indicative of the likely scope of the defence but presently there is scope for the boundaries to be tested by the courts. There are three defences under the Child Abduction Act 1984, s 2(3), two of which (the defendant being, or reasonably believing that he is, the father of a child whose parents were not married at the time of birth) are unlikely to be relevant in trafficking or slavery cases. However, the third is provided for through s 2(3)(b): it is a defence for a defendant to prove that he believed the child to be 16 or over. This belief need not be reasonable, if it is honestly held[96]. Thus, in the context of abduction, if a

92 *Foster v DPP* [2004] EWHC 2955 (Admin), [2005] 1 WLR 1400.
93 *R v A (child abduction)* [2000] 1 Cr App Rep 418 at 422–424.
94 *Foster v DPP* [2004] EWHC 2955 (Admin), [2005] 1 WLR 1400 at [27].
95 *R v Berry* [1996] 2 Cr App Rep 226 at 229.
96 *R v Heys* [2011] EWCA Crim 2112 at [6].

defendant believed the victim was 16 or over then conduct sufficient to amount to kidnapping is required before the defendant's behaviour is criminalised. No offence is therefore established if force or fraud sufficient for a kidnapping has not been proved, and a belief that the victim is 16 or over can be proved by the defendant.

Sentence

9.158

The offence is triable either way, with a maximum sentence of seven years' imprisonment if tried on indictment, and six months' imprisonment if tried summarily[97]. It has been noted that the disparity between this and the maximum life sentence for kidnapping seems illogical, and that in the worst cases of child abduction the maximum sentence may be too low[98]. Although the case of *R v RH* sets out a detailed approach to sentencing child abduction cases in general, akin to a full sentencing guideline[99], little guidance is available for sentencing in cases with slavery or trafficking elements. In such cases more assistance may be gained from the cases already referred to in relation to other offences, with suitable adjustment made for: (a) the increased seriousness of an offence committed against a child; but also (b) the absence of features such as force or fraud.

Immigration offences

9.159

Trafficking can go hand in glove with breaches of immigration law, albeit (as set out above) trafficking does not require a crossing of national borders but simply movement from one location to another for the purposes of exploitation. Immigration offences may be apposite where trafficking occurs from outside the United Kingdom and in certain other circumstances where defendants' actions engage with immigration law. Immigration crime is a minefield. Those prosecuting and defending in immigration crime would be well advised to read the judgment in *R v Boateng*[100]. This case is instructive, it shows the various ways in which mistakes can be made by a prosecutor in indicting immigration offences, as well as ways in which mistakes can be made by defence representatives.

97 Child Abduction Act 1984, s 4(1).
98 *R v Kayani* [2011] EWCA Crim 2871, [2012] 2 All ER 641 at [5] and [16].
99 *R v RH* [2016] EWCA Crim 1754, [2017] 4 WLR 81 especially [7]–[14].
100 [2016] EWCA Crim 57, [2016] 2 Cr App Rep 43.

9.160

The offence of primary importance is s 25 of the Immigration Act 1971, which sets out that:

'(1) A person commits an offence if he—

(a) does an act which facilitates the commission of a breach or attempted breach of immigration law by an individual who is not a national of the United Kingdom,

(b) knows or has reasonable cause for believing that the act facilitates the commission of a breach or attempted breach of immigration law by the individual, and

(c) knows or has reasonable cause for believing that the individual is not a national of the United Kingdom.

(2) In subsection (1) *'immigration law'* means a law which has effect in a member State or the United Kingdom and which controls, in respect of some or all persons who are not nationals of the State or, as the case may be, of the United Kingdom, entitlement to—

(a) enter or arrive in the State or the United Kingdom,

(b) transit across the State or the United Kingdom, or

(c) be in the State or the United Kingdom.'

9.161

It is notable that this section as originally enacted, and in force until as recently as 2003, was concerned with securing or facilitating entry into the UK of illegal entrants, and related matters. The 'immigration law' the breach of which is facilitated must be one which controls entitlement of non-nationals to enter, transit across, be in the state[101] and, since 28 June 2022, arrive in the state[102], so it does not include, for example, laws which create document offences[103]. The breach which the defendant facilitates need not actually be completed by the third party, nor does it need to amount to an offence[104].

---

101 Immigration Act 1971, s 25(2).

102 The Nationality and Borders Act 2022 amended s 25 to cause unlawful arrival into the UK to be a breach of an immigration law. This amendment was aimed primarily at 'small boat' crossings, where arriving at a UK port with an immigration hub or via UK Border Agency interdiction of a small boat would constitute 'arrival', but not 'entry', into the UK; see *R v Bani* [2021] EWCA Crim 1958. The amendment is also of wider application. The 2022 Act also made it a specific offence (s24(D1) Immigration Act 1971) for 'visa nationals' to arrive in the United Kingdom without an entry clearance. Those who arrange this commit the facilitation offence.

103 *R v Kapoor* [2012] EWCA Crim 435, [2012] 2 All ER 1205 at [36].

104 *R v Javaherifard* [2005] EWCA Crim 3231 at [37] and [44].

9.162

There was doubt over whether this offence required that the individual who breached the relevant immigration law (usually the person who entered the UK unlawfully), as well as the facilitator (the person arranging the travel and breach of immigration law) needed to have committed a criminal offence in order for the facilitator to be guilty of an offence under s 25. It was possible to interpret *R v Kaile*[105] so as to infer that both individuals had to commit an offence before the facilitator could be guilty of an offence. However, this has been clarified in later cases: on the facts of *Kaile* criminality by the third party was necessary, since the prosecution case was expressly that the breach facilitated was an offence (including a component of deception committed by the individual) under the Immigration Act 1971, s 24A or 26. However, if the defendant is alleged to have facilitated some other breach, and such a breach (if considered in isolation) can occur without dishonesty on the part of the third party, then the offence under s 25 does not require such dishonesty either[106].

9.163

As a matter of good practice, an indictment for a s 25 offence should specify which immigration law the defendant is said to have breached. The breach will usually be founded on the Immigration Act 1971, s 1 and/or 3, the sections providing the general provisions for regulation and control of being in and entry and stay within the UK[107]. However, a failure to particularise the breach within the indictment will not necessarily be fatal, especially if it is expressly set out in the prosecution's opening[108]. Defence practitioners should therefore be ready to request further particulars if it is not clear which immigration law is said to have been breached/targeted for breach: a lack of such a request has

---

105 [2009] EWCA Crim 2868 at [16].

106 *R v Boateng* [2016] EWCA Crim 57 at [27]. Note: *Boateng* concerned facilitating the entry of a third party without leave, when leave was required. In that case the particulars of the illegal entry in a s 25 offence should have been framed by reference to s 3 of the Immigration Act 1971 (the general prohibition on entry without leave). What of a deceptive entrant (someone gaining leave by deception) when the person whose entry is facilitated is not dishonest himself (eg a child)? It is arguable in such a case that there is no breach of s 3, because leave has been obtained (albeit by deception); so the particulars of the illegal entry in a s 25 offence should not be framed by reference to s 3. On the other hand, the entry into the UK was undoubtedly illegal. The definition of 'illegal entrant' (in the Immigration Act 1971, s 33(1) as amended by the Asylum and Immigration Act 1996], Sch 2, para 4(1)) follows: 'illegal entrant … means a person … entering or seeking to enter [or who has entered the UK] by means which include deception by another person'. Rather than particularising the breach of immigration law by reference to s 3, it is suggested that the breach should be framed by reference to s 33(1). Alternatively, when prosecuting such a case, best practice may well be to invite the Secretary of State to review the grant of leave on the basis that it was obtained by deception with a view to revoking or curtailing leave. In those circumstances, the breach could be framed by reference to s 3.

107 The following wording for particularising a breach of immigration law within the particulars of offence is often appropriate: '… namely the general principles regulating being in the United Kingdom under section 1 of the Immigration Act 1971, and the general provision for the regulation and control of immigration under section 3 of the said Act …'

108 *R v Dhall* [2013] EWCA Crim 1610 at [15].

been held to be relevant when holding that an absence of particulars was not a fatal flaw[109].

9.164

It is possible to facilitate entry by actions occurring immediately after entry has occurred[110]. Facilitating an illegal entrant to 'be' in the UK may cause a breach of immigration law without that breach itself constituting an offence. The s 25 offence is only committed if, with the requisite guilty knowledge, the acts facilitate the commission of a breach of immigration law controlling, in this instance, 'being in the State': that is, being unlawfully in the UK. If an individual provides legal advice about how lawfully and honestly to regularise the stay of someone known to be an illegal entrant, no offence arises: those acts do not facilitate the commission of a breach of immigration law through continued illegal presence; they do the opposite. If someone provides food, money or accommodation to an illegal entrant, knowing or having reasonable cause for believing that such acts facilitate him being in the country as an illegal entrant, he would be guilty of an offence. If food, money or accommodation is supplied to someone known to the provider to be an illegal immigrant, but is not supplied with the knowledge that it will assist his presence as an illegal entrant but instead is supplied knowing that it will assist him simply as a human being, eg to avoid degradation or destitution, there would be no offence. The provision of state support and other statutory benefits is made under the protection of statutory provision if no other defence is available, but it is difficult to see how that would assist someone to remain as an illegal entrant, as opposed to remain while seeking to regularise his stay[111]. Section 25 charges are more likely to be preferred (either alone or as a lesser alternative to a trafficking charge) where evidence of exploitation is less obvious, and thus such a defence more plausible.

Practitioners should be aware of the new offences created by the Border Security, Asylum and Immigration Act 2025 that came into force on 5 January 2026[112]. These relate to the handling and supplying of articles, and collecting information for use in immigration crime[113] (which are similar to the like offences under terrorism legislation) as well as putting the life or limb of another in danger on a 'small boat' crossing[114].

109 Ibid.

110 *R v Javaherifard* [2005] EWCA Crim 3231 at [29]. Although this was a decision on s 25 after it had been amended to (so far as is relevant) its current form, it appears the decision owed a certain amount to the pre-2003 wording (which created offences such as 'facilitating … the entry into the United Kingdom of … an illegal immigrant'). Nonetheless, the principle that acts can be facilitated even after they have been completed, as long as it is sufficiently soon after, could still apply.

111 Ibid at [50].

112 Reg 2 The Border Security, Asylum and Immigration Act 2025 (Commencement No. 1) Regulations 2025.

113 Sections 13, 14 and 16 Border Security, Asylum and Immigration Act 2025.

114 Sections 21 Border Security, Asylum and Immigration Act 2025.

Sentence

9.165

Offences under s 25 are triable either way, with the maximum penalty on indictment being life imprisonment[115]. General guidance on aggravating factors was given in *R v Le, R v Stark* and *AG Ref (Nos 49 & 50 of 2015)*[116]. Such factors included committing the offence for financial gain, duration of the offending when it was not a single incident, and the degree of planning and sophistication[117]. The features of trafficking in these cases were not considered. Of note, aggravating factors have not to date considered the harm, or risk of harm to illegal migrants who are being facilitated, where abuse of vulnerability is no doubt a significant feature. *Le and Stark* was also decided at a time when the maximum sentence for this offence was seven years' imprisonment, so the specific sentences discussed would no longer be relevant. Especially given the increase in the maximum sentence to life imprisonment, sentences in double figures will often be appropriate.

9.166

In *Attorney General's Reference (No 6 of 2004); R v Plakici*[118] the sentence for the illegal entry element of the offending was five years' imprisonment (out of a total of 23 years for criminality which included the commission of serious sexual offences). The court broadly followed the approach of *Le and Stark*, a key sentencing authority for offences of facilitating illegal entry. *Le and Stark* was decided when the maximum sentence was ten years' imprisonment. A sentence for such an offence today would be higher. Of note, in this case the court also considered the sentencing for the offence of kidnapping in the context of trafficking the victims. Ten years' imprisonment was imposed. The defendant had employed between 50 and 75 security guards who were not entitled to be in the country, and had taken advantage of their status to exploit them, paying wages of around £3 per hour. On occasion the defendant required them to work for 24 hours or more. He had forged documents for the workers and made substantial profits over a five-year period. A sentence of four-and-a-half years' imprisonment was increased to eight years'[119].

9.167

There is no Sentencing Guideline currently. Six new draft sentencing guidelines for offenders convicted of immigration offences in England and Wales were

---

115 This was 14 years' imprisonment prior to 28 June 2022 (and after 10 February 2003).
116 [2015] EWCA Crim 1402, [2016] 1 Cr App R(S) 4.
117 [1999] 1 Cr App Rep (S) 422, especially 425.
118 [2004] EWCA Crim 1275, [2005] 1 Cr App Rep (S) 19.
119 *A-G's Reference No 28 of 2014 (R v Okoh)* [2014] EWCA Crim 1723. The conviction was not appealed in this case. It prima facie might have been the subject of an appeal against conviction; however, the defendant had assisted the workers to avoid prohibitions on working in the UK, but not to breach an 'immigration law' as defined by the Act (see para **4.55** above).

published for consultation by the Sentencing Council on 20 March 2024 following changes to the legislation. Although the consultation period closed on 12 June 2024, there is no indication as to when the final guideline will be published.

Offences related to the 'use' of victims of slavery and trafficking

9.168

There are a wide range of purposes for which victims are trafficked, or held in conditions of slavery, servitude, or forced or compulsory labour. Many such purposes are themselves illegal, so even where trafficking or restriction of liberty are not proved, other offences will often arise.

Sexual exploitation

9.169

Perhaps the most widely recognised purpose for trafficking, is that of sexual exploitation, particularly forced prostitution. Several offences may be relevant here: causing or inciting prostitution for gain under the SOA 2003, s 52, and controlling prostitution for gain under s 53. Each carries a maximum penalty of seven years' imprisonment when tried on indictment and both are lifestyle offences for the purposes of the Proceeds of Crime Act 2002. The sexual offences sentencing guideline applies.

9.170

For the s 52 offence to be committed, the defendant must 'intentionally cause or incite another person to become a prostitute'. An element of the offence is that the complainant has not acted as a prostitute before, and also that the defendant knew this[120]. Where, therefore, a woman who worked as a prostitute in her home country is brought to the UK to do the same, there would be a complete defence where trafficking is based on s 52. However, where the sexual services are controlled, it may be relevant for the offence under s 53.

9.171

'Controlling' prostitution under the SOA 2003, s 53 does not require force or coercion, only direction[121]. Both offences include a requirement that the defendant acts 'for or in the expectation of gain for himself or a third

120 *R v Ubolcharoen* [2009] EWCA Crim 3263 at [6].
121 *R v Massey* [2007] EWCA Crim 2664, [2008] 2 All ER 969.

person'[122]. The fact that the gain may not be for defendants themselves highlights that care needs to be taken to consider whether those who are forced into supervisory roles after having been the victims of trafficking themselves should be criminalised (see *R v LM*[123] and *R v EK*[124]). In the latter case the defendant was prosecuted but her culpability was reduced because of her status as a VOT. See also *Attorney General's Reference (Nos 129 and 132 of 2006); R v. Delgado-Fernandez, Zammit and Thi*[125], where the victims were experienced prostitutes before they were trafficked into the UK and had apparently consented to their prostitution: where their services were controlled it was relevant to culpability of the defendant(s) at sentence, and did not preclude a prosecution for trafficking for sexual exploitation[126].

9.172

Where the complainants are children, offences under the SOA 2003, ss 48, 49 and 50 may be charged – these cover causing or inciting sexual exploitation of a child; controlling it; and arranging or facilitating it, respectively. All are triable either way, with a 14-year maximum sentence on indictment. The sexual offences guideline applies.

9.173

'Sexual exploitation' in the context of ss 48, 49 and 50 of SOA 2003 only covers prostitution and the creation of indecent images[127]. In each case, unless the complainant is under 13, it is a defence if the defendant reasonably believed the complainant was 18 – this may often be relevant in cases where the complainant is not previously known to the defendant, perhaps having been picked up off the street, whether in the UK or abroad.

9.174

Those whose sole involvement is as customers who are paying for the services of exploited (adult) prostitutes are likely to be guilty of the strict liability offence under SOA 2003, s 53A, 'paying for sexual services of a prostitute subjected to force etc.', punishable with a level 3 fine. Those who pay for sex from children will commit one of a number of offences under SOA 2003, s 47, which attract higher penalties, up to and including life imprisonment.

---

122 SOA 2003, ss 52(1)(b) and 53(1)(b).

123 [2010] EWCA Crim 2327, [2011] 1 Cr App Rep 135.

124 [2018] EWCA Crim 2961.

125 [2007] EWCA Crim 762.

126 See the commentary above on s 3(3), which shows why consent is irrelevant if the exploitation is for controlling the activities of prostitution for gain.

127 SOA 2003, s 51(2).

Drug offences

9.175

A number of cases have shown that forced or compulsory labour is often used in the production of cannabis and other drugs. It may be difficult to show that those in control of such operations have committed an offence under the Misuse of Drugs Act 1971, s 4(2)(a) (producing a controlled drug); they are more likely to be concerned in the production (under the Misuse of Drugs Act 1971, s 4(2)(b)), or to have conspired with the worker or workers to commit a s 4(2)(a) offence, or an offence of cultivation of cannabis under s 6.

9.176

The maximum sentence varies depending on the class of drug, for cannabis cultivation it is 14 years' imprisonment. These offences are covered by the drug offences sentencing guideline. The defence of lack of knowledge, suspicion or reason to suspect (under the Misuse of Drugs Act 1971, s 28) is likely to be most encountered.

9.177

In recent years, offences of supplying class A drugs using children and vulnerable adults in county lines cases have been successfully prosecuted under MSA 2015 where the evidence proves the elements of trafficking and exploitation. In the case of *R v Karemera*[128], the Court confirmed that prosecution for trafficking in order to secure services from children or vulnerable adults – now under s 3(6) – does not depend upon the ability to call the individual said to have been exploited or the target of exploitation. Where evidence does not support an offence under s 2 of MSA 2015, other offences under the Misuse of Drugs Act 1971, including those dealing with possession and supply of class A drugs under ss 4(3) and 5(3) of the 1971 Act, may be appropriate depending on the criminality or culpability of the suspect in the context of his trafficking (see Chapter 5). These offences carry a sentence up to life imprisonment[129].

Worker exploitation

9.178

A gangmaster is a person who supplies a worker to do agricultural work, gathering shellfish, or the processing and packaging of produce from such

128 [2018] EWCA Crim 1432.
129 See further *R v Zakaria Mohammed* [2019] EWCA Crim 1881.

work[130]. A gangmaster must be licensed, pursuant to the Gangmasters (Licensing) Act 2004, s 6. Acting as a gangmaster without a licence or having false documents to make others believe one is licensed, is punishable with up to ten years' imprisonment[131]. This is clearly a very substantial penalty for an offence which is expressed as being concerned with regulatory failings: the true mischief at which it is aimed is the exploitation of workers, which the licensing scheme seeks to prevent.

9.179

A list of factors relevant to sentencing for a s 6 offence, adapted from those set out in the context of trafficking offences, was provided by the Court of Appeal in *R v Morkunas*[132]. In that case the defendant had systematically exploited a significant number of workers over three years, reinforcing economic exploitation with threats and in some cases the use of violence (including one count of assault occasioning actual bodily harm ('ABH') of which he was convicted), and had profited to the tune of around £100,000[133]. A sentence of seven years' imprisonment was imposed for the Gangmasters (Licensing) Act 2004 offence, after a 12.5% discount for plea with concurrent sentences for the other offences. This sentence was not interfered with (although the court commented that the judge could have taken a lower starting point for the Gangmasters (Licensing) Act 2004 offence and made the sentence for the ABH offence consecutive). This offending would have fallen within the s 1 MSA 2015 paradigm had they been indicted after 31 July 2015. The list of factors will be relevant in a sentence for s 1.

9.180

A gangmaster, whether licensed or not, can be in a position where he is expected to safeguard, or to not act against, the financial interests of his workers, particularly if he collects wages on their behalf. If he makes unwarranted deductions from those wages, an offence of fraud by abuse of position (Fraud Act 2006, s 4) may be committed. This does not mean that all exploitative financial arrangements will amount to fraud: for example, the charging of excessive rents for accommodation that the worker is required to take was discussed and not considered to be sufficient[134].

130 Gangmasters (Licensing) Act 2004, ss 3 and 4.

131 Gangmasters (Licensing) Act 2004, s 12.

132 [2014] EWCA Crim 2750 at [51]. See paras **3.36** and **4.37** for the list of factors for trafficking offences.

133 Ibid at [59]–[61].

134 *R v Valujevs* [2014] EWCA Crim 2888, [2015] QB 745. It may be that other fraud offences could apply – for example, fraud by false representation where a trafficking victim is promised a good life at his destination – but of course the gain or loss involved in a fraud must be in money or property, which will often not apply.

9.181

An offence of failing to pay the national minimum wage is punishable only by way of a fine[135]. It may therefore be an attractive option for defendants to offer as an alternative plea; prosecutors may not accept it where the evidence of wider exploitation is sufficient. Prosecutors should only accept a defendant's plea if the court is able to pass a sentence that matches the seriousness of the offending, particularly where there are aggravating features; if it enables the court to make a confiscation order in appropriate cases; and it provides the court with adequate powers to impose other ancillary orders[136].

Other offences

9.182

There is potential for other offences to be disclosed by complainants that have been perpetrated in order to achieve the trafficking/ exploitation, with violence and dishonesty predominating. In circumstances where a range of different charges may be available, prosecutors should select charges which reflect the seriousness and extent of the offending, give the court adequate powers to sentence and impose appropriate post-conviction orders, allow a confiscation order to be made in appropriate cases and enable the case to be presented in a clear and simple way[137]. If the offences of violence and dishonesty feature materially in the context of trafficking offending, it might be appropriate to indict them separately. Guidance issued to prosecutors specifies that given the seriousness of MSA charges, even where other offences are available, modern slavery charges are most likely to require prosecution:

> 'Given the seriousness of these charges, even where other offences are available, modern slavery charges are most likely to require prosecution. Applying section 6 of the Code for Crown Prosecutors, it is highly likely that these will reflect the seriousness and extent of the offending. The selection of modern slavery charges also means that the court is enabled to impose appropriate ancillary orders including Slavery and Trafficking Reparation Orders and Slavery and Trafficking Prevention Orders (see below). Additional serious charges should also be considered, particularly where they may attract a consecutive sentence: most obviously, where serious offences against the person, sexual offences or drug offences have been committed (in particular in county lines offending)'[138].

135 National Minimum Wage Act 1998, s 31.

136 Paragraph 9 of the Code for Crown Prosecutors.

137 Paragraph 6 of the Code for Crown Prosecutors.

138 Modern Slavery and human trafficking: offences and defences, including the section 45 defence – Part 1 (updated 22 July 2025): https://www.cps.gov.uk/legal-guidance/modern-slavery-and-human-trafficking-offences-and-defences-including-section-45 (accessed 18 August 2025).

9.183

Nearly all cases of exploitation are motivated by greed and financial gain and this should be reflected in the charges – money laundering offences founded on ss 327, 328 and/or 329 of the Proceeds of Crime Act 2002 may be appropriate. Criminal property constitutes the benefit from criminal conduct or represents such a benefit (in whole or part and whether directly or indirectly) where the alleged offender knows or suspects that it constitutes or represents such a benefit[139]. Property can include money, all forms of property or real estate and or things in action and or other intangible or incorporeal property. The definition of criminal property means there is no distinction between the proceeds of the defendant's own crimes and of crimes committed by others. Thus, laundering one's own proceeds is just as much money laundering as laundering someone else's. Sections 327, 328 and 329 are either way offences with a maximum sentence of 14 years' imprisonment or a fine or both.

9.184

Section 327 of the Proceeds of Crime Act 2002 makes concealing, disguising, converting, transferring or removing criminal property from England and Wales an offence.

9.185

Section 328 of the Proceeds of Crime Act 2002 makes it an offence to enter into or become concerned in an arrangement which a person knows or suspects facilitates (by whatever means) the acquisition, retention, use or control of criminal property by or on behalf of another person. This offence potentially includes a large range of involvement in money laundering offences frequently at the layering and integration stage. It will often be apt for the prosecution of those who launder on behalf of others. This offence can encompass persons who work in financial or credit institutions, accountants etc, who in the course of their work facilitate money laundering by or on behalf of other persons.

9.186

Section 329 of the Proceeds of Crime Act 2002 criminalises the acquisition, use and possession of criminal property. This offence can be committed if the accused uses criminal property or passively possesses criminal property. Unlike ss 327 and 328, it does not attract the lifestyle provisions for the purposes of confiscation.

139 Section 340(3).

Orders on conviction

Confiscation

9.187

Any offence where the defendant benefits can be the subject of confiscation proceedings under the Proceeds of Crime Act 2002; this is likely to apply to most slavery and human trafficking cases. A number of the offences discussed above are 'lifestyle offences', listed in the Proceeds of Crime Act 2002, Sch 2, and therefore give rise to the various statutory assumptions in s 10. Offences under the MSA 2015, ss 1 and 2, the Immigration Act 1971, s 25, the SOA 2003, ss 48–50, 52 and 53, and the Misuse of Drugs Act 1971, s 4(2), are all 'lifestyle offences'. It should be noted that the assumptions also apply to any offence which forms part of a course of criminal activity, or is committed over a period of at least six months (provided that the defendant has benefited from it in the sum of at least £5,000)[140].

9.188

Where a confiscation order is made, a court may also impose a slavery and trafficking reparation order under s 8 of the MSA 2015. These orders can only be made against defendants convicted of s 1, 2 or 4 of the MSA 2015. Such an order requires the defendant to pay compensation to the victim for any harm resulting from the offence. Whether or not a confiscation order is made, compensation orders are also available under ss 133–135 of the Sentencing Act 2020.

Forfeiture

9.189

Various forfeiture provisions may be relevant. Under the MSA 2015, s 11, a vehicle used for a trafficking offence under s 2 may be forfeited. The Immigration Act 1971, s 25C provides for a similar power in relation to offences contrary to s 25 of that Act. Section 27 of the Misuse of Drugs Act 1971 provides a wider power, allowing 'anything shown to the satisfaction of the court to relate to the offence' to be forfeited where an offence under that Act has been committed. In all cases, the general power under the Sentencing Code, ss 152–255 allows property in the possession or control of the defendant at the time of his arrest, and used or intended to be used for committing or facilitating any offence, to be taken as part of a deprivation order. Such forfeiture orders are part of the punishment of the offender, so should be taken into account when considering

140 Proceeds of Crime Act 2002, s 75(2).

totality[141]. When defending it is worth bearing in mind that if an asset could form part of a defendant's recoverable amount in confiscation proceedings, by agreeing that they can be deprived of it under s 143, the defendant will be at risk of the state recovering that money twice.

Civil orders

9.190

On or after conviction for an offence listed in the MSA 2015, Sch 1 (which broadly covers offences under the MSA 2015, the predecessors to those offences, and inchoate versions of those offences), the court can impose a 'slavery and trafficking prevention order' ('STPO') (see ss 14–17). Such orders can impose prohibitions on the defendant doing anything described in the order, if necessary, to protect others from harm because of further slavery or trafficking offences. The prohibitions are confined to restricting the activities of each defendant tailored to the role they have played. Examples of possible prohibitions are given in the Explanatory Notes to the Act, including participating in particular kinds of business, acting as a gangmaster, visiting particular places, restricting contact with specified individuals, transporting others in a vehicle, owning more than one mobile phone or working with children[142]. There is no restriction on the kind of prohibition that may be imposed; however, the restriction must relate to the activities of the individual. Unusually they have international reach, and if there is an evidenced agreement and or consent from the other jurisdiction the orders can be imposed both domestically and or internationally.

9.191

The Act makes further provisions as to prohibition on foreign travel, and the requirement to provide one's name and address to police, but orders are not limited to these conditions. A magistrates' court may also impose 'slavery and trafficking risk orders' ('STROs') by virtue of the MSA 2015, s 23 where the defendant has not been convicted, but has acted in a way that shows a risk of committing such offences or to protect others from the risk of harm; these can only be applied for by specified law enforcement agencies. Risk orders can be made for up to five years. Interim ROs may also be made. The interim orders are particularly important where an investigation is on-going and there is a need to protect potential victims of trafficking from a risk of harm. The Home Office has issued guidance on STPOs and STROs, and the forms to be used for applications[143].

141 *R v Buddo* (1982) 4 Cr App Rep (S) 268, [1982] Crim LR 837.

142 Explanatory notes, para 80.

143 Available at www.gov.uk/government/publications/slavery-and-trafficking-prevention-and-risk-orders.

9.192

Serious crime prevention orders ('SCPOs') may be imposed either by the Crown Court on conviction for a serious offence, or by the High Court if satisfied that the person has committed or facilitated the commission of such an offence (or acted in a way likely to do so)[144]. A serious offence is either one listed in the Serious Crime Act 2007, Sch 1, Part 1, which includes the majority of offences discussed in this chapter, or one which, in the particular circumstances of the case, the court considers to be sufficiently serious to be treated as if it were in that schedule[145]. SCPOs may contain a wider range of restrictions, requirements and other terms (as well as prohibitions) than STPOs and STROs, but may not be in force for more than five years (although this does not prevent an application to the High Court for a new order in the same terms as the old one)[146]. They can only be made on application by the DPP (who has delegated authority to specified senior prosecutor roles) or the director of the SFO[147].

9.193

The terms of an order must protect the public by preventing, restricting, or disrupting the defendant's involvement in serious crime[148], and must be commensurate with the risk[149]. They must be precise, practicable and enforceable, and be preventative not punitive[150]. These general comments should, as a matter of principle, also apply to STPOs and STROs. It is important to look beyond the charge to the underlying facts and background circumstances when considering these orders.

9.194

Finally, sexual harm prevention orders (SHPOs) may be imposed on a defendant convicted of any of various sexual and non-sexual offences, listed in the SOA 2003, Schs 3 and 5[151]. These schedules include all the sexual offences discussed above with the exception of the strict liability offence for customers of exploited prostitutes (SOA 2003, s 53A), and also include trafficking under the MSA 2015, s 2, kidnapping, false imprisonment, and child abduction.

9.195

Breach of any of these orders is an either way offence, with a maximum sentence of five years[152]. Guidance on sentencing for breach of an SCPO, likely to be applicable in other cases as well, was given in *R v Koli*[153].

144 Serious Crime Act 2007, ss 1, 2 and 19.
145 Serious Crime Act 2007, s 2(2).
146 Serious Crime Act 2007, s 16.
147 Serious Crime Act 2007, s 8.
148 Serious Crime Act 2007, s 1(1)(b).
149 *R v Hancox* [2010] EWCA Crim 102, [2010] 4 All ER 537 at [10].
150 Ibid at [11]–[12].
151 SOA 2003, s 103A.
152 MSA 2015, s 30 (for STPOs and STROs), Serious Crime Act 2007, s 25 (for SCPOs), and SOA 2003, s 103I (for SHPOs).
153 [2012] EWCA Crim 1869, [2013] 1 Cr App Rep (S) 39.

10 Criminal Defences available to Victims of Trafficking and Modern Slavery

Ben Douglas-Jones KC, Michelle Brewer, Daniel Bunting and Andrew Johnson

Introduction

10.1

It is well established in international and domestic law that victims of exploitation who commit criminal acts because of their exploitation must, in appropriate cases, not be prosecuted.

10.2

This principle is not to be understood as granting immunity from prosecution. Rather, as Lord Judge CJ explained in *R v L and Others*[1]:

> 'The reasoning is not always spelled out, and perhaps we should do so now. The criminality, or putting it another way, the culpability, of any victim of trafficking may be significantly diminished, and in some cases effectively extinguished, not merely because of age (always a relevant factor in the case of a child defendant) but because no realistic alternative was available to the exploited victim but to comply with the dominant force of another individual, or group of individuals.'

10.3

The purpose of this chapter is to provide clear and structured guidance for public authorities and legal practitioners on the application of the non-prosecution and non-punishment framework. It sets out the key principles underpinning this framework and the practical steps required to implement them effectively. Central to this analysis is the critical need to ground each stage of the criminal process in the positive obligations arising under Art 4 of the ECHR. These

---

1 [2013] EWCA Crim 991 at [13].

obligations shape the responsibilities of the police, prosecution, and courts when dealing with individuals whose offending is closely linked to trafficking, slavery, servitude or forced or compulsory labour or the circumstances of their exploitation.

10.4

This chapter examines how these positive obligations arise, how they operate in practice, and the impact they have on decisions to investigate, protect, charge, and prosecute victims and possible victims of exploitation who commit criminal acts. It emphasises that these obligations are not discretionary: they are essential to ensuring that the rights of such individuals under Art 4, and, by extension, their right to a fair trial under Art 6, are fully respected and upheld. Importantly, as explored below, these positive obligations can arise regardless of whether the suspect, or, subsequently, the defendant, discloses that they are a victim and whether or not they propose to rely on s 45 of the Modern Slavery Act 2015 ('MSA 2015') defence.

10.5

Moreover, failures by public authorities to discharge their positive obligations under Art 4 to investigate offences of: (1) trafficking; and (2) slavery, servitude or forced or compulsory labour (together referred to as 'modern slavery') may materially affect a prosecutor's ability to fulfil its prosecutorial function lawfully and/or a defendant's ability to prepare and advance a defence under s 45. These failings must therefore be evaluated within the broader framework of Art 6, procedural fairness, and the State's duties of victim identification and protection, recognising that a trafficking-compliant investigation under Art 4 may be a necessary precondition to ensuring a fair trial for victims and potential victims of trafficking.

Laying the groundwork: international and regional legal bases for the non-punishment principle

10.6

The domestic safeguards in England and Wales concerning victims of human trafficking or modern slavery who are prosecuted for criminal offences which are connected to their trafficking or modern slavery stem from the 'Palermo Protocol'[2]; the Council of Europe Convention on Action against Trafficking in Human Beings 2005[3], ratified by the UK in December 2008 ('ECAT'),

2 The 2000 Protocol to Prevent, Suppress and Punish Trafficking in Persons, especially Women and Children. This protocol supplemented the UN Convention against Transnational Organized Crime. The protocol was ratified by the UK on 9 February 2006.

3 CETS No 197.

specifically Art 26; EU Directive 2011/36/EU on Preventing and Combating Trafficking in Human Beings and Protecting its Victims ('the EU Trafficking Directive'), specifically Art 8; and Art 4 of the European Convention on Human Rights and Fundamental Freedoms (ECHR).

Non-punishment principle: international instrument

Palermo Protocol

10.7

The modern international framework for the protection of victims of trafficking is rooted in the Palermo Protocol[4], which supplements the United Nations Convention against Transnational Organized Crime. The Preamble emphasises that an effective response to trafficking must be comprehensive, encompassing prevention, prosecution, and the protection of victims' human rights.

10.8

The Protocol defines *trafficking in persons* as the recruitment, transportation, transfer, harbouring, or receipt of persons by means such as coercion, abduction, fraud, or abuse of power, for the purpose of exploitation, including slavery. Its scope is limited to transnational trafficking and does not extend to purely domestic cases.

10.9

Although the Protocol itself is silent on the non-punishment principle, the Working Group on Trafficking in Persons (2010) produced a background paper addressing the non-punishment and non-prosecution of victims for offences committed as a direct consequence of their trafficking. This reflects a growing international consensus that victims should not be criminalised for conduct arising from their exploitation.

Non-punishment principle: regional instruments

Council of Europe Convention on Action against Trafficking in Human Beings (ECAT), Art 26

10.10

The Council of Europe Convention on Action against Trafficking in Human Beings (ECAT), ratified in 2008, was implemented domestically

4 Palermo Protocol, Art 1.1.

through policy[5] and the Modern Slavery Act 2015. The protection afforded by Art 26 applies only to individuals who meet the definition of a trafficking victim under Art 4 ECAT.

10.11

Arts 1 and 2 of ECAT set out its core objectives: to prevent and combat trafficking, to protect the rights and dignity of victims, to ensure effective investigation and prosecution, and to promote international cooperation. Unlike the Palermo Protocol, ECAT applies to all forms of trafficking, whether national or transnational.

10.12

Art 26 provides:

> 'Each Party shall… provide for the possibility of not imposing penalties on victims for their involvement in unlawful activities, to the extent that they have been compelled to do so.'

10.13

Following *R v L and Ors*, it was confirmed children did not have to establish compulsion under Art 26. 'Compulsion' should be understood to mean where any of the means listed in Art 4 of ECAT are used to achieve consent (see Explanatory Report[6] to ECAT at [273]).

10.14

For adults, 'compulsion' should be understood to mean where any of the means in Art 4 of ECAT are used to achieve consent to the exploitation (see Explanatory Report[7] to ECAT at [273]). The Explanatory Report (paras 272–274) clarifies that States must adopt measures, whether through substantive or procedural law, and consistent with national legal principles, that allow for the non-punishment of victims who have been compelled to commit offences as a direct consequence of their trafficking.

10.15

Those international safeguards underpin the protection of victims of offences in ss 1 to 4 of the MSA 2015, corresponding to the conduct proscribed under Art 4 of the ECHR.

---

5 This is when the National Referral Mechanism ('NRM') became operational in the UK.

6 Explanatory Report – CETS 197 – Action against Trafficking in Human Beings.

7 Explanatory Report – CETS 197 – Action against Trafficking in Human Beings.

EU Exit and the EU Trafficking Directive

10.16

For the purposes of this chapter, the justiciability of the EU Trafficking Directive in relation to the non-punishment principle is not considered in detail. This is because Art 26 of ECAT has been interpreted by the Court of Appeal as providing similar safeguards against prosecution and punishment for victims of exploitation to those set out in Art 8 of the Directive. Both are underpinned through the protective obligations under Art 4 of the ECHR.

10.17

However, the Directive contains expanded definitions in Art 2 relevant to trafficking in human beings when compared with the equivalent article in ECAT, Art 4. Where these or other definitions in the Directive are material to a case, and the trafficking or modern slavery (ie the cause of action) occurred prior to the end of the Brexit transition period on 31 December 2020, the analysis of the Supreme Court in *Lipton and another v BA Cityflyer Ltd* may require consideration[8]. Beyond that, the Directive may help as an interpretative tool as to how the ECtHR may interpret ECAT.

From principle to practice: the UK's evolving approach to non-punishment

10.18

Historically, the safeguards underpinning the non-punishment principle in England and Wales were implemented through the common law defence of duress, the Crown Prosecution Service's guidance on suspects in criminal cases who may be victims of trafficking or slavery ('the CPS guidance'), and the remedy of abuse of process (examined further below).

10.19

Since the commencement of the MSA 2015 on 31 July 2015, the non-punishment framework in England and Wales has been strengthened by the introduction of the statutory defence under s 45. This defence applies to individuals charged with certain non-excluded offences where they are victims of slavery or slavery related offences (as defined in s 1) or trafficking (s 2), and where there is a demonstrable link between their offending and their exploitation.

8 *Lipton and another v BA Cityflyer Ltd* [2024] UKSC 24.

The four-stage framework for prosecuting potential victims of modern slavery and human trafficking

10.20

While the introduction of the statutory defence under s 45 of the MSA 2015 has strengthened the non-punishment framework, it operates within a broader legal and procedural context. The obligations of the police and the Crown Prosecution Service (CPS) to conduct an independent and impartial investigation of the allegation of trafficking, slavery or related acts for criminal exploitation remain engaged wherever there is *prima facie* evidence of this which falls to be considered by the police/investigative agency and/or the CPS. These duties are reinforced by policing and CPS guidance: Modern Slavery and human trafficking: offences and defences, including the s 45 defence; Part 2 – modern slavery non-prosecution principles and defences, including s 45 ('the CPS guidance')[9], as examined below.

10.21

The CPS guidance is a structured, four-stage approach to inform decision-making in cases involving potential victims of criminal exploitation who commit criminal acts. This framework is intended to ensure that such cases are assessed consistently and lawfully, with appropriate regard to the individual's potential victim status.

10.22

Where this four-stage approach is undertaken in the absence of an effective criminal investigation of the defendant as a victim in accordance with Art 4 of the ECHR and/or where the protective duties owed by the state to the possible victim are not acknowledged or implemented, this may result in a breach of the defendant's right to a fair trial under Art 6. There will be a particular risk of a breach of Art 6 where a prosecutor proceeds in disregard of Art 4 investigative duties (see **10.77** and **10.140–10.157** below).

The four-stage approach to the prosecution decision

10.23

1. Is there a reason to believe that the person is a victim of modern slavery?
   - If yes, move to Question 2.
   - If not, you do not need to consider this assessment further.

9 https://www.cps.gov.uk/prosecution-guidance/modern-slavery-and-human-trafficking-offences-and-defences-including-section#a13 (last accessed 26 November 2025).

2. Is there clear evidence of a credible common law defence of duress?
   - If yes, then the case should not be charged or should be discontinued on evidential grounds.
   - If not, move to Question 3.
3. Is there clear evidence of a statutory defence under s 45 of the 2015 Act?
   - If yes, then the case should not be charged or should be discontinued on evidential grounds.
   - If not, move to Question 4.
4. Is it in the public interest to prosecute? This must be considered even where there is no clear evidence of duress, or all the elements of the statutory defence under s 45, or where the offence is excluded under Schedule 4.

The centrality of Art 4 compliance in the four stage process

Overview

10.24

Before applying the CPS four-stage guidance, the police and prosecution must fully understand and meet their positive obligations under Art 4 ECHR. If they do not, the integrity of the four-stage decision-making process will be undermined and the resulting prosecutorial decision could be unlawful.

10.25

The CPS's structured framework, designed to assess whether a suspect or defendant should be prosecuted in light of their potential victim status, relies on a foundation of timely and effective investigation into trafficking or modern slavery. Without such an investigation, the evidential and public interest assessments at each stage risk being based on incomplete or flawed information. As the ECtHR made clear in *VCL and AN v United Kingdom*[10], a failure to assess credible indicators of trafficking will not only breach the State's positive obligations under Art 4 but may also undermine the fairness of the criminal proceedings, thereby engaging, and giving rise to a significant risk of a breach of Art 6.

10 *VCL and AN v United Kingdom* (2021) 73 EHRR 9. See also *FM and Others v Russia* (App Nos 49848/18 and others, judgment of 10 December 2024), in which the ECtHR for the first time found a violation of Art 14 read with Art 4 in a trafficking case. The Court held that the Russian authorities' failure to investigate and take operational measures to protect five women trafficked for forced labour constituted intersectional discrimination on the grounds of gender, ethnicity and irregular migration status. The judgment is significant for its analysis of how discriminatory state inaction may itself engage Art 4 positive obligations.

10.26

In cases involving offending where the alleged criminality is a manifestation of trafficking or exploitation or the circumstances stemming from exploitation, the duty to conduct an Art 4-compliant investigation is central to the lawfulness and fairness of any prosecutorial decision. The fulfilment of the duty underpins both the assessment of the evidential and the public interest limbs of the CPS Code Test for Crown Prosecutors. This investigation duty is separate and distinct from the positive obligation to identify possible credible victims as such (see **Chapter 4**). Both police and the CPS hold concurrent investigative and protective obligations under Art 4, which are detailed in Chapter 4. As both the domestic courts and ECtHR make clear the duty to *investigate* rests, practically, with law enforcement agencies such as the police and can only be discharged by them. However, the investigative duty applies to prosecutors (as made clear in the CPS guidance) in that prosecutors must fulfil their Art 4 investigative duties by ensuring that the police (or other investigative agency) have conducted an Art 4 compliant investigation.

10.27

It is therefore necessary to understand two interrelated matters: first, the nature of the Art 4 violation that the suspect or defendant claims to have suffered; and second, the corresponding duties which arise for the police and, subsequently, the CPS or other prosecutor in the prosecution of a possible victim.

Gravity of modern slavery and human trafficking in international and domestic law

10.28

Where there is *prima facie* evidence, whether arising from the defendant's account or other sources, including indicators, that the offences being prosecuted are connected to the individual's status as a victim of trafficking, slavery, or related exploitation, the harm in question is considered particularly grave.

10.29

In order to recognise the gravity of modern slavery and human trafficking, it is essential to place these offences within their international law context, as this informs and shapes their recognition and treatment under domestic law.

10.30

Chapter 1 examines the constituent elements of the distinct offences of slavery, servitude, forced or compulsory labour, and human trafficking. A clear understanding of these offences is essential to any proper application of the non-punishment principle and the s 45 MSA statutory defence. As explained in **Chapter 1**, the offences derive from international and regional instruments which inform their meaning for the purposes of Art 4 ECHR and, in turn, inform how domestic law is to be interpreted.

Art 4 Slavery (s 1(a) MSA 2015)

10.31

The prohibition of slavery is firmly established as a *jus cogens* norm, a fundamental principle from which no deviation is permitted. Slavery represents the gravest form of harm within the hierarchy of violations under Art 4 of the ECHR. This is analysed in **Chapter 1**.

Servitude (s 1(a) MSA 2015)

10.32

The prohibition of servitude is likewise recognised as a fundamental part of international law from which no deviation is permitted. Within the hierarchy of Art 4 ECHR violations, servitude occupies a position above forced or compulsory labour in terms of gravity. As examined in **Chapter 1**, where any or all powers attaching to the right of ownership are exercised over a person in servitude this constitutes *de facto* slavery.

Forced and compulsory labour (s 1(b) MSA 2015)

10.33

The prohibition on forced or compulsory labour is absolute. Article 4(3) limits the scope of this offence by defining what does *not* count as 'forced or compulsory labour.' It excludes specific categories of work, such as military service and civic obligations, from the definition, provided they meet established legal criteria. Consequently, any conduct that actually falls within the definition of forced labour is considered a grave violation of fundamental human values, as consistently held by the ECtHR.

Human trafficking (ss 2 and 3 MSA 2015)

10.34

The right to be free from human trafficking is absolute. The exploitation involved in trafficking may include any of the harms prohibited by s 1 of the MSA 2015. The severity of that exploitation corresponds to the hierarchy outlined above.

Negative and positive obligations under Art 4 ECHR

10.35

To guarantee the right under Art 4 ECHR, the European Court of Human Rights (ECtHR) imposes both **negative** and **positive** obligations on States:

- **Negative obligation**:The State must refrain from interfering with the Art 4 right.This includes avoiding acts or omissions that directly contribute to or fail to prevent slavery or related acts.
- **Positive obligations**: The State must take proactive steps to ensure the effective enjoyment of the right not to be held in slavery or servitude or subjected to forced or compulsory labour or trafficking[11]. Simply refraining from abuse ('mere non-interference') is not enough to meet the standard required by the Convention: see *Siliadin v France*[12].

10.36

The ECtHR[13] affirmed that Art 4 ECHR imposes the following substantive and procedural positive obligations on states:

(i) Establish an effective legal and administrative framework to prohibit and penalise trafficking and related abuses (the systems duty).

(ii) Take proactive operational measures to prevent exploitation and to protect victims, potential victims, and individuals at risk of becoming victims (the protective and recovery duty).

(iii) Conduct effective, law enforcement-led criminal investigations capable of identifying and prosecuting perpetrators where there is *prima facie* evidence or a credible suspicion of a violation of Art 4, or where there exists a real and immediate risk of such violations occurring. In addition, there must be access to effective judicial remedies, in accordance with the procedural obligations under Art 4.

(iv) Secure restitution for victims in respect of the harm suffered (the restitution duty).

11 Art 4 ECHR must be read together with Art 1. By Art 1, states must secure the rights and freedoms of the Convention for all individuals within their jurisdictions, including those accused of criminal offences. States must ensure effective protection against violations by both state and private actors.

12 (Application no 73316/01) judgment of 26/07/2005, final on 26/10/2005; (2006) 43 EHRR 16.

13 *SM v Croatia [GC], (2021)* 72 E.H.R.R. 1, [312–320]; *Rantsev v Cyprus and Russia*, (2010) 51 E.H.R.R. 1.

Interdependence of positive obligations under Art 4 ECHR

10.37

In *F.M. v Russia*[14], the ECtHR affirmed that the positive obligations under Art 4 ECHR, to protect victims, prevent trafficking, and prosecute perpetrators, must operate not in isolation but in synergy. Drawing on the Palermo Protocol and ECAT, the Court recognised that these obligations are inextricably linked and must be understood within a comprehensive and integrated framework. The corollary is that a failure to fulfil one or more of these duties may significantly undermine the effectiveness of those obligations that have been met (see *VCL and AN v UK*).

The burden on state authorities

10.38

The ECtHR has emphasised that positive obligations under Art 4 must not impose an unreasonable or disproportionate burden on public authorities. The assessment of what constitutes reasonable protective measures is context-specific and must take into account all relevant circumstances, including the scope of the authorities' powers, the physical safety of the victim, and the rights of others.

10.39

As the Court observed in *F.M v Russia* it is relevant to the consideration of the proportionality of any positive obligation arising in the present case that the Palermo Protocol requires States to endeavour to ensure the physical safety of victims of trafficking while within their territory[15].

10.40

In *MC v Bulgaria*[16] a special protection by the state is owed to children and vulnerable individuals, in which the Court will be particularly demanding in its supervision of a state's existing measures designed to protect individuals from violence by non-state actors. The Court will afford states a narrower margin of appreciation regarding adequacy of measures taken in such contexts. The Court has identified undocumented migrants and those without lawful status as another vulnerable cohort in the context of Art 4 ECHR[17].

---

14 *FM v Russia* (App nos 71671/16 and 40190/18 December 2024 at [280].) ECtHR, 10

15 *FM v Russia* (App nos 71671/16 and 40190/18 December 2024 at [280].) ECtHR, 10; The Court referring to see Rantsev, [286-287], and *SM v. Croatia*, [305].

16 *MC v Bulgaria* at [150], re-affirmed in V.C.L. and *A.N. v UK* at [161].

17 *FM v Russia* (App nos 71671/16 and 40190/18) ECtHR, 10 December 2024 at [342].

The trigger for positive obligations under Art 4 ECHR

10.41

These obligations are triggered where there is a credible suspicion that an individual may be a victim or is at real and immediate risk of becoming a victim of Art 4 abuse. The threshold is low, requiring only that the account or evidence is not inherently implausible[18], and the fact that it was known or ought to have been known to the authorities is sufficient to trigger the positive obligations[19]. This threshold is examined in more detail in **Chapters 4, 14** and **16**.

10.42

There is no requirement for the individual to self-identify or come forward. The duty to act is placed squarely on the State where *prima facie* evidence gives rise to a credible suspicion.

10.43

Both the CPS and the police (or any investigative agency) have an independent duty to investigate. Neither can excuse a failure to act by pointing to mistakes or omissions by the other. This obligation is indivisible and cannot be transferred.

10.44

While cooperation between the CPS and the police is essential for timely, thorough, and lawful investigations, coordination must not become dependency. A joint working relationship does not remove either authority's responsibility to act once the legal threshold is met.

10.45

The police and CPS duties to investigate and protect are not conditional on the NRM process being invoked or on a competent authority decision being made. They do not need to wait for a referral or a formal decision on victim status before acting. This principle was clearly affirmed in *VCL and AN v United Kingdom*[20], where the ECtHR held that at point of arrest, the two Vietnamese putative minors, who were working as gardeners in a makeshift cannabis factory, presented sufficient indicators to give rise to a credible suspicion of trafficking. The circumstances of their discovery constituted *prima facie* evidence of trafficking, because of the well-documented nature of this exploitation.

18 See *R (on the application of TDT) v Secretary of State for the Home Department* [2018] EWCA Civ 1395 for an analysis of what constitutes 'credible suspicion'.

19 *SM v Croatia [GC]*, (2021) 72 E.H.R.R. 1.

20 *VCL and AN v United Kingdom* (2021) 73 EHRR 9.

10.46

A similar conclusion was reached by Lord Justice Underhill in *R (TDT) v Secretary of State for the Home Department*[21], where he observed that even at the NRM referral stage, there were sufficient indicators that TDT matched the profile of a trafficking victim, thereby triggering the credible suspicion threshold.

10.47

Notably, as examined in Chapter 4, the Modern Slavery Statutory Guidance requires both the First Responder and the Competent Authority to share the NRM referral with the police. Where a positive reasonable grounds decision is made, this too must be communicated to the police, along with any additional material the police request[22]. Therefore, where a potential victim suspect is referred into the NRM, the police will be on notice of this.

The credible suspicion threshold and the functional role of a positive reasonable grounds decision

10.48

A positive reasonable grounds decision is not admissible evidence for the defence. However, focusing solely on admissibility is too narrow. It overlooks the decision's critical role in triggering the state's procedural and protective duties under Article 4 ECHR.

10.49

Crucially, a positive reasonable grounds decision acts as formal recognition by the Competent Authority that there are reasonable grounds to believe the individual is a victim. This finding crystallises the state's Art 4 obligations, specifically the duties to investigate, support, and safeguard. It functions as the procedural gateway ensuring the State fulfils these substantive human rights duties; see *VCL and AN v United Kingdom*[23]; *R (on the application of H) v Secretary of State for the Home Department*, per Burnett LJ (as he then was)[24]; and *R (TDT) v Secretary of State for the Home Department*, per Underhill LJ[25]. A positive reasonable grounds decision therefore mandates an effective police investigation. It also

21 *R (TDT) v Secretary of State for the Home Department* [2018] EWCA Civ 1395,

22 Home Office, *National referral mechanism guidance: adult (England and Wales)* (updated 30 September 2025) [accessed 18 October 2025] at [9]-[10] and Home Office, Modern Slavery: Statutory Guidance for England and Wales (under s49 of the Modern Slavery Act 2015) and Non-Statutory Guidance for Scotland and Northern Ireland (Version 4.2, 16 September 2025).

23 *VCL and AN v United Kingdom* (2021) 73 EHRR 9 [162].

24 *R (on the application of H) v Secretary of State for the Home Department* [2016] EWCA Civ 565; Imm AR 1272, [37].

25 For a detailed analysis of 'credible suspicion', see *R(TDT) v Secretary of State for the Home Department* [2018] EWCA Civ 1395, [2018] 1 WLR 4922 and Chapter 2.

requires the police and CPS to implement protective measures, recognising that the duties to investigate and protect are interconnected. Where *prima facie* evidence of trafficking, slavery or related acts is before front line public authorities, including the police, this will trigger their positive obligations irrespective of an identification decision[26].

The dual investigatory duty: pre-trial and during judicial proceedings

10.50

When harm prohibited by Art 4 ECHR (slavery, servitude, forced or compulsory labour, or trafficking) is committed by private individuals, the State is directly obliged to conduct an official investigation. This duty is similar whether the alleged perpetrator is a private individual or a state agent. The investigation obligation is procedural but anchored within Art 4's substantive protections.

10.51

The ECtHR draws a distinction between two key investigatory duties under Art 4:

- Criminal Investigation: States must start an official criminal investigation where *prima facie* evidence arises of modern slavery or trafficking;
- Effective Judicial Proceedings: There must be a judicial mechanism able to establish the facts and events leading to the harm.

10.52

The duty to investigate under Art 4 ECHR extends beyond the initial pre-trial phase to encompass the entirety of judicial proceedings. Crucially, the pre-trial investigation constitutes only the first limb of a broader dual obligation. The second limb is the duty to ensure the conduct of effective judicial proceedings. It is essential to recognise that judicial proceedings cannot substitute for, nor render unnecessary, a thorough and effective investigation by law enforcement authorities [27]. These are distinct but complementary functions.

---

26 See *R (on the application of H) v Secretary of State for the Home Department* (above) and *R(TDT) v Secretary of State for the Home Department* (above).

27 In *VCL and AN v UK*, the ECtHR examined pre-trial up to and including the Criminal Cases Review Commission reference as well as the Court of Appeal judgments both preceding and following that reference. In such cases the Court has adopted a 'particularly thorough scrutiny' (see *SM v Croatia* [315]-[317]).

10.53

The investigative role of law enforcement involves the proactive gathering of evidence and the pursuit of leads to establish the facts and identify those responsible for Art 4 violations. Following the investigation, the CPS must assess whether the evidential threshold is met and whether prosecution is in the public interest.

10.54

In contrast, the judiciary adjudicates; it does not investigate. A fact-finding judge evaluates the evidence, while a trial judge ensures that evidence is presented clearly to the jury. Consequently, the courts rely entirely on the quality of the police investigation. If that investigation is flawed, the court cannot fulfil its own Art 4 obligations.

The rule of law and the duty to investigate under Art 4 ECHR

10.55

The duty to investigate under Art 4 ECHR reflects the well-established investigatory obligations under Arts 2 and 3[28]. The ECtHR has consistently held that states must conduct effective, law enforcement-led investigations into serious breaches of fundamental rights[29].

10.56

This duty is frequently misunderstood. It is not a general obligation of inquiry or identification. Rather, it requires a focused criminal investigation by a law enforcement agency into the harm suffered by the alleged victim. Specifically, the alleged trafficking, slavery, or slavery-related exploitation must be the subject of the investigation.

10.57

At its foundation, this obligation is about the rule of law and the integrity of the justice system. The requirement to investigate allegations of slavery, servitude, forced labour, or trafficking is not merely procedural, it is constitutional in nature. It ensures that states do not appear complicit, indifferent, or tolerant of serious rights violations.

28 *FM v Russia* at [313-314].

29 Ibid. at [310] and consistent with *Secretary of State for the Home Department v Hoang Anh Minh* at [37] and *MS(Pakistan)*.

10.58

The ECtHR has repeatedly stressed that investigating Art 4 abuses is essential to maintaining public confidence, preventing collusion or the perception of collusion, and upholding the credibility of the justice system.

10.59

As Lord Kerr observed in *Commissioner of Police of the Metropolis v DSD and another*[30], concerning the positive obligation to investigate Art 3 harms (rape):

> 'In order to be an effective deterrent, laws which prohibit conduct constituting a breach … must be rigorously enforced and complaints … properly investigated. Strasbourg authority establishes the duty to properly investigate reported offences … summarised in *O'Keeffe v Ireland:*
>
> > "Article 3 requires authorities to conduct an effective investigation … capable of establishing the facts and identifying and punishing those responsible, conducted independently, promptly, and allowing victims effective participation."'

10.60

This principle applies with equal force to Art 4 investigations. A state's failure to investigate trafficking or exploitation allegations not only undermines the rights of the individual but erodes the foundation of lawful governance.

An effective investigation

10.61

The investigative duty under Art 4 ECHR is concerned with the adequacy of the *process*, rather than the *outcome*.

10.62

This means that the State is required to take appropriate steps to investigate whenever there are indications that an individual may have been subjected to treatment contrary to Art 4. The obligation is discharged through the conduct of a serious and effective criminal investigation, even if it does not ultimately result in a prosecution or conviction.

10.63

Once triggered, the investigation must satisfy the following minimum standards:

30 *Commissioner of Police of the Metropolis v DSD and another* [2018] UKSC 11.

- **Independence and impartiality:** The investigating body must be institutionally and practically independent, particularly from those potentially implicated in the alleged abuse.
- **Promptness and reasonable expedition:** Investigations must be initiated and pursued without undue delay, with particular urgency where there is a risk of ongoing harm.
- **Effectiveness:** Authorities must proactively gather evidence and take all reasonable steps to secure relevant material, including, where appropriate, medical evidence. The investigation must be capable of establishing the facts, identifying those responsible, and securing accountability. **The burden must not fall on the victim to initiate or sustain the process.** This is a *duty of means*, not of result; ie the authorities are required to take all reasonable steps to investigate, but they are not required to guarantee a conviction.
- **Victim participation:** Victims or their families must be involved in the investigation to the extent necessary to safeguard their legitimate interests.
- **Proportionality:** The obligation must not impose an impossible or disproportionate burden on the authorities.
- **Discriminatory motivation:** Where there is a credible suspicion that discriminatory attitudes (eg, based on gender or irregular immigration status) may have played a role in the Art 4 harm, the investigation must be conducted with particular vigour and impartiality. This is essential not only to reaffirm society's condemnation of such conduct, but also to maintain the confidence of minority groups in the authorities' ability to protect them from discriminatory violence (see *F.M. v Russia* at [341]).
- **Cross-jurisdictional cooperation:** In cases involving transnational elements, there is a duty to cooperate effectively with the relevant authorities of other States in investigating events that occurred outside the domestic jurisdiction.

10.64

Only significant flaws in the investigative process, those capable of undermining its ability to establish the circumstances of the case or identify those responsible, will amount to a breach of the Art 4 duty. Minor errors or isolated omissions are insufficient to render an investigation ineffective.

Case law illustrations of an Art 4 investigatory breach

10.65

In *S.M. v Croatia*[31], the applicant alleged that a former police officer had forced her into prostitution. Although she was administratively recognised as a potential

31 *SM v Croatia* [2020] ECHR 995.

trafficking victim, the Court held that this was no substitute for a criminal investigation. It found *prima facie* evidence of trafficking, including recruitment via Facebook, use of force, debt bondage, and abuse of vulnerability, but the authorities failed to pursue obvious lines of inquiry and relied excessively on the applicant's testimony without accounting for the impact of trauma.

10.66

In *T.V. v Spain*[32], the Court identified serious shortcomings in the domestic response to an arguable complaint of trafficking and forced prostitution. Similarly, in *B.B. v Slovakia*[33], the authorities were criticised for failing to investigate the applicant's relationship with the alleged trafficker and for not recognising the subtle forms of coercion often present in trafficking cases.

10.67

In *T.I. and Others v Greece*[34], the Court examined both the investigation into alleged exploitation and the visa issuance process. Given the prevalence of trafficking in Russia and Greece, and the seriousness of the allegations, including claims of public official involvement, the authorities were required to act with heightened diligence. They failed to do so: the investigation was excessively delayed, the offences became time-barred, and the applicants were not adequately involved in the proceedings.

10.68

In Šečić v Croatia[35], the ECtHR considered a complaint concerning the ineffective criminal investigation of a racially motivated physical assault. Reiterating its earlier jurisprudence in *MC v Bulgaria*, the Court affirmed that Art 3 ECHR may give rise to a positive obligation on a state to conduct an official investigation (para 53). It emphasised that this obligation is one of means, not of result, citing the Art 2 cases of *Menson v United Kingdom*[36] and *Yaşa v Turkey*[37]. At paragraph 54, the Court observed that the authorities are required to take "all reasonable steps available to them to secure the evidence concerning the incident" and must act with "promptness and reasonable expedition." Upon reviewing the investigative steps taken by the police, the Court concluded at paragraph 59 that "the failure of the state authorities to further the case or obtain any tangible evidence with a view to identifying and arresting the attackers over a prolonged period of time indicates that the investigation did not meet the requirements of Art 3. It therefore found that Art 3 had been breached and that the applicant was entitled to be compensated.

32 *T.V. v Spain* [2022] ECHR 103.
33 *B.B. v Slovakia* [2020] ECHR 123.
34 *T.I. and Others v Greece* [2021] ECHR 232.
35 *Šečić v Croatia* (2009) 49 EHRR 18 (31 May 2007).
36 *Menson v United Kingdom* (2003) 37 EHRR CD220.
37 *Yaşa v Turkey* (1999) 28 EHRR 408.

10.69

In *Beganović v Croatia*[38], at paragraph 75, the Court set out the "minimum standards applicable" to the duty to investigate. These include requirements that the investigation be independent, impartial, and subject to public scrutiny, and that the authorities act with diligence and promptness. The Court reiterated that, for an investigation to be considered effective, the authorities must take all reasonable steps to secure evidence concerning the incident. This includes, *inter alia*, obtaining a detailed statement from the alleged victim, collecting eyewitness testimony, securing forensic evidence, and, where appropriate, commissioning additional medical reports.

Underpinning purpose of protective measures

10.70

Once triggered, the principal objective of the protective duty under Art 4 ECHR is to take reasonable and timely steps to safeguard the potential victim from further exploitation, shield them from threats of harm, and prevent exposure to renewed risk. This duty is not abstract; it imposes concrete operational obligations on public authorities, including the CPS, to act decisively in the face of credible suspicion.

10.71

These protective obligations are integral to a putative victim's capacity or willingness to be involved in an effective investigation and to their access to justice.

10.72

The duty comprises two interdependent dimensions:

(a) The protective duty, which requires proactive measures to prevent further harm to the victim; and

(b) The recovery duty, which entails facilitating the victim's physical, psychological, and social rehabilitation.

10.73

As affirmed by the ECtHR in *VCL and AN v United Kingdom* at [159], these duties are inextricably linked: effective protection cannot be achieved without supporting recovery, and meaningful recovery cannot occur without ensuring safety and stability.

38 (Application No 46423/06) 25 June 2009.

10.74

For the CPS, this means that decisions, whether to prosecute, divert, or discontinue, must be informed by an understanding of these dual obligations. The protective function is not limited to avoiding harm through prosecution; it extends to ensuring that victims are not re-traumatised or placed at further risk through procedural decisions that fail to account for their status and vulnerabilities.

Protective duties: the CPS

10.75

In *VCL and AN v United Kingdom*, the ECtHR found that the CPS had breached its protective obligations under Art 4 ECHR by pursuing a prosecution without conducting a thorough assessment of the defendants' trafficking histories. The failure properly to consider their status as potential victims of trafficking rendered the prosecution incompatible with the state's duty to protect. The following principles emerge from the judgment:

1. **Impact of Prosecution on Recovery and Risk of Re-trafficking**: The Court held that it is axiomatic that the prosecution can seriously impair a victim's recovery and reintegration, obstruct access to support, and increase vulnerability to re-trafficking.

2. **Prompt Identification and Assessment**: Once authorities are, or ought to be, aware of a credible suspicion that a suspect may be a trafficking victim, a prompt assessment by trained professionals is required.

3. **Use of International Criteria**: Assessments should apply the standards set out in the **Palermo Protocol** and **ECAT**. In this regard, see chapter 1 and analysis of the s 2 MSA 2015 offence.

4. **Timing of Prosecutorial Decision**: Decisions to prosecute should, where possible, be deferred until a trafficking assessment has been completed. Notably, the Court envisaged that any such 'assessment' was capable of producing exculpatory evidence (see duty to investigate analysis above).

5. **Weight of the Assessment in Decision-Making**: While prosecutors are not bound by the assessment [NRM decision], any departure must be justified with clear and consistent reasoning aligned with international standards.

10.76

Law enforcement's duty to investigate and duty to protect are inextricably linked as demonstrated by the ECtHR in *FM v Russia* at [330]:

> 'By failing in its duty to carry out an effective investigation, the respondent State fostered a sense of impunity among the traffickers and precluded the applicants' recovery from their traumatic experiences. It also left the applicants without the opportunity to seek compensation in respect of damage suffered by them, including the withholding of earnings from them by their traffickers, as part of ensuring *restitutio in integrum* in the process of upholding their dignity, assisting their recovery and reducing the risks of their again falling victim to traffickers (see *Krachunova v. Bulgaria*, no. 18269/18, 28 November 2023).'

Institutional competence and Art 4 violations underpinning Art 6 breaches

10.77

In *VCL and AN v United Kingdom*[39], the Strasbourg Court declined, on procedural grounds, to examine as a separate complaint the second applicant's contention that the police's failure to conduct an Art 4 compliant investigation constituted a distinct violation of Art 6, noting that this argument had not been properly advanced before the domestic courts[40]. Nevertheless, the Court addressed the same investigative shortcomings within its broader assessment under Art 6. It held that the authorities' failure to carry out a timely evaluation of whether the applicants had been trafficked deprived them of evidence that might have formed a fundamental part of their defence, and that this omission contributed directly to the finding that the proceedings were not fair within the meaning of Art 6(1).

10.78

In cases of trafficking and modern slavery, the failure to undertake an investigation that meets the requirements of Art 4 is not a mere procedural shortcoming lying somewhere in the background. It strikes at the heart of the fairness of the criminal process. As the Court made clear in *VCL and AN*, the absence of a timely and proper assessment of whether the accused had in fact been trafficked deprived them of material capable of forming a fundamental part of their defence. That omission was not incidental: it went directly to the question whether they received a fair trial within the meaning of Art 6(1). The following findings at [195]–[196] reveal the Art 4 violations that underpinned the Court's conclusion that the CPS had breached Art 6:

---

39 *VCL and AN v United Kingdom* (2021) 73 EHRR 9.

40 The rationale for treating this police-investigation limb as procedurally inadmissible is not entirely clear. The judgment records that a written submission on this basis was put to the Court of Appeal [59], but notes that the point was not developed domestically.

'The Court has repeatedly emphasised the importance of the investigation stage for the preparation of the criminal proceedings, as the evidence obtained during this stage determines the framework in which the offence charged will be considered at the trial (see *Salduz v. Turkey* [GC], no. 36391/02, § 54, ECHR 2008, and *Dvorski v. Croatia* [GC], no. 25703/11, § 108, ECHR 2015). It has also recognised that an accused often finds himself in a particularly vulnerable position at that stage of the proceedings, the effect of which is amplified by the fact that legislation on criminal procedure tends to become increasingly complex, notably with respect to the rules governing the gathering and use of evidence…

Although victims of trafficking are not immune from prosecution, an individual's status as a victim of trafficking may affect whether there is sufficient evidence to prosecute and whether it is in the public interest to do so (see paragraph 161 above). **Evidence concerning an accused's status as a victim of trafficking is therefore a "fundamental aspect" of the defence which he or she should be able to secure without restriction.'[emphasis added]**

10.79

The Court went on to conclude there had been a violation of Art 6 at [200]:

'The Court has already found that the authorities' failure to conduct a timely assessment of whether the applicants had in fact been trafficked amounted to a breach of their positive obligations under Article 4 of the Convention (see paragraphs 174 and 183 above). **In the context of Article 6 of the Convention, it considers that the lack of such an assessment prevented them from securing evidence which may have constituted a fundamental aspect of their defence.' [emphasis added]**

10.80

The Court's reasoning in finding the CPS in breach of Art 6 applies with even greater force to the police, given the distinct institutional competencies of the two bodies. The police are the primary investigative authority and bear the initial responsibility for identifying indicators of trafficking and triggering the State's protective and procedural investigatory duties under Art 4. Notably, where the State has failed to discharge its positive obligations under Art 4, the ECtHR case law, and in particular *VCL and AN*, confirms that a guilty plea entered without an Art 4 compliant assessment and an investigation into the allegation cannot validly waive the right to a fair trial in any meaningful sense: the authorities remain responsible for ensuring that the proceedings as a whole are fair and cannot rely on waiver to cure structural defects that go to the rule of law.

Sequencing and institutional responsibility: the investigative duty as a precondition to prosecution

10.81

The purpose of the investigatory duty under Art 4 ECHR is to elicit facts relevant to the trafficking or modern slavery allegation through an effective, law enforcement-led investigation (see police guidance below). This is the institutional responsibility of the police.

10.82

This would be consistent with police guidance:

> 'Every report of modern slavery must be investigated from the point of disclosure or suspicion and should be conducted in accordance with standard investigative practice.
>
> Be aware that offenders may be victims.
>
> Victims may be experiencing mental ill health, for example, Stockholm syndrome, trauma or post-traumatic stress disorder, and it may take months to obtain evidence from them. They may feel empathy and attachment with their exploiters and be unwilling to provide evidence against them. There is also the risk that unless they are sufficiently protected, victims may return to their exploiters.
>
> All potential victims are vulnerable and should, therefore, be interviewed in compliance with Ministry of Justice (2022) Achieving Best Evidence in Criminal Proceedings: Guidance on interviewing victims and witnesses, and guidance on using special measures.'

Police investigatory process guidance[41]

10.83

The primary purpose of a criminal investigation is to identify the suspect and to ensure that they are brought to justice following a professional, ethical and robust investigation. This will help to prevent future offending, to improve public confidence in the police, and to reduce both crime and the fear of crime.

41 College of Policing, *Investigation process* (Authorised Professional Practice, first published 23 October 2013, updated 28 May 2024) <https://www.college.police.uk/app/investigation/investigation-process> accessed 18 October 2025.

10.84

An effective investigation is fundamental to safeguarding. Similarly, safeguarding is central to an effective investigation. Many crimes will involve abuse and exploitation of people who are less able to look after themselves. Offenders will seek to take advantage of vulnerable people or will create vulnerability to enable abuse. Effective investigations will focus on the behaviour of the suspect to build understanding of how a victim's vulnerability was exploited and/or created[42].

10.85

The CPS confirmed in a public statement[43]:

> 'Victims of modern slavery will be identified earlier in criminal investigations – saving them from being wrongly prosecuted…The CPS has previously carefully considered the claim of suspects who say they have offended because they were trafficked. Today's change shifts the focus of this to before a suspect is charged and reminds prosecutors to be alert to the full situation and vigilant to potential indicators of trafficking.
>
> The guidance says that where someone is suspected or claims to be a victim of modern slavery, that they were coerced or directed to commit a crime as a result, as far as possible police or law enforcement will need to fully investigate suspects' situations before the CPS will be able to make a charging decision…Investigations into whether a person is a victim of modern slavery are often raised after charge, which often delays the progression of cases and increases the number of court appearances and adjournments while they were followed up.
>
> The changes will mean that prosecutors can make more informed decisions at point of charge, and reduce the number of cases where a claim is made halfway through a prosecution.'

10.86

Criminal trials do not proceed in the abstract; they are predicated on a factual foundation established through police investigation which has led to a decision to prosecute. That foundation is not optional; it is a legal prerequisite.

42 Ibid. p.9

43 Crown Prosecution Service, '*Victims of modern slavery to be further protected from prosecution by earlier investigation*' (CPS, 2 December 2021) <https://www.cps.gov.uk/cps/news/victims-modern-slavery-be-further-protected-prosecution-earlier-investigation> accessed 18 October 2025.

10.87

Prosecutors do not apply the Full Code Test, particularly the evidential stage, without a police investigation into the underlying criminal allegation. In cases of offending where the alleged criminality is linked to trafficking, slavery, or related exploitation, both the availability of a s 45 defence and the public interest in prosecution depend on the trafficking or modern slavery context. The four-stage test cannot be properly applied without an Art 4-compliant law enforcement investigation into the trafficking or modern slavery offence(s).

10.88

Where *prima facie* evidence of trafficking or modern slavery emerges after charge or during prosecution, the duty to investigate is triggered at that point. The obligation does not depend on the procedural stage of the case. It arises from the moment the authorities know or ought to have credible suspicion or know of *prima facie* evidence, regardless of whether the individual is a victim, suspect, or defendant.

10.89

The investigation must be independent and impartial. Its potential impact on the ongoing prosecution cannot influence the decision on whether to initiate a criminal investigation or the nature of that investigation into the alleged trafficking or modern slavery.

10.90

The CPS guidance sets out what steps a prosecutor should take when a potential victim of trafficking ('PVOT') or a victim of modern slavery is facing charge or prosecution.

10.91

The current CPS policy guidance provides:

> 'The CPS and its prosecutors must act compatibly with Art 4 of the ECHR, its policy recognising that Art 26 of ECAT provides for the possibility of non-punishment principle set out above.
>
> The CPS policy observes that certain public authorities, including the police, have a statutory duty to refer potential victims into the National Referral Mechanism (NRM). The Crown Prosecution Service (CPS), however, is not a first responder and therefore cannot make referrals directly.
>
> In circumstances where a potential victim of modern slavery is identified whether as a victim, witness, suspect, or defendant, CPS policy requires the following steps to be undertaken:

1. the CPS should request that the police make a referral into the NRM and, at minimum, ensure that the question of referral has been properly considered.
2. In such cases, **the police must also be advised to investigate the claim of victimhood**, independently of any NRM referral, if they have not already done so.
3. The prosecutor must satisfy themselves that this investigation has been conducted with sufficient thoroughness. All liaison and correspondence with the relevant Competent Authority should be routed through the police.'

10.92

However, as observed above, the trigger will be *prima facie* evidence, whether that is an NRM referral, a positive NRM decision or evidence from the criminal case (including the circumstances or condition in which a person was apprehended) or the person's antecedents. Prosecutors and defence practitioners must remain alert to cases where representations to the CPS may be appropriate. They should be mindful of the principles established in case law[44], discussed in more detail below.

CPS protective duties and the imperative of Art 4-compliant investigation

10.93

Prosecutors and defence practitioners must remain alert to cases where representations to the CPS may be appropriate. They should be mindful of the principles established in case law, discussed in more detail below. While public authorities may depart from their own published guidance where justified (see Chapter 4), such departures must be legally defensible. Any such departure from published guidance must be assessed in light of the State's positive obligations under Art 4 of the ECHR, which require the protection of victims and the investigation of credible suspicions of trafficking, slavery, or related Art 4 violations.

10.94

CPS policy itself confirms that prosecutorial decisions should be consistent with these obligations. The key question, therefore, is whether the CPS's actions or omissions breached the protective and procedural duties imposed by Art 4.

44 *R v S(G)* [2018] EWCA Crim 1824; [2019] Cr App R 7, *R v AAD* [2022] EWCA Crim 106; [2022] 1 Cr App R 19; [2022] 1 WLR 404, and *R v AFU* [2023] EWCA Crim 23; [2023] 1 Cr App R 16.

10.95

Failures to apply policy should therefore not be assessed only through public law principles but, more fundamentally, through the prism of Art 4 compliance. The legality of the CPS's position must ultimately be grounded in whether its conduct upheld or undermined the State's obligations under Art 4.

10.96

Where CPS guidance refers to the need for an investigation, this must be understood, once a credible suspicion of trafficking arises, as requiring an inquiry that meets the standards demanded by Article 4. Such an investigation must be independent, impartial, and directed specifically to whether the conduct amounts to offences under ss 1 or 2 of the MSA 2015. A failure to carry out such an investigation, or to do so effectively, is not a merely technical omission: as *VCL and AN v United Kingdom* demonstrates, it is liable to bear directly on the fairness of the criminal proceedings. By depriving the defendant of evidence capable of going to liability, culpability and the public interest in prosecution, the absence of an Art 4 compliant investigation may undermine the right to a fair trial protected by Art 6.

10.97

While proceedings should be conducted expeditiously, this must not come at the expense of the defendant's procedural rights[45]. A failure by the police to discharge their investigative obligations under Art 4 undermines the integrity of the prosecutorial process and reinforces the conclusion that a fair trial cannot be ensured in the absence of an effective investigation.

Prosecutorial staged inquiry

10.98

The following staged inquiry must be informed by the Art 4 positive obligations and their bearing on Art 6 as examined above.

10.99

When deciding whether to prosecute:

(a) an adult PVOT (aged 18 or over at time of the offence) who is suspected of committing a criminal offence when compelled to do so as a direct consequence of his situation; or

(b) a child PVOT (under 18) who is suspected of committing a criminal offence as a direct consequence of being a victim of trafficking,

45 *OAO Neftyanaya Kompaniya Yukos v. Russia*, 2011, [540].

prosecutors should adopt the following four-stage assessment when applying the Full Code Test for Crown Prosecutors. This is so even where there is no clear evidence of duress or where the offence cannot attract the s45 defence because it is an excluded offence under Sch 4.

First stage: Is there a reason to believe that the person is a victim of trafficking or slavery?

10.100

The prosecutor is required to consider whether the suspect or defendant is a potential victim of trafficking or modern slavery. **Chapter 1** of this book explores the definition of trafficking and modern slavery, both in respect of adults and children (the definition differs significantly between the two across the offences). **Chapter 4** sets out the identification framework in place for victims of trafficking in the UK, the National Referral Mechanism. Not all victims are referred into this identification framework, as adults must consent and cannot be compelled into being referred.

10.101

The Modern Slavery Statutory Guidance provides indicators of trafficking and modern slavery[46], and all professionals should be alert to the components and indicators of these offences. However, as discussed in **Chapter 1**, the definitions provided are not always consistent with international legal definitions. As confirmed by the ECHR in *VCL and AN v United Kingdom*, Art 4 ECHR compliance requires that the definitions set out in the ECAT and the Palermo Protocol must be followed when assessing whether an individual is a victim.

10.102

There is no requirement for a suspect or defendant to self-identify as a victim before enquiries are initiated[47]. This applies regardless of whether a referral or formal identification decision has been made under the NRM. As the Court of Appeal has recognised, objective evidence of a well-established trafficking model may be sufficient to establish a credible suspicion in an individual case[48].

10.103

The protective and investigatory duties arising under Art 4 ECHR, as outlined above, apply from the point at which authorities know or ought to know of credible indicators of trafficking or modern slavery. These duties are triggered by the evidence, not by procedural stage or formal identification.

46 See *R v HHD* [2018] EWCA Crim 2995 at [21.2]: note that *post*-EU exit the reference to Article 2 of the EU Directive should be read as Article 4 of ECAT.

47 This would be contrary to ECHR, Art 4, see: *Rantsev v Cyprus & Russia* (2010) 51 EHRR 1 at 296, 288 and Recital (1) of the EU Trafficking Directive.

48 See *R(TDT) v Secretary of State for the Home Department* [2018] EWCA Civ 1395, [2018] 1 WLR 4922.

The prosecutor's role

10.104

Prosecutors must assess investigations and evidence in line with CPS guidance. Applying the evidence limb of the Full Code Test with reference to s 45 MSA 2015 alone is insufficient to meet the CPS's obligations under domestic and international law.

10.105

Prosecutors should be familiar with the elements of trafficking under Art 3 of the Palermo Protocol and Art 4 of ECAT, as well as the definitions of slavery, servitude, and forced or compulsory labour (see **Chapter 1**). This will involve consideration of evidence collated from the Art 4 compliant police investigation (see above). They must also understand indicators of trafficking and related offences and make appropriate enquiries with relevant public authorities, such as Single Competent Authority (SCA)[49], Immigration Enforcement Competent Authority (IECA)[50], local authorities, Home Office, victim support providers, and youth offending teams, to determine whether a suspect or defendant may be a potential victim of trafficking or modern slavery.

10.106

In terms of a credibility assessment of the suspect or defendant the Court of Appeal has closely aligned its approach with the statutory guidance[51]. In *R v JXP*[52] the Court accepted the appellant's reasons explaining the late disclosure of trafficking notwithstanding that it was after a criminal trial in which it had not been disclosed. The importance of this is that the Court has recognised the fact that victims of trafficking will often make late disclosure about their trafficking circumstances. The CPS as a public authority should apply the principles and guidance set down in the statutory guidance specific to credibility as to do otherwise could render the decision unlawful[53].

10.107

The complexities of the elements set out in the criminal offences of human trafficking and modern slavery (MSA 2015, ss 1 and 2) are such that the Court

---

49 See Chapter 4: under the NRM there are two competent authorities, the SCA and the IECA. The label "Single Competent Authority" is accordingly a misnomer. Nevertheless, "SCA" is used as an umbrella term encompassing both authorities.

50 *R v HHD* [2018] EWCA Crim 2995. See para 19.

51 Home Office, *Modern Slavery Act 2015 – Statutory Guidance for England and Wales* (v 4.2, 10 October 2025), see Annexes D and E.

52 [2019] EWCA Crim 1280.

53 See Chapters 2 and 3 for discussion of cases where the Courts have held that other public authorities have acted unlawfully when they have failed to consider 'credibility guidance' viz trafficking victims.

of Appeal[54] has endorsed the appropriateness of considering whether or not someone is a PVOT by reference to the regional instruments (Art 4 of ECAT). This is consistent with the approach adopted by the Supreme Court in *MS (Pakistan)*[55] and confirmed by the ECtHR[56]. Where a suspect or defendant is a victim of slavery, servitude or forced and compulsory labour, they may also be a victim of trafficking within the meaning of the international and regional instruments as well.

10.108

At Stage 1 of the CPS guidance, it is appropriate to first assess whether a suspect or defendant is a victim of slavery, servitude, or forced or compulsory labour, followed by an assessment of trafficking in human beings. This approach can assist practitioners, as these forms of exploitation are explicitly recognised within the definition of human trafficking. Starting with slavery-related offences allows for a clearer determination of whether the individual meets the criteria for the s. 45 statutory defence. If they do, it may be unnecessary to further establish that they were trafficked for the purpose of such exploitation. Given the hierarchical nature of slavery and related acts, the severity of harm may also be relevant to both the public interest test and the application of the s. 45 defence.

10.109

In the case of an adult, consider whether each of the three components of trafficking are present:

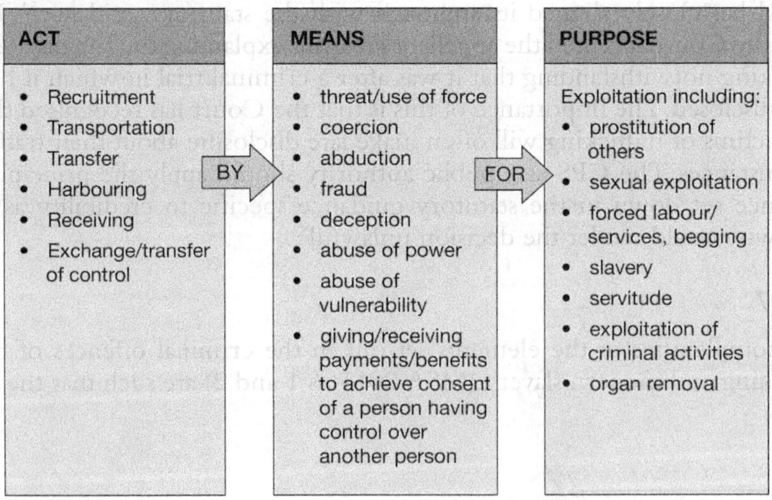

54 *R v HHD* [2018] EWCA Crim 2995 at para 21.2. Note: to assist practitioners, the Court endorsed the suggestions of the Respondent Crown in *R v HHD* without a full discussion of the issues. As set out above, following EU-exit, the reference to Art 2 of the EU directive in this case should be read as a reference to Art 4 of ECAT.

55 *MS (Pakistan) v Secretary of State for the Home Department* [2020] UKSC 9, [2020] 1 WLR 1373.

56 *VCL and AN v UK*.

10.110

In the case of a child (under 18) the means are not necessary. A child is a victim of trafficking if the act and purpose are present:

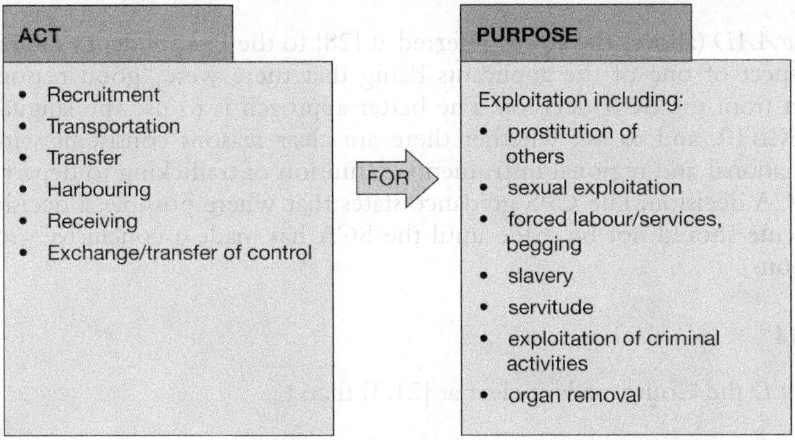

Analysis and departure from a positive NRM decision

10.111

In *R v VSJ*[57] the Court (comprising the Lord Chief Justice, the Vice President of the Court of Appeal Criminal Division and Goss J) considered *R v L* and noted that competent authority decisions are not binding on the Court[58]. The Court held that when reviewing whether or not to prosecute, ' … the cogency of the evidence which may be relied on by the Competent Authority must be subject to thorough forensic examination when the CPS is considering the question of nexus and whether it is in the public interest to prosecute[59]'. As observed by the Supreme Court in *MS (Pakistan)*[60] the identification decision reached by the SCA is a paper exercise[61], albeit with multi-agency involvement.

10.112

As set out below, one of the appellants in *R v VSJ*, VCL, was successful in his application to the ECtHR, where he alleged that the CPS's decision to prosecute him, as upheld by the domestic courts in *R v VSJ*, breached his rights under Arts 4 and 6 of the ECHR. This challenge concerned the CPS analysis of the NRM decision, the judicial scrutiny of the CPS decision-making and

57 [2017] EWCA Crim 36, [2017] 1 WLR 3153.
58 See para 38.
59 See para 39.
60 [2020] UKSC 9.
61 See para 14.

failings of the CPS to discharge their positive obligations under Art 4 ECHR (see above).

10.113

In *R v AAD* (above) the Court referred at [28] to the Respondent's submission in respect of one of the applicants being that there were "good reasons" to depart from the SCA decision. The better approach is to use the language of the ECtHR and to ask whether there are clear reasons consistent with the international and regional instruments' definition of trafficking to depart from the SCA decision. The CPS guidance states that where possible, a decision to prosecute should not be made until the SCA has made a conclusive grounds decision.

10.114

In *R v D* the Court made it clear at [21.3] that:

> '... in cases where there is a suspicion of trafficking or slavery, the CPS guidance requires prosecutors at the first hearing to request that a plea is not formally entered and to apply for an adjournment for further investigation into the defendant's possible status as the victim of slavery or trafficking.'

10.115

The Court went on to note at [24]:

> 'In such cases we recognise that the usual stage timetable for case progression under Better Case Management in the Crown Court and Transforming Summary Justice in the Magistrates' Court cannot apply and stage dates will need to be altered to accommodate the referral. Courts will no doubt wish to ensure that VOT questions are not missed. Conversely, we anticipate that courts will be astute to guard against unfounded attempts to raise a VOT point and so cause delay and disruption. Because of the BCM ramifications, we will pass a copy of this judgment to the Senior Presiding Judge for consideration and, if necessary, action.'

10.116

Prosecutors often face a dilemma: the four-stage decision-making process takes time, yet many suspects who may be potential victims of exploitation present a flight risk. Where such individuals are charged under the Threshold Test and/or remanded in custody, thereby triggering custody time limits, this may lead to a breach of Arts 4 and 6 ECHR.

10.117

In light of these concerns, and in response to issues raised by the Respondent and endorsed by the Court in *R v D*, the Plea and Trial Preparation Form was amended to include in the defence section the question: 'Is the defendant said to be a victim of modern slavery?' This procedural development marks a significant step in aligning criminal practice with the state's protective and investigatory duties under Art 4. By enabling courts to consider adjusting procedural timelines to allow an investigation into a defendant's exploitation status, it seeks to reconcile due process guarantees with compliance obligations under the Convention.

10.118

As explored further in **Chapters 4** and **5**, this procedural adaptation must be complemented by broader safeguarding mechanisms. In particular, provisions such as secure accommodation and other forms of protective support may assist prosecutors in discharging their obligations under Art 4. Achieving this, however, will require a coordinated and multi-agency approach to ensure that the CPS is effectively supported in identifying and responding to potential indicators of exploitation. As stated above an Art 4 ECHR investigation by the police is fundamental to this exercise.

10.119

Despite these reforms, the continuing flow of appeals in the Court of Appeal (Criminal Division) suggests that the protective purpose of the Plea and Trial Preparation Form, as a safeguard against breaches of Art 4, remains neither fully understood nor consistently applied. Importantly, while the form directs the question to the defence, the obligations under Art 4 vest in state authorities. Consequently, a failure by the defence to raise the issue does not absolve the Crown or the police of their own responsibilities where those obligations have been triggered. As reaffirmed by the ECtHR in *VCL v United Kingdom*, failures on the part of the defence cannot relieve state authorities of their positive obligations under Art 4 of the Convention.

Evidentiary value of a positive reasonable or conclusive grounds decision

10.120

Where the SCA makes a reasonable grounds decision, or latterly a conclusive grounds decision that the defendant is either a victim of trafficking or not (see **Chapter 4**), the prosecutor must consider it. In *R v L*[62] the court, when

62 [2013] EWCA Crim 991, [2013] 2 Cr App Rep 247 at para 28.

considering the weight to be applied to the trafficking identification decision taken under ECAT, Art 10, held:

> 'Whether the concluded decision of the competent authority is favourable or adverse to the individual it will have been made by an authority vested with the responsibility for investigating these issues, and although the court is not bound by the decision, unless there is evidence to contradict it, or significant evidence that was not considered, it is likely that the criminal courts will abide by it.'

10.121

This was re-affirmed by the Court in *R v S(G)*[63], where the Court also considered the status of the fact-finding decision of the First-tier Tribunal ('FTT'). However, the SCA decision is not commensurate in weight with a determination of fact made by the Immigration and Asylum Chamber ('IAC') fact-finding tribunal. The determination of the FTT (IAC) will carry a different weight from that of the SCA decision[64]. Any challenge to the FTT decision will require caution bearing in mind the principles of collateral attack of judgments[65] and the Supreme Court's repeated pronouncement of the expertise of the FTT and Upper Tribunal (IAC), the most recent of which post-dates *R v S(G)* and is specific to the identification of victims of trafficking[66].

CPS failures and judicial oversight:

Key Deficiencies Identified by the ECtHR of the analysis of VCL's case in VSJ

10.122

The ECtHR found that the CPS had breached its obligations under both Art 4 and Art 6 ECHR by prosecuting a recognised victim of trafficking without conducting a proper assessment of the trafficking indicators and without providing adequate reasons for rejecting the Competent Authority's conclusive grounds decision.

10.123

Although the Court declined to determine the second applicant's submission that the police's failure to conduct an Art 4-compliant police investigation

63 [2018] EWCA Crim 1824, [2018] 4 WLR 167, [2019] 1 Cr App R 7, [2019] Crim LR 147. See para 76.iii.

64 See *MS (Pakistan) v Secretary of State for the Home Department* [2020] UKSC 9.

65 The FtT's findings are not *res judicata* on the question whether an individual is a victim of trafficking. However, any collateral attack of the finding of the FtT or suggestion of little weight being placed on the findings should be exercised with caution in the light of the dicta in *MS(Pakistan)* and the recognised expertise of that fact-finding tribunal *viz* identification of victims of trafficking.

66 Ibid. *MS(Pakistan)*.

constituted a separate breach of Art 6 on procedural grounds, the reasoning applied to the CPS has broader implications for all public authorities involved in the criminal justice process, in particular the police (see above).

- The CPS did not dispute the nexus between the trafficking of the appellant *VCL* and the offence; rather, it repeatedly asserted that there was no clear evidence the applicant had been trafficked, despite the Competent Authority's conclusive decision.
- The CPS failed to provide clear or reasoned justification for departing from the Competent Authority's findings. The limited explanations offered, such as those provided to a Member of Parliament and the Court of Appeal, were peripheral and did not address the core elements of trafficking.
- The Court of Appeal, in dismissing the applicant's appeal twice, relied on the same inadequate reasoning, failing to engage with the substance of the trafficking determination.
- The CPS could have lawfully disagreed with the Competent Authority's decision if it had provided clear reasons consistent with the definitions in the Palermo Protocol and ECAT. It did neither.
- Despite the applicant being discovered in circumstances that gave rise to a credible suspicion of trafficking, his case was not referred to the NRM, and he was prosecuted without the necessary safeguards.
- The ECtHR concluded that the failure to investigate and assess trafficking indicators undermined the fairness of the proceedings and constituted a breach of both Art 4 (protective and procedural duties) and Art 6 (fair trial rights).

10.124

This case underscores the need for prosecutors to engage meaningfully with trafficking determinations and to ensure that decisions to prosecute are grounded in a proper understanding of the State's obligations under international and domestic law, specifically positive obligations arising in Art 4 (see above).

The crown's assessment on whether to proceed

Initiating criminal proceedings where Art 4 positive obligations are triggered

10.125

Where the prosecution accepts that a defendant is a potential victim of trafficking (VOT) or modern slavery and, applying CPS guidance, determines that prosecution remains appropriate, it may be thought that it is not necessary, merely for the purposes of identification, to delay proceedings pending an NRM referral or decision. The prosecution may, based on available evidence, consider that in recognising the defendant as a VOT, that it can proceed in accordance with CPS policy.

10.126

However, what has not been fully determined in domestic jurisprudence is the procedural consequence of the prosecution accepting that a credible suspicion arises that the defendant is a victim of trafficking or modern slavery, that the trafficking or modern slavery is connected to their criminality and their submission that they were compelled to commit the offence.

10.127

Such a decision triggers the State's procedural obligation under Art 4 ECHR to conduct an effective investigation, one that meets the standard required where a violation of an absolute right is alleged. It also activates the protective duties owed to the individual, as previously outlined.

10.128

Both obligations are binding on the police and the CPS, as confirmed in *F.M. v Russia*. Any decision by the CPS to proceed with prosecution in the absence of an Art 4 compliant investigation risks a violation of Arts 4 and 6 ECHR. First, the decision to prosecute may be made without a prior police investigation capable of establishing all the facts material to the public interest decision, thereby undermining the protective duties articulated in *VCL v United Kingdom*. Second, the absence of such investigation may deprive the defendant of evidence supporting a s 45 defence. The procedural integrity of the prosecution decision, and the fairness of the trial, depend on the proper discharge of these positive obligations. An independent, Art 4 compliant investigation should be carried out before the decision to prosecute is made.

The imperative of an Art 4-compliant investigation

10.129

Where *prima facie* evidence of trafficking or slavery existed at the point of threshold charge or remand in custody, the state's protective and investigatory duties under Art 4 may already have been breached. Consequently, any subsequent decision to pursue prosecution, even where the defendant is accepted to be a victim, risks entrenching those breaches in the manner identified by the ECtHR in *VCL*.

Sequencing obligations and custody time limits

10.130

A further practical tension arises between the state's obligations under Arts 4 and 6 ECHR and the strict custody time limit that applies when a defendant is remanded (which is, itself, informed by the obligations under Arts 5 and 6 ECHR). When someone who might be a victim of trafficking or modern slavery is kept in custody, there is a practical challenge. On one hand, the authorities have a duty properly to investigate whether the person is a victim. On the other hand, the trial must start within a set time limit because the person is being held in custody. This may affect how the defendant makes decisions, since they may not wish to delay their trial or extend custody. It also places pressure on the prosecution, who could face criticism if the case is not ready in time, and on the court, which must ensure compliance with statutory time limits.

10.131

Resolving this tension is complex. Custody time limits cannot justify moving forward with a prosecution without a proper investigation or without considering whether proceeding would breach Articles 4 and/or 6 ECHR. Defence lawyers may have more detailed knowledge of the defendant's account, but the defendant may be fearful of full disclosure or unable to explain the extent of their exploitation. Where exploitation involves an organised criminal network, uncovering the scale and nature of that operation requires a police investigation to obtain the necessary evidence.

Editorial perspectives on the impact of Art 4 breaches on fair trial rights

10.132

There is some divergence of editorial opinion on the impact that a failure to investigate, as required by Art 4, has on the fairness of a trial. This divergence is nuanced, reflecting differences of emphasis and framing rather than fundamentally opposing positions. It is useful to set out these perspectives because, in the experience of the editors and authors of this chapter, alleged breaches of Arts 4 and 6 are frequently cited in grounds of appeal but rarely form the core of oral submissions or appellate reasoning. These views are presented transparently and as a guide, recognising that the issues may require further consideration by the senior courts.

10.133

Ben Douglas-Jones KC's view: In some cases, it may be that proceeding with a trial where there has been a breach of the Art 4 procedural obligation to investigate will not lead to an unfair trial; in other cases, it will. Each case will turn on its own facts. Where the Art 4 breach is a breach of the obligation to investigate a possible offence of slavery, servitude, forced or compulsory labour or trafficking in human beings and/or where a court proceeds when other deficiencies identified in *VCL* (see above) are present it may not lead to a breach of Art 6. However, in other cases it will. In those circumstances, a second limb abuse of process application to stay the case/indictment will be appropriate and any conviction may be unsafe.

10.134

Where a court is considering a situation where there appears to have been a breach of Art 4 and one or both parties are nevertheless inviting the court to proceed with the trial, it is necessary for the judge, irrespective of whether the issue is raised by the parties, actively to consider, hearing submissions from counsel and potentially receiving evidence on a *voir dire*. The judge will in those circumstances need to determine whether it would be unfair in an Art 6 sense for the trial to proceed. This will turn on whether it would or might well be unfair to try the defendant by reference to the CPS guidance (including whether Art 4 positive obligations have been complied with). The unfairness in this sense is governed by *ex parte Bennett* limb 2 principles: see *AAD*.

10.135

The Court of Appeal (Criminal Division) shall allow an appeal against a conviction where the conviction is unsafe and otherwise shall dismiss the appeal; s 2 of the Criminal Appeal Act 1968. Whilst breaches of Convention rights are always relevant in assessing whether a conviction is unsafe, they are never determinative; a breach of Art 6 does not automatically render a conviction unsafe[67].

10.136

As was said by the House of Lords (in relation to a breach of the reasonable time requirement in Article 6):

> 'the court is concerned to reject any argument that a breach of the reasonable time guarantee *automatically* means that the trial proceedings have to be set aside if they have already taken place. There is no right under the Convention to have them set aside in all such cases. Article 13 of the Convention would give a right to have the proceedings set aside only in those (rare) cases where, in the circumstances, it would be an essential element of "an effective remedy" for the violation. In other cases a less drastic remedy, for example, by way of declaration, reduction in sentence or damages, will do; a defendant cannot demand more'[68].

67 *R v Abdurahman* [2019] EWCA Crim 2239.
68 AG Ref (No 2 of 2001) [2003] UKHL 68, [165].

10.137

In three recent cases, the Court was not attracted by arguments founded on Art 4. In *R v Thakoraka-Palmer*[69], the Court held at paragraph 41 that the applicant's submission on "*restoration*" of Art 4 rights was misconceived and that the safety of the conviction should be assessed by reference to whether the CPS properly and lawfully applied its guidance on prosecuting possible victims of exploitation.

10.138

In *Henkoma*[70], at paragraph 35, Carr LJ (as she then was) held that breaches of Art 4 do not, by themselves, render a prosecution unlawful and that the focus must be on the safety of the conviction. In that case the facts of the exploitation were agreed between the parties. The seriousness of the offences (firearms) was such that Art 4 breaches were deemed to add little to the abuse of process argument underpinning the appeal.

10.139

In *FGH*[71], where Art 4 was a standalone ground, the Court rejected its significance, with Farbey J setting out at [42]:

> '[Counsel for the applicant] relied on article 4 of the European Convention on Human Rights (prohibition of slavery and forced labour) to argue that the applicant's prosecution breached the State's procedural obligation to investigate situations of potential trafficking. We are not persuaded that there was any arguable breach of article 4. In any event, this line of argument adds nothing of substance to the other submissions advanced on the applicant's behalf.'

10.140

Michelle Brewer's view: An overarching point to be made is the role of the Court of Appeal (Criminal Division) differs from that of trial courts. The Court of Appeal focuses on whether the prosecution's decision to prosecute was lawful, applying public law principles such as rationality and proportionality. In trafficking and modern slavery appeals against conviction the Court has primarily focused on whether the prosecution's reasons on public interest and culpability are vitiated by public law error. By contrast, trial judges are not limited to that standard. When considering Art 4 'failure to investigate' arguments in abuse of process applications, they are required to assess whether the trial itself would be fair. Domestic authority and ECtHR case law confirm that this is a substantive, merits-based evaluation of trial fairness, not a review confined to public law error.

69 [2023] EWCA Crim 491.
70 [2023] EWCA Crim 808 at [35].
71 [2024] EWCA Crim 1353.

10.141

The Court of Appeal does not prescribe, and certainly does not limit, the approach first-instance courts may take when faced with an abuse of process argument founded on failures in the investigation which breach Art 4 and their impact on a defendant's Art 6 rights.

10.142

The trial judge starts from the principle that Art 4 only imposes a procedural duty to investigate where there is a credible suspicion of trafficking, slavery, servitude, or forced labour. This duty arises as soon as allegations or clear indicators come to the authorities' attention, or ought reasonably to have been known which give rise to a credible suspicion of Art 4 harm (see **Chapter 4** and **14**). It requires prompt, independent inquiries by the police to establish the facts and identify offenders, combined with measures to protect victims, such as early identification by trained specialists and support for their recovery so they can participate effectively in proceedings.

10.143

The judge must decide whether this duty was triggered during the investigation or criminal proceedings and whether it was properly discharged, considering what reasonable steps were required for an Art 4-compliant investigation. Timing is critical: the obligation is judged by what was known or ought to have been known at the time, not by later outcomes. Rejecting that a failure to investigate in compliance with Art 4 based on findings from a flawed investigation risks circular reasoning and undermines scrutiny of credible exploitation, as seen in *VCL and AN*. This is because breaches of Art 4 are not mere procedural defects but structural failures of State responsibility, striking at the integrity of the trial process and, where serious, potentially amounting to an abuse of process. As Lord Kerr explained in *DSD v Commissioner of Police of the Metropolis*[72], failures to investigate allegations of a violation of a fundamental right are failings which are 'structural and constitutional in nature, going to the heart of the rule of law.' This distinguishes them from procedural errors, which may not breach Art 6[73]. Both the Supreme Court and Strasbourg treat failure to investigate a fundamental right as a structural defect that can fatally undermine trial integrity (*VCL*).

72 [2018] UKSC 11.

73 See *Abdurahman* [2019] EWCA Crim 2239, [2020] All ER (D) 13 (Jan), which concerned procedural failings in a terrorism investigation, specifically the absence of caution and denial of legal advice. The analysis in that judgment of *Ibrahim v UK* may now require re-visiting in the light of subsequent ECtHR Grand Chamber judgments, including *Beuze v Belgium* (2019), adopting an approach more aligned with *Cadder v HM Advocate* [2010] UKSC 43, considering *Salduz v Turkey*.

10.144

The trial judge applies Strasbourg principles proactively, assessing whether any failure to investigate under Art 4 so compromises the defendant's ability to have a fair trial, or so undermines the justice system, that continuing would amount to an abuse. This is a fact-sensitive, trial-focused assessment, not a public law review of whether the investigation was lawful or reasonable.

10.145

In some cases, the trial judge may conclude that the standard will be met where the police have complied with s 23 of the Criminal Procedure and Investigations Act 1996 (CPIA) and, in context, that investigation also meets the minimum requirements of an effective Art 4 investigation without being undermined by failures in protective duties[74].

10.146

However, as the Court held in *VCL*, an accused's status as a trafficking victim is a "fundamental aspect" of the defence and must be secured without restriction. Where serious shortcomings in victim protection compromise the victim's ability to contribute to the investigation, or where the investigation fails to pursue lines of enquiry aimed at establishing the facts of the trafficking allegation and identifying offenders, CPIA compliance alone will be insufficient. In such cases, a further investigation may be required to ensure fairness and legality, or, if the process has been irreparably tainted by historical Art 4 breaches, no such investigation may be possible. In those circumstances, the trial judge will have to consider whether the Art 4 failure to investigate gives rise to an Art 6 violation. This is consistent with the analysis in *VCL* and *R v O*[75], where the Court held that the appellant had not been provided with a fair trial (Art 6) because neither the defence nor the prosecution took steps to investigate the appellant's account of trafficking.

Henkoma, Thakoraka Palmer and FGH

10.147

In *VCL and AN v UK*, the Strasbourg Court criticised the Court of Appeal's narrow review, which focused on whether prosecutorial discretion had been

74 The CPIA Code of Practice (Criminal Procedure and Investigations Act 1996, s 23(1), revised March 2015) sets out the procedural framework for recording, retaining, and disclosing material in criminal investigations. Where victims of trafficking are defendants, the Code's obligations regarding recording of all relevant material (paras 4.1–4.4), retention (paras 5.1–5.8), sensitive material handling (paras 6.12–6.14), and revelation to the prosecutor (paras 7.1–7.4) provide the specific statutory mechanism by which Art 4 investigative standards should be met. Failures to comply with the Code in trafficking cases may engage both Art 4 and Art 6 obligations.

75 [2008] EWCA Crim 2835, see para 26.

misapplied rather than examining the State's positive obligations under Art 4 and the impact of their breach on a defendant. The Court held that this approach risks penalising victims for failing to identify themselves and allows authorities to rely on their own failure to fulfil operational duties. As a result, the ECtHR concluded that the proceedings as a whole were not fair and found a violation of Art 6.

10.148

The Court of Appeal has not yet addressed the ECtHR's finding in *VCL and AN*[76] that prosecution itself can breach Art 4 protective duties, a point Strasbourg considered material to the public interest assessment. CPS guidance recognises that decisions to prosecute in trafficking and modern slavery cases must comply with Art 4. A failure to investigate or discharge protective obligations directly affects the public interest limb of that decision and, as in pre–s 45 cases, is highly relevant to the assessment. Applications to stay for abuse of process turn on unfairness, oppression, and illegality. Where continuing a prosecution entrenches Art 4 breaches, particularly where failures in protective duties compromise the defendant's ability to engage in an investigation into their exploitation, these failings may undermine the public interest analysis and, in some cases, justify a stay[77]. *VCL and AN* therefore establishes that where indicators of trafficking or modern slavery have not been properly investigated, later appellate review confined to the traditional abuse-of-process framework will not, in general, suffice to restore compliance with Art 6.

10.149

This distinction of approach highlights the gap between first-instance courts, which can address fairness and legality through abuse-of-process applications, and the narrower appellate role of the Court of Appeal. As *R v Thakoraka Palmer* illustrates, the Court of Appeal has emphasised that its function is not to 'restore' rights or directly to remedy any prior State breach of Art 4. Although the appellant in that case contended that his status as a victim of trafficking rendered his conviction unsafe, the Court held that the State's positive obligations under Art 4 do not provide a free-standing ground of appeal; instead, trafficking was treated as part of the factual matrix informing culpability and prosecutorial discretion. As set out above, the ECtHR, however, considered that such a confined focus on abuse of process and the exercise of prosecutorial discretion failed to remedy the disadvantage arising from the non-recognition of the applicants as trafficking victims, and did not cure the earlier investigative failures. In consequence, the proceedings, viewed as a whole, could not be regarded as fair, leading to a violation of Art 6(1).

76 *VCL and AN v United Kingdom* [159], [161].
77 *AAD, AAH, AAI* and R[2022] EWCA Crim 106 at [127].

10.150

While *VCL and AN v United Kingdom* (ECtHR) preceded this judgment and was raised in argument, the Court did not directly apply or engage with the core principles articulated in *VCL* or *SM v Croatia* concerning the timing and scope of Art 4 duties. In particular, the judgment does not analyse whether, and at what stage, an Art 4 obligation to investigate or protect was triggered during the criminal process, nor whether any failure had procedural consequences under Art 6 as recognised in *VCL*.

10.151

Instead, the Court's reasoning focused on a retrospective assessment of the appellant's credibility absent an Art 4 compliant investigation, the nexus between trafficking and offending, and the seriousness of the criminality. It concluded that there was no abuse of process and that the conviction remained safe. Although trafficking principles were referenced, the judgment leaves open how future domestic appellate decisions will address cases framed squarely on ECtHR concepts such as 'credible suspicion' or 'prima facie indicators', arising during first instance criminal proceedings and whether they will fully reflect *VCL*'s analysis of procedural and fair trial rights where trafficking identification was missed and no Art 4 investigation was undertaken.

10.152

In *Henkoma*, the Court of Appeal acknowledged multiple safeguarding failures and accepted that the appellant was a victim of trafficking linked to the offending. It also recognised breaches of Art 4, including failures to refer the appellant to the National Referral Mechanism. However, these breaches were treated as background facts rather than determinative of the prosecution's legality or the conviction's safety.

10.153

The Court did not consider whether, during the Woolwich or Isleworth proceedings, the threshold of credible suspicion triggered a duty to investigate under Art 4. Instead, as in *Thakoraka Palmer*, it adopted a retrospective approach. This reflects the domestic abuse of process framework but leaves unresolved questions about the operational duty to investigate and its implications for first-instance decision-making and trial fairness.

10.154

Finally, the judgment does not explore the functional content of Art 4 obligations, such as early identification, specialist assessment, and protective measures, which Strasbourg regards as integral to an effective investigation. Nor does it address whether historical safeguarding failures preceding the firearms offences should have informed the legality of the earlier prosecutions. While the Court rightly emphasised the gravity of the offending and the limits of appellate review, its analysis highlights the absence of senior domestic authority directly addressing the constitutional nature of Art 4 breaches and their potential impact on trial fairness. In the case of *Henkoma,* even where the prosecution for the firearms offence remained in the public interest, the quashing of the earlier convictions would likely have had a bearing on sentence.

10.155

The appeal in *R v FGH* was not argued on the basis that failures to investigate under Art 4 gave rise to an Art 6 fair trial violation as analysed by the ECtHR in *VCL and AN v UK.* It was framed purely in domestic abuse-of-process terms, with reference to CPS guidance, rather than as a claim that missed trafficking identification and protection structurally undermined trial fairness.

10.156

Applying *R v S(G)* and *AFU,* the Court asked whether, had the applicant's trafficking status been known, the prosecution would or might well not have been brought, or whether compulsion so reduced culpability that prosecution was not in the public interest. The reasoning was retrospective and focused on culpability and public interest, not on whether Art 4 duties were triggered and discharged or their consequences for Art 6.

10.157

Art 4 obligations were treated as contextual rather than constitutional. The Court did not engage with Strasbourg principles on 'credible suspicion,' the timing of investigative duties as per *SM v Croatia,* or the interplay between an Art 4 and infringement of Art 6 as per *VCL.* This divergence from ECtHR method persists throughout the appellate jurisprudence, however domestic public law cases such as *R (oAo KP) v Secretary of State for Foreign, Commonwealth and Development Affairs*[78], drawing on Supreme Court jurisprudence signal a shift towards more intensive scrutiny where fundamental rights are at stake, which may presage closer alignment with the ECtHR.

Is there clear evidence of duress or of a s 45 defence?

10.158

As above, Art 4 positive obligations outlined above, remain material to these stages of the decision-making.

78 *R (oAo KP) v Secretary of State for Foreign, Commonwealth and Development Affairs* [2025] EWHC 370 (Admin).

10.159

If a suspect or defendant is identified as a victim of trafficking (or slavery, or a slavery related offence) the prosecution must proceed to examine and apply Stages 2 to 4 of the CPS guidance. Stages 2 and 3 are defined steps in the application of the "Evidential Stage" of the Full Code Test for Crown Prosecutors. The Evidential Stage includes the following:

> '**4.6** Prosecutors must be satisfied that there is sufficient evidence to provide a realistic prospect of conviction against each suspect on each charge. They must consider what the defence case may be, and how it is likely to affect the prospects of conviction. A case which does not pass the evidential stage must not proceed, no matter how serious or sensitive it may be.
>
> **4.7** The finding that there is a realistic prospect of conviction is based on the prosecutor's objective assessment of the evidence, including the impact of any defence and any other information that the suspect has put forward or on which they might rely. It means that an objective, impartial and reasonable jury or bench of magistrates or judge hearing a case alone, properly directed and acting in accordance with the law, is more likely than not to convict the defendant of the charge alleged. This is a different test from the one that the criminal courts themselves must apply. A court may only convict if it is sure that the defendant is guilty.
>
> …'

10.160

As such, the reference to 'clear evidence' in the CPS guidance (concerning human trafficking and modern slavery) is shorthand for considering whether, having considered the likely state of the evidence at the end of the defence case, there is a realistic prospect of conviction, when duress (at Stage 2) and s.45 (at Stage 3) are taken into account.

Second stage: Is there clear evidence of duress?

10.161

At Stage 2, the prosecution must ask whether there is "clear evidence" of duress.

10.162

Duress provides a common law protection for victims of trafficking who commit offences. The scope of the defence was reconsidered by the House of

Lords in *R v Hasan*[79]. In that case, Lord Bingham stated, 'I find it unsurprising that the law in this and other jurisdictions should have been developed so as to confine the defence of duress within narrowly defined limits'[80].

10.163

The elements which must be established by a defendant are as follows:

- the defendant believed that there was a threat of death or serious injury[81];
- this belief was reasonable, as well as genuinely held[82];
- the threat was to the defendant, a member of his immediate family, or to a person for whose safety he reasonably regarded himself as responsible[83];
- the defendant's criminal conduct was directly caused by the threat[84]; and
- a sober person of reasonable firmness, having the same characteristics as the defendant, would have responded in the same way[85]; the characteristics which may be taken into account are only those which realistically make a person less able to resist threats: age and possibly sex are relevant, as are pregnancy and physical or mental disabilities; other factors are not[86].

10.164

There are also several factors which preclude a defence of duress from succeeding. Duress is unavailable:

- as a defence to murder, attempted murder, and perhaps to treason involving the death of the sovereign[87];
- if there were some evasive action that the defendant could reasonably have been expected to take, in order to avoid the threat without committing the offence[88]; if the threat were not expected to be carried out almost immediately, 'there may be little if any room for doubt that he could have taken evasive action, whether by going to the police or in some other way'[89]; or

79 [2005] UKHL 22 sub nom *R v Z* [2005] 2 AC 467.
80 At [21].
81 *R v Hasan* [2005] UKHL 22 at [21](2).
82 Ibid at [23].
83 Ibid at [21](3). The inclusion of '… a person for whose safety the defendant would reasonably regard himself as responsible' was not decisively affirmed in *R v Hasan*, but it appeared to Lord Bingham to be consistent with the rationale of the defence. This issue does not arise in these cases.
84 Ibid at [21](5).
85 *R v Graham* (1982) 74 Cr App Rep 235, CA at 241; *Graham* was approved in *R v Howe* (1987) 85 Cr App Rep 32, HL, at 65–66.
86 *R v Bowen* [1996] 2 Cr App Rep 157, CA at 166.
87 *R v Hasan* [2005] UKHL 22 at [21(1)].
88 Ibid at [21](6).
89 Ibid at [28].

- where the defendant voluntarily associated with people engaged in criminality, in circumstances where he foresaw or ought reasonably to have foreseen the risk of being subject to violent compulsion: the 'gang exception'[90].

10.165

While the third factor above is recognised as being the correct position in law, the factual background to the reported cases is such that it may be arguable that where children are recruited by gangs associated with county lines offending, and compelled to supply drugs, duress could be available as a defence. The regional trafficking instruments explicitly recognise the special vulnerability of children to trafficking (see above and **Chapter 1**).

10.166

However, in *R v VSJ*[91] in the submission made to the court by Anti-Slavery International (a charity founded in 1839 to combat slavery), as an intervener, it was urged that the court should take the opportunity to re-assess the approach the courts have taken to victims of trafficking in the context of duress and should develop the common law defence of duress "... in line with the international obligations of the UK so that it applies to victims of trafficking in a manner consistent with the UK's international obligations under Art 26 of the Council of Europe Convention, Art 3 of the Palermo Protocol and Art 4 of the Convention on Human Rights;" see [24] and [25]. Anti-Slavery International's submission was rejected at [27], where the Court held that

> '... the principles in the case law [concerning non-prosecution (ie, at the time, *R v M(L)*[92] and *R v L(C)*[93])] were established by the courts in a way which ensured that the domestic law of England and Wales was in accordance with the obligations under the international conventions: see in particular [7] of M(L).'

10.167

In *R v van Dao*[94], the Court of Appeal considered the case of a victim of trafficking who had been threatened with false imprisonment. The court was invited to expand the defence of duress:

> '... better [to] ensure that domestic (English [and Welsh]) criminal law implemented the United Kingdom's obligations of protecting victims of trafficking contained in the [Convention] and in Article 26[95]'.

90 Ibid at [39]; see also *R v Fitzpatrick* [1977] NILR 20 and *R v Sharp* [1987] QB 853.
91 [2017] EWCA Crim 36, [2017] 1 WLR 3153.
92 [2010] EWCA Crim 237, [2011] 1 Cr App Rep 135.
93 [2013] EWCA Crim 991, [2013] 2 Cr App Rep 247.
94 [2012] EWCA Crim 1717, [2013] Crim LR 234.
95 Ibid at [24](iv).

10.168

The judgment was adjourned to allow the Court to consider the judgment in *R v N; R v L*[96]. Gross LJ (giving the judgment) held:

> 'The furthest we are prepared to go and essentially in deference to the arguments addressed to us, is to express a provisional view: namely, that we would have been strongly disinclined to accept that a threat of false imprisonment suffices for the defence of duress, without an accompanying threat of death or serious injury. We would be minded to regard any such widening of the defence as ill-advised. While accepting that the issue has not been resolved by authority, our provisional view is supported by pointers in the more recent authorities and, more especially, by considerations of policy there highlighted ...'[97].

10.169

The corollary is that the non-punishment principle, whether under s 45 or in an abuse of process submission as considered in *AAD*, should not be conflated with the threshold for duress. The Court noted the observations of Hughes LJ in *LM* and those of Lord Judge CJ in *R v N; R v L*, warning against eliding these concepts. As Lord Judge stated at [12]:

> 'The logical conclusion of such elision would be to create a new form of immunity (albeit under a different name) or to extend the defence of duress by removing the limitation inherent in it. Whatever form of trafficking is under consideration, that approach... would be fallacious.' [Emphasis added]

10.170

Gross LJ concluded that no modification should be made to the defences of duress or duress of circumstances in the context of victims of trafficking facing criminal charges.

Third stage: Is there clear evidence of a s 45 defence?

10.171

Section 45 of MSA 2015 came into force on 31 July 2015. It creates defences available to defendants who are victims of trafficking who commit certain criminal offences. It does not apply to offences which appear in MSA 2015,

96 [2012] EWCA Crim 189, [2012] 1 Cr App Rep 35.
97 [2012] EWCA Crim 1717, [2013] Crim LR 234 at [33].

Sch 4. It also does not apply to offences which were committed before s 45 came into force: *R v. CS and Le*[98].

10.172

Section 45 creates separate statutory defences for adults and children: it is important to ensure the correct defence is identified[99].

10.173

In this section, we consider both the s 45 defence as considered within the prosecutorial decision to prosecute (third stage) and where the statutory defence is run at trial.

10.174

If the offence is not a Sch 4 one, and the prosecutor is not satisfied that there is sufficient evidence to provide a realistic prospect of conviction against a suspect on a particular offence when the statutory defence is considered, the evidential stage of the Full Code Test would not be met; in addition, although in those circumstances it is academic, it would also not be in the public interest to prosecute.

10.175

Even if the offence is a Sch 4 one, the prosecutor will need to consider whether the defence would otherwise have applied, as this would inform the overall decision as to whether to prosecute in the public interest.

Elements of the statutory defence: Adults

10.176

Section 45(1)–(3) provides:

(1) A person is not guilty of an offence if—

  (a) the person is aged 18 or over when the person does the act which constitutes the offence,

  (b) the person does that act because the person is compelled to do it,

  (c) the compulsion is attributable to slavery or to relevant exploitation, and

98 [2021] EWCA 134.

99 See *R v. NHG* [2022] EWCA Crim 859 and *R v. ADG and BIG* [2023] EWCA Crim 1309 as examples of where this did not occur.

(d) a reasonable person in the same situation as the person and having the person's relevant characteristics would have no realistic alternative to doing that act.

(2) A person may be compelled to do something by another person or by the person's circumstances.

(3) Compulsion is attributable to slavery or to relevant exploitation only if—

(a) it is, or is part of, conduct which constitutes an offence under s 1 or conduct which constitutes relevant exploitation, or

(b) it is a direct consequence of a person being, or having been, a victim of slavery or a victim of relevant exploitation.

10.177

Section 45(5) provides (and is applicable to both adults and children):

(5) For the purposes of this section—

'relevant characteristics' means age, sex and any physical or mental illness or disability;

'relevant exploitation' is exploitation (within the meaning of s 3) that is attributable to the exploited person being, or having been, a victim of human trafficking.

10.178

With an adult, the tribunal of law (judge in the Crown Court) must be satisfied there is:

(1) some evidence that the defendant did the act (which would be an offence but for the defence) because he was compelled to do it; and

(2) some evidence that the compulsion is attributable to slavery or to relevant exploitation; and

(3) some evidence for a tribunal of fact (jury in the Crown Court) to be able to infer that a reasonable person in the same situation as the person and having the person's relevant characteristics would have no realistic alternative to doing that act.

Statutory interpretation of s 45 MSA 2015

Common law principles

10.179

Although s 45(1)(c) requires that the compulsion be attributable to 'slavery' or 'relevant exploitation', the broader statutory framework, particularly ss 45(3), 45(5), and 56, makes clear that the s 45 defence may be invoked by a defendant who is, or has been, a victim of any conduct falling within s 1 (slavery, servitude, or forced or compulsory labour) and/or ss 2 and 3 (trafficking offences).

10.180

Section 45(3) specifies that the compulsion must be, or form part of, conduct constituting an offence under s 1 or conduct amounting to 'relevant exploitation'. Section 45(5) defines 'relevant exploitation' as exploitation attributable to the person being, or having been, a victim of human trafficking. Section 56 further clarifies that 'victim of slavery' includes victims of slavery, servitude, or forced or compulsory labour, and that 'relevant exploitation' refers to trafficking under ss 2 and 3.

10.181

For completeness, s 45(3)(b) provides that compulsion is attributable to slavery or relevant exploitation if it is a direct consequence of the person being, or having been, a victim of slavery or trafficking. This reinforces the interpretation that the defence is not limited to narrow categories of exploitation but extends to the full scope of conduct proscribed under ss 1 to 3 although s 2 and s 45 must be read separately[100].

10.182

Section 56 defines 'victim of slavery' in the following way[101]:

> **'Victim of Slavery**
>
> (1) For the purposes of Part 5 of the 2022 Act, "victim of slavery" means a person who has been subjected to **slavery, servitude or forced or compulsory labour**.
>
> (2) In determining whether a person has been subjected to slavery, servitude or forced or compulsory labour, regard may be had to all the circumstances including—
>
> (a) any of the person's personal circumstances (such as the person's age, the person's family relationships, and any physical or mental disability or illness) that significantly impair the person's ability to protect themselves from being subjected to slavery, servitude or forced or compulsory labour;
>
> (b) any work or services provided by the person.
>
> (3) The consent of a person (whether an adult or a child) to any of the conduct alleged to show that the person has been subjected to

100 See *R v How* [2026] EWCA Crim 476 at [37-38].

101 The definition itself is contained in Reg 2 The Slavery and Human Trafficking (Definition of Victim) Regulations 2022, made under s69(1) Nationality and Borders Act 2022.

slavery, servitude or forced or compulsory labour is not relevant to a determination as to whether the person is a victim of slavery.'

10.183

This construction is supported by Hansard[102], which reflects Parliament's intention to ensure that the defence protects victims of all forms of exploitation covered by the Modern Slavery Act. It is also consistent with common law principles of statutory interpretation, and, if necessary, s 3 of the Human Rights Act 1998 would require s 45 to be read and given effect in a way that is compatible with Art 4 ECHR, ensuring that victims are not punished for offences committed as a direct consequence of their exploitation.

Section 3 HRA interpretation

10.184

The ECtHR in *VCL and AN v United Kingdom* confirmed that the non-punishment principle forms part of the State's protective obligations under Art 4. Section 3 of the Human Rights Act 1998 requires courts to construe s 45 compatibly with Convention rights. This means giving effect to Art 4's protective purpose, alongside Art 7's guarantee of legal certainty. Section 45 of the Modern Slavery Act 2015 should therefore be interpreted to cover all the harms proscribed by Art 4 so that victims are not punished for offences they were compelled to commit as a direct consequence of those harms.

Burden and standard of proof: s 45

10.185

In *R v MK and R v Gega*[103], the Lord Chief Justice held that it was for the defendant to raise evidence of each of the elements of the defence and for the prosecution to disprove one or more of them to the criminal standard in the usual way[104].

10.186

Where there is some evidence of all three limbs, it then falls to the tribunal of fact (jury in the Crown Court) to consider whether it is sure that the prosecution has disproved:

102 For the correct modern approach to statutory construction, see *Luckhurst* [2022] UKSC 23; [2022] 1 WLR 3818 at [23].

103 [2018] EWCA Crim 667, [2019] QB 86; [2018] 3 WLR 895, [2018] 3 All ER 566, [2018] 2 Cr App R 14, [2018] Crim LR 922, [2018] CLY 599.

104 See paras 21, 25–28, 31, 36, 39, 44–45 of judgment.

(1) that the defendant did the act (which would be an offence but for the defence) because he was compelled to do it; or

(2) that the compulsion is attributable to slavery or to relevant exploitation; or

(3) that a reasonable person in the same situation as the person and having the person's relevant characteristics would have no realistic alternative to doing that act.

10.187

If the prosecution disproves any of the three limbs, the defence fails.

10.188

It follows that the defendant will not discharge the evidential burden of proof just because they have been identified or accepted as a victim of trafficking. The adult defendant must also show some evidence that they were compelled to commit the criminal act and that a reasonable person in the same situation as the defendant with their "relevant characteristics" would have no realistic alternative to doing that act.

Compulsion and nexus

10.189

A common thread through the variety of non-punishment safeguards within the trafficking instruments and MSA 2015, s 45 is the role of compulsion in the criminality, and whether there is a nexus between the trafficking of the victim and the criminal offending.

10.190

The position of children is dealt with below. It should be highlighted however that with s 45(1) an adult has to show some evidence of *compulsion*.

10.191

The prosecutor then has to satisfy the tribunal of fact so that it is sure that there was no relevant compulsion if the defence is to be attacked on that basis/limb.

10.192

With s 45(4) (the defence for children), all a child has to do is show that there is some evidence that the criminal act was committed as a *direct consequence* of the slavery or trafficking.

10.193

The prosecutor then has to prove that the criminal act was not committed as a direct consequence of trafficking or slavery if the defence is to be challenged on that basis/limb. Compulsion is unnecessary with children. In the context of Stage 4 of the CPS guidance (public interest) compulsion will be the touchstone of a prosecutorial decision to not prosecute or to discontinue proceedings in respect of an adult. With a child, there does not need to be any compulsion before it may not be in the public interest not to prosecute; see *R v VSJ*[105].

10.194

In *R v LM*[106] the court held that the word 'compelled' was not limited to the circumstances in which the English common law defences of duress and necessity apply. However, in *R v AAD*[107], the Court rejected a submission that 'compulsion' should be interpreted as being synonymous with 'causation'. *R v Baniulyte*[108] clarifies that the s 45 MSA 2015 defence and the common law defence of duress are 'not identical' and that s 45 may succeed where duress fails, notably because s 45 does not incorporate the duress requirement that the defendant must not have voluntarily put herself in a position where compulsion was foreseeable. The Court quashed the convictions, finding that the failure to advise the appellant about the s 45 defence denied her 'the opportunity to put forward a defence which quite probably would have succeeded'.

10.195

In *R v L* the court held[109]:

> 'The reasoning is not always spelled out, and perhaps we should do so now. The criminality, or putting it another way, the culpability, of any victim of trafficking may be significantly diminished, and in some cases effectively extinguished, not merely because of age (always a relevant factor in the case of a child defendant) but because no realistic alternative was available to the exploited victim but to comply with the dominant force of another individual, or group of individuals'.

10.196

Compulsion in the context of s 45(1), non-punishment and public interest is not synonymous with the threshold of pressure necessary for duress, the test for which is different and the threshold for which is undoubtedly higher[110].

---

105 [2017] EWCA Crim 36, [2017] 1 WLR 3153, *per* Lord Thomas CJ, at [22] and [37].
106 [2010] EWCA Crim 237, [2011] 1 Cr App Rep 135.
107 [2022] EWCA Crim 106, at [144] and [145].
108 [2025] EWCA Crim 1205.
109 [2013] EWCA Crim 991, [2013] 2 Cr App Rep 247 at para 13.
110 See *R v LM* [2010] EWCA Crim 237, [2011] 1 Cr App Rep 135, in particular Hughes LJ's analysis at [7] to [14].

The term 'compulsion' in the regional trafficking instruments is directed to the particular state of 'trafficking' and to victims of human trafficking. The Explanatory Report to ECAT[111] provides, in respect of non-punishment:

> '273. In particular, the requirement that victims have been compelled to be involved in unlawful activities shall be understood as comprising, at a minimum, victims that have been subject to any of the illicit means referred to in Article 4, when such involvement results from compulsion'.

10.197

Those illicit means include, 'threat or use of force or other forms of coercion, of abduction, of fraud, of deception, of the abuse of power or of a position of vulnerability or of the giving or receiving of payments or benefits to achieve the consent'. The Explanatory Report to ECAT also helpfully sets out what is meant by abuse of position of vulnerability, which is considered at length in Chapter 1 of this book.

10.198

For the purposes of MSA 2015, s 45, when considering whether a reasonable person would have acted as the defendant acted, the jury will have to consider both the nature of the compulsion and compulsion in the context of the seriousness of the offence; see, in the analogous context of public interest and abuse of process, the analysis of the Court of Appeal in *R v VSJ*[112] and *R v S(G)*[113].

10.199

In *R v EK*[114], the appellant had appealed her conviction and sentence on the ground that at the time of her criminality she was a victim of trafficking The appellant had pleaded guilty to conspiracy to control prostitution for gain, possession of false documents and removing criminal property. The Court held that, while she had previously been a victim of trafficking, at the time of her criminal activity her position was such that it did not extinguish her culpability or so diminish it as to cast doubt on the decision to prosecute. The appellant was deemed to be working alongside the trafficker and in a position of power. The Court observed that in such instances although it would not absolve

111 CETS, *Explanatory Report to the Council of Europe Convention on Action against Trafficking in Human Beings*.

112 [2017] EWCA Crim 36, [2017] 1 Cr App Rep 33: see the analysis of the cases ofVSJ and Craciunescu in particular.

113 Above, at [76], where the Court of Appeal Criminal Division recognised in terms that the starting point is to look at the seriousness of the offence before considering the effect on criminality/culpability of the dominant force of compulsion.

114 [2018] EWCA Crim 2961.

individuals from criminal responsibility; it may be reflected in a reduction of sentence passed[115].

10.200

In *R v GB*[116] the Court quashed a trafficking victim's conviction for possession of a false document with intent because of the nexus between the offending and the trafficking, and the level of compulsion that she had been under. In that appeal the Court considered the findings of the FTT (IAC), SCA positive decision and expert reports.

10.201

Where there is a gap in time between the trafficking and the offending, it is likely that there will not be a sufficient nexus between the trafficking and the offending to warrant a decision not to prosecute a suspect in the public interest. An example of where it would or might well not have been in the public interest to prosecute notwithstanding a significant gap in time is the case of A in *R v VSJ*[117]. There, A had been held in domestic servitude for many years as a child and adult. Her offending came several years after the servitude had ended but there was nevertheless a nexus because her offence was committed to obviate the possibility of her being re-trafficked.

10.202

What the above cases illustrate is that they will turn on their own facts and the weight attributed by the Court of Appeal to the findings of the FTT, SCA and conclusions of the experts will be case specific.

Elements of the statutory defence: children (under 18 years old)

10.203

Section 45(4) provides:

'(4) A person is not guilty of an offence if—

(a) the person is under the age of 18 when the person does the act which constitutes the offence,

(b) the person does that act as a direct consequence of the person being, or having been, a victim of slavery or a victim of relevant exploitation, and

115 See also *R v GS* [2018] EWCA Crim 1824.
116 [2020] EWCA Crim 2, [2020] 1 WLUK 128.
117 [2017] EWCA Crim 36, [2017] 1 WLR 3153.

(c) a reasonable person in the same situation as the person and having the person's relevant characteristics would do that act.'

Burden and standard of proof: s 45

10.204

With a child (or a defendant claiming to be a child) the tribunal of law (judge in the Crown Court) must be satisfied there is:

(1) some evidence that the defendant was under the age of 18 when he did the act which constitutes the offence; and

(2) some evidence that the defendant did that act as a direct consequence of the defendant being, or having been, a victim of slavery or a victim of relevant exploitation; and

(3) some evidence from which a tribunal of fact (jury in the Crown Court) is able to infer that a reasonable person in the same situation as the person and having the person's relevant characteristics would do that act.

10.205

As with an adult, with a child or possible child where there is some evidence of all three limbs above, it then falls to the prosecution to disprove the defence so that the tribunal of fact (jury in the Crown Court) is sure one of the components of the defence has been disproved: (1) that the defendant was under 18; (2) that the defendant was or had been a victim of trafficking, slavery, servitude, forced or compulsory labour; (3) that a reasonable person in the same situation as the defendant and having the defendant's relevant characteristics would have done the act.

Age: interplay between s 45(4) and s 45(1)

10.206

Where the prosecution proves this so that the tribunal of fact/jury is sure that the defendant was an adult, the jury should be directed that they should then go on to consider whether the Crown has disproved the three elements in s 45(1) (the adult defence).

Age: generally

10.207

Age is highly unlikely to be in issue where the defendant was born in the UK and has lived in the UK[118], but often arises in the case of third country nationals.

118 This is because there will likely be documentation evidencing age (medical records, birth certificate, school records etc).

The CPS guidance addresses the issue of age and provides that there should be 'due inquiry' into the age of the defendant and, if following this, there remains doubt (see also 'Children as suspects and defendants'[119]), the defendant must be treated as a child (see Guidance).

Age disputes and the s 45 defence

10.208

Chapter 6 of this book sets out the principles applicable where the age of a putative child is in dispute. The prosecution, as a public authority, is expected to be familiar with these principles and to apply them appropriately in any case where age is contested. Where acting for a child and age is put in issue, whether by the prosecution or another public body, this may necessitate a separate legal challenge (see Chapter 6).

10.209

In all cases, legal representatives must be familiar with the principles governing age assessments in the context of putative child victims of trafficking or modern slavery. These principles are essential to ensuring that such individuals are afforded the correct procedural and protective safeguards.

10.210

While there is no formal burden or standard of proof in general age assessments, s 45(4) of the Modern Slavery Act 2015 draws a clear legal distinction between adults and children. Where age is in dispute, the burden of proof lies with the prosecution to establish that the defendant was 18 or over at the relevant time. This is a legal and persuasive burden and must be discharged before the defendant can be treated as an adult for the purposes of the defence[120].

10.211

Where the defendant is said to turn 18 during the offending/indictment period, prosecutors need to frame charges or counts by reference to the defendant's age, with separate counts representing the criminal act committed when the defendant was a child and when they were an adult. In *R v Moussa*[121] the Court rejected the suggestion that directions should have been in accordance with s 45(4) where the indicted conduct took place when the appellant was an adult but the appellant maintained the process of pressure started when he was a child.

119 https://www.cps.gov.uk/legal-guidance/children-suspects-and-defendants, 13 July 2023, accessed 12 February 2025.

120 MK & Gega, [44]. For assessment of age generally in the criminal courts see also s405 Sentencing Act 2020 and s99 Children and Young Persons Act 1933.

121 [2024] EWCA Crim 214.

Victim of trafficking, slavery, servitude, forced or compulsory labour

10.212

As with s 45(1), s 45(4)(b) provides a defence to victims of slavery, servitude and forced or compulsory labour or human trafficking. The position is clearer with s 45(1) than with s45(4) because the expression 'victim of slavery' features in s 45(4), whereas it does not in s 45(1). As set out above, s 56(1) defines 'victim of slavery' to mean '… victim of: (a) conduct which constitutes an offence under s 1; or (b) conduct which would have constituted an offence under that section if that section had been in force when the conduct occurred'. This is addressed in the section of the defence as it applies to adults (see above).

Direct consequence

10.213

If the tribunal of fact/jury is sure that the defendant is a child, and if the prosecution seeks to challenge the defence on the ground that the commission of the act was not a direct consequence of trafficking, slavery, servitude, forced or compulsory labour, the prosecution faces a greater hurdle than with adults where it merely (relatively) has to prove that an adult was not compelled to act. It may be argued that the 'reasonable person' test (see below) does require a child to introduce some evidence of compulsion. However, the expert advisers to the Independent Review of the Modern Slavery Act 2015 Final Report[122] were of the view that compulsion did not feature as a component of s 45(4)(c). Applying the principles of statutory interpretation, taking s 45 as a whole, it is plain that a distinction was made between adults and children. The use of 'compelled' is only found within the requirements for adults not children. On plain reading of the legislation 'compulsion' is not a requirement for children and any attempt to read 'compulsion' into statute would be an impermissible gloss. When directing a jury, Judges should follow the current guidance in the Compendium, and not use the phrase 'menace of penalty'.[123]

Reasonable person in the same situation and having the person's relevant characteristics

10.214

In *DPP v M*[124] the court held that when considering the defence under s 45(4) age is only one factor to consider when considering the situation and relevant characteristics of the defendant for the purposes of subs.(4)(c), and the

122 Presented to Parliament by the Secretary of State for the Home Department, May 2019, at 4.4.3.
123 *R v Finch* [2026] EWCA Crim 477 at [32].
124 [2020] EWHC 3422 Admin; [2021] 1 WLR 1669, DC.

seriousness of the offence will be of less significance than it would in respect of the defence under s.45(1), as a child is more likely than an adult to behave without proper understanding of the nature and consequences of his actions. Note: this case was overturned in so far as it held that Conclusive Grounds decisions of the SCA are admissible at trial. They are not: see below.

Expert evidence: s 45 defence

10.215

For adult defendants to raise the s 45 defence, they must adduce evidence that they were compelled to commit the crime. Compulsion in the context of this statutory defence requires that a reasonable person in the same situation as the defendant with the person's relevant characteristics would have been so compelled. The defence involves both an objective element and a subjective element.

10.216

As with duress, psychiatric evidence might be admissible to show that a defendant was suffering from mental illness or impairment or a recognised psychiatric condition, provided that a reasonable person suffering from such illness might be more susceptible to compulsion. Such evidence might arguably assist the jury in deciding whether a reasonable person suffering from such condition in the same situation as the defendant might have committed the offence.

10.217

The Court of Appeal cases which have considered expert evidence have been varied in the weight placed on the evidence itself. Some cases have placed little weight on expert trafficking or medical evidence[125] supporting the identification of a defendant as a victim of trafficking and other cases have placed significant weight[126] on this evidence.

10.218

Unlike in asylum and human rights proceedings, expert evidence relevant to a defendant's status as a victim of trafficking or modern slavery is rarely deployed in first instance criminal cases. Country evidence may be admissible to show

125 See the commentary of Lord Judge in *R v N; R v L* [2012] EWCA Crim 189, [2013] QB 379 at 86c and the commentary of Lord Thomas in *R v* VSJ [2017] EWCA Crim 36, [2017] 1 Cr App Rep 33 at paras 87 and 88; *R v S(G)* [2018] EWCA Crim 1824, [2018] 4 WLR 167, [2019] 1 Cr App R 7, [2019] Crim LR 147 at 70, *R v EK* [2018] EWCA Crim 2961. See also *R v D* [2018] EWCA Crim 2995.

126 *See R v GB* [2020] EWCA Crim 2, [2020] 1 WLUK 128; *R v JXP* [2019] EWCA Crim 1280; *R v N* [2019] EWCA Crim 984, [2019] 6 WLUK 337; *R v S* [2019] EWCA Crim 1280; and *R v O* [2019] EWCA Crim 1389, [2019] 7 WLUK 537.

or contextualise what a person in the same situation as the defendant was enduring/had endured.

10.219

Expert evidence can be admitted in criminal proceedings if the following requirements are met:

(i) The expert evidence is of assistance and has sufficient probative value, in short, that it can provide the court and the jury with information which is likely to be outwith a judge or jury's knowledge and experience;

(ii) The expert has expertise in the relevant field (see Criminal Procedure Rules, Part 19);

(iii) The expert must be able to provide impartial, objective evidence on the matters within his field of expertise (see Criminal Procedure Rules, Part 19);

(iv) The expert's opinion must in other respects satisfy a threshold of acceptable reliability.

10.220

It is good practice in appropriate cases that defence practitioners, both at first instance and in appellate proceedings, instruct experts to assist the SCA in reaching reasonable and conclusive grounds determinations. Examples of the type of evidence that could be obtained in support of a s 45 defence and an NRM referral are shown in the Court of Appeal authorities[127] and have included physiological and psychiatric evidence, country expert evidence, trafficking indicators evidence (see **Chapters 3** and **4**).

10.221

A trafficking/modern slavery expert could be asked to comment on:

1. modus operandi and exploitation typology;
2. criminal exploitation indicators;
3. indicators of exploitation and trafficking;
4. trafficking account and plausibility;
5. expert opinion on whether the defendant is a PVOT (possible victim) or is a victim;
6. indicators of exploitation;
7. pre-trafficking background;
8. recruitment;

127 Ibid.

9. transportation;
10. control mechanisms;
11. harbouring;
12. transit stages;
13. destination and exploitation;
14. plausibility of trafficking account;
15. outline and analysis of physical, sexual and mental health issues;
16. support recommendations; and
17. aspects and type of debt bondage.

Admissibility of SCA and FTT decisions at trial

10.222

In *R v Brecani*[128] the Court of Appeal held that decisions of the competent authorities are not admissible in evidence at trial. However, they may be received and weighed by a court considering an abuse of process argument at first instance. The Court overturned the Divisional Court's decision of the previous year in *DPP v. M*[129] in that respect. The decision in *Brecani* was upheld in the special court's consideration of the Registrar's questions in *AAD*.

10.223

Decisions of competent authorities may, in an appropriate case, however, be received as fresh evidence under s 23 of the Criminal Appeal Act 1968 on appeal: see *R v. AAD* at [81]. Although their decisions are not binding on the Court, they will usually be respected by the Court in the absence of evidence undermining them: *R v. AFU*[130] at [88]; see *VCL and AN v the UK* (above), where it was said that "clear reasons" were needed to depart from an SCA decision.

10.224

In *R v S(G)*, Gross LJ explained (following the decisions of *R v Sadighpour* and *R v Mateta* in the context of the refugee defence being overlooked in the Crown Court) that a decision of the First-tier Tribunal and a letter from the Home Office could all be received applying the test for fresh evidence in s 23. This was approved in *Brecani* at [41] and in *AAD* at [81].

128 [2021] EWCA Crim 731.
129 [2020] EWHC 344 (Admin).
130 [2023] EWCA Crim 23.

Art 6 ECHR: procedural fairness and the impact of Art 4 failures

10.225

Both police and CPS policy recognise that they must act consistently with their positive obligations under Art 4. Where the Crown argues that a Single Competent Authority (SCA) decision should be departed from in circumstances where the police and CPS have breached their duty to investigate allegations of trafficking or modern slavery, it is difficult to see how a "good reason" can arise to justify departure from that decision.

10.226

The fairness of criminal proceedings may be further compromised because the SCA decision is inadmissible before the jury. In such circumstances, the Crown should not be permitted to rely on its own Art 4 failings, or those of the police, to undermine the Competent Authority's assessment. These failures may justify an abuse of process submission based on an Art 6 violation, regardless of the availability of the statutory defence under s 45. The existence of s 45 does not cure the procedural unfairness caused by institutional failures to fulfil Art 4 duties. Section 45 presupposes that the defendant must provide evidence of trafficking or related exploitation. Imposing this evidential burden in the absence of an Art 4 compliant police investigation may itself amount to a violation of Art 6.

Jury directions and routes to verdict

10.227

Jury directions and routes to verdict often end up highly complex in s 45 cases:

(i) because of the myriad ways in which a defendant may be a victim of 'slavery' (in the broad sense, meaning slavery, servitude, forced or compulsory labour, construed by reference to conduct amounting to an Art 4 ECHR violation) and/or 'exploitation' (within the meaning of ss 2 and 3 of the MSA 2015, where s 2(2) defines exploitation for trafficking by reference to slavery, servitude and forced or compulsory labour); and

(ii) because s 45 was drafted without proper consideration of the burden of proof, so the jury has to consider whether the prosecution has disproved one of the propositions in s 45(1) or (4): this may lead judges to formulate directions including double negatives, which is obviously undesirable.

10.228

When formulating directions for the jury, it is essential to acknowledge the tiered structure of the offences covered by s 1 of the MSA 2015. The crimes are hierarchical, meaning that an individual who is a victim of slavery is invariably also a victim of both servitude and forced or compulsory labour. In the same vein, a victim of servitude is, by extension, a victim of forced or compulsory labour.

10.229

Consequently, in such situations, the jury only needs to be instructed to determine whether the prosecution has proven, to the criminal standard, that the defendant is not a victim of forced or compulsory labour. This approach is sufficient because if the prosecution successfully discharges this burden, it will have logically demonstrated that the defendant cannot be a victim of either servitude or slavery.

10.230

It is also essential to consider what the real issues in any case are. In many cases, it may be appropriate for the prosecutor to concede: (i) that a defendant is a victim; and (ii) that the defendant was compelled to commit the offence but to maintain (iii) that a reasonable person of the defendant's age and sex and in the same situation as the defendant and having the defendant's physical or mental illness or disability would have had a realistic alternative to doing the act alleged.

10.231

Below is a sample route to verdict for an adult and a child defendant.

10.232

Facts relevant to the sample route to verdict: D is arrested supplying heroin and crack cocaine to drug users in a county town. D is indicted with being concerned in the supply of those drugs over a three month period leading up to the arrest date. A handset is seized from D on arrest. Analysis of the handset reveals that D is at the end of a county line. D is based in the county town. D is being directed by an organised crime group based in a city. Messages reveal that D has been threatened with the use of force. D has been supplying drugs for three months. In the last month, D has himself directed others to supply drugs[131].

Step 1

10.233

Direct the jury on the elements of trafficking[132].

131 When the editors of this work formulated directions with the editors of the Crown Court Compendium Part 1 – see 18-6 – it was resolved that the clearest way to direct a jury was first to direct them on the elements of human trafficking and modern slavery (on which the s.45 defence is parasitic), and, second, to direct them in respect of the elements of the defence.

132 See **Chapter 9**.

Step 2

10.234

Direct the jury on the elements of forced or compulsory labour[133].

Adults

10.235

In order to reach your verdict, you will need to answer the following questions in this order:

Question 1

Has the prosecution made you sure that D was not a victim of human trafficking/forced or compulsory labour?

- If the answer is yes, then your verdict will be guilty.
- If the answer is no, go on to consider question 2.

Question 2

Has the prosecution made you sure that D was not compelled to be concerned in the supply of heroin and crack cocaine by reason of being a victim of human trafficking/ forced or compulsory labour?

- If the answer to the question is yes, then your verdict will be guilty.
- If the answer to the question is no, go on to consider question 3.

Question 3

Has the prosecution made you sure that a reasonable person of D's age and sex and in the same situation as D (and having D's physical or mental illness or disability – outline any relevant evidence) would (at any point in the indictment period) have had a realistic alternative to being concerned in the supply of heroin and crack cocaine?

- If the answer to the question is yes, then your verdict will be guilty.
- If the answer to the question is no, then your verdict will be not guilty.

133 Ibid.

Child

10.236

In order to reach your verdict, you will need to answer the following questions in this order:

Question 1

Has the prosecution made you sure that D was not concerned in the supply of heroin and crack cocaine as a direct consequence of being a victim of human trafficking/forced or compulsory labour?

- If the answer to the question is yes, then your verdict will be guilty.
- If the answer to the question is no, go on to consider question 2.

Question 2

Has the prosecution made you sure that a reasonable person of D's age and sex and in the same situation as D (and having D's physical or mental illness or disability – outline any relevant evidence) would not have been concerned in the supply of heroin and crack cocaine (at any point in the indictment period) as D was?

- If the answer to the question is yes, then your verdict will be guilty.
- If the answer to the question is no, then your verdict will be not guilty.

Fourth stage: Is it in the public interest to prosecute?

10.237

The public interest test necessarily turns on the facts of individual cases. In each case it involves a careful analysis of the following:

- the seriousness of the offence: the more serious an offence, the greater the criminality or culpability that attaches to the offending; with a serious offence there will always be a greater need for prosecution in the public interest;
- the level of compulsion: the vulnerability of the defendant is highly relevant to this assessment of culpability; see *R v VSJ*[134] and *R v S(G)*[135].

---

134 [2017] EWCA Crim 36, [2017] 1 WLR 3153.
135 [2018] EWCA Crim 1824, [2018] 4 WLR 167, [2019] 1 Cr App R 7, [2019] Crim LR 147.

- the nexus of compulsion: for a prosecution not to be in the public interest there must usually be a direct link between the trafficking and the offending; where the trafficking is egregious, as in the case of A in *R v VSJ*,[136] an indirect link may suffice; see **para 5.47** above.

10.238

The CPS guidance is key to the public interest question. It helpfully assists in how the prosecution should address its mind to the public interest question in a case where the defendant is a victim of trafficking. It is essential that representatives for the Crown and the defendant consider the CPS guidance in its entirety.

10.239

When considering the public interest test the CPS has used the international and regional instruments' definition of trafficking to ensure that the appropriate international and regional legal obligations are met. The CPS has avoided adopting Parliament's distinction between trafficking and slavery. This approach is consistent with the concern that Parliament's artificial distinction between the two concepts may cause some potential victims of trafficking not to be identified as such[137].

10.240

In *VCL*[138] the Court held that because an individual's status as a trafficking victim may determine both evidential sufficiency and the public interest in prosecution, any decision to prosecute should, wherever possible, follow a trafficking assessment by a qualified authority. This is especially critical for children, given their heightened vulnerability. The Court recognised that prosecuting victims or potential victims of trafficking may, in certain circumstances, conflict with the State's duty under Art 4 to take operational measures to protect them where there is, or ought to be, credible suspicion of trafficking. That duty has two aims: to protect victims from further harm and to facilitate their recovery. The Court held that prosecution undermines both objectives; it exposes victims to the ordeal of criminal proceedings, risks re-trafficking, and may impede access to support and services envisaged by the Anti-Trafficking Convention. It can

136 [2017] EWCA Crim 36, [2017] 1 WLR 3153.

137 The reference to a trafficker having to facilitate the travel of a person to fulfil the elements of an offence of trafficking is, for example, unhelpful in MSA 2015, s 2. The section sets out that the travel may be fulfilled by *inter alia* the receipt or harbouring of a person. However, the international and regional definition of trafficking adopted in the regional instruments binding on the UK (whether under the Palermo Protocol, ECAT or the EU Trafficking Directive) does not require the 'travel' of a person: if he is recruited, received by someone or harboured by someone he will be a victim of trafficking if the other components of the definition are fulfilled. See Chapter 1, which deals with the definition at length.

138 *VCL and AN v UK* remains under enhanced supervision by the Committee of Ministers (1545th meeting, 2–4 December 2025). The UK government's annual report on responding to human rights judgments (December 2025) confirmed that *VCL and AN* remains an open case.

also create lasting barriers to reintegration into society. These considerations are directly relevant to the public interest analysis and reinforce why compliance with Art 4 is integral to ensuring fairness under Art 6.

The public interest and compulsion

10.241

The CPS guidance provides that 'compulsion' is irrelevant insofar as a child's status as a victim of trafficking is concerned. However, the guidance provides that compulsion will be a relevant consideration when considering whether the public interest in prosecuting a child is satisfied (see Code for Crown Prosecutors, para 4.14 b for further guidance).

10.242

The CPS guidance requires that the prosecutor be obliged to comply with their obligations under Art 26 of ECAT. The purpose of the four-stage approach to the prosecutor's decision is to give effect to Art 26 of ECAT. In respect of children, the CPS guidance reads, 'If there was compulsion, then this will reduce the public interest, but it is not a necessary element.' In *R v VSJ and Ors*[139] it was made clear (see above) that compulsion is not necessary to reduce the criminality or culpability of a child to a point where prosecution is not in the public interest. The CPS guidance was amended after *VSJ*. It expressly says that compulsion is relevant – but not necessary – when deciding whether or not to prosecute children; whereas compulsion is not a necessary component of trafficking in the case of a child. It may be appropriate for it to feature at Stage 4 in these terms but it should be underscored that compulsion is not necessary to render the prosecution of a child victim not in the public interest[140].

Abuse of process

10.243

Before s 45 came into force on 31 July 2015, abuse of process had existed as a safeguard in cases where the prosecution's decision to charge a defendant was exercised wrongly. In *R v DS*[141], the Lord Chief Justice, Lord Burnett, held that what had been considered to be a special type of abuse of process should no longer subsist as a safeguard for victims of trafficking and modern slavery because there was sufficient protection in s 45 and on appeal. In *R v AAD* the Court held at [116]:

139 For an analogous policy challenge, see *PK (Ghana) v Secretary of State for the Home Department* [2018] EWCA Civ 98.

140 Article 8 of the Directive includes compulsion as a component of the considerations justifying non-prosecution. In that respect Art 8 does not distinguish between adults and children (unlike Art 2 of the Directive, which defines trafficking in the case of children without reference to compulsion).

141 [2020] EWCA Crim 285.

> '… There is, on the face of it, no incompatibility in [the s 45] defence being available and there also being available the potential (in an exceptional case) for advancing the abuse of process jurisdiction with regard to a decision to prosecute and pursue to trial. Indeed, to retain the availability of the abuse of process jurisdiction for this purpose would seem better to preserve the obligations in the Convention and Directive, which extend not only to VOTs not being punished but also, in appropriate cases, to not being prosecuted.'

10.244

The Court went on to say at [117] that the abuse of process jurisdiction in cases involving the prosecution of victims of trafficking has sometimes been described as 'special' or 'unusual' but that is only really so because of the context. 'Any abuse of process argument has to take into account the context: and here such context necessarily includes the international obligations relating to VOTs and to the very sensitive issues arising with regard to VOTs'. At [118] the Court emphasised that the exceptional availability of abuse of process would complement s 45. At [119] the Court said:

> 'It would therefore follow that where the CPS has taken into account the relevant prosecutorial guidance and has taken into account any conclusive grounds decision (and has a rational basis for departing from a conclusive grounds decision if it has been favourable to the prospective defendant) there is simply no basis for an abuse of process challenge at all: since mere asserted disagreement with a decision to prosecute will never of itself suffice.'

10.245

At [120] it went on to say:

> 'But what if the CPS has failed unjustifiably to take into account the CPS Guidance or what if it has no rational basis for departing from a favourable conclusive grounds decision? That of course, given the terms of the current CPS guidance and given the much greater awareness nowadays of the situation concerning VOTs generally, is, or should be, a highly improbable scenario. But in principle such a scenario would, on ordinary public law grounds, seem to operate to vitiate that prosecution decision: whether by reason of a failure to take a material matter (viz the CPS prosecution guidance) into account or by making a decision to prosecute which is properly to be styled as irrational. Consequently, such a prosecution may, in an appropriate case, be stayed. This aligns with the principle, summarised helpfully in Blackstone's Criminal Practice 2022 at para D2.22 that, generally speaking, a decision to prosecute is not susceptible to judicial review in the Administrative Court because it may be challenged during the trial

process itself, most particularly by an application to stay the proceedings on the grounds of abuse of process. …'

10.246

In *AFU* the import of the decision in *AAD* concerning abuse of process was made clear. The Court found that Counsel had advised the appellant appropriately as to the possibility of deploying a s 45 defence. He pleaded guilty unequivocally. However, the police had failed to discharge their Art 4 operational measures duties to investigate the offence of trafficking and the prosecution failed to comply with the CPS guidance. There were clear indicators of trafficking from the outset, given the circumstances of the appellant's arrival into the UK. Had the guidance been complied with, the prosecution authorities would have discovered several material factors which were in fact overlooked, including that the appellant: (a) had been trafficked to the UK; (b) was required to work in two cannabis factories; (c) was beaten and deprived of sufficient food and his liberty; (d) prior to his arrest, he had been age-assessed as a minor, referred via the NRM as a potential victim of trafficking and had been placed into foster care; (e) had been the subject of a positive reasonable grounds decision; and (f) at the point when he was arrested for the instant offence, had gone missing from foster care and was working at another cannabis farm.

10.247

Therefore, if the guidance had been followed, the prosecution would have been discontinued at Stage 3 and Stage 4: the dominant force of compulsion from trafficking was sufficient to reduce the defendant's criminality or culpability to or below a point where it was not in the public interest for him to be prosecuted. It was an exceptional case where there was a clear abuse of process such that the conviction was unsafe.

10.248

If an abuse is found, then the remedy will not necessarily be a stay of proceedings. Depending on the reasons for an abuse, it may be that the decision to prosecute can be remade without the public law error identified.

10.249

As may be seen from *AFU*[142], the relevance of abuse of process at appellate level is that where the Court of Appeal concludes that the trial court would have

142 See also *R v AAB* [2024] EWCA Crim (26 July 2024), in which the Court of Appeal quashed a 2007 conviction for cannabis production, accepting that the appellant had been trafficked and compelled, and that inconsistencies in the accounts of trafficking victims do not negate the core elements of trafficking and compulsion.

stayed the indictment as an abuse of the process of the court had an application been made, the proper course is to quash the conviction[143].

10.250

Leading cases of historical significance, which retain some of their importance in the context of the *AAD / AFU* landscape include *R v L(C)* and *LM*. In *L(C)* in which Lord Judge, Chief Justice, held[144]:

> '… In the context of an abuse of process argument on behalf of an alleged victim of trafficking, the court will reach its own decision on the basis of the material advanced in support of and against the continuation of the prosecution. Where a court considers issues relevant to age, trafficking and exploitation, the prosecution will be stayed if the court disagrees with the decision to prosecute. The fears that the exercise of the jurisdiction to stay will be inadequate are groundless'.

10.251

In *R v LM*, the court stated[145] 'where trafficking is an obvious possibility, the police should enquire into it'. It arguably follows that, if it can be shown there was either no or inadequate inquiry into whether a defendant is a potential victim of trafficking, the prosecution cannot discharge their responsibility and the decision to prosecute will be flawed. The abuse of process regime concerning prosecutorial discretion in cases involving victims of trafficking who commit offences is akin to a public law challenge to the decision[146].

Excluded offences under Sch 4

10.252

For offences to which s 45 does not provide a defence, because they are excluded by Sch 4 to the MSA 2015, the non-prosecution regime in the CPS guidance and the abuse of process jurisdiction still apply[147]. However, the fact that an offence is excluded from the s 45 defence is a factor that will be taken into account in assessing the public interest in prosecuting.

143 *R v LM* [2010] EWCA Crim 237, [2011] 1 Cr App Rep 135 at §17.
144 [2013] EWCA Crim 991, [2013] 2 Cr App Rep 247 at para 17.
145 [2010] EWCA Crim 237, [2011] 1 Cr App Rep 135 at para 32.
146 *R v LM* [2010] EWCA Crim 2327, [2011] 1 Cr App R 12 [§ 7]; see also: *R v N and R v Le* [2012] EWCA Crim 189, [2012] 1 Cr App R 35; *R v L, N, N & T* [2013] EWCA Crim 991, [2013] 2 Cr App R 23; *R v VSJ* [2017] EWCA Crim 36, as well as AAD and AFU.
147 AAD at [142].

10.253

Schedule 4 contains a selection of offences of varying seriousness, many of which are frequently committed by victims of trafficking, for example: malicious wounding, robbery, offences relating to slavery and human trafficking and sexual offences. If a PVOT is charged with a Sch 4 offence, the PVOT cannot rely on a statutory defence irrespective of whether their offending was a manifestation of or directly linked to their trafficking. Schedule 4 offences are often intimately linked to trafficking, and/or are known as offences caught within forced criminality paradigms. It does not distinguish between offences committed by child victims or adult victims.

10.254

In the Commons debate on second reading, the Home Secretary said[148]:

> 'The [s 45] defence includes substantial safeguards against abuse and it will not apply to a number of serious offences – mainly violent and sexual offences – which are set out in the Bill. However, even in cases where the defence does not apply, prosecutors will still need to look carefully at all the circumstances to see whether it is in the public interest to prosecute victims'.

10.255

Any victim who is caught by the Sch 4 excluded offences cannot be said to come within MSA 2015, s 45 and the MSA 2015 does not apply to them[149].

10.256

It may be inferred from those who spoke in Parliament that it was Parliament's intention that those victims excluded from the statutory defence could rely on prosecutorial discretion as per the CPS guidance. The s 45 MSA 2015 statutory defence arose from the principle that a PVOT should not, in most circumstances, be punished for crimes committed under compulsion which are directly linked to their trafficking. Arguably the exclusion of offences under

---

148 607 HC Official Report (6th series) col 177, 8 July 2014, in the speech of the Home Secretary (Theresa May); see also Commons Committee Stage, 9th sitting, 607 HC Official Report (6th series) cols 365 and 391, 11 September 2014, junior Home Office minister Karen Bradley, and col 387, Sarah Teather.

149 The Crime and Policing Bill (introduced 25 February 2025, passed House of Commons 17 June 2025) was under Lords consideration at the date of writing. The Bill proposes amendments to Sch 4 MSA 2015 adding further excluded offences, including the new child criminal exploitation (CCE) offence, coerced internal concealment (CIC), and further serious sexual and violent offences. A government Equality Impact Assessment (December 2025) acknowledged that adding the CCE offence may disproportionately affect black victims of modern slavery given the demographics of county lines exploitation. The proposed expansion of Sch 4 heightens the tension with the non-punishment principle identified at paras **10.256–10.257**. Note: the Bill had not received Royal Assent at the date of writing.

Sch 4 conflicts with the non-punishment principle. There is no reference of exclusions within the Trafficking Convention (nor the EU Directive). Both the Trafficking Convention and EU Directive 2011/36/EU support the use of a human rights and child rights-based approach. Sch 4 derived from Sch 15 to the Criminal Justice Act 2003, which listed 'Specified offences for purposes of Chapter 5 of Part 12' (ie it was designed for consideration as part of the 'dangerous offenders' sentencing provisions). Those who spoke in Parliament acknowledged the deficiencies in compiling Sch 4 from Sch 15.

10.257

The Group of Experts on Action against Human Trafficking ('GRETA') responsible for monitoring the states' compliance with ECAT state that the scope of the non-punishment provision should cover all offences which victims of trafficking were compelled to commit, including administrative and immigration-related offences[150].

Procedure at Court

10.258

Some of the practice points endorsed in *R v D*[151] have been summarised above. It is helpful to set them out in full here for ease of reference:

> '19. In order to comply with the United Kingdom's international obligations with regard to the prosecution of victims of trafficking, the CPS issued the 2013 Guidance, highlighting the need for prosecutors to be alert to the indicators of trafficking and providing a detailed and structured approach to the decision on whether or not to prosecute in the public interest. The first question is whether there is reason to believe that the person has been trafficked. In determining this question the guidance requires the prosecutor to make proper enquiries and to utilise the National Referral Mechanism ("NRM"). A referral through the NRM will lead to a decision by the competent authority of which prosecutors should take into account.
>
> 20. This plainly did not happen in this case. However, as has previously been said by this court, the obligation to identify whether a suspect might be a victim of trafficking does not rest on the prosecutor alone. It is incumbent on a suspect's legal representatives in an appropriate case to take steps to ascertain if he had been trafficked and to advise him on the relevant provisions. The court should also be alert to ensure that this has been done. The failure of all parties and the court in this

150 Paragraph 186 of the GRETA general report (2016).

151 [2018] EWCA Crim 2995.

regard led to the potentially inappropriate prosecution and conviction of this applicant.

21. In the course of his submissions, Mr Douglas-Jones invited this court to clarify four points for the assistance of practitioners and courts faced with the prosecution of a potential VOT. With the caveat that we have not heard full argument, still less had the opportunity to canvass any views from others involved in the Criminal Justice System, we go some way towards doing so as follows:

1. The latest version of the CPS guidance on the non- prosecution of VOTs is dated 2018. This now sets out a four-stage test which requires inter alia the prosecutor to consider whether there is clear evidence of a statutory defence under section 45 of the Modern Slavery Act 2015. If the answer to that is "yes", then the case should not be charged or should be discontinued on evidential grounds. If not, the guidance requires the prosecutor to go on to decide whether it is in the public interest to prosecute. Thus the guidance still applies to all cases where the statutory defence is not available.

2. It is not always necessary, particularly in the context of domestic trafficking, for there to be movement before a person can be identified as a VOT. When considering the application of the public interest test and how the guidance should be applied, all concerned should consider the definition of "trafficking" in Article 2 of Directive 2011/36/EU of the European Parliament and the Council (5 April 2011) which provides as far as material:

"This Directive is part of global action against trafficking in human beings, which includes action involving third countries as stated in the 'Action-oriented Paper on strengthening the Union external dimension on action against trafficking in human beings; towards global EU action against trafficking in human beings' approved by the Council on 30 November 2009. In this context action should be pursued in third countries of origin and transfer of victims, with a view to raising awareness, reducing vulnerability, supporting and assisting victims fighting the root causes of trafficking and supporting those third countries in developing appropriate anti-trafficking legislation."

3. As a decision has to be taken whether or not to prosecute a VOT, it is of importance that wherever possible those who may be VOTs are identified before any plea is taken at court. Indeed in cases where there is a suspicion of trafficking or slavery, the CPS guidance requires prosecutors at the first hearing to request that a plea is not formally entered and to apply for an adjournment

for further investigation into the defendant's possible status as the victim of slavery or trafficking.

22. The court should be alive to the duties of the prosecution to comply with the guidance where a defendant is a potential credible VOT by reference to the indicators of trafficking published by the UN office on Drugs and Crime (UNODC) and UN Global Initiative to Fight Human Trafficking.

23. Should the matter be raised at the first hearing the judge will need to determine, as a matter of judgment on the facts of the individual case, whether a defendant is a potential credible VOT. If he so determines, the case should be adjourned for an NRM referral to be made. This should take 45 days but in practice may be considerably longer.

24. In such cases we recognise that the usual stage timetable for case progression under Better Case Management in the Crown Court and Transforming Summary Justice in the Magistrates' Court cannot apply and stage dates will need to be altered to accommodate the referral. Courts will no doubt wish to ensure that VOT questions are not missed. Conversely, we anticipate that courts will be astute to guard against unfounded attempts to raise a VOT point and so cause delay and disruption. Because of the BCM ramifications, we will pass a copy of this judgment to the Senior Presiding Judge for consideration and, if necessary, action.

4. We remind all concerned of the need to be alert to the possibility of trafficking and re-trafficking which may arise in a number of different ways, as the present case demonstrates.'

10.259

As is set out above, in the Crown Court, the PTPH Form has a specific box asking 'Is the defendant said to be a victim of modern slavery?', which is under the heading of 'defence information'. In completing the form and drafting any defence statement practitioners will need to remember that a s 45 defence can only arise as an exclusion of liability for someone who has done the act. In other words, by relying on the defence, the defendant will effectively be admitting the elements of the offence. Where there are *indicia* of trafficking (not accepted by a defendant) defence practitioners should highlight this factor as soon as practicable unless to do so might compromise the safety of the defendant, in which case, modified proceedings should be considered; see as an eg *R v M*[152] in which proceedings were held inter partes *vis-à-vis* prosecution and one defendant by *ex parte vis-à-vis* co-defendants.

152 [2021] EWCA Crim 1934, [2024] 1 Cr App R 20.

Immigration offences

Immigration and Asylum Act 1999, s 31

10.260

Many victims of international trafficking enter the UK as refugees (see **Chapter 16** for a fuller exposition of trafficking victims meeting the definition of refugee). Where they do so by deception or where they commit an identity document offence, they may have a defence on the ground of their refugee status under the Immigration and Asylum Act 1999, s 31.

10.261

This is a defence which has frequently been overlooked by practitioners and judges. Lord Thomas CJ made clear his views that where the defence is overlooked a referral of the relevant practitioner to his respective regulator is appropriate; see *R v Al Shabani*[153].

10.262

Section 31 derives from Art 31 of the Convention Relating to the Status of Refugees 1951[154], which provides as follows:

> '1. The Contracting States shall not impose penalties, on account of their illegal entry or presence, on refugees who, coming directly from a territory where their life or freedom was threatened in the sense of Article 1, enter or are present in their territory without authorization, provided they present themselves without delay to the authorities and show good cause for their illegal entry or presence'.

10.263

Section 31 is the domestic provision which incorporates Art 31 of the 1951 Refugee Convention into the law of England and Wales. Section 31 has a limited application in that it only provides a defence to certain offences. Article 31 itself should not be overlooked, because it is broader in scope than s 31. In rare cases, it may be necessary for prosecutors to look beyond the section and consider the scope of Art 31 itself when considering charging a refugee. It may be necessary for defence practitioners (in an appropriately compelling case) to consider abuse of process as a remedy to a refugee being charged with an offence in circumstances where he should have been afforded refugee protection under

153 [2015] EWCA Crim 1924.
154 189 UNTS 150.

Art 31 (but where s 31 does not apply)[155]. The Court of Appeal has observed that s 31 may not provide the full protection encompassed in Art 31[156].

10.264

In cases where a statutory defence is not available to a refugee, the purposive and humanitarian aims of the Refugee Convention should be borne in mind when prosecutors consider the public interest; see *R v Asfaw*[157].

10.265

Since s 31 applies in relation to specific offences only, where a refugee commits any other offence, prosecutors should apply the public interest limb of the Full Code Test for Crown Prosecutors to ensure that proper consideration is given to any entitlement to Art 31 Refugee Convention protection. Relevant public interest factors would include the seriousness of the level of crime involved in securing illegal entry; that the suspect's actions caused harm to others, or placed other persons' life, health or safety at risk; disruption to services, such as those relating to train services in the Channel Tunnel; and economic loss, which may be linked to any disruption of services.

10.266

Section 31 is in the following terms:

'31 Defences based on Article 31(1) of the Refugee Convention

(1) It is a defence for a refugee charged with an offence to which this section applies to show that, having come to the United Kingdom directly from a country where his life or freedom was threatened (within the meaning of the Refugee Convention), he—

(a) presented himself to the authorities in the United Kingdom without delay;

---

155 See *R v Mirahessari* [2016] EWCA Crim 1733, in which refugees were charged with the 19th century offence of obstructing an engine when they breached Channel Tunnel security and tried to walk from Calais to Folkestone. In that case the appellants sought unsuccessfully to deploy abuse of process through their being charged with an offence to which the refugee defence does not attach.

156 In *R v Ordu* [2017] EWCA Crim 4, [2017] 1 Cr App Rep 21 at 4 (Edis J, as he then was, giving the judgment of the Court), it was noted: 'The [Immigration and Asylum Act] 1999 came into force in November 1999 following a decision of the Divisional Court in *R v Uxbridge Magistrates' Court ex p. Adimi* [2001] QB 667, which had been decided on 29 July 1999. Section 31 was an attempt to comply with the treaty obligations of the United Kingdom under Article 31(1) of the Refugee Convention and was introduced by amendment to the Bill which became the Act because of the decision in *Adimi*. Until that date UK criminal law did not comply with the treaty obligations of the UK, and the introduction of s 31 was an attempt by Parliament to rectify the position. It was not, at least initially, successful because the plain words of s 31(2) appeared to remove the defence from those who had stopped over in a safe country while travelling, while Article 31 affords such people protection. That being so, s 31 as so construed failed to comply fully with the treaty obligation.'

157 [2008] UKHL 31, [2008] 1 AC 1061, [2008] 2 WLR 1178, [2008] 3 All ER 775.

(b) showed good cause for his illegal entry or presence; and

(c) made a claim for asylum as soon as was reasonably practicable after his arrival in the United Kingdom.

(2) If, in coming from the country where his life or freedom was threatened, the refugee stopped in another country outside the United Kingdom, subsection (1) applies only if he shows that he could not reasonably have expected to be given protection under the Refugee Convention in that other country.

(3) In England and Wales … the offences to which this section applies are any offence, and any attempt to commit an offence, under—

(a) Part I of the Forgery and Counterfeiting Act 1981 (forgery and connected offences);

(aa) section 4 or 6 of the Identity Documents Act 2010;

(b) section 24A of the 1971 Act (deception); or

(c) section 26(1)(d) of the 1971 Act (falsification of documents).

…

(5) A refugee who has made a claim for asylum is not entitled to the defence provided by subsection (1) in relation to any offence committed by him after making that claim.

(6) 'Refugee' has the same meaning as it has for the purposes of the Refugee Convention.

(7) If the Secretary of State has refused to grant a claim for asylum made by a person who claims that he has a defence under subsection (1), that person is to be taken not to be a refugee unless he shows that he is.

…'

Application of s 31

10.267

In order for a defendant to avail himself of a s 31 defence:

- the defendant needs to satisfy an evidential burden that he was a refugee (a refugee being … a person who has left his own country owing to a well-founded fear of being persecuted for reasons of race, religion, nationality, membership of a particular social group or political opinion'):

see *R v Makuwa*[158]; the legal burden then vests in the Crown to prove that a defendant is not a refugee (if the Crown does not accept that the defendant is a refugee); or alternatively, where the Secretary of State has refused to grant a claim for asylum in respect of a defendant who claims that he has a defence under s 31(1), the legal burden vests in the defendant to show on the balance of probabilities that he is a refugee: see *R v Sadighpour*[159] and *R v Mateta*[160];

- the defendant then needs to prove (on the balance of probabilities) that he did not stop in any country in transit to the UK or, alternatively, that he could not reasonably have expected to be given protection under the Refugee Convention in the countries outside the UK in which he stopped; and, if so:
  - — to prove that he presented himself to the authorities in the UK without delay;
  - — to show good cause for his illegal entry or presence; and
  - — to prove that he made a claim for asylum as soon as was reasonably practicable after his arrival in the UK.

10.268

In *SXH v The CPS*[161], the Supreme Court considered whether a suspect's entry into the UK as an asylum seeker and the decision to prosecute her for entering with false travel documentation (an offence which could attract the s 31 statutory defence) engaged ECHR, Art 8. The Court held that the decision to prosecute did not amount to a breach of Art 8, observing that 'it is difficult to envisage circumstances in which the initiation of a prosecution against a person reasonably suspected of committing a criminal offence could itself be a breach of that person's human rights', at [34].

Section 31(2)

10.269

Section 31(2) is to be construed as providing immunity from prosecution to refugees who, fleeing from their country of persecution, make a short-term stopover in an intermediate country en route to the country of intended

158 [2006] EWCA Crim 175, [2006] 1 WLR 2755 at 37.
159 [2012] EWCA Crim 2669, [2013] 1 Cr App Rep 269 (per Treacy LJ, who gave the judgment of the Court, at 38–40).
160 [2013] EWCA Crim 1372, [2014] 1 WLR 1516 (Leveson and Fulford LJJ and Spencer J) at 10.
161 [2017] UKSC 30.

refuge[162]. In *R v Kamalanathan*[163] Thomas LJ (as he then was), giving the judgment of the Court, said:

> '[4] … A person could be, for example, making a short stopover or be still in the course of flight, if he had to be concealed in the intervening country whilst he was being pursued by foreign agents. It might be, in such circumstances, that the time could be very much more than the 3 hours that had occurred on the facts in *Asfaw*.
>
> [5] The real question is, looking at all the circumstances: is the person in the course of a flight? Is he making a short-term stop over? Is he in transit? Whichever phrase is used, one has to see whether at the material time the person was here, not having come to this country either temporarily or permanently seeking to stop here but was going on. That is a question of fact'.

Presenting without delay / Claiming asylum as soon as reasonably practicable

10.270

In *R v Jaddi*[164] Hughes LJ (as he then was) giving the judgment of the court stated:

> '[26] … In very general terms, it seems to us that in the great majority of cases there will simply be no excuse for a genuine refugee not to make himself known immediately he arrives in the safe place – that is to say the arrivals immigration hall at a United Kingdom airport. Moreover, from the point of view of sensible immigration control, that makes sense. It is a great deal more difficult to discern whether a claim to be a refugee is genuine if it is not made until some time later and especially if it is only made when it is forced on the claimant by discovery that he is living illegally.
>
> [30] … it is certainly open to a tribunal of fact to conclude and in many cases it may be the right conclusion, that there is simply no

162 *R v Asfaw* [2008] UKHL 31, [2008] 1 AC 1061. The House of Lords decided that the IAA 1999, s 31 should be read so that it provided immunity, if the other conditions are fulfilled, from the imposition of criminal penalties for offences attributable to the attempt of a refugee to leave the country in the continuing course of a flight from persecution even after a short stopover in transit. This changed the law as it had previously been understood and explained in *R (on the application of Pepushi) v Crown Prosecution Service* [2004] EWHC 798 (Admin). The development of the law may be seen from *R v Kamalanathan* [2010] EWCA Crim 1335, *R v Abdalla* [2010] EWCA Crim 2400, [2011] 1 Cr App Rep 432, and *R v Mateta* [2013] EWCA Crim 1372, [2014] 1 WLR 1516.

163 [2010] EWCA Crim 1335.

164 [2012] EWCA Crim 2565.

reason for such a traveller not to identify himself the moment he is in friendly official hands'.

10.271

R v Jaddi was considered by the court in *R v Mateta*[165]:

'These observations were not intended to detract from the principles in *R v Asfaw* and *R v Mohamed (Abdalla)* [viz there is no need for a voluntary exonerating act] or the other authorities to which we have referred: they do no more than make clear the very real importance of focusing on the particular facts and circumstances of each case'.

10.272

In *R v Z*[166] HallettVP, giving the judgment of the court, accepted the submissions of the appellant and respondent that:

'27 … it was clearly arguable that the appellant did claim asylum at the first reasonably practicable moment. On any view, she claimed asylum within a matter of hours of landing in the United Kingdom and before she had left the airport …

28. It will be a question of fact in every case as to whether or not there is an excuse for a refugee not to make themselves known immediately they arrive in the immigration hall'.

Good cause

10.273

This condition '… has only a limited role in the article. It will be satisfied by a genuine refugee showing that he was reasonably travelling on false papers'[167].

Article 31

10.274

Article 31 of the 1951 Convention relating to the Status of Refugees[168] provides as follows:

165 *R v Mateta* [2013] EWCA Crim 1372, [2014] 1 WLR 1516.
166 [2016] EWCA Crim 1083.
167 See *R v Uxbridge Magistrates' Court and Another, ex p Adimi* [2001] QB 667 at 679; see also *Mateta* at 21(v).
168 For a discussion on this provision, see: https://www.unhcr.org/3bcfdf164.pdf and https://www.refworld.org/pdfid/59ad55c24.pdf (last accessed on 6 June 2020).

> '1. The Contracting States shall not impose penalties, on account of their illegal entry or presence, on refugees who, coming directly from a territory where their life or freedom was threatened in the sense of Article 1, enter or are present in their territory without authorization, provided they present themselves without delay to the authorities and show good cause for their illegal entry or presence.
>
> 2. The Contracting States shall not apply to the movements of such refugees' restrictions other than those which are necessary and such restrictions shall only be applied until their status in the country is regularized or they obtain admission into another country. The Contracting States shall allow such refugees a reasonable period and all the necessary facilities to obtain admission into another country.'

Anonymity

10.275

The appropriateness of anonymising a possible credible victim of modern slavery or trafficking who is a defendant is now dealt with in *R v Baniulyte*[169], which has fundamentally changed the approach from that set out previously in 2017, which had been followed in a multitude of cases. See **Chapter 8**.

Annex

10.276

Offences in relation to which the MSA 2015, s 45 defence is not available:

- false imprisonment;
- kidnapping;
- manslaughter;
- murder;
- perverting the course of justice;
- piracy;
- the following offences under the Offences against the Person Act 1861:
  - — s 4 (soliciting murder);

169 [2025] EWCA Crim 1205.

— s 16 (threats to kill);

— s 18 (wounding with intent to cause grievous bodily harm);

— s 20 (malicious wounding);

— s 21 (attempting to choke, suffocate or strangle in order to commit or assist in committing an indictable offence);

— s 22 (using drugs etc to commit or assist in the committing of an indictable offence);

— s 23 (maliciously administering poison etc so as to endanger life or inflict grievous bodily harm);

— s 27 (abandoning children);

— s 28 (causing bodily injury by explosives);

— s 29 (using explosives with intent to do grievous bodily harm);

— s 30 (placing explosives with intent to do bodily injury);

— s 31 (setting spring guns etc with intent to do grievous bodily harm);

— s 32 (endangering safety of railway passengers);

— s 35 (injuring persons by furious driving);

— s 37 (assaulting officer preserving wreck);

— s 38 (assault with intent to resist arrest);

- an offence under any of the following provisions of the Explosive Substances Act 1883:

— s 2 (causing explosion likely to endanger life or property);

— s 3 (attempt to cause explosion, or making or keeping explosive with intent to endanger life or property);

— s 4 (making or possession of explosives under suspicious circumstances);

- child destruction;
- cruelty to children (Children and Young Persons Act 1933, s 1);
- control etc of quasi-military organisation (Public Order Act 1936, s 2);
- infanticide (Infanticide Act 1938, s 1);
- an offence under any of the following provisions of the Firearms Act 1968:

— s 5 (possession of prohibited firearms);

— s 16 (possession of firearm with intent to endanger life);

— s 16A (possession of firearm with intent to cause fear of violence);

- — s 17(1); (use of firearm to resist arrest);
- — s 17(2); (possession of firearm at time of committing or being arrested for specified offence);
- — s 18 (carrying firearm with criminal intent);

- an offence under any of the following provisions of the Theft Act 1968:
  - — s 8 (robbery or assault with intent to rob);
  - — s 9 (burglary), where the offence is committed with intent to inflict grievous bodily harm on a person, or to do unlawful damage to a building or anything in it;
  - — s 10 (aggravated burglary);
  - — s 12A (aggravated vehicle-taking), where the offence involves an accident which caused the death of any person;
  - — s 21 (blackmail);
- the following offences under the Criminal Damage Act 1971:
  - — an offence of arson under s 1;
  - — an offence under s 1(2) (destroying or damaging property) other than an offence of arson;
- assisting unlawful immigration to member state (Immigration Act 1971, s 25)[170];
- penalty for fraudulent evasion of duty etc) in relation to goods prohibited to be imported under the Customs Consolidation Act 1876, s 42 (indecent or obscene articles) (Customs and Excise Management Act 1979, s 170);
- hostage-taking (Taking of Hostages Act 1982, s 1);
- an offence under the following provisions of the Aviation Security Act 1982:
  - — s 1 (hijacking);
  - — s 2 (destroying, damaging or endangering safety of aircraft);
  - — s 3 (other acts endangering or likely to endanger safety of aircraft);
  - — s 4 (offences in relation to certain dangerous articles);
- ill-treatment of patients (Mental Health Act 1983, s 127);
- abduction of child by parent etc or others (Child Abduction Act 1984, ss 1, 2);

170 Note that whilst the s25 facilitation offence is included in Sch 4 the s25A offence (which is now in almost effectively identical terms, and with the same maximum penalty, is not).

- riot (Public Order Act 1986, s 1);
- violent disorder (Public Order Act 1986, s 2);
- torture (Criminal Justice Act 1988, s 134);
- causing death by dangerous driving (Road Traffic Act 1988, s 1);
- causing death by careless driving when under the influence of drink or drugs (Road Traffic Act 1988, s 3A);
- an offence under the following provisions of the Aviation and Maritime Security Act 1990:
  - — s 1 (endangering safety at aerodromes);
  - — s 9 (hijacking of ships);
  - — s 10 (seizing or exercising control of fixed platforms);
  - — s 11 (destroying fixed platforms or endangering their safety);
  - — s 12 (other acts endangering or likely to endanger safe navigation);
  - — s 13 (offences involving threats);
- offences relating to Channel Tunnel trains and the tunnel system (an offence under Part 2 of the Channel Tunnel (Security) Order 1994 (SI 1994/570));
- putting people in fear of violence (Protection from Harassment Act 1997, s 4);
- stalking involving fear of violence or serious alarm or distress (Protection from Harassment Act 1997, s 4A);
- racially or religiously aggravated assaults (Crime and Disorder Act 1998, s 29);
- racially or religiously aggravated offences under the Public Order Act 1986, ss 4 or 4A (Crime and Disorder Act 1998, s 31(1)(a) or (b));
- an offence under the following provisions of the Terrorism Act 2000:
  - — s 54 (weapons training);
  - — s 56 (directing terrorist organisation);
  - — s 57 (possession of article for terrorist purposes);
  - — s 59 (inciting terrorism overseas);
- genocide, crimes against humanity and war crimes and ancillary conduct (International Criminal Court Act 2001, ss 1, 2);
- an offence under the following provisions of the Anti-terrorism, Crime and Security Act 2001:

- s 47 (use of nuclear weapons);
- s 50 (assisting or inducing certain weapons-related acts overseas);
- s 113 (use of noxious substance or thing to cause harm or intimidate);

- female genital mutilation and related offences (Female Genital Mutilation Act 2003, ss 1, 2, 3);
- the following Sexual Offences Act 2003 offences:

- s 1 (rape);
- s 2 (assault by penetration);
- s 3 (sexual assault);
- s 4 (causing person to engage in sexual activity without consent);
- s 5 (rape of child under 13);
- s 6 (assault of child under 13 by penetration);
- s 7 (sexual assault of child under 13);
- s 8 (causing or inciting child under 13 to engage in sexual activity);
- s 9 (sexual activity with a child);
- s 10 (causing or inciting a child to engage in sexual activity);
- s 13 (child sex offences committed by children or young persons);
- s 14 (arranging or facilitating commission of child sex offence);
- s 15 (meeting a child following sexual grooming);
- s 16 (abuse of position of trust: sexual activity with a child);
- s 17 (abuse of position of trust: causing or inciting a child to engage in sexual activity);
- s 18 (abuse of position of trust: sexual activity in presence of child);
- s 19 (abuse of position of trust: causing a child to watch a sexual act);
- s 25 (sexual activity with a child family member);
- s 26 (inciting a child family member to engage in sexual activity);
- s 30 (sexual activity with a person with a mental disorder impeding choice);
- s 31 (causing or inciting a person with a mental disorder impeding choice to engage in sexual activity);
- s 32 (engaging in sexual activity in the presence of a person with a mental disorder impeding choice);

— s 33 (causing a person with a mental disorder impeding choice to watch a sexual act);

— s 34 (inducement, threat or deception to procure sexual activity with a person with a mental disorder);

— s 35 (causing a person with a mental disorder to engage in or agree to engage in sexual activity by inducement, threat or deception);

— s 36 (engaging in sexual activity in the presence, procured by inducement, threat or deception, of a person with a mental disorder);

— s 37 (causing a person with a mental disorder to watch a sexual act by inducement, threat or deception);

— s 38 (care workers: sexual activity with a person with a mental disorder);

— s 39 (care workers: causing or inciting sexual activity);

— s 40 (care workers: sexual activity in the presence of a person with a mental disorder);

— s 41 (care workers: causing a person with a mental disorder to watch a sexual act);

— s 47 (paying for sexual services of a child);

— s 48 (causing or inciting child prostitution or pornography);

— s 49 (controlling a child prostitute or a child involved in pornography);

— s 50 (arranging or facilitating child prostitution or pornography);

— s 61 (administering a substance with intent);

— s 62 (committing offence with intent to commit sexual offence);

— s 63 (trespass with intent to commit sexual offence);

— s 64 (sex with an adult relative: penetration);

— s 65 (sex with an adult relative: consenting to penetration);

— s 66 (exposure);

— s 67 (voyeurism);

— s 70 (sexual penetration of a corpse);

- causing or allowing a child or vulnerable adult to die or suffer serious physical harm (Domestic Violence, Crime and Victims Act 2004, s 5);
- an offence under the following provisions of the Terrorism Act 2006:

— s 5 (preparation of terrorist acts);

— s 6 (training for terrorism);

— s 9 (making or possession of radioactive device or material);

— s 10 (use of radioactive device or material for terrorist purposes);

— s 11 (terrorist threats relating to radioactive devices etc);

- slavery, servitude and forced or compulsory labour (Modern Slavery Act 2015, s 1);
- human trafficking (Modern Slavery Act 2015, s 2).

11 Victims of exploitation at the police station

Steven Bird, Michelle Brewer, Philippa Southwell and Ben Douglas-Jones KC

11.1

The first contact that victims of modern slavery, human trafficking and exploitation may have with law enforcement is likely to be on arrest, particularly for those involved in forced criminality. After arrest, they will be taken to a police station and there is an opportunity for early identification of the arrested person as a victim of trafficking which is often missed.

11.2

In any criminal case, the police station stage is extremely important and influences greatly how the case develops. With potential victims of exploitation, this stage of the case is even more important as the police have the opportunity to divert them from the criminal justice system or at least to refer them into the National Referral Mechanism ('NRM') as early as possible.

11.3

This stage of proceedings also provides the potential victim of exploitation, modern slavery or trafficking ('PVOT') with access to legal advice, perhaps for the first time. It is essential that legal representatives are aware of the basic trafficking indicators and can discuss the issues concerning a referral into the NRM at this early stage with their arrested client. All those involved in representing, or dealing with, suspects at the police station stage in proceedings need to be alive to the possibility that suspects may be victims of exploitation. They need to be familiar with the operative duty to identify victims of slavery, servitude, forced or compulsory labour, and human trafficking: the national referral mechanism and Art 4 ECHR (see **Chapters 4** and **10**).

Arrival at the police station

Risk assessment

11.4

The first contact that an arrested PVOT will have with police after their initial arrest will be with the custody officer who is responsible for the welfare of the detained person while in police custody. The custody officer is responsible for initiating a risk assessment to consider whether the detainee is likely to present specific risks to custody staff, any individual who may have contact with the detainee (eg legal advisers, medical staff) or themselves. This risk assessment must include the taking of reasonable steps to establish the detainee's identity and to obtain information about the detainee that is relevant to their safe custody, security and welfare and risk to others[1].

11.5

The current police risk assessment does not include any questions specifically designed to identify whether the arrested person may be a PVOT and the process itself is unlikely to identify much more than whether the individual needs to see a health professional or has any mental health issues that require the services of an appropriate adult.

11.6

Whether the custody officer or arresting officers have any awareness of the issues that may identify the arrested individual as a potential victim of trafficking may depend on the extent of the briefing for the operation that led to the arrest, and the individual officer's experience and training.

11.7

If the operation leading to the arrest was a directed operation at a specific premises or group, it may be that the senior officers have made those engaged in the operation aware of the likelihood that potential victims of trafficking may be present and arrested at the scene. For instance, senior officers involved in the planning of a raid on a known cannabis factory which leads to the arrest of a number of young foreign nationals ought to have identified that possibility in advance. Consequently, the police should be aware that any suspects arrested at the premises might be potential victims of trafficking and the officers subsequently dealing with them whilst in police detention should ensure that the issue is addressed and any necessary safeguards put in place.

11.8

If the arrest is opportunistic (eg a person arrested for pickpocketing on the street having been spotted by an officer), the identification of the individual as a potential victim of trafficking is likely to be more problematic and more reliant on the training of the custody officer or arresting officer to identify the warning signs.

---

1 Police and Criminal Evidence Act ('PACE') 1984, Code C3.6.

Police training and development

11.9

Police recruitment and training in the UK has evolved significantly. While the Certificate of Knowledge in Policing ('CKP') may have been a pathway in the past, new entry routes such as the Police Constable Degree Apprenticeship (PCDA) and the Degree Holder Entry Programme (DHEP) are now prominent[2]. Modern slavery and human trafficking content is increasingly integrated into these initial training programmes to equip new recruits with foundational knowledge from the outset of their careers[3]. The College of Policing's updated Authorised Professional Practice (APP) on modern slavery provides comprehensive guidance for both frontline officers and investigators, reflecting a structured approach to embedding this knowledge[4]. Advice and guidance on modern slavery links across to other relevant APP, including domestic and child abuse APP and operational areas such as custody officer advice.

11.10

The College of Policing continues to provide extensive training on protecting vulnerable people, with its e-learning programmes covering a wide range of issues including child abuse, child sexual exploitation, domestic abuse, female genital mutilation, forced marriage, honour-based violence, modern slavery, prostitution, serious sexual offences, stalking, and harassment[5]. Critically, the College of Policing has introduced two new dedicated courses for police and other law enforcement officers focusing on modern slavery: an awareness-raising course designed for frontline officers to enhance their ability to spot the signs, and a four-day specialist investigator training course aimed at enabling investigators to bring perpetrators to justice[6]. Additionally, other specialist courses including a specialist child abuse investigator development course ('SCAIDP') and specialist sexual assault investigators development course ('SSAIDP') feature matters of modern slavery, where it impacts specifically on children and families (eg domestic servitude, trafficking for child sexual exploitation)[7]. Furthermore, the Home Office offers free e-learning courses, including 'First responder training' and 'Child victims of modern slavery,' providing guidance on identifying indicators, safeguarding processes, and referral to the National Referral Mechanism[8].

2 https://www.college.police.uk/career-learning/joining-police (accessed 22 August 2025).
3 https://www.college.police.uk/app/modern-slavery (accessed 22 August 2025).
4 https://www.college.police.uk/app/modern-slavery (accessed 22 August 2025).
5 https://www.college.police.uk/career-learning/courses/protecting-vulnerable-people (accessed 22 August 2025).
6 https://www.college.police.uk/app/modern-slavery/introduction (accessed 22 August 2025).
7 The editors are grateful to Sharon Stratton, Policing Standards Manager in Vulnerability and Public Protection for the College of Policing, and Joanne Floyd, Trainer – Investigations Learning and Development, West Midlands Police for assisting the editors with this section.
8 https://www.gov.uk/guidance/modern-slavery-and-human-trafficking-training-for-frontline-professionals (accessed 22 August 2025).

11.11

The College of Policing manages the content and delivery of detective training through the Professionalising Investigation Programme (PIP), which provides structured development for investigative skills[9]. Recognising the complexity of these crimes, specific and detailed training for investigators in modern slavery and human trafficking is now firmly established. The College of Policing offers a dedicated Modern Slavery and Human Trafficking (MSHT) investigator learning programme, directly addressing the need for specialised skills in this area[10]. The Metropolitan Police Service, for example, also delivers a dedicated Modern Slavery and Organised Immigration Crime Investigators course, aimed at improving the identification of offences, safeguarding vulnerable persons, and disrupting criminal activity[11]. This specialised training is crucial given the often hidden and complex nature of modern slavery, frequently linked to organised crime groups.

11.12

Improved and targeted training for 'front line' officers and staff has demonstrably led to a greater number of potential victims of trafficking being identified. The number of potential victims referred to the National Referral Mechanism (NRM) has seen a steady rise, reaching 19,125 referrals in 2024, representing a 13% increase compared to 2023 (16,990) and the highest annual number since the NRM began[12]. This underscores that policing and partners are improving at identifying potential victims. The requirement for training early in an officer's career is now met with integrated content and readily available e-learning, and the need for constant updates is reflected in the College of Policing's ongoing review of modern slavery guidance, including incorporating new legislation such as the Nationality and Borders Act 2022 and the Illegal Migration Act 2023, and evolving typologies of exploitation[13]. However, reports still highlight that while training has increased, inconsistencies in police response and support for victims remain across different forces, and some officers may still lack appropriate knowledge even now. This is a critical issue as every criminal justice stakeholder must understand modern slavery, given that exploitation can arise in any case where there is more than one criminal actor, which inherently gives rise to the risk of an imbalance of power, vulnerability, and exploitation[14].

---

9 https://www.college.police.uk/career-learning/investigation/professionalising-investigation-programme-pip (accessed 22 August 2025).

10 https://www.college.police.uk/article/modern-slavery-and-human-trafficking-investigator-learning-programme (accessed 22 August 2025).

11 https://www.met.police.uk/foi-ai/af/accessing-information/met/disclosure-logs/2021/october/modern-slavery-training/ (accessed 22 August 2025).

12 https://www.gov.uk/government/statistics/modern-slavery-national-referral-mechanism-and-duty-to-notify-statistics-uk-end-of-year-summary-2024 (accessed 22 August 2025).

13 https://www.college.police.uk/app/modern-slavery (accessed 22 August 2025).

14 https://www.hims.org.uk/assets/documents/HMICFRS%20Modern%20Slavery%20Report.pdf (accessed 22 August 2025).

This emphasises the ongoing need for a consistent and high-quality training approach across all services.

Provision of rights

11.13

On arrival at the police station, the arrested person will be informed by the custody officer of their legal rights under PACE 1984, which may be exercised at any stage during the period in custody. These rights include:

- the right to consult privately with a solicitor and to have free independent legal advice;
- the right to have someone informed of their arrest;
- the right to consult the Codes of Practice;
- the right to interpretation and translation and the right to communicate with their High Commission, Embassy or Consulate; and
- the right to be informed about the offence and any further offences for which they are arrested whilst in custody and why they have been arrested and detained[15].

11.14

The detainee must also be given a written notice, which contains information to allow them to exercise these rights by setting out:

- the above rights;
- the arrangements for obtaining legal advice;
- the right to a copy of the custody record;
- the right to remain silent as set out in the caution;
- the right to have access to materials and documents which are essential to challenging the lawfulness of their arrest and detention for any offence;
- the maximum period for which they may be kept in police detention without being charged;
- when detention must be reviewed and when release is required;
- the right to medical assistance;
- the right, if they are prosecuted, to have access to the evidence in the case before their trial[16].

15 PACE 1984, Code C3.1.
16 PACE 1984, Code C3.2.

11.15

The notice should also briefly set out the detainee's other entitlements while in custody, by mentioning the provisions relating to the conduct of interviews, the circumstances in which an appropriate adult should be available to assist the detainee, and the statutory right to make representations whenever the need for their detention is reviewed. Finally, the notice should list the entitlements concerning reasonable standards of physical comfort, adequate food and drink, access to toilets and washing facilities, clothing, medical attention, and exercise when practicable, as well as personal needs relating to health, hygiene and welfare concerning the provision of menstrual and any other health, hygiene and welfare products needed by the detainee in question and speaking about these in private to a member of the custody staff[17].

11.16

The custody officer or other custody staff as directed by the custody officer will ask the detainee whether they would like legal advice and want someone informed of their detention, with the detainee asked to sign the custody record to confirm their decisions.

11.17

The custody officer must also determine whether the detainee is, or might be, in need of medical treatment or attention, requires an appropriate adult or help to check documentation or requires an interpreter. The decision in respect of these matters must be recorded on the custody record[18].

11.18

If the detainee appears to be someone who does not speak or understand English, the custody officer must ensure that without delay arrangements are made for the detainee to have the assistance of an interpreter and that the detainee is told clearly about their right to interpretation and translation.

11.19

The written notice given to the detainee must be in a language that the detainee understands and includes the right to interpretation and translation. If a translation of the notice is not available, the information in the notice must be given through an interpreter and a written translation provided without undue delay[19].

17 PACE 1984, Code C3.2.
18 PACE 1984, Code C3.5.
19 PACE 1984, Code C3.12.

11.20

The right to free and independent legal advice will only be effective if it is exercised by the arrested person. Many people detained in the police station will not request the services of a solicitor and may therefore not obtain some of the protections that would be otherwise available to them at the police station. Whether a potential victim of trafficking is more or less inclined to request legal advice than any other detainee is unknown, although it is widely reported by victims of trafficking that they have little understanding of the procedures in the UK, particularly those who have come from isolated communities and they may not take up their entitlement to such advice.

11.21

Should the arrested person request legal advice, the police will ask whether they have a solicitor who they would like to contact. If they do not know a solicitor, the police will arrange for the duty solicitor to attend. In each situation the police will call the Defence Solicitor Call Centre ('DSCC'), who will contact the nominated firm or the duty solicitor.

Criminal Defence Direct

11.22

In some cases, despite asking to speak to a solicitor, the detained person may only be able to speak to an adviser at a call centre known as Criminal Defence Direct ('CDD'). Calls will be sent to CDD where the person is detained:

- in relation to any non-imprisonable offence;
- on a bench warrant for failing to appear and being held for production before the court, except where the existing solicitor acting has clear documentary evidence available that would result in the detainee being released from custody;
- on suspicion of driving with excess alcohol, who is taken to the police station to give a specimen (Road Traffic Act 1988, s 5); failure to provide a specimen (Road Traffic Act 1988, ss 6, 7, 7A); or driving whilst unfit/drunk in charge of a motor vehicle (Road Traffic Act 1988, s 4); or
- in relation to breach of police or court bail conditions[20].

11.23

Even in the above cases, a solicitor will be contacted if:

20 See **Chapter 2** regarding common offences linked to trafficking. Many victims who have been re-trafficked are often in breach of police or court bail.

- the detainee is to be subject to an interview or an identification procedure;
- the detainee is eligible for assistance from an appropriate adult under the PACE Codes of Practice;
- the detainee is unable to communicate over the telephone;
- the detainee complains of serious maltreatment by the police;
- the investigation includes another alleged offence which allows a solicitor to advise;
- the solicitor is already at the same police station;
- the advice relates to an indictable offence; or
- the request is a Special Request[21].

11.24

In the case of potential victims of trafficking, it is likely that one of the exceptions above will apply such that the use of the CDD should be limited. One might expect that the potential victim of trafficking detained might require an appropriate adult or have difficulties in communication.

11.25

If the CDD is deployed, it is unlikely that the detained person would be identified by them as a potential victim of trafficking, given the limited and remote interaction on the telephone. The level of training provided for CDD staff in relation to identifying victims of trafficking is unknown. If the arrested potential victim of trafficking is directed to the CDD, because the offence is not imprisonable or they are in breach of bail, an opportunity to identify them as a potential victim of trafficking is missed.

Duty to attend the police station

11.26

Once called by the DSCC the solicitor will contact the police station by telephone and, if appropriate, also speak to the arrested person. The solicitor has a duty to attend at the police station to provide advice and attend all police interviews with the arrested person in connection with an offence. The

21 A 'Special Request' is a request made to the solicitor by the DSCC to take the case even if it does not fall within the exceptions. Special Requests may include, for example, requests where CDD considers that, because of a conflict of interest, the request should be handled by a solicitor (instead of by a CDD telephone adviser) or considers that Advocacy Assistance is required.

solicitor must also attend at any identification parade, group identification or confrontation, and where the arrested person complains of serious maltreatment by the police[22]. Attendance at video identification parades is discretionary[23].

11.27

In general terms, once there is to be an interview the detained person will have face-to-face advice from a solicitor or accredited police station representative.

Arrival of the legal representative at the police station

11.28

On arrival at the police station the legal representative should obtain and read a copy of the custody record to ascertain the circumstances of the arrest and what has happened up to that point, while the detained person has been in police custody.

11.29

The legal representative should also obtain as much information from the interviewing officer as possible by way of disclosure about the alleged offence and the circumstances of the arrest. The police are not obliged to disclose anything to the representative but will provide at least some limited disclosure in all cases. The legal representative should consider the disclosure provided (usually but not always in written form) and ask further questions of the officer, which may or may not be answered. It is important to note what information is refused as well as what is provided.

11.30

This is an opportunity for the legal representative to gauge whether there may be any potential indicators of human trafficking. Legal representatives should be aware of the basic trafficking indicators and common types of offences where victims are exploited for criminality as well as certain types of victim profile, all of which should give cause for further enquiry. See **Chapter 4** for further explanation on indicators of trafficking and **Chapter 2** for common forms of forced criminality offences.

22 SCC 2025 Specification para 9.34.
23 SCC 2025 Specification para 9.36.

Interaction with the detained person

Interpreters

11.31

Although not the case with every potential victim of trafficking, it is likely that where the victim is a foreign national there will be language difficulties: instructions will need to be taken and advice given via an interpreter. If the custody officer assesses that the suspect does not understand English sufficiently well to be able to communicate effectively, they will seek the services of an interpreter.

11.32

Every interpreter working in the courts and police stations should be selected through the Ministry of Justice Framework Agreement (where the contract is currently with Capita Translation) or from the National Register of Public Service Interpreters (NRPSI) in order to ensure a minimum and measurable standard of training and quality assurance. Such interpreters are subject to a Code of Conduct, standards of competence and professional skills, and disciplinary proceedings.

11.33

The arrangements must comply with the minimum requirements set out in Directive 2010/64/EU of the European Parliament and of the Council of 20 October 2010[24] on the right to interpretation and translation in criminal proceedings. The Directive states that the quality of interpretation and translation provided has to be sufficient to 'safeguard the fairness of the proceedings, in particular by ensuring that suspected or accused persons have knowledge of the cases against them and are able to exercise their right of defence'. Therefore, the suspect must be able to understand their position and be able to communicate effectively with police officers, interviewers, solicitors and appropriate adults in the same way as a suspect who can speak and understand English and who would therefore not require an interpreter[25].

11.34

Equally, a written translation of all documents considered essential for the person to exercise their right of defence and to 'safeguard the fairness of the proceedings' should be provided, which includes any decision to authorise a person to be detained and details of any offence(s) with which the person has been charged or for which they have been told they may be prosecuted.

24 Note: notwithstanding EU Exit, this Directive is given effect through its inclusion in s 13.1A of PACE 1984, Code C.

25 PACE 1984, Code C13.1A.

11.35

All reasonable attempts should be made to make the suspect understand that interpretation and translation will be provided at public expense[26].

11.36

Consideration should be given to the gender and religious or cultural background of the interpreter. The views of the potential victim of trafficking should be taken into consideration, although this is not specifically set out in the PACE 1984 Codes of Practice (with the exception of seeking an alternative interpreter if the detainee complains about the adequacy of the translation from the interpreter in attendance).

11.37

The interpreter used to interpret witness statements should not also be used for the interview and private discussions between the legal adviser and the detainee. The adviser should consider whether there is a tension in using the same interpreter to interpret in the consultation as is used for the interview. It is possible to obtain public funding under the Police Station Advice and Assistance scheme for an interpreter to be obtained by the defence, although in practice there are problems in terms of locating suitable interpreters without an undue delay to the investigation and the time that the detainee remains in custody.

11.38

It is important that the interpreter understands that the discussions between the adviser and the detainee are confidential and subject to legal professional privilege. It would be a serious breach of the interpreter's professional ethics to inform police of what was discussed in such consultation. If such a situation arises, complaint must be made to their professional body, to the police and Ministry of Justice.

11.39

It is important that an interpreter used at a police station or in the course of investigations by other investigating agencies is not engaged to interpret in court. If, however, it is not possible to find another interpreter (for example, where the language is uncommon) the court and all parties must be notified of the intention to use the same interpreter for the court proceedings[27].

26 PACE 1984, Code C13.1B.
27 *R (on the application of Bozturk) v Thames Magistrates' Court* (2001) Times, 26 June.

Initial meeting with the client

11.40

It is important to try to establish a rapport with the client, which is always more difficult via an interpreter. The client should be informed as to the status of the legal representative. If attending as duty solicitor, the representative should explain the nature of the duty scheme, as suspects are often under the impression that the duty solicitor is the 'police solicitor', obtained for them by the police.

11.41

The role of the adviser should be explained, as should the fact that everything said in the consultation is confidential and subject to legal professional privilege and cannot be disclosed to others (except in very limited circumstances). It is also worth explaining that the solicitor is there to advise the suspect on the law and provide advice based on their instructions, if any, and is not there to suggest an account to put forward. Some suspects may not understand the purpose of having an adviser is to assist them and some potential victims of trafficking may be wary or distrustful of their legal adviser. It is important to ensure that the client understands that the legal adviser is completely independent of the police, that they will not divulge information to the police and that the adviser is there to protect the interests of the client while in detention. It must be remembered that non-UK-resident victims of trafficking may come from countries which do not afford fair trial rights in practice, and therefore trust will need to be built with the client.

Identifying the client as a potential victim of trafficking: disclosure

11.42

The adviser should be alert to basic trafficking indicators[28]. The Law Society Practice Note, 'Criminal Prosecutions of Victims of Trafficking'[29], sets out a non-exhaustive list of offences that victims of trafficking are often arrested for at paragraph 6.1, which includes cannabis cultivation, drug importation, immigration offences, document offences, prostitution, dishonesty offences including theft, pick-pocketing and begging.

11.43

The Practice Note also sets out a non-exhaustive list of common factors which may also assist in identifying possible victims, including:

---

28 See **Chapter 4**.

29 Available at www.lawsociety.org.uk/support-services/advice/practice-notes/criminal-prosecutions-of-victims-of-trafficking/, last accessed 22 August 2025.

- the suspected victim is from a place known to be a source of human trafficking;
- the possession of false identity or travel documents;
- showing signs of fear or anxiety;
- exhibiting distrust of the authorities;
- evidence of violence or threats of violence;
- fear of revealing immigration status;
- lack of knowledge of home or work address;
- signs that the individual's movements are being controlled or that they are taking instructions from a third party; and
- inconsistency about name and age.

11.44

If the adviser suspects that the detained person may be a victim of trafficking, the issue should be raised with the client and discussed. It is in the best interests of the suspect to declare that they are a victim of trafficking at this stage so that the legal protections afforded to them can be implemented.

11.45

However, it is common for victims of human trafficking and modern slavery not always to identify as such and not to make such disclosures to their solicitor or to police. They may often mistrust the authorities and their legal representatives (who they may consider to be in a position of authority, especially if called as duty solicitor). Many victims of trafficking will not wish to make such a disclosure to their legal adviser and may deny that they have been acting under the coercion of their trafficker. It is also common for a client to have been coached by the traffickers to give a particular account.

11.46

These discussions will rarely be straightforward. However, if disclosure can be made with the client's consent, it will trigger a duty on the police to investigate the matter and a referral into the NRM at this stage. The adviser should ensure that the notification is placed on the custody record.

11.47

The disclosure may prompt a further review of the safeguarding assessment regarding the medical needs of the suspect and consideration as to whether an appropriate adult is required, should an interview under caution take place.

11.48

While it is likely the police will seek to interview the suspect for the index offence, representations should be made to police that this is inappropriate and that the suspect should be referred into the NRM. Questioning in relation to the index offence will entail questioning as to their exploitation without the safeguards and special measures afforded to the client by an Achieving Best Evidence ('ABE') interview, where the potential victim of trafficking is treated as a potential victim of crime. Not every potential victim of trafficking will choose to co-operate with the ABE interview process.

Instructions not to disclose: the ethical dilemma

11.49

A client who is a PVOT or possible victim of exploitation may either not disclose that they are an exploited individual, in circumstances where the objective evidence is that they have been exploited, or give specific instructions to the legal adviser not to disclose that they have been exploited and have been acting under the influence of their trafficker/ exploiter.

11.50

This situation raises issues of professional ethics and considerable caution is required. A referral of the client into the NRM is likely to be advantageous to the individual in many ways, not least in relation to a positive decision against charge on the index offence or in raising a modern slavery defence in due course should the matter proceed to trial. On the other hand, for a client accused of a criminal offence, exposing their traffickers may involve a significant personal risk.

11.51

Adults cannot be referred into the NRM without their consent. Therefore, with an adult client who is refusing to agree to disclosure being made to police to trigger a NRM referral, the position is clear: no disclosure can be made.

11.52

Consent to be referred into the NRM is not required for a potential victim of trafficking under the age of 18. However, consent must be obtained by the legal representative to contact a first responder, triggering the NRM[30]. The age of the client is not always obvious and at this stage the adviser has little option but to accept the client's instructions as to age.

30 See **Chapter 21** for full details on NRM referrals and confidentiality.

11.53

A solicitor is professionally and legally obliged to keep the affairs of clients confidential. The obligations extend to all matters revealed to a solicitor, from whatever source, by a client, or someone acting on the client's behalf. In exceptional circumstances this general obligation of confidentiality may be overridden. However, certain communications are subject to legal professional privilege ('LPP') and can never be disclosed, unless statute permits it either expressly or by necessary implication[31].

11.54

LPP is a privilege against disclosure which ensures that clients know that certain documents and information provided to lawyers cannot be disclosed at all. It recognises the client's fundamental human right to be candid with their legal adviser, without fear of later disclosure to their prejudice. It is an absolute right and cannot be overridden by any other interest.

11.55

Generally, confidentiality extends beyond LPP, which protects only those confidential communications falling under the definition of advice privilege or litigation privilege. Advice privilege includes communications between a lawyer, acting in their capacity as a lawyer, and a client for the purpose of seeking and providing legal advice.

11.56

It is not always easy to identify what information is subject to privilege (and therefore cannot be overridden without a statutory exception) and what is merely confidential. Not all communications between a lawyer and client are privileged. The protection applies only to those communications which directly seek or provide advice or which are given in a legal context, that involve the lawyer using their legal skills and that are directly related to the performance of the lawyer's professional duties[32].

11.57

Information given to a legal adviser by the client in the consultation prior to a police interview is privileged. As such, if a client discloses that they are a victim of trafficking but specifically instructs the legal adviser not to disclose this information to police, regardless of the client's age, the legal adviser cannot make the disclosure.

31 See https://www.lawsociety.org.uk/topics/anti-money-laundering/anti-money-laundering-guidance last accessed 27 September 2025.

32 *Privilege, Passmore* (5th edn, Chapters 1 and 2, in particular).

11.58

The issue is perhaps more difficult where the adviser believes from their own assessment of the client that the client is a potential victim of trafficking under the age of 18, but the client does not confirm this to be the case. It is arguable that the legal adviser's belief of the client's status is not privileged, but confidential. This is a very fine line.

11.59

The Law Society Practice Note on this subject (above) suggests that if a child client reveals information which indicates continuing sexual or other physical abuse but refuses to allow such disclosure of information to an appropriate authority, a conflict may arise between the duty of confidentiality and the adviser's ability to act with integrity (principle 2 of the SRA Handbook).

11.60

Whether the adviser's duties conflict or not will depend on the materiality of the information in question. The adviser must consider whether the threat to the child's life or health, both mental and physical, is sufficiently serious to justify a breach of the duty of confidentiality[33].

11.61

In the vast majority of cases, it would not be appropriate for the adviser to make a disclosure to police which would lead to a referral to the NRM for a child client who has not specifically given consent for that disclosure. It would be an extremely rare case where the legal adviser makes such a disclosure based on discussions with the client without the client's consent.

11.62

A careful note should be made as to the information obtained and the reasons why no disclosure was made. The client should be encouraged to meet with an appropriate organisation after the police station attendance in the hope that they will subsequently allow a referral to take place.

Advice

11.63

If the legal adviser considers the client to be a potential victim of trafficking, the client should be encouraged to allow disclosure of that fact to the police

33 See www.lawsociety.org.uk/support-services/advice/practice-notes/criminal-prosecutions-of-victims-of-trafficking/, last accessed 22 August 2025.

for referral into the NRM. Such a disclosure imposes on police a duty to investigate the details of the disclosure (see below) and may stop, or at least suspend, the instant investigation. The client should be treated as a victim of crime. Even if the investigation into the index offence continues, the early disclosure will impact on the decision by the prosecuting authorities as to whether to prosecute the matter and may provide a more effective defence under the Modern Slavery Act 2015 ('MSA 2015'), s 45.

11.64

A defence under the MSA 2015, s 45 does not require a NRM referral, but the consequences of such a referral may provide evidence to support the s 45 defence, or any application to stay proceedings as an abuse of process and/or a review of any decision to prosecute either initially or at a later stage. Gathering such evidence may be particularly difficult for defence lawyers, particularly where it may exist by way of intelligence-based sources on the operation of a particular trafficking gang, so the balance will be in favour of the client allowing a referral.

11.65

Anyone advising on a matter where the client may be a potential victim of trafficking should consider the defence provided by the MSA 2015, s 45 and/or duress. A full analysis of the non-prosecution regime and defences is set out in **Chapter 10**.

11.66

A person aged 18 or over at the time of the act which constitutes the offence is not guilty of an offence if they do that act because they are compelled to do it, the compulsion is attributable to slavery or to 'relevant exploitation', and a reasonable person in the same situation as the person and having the person's relevant characteristics would have no realistic alternative to doing that act[34].

11.67

A person may be compelled to do something by another person or by their circumstances[35]. Compulsion is attributable to slavery or to relevant exploitation only if it is, or is part of, conduct which constitutes an offence under the MSA 2015, s 1 or conduct which constitutes relevant exploitation, or it is a direct consequence of a person being, or having been, a victim of slavery or a victim of relevant exploitation[36].

---

34 MSA 2015, s 45(1).
35 MSA 2015, s 45(2).
36 MSA 2015, s 45(3).

11.68

A person under the age of 18 when they do the act which constitutes the offence is not guilty of an offence if they do that act as a direct consequence of being, or having been, a victim of slavery or a victim of relevant exploitation, and a reasonable person in the same situation as the person and having the person's relevant characteristics would do that act[37].

11.69

'Relevant characteristics' means age, sex and any physical or mental illness or disability. 'Relevant exploitation' is exploitation (within the meaning of the MSA 2015, s 3) that is attributable to the exploited person being, or having been, a victim of human trafficking[38].

11.70

The defences set out above do not apply if the offence under investigation falls within the MSA 2015, Sch 4[39]. If the offence under investigation falls within the exceptions set out in Sch 4 (see the full list of exceptions, set out in the annex to **Chapter 10**), it will not preclude the engagement of the non-punishment legal framework or the Crown applying their guidance in deciding whether to prosecute (see **Chapter 10**).

11.71

If an interview is to proceed, the client should be advised as to the best options for dealing with the interview. This may include setting out sufficient information to mount the defence at a later stage or to prepare the groundwork for representations to the prosecuting authority that it would be inappropriate to bring charges.

11.72

Much will depend on whether the client accepts that they are a victim of trafficking and have been acting under the influence of their trafficker. If they accept that, and disclosure has been made, but the interview proceeds, a prepared statement to that effect should be considered, followed by a no comment interview. It would not necessarily be appropriate for the potential victim of trafficking to be probed about their disclosure in an investigative interview of this nature and answering questions may be problematic.

37 MSA 2015, s 45(4).
38 MSA 2015, s 45(5).
39 MSA 2015, s 45(7).

11.73

If the client refuses to disclose, or denies being a potential victim of trafficking, the client would most likely be best advised not to answer questions. Any answers that specifically deny or undermine the potential trafficking defence may be problematic (albeit not fatal) later at trial if by that stage disclosure has been made.

11.74

A refusal to answer questions in interview will invoke the *possibility* of adverse inferences being drawn in any subsequent trial if the jury (or tribunal in the magistrates' or youth court) believes that the fact not mentioned was relied on in the defence of those proceedings and it was a fact which in the circumstances existing at the time the accused could reasonably have been expected to mention when questioned[40].

11.75

Victims of trafficking may not want to disclose details regarding their exploitation for a number of complex cultural, religious and physiological reasons, which can include juju rituals, debt bondage and fear of reprisals. Full details on control methods are explored in **Chapter 2**.

11.76

Whether a jury would subsequently draw an adverse inference from a silent interview cannot be known at the time of the interview. Indeed, in the case of a vulnerable person who may be a victim of trafficking, there will be very good arguments to be deployed at trial that no inference should be drawn and that it was entirely reasonable for that person not to have answered questions and mentioned facts in interview that they later relied on at trial.

11.77

Whether the suspect could reasonably have been expected to mention a fact at the time of the interview or on charge is a question of fact and the court must have regard to 'the actual accused with such qualities, apprehensions, knowledge and advice as they are shown to have had at the time'[41].

11.78

The court will take into account such matters as the time of day that the interview took place, the age of the suspect, their experience, their mental capacity and state of health, their knowledge, personality, and the fact that they had received legal advice before allowing the possibility of an adverse inference being drawn by the jury.

40 Criminal Justice and Public Order Act 1994, s 34.
41 *R v Argent* (1997) 2 Cr App Rep 27.

11.79

A potential victim of trafficking is likely to be able to rely on a number of the above issues in order to justify the reasonableness of a decision not to mention facts in interview. It is possible that, during trial, expert evidence may be required to explain the special vulnerabilities of trafficked individuals, to ensure that the point is fully understood by the court.

11.80

The suspect cannot rely solely on the fact that they were advised to say nothing in interview by his legal adviser in order to avoid an adverse inference being drawn. What is important is not the quality of the advice but the effect of the advice on the suspect, and whether in the circumstances it was reasonable for them to take the advice and not answer questions.

11.81

The fact that the suspect has been advised by their legal representative to remain silent must be given 'appropriate weight' by the court. It is important that the decision to remain silent was genuinely made as a result of legal advice rather than because there was no innocent explanation or none that would stand up to scrutiny[42].

11.82

Once it is shown that the advice (of whatever quality) has genuinely been relied on as the reason for the suspect remaining silent, a jury may still be directed that they may properly draw an adverse inference. It is not necessarily unreasonable to expect the suspect to mention the facts in question notwithstanding the advice received. What is reasonable depends on all the circumstances.

11.83

The fact that advice has been given to remain silent remains an important consideration but not one that automatically excludes an adverse inference. The defendant has a choice to accept or reject the advice and is warned in the caution that a failure to mention any facts that they relied on at trial might harm their defence.

11.84

Circumstances where a suspect could have good reason to rely on advice to remain silent, even if they have an innocent explanation for the allegations,

42 *Condron v United Kingdom* (App No 35718/97) (2000) 31 EHRR 1, [2000] Crim LR 679; *R v Betts* [2001] EWCA Crim 224, [2001] 2 Cr App Rep 257.

would include where the suspect was vulnerable and might have real difficulty getting across what they wanted to say. Potential victims of trafficking are undoubtedly vulnerable and are likely to have understandable reasons as to why they may be reluctant to disclose certain information in interview even where that information may assist them in relation to setting out a defence under the MSA 2015, s 45 or in a wider context.

11.85

In circumstances where a potential victim of trafficking will not consent to a disclosure to police and for a NRM referral, and where they choose to remain silent in interview, it is important that legal representatives make detailed notes of instructions. The legal adviser should try to obtain as much information as possible from the potential victim of trafficking as to their fears and concerns. It may become relevant should the matter go to trial and a slavery defence is subsequently raised.

11.86

In order to rebut any potential adverse inference, the legal representative may be required to provide evidence regarding the instructions they obtained, their advice and the reason that the suspect did not want to answer questions. This *may* require a waiver of privilege, as the reasons for the advice will have to be explained. Any waiver will extend to the whole of the consultation and not merely the discrete piece of advice.

11.87

However, if the adverse inference to be drawn is that the suspect has recently made up an account in order to take advantage of the defence after charge, such inference can be rebutted by the legal adviser providing a statement as to the account given to them in the pre-interview discussion or producing a statement made by the defendant at that time. This will demonstrate that the account has not been made up subsequently and may prevent privilege being waived for the whole of the consultation, or at all[43].

11.88

Clearly such a decision needs careful consideration at trial as there remains a risk that privilege will have to be waived. Such a decision may be dependent on the content of the rest of the consultation and the importance of the jury understanding the reason for the defendant remaining silent in interview.

43 *R v Wilmot* (1988) 89 Cr App Rep 341.

Positive obligations owed to a victim of trafficking by the state

11.89

When a defendant or suspect in criminal proceedings has been identified[44] as a potential victim of trafficking that individual could fall within the scope of the ECHR, Art 4. Article 4 is a prohibition on slavery and servitude (see Chapter 10 for a fuller account of this provision) and in *Rantsev v Cyprus and Russia*[45] the ECtHR held that trafficking in human beings fell within the scope of Art 4[46].

11.90

Article 4 carries with it positive obligations on the state to the victim of trafficking (or potential victim of trafficking). Article 4 requires Member States to penalise and prosecute effectively any act aimed at maintaining a person in a situation of slavery, servitude or forced or compulsory labour[47].

11.91

Article 4 may, in certain circumstances, require a state to take operational and protective measures to protect victims, or potential victims, of trafficking[48]. In order to establish that this positive obligation arises it must be demonstrated that the state authorities were aware, or ought to have been aware, of circumstances giving rise to a reasonable suspicion that an identified individual had been, or was at real and immediate risk of being, trafficked or exploited within the meaning of the Council of Europe Convention on Action against Trafficking in Human Beings ('ECAT'), Art 4(a)[49]. Protection measures include facilitating the identification of victims by trained persons and assisting victims in their physical, psychological and social recovery[50]. The scope of the investigative duty under the ECHR, Art 3 was looked at further in the now leading case of *Commissioner of Police of the Metropolis v DSD*[51]. The claimants were victims of John Worboys, a serial sex offender known as the Black Cab Rapist. The Court held that serious failures (also described by Lord Kerr as 'conspicuous or substantial' and 'egregious and significant') by the police in an investigation into serious offences against the person (described by Lord Kerr as 'serious violence to an individual'), even where these fall short of system failing, will amount to a

44 Self-identification is not a pre-requisite to an individual meeting the definition of trafficking and coming within the scope of the different international, regional and domestic safeguards viz trafficking victims. This identification could be through the NRM (see Chapter 2) or by a statutory agency or other organisation supporting or assisting the potential victim.

45 App No 25965/04 (10 May 2010), paras 277 and 282.

46 See **Chapter 10** and *VCL and AN v UK* Application Numbers 77587/12 & 74603/12; [2021] 73 EHRR 9.

47 *CN v United Kingdom* (2013) 56 EHRR 24, para 66; *Siliadin v France* App No 73316/01 (26 October 2005), para 112 and *CN and V v France* App No 67724/09 (11 October 2012), para 105.

48 *Rantsev* at para 286; *Osman v UK* (App No 87/1997/871/1083) at [115].

49 *Rantsev* at para 286; *CN v United Kingdom*, para 67.

50 *Chowdhury v Greece* App No 21884/15 at para 110.

51 [2018] UKSC 11.

breach of the investigative obligation under Art 3. A credible or arguable claim of serious crime will trigger the duty to carry out an effective investigation.[52]

11.92

There is a significant body of material in the public domain about the typology of trafficking within the UK. If a suspect fits this (eg a Vietnamese child recovered in a cannabis farm), it will be arguable that the Art 4 protection obligations are triggered at an early stage, such as upon arrest, and thus before the decision to charge[53]. See **Chapter 2** for common trafficking victim profiles in the UK.

11.93

Article 4 entails a procedural obligation to investigate where there is a reasonable suspicion that an individual's rights under the article have been violated[54]. The duty to investigate does not depend on a complaint from the victim or next of kin; it is triggered as soon as the matter has come to the attention of the authorities, and the authorities must act of their own motion[55]. This obligation entails the relevant investigatory agencies asking the appropriate questions, making enquiries or further enquiries into the facts and background, and/or parts of the trafficking chain[56]. Early identification as to whether or not a defendant has in fact been trafficked has been recognised by the ECtHR as being of paramount importance in a criminal prosecution or investigation. As soon as the authorities are aware of circumstances giving rise to a credible suspicion that an individual suspected of committing a criminal offence may have been trafficked or exploited, they must be promptly assessed by individuals trained and qualified to deal with victims of trafficking. The Court confirmed that 'given that an individual's status as a victim of trafficking may affect whether there is sufficient evidence to prosecute and whether it is in the public interest to do so, any decision on whether or not to prosecute a potential victim of trafficking should – insofar as possible – only be taken once a trafficking assessment has been made by a qualified person. This is particularly important where children are concerned'[57].

11.94

For the purposes of a criminal investigation, the relevant agencies required to meet this positive obligation will be the police and the Crown. The criminal

52 See Chapters 1 and 4 for further explanation on duty to investigate.

53 See, for example, Association of Chief Police Officers, *Position from ACPO Leads on Child Protection and Cannabis Cultivation on Children and Young People Recovered in Cannabis Farms*, available at http://new.ecpat.org.uk/sites/default/files/acpo_leads_position_on_cyp_recovered_from_cannabis_farms_final.pdf, last accessed 14 December 2017.

54 *Rantsev*, para 286; *CN v United Kingdom* (2013) 56 EHRR 24, para 69; see also *VCL and AN v UK* Application Numbers 77587/12 & 74603/12; [2021] 73 EHRR 9.

55 *Rantsev*, para 288; *J v Austria* App No 58216/12 (17 January 2017) at para 107.

56 *Rantsev*, paras 297, 303.

57 *VCL and AN v UK* Application Numbers 77587/12 & 74603/12; [2021] 73 EHRR 9.

investigation must be effective and capable of leading to the individuals responsible for the trafficking. Reasonable speed and diligence are required, although an investigation must be urgent if it is possible to remove the individual concerned from a damaging situation[58]. Promptness is required to avoid a negative impact on the victim's personal situation[59]. Authorities must take all reasonable steps to secure evidence concerning the incident[60].

11.95

Article 4 positive obligations and whether these have been fulfilled by state agencies is likely to be relevant to any challenge to the removal of a victim of trafficking from the UK or deportation decision (see Chapter 10), any challenge to a negative identification decision by the NRM (see **Chapter 4**) and/or prosecution of a potential victim of trafficking and any onward appeals of these decisions (see **Chapters 12** and **13**).

The NRM and the duty to notify

11.96

The NRM is a framework for identifying and referring potential victims of modern slavery and ensuring they receive the appropriate support. It was implemented in 2009 for victims of trafficking to give effect to obligations arising under ECAT and extended to include victims of modern slavery on 31 July 2015 (see **Chapter 4**).

11.97

The police are first responders under the NRM. They have a further statutory duty under the MSA 2015. The duty applies to specified public authorities to respond to incidents of suspected trafficking and slavery. This is referred to as the duty to notify, and can be found in the MSA 2015, s 52.

11.98

Section 52 of the MSA 2015 is intended to further improve identification of victims by creating a statutory duty for specified public authorities to notify the Secretary of State where they have reasonable grounds to believe that a person may be a victim of slavery or human trafficking. The section requires that where a specified public authority to which the section applies has reasonable grounds to believe that a person may be a victim of slavery or human trafficking, it must notify the Home Office, regardless of whether the individual has consented to enter into the NRM.

58 *Chowdhury v Greece*, para 89.
59 *LE v Greece* App No 71545/12 (21 April 2016), para 68.
60 In the context of Art 3, the positive obligation to secure evidence arose in *J v Austria* at para 107.

11.99

The public authorities currently required[61] to report under the duty to notify are as follows:

- a chief officer of police for a police area;
- the chief constable of the British Transport Police Force;
- the National Crime Agency;
- a county council;
- a county borough council;
- a district council;
- a London borough council;
- the Greater London Authority;
- the Common Council of the City of London;
- the Council of the Isles of Scilly;
- the Gangmasters and Labour Abuse Authority.

Crime recording

11.100

The Home Office Counting Rules ('HOCR') for recorded crime was introduced as of April 2019. All reported cases of modern slavery should be recorded on the force crime system, in accordance with the below provisions and for forces live on the Home Office Data Hub.

N200/01 – reported incident – NRM referral pending reasonable grounds decision

N200/02 – reported incident – NRM referral negative reasonable grounds decision

N200/03 – reported incident – NRM referral – Duty to notify only

N200/04 – reported incident – NRM referral – Positive reasonable grounds/ police referral – Outside England and Wales

N200/05 – reported incident – NRM referral – Negative reasonable grounds – Outside England and Wales

N200/06 – reported incident – NRM referral – Transferred to another force in England and Wales

61 Set out in MSA 2015, s 52.

11.101

General rule: one record for each NRM referral received.

11.102

The incident of modern slavery must be recorded under this classification at the first opportunity, this should be the person receiving the initial report, including call handlers, crime bureaus and specialist units. The College of policing guidance states:

> 'NRM referrals received by the force from the SCA will be recorded initially under classification N200. The N200 record is to be retained pending receipt of the reasonable grounds decision. Once the reasonable grounds decision is received, the recording decision must be made in accordance with the flowchart (see the link to the HOCR in the 'Useful links' section).
>
> For incidents where modern slavery criminality occurred in England and/or Wales, all referrals made by the police into the NRM and/or incidents where victims report to police directly must be subject to a recorded crime of modern slavery. If it is determined that all modern slavery criminality occurred outside England and Wales, an N200/04 must be recorded. Duty to Notify referrals submitted by the police must be subject to a recorded crime.
>
> Reports recorded under this classification must be included in force notifiable crime statistical returns, using the same reporting process as notifiable crimes.
>
> With regards to the NRM, the expectation is that once a reported incident of modern slavery in England and Wales is confirmed by a positive reasonable grounds decision, it will be reclassified as such at the earliest opportunity. There should be no delay for any investigation to occur, beyond establishing the circumstances of the incident to inform the NCRS crime recording decision.
>
> Once recorded and classified, a reported incident of modern slavery will remain recorded as such, unless (or until) it is reclassified as a confirmed crime of modern slavery, in addition to any other notifiable crime, as appropriate. Such reclassification must take place as soon as the reporting officer is satisfied that it is more likely than not that a notifiable crime has been committed, or once a positive grounds decision is returned. The decision to record a crime must not be delayed pending the outcome of the criminal investigation'[62].

62 https://www.app.college.police.uk/app-content/major-investigation-and-public-protection/modern-slavery/national-referral-mechanism/ (updated 24 February 2022; last accessed 22 August 2025).

The police interview

11.103

In a situation where disclosure has been made to police that the client is a potential victim of trafficking but the officer in the case for the index offence continues with the interview under caution, the adviser should place on record at the start of the interview that the suspect has disclosed themselves to police as a potential victim of trafficking and that there is a duty upon the police to refer the client into the NRM and to consider an appropriate assessment[63]. In the light of that process, an interview on the index offence is inappropriate.

11.104

Guidance has been issued, following the implementation of the MSA 2015, by the National College of Policing. It states:

> 'If a person is arrested and so enters the criminal justice system as a perpetrator, and officers discover during the PACE interview that the person committed a modern slavery offence through coercion and may also be a victim, the interview should continue and evidence be obtained. On conclusion of the interview, the person should be referred into the NRM if they consent. If appropriate, the person should be bailed for the offence under investigation. If, however, the person has been arrested for an offence outlined in Schedule 4, is illegally residing in the UK and is likely to abscond, bail should be withheld. Following the referral, a victim debrief and a subsequent interview in line with Achieving Best Evidence in Criminal Proceedings: Guidance on interviewing victims and witnesses, and guidance on using special measures should take place to identify additional perpetrators and to help officers gather further evidence'[64].

11.105

If disclosure is made during the course of the interview when it had not been made previously to the adviser, or in circumstances where the client had refused to disclose it prior to interview, the adviser should consider interrupting the interview and request a further consultation with the client so that the matter can be clarified. At that point, disclosure can be made and representations made that the interview should not continue, regardless of the advice of the National College of Policing.

63 As per *VCL and AN v UK* Application Numbers 77587/12 & 74603/12; [2021] 73 EHRR 9.

64 See www.app.college.police.uk/app-content/major-investigation-and-public-protection/modern-slavery/national-referral-mechanism/#responding-to-perpetrators-who-may-also-be-victims, last accessed 22 August 2025.

Age of potential victim of trafficking

11.106

The age of the potential victim of trafficking may be an issue and may not be known. It is common for victims of trafficking to be groomed to give a certain age if questioned by authority. The age given will depend on the modus operandi of the traffickers: some may be told to say that they are older than they actually are, and others to say that they are younger.

11.107

Generally, if the potential victim of trafficking claims to be an adult, the legal adviser has to act on those instructions. However, if the adviser believes the potential victim of trafficking to be under 18, advice should be given to declare a proper age. Those under the age of 18 are treated more favourably in detention and would be entitled to the support of an appropriate adult.

11.108

The police are under an obligation to treat anyone who appears to be under the age of 18 as a juvenile unless there is clear evidence that they are older[65]. Full details on age assessment are explained in **Chapter 6**.

Appropriate adult

11.109

It is arguable that anyone identified as a potential victim of trafficking is potentially vulnerable and should be afforded the right to an appropriate adult. This is obviously true if the person is, or appears to be, under the age of 18, but should also apply to adults who have made such disclosure or where there is suspicion that they may be a potential victim of trafficking.

11.110

If an officer has any suspicion, or is told in good faith, that a person of any age may be mentally disordered or otherwise mentally vulnerable, in the absence of clear evidence to dispel that suspicion, the person shall be treated as such[66]. It is arguable that a potential victim of trafficking should be considered to be mentally vulnerable, which is defined in the PACE Code C as someone 'who, because of their mental state or capacity, may not understand the significance of what is said, of questions or of their replies'. This definition may fit potential victims of trafficking, but it is suggested that a change to the Code is desirable

65 PACE 1984, Code C1.5.
66 PACE 1984, Code C1.4.

to specifically bring potential victims of trafficking within the definition of 'mentally vulnerable' people.

11.111

An appropriate adult in the case of a juvenile is:

- the parent, guardian or, if the juvenile is in the care of a local authority or voluntary organisation, a person representing that authority or organisation;
- a social worker of a local authority;
- failing these, some other responsible adult aged 18 or over who is not:
  - a police officer;
  - employed by the police;
  - under the direction or control of the chief officer of a police force; or
  - a person who provides services under contractual arrangements (but without being employed by the chief officer of a police force) to assist that force in relation to the discharge of its chief officer's functions, whether or not they are on duty at the time[67].

11.112

An appropriate adult in the case of a person who is mentally disordered or mentally vulnerable is:

- a relative, guardian or other person responsible for their care or custody;
- someone experienced in dealing with mentally disordered or mentally vulnerable people but who is not:
  - a police officer;
  - employed by the police;
  - under the direction or control of the chief officer of a police force; or
  - a person who provides services under contractual arrangements (but without being employed by the chief officer of a police force) to assist that force in relation to the discharge of its chief officer's functions, whether or not they are on duty at the time;
- failing these, some other responsible adult aged 18 or over.

67 PACE 1984, Code C1.7(a).

11.113

In the case of people who are mentally disordered or otherwise mentally vulnerable, it may be more satisfactory if the appropriate adult is someone experienced or trained in the care of such individuals, rather than a relative lacking such qualifications. However, if the detainee prefers a relative to a better qualified stranger, or objects to a particular person, their wishes should, if practicable, be respected[68].

11.114

A detainee should always be given an opportunity, when an appropriate adult is called to the police station, to consult privately with a solicitor in the appropriate adult's absence if they want. An appropriate adult is not subject to legal privilege[69].

11.115

A solicitor or independent custody visitor who is present at the police station and acting in that capacity may not be the appropriate adult[70].

11.116

It is imperative that the adviser is content that the appropriate adult is appropriate. It may be, for example, that a juvenile potential victim of trafficking may request an appropriate adult who is linked to their trafficker. In certain exploitation paradigms, the person who might naturally be an appropriate adult (such as a parent) might in fact be the trafficker or exploiter. Representing the suspect as such may be part of the coercive controlling features of the trafficking itself. Practitioners and police should be alive to this possibility. In such circumstances, it will be very difficult for the adviser or police to ascertain victim status as the client will not have disclosed being a potential victim of trafficking and most certainly would not disclose in the presence of such an adult. The gender of the appropriate adult may be important to the potential victim of trafficking and their views should be taken into account if expressed.

After the interview

11.117

If disclosure of the suspect's status as a potential victim of trafficking has been made to police and the police have followed up with a NRM referral, no decision should be made to charge the suspect with any offences at that point.

68 PACE 1984, Code C Note 1D.
69 PACE 1984, Code C Note 1E.
70 PACE 1984, Code C Note 1F.

Subject to the seriousness of the offence and a suspect's background and previous convictions, it may well be appropriate for representations to be made to the police to the effect that prosecution would not be appropriate on evidential grounds or in the public interest, relying on the CPS guidance 'Modern Slavery and human trafficking: offences and defences, including the section 45 defence'[71] in so far as it relates to the non-prosecution of victims of trafficking. It ought to be for the CPS to make a charging decision in a case where a suspect is a possible credible victim of trafficking, modern slavery or exploitation, given the complexity of the legal landscape and the complicating procedural and evidential features of a NRM referral and assessment. Representatives should also consider drafting written representations to the duty CPS charging lawyer invoking non-prosecution principles, based on the CPS guidance. This is explored in detail in Chapters 10.

11.118

Where a NRM referral has been made by the police, the potential victim of trafficking should be collected and transported by a relevant first responder from the police station to safe and secure accommodation.

11.119

In the period of time between the NRM referral and the reasonable grounds decision being made, police have a responsibility to ensure that the victim is safeguarded. Local authorities also retain a statutory duty to provide housing and officers should contact relevant local authorities and anti-slavery charities to assist[72].

11.120

If the person is destitute or needs immediate support, the Salvation Army may support them.

11.121

The Homelessness code of guidance for local authorities published in 2018 puts an obligation on local authorities to assist victims of modern slavery. Housing authorities are required to:

> '[…] secure that accommodation is available for an applicant if they have reason to believe that the applicant may be homeless, eligible for assistance and have a priority need. If housing authorities believe an individual may be vulnerable as a result of being a victim of modern

71 https://www.cps.gov.uk/legal-guidance/modern-slavery-and-human-trafficking-offences-and-defences-including-section-45 (accessed 22 August 2025).

72 See https://www.app.college.police.uk/app-content/major-investigation-and-public-protection/modern-slavery/national-referral-mechanism/ (accessed 1 February 2026).

slavery following a referral to the NRM housing authorities should ensure that accommodation is available while they are waiting for an initial "reasonable grounds" decision'[73].

11.122

Where the police have not made a NRM referral, legal representatives should take steps to ensure that they contact a first responder and trigger a NRM referral without delay (see **Chapter 2**).

11.123

If the client has not made a trafficking disclosure and is to be charged, the legal adviser may provide further legal advice immediately following charge. However, attendance upon the client thereafter whilst fingerprints, photographs and swabs are taken will not meet the 'sufficient benefit test' for public funding, except where the client requires further assistance owing to their particular circumstances, in which case the relevant factors must be noted on file. It is arguable that such clients would be eligible to have the services of the legal adviser under public funds for this process of further disclosure.

11.124

The adviser may remain at the police station if required to make representations about bail, including conditions that may be attached to any police bail or bail to court following a decision to charge the suspect with criminal offences. For example, it will be important to ensure that bail conditions imposed do not place the client in potential danger from their suspected trafficker.

Police bail

11.125

Where no charging decision has been made but the investigation is continuing, the suspect must be released without bail unless the officer is satisfied that releasing the person on bail is necessary and proportionate in all the circumstances (having regard, in particular, to any conditions of bail which would be imposed), and a custody officer authorises the release on bail (having considered any representations made by the person)[74].

---

73 Updated 18 July 2025: https://www.gov.uk/guidance/homelessness-code-of-guidance-for-local-authorities/chapter-25-modern-slavery-and-trafficking#:~:text=If%20housing%20authorities%20believe%20an%20individual%20may,Grounds%20decision%20and/or%20while%20the%20housing%20authority (accessed 22 August 2025).

74 PACE 1984, s 30A(1) and (1A).

11.126

Police bail conditions cannot include the taking of a security or surety to ensure the person's surrender to custody or any requirement to reside in a bail hostel[75]. Police bail conditions may be imposed only if they appear necessary to secure that the person surrenders to custody, to secure that the person does not commit an offence while on bail, to secure that the person does not interfere with witnesses or otherwise obstruct the course of justice, whether in relation to themself or any other person, or for the person's own protection or, if the person is under the age of 18, for the person's own welfare or in the person's own interests[76].

11.127

Once released on police bail the date on, or police station to, which the person has to surrender can be changed, although the person must be given notice in writing of any changes[77].

11.128

The initial period of police bail cannot exceed three months beginning with the day after the day on which the person was arrested for the offence in relation to which bail is granted[78].

11.129

Police bail conditions can be varied by police[79] and if the person on bail wishes to apply to vary conditions, an application should initially be made to the police. If that is refused, an application can be made to the magistrates' court[80]. Public funding is available (if financially eligible) under the Advocacy Assistance scheme for such applications.

11.130

Police bail can be extended before the three months expires to six months by an officer of at least inspector rank[81]. The police have to inform the person or their legal representative and give them an opportunity to make representations against such a decision[82].

75 PACE 1984, s 30A(3A).
76 PACE 1984, s 30A(3B).
77 PACE 1984, s 30B(6), (6A) and (7).
78 PACE 1984, s 30B(8). In SFO investigations when the initial limit is three months (PACE 1984, s 47ZB(1)(a)).
79 PACE 1984, s 30CA.
80 PACE 1984, s 30CB.
81 PACE 1984, s 47ZD(2).
82 PACE 1984, s 47ZD(3), (4).

11.131

Bail can only be so extended if there are reasonable grounds for:

- suspecting the person in question to be guilty of the relevant offence;
- believing that further time is needed for making a decision as to whether to charge the person with the relevant offence, or otherwise, that further investigation is needed of any matter in connection with the relevant offence;
- believing that the decision as to whether to charge the person with the relevant offence is being made diligently and expeditiously, or otherwise, that the investigation is being conducted diligently and expeditiously; and
- believing that the release on bail of the person in question is necessary and proportionate in all the circumstances (having regard, in particular, to any conditions of bail which are, or are to be, imposed)[83].

11.132

Police bail can be extended up to a further three months on application to a magistrates' court prior to the end of the currently applicable bail period but only if the court has reasonable grounds for believing that:

- further time is needed for making a decision as to whether to charge the person with the relevant offence, or otherwise, that further investigation is needed of any matter in connection with the relevant offence;
- the decision as to whether to charge the person with the relevant offence is being made diligently and expeditiously, or otherwise, that the investigation is being conducted diligently and expeditiously; and
- the release on bail of the person in question is necessary and proportionate in all the circumstances (having regard, in particular, to any conditions of bail which are, or are to be, imposed)[84].

11.133

The court will only increase the bail period if the nature of the decision or further investigations means that that decision is unlikely to be made or those investigations completed if the current applicable bail period in relation to the person is not extended as requested[85].

---

83 PACE 1984, s 47ZC(2)–(5).
84 PACE 1984, s 47ZG.
85 PACE 1984, s 47ZG(8).

11.134

In all other circumstances, where no charging decision has been made but the investigation continues, the person will be 'released under investigation' to which status no conditions can be attached.

11.135

Given these restrictions on police bail, it is likely that any potential victim of trafficking who has made a disclosure and been referred into the NRM will be released under investigation with no specific date to return.

11.136

It is important to keep in contact with the client throughout this period and ensure that they seek assistance from one of the appropriate organisations, whether or not they have disclosed themselves to be a potential victim of trafficking. A referral into the NRM can be made at any time by a relevant organisation and such a referral may well assist the client's case at whatever stage it is made.

11.137

The police may decide to release a potential victim of trafficking on police bail with protective conditions such as release to a suitable safe bail address not near the area of exploitation, although this cannot be a bail hostel. Often potential victims of trafficking go missing straight from their release from police custody as they will not wait to be met by someone from an organisation that might have been requested to help them. Victims may be met at the police station by people connected to their trafficker.

11.138

If bail conditions are imposed, it is important to ensure that they do not put the potential victim of trafficking in potential danger. It would be inappropriate to demand that the potential victim of trafficking sign on at a police station in an area of danger for them that is close to their trafficker or place of arrest. Further protective conditions and safeguarding are discussed in Chapters 8 and 11.

Limits on period of detention without charge

11.139

In the first instance a person shall not be kept in police detention for more than 24 hours without being charged. The time from which the period of detention of a person is to be calculated is the time at which that person arrives at the relevant police station, or the time 24 hours after the time of that person's arrest, whichever is the earlier[86].

11.140

A person who has not been charged within the 24-hour period shall be released either without bail unless the pre-conditions for bail are satisfied, in which case they may be released on police bail[87].

11.141

However, where a police officer of the rank of superintendent or above has reasonable grounds for believing that the detention of that person without charge is necessary to secure or preserve evidence relating to an offence for which they are under arrest or to obtain such evidence by questioning them; an offence for which they are under arrest is an indictable offence; and the investigation is being conducted diligently and expeditiously, they may authorise the keeping of that person in police detention for a period of up to 36 hours after the relevant time[88].

11.142

Any application for a warrant of further detention to detain a suspect beyond 36 hours has to be made to the magistrates' court. Representation at such a hearing is funded by Advocacy Assistance and is not means tested[89]. The maximum time that a person can be kept in detention is 96 hours[90].

The charging decision

11.143

According to the Crown Prosecutors' Guidance the police may charge:

- any summary only offence (including criminal damage where the value of the loss or damage is less than £5,000) irrespective of plea;
- any offence of retail theft (shoplifting) or attempted retail theft irrespective of plea provided it is suitable for sentence in the magistrates' court; and
- any either way offence anticipated as a guilty plea and suitable for sentence in a magistrates' court.

---

86 PACE 1984, s 41.
87 PACE 1984, s 41(7).
88 PACE 1984, s 42(10).
89 PACE 1984, ss 43 and 44.
90 PACE 1984, s 44.

11.144

Good practice dictates that any case which involves indicators of modern slavery should be referred to the CPS for a charging decision as the issues are more complex, even if it might otherwise fall within the police charging remit. Legal advisers should press for this course at the police station by making representations to the investigating officer and the custody officer.

11.145

Publicly funded advice can be provided in the period after release from the police station and while a charging decision is being contemplated. Advice can be provided under the Legal Advice and Assistance scheme but this is strictly means tested and will only add to the fees the solicitors' firm receives for the representation if it takes the firm over the fee threshold into the exceptional fee bracket (see **Chapter 20**). Consequently, although in practice the work is likely not to be remunerated above the Police Station Advice Fixed Fee, funding is technically available for representations to be made to the police or the CPS for the disposal of the case without charge.

11.146

Written representations can be submitted when the matter has been sent to the CPS for a decision on charge. Written representations[91] should include detailed reference to the Crown's obligations under the CPS guidance 'Modern Slavery and human trafficking: offences and defences, including the section 45 defence' Part 2 ('the CPS guidance')[92].

11.147

Defence representatives should endeavour to persuade the CPS that the client is a victim of trafficking and should not be prosecuted in the circumstances. Reference should be made to the availability of the s 45 MSA 2015 defence and the Crown's ECAT obligations not to proceed with the prosecution as not in the public interest (see **Chapters 10** and **12**).

11.148

While victim status does not create a blanket prohibition on prosecution, where the criminality or culpability of victims of exploitation, modern slavery and trafficking is reduced materially by exploitation and its nexus to the offence, prosecution may well run counter to the evidential stage and/or the public interest stage of the Full Code Test for Crown Prosecutors. This is inherent within the CPS guidance, an important document that allows the CPS to fulfil

91 Under The Code of Crown Prosecutors, para 3.3.

92 https://www.cps.gov.uk/legal-guidance/modern-slavery-and-human-trafficking-offences-and-defences-including-section-45 (accessed 22 August 2025).

the state's obligations in England and Wales under ECAT (arts 4, 26 and 10 to 13). The CPS guidance must be considered by the prosecutor pre-charge where there are indicators or possible indicators of exploitation or trafficking present in respect of a suspect. The CPS guidance is relevant irrespective of whether the suspect has self-identified as a victim of trafficking. Indicators of trafficking are sufficient to prompt consideration of the guidance. Prosecutorial obligations are discussed in **Chapter 10**.

11.149

The CPS guidance provides that prosecutors should be alert to particular circumstances or situations where a suspect or defendant might be a victim of trafficking or slavery. The December 2021 iteration of the CPS guidance set out, 'Prosecutors are required to consider whether the suspect or defendant is a [possible victim] and should be alert to particular circumstances or situations where someone suspected of committing a criminal offence might also be a victim of trafficking or slavery':

> 'The most common offences include an unaccompanied foreign national child committing offences, such as pickpocketing or cultivation of cannabis; or the exploitation of UK children in 'County Lines' offending; or in the case of adults, committing offences such as those involving immigration documents or controlling prostitution. Gangs and organised criminal networks involved in exporting illegal drugs into one or more importing areas (within the UK) have also been exploiting children and vulnerable adults by using them to carry out illegal activity on their behalf. This includes moving and storing drugs and money and these criminal networks often use coercion, intimidation, violence (including sexual violence) or weapons against them. For further information, see 'County Lines' guidance'[93].

11.150

The CPS guidance says:

> 'The identification of victims of modern slavery during the course of an investigation and prosecution involves compliance with international and domestic law, the importance of which is codified in treaties and legislation and underlined by international and domestic court decisions.'

11.151

The current version of the CPS guidance does not spell out the duty of inquiry incumbent on the prosecution so as to fulfil its identification obligations

93 Suspects in a Criminal Case who might be Victims of Trafficking or Slavery, December 2021.

following *VCL and AN v UK*[94]. The December 2021 version did. Prosecutors should be reminded that their duty extends to making enquiries as the CPS acknowledged following *VCL and AN v the UK* in the earlier guidance:

> 'In considering whether a suspect might be a victim of trafficking or slavery, as required in the first stage of the assessment, prosecutors should have regard to their duty to make proper inquiries in criminal prosecutions involving individuals who may be victims of trafficking or slavery.
>
> The inquiries should be made by:
>
> - Advising the investigator who investigated the original offence that the suspect's trafficking/slavery situation must be investigated at an early stage if it has not already been done. Note in VCL the ECtHR said that "... the potential scope of [the positive obligation to take operational measures to protect the PVs] extends beyond their identification as victims of trafficking"
> - Prosecutors should satisfy themselves that the investigation has been sufficiently thorough and focussed on the circumstances of the PV/suspect to ensure that the PV/suspects' possible rights as a VOT are recognised and protected. However, if there is reliable and admissible evidence which confirms that the suspect is not a victim of trafficking/slavery there is no requirement to do so; and
> - Advising the investigator to consider referring the suspect to the NRM for victim identification if this has not already been done in the circumstances set out below. All law enforcement officers can refer potential victims of trafficking/slavery to the NRM.
>
> An NRM referral should always be made.
>
> - unless the law enforcement agency is in possession of clear and sufficient evidence to prove that the suspect is not a victim of trafficking/slavery; or
> - unless the prosecutor agrees that the suspect is a VOT/VOS. Where the prosecution agrees that someone is a VOT, that concession should be made and there is then no procedural reason to wait for a SCA decision. Prosecutors should make that admission where appropriate.'

11.152

The Full Code test has two stages: the evidential stage, which if met, is followed by the public interest stage. At the evidential stage, Prosecutors must

94 Application Numbers 77587/12 & 74603/12; [2021] 73 EHRR 9.

be satisfied that there is 'sufficient evidence to provide a realistic prospect of conviction against each suspect on each charge' including taking account of possible defences. Once the evidential stage test has been satisfied, a prosecutor must consider whether a prosecution is required in the 'public interest'. See **Chapter 10** for further details on the CPS guidance and its interplay with abuse of process and the safety of convictions.

Interviews where disclosure has been made

11.153

In circumstances where disclosure has been made to police that the suspect is a potential victim of trafficking and the suspect has been referred into the NRM, a request may be made for the individual to provide an interview about their trafficked status. These interviews should be attended by solicitors and funding is available under the Advice and Assistance Scheme subject to the client being financially eligible (which will likely be the case for the vast majority of potential victims of trafficking).

11.154

There is no obligation to co-operate in such interviews but co-operation may assist in providing information that could be used by authorities confirming the trafficked status of the individual and hence in any further representations that prosecution is inappropriate. However, in circumstances where the potential victim of trafficking has been charged or is still a suspect and is invited to provide an ABE interview whilst still a defendant or suspect in a case, it is routine that the investigating trafficking officer will provide information to the competent authority regarding their separate modern slavery investigation. This can in some cases be adverse and affect the competent authority's determination. The advice on whether a potential victim of trafficking suspect or defendant should co-operate in a parallel investigation is case specific.

11.155

The interviews will be conducted by specially trained officers and will be recorded on video as part of the Achieving Best Evidence process.

Police interviewing techniques with vulnerable witnesses

11.156

A training course called 'Investigative Interviewing' is available for those police officers who are likely to be required to conduct interviews with vulnerable complainants or to manage interviews in serious crime cases. This is based upon the best practice PEACE model[95] (see para **6.150** below).

11.157

The investigative interview process should create a managed conversation with the interviewee. It is not a linear process but should be constantly reviewed, remaining flexible and adaptable to changing circumstances. The process should not be undertaken with urgency, which is a challenge to many police officers who are under considerable pressure in terms of the time available to obtain witness and complainant evidence.

11.158

Investigative interviewing should be approached with an investigative mind-set. Accounts obtained from the person who is being interviewed should always be tested against what the interviewer already knows or what can be reasonably established. The main purpose of obtaining information in an interview is to further the enquiry by establishing facts. Interviewers should think about what they want to achieve by interviewing the complainant, witness or suspect, and set objectives which will help to corroborate or disprove information already known. Investigators should try to fill the gaps in the investigation by testing and corroborating the information by other means where possible.

11.159

The PEACE mnemonic stands for:

- planning and preparation;
- engage and explain;
- account, clarification and challenge;
- closure; and
- evaluation.

11.160

Planning and preparation is one of the most important phases in effective interviewing. Prior to the interview, the interviewer prepares an interview plan containing all the necessary elements, including defining the aims and objects of the interview and assessing what information is available and from where it can be obtained.

95 See College of Policing, at www.app.college.police.uk/app-content/investigations/investigative-interviewing/, last accessed 22 August 2025.

11.161

Planning and preparation should be carried out no matter what type of interview is being considered, whether it is with a witness, complainant or suspect, as it ensures that the investigators are ready to conduct an effective and ethical interview.

11.162

In order to engage, the interview should open with an introduction appropriate to the circumstances in order that a suitable relationship may be formed, with the interviewer showing awareness of and responding to the welfare needs of the witness and any fears and expectations the witness may have. The reasons for the interview should be explained as should the routines to be followed and how it relates to the evidential process.

11.163

The process of 'account, clarification and challenge' involves obtaining from the witness the account, achieving quality information and fine detail. The interviewer summarises and recounts what the witness has said at each stage so that both parties have an agreed understanding of what has taken place.

11.164

The process should allow for 'free recall', letting the subject talk freely without interruption. In the 'Clarification' phase the interviewer seeks to clarify the pertinent parts of the account starting in a chronological fashion, but probing questions should be used as the interview proceeds.

11.165

Challenges are often required as there could be and often are inconsistencies in the account. However, the challenges should be in a structured manner. The interviewer should seek to establish 'the evidence chain' and identify weaknesses and inconsistencies. The challenge process should be conducted with complainants and witnesses in a sympathetic way.

11.166

The interviewer should ensure that there is a planned closure of the process. The complainant or witness should be given an opportunity to ask questions, and explanations where legally available and practical should be provided. This ensures that the complainant or witness knows what will happen next.

11.167

After each interview is completed the event and the material gathered should be fully evaluated. This includes consideration of whether the objectives were achieved, whether any further information is required and the need for any further enquiries or corroboration.

11.168

Where multiple interviews are taking place, the teams should confer to ensure every member is aware of all the facts and decisions taken as to whether re-interviews are necessary.

Achieving Best Evidence interviews

11.169

These interviews are generally conducted using the ABE process and are video recorded[96]. There is guidance to assist those responsible for conducting video-recorded interviews with vulnerable, intimidated and significant witnesses, as well as those tasked with preparing and supporting witnesses during the criminal justice process. The guidance incorporates best practice from local areas and the expertise of practitioners, charities and voluntary groups who support complainants and witnesses at a local level.

11.170

Any video-recorded interview serves two primary purposes: evidence gathering for use in the investigation and in criminal proceedings; and to be used as the evidence-in-chief of the witness should the case go to court.

11.171

The Ministry of Justice guidance document outlines those who are defined as vulnerable. It states, that all children (those under 18) should always be deemed vulnerable. However, in respect of adults the guidance focuses on those adults with physical or mental health disabilities or issues. This follows the statutory definition of a vulnerable adult witness as someone who 'suffers from mental disorder within the meaning of the Mental Health Act 1983, or otherwise has a significant impairment of intelligence and social functioning' or who 'has a physical disability or is suffering from a physical disorder'[97].

11.172

The guidance also outlines the procedures to be used in the case of intimidated witnesses. The assistance of these special measures is available if the court

96 'Achieving Best Evidence in Criminal Proceedings' guidance has been thrsough a number of iterations since 2002. The current (2022) version (updated in June 2023) is produced by the Ministry of Justice and available at https://assets.publishing.service.gov.uk/media/6492e26c103ca6001303a331/achieving-best-evidence-criminal-proceedings-2023.pdf, last accessed 22 August 2025.

97 Youth Justice and Criminal Evidence Act 1999, s 16.

is satisfied that the quality of evidence given by the witness is likely to be diminished by reason of fear or distress on the part of the witness in connection with testifying in the proceedings[98].

11.173

In their determination the court must take into account:

- the nature and alleged circumstances of the offence to which the proceedings relate;
- the age of the witness;
- the social and cultural background and ethnic origins of the witness;
- the domestic and employment circumstances of the witness;
- any religious beliefs or political opinions of the witness;
- any behaviour towards the witness on the part of the accused, members of the family or associates of the accused, or any other person who is likely to be an accused or a witness in the proceedings[99].

11.174

Those who are victims of trafficking would fall within the definition of a witness requiring assistance due to fear or distress. However, the best practice techniques are not always utilised in police investigations and do not seem to have been adopted by the Immigration agencies.

11.175

There are many benefits to an investigator in video recording interviews where disclosure of trafficking has been made. One of the main benefits is the reassurance to the interviewee that by recording their evidence on video, they may not be required to face their exploiter or trafficker in court at a later date. Additional benefits of the process include ensuring an accurate record of the interview, and a reduced likelihood of allegations that the witness was led by the interviewers in delivering their account.

98 Youth Justice and Criminal Evidence Act 1999, s 17(1).
99 Paragraph 1.11.

12 Criminal court process

Paramjit Ahluwalia, Ben Douglas-Jones KC and Philippa Southwell

Introduction

12.1

All criminal practitioners need to be aware of indicators of trafficking and keep an open mind as to whether a suspect/defendant might be a trafficked person/subject to modern slavery. Assumptions should not be made by a prosecutor or defence representative that simply because of the subject's country of origin[1], or the type of alleged offence that considerations of trafficking/modern slavery are not applicable. Equally, criminal practitioners need to be aware of paradigmatic offending common within particular cultural or ethnic groups, which serve as indicators of trafficking, so that victim status is not overlooked. Examples of forced criminality and other types of exploitation may not be immediately obvious.

12.2

It can help practitioners who do not deal with victims of trafficking ('VOTs') (including victims of slavery, servitude or forced or compulsory labour) on a regular basis to ask themselves the question: 'Has my client been *exploited* by someone in connection with the commission of a criminal act?' If the answer is yes, they consider whether their client is or might be a VOT (including a victim of slavery, servitude or forced or compulsory labour) (see **Chapters 1** and **2**). All those involved in the criminal court process need to be alive to the possibility that defendants may be victims of exploitation. They need to be familiar with the operative duty to identify victims of slavery, servitude, forced or compulsory labour, and human trafficking: the national referral mechanism and Art 4 ECHR (see **Chapter 4**).

12.3

The Statutory Guidance[2] under the Modern Slavery Act 2015 ('MSA 2015') outlines that forced criminality is understood as the exploitation of a person to

1 UK nationals are the most commonly referred nationality into the NRM (Albanian nationals; Vietnamese nationals; Sudanese and Eritrean nationals accounting for the next most common nationalities referred into the NRM in 2023) – https://www.gov.uk/government/statistics/modern-slavery-nrm-and-dtn-statistics-end-of-year-summary-2023/annex-key-drivers-of-nrm-referrals-and-dtn-reports-for-potential-victims-of-modern-slavery.

2 Modern Slavery: statutory guidance for England and Wales – updated at 16 January 2025, version 3.12. The guidance is aimed at staff within public authorities and those involved in supporting victims as well as competent authority staff. However it is of particular assistance in highlighting indicators of trafficking.

commit activities that may include 'pick-pocketing, shoplifting, drug trafficking or cultivation, begging, benefit fraud and/or other types of fraud, sham marriage or other similar activities which are subject to penalties and imply financial gain'[3]. Organised crime networks and individuals who use human beings as commodities continually evolve and adapt their modus operandi to evade the attention of the authorities and to increase profitability[4].

12.4

General indicators of trafficking have been published by the United Nations Office on Drugs and Crime. The UN gives further, specific, guidance in relation to children, domestic servitude, sexual exploitation, labour exploitation, begging and petty crime[5]. Criminal practitioners should be familiar with these concepts and indicators, so they know what matters to explore through the police or with clients from the first opportunity onwards.

12.5

To assess the presence of trafficking/modern slavery indicators properly, full background details of a suspect/defendant need to be taken, as well as instructions concerning the alleged offence itself. These are difficult tasks to conduct under the pressure and time limitations associated with practice, particularly in magistrates' or youth courts. Cases are often, if not invariably, listed with many other first appearances. Consideration should be given to the sort of questions that need to be asked when liaising with the police (if prosecuting) or when taking instructions (if defending).

12.6

Trafficked persons/those subject to modern slavery often do not identify themselves or present as victims or avoid making disclosures due to fear of authority or reprisals from traffickers. Often trafficked persons/those subject to modern slavery are coached by their exploiters, as to the accounts they should give following apprehension. When taking instructions, detailed questions should be asked regarding background, methods of compulsion or coercion or control used, such as debt bondage, the impact of cultural aspects of background (such as juju rituals), threats, sexual and physical abuse[6]. Consideration should also be given to whether there are indicators of re-trafficking in the evidence. Internal trafficking within the UK should not be overlooked when taking instructions, particularly in relation to county lines offending where drug lines are being used in relation to drug distribution and related offending from large

---

3 Statutory Guidance, para 2.47.

4 See Chapter 15 for full details on forced criminality, modus operandi and common compelled or coerced criminality offences.

5 Available at: www.unodc.org/pdf/HT_indicators_E_LOWRES.pdf, last accessed 18 August 2025.

6 See **Chapter 2** for control methods and modus operandi. Chapter 1 provides a breakdown of the definition. **Chapters 4** and **8** highlight the particular vulnerabilities of trafficked persons.

cities to towns (see *Karemera)*[7]. Child criminal exploitation and 'cuckooing' (taking over the home of a vulnerable person without their consent for conduct of illegal activities such as drug dealing are anticipated to form distinct offences under the anticipated Crime and Policing Bill)[8] should be carefully considered in relation to exploitation relating to organised and drug crime.

12.7

Child VOTs may find it hard to disclose information. This may be because their stories have been fabricated by their trafficker or that they have been given inaccurate information about the role of authorities by their traffickers and they may have been subject to ongoing grooming. For children, no compulsion is required in terms of the criminal activity to render them victims; and children cannot give informed consent to engage in criminal or other exploitative activity. Child criminal exploitation[9] is defined within the Statutory Guidance as being 'common in county lines and occurs where an individual or group takes advantage of an imbalance of power to coerce, control, manipulate or deceive a child or young person under the age of 18. The victim may have been criminally exploited even if the activity appears consensual. Child criminal exploitation does not always involve physical contact; it can also occur through the use of technology.' As outlined in the Statutory Guidance at 10.9, 'they may relate their experience in an inconsistent way or with obvious errors.'

12.8

The Statutory Guidance at Annex D indicates that trafficked victims' early accounts may be affected by the impact of trauma. This can result in delayed disclosure, difficulty recalling facts, or symptoms of PTSD[10]. VOTs may also be reluctant to self-identify for several other reasons that can make understanding their experiences challenging. Trafficked children may be unable to disclose or give consistent credible accounts on account of matters such as on-going nature of abuse throughout childhood, or loyalty and perceived friendships with exploiters[11]. The Guidance at 10.14 sets out that child victims may find it difficult to recount trauma witnessed or experienced, which may lead to the child providing conflicting accounts of what has happened to them. Further, this should not be used to make judgments on the credibility of the child's account.

12.9

Individuals may be unwilling to self-identify for other reasons[12], including

7 [2018] EWCA Crim 1432.
8 At second reading stage in House of Lords (as at 19 August 2025).
9 Anticipated to form separate offence in Crime and Policing Bill at time of writing.
10 See Chapter 8 for full details on the psychological impact of human trafficking.
11 Statutory Guidance, Annex D, para 13.58.
12 Statutory Guidance – Annex D, para 13.11.

- being in a situation of dependency;
- the stigma attached to trafficking;
- fear of reprisals against them, their families, or friends;
- feeling they are dishonouring their family or community by not continuing in their situation;
- being distrustful of authorities
- being groomed into believing they are complicit in the process;
- fear of being discovered as being in the UK illegally and fear of deportation;
- suffering from 'Stockholm syndrome';
- being romantically 'involved' with their trafficker/exploiter;
- being unable and/or unwilling to view themselves as victims;
- seeing their current situation as temporary and blaming it on a lack of understanding of culture and labour market in UK;
- tolerating their situation as they see it as a stepping stone to a better future;
- being unaware of intentions of trafficker/exploiter to exploit them;
- not understanding what modern slavery means[13].

12.10

It is therefore incumbent on practitioners to look for signs of exploitation. The Statutory Guidance to the MSA 2015 sets out a number of general indicators of modern slavery to consider. Some of these factors highlight that victims may[14]:

- show signs that their movements are being controlled;
- show fear or anxiety;
- be subjected to violence or threats of violence against themselves or against their family members and loved ones;
- suffer injuries that appear to be the result of an assault;
- have false identity or travel documents (or none at all);
- be found in or connected to a type of location likely to be used for exploiting people;
- be forced, threatened or deceived into working in poor conditions;
- be distrustful of authorities;

13 Statutory Guidance, Annex D, para 13.11.
14 Statutory Guidance, 3.10.

- be afraid of revealing their immigration status;
- have had the fees for their transport to the country of destination paid for by facilitators, whom they must pay back by working or by providing services in the destination country;
- have limited contact with their families or with people outside of their immediate environment;
- be under the perception that they are bonded by debt;
- be in a situation of dependence;
- have acted on the basis of false promises.

12.11

Common Indicators of Trafficking for Criminal Exploitation are set out in the Statutory Guidance (at [10.6]) include that victims may:

- be children, elderly persons or disabled migrants who tend to beg in public places and on public transport;
- be carrying and/or selling illicit drugs;
- live with members of their gang;
- travel with members of their gang to the country of destination;
- live, as gang members, with adults who are not their parents;
- have physical impairments that appear to be the result of mutilation;
- be children of the same nationality or ethnicity who move in large groups with only a few adults;
- be unaccompanied minors who have been 'found' by an adult of the same nationality or ethnicity;
- move in groups whilst travelling on public transport: for example, they may walk up and down the length of trains;
- participate in the activities of organised criminal gangs;
- be part of large groups of children who have the same adult guardian;
- be punished if they do not collect or steal enough;
- move daily in large groups and/or over considerable distances;
- be forced to commit benefit fraud.

12.12

It is critical when representing children and young people in relation to county lines exploitation, (which itself constitutes child criminal exploitation) to know what the components or elements of human trafficking are (see **Chapters 9** and **10**) and take careful note of the background circumstances of the case using a lens of modern slavery[15]. It is helpful to apply the indicators set out in the Statutory Guidance, which include[16]:

- persistently going missing from school, home, care, being found out of area and/or children travelling to locations with which they have no obvious connections, including seaside or market towns;
- unwillingness to explain their whereabouts;
- unexplained acquisition of money, clothes or accessories, or mobile phones which they are unable to account for;
- excessive receipt of texts/phone calls and/or having multiple mobile phone handsets and/or SIM cards;
- relationships with controlling/older individuals or groups;
- suspicion of physical assault/unexplained injuries;
- parental concerns;
- carrying weapons;
- gang association or isolation from peers or social networks.

Police station and charge

12.13

Police station advisers need to know the components of human trafficking by reference to Art 4 of the Council of Europe Convention on Action against Trafficking ('ECAT') – see **Chapters 9** and **10**) be alive to indicators of possible trafficking: see above and Chapter 2. They also need to be aware of the protections available for VOTs under the CPS guidance (contained at part 2 of published guidance on 'Modern Slavery and human trafficking'[17] relating to non prosecution principles) and s 45 of MSA 2015 which provide protections from prosecution and a defence for VOTs in certain circumstances. See **Chapter 10**.

12.14

Where a suspect is a potential victim of trafficking ('PVOT'), practitioners should be aware that public authorities, including the police (as specified in

15 See background circumstances in *R v AAJ* [2021] EWCA Crim 1278.
16 Statutory Guidance, para 10.18.
17 CPS – Modern Slavery and human trafficking: offences and defences, including the section 45 defence, updated at 22 October 2024.

s 52 of the MSA 2015), have a statutory duty to notify the Home Office when they come across potential victims of modern slavery.

12.15

There are two Competent Authorities in the Home Office, the Single Competent Authority ('the SCA') and the Immigration Enforcement Competent Authority ('the IECA.')[18]. Referrals by a first responder are only made to the Single Competent Authority, who then allocate the case to the relevant competent authority. The CPS is not a first responder and as a result cannot make a referral into the NRM. Where a prosecutor comes to the conclusion that a suspect should be referred to the Single Competent Authority for a decision to be made as to whether there are reasonable grounds to believe that a suspect is a VOT, this must be done through the police[19]. A child can be referred without their consent, but an adult PVOT must provide their consent for a referral to take place (see **Chapter 2**).

12.16

The following public authorities are first responders:

- police forces;
- certain parts of the Home Office:
  - UK Visas and Immigration;
  - Border Force;
  - Immigration Enforcement;
- National Crime Agency;
- local authorities;
- Gangmasters and Labour Abuse Authority ('GLAA');
- health and social care trusts (Northern Ireland).

18 The SCA was launched in April 2019 and brought together the UK Visas Immigration, other sections of the Home Office and the National Crime Agency into a single organisation. This has now changed and there are currently 2 Competent Authorities – the SCA and the IECA. The IECA is responsible for a specific cohort of adult cases, which include all adult foreign national offenders detained in an Immigration Removal Centre, all adult foreign national offenders in prison where a decision to deport is awaited or has been made; all individuals detained in an Immigration Removal centre managed by National Returns command and non detained adult foreign national offenders where action to pursue deportation is taken in the community.

19 In any written representations made to the Crown concerning a case involving a suspected trafficked person/person subject to modern slavery, reference to the Full Code Test for Crown Prosecutors should also be considered.

12.17

Practitioners should consider whether these organisations have had any dealings with suspects and whether they have fulfilled their statutory duty under s 52 to make a referral via the National Referral Mechanism framework for identifying and referring potential victims of modern slavery and ensuring they receive the appropriate support ('NRM') to the SCA. Having identified indicators of trafficking, practitioners should explore them with a view to triggering an investigation into trafficking circumstances.

12.18

Practitioners should also remember that initial work on identifying VOTs can be done by first responders, who have expertise in what evidence to focus on and collate. By referring a client to a first responder, the first responder will prepare a formal referral to the NRM so that the SCA can consider whether a VOT is assessed as being a VOT on, first, a reasonable grounds (I suspect but I do not know) basis and, if so, second, after a recovery and reflection period, on a conclusive grounds (balance of probabilities) basis. See **Chapter 21** for privilege and ethics considerations.

12.19

As well as the statutory first responders referred to above, the following non-statutory bodies are first responders to whom those representing PVOTs in criminal proceedings should consider referring their clients:

- Salvation Army;
- Migrant Help;
- Medaille Trust;
- Kalayaan;
- Barnardo's;
- Unseen UK;
- NSPCC;
- BAWSO;
- New Pathways;
- Refugee Council;
- Tara Project (Scotland).

12.20

Practitioners should have in mind the *purpose* for identifying suspects as PVOTs. They should be familiar with the issues in **Chapter 10**: if a suspect is a VOT, they may have a defence under s 45 of MSA 2015. Furthermore, the degree of exploitation and the nexus between the trafficking and offending may mean that a VOT should not be prosecuted in the public interest. Practitioners should also be familiar with **Chapter 11**, which addresses VOTs at the police station in greater detail.

12.21

Defence practitioners should have it in mind that the prosecutor must consider the CPS guidance pre-charge, where there are indicators of trafficking, irrespective of whether the suspect has self-identified as a PVOT.

Post-charge

12.22

The CPS guidance continues to apply *post*-charge and throughout a case. Prosecutors and defence practitioners must be alert to any evidence which suggests that a suspect or defendant might be a VOT, so that the s 45 defence may be deployed where appropriate and so that the non-prosecution regime may be invoked where appropriate; see **Chapter 10**.

12.23

Prosecutors and defence practitioners should bear in mind that the police and prosecution may receive information or material during the investigation and preparation of a case which alerts them to the fact that a suspect is a PVOT.

12.24

The revised disclosure manual of the CPS (updated at 14 July 2022) highlights the general duties of the CPS outside the Criminal Procedure and Investigations Act 1996, including duties of disclosure which assist 'the prosecutor, in determining whether a person should be charged with an offence, and with which offence; and the accused, by providing certain material during the early stages of a prosecution'[20].

12.25

The guidance also goes on to state:

> 'In all cases, irrespective of anticipated plea, the officer must comply with the common law disclosure obligations and certify that, to the best of the officer's knowledge and belief, no information has been

20 At Chapter 2 of Disclosure Manual.

withheld which would assist the accused in the preparation of the defence case, including the making of a bail application'[21].

12.26

If material includes evidence of trafficking or exploitation indicators and may be capable of assisting a defendant it ought to be disclosed. Examples of such evidence include matters that assist in:

(1) advancing a defence under s 45 of MSA 2015;

(2) causing the CPS to (re-)consider whether prosecution is in the public interest;

(3) mitigation.

12.27

It is important to bear in mind that for exploitation, re-exploitation, county lines and cannabis production cases that a single police force ought to consider material held by other police forces that assists in consideration of whether an individual has been exploited or re-exploited in other police force areas (see example of re-exploitation and significance of material from other police force areas in *R v AAJ*)[22].

12.28

At all stages of a case, post-charge (even if a guilty plea has been entered) prosecutors have a duty to re-evaluate the evidence in line with the CPS guidance and re-assess the public interest in bringing a prosecution, bearing in mind the State's obligations under international law (see Chapter 5).

12.29

In most areas of law, where a defendant has been advised appropriately about the strength of the evidence, a guilty plea will be unequivocal and a conviction safe. Prosecutors should remember that with a suspect who is a VOT, even an unequivocal guilty plea may not lead to a safe conviction. See for example *R v O*[23]; and *R v LZ*[24] and *R v AFU*[25], where the Court of Appeal held that convictions were unsafe because if the CPS had known at the date of guilty pleas what was apparent at the date of the appeals in terms of indicators and the circumstances of trafficking, the defendants would, or might well, not have been prosecuted (see second category of cases in *R v Tredget*[26] and *R v AAD and*

21 CPS Disclosure Manual Chapter 2.
22 [2021] EWCA Crim 1278.
23 [2011] EWCA Crim 2226.
24 [2012] EWCA Crim 1867.
25 [2023] EWCA Crim 23.
26 [2022] EWCA Crim 108.

others[27] in relation to abuse of process). There is a significant onus on defence practitioners to ensure that indicators of trafficking are explored no matter when they come to light during a case and that the non-prosecution regime is invoked and the s 45 defence deployed where appropriate.

12.30

Where the prosecutor is not the CPS, if the authority has trafficking/slavery guidance, that guidance should be compared against the CPS guidance to see whether it is fit for purpose. If the prosecuting body does not have any guidance, the authority should be invited to apply the CPS guidance.

Magistrates' court

First appearance

12.31

The first appearance in a magistrates' court or youth court is a critical hearing for cases concerning a VOT. In many cases, because VOTs will present a flight risk, they are likely to be produced at court from custody. The hearing usually takes place the day after the individual has been charged by the police if the suspect is remanded in custody.

Assessing the evidence

12.32

The initial details of the prosecution case provided by the CPS to a defence representative will often only consist of a charge sheet, a list of antecedents and a short police case summary[28]. It is critical that defence representatives:

- consider whether there are indicators of trafficking or modern slavery;
- ascertain whether any referral has yet to take place to the SCA[29] by the police or any other first responder; and, if not, to invite a first responder to refer the case, if indicators are present. Consideration will need to be given as to whether the police should act as a first responder as there may be a conflict of interest if the police do not consider indicators of trafficking are present and/or their impetus is to secure a prosecution (consider **Chapter 21** where the client does not consent to an NRM referral);

27 [2022] EWCA Crim 106.
28 MG5 document.
29 See Chapter 2, where the SCA process is set out in detail.

- liaise with the prosecutor at court and ask for a review of the case at this stage in the light of the CPS legal guidance on 'Human Trafficking, Smuggling and Slavery' and the potential for a complete defence under MSA 2015. The prosecutorial decision may be assisted in having detailed representations from the defence to conduct this review. The CPS may need to be invited to prompt the police to refer and/or investigate the trafficking dimension of the case further in order to assist with this prosecutorial review.

Bail application

12.33

Bail is a significant matter to consider, particularly given that the time it takes for a NRM conclusive grounds decision to be made is at least 45 days and in practice far longer[30]. Under the Bail Act 1976, s 4, bail must be granted by a court to a person accused of an offence if none of the exceptions specified in Sch 1 applies.

12.34

The exceptions to the right to bail are where the court is satisfied that there are substantial grounds for believing that the defendant if released on bail would:

- fail to surrender to custody; or
- commit an offence while on bail; or
- interfere with witnesses or otherwise obstruct the course of justice, whether in relation to himself or any other person.

12.35

Representatives should be aware of facilities to protect VOTs in their area to enable appropriate bail decisions to be made that will avoid the potential for re-trafficking. With child (under 18) PVOTs, the local authority with safeguarding responsibility must be contacted, and the PVOT referred to Children's Social Care urgently under child protection procedures. Children and young persons should be bailed to local authority care. It is therefore essential that at the first appearance any disputes as to the age of the defendant needs to be raised by the prosecution or police; see para **12.61** below and **Chapter 11**.

30 The Notes to 'Official Statistics Modern slavery: National Referral Mechanism and Duty to Notify statistics UK, end of year summary 2024' published 6 March 2025 record: 'The average (median) time taken from referral to conclusive grounds decisions made this year across the competent authorities was 637 days, compared to 526 days in the previous year … For conclusive grounds decisions made by the SCA this year, the average time taken was 658 days, and the IECA took an average of 572 days ….'

12.36

In considering any bail application, consideration should be given to the use of electronic tagging. A curfew that has a minimum duration of nine hours amounts to a qualifying curfew under the provisions of the Sentencing Act 2020 ('the Sentencing Code')[31]. If an adult defendant were convicted and sentenced at a later date, then the court must direct that the credit period, which is half the sum of the number of days a person has been on curfew, should count towards sentence[32].

12.37

In terms of any conditions, such as reporting to a local police station, consideration should be given to the level of any travel cost which will be incurred, and to whether the police station is in an area where the victim's exploitation has taken place and in which his traffickers operate. Consideration should also be given to whether any suggested bail address is in such an area. Protective conditions should be considered, such as no unsupervised use of phones or electronic equipment. It is common for victims who are being controlled or in debt bondage to contact their traffickers and be subsequently further trafficked or re-trafficked. For other safeguarding measures and considerations, see **Chapters 8** and **11**.

12.38

In considering whether a defendant would, if released, fail to surrender to custody, practitioners should look at whether the defendant has already been engaging with authorities such as the Home Office (if not British nationals), when considering what reporting condition(s) might be necessary. Furthermore, it may be that the defendant has been co-operating with police who might be investigating the individuals who have trafficked or placed the defendant into a position of modern slavery. In such cases, further reporting conditions might be unnecessary. With children, Youth Offending Services ('YOS') should be contacted (particularly if the YOS is the first responder) to ensure that a supportive bail package can be offered to alleviate any concerns, as well as to offer protective measures for the VOT.

Entering pleas

12.39

At the first appearance at a magistrates' court, suspects/defendants are asked to enter or give an indication of plea. There are significant incentives in terms of

31 The Criminal Justice Act 2003, s 240A applies for offences in respect of an offence of which the offender was convicted before 1 December 2020; see, generally, Youth Court Bench Book at p76 in relation to children and young persons.

32 See Home Office Guidance, *Concordat on Children in Custody* (October 2017). Such measures could include a Children Act 1989, s 47 enquiry/investigation, by the children's services.

credit for pleading guilty to an offence at an early stage. The Sentencing Council 'Reduction in Sentence for a Guilty Plea Definitive Guideline'[33] highlights that 'Defendants who are going to plead guilty are encouraged to do so as early in the court process as possible'. There is separate guidance for magistrates' courts and the Crown Court[34]. For example, if a guilty plea is entered at the first stage of proceedings an individual would normally receive maximum credit, namely one-third reduction from a sentence. The first stage of proceedings is the first appearance at the magistrates' court. For either way offences and indictable only offences, normally at the first hearing in the Crown Court a maximum of 25% credit would apply. A sliding scale then applies with a maximum of 10% on the day of trial.

12.40

If a representative considers that there are trafficking indicators, or a possible defence under s 45 of MSA 2015, then an adjournment of plea arraignment must ordinarily be sought (unless the prosecution agrees that the defendant is a VOT)[35]. Practitioners need to be robust and courts need to understand that the above incentives should not and are not meant to put undue pressure on a defendant whose circumstances need to be explored to see whether he is a VOT. Courts should be alive to the fact, where a defendant is a PVOT, a premature – even *un*equivocal – guilty plea may (exceptionally) lead to a conviction being unsafe (see **Chapter 10**).

12.41

Proper enquiries must be made in cases involving PVOTs. The CPS guidance 'Modern Slavery and human trafficking: offences and defences, including the section 45 defence" states that prosecutors' obligations include duties to make proper enquiries and to ensure a referral is made to the SCA through a first responder as well as to consider defences under MSA 2015 and other potential defences, such as duress.

12.42

Better Case Management forms which are case management forms completed at first appearance hearings now include express provision about whether a defence pursuant to section 45 MSA 2015 is applicable (see *R v BTE*)[36].

33 Guidance in force at 1 June 2017, at: https://www.sentencingcouncil.org.uk/publications/item/reduction-in-sentence-for-a-guilty-plea-definitive-guideline-2/, last accessed 18 August 2025.

34 Ibid fn 24.

35 Note that if an individual at the magistrates' court provides no indication of plea, then this is often recorded a not guilty plea having been entered. Representatives should keep a detailed file note in case the court computer system is inadequate.

36 See [10] of *R v BTE* [2022] EWCA Crim 1597.

12.43

The Sentencing Council 'Reduction in Sentence for a Guilty Plea Definitive Guideline' specifically provides that where 'further information, assistance or advice [is] necessary before indicating plea' which made it unreasonable to expect the defendant to indicate a guilty plea sooner than was done, a reduction of one-third should still be made[37].

12.44

In *R v D*[38] Cutts J, said on behalf of the Full Court, presided over by Gross LJ, that suggestions of Crown Counsel to assist practitioners and judges, should be endorsed:

> 'As a decision has to be taken whether or not to prosecute a VOT, it is of importance that wherever possible those who may be VOTs are identified before any plea is taken at court. Indeed in cases where there is a suspicion of trafficking or slavery, the CPS guidance requires prosecutors at the first hearing to request that a plea is not formally entered and to apply for an adjournment for further investigation into the defendant's possible status as the victim of slavery or trafficking'[39].

12.45

Full credit for any guilty plea should be retained (see above). It is best practice that arraignment should only take place once a (conclusive) trafficking determination has been received from the SCA although this can cause some delay (unless the prosecutor accepts that the defendant is a VOT)[40]. If the determination is negative, this does not mean an MSA defence cannot be raised at trial. Care should be taken in giving advice to clients on plea that a negative decision may be conclusive of the issue. The SCA decision does not determine guilt in a criminal court, although a negative decision may disclose a weak defence if there is evidence that a specific assertion of trafficked status has been negated through a SCA identification process. The SCA decisions can be, and often are, legally challenged by the defendant (see **Chapter 4**).

Custody time limits

12.46

Where there is a referral via the NRM to determine a defendant's trafficking status, representatives should be mindful of custody time limits and should be

37 Ibid fn 24. See exception F1 of the Guideline.
38 [2018] EWCA Crim 2995 at § 21.3.
39 *Idem*, see [20] and [21].
40 *R v DS* [2020] EWCA Crim 285.

proactive in obtaining a decision from the SCA. This obligation rests with both the defence and prosecution. Whilst the guidance gives an estimated timeframe for making a conclusive determination of 45 days[41], many decisions take considerably longer. Representatives should actively consider judicial review when the SCA fails to make a timely identification decision where it has sufficient information to do so.

12.47

Custody time limits ('CTLs') apply to all defendants who are remanded in custody. CTLs apply to each specific charge and not the offender. Each charge attracts its own CTL[42]. A CTL begins the day after the court appearance when the defendant was first remanded[43]. The time limits that apply in relation to adults are as follows:

- summary only offences: the time limit is 56 days, unless extended by a court;
- either way offences: 182 days if and when the court allocates a case for Crown Court trial or if the defendant elects a Crown Court trial (less any time the defendant has spent in custody of the magistrates' court prior to sending).
- indictable only offences: the time limit is 182 days from the date a case is sent to the Crown Court under the Crime and Disorder Act 1998, s 51, less any time spent in custody (if remanded by the magistrates' court) prior to sending.

12.48

The prosecution can apply to extend the custody time limit. The test to be applied, under the Prosecution Offences Act 1985, s 22(3), is whether the court is satisfied that there is a need for an extension (1) because of a good and sufficient cause; and '(2) the prosecution has acted with all due diligence and expedition'. The prosecution must satisfy the court, on the balance of probabilities, that both conditions prescribed by s 22(3) are met[44].

12.49

In a case where an individual's trafficking/modern slavery background has been raised at an early stage, if there have been delays on the part of the authorities investigating the matter or any delay in referral to the SCA, submissions opposing an extension of the custody time limits should include this information.

41 See fn 33 (above).
42 See *R v Wirral District Magistrates Court, ex p Meikle* [1990] Crim LR 801.
43 Prosecution of Offences (Custody Time Limits) Regulations 1987, SI 1987/299, reg 2(2).
44 *R v Manchester Crown Court, ex p McDonald* [1999] 1 Cr App Rep 409.

Case management forms

12.50

Care needs to be taken when completing case management forms: the preparation for effective trial ('PET') for offences to be tried summarily, and better case management ('BCM') forms for offences sent to the Crown Court. These are submitted at the first appearance[45]. The form asks what the 'real issues in the case are'. Such a form is admissible at trial. In *R (on the application of Firth) v Epping Magistrates' Court*[46], the Administrative Court considered that:

> '7. The use of a case progression form is part of this process. It forms part of the court record. It records matters such as the date fixed for the trial, the estimated length of trial, the likely number of defence witnesses, and the names of prosecution witnesses.'

12.51

The form requires advocates to set out what the issues in the case are. In respect of that requirement, the Administrative Court held:

> '22. It does not infringe against the principle that a defendant is not required to incriminate himself for the court to require that the nature of the defence is made plain well before the trial. Of course, any requirement for disclosure of the nature of the defence must be a fair requirement, in the sense that it must not be extracted from a defendant in circumstances where the prosecution have no case and are trying to adopt Star Chamber processes to try to build a case, but the rules are designed to make sure that this does not occur.'
>
> '33. Part of the purpose of early identification of the real issues is to avoid the time, expense and possible inconvenience of having to obtain evidence to prove aspects of the case which are not disputed.'

12.52

It is incumbent on the parties to engage with the issues immediately in all cases. In proceedings involving defendants who might be VOTs, it is particularly important. The failure to engage at the first hearing, where investigation into a defendant's trafficking status and where referral into the NRM is necessary, will cause delays. This is liable to prejudice a defendant *vis-à-vis*:

- bail;
- an early trial date;

45 For example, PET forms and BCM forms will be uploaded to the digital case if transferred to the Crown Court.

46 [2011] EWHC 388 (Admin), [2011] 1 WLR 1818.

- custody time limits;
- preservation of evidence which might be relevant to the CPS's decision to continue with the prosecution or a s 45 MSA 2015 defence.

12.53

The upshot of the above is that when completing the forms, all matters that remain in issue, or that are not agreed, should be raised. If the commission of the act is not accepted, representatives need to be careful not to only state that a s 45 defence may apply. The s 45 defence is only relevant where the defendant has done the criminal act. Therefore, merely referring to a defence under s 45 would imply an admission that the defendant committed the *actus reus*. If essential elements of the offence are to be challenged, that needs to be made clear in the form. Equally, if the defendant accepts having committed the *actus reus*, then that should be made clear.

12.54

It is also best practice to set out in the case management form whether there are trafficking indicators or possible indicators which need investigation and/or warrant NRM referral. This enables the court to monitor any inquiry into, and have an active involvement in, the identification of possible failures by the prosecutor. It will assist in promoting all appropriate enquiries into whether the defendant is a VOT for the purposes of reassessing the decision to prosecute and/or pre-trial case management. Furthermore, it may not be appropriate to refer to a possible s 45 defence at an early stage before inquiries have been conducted. It may not be appropriate to refer to a possible s 45 defence even where there are indicators if at that stage the prosecutorial decision is to be remade.

Age assessments

12.55

Age disputes arise more frequently in trafficking cases than in other case because of the number of trafficked foreign nationals, who do not have genuine identity documents. If the age of a defendant is a disputed issue, then that should be raised within the case management form[47]. If no *appropriate* age assessment has taken place in accordance with Home Office Guidelines[48], this is a matter of the utmost importance to raise with the court, as it will impact upon venue of

47 Full guidance on age disputes can be found in **Chapter 6**.

48 Home Office, *Assessing age* (30 June 2025), at: https://assets.publishing.service.gov.uk/media/672e169e4f7608e424ffdab1/Assessing+age.pdf (accessed 18 August 2025).

trial, bail, NRM referral, the application of the s 45 defence and sentencing. See **Chapter 6** (age assessments and disputes to age).

12.56

Where an asserted minor age of a putative child defendant is not accepted by the SCA, representatives will need to consider bringing judicial review proceedings to challenge the assessed age of the defendant, during the course of criminal proceedings. This is addressed in **Chapter 6**.

Abuse of process

12.57

The abuse of process jurisdiction, through which a decision to prosecute a VOT may be challenged in exceptional circumstances, remains available for all victims of trafficking cases; for matters that both pre-date and post-date the statutory defence under s 45 MSA 2015 coming into force (see **Chapter 10**). The jurisdiction is only 'special' on account of the particular sensitivity to be applied to VOT prosecutions (*R v AAD)*[49]. The Court in *AAD* considered that if the CPS has taken into account relevant prosecutorial guidance[50] and conclusive grounds decision and had rational basis ('good reasons') for departing from it, then there would be no abuse of process. But an abuse of process would exist where the CPS failed unjustifiably to take into account the CPS guidance or had no rational basis for departing from a favourable conclusive grounds decision. However decisions to prosecute are for the CPS. The court would assess this by way of review on grounds 'corresponding to public law grounds'[51].

12.58

Decisions on disputed facts or evaluation of fact are for the jury (*R v AAD*, at [142(3)]).'

12.59

The Court in *AAD* was not considered to have disapproved of the earlier guidance in *S(G)*[52], in *R v AFU* at [118].

12.60

The two-limb process of abuse of process applies to all offences; even if the offence is one to which section 45 MSA 2015 cannot apply on the basis it is

49 *R v AAD and others* [2022] EWCA Crim 106.

50 https://www.cps.gov.uk/legal-guidance/modern-slavery-and-human-trafficking-offences-and-defences-including-section-45 (accessed 18 August 2025).

51 See *R v AFU* [2023] EWCA Crim 23, at [117]. See **Chapter 10** for a full exposition on this topic.

52 [2018] EWCA Crim 1824; [2019] Cr App R 7 at [76].

an offence excluded under Schedule 4 MSA 2015 (see *R v A)*[53]. In *R v A* the Court relected that a serious offence in the circumstances would require an even greater degree of continuing compulsion. And that there would need to be an absence of any reasonable alternative available to a defendant before the court would view it not to be in the public interest to prosecute.

12.61

Where in the course of the criminal proceedings, the police and/or the CPS fail in their positive respective obligations to investigate and to cause the police to investigate pursuant to ECHR,Art 4 (see **Chapter 11**) the decision to prosecute may be vitiated by a breach of Art 4 (see **Chapter 10** and **Chapter 13**). In *R v AFU*, the Court took into account that no full investigation had taken place, despite clear indicators of trafficking from the outset, which led to a conviction being found to be unsafe[54].

12.62

Similarly, If there have been failures by the CPS or the police (or even the SCA or a first responder) to ensure an appropriate age assessment has taken place in accordance with Home Office guidance[55], it may be appropriate at the first appearance to raise the possibility of an application for a stay of proceedings on the grounds of abuse of process.

Section 45

12.63

Section 45 of MSA 2015 provides a defence for victims of slavery or exploitation that is attributable to human trafficking. It came into force from 31 July 2015. It does not apply to those offences listed in Sch 4. For adults (18 and over) s 45(1) provides a defence for defendants who are (1) compelled to do an (otherwise criminal) act; (2) the compulsion is attributable to slavery or exploitation from trafficking; and (3) a reasonable person in the same situation as the defendant, with the defendant's relevant characteristics (age, sex, illness or disability) would have no realistic alternative to doing that act. See **Chapter 10**.

12.64

For children (under 18) s 45(4) provides a defence for a defendant (1) who does an (otherwise criminal) act; (2) he does it as a direct consequence of the defendant being, or having been, a victim of slavery or a victim of exploitation

53 [2020] EWCA Crim 1408.

54 See [135(i)] and [135(ii)] of *AFU* on failures of police to discharge duty as first responders.

55 Home Office, *Assessing age* (30 June 2025), at: https://assets.publishing.service.gov.uk/media/672e169e4f7608e424ffdab1/Assessing+age.pdf (accessed 18 August 2025).

from trafficking; and (3) a reasonable person in the same situation as the defendant and having the defendant's relevant characteristics (age, sex, illness or disability) would do that act. As with s 45(1), see **Chapter 10**, where this topic is discussed more fully.

Summary only offences

12.65

If a charge is summary only, the proceedings are in a magistrates' court. The ethos of magistrates' court proceedings is that they are speedy. Summary only offences are relatively minor and normally lead to no more than a short custodial penalty, at most. Because of these factors, trafficking and modern slavery indicators may be inadvertently ignored or overlooked. The CPS guidance '*Modern Slavery and human trafficking: offences and defences, including the section 45 defence*'[56] applies to summary offences as well as indictable offences.

12.66

Some common summary only offences that might be committed in the context of trafficking and slavery and which may give rise to a s 45 defence are set out in **Chapter 2**. When preparing a case involving trafficking/modern slavery that concerns a summary only offence, or issues of trafficking that need to be litigated in a magistrates' (including youth) court, consideration should be given to applying for a certificate for counsel/higher court advocate with specialist training in trafficking law and procedure, given the complexity of trafficking issues that may be involved. Asking for the matter to be reserved to a district judge rather than a lay bench should also be considered.

Either way offences

12.67

In relation to an either way offence, such as cultivation of cannabis by a trafficked 'gardener', the magistrates will need to consider the most appropriate venue for trial through the 'allocation' procedure. The defendant will be asked to give an indication of plea. If there are still outstanding trafficking or modern slavery determinations to be made, then 'no indication' as to plea can properly be given. A request for the protection of credit for any later guilty plea should be made; see above at para **7.42**.

56 Updated: 22 July 2025; https://www.cps.gov.uk/legal-guidance/modern-slavery-and-human-trafficking-offences-and-defences-including-section-45 (accessed 18 August 2025).

12.68

The Sentencing Council has issued a definitive sentencing guideline on venue/allocation, in accordance with the Coroners and Justice Act 2009, s 122(2) 'Allocation Guideline'[57], which sets out:

> 'In general, either way offences should be tried summarily unless:
>
> (a) the outcome would clearly be a sentence in excess of the court's powers for the offence(s) concerned after taking into account personal mitigation and any potential reduction for a guilty plea;
>
> (b) for reasons of unusual legal, procedural, or factual complexity, the case should be tried in the Crown Court. This exception may apply in cases where a very substantial fine is the likely sentence. Other circumstances where this exception will apply are likely to be rare and case specific; the court will rely on the submissions of the parties to identify relevant cases'.

12.69

Given the complexity of issues that often arise where there are indicators of trafficking, exploitation and modern slavery, the Crown Court may be the more appropriate venue for trying these cases. Practitioners should be aware of the Allocation Guideline when making submissions concerning venue.

12.70

If a summary trial of a case involving issues of trafficking law and procedure is directed, consideration should be given to an application for a certificate for counsel/higher court advocate, particularly in youth court cases, where the seriousness of cases tried summarily will often warrant the grant of a certificate. (see para **7.62**).

Crown Court

12.71

The first appearance at the Crown Court after a case has been sent should be listed within 28 days of the first appearance in a magistrates' court. An indictment and the principal parts of the prosecution case should be served on the Court and the defence at least seven days before the hearing. The hearing

57 Published by the Sentencing Council and to apply to all cases involving adults at the magistrates' court and children/young persons charged with adults dealt with (1 March 2016), at: https://www.sentencingcouncil.org.uk/overarching-guides/magistrates-court/item/allocation/, last accessed 18 August 2025.

is known as a plea and trial preparation hearing ('PTPH') and has a specific form which has been subject to key changes with which practitioners should be familiar[58].

PTPH – form and key issues

12.72

PTPH forms now include a section that asks, 'Is the defendant said to be a victim of modern slavery.' This enables consideration to be given to whether the prosecution should continue and/or whether the defendant is alleging a defence under s 45 of MSA 2015.

12.73

Other matters that need to be included are issues such as abuse of process, dismissal, fitness to plead, severance, arraignment, witness requirements, reporting restrictions and special measures.

12.74

If a defendant is outlining a defence that he has been a trafficked person/ subject to modern slavery, or if other issues of exploitation arise, then early consideration needs to be given to seeking reporting restrictions and/or an anonymity direction for all pre-trial hearings and trial. Under the Criminal Procedure Rules 2025 ('CrimPR'), r 6.2, the procedure for reporting restrictions has been strictly codified. It is no longer sufficient to simply apply to the judge; the applicant is responsible for formally notifying the media via the email distribution lists provided by the Crown and magistrates' courts. These lists are available from court staff. This must be done before the hearing. Failure to provide this notice may lead to the adjournment or dismissal of anonymity requests. See **Chapter 8** for special measures for victims of trafficking.

Fitness to plead: Crown Court

12.75

Early recognition of any concerns as to fitness to plead and/or to stand trial are vital in cases involving trafficked persons/those subject to modern slavery. The usual process in criminal proceedings includes a stage where a defendant is invited to enter a plea, whether guilty or not guilty. Fitness to plead is governed by procedure under the Criminal Procedure (Insanity) Act 1964, supplemented

58 Ministry of Justice PTPH form key changes July 2019, at: http://www.justice.gov.uk/courts/procedure-rules/criminal/forms, last accessed 18 August 2025.

by the Domestic Violence Crime and Victims Act 2004 and CrimPR, r 25.10. The law on fitness to plead is intended to provide a process for defendants in criminal proceedings who lack sufficient ability to participate meaningfully in a trial because of their mental or physical condition. The intention is to balance the rights of a defendant with vulnerabilities as against the need to protect the public. The court can make findings of fact as part of the process. The Law Commission published a Consultation Paper on unfitness to plead ('CP197') in October 2010 and reported in 2016. They concluded that 'the current law in this area is outdated, inconsistently applied and can lead to unfairness'. They also expressed the 'significant concerns' raised by the 'current lack of an effective legal framework for addressing participation difficulties experienced by young defendants in the youth court'. Their recommendations for reform have not, so far, been adopted[59].

The current test for unfitness to plead

12.76

The current test for whether a person is unfit to plead was laid down in *R v Pritchard* in 1836[60] in three parts:

(i) whether the defendant is mute of malice or not;

(ii) whether they can plead to the indictment or not;

(iii) whether they are of sufficient intellect to comprehend the course of proceedings on the trial, so as to make a proper defence. This would include an ability to challenge a juror, to comprehend the evidence and to put forward a defence to the allegations.

12.77

The burden is usually on the defence to establish, on the balance of probabilities, that the defendant is unfit to plead[61]. However, where the issue is raised by the prosecution, the burden must be discharged beyond a reasonable doubt[62]. Over the course of more than a century, this test has been the subject of further clarification as follows:

(i) the test is not limited to the ability to enter a plea but depends on the ability or otherwise to follow a trial[63];

59 Law Commission, *Unfitness to Plead Report 2016* (13 January 2016), and Government interim response, at: https://www.lawcom.gov.uk/project/unfitness-to-plead/, last accessed 18 August 2025.

60 *R v Pritchard* (1836) 7 C & P 303.

61 *R v Robertson* [1968] 1 WLR 1767, [1968] 3 All ER 557.

62 *R v Podola* [1960] 1 QB 325, [1959] 3 All ER 418.

63 *R v Marcantonio* [2016] EWCA Crim 14, [2016] 2 Cr App Rep 81.

(ii) an accused person can be unfit to plead, even if not clinically insane[64];

(iii) that the defendant suffers from a diagnosed mental illness does not mean he is inevitably unfit to plead. An assessment of the *Pritchard* criteria is not dependent on diagnosis, although a significant impairment may be good evidence to support a finding of unfitness[65];

(iv) the defendant does not have to suffer from a diagnosed illness or disorder within the international classification of diseases to be unfit to follow proceedings. There may be a combination of factors[66];

(v) loss of memory does not amount to unfitness to plead, providing the defendant can follow the proceedings[67];

(vi) making bad decisions because of a mental illness does not mean the defendant is unable to follow a trial[68].

12.78

The Criminal Procedure Rules provide for the commissioning of medical reports. Crim PR, r.3.10(2) provides details of when a court may exercise the power to commission a medical report of its own initiative, having regard to an assessment of the defendant's health independently of the parties to assist the court, through representations by a party or observations by the court.

12.79

For example, the Crown Court might invoke CrimPR, r3.10 concerning a defendant's fitness to participate at trial under s 4 Criminal Procedure (Insanity) Act 1964. It must then identify each issue upon which opinion is needed; and give directions for obtaining the report and dates by when a report is to be provided. In relation to issues of privilege and third parties, see **Chapter 21**.

Fitness to plead procedure

12.80

Since this is a special plea, the Crown Court procedure dictates that the judge must decide fitness as soon as it arises, based on a 'rigorous examination' of available evidence as against the *Pritchard* criteria[69]. The judge makes this

64 *Governor of Stafford Prison, ex p Emery* [1909] 2 KB 81, 73 JP 284.
65 *R v Berry* (1977) 66 Cr App Rep 156.
66 *R v Berry* ibid.
67 *R v Podola* [1960] 1 QB 325, [1959] 3 All ER 418; *R v Norman* [2008] EWCA Crim 1810, [2009] 1 Cr App Rep 192.
68 *R v Walls* [2011] EWCA Crim 443, [2011] 2 Cr App Rep 61.
69 *Marcantonio* [2016] EWCA Crim 14, [2016] 2 Cr App Rep 81; *R v Ghulam* [2009] EWCA Crim 2285, [2010] 1 WLR 891.

decision alone on the written or oral evidence of two or more registered medical practitioners, at least one of whom must have been approved by the Secretary of State under s 12(2) of the Mental Health Act 1983 as having special experience in the diagnosis and treatment of mental disorder[70]. An analysis of the contemporary dilemmas includes a lack of normative standards, whether fitness to plead should be disability neutral or whether unfitness requires the presence of a psychiatric diagnosis; and how the courts can insure against the deprivation of liberty of innocent persons while ensuring the public are adequately protected[71].

12.81

Generally, the issue of fitness to plead is decided before trial, although there are cases where it arises during the trial and before disposal, including in cases where a second procedure should have been conducted[72]. If it arises at any time after sentence the procedure does not apply, as the process is concluded[73]. If the defendant is found fit to plead, the trial proceeds in the usual way. Where a decision is made that a defendant is unfit to plead, the appointment of an advocate to put the case for the defendant is mandatory. Such appointment should include an assessment of the advocate's expertise. When the case involves an allegation of trafficking or the defendant is a PVOT, consideration should be given to the advocate's experience and expertise in trafficking cases[74]. There will then be a trial of the fact of the allegation. Where one defendant is unfit and a co-defendant is not, the court must decide whether they should be tried together[75].

12.82

Defence practitioners will need to instruct and obtain expert psychiatric evidence (two separate psychiatrists, if the Crown are unlikely to seek to obtain a separate one) in order to satisfy the conditions under ss 4 and 4A Criminal Procedure (Insanity) Act 1965. Post *R v John M*[76] the Court will need to determine whether the defendant can:

i. understand and rationally reply to the indictment;

ii. exercise their right to challenge jurors;

70 Domestic Violence, Crime and Victims Act 2004, s 22.

71 P Brown, *Unfitness to Plead in England and Wales; Historical Development and Contemporary Dilemmas* (Sage, 2019), at: https://journals.sagepub.com/doi/full/10.1177/0025802419856761, last accessed 18 August 2025.

72 *R (on the application of Hasani) v Blackfriars Crown Court* [2005] EHWC 3016 (Admin), [2006] 1 All ER 817.

73 *R v Webb* [1969] 2 QB 278, [1969] 2 All ER 626; *R v Burles* [1970] 2 QB 191; *R v Grant* [2008] EWCA Crim 1890; *R v B* [2008] EWCA Crim 1997, [2009] 1 Cr App Rep 261; *R v Orr* [2016] EWCA Crim 889, [2016] 4 WLR 132.

74 Criminal Procedure Rules 2025, r 25.9 and 25.10(3).

75 *R v B* [2008] EWCA Crim 1997, [2009] 1 WLR 1545.

76 [2003] EWCA Crim 3452.

iii. understand the details of the evidence as it is given;

iv. instruct legal advisers;

v. give evidence in person – both in examination-in-chief and cross-examination;

12.83

In assessing whether a defendant is unfit to plead, a Court needs to have regard to facilities available to assist in effective participation, such as the use of an intermediary, special measures or a witness companion. In applying the test of fitness to plead, the Court needs to consider the individual's capabilities in the context of the particular proceedings – for example the complexity of the case and what the process will in fact demand of the defendant (see *R v Thomas)*[77].

Trial of the acts or omissions

12.84

Following a decision by a judge that a defendant is unfit to plead, it is then for a jury to decide whether the defendant did the act or omission alleged[78]. Usual rules of evidence apply, including in relation to hearsay and bad character[79]. The prosecution will be required to disprove issues such as self-defence, accident, or mistake as these can be raised on objective evidence[80]. However, it is rarely necessary to prove the mental element unless the act includes some purposive element such as concealing criminal property or voyeurism[81]. It follows that the jury cannot consider diminished responsibility or loss of control as part of their decision on the acts or omissions of the accused[82]. The defendant does not put forward a positive defence or give evidence as he is unfit to do so, although in some circumstances a defendant's police interview may be relevant, subject to whether the defendant understood the caution or not and suitable warnings from the trial judge[83]. If a finding that an accused person is unfit to plead is later quashed by the Court of Appeal, it is not possible to substitute an alternative verdict or order a retrial[84].

---

77 *R v Thomas* [2020] EWCA Crim 117.

78 Criminal Procedure (Insanity) Act 1964, s 4A(2).

79 *R v Chal* [2007] EWCA Crim 2647, [2008] 1 Cr App Rep 247; *R v Creed* [2011] EWCA Crim 144, [2011] Crim LR 644.

80 *R v Wells* [2015] EWCA Crim 2, [2015] 1 WLR 2797.

81 *R v Antoine* [2001] AC 340, [2000] 2 WLR 703; *R v Grant* [2001] EWCA Crim 2611, [2002] QB 1030; *R (on the application of Young) v Central Criminal Court* [2002] EWHC 548 (Admin), [2002] 2 Cr App Rep 178; *R v B* [2012] EWCA Crim 770, [2012] 3 All ER 1093.

82 *R v Antoine* [2001] AC 340, [2000] 2 WLR 703.

83 *R v Swinbourne* [2013] EWCA Crim 2329, (2014) 178 JP 34.

84 *R v McKenzie* [2011] EWCA Crim 1550, [2011] 1 WLR 2807.

12.85

The jury is not asked whether the defendant is guilty or not guilty. It is directed that it must be sure that the defendant 'did the act or made the omission charged against him as the offence'. If the jury is satisfied, it must find accordingly[85]. If not, it must acquit the defendant[86]. The procedure is approached as a method for public protection not a trial, so Art 6 rights have been held not to apply[87].

Disposal rather than sentence

12.86

If a defendant who has been found unfit to plead is then found to have done the act or made the omission charged then the court's powers are limited by the Criminal Procedure (Insanity) Act 1964, s 5 to three orders, as follows:

(i) a hospital order pursuant to the Mental Health Act 1983 ('MHA 1983'), s 37 on the written or oral evidence of two medical practitioners, at least one of whom must have been approved by the Secretary of State as having special experience in the diagnosis and treatment of mental disorder. An interim order can be made pending the paperwork. To make a hospital order, the court must be satisfied on the evidence of the approved clinician who would be in charge of the offender that suitable arrangements have been made for admission and treatment. A hospital order can be made with a restriction on release pursuant to the MHA 1983, s 41 if the court is satisfied that a restriction is necessary for the protection of the public. A restriction is usually made without limit of time and continues if the patient is subject to conditional release as part of treatment[88];

(ii) a supervision order;

(iii) an absolute discharge.

Fitness to plead: magistrates' and youth courts

12.87

There is no specific procedure as to how a defendant's fitness to plead may be determined in a magistrates' court (for ss 4 and 4A of the Criminal Procedure

85 Criminal Procedure (Insanity) Act 1964, s 4A(2) and (3).

86 *R v McKenzie* [2011] EWCA Crim 1550, [2011] 1 WLR 2807; *R v Chal* [2007] EWCA Crim 2647, [2008] 1 Cr App Rep 247.

87 *R v M* [2002] EWCA Crim 2024, [2002] 1 WLR 824; *R v H* [2003] UKHL 1, [2003] 1 All ER 497.

88 *R v Blackwood* (1974) 59 Cr App Rep 170; *R v Lincolnshire (Kesteven) Justices, ex p O'Connor* [1983] 1 All ER 901; *R v Barker* [2002] EWCA Crim 1508, [2003] 1 Cr App Rep (S) 212; *R v Khelifi* [2006] EWCA Crim 770, [2006] 2 Cr App Rep (S) 650; *R v Vowles* [2015] 2 Cr App Rep (S) 39; *R v Turner* [2015] EWCA Crim 1249; *R v Marshall* [2015] EWCA Crim 474.

(Insanity) Act 1964 apply only to trial on indictment). The defence have various options:

i. a defendant could seek to elect trial and have fitness to plead determined in the Crown Court;

ii. a defendant could seek to plead not guilty if the offence is summary only and as a result put the prosecution to proof – which may be difficult should the offence type require mens rea;

iii. ask the Court to consider using their powers under s 37(3) of the 1983 Act which provides that:

> 'where a person is charged before a magistrates court with any act or omission as an offence and the court would have power, on convicting him of that offence to make an order under subsection (1) above in his case then, if the court is satisfied that the accused did the act or made the omission charged, the court may, if it thinks fit, make such an order without convicting him.'

12.88

However, with options ii and iii, the magistrates' court, under s 11(1) Powers of Criminal Courts (Sentencing) Act 2000, will need to first determine if it is satisfied that the defendant did the act or made the omission charge; before it goes on to consider whether it is of the opinion that an inquiry ought to be made into the defendant's physical or mental condition, before the method of dealing with them is determined.

12.89

Concerning youth defendants, this may mean that case preparation will not routinely include obtaining the types of assessments that would be required under the fitness to plead procedure in the Crown Court. If a defendant is unable effectively to participate in the trial process, this will affect the fairness of proceedings and could affect the welfare of any child defendant[89].

12.90

Where the defendant lacks capacity and is a trafficked person/subject to modern slavery, the processes that have developed in the Crown Court and in the appellate courts ought to steer the lower courts[90].

89 Children and Young Persons Act 1933, s 44.

90 *CPS v P* [2008] 4 All ER 628 and see M Bevan, *Unfit To Plead in the Magistrates' and Youth Courts?*, at: www.criminallawandjustice.co.uk/features/Unfit-Plead-Magistrates-and-Youth-Courts (accessed 18 August 2025).

12.91

Unfit defendants who are also trafficked persons/subject to modern slavery would fall into the category of persons who would be protected according to international law and should not face a trial process, unless it is in the public interest for them to be tried. It may be appropriate to rely on evidence concerning aspects of a PVOT's trafficking status and circumstances to support an abuse of process application predicated primarily on unfitness.

12.92

When considering an abuse of process application or alternative arrangements to accommodate a defendant VOT who lacks capacity, practitioners may consider the Law Commission's Unfitness to Plead Project[91]. This exposed significant concerns over the inadequacies of the procedures to address unfitness to plead in magistrates' and youth courts and the continuing need for better protection for defendants who lack capacity to engage in the trial process. Despite these observations, there has been no legislative change in this regard.

12.93

The following, taken from the Law Commission Report Volume 1, may be of assistance in simplifying and streamlining proceedings as a matter of case management to ensure a defendant who is a victim of trafficking lacking capacity is not tried at all. If the defendant is tried, it should ensure that the trial process is fair and accommodates any vulnerabilities, or that the defendant is diverted away from the criminal justice system through referral mechanisms[92]:

12.94

> **'AN OVERVIEW OF OUR APPROACH**
>
> **Full trial wherever fair and practicable**
>
> 1.11 At the heart of our recommendations lies our belief that the normal criminal trial is the optimum process where a defendant faces an allegation in our criminal justice system. We consider that full trial is best not just for the defendant, but also for those affected by an offence and society more generally. This is because the full criminal process engages fair trial guarantees for all those involved, under article 6 of the European Convention on Human Rights ("ECHR"), and allows robust and transparent analysis of

91 https://lawcom.gov.uk/project/unfitness-to-plead/ (accessed 18 August 2025).

92 Law Commission 2016, *Unfitness to Plead Volume 1* (LAW COM 364), at: https://webarchive.nationalarchives.gov.uk/ukgwa/20241223105401mp_/https://cloud-platform-e218f50a4812967ba1215eaecede923f.s3.amazonaws.com/uploads/sites/30/2016/01/lc364_unfitness_vol-1.pdf (accessed 18 August 2025).

all the elements of the offence and any defence advanced. It also offers the broadest range of outcomes in terms of sentence and other ancillary orders.

1.12 Removing any defendant from that full trial process should, we consider, only be undertaken as a last resort. The decision to adopt alternative procedures should be made with great caution and only where it is in the best interests of the defendant, because he or she lacks the capacity to participate effectively in his or her trial. We consider that every effort should be made to afford a defendant whose capacity may be in doubt such adjustments to the proceedings as he or she reasonably requires to be able to participate in the full criminal process, and to maintain that capacity for the whole of the process. However, we do acknowledge that a very small number of defendants will never have the capacity to participate effectively in a trial. (We consider these issues in Chapter 2).

Accurate and efficient identification of defendants who cannot participate effectively in their trial

1.13 We consider that the most important element of a framework to address issues of unfitness to plead is a legal test which accurately and efficiently identifies those defendants who, even considering available adjustments to trial, have such impairments in their ability to participate in proceedings that they could not fairly be tried. The current Pritchard test10 used to assess unfitness to plead requires updating and is not consistently understood or applied by clinicians, legal practitioners and the courts. We also consider it essential that those who, although unable to engage with the full trial process, have sufficient understanding and decision-making capacity to enter a plea of guilty, should be enabled to do so. (We address the legal tests in Chapter 3).

1.14 Assessment of such defendants is currently a time-consuming process and in some cases three or more expert reports are prepared, generally by psychiatrists or psychologists, before a defendant is found unfit to plead. The current arrangements often lead to substantial delays, causing uncertainty and anxiety to complainants, witnesses and the defendant. We consider that arrangements can be made to streamline this process, saving time and precious resources, without compromising the robustness or fairness of the outcome. (We discuss these recommendations in Chapter 4).

Diversion out of the criminal process where appropriate

1.15 Following a finding by the court that a defendant lacks the capacity to participate effectively in the full criminal process, we

> take the view that the court should have the option not to embark on the alternative procedures for scrutinising the allegation. We have in mind, in particular, cases where a disposal11 imposed by the court is not necessary to protect the public, or to support the individual to avoid future concerning behaviour, and where it is concluded that it is not in the public interest for any further criminal hearing on the matter. We take this position because any procedure which protects the interests of the vulnerable individual, but appropriately scrutinises the allegation in order to justify imposing disposals on that individual, will inevitably be complex, and demanding of jurors, witnesses and defendants alike. In addition, such alternative procedures cannot result in conviction, because the defendant who cannot participate effectively is unable properly to defend him- or herself. As a result, the disposals available to the court are inevitably limited, and cannot involve punishment of the defendant.
>
> 1.16 For many individuals who are unfit to plead, the low level of seriousness of the original allegation and the arrangements which can be made in the community, without the court's intervention, mean that further action by a criminal court is unnecessary. We therefore recommend that diversion of such individuals out of the criminal justice system, once they have been found to lack capacity for trial, should be available where the court is satisfied that such an approach is in the interests of justice....

Disposal of defendants suffering from a mental disorder – magistrates' court

12.95

Expert evidence is admissible in criminal proceedings if it is relevant to a matter in issue in proceedings and if it is needed to provide the court with information outside the court/jury's own knowledge and experience (see *R v AAD*)[93]. Expert evidence must comply with CrimPR, part 19 and must not be used to usurp the jury's fact finding function on matters such as plausibility and credibility in relation to the statutory defence under s 45 MSA 2015. The types of expert evidence relevant in cases concerning VOTs and s.45 MSA 2015 relate to the modus operandi of trafficking gangs; cultural nature matters such as juju; or evidence of a defendant's psychiatric or psychological state. See **Chapter 10**. In relation to age, it is generally accepted that trafficked children will not necessarily have any correct identifying documents, some may not know their exact age, others will have been told to lie. When age is not clear,

93 *R v AAD* and others [2022] EWCA Crim 106.

the presumption is that the person is under 18[94], although courts are expected to make 'due enquiry' using any available documentation, fingerprint record and oral evidence, including any expert assessment. A declaration as to age by a court is then regarded as the true age. See **Chapter 6** in respect of the due process to be adopted in establishing age[95].

12.96

Expert evidence is to be preferred over and above a 'myths direction' although it may also be helpful or necessary, particularly in cases involving sexual exploitation, for a judicial direction to deal with common misconceptions[96].

12.97

Where a s 45 MSA 2015 defence is relied on, expert evidence may be admissible in relation to the issue of 'relevant characteristics', which are defined as 'age, sex and any physical or mental illness or disability'. Although 'reasonable person' is a fixed objective standard, it is informed by the subjective elements included within 'relevant characteristics'. The type of expert evidence that could be admissible relates to psychiatric or psychological evidence for example in relation to mental health conditions – one example relating to post traumatic stress disorder. Once there is some evidence of all limbs of the defence, it will be a matter for the Crown to disprove one of those limbs (see **Chapter 10** for the interplay between the evidential and legal burdens of proof in the context of s 45). To represent a defendant properly, defence representatives should ensure that they assume the responsibility for obtaining evidence relevant to what was reasonable in the circumstances. Defence practitioners should consider whether regional trafficking experts'[97] reports might be admissible (or capable of agreement in agreed facts in whole or in part)[98].

Adducing expert evidence

12.98

Adducing expert evidence is dealt with in Part 7.1 of the Criminal Practice Direction ('CPD')[99]. It is the duty of an expert to help the court to achieve the

94 ECAT, Art 10.

95 Children and Young Persons Act 1933, s 99 and Magistrates' Courts Act 1980, s 150.

96 CPS, *Guidance 'Rape and Sexual Offences – Chapter 4: Tackling Rape Myths and Stereotypes'*; 21 May 2021:: https://www.cps.gov.uk/legal-guidance/rape-and-sexual-offences-chapter-4-tackling-rape-myths-and-stereotypes (accessed 18 August 2025).

97 Those with expertise of trafficking in particular geographical settings.

98 *MK v R* [2018] EWCA Crim 667.

99 Criminal Practice Direction (2023), at: https://assets.publishing.service.gov.uk/media/67e4098bd052ace7e897768f/criminal-practice-directions-2023.pdf, last accessed 18 August 2025. (NB the link directly to Crim PR 19 now ishttps://www.legislation.gov.uk/uksi/2020/759/part/19 (accessed 18 August 2025).

overriding objective that justice should be achieved[100]. This duty overrides the duty owed to the party providing the instructions or payment[101]. An 'expert' is described as 'a person who is required to give or prepare expert evidence for the purpose of criminal proceedings, including evidence required to determine fitness to plead or for the purpose of sentencing'[102]. Expert evidence is opinion evidence which must be objective and unbiased, and within the expert's area or areas of expertise[103]. See Chapter 5 for detailed guidance on instruction of experts.

12.99

Under Crim PR 19.9, a party seeking to introduce expert evidence under r 19.3(3) may apply to the court to withhold information from another party, in relation to expert evidence on the basis that it would be 'in the public interest to withhold that information'. Such an application needs to be served on the court officer, explaining why it would be in the public interest to withhold it and why the information or extracts have been omitted. The application must also be served on the other party but will omit anything which would reveal what the party thinks ought to be omitted. Examples might include sensitive medical information about a defendant; or, in the context of trafficking, it might include matters which could compromise a defendant's safety. Such application must be heard in private by the court. At a hearing, representations would first be given by the applicant, followed by the other party (in both parties' presence), and then any further representations in the absence of the party from whom the information is withheld: see *R v M*[104] for the approach of a defendant in an analogous situation when seeking to withhold material from co-accused on the grounds of personal safety.

Admissibility of expert evidence

12.100

To be admissible, expert opinion evidence must be relevant to the issue which the court is called upon to decide[105]. It must be logically probative or disprobative of some matter which requires proof[106]. A competent expert can only provide opinion evidence which is outside the knowledge and experience of the court[107] where there is a reliable scientific basis for the opinion[108]. Reports

100 CrimPR, r 19.2.
101 *The Ikarian Reefer* [1993] 2 Lloyds Rep 68; *R v Harris* [2005] EWCA Crim 1980.
102 CrimPR, r 19.1.
103 CrimPR r 19.2.
104 [2021] EWCA Crim 1934; [2024] 1 Cr.App. R. 20.
105 *O'Brien v Chief Constable of South Wales Police* [2005] UKHL 26 at para 3; *R v AAD* [2022] EWCA Crim 106; [2022] 1 WLR 4042 at [85]-[87].
106 Per Lord Simon of Glaisdale in *DPP v Kilbourne* [1973] AC 729.
107 Crim PD, 19 A.1.
108 *R v Dlugosz* [2013] EWCA Crim 2.

must comply with the Criminal PR, r 19.4 giving detail of the expert's 'qualifications, relevant experience and accreditation' and setting out the basis of the opinion'[109].

12.101

In *R v AAD*[110] the Court gave the following guidance on when expert evidence in the context of trafficking might be admissible:

> '86 We would add that it does not matter that the members of the jury have not shared the suggested experiences described by the defendant in a human trafficking or modern slavery case. Indeed, this applies in all criminal trials regardless of the nature of the charge. Few jurors will have been subjected, for instance, to duress leading to their participation in an armed robbery or will have found themselves caught up or involved in a city centre riot. This lack of first-hand experience of the circumstances of offences such as these does not require a witness … to express a view as to whether the account of the defendant is consistent with how someone would behave if placed under duress to commit armed robbery or if caught up in a riot. The jurors will be well placed to form their own conclusions on these questions. It follows that we reject [the] submission that a trafficking expert can express an opinion in evidence before the jury as to the plausibility and consistency of the defendant's account. Similarly, we disagree with the suggestion that a trafficking expert during a trial can comment on the vulnerability of the defendant. It is equally impermissible for an expert in a trafficking trial to express a view as to whether a given set of facts meets the legal definition of trafficking, acting thereby as an expert on the law of England and Wales. None of these situations come within the well-known exceptions, such as with diminished responsibility, when an expert is permitted to give evidence on the "ultimate issue" (see *Director of Public Prosecutions v A and BC Chewing Gum Ltd* [1968] 1 QB 159, 164). As observed by the editors of Phipson on Evidence, 19th ed (2017), para 33-12, this is because the expert's opinion is valueless, even unintelligible, if he or she is prohibited from expressing their view merely because the trier of fact will be called upon to decide the same question. In a similar vein, the secondary transfer of cellular material in the context of DNA evidence is an example of when it is necessary for the expert to know and comment on the factual circumstances in question, to enable him or her to give relevant evidence.
>
> 87 This is not, we emphasise, to overlook those instances in trafficking cases when there may be discrete issues that properly require explanation by way of expert evidence, for instance as to the defendant's psychiatric

109 *R v H* [2014] EWCA Crim 1555, para [44].
110 [2022] EWCA Crim 106; [2022] 1 WLR 4042.

or psychological state or the detailed mores of people trafficking gangs operating in countries that are outside the court's own knowledge and experience. We stress that in the latter instance, this does not require any comment by the expert as to the consistency of the account given by the defendant, whereas in the former the psychiatrist or psychologist may express a view as to the detail and content of the defendant's account as a necessary step to reaching a diagnosis.'

12.102

As to the admissibility of a conclusive grounds' decision and/or the underlying material it is founded on, see **Chapter 10**.

12.103

Expert evidence may also assist the court when considering pre-trial applications such as severance, special measures and applications for anonymity or to move proceedings. Funding for prior authority for such reports should be applied for as soon possible after the first appearance.

Indictment and severance

12.104

Where a defendant has used or been advised to use an alias name, practitioners should ensure that his name is correctly spelt and that the correct name is used on the indictment. In a case where anonymisation is appropriate, care should be taken to ensure that the defendant's name is not released into the public domain.

12.105

If a PVOT is charged with others, careful consideration needs to be given to whether the defendant has or might have been charged with individuals responsible for trafficking, exploiting or exerting a form of control over him or persons linked to the network responsible for his exploitation. Where there is an application for severance, this should in normal circumstances be raised as soon as possible. The CrimPR, r 3.29 outlines that the application must be served as soon as practicable after becoming aware of the grounds for doing so, and that such an application has to be served on the court and each of the other parties. When considering the practicability of raising severance, it is suggested that care needs to be taken to ensure that the raising of the issue does not itself expose the defendant to risk.

12.106

The Indictments Act 1915, s 5 gives a discretion to the Crown Court to order severance. In circumstances where a s 45 MSA 2015 defence is being raised and an allegation of trafficking/modern slavery is being made against a co-defendant it is advisable to request a separate listing for mention to address pre-trial issues, including severance, and any ancillary applications without the co-defendant(s) or their legal representative being present.

12.107

Judges have detailed guidance from the Judicial College about how to deal with any suggestion that a defendant has been trafficked. If the SCA has not reached a decision, then the judge should adjourn for this to happen. Those representing the defendant should be aware of the risks to the defendant once the basis for severance has been disclosed – the safety of the defendant, including in custody, needs to be ascertained and, if necessary, safeguarding measures should be adopted in prison, particularly where the defendant is detained in the same prison as his co-defendants or others connected to the organised criminal network. Safeguarding issues should be raised with the court and prison service, if the remand prison is the same, to avoid the trafficked defendant and co-defendant being transported to and from court together. Where a defendant is remanded on bail, consideration should be given to whether it is appropriate to refer to any address of a PVOT defendant in court or in a defence statement when it might be seen by a co-defendant. Other protective measures could be sought for those on bail, such as non-contact with the co-defendant. If an application to sever is unsuccessful, other practical issues should be considered, such as how a defendant who has raised his trafficked status should be produced at court, and, in court whether a dock officer should sit between the defendants. In general, the Court of Appeal will only interfere with the exercise of discretion for a refusal of severance as a ground of appeal, only if it can be shown that the trial judge took into account irrelevant considerations, ignored relevant issues and/or arrived at a manifestly unreasonable decision[111].

Arraignment

12.108

If at arraignment no decision on a PVOT defendant's trafficking status has been received from the SCA, then arraignment must in most circumstances (unless the prosecutor agrees that the defendant is a VOT)[112] be postponed pending this decision. As set out above, a request should be made so that full credit for a guilty plea is retained, where appropriate, until after that decision has been made. The reason for this is that:

> 'the decision of the competent authority as to whether a person had been trafficked for the purposes of exploitation is not binding on the

111 *R v Moghal* (1977) 65 Cr App Rep 56.

112 In many cases, prosecutors remain reluctant to concede that a PVOT defendant is a VOT even where the components of trafficking are impliedly conceded in case summaries. See **Chapter 10**.

court but, unless there was evidence to contradict it or significant evidence that had not been considered, it is likely that the criminal courts will abide by the decision'[113].

Defence statements

12.109

Service of a defence statement occurs 28 days after the disclosure of the material from the prosecution at Stage 1 of the Crown Court proceedings[114]. Under the Criminal Procedure and Investigations Act 1996, s 6A, the defence statement should set out:

- the nature of the defence including any particular defences on which they intend to rely;
- what matters of fact 'on which [the defendant] takes issue with the prosecution';
- why they take issue with it;
- any matters of fact they rely on for the purposes of their defence;
- any point of law, including any point as to the admissibility of evidence or an abuse of process, which they wish to take and any authority on which they intend to rely for that purpose;
- if an *alibi* is to be relied upon, details of the alibi (including name, address and date of birth of alibi).

12.110

If a s 45 defence is to be raised, this should be included in a defence statement. It should be made clear whether the alleged offence is admitted, subject to the trafficking issues, otherwise the omission of any other live issue could give rise to an adverse inference. If, at the stage of serving a defence statement, the trafficking/modern slavery issues have not been investigated or an SCA decision has not been received, then the defence statement can be used as a further mechanism to trigger such investigation and referral. The need to investigate and refer the defendant should be expressly particularised and reference should be made to positive obligations the State are under in relation to Article 4 of the ECHR.

113 *R v VSJ* [2017] EWCA Crim 36, para [28].

114 Criminal Procedure and Investigation Act 1996 (Defence Disclosure Time Limits) Regulation 2011, SI 2011/209 (in force from 28 February 2011). The time limit for providing information within a defence statement in a magistrates' court is 14 days after initial prosecution disclosure (or notice from the prosecutor that there is no material to disclose): there is no obligation on a defendant to provide a defence statement in a magistrates' court but if one is given, that time limit applies.

Disclosure requests

12.111

Defence practitioners should consider seeking the following in relation to a case involving trafficking/modern slavery:

- copies of all competent authority and SCA decisions and minutes concerning the defendant;
- a copy of the NRM referral form;
- copies of historical NRM referral form/s;
- communication by the police to the SCA if they were first responder;
- details of which officer/agency completed it;
- date of when the NRM referral form was in fact sent;
- copies of all items sent to the SCA with the NRM referral, for example, expert trafficking reports;
- all contemporaneous notes from the date of arrest;
- any body-worn camera footage from officers at the point of arrest/ scene photographs – as these may highlight crucial evidence as to the demeanour of the defendant, his physical condition, living conditions, and indicators of mental illness and/or vulnerabilities at the time;
- details of all investigations conducted by police (of any constabulary area) into the defendant's trafficking/slavery situation;
- inclusion of all witness statements taken in any investigation/enquiries into a defendant being in a trafficking/slavery situation;
- consideration of when the police (and which officer(s)) spoke to the defendant, and whether an interpreter was used (and, if so, who);
- details of any police intelligence to do with the premises at which the defendant was arrested, for example any reports by neighbours, or previous incidents of other individuals having been arrested at the address (this may lead to issues of public interest immunity which will need to be considered), including briefing notes from any police operation(s) relevant to the allegation;
- previous reports/allegations concerning places used to harbour or receive VOTs or where slavery or servitude has taken place;
- if the circumstances focus upon a household in which the defendant was held, then information should be sought as to all previous reports made to

the police in relation to that particular address, or linked to the individuals exerting control over the defendant;

- records of Youth Offending Services in relation to county lines cases, including whether any trafficking indicators have been previously noted;
- Social Services records, if the individual is a child in care or in respect of whom Social Services have had contact, consideration to any indicators of exploitation and/or periods where individual reported as missing;
- reports with Home Office 'opening codes':
  - N200/01 – reported incident – NRM referral pending reasonable grounds decision[115];
  - N200/02 – reported incident – NRM referral negative reasonable grounds decision;
  - N200/03 – reported incident – NRM referral – Duty to notify only;
  - N200/04 – reported incident – NRM referral – Positive reasonable grounds/police referral – Outside England and Wales;
  - N200/05 – reported incident – NRM referral – Negative reasonable grounds – Outside; England and Wales;
  - N200/06 – reported incident – NRM referral – Transferred to another force in England and Wales;
- Communications data, cell site information;
- Automatic Number Plate Recognition ('ANPR') evidence showing movements around the UK;
- travel tickets;
- evidence from financial investigation, including bank accounts;
- airport manifests showing suspects/travel/flight bookings with airlines.

12.112

Practitioners should adopt caution when evaluating third party disclosure (eg Home Office records concerning the defendant), particularly if adverse credibility issues or inconsistent instructions arise in these documents. It is highly likely that the Home Office interviews in the context of an asylum claim or immigration application will not have been done under caution. These interviews are unlikely to have been recorded and often the individual

115 From April 2019, the Home Office Counting Rules ('HOCR') for recorded crime has introduced the N200 set of rules for modern slavery offences. All reported incidents of modern slavery should be recorded on the force crime system, see: https://www.app.college.police.uk/app-content/major-investigation-and-public-protection/modern-slavery/national-referral-mechanism/#making-a-referral, last accessed 18 August 2025.

will have had no legal representation present at time of interview. These interviews do not adopt the 'Achieving Best Evidence' model. Following the commencement of s 22 Border Security, Asylum and Immigration Act 2025, police now have statutory authority to retain electronic devices seized during immigration investigations. Because these devices are now held under 'immigration crime' powers rather than PACE, defence practitioners must be proactive in making s 8 CPIA requests and applications for the download of data, specifically seeking communications that prove coercion or threats from traffickers.

Bad character applications

12.113

The Crown may seek to introduce bad character against a defendant under the provisions of the Criminal Justice Act 2003, s 101.

12.114

One of the aspects of re-trafficking is that a person can be continually moved between different locations and in addition, even post-sentence, be at risk of being re-trafficked. It is not uncommon in trafficking and modern slavery for an individual to have unchallenged previous convictions that are, on any proper analysis, unsafe: sometimes these are the consequence of guilty pleas or findings where representatives have failed (or failed adequately) to raise a VOT's circumstances which were pertinent to whether or not he should have been prosecuted in the public interest (or convicted in light of a s 45 defence). It is also often the case that criminal acts historically committed by VOT defendants should not be treated as *criminal* or acts of which the defendant was *culpable* (see *R v L)*[116]. Furthermore, often historical sentencing exercises may have been flawed and judges may not have applied appropriate weight to the defendant being a VOT or there having been indicators of trafficking present.

12.115

It follows that, if the prosecution are seeking to introduce 'bad character' evidence, consideration should be given to whether the bad character allegations assist in illustrating previous exploitation in the way in which they would if the defendant was not a VOT and whether they are admissible. Much will depend on relevance and seriousness.

116 [2013] EWCA Crim 991, [2013] 2 Cr App Rep 247 at para 13; and *R v AFU* (above).

12.116

The Criminal Justice Act 2003, s 101(1) governs the test for admissibility of a defendant's bad character. It is admissible:

'if, but only if–

(a) all parties to the proceedings agree to the evidence being admissible,

(b) the evidence is adduced by the defendant himself or is given in answer to a question asked by him in cross-examination and intended to elicit it,

(c) it is important explanatory evidence,

(d) it is relevant to an important matter in issue between the defendant and the prosecution,

(e) it has substantial probative value in relation to an important matter in issue between the defendant and a co-defendant,

(f) it is evidence to correct a false impression given by the defendant, or

(g) the defendant has made an attack on another person's character.'

12.117

Aspects that should be considered when seeking to exclude any bad character are:

- Criminal Justice Act 2003, s 101(3): this provides that the court must not admit evidence under s 101(1)(d) or (g) if, on an application by the defendant to exclude it, it appears to the court that the admission of the evidence would have such an adverse effect on the fairness of the proceedings that the court ought not to admit it;
- consideration should be given to how long ago the bad character subject matter was: see Criminal Justice Act 2003, s 101(4);
- in addition, it will be critical to examine in cases of a disputed age assessment whether or not the age assessments were lawfully made at the time of the convictions (ie not vitiated by a public law error: see **Chapter 6**);
- whether the alleged 'bad character' evidence is being used to prove a tendency to act in a particular way or to rebut a coincidence.

12.118

By s 74(3) of the Police and Criminal Evidence Act 1984:

'74.— Conviction as evidence of commission of offence.

...

(3) In any proceedings where evidence is admissible of the fact that the accused has committed an offence, [...] if the accused is proved to have been convicted of the offence—

(a) by or before any court in the United Kingdom;

… he shall be taken to have committed that offence *unless the contrary is proved*' [Emphasis added].

12.119

It follows that if a defendant seeks to challenge a conviction on the ground that he should not have been prosecuted in the public interest or a s 45 defence was overlooked (see **Chapter 10**) and the conviction is unsafe, he can challenge it. It will be an exceptional course[117].

12.120

Where the facts of a conviction are not accepted, see *R v Ainscough*[118]:

> 'when there is a dispute about the facts supporting previous convictions, in almost all cases it should be possible for the matter to be dealt with in accordance with *Humphris*[119], where bad character evidence was introduced under the hearsay provisions of the Criminal Justice Act 2003, s 117. However, one appreciates that there may be cases where the position is simply too complicated. Whatever the complainant may have said in a statement at the time of the earlier conviction, or may say now in evidence to the court, it may be that a current defendant was sentenced on a different basis as a result of a basis of plea proffered and accepted by the prosecution and by the judge. In other words, where these matters are in dispute there is a need for caution, there is a need to have regard to what was said in *Humphris* and there is a need to ensure that a current trial does not give rise to numerous satellite issues about what did or did not happen in some cases many years ago. It goes without saying that that is particularly to be avoided where what is taking place now is a relatively short trial on a simple issue'[120].

Trial issues

12.121

A s 45 MSA 2015 defence can be advanced regardless of whether negative Reasonable Grounds or negative Conclusive Grounds decisions have been made by the Single Competent Authority, However, practitioners may wish to carefully consider discrepancies and inconsistencies set out within any

117 See *R v Zawadzka* [2016] EWCA Crim 1712, para 25.
118 [2006] EWCA Crim 694.
119 [2005] EWCA Crim 203.
120 Ibid at [19].

consideration minute by the Competent Authority and review advice on merits to an individual defendant on receipt.

12.122

The decision of the relevant Single Competent Authority (IECA or SCA) is not admissible before the jury at trial – this is regardless of whether the decision is positive or negative (see **10.222** and following).

12.123

It is crucial to analyse what evidence considered by the SCA, whether it be admissible at trial (see **Chapters 4** and **10**) and what further evidence could be obtained in support of a s 45 defence.

Questioning of the 'officer in the case'

12.124

An Officer in the Case is the police officer with responsibility for day-to-day decisions during an investigation. Careful consideration should be given to the need to cross-examine such officer; particularly in relation to aspects of whether positive obligations under Article 4 ECHR have been complied with and any potential asserted failures to investigate the trafficking status of the defendant. The College of Policing Guidance Authorised Professional Practice 'Taking a Report'[121] highlights that it is:

> 'the duty of a local police force (the primary legislative agency) to begin an investigation as soon as they believe a modern slavery crime may have been committed, regardless of whether a victim makes an allegation, whether a report is made, or whether consent to be entered into the national referral mechanism is provided or refused. A modern-day slavery crime MUST NOT be approached as an employment or immigration issue at this stage'.

12.125

In cases involving human trafficking/modern slavery, there may well be questions as to the following aspects of the case which can be asked in advance so that the prosecution position is known pre-trial:

- whether there was any consideration of trafficking or modern slavery pre-arrest in the pre-planning stages undertaken by the police, including the potential recovery of victims during the police operation (for instance,

121 https://www.college.police.uk/app/major-investigation-and-public-protection/modern-slavery/taking-report (accessed 18 August 2025).

there are often pre-planning briefings when cannabis farms are raided on a large scale);

- whether there was any surveillance of any property that may establish that the defendant never left/did not feel able to leave or that there was limited movement from the property, or movement under escort;
- whether there was any consideration by the police of trafficking or modern slavery indicators at the point of the defendant's arrest;
- whether there is any evidence or information of an organised crime network, its hierarchy and whether the police have actively analysed this evidence;
- whether there have been investigations into telephones;
- whether telephone applications show matters such as whether a trafficker has regularly contacted or controlled the defendant;
- whether the defendant was interviewed, when a suspect, as a PVOT;
- at what stage any SCA referral was made;
- whether an SCA referral resulted in a crime record being set up (NB: this would contravene Home Office 'counting rules')[122];
- if no crime record was created, confirmation as to why one had not been made;
- what investigation of others linked to the address or as having controlled the defendant had been conducted;
- what investigation there had been, if any, of re-trafficking issues.

12.126

Policing trafficking experts may be able to provide expert evidence on what indicators of trafficking the police should have been alive to during the police operation and/or arrest and interview. Defence practitioners should consider whether such an expert might be able to evaluate the quality of the investigation into the trafficking of the defendant as undertaken by the police. This expert evidence can assist in formulating the cross-examination of an investigating officers, making an abuse of process application or in deploying a s 45 defence.

12.127

Practitioners may find it useful to consider principles in relation to positive procedural and substantive obligations under Article 4 ECHR in *TV v Spain*[123]

---

122 Home Office Crime Recording Rules for frontline officers and staff which provide a national standard for the recording and counting of 'notifiable' offences recorded by police forces in England and Wales (known as 'recorded crime').

123 Application No. 22512/21 (10 October 2024).

and *BB v Slovakia*[124] in preparing relevant and appropriate questions for cross-examination of the officer in the case at trial (See commentary at Crim LR 2025, Issue 2, p93). If an abuse of process application relates to questions concerning the conduct or failings of the investigating officers; then it may be relevant to consider if a voir dire is required in advance of the abuse of process application.

Exclusion of interview

12.128

If the police interview took place without an appropriate adult in place, and the defendant is considered to be a child or young person under 18, then it may be that exclusion of the police interview is appropriate, for example, under the Police and Criminal Evidence Act 1984, ss 78 and/or 76 and the PACE Code provisions, in particular, Code C.

Adverse inferences from failure to mention facts in police interview

12.129

Under the Criminal Justice and Public Order Act 1994, s 34, a power exists which allows a court (magistrates or jury) to draw an adverse inference if an individual fails to mention facts that they later come to rely on in their defence. Such an adverse inference applies only when this failure to mention facts occurs in the following circumstances: 'at any time before he was charged with the offence, on being questioned under caution by a constable trying to discover whether or by whom the offence had been committed … [or] on being charged with the offence or officially informed that he might be prosecuted for it …'. Section 34(1) provides that the inference can only be drawn where it concerns a 'fact which in the circumstances existing at the time the accused could reasonably have been expected to mention when so questioned, charged or informed'.

12.130

The prosecution and defence should consider before the start of the trial whether an adverse inference should be sought by the prosecution where there are background issues of trafficking or modern slavery. Where an individual has faced difficult circumstances of exploitation, coercion or is in fear of authority figures such as police or immigration officers, there may be reasons why an individual did not set out details of his full background circumstances or raise facts relevant to a s 45 defence within the police interview or post-caution (see **Chapter 4** regarding late disclosure).

124 Application No. 48587/21 (24 October 2024).

12.131

In *R v Argent*[125] Lord Bingham highlighted that 'in the circumstances' should not be construed restrictively when assessing the application of s 34. Lord Bingham said:

> 'The time referred to is the time of questioning, and account must be taken of all the relevant circumstances existing at that time. The courts should not construe the expression "in the circumstances" restrictively: matters such as time of day, the defendant's age, experience, mental capacity, state of health, sobriety, tiredness, knowledge, personality and legal advice are all part of the relevant circumstances; and those are only examples of things which may be relevant. When reference is made to "the accused" attention is directed not to some hypothetical, reasonable accused of ordinary phlegm and fortitude but to the actual accused with such qualities, apprehensions, knowledge and advice as he is shown to have had at the time.
>
> 'Like so many other questions in criminal trials this is a question to be resolved by the jury in the exercise of their collective common-sense, experience and understanding of human nature. Sometimes they may conclude that it was reasonable for the defendant to have held his peace for reasons, such as, that he was tired, ill, frightened, drunk, drugged, unable to understand what was going on, suspicious of the police, afraid that his answer would not be fairly recorded, worried at committing himself without legal advice, acting on legal advice, or some other reason accepted by the jury.
>
> '… This is an issue on which the judge may, and usually should, give appropriate directions. But he should ordinarily leave the issue to the jury to decide.'

12.132

Where the prosecution seeks an adverse inference direction under s 34 in the context of a defendant who contends that he is a victim of exploitation, the circumstances of the defendant's arrest and the demeanour of the defendant at the time of interview may be relevant matters to consider when questioning witnesses at trial, including officers present at the defendant's arrest and the defendant, should s/he decide to give evidence. In addition, this evidence may be the legitimate province of expert psychological, psychiatric or, trafficking evidence.

12.133

Further, consideration should be given to the state of health and/or fitness for interview of any defendant recovered in cannabis farms. The policing

125 [1997] 2 Cr App Rep 27.

guidance[126] clearly sets out the high levels of toxicity in premises modified for cannabis cultivation, which will have an impact on any individual exposed to this toxicity. As good practice any individual recovered in such premises should be evaluated by a Forensic Medical Examiner to ensure fitness to be interviewed.

Defendant giving evidence

12.134

There may be a real concern in a case where a defendant has a background of being subjected to trafficking or modern slavery exploitation about his ability to give evidence at trial safely and without fear. Special measures for vulnerable suspects/defendants are addressed in Chapter 8.

12.135

The Equal Treatment Bench Book (revised May 2025)[127] sets out that 'victims of modern slavery are likely to be vulnerable witnesses, considerably damaged by their experiences and wary of authority figures. Patience as well as sensitivity will be required.'

12.136

The Bench Book outlines that protected questioning techniques may be appropriate, such as:[128]

- No repeated questions.
- Short, single-strand questions, ie one matter raised in the question at a time.
- Giving structure to the questions.
- Focused questions on the matters in dispute.
- Reduction in the use of leading questions.
- Reduction in the use of tag questions.

---

126 Home Office Guidance 2015, at: https://assets.publishing.service.gov.uk/media/5a807f9b40f0b62302693dcc/Guidance_for_local_authorities_on_taking_action_against_10.03_15.pdf, last accessed 18 August 2025.

127 https://www.judiciary.uk/about-the-judiciary/diversity/equal-treatment-bench-book/ page 132 (accessed 18 August 2025).

128 *Idem*, page 134.

12.137

A psychologist or psychiatrist might appropriately be instructed to provide an opinion on the ability of the defendant effectively to participate in a trial, and, in particular, whether any adjustments to the trial process should be made to accommodate trauma or other vulnerabilities (for example the defendant not sitting in the dock, the use of an intermediary or a greater number of breaks, etc): see Chapter 8.

12.138

Crim PR, r 3.9(6) needs to be considered as it specifically provides that 'facilitating the participation of any person includes giving directions for the appropriate treatment and questioning of a witness or the defendant, especially where the court directs that such questioning is to be conducted through an intermediary.'

12.139

Crim PR, r 3.8(6) provides that:

> 'Facilitating the participation of any person includes –
>
> (a) giving directions for someone to accompany a witness if the witness so wishes while the witness gives evidence and at any other hearing; and
>
> (b) giving directions for the appropriate treatment and questioning of a witness or the defendant, especially where the court directs that such questioning is to be conducted through an intermediary.'

12.140

Those ground rules may include things such as the manner and duration of questioning, directions about questions that may or may not be asked, the use of models or body maps, and the allocation amongst defendants of topics that can be asked of a witness[129].

12.141

Account needs to be taken of language needs, which may be overcome by use of an interpreter. Also, any learning difficulties or literacy issues a defendant may have should be addressed. An intermediary will usually be able to assist with this.

---

129 See: *The Advocate's Gateway* and the Toolkits for questioning witnesses there and Crim PR part 3.8(9)b.

12.142

It is important at an early stage of proceedings to gauge the educational and cultural background of a defendant. It may well impact on the style of questions asked of a defendant and the ability to understand questions and assimilate documents or schedules.

Absconders

12.143

In all criminal cases defendants are advised that a trial can proceed, and indeed that they can be convicted, in their absence. In *R v Jones*[130], the House of Lords considered that a judge has a discretion to start or continue a trial in a defendant's absence, but that this power was to be exercised with great caution, and with close regard to the overall fairness of the proceedings. The circumstances that a judge should have regard to are:

(i) the nature and circumstances of the defendant's behaviour in absenting himself from trial and whether the behaviour was voluntary;

(ii) whether an adjournment would resolve the matter;

(iii) the likely length of such an adjournment;

(iv) whether the defendant, though absent, wished to be represented or had waived his right to representation;

(v) whether the defendant's representatives were able to receive instructions from him, and the extent to which they would be able to present his defence;

(vi) the extent of the disadvantage to the defendant in not being able to present his account of events;

(vii) the risk of the jury reaching an improper conclusion about the absence of the defendant;

(viii) the general public interest that a trial should take place within a reasonable time;

(ix) the undesirability of having separate trials if there were co-defendants.

12.144

The Court emphasised the decision to proceed with a trial in the absence of an accused was one to be approached with the utmost care (*R v Lopez)*[131].

130 [2002] UKHL 5, [2003] 1 AC 1.
131 *R v Lopez* [2013] EWCA Crim 1744.

12.145

Crim PR, r 25.2 states:

'(b) the Court must not proceed if the defendant is absent, unless the court is satisfied that—

(i) the defendant has waived the right to attend, and

(ii) the trial will be fair despite the defendant's absence'.

12.146

It is crucial to consider the position of individuals who may have been re-trafficked and who therefore may not have voluntarily chosen to absent themselves from trial. This is particularly important with children and young persons, given their high risk of re-trafficking. These are all factors which a court needs to take into consideration in the determination of whether a trial can proceed in their absence.

12.147

If, for example, at date of trial, a representative has written instructions that have been signed, such as a proof of evidence, it will be a question for him if he considers the extent to which he is able to present the defence for the defendant. Without a signed proof of evidence, and a signed defence statement, it may be extremely difficult for a representative to continue at trial and as a result he would have to withdraw.

12.148

In some instances, a representative may become aware that his client has absconded in advance of trial. When an individual has been re-trafficked in advance of a defence statement being due to be submitted to the court it is best practice to notify the court if there are in effect 'non-compliance' issues. It would not be appropriate to wait until the day of trial to set out non-compliance issues; if, for example, a client has failed to engage in attending any appointments/conferences with a solicitor from PTPH until trial and he cannot be contacted, this should trigger a notification.

12.149

Although *R v Okedare*[132] related to the position of absconders in the context of post-trial appeals against convictions and sentence, the case is relevant and should be considered in the context of individuals absconding at trial date. The court in *Okedare* dealt with one applicant, K, who had been arrested in relation to cannabis cultivation. The court considered that he 'may well have

132 [2014] EWCA Crim 228.

been re-trafficked'. Because there had been written confirmation to the defence representatives to wish to appeal against conviction, there was nothing to suggest that the applicant wished to withdraw his appeal.

12.150

The court, in assessing the case, evaluated that 'In any event there remains the possibility that his disappearance was not his fault.' On account of this, the Court of Appeal considered that it had no option but to stay the application for permission to appeal, until the applicant was able to satisfy the evidential requirements as to whether or not he had in fact been trafficked and if he had been compelled to commit the offence for which he was tried.

12.151

The above is highly pertinent when the Crown Court or a magistrates' court is considering whether a trial in absence should take place, where an individual 'may well have re-trafficked or simply absconded'. The issues at trial in relation to a defence under the MSA 2015 almost invariably cannot properly be dealt with without the defendant giving evidence as to the compulsion they experienced. As a result, *Okedare* provides a basis for highlighting the need for an application to stay the proceedings or adjourn them *sine die* in those circumstances.

Pre-sentencing application to vacate a guilty plea

12.152

If, after a guilty plea but before sentence, it becomes apparent that an individual was a trafficked person subject to modern slavery, or had a defence available under MSA 2015, s 45, but this was unknown for a good reason, then it might be appropriate for a court to hear an application to vacate the guilty plea.

12.153

A defendant may apply at any time before sentence to vacate a plea of guilty, and it is for the court to decide whether justice requires that that should be permitted[133]. Where the plea was in a magistrates' court and the case was committed for sentence, the sending to the Crown Court renders the magistrates' court *functus officio*. The Crown Court may send the case back to a magistrates' court before sentence[134]. Following sentence, it is suggested that the only route available to a defendant is appeal and where his plea was entered in a magistrates' court before sending to the Crown Court for sentence, a referral

133 *S (an infant) v Manchester City Recorder* [1971] AC 481.

134 See *R v Rochdale Justices, ex p Allwork* (1981) 73 Cr App R 319 at 323.

from the Criminal Cases review Commission ('CCRC') to the Crown Court (see **Chapter 13**, at para **13.7**).

12.154

Criminal PR, r 25.5 states that a party must apply to vacate a plea in writing to both the Crown and the court 'as soon as practicable after becoming aware of the grounds for doing so'.

12.155

The principles, as set out within *DPP v Revitt*[135], are that:

> 'it is likely to be appropriate to permit the withdrawal of an unequivocal plea of guilty if it becomes apparent that the defendant did not appreciate the elements of the offence to which he was pleading, or if it becomes apparent that the facts relied upon by the prosecution do not add up to the offence charged.'

12.156

The application must set out the following matters (see Crim PR, r 25.5(3)):

(a) why it would be unjust for the guilty plea to remain unchanged;

(b) what, if any, evidence the applicant wishes to call;

(c) identify any proposed witness;

(d) indicate whether legal professional privilege is waived, specifying any material name and date.

Sentencing

12.157

When a VOT is convicted of an offence, the background of trafficking, modern slavery or exploitation need not be completely rejected. It can still be key to mitigation. A defendant may not have acted under duress, may not be able to rely on MSA 2015, s 45 to provide a defence, and may not have been able to cause the prosecution to discontinue the case in the public interest but may nonetheless have been vulnerable and even trafficked but without a nexus to the alleged offence or where the dominant force of compulsion from trafficking does not erode criminality significantly notwithstanding there being a nexus between the trafficking and offending.

135 [2006] EWHC 2266 (Admin), [2006] 1 WLR 3172.

12.158

The significance of such mitigation is exemplified in *R v N; R v L*[136]. There, sentences of an 18-month detention and training order and 20 months' detention in a Young Offender Institution were imposed in the separate cases in the Crown Court. They were reduced to a four-month DTO and 12 months' custody respectively: see [93] and [113].

12.159

In *R v L*[137] the court emphasised that where trafficked persons commit offences that are unconnected with their trafficking status, the facts of the trafficking can still amount to mitigation:

> 'These defendants are not safeguarded from prosecution or punishment for offences which were unconnected with the fact that they were being or have been trafficked, although we do not overlook that the fact that they have been trafficked may sometimes provide substantial mitigation.'

12.160

This spectrum of culpability was again highlighted when the court said that 'due allowance [was] to be made in the sentencing decision for their diminished culpability' (at [33]). This can be contrasted by those cases where the 'fact that the defendant was a trafficked person will provide no more than a colourable excuse for criminality which is unconnected to and does not arise from their victimisation.'

12.161

For many offences, Sentencing Guidelines apply. Section 59 of the Sentencing Act 2020 provides that:[138]

> 'Every court—
>
> (a) must, in sentencing an offender, follow any sentencing guideline which is relevant to the offender's case, and
>
> (b) must, in exercising any other function relating to the sentencing of offenders, follow any sentencing guidelines which are relevant to the exercise of the function,
>
> unless the court is satisfied that it would be contrary to the interests of justice to do so.'

136 [2012] EWCA Crim 189, [2012] 1 Cr App Rep 35, Judge LCJ giving the judgment of the Court.
137 [2013] EWCA Crim 991, [2014] 1 All ER 113 at para [14].
138 Offences committed after 6 April 2010.

12.162

Notably, sentencing guidelines for drug mules was specifically revised after an academic research project[139].

12.163

A judge will need to determine the appropriate classification of an offence, in terms of the 'category of harm' and in addition the 'culpability demonstrated by the offender's role'. As highlighted by *R v L*[140], the backdrop of trafficking and modern slavery is pertinent to the issue of culpability.

12.164

Typical factors highlighting a lesser role (such as those in the drugs sentencing guideline) overlap with some of the issues that face those who have been subject to a backdrop of trafficking/exploitation:

- performs a limited function under direction;
- engaged by pressure, coercion, intimidation;
- involvement through naivety/exploitation;
- no influence on those above in a chain.

12.165

In the Sentencing Council Definitive Guideline on Supplying or offering to supply a controlled drug/ Possession of a controlled drug with intent to supply it to another[141], exploitation is relevant both to culpability demonstrated by the offender's role and mitigation (offender's vulnerability was exploited). In the Sentencing Council publication 'Assessing the impact and implementation of the Sentencing Council's Drug Offences Definitive Guideline'[142] specific provision is discussed for the imposition of more lenient sentences on individuals who have been subjected to exploitation by gangs and criminals heavily involved in the drugs trade, such as drug mules.

12.166

The first question for the sentencing court to resolve will be whether there is evidence to support the submission that the defendant was a trafficked person/

139 Twelve case studies, at: https://www.sentencingcouncil.org.uk/wp-content/uploads/Drug_mules_bulletin.pdf, last accessed 18 August 2025.

140 [2013] EWCA Crim 991, [2014] 1 All ER 113.

141 https://www.sentencingcouncil.org.uk/offences/magistrates-court/item/supplying-or-offering-to-supply-a-controlled-drug-possession-of-a-controlled-drug-with-intent-to-supply-it-to-another/ (accessed 18 August 2025).

142 https://www.sentencingcouncil.org.uk/wp-content/uploads/Drug-offences-guideline-assessment.pdf (accessed 18 August 2025).

subject to modern slavery on the relevant occasion and acting under the control of traffickers when s/he committed the offence[143].

12.167

In principle, the courts should consider non-punishment or reduced punishment having regard to the obligations under ECAT, Art 26 so there can be greater consideration of absolute or conditional discharges, community penalties or suspended sentences.

12.168

Sentencing outcomes will depend on the nature of the offence charged, which sentencing guidelines apply, including the guideline on a reduction for a guilty plea and guidelines on sentencing children. There is no Sentencing Council guideline which deals with victims of trafficking who commit a crime while they are victims. It is also worth noting that powers under the Serious Organised Crime and Police Act 2005 provide immunity from prosecution or sentence discounts for those who co-operate with the authorities. Overall, sentencing judges should take into account the age of the defendant when he became involved in the enterprise, the level of participation and the level of exploitation, taking a structured approach to the victims' relative involvement and culpability[144].

12.169

More broadly, courts should consider the following: trafficked persons are necessarily the subjects of duress, coercion, or compulsion even where such a dominant force does not amount to a defence. Where such a defence is not available, for sentencing purposes, the influence of others in the commission of a crime may give rise to relevant mitigation. It may be appropriate to submit a basis of plea to ensure the background circumstances of trafficking are properly set out. Where that influence causes a defendant to be the subject of conduct amounting or akin to slavery or servitude, and/or where the individual may have been subject to oppression[145], material mitigation will be present. When considering mitigation in the context of exploitation it is helpful to consider the criteria used to sentence a *perpetrator* of offences of trafficking, slavery, or servitude. In the same way that aggravating features of such an offence will increase the culpability of a defendant who is to be sentenced for trafficking offences, those aggravating features will serve to mitigate the criminal conduct of a victim of exploitation/trafficking[146]. Similarly, aggravating features of sexual offending are focused in part on victim vulnerability[147]. Where an offender has a

143 *R v Khalifa* [2016] EWCA Crim 1967.
144 *R v N; R v L* [2012] EWCA Crim 189, [2013] QB 379.
145 *R v SK* [2011] EWCA Crim 1691, [2012] 1 All ER 1090.
146 *R v N; R v L* [2012] EWCA Crim 189, [2013] QB 379.
147 *A-G's Reference (No 126 of 2014) (Jumale)* [2015] 1 Cr App Rep (S) 65.

particular vulnerability, this can amount to a mitigating factor. Information as to the individuals subject to trafficking and modern slavery ought to be provided to probation in advance of any pre-sentence report being prepared. Past reports such as psychological reports, the reasonable grounds or conclusive grounds decision (and consideration minute) or independent trafficking expert reports might also assist a court in understanding the full complexity of an individual's exploitation prior to the commission of an offence.

12.170

The Court in *R v Haslam*[148] upheld a deferred sentence that had been imposed on an appellant who had pleaded guilty to a third possession with intent to supply drugs offence. The Court upheld the finding made by the sentencing judge of there being exceptional circumstances such that Haslam should not receive a minimum seven-year sentence. The appellant did not put forward a specific statutory defence under s 45 MSA 2015, but had a background of being placed in care; no formal education since the age of ten; and owed a drug debt to a dealer and became drawn and groomed into county lines offending.

12.171

In *R v Orlu*[149], the Court carefully considered the independent evidence that existed from Social Services reports concerning an individual's drug debt to a gang and the exploitation he had been under, being in bondage debt to a gang. This had been set out in a basis of plea and the sentencing Judge had not ordered a *Newton* hearing. As a result the Court considered it was obliged to consider the basis of plea as factually correct; and reduced somewhat their culpability.

12.172

Even in cases that fall within exclusions under Sch 4 MSA 2015, background factors that they had been victims of modern slavery may be relevant mitigation (see *R v Kurmekaj*[150] in relation to a sentence for conspiracy to facilitate a breach of UK Immigration law).

12.173

A practical approach to mitigation on behalf of a trafficked person who has committed a criminal offence may include consideration of elements akin to the criminal offence of coercive control; see the Serious Crime Act 2015, s 76. The essential elements of the offence set out features of a trafficker or exploiter's criminal behaviour. Those elements may be useful factors to frame as mitigating features of a trafficking victim's behaviour:

148 [2024] EWCA Crim 404.
149 [2024] EWCA Crim 171.
150 [2024] EWCA Crim 1666.

- Is the coercion the product of repeated or 'continuous'[151] behaviour towards the defendant?
- Is the coercing person/exploiter personally connected to the defendant (ie do they live together as members of the same family or have they previously been in an intimate personal relationship with each other)?
- Has the behaviour had a serious effect on the defendant?
- Did the exploiter know or ought he to have known that the behaviour would have a serious effect on the defendant?

12.174

Further, it is a useful to look at the following components of coercive behaviour when sentencing victims of trafficking who commit crime. Coercive behaviour is a continuing act or a pattern of acts of assault, threats, humiliation and intimidation or other abuse that is used to harm, punish or frighten the victim and can capture a wide range of behaviour including isolation, monitoring, controlling movement, financial abuse, threats and force, including where it causes child neglect. The behaviour does not have to have occurred within a domestic setting, eg the home. Trafficked persons are commonly monitored remotely by phone, social media or even spyware.

12.175

Under sentencing guidelines for young offenders, immaturity may be as important as chronological age[152]. However, when a young person has committed a serious offence, immaturity when balanced against age may not result in a reduced sentence[153]. Following conviction and sentence, victims of trafficking may face a number of potential ancillary orders, including:

- a recommendation for deportation from the Criminal Court if sentence is under 12 months imprisonment (or alternatively may well end up being subject to automatic deportation provisions);
- confiscation;
- compensation;
- slavery and trafficking reparation orders: orders requiring the persons against whom they are made to pay compensation to the victim of a relevant offence for any harm resulting from that offence: MSA 2015, s 8;
- forfeiture and detention of vehicles, ships or aircraft: this applies to vehicles used or intended to be used in connection with an offence: see MSA 2015, ss 11 and 12;

---

151 *Sic*: this should perhaps be read as 'continual' or 'continuing'.
152 *R v N* [2010] 2 Cr App Rep 97.
153 *Asi-Akram* [2006] 1 Cr App Rep (S) 260; *R v B* [2006] EWCA Crim 330.

- slavery and trafficking prevention orders: post-conviction orders necessary for protecting persons from the physical or psychological harm which would be likely to occur if the defendant committed a slavery or human trafficking offence: see MSA 2015, ss 14–17;
- slavery and trafficking risk orders: orders where a person has acted in a way which means that there is a risk that he will commit a slavery or human trafficking offence to protect persons from the physical or psychological harm which would be likely to occur if the defendant committed a slavery or human trafficking offence: see MSA 2015, ss 23 and 24;
- sexual harm prevention orders and sexual risk orders, etc: see Anti-social Behaviour, Crime and Policing Act 2014, s 113(1), Sch 5, paras 1, 5;
- serious crime prevention orders: the Serious Crime Act 2007, ss 19(5) and 1(3) empower the Crown Court and High Court respectively to impose conditions considered appropriate for the stated purpose of protecting the public from serious crime: this is supplemented by the examples of the types of prohibitions, restrictions or requirements provided in the Serious Crime Act 2007, s 5;
- cash seizure and forfeiture orders;
- restraint orders: these have the effect of freezing property anywhere in the world that may be liable to be sold to satisfy a confiscation order;
- deprivation of property orders: these enable the court to deprive an offender of property, used, or intended to be used to commit an offence, for example a vehicle;
- restraining orders on acquittal: these can be made if the court considers it necessary to do so to protect a person from harassment from the defendant: see Protection from Harassment Act 1997, s 5A;
- registration on the sex offenders' register: see the Sexual Offences Act 2003 (Notification Requirements) (England and Wales) Regulations 2012. The Home Office has introduced measures which will extend and strengthen the system of notification requirements placed on registered sex offenders (commonly referred to as the sex offenders' register). These measures came into force on 13 August 2012 and require all offenders subject to the notification requirements under the Sexual Offences Act 2003 to notify to the police.

13 Criminal appeal process for victims of exploitation who commit criminal acts

Andrew Johnson and Paramjit Ahluwalia

Introduction

13.1

It is a common occurrence that aspects of cases involving victims of human trafficking, modern slavery and exploitation who commit criminal acts are overlooked by the criminal justice system, when their exploitation is such that their criminality or culpability should be regarded as expunged or materially reduced (see **Chapter 10**). This was identified as a problem in the seminal case of *R v O*[1] in 2008 and has subsisted as such following the coming into force of the Modern Slavery Act 2015 ('MSA 2015')[2]. This is often because victims do not make disclosures regarding their exploitation until after conviction, or because exploitation indicators are overlooked by their legal representatives, the prosecution, and the courts at the time of conviction. Human trafficking, modern slavery and exploitation represent very serious evils, both in the UK and worldwide. The number of cases coming before the appellate courts demonstrates the underlying complexities which those evils pose to the criminal justice system and how systemic failures continue to occur in such cases.

13.2

It is important that prima facie unsafe convictions are challenged as soon as they come to light for several reasons. Many foreign national victims will be subject to immigration proceedings, such as automatic deportation or deportation as conducive to the public good, which is triggered by the conviction[3]. The criminal court could order a recommendation for deportation[4]. British nationals may be deprived of their British citizenship[5]. Many victims who decide to cooperate with the authorities about their trafficking situation and background circumstances may have unchallenged convictions as a result of

1 [2008] EWCA Crim 2835.
2 See statutory defence under s 45 MSA 2015.
3 UK Borders Act 2007, s 32 and Immigration Act 1971, s 3(5)(a).
4 Immigration Act 1971, s 3(6).
5 British Nationality Act 1981, s 40.

their exploitation and may be treated as having bad character for any subsequent criminal case against their traffickers, where they are a complainant or in any prosecution they face themselves. These convictions should be scrutinised with a view to challenging them, even if they are significantly out of time, or spent[6].

13.3

Setting aside unsafe convictions plays an important part in the rehabilitation and self-identification process for victims. Many may go on to enter education or employment[7], certain types of convictions will directly affect eligibility onto a course or employment and hinder a victim's re-integration back into society. It is also necessary for convictions to be set aside before a defendant may qualify for compensation under the various schemes (see **Chapter 15**).

Appeals to the Crown Court

13.4

A defendant convicted in the magistrates' court may appeal against their conviction to the Crown Court (under s 108 of the Magistrates' Courts Act 1980 ('MCA 1980')):

(i) If the defendant pleaded guilty, against their sentence;

(ii) If the defendant pleaded not guilty and was convicted after trial; then against conviction and sentence.

13.5

No leave to appeal is required if the application is lodged in time and the appeal that takes place is by way of a 're-hearing.'

13.6

The same mechanism of appeal applies to the youth court, due to the provisions under s 148(1) of the MCA 1980.

13.7

In general, once a defendant has pleaded guilty in a magistrates' court, no appeal against conviction is available in the Crown Court. The exception to this is when the guilty plea is found by the Crown Court to have been equivocal[8].

---

6 See **Chapter 20** on funding and the sufficient benefit test.

7 Example of employment opportunities and progression as a carer being hindered by conviction – *R v GB* [2020] EWCA Crim 2.

8 See *Durham Quarter Sessions, ex parte Virgo* [1952] 2 QB 1; *Blandford Justices, ex parte G* [1967] 1 QB 82.

13.8

An appeal notice must be served on the magistrates' court/youth court officer and every other party[9]. The appeal notice needs to identify the issues, give notice of which witnesses the appellant would seek to question and set out the issues in the case; whether the issues in the Crown Court differ from those in the magistrates' court[10], which witnesses are sought to be called; and details of whether evidence is sought to be introduced for example that involves hearsay or bad character. In addition, the application should set out any extension of time limit sought.

13.9

Notices of appeal[11] must be served not more than 15 business days after sentence if the appeal is against sentence. If the appeal is against conviction, then notice of appeal should be not more than 15 business days after sentence, the date sentence is deferred or date of committal for sentence (whichever is earlier)[12].

13.10

The Crown is required to serve a respondent's notice not more than 15 business days after service of the appeal notice for appeals against conviction if the appeal is contested[13].

13.11

The limited scope of an appeal where the defendant pleaded guilty in the magistrates' court is a significant issue for victims of trafficking for criminal exploitation.Victims of modern slavery/trafficking for criminal exploitation are frequently advised to plead guilty by trial representatives or have entered pleas when unrepresented.

13.12

The interplay between s 108 of the MCA 1980 (appeals against conviction to the Crown Court following trials but not guilty pleas and against sentence) and s 11 of the Criminal Appeal Act 1995 empowers the CCRC to oblige the Crown Court to hear an appeal; see *R v Nori*; *R v YY (Practice Note)*[14] and *R (oAo Crown Prosecution Service) v Preston Crown Court*[15]. The words in s 11(2) 'shall be treated for all purposes as an appeal … (whether or not [the appellant] pleaded guilty)' mean that, following a CCRC reference, an appeal in the Crown Court

9 Crim PR, 34.2.
10 See Crim PR 34.3.
11 See https://www.gov.uk/guidance/criminal-procedure-rules-forms#appeal (accessed 9 October 2025).
12 CrimPR 34.2(2).
13 CrimPR 34.2(5).
14 [2016] EWCA Crim 18; [2016] 1 Cr.App. R. 28 at [42].
15 [2023] EWHC 1957 (Admin); [2023] 2 Cr.App. R. 18.

proceeds by way of rehearing[16]. In the same case it was held that a guilty plea amounted to a confession and was potentially admissible[17]. In *R v Nori and R v YY (Practice Note)*[18], Sir Brian Leveson P giving the judgment of the Court recognised the importance of CCRC referrals to the Crown Court, when setting out a directive that the CCRC should ordinarily not be involved in appeals to the Court of Appeal Criminal Division unless there had been a prior, unsuccessful, appeal:

> 'We recognise that appeals from the magistrates' court to the Crown Court after a plea of guilty have to be processed through the CCRC because of the constraints placed on the Crown Court (sitting on appeal) in relation to unequivocal pleas of guilty: see s.108(1) of the Magistrates' Courts Act 1980 and decisions such as *R. v McNally* (1954) 38 Cr. App. R. 90 and *S (An infant) v Recorder of Manchester* [1971] A.C. 481.'

Applications to re-open cases under s 142

13.13

Section 142 of the MCA 1980 confers upon the magistrates' court a power to rectify mistakes. Thus, s 142(2) enables a convicted defendant (whether he pleaded guilty or not guilty) to ask the magistrates to set the conviction aside. However, it does not provide a general power of review: *H v. DPP*[19]. It is therefore unlikely that it will be able to be invoked on the basis of an argument that a defendant convicted summarily should not have been convicted because they are a victim of trafficking.

Committal for sentence – equivocal pleas

13.14

Even after a case is committed for sentence, if a guilty plea has been entered in a magistrates' court, a Crown Court judge may remit the case to the magistrates' court if they receive credible evidence that the plea was equivocal[20]. Those instructed to deal with committals for sentence should be alive to the need to consider whether any trafficking issue might have been overlooked in the lower court.

16 See *Preston* (above), *per* Bennathan J, with whom Edis LJ agreed, at [37]–[41], [43], [47], [49] and [50].
17 At [45].
18 [2016] 1 Cr App R 28, 435 at 446.
19 [2021] EWHC 147 (Admin).
20 *R v Rochdale Justices, ex p Allwork* (1981) 73 Cr App R 319 at 323; see also *R v Mutford and Lothingland Justices, ex p Harber; R v East Suffolk Quarter Sessions, ex p Harber* (1971) 55 Cr App R 57.

Appeals to the Court of Appeal

Preparation of appeals and disclosure – defence enquiries

13.15

Defence enquiries play a vital part in the prospects of a successful appeal predicated on a potential victim of trafficking ('PVOT') claim to have committed offences because of or in connection with their trafficking status or circumstances. In appeals involving victims of slavery, human trafficking and exploitation, a significant amount of preliminary work must be conducted by the defence. The objective of such preparation is often to obtain material which can be used as fresh evidence in support of a prospective applicant's human trafficking and modern slavery claim to be or to have been a victim.

13.16

Victims may not be able to recall many details about the previous proceedings, or who their trial representatives were. The first step is to contact the convicting court to try to obtain as much information as possible. It is not necessary to ask for a certificate of conviction, although this document may contain useful information. The Court should be asked to provide basic information needed for an applicant's representative, such as:

(i) details of trial representatives;

(ii) date of conviction;

(iii) date of sentence;

(iv) sentence received;

(v) number of days spent on remand;

(vi) details of Court transcribers;

(vii) case number;

(viii) confirmation of whether a pre-sentence report was ordered.

13.17

When contacting previous trial lawyers for their files, it is important to obtain a complete set of papers, including the following:

- case papers (including access to the Crown Court Digital Case System ('DCS' or 'Case-lines'), if available);
- all witness statements and exhibits;
- interview tape/disc or full transcript of interview;

- copy of co-defendants' interviews[21]:
- unused material;
- any expert reports;
- copy of PTPH form to see the issues raised before trial and ostensible trial issues (including the question of whether the defendant is a victim of modern slavery)[22]:
- defence statement;
- agreed facts;
- any basis of plea;
- pre-sentence report if one was prepared;
- correspondences and working file;
- police station notes including notes of internal conferences with accused beforehand;
- instructions;
- all attendance notes;
- counsel's notebooks and notes;
- any signed endorsements;
- any previous advice on appeal.

13.18

Where an individual has potentially been subjected to re-exploitation and prosecuted in previous criminal cases, then it is advisable to seek the above for those matters – given they may provide supporting information concerning indicators of re-trafficking or a cycle of re-exploitation that impacts on the safety of the conviction[23].

13.19

In cases where previous representatives confirm they have destroyed the file, it is advisable to ask both solicitors and counsel if they hold anything electronically by way of emails or on their digital case management system.

21 Examples might be where this may be of value is where a co-defendant described at the date of interview the circumstances of exploitation.

22 See PTPH 2 guidance. As of July 2019, PTPH forms require the defence to identify defendants who are a victim of modern slavery so that appropriate orders or investigations can be made at PTPH.

23 See *R v AAJ* [2021] EWCA Crim 1278.

13.20

Subject access requests will also be necessary in cases where an applicant was either unrepresented or, in older cases, where the trial lawyers are no longer in possession of their file: the obligation is only to keep a file for six years[24].

13.21

Subject access requests under the Data Protection Act 2018 can be made to the police, Ministry of Justice, CPS and Home Office. Material which contains personal information about a client can be obtained through making an application under the Data Protection Act 2018[25]. If making a request on behalf of a client, a signed authority is needed: it is likely that certified copies of an identity document and proof of address of the client will be required when making such an application. Most bodies will have specific subject access request forms that will need to be completed. Applications for data held by police authorities that do not fall under the Data Protection Act 2018, Pts 2 and 3 and Ch 3, can be made under the Freedom of Information Act 2000, s 1.

13.22

If any other litigation or proceedings are ongoing, such as immigration proceedings, claims against public authorities or judicial review proceedings, any witness statement taken or served in those proceedings should be obtained, and discussion with the other legal teams should take place to determine what material they hold which may be served as fresh evidence. A multi-professionals' meeting will usually be beneficial, where there is ongoing litigation to discuss fresh evidence, witness statements, legally privileged material, and timetables.

13.23

Representatives should also consider obtaining the following documents from other legal representatives or via DPA subject access requests to the relevant bodies:

(i) the competent authority file, including National Referral Mechanism ('NRM') referral form, all material relied upon in making the determination, interview notes, a full copy of the reasonable and conclusive grounds determinations and full reasoning, including full trafficking consideration minutes of reasonable and conclusive grounds decisions. The relevant public body is the Home Office;

(ii) prison and probation files;

(iii) a client's immigration file;

24 See *R v Ealing Magistrates' Court, ex p Sahota* (1997) 162 JP 73, [1997] 45 LS Gaz R 29, QBD.
25 See Pts 2 and 3 and Ch 3 of the Act.

(iv) medical notes, including any psychological or psychiatric reports;

(v) Home Office file;

(vi) First-tier Tribunal (Immigration and Asylum Chamber) decisions, Upper Tribunal decisions or Judicial Review judgments;

(vii) material relied on for any judicial review application or claim;

(viii) asylum interview;

(ix) screening asylum interview and decisions made by the Secretary of State for the Home Department on the claim (i.e. the Reasons for Refusal Letter);

(x) all witness statements and accounts given in related proceedings;

(xi) social services records if the individual was under 18 or under leaving care provisions at any material time.

13.24

A statement from the applicant should be taken, and a decision should be made as to whether this is served as fresh evidence. The statement should cover the background history prior to their trafficking; their trafficking; life in the UK and personal circumstances; details of the offending; any nexus between the particular offence/s and the exploitation; instructions on what advice the applicant was given during the original proceedings and instructions on extension of time requests.

13.25

It should also be considered best practice to work from any pre-existing witness statement, already recently taken regarding the trafficking background and exploitation in other live proceedings such as an asylum claim or judicial review claim. It is common that during the process of preparing a criminal appeal an applicant will be engaging with numerous lawyers, such as immigration, public law, and community care lawyers. By taking a joint statement, the risks of exposing a victim of exploitation to unnecessary trauma and/or the risk of generating inconsistencies and inaccuracies as a by-product of exploitation can be avoided or minimised.

13.26

Transcripts of the summing up, sentencing remarks and mitigation should be obtained. Consideration should be given to obtaining a transcript of the prosecution opening for sentence, as often the discussion between a prosecutor and a judge will reveal a failure to identify a VOT. Each court will have an exclusive provider of transcription services. The requests for transcripts will need to be made through the relevant transcriber company. Permission to obtain the transcript from the court is now generally needed via the submission of a form EX107[26].

13.27

As shown in *R v N*[27], it is critical to consider the factual basis set out in the plea in mitigation by the advocate. In *N*, the mitigation referenced clear trafficking indicators, for example, the applicant being taken to the cannabis factory and told he would have to pay off the cost incurred for passage to the UK. Further in mitigation, it was explained he was not allowed to leave the property and was exploited. The court considered that it should have been apparent to the defence advocate, the CPS, and the judge that the applicant was a possible credible victim of trafficking. In the court's view the prosecutor should have followed published guidance, and should have sought an adjournment, in order to fulfil its duties to make proper enquiries and to refer the defendant through the NRM to the competent authority.

Test – whether conviction is unsafe

13.28

Under s 1(1) Criminal Appeal Act 1968, an Applicant convicted of an offence may appeal to the Court of Appeal against their conviction, either with the leave of the Court of Appeal (s 1(2)(a)); or by being granted a certificate that the case is fit for appeal by the judge of the court of trial (s 1(2)(b)). An appeal notice must be served not more than 28 days after the conviction if appealing from the Crown Court; and not more than 20 business days after the Registrar serves notice that the CCRC has referred a conviction to the Court of Appeal[28].

13.29

There is a single test for allowing an appeal against conviction: if the Court of Appeal thinks that the conviction is unsafe (s 2(1)(a) CAA 1968).

13.30

In drafting grounds of appeal, the Guide to Proceedings in the Court of Appeal, Criminal Division must be followed[29]. Advocates should not settle or sign grounds of appeal unless they consider that they are properly arguable. It is necessary to lodge grounds of appeal with the Court of Appeal itself, rather

26 See guidance of October 2024 – https://www.gov.uk/government/publications/order-a-transcript-of-court-or-tribunal-proceedings-form-ex107/guidance-for-requesting-a-transcript (accessed 20 August 2025).
27 [2019] EWCA Crim 984 at [38]-[40].
28 See Crim P.R. part 39.2 (last updated October 2023).
29 (January 2024) https://www.judiciary.uk/wp-content/uploads/2023/05/Guide-to-proceedings-in-the-CACD-Jan-2024-Final.pdf.(accessed 20 August 2025).

than the original Crown Court. A summary of the grounds should be set out within the first 2 pages of the grounds document.

13.31

The Registrar may serve on any party directly affected by the appeal the appeal notice. If the Respondent (normally the CPS Appeals and Review Unit) wishes to make representations to the court (or is directed to by the Court), then a Respondent's Notice must be served not more than 10 business days after the Registrar serves the appeal notice/directions to provide a Respondent's notice[30].

13.32

Practitioners must use the revised procedures in CrimPR 2025 Part 39 when appealing against conviction and sentence and Part 42 when appealing against confiscation decisions linked to trafficking convictions. These new rules consolidate the timelines for appealing ancillary financial orders alongside the substantive conviction.

Common grounds of challenge on appeal against conviction

13.33

Common scenarios where an appeal is brought by a defendant, who is a victim of trafficking, have historically been as follows:

13.34

Scenario 1:

(i) the defendant presented with trafficking indicators during the course of the criminal proceedings but

(ii) the CPS failed adequately, or at all, to review whether the prosecution of the defendant was in the public interest in accordance with the CPS non-prosecution guidance[31]: and/or

(iii) legal representatives of the defendant did not advise adequately at all on the non-prosecution protection of the CPS guidance (predicated on ECAT[32], Art 26 and/or historically the EU Anti-Trafficking Directive[33].

30 Crim PR part 39.6.

31 Part 2 of Modern Slavery and human trafficking: offences and defences, including the section 45 defence (https://www.cps.gov.uk/legal-guidance/modern-slavery-and-human-trafficking-offences-and-defences-including-section-45; (accessed 20 August 2025).

32 Council of Europe Convention on Action against Trafficking in Human Beings.

33 Directive (EU) 2024/1712 of the European Parliament and of the Council of 13 June 2024 amending Directive 2011/36/EU on preventing and combating trafficking in human beings and protecting its victims.

Art 8) and they failed to make either public interest representations to the Crown and/or they failed to advance an abuse of process application (see **Chapters 10** and **12**); and

(iv) the appellant was therefore prosecuted in circumstances where their prosecution was (or might well not have been) in the public interest.

13.35

The Court of Appeal requires that applications be only made to the Court after due diligence has been effected by those seeking to appeal[34]. It is therefore necessary that any new legal appellate team apprises itself fully of what happened during the criminal proceedings that might be relevant to the grounds of challenge, and ensures the facts are correct[35]. In pleading this ground, either actual or implied allegations of incompetence by previous legal representatives may have to be made. It is therefore necessary that enquiries are made of the previous lawyers concerning the particulars of implied or actual incompetence and that they are made aware of any allegations (see para **9.45**). Further, where appropriate, it is important to secure other objective and independent evidence to substantiate the allegations made[36]. This species of ground of appeal will almost invariably require the applicant to waive privilege.A formal waiver form should be lodged with the grounds, or the Court should be informed if the applicant is unwilling to give a waiver.

13.36

Scenario 2:

(i) the defendant did not disclose that he was or self-identify as a victim of trafficking at the time of the defendant's criminal proceedings (first instance) and there were no or few indicators present of trafficking during the criminal proceedings;

(ii) after conviction, the defendant is identified either through experts, supporting organisations or by the competent authority, other statutory agencies or in other legal proceedings (i.e. immigration appeal hearings) as a victim of trafficking;

(iii) the defendant's conviction is then challenged as unsafe on the premise that had the prosecutor known at the time of the conviction what is known

34 *R v A* [2014] EWCA Crim 567.

35 *R v McCook* [2014] EWCA Crim 734, [2016] 2 Cr App Rep 388; see further *R v Grant-Murray* [2017] EWCA Crim 1228, [2017] All ER (D) 62 (Aug), para 131.

36 In a different context, in *R v James Lee* [2014] EWCA Crim 2928 the court highlighted that as well as approaching the trial representatives, steps should be taken to obtain objective and independent evidence in support of the grounds in order to establish the facts. In some appeals brought on behalf of exploitation victims who commit criminal acts, a SCA CG decision and a witness statement from the applicant may suffice as fresh evidence in support of the application for leave to appeal.

at the time of appeal about the applicant's exploitation circumstances[37], he would or might well not have been prosecuted in the public interest[38].

13.37

Scenario 3:

The prosecution's public interest review is flawed by a failure on the part of the police to investigate the allegation of trafficking, thereby violating ECHR, Art 4 (specifically positive obligations such as the procedural measures' obligation to investigate a credible suspicion of trafficking)[39] and ECHR, Art 6; see the seminal case of *VCL and AN v the United Kingdom*[40].

Prosecutorial failings and abuse of process

13.38

It remains possible, following the coming into force of the MSA 2015, to argue at first instance that prosecutorial failings in discharging their duties in relation to victims of trafficking render the prosecution an abuse of process, and to advance an argument on appeal to the effect that the conviction is unsafe and the prosecution was an abuse of process (whether or not abuse has been raised at first instance): see *R v AAD*[41] at [106] and [142] and *AFU*[42] at [81] to [119], rejecting the approach taken in *R v DS*[43] and *R v A*[44].

13.39

The correct approach for the Court on appeal remained as formulated in *GS*[45]:

---

37 Whether by invoking the CPS non-prosecution guidance or ECAT, Art 26 or EU Directive, Art 8. The protection of the regional instruments (ECAT and historically the EU Directive) and Arts 4/6, ECHR will usually derive from the CPS non-prosecution guidance and its application); see *R v Thakoraka-Palmer* [2023] EWCA Crim 491 at [2] and [41].

38 *R v O* [2011] EWCA Crim 2226 and *R v LZ* [2012] EWCA Crim 1867; *R v T(O)* [2013] EWCA Crim 2405; and *R v Y* [2015] EWCA Crim 123. These cases are of great historical significance as the Court accepted that, notwithstanding unequivocal guilty pleas these appellants should not have been prosecuted. The international law context meant that their convictions were unsafe. The basis for allowing these appeals arose for no fault of the practitioners or judges involved. Now they would be likely to be decided in a different way. The nuanced understanding of indicators of exploitation expected of those working in the criminal justice sector is now such that the facts of all of these cases would now be likely to imply criticism of those who failed to recognise that they might be exploitation victims. See also *AFU* (above).

39 See *TV v Spain* (App No 22512/21) and *BB v Slovakia* (App No 48587/21, 24 October 2024) and case commentary in Criminal Law Review 2025, Issue 2, p 93.

40 (2021) 73 EHRR 9.

41 [2022] EWCA Crim 106; [2022] 1 Cr App R 19; [2022] 1 WLR 404.

42 [2023] EWCA Crim 23; [2023] 1 Cr App R 16.

43 [2020] EWCA Crim 285.

44 [2020] EWCA Crim 1408.

45 [2018] EWCA Crim 1824; [2019] Cr App R 7, at [76(v)].

> 'As always, the question for this Court goes to the safety of the conviction. However, in the present context, that inquiry translates into a question of whether in the light of the law as it now is (this being a rare change in law case) and the facts now known as to the Applicant (having regard to the admission of fresh evidence) the trial court should have stayed the proceedings as an abuse of process had an application been made. This question can be formulated indistinguishably in one of two ways which emerge from the authorities: was this a case where either: (1) the dominant force of compulsion, in the context of a very serious offence, was sufficient to reduce the Applicant's criminality or culpability to or below a point where it was not in the Public Interest for her to be prosecuted? or (2) the Applicant would or might well not have been prosecuted in the Public Interest? If yes, then the proper course would be to quash the conviction. As explained in Joseph (Verna) at [20 iii)], the Court's power to stay is "a power to ensure that the State complied with its international obligations and properly applied its mind to the possibility of not imposing penalties on victims".'

13.40

In *AAD* it was emphasised that the jurisdiction was only 'special' on account of the particular sensitivity to be applied to VOT prosecutions. It is not, however, 'for the appellate court to substitute its own view, but rather to review the decision to prosecute by reference to considerations of including those of rationality and procedural fairness': *AFU* at [117]. As emphasised by the Court in *AAD* at [142(3)], 'decisions to prosecute are for the CPS. Decisions on disputed facts or evaluation of fact are for the jury.'

13.41

The abuse of process doctrine applies thus to both cases pre-dating enactment of the MSA 2015 and those that post-date the MSA 2015. It also applies to offences under Schedule 4 MSA 2015. However, the Court in *A*[46] reflected that before it would be deemed not in the public interest to prosecute an individual suspected of carrying out an offence included in Schedule 4; that a greater degree of continuing compulsion and absence of any reasonably available alternatives to the defendant would be required (at [64]).

13.42

On appeal:

A*ppropriate deference*' should be afforded to retrospective consideration by a prosecutor of whether a victim of trafficking would have been prosecuted: *R v Henkoma*[47].

46 [2020] EWCA Crim 1408.
47 [2023] EWCA Crim 808 at [38].

Failure to advise on statutory defence

13.43

Appeals against conviction have been founded on the ground that[48]:

(1) s 45 provided a defence; but

(2) the appellant's representatives overlooked its availability; and

(3) did not advise the appellant that he could have deployed the defence; and

(4) that deficient advice prompted the appellant to plead guilty; therefore

(5) the plea was equivocal or a nullity and the conviction unsafe.

13.44

These appeals mirror the appeals which followed the enactment of s 31 of the Immigration and Asylum Act 1999 (the provision providing a defence to refugees who commit certain document offences). That 'refugee defence' was frequently overlooked by representatives, who proceeded to advise clients to plead guilty, when the defence was available to them, without advising them about the defence[49]. Appeals founded on a failure to advise an appellant on s 31 and s 45 are a product of the statutory defence appearing in legislation separate from the legislation defining the offence. In *R v Dastjerti*[50] the Court of Appeal Criminal Division adopted a checklist for use by an appellate court determining whether a conviction was safe following a guilty plea, where it was alleged on appeal that a defendant had not deployed a defence which had been open to him[51].

13.45

Tailored to s 45(1) of MSA 2015 (the defence which applies for adults), the *Dastjerdi* checklist reads:

> '(1) That the applicant should have been advised about the possibility of availing himself of the [section 45] defence;
>
> (2) That the applicant was not so advised;
>
> (3) That, had [the applicant] been so advised, it was open to him to advance the defence;

48 See BTE [2022] EWCA Crim 1597.

49 See *R v Mateta* [2013] EWCA Crim 1372, [2014] 1 WLR 1516; and *R v AM, MV, RM and MN* [2010] EWCA Crim 2400, [2011] 1 Cr App R 35.

50 [2011] EWCA Crim 265 at [9].

51 The *Dasjerti* checklist was adapted to the facts of *R v PK* [2017] EWCA Crim 486 (Sir Brian Leveson P giving the judgment of the Court), *at* [13] *and R v Idahosa* [2019] EWCA Crim 1953, at [59]. *As with R v Dasjerti* itself, those cases concerned the refugee defence under s 31 of the Immigration and Asylum Act 1999.

(4) That the prospect that [the applicant] would have been able to advance such a defence were good'[52].

For full details of s 45, as applied to both adults and children, see **Chapter 10**.

13.46

R v Webb and Somerset-How[53] may provide a new focus for appealing against historical convictions under MSA 2015, s 1. If a trial judge directed a jury that 'domination' alone sufficed for a servitude conviction without proving a distinct 'service element', that conviction may be unsafe. Practitioners should review past cases where coercive control was present but traditional forced labour was not.

Appeal following a guilty plea in the Crown Court

13.47

Most of the notable cases which have been brought before the Court of Appeal Criminal Division to date concerning non-punishment of victims of human trafficking have been cases where the applicants entered guilty pleas. A guilty plea does not preclude an appeal against conviction. The court has allowed appeals against conviction following guilty pleas following flawed advice. Significantly, where the appeal relates to the public interest limb of the CPS Full Code not being applied, the fact that a guilty plea was unequivocal will not necessarily prevent a successful appeal[54].

13.48

In *R v Tredget*[55], the Court set out three categories of cases in which a conviction can be overturned notwithstanding a guilty plea had been entered:

(i) The first are cases in which the guilty plea is vitiated, which can occur in a range of circumstances including the appellant being under the influence of controlled drugs at the time he changed his plea, the plea being compelled by an adverse and incorrect ruling of law, the plea being vitiated by improper pressure from the judge, or the plea resulting from

---

52 See *R v AFU* at [99]; see also the submissions at [70]. 'Good' prospects is, it is suggested, shorthand for the court needing to find (pursuant *to R v Boal* (1992) 95 Cr. App. R. 272; [1992] Q.B. 591, CA; and *R. v PK* [2017] EWCA Crim 486; [2017] Crim. L.R. 716) that it was (at least) quite probable that the applicant would have been able (a) to adduce *some evidence* of *all* of the limbs of the defence and (b) that the prosecution would *not have been able to disprove to the criminal standard any one* of the following limbs of the defence. For another example of the modified *Dastjerdi* checklist being applied in the context of an alleged VOT, see *R v BRP* [2023] EWCA Crim 40.

53 [2025] EWCA Crim 1491.

54 See *R v O* [2011] EWCA Crim 2226 and *R v LZ* [2012] EWCA Crim 1867; *R v T(O)* [2013] EWCA Crim 2405; and *R v Y* [2015] EWCA Crim 123, discussed above; see also *R v AFU*.

55 [2022] EWCA Crim 108.

incorrect legal advice that deprived the defendant of a defence that quite probably would have succeeded such that a clear injustice had been done.

(ii) The second are cases where there is a legal obstacle to the appellant being tried, including cases where the prosecution amounts to an abuse of process.

(iii) The third is a 'small residual' category where it is established that the appellant did not commit the offence, 'in other words that the admission made by the plea is a false one'.

Fresh evidence

13.49

Section 23 of the Criminal Appeal Act 1968 ('CAA 1968') provides for the receipt of fresh evidence by the Court of Appeal Criminal Division. The admission of evidence under this section is at the Court's discretion and evidence will be admitted if it is necessary or expedient in the interests of justice (s 23(1)). The Court also has powers under s 23(1)(a) to order for the production of any document or exhibit which appears to them necessary for determination of the case; and under s 23(1A) order any witness to attend for examination and to be examined before the Court, regardless of whether they were called at first instance proceedings. Importantly, in considering whether to receive any evidence the Court has regard to factors within s 23(2) which include:

(a) whether the evidence appears to the Court to be capable of belief;

(b) whether it appears to the Court that the evidence may afford any ground for allowing the appeal;

(c) whether the evidence would have been admissible in the proceedings from which the appeal lies on an issue which is the subject of the appeal; and

(d) whether there is a reasonable explanation for the failure to adduce the evidence in those proceedings.

13.50

It is important within the grounds of appeal to set out what fresh evidence is sought to be introduced in the appeal and how it is said that the constituent ingredients within s 23(2) CAA 1968 have been satisfied. **Chapters 9** and **10** set out the types of expert evidence relevant to appeals brought by victims of trafficking. A large proportion of fresh evidence in trafficking cases will be the competent authority trafficking identification decision (see **Chapter 4**), expert evidence adduced in support of an asylum claim and findings made by immigration tribunals and any witness statements served in those proceedings. All fresh evidence needs to be accompanied by a Form W with a supporting '*Gogana* statement'[56] setting out how this new evidence was obtained and why it was not deployed in the original Crown Court proceedings. Applications to adduce fresh evidence will now usually require inquiries by the court as to whether privilege has been waived. If not, then an explanation should be provided as to why it is not necessary. Recommendations to the single judge as to the steps to be followed in deciding whether to grant leave in out of time cases where 'fresh evidence' is said to apply, are set out in *R v Singh*[57]:

> '50. First, single judges faced with an application for leave to appeal based on fresh evidence, before making any decision, should inquire whether privilege has been waived and, if not, an explanation should be provided as to why it is not necessary.
>
> '51. Second, if an application reaches the single judge without a Respondent's Notice and the single judge would be assisted by one, the single judge should direct the Respondent to consider the application and submit a response.
>
> 52. Third, the single judge should not simply refer an application based on fresh evidence to the full court without any consideration. Once the single judge has ascertained the position from trial representatives and the Respondent, he or she may be able to determine whether the application is potentially arguable. If it is not, the application can be rejected at that stage. If it is potentially arguable, the single judge should normally not grant applications for leave or an extension of time but should refer them to the full court.
>
> 53. Fourth, if the single judge decides to refer an application to the full court, he or she should follow the course adopted by the single judge in this case and refer it for directions. The parties should then seek to agree those directions and submit them to the Registrar for approval by the court. Only if agreement cannot be reached should it be necessary for there to be an oral hearing in relation to them.'

13.51

When preparing an application for leave to appeal, the applicant's representatives should consider their duty of candour to the court, in disclosing material which may undermine their application. It is best practice to provide a condensed bundle of core fresh evidence material and annex any surplus material which may assist the Crown and Court.

56 *R v Gogana* (1999) Times, 12 July.
57 [2017] EWCA Crim 466.

13.52

The Crown will also need to consider their disclosure obligations for post-conviction cases. In *R (Nunn) v Chief Constable of Suffolk Constabulary*[58] the Supreme Court held that the common law duty of disclosure exists in addition to the statutory duty of trial disclosure created by the Criminal Procedure and Investigations Act 1996 ('CPIA 1996'). The basis of the common law duty is fairness, and what fairness requires varies depending on the stage reached by the proceedings. There is no basis for the submission that the full 'trial' duty of disclosure and investigation continues indefinitely: this would be contrary to the public interest in finality and to the need for finite police resources to be appropriately applied. The extent of the common law duty post-appeal is provided in the Attorney-General's Guidelines: any material coming to light that might cast doubt on the safety of the conviction should be disclosed. However, the Criminal Cases Review Commission can, in appropriate cases, make enquiry to see whether a reasonable prospect of a conviction being quashed can be demonstrated, which includes a power to direct new scientific tests and similar. Moreover, the police and prosecutors can choose to accede to representations for further enquiry made on behalf of convicted persons and should exercise sensible judgment in relation to such representations.

Expert evidence in appeals

13.53

The court's approach to receiving expert evidence has varied over the past decade. In *R v EK*[59] the court was prepared to admit evidence that an applicant was suffering from a 'freeze response' deriving from 'Stockholm Syndrome'. However, the court highlighted that when it came 'to the credibility of accounts given by an applicant or appellant, it is for a jury or this court to evaluate them. It is not the function of experts to do so. When it comes to the correctness of a decision to prosecute, expert evidence is ordinarily unlikely to assist.' After a number of cases in which the Court was prepared to attach greater weight to expert evidence supporting an identification of trafficking status and circumstances of criminal exploitation[60], in *R v. AAD*[61] the Court reaffirmed that expert evidence has to be 'truly expert' and deal with issues 'outside the knowledge of the jury, such as providing 'context of a cultural nature'. The court rejected that evidence could be adduced purely because 'members of the jury have not shared the suggested experiences described by the defendant, noting

58 [2014] UKSC 37.

59 [2018] EWCA Crim 2961.

60 *See R v GB* [2020] EWCA Crim 2, [2020] 1 WLUK 128; *R v JXP* [2019] EWCA Crim 1280; *R v N* [2019] EWCA Crim 984, [2019] 6 WLUK 337; *R v S* [2019] EWCA Crim 1280; and *R v O* [2019] EWCA Crim 1389, [2019] 7 WLUK 537.

61 [2022] EWCA Crim 106; [2022] 1 Cr App R 19; [2022] 1 WLR 404, at [82] to [89].

that few juries would, for example, have been 'subjected…to duress leading to their participation in an armed robbery or will have found themselves caught up or involved in a city centre riot'.

13.54

Another example of admissible expert evidence on appeal includes psychiatric evidence. For example, fresh evidence that relates to the opinion of a psychiatrist as to a mental illness suffered at the time of the index offending may be of direct relevance to the safety of conviction, if it forms part of 'relevant characteristics' under s 45(5) MSA 2015.

13.55

When considering whether expert evidence might assist the Court of Appeal, similar considerations apply to those which apply in the Crown Court; see **Chapter 5**. It is crucial to ensure that an expert understands the limitations of his or her duty. One of the possible reasons for the Court of Appeal's reluctance to receive expert evidence is likely to have been that experts have provided an opinion on the 'ultimate issue' that an applicant is a VOT, rather than highlighting *indicia* of trafficking revealed through their expertise.

13.56

However, as observed by the Court of Appeal[62] the application of the 'ultimate issue rule' is vexed. Lord Taylor LCJ stated:

> 'The rationale behind the supposed prohibition is that the expert should not usurp the functions of the jury. But since counsel can bring the witness so close to opining on the ultimate issue that the inference as to his view is obvious, the rule can only be … a matter of form rather than substance. In our view, an expert is called to give his opinion and he should be allowed to do so. It is, however, important that the Judge should make clear to the jury that they are not bound by the expert's opinion, and that the issue is for them to decide'.

Decisions of Competent Authority

13.57

At trial, reasonable grounds and conclusive grounds decisions of the Competent Authority are not admissible[63] (see **Chapter 10**). However, in the context of appeals, the Court in *R v AAD*[64], in which the Registrar had directed that three

62 *R v Stockwell* (1993) 97 Cr App R 260.
63 See *R v Brecani* [2021] EWCA Crim 731; and *R v AAD* (above) at [90] to [106].
64 Above, at [81].

cases be listed together in a 'special court' with a view to providing further guidance in cases involving victims of trafficking, held:

> ' ... although the context and the issues will determine whether a conclusive grounds decision should be received in evidence in the Court of Appeal Criminal Division ..., there is no doubt that such decisions can potentially be adduced on an application for leave or an appeal. Section 23 provides the court with considerable flexibility in this regard ...'

13.58

The court found in *R v AAD* that this was not inconsistent with the decision in *R v Brecani*[65] This approach also accorded with the decision of the court in *R v AAJ*[66], which observed in this context at [39]:

> '(vii) The decision of the competent authority as to whether or not a person has been trafficked for the purpose of exploitation is not binding on the court, but, unless there is evidence to contradict it or significant evidence that has not been considered, it is likely that the courts will respect the decision; ...'[67].

13.59

While not binding on the CACD, 'clear reasons' are needed to depart from such a decision; see *VCL and AN v the United Kingdom*[68].

13.60

In *R v JXP*[69], the court considered the fact that the Competent Authority was a specialist authority with particular expertise and knowledge in the area of trafficking. In that case, it considered that the minute set out in considerable detail the applicant's account. It clearly analysed whether that account met the requirements of trafficking and concluded that it did. The court therefore accorded weight to the decision of this 'specialist authority.'

13.61

In contrast, in *R v V*[70], the court of accepted a submission that a decision minute was wholly lacking in an analysis of the evidence that pointed towards or against the applicant's assertions about his circumstances and the extent to which he was forced to remain at the property and forced into criminality, but

65 [2021] EWCA Crim 731.
66 [2021] EWCA Crim 1278.
67 At [39]; see in this context *R v AFU* [2023] EWCA Crim 23, at [88].
68 (2021) 73 E.H.R.R. 9, at [162]; and see *R v Brecani*, at [65]; and *R v AAD*, at [102]. In *Brecani* and *AAD* the expression 'good reason', rather than 'clear reasons' was used.
69 [2019] EWCA Crim 1280.
70 [2020] EWCA Crim 1355.

rather recounted the applicant's account and accepted it. As a result the material aspect of the decision could be regarded as lacking cogency and carrying little weight, whether it was admitted in evidence or not.

Oral evidence of the appellant

13.62

It has become increasingly common for the respondent to an appeal to submit that the applicant should give oral evidence in order to be cross examined on the contents of a witness statement they have made in support of the appeal and to allow the Court of Appeal to reach credibility findings on matters pertinent to the value of the fresh evidence relied on for an appeal.

13.63

In *R v AAD*, the Court held that:

> 'if the suggested trafficking is based, for instance, on unsatisfactory and untested hearsay evidence from the appellant, the court may express the view that it would be preferable for the appellant to give evidence for the proper resolution of the issues on the appeal, thereby enabling his or her account to be appropriately tested'[71].

13.64

Before the hearing of an appeal (usually an application for leave to appeal listed as a rolled up hearing where the application for leave to appeal and appeal against conviction will be heard concurrently) it is likely to assist the parties and the court if advocates for the applicant and respondent liaise as to the aspects of the applicant's evidence which are to be the subject of challenge in cross examination. They parties should consider whether special measures or ground rules are necessary. Cases have been listed to assist possible victims of exploitation so as to enable them to give evidence. Should any interpreter be required for the appeal hearing; or application for an intermediary be sought, then such applications should be made well in advance of the appeal hearing and form part of any directions hearing.

McCook correspondence

13.65

The guidance by the Lord Chief Justice in *R v McCook*[72] makes clear that in any case where fresh representatives are instructed to advise on appeal, it is

71 At [108].
72 [2014] EWCA Crim 734.

necessary for them to approach the solicitors and/or counsel who acted in the Crown Court to ensure that the factual basis upon which the grounds are premised is correct. As soon as grounds are drafted, it is best practice to send a copy of the draft grounds of appeal to the previous legal representatives. *McCook* correspondence should be provided in both appeals against conviction and sentence. Even if no criticism is made of previous representatives' conduct, *McCook* correspondence needs to take place for the reasons set out in *R v McGill*[73]:

> 'new advocates instructed in a case whether or not they believe the grounds involve criticism of the trial representatives, must make all proper and diligent enquiries of previous counsel, advocates and solicitors, so that they have all the information properly to understand what took place prior to and during the trial.'

13.66

As the Court in *R v Grant-Murray*[74] highlighted:

> 'it is a wholly inadequate compliance with this duty to send the lawyers instructed at the trial the grounds of appeal and to ask for comments. Inevitably the application will be made sometime after the trial and those representing the applicant at the trial must have identified for them the issues that relate to the conduct of the trial which are relevant to the appeal. Specific questions must be formulated and specifically put. Some questions will simply be for information that is not apparent from the papers. In other cases there will be implicit criticism; in such a case there can be no shying away from putting fairly and squarely the implicit criticism of those then acting for the applicant at the trial so that the appellate court has all the information before it when it commences the consideration of the application. The fact that a trial lawyer might have retired or left the profession to take up office or for some other reason does not excuse the newly instructed advocate from pursuing such inquiries with that person.'

13.67

Any application lodged by fresh representatives should be accompanied by a declaration that due diligence in accordance with *McCook* has been complied with and must be confirmed within the form NG and grounds of appeal.

13.68

Questions to previous representatives will be case-specific and dependent on the grounds being argued, however, examples of types of questions to include:

73 [2017] EWCA Crim 1228 at [13].
74 [2017] EWCA Crim 1228; para [133].

- What advice, if any, was given to the applicant regarding an NRM referral?
- What representations, if any, were made to the CPS to review the prosecution?
- Was the applicant advised that he had a potential defence pursuant to s 45 of the MSA 2015?
- What were the terms of any advice that was given to the applicant?
- Was any consideration given to a potential abuse of process application being made?

Appeal against sentence

13.69

Under the Criminal Appeal Act 1968 ('CAA 1968'), s 9, a defendant may appeal to the Court of Appeal against a sentence imposed by the Crown Court on indictment[75]:

> '(3) On an appeal against sentence the Court of Appeal, if they consider that the appellant should be sentenced differently for the offence for which he was dealt with by the Court below may—
>
> (a) quash any sentence or order which is the subject of the appeal; and
>
> (b) in place of it pass such a sentence or make such an order as they think appropriate for the case and as the court below had the power to pass or make when dealing with him for the offence,
>
> but the Court shall so exercise their powers under this subsection that, taking the case as a whole, the appellant is not more severely dealt with on appeal than he was dealt with by the court below'[76].

13.70

In *R v L*[77] the Lord Chief Justice recognised the spectrum of culpability or criminality of victims of trafficking that applied. The court emphasised, at para 14, that offences committed which were unconnected with the status of an individual as a victim of trafficking could still amount to mitigation:

75 In certain circumstances a defendant may appeal against sentence imposed by the Crown Court following conviction in the magistrates' court, including summary offences sent to the Crown Court under the Criminal Justice Act 1988, s 41.

76 Criminal Appeal Act 1968, s 11(3).

77 [2013] EWCA Crim 991, [2014] 1 All ER 113.

> 'These defendants are not safeguarded from prosecution or punishment for offences which were unconnected with the fact that they were being or have been trafficked, although we do not overlook that the fact that they have been trafficked may sometimes provide substantial mitigation.'

13.71

This spectrum of culpability was again highlighted in *R v L*, at [33], where the Court said that 'due allowance [was] to be made in the sentencing decision for their diminished culpability.'

13.72

It is possible that victims will not be recognised as victims of human trafficking during sentencing, they may not have been referred into the NRM at that stage, and therefore no mitigation evidence concerning trafficking would have been placed before the sentencing court. It is possible for the Court of Appeal to consider material which the sentencing judge did not have access to, or which was not in existence at the time.

13.73

Even in cases where the criminality is not directly linked to exploitation, or in cases where an MSA 2015, s 45 defence would not apply (see **Chapter 10**), it may be possible to appeal against a sentence where fresh evidence regarding the defendant's victim status has come to light.

13.74

In general, the Court will be prepared to consider fresh evidence concerning the trafficking status of an applicant/appellant and the principles within s 23 of the CAA 1968 need to be considered, if fresh material is being sought to be introduced on appeal. A cogent explanation is, in practice, needed as to why the evidence was not placed before the Crown Court.

13.75

While this would be an exceptional course in practice, the court could order a probation report where it felt it would assist, even in cases where no previous report was prepared in the Crown Court.

Grounds of appeal against sentence

13.76

When making an application for leave to appeal against sentence, an applicant should include the ground on which the sentence is being challenged, eg 'manifestly excessive' or 'wrong in principle'.

13.77

Sentencing Council Guidelines, for example, those relating to possession of a controlled drug with intent to supply[78], set out that one factor indicating 'lesser role' in relation to culpability includes 'involvement through naivety, immaturity or exploitation.'

13.78

It is important to note when dealing with victims of trafficking, a reduction in sentence may impact upon other proceedings, such as deportation proceedings; especially if the sentence imposed is one of over 12 months' imprisonment.

13.79

Following the coming into force of s 32 UK Borders Act 2007, it is unusual for recommendations for deportation to be imposed. However in cases where a Crown Court judge does pass a recommendation for deportation, it is important to note that such recommendation in itself can be the subject of an appeal against sentence.[79].

Extensions of time

13.80

An application for leave to appeal must be lodged no later than 28 days after the conviction or sentence the subject of the appeal.[80] The Court has the power to grant an extension of time if it decides there is merit to the application for leave. A significant number of appeals brought by victims of trafficking against their convictions are brought out of time and therefore an application for an extension of time must be set out in the body of the grounds and set out in form NG. In most instances there will be new lawyers instructed to advise on appeal; the investigation of the facts by the new representatives and preparation of the grounds of appeal and application for leave to appeal out of time will usually take a considerable time. However, there is always a need to show expedition. It is important to set out either within the body of the grounds the steps taken to prepare the application for leave to appeal, or for solicitors to set out a chronology in Criminal Justice Act 1967, s 9 format to serve with the application to justify the extension of time needed.

78 Sentencing Guideline in relation to Drug Offences effective from 1st April 2021 – https://www.sentencingcouncil.org.uk/offences/crown-court/item/supplying-or-offering-to-supply-a-controlled-drug-possession-of-a-controlled-drug-with-intent-to-supply-it-to-another/

79 See *R v Kluxen and others* [2010] EWCA Crim 1081.

80 Criminal Appeal Act 1968, s 18(2) and Crim PR 39.2.

13.81

Where an application for leave to appeal against conviction is founded on a change in law or a change in understanding of the law, a 'substantial injustice' must be shown to warrant the grant of exceptional leave[81].

13.82

In cases concerning trafficked victims it has historically been possible to overcome the hurdle of showing that exceptional leave should be granted. However, where an application for leave to appeal against conviction arises because the law has changed, or because there has been a change in practitioners' and the courts' understanding of the law since the conviction, the test for granting exceptional leave to appeal out of time is different. If leave to appeal is sought out of time on the ground that a guilty plea led to an unsafe conviction because an applicant failed to reveal his trafficking status or that the applicant's representative failed to identify his trafficking status and/or failed to take steps to invoke the non-prosecution protection regime or failed to deploy a s 45, MSA 2015 defence, leave will be granted where there is a 'clear injustice' (see *R v Mateta*[82] and *R v Boal*)[83].

13.83

The significance of the difference between the *Mateta* and *Boal* 'clear injustice' test and the 'substantial injustice' test was laid bare in *R v Ordu*[84]. This was not a trafficking case but a document offence case in which the refugee defence under s 31 of the Immigration and Asylum Act 1999 ('s 31') had been available to the applicant. However, the applicant had pleaded guilty to the offence, not having been advised properly about the existence of that defence. He had had a good defence under s 31. The plea was equivocal. It was conceded by the Crown that – if leave to appeal were granted – a 'clear injustice' could be shown and that the conviction would be unsafe. However, the failure to appreciate the law by the applicant's representative in the Crown Court was a product of the law changing – so that by the time of the appeal the scope of s 31 was clearer than it had been at the time. Therefore, because of that change in the understanding of the law, before the appeal could be considered, the applicant had, first, to secure leave by showing a 'substantial injustice'. The applicant could not show a substantial injustice and leave was refused. See also *Musa*[85].

81 See *R v Jogee* [2017] AC 387, [2016] 1 Cr App Rep 31; and *R v Johnson* [2016] EWCA Crim 1613, [2017] 1 Cr App Rep 12 (the well-known joint enterprise authorities).
82 [2013] EWCA Crim 1372, [2014] 1 WLR 1516.
83 [1992] QB 591.
84 [2017] EWCA Crim 4; [2017] 1 Cr App R 21; [2017] Crim. LR 396.
85 2024] EWCA Crim 307.

13.84

When considering what cases might be 'change in law' cases for the purposes of an application for leave to appeal against conviction based on a defendant's exploitation status having been overlooked, *R v GS*[86] is important. This was a case where the applicant contended, he should not have been prosecuted in the public interest as a victim of trafficking. The Court, when dealing with a conviction dating back to 2007, considered that there had been a material change in the legal recognition of the rights of VOTs between 2007 and 2018. It considered there to have been limited awareness of such rights at the time and that the detailed provisions of Art 26 of ECAT and Art 8 of the EU Directive had not been in force. Furthermore, it held the contrast between the 2007 and 2013 CPS Guidance was stark. In the court's view, it could not be argued that the law and practice as understood in 2007 would have led to a conclusion that it was an abuse of process to proceed with the prosecution but looked at through the later understanding of the law and procedure, an abuse of process argument would or might well have succeeded. Because the case turned on the change in understanding of law, the court held that exceptional leave would need to be shown, namely that to refuse leave would cause 'substantial injustice'.

13.85

This approach to the grant of leave to appeal out of time should be contrasted with similar cases where legal advice was deficient, but not because of a change in law or a change in the understanding of law: in *R v K(P)*[87]. it was said *obiter* that all that was necessary for the grant of leave to appeal out of time was for an applicant to show that there would be a clear injustice. This was approved in *R v H*[88] as part of the ratio decidendi of the decision.

13.86

This accords with the Court of Appeal's approach to appeals where s 31 has been overlooked by representatives because of negligent omission, as opposed to an omission in advice exposed by a change in the understanding of the law[89]. It also accords with the Court of Appeal's approach to the safety of convictions in trafficking cases in the Court of Appeal Criminal Division, where the issue on appeal has been confined to ignorance of the non-prosecution procedure; see Chapter 5.

86 [2018] EWCA Crim 1824.
87 [2017] EWCA Crim 486.
88 20 October 2017 (CAO Reference 201604765B5).
89 See the approach to the individual appeals in *R v Mateta* [2013] EWCA Crim 1372, [2014] 1 WLR 1516.

13.87

R v O[90] was a 2019 case, which concerned a nine-year-old-conviction. The Court considered that the appeal did not turn on a 'change in law'. Unlike in *R v S(G)*, the conviction was unsafe because the CPS would (or might well) have decided not to maintain O's prosecution had they properly applied the 2007 CPS Guidance. The outcome of the decision on appeal did not turn on any change in law between 2007 and the date of the application. Therefore, 'exceptional leave' was not required. An extension of time was granted: the appellant had been refused indefinite leave to remain in the UK as a direct consequence of her convictions; it was only this which had alerted her to a potential criminal appeal against conviction.

13.88

Plainly there is a different threshold for appeals based on a change in law and those based on inadequate advice. Therefore, if an applicant can show that a conviction is based on inadequate advice, it is easier to secure leave: while some exceptionality should be shown, it is not necessary to show 'substantial injustice'.

13.89

In *R v Khodamoradi*[91], the Court emphasised that applications for extensions of time must be supported by evidence, irrespective of whether the Respondent opposes an extension being granted.

Further applications that may be made with an application for leave to appeal

Applications for bail on appeal

13.90

Either the Single Judge or the Full Court can grant bail pending an appeal in exceptional circumstances, where it is necessary to do justice in the case[92]. The application should be made at the same time as the application for leave or prior to leave being determined. The Crown Court can also grant bail if, exceptionally, it certifies the case as fit for appeal[93].

90 [2019] EWCA Crim 1389 at [41].
91 [2022] EWCA Crim 37.
92 Criminal Appeal Act 1968, ss.19 and 31(2)(e).
93 Senior Courts Act 1981, s.81(1)(f).

13.91

The application should be made with a Form B and ensure compliance with Crim PR r 39.8. In exceptional cases, where the applicant's sentence is short or he is in very ill health, then a note should be sent to the Registrar, highlighting the immediate issues, particularly if the VOT has any mental health issues. If bail is being applied for, practitioners should liaise with the relevant first responder and support organisation where appropriate to ensure a suitable bail address can be put forward (see **Chapters 5** and **12** for further considerations regarding bail).

Anonymity for applicants in the Court of Appeal Criminal Division

13.92

Reporting restrictions operate to restrict what the media can report what has been said in open court; as opposed to anonymity orders which restrict what is said in open court. Requests for anonymity should always be considered when making an application for leave to appeal where the applicant is a VOT. The main issues to consider in assessing principles governing anonymity orders in criminal appeals can be found within *R v Baniulyte*[94] (see **Chapter 8** for the full guidance)and *R v L; R v N*[95]. An applicant's VOT status does not trigger automatic anonymity. The Court of Appeal continues to deal with applications for anonymity on a case-by-case basis.

13.93

Automatic lifetime reporting restrictions apply to all 'victims' of section 2 (human trafficking) offences, but not those who are victims of section 1 offences, under s 2(1)(db) Sexual Offences (Amendment) Act 1992. However, such automatic reporting restrictions are rarely, if ever, applied to defendants who set out within their defence that they are victims of human trafficking offences. Defence practitioners should be alert to the fact that their clients may be entitled to anonymity.

General principles viz concerning anonymity orders

13.94

Consideration should be given to the potential risk to the victim of exploitation of publishing their name and whether to do so might engage European Convention on Human Rights protections, in particular, those under Arts 2

94 [2025] EWCA Crim 1205.
95 [2017] EWCA Crim 2129. See *R v AFU* [2023] EWCA Crim 23; [2023] 1 Cr App R 16, at [1].

(right to life), 3 (prohibition on torture), 4 (prohibition on slavery and forced labour (ie re-trafficking)) or 8 (right to respect for private and family life), or protections under ECAT and/or the EU Trafficking Directive (see Chapter 8).

13.95

Where such a risk of harm is ruled to outweigh ECHR, Art 10 and open justice, a practice has developed in the Court of Appeal Criminal Division whereby the name of the applicant is 'withheld' (not mentioned) in the proceedings and an order is made under the Contempt of Court Act 1981, s 11 prohibiting the publication of their name in connection with the proceedings. Section 11 of the Contempt of Court Act 1981 provides that:

> 'In any case where a court (having power to do so) allows a name or other matter to be withheld from the public in proceedings before the court, the court may give such directions prohibiting the publication of that name or matter in connection with the proceedings as appear to the court to be necessary for the purpose for which it was so withheld.'

13.96

The interplay between the withholding of a name or other matter and s 11 is explored further in paras **13.105** et seq, below.

13.97

A leading authority dealing with anonymity orders by reason of risk to the appellant is the decision of the Supreme Court in *A v BBC*[96] which involved an application by the BBC to set aside an anonymity order. Lord Reed, giving the only judgment, explained the general approach as follows:

> '47 … the right to receive and impart information, which is guaranteed by article 10(1), may be engaged where measures are taken in relation to court proceedings to prevent information from becoming publicly available. The right guaranteed by article 10(1) is however qualified by article 10(2) …
>
> 48 These qualifications reflect the fact that freedom of expression may conflict with other important values, including the rights to life and to bodily security protected by articles 2 and 3 of the Convention, the integrity of legal proceedings and the rights of litigants and accused persons, protected by article 6, and the right to respect for private life, protected by article 8 . Where there is a conflict between the right of the media to report legal proceedings and the rights of litigants or others under a guarantee which is itself qualified, such as article 8, a balance

96 [2014] UKSC 25, [2015] AC 588.

must be struck, so as to ensure that any restriction upon the rights of the media, on the one hand, or of the litigants or third parties, on the other hand, is proportionate in the circumstances. Lord Steyn in *In re S (A Child) (Identification: Restrictions on Publication)* [2004] UKHL 47; [2005] 1 AC 593, and by Lord Rodger in *In re Guardian News and Media Ltd* [2010] UKSC 1; [2010] 2 AC 697.

49 Where the conflict is between the media's rights under article 10 and an unqualified right of some other party, such as the rights guaranteed by articles 2, 3 and 6(1), there can be no derogation from the latter. Care must nevertheless be taken to ensure that the extent of the interference with the media's rights is no greater than is necessary. The need for such care reflects the important role of the media in a democratic society in scrutinising the administration of justice generally, as well as their role as the conduit of information about particular proceedings which may be of public interest.

50 Article 10(2) specifically identifies "maintaining the authority and impartiality of the judiciary" as a legitimate aim which may justify interference with freedom of expression.'

13.98

Note there is no balancing exercise to be conducted between Art 3 and Art 10 in contrast to the Art 8/Art 10 balancing exercise.

13.99

Anonymity orders and other regulation of the court's procedures, pursuant to inherent or Human Rights Act 1998 ('HRA 1988') powers, concern restrictions that a court can impose on what may be said in open court, whilst reporting restrictions concern what the media can report about what has already been aired in open court. As was recognised in *Khuja (formerly known as PNM) v Times Newspapers Ltd*[97], 'The distinction between these two aspects [of open justice] is not always recognised in the case law'[98]. In *D (In the matter of D)*[99], Dyson J held that the same test applies both for conducting proceedings 'in camera' (i.e. excluding the public) and for imposing reporting restrictions although that '*same test could be more easily satisfied where anonymity is sought than where what is applied for is that the proceedings be held in camera*'.

13.100

Recognising that open justice has never been absolute, the Supreme Court in *Khuja* set out examples of the historic exceptions to open justice, in the context

97 [2017] UKSC 49, [2017] 3 WLR 351 at [16].
98 See *R v N; R v L* [2012] EWCA Crim 189, [2013] QB 379, at [12].
99 1 CCLR 190.

of the court regulating its procedures, in particular the inherent power to sit in private. The Court stated that:

> 'The inherent power of the courts extends to making orders for the conduct of the proceedings in a way which will prevent the disclosure in open court of the names of parties or witnesses or of other matters, and it is well established that this may be a preferable alternative to the more drastic course of sitting in private: see *R v Socialist Worker Printers and Publishers Ltd, ex p Attorney General* [1975] QB 637, 652; *Attorney General v Leveller Magazine Ltd* [1979] AC 440, 451–452 (Lord Diplock), 458 (Viscount Dilhorne), 464 (Lord Edmund-Davies)'[100].

13.101

As far as the criminal courts are concerned, the Supreme Court confirms later in that same paragraph that:

> '…the court retains the power which it has always possessed to allow evidence to be given in such a way that the identity of a witness or other matters is not more widely disclosed in open court, if the interests of justice require it. Where a court directs that proceedings before it are to be conducted in such a way as to withhold any matter, the Contempt of Court Act 1981, s 11 allows it to make ancillary orders preventing their disclosure out of court. Measures of this kind have consistently been treated by the European Court of Human Rights as consistent with article 6 of the Convention if they are necessary to protect the interests of the proper administration of justice: *Doorson v The Netherlands* (1996) 22 EHRR 330, para 71; *V v United Kingdom* (1999) 30 EHRR 121, para 87; cf *A v British Broadcasting Corpn* [2015] AC 588, paras 44–45 (Lord Reed).'

13.102

Importantly, the Supreme Court confirmed 'that necessity remains the touchstone of this jurisdiction'[101]. The court stated (at [15]) that two factors have combined to broaden the scope of the exceptions to the open justice principle, namely civil and criminal litigation raising issues of national security and the recognition of rights derived from the ECHR, which by the HRA 1998, s 6, bind the courts as public authorities. In relation to the latter, the Supreme Court said:

> 'The Convention right most often engaged in such cases is the right under article 8 to respect for private and family life. Article 8 rights are heavily qualified by the Convention itself, and even when they are made good they must be balanced in a publication case against

100 At para [14].
101 At para [14].

> the right to freedom of expression protected by Article 10. But other Convention rights may occasionally be engaged which are practically unqualified, such as the right to life under article 2 and to protection against serious ill-treatment under Article 3: *A v British Broadcasting Corpn* [2015] AC 588. These countervailing interests have become significant, not just because they have come to be recognised as legal rights, but because the resonance of what used to be reported only in the press and the broadcasting media has been greatly magnified in the age of the internet and social media'.

13.103

An anonymity order can usually only be justified where it is strictly necessary. As Lord Roger indicated in *Re Guardian News and Media Ltd*[102]:

> '… in an appropriate case, where threats to life or safety are involved, the right of the press to freedom of expression obviously has to yield: a newspaper does not have the right to publish information at the known potential cost of an individual being killed or maimed. In such a situation the court may make an anonymity order to protect the individual'.

13.104

Insofar as the HRA 1998 is concerned, Lord Roger in his judgment in *Re Guardian News and Media Ltd*[103] addressed anonymity orders giving effect to ECHR rights as follows:

> 'States are, of course, obliged by Articles 2 and 3 to have a structure of laws in place which will help to protect people from attacks on their lives or assaults, not only by officers of the state but by other individuals. Therefore, the power of a court to make an anonymity order can be seen as part of that structure'.

13.105

See also *Re Trinity Mirror plc*[104] by way of example, in which the power was also said to arise from the HRA 1998, s 6.

Anonymity orders in criminal appeals

13.106

Anonymity is achieved in the Court of Appeal Criminal Division through the interplay of the power under common law and/or the HRA 1998,

102 [2010] UKSC 1, [2010] 2 AC 697 at para 26.
103 [2010] UKSC 1, [2010] 2 AC 697 at para 26.
104 [2008] EWCA Crim 50, [2008] QB 770 at para 26.

s 6 to cause the name of the appellant not to be mentioned during the appeal hearing and the further power under the Contempt of Court Act 1981, s 11 prohibiting the publication of that name in connection with the proceedings[105] (see above). It is therefore essential, if a s 11 order is to be sought, that an application for anonymity is made before the hearing, so that the case can be called on by a cypher assigned to the case and not by the name of the applicant. Anonymity is in that way preserved until the application is considered by the Full Court.

13.107

The Court of Appeal in *R v L; R v N*[106] considered that in light of the need for consistency and the UK's obligations generally it would be desirable in principle for the Criminal Division of the Court of Appeal to follow the practice adopted in the Civil Division and Immigration Tribunal of anonymising the applicant in cases raising asylum and international protection issues. However, the court (as set out above) declined to give guidance, without argument from the press because of the importance of open justice in criminal proceedings.

13.108

The court considered whether the applicants' Arts 2 and 3 rights were or were potentially engaged. On balance the court decided that anonymity should be afforded for these victims of trafficking. If their accounts were accepted, they may have a genuine or well-founded fear of reprisals on them or on their families at home. Additionally, the court found that if it did not grant anonymity, it would undermine the anonymity orders in the Immigration Tribunal and in related Administrative Court proceedings.

13.109

Consideration needs to be given as to whether the applicant was a victim of trafficking for sexual exploitation (see *R v O*[107] and *R v GB*)[108]. In *R v O*[109], the Court of Appeal granted anonymity based on the applicant's Art 3 rights being engaged, given the threats to kill and violence to which she was subjected and repercussions faced by her in Italy. The court considered both the risk to her, as well as her family. In *R v S(G)*[110], the court stressed that any application for anonymity 'should always be closely scrutinised and should not be granted unless strictly necessary.'

105 See *Khuja* (above) at [14].
106 [2017] EWCA Crim 2129.
107 [2019] EWCA Crim 1389.
108 [2020] EWCA Crim 2.
109 [2019] EWCA Crim 1389 at [3].
110 [2018] EWCA Crim 1824 at [5].

13.110

Although in *R v AAC*[111] the Court made an anonymity order on the basis that the Appellant had alleged that she was a victim of sexual offending and therefore fell within s 1 of the Sexual Offences (Amendment) Act 1992. The Court did not address the provisions of s 1(4) which exclude reporting of proceedings other than those related to the allegation: see *Beale*[112] at [14] and Sana Musharraf[113] at [15].

13.111

Considering the high hurdle that needs to be overcome before anonymity will be granted, consideration should also be given to lesser measures, such as aspects of reporting restrictions, which might serve to protect VOTs[114].

13.112

The checklist in *Marine A*[115] provides an essential tool for the application of anonymity principles (as reaffirmed in *Khuja* above). In *Marine A* the Court Martial board found Marine A guilty of murder[116] but acquitted Marines B and C. The judge advocate then lifted the prohibition on identification of the marines, on the ground that identification would not create or increase an immediate risk to their lives, although he stayed the order pending appeal. The marines applied for leave to appeal against the order lifting the prohibition on their identification and the media parties applied for leave to appeal against the rulings denying them access to the video clips and the stills which showed the fatal shooting of the victim, a wounded Afghan insurgent which had not been made available. In a joint judgment to which Lord Thomas of Cwmgeidd CJ and Tugendhat J contributed, the Court held:

> '84 … a defendant in a criminal trial must be named save in rare circumstances.
>
> 85 However, the court has a power to withhold the name and address of a defendant in cases where circumstances justify that …'

13.113

The Court went on to say under the heading 'A structured approach to restrictions on open justice in the reporting of criminal trials':

111 [2023] EWCA Crim 15.
112 [2017] EWCA Crim 1012.
113 [2022] EWCA Crim 678.
114 See *R v N*; *R v L* [2012] EWCA Crim 189, [2013] QB 379 at [15].
115 Although *R v Marine A* was not mentioned in *GL and N*, the court in *GL and N* was referred to it.
116 Later reduced to manslaughter on the ground of diminished responsibility.

'86 In our view, applications to restrict reporting of criminal proceedings should be approached in a structured way. For example, in considering whether reporting restrictions should be imposed, the Court of Appeal (Criminal Division) set out in *Ex p The Telegraph Group plc* [2001] 1 WLR 1983, para 22 a three-stage test. That was approved in *Independent Publishing Co Ltd v Attorney General of Trinidad and Tobago* [2005] 1 AC 190, para 69 by the Privy Council:

> "in considering whether it was 'necessary' both in the sense under section 4(2) of the 1981 Act of avoiding a substantial risk of prejudice to the administration of justice and therefore of protecting the defendants' right to a free trial under article 6 of the Convention and in the different sense contemplated by article 10 of the Convention as being 'prescribed by law' and 'necessary in a democratic society' by reference to wider considerations of public policy, the factors to be taken into account could be expressed as a three-part test; that the first question was whether reporting would give rise to a not insubstantial risk of prejudice to the administration of justice in the relevant proceedings, and if not that would be the end of the matter; that, if such a risk was perceived to exist, then the second question was whether a section 4(2) order would eliminate the risk, and if not there could be no necessity to impose such a ban and again that would be the end of the matter; that, nevertheless, even if an order would achieve the objective, the court should still consider whether the risk could satisfactorily be overcome by some less restrictive means, since otherwise it could not be said to be 'necessary' to take the more drastic approach; that, thirdly, even if there was indeed no other way of eliminating the perceived risk of prejudice, it still did not follow necessarily that an order had to be made and the court might still have to ask whether the degree of risk contemplated should be regarded as tolerable in the sense of being the lesser of two evils; and that at that stage value judgments might have to be made as to the priority between the competing public interests represented by articles 6 and 10 of the Convention …"

87 We consider that the court should approach the making of an order that a defendant be not identified in a similar way. The starting point is, in our judgment, the duty of the court, as a public authority, to ensure compliance with the principles (1) of open justice, and (2) that there be no interference with an individual's rights under articles 2 and 3, and (3) no unnecessary or disproportionate interference with (a) the rights of the public under article 10 (having regard to the position of the media under section 12 of the Human Rights Act 1998), and (b) of any relevant individuals under article 8.

88 As open justice is so important a principle, an order that a defendant be not identified will not be necessary if some other measure is available

to protect those rights of the individuals, and that other measure would be proportionate. In other cases, alternative measures have been taken, most notably in *Venables v News Group Newspapers Ltd* [2001] Fam 430. No order was made at the trial of Venables and Thompson that they be not named (there was an order restricting reporting of their names, which was lifted at the end of the trial). Subsequently those defendants changed their names, and orders were made to prohibit the disclosure of their identities under their new names.'

13.114

In the context of Art 8, ECHR, consideration should be given to *R (Marandi) v Westminster Magistrates' Court*[117] in relation to the threshold question of whether measure in question would amount to an interference with the claimant's right to respect for their private and family life. The next stage was a balancing exercise, on whether the consequences of disclosure would be so serious an interference with the claimant's rights that it was necessary and proportionate to interfere with the ordinary rule of open justice. In *SFO v Bluu Solutions Ltd*[118], the Court stressed at [27] that the question was not 'whether it is necessary to publish the identity of individuals in order for there to be proper public scrutiny of the approval process; rather it is the extent to which the individual seeking anonymity has established that it is necessary for the proper protection of his Article 8 rights that his identity continues to be withheld following his acquittal.'

Requests to expedite the hearing

13.115

VOT applicants are some of the most vulnerable. Practitioners should consider submitting a note attached to the application for leave to appeal highlighting that the case concerns a victim of modern slavery/trafficking and asking that the Registrar consider expediting the hearing. The Registrar has the power to refer the case to the full court immediately for a hearing, where the application for leave and final appeal can be determined together.

Applications for funding

13.116

When applying for leave to appeal, representatives must indicate on the form NG if they are applying for a funding certificate, which ordinarily will only be

117 [2023] EWHC 587 (Admin).
118 [2024] EWHC 500 (KB).

granted for counsel if leave is granted. See **Chapter 20** on funding. It is also possible for the court to grant a retrospective representation order, particularly where there has been continued involvement of the applicant's solicitor after lodging the application for leave to appeal[119].

Request for transcripts

13.117

It is likely in most cases where slavery or human trafficking is put forward as a ground of appeal that a transcript will have been obtained in preparation for making the application, particularly where there are new representatives. However, the Registrar routinely obtains copies of the summing up, sentencing remarks and the prosecution opening of the facts where relevant. If the application seeks any other transcripts of part of the proceedings, representatives should indicate why they are being requested[120].

Request for an oral leave hearing

13.118

An application for an oral hearing to argue grounds of appeal is rarely made and, if made, rarely, granted, although historically in cases concerning victims of human trafficking the court has allowed such applications.

Absconding/missing

13.119

It is important to appreciate that there are risks of a victim of trafficking applicant being re-trafficked. The Court of Appeal, Criminal Division, provided guidance as to the approach to be taken when defendants' representatives apply for leave to appeal or appeal against conviction and/or sentence in circumstances where the defendant has absconded during the appeal process. First, it allows legal representatives to lodge appeals even in the absence of their clients, providing that they have actual or implied authority or where, in any event, the court may wish to intervene in the public interest. It is, however, incumbent upon representatives to notify the Registrar of the position. In *R v Okedare*[121], the applicant went missing/absconded before the application for leave to appeal against conviction was lodged. The court considered that he 'may well have been

119 *R v Singh* [2017] EWCA Crim 466.
120 Crim PR, r 5.5.
121 [2014] EWCA Crim 228, [2014] 1 WLR 4071.

re-trafficked or simply absconded.' There had been written consent provided to the defence representatives from that appellant that he wished to appeal against the conviction. This consent was in the absence of anything to suggest that the applicant wished to withdraw his appeal. The court, in assessing the case, said that 'in any event there remains the possibility that his disappearance was not his fault'. On account of this, the Court of Appeal considered that it had no option but to stay the application for permission to appeal *sine die*[122], until the applicant was able to satisfy the evidential requirements as to whether or not he had in fact been trafficked and/or whether he had been compelled to commit the offence.

13.120

If leave has been granted and a waiver of legal privilege has been signed, it is possible to continue with the determination of the appeal in the absence of the appellant. Representatives will, however, need to notify the court as to the applicant's status[123]. In circumstances where a victim of trafficking has absented himself, representatives should ensure they obtain evidence to submit to the court regarding the circumstances of the appellant going missing. For those appellants who are minors, the local authority and police will be engaged, and the appellant's legal team should obtain a crime reference number and information regarding the circumstances of the child going missing. Other evidence can be obtained from the support organisation or first responder involved in the care of the victim of trafficking.

13.121

If a missing victim of trafficking, whose appeal has been stayed, subsequently comes into contact with the authorities, the Court of Appeal and defence representatives will not automatically be made aware of this and the stay may be left in place for many years, even if the applicant is again known to the authorities. Many victims who have been re-trafficked will continue in a cycle of further criminalisation and prosecution. In cases that are adjourned *sine die*, the court may direct the police to put an intelligence marker against the applicant's details on the Police National Computer, so that in the event of an apprehension or arrest of the applicant the Court of Appeal and their representatives can be notified. The Court in *R v VSJ*[124] in relation to a missing applicant ('N') held that 'should he still be in this country and he comes to the attention of the police then this Court is to be notified forthwith so that these applications may be then heard as speedily as possible'. The court relisted N's case in November 2018 to reconsider whether the adjournment *sine die* should continue. It determined that that was appropriate.

122 See also *R v Joseph* [2017] EWCA Crim 36, [2017] 1 WLR 3153.
123 *R v L* [2013] EWCA Crim 991, [2014] 1 All ER 113.
124 [2017] EWCA Crim 36, [2017] 1 WLR 3153.

Applications to the Criminal Cases Review Commission

13.122

The CCRC is a body corporate created under the auspices of the Criminal Appeal Act 1995[125]. It should consist of at least 11 commissioners, at least two thirds of whom must appear to the prime minister to have knowledge of the criminal justice system.

13.123

Where a person has been: (1) convicted on indictment in England and Wales; (2) sentenced following conviction; (3) found not guilty by reason of insanity; or (4) found to be under a disability, and that he did the act or made the omission charged against him the CCRC may refer the case to the Court of Appeal[126]. A reference is then taken as if leave to appeal had been granted by the Court of Appeal (see s 9(2) Criminal Appeal Act 1995). In addition, no extension of time is required post a referral by the CCRC (see *Malkinson*, at [36])[127].

13.124

Where a person has been convicted of an offence by a magistrates' court in England and Wales the CCRC may at any stage refer the conviction to the Crown Court. It may also refer any sentence imposed following the conviction to the Crown Court[128]. The reference to the Crown Court is treated as an appeal under the Magistrates' Courts Act 1980, s 108, even where the appellant had entered a guilty plea. It is not necessary to apply to vacate that plea. The plea is evidence that the prosecution may seek to adduce on the appeal, subject to the exclusionary discretion available to the court: *R (DPP) v Crown Court at Preston*[129]. The Crown Court cannot impose a more severe penalty than was originally imposed following the reference. It may grant bail pending the hearing.

13.125

The CCRC can only make a reference if[130]:

(i) the CCRC 'considers that there is a real possibility that the conviction, verdict, finding or sentence would not be upheld were the reference to be made';

125 Criminal Appeal Act 1995, s 8.
126 Criminal Appeal Act 1995, s 9.
127 [2023] EWCA Crim 954.
128 Criminal Appeal Act 1995, s 11.
129 [2023] EWHC 1957 (Admin).
130 Criminal Appeal Act 1995, s 13.

(ii) because of an argument, or evidence, not raised in the proceedings which led to the conviction, verdict, finding or sentence or in the case of a sentence, because of an argument on a point of law, or information, not raised; and an appeal has been determined or leave to appeal against it refused;

(iv) however, nothing prevents the CCRC from making a reference 'if it appears to the Commission that there are exceptional circumstances which justify making it'.

13.126

Exceptional circumstances can bypass the need for a previous appeal to have been made in relation to a conviction, verdict, finding or sentence. In *R v Mateta*[131] the Court of Appeal praised the CCRC for its work in identifying wrongful convictions in the context of refugees whose possible defences under the Immigration and Asylum Act 1999, s 31 had been overlooked. Four of the five cases in that combined appeal were CCRC references where the exceptionality provision had been invoked[132]. However, in *R v YY; R v Nori*[133] the Court of Appeal invited the CCRC to consider a 'triage system' so that the exceptional procedure was not deployed as a matter of routine in cases where a defence had been overlooked in the Crown Court, where the Registrar could refer the consideration of leave to the Full Court. This was by way of an '… attempt to ensure that those cases in which there is no available means of redress other than through the CCRC are investigated and dealt with as expeditiously as possible'[134]. The court noted that the exceptional procedure should be available to defendants seeking a reference to the Crown Court following a guilty plea in the magistrates' court because of the '… constraints put on the Crown Court (sitting on appeal) in relation to unequivocal pleas of guilty'[135].

13.127

The CCRC must have regard to matters including '… any application or representations made to the Commission by or on behalf of the person to whom it relates'[136]. Following *R v YY; R v Nori* it will almost invariably be appropriate for first appeals to be the subject of an application for leave to appeal to the Court of Appeal.

131 [2013] EWCA Crim 1372, [2014] 1 WLR 1516.
132 See para 57.
133 [2016] EWCA Crim 18, [2016] 1 Cr App Rep 435.
134 See paras 38–45.
135 See para 42 and the Magistrates' Courts Act 1980, s 108.
136 Criminal Appeal Act 1995, s 14(2).

13.128

Where an application is made to the CCRC, there is a form to complete which provides for details of the application to be set out[137], but it will assist the Commission and the prospective appellant if submissions akin to grounds of and an advice on appeal and a chronology are sent to the Commission, as this will (by the Criminal Appeal Act 1995, s 14(2)) inform the way the CCRC approaches the review of the case. From a practical perspective the case managers at the CCRC will provide advice on procedure. Exceptionally, it may be of assistance for the assigned Commissioner to meet with the applicant's legal representative. While there is no right to an 'oral hearing' before the CCRC, the Commission may decide that oral submissions to the Commission are appropriate[138].

13.129

Whether the CCRC sees fit to refer a case to the Court of Appeal (or Crown Court)[139] or not, it will prepare a statement of reasons[140]. An applicant aggrieved by the decision of the CCRC not to refer a case (or in relation to an interim issue) may be able to apply for permission to bring a judicial review in the event that the decision is unlawful in a public law sense (ie *Wednesbury* unreasonable, perverse, etc). It will rarely be the case that such a challenge will be successful, as there is a very high threshold for such challenges[141].

13.130

Representatives submitting applications to the CCRC should be alive to the power of the CCRC to conduct investigations for the Court of Appeal[142]. The Court of Appeal may direct the CCRC to conduct inquiries into matters directed to it and report back to the Court of Appeal. Such investigations may have broad scope and are not restricted to cases where a reference is applied for[143]. Practitioners should have in mind that the CCRC has the power to obtain '… a document or other material which may assist the Commission in the exercise of any of their functions'[144]. Where it is 'reasonable to do so', the Commission may require the appropriate person in relation to a public body to produce the document or other material to the Commission or to give the Commission access to it and take away the material to copy or take away a copy

137 https://ccrc.form.service.justice.gov.uk/?analytics=accepted.

138 *R v Criminal Cases Review Commission, ex p Pearson* [1999] 3 All ER 498, [2000] 1 Cr App Rep 141.

139 Should a referral to the Crown Court be made by the CCRC under s.11 Criminal Appeal Act 1995, part 34 of the Crim P.R. applies – see [9.5] above.

140 Criminal Appeal Act 1995, s 14(4) in respect of a positive decision to refer and s 14(6) in respect of a decision not to refer.

141 *R (on the application of Cleeland) v Criminal Cases Review Commission* [2009] EWHC 474 (Admin) at 48.

142 Under s.23A(1) of the Criminal Appeal Act 1968 or section 25A (1) of the 1980 Act.

143 Criminal Appeal Act 1995, s 15. See, eg, *Coles (unreported)* (960227313) 11 November 1997.

144 Criminal Appeal Act 1995, s 17.

of it. The Commission may also direct that person that the document or other material must not be destroyed, damaged, or altered.

13.131

The documents and other material include, in particular, items obtained or created during an investigation or proceedings relating to the case being considered by the CCRC and any other case which may be in any way connected with that case (whether or not any function of the Commission could be exercised in relation to that other case)[145]. The duty to comply with a CCRC requirement is not affected by secrecy or any limitation on disclosure[146].

Appeals by a prosecutor against a 'terminating' ruling

13.132

Section 58 of the Criminal Justice Act 2003 provides the prosecution with a right of appeal in relation to a 'terminating' or 'terminatory' ruling, namely a ruling where the prosecution agrees to the defendant's acquittal if the appeal is not successful.

13.133

The prosecution must inform the court that it intends to appeal or request an adjournment to consider whether to appeal, which will be until the next business day.

13.134

Leave to appeal can be sought from the trial judge immediately after the ruling or the granted adjournment (CrimPR r 38.5). Leave should only be granted where the judge considers there is a real prospect of success. If the judge expedites the appeal, then the notice and application to appeal (Form NG- Pros) must be served on the Crown Court, Registrar and every defendant affected by the ruling the next business day. If the judge does not expedite the appeal, the Crown has five days after telling the judge of the decision to appeal to serve the appeal notice.

13.135

The defence must provide grounds of opposition in a respondent's notice and serve this the next business day if the trial judge has expedited the appeal, or within five business days if not expedited.

145 Criminal Appeal Act 1995, s 17(3).
146 Criminal Appeal Act 1995, s 17(4).

13.136

R v DS[147] is an example of such an appeal in the context of a terminating ruling concerning a defendant VOT.

Appeals to the Supreme Court

13.137

Any party can appeal an adverse decision of the Court of Appeal (Criminal Division) to the Supreme Court, but only where the Court of Appeal certifies that their decision involves a point of law of general public importance and either the Court of Appeal or the Supreme Court grants permission to appeal[148]. An application for a certificate that a point of law of general public importance is involved and for leave to appeal must be made no more than 28 days after the Court of Appeal gives its decision or reasons for its decision. An application for leave to appeal to the Supreme Court must be made within 28 days of the Court of Appeal refusing to grant leave. Both Courts have the power to extend time[149].

13.138

The lack of a right to an oral hearing of an application for a certificate does not infringe Art 6 ECHR: *R v Steel*[150].

147 [2020] EWCA Crim 285.
148 Criminal Appeal Act 1968, s 34.
149 In each case, the 28 days includes the day of judgment hand-down, so it is in fact 27 days.
150 [2006] EWCA Crim 2000.

14 Trafficking, slavery, and extradition – the current legal landscape and obligations under Art 4 ECHR

Michelle Brewer, Amelia Nice, Hina Rai and Louise Willocx

Introduction[1]

14.1

With the rise of global organised crime[2], international cooperation in combating human trafficking, slavery, servitude, and forced or compulsory labour is essential. Extradition plays a vital role in that cooperation, facilitating the return of individuals to face prosecution or serve sentences, provided their fundamental rights are adequately protected.

14.2

This chapter does not aim to provide a procedural guide to extradition. Instead, it examines the potential relevance of Art 4 ECHR in extradition proceedings, focusing on the positive obligations that form the substantive core of the European Court of Human Rights' (ECtHR) jurisprudence in this area. These obligations may be engaged where there is a credible suspicion that the requested person is a victim of trafficking or modern slavery. As such, they are central to the Convention's protective framework and may have direct implications for the lawfulness of extradition in individual cases.

Structure of the chapter

14.3

- **Part 1** outlines the legal framework governing extradition in the United Kingdom.

1 The first and second editions of this chapter were authored by Mary Westcott.

2 'Modern slavery' is an umbrella term for slavery, servitude, and forced or compulsory labour. The terms 'trafficking, slavery and related offences' will be used throughout this chapter to refer to human trafficking and modern slavery. The legal definitions of these concepts are set out in **Chapter 1**.

- **Part 2** outlines the legal framework governing Modern Slavery in the United Kingdom.
- **Part 3** analyses the principles developed by the European Court of Human Rights (ECtHR), including the State's protective and procedural obligations under Art 4 ECHR and their expression in domestic legislation and jurisprudence.
- **Part 4** draws out the key principles emerging from existing extradition case law in which the requested person resists extradition on the grounds of being a victim of trafficking. It outlines the common issues raised and the arguments typically advanced in such cases, highlighting how courts have approached the interplay between Art 4 ECHR obligations and the extradition framework.
- **Part 5** considers where positive obligations under Art 4 ECHR may be relevant to issues arising in extradition cases.
- **Part 6** identifies and discusses common legal and procedural challenges arising in cases involving victims or potential victims of trafficking in the extradition context.

14.4

The risk arising on extradition of further trafficking, slavery or related offences is addressed to a very limited extent in this chapter; this analysis should be read alongside **Chapter 16** (International Protection). The scope of the delimitation of Art 4(3) ECHR is examined in **Chapter 1**. For a fuller treatment of the legal definitions of trafficking, slavery, and other Art 4 harms, as well as the UK's identification procedures, including the National Referral Mechanism (NRM), reference should be made to **Chapters 1** and **4**.

Part 1 The UK extradition framework and legal principles

Governing legislation: the Extradition Act 2003

14.5

Extradition in the UK is governed by a single codified Act: the Extradition Act 2003 ('the 2003 Act'). The Act separates its extradition partners into one of two categories: Category 1 and Category 2.

14.6

Part 1 of the Act deals with Category 1 territories (Part 1 cases), namely member states of the European Union (EU).

14.7

Part 2 of the Act deals with Category 2 territories (Part 2 cases), namely non-EU countries with whom the UK has a formal extradition arrangement[3].

Post-Brexit Changes: From EAW to the Trade and Cooperation Agreement (TCA)

14.8

For many years the UK's extradition arrangements with EU countries were based on a European Arrest Warrant (EAW) system pursuant to Part 1 of the 2003 Act[4].

14.9

Following the UK's exit from the EU, the Transition Period ended on 31 December 2020, and the EAW system ceased to apply.

14.10

As of 1 January 2021, a new agreement called the Trade and Cooperation Agreement (TCA) came into effect providing a streamlined arrangement seeking to achieve a broadly similar approach based on a warrant system[5]. The TCA refers to 'Arrest Warrants' (AW) rather than EAWs[6].

14.11

Where a requested person was arrested prior to 11pm on 31 December 2020, proceedings continue to be governed by the EAW framework[7]. EAWs issued before 31 December 2020 will still be valid in the UK and EU Member States but will be governed by the provisions ofTCA when the individual is eventually arrested and brought before the UK court.

3 See the Extradition Act 2003 (Designation of Part 2 Territories) Order 2003 for full list of countries.

4 The EA 2003, giving effect to the Council Framework Decision on the European Arrest Warrant and the surrender procedures between Member States of 13 June 2002 (2002/584/JHA) ('EAW Framework Decision'), the duty of consistent interpretation noted in *Assange v Swedish Prosecution Authority (Nos 1 and 2)* [2012] UKSC 22, [2012] 2 AC 471, and arguably more robustly since 1 December 2014, after the UK's opt-back into the Framework Decision under Protocol No 36 to the Treaty of Lisbon and Case C-105/03 *Criminal Proceedings against Pupino* [2006] QB 83.

5 As implemented by the European (Future Relationship) Act 2020.

6 ART 598 TCA.

7 Art 62 of the Withdrawal Agreement; *Polakowski v Westminster Magistrates' Court* [2021] EWHC53 (Admin).

Export and import extradition requests

14.12

Most extradition proceedings concern individuals arrested in this jurisdiction, wanted for prosecution or custodial punishment elsewhere, so-called 'export' extradition.

14.13

'Import' extradition requests issued from this jurisdiction, justifying arrest elsewhere and requesting extradition to our courts do not involve proceedings in open court, so will only become public during consequent criminal proceedings. In those circumstances, the interaction of the trafficking, slavery or related acts with extradition proceedings will either be dealt with in the requested state or this country during the criminal trial or both.

The designated central authorities

14.14

In England and Wales, the National Crime Agency ('NCA') is the designated 'Central Authority'[8] for the receipt and certification of AWs for Part 1 extradition requests. The UK Central Authority (UKCA) in the Home Office is the central authority for receiving Part 2 extradition requests from non-EU member states. The NCA has a power to refuse to certify an AW in very limited circumstances, particularly following the introduction of a proportionality test[9] under the TCA.

14.15

The NCA is a recognised First Responder under the National Referral Mechanism (NRM) and can refer potential victims into the NRM (see **Chapter 4**)[10]. Separately, the NCA has a statutory duty to notify the Home Office if it has reasonable grounds to believe a requested person is a victim of trafficking or modern slavery[11]. Where a referral is made into the NRM, they should be referred to the police. This can be on the victim's behalf if they give consent, or as a third party referral if they do not give consent. The police will then determine what action is appropriate, in line with Home Office Counting

8 EAW Framework Decision, Art 7.

9 TCA Art 597; s 157 Anti Social Behaviour, Crime and Policing Act 2014.

10 Home Office, *National referral mechanism guidance: adult (England and Wales)* (updated 30 September 2025) at [4] https://www.gov.uk/government/publications/human-trafficking-victims-referral-and-assessment-forms/guidance-on-the-national-referral-mechanism-for-potential-adult-victims-of-modern-slavery-england-and-wales#Section-1 accessed 14 October 2025.

11 MSA 2015, s 52(5).

Rules. The victim is under no obligation to cooperate with the police to receive support through the NRM.[12]

14.16

There are no statistics recording the number of potential victims of trafficking, slavery and related offences or NRM[13] referrals made in the context of extradition proceedings.

14.17

While extradition proceedings in Scotland and Northern Ireland fall outside the scope of this chapter, the Crown Office and Procurator Fiscal Service (COPFS) handles all requests in Scotland. In Northern Ireland, proceedings are managed by the Crown Solicitor's Office, with operational duties carried out by the Police Service of Northern Ireland (PSNI)[14].

Facilitating communication with requesting judicial authorities

14.18

The NCA also facilitates communication between the Crown Prosecution Service ('CPS') and the requesting judicial authority throughout the extradition process in a Part 1 case, for example, notifying the judicial authority of the date of arrest, transmitting requests for further evidence and details of remand time, and liaising regarding practical removal arrangements. NCA communications will usually be via the CPS and not directly with individuals or their representatives.

The CPS as agent for the requesting judicial authority

14.19

The CPS Extradition Unit and the NCA have key roles in all extradition cases.

14.20

The CPS acts as an agent for the requesting judicial authority[15], making representations in court in favour of extradition. In this role, the CPS will not typically act outside instructions from the judicial authority on whether to 'take

12 Ibid. s 9.

13 **Chapter 4** sets out the identification process under the NRM.

14 Home Office, *National referral mechanism guidance: adult (Northern Ireland and Scotland)* (updated 30 September 2025) <https://www.gov.uk/government/publications/human-trafficking-victims-referral-and-assessment-forms/national-referral-mechanism-guidance-adult-northern-ireland-and-scotland> accessed 14 October 2025.

15 *R v Director of Public Prosecutions ex parte Thom* [1996] Crim.L.R. 116; *Government of Germany Kleinschmidt* [2005] EWHC 1373 (Admin).

a view' about whether to pursue a prosecution, as it might in routine criminal proceedings. That said, the CPS Extradition Unit advises foreign authorities, where appropriate, on the content and validity of extradition requests received via the NCA or Home Office, as well as on ongoing or proposed extradition proceedings[16].

14.21

The CPS has published comprehensive guidance on the non-prosecution principles and available defences in cases involving modern slavery, including the statutory defence under s 45 of the Modern Slavery Act 2015[17]. The guidance affirms that the CPS must act compatibly with Art 4 of the ECHR and sets out its role in relation to the NRM and the Competent Authorities, specifically stating that:

> 'Certain public authorities, including the police, have a statutory duty to refer potential victims into the NRM. The CPS cannot make referrals: it is not a first responder. Where there is a potential victim of modern slavery, however, the CPS should ask the police to make a referral and ensure at the least that the police have considered the question of referral. This is the case whether the person is a victim, witness, suspect or defendant. The police must be advised to investigate the claim, in addition to any NRM referral, if it has not been already. The prosecutor must satisfy themself that this investigation is sufficiently thorough. All liaison and correspondence with the relevant competent authority should be conducted through the police.
>
> A prosecutor must be alert to Indicators of trafficking. A prosecutor may consider that someone is a potential victim of modern slavery based on their own assessment of the case, or following defence representations, or observations from the court or other authority. The obligation exists whether or not the suspect makes a disclosure to this effect or provides any information or evidence of it. Prosecutors should use the statutory guidance to inform their assessment. The police should always be asked to make a referral, unless the police are in possession of clear and sufficient evidence to prove that the suspect is not a victim of modern slavery.'
>
> ….
>
> To support the competent authority in prioritising cases effectively, the prosecutor should ensure that the police have provided the following

16 Crown Prosecution Service, *Extradition from the UK* (Updated 20 February 2023) https://www.cps.gov.uk/legal-guidance/extradition-from-uk accessed 30 September 2025.

17 https://www.cps.gov.uk/prosecution-guidance/modern-slavery-and-human-trafficking-offences-and-defences-including-section.

information to the relevant competent authority, together with the relevant factors of each case:

- Defendant's full name
- Date of birth
- Nationality if known
- NRM reference number
- Court and next hearing date
- CTL expiry date
- If the defendant is a youth

The police should be asked to confirm what information has been supplied to the relevant competent authority and that the relevant competent authority has been informed of the significant dates applicable, such as court hearing dates and the timescales by which a response or decision is required from them. Timescales should be agreed between the prosecutor and the police for the police to notify the prosecutor of the relevant competent authority's decision. If the information has not been provided by the agreed dates, the prosecutor should ensure this has been escalated by the police with the relevant competent authority.

The relevant competent authority should be updated immediately, by the police, as the case develops (for example, if someone is later remanded into custody, or if a trial date is set / brought forward). Prosecutors should ensure the police have relevant information to do so and advise the police on the need for close engagement with the relevant competent authority and the need to record all contact, should the court require assurance and in the event that a custody time limit extension application is required.'

Extradition court proceedings

14.22

Whether dealing with a Part 1 or Part 2 case, following arrest in this jurisdiction, the 2003 Act requires production in custody at Westminster Magistrates' Court[18] for an 'initial hearing'[19].

18 Excluding Scotland, where it must be a sheriff at the sheriff's court.
19 Eg 2003 Act, ss 7–8 in Part 1 cases. Discussion about devolving extradition to equivalent first instance courts in regional centres such as Birmingham, Cardiff, Leeds and Manchester have not thus far been progressed.

14.23

No police interview will have been conducted prior to the first court appearance.

Initial hearing

14.24

The requested person must have been served with the AW as soon as practicable after their arrest[20]. If this has not been done the requested person may apply for a discharge at the initial hearing. The judge may exercise their discretion to grant a discharge. The Judge must determine, on the balance of probabilities, whether the person before the court is the individual named in the extradition warrant. If the Judge is not satisfied of this, the person must be discharged[21].

14.25

Assuming the preliminary requirements are met, the Judge must inform the requested person of the contents of the warrant and give them the required information about consent.[22] A requested person can also be arrested provisionally, subject to a 'provisional arrest'[23]. In provisional arrest cases, the Judge will not have the Part 1 warrant / Part 2 extradition request and the certificate and will have to set a date to receive them. If those papers are not received by the relevant date, the requested person must be discharged[24].

14.26

If the requested person does not consent to extradition, the Judge identifies the issues and deals with case management. A date is fixed for the extradition hearing taking account the statutory requirement that the date cannot be later than the end of the permitted period, which is 21 days starting with the date of arrest in a Part 1 case and two months starting with the date on which the requested person is brought before the court in a Part 2 case[25]. In order to avoid this issue, the proceedings are formally opened at the initial hearing and adjourned. The final decision the judge has to make at the initial hearing is regarding bail.

14.27

If the requested person consents to extradition, they will be required to sign the consent form and their consent will be irrevocable.[26] The requested person

20 EA 2003, ss 4(2), 72(2).
21 EA 2003, s 7.
22 EA 2003, s 8.
23 EA 2003, ss 5, 74.
24 EA 2003, ss 6, 74.
25 EA 2003, s 8(4), 75(2) .
26 EA 2003, s 45.

will be extradited within 10 days for Part 1 and 28 days for Part 2 cases and will waive their appeal rights[27].

The Extradition Hearing

14.28

At the hearing, the court must consider:

- In Part 1 cases whether the warrant was issued by a Judicial Authority and whether the conduct in the extradition request amounts to an extradition offence.
- Whether any statutory bars to extradition apply under ss 11–19B of the 2003 Act;
- whether extradition would be compatible with the European Convention on Human Rights under section 21
- In Part 2 cases whether the judge has received the request and certificate from the Secretary of State, whether there are sufficient particulars of the requested person and the offence alleged and whether there is an arrest warrant or certificate of conviction. –
- whether extradition would be compatible with the European Convention on Human Rights under ss 21 and 87 of the 2003 Act.

Time limits in extradition proceedings

Statutory emphasis on expedition

14.29

The statutory framework emphasises expedition[28] but provides some flexibility where an adjournment is required in the interests of justice[29] or where the person is charged with an offence in the UK or serving a domestic sentence[30].

14.30

As in any litigation, common causes of delay include legal aid, obtaining evidence on behalf of the requested person, particularly expert evidence, the CPS seeking evidence in reply from the requesting judicial authority or state, and the preparation of first instance judgments. Nevertheless it is important for

27 EA 2003, s 47.
28 Eg Criminal Procedure Rules, 50.2 and Criminal Practice Directions 50A(1).
29 EA 2003, ss 8(5) and 75(3) and 76(4).
30 EA 2003, ss 8A, 8B, 76A, 76B.

practitioners to be aware of the 60 day time limit. In practice, an extradition case, including the exercise of a statutory appeal right (further protracted by a permission stage), will often be far in excess of the 60-day time limit applying to Part 1 cases.

Appeals from first instance proceedings

14.31

Applications for leave to appeal against a decision to extradite or discharge a requested person, whether made by the magistrates' court or the Secretary of State, must be filed with the High Court. The procedural requirements for such appeals are set out in Part 50 of the Criminal Procedure Rules 2025[31].

14.32

Appeals may be brought on a question of fact or law but require the permission from the High Court[32].

14.33

The time limits are strict:

- Seven days from the date of the judge's extradition or discharge order;
- Fourteen days from the date of the Secretary of State's extradition or discharge order.

14.34

In Part 2 cases, where the requested person appeals both the judge's decision to send the case to the Secretary of State and the Secretary of State's decision to order extradition, the appeals are heard together, subject to permission being granted.

14.35

If the High Court dismisses the appeal, the requested person or the requesting state may seek leave to appeal to the Supreme Court. This must be done within 14 days of the High Court's decision. Such an appeal may only proceed if the High Court certifies that the case raises a point of law of general public importance.

31 Criminal Procedure Rules 2025, SI 2025/909 (L. 7), pt 50 https://www.legislation.gov.uk/uksi/2025/909/part/50/crossheading/7 accessed 30 September 2025.

32 Extradition Act 2003, Part 1 Appeals (ss 26, 28-32) and Part 2 Appeals (ss 103.105, 108-114).

Legal framework governing extradition decisions

Prima facie requirement

14.36

The *prima facie* evidential requirement does not apply to Part 1 extradition cases (ie EU Countries).

14.37

In certain Part 2 cases, however, the court must assess whether sufficient admissible evidence exists to justify a trial, had the alleged offence occurred in the UK. This involves determining whether the prosecution case, taken at its highest, could properly be left to a jury (see *R (Harkins) v Secretary of State for the Home Department*[33] and *R v Galbraith)*[34].

14.38

The 2003 Act imposes strict requirements to ensure the court receives adequate detail regarding the alleged offences, convictions, or proceedings. States party to the European Convention on Extradition 1957 (ECE), along with the USA, Canada, Australia, New Zealand, and other designated territories[35], are exempt from the prima facie requirement. These countries must nonetheless provide sufficient 'information' about the accusation or conviction, typically in the form of an affidavit.

Statutory bars to extradition

14.39

A number of statutory bars may prevent extradition under the 2003 Act. These bars reflect fundamental legal safeguards and must be considered by the court before ordering extradition. The main bars are set out below.

14.40

Dual criminality requires that the alleged conduct would constitute a criminal offence under UK law.[36] The double jeopardy bar applies where the requested person has already been prosecuted for the same offence[37]. Further, the absence

33 *R (Harkins) v Secretary of State for the Home Department* [2007] EWHC 639 (Admin).
34 *R v Galbraith* [1981] 1 WLR 1039.
35 Home Office, *Extradition: Processes and Review* (gov.uk, updated 30 August 2023) https://www.gov.uk/guidance/extradition-processes-and-review#extradition-from-the-uk-category-1-territories accessed 30 September 2025.
36 EA 2003, s 10.
37 EA 2003, ss 12, 80.

of a prosecution decision may prevent extradition where the requesting state has not yet decided to charge or try the individual[38]. Extraneous considerations arise where the request is improperly motivated, for example, by the person's race, religion, nationality, gender, sexual orientation, or political opinions, or where extradition would expose them to prejudice on such grounds[39]. The passage of time bar may be engaged where delay renders extradition unjust or oppressive due to the time elapsed since the offence or since the person became unlawfully at large following conviction[40].

14.41

A person's extradition may be refused where it appears to the judge that the physical or mental condition of the Requested Person is such that it would be unjust or oppressive to extradite him. 'Unjust' relates to the risk of prejudice to the requested person in the conduct of the trial itself[41]. 'oppressive' relates to the requested person's personal circumstances[42].This is a highly fact specific exercise.

14.42

The forum bar allows the court to refuse extradition where a substantial part of the alleged conduct occurred in the UK, and having considered the statutory factors, extradition would be contrary to the interests of justice[43]. In conviction *in absentia* cases, extradition will be barred if the person was convicted without being deliberately absent and would not be entitled to a retrial upon return[44].

Extradition and European Convention on Human Rights

14.43

In all extradition cases, the judge must assess whether extradition would be compatible with the requested person's rights under the ECHR. If extradition would breach those rights, the judge must discharge the person. Common challenges arise under Art 3, concerning prison conditions in the requesting state, and Art 8, relating to interference with private and family life in the UK.

14.44

The TCA includes a fundamental rights clause which provides that where there are substantial grounds for believing that the surrender of the requested

38 EA 2003, s 12A.
39 EA 2003, ss 13, 81.
40 EA 2003, ss 14, 82.
41 *Kakis v Government of the Republic of Cyprus* [1978] 1 WLR 799 [p782].
42 *Government of the United States v Tollman* [2008] EWHC 184 (Admin) [47-50] [110].
43 EA 2003, ss 19B, 83A.
44 EA 2003, ss 20, 86.

person would pose a real risk to the protection of their fundamental rights, the executing judicial authority may, where appropriate, seek additional guarantees concerning the treatment of the person following surrender. These guarantees may inform the authority's decision on whether to execute the arrest warrant.

14.45

All Council of Europe countries are signatories to the ECHR, therefore there is a presumption that such countries will be capable of offering adequate protection of the requested persons human rights, subject to evidence that the presumption is rebutted. The presumption of adequate protection also applies to non signatory countries[45]. This is a rebuttable presumption and remains a central issue in extradition proceedings, as illustrated in *SLP v Prosecutor General of the Republic of Latvia (Rev1)*[46].

14.46

Slavery and servitude, as prohibited under Art 4(1) ECHR, are recognised as *jus cogens* norms operating *erga omnes*. This status is significant in two respects. First, it supports a presumption, consistent with the bedrock principles of extradition, namely mutual trust, confidence, and international cooperation, that the requesting state can uphold these fundamental protections. Second, it reflects the elevated level of international concern and obligation attached to these norms, which may justify heightened scrutiny in extradition proceedings involving allegations of trafficking, slavery or related harms proscribed by Art 4 ECHR.

Rebuttable presumption

14.47

The presumption is typically subject to the staged approach identified by the CJEU in *Criminal Proceedings Against Aranyosi and Căldăraru*[47]. This case concerned prisons conditions in the requested state.

14.48

Stage 1 involves the court determining whether there is a real risk of inhuman or degrading treatment by assessing objective, reliable, specific and properly updated evidence. Where such a risk is identified, the court is required to proceed to stage 2.

45 *Ahmed v Government of United States* [2006] EWHC 2927 (Admin) [101].
46 *SLP v Prosecutor General of the Republic of Latvia (Rev1)* [2025] EWHC 298 (Admin) at [26].
47 *Proceedings Against Aranyosi and Căldăraru* [2016] QB 921 [880]-[104]; *Mohammed v Portugal* [2017] EWHC 3237 (Admin) [15].

14.49

At this point the court must make a specific assessment as to whether there are substantial grounds to believe that the individual concerned will be exposed to the relevant risk. To that end, it must request the issuing authority to provide as a matter of urgency all necessary supplementary information on the conditions in which it is envisaged the requested person will be detained.

14.50

Stage 3 then deals with the position after the information is provided. If the executing authority finds that, for the individual concerned, there is a real risk of a violation, execution of the warrant may not proceed. The court may consider postponing the warrant, rather than refusing it.[48]

Art 3 – Prohibition on torture, inhuman or degrading treatment and extradition

Extradition, expulsion and the Soering principle

14.51

Although the ECtHR has not drawn a formal distinction between extradition and expulsion (including deportation and administrative removal) in its case law concerning the engagement of rights under the ECHR, the two procedures are distinct in terms of their statutory frameworks and public purposes. However, where fundamental rights are engaged, the legal tests applied are treated equivalently[49].

14.52

To engage Art 3, the alleged ill-treatment must reach a minimum level of severity. This threshold is relative and depends on the circumstances[50]. Treatment will breach Art 3 if the suffering or humiliation exceeds what is inherent in lawful detention or punishment. A breach of Art 3 arises where removal would expose the individual to a real risk of torture or inhuman or degrading treatment.

14.53

In addition to jurisdictional developments, the ECtHR in *Soering v United Kingdom*[51] established what is now known as the Soering principle. The Court held that where extradition would have consequences that are not too remote and adversely affect the enjoyment of a Convention right, the extraditing

48 *Proceedings Against Aranyosi and Căldăraru* [2016] QB 921 [880]-[104;]*Mohammed v Portugal* [2017] EWHC 3237 (Admin) [15].
49 *R (Ullah) v Special Adjudicator* [2004] UKHL 26 at [33].
50 *Saadi v Italy* App no 37201/06 (ECtHR, 28 February 2008); also reported as (2009) 49 EHRR 30.
51 *Soering v United Kingdom* (Application No. 14038/88) [1989] ECHR 14.

State's obligations under the Convention may be engaged. It concluded that a Contracting State may violate Art 3 where substantial grounds exist for believing that extradition would expose the person to a real risk of torture or inhuman or degrading treatment or punishment.

14.54

The rigorous standard of Art 3 applies uniformly, regardless of whether the removal is affected by expulsion, deportation, or extradition. The nature of the legal mechanism does not dilute the absolute protection afforded by Art 3. The absolute nature of Art 3 ECHR was affirmed in *Chahal v United Kingdom*[52], where the ECtHR held that public safety concerns or criminal allegations cannot override the prohibition against torture and inhuman or degrading treatment.

Assessment of risk, burden of proof and standard of proof

Independent and rigorous scrutiny

14.55

Art 13 of the ECHR requires the availability of an effective remedy at the domestic level, both in law and in practice. This entails a procedure that provides independent and rigorous scrutiny of the claim that substantial grounds exist for fearing a real risk of such treatment.

Disregard of conduct

14.56

When assessing whether extradition or expulsion would breach Art 3, the court must disregard the individual's conduct or the seriousness of the offence. The risk of such treatment is paramount and cannot be balanced against public interest or any other justification for removal. The analysis focuses on the foreseeable consequences of removal, requiring a careful evaluation of both:

- The general situation in the receiving State; and
- The individual circumstances of the person concerned.

Burden of proof

14.57

Where a requested person raises an arguable claim that removal would expose them to treatment contrary to Art 3 of the Convention, it is, in principle, for

52 *Chahal v United Kingdom* (Application No. 22414/93)[1996] ECHR 1996-V.

the requested person to adduce evidence capable of demonstrating that there are substantial grounds for believing that, if the removal were carried out, they would face a real risk of treatment contrary to Art 3. Once such evidence is presented, the burden shifts to the State to dispel any doubts raised by the material relied upon[53].

Individual assessment of risk

14.58

Risk may arise from the requested person's personal characteristics, such as gender, age, ethnicity, health or membership of a vulnerable group. This is relevant in an Art 4 ECHR context as explored below because of objectively identifiable groups vulnerable to trafficking, slavery and related harms (ie women, those with disabilities and particular racial groups such as those from the Roma community)[54]. Although a number of individual factors may not, when considered separately, constitute a real risk, the same factors may give rise to a real risk when taken cumulatively and when considered in a situation of a vulnerable group.

14.59

In respect of the latter, where a requested person alleges membership of a group that is systemically exposed to ill-treatment, Art 3 is engaged once the requested person demonstrates, where necessary, by reference to available sources, that there are serious reasons to believe both in the existence of the alleged practice and in their membership of the group concerned. In such cases, individualised risk need not be shown unless the State seeks to argue that the applicant falls outside the scope of the group-based risk.

Past ill-treatment

14.60

Established past ill-treatment contrary to Art 3 in the receiving State is a strong indicator of a future real risk of similar treatment. In such circumstances, the burden shifts to the State to dispel any doubts as to the existence of that risk. At the same time, the absence of past persecution or ill-treatment is not

53 *Khasanov and Rakhmanov v. Russia* [GC] (Applications nos 28492/15 and 49975/15) [109] (2022).

54 Lorena Molnar, 'The Imperative Need for Criminological Research on the European Roma: A Narrative Review' (2023) 24(2) *Trauma, Violence, & Abuse* 1016. Anti-Slavery International, *Trafficking for Forced Criminal Activities and Begging in Europe: Exploratory Study and Good Practice Examples* (2014) <https://www.antislavery.org/wp-content/uploads/2017/01/trafficking_for_forced_criminal_activities_and_begging_in_europe.pdf> accessed 2 October 2025.

determinative and does not preclude a finding of future risk, particularly where new or evolving circumstances are shown.

Art 3 violation – failing to protect a vulnerable complainant

14.61

In *N.Ç. v Turkey*[55], a case concerning the sexual abuse and exploitation of a minor complainant, the ECtHR found a violation of Art 3 arising from the State's failure to adequately protect the applicant during criminal proceedings. These included the absence of psychological and welfare support, exposure to intimidating confrontations with defendants, humiliating and unjustified reconstructions of the assaults, excessive and intrusive medical examinations, and a lack of security measures against threats from defendants' relatives. Taken together, these procedural shortcomings constituted inhuman and degrading treatment, breaching the State's obligations to safeguard the dignity and integrity of a vulnerable child victim.

Art 3 risk emanating from non-state authorities

14.62

Art 3 of the Convention applies not only to the danger emanating from State authorities but also where the danger emanates from persons or groups of persons who are not public officials. However, it must be shown that the risk is real and that the authorities of the receiving State are not able to obviate the risk by providing appropriate protection[56]. In this context, the possibility of protection or relocation of the applicant in the State of origin is also of relevance.

Art 3 arguable claim, suspension of removal and Art 13 ECHR

14.63

Article 13 remedy in removal cases provides that where an arguable claim of Art 3 is raised, this operates to have automatic suspensive effect, ensuring that removal is stayed while the claim is under consideration[57]. These procedural

55 *NÇ v Turkey* App (Application No 40591/11) (2021)[Section II].

56 *JK and Others v. Sweden* [GC], 2016, [80]. *Bagdanavicius v Secretary of State for the Home Department* [2005] UKHL 38.

57 *MSS v Belgium and Greece* [GC], (Application No 30696/09) (2011) [286–322, 293]; *Abdolkhani and Karimnia v Turkey* (Application No 30471/08) (2009)[107–117]; *Gebremedhin [Gaberamadhien] v France* (Application No 25389/05 (2007)[53–67]; *I.M. v France* (Application No 9152/09) (2012) (2 February 2012); *Chahal v United Kingdom* [GC] (Application No 22414/93) (1996) ([147–154]; *Shamayev and Others v Georgia and Russia* (Application No 36378/02) (2005) [460].

guarantees are firmly established in the jurisprudence of the ECtHR, which has consistently emphasised that the effectiveness of the remedy depends not only on its formal availability but also on its practical operation in protecting individuals from irreparable harm.

Assessment of the evidence

14.64

In assessing whether removal would expose an individual to a real risk of treatment contrary to Art 3, the Court has consistently held that the existence of such risk must be evaluated primarily by reference to the facts known or reasonably knowable to the Contracting State at the time of removal.

14.65

The State is required to consider not only the evidence submitted by the applicant but also all other relevant material, including publicly available and credible country information. In evaluating such material, particular weight is given to the reliability, objectivity, and corroboration of the sources.

Extradition and Arts 5 and 6 ECHR

14.66

The ECtHR has recognised that Art 5 may also be engaged in extradition cases, particularly where detention follows a flagrantly unfair trial. In *Othman v United Kingdom*[58], the Court considered the overlap between Arts 5 and 6, noting that a breach of Art 6 may render subsequent detention contrary to Art 5(1)(a). An extraditing State may bear responsibility indirectly where a flagrant denial[59] of the standards of a fair trial, gives rise to breaches of Arts 5 and 6 ECHR.

14.67

In *Soering*, the applicant argued that the absence of legal aid in Virginia would prevent him from securing legal representation, contrary to Art 6(3)(c). The ECtHR acknowledged the importance of the right to a fair trial and stated (at [113]) that:

> 'The Court does not exclude that an issue might exceptionally be raised under Art 6 by an extradition decision in circumstances where

58 *Othman v United Kingdom* (Application No 8139/09)(2012) 55 EHRR 1.

59 Ibid, [260]. 'What is required is a breach of the principles of fair trial guaranteed by art 6 which is so fundamental as to amount to a nullification, or destruction of the very essence, of the right guaranteed by that Art.'

the fugitive has suffered or risks suffering a flagrant denial of a fair trial in the requesting country.'

14.68

Although the facts did not disclose such a risk, this passage laid the foundation for the flagrant denial of justice test, now well-established in Strasbourg jurisprudence.

14.69

When addressing Art 6, the ECtHR considered both the harm already suffered by the Requested Person and the potential future harm.

14.70

The standard of proof differs depending on whether the case concerns a risk of future harm or a past violation:

- In accusation cases, where the individual is sought to stand trial, the test is whether there are substantial grounds for believing that the person would face a real risk of a flagrant denial of justice.
- In conviction cases, where the individual has already been tried, the question is whether a flagrant violation of Art 6 occurred, and this must be proved on the balance of probabilities.

14.71

This distinction was affirmed in *Popoviciu (Respondent) v Curtea De Apel Bucharest (Romania) (Appellant)*[60], where the Supreme Court held that the High Court had misdirected itself by applying the wrong standard.

The Othman exception

14.72

While the assessment of a flagrant denial of justice under Art 6 in extradition cases ordinarily concerns past events and must be proved as a matter of historical fact, an exceptional evidential approach applies where the allegation involves evidence obtained by torture. In such cases, the Court has recognised that the unique gravity and moral abhorrence of torture, prohibited as a *jus cogens* norm under international law, justifies a relaxation of the standard of proof. The use of torture-tainted evidence in criminal proceedings is, in itself, sufficient to constitute a flagrant denial of justice, irrespective of its reliability. This principle

60 *Popoviciu (Respondent) v Curtea De Apel Bucharest (Romania) (Appellant)* [2023] UKSC 39.

reflects the imperative to safeguard the integrity of the trial process and uphold the rule of law, as affirmed in *Othman v United Kingdom* and *Gäfgen v Germany*[61].

The Othman *exception and inhuman and degrading treatment*

14.73

In *Popoviciu v Curtea de Apel Bucharest (Romania)*[62], Lord Lloyd-Jones observed that the Strasbourg Court, in *Othman v United Kingdom*[63], recognised an exception to the general approach under Art 6 ECHR in cases involving evidence obtained through torture. He further noted that, while the point was not definitively resolved, the ECtHR did not exclude the possibility that similar considerations might apply to evidence obtained through other forms of ill-treatment, even if falling short of torture.

Art 8 of ECHR and the Celinski principles

14.74

Lord Thomas CJ in *Polish Judicial Authorities v Celinski*[64] distilled a series of principles which continue to provide the structure through which extradition courts assess competing interests, particularly where statutory bars, most commonly Art 8 ECHR or injustice or oppression arising from mental or physical health, are engaged.

14.75

There are several differences between the EAW Framework Decision and the EU–UK Trade and Cooperation Agreement (TCA). Foremost is the absence in the TCA of the principle of 'mutual trust and confidence', a principle that was central to the operation of the EAW. The TCA states at Art 524(1):

> 'The cooperation provided for in this Part is based on the Parties' and Member States' longstanding respect for democracy, the rule of law and the protection of fundamental rights and freedoms of individuals, including as set out in the Universal Declaration of Human Rights and in the European Convention on Human Rights, and on the importance of giving effect to the rights and freedoms in that Convention domestically.'

---

61 App No. 22978/05 (ECHR 1 June 2010).

62 *Popoviciu (Respondent) v Curtea De Apel Bucharest (Romania) (Appellant)* [2023] UKSC 39 at [64].

63 *Othman v United Kingdom* (2012) 55 EHRR 1

64 *Polish Judicial Authorities v Celinski* [2015] EWHC 1274 (Admin); *HH v Italy* et al [2013] 1 AC 338 and *Norris v USA (No 2)* [2010] 2 AC 487 and *Andrysiewicz v Poland* [2025] UKSC 23.

14.76

Neverthless, the principle of mutual trust between judicial authorities continues to apply.[65] In extradition proceedings, the courts in England and Wales presume the competence, integrity, and good faith of the requesting state, particularly in Part 1 cases. This presumption includes confidence that the requesting authority will address legal issues, safeguard rights, and follow due process within its own jurisdiction, absent compelling evidence to the contrary[66].

14.77

High public interest in honouring extradition arrangements: the public interest in upholding extradition arrangements remains a weighty consideration. The United Kingdom must not be perceived as a haven for fugitives. Judicial reasoning must expressly engage with this dimension of the public interest.

14.78

Prosecutorial independence: Courts in England and Wales will ordinarily defer to the prosecutorial decisions of the requesting state, reflecting the principle of mutual trust and confidence between judicial authorities, particularly under the EA 2003, and Part 1 in relation to EU and former EAW states. In that vein, it is for the requesting state to determine whom to prosecute and whether to treat an individual as a victim or defendant. The English court's role is to assess whether the request engages any statutory bars, proportionality concerns, or human rights issues, not to evaluate the merits of the foreign prosecutorial decision, absent clear evidence of bad faith, abuse of process, or a denial of justice.

14.79

Culpability and sentencing are primarily for the requesting state: it is for the requesting court to assess the impact of mitigating factors on culpability and sentence. In accusation cases, the extradition court must proceed on the basis that such matters will be properly ventilated at trial. In conviction cases, the sentencing approach of the requesting state should not be second-guessed, provided it complies with Convention standards. In cases involving the potential separation of a requested person from his or her children, the likely sentence which might be imposed in this country in equivalent circumstances may also be relevant[67].

14.80

Limited role of Courts in England and Wales reviewing sentencing practices abroad: courts are not equipped to conduct a detailed review of

65 *Banica v Romania* [2023] EWHC 405 (Admin).

66 TCA Art 524(1), Case C-202/24, *Alchaster, Banica v Romania* [2023] EWHC 405 (Admin), *Prusianu v Romania* [2022] EWHC 1929 (Admin).

67 *HH v Italy* et al [2013] 1 AC 338 [132].

foreign sentencing practices, which may reflect different policy choices, including the use of suspended sentences or rehabilitative measures. The extradition court must avoid substituting its own view of the appropriate sentence.

14.81

Structured and reasoned approach to Art 8 analysis: where it is submitted that Art 8 is engaged, the court must adopt a structured approach, identifying and balancing the relevant factors for and against extradition. These may include the individual's vulnerability and the adequacy of protective measures in the requesting state.

Part 2: UK legal architecture on modern slavery

Modern Slavery Act 2015

14.82

The Modern Slavery Act 2015 ('MSA 2015') is a multi-dimensional statute that integrates criminal, civil, regulatory, and victim protection frameworks into a single legislative instrument. While its core purpose is to consolidate and strengthen criminal offences relating to slavery, servitude, forced labour, and human trafficking, the Act goes beyond criminalisation to establish mechanisms for prevention, enforcement, and victim support.

14.83

The criminal offences set out in s 1 of the MSA 2015, namely slavery, servitude, and forced or compulsory labour, are to be interpreted and applied in accordance with Art 4 of the ECHR, which prohibits slavery, servitude and forced labour. Sections 2 and 3 of the Act establish the offence of human trafficking (see **Chapter 1**).

14.84

Described as world-leading, the Act aimed to ensure perpetrators face severe penalties, including life imprisonment, while enhancing protections for victims. It imposed obligations on businesses to address slavery in their supply chains and empowered courts to restrict individuals where necessary to prevent harm.

14.85

Key provisions included the creation of an Independent Anti-Slavery Commissioner to improve coordination, a statutory defence for victims compelled to commit offences, and duties on the Secretary of State to issue guidance and regulations on victim identification and support. The Act also provided for Independent Child Trafficking Advocates, introduced reparation orders to compensate victims from confiscated assets, and granted law enforcement powers to intercept vessels suspected of trafficking.

Modern slavery statutory guidance

14.86

Section 49(1)(d) of the MSA 2015 requires Statutory Guidance to provide a framework and arrangements for the identification and protection of victims and potential victims of trafficking, slavery, and related offences, with broad application across the criminal justice and asylum systems (see **Chapter 4**). It details the functions of the National Referral Mechanism and obligations of agencies including the CPS, police, and immigration authorities, and sets clear expectations for inter-agency cooperation and the handling of victims who are also defendants or asylum applicants.

14.87

The Modern Slavery Statutory Guidance confirms that for the purposes of the NRM, slavery, servitude, forced and compulsory labour are to have the same meaning as they do under Art 4 ECHR. This is consistent with the Slavery and Human Trafficking (Definition of Victim) Regulations 2022.

Nationality and Borders Act 2022

14.88

Although the Nationality and Borders Act 2022 ('NABA 2022') is principally directed at immigration control, it contains provisions which amend or supplement other statutory frameworks, including the Modern Slavery Act 2015, and therefore operates with both sector-specific and cross-sectoral effect.

14.89

Part 5 of the NABA 2022[68] introduced a suite of amendments to the Modern Slavery Act 2015, placing key aspects of victim identification, support, and procedural safeguards on a statutory footing. While some provisions apply specifically to non-UK nationals[69], particularly those engaging with the asylum or immigration system, others extend to all victims of modern slavery and trafficking.

68 Note that ss. 58-67 have not yet entered into force.

69 Sections 58,59 and 63 of NABA 2022.

14.90

The Act empowers the Secretary of State to issue information notices requiring timely disclosure of victim-related evidence[70] and introduces consequences for unjustified delay for those seeking international protection. It clarifies the threshold for identifying victims, replacing the 'may be' test with 'is' and confirming the civil standard of proof for conclusive grounds decisions. Section 50 (not yet enacted) is an enabling provision for regulations on victim identification and support.

14.91

Sections 61 and 64 provide for the entitlement to a recovery period and embed the duty to provide assistance and support during that time. These sections were introduced to give effect to Art 13 of the Council of Europe Convention on Action against Trafficking in Human Beings ECAT (see explanatory report to the Act.). Section 50A of the MSA 2015, inserted by s 64 of NABA 2022, reinforces the statutory framework by imposing a duty on the Secretary of State to secure 'necessary assistance and support' for potential victims during the recovery period defined in s 61. As discussed in Part 3, Art 13 of ECAT has directly informed the protective and procedural obligations arising under Art 4 ECHR (see *Chowdhury v Greece*[71]). Read together, the MSA 2015 and NABA 2022 have placed a number of ECAT provisions on a statutory footing.

Domestic statutory framework for trafficking and its interaction with immigration control

14.92

In *R (CTK) v Secretary of State for the Home Department*[72], the Court of Appeal identified two key statutes that form the domestic legal framework for addressing trafficking: the MSA 2015 and the NABA 2022. While the United Kingdom is a signatory to ECAT, its provisions were not initially reflected in domestic statute. The MSA 2015 marked the first comprehensive legislative response, creating criminal offences, establishing the Independent Anti-Slavery Commissioner, and setting out victim protection measures.

14.93

As the Court describes, the MSA 2015 was subsequently amended by NABA 2022, which gave statutory effect to certain provisions of ECAT for

70 Section 58 of NABA 2022.

71 App no 21884/15 (ECHR, 30 March 2017).

72 *R (CTK) v Secretary of State for the Home Department* [2025] EWCA Civ 1264.

the first time. Notably, the Court observed that NABA introduced a statutory immunity from removal for individuals who receive a positive reasonable grounds decision.

14.94

As is evident, Part 5 of NABA 2022 engages directly with both immigration control and the modern slavery framework, contributing to a more integrated statutory scheme. While the MSA 2015 continues to provide the structural foundation for criminal enforcement, regulatory oversight, and victim support, NABA 2022 introduces procedural and evidential requirements that significantly shape how protections under the MSA 2015 are accessed.

14.95

These provisions are set out in a distinct section of the NABA 2022 titled 'Modern Slavery' and include measures that are not exclusively tied to immigration legislation. This reflects a broader legislative approach in which NABA 2022 influences the operation of the MSA 2015 beyond immigration matters, introducing objective evidence thresholds, time-limited recovery periods, and statutory decision-making criteria. Collectively, these developments signal a shift towards a more coherent and cross-cutting legal framework, where victim protection and immigration enforcement are increasingly interlinked.

Part 3: State obligations under Art 4 ECHR

The absolute and hierarchical status of Art 4 ECHR

14.96

Article 4 of the ECHR, alongside Arts 2 and 3, enshrines a core value of democratic societies. Unlike Art 8 ECHR, which is a qualified right subject to proportionality and justification, Art 4 is absolute in nature.

14.97

Article 4 ECHR provides that *'no one shall be held in slavery or servitude'* and that *'no one shall be required to perform forced or compulsory labour.'* The ECtHR has confirmed that human trafficking falls within the scope of Art 4, and its prohibition is absolute. In the case of slavery and servitude, this prohibition forms part of *jus cogens* norms, universally accepted and non-derogable principles of international law. Slavery gives rise to *erga omnes* obligations (see **Chapter 1**) and is further classified as a crime against humanity under Art 7 of the Rome Statute of the International Criminal Court, placing it within the highest category of international legal concern.

14.98

While the prohibition of forced or compulsory labour is not classified as *jus cogens*, it remains absolute under Art 4 ECHR. The provisions of Art 4(3) properly interpreted delimit the material scope of the protection afforded, rather than constitute exceptions to the right itself (see **Chapter 1**).

Scope and structure of Arts 4(2) and (3): forced or compulsory labour

14.99

Article 4(2) ECHR prohibits forced or compulsory labour, while Art 4(3) delimits the content of this right only in prescribed circumstances. These classifications underscore the absolute and hierarchical nature of the right. This is examined in **Chapter 1**, including as it applies to extradition.

Art 4 ECHR positive obligations

14.100

Article 4 ECHR imposes positive obligations on member states to ensure that the rights it guarantees: freedom from slavery, servitude, forced or compulsory labour and trafficking, are given practical and effective protection. These obligations require states not only to refrain from violating the right, but to take active operational and procedural measures to prevent, identify, and respond to abuses falling within its scope. Positive obligations are to be interpreted in such a way as not to impose an excessive burden on the authorities.

14.101

The ECtHR interprets Art 4 in line with Arts 2 and 3, recognising that the positive duties under Art 4 share common ground with those protecting the right to life and the prohibition of torture and inhuman or degrading treatment. The ECtHR applies similar reasoning across these provisions, which it has described as reflecting 'basic values', a characterisation affirmed in *SM v Croatia*[73] and further supported in *Rantsev v Cyprus and Russia*[74]. As such, the jurisprudence under Arts 2 and 3 is directly relevant.

73 *SM v Croatia* [GC], App No 60561/14, [305].
74 *Rantsev v Cyprus and Russia*, App No 25965/04, [283–289].

Positive obligations under Art 4 ECHR: framework, interpretation, and procedural implications

Overview

14.102

The contours of the State's positive obligations under Art 4 ECHR have evolved incrementally through the Strasbourg Court's jurisprudence. Their scope is not static: these duties continue to develop as the case law responds to new contexts and forms of exploitation. The emergence and expansion of positive obligations has been a defining feature of the Court's interpretative approach to the Convention. They have often been analysed within particular subject areas, most notably domestic violence and human trafficking, and have been organised in various ways, including distinctions between substantive and procedural duties, explicit and implied procedural requirements, and obligations with preventive as opposed to remedial functions. Such classifications assist in clarifying both the nature of the measures required of States and the circumstances in which a breach may arise.[75]. Because positive obligations impose legally enforceable responsibilities on public authorities, clarity as to their content and operation is essential. The framework set out here should be read alongside the broader discussion of positive obligations in **Chapters 4** and **10**.

The principal obligations identified in the authorities, including *SM v Croatia* and *Rantsev v Cyprus and Russia,* may be summarised as follows. First, States must maintain an effective legislative and administrative framework capable of prohibiting, preventing and penalising Art 4 violations (the systems duty). Secondly, they are required to take reasonable operational steps to prevent Art 4 violations and to protect individuals who may be at risk (the protective duty). Thirdly, they must conduct effective investigations capable of identifying and, where appropriate, prosecuting alleged perpetrators, and must secure access to remedies where there is a credible suspicion of an Art 4 breach or a real and immediate risk that such a breach may arise (the procedural duties). Fourthly, the obligation to ensure that victims are afforded restitution in respect of the harm suffered (the restitution duty).

Two-stage assessment under Art 4 ECHR

14.103

Save for the systems duty, the ECtHR assesses compliance with these positive obligations through a two-stage inquiry.

75 Vladislava Stoyanova, 'Framing Positive Obligations under the European Convention on Human Rights Law: Mediating between the Abstract and the Concrete' (2023) 23 *Human Rights Law Review* 1, https://doi.org/10.1093/hrlr/ngad010.

Stage One: Awareness of risk

14.104

The first question is whether the authorities knew, or ought to have known, of a credible suspicion that an individual was, or was at real and immediate risk of being[76], subjected to slavery, servitude, forced or compulsory labour, or trafficking.

Stage Two: Scope of the state's obligations

14.105

The second is whether the State took reasonable steps, within the powers available to it, to prevent the Art 4 violation or to respond appropriately once a credible suspicion of an Art 4 violation has arisen, the next step is to determine what positive obligations flow from it.

The framework under Art 4 includes:

- Operational obligations: the duty to take protective measures to prevent Art 4 violations and safeguard potential victims. The Protection and Recovery Duties.
- Investigative obligations: the duty to conduct an effective investigation into credible allegations of Art 4 violations. The Investigatory Duty or Procedural Duty.
- Restitution for harm caused. The Restorative or Restitution Duty.

The credible suspicion threshold: triggering the protection and investigation duties under Art 4 ECHR

14.106

This section examines how the threshold of credible suspicion operates as the legal trigger for two distinct but interrelated obligations under Art 4 ECHR: the Protection Duty, which requires safeguarding victims (potential or established) from further harm and facilitates recovery, and the Investigation Duty, which mandates a prompt and effective investigation.

76 See **Chapter 4** for discussion on the interpretation of 'real and immediate risk' as it arises in Art 4 and as understood in the context of the Othman exception.

The threshold of credible suspicion

14.107

The State's positive obligations under Art 4 are engaged once a credible suspicion exists that a person has been, or is at real and immediate risk of being, subjected to trafficking, slavery, servitude or forced or compulsory labour. The threshold is deliberately low. It is satisfied where the account or indicators are not inherently implausible and the information was, or ought reasonably to have been, within the knowledge of the authorities.

14.108

These duties do not depend upon the individual self-identifying as a victim or making a formal complaint. The obligations arise automatically once the matter is known, or to be known, to state authorities attention, requiring proactive engagement by the State.

In the United Kingdom, a positive reasonable grounds decision under the National Referral Mechanism (NRM) will ordinarily indicate that the credible suspicion threshold has been met. In *Secretary of State for the Home Department v Hoang Anh Minh*[77], Lord Justice Burnett confirmed that the 'reasonable grounds' test applied by the Competent Authority is substantially aligned with the Art 4 'credible suspicion' standard. He observed that a reasonable grounds decision effectively operates at the same threshold.

However, the State's obligations may be activated even earlier: the circumstances of a referral into the NRM, or other information held by frontline bodies, may themselves amount to the ***prima facie*** evidence giving rise to a credible suspicion[78] (see **Chapter 4**).

Accordingly, Art 4 obligations may be engaged at multiple institutional points: through frontline staff at the moment of referral; through information already held by agencies such as the police, CPS, the NCA, or other safeguarding bodies; or through judicial observations arising in proceedings. This broader conception reflects the Strasbourg Court's position that the protective purpose of Art 4 requires early and coordinated action whenever reliable indicators of exploitation arise. This principle has been affirmed in cases such as *VCL and AN v United Kingdom*[79] and *NC v Turkey*[80], where the Court emphasised that the failure to engage with trafficking indicators or to undertake an assessment appropriately before the instigation of criminal proceedings, or during the course of proceedings may itself constitute a breach of Arts 4 and 6. These decisions underscore the imperative for national authorities, including courts

77 *Secretary of State for the Home Department v Hoang Anh Minh* [2016] EWCA Civ 565 [37].
78 *R (TDT) v Secretary of State for the Home Department* [2018] EWCA Civ 1395.
79 App nos. 77587/12 and 74603/12, ECHR 2021 (16 February).
80 App no 40591/11 (ECHR, 9 February 2021).

and prosecuting bodies, to respond proactively and with due diligence once potential Art 4 indicators are present.

The assessment of indicators must also be undertaken with proper regard to the impact of trauma, fear, coercion and vulnerability, factors which may inhibit disclosure or make an individual's account appear fragmented (see **Chapter 3**). This approach accords with the practice of the UK's senior courts and ensures that the threshold for engagement is applied with the necessary sensitivity.

The operational duties

Dual aims

14.109

In *VCL and AN v United Kingdom*[81], the ECtHR held that the duty to take operational measures under Art 4 has two principal aims:

- Protective Duty: to protect the victim from further harm; and
- Recovery Duty: to facilitate his or her recovery.

Extraterritorial scope of protection

14.110

Notably the *protective* obligations are not contingent on the exploitation having occurred within the jurisdiction where the victim is identified[82].

Burden and reasonableness

14.111

Rantsev emphasises that the duty to take 'appropriate measures' to protect victims or potential victims must be interpreted 'in a way which does not impose an impossible or disproportionate burden on the authorities.' The State is only required to take reasonable measures. The factor of reasonableness for the assessment of breach necessarily presupposes a context-specific assessment.

81 Ibid.
82 Ibid. and *J v Austria*.

The protective duty

Identification

14.112

Protection measures under Art 4 ECHR include facilitating the identification of potential victims by qualified professionals[83] (see **Chapter 4**). While the ECtHR recognises a duty to identify,[84] it does not prescribe how that duty must be implemented, leaving the method to the discretion of the member state. Assessing whether there has been a breach of this duty requires first establishing its existence and then evaluating the significance of the breach by reference to the content and purpose of the duty itself[85]. As explained in **Chapter 4**, the protective measures contained in the Council of Europe Convention on Action against Trafficking in Human Beings (ECAT) do not map precisely onto the positive obligations arising under Art 4 of the Convention. Instead they should be understood, as confirmed by the Strasbourg Court, as a valuable interpretive aid, which the ECtHR draws upon to illuminate both the scope and the practical content of the State's duties under Art 4.

14.113

As noted at [127] of the Explanatory Report to ECAT, failure to correctly identify a victim is likely to result in the continued denial of that individual's fundamental rights and may also deprive the prosecution of a key witness necessary to secure a conviction against the trafficker or perpetrator of modern slavery offences. The identification process requires competent authorities to seek out and evaluate a range of circumstances by which a person may be considered a victim of trafficking or modern slavery. This underscores the centrality of accurate and timely identification to both the protective and prosecutorial aims of the Convention.

14.114

The duty to identify is an enabling duty which informs and triggers the recovery duty and investigatory duty.

83 *Chowdury and Others* v Greece, [10] and *VCL* and *AN v UK*.

84 See **Chapter 4** for an analysis of R(ABW) v Secretary of State for the Home Department [2025] EWHC 3280 (Admin); *AYA v Secretary of State for the Home Department* [2026] EWHC 552 (Admin).

85 Vladislava Stoyanova, 'Framing Positive Obligations under the European Convention on Human Rights Law: Mediating between the Abstract and the Concrete' (2023) 23 *Human Rights Law Review* 1, [11] https://doi.org/10.1093/hrlr/ngad010.

Assessment of risk and ECAT

14.115

The obligation to take preventive operational measures to address risk of further harm has been most extensively articulated in the domestic-violence case law, where the ECtHR has developed a detailed framework of positive duties. Although grounded in a different context, the parallels with human trafficking and other Art 4 harms are clear. Art 4 harm, like domestic abuse, is rarely a single event; it typically consists of a sustained pattern of coercion and exploitation, often giving rise to a recognised and heightened risk of re-trafficking or other Art 4 violations. The protective architecture in ECAT, including mechanisms for early identification, safety planning and risk mitigation, is designed precisely to support victims in leaving exploitative environments and to reduce the likelihood of recurrence.

Against that background, the positive obligations arising under Art 4 support a more flexible reading of the *Othman* standard, mirroring the approach taken in the domestic-violence cases. The Court has made clear that the immediacy or risk requirement must be understood in the light of the typical trajectory of escalation in such settings, where serious harm may be ongoing or foreseeable without the ability to pinpoint the precise moment an incident will occur. What matters is that the authorities are, or ought to be, aware of circumstances which indicate a real and continuing risk. Exact predictability of time, place or method is not required for the State's preventive duty to be triggered.

This reasoning applies with equal, if not greater, force to Art 4 risks. The dynamics of trafficking and other Art 4 harms, including control, dependency, intimidation, ongoing debt bond and cycles of re-exploitation, create a context in which harm may intensify over time or is repeated. The preventive obligations under Art 4 must therefore be interpreted in a manner that captures these realities and enables the State to intervene effectively before further exploitation occurs.

Recovery

14.116

The recovery duty includes an obligation to assist victims in their physical, psychological, and social recovery, and to provide appropriate support and treatment for the consequences of past ill-treatment. In *Begum v Secretary of State*, [86] Lady Carr, LCJ observed that, to date, this duty has been recognised as arising only where the victim is present within the jurisdiction of the State.

86 *Begum v Secretary of State for the Home Department* [2024] EWCA Civ 152.

14.117

The ECtHR clarified in *J v Austria*[87], the fact that authorities treat individuals as potential victims of trafficking does not presuppose official confirmation that the offence has been established. Support must be provided even before the offence is formally confirmed, as withholding assistance until a criminal finding is made would undermine the very purpose of victim protection in Art 4 cases.

The recovery and reflection period under Art 13 ECAT

14.118

In *MN & IXU v Secretary of State for the Home Department*[88], Lord Justice Underhill observed that ECAT provided a 'recovery and reflection period' under Art 13 of ECAT where there are reasonable grounds to believe that the person concerned is a victim. The Court described this provision as having two core elements: first, that the individual must not be removed from the territory during the recovery and reflection period; and second, that they are entitled to support and protection in accordance with Art 12(1) and (2). The Court noted that these entitlements also arise under Art 10(2) – identification.

14.119

The identified purpose of the recovery and reflection period is twofold: to allow the individual time to recover from the trauma they may have experienced, and to provide an opportunity to consider cooperating with the investigation and prosecution of their traffickers.

14.120

In *Chowdhury v Greece*[89], as considered by the Supreme Court in *MS (Pakistan)*, the ECtHR treats Art 13 of ECAT as integral to fulfilling the procedural obligation to investigate under Art 4 ECHR. The Court held that the failure to grant a recovery and reflection period undermined both the effectiveness and lawfulness of the investigation, amounting to a breach of the procedural duty. As the Supreme Court observed, the ECtHR draws on ECAT, including Art 13, to help define the scope and content of the positive obligations under Art 4. Accordingly, the requirements of Art 13 ECAT may serve as a benchmark in assessing whether the duty to conduct an effective investigation into alleged Art 4 violations has been met.

87 *J v Austria* (2017) no. 58216/12.
88 [35]-[36].
89 App No 21884/15 (ECHR, 30 March 2017).

14.121

The ECtHR did not consider Art 13 ECAT in the context of the protective obligations of assistance and recovery, however, in the light of Lord Justice Underhill's delineation of the two distinct purposes of Art 13, arguably this could be characterised as integral to the protective duties under Art 4 of ECHR, not just the procedural obligation to investigate (see **Chapter 4**).

Non-removal: is it a core protective obligation under Art 4 read with ECAT obligations?

14.122

The ECtHR has shaped the content of Art 4's protective duties by regularly relying on ECAT and on its interpretation by GRETA, the Convention's monitoring body. Against that background, the following points can be distilled:

'1. Identification and the Duty to Prevent Premature Removal

As the Explanatory Report to ECAT makes clear, once the competent authorities have 'reasonable grounds' to believe that a person may be a victim of trafficking, the duty not to remove arises under Art 10 ECAT. This obligation applies before the identification process concludes, recognising that identification is often complex, time-consuming, and may require cooperation with other states or support agencies. Many victims are unlawfully present and at immediate risk of removal; ECAT explicitly seeks to prevent premature expulsion before victim status can be properly assessed.

Art 10 ECAT contains no such public order exemption permitting expulsion before the identification process has concluded, reinforcing the primacy of non-removal during the identification process.

2. Recovery and Reflection Period: Art 13 ECAT

Under Art 13 ECAT, individuals with reasonable grounds to be considered victims are entitled to a recovery and reflection period. As observed by Lord Justice Underhill in *MN & IXU v SSHD*, this period serves two purposes:

- To allow the individual time to recover from trauma.
- To enable consideration of cooperation with criminal investigations.

During this period, the individual must not be removed and must receive support under Arts 12(1) and (2).

Art 13(3) permits expulsion on public order grounds, this is a limited exception and must be interpreted narrowly.

3. Primacy and Realism of Non-Removal

The rights conferred under ECAT's Chapter III, support, assistance, and access to justice, may be rendered illusory if a person is removed before identification is reasonably possible. ECAT does not require certainty; 'reasonable grounds' are sufficient to trigger protection. This pragmatic threshold ensures that potential victims are safeguarded while their status is assessed.

4. GRETA's Interpretation and ECtHR Endorsement

GRETA, the Convention's monitoring body, has affirmed that identification is a key obligation, requiring states to ensure that the recovery and reflection period is not terminated without proper consideration of the individual's circumstances. GRETA also confirms that non-removal applies to both returns to the country of origin and transfers to third countries. This reflects that early and proactive non-removal is integral to the effective protection of trafficking victims. In *Chowdhury v Greece*, the ECtHR confirmed it would be informed by GRETA's interpretation, using ECAT as the substantive framework for assessing compliance with Art 4 ECHR.

5. Independence from Criminal Proceedings

The identification process is independent of any criminal investigation. It centres on the rights and recovery of the individual, not their utility to prosecution. This ensures that protection is not contingent on cooperation or evidentiary value, but on the existence of reasonable grounds to believe the person may be a victim.'

14.123

The question of whether non-removability pending the conclusion of the victim identification process constitutes a protective obligation under Art 4 ECHR remains unresolved by both the domestic courts and the ECtHR.

Arts 10 and 13 ECAT impose a duty not to remove individuals from the territory during the identification process and throughout the recovery and reflection period. Unlike Art 10, Art 13 includes a public order exception. Whether, and if so how, these provisions fall within the scope of the State's positive obligations under Art 4 ECHR was considered in part in *R (ABW) v Secretary of State for the Home Department*[90]. The High Court addressed the legality of the Public Order Disqualification (POD) in NABA s 63, which curtails support, assistance and identification where particular criteria are met. Where a POD is in place and the individual is a non-UK national, they may be removed. However, *R (ABW)* did not concern removability during the course of the identification process itself, but rather whether the protective duties under Arts 10 and 13 of ECAT, as

90 *R (ABW) v Secretary of State for the Home Department* [2025] EWHC 3280 (Admin).

given effect in domestic law, could be suspended up to the point of removal, the Court concluded that identification could not be suspended pending removal. However, the Court went on to reject that a positive obligation to identify arises in all cases where there is a credible suspicion of an Art 4 violation. That judgment, and its implications, are examined at length in **Chapter 4**, the editorial view is that the analysis of the Court is arguably incorrect. There is currently a pause in decision-making on PODs following *R (ABW)*[91].

Art 4, like Art 3, protects one of the core values of the Convention. The Court has repeatedly held that, where there is an arguable Art 3 claim in a removal case, removing the person before that claim is decided may deprive them of an effective remedy under Art 13 ECHR, so removal must be suspended. Although those cases usually concern a future risk of ill-treatment under Art 3, the same logic can apply where there is a substantive Art 4 issue. By analogy, if there is an arguable (*prima facie*) claim that removal would expose a person to trafficking, slavery or forced labour contrary to Art 4, the same procedural safeguard, a suspension of removal to secure the effectiveness of the remedy, may be thought to apply.

The non-punishment principle and the protective duty under Art 4 ECHR

14.124

The ECtHR has clarified that neither ECAT nor any other international instrument establishes a general prohibition on the prosecution of victims of Art 4 violations. However, the prosecution of individuals who are, or may be, victims of Art 4 violations may, in certain circumstances, be incompatible with the State's duty to take operational measures to protect them under Art 4 ECHR.

14.125

In *VCL and AN v United Kingdom*, the Court found the UK to be in breach of its protective obligations under Art 4, having regard to the following principles:

1. **Impact of prosecution on recovery and risk of re-trafficking**: It is axiomatic that prosecuting victims can seriously impair their physical, psychological, and social recovery. A criminal conviction may hinder reintegration and obstruct access to the support and services envisaged by ECAT, while increasing vulnerability to re-trafficking.

91 Following the handing down of *R (ABW) v Secretary of State for the Home Department* [2025] EWHC 3280 (Admin) on 17 December 2025, the Secretary of State applied for permission to appeal and for a stay of the judgment's effects. An application to stay the interim effects of the judgment was refused on 17 December 2025, with the substantive application for permission to appeal and stay to be considered in the New Year 2026. The outcome of the permission to appeal application remains relevant to the status of the Public Order Disqualification framework at para **14.123**.

2. **Prompt identification and assessment**: Once the authorities are aware, or ought reasonably to be aware, of circumstances giving rise to a credible suspicion that an individual suspected of committing a criminal offence may have been trafficked or exploited, that individual must be promptly assessed by professionals trained and qualified to identify victims of Art 4 harm.

3. **Use of international criteria**: In trafficking cases, such assessments should be conducted using the criteria set out in the Palermo Protocol and ECAT, ensuring consistency with international standards.

4. **Timing of prosecutorial decision**: Given that victim status may affect both the evidential sufficiency and the public interest in prosecution, any decision to prosecute should, insofar as possible, be deferred until a trafficking assessment has been completed by a qualified person.

5. **Weight of the assessment in decision-making**: Once an assessment has been made, it must be taken into account in any subsequent prosecutorial decision. While prosecutors are not bound by the findings, any departure must be supported by clear and consistent reasoning, aligned with the definitions and standards in ECAT and the Palermo Protocol.

The Court made clear that State authorities cannot abdicate its duties by relying on the failings of defence legal representatives, nor on the silence of defendants, particularly minors, who may be unaware of their status or too afraid to disclose it. The Court focused on the protective obligations under Art 4 rather than on whether the threshold in Art 6(3)(c) had been met. It found that the CPS's failure to carry out a timely trafficking assessment, consistent with its positive obligations, deprived the applicants of the opportunity to secure evidence that might have formed a fundamental element of their defence, and thus breached Art 6. The Court analysed the Art 6 violation in the light of a breach of Art 4 protective obligations, but in the context of Art 6 refer to an investigatory duty.[92] The judgment considered that a failure to investigate where there is a credible suspicion of Art 4 harm may itself lead to a breach of Art 6, particularly where this deprives the individual of access to potentially exculpatory evidence.

This link between the Art 4 investigatory duty and the fair-trial guarantees under Art 6 is of particular importance in the extradition context. Evidence of trafficking status may be central to resisting removal. Where jurisdiction is engaged, a failure by the authorities to investigate, despite clear indicators, may deny the person evidence that is fundamental to the fairness of the proceedings, thereby giving rise to a risk of an Art 6 breach.

92 *VCL and AN v UK* at [194].

No extension of the non-punishment principle

14.126

In *Begum v Secretary of State for the Home Department*,[93] the Court considered, but declined to adopt, submissions inviting it to extend the non-punishment principle to national security deprivation-of-citizenship decisions. It emphasised the limits of judicial intervention in such decisions and held that the non-punishment principle does not presently apply in this context.

14.127

Applying the approach set out in *R (AB) v Secretary of State for Justice*[94], the Court held that it could not be said with confidence that the Strasbourg Court would adopt the broader interpretation of the non-punishment principle advanced by Professor Mullally, the UN Special Rapporteur on Trafficking[95]. As Lord Reed PSC had explained in *R (AB)*, the conditions for recognising a new positive obligation under Art 4 ECHR must be satisfied and any development must be incremental and consistent with established Strasbourg jurisprudence. The Court concluded that extending the non-punishment principle to administrative decisions of this nature would go beyond incremental development, and therefore falls outside the scope of the current legal framework.

Restitutionary duty

14.128

Where a breach of an obligation under the ECHR is established, the State is under a duty to bring the violation to an end and to provide reparation that, so far as possible, restores the position that would have prevailed had the breach not occurred. This principle was clearly articulated by the ECtHR in *Papamichalopoulos v Greece*[96], where the Court stated at [34]:

> 'A violation of the Convention imposes on the respondent State a legal obligation to put an end to the breach and make reparation for its consequences in such a way as to restore as far as possible the situation existing before the breach.'

14.129

This obligation is described as a restitutionary duty and forms part of the Court's remedial approach to Convention violations, including under Art 41.

93 *Begum v Secretary of State for the Home Department* [2021] UKSC 7.
94 [2021] UKSC 28; [2022] AC 487.
95 Siobhán Mullally, *Report of the Special Rapporteur on trafficking in persons, especially women and children: Implementation of the non-punishment principle* (21 June–9 July 2021) UN Doc A/HRC/47/34.
96 *Papamichalopoulos v Greece* App no 14556/89 ECHR 28.

14.130

However, no restitutionary duty arises unless a breach is established. A mere possibility or arguable breach is insufficient to trigger this obligation. Even where a breach is found, the ECtHR has consistently held that States retain discretion in determining the appropriate form of reparation; it is for the State concerned to decide how to discharge its obligation within its domestic legal system.

14.131

This latitude reflects the subsidiarity principle and the margin of appreciation afforded to States in implementing Convention rights. The form of reparation may vary, including restitution, compensation, or other measures, depending on the nature of the breach, the harm suffered, and the domestic legal and institutional context.

The Procedural Duty: The Duty to investigate under Art 4

14.132

In *Rantsev v Cyprus and Russia*[97], the ECtHR held that ECAT explicitly requires each State Party to establish jurisdiction over any Art 4-type offence committed in its territory. This is a logical consequence of the procedural obligation under Art 4 to investigate alleged offences. The Court distinguishes between two types of duties that must be kept conceptually separate: an official criminal investigation, and an effective judicial mechanism capable of elucidating the circumstances and sequence of events said to have led to the alleged harm.[98]

14.133

The ECtHR has held that the ECHR does not impose procedural obligations to investigate matters that fall outside a State's jurisdiction for the purposes of Art 1[99]. There is therefore no duty to investigate Art 4 offences which have occurred within the exclusive jurisdiction of other States (whether or not they are parties to the ECHR). In such cases, the limit of the obligation is to cooperate with those States, in particular through mutual legal assistance and other forms of international cooperation.

97 App no 25965/04, ECHR 2010.
98 *Ribcheva and Others v Bulgaria* no 37801/16, 30 March 2021, [139]; *Anna Todorova v Bulgaria* no 23302/03, 24 May 2011, [74].
99 *Rantsev v Cyprus and Russia* App no 25965/04, ECHR 2010 [289].

14.134

As the Supreme Court confirmed in *MS(Pakistan)*[100] the duty must be discharged by the police, not the Competent Authority. Lord Justice Burnett in *Secretary of State for the Home Department v H*[101] stated this duty rested with the CPS and Police. A duty triggered not by the lodging of a complaint but by circumstances giving rise to a credible suspicion of trafficking, slavery or related offences.

14.135

The ECtHR has confirmed that this investigatory duty extends to prosecutors[102] and the judicial authorities[103]. In respect of judicial authorities, the ECtHR otherwise frames this as a failure of effective judicial response.

Autonomous nature of the procedural obligation

14.136

Under Arts 2 (right to life) and 3 (prohibition of torture, inhuman or degrading treatment), the ECtHR has consistently held that the obligation to conduct an effective investigation, the 'procedural obligation', is distinct and autonomous from the substantive duty not to take life or inflict ill-treatment. This procedural duty may be triggered even in the absence of any allegation or evidence that the State is directly responsible for the underlying harm. The Court has modelled the positive obligations under Art 4 on those under Arts 2 and 3, as all three protect 'basic values of society.'

In practice, the Court may find a violation of the procedural obligation to investigate a potential loss of life or ill-treatment even where there is no complaint, and no finding, that the State has breached the substantive right. The purpose of the procedural obligation is to ensure accountability and transparency in response to credible allegations or circumstances suggesting a possible breach, irrespective of whether the State's own conduct is at issue. Without an effective investigation, it is not possible to determine whether there has been a breach of Arts 2, 3 or 4: it is the investigative process which serves to elucidate the relevant facts. [104] This obligation to investigate is therefore underpinned by the rule of law (see **Chapter 10**).

100 *MS (Pakistan) v Secretary of State for the Home Department* [2020] UKSC 9.
101 *Secretary of State for the Home Department v Hoang Anh Minh* [2016] EWCA Civ 565; [2016] Imm AR 1272.
102 See *Secretary of State for the Home Department v Hoang Anh Minh* [2016] EWCA Civ 565; Imm AR 1272, [39].
103 *Chowdury and Others v Greece*.
104 *M.H. and Others v Croatia*, no 15670/18 and 43115/18, 18 November 2021, [165].

Standards for an effective investigation

14.137

Art 4 ECHR is engaged as soon as the matter comes to the attention of the authorities. Once triggered, the investigation must meet the following standards:

- Independence and impartiality of the investigating body;
- Promptness and reasonable expedition, with urgency where there is a possibility of removing the individual from a harmful situation;
- Effectiveness, meaning the investigation must be thorough, involve the victim, capable of leading to the identification and punishment of those responsible, this is an obligation concerning the means to be employed, not the results to be achieved;
- Evidence gathering, requiring authorities to take all reasonable steps available to secure evidence concerning the incident. This should not depend on an initiative of the applicant to take the responsibility for the conduct of any investigatory procedures[105];
- Proportionality, ensuring that the obligation is not interpreted in a way that imposes an impossible or disproportionate burden on the authorities.

Justiciability of ECAT provisions and Art 4 ECHR compliance

14.138

The justiciability of the ECAT within UK law is contingent upon the manner and extent to which its provisions are incorporated into domestic legislation or arise as part of a positive obligation under Art 4.

Statutory incorporation and public law

14.139

Where it is asserted that ECAT provisions are expressly embedded in primary or secondary legislation, such as the MSA 2015 or the NABA 2022, they are enforceable as statutory rights. The court's task is to ascertain the objective intention of Parliament, as manifested by the language it has chosen to use, interpreted in the context of the legislation as a whole and with due regard to its underlying purposes, so far as those purposes can reliably be obtained from admissible material.

105 *S M. v Croatia* [GC], [336].

14.140

Only where ambiguity remains and where Convention rights are engaged, does the interpretative obligation under s 3 of the HRA 1998 arise. Section 3 requires courts to interpret legislation compatibly with Convention rights 'so far as possible,' but *Secretary of State for Business and Trade v Mercer*[106] confirms that this obligation does not extend to altering the fundamental architecture of a statutory scheme. Judicial interpretation must respect the legislative intent and structural coherence of the statute.

Unincorporated ECAT duties and statutory guidance

14.141

Absent statutory incorporation, ECAT does not confer directly enforceable rights in domestic law unless they find voice in the positive obligations under Art 4. The Supreme Court has consistently held that unincorporated treaties are not a source of justiciable obligations. However, where government policy expressly purports to implement ECAT, such policy may be challengeable on public law grounds. The courts have recognised, in cases such as *EOG & KTT*[107], that failure to adhere to self-imposed policy commitments may constitute a reviewable error, but only while the policy remains in force and only to the extent that it aligns with ECAT.

14.142

Should the government withdraw or disclaim its intention to comply with ECAT, the courts would lack jurisdiction to enforce the treaty's provisions independently unless the ECAT measure is integral or constitutes a positive obligation under Art 4 ECHR.

ECAT as an interpretative tool for Art 4 ECHR Positive obligations

14.143

Both the ECtHR[108] and the UK Supreme Court[109] have affirmed that the content of the positive obligations under Art 4 ECHR are informed by ECAT as interpreted by GRETA, its monitoring body. The ECtHR relies on ECAT to provide the substantive framework for understanding the nature and scope of the positive obligations owed to victims. This interpretative approach is

106 *Secretary of State for Business and Trade v Mercer* [2023] UKSC 12.
107 [2022] EWCA Civ 307.
108 *Chowdhury v Greece* [104].
109 *MS(Pakistan) v Secretary of State for the Home Department* [2020] UKSC 9[25] and [27].

consistent with the Court's broader interpretative principle that the ECHR must not be read in isolation, but should, so far as possible, be interpreted harmoniously with other rules of international law of which it forms part (see **Chapter 1**). The Supreme Court has not yet been required to resolve the issue of whether all the obligations in ECAT are incorporated into a State's positive obligations under Art 4.[110]

14.144

Where the Strasbourg court has not yet decided whether a particular ECAT provision corresponds to, or helps define, a positive obligation under Art 4, it falls to the domestic courts to identify the scope of that obligation for themselves. This is consistent with s 2 of the Human Rights Act 1998, which requires courts to take account of ECtHR case law but does not require them to follow it in every respect. As Lord Dyson explained in *Rabone v Pennine Care NHS Trust*[111] in relation to the evolving operational duty under Art 2, the Strasbourg jurisprudence in a developing area may be incomplete and its contours will often emerge only incrementally, in a way that resembles the gradual evolution of the common law of negligence. The same dynamic can arise under Art 4 (see **Chapter 1**), recent domestic authority has emphasised that any extension of Art 4 obligations must be approached with particular caution, as illustrated by *Begum v Secretary of State for the Home Department*[112].

Part 4: Trafficking, slavery, and extradition — legal framework and case law

Modern slavery and trafficking: substance and limits of extradition bars

14.145

As set out above, the question of whether a person's extradition is barred by reason of one of the heads raised in challenge to extradition is to be considered by the judge at the extradition hearing. A number of arguments may be relevant in the context where the requested person is a victim of trafficking or modern slavery and typically there is an overlap between the issues raised.

14.146

In some cases, a person's identification as a victim, *might* explain or be connected to the commission of the extradition offence. However, scenarios where there is a causal link between the requested person's extradition offence

110 Ibid, [27].
111 See *Rabone v Pennine Care NHS Trust* [2012] UKSC 2.
112 *Begum v Secretary of State for the Home Department* [2021] UKSC 7.

(whether convicted or merely accused) and trafficking or modern slavery are comparatively rare. Rather a requested person's status as a victim more often arises where there is no connection to the criminality which prompted an extradition request.

14.147

Extradition courts have been sensitive to issues of trafficking, slavery and related offences but have chosen to do so within the framework of traditional challenges, often in the context of potential prospectives breaches of Art 8 or on the basis of injustice or oppression given a requested person's mental or physical health. *Ministry of Justice of Lithuania v AI*[113] considered and placed significant weight upon the evidence of AI's trafficking and the psychological harm that had been caused as a consequence. The court concluded in the face of this evidence that there would be a real risk that AI's rights under ECHR, Art 3 would be breached if she were extradited to Lithuania. In *AI* the trafficking had no nexus to the offending which was the subject of the extradition and had post-dated the offending. A point which could be made in a case like this is whether extradition would have breached Art 4 ECHR: extradition would have deprived her of assistance to recover from the trafficking and would have interfered with the investigation into her trafficking[114].

14.148

Where Art 4 ECHR is raised as a distinct ground in extradition, it typically forms part of broader submissions or an allegation of a risk of trafficking or re-trafficking if extradited. There remains limited engagement in extradition appeals with the UK's positive and procedural obligations under Art 4 ECHR and their bearing on the principles articulated in *Celinski* or as a standalone ground of challenge on human rights grounds (see Part 3)[115]. As awareness of States' positive obligations towards victims has increased, further judicial clarification may assist in defining their scope and practical effect. At present, there also appears to be a lack of alignment between the approach taken in criminal prosecutions,[116] where the status of a potentially trafficked defendant should, in principle, be resolved before plea. At least until *KTT v Secretary of State for the Home Department*,[117] Home Office practice had the effect that protection was, in substance, withheld from confirmed victims with trafficking-related asylum claims unless and until their status was recognised in a way that permitted the grant of leave. That approach was found to be unlawful.

113 [2010] EWHC 2299 (Admin) 2010 WL 3515648.

114 *F.M. v Russia*, App. No 71671/16 40190/18, 10 December 2024, paras 280 and 307; *Chowdhury v Greece*, App. No 21884/15, 30 March 2017, paras 110 and 116.

115 *Ministry of Justice of Lithuania v AI* [2010] EWHC 2299 (Admin); *Z v Poland* [2014] EWHC 1242 (Admin); and *NV v Czech Republic* [2020] EWHC 409 (Admin).

116 *R v D* [2018] EWCA Crim 2995: The status of any potentially trafficked defendant should preferably be determined before any plea is entered.

117 *KTT v SSHD* [2021] EWHC 2722 (Admin)

Timing and identification of victim status

Early identification and evidence gathering

14.149

For a requested person to rely on their status as a victim or potential victim of modern slavery or human trafficking to resist extradition, it is essential that legal representatives identify any trafficking or modern slavery related issues at the earliest opportunity and substantiate them promptly with appropriate evidence. Early engagement enables the necessary procedural safeguards to be triggered and ensures that the court is fully informed of the potential implications under Art 4 ECHR. This, in turn, requires a clear understanding of the legal definitions of slavery, servitude, forced or compulsory labour, and human trafficking (see **Chapter 1**), as well as familiarity with the National Referral Mechanism process (see **Chapter 4**). A trauma-informed approach to client interaction and evidence-gathering is also crucial (see **Chapter 3**), given the vulnerabilities and complexities that frequently arise in such cases.

14.150

If concerns about trafficking or related acts are not identified early, they may be met with scepticism later in proceedings, and there may be insufficient time to gather supporting evidence. While the Statutory Guidance offers caution against dismissing late disclosures, extradition courts are particularly sensitive to perceived delaying tactics, especially in conviction cases, where time spent in custody may be deducted from the sentence imposed by the requesting state.

14.151

Where an individual resists extradition based on having experienced trafficking, slavery, or related exploitation, they may be required to provide detailed evidence of the alleged Art 4 abuse. Consideration will be required as to whether special measures are necessary (see **Chapters 3** and **8**).

14.152

As recognised in *VCL and AN v United Kingdom*, the applicants were required to proceed with the criminal trial when there had been no Art 4 compliant investigation into their trafficking (see **Chapter 10**). The ECtHR held that this denied them access to potentially exculpatory evidence which was fundamental to their defence. The Court concluded that this breached the applicants Art 6 ECHR rights.

14.153

Where *prima facie* evidence of trafficking or modern slavery arises, the parties and the court will be required to consider the following issues in light of Art 4 of the ECHR:

(a) What positive obligations are engaged under Art 4 ECHR, including the duty to take operational measures to protect individuals from trafficking and exploitation and investigate the allegation;

(b) Which state authority or authorities bear responsibility for discharging those obligations, whether in the context of identification, protection, investigation, or prevention;

(c) Whether those positive obligations have been fulfilled, having regard to the procedural and substantive duties imposed by Art 4;

(d) If the obligations have not been met, how this affects the requested person's ability to effectively present their case resisting extradition, including any risk of further Art 4 harms, lack of protection, ongoing investigation or inability to access recovery or remedies in the receiving state.

14.154

The judgment in *VCL and AN v the United Kingdom* establishes a series of interrelated principles that underscore the State's positive obligations in cases involving potential victims of trafficking:

1. **Early identification is paramount**

   The timely identification of victims is essential to ensuring that their rights under Art 4 ECHR are respected. Delay or failure in this regard risks undermining the fairness of any subsequent legal proceedings.

2. **Trigger for assessment**

   Where the authorities are, or ought reasonably to be aware of circumstances giving rise to a credible suspicion that an individual suspected of committing a criminal offence may have been a victim of an Art 4 violation, there is a duty to ensure that the individual is promptly assessed by professionals trained and qualified in identifying and supporting victims of trafficking and modern slavery.

3. **Standards for assessment**

   For trafficking any such assessment must be conducted in accordance with the criteria set out in the Palermo Protocol and ECAT. These instruments define trafficking by reference to acts (eg recruitment, transportation), means (eg coercion, deception), and purpose (exploitation), with the important caveat that the element of coercion is not required in the case of children. In respect of slavery, servitude or forced labour the assessment must be consistent with Art 4 (see **Chapter 1** defining these acts).

4. **State responsibility independent of defence conduct**

   While criminal defence lawyers must remain alert to indicators of trafficking or modern slavery, their failure to recognise the indicators, does not relieve the State of its independent responsibility. The obligation to identify and protect victims of trafficking or modern slavery lies with the competent national authorities and other public authorities. Where legal representation is publicly funded, the State must intervene in the event of a manifest failure by counsel to provide effective representation (see *Daud v Portugal*, 21 April 1998, [38]), which can encompass a failure recognise indicators of Art 4 violations.

5. **Failure to conduct a timely investigation**

The authorities' failure to conduct a timely investigation into whether the applicants had been trafficked, despite clear circumstances giving rise to a credible suspicion, breached the State's positive obligations and, in the context of Art 6, deprived the applicants of the opportunity to secure evidence that could have formed a fundamental aspect of their defence.

Victim identification in the extradition context

14.155

In extradition proceedings, the identification of potential victims of trafficking or modern slavery frequently depends on the individual raising a concern themselves. This reactive model stands in contrast to the proactive obligations articulated by the ECtHR in *VCL and AN v United Kingdom*, which emphasise that where there is credible suspicion of an Art 4 violation, prompt assessment by trained professionals is required.

The arrest that initiates extradition proceedings may be the first occasion on which the requested person comes into contact with UK authorities. It cannot therefore be assumed that trafficking or modern slavery indicators have previously been identified or recorded. Although the NCA is a designated first responder under the National Referral Mechanism (NRM) (see **Chapter 4**), its direct contact with requested persons in extradition cases is often limited. Even where an NRM referral exists, there is no certainty that it will have been communicated to the legal representative in the extradition proceedings, who may be a duty solicitor with little or no access to earlier information.

Against this backdrop, it is often defence representatives who, in practice, bear the immediate responsibility for recognising and raising potential trafficking or modern slavery issues and requesting that a first responder refer their client into the NRM. This may be beneficial for the requested person, particularly where trust and rapport have been established, however it underscores the practical reality that the initial identification process may depend on actors whose institutional role falls outside the formal first-responder framework. That said, although defence lawyers are not designated first responders under the NRM, they may request that a first responder organisation make a referral on behalf of their client. In practice, they retain significant scope to shape and support that process and should work proactively with the first responder once a referral is made to the NRM (see **Chapter 4**).

However, defence lawyers cannot replicate the institutional connections, statutory powers, or operational reach of those who are. Although the CPS is likewise not a first responder, its role is fundamentally different: as part of the criminal justice system, it works directly with law-enforcement agencies, receives investigative material, and can initiate or shape investigative action where appropriate (see **Chapter 10**). Defence representatives, by contrast, lack access to the institutional pathways that enable the State to discharge its investigative obligations.

Where an alleged Art 4 violation falls within the jurisdiction of the United Kingdom, effective engagement between designated first responders, the police, and the CPS is essential to ensuring the prompt and effective investigation required by Art 4 ECHR. These investigative duties lie squarely with the State, not with the defence. Defence involvement can assist in facilitating disclosure, supporting the requested person, and ensuring trauma-informed coordination with safeguarding professionals (see **Chapter 3**), but it cannot substitute for the law-enforcement functions and investigatory responsibilities that underpin the State's positive obligations.

The current reliance on defence representatives to trigger identification mechanisms, in the absence of a formalised institutional process within extradition proceedings, raises questions about the extent to which existing practice aligns with the State's positive obligations under Arts 4 and 6 ECHR as interpreted in *VCL and AN v UK*.

Significant difficulties can arise where defence representatives do not identify potential indicators or fail to advise the requested person about grounds for resisting extradition that derive from alleged Art 4 violations. As the Court made clear in *VCL and AN v UK*, public authorities cannot disregard their positive obligations merely because the defence has not raised the issue, provided there is a credible suspicion of trafficking or modern slavery. In circumstances where the defence does not proactively engage, responsibility will fall to the prosecution to ensure that relevant trafficking or modern slavery indicators are raised before the court (see **Chapter 10**).

There remains the wider principle that the duty of identification applies not only to executive agencies but also to judicial authorities. As confirmed in *Chowdhury v Greece* and *VCL and AN v UK*, judges must themselves remain alert to indicators of trafficking or modern slavery and cannot rely solely on formal designation processes.

It will therefore be permissible for a judge to raise with the parties the possible presence of trafficking or modern slavery indicators where these appear, on one view of the evidence, to arise. A judge may do so while making clear that the credibility, weight, and ultimate significance of any indicators remain matters for determination at the appropriate stage, thereby avoiding any descent into the arena. This approach accords with the authorities confirming that judges may exercise robust case management without prejudging contested matters.

However, the limits of judicial intervention are well established. In *Re Q*[118], the Court of Appeal held that comments made by the judge gave rise to a danger of apparent bias, highlighting the distinction between 'robust active case management' and 'premature adjudication.' Similarly, in *Dorman & Ors v Clinton Devon Farms Partnership*[119], Mr Justice Saini allowed an appeal against a refusal to recuse, finding that vigorous case management had crossed into apparent bias. These authorities reinforce the need for judges to remain scrupulously neutral while ensuring that relevant indicators are properly ventilated.

Given these strict confines on the judicial role, the effectiveness of safeguarding obligations in extradition proceedings depends heavily on the proactive engagement of the parties. It is ultimately for those appearing before the court, both prosecution and defence, to identify, articulate, and substantiate potential trafficking or modern slavery concerns at the earliest opportunity. Only through such proactive participation can the court be placed in a position to discharge its own procedural obligations under Art 4 ECHR while maintaining the necessary neutrality of the judicial role.

14.156

The extradition court may be called upon to consider an abuse of process application where allegations under Arts 4 and 6 of the ECHR raise fair trial issues within the domestic extradition proceedings. In an extradition context this requires the court to strike a delicate balance of complying with its own procedural obligations under Art 4, while respecting the adversarial nature of the proceedings.

14.157

However, unlike in domestic criminal proceedings, the abuse jurisdiction in extradition does not extend to the way the requesting state conducts or will conduct its proceedings; such matters are only justiciable where they amount to a flagrant denial of Art 6 rights.[120]

NRM decisions

14.158

Once legal representatives have referred a requested person to a first responder to trigger the NRM mechanism, the respective reasonable grounds and conclusive decisions will be awaited.

This process involves consideration of two key issues:

118 [2014] EWCA Civ 91.
119 [2019] EWHC 2988 (QB).
120 *Hafeez v Government of the United States of America* [2020] EWHC 155 (Admin) at [73].

- The admissibility and status of the NRM decisions;
- The extent to which courts will adjourn pending these decisions.

Status of NRM decisions

14.159

Two years after the judgment in *Celinski,* Thomas CJ presiding in *R v Joseph, VCL & Ors*[121] confirmed

> 'The decision of the competent authority as to whether a person had been trafficked for the purposes of exploitation is not binding on the court but, unless there was evidence to contradict it or significant evidence that had not been considered, it is likely that the criminal courts will abide by the decision (see *R v L(C), N, N & T, 2013* at paragraph 28)[122].'

In criminal proceedings, a positive reasonable or conclusive grounds decision that a defendant is a victim of trafficking or modern slavery does not compel the prosecution to discontinue the case.[123] However, any decision to depart from such a finding must be supported by good reasons that are consistent with the UK's obligations under the relevant international trafficking instruments and with the prosecution's own guidance, which is framed in light of the State's positive duties under Art 4 ECHR. A central consideration, reflected in the CPS guidance, will be whether the police have discharged the procedural duty to investigate where the alleged trafficking or modern slavery occurred within the UK (see **Chapter 10**).

The same principle applies to judicial decision-making: a fact finding judge, whether in criminal or extradition proceedings, is not bound by a reasonable or conclusive grounds decision, but any decision to depart from it must be reasoned, justified, and compatible with the obligations identified in *VCL and AN v UK*[124]. As the ECtHR held in *VCL and AN v UK* at [196]:

> 'Although victims of trafficking are not immune from prosecution, an individual's status as a victim of trafficking may affect whether there is sufficient evidence to prosecute and whether it is in the public interest to do so (see paragraph 161 above). Evidence concerning an accused's status as a victim of trafficking is therefore a 'fundamental aspect' of the defence which he or she should be able to secure without restriction.'

121 *R v Joseph & Ors* [2017] EWCA Crim 36.

122 Ibid. [20 viii].

123 *R v AAD, AAH and AAI* [2022] EWCA Crim 106 para 142(4); *Brecani* [2021] EWCA Crim 731, para 9; V.C.L. and A.N. v UK, App. nos 77587/12 and 74603/12, 16 February 2021, para 162.

124 V.C.L. and A.N. v UK, App. nos 77587/12 and 74603/12, 16 February 2021, para 172 and 181.

14.160

The competence of the courts and tribunals to make findings of fact on the question of whether an individual is a victim of trafficking or modern slavery has been confirmed by the Supreme Court in *MS(Pakistan) v Secretary of State for the Home Department*, this will necessarily include determining the admissibility or weight given to an NRM decision. The veracity of the evidential value of the NRM decisions in criminal cases has been considered by the senior courts, including the Court of Appeal Criminal Division (CACD)[125]. The decisions of *SLP v Prosecutor General of the Republic of Latvia (Rev1)* [126] and *Koceku v Albania*[127] are to be understood against that backdrop.

14.161

However, for the purposes of this section, it is not the evidential value of the NRM decision of itself that is considered, but rather the procedural implications arising from the making of that decision. It is the fact and context of the decision itself, not its substantive weight, that may warrant further consideration.

The threshold of a positive NRM reasonable grounds decision

14.162

The ECtHR does not prescribe to member states how they should comply with their systems duty to put in place mechanisms to prevent Art 4 harms, protect victims or prosecute offences.

14.163

In *Secretary of State for the Home Department v H*[128], Lord Justice Burnett held that the UK does not operate a single body responsible for fulfilling all the obligations arising under Art 4 ECHR. As observed by Lord Justice Underhill in *R(TDT) v Secretary of State for the Home Department*[129], a victim of an Art 4 offence can be 'identified' as a victim absent an NRM decision, because evidence giving rise to a credible suspicion of trafficking could be present and known or ought to be known by the relevant public authorities (in that case the Home Office) prior to a decision being reached under the NRM framework.

125 See *R v ADD* & Ors [2022] EWCA Crim 106 and Ors at [85iv].

126 *SLP v Prosecutor General of the Republic of Latvia (Rev1)* [2025] EWHC 298 (Admin) at [26].

127 *Koceku v Albania* [2024] EWHC 1028 (Admin).

128 *Secretary of State for the Home Department v Hoang Anh Minh* [2016] EWHC 299 (Admin); *Secretary of State for the Home Department v Hoang Anh Minh* [2016] EWCA Civ 565.

129 *R (TDT) v Secretary of State for the Home Department* [2018] EWCA Civ 1395.

14.164

The statutory framework underpinning the National Referral Mechanism (NRM) is set out in Part 2 above and examined at length in **Chapter 4**.

To understand the procedural significance of the reasonable grounds decision made by the Competent Authority, the starting point is Lord Justice Burnett's analysis in *Secretary of State for the Home Department v Hoang Anh Minh,* that the threshold applied in a reasonable grounds decision-making is substantially aligned with the 'credible suspicion' standard recognised in Art 4 jurisprudence. He went on to observe that where the Competent Authority concludes that there are reasonable grounds to believe an offence under Art 4 ECHR has been committed, it is required to notify the police. Its role in any potential criminal investigation is limited to this notification function following a positive reasonable grounds decision. Importantly, Lord Justice Burnett noted that a failure by the Competent Authority to notify the police, resulting in the individual's removal from the UK before a justiciable offence could be investigated, may give rise to a successful complaint under Art 4 ECHR.

14.165

As Lord Justice Underhill held in *R(TDT) v Secretary of State for the Home Department*[130] at [35]:

> 'I turn to the protection duty under Art 4 of the ECHR, as articulated in *Rantsev.* As held by Burnett LJ in *Hoang* (see para. 31 (2) above), **the 'reasonable grounds' test to be applied by the Competent Authority is substantially equivalent to the 'credible suspicion' threshold under Art 4. But it does not follow that that threshold may not, on the facts of a particular case, have been crossed before the case comes before the Competent Authority** – that is, at the earlier stage when a member of the Home Office front-line staff decides to refer. **Indeed that will be so in most cases where a positive reasonable grounds decision is subsequently made: if the case crossed the credible suspicion threshold when considered by the Competent Authority it will also have done so at the point when it was referred. Accordingly, the Secretary of State will have come under the protection duty under Art 4 sometime before the Competent Authority makes its decision**. It should be noted that the designation of the Competent Authority under the UK system – whether it be the UKHTC or part of the Home Office – is a purely domestic construct: the Court in Rantsev and Chowdhury refers simply to 'the State authorities', which would embrace front-line staff as much as the authorities further up the chain of referral.' [Emphasis added]

130 Ibid.

14.166

In light of Lord Justice Underhill's analysis above, a positive reasonable grounds decision, being a determination by a State authority that the credible-suspicion threshold has been met, serves as the point at which the State's positive obligations under the ECHR are triggered (see Part 3). The ECtHR reaffirmed this in *VCL and AN v UK*, emphasising that such a decision engages the procedural duties arising under Art 4 whenever there is a credible indication that an individual may have been a victim of trafficking or modern slavery.

The rule of law requires that the substantive protections guaranteed by Arts 2, 3 and 4 are rendered effective through the rigorous enforcement of criminal law and the proper investigation of complaints. As Lord Kerr observed in *DSD*[131], the Strasbourg Court has consistently held that investigations must be independent, prompt and capable of establishing the relevant facts and identifying and punishing those responsible, while ensuring effective participation of the victim, principles summarised in *O'Keeffe v Ireland*. Read together with the ECtHR's judgment in *VCL and AN v UK*, these authorities make clear that once a positive reasonable grounds decision is made by the competent authority, the State's protective and procedural obligations under Art 4 are firmly engaged. Ensuring that these duties are discharged with diligence and expedition is not merely good practice; it is essential to upholding the rule of law and ensuring the Convention's guarantees have practical effect.

Positive obligations in the extradition context: matters for consideration

14.167

The extent of the procedural duty to investigate will depend on the location of the alleged Art 4 abuse.

14.168

By contrast, the protective duty to provide assistance and support to enable recovery requires an individualised assessment, and access to such support is not contingent upon where the abuse occurred (see **Chapters 4** and **5**).

14.169

As examined in above, the ECtHR can find a violation of the procedural duty to investigate, even if there is no complaint or finding that the State actually breached the underlying substantive right. The procedural obligation exists to ensure accountability and transparency whenever credible allegations or

131 *Commissioner of Police of the Metropolis v DSD & NBV* (Rev 1) [2018] UKSC 11, [2019] AC 196 at [24].

circumstances suggest a potential breach, regardless of whether the State's own actions or omissions are at issue.

14.170

As the Court held in *Begum*[132], it requires a two-step process (i) was the credible threshold met for Art 4; and (ii) what positive obligations arise. In extradition cases, the third question may be, which state is responsible (or was responsible) for meeting those positive obligations.

Celinski, SLP and Koceku: Judicial autonomy, status and admissibility of NRM decisions in Extradition Proceedings

14.171

Any application for an adjournment to allow for an NRM referral and decision-making to take place must be considered in light of the duty on public authorities, which includes the court, to act compatibly with Convention rights.[133] This will require consideration of the procedural consequences of such a decision on the extradition proceedings.

14.172

In *Polish Judicial Authorities v Celinski and Others*, Mr Cambal resisted extradition in part on the basis that he had been trafficked. He gave evidence before the District Judge that, following an initial court appearance for criminal offences in Slovakia, he had been trafficked to the United Kingdom for the purposes of sexual and labour exploitation, from which he later escaped. He had been convicted and sentenced *in absentia*. Before the extradition proceedings commenced, he had been referred into the National Referral Mechanism (NRM) as a potential victim of trafficking.

The District Judge rejected his account and concluded that there was no real risk of a breach of his rights under Art 4 ECHR; his discharge was ordered on unrelated grounds. On appeal by the requesting state, Mr Cambal relied on a positive conclusive grounds decision that he was a victim of trafficking issued by the UK Competent Authority, contending that the extradition request required re-examination in light of that determination. Lord Thomas CJ held that the Competent Authority's positive finding made no difference because the extradition judge had heard his evidence and rejected it, and those facts must be respected. The Court also emphasised that extradition hearings should not normally be adjourned pending NRM referrals or deferred pending Competent Authority decisions.

132 *Begum v Secretary of State for the Home Department* [2021] UKSC 7.
133 Section 6 of the Human Rights Act 1998.

It remains for the judge to determine the issue of trafficking assisted by the CPS and the UK Competent Authority providing the relevant evidence underlying that decision[134].

Points now arising in light of subsequent jurisprudence

14.173

Several points must be made about *Celinski* in the current legal landscape.

First, Lord Thomas CJ's judgment in *Celinski* preceded his later decision in *R (Joseph and Others)*[135], in which, following consideration of Lord Judge CJ's earlier analysis in *R (L and Others)*[136] (a judgment not referred to in *Celinski*), he confirmed that a decision-maker may depart from a positive identification decision of the Competent Authority only where there is a *good reason* to do so.

14.174

Secondly, *Celinski* predates the sequence of domestic and Strasbourg authorities that now define the Art 4 framework in cases involving trafficking or modern slavery indicators (see **Chapters 4** and **10**). Following *Celinski*, the analysis of Lord Justice Burnett (as he then was) in *Secretary of State for the Home Department v H*[137] clarified that a positive reasonable grounds decision by the Competent Authority meets the credible suspicion under Art 4 ECHR. Lord Justice Underhill sub*sequently confirmed that position in R(TDT) v Secretary of State for the Home Department*[138] and held that such a decision(reasonable grounds) would trigger the State's protective and procedural obligations, but went further, emphasising that the Art 4 positive obligations may arise even in the absence of a reasonable grounds decision where the indicators of trafficking or modern slavery are present and known, or ought to have been known, to the relevant public authorities. In *VCL and AN v United Kingdom*, consistent with that approach, the ECtHR held that: (a) a positive reasonable grounds decision engaged Art 4 positive obligations; (b) credible suspicion may arise earlier, before any formal decision, where the information justifies it; and (c) failures to identify, investigate and safeguard victims of violations of Art 4 gave rise to a breach of Art 6, compromising the fairness of the criminal proceedings. Separately, the Supreme Court in *MS (Pakistan)*[139] recognised that, on the facts of a given case, Art 4 procedural obligations may require that a potential victim is not removed from the United Kingdom where removal would risk a breach of Art 4 duty to investigate.

134 See also, *SNT v Poland* [2024] EWHC3349 (Admin).

135 [2017] EWCA Crim 36.

136 [2013] EWCA Crim 991, [2014] 1 All ER 113.

137 *Secretary of State for the Home Department v Hoang Anh Minh* [2016] EWCA Civ 565.

138 *R (TDT) v Secretary of State for the Home Department* [2018] EWCA Civ 1395.

139 *MS (Pakistan) v Secretary of State for the Home Department* [2020] UKSC 9.

14.175

Thirdly, and in that regard, Lord Thomas CJ's judgment in *R(Joseph and Others)* must be read in the light of the ECtHR's decision in *VCL and AN v United Kingdom. VCL* was an appellant in *R(Joseph and Others).* The decision in *R (Joseph & Others)* concerned the choice of the prosecution to continue with criminal proceedings notwithstanding a positive identification by the Competent Authority. The Court of Appeal (Criminal Division) upheld that decision. When considered by analogy in the extradition context, its reasoning must now be read alongside the ECtHR's judgment in *VCL and AN v United Kingdom.* As set out above, the Strasbourg Court held that the United Kingdom, including its courts, had breached Arts 4 and 6 by failing to engage with the positive obligations arising from a positive identification decision. That analysis is directly relevant to understanding *Joseph*: where a positive identification has been made, the decision to proceed, whether with a prosecution or, in the extradition context, without adjournment or further inquiry, requires the authorities and the courts to address the Art 4 procedural and protective duties that arise and to justify proceeding, if they do so, when these obligations have not been discharged.

These later authorities were not before the court in *Celinski.*

SLP ,Art 13 and the evidential status of NRM decisions

14.176

In *SLP v Prosecutor General of the Republic of Latvia (Rev 1)*[140], Mr Justice Dexter Dias summarised the position on decisions made by the Single Competent Authority (SCA). He observed that conclusive grounds decisions are made on the balance of probabilities, on the papers, and are not binding on the extradition judge. The judge must reach an independent view on whether the person is a victim and may disagree with the SCA. Extradition proceedings should not ordinarily be delayed to accommodate referrals or pending decisions, though an adjournment may be justified on the facts.

It is important to recognise the limits of what *SLP* decided. In this case a positive reasonable grounds decision had been made. The issue before the court was whether s 61 of the Nationality and Borders Act 2022, which implements the United Kingdom's obligations under Art 13 of the Council of Europe Convention on Action against Trafficking in Human Beings (ECAT), created a bar to extradition by reason of an NRM decision, an ongoing identification process, or the operation of the statutory recovery and reflection period. The court therefore analysed s 61 for what it expressly does: it prohibits removal during the recovery period and requires the person to be permitted to remain

140 [2025] EWHC 298 (Admin), KBD.

in the United Kingdom for its duration, unless public order provisions apply (s 63 of NABA 2022[141]).

14.177

The Court in its analysis was assisted by the Explanatory Notes to NABA 2022, which confirm that s 61 was enacted 'to give effect to Article 13 ECAT' and that the recovery period is designed to ensure that, once reasonable grounds exist, the potential victim 'must not be removed from the UK' and is afforded time to recover and decide freely whether to cooperate with the authorities.

Mr Justice Dexter Dias concluded that a requested person could not avail themselves of s61 of NABA 2022 because this was directed at those subject to removal under immigration powers not extradition proceedings, concluding that NABA 2022 was legislation concerned with those subject to immigration control not extradition.

This case concerned a complex legal framework which traversed ECAT, Art 4 and domestic legislation intended to give effect to the former and which was silent on the latter. It is against that backdrop that the following analysis should be understood.

Art 13 of ECAT

14.178

Art 13 of ECAT makes clear that the recovery and reflection period is a 'distinct and powerful' measure and during this period it should not be possible to enforce any expulsion[142] against the potential victim. GRETA[143] has provided commentary on the purpose of this measure:

Recovery. The first purpose is to afford the presumed victim time and space to recover and to escape the influence of traffickers. This protected interval is intended to stabilise the individual and support access to assistance.

Reflection and informed choice. The second purpose is to enable an informed decision about cooperation with the authorities. 'Informed' presupposes calm decision-making with access to legal information and support, free from pressure.

Identification and investigation. Once there are reasonable grounds to believe a person is a victim, the period must be provided, expulsion must not be enforced, and the person must be authorised to stay. This facilitates

141 See **Chapter 4**, as decision-making under s63 has been paused.

142 ECAT uses the term 'expulsion' not removal or deportation.

143 GRETA (Group of Experts on Action against Trafficking in Human Beings), *Guidance Note on the Recovery and Reflection Period (Article 13 of the Council of Europe Convention on Action against Trafficking in Human Beings)*, THB-GRETA(2024)14 (Council of Europe 2024).

completion of victim identification and, by building trust in a safe environment, may improve willingness to give evidence and assist investigations.

Non-conditionality. The only pre-requisite is the 'reasonable grounds' threshold. Granting the period is not contingent on cooperation with investigators or prosecutors.

Non-discrimination. The measure is victim-centred and not confined to irregular migrants; it is available to any presumed or identified victim, including EU nationals, where the threshold is met.

Link to the non-punishment principle. The period sits alongside the Convention's non-punishment principle (Art 26), reinforcing a protective approach that avoids penalising victims for conduct arising from their exploitation.

It provides that *once there are reasonable grounds to believe the person is a victim,* this is the same threshold that triggers the Art 4 positive obligations (see *VCL and AN*; Underhill LJ in *R(TDT)*). During this period, ECAT requires that no expulsion be carried out, unless public order grounds apply (see **Chapter 4** for the strict interpretation of Art 13(3)) and the Explanatory Report to ECAT confirms that States must create a legal framework ensuring the person can remain for the duration.

14.179

Although Art 13 emerged within migration-related contexts, both the drafting history and subsequent commentary[144] make clear that its protective purpose is not confined to irregular migrants. Its safeguards are directed to anyone whose circumstances render them vulnerable to exploitation or for whom removal would impede recovery or informed decision-making. GRETA has therefore emphasised that Art 13 functions as a victim-empowerment measure, intended to support 'any presumed or identified victim,' including EU nationals, in regaining autonomy and escaping the influence of traffickers.

14.180

This broader protective purpose is reflected in the travaux préparatoires. During the meetings of the Council of Europe's Ad Hoc Committee on Action against Trafficking in Human Beings (CAHTEH) from 2003 to 2005, the drafters confirmed the fundamental principle of non-conditionality. At the third meeting, the Committee agreed that the recovery and reflection period must not depend on cooperation with investigative or prosecuting authorities. Its aim was to provide victims with the time and space necessary to recover and to assess the options available to them. As the meeting report explained, 'informed'

144 Helmut Sax, 'Article 13 Recovery and Reflection Period' in Julia Planitzer and Helmut Sax (eds), *A Commentary on the Council of Europe Convention on Action against Trafficking in Human Beings* (Edward Elgar Publishing 2020).

decision-making requires that the victim be able to take decisions calmly, with access to information about possible legal action, available protection, and assistance, and free from the continuing influence of traffickers. The drafters also clarified that, to serve these purposes, victims should not be placed at risk of expulsion during that period. States were free to choose the mechanism by which this protection was secured. GRETA has repeatedly stressed that Art 13 is a victim-empowerment measure, grounded in the need for recovery and independent decision-making, and should be accessible to 'any presumed or identified victim,' including EU nationals.

Art 13 of ECAT and Art 4 ECHR

14.181

Absent from the judgment in *SLP*, is the further and necessary step: the connection between Art 13 ECAT, now incorporated into domestic law, and the positive obligations arising under Art 4 ECHR. In this appeal, the positive obligations were triggered by the positive reasonable grounds decision. Further, the Strasbourg Court has treated Art 13 ECAT as informing the scope and content of those obligations (see *Chowdhury v Greece* and **Chapter 4**). In particular, Art 13 reflects the principle that, once there are reasonable grounds to believe someone is a victim of trafficking, the State must create a protected space in which the person can recover, escape the influence of traffickers, access assistance, and take decisions free from pressure. Those safeguards are closely aligned with the investigative and protective duties that arise under Art 4, and the reasonable grounds threshold is a trigger for those obligations.

14.182

Although Art 13 ECAT was addressed, the court does not appear to have been presented with the wider legal framework bearing on the State's positive obligations under Art 4 ECHR. In particular, the connection between Art 13 and those obligations was not explored, notwithstanding that the threshold for engagement had been met. That argument could have been advanced either as a standalone submission under Art 4 or as an interpretative aid to s16 of the NABA 2022, read pursuant to s 3 of the Human Rights Act 1998.

14.183

On the facts of *SLP*, no Art 4 duty to investigate arose for the United Kingdom because the alleged trafficking occurred in Latvia. A duty of co-operation with the Latvian authorities did arise, and investigative obligations may have arisen in Latvia, particularly if indicators were, or ought to have been, known and in any event will likely have been triggered by the UK's positive reasonable-grounds decision. However, the implications of these matters for the positive obligations under Arts 4 and 6 were not developed in argument. Likewise, no submission appears to have been made that extradition would breach Art 4 because the United Kingdom's protective obligations remained undischarged and because Latvia would not, on the evidence, discharge the investigative duty. This lacuna is examined further below.

14.184

Notably, following the dismissal of W's appeal in *W v Spain*[145], a reasonable-grounds decision was subsequently made identifying W as a potential victim of trafficking. In subsequent proceedings, Mr Justice Fordham granted an injunction restraining removal to allow the NRM identification process to run its course. He identified the central question as the applicability of *MS (Pakistan)* to the extradition context and invited the Judicial Authority to provide any 'knock-out answer' to that proposition; none was forthcoming. Before the adjourned hearing, the Judicial Authority accepted that the conclusive-grounds process should be allowed to run to conclusion. In light of the reasonable-grounds finding, the positive obligations engaged included the protective duties of identification and recovery and the procedural duty to investigate; it was the investigative duty that was material to the application of *MS (Pakistan)*[146].

Inadmissibility of brief NRM decisions: the position in Koceku v Albania

14.185

In *Koceku v Albania*[147], the appellant relied on a conclusive grounds decision identifying him as a victim of modern slavery in the United Kingdom. Mr Justice Julian Knowles declined to admit that decision into evidence. The document consisted of a single sentence, without any accompanying reasoning or factual analysis, and appeared inconsistent with the appellant's own account before the District Judge. The court also held that the alleged exploitation took place in the United Kingdom after the appellant's arrival, and was therefore immaterial to the Art 8 proportionality assessment in the extradition proceedings. On that basis, the court concluded that the NRM decision did not assist in determining whether extradition would result in an unjustified interference with the appellant's rights.

14.186

Two points arise from this.

First, in both *Celinski* and *Koceku*, it appears that the underlying minute or reasoning supporting the conclusive grounds decision had not been disclosed

145 [2020] EWHC 2278 (Admin).
146 See *MS(Pakistan)*paras 34-36.
147 [2024] EWHC 1028 (Admin).

to the court. That document is not ordinarily provided to the individual but may be disclosed by the Competent Authority where directed by a court or tribunal. It is unsurprising that this possibility was not explored in those cases: the Modern Slavery Statutory Guidance does not refer expressly to extradition proceedings. The Guidance does, however, recognise duties to disclose reasonable and conclusive grounds minutes in appropriate circumstances, including legal proceedings (see **Chapter 4**). It is to be hoped that these documents will become more readily available.

Second, as Mr Justice Dexter Dias clarified in *SLP v Prosecutor General of the Republic of Latvia (Rev 1)*, the judgment in *Koceku* should not be read as establishing that conclusive grounds decisions are, as a category, inadmissible in extradition proceedings. The refusal to admit the document in *Koceku* was fact-specific, turning on its brevity, lack of reasoning and apparent inconsistency with the appellant's own evidence.

14.187

It is also important to recognise the limits of the issue that arose before Julian Knowles J. The argument advanced in *Koceku* concerned the evidential weight and admissibility of the decision. The court was not asked to consider, and therefore did not determine, the consequences of a reasonable grounds or conclusive grounds decision for the State's procedural and protective obligations under Art 4 ECHR. Those obligations, and the point at which they are triggered, were not raised as an issue in that case. As earlier noted, subsequent authorities have established that a positive reasonable grounds decision meets the threshold of credible suspicion, thereby engaging the State's investigative (where jurisdiction is engaged) and protective duties, and that those duties may arise even in the absence of such a decision where indicators are present and known, or ought to have been known, to the competent public authorities. Nothing in *Koceku* addresses, still less displaces, those principles.

14.188

None of the above dictates that extradition must be delayed in every case. The Framework Decision and the Trade and Cooperation Agreement favour expedition; and courts retain a discretion to refuse adjournments where they are not justified. But where credible suspicion exists and reasonable grounds are (or are likely to be) established, the Art 13 recovery period, now reflected in s 61 NABA 2022, is an important indicator of what Art 4 requires in practice. In that setting, a short adjournment to permit the recovery period enabling protective and investigative steps may be necessary; where an adjournment is refused, the fact-finder should proceed with particular care, mindful that the investigation envisaged by Art 4 has not yet been completed and the consequences that may have on the requested person's right to a fair trial under Art 6 (see **Chapter 10**).

Trafficking or modern slavery status and traditional bars to extradition

14.189

The fact of a requested person being, or potentially being, a victim of trafficking or modern slavery may be relevant to some of the statutory bars to extradition, most commonly arguments relating to oppression under passage of time or physical and mental health and in the context of human rights arguments.

Article 8

14.190

In a number of cases, courts have acceded to a requested person's arguments on the basis of Art 8 ECHR. In *R v Poland*[148], the court held that being a victim of trafficking *"is a matter which needs to be taken into account"* in the Art 8 context. The case illustrates the way such an experience may be given weight in the balancing exercise.

> '29. In the circumstances of the present case, this appellant was trafficked and clearly suffered significantly as a result, both in terms of the ill-treatment which he received at the hands of those who trafficked him and also in terms of the impact on his mental health. Furthermore, it was, in my judgment, relevant that he is a recovering and supported victim of trafficking, which also is relevant to the strength of theArticle 8rights which he has established in terms of his private life alongside the fact that he has, by contrast with the tentative conclusions of the district judge, clearly co-operated in bringing those he says are responsible for trafficking him to justice. Thus, I am satisfied that the balance which was struck by the district judge did not afford significant weight to the factors which I have identified above and afforded too much weight to the sentence, in that she took into account an inaccurate length of sentence.'

14.191

Similarly, in *IM v Bulgaria*, whilst the court rejected the argument that extradition would lead to the requested person being 're-trafficked', it nevertheless went on to conclude that extradition to Bulgaria 'would involve a disproportionate effect on his right to respect for private life'. This was given the 'combination of circumstances […] the nature of the alleged offences, the passage of time, the fact that the Appellant has been the victim of trafficking, his mental health

148 [2018] EWHC 3696 (Admin).

and vulnerability, and the real problems he would now face if he were sent to Bulgaria'[149].

14.192

A number of cases have also been discharged at first instance where the requested person's trafficking status has been a central issue to Art 8 and not appealed by the CPS. However, these cases tend not to be published.

14.193

Oppression arising from passage of time or as a result of physical or mental ill-health will be of relevance to victims of trafficking or modern slavery where their experience has left them with poor health or otherwise in a situation which can be described as more than one of hardship.

In *Baranik v Poland*[150], the appellant, who had a conclusive grounds decision recognising him as a victim of modern slavery in the UK, adduced fresh medical evidence. He suffered from post-traumatic stress disorder and other mental health conditions, and it was contended that extradition would have an exceptionally severe effect on his mental health, significantly exacerbating his depression, anxiety, and PTSD. On appeal, the court held that extradition would be disproportionate under Art 8 ECHR. In those circumstances, it was unnecessary to determine the case under s 25 of the Extradition Act 2003, although there was plainly a substantial overlap in the considerations.

14.194

In *NV v Czech Republic*[151], the Divisional Court considered an appeal against extradition on two principal grounds: whether extradition would be oppressive under s 25 of the EA 2003 in light of NV's mental health condition, and whether it would be disproportionate under Art 8. The requested person was a fugitive and his extradition was sought in relation to offences of people trafficking and supply of drugs. The Court acknowledged that a conclusive grounds decision remained outstanding and took account of NV's history as a victim of trafficking, including medical evidence of severe PTSD and a risk of suicide. However, in dismissing the appeal, the Court reiterated that the statutory threshold for oppression under s 25 is high. While the mental health evidence was serious, it was not considered sufficient to meet that threshold. As to Art 8, the Court found that any interference with NV's rights was justified by the public interest in extradition for serious offending. It further noted that appropriate medical treatment could be accessed in the Czech Republic. This case is examined further below in the context of Art 4 ECHR.

149 *IM v Bulgaria* [2019] EWHC 602 (Admin), para 45.
150 [2019] EWHC3520(Admin), para 56.
151 *NV v Czech Republic* [2020] EWHC 409 (Admin).

Article 4

14.195

The ECtHR has not articulated a fixed framework of positive obligations under Art 4; instead, these obligations have emerged incrementally through its jurisprudence, shaped by the specific facts of individual cases. Therefore, to distil the positive obligations attached to the rights, understanding their contours and boundaries requires extensive interpretive effort[152]. How such obligations may bear on extradition proceedings is a matter for determination by the extradition courts and, where appropriate, the senior appellate courts.

Fugitive status

Fugitive, consent, and Art 4

14.196

Whether a requested person is a fugitive is often contested. This issue is relevant not only to bail but also to the substantive proceedings (see **Chapters 1, 4, 8** and **10**). Notably, fugitivity, if proved to the criminal standard, may preclude reliance on the passage of time bar. A finding that the individual has used the UK as a safe haven may also strengthen the public interest in favour of extradition under Art 8.

14.197

In cases where the requested person is a putative victim of trafficking, slavery or related offences, the voluntariness of their departure from the requesting state, and of their subsequent stay in the United Kingdom, is frequently in issue.

Definition

14.198

Fugitive is not defined in the Extradition Act 2003.

14.199

In *Wisniewski v Poland*[153], Lord Justice Lloyd Jones described 'fugitive' as a judicial concept denoting a status which, in the context of Part 1 of the 2003 Act, precludes reliance on the passage of time under s 14. At [59] he held that

152 For an extensive developed analysis see Vladislava Stoyanova, *Positive Obligations under the European Convention on Human Rights: Within and Beyond Boundaries* (Oxford University Press, 8 September 2023).

153 *Wisniewski v Poland* [2016] EWHC 386 (Admin).

a person who has knowingly placed themselves beyond the reach of a legal process cannot invoke the passage of time resulting from that conduct in order to rely on the statutory bar. Rather than attempting an exhaustive definition, *Wisniewski* emphasises a fact-sensitive application of that principle addressed the concept of fugitive status.

14.200

This approach has been applied in subsequent authority, including *Pillar-Neumann v Public Prosecutor's Office of Klagenfurt, Austria*[154], where the court reiterated that the essential inquiry is whether the requested person has knowingly placed themselves beyond the reach of legal process, whether by fleeing the country, concealing their whereabouts, or evading arrest.

Deliberate flight

14.201

In *Krzyzsowski v Circuit Court in Gliwice, Poland*[155], Longmore LJ held that where 'deliberate flight' would, in practice, almost automatically defeat reliance on section 14, the question whether the defendant deliberately fled must be proved by the requesting state to the criminal standard. Drawing an analogy with the 'deliberate absence' provisions in sections 20(3) and 85(3), he rejected the contention that the burden should fall on the requested person to prove the absence of deliberate flight.

14.202

In *R v Noye*[156], Lord Judge CJ, considering sentence credit for time spent in custody abroad, treated a deliberate and organised decision to leave the jurisdiction to evade justice as paradigmatic of 'flight' from the legal process. That analysis underlines that fugitivity is concerned with intentional and autonomous evasion, rather than mere physical absence.

Consent and the relevance of trafficking to fugitive status

14.203

As analysed in **Chapter 1**, international and domestic law now start from a common premise: what matters is whether there is free and informed consent, not a bare appearance of agreement. Where consent is procured through force, threats, deception, coercion, or abuse of a position of vulnerability, it is neither

154 *Pillar-Neumann v Public Prosecutor's Office of Klagenfurt, Austria* [2017] EWHC 3371 (Admin).
155 *Krzyzsowski v Circuit Court in Giliwice, Poland* [2007] EWHC 2754 (Admin).
156 *R v Noye* [2013] EWCA Crim 510 at [19].

free nor informed and is therefore legally irrelevant to the question whether slavery, servitude, forced or compulsory labour or trafficking has occurred.

14.204

The Palermo Protocol and ECAT structure trafficking around three elements – act, means and purpose – and make explicit that where any of the listed 'means' are used to obtain consent to exploitation (including abuse of a position of vulnerability), that consent shall be irrelevant. The concept of 'abuse of a position of vulnerability' is central: it captures situations in which the trafficker intentionally capitalises on homelessness, poverty, destitution, immigration status or other acute disadvantages to secure the victim's apparent agreement. In such circumstances, the very quality of the consent is vitiated.

14.205

UK criminal law reflects this structure. Lack of consent is not an element of offences under ss 1–4 of the Modern Slavery Act 2015, and s 1(5) expressly provides that apparent consent does not preclude a finding of slavery, servitude or forced or compulsory labour. In cases such as *R v Khan, R v Connors and R v Rooney* (see analysis in **Chapter 1**) the courts have treated adult victims' apparent "choices" to travel and thereafter to work or reside in exploitative conditions as evidentially and legally weak where those choices were shaped by homelessness, destitution, learning disability, addiction or other vulnerabilities deliberately exploited by the perpetrators. Similarly, in cases of servitude, such as the category 'serfdom' or modern equivalent 'domestic servitude', this requires the individual to believe their situation is inescapable or permanent.

14.206

International criminal jurisprudence on enslavement and sexual slavery takes the same approach (see **Chapter 1**). In *Kunarac* and in the ICC's Elements of Crimes and sexual-slavery case law, a victim's apparent acquiescence is irrelevant where domination is enabled by a coercive environment, or secured through force, threats, or abuse of power; the legal focus is on domination, not agreement.

14.207

This has a direct bearing on fugitivity. The authorities frame the test not only in terms of whether a person has 'knowingly' placed themselves beyond the reach of legal process, but whether they have done so deliberately, a formulation which presupposes a free and informed choice to evade justice. In *Krzyzsowski,* Longmore LJ stressed that 'deliberate flight', which in practice will almost automatically defeat reliance on s 14, must be proved by the requesting state to the criminal standard, in line with the 'deliberate absence' provisions in ss 20(3) and 85(3). Read alongside international and domestic principles on consent, this means that 'deliberate' flight cannot be established where the apparent decision to leave is itself the product of abused vulnerability: where homelessness, destitution or other structural vulnerabilities are intentionally exploited to secure agreement to travel, that agreement cannot constitute free and informed choice in the sense understood in **Chapter 1**, and thus cannot supply the autonomous decision-making that deliberate evasion requires.

14.208

The essence of slavery is the domination of another person's life so that they are deprived of any real personal autonomy. They are deprived of important freedoms by the coercion and controlling behaviour of another person. Particular features, such as control over movement, residence, labour, or relationships, are indicia, not requirements; they help show the extent of domination, but need not all be present. Where that level of domination exists, it is difficult to characterise departure from the jurisdiction as a deliberate act of evasion for the purposes of fugitivity.

14.209

Similarly, in servitude, specifically serfdom, the individual is compelled to provide services and is often required to live in accommodation controlled by another, under conditions that they perceive as inescapable or enduring. In such situations, a court considering fugitivity may have to assess whether the conditions at the time of departure permitted the requested person sufficient real autonomy to make a deliberate decision to evade legal process, bearing in mind that international law treats apparent consent, obtained through exploitation of vulnerability, as legally vitiated. This analysis would extend to the other traditional forms of servitude: debt bondage, servile marriage and child exploitation.

Trafficking, consent and fugitivity in R v Poland

14.210

The interaction between these principles and fugitivity arose directly in *R v Polish Judicial Authority*,[157] where the appellant had been conclusively recognised by the UK authorities as a victim of trafficking. He was homeless, destitute and without shelter when approached by men offering work in the United Kingdom, and the conclusive grounds decision and psychiatric evidence indicated that he had been recruited and transported for the purpose of exploitation through deception, fraud and abuse of his position of vulnerability.

157 [2018] EWHC 3696 (Admin) para 21.

14.211

The district judge's characterisation of his decision to travel as 'voluntary and without coercion' failed to engage with this legal framework. It overlooked that, under the Palermo/ECAT definition and the domestic offences, consent obtained by abusing a position of vulnerability is not free and informed consent at all, and is treated as legally irrelevant to whether an individual has been trafficked. On appeal, Mr Justice Dove accepted that the district judge's formulation was an overstatement and that the appellant's decision was made under the influence of deception and in the context of acute vulnerability.

14.212

However, Mr Justice Dove then drew a distinction between consent to exploitation and the decision to leave Poland. He held that, notwithstanding the trafficking determination, the appellant retained sufficient decision-making capacity to choose to travel to the UK while knowing that he had an outstanding custodial sentence and a retrial to face, and that by doing so he knowingly placed himself beyond the reach of the Polish criminal process. On that basis, the appellant was found to be a fugitive and could not rely on the s 14 passage of time bar.

14.213

Viewed through the lens of free and informed consent developed in **Chapter 1**, *R v Poland* illustrates both the importance and the limits of trafficking status in the fugitivity analysis. On the one hand, the High Court accepted that the elements of trafficking were satisfied, including abuse of vulnerability, which, in international and domestic law, renders the appellant's consent to exploitation legally irrelevant. On the other, the court treated his homelessness and destitution as background to, but not determinative of, his capacity to make a separate, informed choice to evade justice by leaving Poland.

14.214

Applying the combined *Wisniewski/Krzyzsowski* test together with the international and domestic law principles on consent, a different view is arguable. If 'deliberate' flight presupposes a free and informed choice, and if the same homelessness and destitution that enabled the exploitation are precisely the vulnerabilities intentionally exploited to secure his agreement to travel, then that agreement cannot, on the **Chapter 1** analysis, constitute free and informed consent in the relevant sense even in the absence of his knowledge that he was to be exploited. On this view, the very factors that would make his consent to exploitation legally irrelevant also undermine the autonomy necessary for a truly deliberate decision to travel to the UK and thereby evade legal process, casting doubt on whether the fugitivity threshold is met.

14.215

R v Poland ultimately resolves this tension in favour of finding fugitivity, holding that a person may, on specific facts, be both a victim of trafficking and yet retain sufficient awareness and autonomy to place themselves deliberately beyond the reach of the criminal justice system. The jurisprudence to date does not conclusively determine how far abused vulnerability should cut down the notion of 'deliberate' flight, but any assessment of fugitivity in trafficking cases should, at minimum, engage explicitly with the quality of the requested person's consent in light of their vulnerability, rather than treating trafficking as a merely background factor. This has to be understood also within the framework of culpability, as examined below.

Compulsion, non-punishment and deliberate flight

14.216

In trafficking cases, a victim's departure from the jurisdiction may itself constitute the recruitment or transportation stage of trafficking, brought about by the recognised 'means' (deception, fraud, coercion, or abuse of a position of vulnerability). As explained above, apparent consent to those acts is treated as legally irrelevant to the existence of trafficking. This has particular importance for Art 26 ECAT, which requires States to provide for the non-punishment of victims for unlawful acts to the extent they were compelled to commit them. 'Compulsion' will often be satisfied where one or more of the trafficking 'means' has been used, and the scope of relevant offences extends to acts at the outset of the process, including offences linked to the act of transportation itself (for example, possession of false documents or unlawful entry carried out under traffickers' control). The Convention's protective emphasis, placing victims' rights and recovery at the forefront, supports treating such acts as compelled, so that apparent acquiescence in being recruited, transferred or transported does not restore genuine autonomy of decision-making.

14.217

For fugitivity, the question is whether the requested person deliberately and knowingly took a decision to take themself beyond the reach of the legal process. That presupposes a free and informed choice at the point of departure.

In *R v Polish Judicial Authority*, Mr Justice Dove accepted that the appellant was recruited and transported to the UK for exploitation by deception/fraud and abuse of vulnerability (homelessness, destitution), and observed that the Judge's 'voluntarily and without coercion' formulation was 'at least questionable and an overstatement.' This critique was directed at the initial decision to go with the traffickers. On those facts, applying the terminology of ECAT, the appellant was arguably compelled to travel to the UK.

14.218

Nevertheless, the court held that the requested person knew of his outstanding sentence and retrial and decided to place himself beyond the Polish process; it therefore found him a fugitive. The difficulty with that analysis is that it risks disaggregating what international law treats as a continuous trafficking process. If compulsion (via deception and abuse of vulnerability) is found to have secured the transfer out of the jurisdiction, it is at least arguable that the same compulsion undermines the autonomy required for a deliberate and knowing decision to leave the jurisdiction and thereby evade justice. Put shortly: if, in law, he did not consent to his transportation of the jurisdiction and is treated as compelled, it sits uneasily with a simultaneous finding that he deliberately chose to flee. The answer will depend on the evidence at the moment of departure; but where the trafficking 'means' were already operating to bring about the transfer, the State may struggle to prove deliberate flight to the criminal standard.

Art 4 ECHR: Real risk or Flagrant Breach?

14.219

Unlike Art 8 ECHR, which is a qualified right subject to proportionality and justification, Art 4 is absolute and non-derogable. Its core prohibitions, particularly against slavery and servitude, are recognised as *jus cogens* norms under customary international law and give rise to *erga omnes* obligations (see **Chapter 1**). These classifications underscore the hierarchical and inviolable nature of the right. Slavery is expressly recognised as a crime against humanity under Art 7 of the Rome Statute of the International Criminal Court, placing it within the same category of international concern as torture and other inhuman treatment prohibited under Art 3 ECHR. Art 4(2) prohibits forced or compulsory labour and has been treated in the Strasbourg case law as effectively absolute, with Art 4(3) operating not as a limitation or exception but as a definitional clause: it identifies forms of labour which, by definition, do not fall within 'forced or compulsory labour' and thus delimits the scope of the prohibition rather than carving out justified interferences.

14.220

In *Grecu v Gorj County Court (Romania)*[158], the appellant resisted extradition on the basis that it would breach her rights under Arts 4 and 8 ECHR. She had been convicted in Romania of trafficking minors for sexual exploitation and sentenced to seven years and six months' imprisonment. While in the UK custody, she was referred to the National Referral Mechanism (NRM), which issued a positive reasonable grounds decision but later reached a negative

158 *Grecu v Gorj County Court (Romania)* [2022] EWHC 2056 (Admin).

conclusive grounds decision (ie the Competent Authority was not satisfied to the civil standard that Ms Grecu was a victim of trafficking).

14.221

Mrs Justice Thornton noted the unsettled threshold for Art 4 ECHR, specifically whether a flagrant breach is required or whether the Art 3 'real risk' standard applies. She upheld the District Judge's findings, including the rejection of the appellant's credibility regarding alleged coercion and violence from her brother and ex-partner. The absence of corroborative evidence, her conviction as a perpetrator, and the negative conclusive grounds decision weighed against her claim. The Court relied on the presumption of Romania's compliance with its international obligations and dismissed the Art 4 argument.

14.222

The observation that the 'real risk' test might apply reflects both the structure of the Convention and the broader framework of international law. While Art 4(3) ECHR delimits the scope of 'forced or compulsory labour' by identifying forms of work which do not fall within that concept, it does not create a licence to justify interferences with Art 4(2), and it does not touch the absolute prohibitions on slavery and servitude in Art 4(1). Both Arts 3 and 4 are drafted in absolute terms, share non-derogable status under Art 15(2), and protect core aspects of human dignity. The ECtHR has repeatedly underlined the foundational importance of Art 4 and has treated trafficking in human beings – as a combination of acts, means and purpose – as falling squarely within the scope of that absolute protection.

14.223

The editorial standpoint is that given the gravity of the harms addressed by Art 4, its status in international law, and its close alignment with the types of violations protected under Art 3, there is considerable force in Mrs Justice Thornton's indication that a 'real risk' threshold may be appropriate. On the analysis advanced here, the structure and case law of the Convention support the conclusion that, in extradition and expulsion cases engaging Art 4, including in relation to trafficking, the applicable standard should mirror that under Arts 2 and 3: it is sufficient to show a real risk of treatment contrary to Art 4 in the requesting State, and no additional 'flagrant breach' test is required. Framing Art 4 in this way preserves its absolute, non-derogable character, reflects the Court's treatment of trafficking as falling within the ambit of Art 4, and ensures that the Convention's safeguards remain effective in addressing serious and often hidden forms of exploitation.

14.224

What follows is a non-exhaustive outline of issues that may merit further consideration.

Prospective breaches of Article 4 positive obligations in extradition

14.225

Any argument that extradition would breach Art 4 ECHR because of a failure to discharge positive obligations must be evidence-based. Where a credible suspicion arises that the requested person is a victim of slavery, servitude, forced or compulsory labour or trafficking, the court must assess the future risk that either the United Kingdom or the requesting state will fail to fulfil their identification, protection, and investigative duties if extradition proceeds, taking into account current information and context rather than only past events. In all cases, the court must consider whether the relevant authorities have taken, or will take, reasonable and appropriate steps to discharge their obligations, having regard to the nature of the risk, the individual's vulnerability, and the procedural safeguards in place. The task is a forward-looking evaluation of what measures should be taken to prevent an Art 4 breach, not merely a retrospective audit of what has already occurred.

Historical breach by the requesting state

14.226

The Court may, in certain cases, be required to consider whether the requesting state has previously failed to discharge its protective, recovery, or investigatory duties under Art 4 (or Art 3) ECHR in relation to the requested person. This assessment typically arises where:

(a) the requesting state knew or ought to have known that there was a credible suspicion that the requested person was a victim of harm contrary to Art.4,

(b) they were under a duty to identify when positive obligations were triggered by a credible suspicion of trafficking. This, in turn, requires an examination of what those duties entailed, when they were said to arise, and an assessment of whether, and in what respects, those obligations may have been breached, and

(c) materiality of these breaches in the extradition proceedings.

14.227

This evaluative task reflects the approach taken by the ECHR, which considers alleged breaches of positive obligations *post factum*, in light of the circumstances and evidence available.

Historical breach by UK authorities

14.228

Any past failure by UK authorities to comply with positive obligations may also warrant consideration, especially where such failure is said to have impacted the mental health of the requested person. This may be particularly relevant in circumstances where the UK is alleged to have ongoing positive obligations, whether protective, recovery-related, or restitutive in nature. Where investigative duties are engaged, the question may arise as to whether those obligations were appropriately triggered and discharged in accordance with applicable standards[159].

Ongoing breach by either state

14.229

The court may, in certain circumstances, be required to consider the relevance of a putative ongoing or unresolved breach of positive obligations under Art 4 by the requesting state and/or the UK, and how this bears on extradition. This may arise where the UK Competent Authority has made a positive identification decision, or where the available evidence establishes a credible suspicion of trafficking, slavery, or a related offence which took place in either the UK or the requesting state or the trafficking occurred from the requesting state to the UK.

14.230

In such cases, issues may arise regarding the extent to which the UK is acting consistently with its protection and procedural (investigative) duties under Art 4 ECHR. It may be submitted that compliance with the investigatory duty (by both or either the requesting state and the UK) is relevant to the assessment of risk on return, including the potential for re-trafficking, or to the existence of nexus offending. A failure to discharge that duty may also be said to affect the fairness of the domestic extradition proceedings, in line with the reasoning in *VCL and AN v United Kingdom*.

14.231

In *NV (Vietnam) v District Court in Plzen-Mesto, Czech Republic*[160], no Art 4 submissions were advanced. On the facts, however, it is a paradigm example of a case in which Art 4 was arguably engaged. The appellant described being in debt bondage to an organised criminal network in Vietnam, trafficked to the Czech Republic, imprisoned in a basement, regularly beaten, and forced to deliver

159 *EK (Art 4: Anti-Trafficking Convention) Tanzania* [2013] UKUT 00313 (IAC).
160 [2020] EWHC 409 (Admin) (25 February 2020).

a package (one of the index offences) without knowledge that it contained cannabis. After serving a custodial sentence, he reported being re-trafficked and forced into further criminal activities, including people trafficking, and subjected to severe violence and abuse. He eventually was trafficked to the UK, where he was again exploited, then stopped by police and referred into the NRM; he received a positive reasonable-grounds decision but no conclusive-grounds decision before the extradition hearing.

14.232

The evidence before the court included significant mental health difficulties, flashbacks, nightmares, panic attacks, fear of re-trafficking, and his belief that he would "die" if returned to the Czech Republic. The responses from the Czech authorities focused on fair-trial guarantees, the possibility of reopening proceedings and varying sentence, and mechanisms to address mental health in the execution of any custodial term. On the face of the judgment, they did not address past or prospective compliance with Art 4 obligations or any risk of re-trafficking, nor did they engage with the implications of the UK's positive reasonable-grounds decision for their own Art 4 duties.

14.233

GRETA[161] has criticised the Czech Republic for failing explicitly to recognise criminal exploitation as a form of exploitation and for rarely identifying such victims, raising concerns about systemic under-identification and under-protection. Against that background, and consistently with *VCL and AN*, it is at least arguable that NV's extradition exposed him to a real risk of violations of his Art 4 rights in the requesting state and that the UK's decision to extradite a potential victim with serious mental health issues, before completion of the identification process and no indication of any investigation in his trafficking by the requesting state, may have breached its own positive protective obligations under Art 4.

14.234

Critically, Art 4 and its positive obligations were not advanced as a distinct ground in NV, so the court did not undertake a structured examination of the UK's duties once a credible suspicion of trafficking had arisen, nor did it assess whether the Czech Republic's record raised a real risk of future Art 4 violations or historical violations. On the approach in *VCL and AN* and *Rantsev*, however, the editorial analysis suggests that, in any future case with comparable facts, domestic courts should, of their own motion, identify and require the parties to address the issues concerning positive obligations engaged by Art 4, including

161 GRETA, Report concerning the implementation of the Council of Europe Convention on Action against Trafficking in Human Beings by the Czech Republic, 11 February 2020.

the risk of onward violations in the requesting state and any prior failures of identification, investigation or protection attributable to either state[162].

Prospective breaches of Article 4: re-trafficking risk, cross-border identification, and evidential burdens in extradition

14.235

The risk that the requested person might be vulnerable to being re-trafficked, including the risk of being coerced back into forced criminality, is potentially relevant in this context. The evidential threshold is high. The issue was litigated in *C v The Prosecutor General's Office of the Republic of Latvia*[163], albeit framed as a further factor to be required to satisfy an Art 8. However, the court refused the appeal, rejecting arguments that she would be at risk of being re-trafficked and noted:

> 'A direct appeal to Article 4 ECHR would require a requested person to rebut by evidence the strong presumption that the country concerned would abide by its international obligations under the ECHR : *Krolik v Poland* [2012] EWHC 2357 (Admin); [2013] 1 WLR 490. Alternatively, and by analogy with cases under Article 3 when the risk of ill-treatment etc. comes from non-state actors, a requested person may, at least in theory, be able to show by reference to the circumstances of his case that the requesting state cannot provide sufficient protection: see the discussion in *R (Bagdanavicius) v Secretary of State for the Home Department* [2005] UKHL 38; [2005] 2 AC 668.'

14.236

In order to consider whether or not the requested person might be at risk of being re-trafficked, consideration must first be given to reciprocity, or otherwise, of victim identification in the requesting state.

Extraterritorial scope of NRM Decisions and non-reciprocal arrangements

14.237

Art 4 ECHR requires that the acts it proscribes must be provided for as specified criminal offences. Issues may arise where the requested person would not be recognised in the requesting state as a victim of Art 4 abuse because their form

162 *VCL and AN v UK*, App. nos 77587/12 and 74603/12, 16 February 2021, paras 198–199.
163 [2016] EWHC 2211 (Admin).

of exploitation is not recognised. The Court may be called upon to consider specifically of legislative gaps[164] or systemic deficiencies[165].

14.238

The UK's NRM decision-making is not territorially confined. The Competent Authority may issue positive reasonable grounds decisions in respect of suspected trafficking or Art 4 ECHR harms occurring outside the UK. In such cases, for the purposes of Art 4, consideration of whether the requesting state has a non-reciprocal arrangement on identification decisions may be relevant. Whether the UK NRM decision is treated as *prima facie* evidence that an Art 4 offence occurred within the requesting state's jurisdiction. In an ECtHR context, it is likely that an identification decision consistent with Art 10 of ECAT, such as a positive reasonable grounds decision, will be sufficient to trigger the credible suspicion threshold in Art 4, recalling that the measures in ECAT create a cooperative framework within which states address trafficking and the protection of victims.

14.239

GRETA has noted that identification and protection mechanisms are established in internal law and implemented nationally, with significant variation across States Parties; it has repeatedly urged clearer, statutory frameworks and consistent practice. There is no mechanism of formal mutual recognition for victim-identification decisions comparable to mutual recognition in criminal justice instruments. As a result, recognition of status in one state does not automatically carry over to another, and a person may be required to undergo a fresh identification when moving or being transferred, with attendant risks of gaps in access to assistance and protection[166].

Implications for Arts 4 and 3 ECHR.

14.240

These features are relevant to a court's assessment of the State's positive obligations under Art 4, including the need for prompt, effective identification and protection. The Strasbourg case law, read together with ECAT, treats the recovery and reflection safeguards and early identification duties as informing the scope and content of Art 4 obligations; the Court has emphasised that victims must be able to participate effectively and that authorities should not expect immediate self-reporting in the face of trauma. Where continuity of

164 *Aranyosi and Căldăraru.*

165 Court of Justice, judgment of 21 December 2011, joined cases C-411/10 and C-493/10, N.SThe systemic deficiency threshold is substantively the same as that considered by the ECtHR in *MSS v Greece and Belgium*.

166 E.g. *IM v Regional Prosecutor's Office of Ruse, Bulgaria* [2019] EWHC 6012 (Admin), para 40.

protective measures is at issue, the court may need to consider whether the requesting state's identification process is human-rights compliant and whether requiring a fresh process would risk re-traumatisation, potentially engaging Art 3 as well as Art 4.

The court should consider whether the requesting state's victim-identification process is human-rights compliant, and whether requiring the requested person to undergo that process would risk re-traumatisation. The latter may engage Art 3 (see the fact-specific illustration in *The Government of Lithuania v AI)*[167] and Art 4, given the State's positive obligations to protect victims and to assist their recovery.

14.241

In *SLP v Prosecutor General of the Republic of Latvia (Rev1)*[168] the Court analysed the evidential framework applicable to Art 4 ECHR claims in extradition, drawing on Lord Burnett CJ's reasoning in *Olga C v The Prosecutor's General Office of the Republic of Latvia*[169].

14.242

The Court observed that there is a strong but rebuttable presumption that Council of Europe member states will comply with their obligations under Art 4.

In practice, this presumption can be understood as operating primarily at the level of the systems duty: the court proceeds on the basis that, absent cogent evidence to the contrary, a Council of Europe state has in place an adequate legislative and institutional framework to prevent, protect against and prosecute trafficking, slavery and related exploitation. GRETA country evaluation reports will often be central in testing that assumption in a given case, since they directly scrutinise a state's implementation of ECAT obligations and highlight systemic gaps or failures.

14.243

On the editorial analysis advanced here, however, that systems-level presumption does not exhaust the obligations arising under the Convention. Article 1 ECHR requires Contracting Parties to 'secure to everyone within their jurisdiction' the rights and freedoms defined in the Convention, and the ECtHR has consistently treated this as generating individual-focused positive obligations under Article 4, in addition to any general systems duties; once a credible suspicion of trafficking or related exploitation arises, those operational duties must be examined separately from, and not assumed satisfied by, the mere existence of an ostensibly adequate framework.

167 [2010] EWHC 2299 (Admin), 2010 WL 3515648.
168 *SLP v Prosecutor General of the Republic of Latvia (Rev1)* [2025] EWHC 298 (Admin) at [26].
169 *Olga C v The Prosecutor's General Office of the Republic of Latvia* [2016] EWHC 2211 (Admin).

The State may, in an individual case where the credible-suspicion threshold is met, be required to take operational measures to identify, protect and support the person and to investigate the underlying exploitation. The investigative duty, in particular, rests on the State or States in whose jurisdiction the substantive Art 4 harm is said to have occurred.

14.244

The question for an extradition court is therefore threefold: (i) whether, on the evidence, the United Kingdom's operational duties have arisen and, if so, whether they have been discharged; (ii) whether, on the evidence, corresponding operational duties arise in the requesting state and are capable of being engaged and 'animated' in respect of the individual concerned; and (iii) whether, taking into account the specific facts of the case and any country material (including GRETA reports), there is a real risk that those duties will not be fulfilled, thereby giving rise to future violations of Art 4.

In *SLP*, the court applied this framework but found no evidential basis to rebut the systems-level presumption. Latvia was not alleged to be complicit in trafficking, had enacted an appropriate legislative framework, and the international material, while identifying areas for improvement, fell short of demonstrating systemic non-compliance with Art 4 duties or an inability or unwillingness to protect the appellant from non-state actors. In the absence of case-specific evidence indicating that Art 4 positive obligations would not be animated or fulfilled in his particular circumstances, the presumption remained intact. The Court concluded that where the alleged risk arises from non-state actors, such as the 'Russian Mafia', the burden lies on the requested person to demonstrate that the requesting state is unwilling or unable to provide reasonable protection.
Against that evidential background, the court held that the claim of prejudice had to be assessed on the material actually before it and that it was not required to adjourn or defer its decision pending the outcome of the NRM process.

14.245

Extradition may bear directly on the duty to investigate. It may be said that no effective investigation can occur if the requested person is removed and held in custody abroad pending trial, or that expecting UK authorities to investigate in those circumstances would impose a disproportionate and unrealistic burden. Crucially, these procedural obligations arise once there is a credible suspicion of trafficking or modern slavery; they do not depend on a reasonable-grounds or conclusive-grounds decision being in place.

The editorial analysis advanced in this book, advances that the Court's approach in *SLP* sits uneasily with the combined effect of Art 13 ECAT, Art 4 ECHR and Art 1 ECHR. Once a positive reasonable-grounds decision has been made, Art 13 (as incorporated domestically) and the Strasbourg case law treat that threshold as triggering positive obligations under Art 4 to create a 'protected space' in which the potential victim can recover, access assistance and make decisions free from the influence of traffickers, and to investigate the underlying exploitation (in this case Latvia). Those safeguards are closely aligned with the investigative and protective duties under Art 4 and, properly understood, are part of the framework within which the extradition court must evaluate whether the State's (or States) positive obligations under Art 4 have been, and can be, discharged in the individual case.

In that context, the evidential burden cannot rest exclusively on the requested person (see *VCL and AN v UK*, *SM v Croatia* and *FM v Russia*). Art 1 requires Contracting Parties to 'secure' Convention rights to everyone within their jurisdiction, and the ECtHR in *VCL and AN* emphasised that once the authorities are, or ought to be, aware of circumstances giving rise to a credible suspicion of trafficking, it is for the State to take operational measures of its own motion to identify, protect and support the victim and to investigate their trafficking. Where positive obligations under Art 4 are triggered, institutional responsibility lies with the relevant State authorities, here, both the United Kingdom and the requesting State, to obtain, generate and assess the material necessary to fulfil their protective and procedural duties. A rebuttable presumption of systems compliance in a Council of Europe State may operate at a general level, but it cannot relieve States of their own obligation, once put on notice of a credible suspicion, to ensure that the evidential record before the extradition court is sufficient to allow a proper assessment of the risks of Art 4 violations and of whether their positive obligations, on both sides of the extradition equation, will in fact be met, as owed to the appellant.

Non-punishment and nexus offending and positive obligations

14.246

In *VCL and AN v UK*, the ECtHR recognised for the first time that in certain circumstances, the prosecution of victims of trafficking would amount to a violation of Art 4.[170]

14.247

The senior courts have not yet determined whether extradition can violate Art 4 ECHR by failing to give effect to the non-punishment principle, that is, the protective and procedural obligations owed to victims of trafficking in respect of criminal conduct committed under compulsion.

170 *VCL and AN v UK*, App. nos 77587/12 and 74603/12, 16 February 2021, para 157–162.

14.248

The ECtHR has recognised that the prosecution of a victim of trafficking may fall within the protective obligations under Art 4. It follows that there is no blanket immunity from prosecution for victims of trafficking, slavery, or related exploitation; rather, bringing or continuing a prosecution may engage, and, in some circumstances, breach, the State's Art 4 duties if those obligations are not met. In particular, a failure by the authorities with institutional responsibility to investigate an arguable Art 4 violation may also give rise to a violation of Art 6, where the missing investigative steps could have yielded exculpatory material capable of assisting the victim at trial.

14.249

The complexities involved in applying this principle within an Art 4 framework are illustrated in *VCL and AN v United Kingdom*[171] and *GS v United Kingdom*[172]. In both accusation and conviction cases involving nexus offending, where the criminal conduct constitute the Art 4 harm itself (eg debt-bonded criminality, forced labour, or trafficking for criminal exploitation; see **Chapter 1**), prior breaches of positive obligations may be relevant to the analysis of extradition bars or risk on return, this includes consideration of the protective, recovery, and investigatory duties under Art 4.

14.250

In such contexts, it may be necessary to examine whether any protective duties or an Art 4-compliant investigation were triggered and adequately discharged in the requested state, or whether any prior investigation or trial fell short of the required standards.

14.251

In some extradition cases, it is possible to argue that inadequate non-punishment provisions exist in the requesting state and/or that the case for non-punishment upon extradition is so strong, extradition should not go ahead. As to the latter, extradition to serve no sentence (either because it has been served in this jurisdiction or because a prison sentence would be unlikely) would be disproportionate and in certain contexts an abuse of process.[173]

14.252

The court in *Z v Poland*[174] considered the possibility of extradition being oppressive by reference to the non-punishment of trafficked offenders. Whilst

171 (2021) 73 EHRR 9; App nos. 77587/12 and 74603/12.

172 (2021) App no. 7604/19.

173 *Wysocki v Poland* [2010] EWHC 3430 (Admin) *Kupczynski v Poland* [2012] EWHC 3332 (Admin) *USA v Shlesinger* [2013] EWHC 2671 (Admin) *Antochi* [2020] EWHC 3092 (Admin).

174 [2014] EWHC 1242 (Admin).

not deciding the point, it noted that had the requested person's trafficking been investigated by the requested state 'a real question of oppression would have arisen because there would have had to have been balanced against the long but sad and unfortunate life that the Appellant has experienced in the United Kingdom, the possibility or probability that, by applying Art 8 of the Directive, she would not have been prosecuted for this offence now whatever the situation may have been in 1997'[175].

14.253

In *SNT v Poland*[176], the court dismissed the appeal, finding as a matter of fact that the requested person was not a victim of trafficking. Given that there was a credible suspicion of trafficking (a positive identification decision) but no Art 4-compliant investigation, the rejection of his account without first discharging the investigatory duty is arguably capable of breaching Arts 4 and 6[177]. As the court found he was not a victim, the non-punishment issue did not arise for decision; nevertheless, the court observed that there were "powerful arguments" that the District Judge ought to have found Poland's non-punishment provisions inadequate.[178]

14.254

In relation to non-punishment provisions in the requesting state, evidence from GRETA and, where appropriate, other experts will often be required to assess how those provisions operate in practice. This is particularly important in Part 1 (European) cases, where there is a strong presumption that Council of Europe states have implemented non-punishment measures in line with ECAT. That presumption, however, goes to the systems duty, the existence of an adequate legislative and institutional framework, and should not be conflated with the operational duties which may be owed to individuals once the credible-suspicion threshold has been met. As examined above, the rebuttable presumption concerns the general adequacy of the system, not the separate question whether, in the specific case, the Art 4 positive obligations to identify, protect and refrain from punishing a victim (or potential victim) will in fact be discharged.

14.255

Nexus offending presents complex legal and factual issues. The English court's role in extradition proceedings is limited: it does not assess the merits of the foreign prosecutorial decision, matters of mitigation, or the culpability of the requested person, save in exceptional cases involving clear bad faith, abuse of process, or a flagrant denial of justice. Within that framework, however, the court

175 [2014] EWHC 1242 (Admin), para 17.
176 [2024] EWHC 3349 (Admin).
177 *VCL and AN v UK*, App. nos 77587/12 and 74603/12, 16 February 2021, paras 160–162.
178 Para 74.

may still need to examine, after the event, whether a failure by the requesting state to investigate potential trafficking or related exploitation has given rise to a real risk of an Art 4 violation, or contributed to a flagrant denial of justice, for the purposes of the statutory human-rights bar.

14.256

This may also be particularly relevant where such a failure has resulted in the absence of potentially exculpatory evidence central to the defence, as illustrated in *VCL and AN v United Kingdom*[179] (breaches of Arts 4 and 6 ECHR). In that case, the ECtHR found that the failure to identify and investigate trafficking allegations had a direct impact on the fairness of the criminal proceedings under Art 6, due to the lack of evidence that might have supported the defence.

Cross border

14.257

In cross-border cases where the continuum of the trafficking process extended from the requesting state to the UK, the investigatory duties may be triggered in both the requesting state and in the UK, from the point *prima facie* evidence is known or ought to be known by one of the states[180]. In some cases the evidence may only arise in the UK (i.e. a positive reasonable grounds decision). This may require the Court to consider the bearing any ongoing investigatory duty may have on the extradition proceedings and the matters in issue.

Assurances and trust

14.258

The assessment of diplomatic assurances in extradition cases is guided by the principles set out in *Othman v United Kingdom*[181] which require the court to determine whether the assurance sufficiently mitigates the relevant risk. This involves evaluating both the legal and practical effect of the assurance, with reference to the reliability of the state and officials providing it. The *Othman* principles, though not a checklist, have been consistently applied in this jurisdiction, including in *Dean (Zain Taj) v Lord Advocate*[182], where the Supreme Court affirmed that courts are ordinarily entitled to assume good faith and that the requesting authorities will make genuine efforts to comply[183].

179 *VCL; see SM v Croatia* [GC}; *TV and Spain and BB v Slovakia*, 2024 at [99].
180 *Zoletic and others v. Azerbaijan* [156], [191]; *Rantsev v Cyprus and Russia, 2010* [289], [308].
181 (2012) 55 EHRR 1 at [188]–[189].
182 *Dean (Zain Taj) v Lord Advocate* [2017] UKSC 44.
183 *Georgiev v Bulgaria* [2018] EWHC 359 (Admin) at [8(vii)].

14.259

In the context of Art 4 ECHR, this principle was applied in *Grecu v Gorj County Court (Romania)*, Mrs Justice Thornton, in dismissing the appeal, considered and placed weight on the principle of mutual recognition and trust[184]. To date, assurances regarding Art 4 have not been in issue. Should this be developed, the substantial body of caselaw on the use and reliance upon assurances in the Art 3 context will provide guidance.

Abuse of process

14.260

Abuse of process is a residual jurisdiction which may be considered after the mandatory issues have been determined by the court[185].

14.261

UK courts have the power to prevent abuse of process in extradition proceedings. As confirmed in *Tollman*[186], this jurisdiction must be exercised in line with the framework and purpose of the 2003 Act. In *R (Bermingham) v Director of the SFO*[187], the Divisional Court emphasised that any claim of abuse must be assessed with reference to the structure of the Act.

14.262

Some statutory bars to extradition, such as those based on human rights or improper motives, may overlap with the abuse of process jurisdiction. As noted in *Tollman* at [82], conduct by prosecutors or judicial authorities that amounts to oppression or unfair prejudice may be treated as abuse, reflecting principles from domestic criminal law. Where a statutory bar is available and engaged, however, it will usually be unnecessary to invoke abuse of process in addition.

14.263

In domestic proceedings, abuse of process typically arises where a fair trial is impossible or where it is necessary to protect the integrity of the justice system (*R v Maxwell*[188]; *R v Crawley*[189]). In extradition cases, the 2003 Act provides specific safeguards to ensure fairness, including protection against removal to face an unfair trial. As a result, most abuse arguments in extradition focus on preserving the integrity of the process, particularly where the conduct of the

184 *Grecu v Gorj County Court (Romania)* [2022] EWHC 2056 (Admin).

185 *R (Bermingham) v Director of the SFO* [2007] QB 727; *Symeou v Greece* [2009] 1 WLR 2384; *Belbin v France*[2015] EWHC 149 (Admin), *Tollman v USA* [2007] 1 WLR 1157.

186 *Tollman* [2008] EWHC 184 (Admin) at [80]–[82].

187 *R (Bermingham) v Director of the SFO* [2006] EWHC 200 (Admin); [2007] QB 727) at [98].

188 *R v Maxwell* [2010] UKSC 48.

189 *R v Crawley* [2014] EWCA Crim 1028.

requesting state or the nature of the request raises concerns about fairness or legitimacy.

14.264

In *AAD, AAH, AAI v R*[190], Lord Justice Fulford VP, sitting on appeal against conviction, noted that the surrounding circumstances are central to any abuse of process analysis. These may include the United Kingdom's international obligations and the complex, sensitive issues typically engaged in trafficking or modern slavery cases.

Evidence

Proof of evidence, expert evidence and special measures

14.265

It is standard practice for a requested person to provide a signed proof of evidence early in proceedings, enabling the CPS to seek instructions from the requesting authority. However, this may be challenging without access to NRM materials. Legal representatives must balance the need for a full account with the importance of consistency across NRM and extradition proceedings. Awareness of the nuances of trafficking, slavery, and related offences, including forced criminality, is essential.

14.266

Where an account develops over time, the court should consider whether this may be explained by trauma, distrust of authorities, or deception, as recognised in *MN and IXU v SSHD*. It may be necessary to obtain expert psychiatric and/or psychological evidence to assess the impact of trafficking and the risk of further abuse, as well as any potential breach of the State's positive protective obligations under Arts 3 and 4 ECHR (see **Chapter 3**). Any such report should meet the standards and methodological requirements set out in Chapter 3. It may also be preferable to defer taking full instructions for a proof of evidence until that assessment is complete. This is particularly important to ensure a trauma-informed approach and to avoid unnecessary re-traumatisation of the individual.

14.267

The use of intermediaries may also be appropriate, not only in cases involving cognitive impairment, but where expert evidence demonstrates that the requested person's memory or ability to process information has been affected (see **Chapters 3** and **8**). In such cases, analogies may be drawn from immigration and criminal jurisprudence where intermediaries have been authorised.

190 *AAD, AAH, AAI v R* [2022] EWCA Crim 106, [117].

14.268

Fear of retaliation may hinder disclosure, particularly given the open nature of extradition proceedings and the potential transmission of information to the requesting state. While closed proceedings are possible, they remain rare. **Chapter 8** provides further guidance on protective measures available to accommodate victims in legal proceedings.

14.269

In parallel, jurisprudence under Arts 3 and 8 ECHR, particularly *NC v Turkey,* underscore the importance of procedural safeguards for victims giving evidence in cases involving serious exploitation. The ECtHR has held that States must take steps to prevent secondary victimisation, including providing psychological and welfare support, shielding victims from intimidating environments, and avoiding unnecessary or intrusive evidentiary practices.

14.270

These principles and their application in the extradition context may require judicial consideration, particularly where the requested person's account of Art 4 harm is central to resisting removal. Consideration of procedural and protective obligations under Arts 4 and 6, including whether the individual has been adequately supported in presenting their account is addressed (see **Chapters 3** and **8**). Guidance from the senior courts on the assessment of the credibility of a victim of trafficking is examined in **Chapter 4**.

Objective evidence

14.271

In carrying out an assessment on whether extradition would breach the requested person's fundamental rights, the court will also typically require objective, reliable, specific, and properly updated evidence on the general legal and practical framework concerning the requesting state's compliance with Art 4 positive obligations, combined with the individual circumstances of the request person.

14.272

Such evidence may include:

1. **Art 4 jurisprudence from the ECtHR on the country in question**

   In *Aranyosi and Căldăraru*[191], the CJEU identified judgments of the ECtHR as a source of country-specific insights into how Council of

191 *Aranyosi and Căldăraru* [89]-[91].

Europe member states have been found to breach their obligations. These judgments illuminate the factual circumstances, systemic failures, and omissions that have led to findings of violations, and offer a useful reference point for understanding the practical application of Art 4 obligations in particular jurisdictions.

2. GRETA country reports

GRETA, the monitoring body under the ECAT, publishes country-specific evaluations of compliance with the Convention. These reports assess prevention, protection, prosecution, and partnership efforts, and are particularly valuable for identifying structural weaknesses, strengths and identifying gaps in implementation.

GRETA's observations on gaps in legal and policy frameworks

GRETA has noted in its evaluations that certain forms of exploitation are not always explicitly recognised within the legal, policy, or operational frameworks of some Council of Europe member states. Specific areas identified include forced begging, forced and sham marriage, trafficking for the purpose of organ removal, and the sexual exploitation of men and boys. These forms of exploitation are, in some instances, absent from national definitions of trafficking and from procedures for victim identification.

Implementation challenges in applying the non-punishment principle

GRETA has observed that several Council of Europe member states face challenges in giving full effect to the non-punishment principle under Art 26 of ECAT, which provides that victims of trafficking should not be penalised for unlawful acts committed as a direct consequence of their exploitation. While this principle is reflected in domestic law in many jurisdictions, GRETA's evaluations highlight gaps in both legal safeguards and practical implementation. Common issues identified include limited statutory protections, failure to identify victims before criminal proceedings are initiated, and judicial reluctance to apply the principle, particularly in cases involving criminal exploitation such as forced theft or drug-related offences. GRETA has documented instances where victims were prosecuted or detained for conduct linked to their trafficking experience.

Under-recognition of labour and criminal exploitation

GRETA has noted that forms of exploitation such as labour exploitation, debt bondage, domestic servitude, and coercion into criminal activity (eg 'county lines') may be under-identified in practice in country reports. Observing that although included in domestic legislation, detection is often limited due to gaps in awareness, training, and coordination among authorities. This under-recognition has been linked to narrow legal interpretations, a focus on sexual exploitation, limited outreach to marginalised groups, and fragmented multi-agency responses, which may reduce access to support and justice.

3. **Country visit reports by the UN Special Rapporteur on trafficking in persons**

Country visits are a core component of the Special Rapporteur's mandate, aimed at gaining a detailed understanding of national contexts and responses to trafficking in persons. A comprehensive country visit report is presented to the Human Rights Council during its March session, outlining observations, concerns, and recommendations for strengthening anti-trafficking measures in line with international standards.

4. **US Trafficking in Persons (TIP) reports**

The annual TIP reports rank countries by tier and provide detailed assessments of their efforts to combat trafficking. These reports are widely cited and offer a comparative overview of legislative, enforcement, and victim protection measures.

5. **Upper Tribunal (Immigration and Asylum Chamber) Country Guidance decisions**

Country Guidance decisions issued by the Upper Tribunal (Immigration and Asylum Chamber) serve a vital role in the adjudication of asylum and human rights appeals.[192] These decisions are intended to establish authoritative findings binding on the First-tier Tribunal on country conditions that are relevant to assessing risk on return, particularly in cases involving claims under Arts 3, and 4 of the ECHR. They will be binding on judges in the First-tier Tribunal unless there is a material change in circumstances or credible new evidence that justifies departure.

Country Guidance decisions are typically the product of detailed proceedings before a panel of Upper Tribunal judges, involving extensive country evidence, expert reports, and legal submissions. Their primary function is to promote consistency and predictability in asylum and human rights adjudication, reducing the need for repetitive litigation on country-specific factual issues. Although not binding on higher courts such as the High Court or Court of Appeal, nor on the extradition court, which operates under a distinct statutory framework, such decisions may nonetheless illuminate relevant issues in Art 4 ECHR cases. This is particularly so in relation to countries outside the European Union, including Council of Europe member states, where risks of re-trafficking or failures of protective mechanisms may be material to the assessment of

192 Upper Tribunal (Immigration and Asylum Chamber), *Decisions* (Judiciary of England and Wales) https://www.judiciary.uk/courts-and-tribunals/tribunals/upper-tribunal/upper-tribunal-immigration-and-asylum-chamber/upper-tribunal-immigration-and-asylum-chamber-decisions/ accessed 1 October 2025.

whether extradition would give rise to a real risk of harm or breach of the United Kingdom's positive obligations under the Convention.

Country Guidance decisions may also assist legal representatives in extradition proceedings to consider whether a requested person ought to seek legal advice regarding a potential claim for international protection (see Chapter 16). Where the factual matrix suggests a risk of trafficking, servitude, or other Art 4 ECHR violations, such guidance may help identify whether the individual's circumstances engage the Refugee Convention or other protection frameworks. Expert advice will be essential in this regard, as the statutory framework governing international protection differs significantly dependent on whether the country of return is an EU Member State (see Chapter 16). Notably, there are country guidance decisions which have concluded a risk of return and breaches of Arts 3 and 4 where the return is to countries within the Council of Europe, which are not EU Member States[193].

193 *AM and BM (Trafficked women) Albania CG* [2010] UKUT 80 (IAC); *TD and AD (Trafficked women) CG* [2016] UKUT 92 (IAC). There is a pending Country Guidance appeal on the return of trafficked men to Albania (see Judiciary of England and Wales, *Pending Country Guidance Cases and Issues* (1 September 2025) https://www.judiciary.uk/wp-content/uploads/2025/09/Pending-Country-Guidance-Cases-and-Issues-1-Sept-2025.pdf accessed 1 October 2025.)

15 Compensation for victims of trafficking and modern slavery

Maya Sikand KC and Louise Price

Introduction

15.1

As recognised by professionals working in the field of human trafficking and modern slavery[1], effective compensation has an important role to play in the recovery process of survivors. Focus on Labour Exploitation ('FLEX') put it this way in its working paper *Access to Compensation for Victims of Human Trafficking*:

> 'Compensation awards can provide economic empowerment, facilitating reintegration into society and reducing individual victims' vulnerability to re-trafficking. Obtaining fair compensation can contribute to a sense of justice and closure and can play an important role in a survivor's psychological recovery'[2].

15.2

The Strasbourg Court has said that redress for the victim should be the overarching consideration from a human rights perspective[3]

15.3

However, the available routes to compensation can present very specific challenges to victims of trafficking and modern slavery ('victims'), in particular where there has been no, or no successful, criminal prosecution of the alleged perpetrators. Where there are successful criminal prosecutions for a modern slavery or human trafficking offence, there is the possibility of the court making a compensation order for the benefit of the victim(s) or a Slavery and Trafficking Reparation Order ('STRO') pursuant to the Modern Slavery Act 2015 ('MSA 2015'), s 8. The very small number of such convictions annually

1 See **Chapter 1** for the legal definitions of human trafficking and offences which constitute modern slavery.

2 FLEX (July 2016).

3 *Krachunova v Bulgaria,* Application no 18269/18, 28 November 2023.

means that practitioners must find alternative, creative solutions to obtain compensation for most victims.

15.4

This chapter will examine the following potential routes to compensation:

- compensation available in criminal proceedings;
- the Criminal Injuries Compensation Scheme;
- statutory claims for miscarriages of justice;
- Human Rights Act 1998 claims against public bodies;
- claims against traffickers.

Compensatory obligations: Art 4 of the ECHR

15.5

Art 4 (prohibition on slavery, servitude and forced labour) of the European Convention on Human Rights (ECHR) did not historically go as far as to impose a positive obligation on States to facilitate compensation for victims[4]. However, in the recent case of *Krachunova v. Bulgaria*[5], the European Court of Human Rights (ECtHR) concluded that Art 4, interpreted in a way that rendered its safeguards practical and effective, laid down a positive obligation on the part of Contracting States to *enable* victims of trafficking to claim compensation *from their traffickers in respect of lost earnings*. On the facts in *Krachunova*, the applicant was a victim of sexual exploitation, claiming the proceeds retained by her trafficker ('pimp'), which the Court found were derived from her unlawful exploitation for coerced prostitution, and with which her trafficker had unjustly enriched himself. The applicant sought an order for compensation from him, post-conviction, which included loss of earnings. The domestic court in Bulgaria refused to order compensation for loss of earnings on public policy grounds ie she could not recover money from him that was 'immorally' earned, but she was entitled to non-pecuniary compensation.

15.6

The positive obligation identified by the Court in *Krachunova* enhanced the protection of the rights already enshrined in that article in light of present-day realities and brought that protection into line with the increasingly high standard required in that domain and with the changed social context in which that Art now needed to be applied. The Court applied an interpretative

4 *A and B v Criminal Injuries Compensation Authority and another* [2021] UKSC 27; [2021] 1 WLR 3746.
5 Application no 18269/18, 28 February 2024.

approach which recognised the increasing, global phenomenon of trafficking in finding at [172] that

> 'Making it possible for victims to recoup lost earnings from their traffickers would go some way towards ensuring that those traffickers are not able to enjoy the fruits of their offences, thus reducing the economic incentives to commit trafficking offences. Indeed, the recent trend in law enforcement more generally has been to target not only the persons of criminals but also the proceeds of their offences, and then to use (at least a portion of) those proceeds to compensate victims. This can also reduce the burden on the public resources sometimes used to support the recovery of trafficking victims. Moreover, it can give victims an additional incentive to come forward and expose trafficking, thereby increasing the odds of holding human traffickers accountable and thus preventing future instances of it.'

15.7

Under international law, the UK does have compensatory obligations to victims of trafficking and modern slavery, as set out in Council of Europe Convention against Trafficking in Human Beings (2005) (ECAT), a treaty that is binding in international law but not fully incorporated into domestic law (see **Chapters 1, 4** and **5** for a full discussion as to ECAT's legal effect). The relevant parts are set out below:

> **Art 15 of ECAT**[6]
>
> **'Compensation and legal redress**
>
> 1 …
>
> 2 …
>
> 3 Each Party shall provide, in its internal law, for the right of victims to compensation from the perpetrators.
>
> 4 Each Party shall adopt such legislative or other measures as may be necessary to guarantee compensation for victims in accordance with the conditions under its internal law, for instance through the establishment of a fund for victim compensation or measures or programmes aimed at social assistance and social integration of victims, which could be funded by the assets resulting from the application of measures provided in Art 23'[7].

6 The Council of Europe Convention on Action against Trafficking in Human Beings ('ECAT').
7 ECAT, Art 23 deals with the provision of sanctions and measures, both criminal and non-criminal, including confiscation, for those who are criminally liable for trafficking in human beings.

15.8

The United Kingdom's senior courts have concluded, while Art 4 of the ECHR imposes a positive obligation on Contracting States to ensure that victims can access compensation from their perpetrators, it does not extend to requiring Contracting States themselves to compensate victims for acts committed by private individuals. Moreover, Art 15(4) of ECAT, when properly construed, does not impose such an obligation either[8].

15.9

That said, the United Kingdom satisfies its obligations under Art 15(4) ECAT through the Criminal Injuries Compensation Scheme. The approach adopted in *Krachunova* aligns with the requirements of Art 15(3). Arts 15(3) and 15(4) are broadly framed, and although multiple avenues for redress exist, the practical accessibility of these rights is often limited, rendering them more illusory than real[9].

Compensation in criminal proceedings

Compensation Orders

15.10

Compensation Orders[10] are governed by the Sentencing Code[11], ss 133–146. The discretionary power to make an order arises upon conviction of *any* offence (subject to the special rules for road accidents in s136) (s 134). It does not require a victim to apply to the court for an order to be made[12]. Section 55 of the Sentencing Code requires the court to give reasons if it does not make a Compensation Order where one is available.

15.11

Where the court makes a Compensation Order under the Sentencing Code, a Slavery and Trafficking Reparation Order cannot be made. The current

8 *A and B v Criminal Injuries Compensation Authority and another* [2021] UKSC 27; [2021] 1 WLR 3746 at [27]-[33] and *R (HJK and others) v Director of Legal Aid Casework* [2025] EWHC 774 (Admin) (Criminal Injuries Compensation Authority intervening) at [120]-[133].

9 For an analysis of the compensatory provisions in the Palermo Protocol see United Nations Office on Drugs and Crime, *Legislative Guides for the Implementation of the United Nations Convention against Transnational Organized Crime and the Protocols thereto* (United Nations publication, Sales No. E.05.V.2, 2004) <https://www.unodc.org/documents/human-trafficking/Toolkit-files/08-58296_tool_8-17.pdf.

10 See Sentencing Council, *Slavery, Servitude and Forced or Compulsory Labour / Human Trafficking – Sentencing Guideline* (effective from 1 October 2021) https://www.sentencingcouncil.org.uk/offences/magistrates-court/item/slavery-servitude-and-forced-or-compulsory-labour-human-trafficking/ (accessed 22 August 2025).

11 Sentencing Act 2020, s 1(1).

12 *Holt v DPP* [1996] 2 Cr App Rep (S) 314, [1996] Crim LR 524.

CPS guidance[13] states that a Slavery and Trafficking Reparation Order under s 8 of MSA 2015 'may only be made in conjunction with a fine and/or a compensation order if the defendant has sufficient means to pay all financial orders.' This appears to be misleading. Section 10(1) of the Act expressly prohibits the making of a Slavery and Trafficking Reparation Order where a Compensation Order under s 134 of the Sentencing Code has already been made. The statutory framework therefore requires the court to choose between the two, rather than permitting both to be imposed concurrently.

15.12

The order is for compensation 'for any personal injury, loss or damage resulting from that offence or any other offence which is taken into consideration by the court when determining sentence…' (s 133(a)). Courts will order compensation for a specified amount, and that amount must be the amount that the court considers appropriate, having regard to any evidence and any representations that are made by or on behalf of the offender or the prosecution, as well as the offender's means (s135). Notably, in *R v ANZ*[14], a compensation order of £10,000 to be paid at the rate of £400 per month, made against the appellant following his convictions for four counts of sexual activity with a child and one of cruelty to a person under 16, committed against his daughter, was set aside, because the sentencing judge had made no attempt to enquire into the appellant's means in any respect, contrary to the mandatory requirement under s 135, and so the appellant's counsel had had no opportunity to make representations under s 135(2). The suggested starting points for compensating physical and mental injury are set out by the Sentencing Council[15] and have been developed to be consistent with the approach in the Criminal Injuries Compensation Scheme (2012). The maximum amount a magistrates' court can order in relation to a young offender is £5,000 per charge (s 139)[16].

15.13

To maximise a compensation application, prosecutors (via the police) should seek evidence in support. Distress and anxiety are recoverable losses[17] but evidence is necessary[18].

15.14

Historically the criminal courts have only made Compensation Orders in a 'simple, straightforward case where the amount of compensation can be readily

13 See Crown Prosecution Service, *Sentencing – Ancillary Orders* (updated 2024) https://www.cps.gov.uk/legal-guidance/sentencing-ancillary-orders#a16 accessed 22 August 2025.

14 [2025] EWCA Crim 778.

15 https://www.sentencingcouncil.org.uk/explanatory-material/magistrates-court/item/fines-and-financial-orders/compensation/2.

16 Which also sets out the position in relation to offences taken into consideration.

17 *R v Godfrey* (1994) 15 Cr App Rep (S) 536.

18 *R v Vaughan* (1990) 12 Cr App Rep (S) 46.

and easily ascertained'[19], avoiding the technicalities of claims for loss in the civil courts. In some cases, a more modern approach has been adopted, given the criminal courts' familiarity with more complex financial assessment in confiscation proceedings[20]. However, in *R v Bewick*[21] the Court of Appeal held that since the sentence can only hear submissions from the prosecution and the defence, not third parties (including victims)[22], policy demands that complex issues should not be dealt with in the criminal courts. This was reiterated in *ANZ*[23] where the Court of Appeal said that such orders are designed to be used only in clear and straightforward cases, insisting that the criminal injuries compensation scheme was the best forum for assessing an award for a victim of historic sexual abuse.

15.15

Following *Krachunova*, it may well be that the criminal courts will have to grapple with 'loss' that includes loss of earnings, where that loss results from the trafficking or modern slavery offence in question.

15.16

Victims of offences will not receive the compensation ordered until there is no further possibility of an appeal in which the Compensation Order could be varied or set aside (s 141(1)). Further, the offender can apply to the magistrates' court, any time before the whole amount has been paid, to vary or discharge the amount ordered on several grounds (see s 143). Enforcement of a Compensation Order is the function of the magistrates' courts, which can impose a period of imprisonment in default of payment.

15.17

As the above demonstrates, this is very unlikely to be a fruitful source of compensation for the majority of victims not just because it requires a successful prosecution of a trafficker or perpetrator of a modern slavery offence (see s 1 of the MSA 2015) with identifiable means as well as full co-operation with the police by victims, but also because it requires revelation of the details of loss to the trafficker himself, with only a remote prospect of receiving the money within any reasonable period of time, if at all.

---

19 *R v Donovan* (1981) 3 Cr App Rep (S) 192.

20 See for example *R v Pola* [2009] EWCA Crim 655, [2010] 1 Cr App Rep (S) 32.

21 [2007] EWCA Crim 3297, [2008] 2 Cr App Rep (S) 184.

22 The criminal court should consider and take into account a Victim's Personal Statement and any evidence in support, prior to passing sentence, see *R v Perkins; Bennett; Hall* [2013] EWCA Crim 323, [2013] Crim LR 533.

23 [2025] EWCA Crim 778.

Slavery and trafficking reparation orders

15.18

Section 8 of the MSA 2015 introduces Slavery and Trafficking Reparation Orders ('STROs') against defendants convicted of an offence under ss 1, 2 or 4 of the Act (as to which see **Chapters 1** and **9**) *and* where a Confiscation Order[24] is made[25]. A STRO requires the defendant to pay compensation to the victim for *any* harm resulting from the offence (s 9(1) of the Act) but must not be made if a Compensation Order has been made under the Sentencing Code, s 134[26], for the same offence (see para **15.11** above). In any case in which the court has power to make a STRO, it must consider making one, whether or not the prosecutor applies for one to be made, and it must give reasons if it does not make one (s 8(7) of the Act).

15.19

Like Compensation Orders, courts will order compensation for such amount as the court considers appropriate, having regard to any evidence and representations made by or on behalf of the accused or the prosecutor (s 9(3)). The maximum amount cannot exceed the amount the convicted person is required to pay under the Confiscation Order (s 9(4)) and the court must have regard to the person's means (s 9(5)). Section 10(3) imports the same powers to appeal, review etc a Compensation Order available under the Sentencing Code, ss 141–144. Section 10 of the MSA 2015 demonstrates that the Confiscation Order and STRO are to be dealt with in tandem: if the Confiscation Order is varied, discharged, or quashed, so can the STRO be dealt with in the same way. Where the court makes both a Confiscation Order and an order for compensation, whether a Compensation Order or a STRO, and considers that the offender will not have sufficient means to satisfy all financial orders in full, it must direct that compensation be paid out of the sums recovered under the Confiscation Order[27].

15.20

Given the low number of successful prosecutions under the MSA 2015 to date and the difficulties already identified in relation to Compensation Orders, this is also unlikely to be a fruitful source of compensation for most victims of trafficking or modern slavery. The Independent Review into the MSA 2015 (May 2019), noted as follows:

24 Part 2 of the *Proceeds of Crime Act 2002*. A Confiscation Order can only be made by the Crown Court.
25 See Crown Prosecution Service, *Sentencing – Ancillary Orders* (updated 2024) https://www.cps.gov.uk/legal-guidance/sentencing-ancillary-orders#a16 accessed 22 August 2025 (cited at fn 13 above).
26 Section 10(1) of the Modern Slavery Act 2015.
27 See Proceeds of Crime Act 2002, s.13(5), which provides that where a compensation order is made alongside a confiscation order, the court must direct that the compensation be paid from the amount recovered under the confiscation order if the offender's means are insufficient to satisfy both.

'We were disappointed to note that between the coming into force of the Modern Slavery Act to December 2017 (latest available data) no Reparation Orders were made. Although we have been informed anecdotally of at least two cases in which a Reparation Order has been made, which we expect to be evidenced in future data releases, it is clear that this intention is not being realised. The lack of Reparation Orders also means it has not been possible for us to assess their effectiveness[28].'

15.21

In 2022, the Independent Anti-Slavery Commissioner identified significant shortcomings in the use of financial remedies for victims of trafficking. Data recorded on the Joint Asset Recovery Database (JARD), administered by the National Crime Agency, revealed that since 2015, 206 Confiscation Orders totalling over £5.8 million had been granted in cases where slavery or trafficking was the primary offence. However, only 41 Compensation Orders and eight STROs had been made. This disparity was described as very poor performance, particularly given the challenges in identifying realisable assets due to offenders' criminal lifestyles[29].

15.22

The report noted that the number of Compensation Orders had doubled since August 2019 but suggested that underreporting may be occurring due to police forces failing to update JARD. It recommended that the Home Office publish annual data on compensation and reparation payments to victims, which would encourage better record-keeping and accountability.

The Criminal Injuries Compensation Scheme

15.23

The first Criminal Injuries Compensation Scheme (CICS) was introduced in 1964. It was non-statutory and provided for *ex gratia* payments. The Criminal Injuries Compensation Act 1995 was enacted and schemes from that time have been statutory, pursuant to the Act. The schemes are government funded and designed to compensate 'blameless' victims of violent crime. The current scheme

28 See https://www.gov.uk/government/publications/independent-review-of-the-modern-slavery-act-final-report last accessed 10 December 2025.

29 Independent Anti-Slavery Commissioner, *Access to Compensation and Reparation for Survivors of Trafficking: Policy Paper* (April 2022) https://www.antislaverycommissioner.co.uk/media/pihjjclk/iasc-policy-paper-access-to-compensation-and-reparation-for-survivors-of-trafficking-april-2022-final.pdf accessed 22 August 2025.

is the Criminal Injuries Compensation Scheme 2012[30], which came into force in September 2012[31]. It is administered by the Criminal Injuries Compensation Authority('CICA'). There is a right of appeal to the First-tier Tribunal.

15.24

The Scheme specifically contemplates victims of trafficking and modern slavery and on the face of it meets the requirements of ECAT set out above. Whilst it does not require a criminal conviction of an assailant as a condition precedent, the Scheme poses other significant difficulties for victims of trafficking or modern slavery.

Eligibility criteria

15.25

Paragraph 4 of the 2012 Scheme provides that:

> 'A person may be eligible for an award under this Scheme if they sustain a criminal injury which is directly attributable to their being a direct victim of a crime of violence committed… The meaning of 'crime of violence' is explained in Annex B …'

Criminal injury

15.26

'Criminal injury' means an injury which appears in Part A or B of the tariff in Annex E:

- Part A. physical and psychological injuries;
- Part B: physical and sexual abuse.

15.27

The accompanying note states that 'mental injury' must be disabling and does not include temporary mental anxiety and similar temporary conditions. A mental injury is disabling if it has a substantial adverse effect on a person's ability to carry out normal day-to-day activities for the time specified (eg impaired work or school performance or effects on social relationships or sexual dysfunction).

30 The Criminal Injuries Compensation Scheme 2012 (CICA 2012) was recently under review, but the UK Government decided in July 2025 to drop the full review. See here for a 2025 House of Commons Library Research Briefing: https://commonslibrary.parliament.uk/research-briefings/cdp-2025-0085/ , last accessed 10 December 2025.

31 *Criminal injuries compensation: a guide* (March 2014, updated 14 June 2024) is available at www.gov.uk/guidance/criminal-injuries-compensation-a-guide, last accessed 28 February 2025.

Crime of violence

15.28

The CICS compensates for violent crimes only and those must have been committed in Scotland, England and Wales[32].

15.29

The 2012 version of the Scheme was the first to define the term 'crime of violence', with paragraph 2(1) of Annex B listing qualifying acts, including: a physical attack; any other act or omission of a violent nature causing physical injury; a threat causing fear of immediate violence in circumstances that would affect a person of reasonable firmness; and a non-consensual[33] sexual assault[34]. Any criminal injury sustained must be directly attributable to that threat.

15.30

In *RN v Criminal Injuries Compensation Authority*[35], the Court of Appeal ruled that victims of non-touching sexual abuse are eligible for compensation under the CICS. RN's application was rejected on the basis that he had not suffered physical injury and had not been placed in fear of immediate harm. That reasoning was upheld by both the First-tier Tribunal and the Upper Tribunal, which found that RN had not been subject to a criminal assault, sexual assault, or an act or omission of a violent nature resulting in physical (as opposed to mental) injury.

15.31

The Court of Appeal overturned those decisions. It held that RN had been subject to a crime of violence as defined by paragraph 2(1)(c): A threat against a person, causing fear of immediate violence in circumstances which would cause a person of reasonable firmness to be put in such fear. The Court interpreting 2(1)(c) in line with the criminal law of common assault[36], confirming that there is no requirement under common law for an absence of physical space or time between a threat and the resulting fear. The requirement of 'fear of immediate

32 Northern Ireland has its own scheme.

33 The language of Annex B appears to deliberately include the need for lack of consent even when referring to a sexual assault– this is presumably because someone can commit a sexual offence against children and young adults even if they say they consented. This requirement is controversial as it tends to suggest that a person can be complicit in their own sexual assault, whilst the criminal law recognises, for example, that children under 16 cannot consent. See here for calls for change from All-Party Parliamentary Group for Adult Survivors of Childhood Sexual Abuse: https://static1.squarespace.com/static/5c8faf788d97401af928638c/t/5e4189062488d55edc679042/1581353239794/EMBARGOED+TO+11.2+-+%27Can+adult+survivors+access+justice+and+support%27.pdf , accessed 10 December 2025.

34 Parliament legislated to align the meaning of 2(1)(d) with the definition of a sexual assault under s.3 of the Sexual Offences Act 2003, which requires touching.

35 *RN v CICA* [2023] EWCA Civ 882.

36 Applying *R v Ireland* [1998] AC 147 and *R v Constanza* [1997] 2 Cr App R 492.

violence' encompasses fear of violence occurring at any time, including the immediate future and the victim does not need to know the exact form of the threatened violence, only to fear that violence might be used against them.

15.32

The Court did not determine whether a crime of violence under 'act or omission of a violent nature which causes physical injury to a person' under paragraph 2(1)(b) permits a reading of physical injury to include psychiatric injury. For the Appellant, it was submitted that, both criminal[37] and personal injury law[38] have long rejected a distinction between physical and psychiatric injury when determining 'bodily harm'. The CICA submitted that while the Scheme provides a tariff for both physical and mental injuries, this tariff is only engaged once a crime of violence under Annex B has been established and paragraph 2(1)(b) refers specifically to 'physical injury' when defining a crime of violence, contrasting with the broader term 'criminal injury' used elsewhere in the Scheme's eligibility provisions. The Court acknowledged the complexity of the issue and the strength of arguments on both sides but concluded that resolution should await a case where the point is determinative.

15.33

As international criminal law illustrates, physical violence is not a required element of the offence of slavery (see **Chapter 1**). On the CICA's interpretation of the CICS, an international crime against humanity, one recognised as a *jus cogens* (peremptory) norm and giving rise to obligations *erga omnes* (towards everyone), may nonetheless fall outside the definition of a '*crime of violence*' under Annex B. This highlights a potential inconsistency between domestic compensation frameworks and the gravity of internationally recognised harms, particularly where those harms result in psychiatric rather than physical injury.

Residence

15.34

In relation to those who are not ordinarily resident in the UK, para 10(c) of the Scheme provides that:

---

37 In the context of violent crimes, the courts have held that 'bodily harm' includes psychiatric injury. In *R v Chan-Fook* (*'Chan-Fook'*) [1994] 1 WLR 689, Hobhouse LJ at 695G stated: 'The body of the victim includes all parts of his body, including his organs, his nervous system and his brain. Bodily injury therefore may include injury to any of those parts of his body responsible for his mental and other faculties.'

38 In *Bourhill v Young* [1943] AC 92, Lord Macmillan at 103 stated: 'The crude view that the law should take cognizance only of physical injury resulting from actual impact has been discarded, and it is now well recognised that an action will lie for injury by shock sustained through the medium of the eye or the ear without direct contact. The distinction between mental shock and bodily injury was never a scientific one…'

> 'A person is eligible for an award under this Scheme only if: …One of the conditions in paragraph 13 is satisfied in relation to them on the date of their application under this Scheme'.

15.35

Paragraphs 13–16 provide:

> '13.The conditions referred to in paragraph 10(c) are that the person has:
>
> (a) been referred to a competent authority as a potential victim of trafficking in human beings; or
>
> (b) made an application for asylum under Immigration Rules made under section 3(2) of the Immigration Act 1971.
>
> 14. A person who has made an application under this Scheme and satisfies a condition in paragraph 13 may request that their application under this Scheme is deferred until a final decision has been taken in relation to the referral or application mentioned in that paragraph.
>
> 15.Where a person is eligible for an award under this Scheme by virtue of paragraph 10 only because a condition in paragraph 13 is satisfied in relation to them, that person will not be eligible for an award unless, as a result of the referral or application mentioned in paragraph 13, they have been:
>
> (a) conclusively identified by a competent authority as a victim of trafficking in human beings; or
>
> (b) granted temporary protection, asylum, or humanitarian protection.
>
> 16. In paragraphs 13 and 15:
>
> (a) a person is conclusively identified as a victim of trafficking in human beings when, on completion of the identification process required by Art 10 of the Council of Europe Convention against Trafficking in Human Beings (CETS No.197, 2005), a competent authority concludes that the person is such a victim;
>
> (b) 'competent authority' means a person who is a competent authority of the United Kingdom for the purpose of that Convention; and
>
> (c) 'victim of trafficking in human beings' has the same meaning as under that Convention.'

Time limits

15.36

If the applicant is an adult at the time of the incident, he must apply as soon as reasonably practicable and no later than two years after it occurred[39]. If the

39 Paragraph 87 of CICS.

applicant was under 18 at the time of the incident, later applications may be considered (particularly in historic child sexual abuse cases). Paragraph 89 of the Scheme states that time may be extended where the claims officer is satisfied that:

'(a) due to exceptional circumstances the applicant could not have applied earlier; and

(b) the evidence presented in support of the application means that it can be determined without further extensive enquiries by a claims officer.'

15.37

In *MJ v FTT (No 3)*[40], a case decided under the old test for extension in the 2008 Scheme, the Upper Tribunal held that (a) and (b) were conditions precedent for the exercise of a discretion to waive the time limit, not exceptions to it. Where a decision-maker accepted that (a) and (b) were both satisfied, then there would have to be good reasons to justify not exercising discretion in the applicant's favour. The Upper Tribunal said that where a claim was made in respect of historic sexual abuse of a child, it was not enough simply to decide that the application was out of time. That would be to ignore the very real reasons such an individual would have for not disclosing either the abuse itself, or the full extent of such abuse, and the time that it takes to begin to come to terms with such traumatic experiences, citing *JM, petitioner*[41].

15.38

As to whether ignorance of the Scheme could amount to 'exceptional circumstances', see *R(JA) v First-tier Tribunal*[42], in which the Upper Tribunal found that there can be no *a priori* exclusion of a person being ignorant of law from the exceptional circumstances which *may* show they were not able to apply to CICA any earlier than they did.

15.39

In *R (HJK and others) v Director of Legal Aid Casework*[43], the High Court recognised that victims of trafficking or modern slavery face significant and predictable barriers to accessing the CICS, particularly in making timely applications. The Court observing that the two-year time limit under the Scheme is especially problematic for victims of trafficking or modern slavery, whose exploitation typically occurs over extended periods and involves repeated abuse; with many are unaware of their right to claim compensation until well after the deadline has passed.

40 [2014] UKUT 279 (AAC).
41 [2013] CSOH 169, 2014 SLT 475.
42 [2024] UKUT 121 (AAC).
43 [2025] EWHC 774 (Admin).

15.40

The judgment highlighted that trauma, mental health conditions, language barriers, trust issues and lack of support networks often prevent victims from engaging with legal processes. These factors also inhibit their ability to provide the detailed evidence required to justify an out-of-time application under CICS strict criteria. The application process, especially for out-of-time claims, was complex and required detailed evidence. The Court rejected the notion that victims could simply submit minimal information to 'get a foot in the door,' finding this approach ineffective and unfair.

15.41

Online guidance and telephone support were deemed inaccessible for victims with language and trust issues. The Court held that legal assistance was essential from the outset to ensure meaningful access and participation in the compensation process. The Court concluded that, in such circumstances, the refusal to grant Exceptional Case Funding (ECF) for legal assistance breached the claimants' Art 6 ECHR rights, as they could not participate effectively or fairly in the compensation process without legal support.

Grounds for withholding or reducing an award

15.42

Paragraph 86 of the Scheme provides that 'An application for an award will be determined by a Claims Officer in the authority in accordance with this Scheme.' Paragraphs 22–29 set out grounds for withholding or reducing an award from those who would otherwise have been entitled to one pursuant to paras 4–21. Paragraphs 22–29 reflect the requirements of s 3(1) of the Act, which provides

> 'The Scheme may, in particular, include provision –
>
> a. As to the circumstances in which an award may be withheld or the amount of compensation reduced …'

15.43

The grounds for withholding an award are:

- a failure to report the incident to the police as soon as reasonably practicable (in deciding whether this requirement is met, particular account will be taken of: (a) the age and capacity of the applicant at the date of the incident; and (b) whether the effect of the incident on the applicant was such that it could not reasonably have been reported earlier);
- a failure to co-operate as far as reasonably practicable in bringing the assailant to justice.

15.44

Where victims have been referred into the National Referral Mechanism ('NRM'), it may be arguable that they reported and/or co-operated sufficiently.

15.45

The grounds for withholding or reducing an award include:

- where the applicant fails to take all reasonable steps to assist a claims officer or other body or person in relation to consideration of his application. Such failure includes repeated failure to respond to communications sent to the address given by the applicant;
- where the conduct of the applicant before, during or after the incident giving rise to the criminal injury makes it inappropriate to make an award or a full award. For this purpose, conduct does not include intoxication through alcohol or drugs to the extent that such intoxication made the applicant more vulnerable to becoming a victim of a crime of violence;

15.46

The recognised vulnerabilities identified by the Court in *R (HJK and others) v Director of Legal Aid Casework*[44] would be relevant to grounds for withholding or reducing an award (see above).

15.47

A further ground to withhold or reduce an award under CICS is where the applicant to whom an award would otherwise be made has unspent convictions[45]. The award will be withheld entirely if the applicant received a sentence listed in paragraph 3 of Annex D, including a community order, and reduced if a different sentence.

15.48

In *A v Criminal Injuries Compensation Authority*[46], the claimants argued that the provisions of the Scheme impose an unlawful 'blanket ban' on awards being made under the Scheme to those with an unspent conviction which led to a custodial or a community sentence and that such an exclusionary rule amounted to unjustified discrimination in breach of ECHR, Art 14 (prohibition of discrimination) read in conjunction with ECHR, Art 4 (prohibition of slavery and forced labour). On the facts, the convictions in question were unconnected with the trafficking). The appellants contended that as victims of trafficking with relevant unspent convictions, they had to be treated differently from victims of

44 [2025] EWHC 774 (Admin).
45 Paragraph 26 and Annex D of CICS.
46 [2021] UKSC 27; [2021] 1 WLR 3746.

other crimes with relevant unspent convictions. The Supreme Court disagreed holding that there were no features of the offence of people trafficking which could require preferential treatment to be accorded to victims of trafficking over victims of other serious crime. The appellants alternatively submitted that in excluding from the scheme victims of trafficking with unspent convictions which resulted in custodial or community sentences, but not other victims of trafficking, the scheme discriminated on grounds of other status. The Court agreed that there was clearly a difference in treatment, but such treatment was justified: seeking to ensure that limited funds should be directed towards those who were considered blameless and who had not inflicted loss on society through their offending behaviour was a legitimate aim. In the context of the Scheme, a bright line rule could be justified as it had the advantages of clarity and consistency.

15.49

Notably, the appellants were not 'nexus offenders', that is, their criminal conduct was not connected to their experiences of trafficking or modern slavery. The Court acknowledged that it was arguable that nexus offenders might be entitled to different treatment. However, it noted that the non-punishment principle was not directly at issue in the case before it. The application of the exclusionary rule to nexus offenders remains a live and significant issue, particularly considering the ECtHR's judgment in *VCL and AN v United Kingdom*[47], which affirmed that the non-punishment principle falls within the scope of the positive protective obligations under Art 4 ECHR (see **Chapter 10**).

Other barriers for victims under the CICS

15.50

If a decision to award a claim is initially refused or reduced (which is common), the appeal to the First-tier Tribunal will usually require a victim to give evidence and be subject to cross-examination by CICA and/or questioning from the tribunal itself (albeit a relatively informal jurisdiction). Those who are traumatised and/or suffering with significant psychiatric conditions because of their experience may not wish to be pressed about their injuries and the details of how they were sustained. In such circumstances **Chapter 3**: Trauma informed approach and **Chapter 8**: Special Measures in legal proceedings should be considered[48].

47 *V.C.L. and A.N. v United Kingdom* (2021) 72 EHRR 2.

48 See ATLEU / After Exploitation, *'Life-changing': The Impact of Criminal Injuries Compensation* (November 2025), a systemic review of CICS as applied to modern slavery victims, which recorded refusal rates of 82-100% for trafficking victims in the period reviewed and identified structural barriers including the immigration exclusion, the 'same roof rule', and delays. The report provides evidence of transformative impact when awards are made.

Level of awards

15.51

Section 2(1) of the Criminal Injuries Compensation Act 1995 provides 'The amount of compensation payable under an award shall be determined in accordance with the provisions of the Scheme'. The value of the payments made is calculated by reference to a Parliament-set tariff of injuries (Annex E to the Scheme). The size of the award will be altered to reflect the seriousness of the injury.

15.52

Types of payment which can be made include:

- injury payments;
- loss of earnings payments: where the applicant has no/limited capacity to work as a direct result of a criminal injury (Annex F sets out the multiplier tables);
- special expenses payments.

15.53

The maximum award which can be made, before any reductions, is £500,000. The amount of any injury payment will be determined according to the tariff. For a recent illustration of the potential scale of CICS awards in modern slavery cases, see the award of £208,971 to a forced labour victim who sustained life-changing physical injuries inflicted by traffickers, reported by Hope for Justice in April 2025[49]. Where an application concerns two separate injuries, the award will be for the full tariff amount for the injury with the highest payment, and 30 per cent of the tariff for the second injury. Where there are three or more criminal injuries, it will be 15 per cent of the tariff amount for the criminal injury with an equal or third highest payment. Where a person has sustained a mental injury as a result of a sexual assault, the victim will be entitled to an injury payment for whichever of the sexual assault or the mental injury would give rise to the highest payment under the tariff. If an injury does not fall within the tariff, the claims officer may refer it to the Secretary of State for inclusion if considered of equivalent seriousness.

The Miscarriage of Justice Application Scheme

15.54

The Miscarriage of Justice Application Scheme is a discretionary compensation scheme administered by the Secretary of State for Justice. It provides

49 https://hopeforjustice.org/news/208k-compensation-for-man-who-traffickers-left-with-life-changing-injuries/.

compensation for those who have been wrongfully convicted and punished, pursuant to the Criminal Justice Act 1988, s 133[50]. The Ministry of Justice has paid £2,380,700 in compensation under the Miscarriage of Justice Application Service in the period 2016/17 to 2023/24[51].

15.55

Section 133 was enacted to give effect to the UK's international obligations under Art 14(6) of the International Covenant on Civil and Political Rights 1966, which was ratified by the UK in May 1976. There is an almost identical provision in Art 3 of the Seventh Protocol of the ECHR. Section 133 of the Criminal Justice Act 1988 was very significantly amended by the Anti-social Behaviour, Crime and Policing Act 2014, so as to require an applicant to effectively prove innocence (as opposed to show that their conviction has been set aside because fresh evidence so undermined the case against him such that no conviction could possibly be based upon it[52]).

15.56

Section 133(1) of the Criminal Justice Act 1988 provides that:

> '... when a person has been convicted of a criminal offence and when subsequently his conviction has been reversed or he has been pardoned on the ground that a new or newly discovered fact shows beyond reasonable doubt that there has been a miscarriage of justice, the Secretary of State shall pay compensation for the miscarriage of justice to the person who has suffered punishment as a result of such conviction or, if he is dead, to his personal representatives, unless the non-disclosure of the unknown fact was wholly or partly attributable to the person convicted.'

15.57

Section 133(1ZA), as inserted by the Anti-social Behaviour, Crime and Policing Act 2014, s 175, provides there will have been a miscarriage of justice 'if and only if the new or newly discovered fact shows *beyond reasonable doubt that* the person *did not commit the offence.*'

50 Guidance on how the Scheme operates is available at https://hmctsformfinder.s3.amazonaws.com/forms/guidance/index.htm, last accessed 28 February 2025.

51 https://www.gov.uk/government/publications/miscarriage-of-justice-application-service-mojas-claims-management-information/miscarriage-of-justice-application-service-mojas-claims-management-information#summary-of-findings, last accessed 10 December 2025.

52 See *R (on the application of Adams) v Secretary of State for Justice* [2011] UKSC 18, [2012] 1 AC 48.

15.58

Following that amendment, in *R (on the application of Nealon) v Secretary of State for Justice*[53] the appellants contended that s 133 (as amended) was incompatible with the presumption of innocence enshrined in ECHR, Art 6(2). The Court of Appeal accepted that Art 6(2) was engaged, but not that the amended s 133 is incompatible with it. The court said that s 133 does not require the applicant to prove his innocence generally but focuses on 'the effect of the new or newly discovered fact and nothing else' (para 50). Any denial of compensation does not undermine his acquittal or the presumption of innocence. By a majority of 5:2, the Supreme Court[54] dismissed the appellants' appeals. The majority found that although ECHR, Art 6(2) had been engaged, it does not automatically follow that the ECtHR would find a violation; s 133 was compatible. In *Nealon and Hallam v UK*[55], the Grand Chamber decided in the majority (12:5) that whilst Art 6 (2) did apply to compensation proceedings following acquittal, s 133(1ZA) did not breach the presumption of innocence.

15.59

The test as currently enunciated is a high threshold to cross[56], given the very narrow definition of miscarriage of justice. However, if the test is satisfied (as to which see below), there are many advantages for those victims of trafficking or modern slavery who have been wrongly prosecuted, convicted and incarcerated to apply under this scheme rather than trying to bring a civil claim against a public authority that failed to protect him. This is because a similar approach is used by the Independent Assessor to quantify damages as in tortious claims, and as the assessment is made on written evidence, the victim of trafficking will not have to go through the trauma and stress of giving evidence in court where tortious claims do not settle. Also, Legal Help is available to assist in making the initial application, and if accepted on the Scheme, legal costs are recoverable, including counsel's fees (see **Chapter 20** on funding).

Are victims of trafficking who have had their convictions set aside eligible under the Scheme?

15.60

An applicant will be eligible if the two conditions of s 133 are met:

- the applicant's conviction has been reversed, or he has been granted a free pardon; and

53 [2015] EWHC 1565 (Admin), 165 NLJ 7657.
54 [2019] UKSC 2, [2020] AC 279.
55 Applications nos. 32483/19 and 35049/19, 11 June 2024.
56 See for example the recent case of *Ali v Secretary of State for Justice* [2023] EWHC 3059 (Admin).

- the conviction must have been reversed, or the pardon granted, on the ground that a new or newly discovered fact shows beyond reasonable doubt that the person did not commit the offence.

15.61

Historically, criminal convictions of victims of trafficking, where there was a sufficient nexus between the offending and the offender's trafficked status, were set aside by the Court of Appeal Criminal Division not because no offence was committed but because, under ECAT, Art 26 (echoed in the EU Trafficking Directive, Art 8, which is no longer directly effective post-withdrawal from the EU), criminal proceedings should or would not have been brought at all if the prosecuting authorities had known at the time that the defendant was a victim of trafficking or modern slavery whose offending was inextricably linked with their trafficked status. Since the implementation of the MSA 2015, such convictions are often set aside because of the failure to properly advise a victim of trafficking or modern slavery about the availability of a defence pursuant to the MSA 2015, s 45(1), where a person[57] is not guilty if the compulsion is attributable to slavery or relevant exploitation. This failure to advise can be compounded by a failure to identify a person as a victim of trafficking or modern slavery, denying them the opportunity of relying upon the statutory defence in s 45 (see **Chapters** 4 and **10**).

15.62

Thus, for the purposes of the Scheme, the newly discovered fact is the fact that the person was a victim of trafficking or modern slavery (see Chapter 1) who, if an adult, was *compelled* to commit the offence they did and thus the criminality of the defendant was effectively extinguished[58]. Whilst the ECAT Art 26 protection is about prosecutorial discretion, and so reflected in CPS policy (as to which see **Chapter 10**), the victim of trafficking was arguably innocent (or not guilty) if the newly discovered fact shows that they would have had a common law defence of duress or necessity available to them at trial or post-commencement, a statutory defence pursuant to the MSA 2015, s 45. The words 'did not commit the offence' in s 133(1ZA) must, by definition, include those who are not guilty of the offence by reason of having a common law or statutory defence. In cases where the conviction is set aside by the Court of Appeal on the wider basis that the CPS may not have prosecuted on public interest grounds, the basis of eligibility will turn on the specific facts.

---

57 The elements of the defence are different in relation to child victims of trafficking: see **Chapter 10**.
58 See *R v L* [2013] EWCA Crim 991, [2014] 1 All ER 113 at [13].

Procedure

15.63

The applicant must submit a written application to the Miscarriages of Justice Team, along with copies of the NG form 2, Court of Appeal judgment, perfected grounds of appeal and any CCRC Statement of Reasons. The application form (which is available online) requires a clear exposition of the applicant's personal details, case details, appeal details, and reasons for applying.

15.64

There is a two-year time limit for applications under s 133 of the Criminal Justice Act 1988, which begins on the date the applicant is either pardoned or their conviction is quashed. Under s 133(2A), an application submitted outside this period may still be considered if there are exceptional circumstances that justify doing so. However, the Act does not define what constitutes 'exceptional circumstances' nor legislate for statutory guidance on the matter.

15.65

The Ministry of Justice guidance for the Scheme, states:

> 'The Secretary of State may consider an application made outside the two-year limit. Generally, not being aware of the scheme would not count as exceptional circumstances, but each application received out of time would be considered on its own merits.'

15.66

In *R (HJK)*[59], the Court observed that the claimants' ignorance of the CICS was linked to their specific vulnerabilities and explained the delay in making an application.

15.67

Importantly, the guidance cannot fetter the discretion conferred by s 133(2A), nor can it be used to interpret to limit the scope of that provision. Its role is limited to acknowledging that each out-of-time application must be assessed on its individual merits.

15.68

Following a decision of eligibility (which falls solely to the Secretary of State under s 133(3)), the Independent Assessor[60] will determine the amount of the

59 *R (HJK & Ors) v Director of Legal Aid Casework* (CICA intervening) [2025] EWHC 774.

60 Ministry of Justice, *Independent Assessor of Compensation for Miscarriages of Justice Reappointed* (Gov.uk, 17 August 2023) https://www.gov.uk/government/news/independent-assessor-of-compensation-for-miscarriages-of-justice-reappointed accessed 22 August 2025.

award. The applicant must put in their submissions to the Miscarriages of Justice Team within six months from the date of the notice of eligibility. Funding for a barrister to draft these can be approved by the Assessor.

15.69

The onus is on the applicant to quantify all relevant losses flowing from the miscarriage of justice, and to support it with documentary evidence (including loss of earnings and medical and expert reports). Funding for such reports can be approved by the assessor in advance. The applicant must provide signed and dated statement of evidence, including a brief personal history, account of his time in prison and any resultant difficulties, and an account of their life since release. The assessor will then aim to make final assessment of the applicant's case within three months.

The award

15.70

The total amount of compensation payable cannot exceed the overall compensation limit: £1 million for cases where the applicant has been detained for at least ten years (s 133B) and £500,000 in any other case. Interim payment may be granted, depending on the information available to the assessor on the miscarriage of justice, and attendant consequences.

15.71

There are two parts to the award:

- non-pecuniary: loss of liberty (which can include any period of immigration detention[61] that flows directly from the conviction), hardship, distress and injury to feelings, inconvenience, damage to reputation and possible psychiatric damage;
- pecuniary: loss of past/future earnings, expenses and legal costs related to the miscarriage of justice. Claims for loss of earnings for any one year limited to 1.5 times the median annual gross earnings at the time (s 133A(6)). The assessor may make a deduction from any pecuniary award for saved living expenses – the cost an applicant would have had to pay for essentials from their net income, had they not been wrongly imprisoned[62].

61 Where there has been recovery via other litigation (for eg claims against the Home Office) for loss of liberty and / or psychiatric loss, there is a need to avoid double counting. The fact of such recovered has to be disclosed to the IA.

62 *R (on the application of O'Brien) v Independent Assessor* [2007] UKHL 10, [2007] 2 AC 312.

15.72

The overall objective of s 133, as described by Lord Bingham is 'that the State representing the public at large should make fair recompense to victims of miscarriages of justice'[63]. In assessing the amount payable to the applicant, the Independent Assessor will have particular regard to the seriousness of the offence of which the applicant was convicted, the severity of the punishment suffered as a result, and the conduct of the investigation and prosecution of the offence (s 133A(2)). It is open to the Assessor to reduce the award if they believe that the applicant has contributed towards their circumstances or has a bad criminal record.

Non-pecuniary loss

15.73

In making an award, the Assessor must have regard to the amounts awarded by the courts in personal injury cases, although no direct analogy can be drawn between physical injuries and the effect of a miscarriage of justice. The Assessor also needs to be aware of the awards made in civil wrong cases, in particular malicious prosecution and false imprisonment (including immigration detention cases)[64].

15.74

In assessing an award for loss of liberty, the assessor will have regard to cases decided in the context of false imprisonment by the police and other detaining authorities, such as *Thompson v Metropolitan Police Comr*[65] and *Muuse v Secretary of State for the Home Department*[66]. For longer periods of imprisonment (here, 20 months), *AXD v The Home Office* is a useful reference point[67]. The figures will need to be uprated using the Kemp & Kemp PI Inflation calculator and applying the *Simmons v Castle*[68] 10% uplift in pre-2013 cases. An applicant can also be awarded a sum for any features that aggravated the loss of liberty.

15.75

In *Thompson* Lord Woolf MR recommended the following brackets for basic damages: £500 for the first hour of detention, £3,000 for the first day, with a progressively reducing rate thereafter. These figures need to be adjusted for inflation. The *Thompson* guidelines were approved in *R (on the application of*

63 Ibid.
64 *R (on the application of Miller) v Independent Assessor* [2009] EWCA Civ 609.
65 [1998] QB 498, [1997] 2 All ER 762.
66 [2010] EWCA Civ 453.
67 [2016] EWHC 1617 (QB).
68 [2012] EWCA Civ 1039.

Miller) v Independent Assessor in relation to any s 133 assessment. The respondent submitted that *Thompson* did not indicate the scale of any tapering award, and that any extrapolation from a period of relatively short detention would presume an artificial tariff. However, it was held that the guidelines were an 'essential starting point', from which a longer period of detention had to be related proportionately, 'not by means of a simple arithmetical progression'[69].

15.76

In *Muuse*, an award of basic damages for £25,000 (to be uprated) was made for a period of 128 days' (just over four months) unlawful detention. This award accounted for the fact that the claimant had been lawfully imprisoned for 147 days prior to this period, pursuant to criminal justice powers. The relevance of any preceding period of lawful detention was affirmed in *R v Governor of Brockhill Prison, ex p Evans (No 2)*[70], where the House of Lords upheld the Court of Appeal's award of £5,000 (to be uprated) for a 59-day detention of a prisoner whose release date was miscalculated. One of several factors justifying this lower level of damages was the fact that the unlawful extension of detention occurred in the context of a custodial sentence of two years, of which ten months had been served following a proper conviction. As such, the appellant had 'already made the necessary adjustments to serving a prison sentence'[71].

15.77

However, as held in *Adegboyega v Secretary of State for the Home Department*[72] the assessment of the basic award in cases of unlawful detention is fact-sensitive and should not be approached mechanistically. HHJ Richard Roberts explained that, as a general principle, the court applies a progressively reducing scale of awards as the period of unlawful detention lengthens. However, that approach was not appropriate in the present case, as Mr Adegboyega's psychological injury and distress remained constant throughout his detention, as did the persistent threat of deportation. In reaching its conclusion, the court considered the effects *of R (Diop) v Secretary of State for the Home Department*[73].

15.78

When calculating damages under the Scheme, it is important to recognise that victims of trafficking or modern slavery who are non-British nationals and have received custodial sentences will either be subject to automatic deportation provisions or at risk of deportation under discretionary powers. British nationals may also face deprivation of citizenship in certain circumstances.

---

69 At para 46.

70 [2001] 2 AC 19, [2000] 4 All ER 15.

71 [1999] QB 1043 at 1060D.

72 *Adegboyega v Secretary of State for the Home Department* [2024] EWHC 2365 (KB).

73 *R (Diop) v Secretary of State for the Home Department* [2018] EWHC 3420 (Admin).

15.79

In assessing an award for psychiatric damage, the assessor has no power to make an award for compensation for the effects of the trafficking but rather must focus solely on the effect of the wrongful conviction and sentence. Where an applicant has suffered psychiatric damage because of their trafficking, any expert report must address to what extent the conviction and sentence exacerbated or caused any psychiatric condition. In *Adegboyega*, the medical evidence of moderate PTSD was accepted, and the claimant's damages for psychiatric injury were assessed according to the Judicial College Guidelines for personal injury[74].

15.80

Deptka and another v Secretary of State for the Home Department[75] was considered in *Adegboyega*, and it was held that additional humiliation and injury to dignity merited an award of £15,000 aggravated damages in favour of Mr Adegboyega. The judge rejected the submission that it was not proportionate to award aggravated damages where a basic award and an award for psychiatric injury was made but ensured that the psychiatric injury was not double counted when assessing aggravated damages.

15.81

Any final award is not to be negotiated but can be challenged by way of judicial review. Of course, if there is a Human Rights Act 1998 claim made for a failure to investigate (see below), which in turn resulted in incarceration, there cannot be double recovery for the same loss (ie for incarceration). The same applies in relation to any civil claim brought against the Home Office or the CPS or police for false imprisonment/unlawful detention for any periods of detention which also include the period of imprisonment for sentence. The current 'Notes for Guidance' sent to those accepted on to the Scheme includes the warning that 'The award may be declined or reduced in so far as it compensates for or relates to an impact, loss, damage, detriment, or other circumstance that has previously been the subject of compensation or payment outside the MOJAS scheme and where it relates to the same matter and arising from the same set of circumstances' and that 'An applicant must inform the MOJAS team of any claim or proceedings that may be relevant in deciding the amount of compensation to award'. If a claim from another source is outstanding, it may have the effect of pausing any application to MOJAS.

---

74 Judicial College, *Guidelines for the Assessment of General Damages in Personal Injury Cases* (17th edn, OUP 2024).

75 *Deptka and another v SSHD* [2019] EWHC 503.

Human Rights Act 1998 claims against public bodies

15.82

In deciding whether to bring such a claim, it is important to bear in mind, that HRA 1998 claims have a short limitation period of one year, subject to the court finding it equitable to extend the period. Section 7(5) of the HRA 1998 provides that:

> '(5) Proceedings under subsection 1(a) must be brought before the end of—
>
> (a) the period of one year beginning with the date on which the act complained of took place; or
>
> (b) such longer period as the court considers equitable having regard to all the circumstances,
>
> but that is subject to any rule imposing a stricter time limit in relation to the procedure in question.'

15.83

Notably, in *O'Connor v Bar Standards Board*[76], the Supreme Court addressed the issue of limitation where the alleged breach constituted a continuing act, in that case, disciplinary proceedings. The Court held that section 7(5)(a) of the Human Rights Act 1998 should not be interpreted narrowly, but rather in a manner that provides an effective and workable rule for situations where the infringement arises from a course of conduct. It concluded that, in such cases, time begins to run from the date the continuing act ceases.

15.84

The general approach to 'all the circumstances' in s 7(5)(b) was examined in *Solaria Energy UK Ltd v Department for Business, Energy and Industrial Strategy*[77]:

> '57. What are 'all the circumstances' relevant to the enquiry envisaged by section 7(5)(b)? They are any circumstance which is or might be relevant to the question of whether it is equitable to allow the claim to be brought in the 'longer period'. Whilst there can be no limit on the circumstances which are or may be relevant to that inquiry, it is common sense to observe that what the court will primarily be looking at are those circumstances which are or may be relevant to the delay, which has resulted in a claim being brought after the expiry of the one year stipulated by section 7(5)(a).

76 *O'Connor v Bar Standards Board* [2017] UKSC 78.
77 [2021] 1 WLR 2349.

> 58. Such questions will usually include: what is the overall period of delay on the part of the claimant? Why did it occur? Is there a good reason for it? What was the conduct of the defendant during that period of delay? What effect did the delay have on both parties and any future trial? Those are the sorts of questions which civil judges regularly ask themselves in all manner of interlocutory applications, most regularly in applications for relief from sanctions. They are therefore part of an analysis which civil judges are well-used to undertaking.
>
> 59. In addition, I note that these are also the questions which the judge must ask under section 33(3) of the Limitation Act 1980, which deals with the discretionary exclusion of the time limit in certain personal injury claims, and where the word 'equitable' is also used in the statute to determine the court's approach.'

15.85

Although the decided cases on extensions under the HRA 1998 are generally unhelpful[78], in *R (on the application of D) v Metropolitan Police Comr*[79], Eady J overturned Master Leslie's refusal to exercise his discretion under s 7(5)(b) to extend time to allow a claim to be brought under the ECHR, Art 3. D claimed that the police had infringed her Art 3 rights by failing to properly investigate her complaint of rape. The man whom D had accused had been arrested, tried, and acquitted in 2006. The trial judge criticised the police for serious failings in their evidence gathering.

15.86

The essence of D's complaint was that the unit responsible for investigating rape and other serious sexual offences was under-resourced and inadequately staffed, and the trainee in charge of her case was inexperienced, untrained, and overworked. She brought proceedings in February 2010, three years after the expiry of the one-year time limit. The Master in the QBD focused on the delay between March 2009 (when he found that D had become aware of the potential claim), and February 2010. D argued that during that period she had suffered from depression, domestic violence and struggled with drug-taking, as well as twice attempting suicide. In October 2009, D applied for legal aid and issued proceedings when it was granted. The Master found that D need not have waited for the legal aid determination before issuing the claim and expressly based his decision solely on that finding. However, Eady J found that, while it was a 'relatively simple matter' to issue a claim form, it was reasonable to wait to have legal representation before making an application for anonymity. D had, in addition, wished to avoid committing herself to any costs liability while awaiting the legal aid grant.

78 See for eg *AP v Tameside MBC* [2017] EWHC 65 (QB).
79 [2012] EWHC 309 (QB).

15.87

A potential disadvantage (as compared with the statutory scheme) is that, like all such civil claims, unless the claim settles, victims of trafficking or modern slavery will need to be advised that they will have to give evidence at trial and likely to be subject to cross-examination. In such circumstances early consideration should be given to the need to apply for special measures (see **Chapter 8**, read with **Chapter 3**).

The investigative duty

15.88

In *Rantsev v Cyprus and Russia*[80], the ECtHR held that '[l]ike Arts 2 and 3, Art 4 also entails a procedural obligation to investigate situations of potential trafficking' (recently reaffirmed in *VCL and AN v UK*[81]).

15.89

In *B.B. v Slovakia*[82], the ECtHR confirmed that the threshold of a 'credible suspicion' of human trafficking, sufficient to trigger the State's procedural obligation to investigate under Art 4 ECHR, was met where there is *prima facie* evidence of the constituent elements of trafficking, namely the act, the means, and the purpose. In *AM (Zimbabwe) v Secretary of State for the Home Department*[83], the Supreme Court cited with approval the formulation by Sales LJ (as he then was) in the court below, where he described a *prima facie* case as one in which the applicant presented evidence capable of establishing a potential infringement, if not challenged or countered.

15.90

The investigation must be effective, and, in that regard, the Court in *Rantsev* held as follows[84]:

> '[…] For an investigation to be effective, it must be independent from those implicated in the events. It must also be capable of leading to the identification and punishment of individuals responsible, an obligation not of result but of means. A requirement of promptness and reasonable expedition is implicit in all cases but where the possibility of removing the individual from the harmful situation is available, the investigation

80 (2010) 51 EHRR 1.

81 *Applications nos. 77587/12 and 74603/12*, 16 February 2021.

82 *BB v Slovakia* App no 48587/21 (ECtHR, 24 October 2024) [79] and *S.M. v Croatia* App no 60561/14 (ECtHR, 25 June 2020) [113]–[114], [303].

83 [2020] UKSC 17, [2020] 1 WLR 4188, [16].

84 At 288–289.

must be undertaken as a matter of urgency. The victim or the next-of-kin must be involved in the procedure to the extent necessary to safeguard their legitimate interests.

Finally, the Court reiterates that trafficking is a problem which is often not confined to the domestic arena. When a person is trafficked from one state to another, trafficking offences may occur in the state of origin, any state of transit and the state of destination. Relevant evidence and witnesses may be located in all states. Although the Palermo Protocol is silent on the question of jurisdiction, [ECAT] explicitly requires each Member State to establish jurisdiction over any trafficking offence committed in its territory. Such an approach is, in the Court's view, only logical in light of the general obligation, outlined above, incumbent on all states under Art 4 of the Convention to investigate alleged trafficking offences. In addition to the obligation to conduct a domestic investigation into events occurring on their own territories, Member States are also subject to a duty in cross-border trafficking cases to co-operate effectively with the relevant authorities of other states concerned in the investigation of events which occurred outside their territories. Such a duty is in keeping with the objectives of the Member States, as expressed in the preamble to the Palermo Protocol, to adopt a comprehensive international approach to trafficking in the countries of origin, transit and destination. It is also consistent with international agreements on mutual legal assistance in which the respondent states participate in the present case.'

15.91

A failure to effectively investigate is likely to sound in damages, albeit modest amounts (as to which see further below).

15.92

In *OOO v Commissioner of Police for the Metropolis*[85] the claimants (young Nigerian women) claimed that the police had infringed their rights under the ECHR, Arts 3 and 4. Each of the claimants was trafficked into the UK from Nigeria when a girl, for the purpose of domestic servitude and each alleged that thereafter and over a number of years they were made to work for no pay in a household in and around London and subjected to physical and emotional abuse by the householders. They argued that their treatment over these years was such that they were subject to inhuman and degrading treatment and that they were held in slavery or servitude contrary to Arts 3 and 4 respectively of the ECHR. The claimants' complaints against the police were essentially that when officers of the Metropolitan Police were asked to investigate the treatment that had been meted out to them, they had failed to undertake any

85 [2011] EWHC 1246 (QB).

such investigation. It was the first time the domestic courts had to consider the scope of the *investigative* duty under Arts 3 and 4.

15.93

The police contended that whilst the householders had breached the claimants' Arts 3 and 4 rights, the scope of the investigative duty was such that it had not been breached. The High Court found that the view of the ECHR upon the scope of the investigative duty arising under Arts 3 and 4 of the Convention was sufficiently explained by reference to the decision in *Rantsev*, in that the police were under a duty to carry out an effective investigation of an allegation of a breach of Art 4 once a credible account of an alleged infringement had been brought to their attention. The trigger for the duty would not depend upon an actual complaint from a victim or near relative of a victim. The investigation, once triggered, will have to be undertaken promptly.

The scope of the investigative duty

15.94

The scope of the investigative duty under the ECHR, Art 3 was revisited in the watershed judgment of *Commissioner of Police of the Metropolis v DSD*[86]. The claimants were victims of John Worboys, a serial sex offender known as the Black Cab Rapist and thought to be responsible for the drugging and sexual assault of over 100 women. Both NBV and DSD reported their assault to the police, and in NBV's case Worboys was quickly arrested as a suspect but released without charge. In DSD's case, he was never identified. Worboys was eventually charged with 23 offences relating to 14 victims and convicted of 19 counts (including the assault on NBV). Both women brought damages proceedings against the police, alleging failure to carry out effective investigations into their complaints that amounted to inhuman or degrading treatment contrary to Art 3. In the High Court[87], Green J found that there had been a series of systemic and operational errors, which included the following:

(i) a substantial failure to train relevant officers in the intricacies of sexual assaults and, in particular, drug-facilitated sexual assaults;

(ii) serious failures by senior officers properly to supervise investigations by more junior officers and to ensure that investigations were being conducted in accordance with standard procedure;

(iii) serious failures in the collection and use of intelligence sources to cross-check complaints to see if there were linkages between them;

86 [2018] UKSC 11.
87 [2014] EWHC 436 (QB).

(iv) failures to allocate proper resources to sexual assaults including pressure from borough management to focus resources on other allegations; and

(v) a failure to maintain the confidence of victims in the integrity of the investigative process.

15.95

The police argued that insofar as a duty to investigate arose at all it was a limited duty which arose only where the State was in some way *itself* complicit in a breach of Art 3. Green J rejected this argument and found that the claimants' Art 3 rights had been breached. In a separate judgment (as to which see below), he also awarded damages. The Court of Appeal dismissed the police's appeal[88]. The Supreme Court considered the following two issues:

(i) whether there is an obligation under the HRA 1998, s 6, read with ECHR, Art 3, to investigate ill-treatment which has been perpetrated by a private individual without any complicity of a public authority; and/or

(ii) whether in the case of such ill-treatment any positive obligation is confined to a requirement to put in place the necessary structure to enable such investigation to be conducted but does not extend to the conduct of an individual investigation into a particular alleged crime.

15.96

The argument that the investigative duty does not apply in the absence of state complicity was roundly rejected by the Supreme Court. The majority judgment, given by Lord Kerr, held that the ECHR, Art 3 investigative duty (and by analogy, Art 4) did not require State complicity and applied to both systemic and operational failures. There was a clear and consistent line of Strasbourg authority on the nature and scope of the investigative duty and there was no good reason for the Supreme Court to depart from it. The Court held that serious failures (also described by Lord Kerr as '*conspicuous or substantial*' and '*egregious and significant*') by the police in an investigation into serious offences against the person (described by Lord Kerr as '*serious violence to an individual*'), even where these fall short of a structural or system failing, will amount to a breach of the investigative obligation under Art 3. A credible or arguable claim of serious crime will trigger the duty to carry out an effective investigation. In the Art 4 context, a credible or arguable claim of a trafficking or modern slavery offence will suffice[89].

---

88 *DSD v Metropolitan Police Commissioner* [2015] EWCA Civ 646, [2016] QB 161.

89 In an Art 4 ECHR context see *F.M. v Russia* (App nos 71671/16 and 40190/18) ECtHR, 10 December 2024.

Just satisfaction for investigative duty breaches

15.97

Damages are not automatically recoverable for a failure to investigate. In *OOO v Commissioner of Police for the Metropolis*[90], Wyn Willams J awarded £5,000 (to be uprated) to each of the claimants for the significant frustration and distress (none had psychiatric conditions), over and above a declaration that Art 4 had been breached.

15.98

In the quantum decision of *DSD v Commissioner of Police for the Metropolis*[91], a decision that was not appealed and was expressly commended by Lord Hughes in the Supreme Court judgment, the essential question for the court was whether it was 'necessary' to award damages in order to 'afford just satisfaction' to DSD and NBV within the meaning of the HRA 1998, s 8. Green J reviewed the relevant Strasbourg authorities in this area and awarded both women damages. He said at [118]:

> 'The main factors that I take into account are: the nature of the harm suffered and treatment costs; the duration of the breach by the Defendant; the nature of the failings and whether they were operational and/or systemic; the overall context to the violations; whether there was bad faith on the part of the Defendant or whether there is any other reason why an enhanced award should be made; where the award sits on the range of awards made by Strasbourg and in similar domestic cases; other payments; totality and 'modesty''.

15.99

He awarded to DSD the sum of £22,500[92] comprising a sum (£20,000) for (more general) non-pecuniary harm which was calculated to cover the period to the date of judgment and a small incremental component (£2,500) for *future* treatment. He awarded NBV the sum of £19,000. This comprised £17,000 for the fact of the rape and the post-rape psychological harm to the date of judgment, and £2,000 as a contribution to future treatment costs (these sums need to be uprated in line with inflation).

15.100

Whilst the damages in *DSD* were primarily about the psychiatric harm caused by the investigative failure (which was separate from the harm caused by the sexual violence itself), in victims of trafficking or modern slavery cases, there

90 [2011] EWHC 1246 (QB), [2011] HRLR 29, [2011] UKHRR 767.
91 [2014] EWHC 2493 (QB).
92 Figures need to be uprated to reflect the inflationary increase.

may be the additional element of a prosecution and incarceration of a victim who commits an offence and should have had the non-prosecution/ non-penalty protection (see **Chapter 10**). In *VCL and AN v UK*[93] the Strasbourg Court awarded EUR 25,000 to each applicant for 'procedural breaches' of the Art 4 operational duty as well as Art 6 (which included distress and 'obstacles' caused by their criminal conviction). If the loss of liberty can be shown to flow directly from the failure to investigate, then damages for that loss can be included. The approach to loss of liberty damages is dealt with above.

15.101

Importantly, in *DSD*[94], the Supreme Court confirmed that the award of compensation was not affected by the fact that the victims had received compensation from CICA, and a civil claim against Worboys himself. Lord Kerr explained at [64]–[65] that different wrongs were being compensated:

> 'It is well settled … that the award of compensation for breach of a Convention right serves a purpose which is distinctly different from that of an order for the payment of damages in a civil action. As Lord Brown said in *Van Colle* at para 138:
>
> '… Convention claims have very different objectives from civil actions. Where civil actions are designed essentially to compensate claimants for their losses, Convention claims are intended rather to uphold minimum human rights standards and to vindicate those rights. That is why time limits are markedly shorter. … It is also why section 8(3) of the [HRA] provides that no damages are to be awarded unless necessary for just satisfaction …'
>
> Laws LJ said in para 68 of his judgment in the Court of Appeal [in *DSD*], that the inquiry into compliance with the Art 3 duty is 'first and foremost concerned, not with the effect on the claimant, but with the overall nature of the investigative steps to be taken by the State'. I agree with that. The award of compensation is geared principally to the upholding of standards concerning the discharge of the state's duty to conduct proper investigations into criminal conduct which falls foul of Art 3. In paras 72-78 of his judgment, Laws LJ set out the systemic and operational failures of the appellant, quoting extensively from the judgment of Green J as to the first of these. That catalogue of failures was considered to warrant the award of compensation to the respondents, irrespective of the fact that they had received damages from both Worboys and CICA. I cannot find any flaw in the judge's

93 *Applications nos. 77587/12 and 74603/12*, 16 February 2021.
94 [2018] UKSC 11.

decision to award that compensation nor in the Court of Appeal's decision to uphold that decision.'

15.102

The interplay between damages for breaches of Convention rights and CICA damages was considered in detail in *R (AXO) v FTT (Social Entitlement Chamber) & CICA*[95]. The Court of Appeal found that whether there is double recovery in any case depends on an analysis of the CICA award (and what it was for) alongside an analysis of the Convention award (and what it was for). The first question is whether either or both awards contained an element for pecuniary loss. If so, then the comparison between them should be relatively straightforward. The Court recognised that awards for non-pecuniary losses are less readily comparable but dictated that the comparison should be carried out.

Claims against perpetrators of trafficking or modern slavery

Tortious claims against individual perpetrators

15.103

Whilst civil claims against perpetrators of trafficking or modern slavery for a host of torts (for example, false imprisonment, harassment, assault, battery) are available in theory, such claims are rare, not least because victims are usually terrified of the perpetrators and the reprisals that would follow if a civil claim was initiated, and even if they were successful, enforcing any judgment would be problematic.

15.104

The case of *R (on the application of Tirkey) v Director of Legal Aid Casework*[96] is a chilling demonstration of how the statutory charge can wipe out even a large award for damages. The claimant was an Indian national who was trafficked into the UK by an Indian couple, for whom she was forced to work in conditions of servitude. She brought proceedings against them in the employment tribunal for which she was granted exceptional case funding by the Legal Aid Agency. The claim was successful and resulted in a substantial award of damages (£266,536.14) but, owing to delays by Central London County Court in dealing with an application by the claimant's solicitor for an interim charging order, the couple dissipated their assets before a charge could be obtained over them. The total sum ultimately recovered by the claimant was £35,702.80, and once the Legal Aid Agency had exercised its statutory charge under s 25 of the

95 [2024] EWCA Civ 22.
96 [2017] EWHC 3403 (Admin).

Legal Aid, Sentencing and Punishment of Offenders Act 2012 to recover the cost of the legal aid provided to the claimant, she was left with nothing. Her judicial review, relying on the EU Charter of Fundamental Rights, ECAT and the ECHR failed on all grounds.

15.105

In *AT v Dulghieru*[97], the only known civil claim of its kind, four Moldovan women in their twenties brought claims based on their allegation that they were victims of an unlawful conspiracy to traffic them into the UK from Moldova for the purposes of sexual exploitation and prostitution. The two defendants were significant players in that conspiracy and each of them has been convicted of criminal offences and sentenced to long terms of imprisonment. In this case, the claimants were granted anonymity and eventually judgment was entered in default of a proper defence. The judgment turns on the assessment of damages after hearing from each claimant (which fortuitously for them was in the absence of either defendant, who, although invited by the court to participate, did not). The total amount awarded to the claimants against the defendants, who were liable jointly and severally, was, in the case of AT £175,000, NT £162,000, in the case of ML £132,000 and in the case of AK £142,000[98]. However, it is unlikely that those damages were ever recovered from the defendants, given that they were incarcerated, and any assets would be difficult to trace[99].

Tortious and other claims against a company

15.106

In *Galdikas v DJ Houghton Catching Services Ltd*[100], the first civil case of its kind, the claimants, six individuals who alleged they were trafficked from Lithuania and subjected to severe labour exploitation, brought civil claims against a limited company engaged in the supply of labour to chicken farms in the UK. The claimants were recognised by the NRM as victims of trafficking. The claims encompassed claims in, inter alia, breach of contract, breach of the Agricultural Wages Act 1948, negligence, harassment, and assault. The claimants alleged that they suffered loss and damage, including personal injury, distress, and unpaid wages, because of the defendants' wrongful acts. They also joined the Gangmasters and Labour Abuse Authority (GLAA) (a statutory regulatory body responsible for the licensing of gangmasters and the investigation of

97 [2009] EWHC 225 (QB).
98 Figures to be uprated.
99 For a detailed analysis of this litigation see J Luqmani, 'Traffickers in the UK Courts for Harm Associated with Trafficking' in P Chandran (ed), *Human Trafficking Handbook* (LexisNexis, 2011).
100 [2016] EWHC 1376 (QB), [2016] IRLR 859.

labour abuse) as a defendant[101]. The judgment deals with various preliminary applications for strike out/summary judgment by both the claimants and DJ Houghton (the latter failed). The claimants were granted summary judgment in relation to their claims for breaches of the Agricultural Wages Orders and the Gangmasters (Licensing Conditions) Rules 2009[102] relating, inter alia, to their inadequate wages and unlawful withholding of wages and inadequate working facilities. The case settled in December 2016, some four years after the claimants were exploited[103].

Employment tribunal claims

15.107

Claims against traffickers may be brought in the employment tribunal for employment-related abuses such as failure to pay the minimum wage, failure to pay holiday pay, breaches of the Working Time Regulations1998 and race or sex discrimination. The commentary below focuses on common arguments or issues that occur in respect of employment claims in relation to workers or employees who are victims of trafficking or modern slavery, rather than a general guide to employment law.

Illegality as a defence

15.108

Prior to 2016, it was generally assumed that contracts that were statutorily illegal or which were illegal under common law were void and unenforceable[104], barring some exceptions such as discrimination claims, which, as statutory torts, do not arise out of the contract of employment.

15.109

One example of an exception in the context of trafficking was the decision in 2014, of the Supreme Court, in *Hounga v Allen*[105]. Miss Hounga knowingly

101 The Employment Rights Act 2025 created the Fair Work Agency (FWA), which consolidated the Gangmasters and Labour Abuse Authority (GLAA), the Employment Agency Standards Inspectorate, and HMRC's National Minimum Wage enforcement team with effect from 7 April 2026: see CIPD, *Employment Rights Act 2025 — Fair Work Agency* (https://www.cipd.org/uk/knowledge/employment-law/employment-rights-act-2025-fair-work-agency/). Accordingly, complaints and enforcement actions formerly directed to the GLAA will, from that date, fall within the FWA's remit; practitioners advising victims of labour trafficking and exploitation should consult the FWA as the new primary enforcement body.

102 SI 2009/307.

103 See www.leighday.co.uk/News/News-2016/December-2016/Joy-for-trafficked-workers-while-UKs-Worst-Gangma, last accessed 28 February 2026.

104 The basis for this principle is recorded in cases as early as *Holman v Johnson 1775 1 Cowp 341*, Court of King's Bench, that 'no court will lend its aid to a man who founds his cause of action upon an immoral or illegal act'.

105 [2014] UKSC 47, [2014] 1 WLR 2889.

illegally entered the UK from Nigeria in January 2007, when aged 14. For the following 18 months Miss Hounga lived in the home of Mrs Allen and of her husband (who had facilitated her illegal entry). Although Miss Hounga had no right to work in the UK, and after July 2007 no right to remain in the UK, Mrs Allen employed her, unpaid, to look after her children in the home. There Mrs Allen inflicted serious physical abuse on Miss Hounga and threatened her if she reported the abuse. In July 2008, Mrs Allen forcibly evicted Miss Hounga from the home and thereby dismissed her from the employment. The appeal proceeded on the basis that, by dismissing her, Mrs Allen discriminated against Miss Hounga on racial grounds, namely on ground of nationality, she treated Miss Hounga less favourably than she would have treated others. The Court of Appeal held that the illegality of the contract of employment formed a material part of Miss Hounga's complaint and that to uphold it would be to condone the illegality.

15.110

The Supreme Court unanimously allowed Ms Hounga's appeal in relation to her claim for the statutory tort of discrimination, committed during dismissal. The majority in the Supreme Court held that it would be an affront to current anti-trafficking public policy to allow an employer to evade liability to an employee by reference to the illegality of the contract of employment entered into between them, where the employer had trafficked the employee for domestic servitude. The UK authorities are striving in various ways to combat trafficking and to protect its victims. The public policy in support of the application of the defence of illegality, to the extent that it exists at all, should give way to the public policy to which its application is an affront.

15.111

Then, in *Patel v Mirza*[106], decided in 2016, the Supreme Court completely revised the approach to the defence of illegality. Overruling previous case law, it held by a majority that, in cases where illegality is an issue, the key question is not whether the contract should be considered tainted by illegality but whether, in the circumstances of the case, the relief claimed should be granted. Consequently, the mere fact that a contract is deemed 'illegal' does not, on its own, determine whether the contract is void or unenforceable. Instead, in assessing whether allowing a claim would undermine the integrity of the legal system, the court stated that it is necessary to consider the following: (a) the underlying purpose of the law that has been breached and whether that purpose would be advanced by refusing the claim; (b) any other relevant public policy that might be affected by denying the claim; and (c) whether denying the claim would be a proportionate response to the illegality, keeping in mind that punishment is a matter for the criminal courts.

106 [2016] UKSC 42.

15.112

Lord Toulson did not wish to specify which factors would be relevant in assessing proportionality, given the wide diversity of cases that could be affected by illegality. However, he did rule that a range of factors would be relevant, which could include: (a) the seriousness of the illegal conduct; (b) its centrality to the contract; (c) whether it was intentional, and (d) whether there was a marked disparity in the parties' respective culpability.

15.113

There is no doubt that this new approach is likely to assist claims for compensation based on contract or the statutory tort of discrimination, where the contract of employment or engagement is tainted with illegality. This is evident from the fact that *Hounga,* was cited by the Supreme Court in *Patel* as an example of a case where countervailing public interest considerations had to be balanced against the public interest in applying the illegality defence.

15.114

The new approach was further clarified in *Stoffel & Co v Grondona*[107], in which Lord Lloyd-Jones clarified the application of the '*trio of necessary considerations'* namely, whether the underlying purpose of the illegality would be enhanced by denying the claim; whether denying the claim might have an impact on other public policies; and whether denying the claim would be a proportionate response to the illegality. A court should first identify the policy considerations for the first two points at a general level (but not evaluate them) and determine whether enforcing a claim tainted by illegality would be inconsistent with those policies or, where the policies compete, where the overall balance lies. If it concludes that the claim should not be barred by illegality, there is no need to consider proportionality; proportionality should be considered only if the balancing of policies suggests a denial of the claim.

15.115

Lord Toulson's references in *Patel* to illegality as a potential defence in claims relating to property, tort, and unjust enrichment, as well as contract, and his lengthy reference to the Supreme Court's decision in *Hounga suggest* that the *Patel* approach should also be adopted in discrimination claims where illegality is an issue.

Immigration status and race discrimination

15.116

In *Taiwo v Olaigbe*[108], the Supreme Court held that those who are exploited due to their vulnerable immigration status cannot bring a race discrimination

107 [2020] UKSC 42, SC.
108 [2016] UKSC 31, [2016] 1 WLR 2653.

claim, as immigration status (as distinct from nationality) is not a protected characteristic within the meaning of the Equality Act 2010.

15.117

Ms Taiwo had entered the UK on a false basis, had her passport taken from her by her employer and she was expected to work during most of her waking hours for minimal wages. She was starved and subject to physical and mental abuse. She escaped and brought successful claims in the employment tribunal for the failure to pay her the minimum wage, for unlawful deductions from wages, for failure to provide rest periods and to give her written terms of employment. She was awarded compensation in respect of these claims but her claim for race discrimination, which would have entitled her to damages for the fear and distress she suffered, was dismissed. The tribunal found that her mistreatment was because she was a vulnerable migrant worker who was reliant on the respondents for her continued employment and residence in the UK, not because she was Nigerian. The Supreme Court dismissed her appeal (as well as that of another related appellant). Lady Hale noted that the present law does not offer redress for all the harm suffered by the appellants. She stated that Parliament might wish to consider extending the remedy available under the MSA 2015 to give employment tribunals jurisdiction to grant compensation for ill-treatment meted out to workers.

Caste discrimination

15.118

In *Tirkey v Chandok*[109] the claimant was recruited by a couple to work as their cleaner and nanny. It was argued that the claimant was chosen from Bihar in India because of her low hereditary caste (as defined in India) and inability to speak English. The claimant was made to work 18-hour days, seven days a week. She had her passport taken off her and was not allowed to contact her family. She was paid less than minimum wage. She was given second-hand clothes to wear and slept on a foam mattress on the floor for four and a half years. She was not allowed to bring a bible with her or to go to church.

15.119

The claim was made on the basis of race discrimination. The respondent sought to strike out the claim as caste did not fall within the definition of race set out in section 9 of the Equality Act 2010. The tribunal held that although 'caste' is an autonomous concept that did not presently come within s.9(1) many of the facts relevant in considering caste in many of its forms might be capable of doing so, since 'ethnic origins' in s.9(1)(c) had a broad and flexible ambit,

109 [2014] UKEAT/0190/14/KN.

including characteristics determined by 'descent'. It became common ground during the argument that it was possible that the facts found in hearing the present claim might come within the scope of that phrase. The claim, therefore, proceeded.

15.120

The tribunal found that the claimant's living and working conditions were a 'clear violation of her dignity' that 'created an atmosphere of degradation which was offensive'. The Tribunal found that the claimant was not paid in line with national minimum wage and, therefore, awarded her £183,773.53 as back pay. On top of this, the Tribunal also awarded the claimant £27,500 for direct race discrimination, £7,500 for indirect discrimination and £13,500 for psychiatric injuries, as well as £7,500 in aggravated damages.

Diplomatic immunity

15.121

In *Reyes v Al-Malki*[110], a domestic worker who alleged that she was a victim of trafficking brought claims for direct and indirect discrimination, unlawful deductions from wages (failure to pay the national minimum wage), and breach of the Working Time Regulations 1998 against a Saudi Arabian diplomatic agent and his wife. Mr and Mrs Al-Malki left the UK when Mr Al-Malki's posting came to an end. The Court of Appeal held that the Employment Tribunal had no jurisdiction because Mr Al-Malki was entitled to diplomatic immunity under Art 31 of the Vienna Convention on Diplomatic Relations, and Mrs Al-Malki was entitled to a derivative immunity under Art 37(1) as a member of his family. The Supreme Court unanimously allowed the appeal but on a narrow basis. In short, it held that once a diplomat's posting has come to an end, his immunity after leaving the receiving state is ordinarily limited to a 'residual immunity' under Art 39(2). That residual immunity applies only to acts performed in the exercise of 'official functions'. Acts performed in the exercise of a diplomat's official functions are limited to acts which are part of the diplomatic functions of the diplomatic mission, performed on behalf of the state which that diplomat represents. Mr and Mrs Al-Malki left the UK at the end of Mr Al-Malki's posting, so the only potentially relevant immunity is the 'residual immunity' in respect of official acts. The employment of Ms Reyes to carry out domestic tasks in the residence of Mr and Mrs Al-Malki was not an act in the exercise of the diplomatic functions of the mission. Nor was it done on behalf of Saudi Arabia, even though it assisted Mr Al-Malki in the performance of his official functions. It was not there the exercise of an official function. Consequently, neither Mr Al-Malki nor Mrs Al-Malki could rely on that residual immunity.

110 [2017] UKSC 61, [2019] AC 735.

15.122

The issue of state and diplomatic immunity was then considered by the Supreme Court in *Benkharbouche v Secretary of State for Foreign & Commonwealth Affairs: Janah v Libya*[111]. Moroccan nationals who had been employed as domestic workers by the Sudanese and Libyan embassies in London. Both had been recruited overseas and only one had acquired permanent resident status in the UK. Both were dismissed from their employment and brought claims in the employment tribunal. Some of their claims were based on UK law, some on EU law. In each case, the employment tribunal dismissed all the claims on the basis that they were barred by ss 4(2)(b) and 16(1)(a) of the Act. The EAT upheld the dismissal of the domestic law claims but allowed the EU law claims to proceed. The Court of Appeal affirmed the EAT's judgment, disapplying ss 4(2)(b) and 16(1)(a) so far as they applied to the EU law claims and declaring them to be incompatible with the right to access a court guaranteed by ECHR, Art 6. The Supreme Court held that insofar as the State Immunity Act 1978 ss 4(2)(b) and 16(1)(a) conferred immunity on states in respect of employment claims brought against them by members of their embassy staff, they were found to be incompatible with the Claimant's right to access a court or tribunal under Art 6 ECHR and also discriminatory, contrary to Art 14 ECHR. It reasoned that state immunity was not absolute. The rule of customary international law was that a state was entitled to immunity only in respect of acts done in the exercise of sovereign authority. Thus, there would only be state immunity in an employment claim if the claim arose from an inherently sovereign act. Whether there had been such an act depended on the nature of the employment relationship, which in turn depended on the functions that the employee was employed to perform. While the character of the employment would not necessarily be decisive, an embassy's employment of purely domestic staff was not inherently governmental but was an act of a private law character. There was no basis in customary international law for the application of state immunity to acts of a private law character in an employment context.

15.123

The employment of the two respondents was not an exercise of sovereign authority; nothing about their alleged treatment engaged the sovereign interests of their employers, and they were not seeking reinstatement in a way that would restrict their employers' right to decide whom to employ. As a matter of customary international law, Sudan and Libya were not entitled to immunity, and insofar as ss 4(2)(b) and 16(1)(a) conferred it, they were incompatible with Art 6.

111 *Benkharbouche v Secretary of State for Foreign & Commonwealth Affairs: Janah v Libya* [2017] UKSC 62.

15.124

The same claim then proceeded to the ECtHR[112] in respect of the UK government's proposed remedy to the incompatibility found by the Supreme Court. The Court refused the UK Government's application to strike out two claims made by former embassy staff who had worked for the Sudanese and Libyan embassies in the UK. The ECtHR concluded that the Government's declaration, that it would make a remedial order to amend the 1978 Act and pay damages to the claimants, afforded inadequate redress to the claimants since it was unclear whether their employment claims would be allowed to proceed and the damages offered fell significantly short of the value of their claims.

15.125

In *Basfar v Wong*[113] it was made clear that a diplomatic immunity will not bar the hearing of a complaint brought by a Claimant alleging modern slavery. A migrant domestic worker who had been employed by a Saudi Arabian diplomat to the UK appealed against the striking out, based on diplomatic immunity, of proceedings she had issued against him in the employment tribunal.

15.126

The worker, a national of the Philippines, had been brought to the UK by the diplomat to work in his diplomatic household. She claimed that she was the victim of human trafficking and modern slavery and she brought proceedings in the employment tribunal complaining of breaches of her employment rights. The diplomat applied to strike out the proceedings on the basis that he had immunity from suit under the Vienna Convention on Diplomatic Relations 1961. For the purposes of that application, the employment tribunal assumed the facts alleged by the employee to be true. The issue was whether the exception to immunity set out in Art 31(1)(c) of the Convention applied. That Art provided that immunity would not be available in respect of 'commercial activity exercised by the [diplomat]' outside his official functions. The issue was thus whether exploiting a domestic worker in the manner alleged constituted the 'exercise' of a 'commercial activity', thereby taking the diplomat outside the scope of immunity. Relying on the majority reasoning of the Supreme Court in *Reyes v Al-Malki*[114], the employment tribunal found that the diplomat's conduct amounted to the exercise of commercial activity and that he did not have immunity. The EAT overturned its decision, holding that the Court of Appeal's judgment in Reyes (*Al-Malki v Reyes*[115]) and the minority judgment in the Supreme Court represented the current state of the law.

112 *Benkharbouche v United Kingdom* (19059/18) [2022] 4 WLUK 104.
113 [2022] UKSC 20.
114 [2017] UKSC 61, [2019] AC 735, [2017] 10 WLUK 394.
115 [2015] EWCA Civ 32, [2016] 1 WLR 1785, [2015] 2 WLUK 170.

15.127

A diplomat to the UK who had allegedly trafficked a domestic worker and forced her to work in conditions which amounted to modern slavery did not have diplomatic immunity from proceedings brought against him by the worker in the employment tribunal. Assuming that the allegations were true, the diplomat's treatment of the worker constituted a commercial activity exercised by him outside his official functions for the purpose of the exception to immunity set out in the Vienna Convention on Diplomatic Relations 1961 Art 31(1)(c).

More recently, in *COL v United Arab Emirates*[116], the first UK case in which a foreign State was held liable for modern slavery committed by one of its diplomats on UK soil, a Filipino domestic worker, who had been trafficked to the UK and forced to work without pay for a UAE diplomat, was awarded £262,292.76 in damages comprising false imprisonment, injury to feelings, PTSD damages and exemplary damages. Lavender J held that the employing State, the UAE, did not have immunity from civil liability in modern slavery claims brought against it by the victim, and that sub-clinical distress was actionable as a compensable tort. The judgment extends the principles established in *Basfar v Wong*[117] by confirming that the employing State, not only the diplomat personally, may be held liable in modern slavery claims where the trafficking arises in the context of a diplomatic posting.

National Minimum Wage – concurrent jurisdiction

15.128

Ayaji v Abu[118] is an example of a claim for unpaid national minimum wage being brought successfully in the High Court, as there is concurrent jurisdiction between the High Court and the Employment Tribunal, depending on how the claim is put. This is because a right to the national minimum wage is implied by statute into every contract of employment, so a claimant can bring a claim for breach of contract, in the High Court. The claimant also brought a claim for harassment as defined in the Protection from Harassment Act 1997 and was awarded £39,000 in damages, including for psychiatric injury.

Time limits

15.129

In most breach of contract claims in the civil courts, there is an absolute bar on recovery for damages suffered more than six years before the claim was

116 [2026] EWHC 86 (KB). For analysis of the strategic implications of *COL v UAE*, see Sopher+Co (2–3 March 2026): https://sopherco.com/why-disregarding-the-minimum-wage-constitutes-modern-slavery/ (accessed 2 March 2026]).

117 [2022] UKSC 20.

118 [2017] EWHC 3098 (QB).

issued. Unlike in the employment tribunal, there is no general discretion for the courts to dis-apply the time limit. Time limits in which all claims in the employment tribunal must be brought are set out in the various relevant statutes (for example, section 111 of the Employment Rights Act 1996 for a claim for unfair dismissal, section 123 of the Equality Act 2010 for discrimination claims). The time limits for bringing claims are short, most being either three or six months. In the employment tribunal, if the claim is presented outside the time limit, the tribunal simply does not have jurisdiction to hear it. Generally, time runs from the act complained of. In some cases[119], the tribunal has discretion to exercise a power to extend the time limit if the relevant statutory test is met. For example, claims for unfair dismissal[120] or unauthorised deductions from wages, the test is whether within such further period as the tribunal considers reasonable in a case where it is satisfied that it was not reasonably practicable for the complaint to be presented before the end of the period of three months. For a claim for discrimination under the Equality Act 2010 the test is whether it would be just and equitable to extend the time limit[121].

15.130

In *Ayaji* however, the court accepted the claimant's argument that the time limit should not apply because her traffickers had deceived her. The court agreed that where any fact relevant to the right of action has been deliberately concealed from the claimant by the defendant, the period of limitation shall not begin to run until the claimant has discovered the concealed information or could have done so with reasonable diligence.

Mitigation of loss

15.131

The claimants before the employment tribunal are often under a duty to mitigate their loss, this usually takes the form of finding new employment. In claims for unfair dismissal, this duty stems from section 123(4) of the Employment Rights Act 1996, which applies the common law duty of a person (the claimant) to mitigate her loss when assessing the compensatory award for unfair dismissal.

15.132

In *Beijing Ton Ren Tang (UK) Ltd v Wang*[122] the Employment Appeal Tribunal held that when deciding whether an employee has acted reasonably in seeking

119 But not for all types of claim. See for example, claims for interim relief under the Trade Union and Labour Relations (Consolidation) Act 1992, where there is no discretion to extend the time limit for bringing a claim.
120 Section 111 (2) (b) of the Employment Rights Act 1996.
121 See section 123(1)(b) of the Equality Act 2010.
122 [2009] UKEAT/0024/09.

to mitigate loss, a tribunal must take into account the circumstances of the particular employee. In that case the tribunal concluded that '..this Claimant; ...was greatly shocked by her sudden dismissal; that she felt isolated in this country; she spoke no English and did not know any part of the country outside London. She had been recruited in China to do a particular job here and expected to be allowed to do it until 31 December 2008 at the earliest. The expectation was that she would then return to China. Accordingly she was left in an unusual and vulnerable position when she was unfairly dismissed' [17] and that 'We think that this is one of those unusual cases where, despite that factual state of affairs, the Employment Tribunal was entitled to conclude that in all the circumstances the Respondent has not shown that this Claimant acted unreasonably in failing to obtain alternative employment' [18].

Interim relief

15.133

Interim relief in the employment tribunal is limited. It can be provided under section 130 of the Employment Rights Act 1996 when the threshold set out in section 129 is met. The power is restricted to a continuation of contract order. The threshold for making such an order is when

> '...it appears to the tribunal that it is likely that on determining the complaint to which the application relates the tribunal will find—
>
> (a) that the reason (or if more than one the principal reason) for the dismissal is one of those specified in—
>
> (i) section 100(1)(a) and (b), 101A(1)(d), 102(1), 103 or 103A, or
>
> (ii) paragraph 161(2) of Schedule A1 to the Trade Union and Labour Relations (Consolidation) Act 1992, or
>
> (b) that the reason (or, if more than one, the principal reason) for which the employee was selected for dismissal was the one specified in the opening words of section 104F(1) and the condition in paragraph (a) or (b) of that section was met'.

15.134

There is limited authority concerning the interpretation of sections 130 and 131 and in particular the nature of the relationship established by a continuation of the contract order. This latter point was considered in *Langton v Secretary of State for Health*[123], where HHJ Peter Clark stated, '*As Burton P clarified in Dowling*

123 *Langton v Secretary of State for Health* [2013] UKEAT 0376_13_0110.

v ME Ilic Haulage[124], the effect of a continuation order is not to establish a new contract of employment, as the old contract necessarily ends before an interim relief application can arise, but rather to preserve the claimant's rights to pay and other benefits enjoyed under the terminated contract of employment, and to address, if necessary, the question of continuity of employment (see section 130(1)).'

15.135

In *Rathod v Clinica Private Healthcare Ltd*[125] the Tribunal ruled that it can lawfully make an order for interim relief in situations where the claimant was employed in the UK under a certificate of sponsorship, that had been cancelled by the respondent.

15.136

The respondent argued that the claimant's right to work in the UK was contingent upon having a sponsor and a certificate of sponsorship. As the first respondent ceased sponsoring the claimant on 8 November 2023 and ceased holding a licence to sponsor any workers on 3 June 2024, reinstating or re-engaging the claimant would breach immigration rules. Although both parties agreed that the respondent could not legally employ migrant workers in the claimant's position once its sponsorship ended, the EAT concluded that the continuation of the contract order did not create a new employment relationship, and therefore, it did not prevent such an order from being made.

Family worker exemption from the National Minimum Wage Regulations

15.137

In *Thukalil v Puthenveettil*[126] the first respondent worked as a domestic worker in the appellants' home from 2005 to 2013. Under regulation 2 (2) of the National Minimum Wage Regulations 1999, she was not entitled to the minimum wage[127]. The claim challenged the application of regulation 2 (2) on the ground that it indirectly discriminated against women, because the majority of domestic workers were women, contrary to directly effective EU law rights.

---

124 [2004] ICR 1176.

125 *Rathod v Clinica Private Healthcare Ltd* (ET Case No 2216407/2023) https://www.gov.uk/employment-tribunal-decisions/mr-k-b-rathod-v-clinica-private-healthcare-ltd-and-ms-t-farquar-2216407-slash-2023 (accessed 28 February 2026).

126 [2023] EAT 47.

127 Regulation 2 (2) provides, (2) In these Regulations *'work'* does not include work (of whatever description) relating to the employer's family household done by a worker where the conditions in sub-paragraphs (a) or (b) are satisfied.

(a) The conditions to be satisfied under this sub-paragraph are–

(i) that the worker resides in the family home of the employer for whom he works,

(ii) that the worker is not a member of that family, but is treated as such, in particular as regards to the provision of accommodation and meals and the sharing of tasks and leisure activities.

15.138

The tribunal agreed that regulation 2(2) of the National Minimum Wage Regulations 1999 (the family worker exemption) was indirectly discriminatory. It further concluded that regulation 2 (2) was contrary to the claimant's directly effective EU law right to equal pay under Art 157 of the Treaty on the Functioning of the European Union[128] and that it was bound by the European Communities Act 1972 Pt I s.2(1) to disapply it.

15.139

On appeal, the appellants argued that Art 157 only applied where there was a disparity of pay between a male and a female who did equal work or work of equal value and where the disparity could be attributed to a single source, and since domestic and family workers affected by reg.2(2) worked for different employers, there was no such single source. The tribunal applied *Jenkins v Kingsgate (Clothing Productions) Ltd*[129] and *Bilka-Kaufhaus GmbH v Weber von Hartz*[130] and held that Art 157 could apply where unequal pay as between men and women was caused by an indirectly discriminatory legislative provision such as regulation 2 (2).

---

128 Art 157 provides '1. Each Member State shall ensure that the principle of equal pay for male and female workers for equal work or work of equal value is applied. 2. For the purpose of this Art , 'pay' means the ordinary basic or minimum wage or salary and any other consideration, whether in cash or in kind, which the worker receives directly or indirectly, in respect of his employment, from his employer. Equal pay without discrimination based on sex means: (a) that pay for the same work at piece rates shall be calculated on the basis of the same unit of measurement; (b) that pay for work at time rates shall be the same for the same job. 3. The European Parliament and the Council, acting in accordance with the ordinary legislative procedure, and after consulting the Economic and Social Committee, shall adopt measures to ensure the application of the principle of equal opportunities and equal treatment of men and women in matters of employment and occupation, including the principle of equal pay for equal work or work of equal value.4. With a view to ensuring full equality in practice between men and women in working life, the principle of equal treatment shall not prevent any Member State from maintaining or adopting measures providing for specific advantages in order to make it easier for the underrepresented sex to pursue a vocational activity or to prevent or compensate for disadvantages in professional careers'.

129 (96/80) EU:C:1981:80, [1981] 1 WLR 972, [1981] 3 WLUK 245.

130 (170/84) EU:C:1986:204, [1986] ECR 1607, [1986] 5 WLUK 96.

16 International protection and human rights claims by victims of human trafficking and modern slavery

Michelle Brewer, Catherine Meredith and Zoe Harper

The Domestic Concept of 'Modern Slavery'[1]

16.1

'Modern slavery' is a domestic legal construct, introduced in s 1 of the Modern Slavery Act 2015 (MSA 2015), which serves as an umbrella term encompassing the distinct offences of slavery, servitude, and forced or compulsory labour. Confusingly, the term *modern slavery* is used more broadly in the Modern Slavery Statutory Guidance[2], where it also includes human trafficking.

16.2

Importantly, *modern slavery* is not a term derived from international law. Its adoption in UK legal and political discourse followed the ratification of the Council of Europe Convention on Action against Trafficking in Human Beings (ECAT) and reflects a domestic framing rather than an internationally recognised legal category.

16.3

It is essential that the use of the term *modern slavery* does not obscure the conceptually and legally distinct harms of slavery, servitude, and forced or compulsory labour. As legal scholars[3] have consistently warned, each of these

1 The first and second editions of this chapter were authored by Michelle Brewer and Gemma Loughran.

2 Modern Slavery: statutory guidance for England and Wales (under s 49 of the Modern Slavery Act 2015) and non-statutory guidance for Scotland and Northern Ireland.

3 See Jean Allain, '*The International Legal Regime of Slavery and Human Exploitation and its Obfuscation by the Term of Art Slavery-like Practice' (2012) CRDF 27–42 and Vladislava Stoyanova, United Nations Against Slavery: Unravelling Concepts, Institutions and Obligations*, 38 MICH. J.L. 359 (2017). https://repository.law.umich.edu/mjil/vol38/iss3/2/ [accessed 14 October 2025].

offences must be understood in its own right. Failure to do so risks diluting the gravity of the most serious of these harms, namely, slavery.

16.4

While the detailed legal definitions and constituent elements of these offences are set out in **Chapter 1**, it is important to emphasise here that all four offences, slavery, servitude, forced or compulsory labour, and human trafficking, are prohibited under Art 4 of the European Convention on Human Rights (ECHR).

Scope and structure of the chapter

16.5

This chapter does not aim to provide a comprehensive analysis of refugee law as it generally applies in the UK, nor of human rights law in the context of asylum and human rights appeals. Rather, this chapter focuses on the key substantive and procedural issues that arise in trafficking and modern slavery-related international protection and human rights appeals before the First-tier Tribunal (FTT) and the Upper Tribunal (UT) in the Immigration and Asylum Chamber (IAC).

16.6

It focuses on the intersection between trafficking and modern slavery and claims brought under the Refugee Convention and on human rights grounds. While the legal definitions of trafficking, slavery, servitude, and forced or compulsory labour are set out in **Chapter 1**, this chapter considers how such experiences may give rise to protection claims and how the positive obligations under Art 4 ECHR may influence their assessment or form the basis of standalone human rights claims.

16.7

The formal identification of victims of trafficking and modern slavery through the National Referral Mechanism (NRM) is addressed in detail in **Chapter 4**.

16.8

The chapter does not deal with onward appeal rights in detail or certification decisions (in the case of clearly unfounded, safe third country, or late claims certificates) which preclude a right of appeal within the UK and require any appeal to be made from outside the UK (eg under s 94, 94B or 96 of the Nationality, Immigration and Asylum Act 2002 ('NIAA 2002'))[4]. In such cases,

4 Home Office 'Rights of appeal', Version 16.0, 4 June 2025, Guidance on when there is a right of appeal against decisions in immigration cases including mechanisms to prevent repeat rights of appeal and prevent delay from appeals against unfounded claims.

the remedy lies in an application for judicial review, which is beyond the scope of this chapter.

16.9

The chapter is structured as follows:

- **Part 1** – The Significance of Art 4 ECHR and Its Positive Obligations
- **Part 2** – The Refugee Convention and Victims of Trafficking and Modern Slavery
- **Part 3** – Human Rights claims based on Trafficking and Modern Slavery
- **Part 4** – Asylum and the NRM: Identification, Support and Procedural Intersections
- **Part 5** – Procedural Issues in Trafficking and Modern Slavery Appeals.

Part 1 The significance of Art 4 ECHR and its positive obligations

The Legal Weight of Art 4 ECHR and Its Positive Obligations

16.10

A proper understanding of the legal gravity of slavery, servitude, forced or compulsory labour, and human trafficking is essential to situating these harms within the framework of international protection and human rights law. This section provides an overview of the key principles underpinning Art 4 of the ECHR, with a detailed analysis of definitions and international legal sources set out in **Chapter 1**.

The absolute and non-derogable nature of Art 4 ECHR and hierarchy of international norms

16.11

Art 4 ECHR provides that 'no one shall be held in slavery or servitude' or subjected to forced or compulsory labour. The European Court of Human Rights (ECtHR) has held that human trafficking comes within the scope and protections of Art 4. Their prohibition is absolute, and, in the case of slavery and servitude, forms part of *jus cogens* norms, and is universally accepted and non-derogable. Slavery is classified as a crime against humanity under Art 7 of the Rome Statute of the International Criminal Court (ICC), placing it within the highest category of international legal concern.

16.12

The prohibition of forced or compulsory labour, while not classified as *jus cogens*, is nonetheless absolute under Art 4 of the ECHR; the provisions in Art 4(3)[5] should be understood as defining the material scope of the protection afforded, rather than as exceptions to the right itself.

Positive obligations under Art 4 ECHR

Art 1 ECHR and the development of positive obligations in ECtHR jurisprudence

16.13

Under Art 1 of the ECHR, States are required not only to refrain from infringing the rights guaranteed by the Convention, but also to take active steps to ensure their effective protection. This obligation encompasses both the prevention of harm and the provision of appropriate responses when rights are at risk or have been violated. These duties, referred to as positive obligations, have been progressively shaped by the jurisprudence of the ECtHR, particularly in areas such as domestic violence and human trafficking.

16.14

The Court has categorised these obligations in various ways, distinguishing between substantive and procedural duties, those that are expressly stated and those implied, and obligations aimed at prevention versus those focused on remedy. These frameworks help define the scope of State responsibility and the conditions under which inaction may result in a breach of the Convention.

16.15

In assessing whether a State has fulfilled its obligations under the ECHR, the ECtHR has consistently affirmed that the Convention is intended to guarantee rights that are not theoretical or illusory, but practical and effective[6]. This principle of effectiveness plays a central role in justifying the existence of positive obligations and in shaping their content and scope.

The presumptive nature of positive obligations under Arts 2, 3 and 4 ECHR

16.16

In contrast to Art 8 of the ECHR (a derogable right), where the recognition of positive obligations often depends on the specific circumstances of the case and the balance between individual rights and public interests, the Court's

5 This is subject to strict parameters about the nature and conditions of work – see **Chapter 1**.
6 *Tyrer v. United Kingdom*, App no 5856/72, 25 April 1978.

approach under Arts 2 and 3 begins from the principle that States have inherent positive duties. These include obligations to prevent and respond to violations of the right to life and the prohibition of torture and inhuman or degrading treatment. Art 4 similarly imposes positive obligations on States. The ECtHR has developed these obligations through its jurisprudence, frequently drawing on the reasoning established under Arts 2 and 3 in Art 4 cases. This reflects a consistent approach to the protection of fundamental rights, whereby States are required to take proactive measures to prevent exploitation and abuse, and to provide effective remedies when such rights are violated[7].

Threshold for engaging Art 4 duties

16.17

These duties are triggered where there is a credible suspicion that a person has been a victim of an Art 4 abuse or is at real and immediate risk of an Art 4 abuse, which the state authorities knew or ought to have known about the harm or risk of future harm.

16.18

In *Rantsev v Cyprus and Russia*[8] and *VCL and AN v United Kingdom*[9], the ECtHR held that abstract knowledge derived from published reports, when considered alongside individual circumstances that reflect characteristics identified in those reports, meant that there were sufficient indicators available for the authorities to be aware of a real risk of trafficking or exploitation. Similarly, this mirrors the approach adopted by Lord Justice Underhill in *R (TDT)*[10], where the Court emphasised that the assessment of risk must be informed by both generalised country information and the individual's specific circumstances. This approach underscores the importance of contextualising personal vulnerability within broader patterns of harm, particularly in cases involving trafficking and exploitation.

The systems, protective, procedural and restitution duties

16.19

In *SM v Croatia*[11] and *Rantsev v Cyprus and Russia*[12], the Court affirmed that Art 4 ECHR encompasses both substantive and procedural obligations including duties to:

7 Stoyanova, V. (2025). Positive Obligations. In K. Istrefi, Z. Ratniece, K. Tamuzs, & K. Kamber (Eds.), Companion to the European Convention on Human Rights (Brill).

8 App. no. 25965/04 (ECtHR, 7 January 2010) (2010) 51 EHRR 1, at [296, 298].

9 (2021) 73 EHRR 9.

10 *R (TDT) v The Secretary of State for the Home Department* [2018] EWCA Civ 1395, [2018] 1 WLR 4922 at [80].

11 *SM v Croatia* (2021) 72 EHRR 1.

12 *Rantsev v Cyprus and Russia* (2010) 51 EHRR 1.

- Establish an effective legal and administrative framework to prohibit and penalise trafficking and related abuses (the systems duty).
- Take operational measures to prevent exploitation and protect potential victims (the protective or operational duty).
- Conduct effective criminal investigations into credible allegations of Art 4 violations and ensure effective judicial mechanism capable of elucidating the circumstances and sequence of events that are said to have led to the alleged harm (the investigatory duty).
- Ensure that there has been restitution to the victim for the harms caused (the restitution duty).

16.20

These obligations are assessed through a two-stage test:

1. Awareness of Risk: Whether the state knew or ought to have known of a credible suspicion that an individual was, or was at real and immediate risk of being, subjected to slavery, servitude, forced or compulsory labour, or trafficking.
2. State Response: Whether the state took appropriate and reasonable steps, within its powers, to prevent or respond to that risk.

16.21

Notably, positive obligations must be interpreted in a manner that does not impose an unreasonable or excessive burden on the authorities[13]. The determination of what constitutes reasonable protective measures must be undertaken on a case-by-case basis, with careful consideration of all relevant circumstances. The ECtHR has identified factors such as the scope of the authorities' powers, the physical safety of the victim, and the fundamental rights of others as central to this assessment[14].

16.22

The scope and application of these obligations are central to understanding how Art 4 ECHR informs and shapes international protection and human rights appeals, particularly where trafficking or modern slavery is raised as a basis for such claims. These are also examined at length in **Chapter 14**.

13 *O'Keeffe v. Ireland* [GC], App no. 35810/09, 28 January 2014, at [144].

14 *Osman v United Kingdom*, App. no 23452/94 (ECtHR, 28 October 1998), [116]; *Chowdury and Others v Greece*, App no 21884/15 (ECtHR, 30 March 2017), [88]; *Rantsev v Cyprus and Russia*, App no 25965/04 (ECtHR, 7 January 2010), [287].

Dual aims of the protective duty

16.23

In *VCL* and *AN v United Kingdom*[15], the ECtHR held that the duty to take operational measures under Art 4 has two principal aims:

- Protective Duty: to protect the victim from further harm; and
- Recovery Duty: to facilitate his or her recovery.

Two types of investigatory duties

16.24

The ECtHR identifies two types of investigatory duties that require separation:

1. An official criminal investigation.
2. An effective judicial mechanism capable of elucidating the circumstances and sequence of events that are said to have led to the alleged harm[16].

Standards for an effective investigation

16.25

Art 4 imposes a procedural duty to investigate potential Art 4 abuses, this obligation echoes that in Arts 2 and 3. This duty arises independently of any formal complaint.

16.26

Significantly, once the matter has come to the attention of the authorities, they are under a duty to act of their own motion[17]. As with Arts 2 and 3, the investigative obligation under Art 4 is triggered immediately upon the authorities becoming aware of circumstances that may engage the provision.

16.27

Once triggered, the investigation must meet the following standards:

- Independence and impartiality of the investigating body.

15 *VCL and AN v United Kingdom* (2021) 73 EHRR 9.

16 *Ribcheva and Others v Bulgaria,* App no 37801/16, 30 March 2021, [139]; *Anna Todorova v Bulgaria.* App no 23302/03, 24 May 2011, [74].

17 *CN v the United Kingdom*, App. no. 4239/08, 13 November 2012, [69]; *Chowdury and Others v Greece*, App no 21884/15, 30 March 2017, [116]; *J and Others v Austria,* App. no 58216/12, 17 January 2017, [107]; *Zoletic and Others v Azerbaijan*, App no. 20116/12, 7 October 2021, [185].

- Promptness and reasonable expedition, with urgency where there is a possibility of removing the individual from a harmful situation.
- Effectiveness, meaning the investigation must be thorough, involve the victim, capable of leading to the identification and punishment of those responsible, this is an obligation concerning the means to be employed, not the results to be achieved.

16.28

Although often referred to as a procedural duty, the criminal investigatory obligation serves a substantive purpose: to uncover the facts of the alleged abuse, identify those responsible, and, where possible, facilitate their prosecution.

16.29

The duties are not static or isolated; rather, they are interrelated and mutually reinforcing. Each informs the scope and execution of the others, operating in a dynamic and symbiotic manner to ensure that the State's obligations under the Convention are effectively discharged.

Legal and practical implications of breach

16.30

Recovery is a fundamental component of both protection and prevention. Without it, victims remain exposed to the very harms from which they have escaped. Reintegration is not simply a humanitarian concern; it is a legal and safeguarding obligation. Effective systems must go beyond identifying and removing individuals from exploitation, they must also provide sustained support to help survivors rebuild their lives and prevent their return to exploitative environments.

16.31

Understanding the significance of these duties in the context of trafficking and modern slavery requires consideration of the consequences of non-compliance. Failure to meet these obligations not only compromises the protection owed to victims but may also amount to a breach of the State's responsibilities under the ECHR.

Insufficient recovery and the risk of re-exploitation: a critical gap in trafficking or modern slavery response

16.32

Recovery and reintegration are not optional add-ons in the fight against human trafficking or modern slavery, they are central to preventing re-trafficking or a repeat of slavery, servitude or forced or compulsory labour[18]. The purpose is to ensure long-term safety and dignity for victims and non-repetition. Insufficient recovery leaves victims vulnerable to repeated cycles of exploitation.

Recovery is not linear and it is not guaranteed

16.33

Victims of modern slavery and trafficking survivors often emerge from exploitation with complex trauma, disrupted identities, and fractured trust in institutions (see **Chapter 3**). Recovery is not a single event but a long-term process requiring tailored, trauma-informed support. When this process is rushed, under-resourced, or poorly coordinated, survivors may be left without the emotional, psychological, and practical tools needed to rebuild their lives.

Recovery must be holistic

16.34

It is well recognised that addressing physical and mental health, legal status, housing, education, and employment is essential to effective recovery. Without these foundations, victims may find themselves in precarious situations that mirror the vulnerabilities which led to their initial exploitation.

The risk of re-trafficking is real and recognised

16.35

One of the most sobering realities in trafficking response is the phenomenon of re-trafficking. Victims who have not received adequate support are at heightened risk of being exploited again, sometimes by the same networks, sometimes through new vulnerabilities. This risk is not hypothetical; it is well-documented in international guidance and case studies.

16.36

Factors contributing to re-trafficking include, in particular:

- Lack of secure housing or legal status
- Economic hardship and unemployment
- Social isolation and stigma
- Inadequate mental health support
- Fear or distrust of authorities

18 *Krachunova v Bulgaria* App no 18269/18, judgment 28 November 2023, [169]–[171].

16.37

These risks are compounded when survivors are returned to the circumstances which gave rise to trafficking in the first place, environments where exploitation occurred, or where state protection is weak or inaccessible.

Art 4 positive obligations and the legal significance of NRM decisions in protection appeals

16.38

Understanding the legal and procedural implications of a positive NRM decision is essential in the context of asylum and human rights appeals. While an NRM decision is not determinative of the outcome of such appeals, it carries significant procedural consequences and evidentiary weight.

16.39

Although the NRM process may run concurrently with an international protection or human rights claim, it operates independently. As confirmed in *MS (Pakistan)*[19], the tribunal must make its own findings on the relevant facts and is not bound by an NRM decision. Nor is it required to identify public law errors in that decision.

16.40

That being said, the Supreme Court in *MS (Pakistan)*[20] addressed the legal effect of a **negative** NRM decision on the fact-finding tribunal. By contrast, a **positive** reasonable or conclusive grounds decision carries distinct legal and procedural significance, both generally and within the specific context of international protection and human rights appeals, as explored below.

Procedural significance of a positive reasonable grounds decision

16.41

The reasonable grounds decision made by the Competent Authority under the NRM is not determinative of an asylum or human rights appeal. However, it does have significant procedural consequences.

16.42

The ECtHR does not prescribe how states must structure their mechanisms for preventing Art 4 harms or protecting victims. In *Secretary of State for the Home*

19 *MS (Pakistan) v Secretary of State for the Home Department* [2020] UKSC 9, [2020] 1 WLR 1373.
20 Ibid.

Department v H[21], Lord Justice Burnett confirmed that the UK does not operate a single body responsible for fulfilling all Art 4 obligations.

16.43

Lord Justice Burnett, held in *Secretary of State for the Home Department v H* that the reasonable grounds threshold applied by the Competent Authority is substantially aligned with the credible suspicion standard recognised in Art 4 jurisprudence. As he noted, a positive reasonable grounds decision requires notification to the police, and failure to do so, particularly where it results in removal before a potential criminal offence is investigated, may amount to a breach of Art 4.

16.44

Lord Justice Underhill re-affirmed this threshold analysis in *R (TDT) v Secretary of State for the Home Department*[22], while clarifying it could be triggered even before a positive reasonable grounds decision is made because what is required is *prima facie* evidence known or ought to be known to a public authority, including Home Office officials, that the individual is a victim.

16.45

The current National Referral Mechanism Guidance: Adult (England and Wales)[23] provides that First responders should provide the NRM referral to the police either on the victim's behalf with consent or as a third-party referral where it does not breach common law obligations of confidence.

16.46

As the Modern Slavery Statutory Guidance[24] makes clear the NRM extends to identification of victims of slavery, servitude and forced or compulsory labour and these terms should be understood as having the same meaning as they do under Art 4 ECHR[25]. Accordingly, a positive reasonable grounds decision represents formal recognition by a state authority that the *credible suspicion*

21 [2016] EWCA Civ 565.
22 [2018] EWCA Civ 1395, [2018] 1 WLR 4922.
23 Home Office, *National referral mechanism guidance: adult (England and Wales)* (updated 30 September 2025) at [9] <https://www.gov.uk/government/publications/human-trafficking-victims-referral-and-assessment-forms/guidance-on-the-national-referral-mechanism-for-potential-adult-victims-of-modern-slavery-england-and-wales> accessed 14 October 2025.
24 The Statutory Guidance is published under section 49(1) of the MSA 2015.
25 Home Office, *Modern slavery: statutory guidance for England and Wales (under s49 of the Modern Slavery Act 2015) and non-statutory guidance for Scotland and Northern Ireland* (updated December 2025) [2.77]-[2.106] <https://www.gov.uk/government/publications/modern-slavery-how-to-identify-and-support-victims/modern-slavery-statutory-guidance-for-england-and-wales-under-s49-of-the-modern-slavery-act-2015-and-non-statutory-guidance-for-scotland-and-northe#what-is-modern-slavery> accessed 1 February 2026.

threshold has been met. For statutory agencies such as the Crown Prosecution Service (CPS), this role is explicitly identified in published guidance[26].

16.47

Where the decision is made by the Single Competent Authority within the NRM framework, it is difficult to conceive of circumstances in which such a decision would not engage the state's positive obligations under Art 4 of the ECHR, given that the credible suspicion threshold has been triggered.

16.48

It is against this backdrop that removal during which ongoing positive obligations under Article 4 ECHR arise may constitute a breach of those obligations, as outlined above and examined in detail in **Chapter 14**. Such a breach may occur particularly where the procedural duty to investigate potential exploitation is not fulfilled (see *MS (Pakistan)*)[27]. These positive obligations are borne by all UK public authorities, including courts and tribunals.

Evidentiary significance of positive NRM decisions

16.49

A positive decision under the NRM, whether at the reasonable grounds or conclusive grounds stage, will also carry evidentiary significance in asylum or human rights appeals. This decision has been made by the Competent Authority (the Home Office in cases involving non-British nationals; see **Chapter 4**) and thus amounts to a concession of fact that the appellant is a victim of trafficking, slavery, or related harms. In such cases, the tribunal cannot go behind the positive concession of fact or reassess the facts already accepted by the Competent Authority unless it has good reason to[28]. This remains the case even where the NRM decision is not expressly referred to in the Home Office's decision under appeal.

---

26 See Crown Prosecution Service, *Modern Slavery and human trafficking: offences and defences, including the section 45 defence* (Legal Guidance, updated 22 July 2025) <https://www.cps.gov.uk/legal-guidance/modern-slavery-and-human-trafficking-offences-and-defences-including-section-45-defence> accessed 14 October 2025.

27 *MS (Pakistan) v Secretary of State for the Home Department* [2020] UKSC 9, [2020] 1 WLR 1373.

28 See *R (on the application of Ganidagli) v Immigration Appeal Tribunal* [2001] EWHC 70 Admin; *Carcabuk and Bla (00TH01426)* (18 May 2000, unreported), IAT. In *Davoodipanah v Secretary of State for the Home Department* [2004] EWCA Civ 106, [2004] INLR 341, [2004] All ER (D) 285 (Jan), the Court of Appeal held that a concession made by either party may be formally withdrawn on appeal if the appeal court considers that there is good reason to take that course, but otherwise, the appeal court should not revisit issues relevant to a concession clearly made to a first instance immigration judge who had relied on it. If the Home Office attempts to withdraw a concession fairness requires time and opportunity to make representations including as to the prejudice caused: see also *NR (Jamaica) v Secretary of State for the Home Department* [2009] EWCA Civ 856, [2010] INLR 169, [2009] All ER (D) 43 (Aug); and *CD (Jamaica) v Secretary of State for the Home Department* [2010] EWCA Civ 768, [2010] All ER (D) 34 (Feb).

16.50

The Modern Slavery Statutory Guidance[29] provides that the consideration minute of a positive reasonable or conclusive grounds decision is disclosable. Additionally, the minutes (and other personal data) should also be disclosed under any Subject Access Request under the Data Protection Act 2018 or the duty of candour.

16.51

This must be understood not only in light of domestic case law on concessions of fact, but also because a positive identification decision under the NRM engages the positive obligations under Art 4 ECHR. Where such a decision has been made, any attempt by a public authority, including a tribunal, to go behind it, without first ensuring compliance with the protective duties (such as support and assistance) or the procedural duty to investigate potential criminal conduct, gives rise to a significant risk of an Art 4 violation. This position is supported by the ECtHR's reasoning in *VCL and AN v United Kingdom* and *Chowdhury v Greece*[30].

Part 2 Refugee Convention

International legal obligations and the right to asylum

16.52

The Palermo Protocol[31] and ECAT[32] both expressly provide that they do not affect individuals' and states' rights, obligations, and responsibilities under international law and under the 1951 Refugee Convention[33] and its 1967 protocol[34]. The explanatory report to ECAT explains that State Parties are required to ensure that victims of trafficking have access to fair and efficient asylum procedures and to take whatever steps are necessary to ensure full respect for the principle of *non-refoulement*[35]. In respect of women and girls,

29 [14.212] of Home Office, *Modern slavery: statutory guidance for England and Wales (under s49 of the Modern Slavery Act 2015) and non-statutory guidance for Scotland and Northern Ireland* (updated 10 December 2025) https://www.gov.uk/government/publications/modern-slavery-how-to-identify-and-support-victims/modern-slavery-statutory-guidance-for-england-and-wales-under-s49-of-the-modern-slavery-act-2015-and-non-statutory-guidance-for-scotland-and-northe#what-is-modern-slavery> accessed 12 October 2025.

30 *VCL and AN v United Kingdom (2021) 73 EHRR 9; Chowdury and others v Greece*, App. no. 21884/15, 30 March 2017.

31 Protocol to Prevent, Suppress and Punish Trafficking in Persons, especially Women and Children, supplementing the United Nations Convention against transnational organised Crime 2000, Art 14(1).

32 Council of Europe Convention on Action against Trafficking in Human Beings 2005, Art 40(4).

33 1951 Convention relating to the Status of Refugees, UN Treaty Series vol.189, p.137.

34 1967 Protocol Relating to the Status of Refugees, UN Treaty Series vol.606, p.267.

35 Explanatory Report to the Council of Europe Convention on Action against Trafficking in Human Beings, Council of Europe Treaty Series No.197, [377].

the Istanbul Convention[36] places particular duties on States Parties to ensure a gender-sensitive approach to the process and determination of refugee status[37] which is already being undertaken in international state practice[38].

Definition of a refugee

The international legal definition of a refugee

16.53

The legal definition of the term 'refugee' is set out at Art 1A(2) of the Refugee Convention, which defines a refugee as a person who:

> 'Owing to well-founded fear of being persecuted for reasons of race, religion, nationality, membership of a particular social group or political opinion is outside the country of his nationality and is unable or owing to such fear, is unwilling to avail himself of the protection of that country; or who, not having a nationality and being outside the country of his former habitual residence is unable or, owing to such fear, unwilling to return to it.'

16.54

The Refugee Convention has an autonomous, international meaning as a treaty which may be derived with reference to provisions within Art 31 of the Vienna Convention on the Law of Treaties[39] and there is, in principle, only one true interpretation of a treaty. This was confirmed in *R (Adan) v Secretary of State for the Home Department*[40] before the House of Lords which also concluded that where there is disagreement on the meaning of the Refugee Convention, it is in practice left to national courts to resolve it but, in doing so, they must search for the true autonomous and international meaning of the treaty, untrammelled by their national legal culture[41].

36 Council of Europe Convention on preventing and combating violence against women and domestic violence, Council of Europe Treaty Series No.210 ('Istanbul Convention'), ratified by the UK on 21 July 2022.

37 Istanbul Convention, Art 60.

38 Explanatory Report to the Council of Europe Convention on preventing and combating violence against women and domestic violence ('Istanbul Convention'), Council of Europe Treaty Series No.210, [311].

39 Vienna Convention on the Law of Treaties 1969, UN Treaty Series vol. 1155, p.331.

40 *[2000] UKHL 67, [2001] 2 AC 477*, see particularly *per* Lord Steyn at 516–517.

41 *R (Adan) v Secretary of State for the Home Department* [2000] UKHL 67, [2001] 2 AC 477, see particularly *per* Lord Steyn at 516–517.

Statutory definitions under the Nationality and Borders Act 2022: procedural application and implications for refugee law

16.55

The Nationality and Borders Act 2022 (NABA 2022) introduced statutory provisions proposing definitions of key concepts within the Refugee Convention[42]. The Explanatory Notes to the Act stated that the Refugee Convention contained broad concepts and principles which were open to some degree of interpretation in practice and that the government's intention was to consolidate the legislation underpinning which is derived from a range of sources, including international and European law primary and secondary legislation and a substantial body of case law[43]. The Explanatory Notes further stated that the UK's departure from the EU provided an opportunity to define key elements of the Refugee Convention in UK domestic law in a unified source[44].

16.56

Section 30(4) NABA 2022 therefore repealed The Refugee or Person in Need of International Protection (Qualification) Regulations 2006 (SI 2006/2525), which was the domestic secondary legislation which transposed the provisions of the EU Qualification Directive[45], introduced to establish minimum standards for the identification of persons in need of international protection within the EU.

NABA 2022: definitions applicable to post-28 June 2022 asylum claims

16.57

NABA 2022 introduces definitions for key concepts within Art 1A(2) of the Refugee Convention (above).

16.58

They apply only to the determinations of asylum claims where the claim was made on or after 28 June 2022[46], with transitional provisions set out in policy to include easements where, for example, an applicant is provided an appointment to register their claim before 28 June 2022 but is given and attends an appointment scheduled after that date[47].

42 Sections 30–38 NABA 2022.
43 Explanatory Notes to the NABA 2022 [318–319].
44 Explanatory Notes to the NABA 2022 [322–323].
45 Council Directive 2004/83/EC of 29 April 2004 on minimum standards for the qualification and status of third country nationals or stateless persons as refugees or as persons who otherwise need international protection and the content of the protection granted.
46 Section 30(5) NABA 2022 read with s 87(5)(d) on the commencement of these provisions.
47 Home Office, *Assessing credibility and refugee status in asylum claims lodged on or after 28 June 2022*, version 1.0, 28 June 2022.

16.59

They include definitions for:

- persecution (s 31);
- well-founded fear (s 32);
- reasons for persecution (s 33);
- protection from persecution (s 34); and
- internal relocation (s 35).

16.60

It also introduces other provisions within the Refugee Convention including Art 1F regarding:

- immunity from penalties on account of illegal entry or presence (s 37);
- disapplication on grounds of war crimes, crimes against humanity, serious non-political crimes etc (s 36); and
- Art 31(1) regarding or Art 33(2) dealing with expulsion of refugees on grounds of national security or public order (s 38).

16.61

The Border Security, Asylum and Immigration Act 2025 does not amend those sections of NABA 2022[48].

Concerns over Consistency in Refugee Convention Interpretation Post-NABA 2022

16.62

Concerns have been raised that the definitions introduced by the NABA 2022 may depart from established UK case law interpreting key concepts of the Refugee Convention. Critics suggest that this divergence could create legal uncertainty, as differing interpretations of the Convention may ultimately require judicial clarification to determine its autonomous meaning. This has led to a distinction in how asylum claims are assessed, with separate Home Office policies applying to claims lodged before and after 28 June 2022[49].

48 At the time of writing, the Border Security, Asylum and Immigration Bill introduced to Parliament on 30 January 2025 has completed its passage in the House of Commons, has had its second reading in the House of Lords and resumed its Committee stage in the House of Lords on 3 September 2025.

49 Home Office, *Assessing credibility and refugee status in asylum claims lodged before 28 June 2022*, version 10.0 (28 September 2023).

16.63

It has been argued that applying different interpretations of the Refugee Convention to claims based on their date of submission may be incompatible with the Convention itself, which, as confirmed in *Adan*, admits only one correct interpretation. As claims lodged prior to 28 June 2022 are only beginning to reach the Tribunal and higher courts in significant numbers, there has been limited judicial consideration of the extent to which NABA 2022 affects the settled case law and the proper interpretation of the Convention. However, in unreported decisions, the Upper Tribunal has identified errors of law where First-tier Tribunal judges applied NABA 2022 definitions to pre-28 June 2022 claims, contrary to established legal principles.

JCK (Botswana) v Secretary of State for the Home Department[50]

16.64

In *JCK (s.32 NABA 2022) (Botswana) v Secretary of State for the Home Department*, the first reported Upper Tribunal decision to consider the application of ss 31–36 of the NABA 2022 in a Refugee Convention appeal, the Tribunal held that those provisions apply to international protection claims made on or after 28 June 2022 and that, in such appeals, decision-makers must address the questions in s 32 sequentially, applying the balance-of-probabilities standard to Convention grounds and subjective fear under s 32(2), and the lower 'reasonable degree of likelihood' standard to future risk, protection and internal relocation under ss 32(3)–(4).

16.65

The Upper Tribunal noted that the standard of proof applied in protection claims had been consistent for some thirty-five years[51], it was not invited to consider and therefore did not provide further analysis, as to whether it was lawful or correct to apply a different interpretation of that standard with reference to NABA 2022.

16.66

The interpretation of the Refugee Convention within the framework of NABA 2022, along with concerns regarding potential inconsistencies and the possibility of unequal outcomes arising from certain provisions, are matters that may be subject to further legal examination and judicial consideration (as examined below concerning Particular Social Group).

50 [2024] UKUT 00100 (IAC), headnote.
51 Ibid, [6].

NABA 2022 standard of proof and Arts 3 and 4 ECHR

16.67

Notably, the approach to the assessment of past facts and the appropriate standard of proof for the purpose of assessing the risks of serious harm and breaches of Arts 3 and 4 ECHR remain unchanged.

16.68

It is therefore possible that a claim which does not meet the criteria for recognition under the Refugee Convention may nonetheless succeed on the same factual basis when assessed under humanitarian protection or human rights grounds pursuant to the ECHR (see further below). This does not however equate to refugee status, which remains an internationally recognised legal designation carrying specific rights and protection.

Routes to protection: how victims engage with the UK asylum and human rights systems

16.69

Claims for international protection and/or human rights protection in the UK based on trafficking or modern slavery typically arise in one of three ways:

1. The individual experienced trafficking, slavery, or related abuses outside the UK (in their home country and/or in transit) and has sought refuge in the UK.

2. The individual was trafficked into the UK from overseas and escaped, was recovered or arrested in the UK, coming to the attention of the UK authorities.

3. The individual was trafficked or subjected to slavery or related harms solely within the UK.

16.70

Victims of trafficking or modern slavery may face serious risks if returned to their country of origin. These include re-trafficking or re-exploitation by the same or other perpetrators, especially where the conditions that led to their exploitation persist or have worsened. A lack of support, ongoing vulnerability, and the effects of trauma may further increase the risk, including the possibility of serious mental health deterioration or suicide. These risks may arise individually or in combination.

Key legal considerations in trafficking and modern slavery asylum and human rights appeals

16.71

The following issues are examined below:

- Slavery, Servitude, Forced or Compulsory Labour, and Trafficking as Forms of Persecution
- Past Persecution
- Well-Founded Fear, the Availability of State Protection and Breaches of Art 4 Obligations
- Trafficking and Modern Slavery as a Particular Social Group
- Human Rights Claims
- *MST and Others (national service – risk categories) Eritrea CG*[52]

Clarifying the legal boundaries of 'modern slavery' and trafficking: distinct harms under Art 4 ECHR

16.72

While UK legislation employs the term of art 'modern slavery', this functions as an umbrella label encompassing the distinct and conceptually separate harms of slavery, servitude, forced or compulsory labour. When determining whether an individual has previously suffered an Art 4 ECHR violation, ie past persecution, it is essential to maintain conceptual clarity regarding the specific harm experienced (see **Chapter 1**). These forms of harms exist within a hierarchy of severity, and accurate classification is necessary to uphold objective and coherent standards of protection. Moreover, as developed below, the precise nature of the harm may be material to assessing the reasonableness of the protective obligations owed to the victim[53].

Trafficking and modern slavery as inherently persecutory treatment

16.73

As observed by Lord Justice Laws in *Sepet v Secretary of State for the Home Department*[54], certain forms of conduct are so clearly and universally condemned

52 [2016] UKUT 00443 (IAC).

53 See Vladislava Stoyanova, '*Framing Positive Obligations under the European Convention on Human Rights Law: Mediating between the Abstract and the Concrete*' (2023) 23 *Human Rights Law Review* 1 <https://doi.org/10.1093/hrlr/ngad010> accessed 14 October 2025, at p.19.

54 *Sepet v Secretary of State for the Home Department* [2001] EWCA Civ 681, [2001] INLR 376, 403 at [63].

in national and international law that they will, by their nature, satisfy the definition of persecution within the meaning of the Refugee Convention.

16.74

Section 31(2)(a) NABA 2022 defines persecution as:

> 'sufficiently serious by its nature or repetition as to constitute a severe violation of a basic human right, in particular a right from which derogation cannot be made under Article 15 of the Convention for the Protection of Human Rights and Fundamental Freedoms'.

16.75

As outlined above, slavery, servitude, and forced or compulsory labour are categorically recognised in international law as serious human rights violations [55]. Their prohibition is absolute, and, in the case of slavery and servitude, forms part of *jus cogens* norms, universally accepted and non-derogable. The prohibition of forced or compulsory labour, while not classified as *jus cogens*, is nonetheless absolute under Art 4 of the ECHR; the provisions in Art 4(3)[56] should be understood as defining the material scope of the protection afforded, rather than as exceptions to the right itself.

16.76

Therefore, by their very nature and legal standing, these practices constitute 'persecution' for the purposes of the Refugee Convention[57]. Any individual subjected to such treatment faces a grave and systematic denial of basic rights. Where the persecution is connected to a Convention ground, it will meet the threshold for refugee protection under Art 1A(2) of the 1951 Convention.

Past persecution as a lens for future risk: enhanced relevance in trafficking and modern slavery appeals

16.77

There is no requirement under refugee law that persecution must have occurred in the past; however, past persecution is recognised as a serious indication of a well-founded fear of future harm, unless there are good reasons to believe it will not be repeated[58].

55 ECAT, preamble.

56 This is subject to strict parameters about the nature and conditions of work – see Chapter 1.

57 UNHCR 'Guidelines on International Protection: The application of Art 1(A)2 of the 1951 Convention and/or Protocol relating to the status of refugees to victims of trafficking and persons at risk of being trafficked' (2006) HCR/GIP/06/07, [15].

58 Immigration Rules 339K, reflecting the principle in *Demirkaya v Secretary of State for the Home Department* [1999] INLR 441 at 449D.

16.78

Past persecution is a recognised indicator of future risk, and in the context of trafficking and modern slavery, this risk is heightened by the victim's vulnerability and the potential failure of protective duties (examined further below).

16.79

As the Upper Tribunal has observed, a person who has previously been trafficked may be particularly susceptible to re-trafficking, having already been conditioned to comply, the 'breaking in' period having already occurred[59].

16.80

Trafficking by its nature can (albeit is not required to be) across borders. The continuum of the trafficking experience needs to be considered including where trafficking has occurred entirely outside the country of origin. It is well recognised that a risk of trafficking, slavery or related harms is heightened where a person has already been subject to that abuse previously.

Well-founded fear and the availability of state protection

16.81

A well-founded fear of persecution requires two elements: first, that the claimant genuinely fears persecution (the subjective element); and second, that this fear is supported by objective evidence demonstrating a real risk of persecution (the objective element)[60]. Fear of persecution is well-founded if there is a 'reasonable degree of likelihood' that it will materialise[61].

16.82

The next step in the analysis is to determine whether the acts of slavery, trafficking, or related Art 4 abuses are state-sanctioned, or whether the harm is inflicted by non-state actors. This distinction is critical to assessing the availability and sufficiency of protection in the country of origin.

State-sanctioned slavery and Art 4 abuses

16.83

As Lord Clyde observed in *Horvath v Secretary of State for the Home Department*[62], where the State itself, through its agents, is responsible for the persecution, the

59 *AZ (Trafficked women) Thailand CG* [2010] UKUT 118 (IAC) at [150].

60 *R v Secretary of State for the Home Department, ex parte Singh* [1987] Imm AR 489.

61 *R v SSHD, ex p Sivakumaran* [1988] AC 958, per Lord Goff at 1000F–G.

62 [2000] UKHL 37, [2001] 1 AC 489.

question of protection does not arise. Active persecution by the State is the antithesis of protection. It is only in cases involving non-state actors that the issue of State protection becomes central to the assessment of a well-founded fear of persecution.

16.84

State-sanctioned slavery and related Art 4 violations may occur where governments are directly involved in or facilitate slavery and related abuses [63]. Notable examples include:

- The widespread forced labour schemes targeting Uyghur and other Turkic Muslim minorities in the Xinjiang Uyghur Autonomous Region of China.
- State-controlled cotton production involving forced labour in Turkmenistan and, until recently, Uzbekistan.
- North Korea's extensive system of forced labour, both domestically and through overseas deployments.
- Enforced national service programmes, such as those reported by the ILO in Myanmar[64]. *MST and Others (national service – risk categories) Eritrea CG* is considered below in the section on human rights[65].
- State involvement in trafficking and exploitation through labour brokerage or diplomatic channels.

Organised criminal networks and state responsibility: blurring the line between non-state and state actors

16.85

The distinction between state and non-state actors is not binary; the Court of Appeal in *Svazas*[66] recognised a spectrum of state involvement in ill-treatment. At one end are cases involving harm inflicted by non-state actors; at the other,

63 These examples are likely to constitute an internationally wrongful act entailing the international responsibility of that State under the International Law Commission (ILC) Articles on the Responsibility of States for Internationally Wrongful Acts (ARSIWA). See Philippa Webb and Rosana Garciandia, *State Responsibility for Modern Slavery: Uncovering and Bridging the Gap* (King's College London 2019) <https://www.kcl.ac.uk/archive/news/law/ria-assets/kmodern-slavery-report-en.pdf> accessed 11 October 2025.

64 Governing Body, *Follow-up to the report of the Commission of Inquiry established in accordance with article 26 of the ILO Constitution concerning the non-observance by Myanmar of Conventions Nos 87 and 29, and to the resolutions concerning Myanmar adopted by the International Labour Conference at its 102nd (2013) and 109th (2021) Sessions* (Institutional Section INS, 352nd Session, Geneva, 28 October–7 November 2024, 9 October 2024).

65 *MST and Others (national service – risk categories) Eritrea CG* [2016] UKUT 00443 (IAC).

66 *Svazas v Secretary of State for the Home Department* [2002] EWCA Civ 74, [2002] 1 WLR 1891.

situations where the state is wholly complicit in the persecution. Between these extremes lies a nuanced assessment of whether the state provides 'sufficient protection.' As Chief Justice Gleeson said in *Minister for Immigration and Multicultural Affairs v Khawar*[67] at [30]:

> 'Persecution may result from the combined effect of the conduct of private individuals and the State or its agents; and a relevant form of State conduct may be tolerance or condonation of the inflicting of serious harm in circumstances where the state has a duty to provide protection against such harm.'

16.86

This requires contextual analysis, with particular attention to the degree of involvement and seniority of state actors in the harm, as well as the political will and operational capacity of the state to prevent or respond to such abuse.

16.87

The involvement of Organised Criminal Networks (OCNs) in trafficking, slavery, and related Art 4 abuses necessitates a more nuanced analysis. Studies show that OCNs, particularly those operating transnationally, may exert influence so extensive and entrenched that they function as *de facto* agents of the State. In Southeast Asia and parts of China, criminal networks have been documented operating with tacit approval, material support, or strategic alignment from state actors, including law enforcement, military units, and political elites[68].

16.88

This convergence of criminal and state interests, whether through corruption, shared geopolitical objectives, or economic interdependence, may inform whether the principles in *Horvath*[69] apply. Where OCNs act with the complicity or protection of the State, the harm may be attributable to the State itself, thereby negating the need to assess sufficiency of protection. Even in the absence of formal state involvement, the inability or unwillingness of the State to protect victims from such powerful and embedded networks remains central to the assessment of a well-founded fear of persecution. *UNHCR Trafficking Guidelines*[70] make clear, where state officials are acting corruptly on the basis

67 *Minister for Immigration and Multicultural Affairs v Khawar* [2002] HCA 14 (Australia).

68 Vanda Felbab-Brown, Diana Paz García and Vibha Bajji, *Chinese Crime and Geopolitics in 2024* (Brookings Institution, 29 January 2024) <https://www.brookings.edu/articles/chinese-crime-and-geopolitics-in-2024/> accessed 11 October 2025. USIP Senior Study Group, *Transnational Crime in Southeast Asia: A Growing Threat to Global Peace and Security* (United States Institute of Peace, 13 May 2024) <https://www.usip.org/publications/2024/05/transnational-crime-southeast-asia-growing-threat-global-peace-and-security> accessed 11 October 2025.

69 *Horvath v Secretary of State for the Home Department* [2000] UKHL 37 [2001], 1 AC 489.

70 UNHCR, *Guidelines on International Protection: The application of Article 1A(2) of the 1951 Convention and/or 1967 Protocol relating to the Status of Refugees to victims of trafficking and persons at risk of being trafficked*, 7 April 2006, HCR/GIP/06/07.

of the positions of authority they occupy within governmental structures, a situation of de facto toleration or condonation arises, such that the persecution can be seen to emanate from the state itself. The UNHCR distinguishes this from circumstances in which officials are acting in their *personal capacity* outside the framework of government authority.

Borderless organised criminal networks

16.89

Trafficking, slavery, or related harms perpetrated by an OCN, particularly one with the capacity to operate across borders, are especially relevant where a victim's claim is based on an inability or unwillingness to avail themselves of State protection. Europol reports that 821 criminal networks currently operate in or impact all 27 EU member states, with 68% comprising members of multiple nationalities and ties to 112 nationalities overall. These networks form interconnected, multinational ecosystems, and 76% of the most threatening groups are active in two to seven countries, confirming that the most dangerous OCNs run borderless criminal operations[71].

16.90

This operational profile is indicative of sophisticated, entrenched criminal networks with a wide sphere of influence, often beyond the reach of national law enforcement. The estimated global revenue generated by such networks underscores their capacity to undermine governance and evade accountability, reinforcing the need for a robust and context-sensitive analysis of State protection obligations under Art 4 ECHR.

16.91

As the Court of Appeal observed in *PO (Nigeria)*[72], 'gang' and 'network' are elusive concepts and no more than shorthand for the ability, resources and ruthlessness to exercise illegal power over individuals on a significant scale.

Non-state actors, sufficiency of protection and Art 4 obligations

16.92

In trafficking and modern slavery cases where the feared harm originates from non-state actors, the following issues require careful consideration:

71 Europol (2024), Decoding the EU's most threatening criminal networks, Publication Office of the European Union, Luxembourg. https://www.europol.europa.eu (accessed 11 October 2025).
72 *PO (Nigeria) v Secretary of State for the Home Department* [2011] EWCA Civ 132 at 31.

1. Is the State able and willing to provide protection sufficient to counter the risk upon return?

2. Where such protection exists, is the victim unable or unwilling to avail themselves of it?

16.93

Section 34(1) NABA 2022 provides:

> '**Article 1(A)(2): protection from persecution**
>
> (1) For the purposes of Article 1(A)(2) of the Refugee Convention, protection from persecution can be provided by—
>
> (a) the State, or
>
> (b) any party or organisation, including any international organisation, controlling the State or a substantial part of the territory of the State.
>
> (2) An asylum seeker is to be taken to be able to avail themselves of protection from persecution if—
>
> (a) the State, party or organisation mentioned in subsection (1) takes reasonable steps to prevent the persecution by operating an effective legal system for the detection, prosecution and punishment of acts constituting persecution, and
>
> (b) the asylum seeker is able to access the protection.'

16.94

The absence of 'unwillingness' in s 34(2)(b) is examined below.

16.95

While it is essential to consider whether the perpetrators form part of an OCN in light of the enhanced risk to victims, the court in *PO (Nigeria)* found that it imposed too high a burden for an individual to prove that a gang was involved as a necessary element in establishing risk on return, noting that this would impose an inappropriate burden than honest and meritorious victims would often be unable to discharge[73]. In circumstances where the trafficker is not affiliated with a wider organisation, their influence, reach, and capacity to re-engage the victim must be carefully evaluated. However, the risk of re-trafficking can arise absent a risk from the original trafficker as is examined below.

73 *Ibid*, *per* Maurice Kay, LJ at 64.

Relevant considerations

16.96

In assessing sufficiency of protection and ability to access this in cases of trafficking and modern slavery, this may include consideration of:

- The effectiveness and accessibility of protection mechanisms in the country of origin.
- The victim's personal circumstances, including trauma, stigma, and social isolation.
- The likelihood of re-trafficking or further exploitation, particularly where the individual is known to traffickers or vulnerable due to prior experiences.
- The State's compliance with positive obligations under Art 4 ECHR, including any historical or anticipated breaches.
- The UK's compliance with positive obligations under Art 4 ECHR, and consideration of any breaches which may bear on the question of risk.
- The capacity of the State to protect against powerful or embedded Organised Criminal Networks (OCNs), especially those with transnational reach (see above).

Assessing 'effective protection' in trafficking and modern slavery claims: beyond systemic frameworks

16.97

The decision in *R (Bagdanavicius) v Secretary of State for the Home Department*[74] is of particular relevance in cases involving victims of trafficking. A claimant may be able to demonstrate that, although a general insufficiency of state protection cannot be established, the authorities in their country of origin are nonetheless unlikely to provide the additional protection reasonably required in light of their individual circumstances, particularly where they have already been subjected to persecution[75].

16.98

The protective obligations under Art 4 of the ECHR are designed to prevent further violations of the prohibition against slavery, servitude, and forced or compulsory labour. These positive obligations extend beyond the mere existence

74 *R (Bagdanavicius) v. Secretary of State for the Home Department*, [2005] UKHL 38; [2005] 2 AC 668, [2005] 2 WLR 1359.

75 *AW (sufficiency of protection) Pakistan* [2011] UKUT 31(IAC) at [34–35, 39–40].

of a general protective framework (the systems duty); the ECtHR assesses the specific circumstances of the victim's case to determine the nature and scope of the protection required. The measures adopted must be both effective in safeguarding the individual and reasonable in their implementation, without imposing an excessive burden on the authorities.

16.99

Similarly, ECAT distinguishes between systemic obligations (Chapter II) and victim-specific protective measures (Chapter III). As explained in the Explanatory Report to ECAT, Chapter III is central to the Convention's purpose and reflects the protective approach set out in the United Nations Recommended Principles and Guidelines on Human Rights and Human Trafficking: 'The human rights of trafficked persons shall be at the centre of all efforts to prevent and combat trafficking and to protect, assist and provide redress to victims.'

16.100

Embedded within the frameworks above is an understanding that effective protection against re-trafficking must involve the guarantee of socio-economic rights in a manner that responds to the individual's specific vulnerabilities and removes the need to seek economic security through re-trafficking.

16.101

Reflecting the frameworks above, where the risk upon refoulement involves slavery, servitude, forced or compulsory labour, or human trafficking, the assessment of risk must focus on whether the protective measures that are said to be in place will have a tangible and practical effect in reducing the individual's risk of exploitation, rather than those which are theoretical or illusory.

16.102

This requires more than the existence of systemic frameworks or general anti-trafficking efforts; it demands a practical and victim-centred assessment of whether protection deters or prevents the specific harm feared. Measures that appear to address trafficking in theory but fail to mitigate the actual risk from the trafficked person's perspective do not meet this threshold[76].

16.103

This principle was affirmed in *HD (Trafficked Women) Nigeria CG*[77], where the Upper Tribunal cited *Kacaj (Article 3 – Standard of Proof – Non-State Actors)*

76 See Maja Grundler, 'The Locus of Persecution Reconsidered: Risk of Re-Trafficking, Cumulative Harm, and Failure of State Protection' (2023) 35 *International Journal of Refugee Law* 441 <https://doi.org/10.1093/ijrl/eeae016>.

77 [2016] UKUT 00454 (IAC).

Albania[78], clarifying that *Horvath*[79] should not be interpreted as establishing sufficiency of protection merely because the authorities are making efforts to combat trafficking. If those efforts are demonstrably ineffective, the State may be found unable to provide the necessary protection. The assessment must therefore focus not on institutional intent, but on the real-world impact of protective measures in preventing further harm[80]. As articulated in the Country Guidance case *AZ (Thailand)*[81], the effectiveness of protection must be judged by its ability to 'deter and/or to prevent the form of persecution of which there was a risk, not just punishment of it after the event.'

16.104

In *TD and AD (Trafficked women) Albania CG*[82] the Upper Tribunal observed that notwithstanding systemic sufficiency of state protection in the receiving state, an appellant may still have a well-founded fear of persecution if she can show that the authorities know or ought to know of circumstances particular to her case giving rise to her fear, but are unlikely to provide the additional protection her particular circumstances reasonably require. In the case of Albanian trafficked women, the Upper Tribunal set out a non-exhaustive list of individual circumstances that must be considered in determining whether they are able to access sufficiency of protections:

1. The social status and economic standing of her family.
2. The level of education of the victim of trafficking or her family.
3. The victim of trafficking's state of health, particularly her mental health.
4. The presence of an illegitimate child.
5. The area of origin.
6. Age.
7. What support network will be available[83].

Reception and re-integration

16.105

Reception and reintegration measures may be able to address the need for post-return support. However, they will be ineffective in key respects if they fail to

78 *Kacaj (Article 3 – Standard of Proof – Non-State Actors) Albania** [2001] UKIAT 00018.
79 *Horvath v Secretary of State for the Home Department* [2000] UKHL 37 [2001] 1 AC 489.
80 *HD (Trafficked women) Nigeria CG* [2016] UKUT 00454 (IAC) at [70]-[73].
81 *AZ (Trafficked women) Thailand v. Secretary of State for the Home Department, CG* [2010] UKUT 118 (IAC) at [59].
82 [2016] UKUT 00092 at [114].
83 The Tribunal maintained most of the guidance in *AM & BM (Trafficked women) Albania CG* [2010] UKUT 80 (IAC) including factors (1)-(6), and added (7) available support. See headnote.

engage with the complex factors that influence a person's vulnerability to re-trafficking. An analysis which must examine whether shelters and reintegration assistance genuinely mitigate those vulnerabilities for that individual victim. Without a deeper understanding of the socio-economic, psychological, and structural barriers faced by trafficked persons, such measures risk being superficial and inadequate. This concern was echoed in *HD (Trafficked Women) Nigeria CG*[84], where the Tribunal emphasised that it was not poverty or vulnerability itself that grounds the protection claim, but the harm arising from that vulnerability, namely the risk of further exploitation. This risk may stem not only from the original trafficker but also from being returned to an environment that exacerbates vulnerability.

16.106

In *AM and BM (Trafficked Women) Albania CG*[85], the Tribunal recognised that stigma associated with having been trafficked may prevent victims from accessing family or community support. It also acknowledged that trauma may impair the individual's ability to reintegrate. Furthermore, reliance on government-run facilities may expose victims to further risk, as traffickers are known to target such locations.

16.107

Where reception and reintegration services are provided by non-state actors, such provision does not constitute protection emanating from the state. Reliance on such arrangements as 'effective protection' for the purposes of the Refugee Convention may be open to challenge, as it arguably departs from the principle that protection must be afforded by the state itself, and that such protection must be both durable and meaningful in nature.

16.108

The case of *TSN v Secretary of State for the Home Department*[86], concerning a Vietnamese man trafficked to the UK, illustrates that reintegration support may not always offer effective protection against re-trafficking. *TSN* was first trafficked to the UK in 2009 and removed in 2014, only to be re-trafficked into the UK in 2015. The Upper Tribunal found that although he had received financial assistance under the Facilitated Returns Scheme on a previous return to Vietnam, this had not prevented his re-trafficking. The Tribunal concluded that he was eligible for refugee status. This case underscores the importance of reintegration measures that go beyond financial support and address the broader vulnerabilities, such as housing, health, employment, and trauma that contribute to the risk of re-trafficking.

---

84 [2016] UKUT 454 (IAC) at [171].
85 [2010] UKUT 80 (IAC).
86 *TSN v Secretary of State for the Home Department* [2019] UKUT (IAC) PA/07665/2017 (unreported).

Inability or unwillingness to avail themselves of protection

16.109

In *VCL and AN v United Kingdom*[87], the ECtHR underscored that 'early identification is of paramount importance' to ensure that victims are not subjected to further exploitation.

16.110

Tribunals may be required to consider risks that arise where a victim of trafficking, slavery, or related harms is unable or unwilling to avail themselves of state protection on return.

16.111

In *Svazas*[88], Lord Justice Sedley considered the notion of unwillingness, in the context of German Jews who had been attacked by the Brownshirt thugs in 1938 at a time when the Nazi authorities were pretending such attacks were beyond their control. He observed at [22]:

> ' … even though the home state may be able to provide protection, the fear now justifiably felt by the individual may be such that he is unwilling to rely on the state to protect him. The latter, which is barely explored in our jurisprudence, is capable of mattering in cases such as the present. Whether or not Mr Svazas is "able" to avail himself of the Lithuanian state's protection, such as it is, against police brutality, he may be justifiably unwilling to try.'

16.112

In assessing whether the victim is unable or justifiably unwilling to avail themselves of protection on return, the following factors may be material considerations:

1. **The history of Art 4 harms and State Authority responses:** At the heart of slavery and related abuses is the victim's loss of agency, resulting from the control exerted over them. These harms often occurred over prolonged periods without intervention or protection from state authorities. In cases involving cross-border trafficking, the absence of state action may have reflected, or been perceived to reflect, collusion, disbelief, or passive indifference. This may entail consideration of evidence where situations such as that of the victim are tacitly tolerated by the authorities (eg child domestic servitude, other worst forms of child labour, or servile marriage).

87 *VCL and AN v United Kingdom* (2021) 73 EHRR 9.
88 *Svazas v Secretary of State for the Home Department* [2002] EWCA Civ 74, [2002] 1 WLR 1891.

This analysis must be situated within the broader justifications invoked by the ECtHR for the triggering of the procedural obligation to investigate under Art 4 ECHR. The Court has consistently emphasised that the effectiveness of the investigation and the accountability of state authorities are central to this obligation. Notably, such investigations are essential for *'maintaining public confidence in the State's adherence to the rule of law and in preventing any appearance of collusion or tolerance of unlawful acts*[89]*.'*

2. **Fear of Reprisal:** It is not uncommon for victims to have been punished for failing to comply with the trafficker's or perpetrator's orders, or to have witnessed reprisals against others. In some instances, such reprisals have involved serious violence or even murder, carried out with apparent impunity. These experiences, alongside the factors identified in paragraph (1) above, may contribute significantly to the victim's subjective fear and unwillingness to avail themselves of state protection. Such factors, may for the victim, preclude accessing state protection on return. The perception of the victim will inform their ability to seek out protection. If the perception of the victim is that the trafficker will be able to find them if they seek out state protection then this must be considered in the context of their vulnerability and mental health. By analogy as Lord Boyd of Duncansby in *JM v Advocate General for Scotland*[90], observed:

> '…On the contrary; those who have presided over trials of historic sex abuse of children are only too aware of the deep psychological and emotional trauma that surrounds such criminal activity. In order to carry off such abuse the victim has to be cowed or otherwise subdued into remaining silent. That is a continuing effect of the crime. Disclosure may be made years or even decades after the abuse has ended. As Sedley J remarked in *R* v *Criminal Injuries Compensation Board* at 702, one of the fruits of crimes of sexual violence is the silence of the victim. That is a direct consequence of the crime and is widely recognised as such in the criminal justice system. To suggest that this effect disappears once the child has reached adulthood is to misunderstand the pervasive nature of the trauma which victims of childhood sexual abuse invariably suffer.'

3. **Non-reciprocal victim identification frameworks:** Recognition of victim status is often not reciprocal between States, including within Europe (see GRETA Country Implementation Reports).

4. **Conditional access to support as part of the protection package:** In many jurisdictions, access to support services is contingent on the victim self-reporting to State authorities. This presents significant barriers, particularly for traumatised individuals (see **Chapter 3**). Significant trauma caused by trafficking can severely limit a victim's capacity to engage with

89 *Nikolova and Velichkova v Bulgaria* no 7888/03, 20 Dec 2007 at [57].
90 *JM v Advocate General for Scotland* [2013] CSOH 169; 2014 SLT 475.

authorities, especially if disclosure would retraumatise them or exacerbate their mental health symptoms. Academic literature and clinical studies confirm that trauma from trafficking often results in post-traumatic stress disorder (PTSD), anxiety, depression, and distrust, which undermine victims' ability to provide coherent testimony, make decisions, or fully understand their legal options[91]. As was recognised in *R (HJK & Ors) v Director of Legal Aid Casework*[92] claimants with trauma-induced cognitive and psychological impairment cannot be expected to navigate complex procedures, and specific support is required for meaningful participation.

5. **Support provision restrictions:** Some states will not accept responsibility for supporting a returning national who was subjected to Art 4 harms unconnected with the home country.

6. **State implementation of support frameworks:** The scope and effectiveness of identification and support mechanisms depend on the State's implementation of its international obligations. Resources such as the US State Department Trafficking in Persons Reports, UN Special Rapporteur on Trafficking in Persons findings, and International Labour Organization (ILO) reports provide insight into these systems. As identified above, consideration is needed at a granular level to understand whether protection will effectively prevent re-trafficking or other harms.

7. **Non-criminalisation or low prosecutions:** Certain types of exploitation, such as criminal exploitation, servile marriage, or child domestic servitude, may not be classified as slavery, servitude, forced or compulsory labour or trafficking under the domestic law of the receiving State. This will be relevant to protection from further harm and access to support and assistance.

8. **Support measures and breaches of fundamental rights:** Leading experts[93] have criticised the practice of detaining trafficking victims in closed shelters, noting that such measures may violate fundamental rights and undermine recovery. Although sometimes justified on grounds of securing availability for criminal proceedings or under the guise of protection, such detention may amount to unlawful deprivation of liberty,

91 Cornelius Katona and Louise Howard, *The mental health difficulties experienced by victims of human trafficking (modern slavery) and the impact this has on their ability to provide testimony: Briefing Paper* (Helen Bamber Foundation and King's College London, 2021). Cathy Zimmerman, Mazeda Hossain and Ligia Kiss, 'Mental health and human trafficking: responding to survivors' needs' (2018) 12 *Health and Human Rights Journal* <https://doi.org/10.1017/S2047102517000301> accessed 11 October 2025.

92 *R (HJK & Ors) v Director of Legal Aid Casework* [2025] EWHC 774 (Admin).

93 Anne Gallagher and Elaine Pearson, *Detention of Trafficked Persons in Shelters: A Legal and Policy Analysis* (La Strada International, 2008) <https://documentation.lastradainternational.org/lsidocs/781%20Detention%20of%20trafficked%20persons%20(Pearson&Gallagher).pdf> accessed 11 October 2025. Marika McAdam, *Freedom of Movement for Persons Identified as Victims of Human Trafficking: An Analysis of Law, Policy and Practice in the ASEAN Region* (ASEAN-ACT, 2021) <https://www.aseanact.org/wp-content/uploads/2021/04/Freedom-of-movement-for-persons-identified-as-victims-of-human-trafficking-1.pdf> accessed 11 October 2025.

particularly when imposed without consent or judicial oversight. The risk of re-traumatisation, deterioration in mental health, and exposure to further harm must be carefully weighed in assessing compliance with the Convention.

Assessment of breach of positive obligations under Art 4 ECHR in the context of risk on return

16.113

The following considerations may be relevant to the Tribunal's assessment of whether there has been a breach of the positive obligations imposed by Arts 3 or 4 of the ECHR, either historically or on an ongoing basis:

Historical breach by state authorities in the home country

16.114

The Tribunal may be required to determine whether the state authorities in the home country previously failed to discharge their protective, recovery, or investigatory duties under Art 4 (or Art 3) of the ECHR in relation to the victim. This may be material to an assessment of effectiveness of protection on return.

16.115

As held by Chief Justice Gleeson and Mr Justice Kirby in *Minister for Immigration and Multicultural Affairs v Khawar*[94], where state authorities fail to enforce the criminal law against perpetrators of domestic violence, thereby withholding protection that victims are entitled to expect, such inaction may amount to toleration or condonation of the abuse. As outlined above, this reasoning aligns with the ECtHR's approach under Art 4 ECHR, which emphasises that failure to investigate or respond to credible indicators of violations of absolute rights can give rise to the appearance of collusion or tolerance of unlawful acts, thereby violating the state's positive obligations[95].

16.116

In assessing historical breaches, consideration may be given to:

- Whether there was *prima facie* evidence available to the authorities in the appellant's country of origin indicating that the appellant was a victim of abuse proscribed under Art 4 ECHR; and

94 *Minister for Immigration and Multicultural Affairs v Khawar* [2002] HCA 14 (Australia) at [116].
95 *Nikolova and Velichkova v Bulgaria* no 7888/03, 20 Dec 2007 at [57].

- Whether the state authorities failed to discharge the positive obligations owed to the appellant under Art 4, and the manner in which those obligations were breached.

16.117

This evaluative exercise reflects the approach adopted by the ECtHR, when assessing alleged breaches of positive obligations retrospectively, having regard to the circumstances and evidence that was known, or ought to have been known, to the state authorities at the relevant time.

Historical breach by UK authorities

16.118

Any past failure by UK authorities to comply with their positive obligations may also warrant consideration, particularly where such failure is said to have impacted the victim's mental health. This may be especially relevant in cases where the UK is alleged to have ongoing obligations, whether protective, recovery-related, or restitutive in nature. Where investigative duties are engaged, the Tribunal may need to assess whether those obligations were appropriately triggered and discharged in accordance with applicable standards (see ongoing breach below).

Ongoing breach by either state

16.119

In certain circumstances, the Tribunal may be required to consider the relevance of a putative ongoing breach of positive obligations under Art 4 and its bearing on the ongoing appeal proceedings. This may arise where:

- The identification process remains active following a reasonable grounds decision; or
- The available evidence establishes a credible suspicion of trafficking, slavery, or a related offence.

16.120

In such cases, the Tribunal may be required to consider whether the UK has acted in accordance with its recovery and investigative duties under Art 4 ECHR[96]. For instance, where an individual has been trafficked into or within the UK, but no effective identification or investigation has taken place despite

96 *EK(Article 4: Anti-Trafficking Convention) Tanzania* [2013] UKUT 00313 (IAC).

the existence of *prima facie* evidence, this may have deprived the appellant of access to corroborative material necessary to substantiate their protection claim. It may be submitted that compliance with the investigatory duty is directly relevant to an assessment of risk on return, including the potential for re-trafficking. A failure to discharge that duty may also be said to undermine the fairness of the domestic asylum appeal proceedings (see *VCL and AN v United Kingdom*[97]; *Chowdury v Greece*[98]). The investigatory duty is examined at length above. As was held in *MS (Pakistan)*[99], any removal of the appellant before an Art 4 compliant investigation would breach the UK's obligations under Art 4.

Reasons for persecution: membership of a particular social group

16.121

Membership of a 'Particular Social Group' is among the most frequently litigated grounds under the Refugee Convention. Its interpretation, shaped by evolving jurisprudence, reflects the Convention's character as a living instrument, constant in its protective purpose, yet adaptable in form[100]. This dynamic quality is especially significant in claims where identity, past harm, and social perception intersect to establish group membership.

16.122

Lord Steyn in *Shah and Islam*[101], applying the statutory interpretation principle of *ejusdem generis* ('of the same kind') to this term, approved the following passage of the US Board of Immigration Appeals in *Acosta*[102],

> 'We find the well-established doctrine of *ejusdem generis*….. to be most helpful in construing the phrase….Each of [the other grounds] describes persecution aimed at an immutable characteristic: a characteristic that either is beyond the power of an individual to change or is so

97 *VCL and AN v United Kingdom* (2021) 73 EHRR 9.

98 *Chowdury and others v Greece*, Application No. 21884/15, 30 March 2017.

99 *MS (Pakistan) v Secretary of State for the Home Department* [2020] UKSC 9.

100 *R v Immigration Appeal Tribunal and Secretary of State for the Home Department, ex p Shah* [1997] Imm AR 145 at [152]. Sedley J's framing of the Convention in this way was approved by the House of Lords.

101 *R v Immigration Appeal Tribunal and Secretary of State for the Home Department, ex p Shah; Islam v Secretary of State for the Home Department* [1999] 2 AC 629, [1999] Imm AR 283, [1999] INLR 144. See also UNHCR, Guidelines on International Protection: The application of Article 1A(2) of the 1951 Convention and/or 1967 Protocol relating to the Status of Refugees to victims of trafficking and persons at risk of being trafficked, 7 April 2006, HCR/GIP/06/07, paragraph 37; UNHCR, Guidelines on International Protection: Membership of a Particular Social Group within the context of Article 1A(2) of the 1951 Convention and the 1967 Protocol relating to the Status of Refugees, HCR/GIP/02/02, 7 May 2002, [11].

102 (1985) 19 I & N 211.

> fundamental to individual identity or conscience that it ought not be required to be changed…'

16.123

It has been the subject of judicial and academic debate whether both limbs of the Particular Social Group test, immutability and social perception, must be satisfied. In *K & Fornah v Secretary of State for the Home Department*[103], the House of Lords held that it is sufficient for one limb to be met.

16.124

The debate distinguishes between two approaches to defining a PSG: the 'social perception' approach, which focuses on how the group is perceived and treated by society at large, and the 'protected characteristics' (or *eiusdem generis*) approach, which defines the group by reference to inherent or immutable traits of its members. The former centres on external recognition; the latter on internal identity.

16.125

In *K & Fornah*, the House of Lords accepted that either approach may be appropriate, depending on the context. Lord Bingham, observed in respect of Art 10 of the EU Council Directive 2004/83/EC of 29 April 2004:

> 'Read literally, this provision is in no way inconsistent with the trend of international authority. When assessing a claim based on membership of a particular social group national authorities should certainly take the matters listed into account. I do not doubt that a group should be considered to form a particular social group where, in particular, the criteria in sub-paragraphs (i) and (ii) are both satisfied. Sub-paragraph (iii) is not wholly clear to me but appears in part to address a different aspect. **If, however, this article were interpreted as meaning that a social group should only be recognised as a particular social group for purposes of the Convention if it satisfies the criteria in both of sub- paragraphs (i) and (ii), then in my opinion it propounds a test more stringent than is warranted by international authority. In its published Comments on this Directive (January 2005) the UNHCR adheres to its view that the criteria in sub-paragraphs (i) and (ii) should be treated as alternatives, providing for recognition of a particular social group where either criterion is met and not requiring that both be met.**' [emphasis added]

103 *K & Fornah v Secretary of State for the Home Department* [2006] UKHL 46, [2007] 1 AC 412.

16.126

This position was subsequently affirmed by the Upper Tribunal in *DH (Particular Social Group: Mental Health) Afghanistan*[104], where it was confirmed that the two approaches may suffice to establish Particular Social Group membership under Art 1A(2) of the Refugee Convention.

Membership of a particular social group as defined in NABA 2022

16.127

For asylum claims made on or after 28 June 2022, NABA 2022 provides:

> '33. Article 1(A)(2): reasons for persecution
>
> (1) For the purposes of Article 1(A)(2) of the Refugee Convention –
>
> (2) A group forms a particular social group for the purposes of Article 1(A)(2) of the Refugee Convention only if it meets both of the following conditions.
>
> (3) The first condition is that members of the group share –
>
> (a) an innate characteristic,
>
> (b) a common background that cannot be changed, or
>
> (c) a characteristic or belief that is so fundamental to identity or conscience that a person should not be forced to renounce it.
>
> (4) The second condition is that the group has a distinct identity in the relevant country because it is perceived as being different by the surrounding society.'

16.128

Under NABA 2022, Particular Social Group for the purposes of Art 1(A)(2) of the Refugee Convention is established only where both of the following conditions are satisfied: (i) the group shares a characteristic that is either immutable or so fundamental to human dignity that individuals should not be required to change it; and (ii) the group is perceived as distinct by society.

Statutory interpretation principles: public international law

16.129

The senior courts have observed that the Refugee Convention should be interpreted in line with its broad humanitarian purpose and the principles set

104 *DH (Particular Social Group: Mental Health) Afghanistan* [2020] UKUT 223 (IAC).

out in its preamble: that all individuals are entitled to fundamental rights and freedoms without discrimination, and that refugees should be able to exercise those rights as fully as possible. As an international treaty without a supranational court to provide authoritative interpretation, the views of other States Parties, while not binding, are relevant to understanding its scope. Where the meaning of a provision is unclear, Arts 31–33 of the Vienna Convention on the Law of Treaties (VCLT)[105] may assist in resolving ambiguity[106].

16.130

The starting point for interpretation remains the text of the Convention itself, as it reflects the agreement reached by the contracting parties (Art 31(1) VCLT). Although application of the Vienna Rules is not usually limited to Art 31(1) and it requires extensive analysis and inquiry and all four paragraphs of Art 31. As confirmed in *Januzi v Secretary of State for the Home Department*[107], and the authorities cited by the Court, the Convention is to be understood as a living instrument, its meaning informed by evolving understandings of protection, but grounded in the language agreed by its signatories.

16.131

The Supreme Court in *Al-Sirri v Secretary of State for the Home Department*[108] observed at [36]:

> 'As Lord Steyn said in *R v Secretary of State for the Home Department, Ex p Adan* [2000] UKHL 67, [2001] 2 AC 477, 'In principle, there can be only one true interpretation of a treaty'. There is, at least as yet, no specialist international court or other body to adjudicate upon Member States' compliance with the Refugee Convention. The guidance given by the UNHCR is not binding, but 'should be accorded considerable weight', in the light of the obligation of Member States under article 35 of the Convention to facilitate its duty of supervising the application of the provisions of the Convention (see *R v Asfaw* [2008] AC 1061, per Lord Bingham at para 13, and *R v Uxbridge Magistrates' Court, Ex p Adimi* [2001] QB 667, 678). Within the European Union the Qualification Directive is designed to lay down minimum standards with which Member States must comply. Sedley LJ correctly concluded that 'the adoption by section 54(2) of the 2006 Act of the meaning of terrorism contained in the 2000 Act has where necessary to be read down in an article 1F[(c)] case so as to keep its meaning within the scope of article 12(2)(c) of the Directive.'

105 Treaty Series No.58 (1980) (Cmnd 7964).

106 *R (Adan) v Secretary of State for the Home Department [2000] UKHL 67, [2001] 2 AC 477*, 508–509, 515–518, 524–527, 528–531.

107 *Januzi v Secretary of State for the Home Department* [2006] UKHL 5, [2006] 2 WLR 397 at [4].

108 *Al-Sirri v Secretary of State for the Home Department; DD (Afghanistan) v Secretary of State for the Home Department* [2012] UKSC 54; [2013] 1 AC 745.

Divergence in the definition of 'particular social group' under NABA 2022

16.132

Section 33 of NABA 2022 defines 'Particular Social Group' in terms that depart from the approach adopted by Lord Bingham in *K and Fornah v Secretary of State for the Home Department*[109] as well as by the Upper Tribunal in *DH (Afghanistan)*[110]. In *DH (Afghanistan)*, the Tribunal held that the Refugee Convention does not require both limbs of the 'Particular Social Group' definition, immutability and social perception, to be satisfied, drawing on Lord Bingham's analysis in *K* and *Fornah*.

16.133

Paragraph [343] of the Explanatory Report to NABA 2022 states that s 33 provides a definition of 'Particular Social Group' as used in the Refugee Convention. On its face, s 33 appears to incorporate and give effect to Art 1(A)(2) of the Convention within domestic law. If that position is established, it will fall to the Upper Tribunal, and, in due course, potentially the senior appellate courts, to interpret the scope and application of this provision in NABA 2022 in compliance with the Refugee Convention.

16.134

While the legal position under NABA 2022 remains unsettled, the factual assessment of whether and how victims of trafficking or modern slavery are perceived as distinct within their country of origin is likely to assume increased importance.

Membership of a particular social group: trafficking and modern slavery

16.135

Art 1(A)(2) of the Refugee Convention requires a nexus, that is, a causal link, between the applicant's membership of the Particular Social Group of former victims of trafficking in human beings and a well-founded fear of persecution, or a lack of effective protection against such persecution.

16.136

Drawing on *Shah v Islam*[111], *K & Fornah v Secretary of State for the Home Department*[112], and *Hoxha*[113], existing jurisprudence indicates that former victims of trafficking,

109 *K & Fornah v Secretary of State for the Home Department* [2006] UKHL 46, [2007] 1 AC 412.
110 *DH (Particular Social Group: Mental Health) Afghanistan* [2020] UKUT 00223 (IAC).
111 *Islam v Secretary of State for the Home Department; R (Shah) v Immigration Appeal Tribunal* [1999] UKHL 20, [1999] 2 AC 629.
112 *K & Fornah v Secretary of State for the Home Department* [2006] UKHL 46, [2007] 1 AC 412 at [10].
113 *Hoxha and Another v Secretary of State for the Home Department*, [2005] UKHL 19, at [37].

slavery, or servitude may fall within the scope of a Particular Social Group (PSG) under Art 1A(2) of the Refugee Convention. In *Hoxha*, it was recognised that a past experience of victimisation may constitute an immutable characteristic, that is, a characteristic beyond the power of an individual to change, and when shared with others who have experienced similar harm, may form a common background that is both fundamental and unchangeable. This reasoning has been considered relevant to the assessment of Particular Social Group membership in cases involving individuals who have experienced serious exploitation.

16.137

This reasoning has been found to encompass enduring experiences such as having been trafficked or enslaved. As clarified in *K & Fornah*, the Convention is concerned not with all forms of harm, but with persecution arising from discriminatory treatment that violates fundamental human rights. The group defined by such shared experience exists independently of the persecution feared, but that experience may nonetheless form the basis on which persecution arises. The enduring stigma and vulnerability that follow exploitation can render former victims of trafficking socially distinguishable within their home society. This may satisfy both limbs of the PSG test: immutability and social perception, consistent with contemporary interpretations of the Refugee Convention.

16.138

Where PSG is interpreted to require that only one limb applies (adopting the analysis of Lord Bingham in *K & Fornah*), a history of trafficking or enslavement is a common background that cannot be changed.

Male victims of trafficking or modern slavery

16.139

It has been argued that there is no principled basis for excluding male victims from Particular Social Group where the relevant criteria, immutability and/(or)[114] social perception, are met, then the protection afforded by the Refugee Convention should apply irrespective of gender[115].

16.140

Academic commentary[116] has observed that trafficked men may face distinct legal and procedural barriers when seeking protection under the Refugee

114 Dependent on the interpretation of PSG.

115 Noemi Magugliani, 'Trafficked adult males and their recognition as members of a particular social group in the United Kingdom's Upper Tribunal' (Refugee Law Initiative Blog, 9 November 2020) https://rli.sas.ac.uk/blog/trafficked-adult-males-and-their-recognition-members-a-particular-social-group-united-kingdoms accessed 12 October 2025.

116 Noemi Magugliani, *Trafficked adult males, gendered constructions of vulnerability and access to protection* (PhD thesis, National University of Ireland Galway 2021).

Convention. It has been suggested that legal reasoning in asylum decisions may not consistently engage with the socio-economic and psychological dimensions of male victimhood, especially in cases involving forced labour or criminal exploitation. These observations have led to calls for a re-examination of the trafficking-asylum nexus, with a view to promoting a more inclusive interpretation of international protection standards that reflects the full spectrum of exploitation and the diverse experiences of male victims.

16.141

It may also be considered significant that an individual subjected to slavery, a violation of a *jus cogens* norm with *erga omnes* effect, which entails the stripping of juridical personality and the reduction of the individual to a status akin to property, might nonetheless be denied refugee status where the legal analysis does not engage with the implications of such dehumanisation in relation to group membership and vulnerability. This concern is particularly relevant in cases involving male victims and may warrant further judicial scrutiny.

16.142

The Upper Tribunal has reached varying conclusions in individual unreported cases on whether male victims of trafficking and modern slavery may constitute a Particular Social Group for the purposes of refugee protection. Independent and expert country evidence continues to play a critical role in understanding the experiences of male victims and how they may be perceived differently in specific factual contexts.

16.143

For example, in certain country settings, prevailing gender norms may prevent male victims from being recognised as such, thereby limiting their access to protection. Additionally, the forms of harm they have suffered may be so heavily stigmatised that their ability to fully disclose their experiences for the purpose of accessing treatment and recovery is significantly compromised. In an unreported decision, *ES v Secretary of State for the Home Department*[117] the Upper Tribunal accepted that a male Albanian trafficking victim was at risk of re-trafficking and identified the sole issue as whether he met the "distinct identity" limb in s 33(4) NABA 2022. Relying on the CPIN material, the 2022 Fact-Finding Mission, the Asylos report and other background evidence, and without expert evidence, the Tribunal found that male Albanian victims of trafficking may form a group with a distinct identity because they are perceived as different within Albanian society. It concluded that ES was a member of such a group and therefore a refugee. A pending country guidance case, LR (Albania – trafficked men), is expected to provide authoritative guidance.

117 UI-2025-000360 at 4-8, 27 and 39.

16.144

While these issues are increasingly recognised, the question of whether male victims of trafficking constitute a Particular Social Group remains one for further judicial consideration. Ultimately, it will fall to the Upper Tribunal or senior appellate courts to clarify the required limbs of Particular Social Group, and protection of male victims in light of evolving understandings of vulnerability and group identity within refugee law.

Kidnap for ransom as exploitation and its relevance to particular social group analysis

16.145

In *R (AAM) v Secretary of State for the Home Department*[118], the High Court considered whether the Claimant's experience of kidnap for ransom constituted exploitation within the meaning of Regulation 3 of the Nationality and Borders Act 2022 Regulations. The court found that the Secretary of State had failed to properly apply the domestic legal framework, particularly the broader definitions of 'means' and 'exploitation' set out in the 2022 Regulations.

16.146

Under Regulation 3(5)(ii), *kidnap* is expressly recognised as a means by which a person may be trafficked. The court emphasised that Parliament's inclusion of 'kidnap', defined in the Oxford English Dictionary as 'carry off (a person etc) by illegal force or fraud esp. to obtain a ransom,' was deliberate and meaningful. It was not limited to abduction for sexual or labour exploitation but extended to scenarios where the victim is kidnapped with a view to obtaining a benefit, such as ransom or extortion.

16.147

The court held that Regulation 3(6) does not require actual exploitation to have occurred. Instead, it is sufficient that the victim was subjected to force, threats or deception designed to induce them to provide services or enable another person to acquire benefits. In the Claimant's case, the kidnap was undertaken with a view to obtaining a ransom, which falls squarely within the scope of exploitation as defined in the Regulations.

16.148

The Defendant's reliance on Art 4 of ECAT, which refers only to 'abduction' and provides a narrower list of exploitation types, was found to be inadequate.

118 *R (AAM) v Secretary of State for the Home Department* [2025] EWHC 447 (Admin).

The court noted that the 2022 Regulations go further than ECAT and the Palermo Protocol by including 'abduction, kidnap and false imprisonment' as recognised means, and by offering a more detailed and subdivided definition of exploitation. The domestic framework is designed to capture other forms of exploitation, including those not explicitly listed in ECAT.

16.149

The judgment confirms that kidnap for ransom may, depending on the facts, constitute exploitation for the purposes of identifying a victim of trafficking. This interpretation aligns with the ECAT Explanatory Report, which acknowledges that domestic legislation may target additional forms of exploitation beyond those enumerated in international instruments.

Implications for particular social group analysis

16.150

A question arises as to whether individuals who are targeted for kidnap for ransom may constitute a particular social group. The recognition of kidnap for ransom as a form of exploitation under the 2022 Regulations strengthens the argument that victims of such treatment may share an innate characteristic or common background, such as ethnicity, socio-economic status, or regional origin, that renders them vulnerable to targeting (see *FM v Russia* and the court's discrimination analysis).

16.151

The court's recognition of kidnap for ransom as exploitation provides a legal foundation for such claims to be properly considered within the international protection framework.

Disability as a ground for refugee protection

16.152

This section should be read with **Chapter 3**.

16.153

It was established in *DH (Particular Social Group: Mental Health) Afghanistan*[119] that a person living with disability or mental ill health may qualify for refugee

119 [2020] UKUT 00223 (IAC).

protection as a member of a particular social group[120]. The decision in *DH* was not appealed by the SSHD.

16.154

Establishing that an applicant belongs to a Particular Social Group, such as persons living with a specific disability or medical condition, is not sufficient to qualify for refugee status. The other inclusion criteria under Art 1(A)(2) of the Refugee Convention must also be met. There must be a nexus, that is, a causal link, between the applicant's membership of the group and a well-founded fear of persecution, or a lack of effective protection against such persecution.

The definition of disability

16.155

Under s 6 of the UK's Equality Act 2010, a person is considered disabled if they have a physical or mental impairment that has a substantial and long-term adverse effect on their ability to carry out normal day-to-day activities. 'Substantial' means more than minor or trivial, and 'long-term' means it has lasted or is likely to last for at least 12 months or is likely to last for the rest of the person's life.

16.156

The UN Convention on the Rights of Persons with Disabilities (UNCRPD) defines persons with disabilities as:

> 'Persons with disabilities include those who have long-term physical, mental, intellectual or sensory impairments which in interaction with various barriers may hinder their full and effective participation in society on an equal basis with others'[121].

DH (Particular Social Group: Mental Health) Afghanistan

16.157

Having determined that it is sufficient to satisfy either the common characteristic or social perception limb of the test for a particular social group (see above), the Tribunal recognised that individuals with disabilities or mental ill health may qualify as such a group. This may be due to the shared characteristic of their condition, which distinguishes them from others, or because they are perceived

120 *DH (Afghanistan)*, Headnote, [1].
121 Art 1 of the UNCRPD.

as different by society, thereby forming a distinct identity within their country of origin. Whether individuals are treated as a cognisable group based on mental health or perceived deviation from social norms is a question of fact.

16.158

The Tribunal adopted an inclusive approach, considering a wide spectrum of mental health conditions, learning disabilities, and neurodiversity. In assessing claims, there must be cogent evidence establishing that the individual suffers from serious mental illness. While such cases may be relatively rare, the central issue is how the person is perceived by potential persecutors. Even those with less severe conditions may face real risks due to societal ignorance or stigma. This requires a fact-specific inquiry into the nature and manifestation of the illness, and prevailing country conditions. Importantly, the absence of a formal diagnosis does not preclude entitlement to international protection.

16.159

Assessment must also address whether the individual faces persecution or serious human rights violations, and whether the State can offer effective protection. The mere existence of a healthcare system is not determinative; societal attitudes and institutional practices may still expose individuals to harm. Treatment may be unavailable, inaccessible, unaffordable, or inadequate, and in some cases, may itself constitute persecution, such as detention, isolation, chaining, beating, or other abusive practices.

16.160

In *DH (Afghanistan)*[122], the appellant suffered from serious mental illness without a formal diagnosis, manifesting in sexually disinhibited behaviour and alcohol misuse. The Tribunal found that in Afghanistan, individuals with mental health conditions faced severe social stigma, risks of being chained or subjected to mob violence, and lacked institutional protection. DH was accordingly recognised as a refugee.

16.161

DH (Afghanistan) pre-dated the introduction of NABA 2022. It is likely that the evidence related to the applicant's mental health presentation, and how mental health may manifest in behaviour, and the country evidence obtained to support the necessary fact-specific assessment of the treatment of individuals with mental health difficulties would support both limbs of the definition of 'membership of a particular social group' proposed by s 33 NABA 2022 (see further above).

122 *DH (Particular Social Group: Mental Health) Afghanistan* [2020] UKUT 00223 (IAC).

Compounded risks at the intersection of trafficking, slavery, and disability

16.162

Art 10 UNCRPD requires States Parties to take all appropriate measures to protect persons with disabilities, both within and outside the home, from all forms of exploitation, violence and abuse, including those with gendered dimensions. Where individuals have been subjected to such harm, States are also required to promote their physical, cognitive and psychological recovery, rehabilitation, and social reintegration, including through the provision of protection services[123].

16.163

Certain disability-related characteristics may increase vulnerability to specific forms of exploitation. For example, persons with visible physical disabilities may be at heightened risk of being trafficked into forced begging, as visible impairments may elicit greater public sympathy. Women and girls with intellectual or psychosocial disabilities may be at increased risk of sexual exploitation, as traffickers may perceive them as easier to manipulate, less likely to self-identify as victims, or less likely to be believed when reporting abuse. The Committee on the Rights of Persons with Disabilities[124] has expressed concern over various forms of trafficking affecting persons with disabilities, including sexual exploitation (particularly of women and children), organ trafficking, trafficking for labour and forced labour, and forced begging[125].

16.164

Research highlights a direct link between certain forms of disability and specific patterns of trafficking, including forced begging and exploitative labour practices. In some instances, the trauma endured by victims may result in serious mental health conditions that themselves give rise to a real risk of harm. More broadly, the manifestation of mental illness may influence risk in nuanced ways, for example, affecting how a person responds under questioning, particularly if they fear disclosing aspects of their background such as experiences of trafficking. It may also impair their ability to recognise danger, protect themselves from exploitation, or navigate interactions with potential persecutors[126]. These factors underscore the need for a careful, individualised assessment of vulnerability and risk.

---

123 Art 16 of the UNCRPD.

124 Information on the Committee and its work available at: https://www.ohchr.org/en/treaty-bodies/crpd accessed 12 October 2025.

125 Thematic study on the issue of violence against women and girls and disability – Report of the Office of the United Nations High Commissioner for Human Rights (2012) A/HRC/20/5.

126 By analogy *RT (Zimbabwe) & Ors v Secretary of State for the Home Department* [2012] UKSC 38 [26 and 42], KK and RS (Sur place activities, risk) Sri Lanka (CG) [2021] UKUT 130 (IAC) [520-521].

16.165

In *IC v The Republic of Moldova* [127], the ECtHR found that the legal framework in place at the relevant time failed to provide practical and effective protection against trafficking and servitude for persons with intellectual disabilities who had been deprived of legal capacity. The applicant, a woman with intellectual disabilities, was removed from State care and placed with a family, where she was subjected to forced labour without pay. The Court concluded that the absence of safeguards in the deinstitutionalisation process directly contributed to her exposure to exploitation.

16.166

In *R (NO) v SSHD*[128], the Court of Appeal accepted that people with mental illness who risked inhuman or degrading treatment in breach of Art 3 ECHR would qualify for humanitarian protection. In the context of that decision the Court considered shortages of mental health treatment facilities, significant unmet need, and societal attitudes that hampered access to treatment, the court found that there was a real risk that the appellant, who suffered from PTSD, would be shunned, become homeless and destitute or fall victim to those who used inhumane methods (exorcism) to treat his illness, and qualified for humanitarian protection on that basis[129].

16.167

Country Guidance decisions of the Upper Tribunal that assess the risk to victims of trafficking upon return to their country of origin frequently identify a nexus between the vulnerabilities arising from the trafficking experience and the risk of re-trafficking or other harm on return.

Burden and standard of proof under the refugee convention and NABA 2022

16.168

Under the Refugee Convention, the burden of establishing a well-founded fear of persecution lies with the applicant. The established standard is whether there is a 'real and substantial risk' or a 'reasonable degree of likelihood' of persecution for a Convention reason[130]. This is a lower threshold than the civil standard of the balance of probabilities.

127 *IC v The Republic of Moldova* App no 36436/22 (ECHR, 27 February 2025), at [152–157].
128 [2016] EWCA Civ 876.
129 *R (NO) v Secretary of State for the Home Department* [2016] EWCA Civ 876, [32, 38, 44–45].
130 *R v Secretary of State for the Home Department, ex p Sivakumaran* [1988] AC 958.

16.169

The approach to assessing past events was authoritatively set out by the Court of Appeal in *Karanakaran*[131], which applies to accounts of past persecution, including trafficking. The Court held that:

> 'There may be circumstances in which a decision-maker must take into account the possibility that alleged past events occurred even though it finds that these events probably did not occur. The reason for this is that the ultimate question is whether the applicant [in an asylum case] has a real substantial basis for his fear of future persecution. The decision-maker must not foreclose reasonable speculation about chances of the future hypothetical event occurring.'

16.170

Section 32 of NABA 2022 introduces a revised framework, raising the standard of proof for certain elements of the asylum claim. The Explanatory Notes to NABA 2022 confirm that s 32 establishes a two-limb test for assessing whether an asylum seeker has a well-founded fear of persecution, applying the balance of probabilities to the initial elements of the claim.

Interpretation of s 32(2) NABA 2022

16.171

Under s 32(2) NABA 2022, the decision-maker must determine, on the balance of probabilities:

1. Whether the asylum seeker has a characteristic that could cause them to fear persecution for a Convention reason (or has such a characteristic attributed to them by the persecutor); and
2. Whether the asylum seeker does in fact fear such persecution in their country of nationality (or former habitual residence).

16.172

In *JCK*[132], the Upper Tribunal interpreted this provision as requiring the civil standard of proof to be applied to both the existence of a Convention ground and the claimant's subjective fear. The Tribunal noted that this may be straightforward in cases involving obvious characteristics (eg race or gender), but more complex where persecution arises from membership of a particular social group, requiring careful analysis of the country context.

131 *Karanakaran v Secretary of State for the Home Department* [2000] 3 All ER 449.
132 *JCK (Botswana) v Secretary of State for the Home Department* [2024] UKUT 00100 (IAC), at [13-14].

16.173

The Home Office guidance suggests that s 32(2)(b) relates to the assessment of material facts; the Tribunal found that the provision simply requires consideration of whether the applicant has a genuinely held subjective fear, which is a discrete exercise from assessing whether past events occurred.

Burden of proof and the state's protective and procedural duties under Art 4 ECHR

16.174

An issue that may arise in asylum claims is where the appellant bears the burden of establishing, to the civil standard, that they were previously subjected to slavery or related acts and fear further harm contrary to Art 4 ECHR upon return, in circumstances where the UK authorities have failed to discharge their positive obligations, namely, to identify and/or investigate[133] indicators of trafficking or exploitation.

16.175

By analogy, in *VCL and AN v United Kingdom*[134], the ECtHR held that where the investigatory authorities (in that case the prosecution) had failed to extensively examine the applicants' allegations of trafficking prior or during the course of prosecuting them, this breached the protective obligations under Arts 4 and 6 ECHR. The Court emphasised that evidence concerning an accused's status as a victim of trafficking constitutes a 'fundamental aspect' of the defence, which must be accessible without restriction.

16.176

As confirmed by the Supreme Court in *MS (Pakistan)*[135], the investigatory duty under Art 4 ECHR is one that must be discharged by the police, not the Competent Authority. Similarly, in *Secretary of State for the Home Department v Hoang Anh Minh*[136], Lord Justice Burnett identified that this duty rests with the Crown Prosecution Service and the police.

133 The UK's procedural obligation to investigate only arises if the individual was trafficked into the UK; was subject to Art 4 abuse within the UK or a UK national subjected them to Art 4 abuse outside of the UK. This investigatory duty lies with the police, the prosecution and latterly with the tribunal and courts (effective judicial response).

134 *VCL and AN v United Kingdom (2021) 73 EHRR 9* at [196].

135 *MS (Pakistan) v Secretary of State for the Home Department* [2020] UKSC 9, [2020] 1 WLR 1373.

136 [2016] EWCA Civ 565 at [38].

16.177

The ECtHR has further clarified that the investigatory obligation under Art 4 extends to judicial authorities, the Court has characterised failures of the Court to act as a lack of effective judicial response.

Objective risk assessment under s 32(4) NABA 2022

16.178

Following the determination of subjective fear, s 32(4) NABA 2022 requires the decision-maker to assess, on the lower standard of proof (reasonable likelihood):

(a) Whether the applicant would be persecuted as a result of the Convention characteristic; and

(b) Whether they would be protected as described in s 34.

16.179

Section 32(5) further requires consideration of internal relocation under s 35.

16.180

The Tribunal has cautioned against conflating the assessment of subjective fear with the evaluation of objective risk. Decision-makers must consider country background material twice: first, to contextualise the subjective fear, and second, to assess the objective risk. The Tribunal emphasised that navigating between varying standards of proof is an intellectual exercise requiring discipline, but it does not alter the fundamental task of taking a holistic view of the evidence.

16.181

To aid clarity, the Tribunal summarised the five questions to be addressed:

1. **Convention Ground**: On the balance of probabilities, does the claimant have a characteristic that could cause them to fear persecution for a Convention reason?

2. **Subjective Fear**: On the balance of probabilities, does the claimant genuinely fear such persecution?

3. **Risk of Harm**: Is there a reasonable likelihood of persecution on return?

4. **State Protection**: Is there a reasonable likelihood that the applicant would not be protected?

5. **Internal Relocation**: Is there a reasonable likelihood that internal relocation is not a viable alternative?

Comparison with ECAT standard of proof

16.182

In *MN and IXU*[137], the Court of Appeal considered the standard of proof under ECAT. The Court rejected the analogy with the Refugee Convention standard, stating:

> 'We do not believe that the analogy with the test for establishing refugee status is a good one… The risk of a victim of trafficking coming back under the influence of his or her traffickers, particularly after a protected recovery and reflection period, is not to be compared with the risk to a victim of persecution if they are returned to their country of origin. If the drafters of ECAT had intended that a similar standard of proof should be applied they could and would have made express provision'[138].

16.183

This distinction highlights the importance of interpreting the provisions of the NABA 2022 in a manner that is consistent with the United Kingdom's international obligations, including the protective purposes of the Refugee Convention and ECAT. It is likely that questions of interpretation arising under NABA 2022 will require judicial consideration, particularly in relation to the protection of individuals who may fall within the scope of these instruments. The interaction between differing standards of proof, the definition of Convention grounds, and the factual complexity of trafficking-related claims will continue to play a significant role in ensuring fair and lawful decision-making.

Internal relocation

General principles

16.184

As outlined above, the Refugee Convention provides international protection to individuals who cannot obtain protection in their country of origin. Consequently, a risk that is purely localised will generally not suffice to establish refugee status, as the individual may be able to relocate to another part of their country. However, where the risk of re-trafficking is not confined to a specific geographical area, internal relocation is unlikely to be a viable alternative. Even if the Home Office identifies a potential place of relocation, it must still assess whether relocation is reasonable.

---

137 *MN & IXU v Secretary of State for the Home Department* [2020] EWCA Civ 1746, [2021] 1 WLR 1956.
138 Ibid, [95].

16.185

The established approach to internal relocation was affirmed by the House of Lords in *AH (Sudan) v Secretary of State for the Home Department*[139].

16.186

Lord Bingham, reiterating his earlier judgment in *Januzi v Secretary of State for the Home Department*, stated[140]:

> 'The decision-maker, taking account of all relevant circumstances pertaining to the claimant and his country of origin, must decide whether it is reasonable to expect the claimant to relocate or whether it would be unduly harsh to expect him to do so.'

16.187

In *AH (Sudan)* at [5], Lord Bingham emphasised:

> 'It is, or should be, evident that the enquiry must be directed to the situation of the particular applicant, whose age, gender, experience, health, skills and family ties may all be very relevant. There is no warrant for excluding, or giving priority to, consideration of the applicant's way of life in the place of persecution. There is no warrant for excluding, or giving priority to, consideration of conditions generally prevailing in the home country.'

16.188

Lord Hope added at [47]:

> 'The words "unduly harsh" set the standard that must be met for this to be regarded as unreasonable. If the claimant can live a relatively normal life there judged by the standards that prevail in his country of nationality generally, and if he can reach the less hostile part without undue hardship or undue difficulty, it will not be unreasonable to expect him to move there.'

16.189

In *AB (Jamaica)*[141], Lloyd LJ clarified:

> '[31] It is plain from what Lord Bingham said that the test … which has in itself made reference to 'a relatively normal life', is one which needs

139 [2007] UKHL 49, [2008] 1 AC 678.
140 [2006] UKHL 5, [2006] 2 AC 426, at [21].
141 *AB (Jamaica) v Secretary of State for the Home Department* [2008] EWCA Civ 784.

to be addressed by decision makers in relation to the facts of a particular case and, accordingly, by reference to those aspects of the facts which are said to … be relevant to the question of unreasonableness or undue harshness …

[35] … to say that 'destitution is the test' is oversimplified and could lead into error a reader who did not pursue the cross-reference to *Januzi*.'

16.190

In *AS (Afghanistan)*[142], the Court of Appeal rejected the Secretary of State's argument that the test should be relativised by reference to whether a 'significant minority' of the population live in similarly poor conditions. The Court accepted the appellant's and UNHCR's submissions that there exists a threshold below which conditions render relocation unreasonable.

Internal relocation and NABA 2022

16.191

Section 35(1) NABA 2022 states that an asylum seeker is not to be taken to be a refugee if (a) they would not have a well-founded fear of being persecuted in a part of their country nationality (or in a case where they do not have a nationality, the country of their former habitual residence), and (b) they can reasonably be expected to travel to and remain in that part of the country. Section 35(2) NABA 2022 continues that in considering whether an asylum seeker can reasonably be expected to travel to and remain in a part of a country, a decision maker must have regard to: (i) the general circumstances prevailing in that part of the country; and (ii) the personal circumstances of the asylum seeker, and must disregard any technical obstacles relating to travel to that part of the country.

Internal relocation of victims of trafficking or modern slavery: current jurisprudence

16.192

Special considerations apply when assessing the internal relocation of trafficking victims. In *AA (Uganda)*[143], the Court of Appeal applied the *AH (Sudan)* factors to a female appellant, noting that she faced not only poverty and homelessness but also the risk of being driven into prostitution. Buxton LJ concluded that enforced prostitution in the place of relocation would be 'unduly harsh'.

142 *AS (Afghanistan)* [2019] EWCA Civ 873.
143 *AA (Uganda)* [2008] EWCA Civ 579.

16.193

Similarly, in *HD (Trafficked women) Nigeria CG*[144], the Upper Tribunal held that the assessment must consider both the individual's personal circumstances and how those characteristics interact with the conditions in the proposed area of relocation. The Tribunal examined the prevalence of internal trafficking in Nigeria and the visibility of victims as outsiders in new locations. It concluded:

> 'It is not possible to state, on the evidence before us, that internal relocation is never a viable option. An individual factual analysis will always be required of a victim of trafficking's vulnerability and its impact on the possibility of internal relocation if she is at real risk of being persecuted in her home area. However, the evidence before us indicates that where an individual has been identified as being at real risk of being trafficked, the possibility of internal relocation will be severely limited; particularly where she is vulnerable to abuse because of lack of skills, mental and psychological problems and isolation.'

16.194

In *TD and AD (Trafficked women) Albania CG*[145], the Upper Tribunal stressed that the assessment must include the claimant's personal history and its relevance in the context of the society to which she would relocate. As Wilson LJ (as he then was) observed in *VNM*[146]:

> 'It is obvious that the reasonableness of her relocation in a different part of Kenya requires consideration of the practicability of her settling elsewhere; consideration of her ability convincingly to present to those in her new milieu a false history relating to herself and to her daughter, including the latter's paternity, and a false explanation for their arrival there; and, in the light of her substantial psychological vulnerability, consideration of her ability to sustain beyond the short term a reasonable life for them both on that false basis.'

Positive obligations under Art 4 ECHR and the implications for internal relocation

16.195

Art 4 of the ECHR, as interpreted in landmark judgments such as *Rantsev v Cyprus and Russia*[147] and *VCL & AN v United Kingdom*[148], imposes positive

144 *HD (Trafficked women) Nigeria CG* [2016] UKUT 454 (IAC).
145 *TD and AD (Trafficked women) Albania CG* [2016] UKUT 92 (IAC).
146 *VNM v Secretary of State for the Home Department* [2006] EWCA Civ 47 at [25].
147 App. no. 25965/04 (ECtHR, 7 January 2010).
148 *VCL and AN v United Kingdom* (2021) 73 EHRR 9.

obligations on states to protect victims of trafficking and modern slavery, prevent future harm, and facilitate their physical, psychological, and social recovery. These obligations encompass not only protection from re-trafficking but also the provision of effective support for rehabilitation and reintegration.

16.196

Considering these duties, requiring a victim of trafficking or modern slavery to relocate internally, particularly to areas where protective and recovery mechanisms are absent or inadequate, risks undermining the UK's ability to fulfil its obligations to a victim identified in the UK. Such relocation may breach the operational duty to prevent re-trafficking and frustrate the recovery and restitution obligations, which extends beyond ensuring physical safety to include access to trauma-informed care, safe accommodation, social support that enable recovery.

16.197

Where credible evidence indicates that internal relocation would result in the denial or serious impairment of access to these essential services, the relocation should arguably be deemed unreasonable. The jurisprudence under Art 4 ECHR, alongside obligations under Art 4 ECAT and relevant UN guidelines, arguably supports the position that internal relocation cannot be considered reasonable where the UK authorities have not discharged their duties to protect, rehabilitate, and prevent re-trafficking or re-victimisation and conditions of return do not provide the recovery and protective mechanisms required.

Credibility

16.198

Whether a victim of trafficking or modern slavery can discharge the burden of proof will require an assessment of the putative victim's credibility.

16.199

Where the Single Competent Authority (SCA) within the Home Office has made a decision accepting that there are conclusive grounds that a person is a victim of trafficking, Home Office asylum caseworkers usually accept that the individual is a victim of trafficking unless there is clear evidence to the contrary[149]. As the decision is made by the SCA within the Home Office, and is made on the balance of probabilities, (which is a higher standard of proof applied to pre-NABA 2022 cases and human rights claims) and the same standard of

149 Home Office, *Assessing credibility and refugee status in asylum claims lodged on or after 28 June 2022*, v.13 (28 September 2023), p.49; Home Office, *Assessing credibility and refugee status in asylum claims lodged before 28 June 2022*, v.10 (28 June 2022), p.49.

proof applied to NABA 2022 cases on the above analysis, the decision should be treated as a concession in the context of the asylum claim (see above).

16.200

The Modern Slavery Statutory Guidance accepts that the identification decision-making process may be influenced by the views of experts[150]. The statutory guidance recognises that there may be 'valid reasons' why aspects of a potential victim's account are 'inconsistent or lack sufficient detail'[151] and that it is 'vital' for decision makers to understand reasons why a potential victim of slavery is 'incoherent, inconsistent or delays giving details of material facts'[152]. The guidance directs that the competent authority must take account of such reasons when considering the credibility of the claim[153]. In particular, the guidance states that such factors may include[154]:

- The impact of trauma including on early accounts, delayed disclosure, difficulty recalling facts, and memory difficulties;
- Barriers to disclosure;
- Victims may not recognise themselves as a victim of modern slavery or may be reluctant to be identified as such;
- Mistrust of authorities;
- Lack of awareness of their situation as exploitative, harmful or abnormal;
- Impact of types of exploitation on disclosure and the need to develop a relationship of trust.

16.201

Children may be unable to disclose or give a consistent, credible account due to additional factors such as[155]:

- Their developmental stage (noting also their developmental age may not match what may be expected for the child's chronological age)[156];
- The on-going nature of abuse throughout childhood and/or grooming;
- Loyalty or perceived friendships with exploiters;

150 Home Office, *Modern Slavery: Statutory Guidance for England and Wales under s49 of the Modern Slavery Act 2015 and Non-Statutory Guidance for Scotland and Northern Ireland* (Version 4.2, September 2025) https://www.gov.uk/government/publications/modern-slavery-how-to-identify-and-support-victims/modern-slavery-statutory-guidance-for-england-and-wales-under-s49-of-the-modern-slavery-act-2015-and-non-statutory-guidance-for-scotland-and-northe accessed 12 October 2025. Annex E, [14.24].

151 Ibid, Annex E, [14.6].

152 Ibid, Annex E, [14.5].

153 Ibid, Annex E, [14.6].

154 Ibid, Annex E [14.72].

155 Ibid, Annex D, [13.61].

156 Ibid, Annex D, [13.62].

- Fear of traffickers or exploiters, violence or witchcraft.

16.202

Whilst the guidance acknowledges the reasons why a victim of trafficking may be incoherent, inconsistent or delay in giving material facts, the guidance also directs that it is 'reasonable to assume that a potential victim who has experienced an event will be able to recount the central elements in a broadly consistent manner' and an ability to remain consistent throughout may lead the competent authority to disbelieve his claim[157].

16.203

A negative reasonable or conclusive grounds decision which fails to take into account either the indicators pointing in favour of a positive trafficking decision or a failure of the SCA to consider the statutory guidance specifically on credibility and factors which may impact on the ability to provide a consistent or coherent account, will likely be unlawful[158]. The Court of Appeal in *MN and IXU v Secretary of State for the Home Department*[159] provided guidance on the treatment of expert evidence[160], the need for a structured approach to considering the evidence (rather than adopting a view and seeking 'mitigating' factors)[161], and held that full weight must be given to the evidence (and guidance) about the difficulties that victims of trafficking have in telling their stories, not only because of the effects of trauma but because their experiences often engender distrust of authority and sometimes entangle them in deceptions of various kinds from which it is difficult to escape[162].

16.204

If a decision refusing an asylum claim adopts the reasoning of the SCA in a negative reasonable or conclusive grounds decision, it is good practice to consider whether the SCA properly considered the evidence, placed weight on the indicators of trafficking and/or specifically considered the factors identified above.

16.205

In decisions on international protection claims made by victims of trafficking, the Home Office has invoked s 8 of the Asylum and Immigration (Treatment of Claimants, etc) Act 2004 to argue that delayed disclosure or a delayed claim for

157 Ibid, Annex E, [14.13].
158 See *R(SF) v Secretary of State for the Home Department* [2015] EWHC 2705 (Admin); *R(FK) v Secretary of State for the Home Department* [2016] EWHC 56 (Admin) and *R(EK) v Secretary of State for the Home Department* [2019] EWHC 1696 (Admin).
159 [2020] EWCA Civ 1746.
160 Ibid, [121].
161 Ibid, [126].
162 Ibid, [253].

asylum by a victim of trafficking should be treated as damaging their credibility for the purpose of their refugee or human rights claim. It is well-established that the weight to be given to s 8 is a matter for the tribunal which must undertake a global assessment of credibility[163]. Where an individual has been recognised as a victim of trafficking on conclusive grounds, such a finding can often be at odds with the assessment of credibility by the SCA or relates to a period when the SCA accepted that an individual was subject to control by a trafficker. The analysis may also be unsustainable as inconsistent with Modern Slavery statutory guidance which recognises that potential victims may be reluctant to come forward or not recognise themselves as victims[164] and the significant barriers faced by victims to disclosure[165].

Consent in the context of trafficking and modern slavery appeals

16.206

The issue of consent frequently arises in trafficking and modern slavery appeals and is examined in detail in **Chapter 1**.

16.207

In its jurisprudence under Art 4 of the ECHR, the ECtHR has consistently applied Art 4(b) of ECAT, which provides that consent is irrelevant where any of the means in the definition of trafficking have been employed. It is not determinative that an individual may have initially consented to their situation, nor that they could have escaped earlier[166].

16.208

The ECtHR's approach to consent is grounded in an objective assessment of the circumstances. As the Court has observed, 'where an employer abuses his power or takes advantage of the vulnerability of his workers in order to exploit them, they do not offer themselves voluntarily.' While consent is often referenced in discussions of forced or compulsory labour, the Court does not examine the victim's subjective state of mind. Instead, it evaluates whether the factual circumstances reveal abuse of power or excessive demands indicative of exploitation[167].

163 *JT (Cameroon) v Secretary of State for the Home Department* [2008] EWCA Civ 878.

164 Home Office, *Modern Slavery Act 2015 – Statutory Guidance for England and Wales*, v.4.1 (11 August 2025), [3.1, 3.6, 13.11].

165 Ibid, [13.18].

166 *Krachunova v Bulgaria,* App no 18269/18, judgment, 28 November 2023, [153]; *Chowdury and others v Greece,* App no 21884/15, judgment 30 March 2017, [96].

167 See Stoyanova, V. (2025). Positive Obligations. In K. Istrefi, Z. Ratniece, K. Tamuzs, & K. Kamber (Eds.), Companion to the European Convention on Human Rights Brill.

Humanitarian protection

16.209

Where a victim of trafficking is not a refugee, they may be entitled to humanitarian protection if there are substantial grounds for believing that they will face a real risk of 'serious harm' under the Immigration Rules[168]. Such harm includes torture or inhuman or degrading treatment or punishment in the country of origin, corresponding to Art 3 ECHR, among other forms of harm[169]. Unlike the Refugee Convention, there is no requirement for the risk of serious harm to be due to any specific reason (such as race, religion, nationality, political opinion or membership of a particular social group) to qualify for humanitarian protection.

16.210

The lower standard of proof of 'real risk' or 'reasonable likelihood' applies to all elements of the claim, both the assessment of past facts and the assessment of future risk of serious harm, when considering whether a person qualifies for humanitarian protection. This remains the case in the context of changes created by NABA 2022 for the consideration of asylum applications made on or after 28 June 2022 with reference to the Refugee Convention (see above). In such cases, if the refugee claim is rejected with reference to s 32 NABA 2022, the humanitarian protection claim must be assessed in a second-stage assessment where all elements of the claim are considered under the lower standard of proof[170].

16.211

The assessment of risk on return is carried out by reference to the applicant's personal history and to the human rights conditions in the country of origin in much the same way as the Refugee Convention assessment. The case law on the assessment of state protection and internal relocation outline above is applied with reference to claims engaging humanitarian protection and Art 3 ECHR.

16.212

Separate guidance has been issued for the consideration of claims lodged before 28 June 2022 (or considered as such under transitional arrangements)[171] and those lodged on or after 28 June 2022[172] following the implementation of the Nationality and Borders Act 2022.

---

168 Immigration Rules, 339C.

169 Immigration Rules, 339CA.

170 Home Office, *Humanitarian protection in asylum claims lodged on or after 28 June 2022*, v.9.0, updated 1 August 2023.

171 Home Office, *Humanitarian protection in asylum claims lodged before 28 June 2022*, v.6.0 (1 August 2023).

172 *UKVI Guidance, Humanitarian protection in asylum claims lodged on or after 28 June 2022*, v.9.0, (1 August 2023).

Part 3: Human rights claims based on trafficking and modern slavery

16.213

Chapter 1 provides a detailed examination of the legal definitions and conceptual boundaries of *slavery*, *servitude, forced or compulsory labour*, and *human trafficking*, drawing on international instruments and jurisprudence. Chapters 4, 10, and 14 explore the positive obligations arising under Art 4 of the ECHR, including the duty to prevent, investigate, and protect against these forms of exploitation.

16.214

This section of the chapter focuses specifically on the interpretation and application of Art 4 ECHR in the Country Guidance case of *MST and Others (national service – risk categories) Eritrea CG*, analysing how the Upper Tribunal approached the concepts of slavery, servitude, and forced labour in the context of Eritrea's national service programme[173].

Substantive Arts 3 and 4 claims

16.215

The ECtHR has aligned Art 4 with Arts 2 and 3. In *IC v Moldova*[174] the ECtHR held that 'the issues raised … cannot be addressed solely from the perspective of Art 4 of the Convention. This is so because the present case also concerns sexual violence which is alleged to have occurred partly in the context of trafficking, but may not necessarily have been inflicted for the purpose of trafficking and exploitation[175].' An examination of the authorities' approach to complaints about rape and abuse was warranted, separately from allegations concerning potential human trafficking, forced labour or servitude[176]. The Court found a violation of Art 4 (positive obligations) in relation to trafficking and/or servitude, Arts 3 and 8 (in relation to rape and sexual abuse). It also found a violation of Art 14 read in conjunction with Arts 3, 4 and 8 ECHR (due to a difference in treatment as a woman with disabilities, in particular lacking capacity).

16.216

In *Rantsev v Cyprus and Russia*[177] the Court held that the ill-treatment was '*inherently linked to the alleged trafficking and exploitation.*' Consequently, the Court assessed it was not necessary to consider a violation of ECHR, Art 3 separately.

---

173 *MST and Others (national service – risk categories) Eritrea CG* [2016] UKUT 00443 (IAC).
174 *IC v The Republic of Moldova*, App no 36536/22 (ECHR 27 February 2025).
175 *IC v The Republic of Moldova*, App no 36436/22 (ECHR, 27 February 2025), para 92.
176 *Ibid*, para 92.
177 (2010) 51 EHRR 1.

Art 3 ECHR: The absolute prohibition on torture and inhuman or degrading treatment

16.217

Chapter 14 examines in detail Art 3 case law in expulsion cases.

16.218

Art 3 of the ECHR states that 'no one shall be subjected to torture or to inhuman or degrading treatment'. The right not to be tortured or subjected to inhuman or degrading treatment is an unqualified right and can never be balanced or given way to other competing considerations[178].

16.219

The ECtHR has repeatedly held that the benchmark for the necessary level of severity required to prove torture or inhuman and degrading treatment is relative and depends on factors including the duration of the treatment, its physical or mental effects, and the age, sex, vulnerability and state of health of the victim[179]. It could include the risk of reprisals or re-trafficking from the victim of trafficking's former traffickers and/or other forms of exploitation from others.

16.220

The basis of an Art 3 entitlement in a removal case is that the claimant, if sent to the country in question, would be at risk there of Art 3 ill-treatment. A risk of sexual abuse and gang attacks has been held to engage Art 3[180].

16.221

In *Opuz v Turkey*[181] the Court held that the physical injuries and psychological pressure committed by the applicant's husband amounted to ill-treatment within Art 3. In *Giorgi v Italy*[182], threatening behaviour causing fear of repetition of a domestic assault over a long period, including controlling and coercive behaviour, surveillance of movements, harassments and threats to kill engaged Art 3[183]. Concerning children, the Committee on the Rights of the Child defines torture and inhuman or degrading treatment or punishment as 'violence in all its forms against children in order to […] punish children for unlawful or

178 See *MSS v Belgium and Greece* (2011) 53 EHRR 28.
179 For example, see *Soering v UK* (1989) 11 EHRR 439 at 100.
180 *A v Secretary of State for the Home Department* [2003] EWCA Civ 175, [2003] All ER(D) 151 (Jan) at [32].
181 *Opuz v Turkey,* App No 33401/02, 9 June 2009.
182 *Giorgi v Italy,* European Court of Human Rights, Application no. 23735/19, 16 September 2022.
183 Ibid, [62–66].

unwanted behaviours, or to force children to engage in activities against their will'[184]. The threshold for children is lower than for adults.

16.222

The ECHR does not provide a definition of torture, but the acts must be deliberately inflicted and must cause suffering to a high degree of intensity. Severe pain or suffering can be inflicted by physical acts, but also by non-physical acts. There are two types of torture, physical and psychological. Psychological or mental torture includes, for example, threats to kill or torture relatives, being kept in constant uncertainty in terms of space or time and the threat of torture in and of itself can be a form of psychological torture[185]. The ECtHR does not require that these acts be instigated or undertaken by public officials[186]. There is no requirement that the treatment be inflicted to obtain information for a finding of torture[187]. Rape[188] has been recognised as torture. The UN Committee against Torture has also acknowledged that forms of gender-based violence such as rape and trafficking may amount to torture in its analysis of the due diligence duties of States Parties to the UN Convention against Torture in preventing, investigating, prosecuting and punishing such forms of harm[189] and in its examination of State reports with regard to their duties[190].

Art 3 ECHR: Suicide risk and mental health deterioration

16.223

The ECtHR recognised that there were very exceptional cases in which removal of a person suffering from a serious mental or physical illness could give rise to compelling humanitarian considerations that engage the responsibilities of States under Art 3 ECHR[191]. In *Paposhvili v Belgium*, the ECtHR clarified in the context of its evolving approach that 'such other very exceptional cases'

184 UN Committee on the Rights of the Child, CRC General Comment No.13: The right of the child to freedom from all forms of violence, CRC/C/GC/13 (18 April 2011), [26].

185 *Gafgen v Germany* (2011) 52 EHRR 1, para 108; UN Economic and Social Council, Commission on Human Rights, *Report by the Special Rapporteur on torture and other cruel, inhuman or degrading treatment or punishment*, P Koojmans, E/CN.4/1986/15(1986), [.118–119] and C Ingelese, the *UN Committee against Torture – An Assessment* (2001), p 226.

186 *HLR v France* (1997) 26 EHRR 29, [40].

187 *Selmouni v France* (1999) 29 EHRR 403, para 101; *R v Secretary of State for the Home Department, ex p Singh* [1999] INLR 632 at [637].

188 *Aydin v Turkey* (1998) 25 EHRR 251, [80-87].

189 See UN Committee against Torture, Convention against Torture and other Cruel, Inhuman or Degrading Treatment or Punishment, General Comment No.2: Implementation of article 2 by States Parties, CAT/C/GC/2, 24 January 2008.

190 See Manfred Nowak et al (eds) (2019) T*he United Nations Convention against Torture and its Optional Protocol: A Commentary*, 2nd edition, Oxford University Press: Oxford Commentaries on International Law, sections 3.1.6.3 (particularly at 131) and 3.1.2.8.

191 *N v United Kingdom* [2008] 47 EHRR 39, [43].

should be understood to refer to 'situations involving the removal of a seriously ill person in which substantial grounds have been shown for believing that he or she, although not at imminent risk of dying, would face a real risk, on account of the absence of appropriate treatment in the receiving country or the lack of access to such treatment, of being exposed to a serious, rapid and irreversible decline in his or her state of health resulting in intense suffering or to a significant reduction in life expectancy'[192].

16.224

In considering whether the treatment and care available in the country of origin is sufficient and appropriate to prevent any breach of Art 3 ECHR, the returning State must also consider the extent to which the applicant will actually have access to the treatment, including with reference to its cost, the existence of a social and family network, and the distance to be travelled in order to have access to the required care[193].

16.225

The ECtHR in *Paposhvili* also set out procedural obligations on the State for assessing the risks under Art 3 ECHR in such cases. The Supreme Court in *AM (Zimbabwe)*[194] observed that 'it is for the applicant to raise a *'prima facie case'* of potential infringement of Art 3. This means a case, which, if not challenged or countered, would establish the infringement.' Once the applicant has presented evidence to establish a *prima facie* case of infringement it will be for the returning state to counter it in the manner outlined in the *Paposhvili v Belgium* case. If, following examination of the relevant information, serious doubts continued to surround the impact of removal, the returning state had to obtain an individual assurance from the receiving state that appropriate treatment would be available and accessible to the applicant[195]. Further clarification was given by the Upper Tribunal in *AM (Art 3; health cases) Zimbabwe*[196] identifying an intermediary step[197] by which the SSHD may provide evidence to dispel 'any serious doubts' about the appellant's evidence and, if it does, the obligation to seek assurances will not arise.

16.226

In *Savran v Denmark*[198], the ECtHR Grand Chamber confirmed that the threshold test described in *Paposhvili* also applied to people with mental illness[199],

192 *Paposhvili v Belgium* [2017] Imm AR 867, [183].
193 *Paposhvili v Belgium*, para 190.
194 *AM (Zimbabwe) v Secretary of State for the Home Department* [2021] AC 633.
195 Ibid, [191].
196 [2022] UKUT 00131 (IAC), [16-29].
197 Applying *Savran v Denmark* [2022] Imm.A.R. 485, [130 (b)-(d)].
198 [2022] Imm.A.R. 485.
199 Para 137.

and was sufficiently flexible to be applied in all situations involving the removal of a seriously ill person[200].

16.227

The UK courts have considered claims where mental health conditions may give rise a real risk of suicide on return to the country of origin. In *J v Secretary of State for the Home Department*[201], the Court of Appeal found that Art 3 may be breached if there is a real risk of committing suicide as a foreseeable consequence of the decision to remove, whether on being informed of the removal direction, during removal or after arrival in the country of origin. The court drew a distinction between 'domestic cases' and 'foreign cases'. The risk of suicide on being informed of an adverse immigration decision and in the course of being removed from the UK (both of which are 'domestic cases'), the tribunal would be entitled to assume that the UK authorities would take all reasonable steps in accordance with its obligations under the Human Rights Act 1998 to protect the individual from self-harm, including by the practice of arranging escorts to accompany the person on removal. A real risk that the person would commit suicide after arrival in the receiving State might not be sufficient to establish an Art 3 breach, because what happens to the person on and after arrival is treated as a 'foreign case' (ie one in which the alleged violation takes place outside of the jurisdiction of the sending State), making the Art 3 threshold particularly high. An issue of considerable relevance in this context is whether the removing and the receiving states have effective mechanisms for reducing the suicide risk and whether those mechanisms are accessible to the individual.

16.228

In *Y (Sri Lanka) v Secretary of State for the Home Department*[202], the Court of Appeal held that the removal of a brother and sister to Sri Lanka would breach Art 3. This was in circumstances where they had both been tortured and the sister raped, where they subjectively feared similar treatment if returned, notwithstanding that their fear was not objectively well-founded, and where they would have no family or other social support, created such a likelihood that they would commit suicide in order to escape isolation and fear.

16.229

The Court of Appeal confirmed in *RA (Sri Lanka) v Secretary of State for the Home Department* that cases giving rise to the increased risk of suicide are analogous to cases of physical illness for the purposes of the application of Art 3 ECHR[203]. In *AXB (Art 3 health: obligations; suicide) Jamaica*[204], the Upper

200 Para 139.
201 [2005] EWCA Civ 629, [2005] Imm AR 409.
202 [2009] EWCA Civ 362, [2009] HRLR 22.
203 [2008] EWCA Civ 1210, [49].
204 [2019] UKUT 00397 (IAC).

Tribunal explained that the factors in *J* are merely an expression of how that exceptional circumstances test within the Strasbourg caselaw should be applied. A similar approach has been taken since *Paposhvili* and its consideration by the UK Supreme Court in *AM (Zimbabwe)*. The Upper Tribunal in *MY (Suicide risk after Paposhvili)*[205] concluded that *Paposhvili* applied to cases involving risk of suicide[206] and that the factors in J do not impose any test or burden on an applicant but are simply guidance on how to deal with subjective fear when considering mental health cases following *Paposhvili*[207]. In *MY's* individual case the appeal was allowed on Art 3 grounds.

16.230

The threshold of severity required to come within the scope of the prohibition of Art 3 ECHR for children, is lower, having regard to all the circumstances of the case, including importantly, the child's needs, best interest, 'extreme vulnerability', and to ensure that conditions do not 'create… for them a situation of stress and anxiety, with particularly traumatic consequences[208].'

Art 4: MST and Others (national service – risk categories) Eritrea CG[209]

16.231

The analysis below should be read in conjunction with **Chapters 1** (*Legal Definitions*) and **18** (*Prosecuting and Defending in the ICC*). This section focuses exclusively on the legal reasoning adopted by the Upper Tribunal in *MST* and does not engage with the specific factual matrix or evidential material considered in that case[210]. The following issues are addressed[211]:

- The Upper Tribunal's interpretation of slavery;
- The Upper Tribunal's interpretation of servitude,
- The Tribunal's approach to threshold distinctions between harms under Art 4(1) (slavery and servitude) and those arising under Art 4(2), read with Art 4(3) (forced or compulsory labour).

205 [2021] UKUT 00232 (IAC).

206 A finding the Tribunal indicated (para 118) was also supported by the individual chamber decision in *Savran v Denmark* (application 57467/15) (ECHR), the Grand Chamber decision then being awaited, and the decision of Sir Duncan Ouseley in *R (Carlos) v Secretary of State for the Home Department* [2021] EWHC 986 (Admin).

207 *MY (Suicide risk after Paposhvili)* [2021] UKUT 232, para 123.

208 *Tarakhel v Switzerland*, App no 29217/12, Grand Chamber judgment, 4 November 2014, paras 118–119.

209 [2016] UKUT 00443 (IAC).

210 *MST and Others (National Service – Risk Categories) Eritrea CG* [2016] UKUT 00443 (IAC).

211 See academic analysis: Sara Arapiles, 'Slave Soldiers and their Protection under International Refugee Law' (Refugee Law Initiative Blog, 18 June 2025) <https://rli.blogs.sas.ac.uk/2025/06/18/slave-soldiers-and-their-protection-under-international-refugee-law/> accessed 20 October 2025.

16.232

It is important to note that this was the first occasion on which the Upper Tribunal was called upon to consider the concept of *slavery de facto* in any depth. The issue has not yet been substantively addressed by the senior domestic courts and has only received cursory treatment within the jurisprudence of the ECtHR. The emphasis throughout this section remains on the legal framework and analytical approach adopted by the Tribunal in relation to these concepts, recognising the complexity and evolving nature of the legal landscape in this area.

Slavery de jure

16.233

The Upper Tribunal in *MST* considered whether the obligation to perform military or national service in Eritrea amounted to slavery *de jure,* that is, the legal ownership of a person capable of recognition before a court of law. The Tribunal concluded that it did not, as there was no exercise by the Eritrean state of a genuine right of legal ownership over conscripts. This conclusion is unsurprising, given that slavery is a *jus cogens* norm, peremptory in nature, operating *erga omnes* (owed to all), and is universally prohibited under international law.

Slavery de facto and the tribunal's conflation

16.234

The Tribunal's analysis of slavery *de facto,* the exercise of powers attaching to ownership in practice, raises a conceptual difficulty. The Tribunal appeared to conflate the legal test for establishing slavery under Art 4(1) of the ECHR with the threshold required to establish a crime against humanity under Art 7(1) of the Rome Statute. Specifically, it held that for slavery to be established in the context of an international protection claim, the appellants must show both: (i) a real risk of being subjected to slavery upon return; and (ii) that slavery in Eritrea is part of a 'widespread or systematic attack directed against any civilian population.'

16.235

This approach conflates two distinct legal standards. The first relates to the risk of a rights violation under the ECHR, which requires only a real risk to the individual. The second pertains to international criminal law, where the classification of an act as a crime against humanity requires proof of its widespread or systematic nature. These thresholds serve different purposes and should not be merged. For example, torture is a violation of Art 3 ECHR if an individual faces a real risk of being tortured, regardless of whether torture is widespread or systematic in the country of return. However, it will only constitute a crime against humanity triable before the International Criminal Court if it was part of a widespread systematic attack in the terms identified in the preceding paragraph. The same principle applies to slavery under Art 4.

16.236

The central point is this, both the ECtHR (under Art 4(1)) and the ICC (under Art 7(2)) adopt the definition of slavery in international law; Art 1 of the 1926 Slavery Convention: 'the status or condition of a person over whom any or all of the powers attaching to the right of ownership are exercised.' This definition does not require that slavery be shown to be widespread or systematic. This position is supported by domestic and international jurisprudence, including *Queen v Tang*[212] (High Court of Australia) and *Basfar v Wong*[213] (UK Supreme Court), and this is reflected in the domestic offence of slavery under section 1 of the Modern Slavery Act 2015, as now confirmed by the Court of Appeal in *R v Webb-Johnson*[214].

16.237

In summary, the Tribunal's requirement that slavery must meet the crime against humanity threshold to be established for the purposes of Art 4 ECHR protection claims imposes an unduly high and legally incorrect burden. The two concepts, individual risk of slavery and classification of slavery as a crime against humanity, must be kept analytically distinct.

Establishing slavery crimes: legal focus and evidentiary thresholds

16.238

As examined in **Chapters 1** and **18**, in assessing slavery crimes, the legal focus lies squarely on the mental state and conduct, acts or omissions, of the perpetrator, rather than on the consent, mental state, reactions, or actions of the victim or survivor. Crucially, slavery or enslavement does not require the presence of force, threat, compulsion, or lack of volition, although such elements may frequently accompany the offence[215].

16.239

Similarly, the existence of work, labour, sexual violence, reproductive harm, or other forms of exploitation or physical or psychological injury are not required

---

212 [2008] HCA 39 (Australia).
213 [2022] UKSC 20, [2023] AC 33.
214 [2025] EWCA Crim 1084.
215 Office of the Prosecutor, *Policy on Slavery Crime* (International Criminal Court, December 2024).

to establish the crime of slavery, though they may often be present. A person may be well-fed, clothed, and housed, and yet still be enslaved[216].

16.240

While the above factors may serve as *indicia* of slavery, the defining feature of the offence is the domination of one person's life by another to the point that the victim is deprived of real personal autonomy. This level of control, enabled by coercion, threats, or a broader coercive environment, captures what contemporary law understands as the essence of slavery, irrespective of the victim's circumstances or any apparent acquiescence.

Servitude: The tribunal's analysis and conceptual oversight

16.241

In paragraph [405] of its decision in *MST*, the Upper Tribunal considered whether the Eritrean system of military and national service amounted to servitude under Art 4(1) of the ECHR. While acknowledging the system's oppressive features, the Tribunal concluded that it did not resemble the paradigm of servitude identified by the European Court of Human Rights in *Siliadin v France,* namely, 'the obligation for the 'serf' to live on another person's property and the impossibility of altering his condition.' The Tribunal emphasised that, even for those subjected to lengthy service, individuals could not sensibly be described as compelled to live permanently on government property. It further noted that, although opportunities for exemption or *de facto* demobilisation were limited, it could not be said that there was an impossibility of altering one's condition.

16.242

However, this analysis arguably overlooks a key dimension of servitude recognised in ECtHR and ICC jurisprudence: the victim's perception of their condition. Servitude, as defined in Art 1(b) of the 1956 Supplementary Convention, and interpreted in *Siliadin*[217], encompasses not only physical constraints but also psychological coercion; but the individual's belief that their situation is permanent and inescapable. The ECtHR has consistently recognised that servitude involves a particularly grave denial of liberty, which may not manifest as physical confinement but nonetheless deprives the individual of autonomy.

216 Ibid. The Policy at [62], referring to *United States of America v Oswald Pohl* et al, Judgment, International Military Tribunal, 3 November 1947 at [15].

217 *Siliadin v France* (2005) 43 EHRR 287.

16.243

In *Siliadin*, the applicant, a minor without legal status, was found to be in servitude due to her complete dependency, lack of pay, inability to leave, and fear of arrest. The Court held that her belief that her condition was unchangeable was central to the finding of servitude. Similarly, in *FM v Russia*, the exploitation of women over extended periods in retail settings was found to constitute servitude, despite the absence of overt physical restraint.

16.244

The Tribunal's analysis in *MST* did not engage with this core subjective dimension, namely, whether individuals perceive their condition as indeterminate and incapable of change. This omission is significant, as it risks underestimating the psychological and coercive dynamics that underpin modern forms of servitude.

Delimitations under Art 4 ECHR

16.245

Art 4(2), which states that 'no one shall be required to perform forced or compulsory labour,' must be read together with Art 4(3). The latter does not 'limit' the exercise of the right, but rather 'delimits' the very content of forced or compulsory labour.

16.246

As clarified by the Grand Chamber in *Stummer v Austria*[218], Art 4(3) specifies what is not to be regarded as 'forced or compulsory labour,' this includes:

> 'Art 4(3)(b) is any service of a military character or, in case of conscientious objectors in countries where they are recognised, service exacted instead of compulsory military service.'

Delimiting the right against forced labour: Art 4(3) ECHR and ILO Convention No 29

16.247

The relationship between Art 4(3) of the ECHR and its origins in the International Labour Organisation (ILO) Forced Labour Convention, 1930 (No. 29) reflects a deliberate legal architecture in which historical reasoning informs the substantive delimitation of rights. Art 4(3) does not merely carve

218 *Stummer v Austria* (2011) 54 EHRR 11 at [120].

out exceptions to the prohibition of forced or compulsory labour; rather, it defines the outer boundaries of what does not fall within the scope of the protected right.

16.248

This interpretive approach was first articulated in *W, X, Y. and Z v the United Kingdom*[219], where the European Commission of Human Rights recognised that the exclusions listed in Art 4(3) ECHR were drawn directly from Art 2(2) of the ILO Convention. The Commission emphasised that these exclusions must be narrowly construed and assessed considering the specific character and voluntariness of the service in question.

16.249

The ILO's foundational framework thus provides both the historical context and the normative basis for delimiting the right not to be subjected to compulsory military labour. It ensures that only those forms of labour strictly contemplated by the drafters, such as military service of a purely military character or emergency service in exceptional circumstances, are excluded from protection. All other forms of labour, particularly those involving coercion, indefinite duration, or economic exploitation, remain subject to judicial scrutiny for potential violations of the right.

The ECtHR's approach in Chitos v Greece: Art 4(2) and the scope of Art 4(3)(b)

16.250

In *Chitos v Greece*[220], the ECtHR found a violation of Art 4(2) of the Convention, without needing to rely on the delimitation provided in Art 4(3). The Court clarified that sub-paragraph 3 is not intended to limit the exercise of the right guaranteed by sub-paragraph 2, but rather to define its scope. Arts 4(2) and (3) form a unified provision, with sub-paragraph (3)(b) indicating what is not considered forced or compulsory labour.

16.251

Sub-paragraph (3)(b) excludes from the scope of Art 4(2) 'any service of a military character or, in the case of conscientious objectors in countries where they are recognised, service exacted instead of compulsory military service.' The Court interpreted this provision strictly, in line with the principle that exceptions to fundamental rights must be narrowly construed. It held that the

219 (nos 3435/67 and others, Commission decision of 19 July 1968, Collection 28).
220 App no 51637/12, Judgment 4 June 2015.

reference to conscientious objectors and compulsory military service clearly indicates that the exception applies only to conscripts, not to professional or career military personnel.

16.252

This interpretation was reinforced by reference to Art 2(2)(a) of ILO Convention No. 29, which similarly excludes 'work or service exacted in virtue of compulsory military service laws for work of a purely military character.' The Court also drew support from the European Committee of Social Rights and Recommendation CM/Rec (2010)4 of the Committee of Ministers, both of which emphasise that excessive service obligations imposed on regular armed forces personnel may amount to forced labour.

Disproportionate burden and voluntariness

16.253

The Court's analysis began by asking whether the applicant had 'offered himself voluntarily' for the work in question, with full knowledge of its consequences, and whether his decision to leave early was affected by 'the menace of a penalty.' The key issue was whether the applicant had been subjected to a disproportionate burden, which could render the service involuntary and thus fall within the scope of Art 4(2).

16.254

In *Chitos*, the applicant, a career army officer, was required to pay a substantial sum to the State in order to resign before completing his contracted service period While the Court accepted that it was legitimate for States to require obligatory service periods and compensation for early resignation, particularly to recover the costs of military education, it found that the burden imposed on the applicant was disproportionate in the specific circumstances of the case. Accordingly, it held that the obligation constituted forced labour within the meaning of Art 4(2).

16.255

This reasoning aligns with the Court's earlier decision in *Van der Mussele*, where it held that a service required to access a profession may amount to forced labour if the burden imposed is excessive relative to the advantages of entering that profession. In *Chitos*, the Court assessed the situation at the time the applicant sought to resign, rather than when he entered military service, and found that the amended legislative framework imposed an unreasonable obligation.

Delimitation and the absolute nature of Art 4 ECHR

16.256

The ECtHR has consistently affirmed that certain rights under the Convention are absolute, most notably Art 3, which prohibits torture and inhuman or degrading treatment or punishment. As stated in *Ireland v United Kingdom*[221], the Convention prohibits such treatment 'in absolute terms.' This principle has been reiterated in *Chahal v United Kingdom*[222] and *Al-Adsani v United Kingdom*[223].

16.257

While Art 4 ECHR is structurally different, the ECtHR has clarified that paragraph 3 does not limit the right in paragraph 2 but rather delimits its content. As held in *Van der Mussele v Belgium* and reaffirmed in *Zarb Adami v Malta*[224], the exclusions in Article 4(3) are not derogations but interpretative aids. They define what does not constitute 'forced or compulsory labour,' grounded in principles of general interest, social solidarity, and normal civic obligations.

16.258

This distinction is critical. If a form of labour does not fall within the scope of the exclusions in Art 4(3), then it is not excluded from the protection of Art 4(2). In such cases, the right not to be subjected to forced or compulsory labour becomes absolute, and the threshold for its engagement should be aligned with that of Art 4(1), which prohibits slavery and servitude without qualification.

16.259

As Lord Bingham observed in *R (Ullah) v Special Adjudicator*[225], it would be contrary to the spirit of a human rights convention to deny protection under Art 4 simply because Art 3 might also be engaged. The Convention must be interpreted to give effect to each right independently, and not to subordinate one to another. The ECtHR's decision in *Soering v United Kingdom*[226], although concerning extradition, established that returning an individual to face treatment contrary to fundamental rights would violate the Convention's core values. This principle applies equally to expulsion and asylum cases, as confirmed in *Chahal*.

16.260

Therefore, where the delimitation in Art 4(3) do not apply, the protection under Art 4(2) must be treated as absolute, and the threshold for engagement should

221 (1978) 2 EHRR 25 at [163].
222 (1996) 23 EHRR 413 at [96].
223 (2001) 34 EHRR 11 at [59].
224 (2006) ECHR 2006-VIII at [44].
225 [2004] UKHL 26 at [41].
226 (1989) 11 EHRR 439.

reflect the seriousness of the harm, akin to the standard applied under Art 4(1). This ensures consistency in the Convention's protective framework and avoids the dilution of rights through artificial thresholds or misplaced reliance on alternative provisions.

Conscription and forced labour under international law: legal delimitations and Eritrea's national service system

16.261

Under international labour law, the right not to be subjected to forced or compulsory labour is a fundamental protection, and any permissible limitations must be narrowly and precisely delimited. Art 2(2)(a) of the ILO Forced Labour Convention No. 29 (1930) provides that compulsory military service may fall outside the scope of forced labour only when it involves work of a *purely military character*. This delimitation is strictly construed. The ILO has consistently affirmed that this provision does not extend to conscripted civilians performing non-military tasks, nor does it permit the use of conscription as a disguised method of labour mobilisation for public works or economic development.

16.262

The ILO's 2012 General Survey [280] further clarifies that work imposed under the guise of emergency service must be genuinely exceptional, sudden, and unforeseen, with strict limitations on its duration, scope, and purpose. Similarly, the Inter-American Commission on Human Rights (IACHR) has emphasised that conscription must be prescribed by law, implemented in a non-arbitrary and non-discriminatory manner, and subject to judicial oversight (see *Fourth Report on the Situation of Human Rights in Guatemala*, 1993; *Piché Cuca v Guatemala*, 1993).

16.263

The ILO Committee of Experts has repeatedly raised concerns about Eritrea's system of compulsory national service, particularly its indefinite duration and the inclusion of both military and civilian components. In its 2025 observation (CEACR)[227], the Committee noted that while conscripts engaged in purely military service are excluded from collective bargaining rights, those assigned to state-owned enterprises are said to enjoy bargaining rights equivalent to other workers. However, for conscripts performing civil service roles, the Committee observed that the 2015 Civil Code imposes restrictions on collective bargaining, effectively depriving most national service participants of this right.

227 International Labour Organisation (ILO), *Observation (CEACR) – adopted 2024, published 113rd ILC session (2025), Right to Organise and Collective Bargaining Convention, 1949 (No. 98) – Eritrea (Ratification: 2000).*

16.264

The Committee recalled that the right to collective bargaining must be upheld beyond the narrowly delimited circumstances set out in Arts 5 and 6 of the Right to Organise and Collective Bargaining Convention, 1949 (No. 98). It expressed concern that the Government's response merely reiterated previous positions, without addressing the substantive issue. Referring to the 2024 report of the UN Special Rapporteur on the Situation of Human Rights in Eritrea (A/HRC/56/24), the Committee highlighted that the indefinite nature of national service, unchanged since the 1998 state of emergency, continues to undermine the right to organise and bargain collectively.

16.265

In parallel, the Committee[228] has long maintained that Eritrea's national service system exceeds the permissible delimitation of compulsory labour under Convention No. 29. Governed by Proclamation No 82/1995, the system includes not only military duties but also development tasks aimed at economic reconstruction. These include work in agriculture, construction, mining, education, and administration, often for indefinite periods and under coercive conditions. The Committee has emphasised that such use of conscripted labour violates Art 1(b) of the Abolition of Forced Labour Convention, 1957 (No 105), which prohibits the use of compulsory labour 'as a method of mobilising and using labour for purposes of economic development.'

16.266

Despite the 2018 peace agreement with Ethiopia, the Committee noted that Eritrea has not undertaken meaningful reforms or demobilisation. Instead, conscripts continue to be subjected to forced labour, minimal pay, and no choice in profession or work location. Draft evaders and deserters face punitive detention and, in many cases, torture or inhuman treatment (A/HRC/50/20).

16.267

While acknowledging Eritrea's stated security concerns, the Committee reiterated that any compulsory labour must be strictly limited to military service or emergency situations, with conditions and duration proportionate to the exigencies. It urged the Government to reform the national service programme to ensure that civil service functions are undertaken voluntarily and that the work imposed aligns with the narrowly delimited circumstances permitted under the Conventions.

---

228 International Labour Organisation (ILO), *Observation (CEACR) – adopted 2021, published 110th ILC session (2022), Forced Labour Convention, 1930 (No. 29) – Eritrea (Ratification: 2000)*; International Labour Organisation (ILO), *Observation (CEACR) – adopted 2022, published 111st ILC session (2023), Forced Labour Convention, 1930 (No. 29) – Eritrea (Ratification: 2000).*

Art 8 ECHR: The right to private and family life in removal cases

16.268

Art 8 of the ECHR provides a right to respect for one's 'private and family life, his home and his correspondence', subject to certain restrictions that are 'in accordance with law' and 'necessary in a democratic society'. Accordingly, the victim of trafficking's private life will need to be balanced against the interests of immigration control in considering whether his removal would breach their Art 8 rights.

16.269

On 13 June 2012, the Secretary of State laid amendments to the immigration rules, which came into force on 9 July 2012. These were intended to define the ambit of ECHR, Art 8. The provisions setting out the circumstances in which the Secretary of State will grant leave to remain in the UK on the ground of private life are now set out in Appendix Private Life[229]. This contains the provision that 'where the applicant is aged 18 or over on the date of application [...] and where the applicant has not been continuously resident in the UK for more than 20 years, the decision maker must be satisfied that there would be very significant obstacles to the applicant's integration into the country where they would have to live if required to leave the UK'[230].

16.270

Home Office guidance to its caseworkers on the provision[231] states that: 'A 'very significant obstacle to integration' means something which would prevent or seriously inhibit the applicant from integrating into the country of return'. Decision makers are required to consider 'all relevant factors in the person's background and the conditions they are likely to face in the country of return'. The guidance states they must also consider obstacles raised by the applicant and further that: 'These obstacles will need to be assessed individually as well as cumulatively. While individual factors may be insufficient alone, several factors considered together 'in the round' may create a very significant obstacle to integration outside the UK.' The guidance notes that decision makers should consider whether the applicant has the ability to form an adequate life by the standards of the country of return and not by UK standards.

16.271

There are clear reasons why there may be very significant obstacles to a victim of trafficking integrating into the country of origin, even if they were not

229 For applications made on or after 20 June 2022. Applications made prior to that date, are governed by para 276 ADE.

230 Immigration Rules, Appendix Private Life, PL5.1.

231 Home Office, *Private life: caseworker guidance*, v.4.0 (6 May 2025).

at risk. These include, but are not limited to, their physical or mental health, the stigma and discrimination they may suffer from their family members, community or wider society. An individual found to be at risk on return is also likely to succeed on human rights grounds, where the determination of whether there are 'significant obstacles to removal' depends on the same or similar facts relied upon to show that internal flight would be 'unduly harsh'[232]. If the criteria under the Immigration Rules are met then an appeal under Art 8 ECHR should succeed on that basis: *TZ (Pakistan) and PG (India) v Secretary of State for the Home Department*[233].

16.272

In any event, it is now clear that whilst the Immigration Rules are a 'relevant and important' consideration which decision-makers are required to take into account in assessing proportionality, they are not a complete code that defines the ambit of the ECHR, Art 8[234]. The Immigration Rules and ECHR, Art 8 are not coterminous. Cases can succeed outside the Immigration Rules under Art 8 even when they fail under the Immigration Rules[235]. In doing so, the public interest in meeting the rules may be a relevant factor in relation to the maintenance of immigration control for the purpose of the balancing exercise under Art 8(2) but not determinative[236].

16.273

The Secretary of State introduced statutory Art 8 public interest considerations, which apply and must be considered in all cases where a court or tribunal is required to determine whether a decision made under the Immigration Acts breaches a person's rights under Art 8[237]. These include provisions stating that it is in the public interest for effective immigration controls to be maintained[238], for persons seeking to enter or remain in the UK to speak English[239], are financially independent[240], and that little weight should be given to a private life established in the UK by a person at a time when the person's immigration status is precarious[241].

---

232 *TD and AD (Trafficked women) (CG)* [2016] UKUT 92 (IAC), [126]. The UT observing that whilst the legal tests are not to be equated, on the facts of the case the outcome may be the same.

233 [2018] EWCA Civ 1109, [2018] Imm AR 1301.

234 *Hesham Ali v Secretary of State for the Home Department* [2016] UKSC 60.

235 *MM v Secretary of State for the Home Department* [2017] UKSC 10.

236 *Hesham Ali v Secretary of State for the Home Department* [2016] UKSC 60; *R (Agyarko) v Secretary of State for the Home Department* [2017] UKSC 11.

237 Nationality, Immigration and Asylum Act 2002, ss 117A and 117B, which are found in Part 5A, headed 'Art 8 ECHR: Public Interest Considerations'.

238 Nationality, Immigration and Asylum Act 2002, s 117B(1).

239 Ibid, s 117B(2).

240 Ibid, s 117B(4).

241 Ibid, s 117B(5).

16.274

This provision can have an impact on victims of trafficking. However, the public interest considerations detailed in the Nationality, Immigration and Asylum Act 2002 are not exhaustive[242]. Consideration of the public interest factors within the context of Art 8 does afford decision-makers a degree of flexibility, even if private life was established when the applicant's status was precarious or other factors apply, to ensure that an end result is reached that is consistent with Art 8[243]. A victim of trafficking's Art 8 claim may be prefaced on the need to rehabilitate from his trafficking experience or premised on the support network they have developed in the UK as a part of that process and considered together with any other factors including obstacles to integration in the country of origin. Both in criminal and employment claims the Supreme Court and the Criminal Court of Appeal (presided over by the Lord Chief Justice) have considered public interest in favour of victims in the context of trafficking[244].

16.275

In the case of children, the best interests of the child are an integral part of the proportionality assessment under Art 8 ECHR and must be a primary consideration[245]. A careful and orderly examination of all relevant factors is required to avoid the risk of undervaluing the best interests of a child in an Art 8 ECHR assessment.

16.276

Art 8 ECHR includes substantive and procedural guarantees to victims of trafficking in the context of applications for leave to remain, and recovery from exploitation[246].

Art 8 ECHR: mental health

16.277

While deterioration in mental health may in principle breach Art 8 ECHR where the threshold in Art 3 is not reached[247], the UK courts have not found

242 *Forman (ss 117A-C considerations)* [2015] UKUT 00412 (IAC).

243 *R (Rhuppiah) v Secretary of State for the Home Department* [2018] UKSC 58 at [36, 49]; *GM (Sri Lanka) v Secretary of State for the Home Department* [2019] EWCA Civ 1630, at [28].

244 In *Hounga v Allen* [2014] UKSC 47 Lord Wilson (with whom the majority agreed) found that the Court of Appeal's decision to uphold a defence of illegality to a complaint by an employee that an employer had discrimination against her ran *'counter to the prominent strain of current public policy against trafficking and in favour of its victims'* and allowed the employee's appeal at 52. In *R v L* [2013] EWCA Crim 991, [2014] 1 All ER 113 at [13], the public interest to prosecute must be considered against the culpability of the appellant, whose criminality may be effectively extinguished or significantly reduced because the criminality was a manifestation of the trafficking of the appellant.

245 *Zoumbas v Secretary of State for the Home Department* [2013] UKSC 74 at [10(4)].

246 *XY v Secretary of State for the Home Department* [2024] EWHC 81 (Admin), [6-97].

247 *Bensaid v United Kingdom* [2001] 33 EHRR 10; *R (Razgar) v Home Secretary* [2004] 2 AC 368.

such a breach in any such health case. In *MM (Zimbabwe)*[248], the court considered that the absence of adequate medical treatment in the country to which a person is to be removed is likely to be relevant to Art 8 ECHR where it is an additional factor weighed in the balance, with other factors which by themselves engage Art 8 ECHR. Issues of trauma, mental illness, access to treatment and care, stigma and discrimination are also likely to be relevant to consideration of Art 8 ECHR, both as very significant obstacles to integration within the immigration rules and the right to private life considered more broadly (see further above).

16.278

Where children are concerned there must be a proper consideration of the child's '*medical conditions and treatment in the context of his best interests*'[249].

Art 6 ECHR

16.279

As examined in **Chapter 4**, State failures to identify victims of trafficking or modern slavery may undermine the fairness of criminal proceedings[250]. Though Art 6 ECHR is inapplicable in immigration cases, the requirements of fairness applies through the Art 4 procedural obligation of an effective judicial mechanism capable of elucidating the circumstances and sequence of events that are said to have led to the alleged harm and Art 8 ECHR[251].

Art 14 ECHR

16.280

Art 14 ECHR the prohibition of discrimination provides:

> 'The enjoyment of the rights and freedoms set forth in [the] Convention shall be secured without discrimination on any ground such as sex, race, colour, language, religion, political or other opinion, national or social origin, association with a national minority, property, birth or other status.'

248 [2012] EWCA Civ 279, *per* Moses, LJ with whom McFarlane LJ and the Master of the Rolls agreed, [22-23].

249 *R (SQ (Pakistan) & Anor) v The Upper Tribunal Immigration and Asylum Chamber & Anor* [2013] EWCA Civ 1251 at [20 and 23].

250 *VCL and AN v United Kingdom (2021)* 73 EHRR 9, [196, 199-201].

251 *Gudanaviciene & Ors, R (on the application of) v The Director of Legal Aid Casework & Or* [2014] EWCA Civ 1622 para 69 'The fact that immigration decisions do not involve the determination of civil rights means that Art 6(1) cannot be invoked in relation to such decisions. But it does not follow that the procedural obligations of Art 8 do not apply to immigration decisions.'

16.281

Art 14 of the Convention enshrines the right not to be discriminated against in 'the enjoyment of the rights and freedoms set out in the Convention'. This means that Art 14 must be read in conjunction with another substantive provision of the Convention, ie it has an ancillary nature. It does not however require a violation of another substantive right[252].

16.282

A detailed discussion of the equality law is beyond the scope of this chapter. The following outlines key concepts and their application in the trafficking, asylum and immigration context.

Characteristics and 'other status'

16.283

Art 14 does not prohibit all differences in treatment but only those based on an identifiable, objective or personal characteristic, or 'status' distinguishing a person or group from another[253]. In addition to grounds expressed in Art 14, 'other status' has been found to include refugee status (*Hode and Abdi v the United Kingdom*[254]) or subsidiary protection status (*MT & Others v Sweden*[255]).

The rubric of Art 14 ECHR

16.284

There is a well established rubric for the application of Art 14 ECHR:

(1) the treatment falls within the ambit of a Convention right;

(2) there is discrimination based on a recognised ground or other status;

(3) those with the relevant status are treated differently from those without it;

(4) the question is whether the state can discharge the burden it bears to justify the proportionality of the difference in treatment[256].

252 *Marckz v Belgium, App no 6833/74, judgment 13 June 1979; Nachova & Ors v Bulgaria* [GC], Apps. No.43577/98 and 43579/98, judgment 6 July 2005.

253 *Kiyutin v Russia,* App no 2700/10, judgment 10 March 2011, [56].

254 *Hode and Abdi v United Kingdom* (2013) 56 EHRR 27.

255 *MT and others v Sweden* (2023) 76 EHRR 29, [111, 117].

256 *R (TP, AR & SXC) v Secretary of State for Work and Pensions* [2020] EWCA Civ 37, para 187, *In re Brewster* [2017] 1 WLR 519, para 66, *Re McLaughlin* [2018] UKSC 48, [15], JP, *R (On the Application Of) v Secretary of State for the Home Department* [2019] EWHC 3346 (Admin), [145], *Secretary of State for the Home Department v S* [2025] EWCA Civ 18, *Langford v Secretary of State for Defence* [2020] 1 WLR 537.

16.285

There are a number of cases which have held that the government failed to discharge that burden, because it did not produce evidence to prove the discrimination was justified[257]. For example, an immigration rule was not justified where there was no evidence before the original decision maker or the court to show that it achieved its stated purpose, the deterrence of forced marriage[258]. See further, *JP*, below in the trafficking context.

Art 14 and trafficking and modern slavery cases

16.286

In *IC v The Republic of Moldova,* the applicant was a woman with intellectual disabilities, and a victim of human trafficking and sexual abuse at the hands of the family with which she was placed following her release (deinstitutionalisation) from a State-run asylum. The ECtHR held that the authorities failed to assess and give weight to her vulnerability due to her gender, intellectual disability and lifelong institutionalisation[259]. The domestic courts also used inappropriate stereotypes which discounted the severity of her treatment. There was a general institutional passivity and/or lack of awareness of the phenomenon of violence against women with disabilities in Moldova. Moreover, the Court considered that the domestic authorities failed to make reasonable adjustments or accommodation to enable access to justice. It concluded to a violation of Art 14 taken together with Arts 3, 4 and 8[260].

16.287

In *B.S. v. Spain*[261], a female sex worker of Nigerian origin and legally resident in Spain alleged that the Spanish police abused her physically and verbally on the basis of her race, gender and on the basis that she was a sex worker. The Court considered that the decisions made by the domestic courts failed to take account of the applicant's particular vulnerability inherent in her position as an African woman working as a sex worker (para 62) and found a violation of Art 14 in conjunction with Art 3.

257 Eg Re. Brewster [2017] UKSC 8; [2017] 1 WLR 519, para 62; *R (TP) v Secretary of State for Work and Pensions* [2020] EWCA Civ 37; [2020] PTSR 1785; *Bayev v Russia* (2018) 66 EHRR 10, para 78; *Re A (Children)(Contact: Ultra-Orthodox Judaism: Transgender Parent)* [2017] EWCA Civ 2164; [2018] 4 WLR 60, para 109; *Langford v Secretary of State for Defence* [2019] EWCA Civ 1271; [2020] 1 WLR 537.

258 *R (Quila) v Secretary of State for the Home Department* [2011] UKSC 45; [2012] 1 AC 621 [50, 58].

259 *IC v the Republic of Moldova* App no 36436/22 (ECHR, 27 February 2025), [217].

260 *IC v the Republic of Moldova* App no 36436/22 (ECHR, 27 February 2025), [221-223].

261 *BS v Spain* App no 47159/08 (ECHR, 24 July 2012).

16.288

In *FM v Russia*[262] the Court found a violation of Art 14 taken in conjunction with Art 4 ECHR. In its reasoning the Court set out a number of general principles governing the application of Art 14 and made factual and legal findings under Art 4 said to be 'equally pertinent to the assessment under Art 14'. The Court concluded that the inaction of the authorities in relation to positive obligations under Art 4 'amounted to repeatedly condoning trafficking, labour exploitation and related gender-based violence and reflected a discriminatory attitude towards the applicants as women who were foreign workers with an irregular immigration status. The respondent State authorities' general and discriminatory passivity created a climate that was conducive to their trafficking and exploitation.'

16.289

This is an important case on intersectional discrimination, which took account of other international instruments on the discrimination of victims of trafficking. This included the updated legislative guide on the Palermo Protocol, published by the UNODC in 2020[263], and its provisions on discrimination, ie:

> '63. The link between discrimination and trafficking lies in the fact that measures taken by States to prevent and suppress trafficking can perpetuate discrimination or violate the prohibition against discrimination. This is particularly acute in cases involving non-nationals and in the context of gender-based discrimination. Even if they are outside their country of residence, international law is clear that victims of trafficking in persons cannot be discriminated against simply because they are non-nationals …
>
> '65. It is widely accepted that the principle of non-discrimination extends to indirect discrimination, where a practice or requirement is neutral on the face but impacts disproportionately upon particular groups.'

16.290

The Court also had regard to the CEDAW Committee affirmed in its General Recommendation No. 38 (2020) on trafficking in women and girls in the context of global migration[264]. This recognises 'the gender-specific nature of

---

262 *FM v Russia,* [2024] 58 BHRC 384, para 182.

263 United Nations Office on Drugs and Crime, Legislative Guide for the Protocol to Prevent, Suppress and Punish Trafficking in Persons, Especially Women and Children, Vienna, 2020 at https://www.unodc.org/unodc/en/treaties/CTOC/legislative-guide.html [accessed 12 October 2025].

264 UN Committee on the Elimination of Discrimination against Women, General recommendation No.38 (2020) on trafficking in women and girls in the context of global migration, CEDAW/C/GC/38, 20 November 2020 at https://www.ohchr.org/en/documents/general-comments-and-recommendations/general-recommendation-no38-2020-trafficking-women [accessed 12 October 2025].

the various forms of trafficking in women and girls and their consequences, including with regard to harms suffered and that 'trafficking and [sexual exploitation] of women and girls is unequivocally a phenomenon rooted in structural, sex-based discrimination, constituting gender-based violence, and is often exacerbated in the contexts of displacement, migration …' Further this states:

> '20. Trafficking in women and girls is rooted in sex-based and gender-based discrimination, gender-based structural inequality and the feminization of poverty. The women and girls who are most vulnerable to being trafficked are those belonging to marginalized groups, such as women and girls living in rural and remote areas, those belonging to indigenous and ethnic minority communities, women and girls with disabilities, women and girls with an irregular migration status …'

16.291

The Court noted that the CEDAW Committee reiterated in its General Recommendation No. 35 (2017)[265] stated that 'discrimination against women was inextricably linked to other factors that affected their lives, such as, *inter alia*, their ethnicity/race, indigenous or minority status, colour, socio-economic status, language, national origin, age, urban or rural location, migration status, being deprived of liberty and being subjected to trafficking. …It recommended that States Parties should ensure that all legal proceedings, protective and support measures and services concerning victims/survivors respected and strengthened their autonomy, were accessible to all women, in particular those affected by intersecting forms of discrimination, took into account any specific needs of their children and other dependants, were available throughout the State Party and were provided irrespective of residency status or ability or willingness to cooperate in legal proceedings against the alleged perpetrator[266].'

16.292

In *JP v Secretary of State for the Home Department*[267] the Administrative Court held that a policy which told caseworkers not to make a decision on whether to grant ECAT leave to a victim of trafficking until it is determined that the victim does not qualify for another form of leave (ie the 'scheduling rule') was discriminatory, contrary to Art 14 ECHR, read in conjunction with Arts 4, Art 8 and Art 1 Protocol No 1. The rule fell within the ambit of Art 4 as leave fell within the package of protective measures for victims of trafficking (eg aimed

265 UN Committee on the Elimination of Discrimination against Women, General recommendation No.35 (2017) on gender-based violence against women, updating general recommendation No. 19 (1992) CEDAW/C/GC/35, 26 July 2017 at https://www.ohchr.org/en/documents/general-comments-and-recommendations/general-recommendation-no-35-2017-gender-based [accessed 12 October 2025].

266 *FM v Russia* [2024] 58 BHRC 384, [205].

267 [2019] EWHC 3346 (Admin) [144–164].

at their recovery), Art 8 ECHR, the right to respect for private and family life, as ECAT leave is a means by which a victim's right to live, work and study is promoted, and Art 1 Protocol No 1 on the basis that ECAT leave enabled access to mainstream benefits and support. The Administrative Court found that victims seeking ECAT leave with an asylum claim were in an analogous position to a victim seeking ECAT leave, not claiming asylum. It also accepted that being an 'asylum seeker' fell within the 'other status' for the purpose of the ECHR. Finally, there was no sufficient or objective justification for the difference in treatment.

16.293

Secretary of State for the Home Department v S and VLT[268] concerned a challenge to the Discretionary Leave policy for victims of trafficking on the basis that it unjustifiably excluded victims of trafficking from eligibility if subject to deportation proceedings. The Court of Appeal found that this did not constitute a breach of Art 14 ECHR. The Court was prepared to accept that the refusal of a residence permit (leave) was 'within the ambit' of Art 4 or 8 ECHR and was prepared to assume that being subject to a deportation order or proceedings was a protected status. The Court of Appeal held that victims subject to a deportation order or proceedings were not in an analogous situation to other victims of trafficking who were entitled to discretionary leave. The reason was because they had been convicted of criminal offences in the UK and sentenced to imprisonment, and also because they were subject to a deportation order. The Supreme Court refused permission to appeal.

16.294

The Tribunal must have due regard must be taken to protected characteristics under the ECHR, in substantive decision-making and procedurally, eg by special measures (see **Chapter 8**). The substantive relevance of Art 14 ECHR will need to be established in individual human rights appeals. It may potentially arise as a free-standing issue. Discrimination on grounds of age, gender, disability, trafficking or other status, may also be relevant factors in the assessment of compassionate or compelling circumstances under Art 8 ECHR.

Part 4 Asylum and the National Referral Mechanism: identification, support and procedural intersections

16.295

The National Referral Mechanism is examined at length in **Chapter 4**.

268 [2025] EWCA Civ 188.

16.296

The UKVI[269] is a First Responder Organisation with a formal Duty to Notify the Home Office where they encounter a potential victim of trafficking or modern slavery[270]. They must refer child victims into the NRM and they must refer adult victims into the NRM where they give informed consent or notify the Home Office that they have encountered a potential victim of trafficking where an adult does not give consent to enter the NRM. Accordingly, UKVI staff should be familiar with indicators of trafficking and need to know and understand the signs which may indicate a person is a victim of trafficking in order to decide to refer a case to the NRM[271].

16.297

In *R (TDT)*[272] the Court of Appeal considered the Secretary of State's positive obligation to identify victims of trafficking, holding that the threshold for frontline staff to refer into the NRM was *'very low'* involving *'any suspicion or any claim'* and the subsequent duty of investigation required the low threshold of a *'credible suspicion'*, that a person has been trafficked. It was accepted that falling into a class of individuals particularly vulnerable to trafficking, in that case young Vietnamese males, could give rise to a credible suspicion that a person had been trafficked to the UK.

16.298

Knowledge of specific trafficking contexts was also relevant in *DA v SSHD*[273] in which Fordham J gave a decision on interim relief accepting that there was a strong *prima facie* case that the omission of questions about a person's journey to the UK in screening interviews gave rise to a serious risk that potential victims of trafficking would not be identified noting the SSHD's duty to identify potential victims from indicators, the evidence of the particular risk to migrants of being forced into modern slavery whilst in Libya, and evidence of problems of identification in only asking a direct question about exploitation[274].

16.299

Home Office guidance to UKVI caseworkers' states that if at any stage of the process there are indicators to suggest an adult could be a potential victim of slavery, they must consider making a referral into the NRM in accordance

269 Along with other Home Office agencies, Border Force, responsible for maintaining the security and integrity of the border, and Immigration Enforcement, responsible for enforcing immigration law.

270 Home Office, *Modern Slavery – Statutory Guidance for England and Wales*, v.4.2 (10 October 2025), [4.10].

271 Ibid, 3.3.

272 *R (TDT) v The Secretary of State for the Home Department* [2018] EWCA Civ 1395, [2018] 1 WLR 4922.

273 [2020] EWHC 3080 (Admin).

274 The substantive case was subsequently settled.

with the UK's obligations under ECAT. They must be vigilant and aware that indicators can present themselves at any stage of the process. If they are unsure if indicators are present and a referral into the NRM is needed, they must refer to a senior caseworker or technical specialist[275].

16.300

Home Office statutory guidance recognises that where UKVI staff conduct screening interviews, they may be the first to have contact with potential victims of modern slavery. The guidance highlights the importance of awareness of indicators as applicants may not identify themselves as victims of trafficking[276]. The statutory guidance recognises that 'it would not be appropriate to conduct a full interview at the screening stage'[277]. As UKVI staff may encounter potential victims of trafficking initial screening interviews or substantive interviews, they are reminded in both cases that such claimants may be reluctant to go into much detail about the full facts of their case[278] and referred to guidance on 'victims who are reluctant to self-identify'[279]. The statutory guidance further provides:

16.301

There are no minimum indicators required for making an NRM referral. At the substantive interview stage, interview questions must be open and without assumptions to establish what happened.

16.302

Each officer should engage their professional curiosity to understand the needs of the individual – identifying potential vulnerabilities early in the process will likely significantly influence how that person is managed, both in terms of the need of any immediate safeguarding steps but also in the longer term in respect of decisions around their application.

16.303

If staff consider the person is a potential victim of modern slavery, they should act as the First Responder and follow the steps on handling potential victims of modern slavery including referral to the NRM. However, responding appropriately to discharge their duty of care could be as simple as alerting a line

---

275 Home Office, Assessing credibility and refugee status in asylum claims lodged on or after 28 June 2022, v.10 (28 September 2022); Home Office, *Assessing credibility and refugee status in asylum claims lodged on or after 28 June 2022,* v.13.0 (28 September 2023).
276 Home Office, *Modern Slavery – Statutory Guidance for England and Wales*, v.4.1 (11 August 2025), [4.10].
277 Ibid, 12.40.
278 Ibid, 12.38.
279 Ibid, 12.38.

manager, speaking to a colleague for advice, or referring to a senior case worker, officer in charge or Vulnerability Champion in first instance[280].

16.304

Legal representatives or other agencies who identify potential victims of trafficking or modern slavery during the asylum process or their work more generally may also support victims in accessing the NRM by making a referral to one of the First Responder Organisations permitted to refer potential victims of trafficking into the NRM (see **Chapter 4**). First Responder Organisations include specific NGOs as well as statutory agencies such as local authorities and UKVI[281].

Asylum interviews and decision-making

16.305

This section should be read alongside **Chapter 3**, which sets out best practice for conducting interviews in cases involving trafficking and modern slavery.

16.306

Victims of trafficking or modern slavery are entitled to a Recovery Period for 30 days from the date that a positive decision is made that either there are reasonable grounds that they may be a victim of trafficking or that there are conclusive grounds that they are a victim of trafficking, whichever is the sooner, and during which they may not be removed from or required to leave the UK[282]. This applies whether they were referred into the NRM prior to any asylum claim or whether they were identified during the asylum process. In practice, however, the asylum consideration period is not paused during this period, either to await a reasonable grounds decision or to allow for a period of recovery. Interviewing asylum applicants who are potential victims of trafficking without the benefit of an appropriate rest and recovery period may give rise to risks of re-traumatisation and harm and be inconsistent with the UK's legal obligations under ECAT.

16.307

The current interpretation by both the Home Office and the courts is that there is nothing to prevent either an asylum screening interview (a status interview determining identity, nationality or citizenship, and journey details)

280 Ibid, 12.40-12.42.
281 The full list of first responder organisations is set out in Home Office, *National Referral Mechanism guidance: adult (England and Wales)*, 20 October 2024.
282 NABA 2022, s 61.

or a substantive asylum interview taking place prior to completion of the identification process[283].

16.308

Under the mainstream asylum determination process for adults, after an application for asylum has been made and the initial asylum screening interview has taken place, an individual will be invited to attend a substantive interview to give details about their reasons for needing protection[284]. The process is modified for unaccompanied children to provide for an initial welfare interview in place of a screening interview, a case review process for liaison with the child's social worker with responsibility for facilitating the appointment of a legal representative for the child, the submission of a written Statement of Evidence Form (SEF), and consideration of whether an interview is required based on the information received[285].

16.309

The substantive interview may be delayed following representations to allow time for obtaining and submitting medico-legal evidence[286], or in response to submissions on any safeguarding issues raised by the legal representative. The Home Office does not routinely consider whether any reasonable adjustments are appropriate in place of its standard interviewing process, either to consider whether an interview should not take place to prevent risks of re-traumatisation and harm or whether information may be obtained by alternative means, in the form of a statement prepared with a legal representative, nor is this addressed in its guidance. As a result, any submissions on adjustments required may need to be strongly argued and supported with clear medical evidence. The Home Office has duties in respect of persons with mental health disabilities under the Equality Act 2010 and, following *NC v Turkey*[287], where there are insufficient special measures or prior reasonable adjustments which give rise to a real risk of secondary trauma, this may engage Art 3 (inhumane treatment), Art 4 (breach of protective duty and investigatory duty) and Art 8 (physical and moral integrity: mental health) of the ECHR (see **Chapter 3**).

16.310

Home Office statutory guidance states that UKVI interviewers need to know how to engage with potential victims of modern slavery they may meet during an asylum interview and notes that such claimants may be reluctant to go into

---

283 *R (XYL) v Secretary of State for the Home Department* [2017] EWHC 773 (Admin) at para 22.

284 A streamlined asylum process was introduced place for applications made before 7 March 2023 for applicants from specified countries with a high grant rate of refugee status or humanitarian protection under which a personal questionnaire is issued and an applicant only invited to a shorter personal interview if necessary. See Home Office, *Streamlined asylum processing*, (2 May 2024).

285 Home Office, *Processing children's asylum claims*, v.5.0 (22 January 2025).

286 Home Office, *Medical evidence in asylum claims: caseworker guidance*, v.2.0, 30 August 2022.

287 European Court of Human Rights, Application no.40591/11. See particularly paras 94–96.

much detail about the full facts of their case and refers UKVI caseworkers to guidance on 'Victims who are reluctant to self-identify'[288]. The guidance states that asylum interviewers should be careful not to cause undue distress during interviews and refers them to guidance on 'Interviewing people who have experienced trauma' and 'Trauma-informed practice' for further information[289]. At the same time, the guidance encourages interviewers to aim to obtain as full an account as possible[290].

16.311

Increasingly, UKVI undertakes substantive asylum interviews by video conferencing. Its guidance states that if remote interviewing would not be suitable an individual applicant then the claimant or legal representative must contact the Home Office to provide reasons why this would not be suitable in their case. Its guidance states that staff need to consider whether the claimant has any sight or hearing impairment, mental health issues, learning disabilities or difficulties, or if there are other factors that may prevent a claimant disclosing particularly sensitive information in a video conferencing interview. It further states that:

> 'This does not mean that [video-conferencing] will not be appropriate, but any reasons given by the claimant for not wanting an interview to be conducted by [video-conferencing] must be carefully considered. This may include, but is not limited to, cases involving sexual orientation or gender identity, victims of torture or other trauma where recording was part of the persecution, victims of sexual violence or other forms of gender-based persecution, victims of modern slavery or claimants with mental health conditions. A decision to continue with a [video-conferencing] interview despite a request to the contrary from the claimant should be fully justified and recorded in the claimant's records.'

16.312

It is unlikely that an asylum interview undertaken by remote interviewing will provide adequate safety for disclosure and engagement by potential victims of trafficking unless specifically requested by the applicant as a preference or adjustment, or unless significant additional safeguards are put in place.

16.313

It was previously Home Office practice not to take any negative asylum decision where there were reasonable grounds for believing a person was a victim of

288 Home Office, *Modern Slavery – Statutory Guidance for England and Wales*, v.4.1 (11 August 2025), [12.38].
289 Ibid, 12.39.
290 Ibid, 12.39.

trafficking until the conclusive grounds decision was made as that decision could have a bearing on the asylum claim[291]. However, decisions by the SCA within the NRM as to whether there are conclusive grounds that an individual is a victim of trafficking were, and continue to be, subject to very significant delays[292]. The policy has since changed to remove the pause on asylum decision-making during the NRM identification process[293]. Since the change in policy, it is now common for an asylum decision to be made before the formal identification of an individual as a victim of trafficking within the NRM. Despite the potential relevance of the Single Competent Authority decision to trafficking risks on return considered within the asylum claim, the change in policy may reduce the delays that victims face in accessing protection, in a context where it is recognised that a prolonged period of uncertainty is liable to be inimical to the social and psychological recovery that ECAT is designed to promote[294] and the Tribunal is competent to make findings as to whether an individual is a victim of trafficking. In specific, individual cases, however, it may be appropriate to make representations to the Single Competent Authority for expedition of the NRM decision so that this may be obtained before the asylum decision is made. The Competent Authority's decision minute setting out its written assessment of how a person's situation meets the definition of a modern slavery victim is disclosable in proceedings before the Tribunal[295].

Asylum, trafficking and modern slavery support and recovery

16.314

This is examined at length in **Chapters 4** and **5**.

16.315

Asylum seekers who are potential or confirmed adult victims of trafficking within the NRM process may access support services through the Modern

---

291 See for example archived policy, *Home Office, Victims of modern slavery – Competent Authority guidance*, v.5.0 (21 January 2019).

292 For example, an average of 588 days in 2023, the most recent full year for which data is available: *Modern Slavery: National Referral Mechanism and Duty to Notify statistics UK, end of year summary 2023*, 7 March 2024.

293 The archived policy, Home Office, *Modern Slavery: Statutory Guidance for England and Wales*, v.2.5 (8 November 2019) stated: 'Appropriate immigration teams should consider any outstanding immigration cases, such as an outstanding asylum application, following a negative Reasonable Grounds decision or any Conclusive Grounds decision' ([14.208]). This was removed from the archived version of the policy v.2.6 (1 February 2022) and subsequent versions.

294 *EOG & Anor v SSHD* [2022] EWCA Civ 307 (17 March 2022), para 40.

295 [14.212] of Home Office, *Modern slavery: statutory guidance for England and Wales (under s49 of the Modern Slavery Act 2015) and non-statutory guidance for Scotland and Northern Ireland* (updated 10 October 2025) https://www.gov.uk/government/publications/modern-slavery-how-to-identify-and-support-victims/modern-slavery-statutory-guidance-for-england-and-wales-under-s49-of-the-modern-slavery-act-2015-and-non-statutory-guidance-for-scotland-and-northe#what-is-modern-slavery> accessed 12 October 2025.

Slavery Victim Care Contract (MSVCC) and other support services instead of, or in addition to, asylum support provision. Following a positive reasonable grounds decision within the NRM that an adult may be a victim of trafficking, that individual will be entitled to the rate of financial support provided under the MSVCC to facilitate recovery in addition to the subsistence rate of asylum support and alongside other forms of support provided under the MSVCC[296].

Grants of leave to remain

Refugee leave and humanitarian protection

16.316

Refugee leave is granted where an individual meets the definition of a refugee within Article 1 of the 1951 Refugee Convention and meets the requirements of paragraph 334 of the Immigration Rules. Refugee Status is an internationally recognised status with established rights under the Convention. In the UK, leave to remain is granted for a period of five years which is renewable upon application where the person remains eligible for refugee protection following a safe return review, and a person may apply for indefinite leave to remain (or 'settlement') after a period of five years[297]. Entitlements to family reunion for those recognised as refugees or humanitarian protection are currently under review and restrictions on those rights may be the subject of future legal challenges.

16.317

Humanitarian protection is a status established in domestic law under paragraph 339C of the immigration rules. The provisions for leave to remain are currently aligned with those for refugee leave, and humanitarian protection is currently granted for a period of five years renewable under the same review process as for refugee leave[298].

296 Home Office, *Modern Slavery Statutory Guidance for England and Wales (under s49 of the Modern Slavery Act 2015) and non-statutory guidance for Scotland and Northern Ireland*, v. 4.2, 10 October 2025, Appendix F; asylum seekers who are potential victims of trafficking are not treated differently from other potential victims of trafficking with regard to the level of financial support following the settled case of *R (YH) v SSHD*, CO/4801/2022.

297 See Home Office, *Refugee and humanitarian protection leave in asylum claims lodged before 28 June 2022*, v.1.0, 28 June 2022, at https://www.gov.uk/government/publications/asylum-under-immigration-rule-334-process [accessed 12 October 2025]; Home Office, *Permission to stay on a protection route for asylum claims lodged on or after 28 June 2022*, at https://www.gov.uk/government/publications/permission-to-stay-on-a-protection-route-caseworker-guidance [accessed 12 October 2025].

298 The significant change to humanitarian protection announced by the Statement of Immigration Rules: HC17, 11 May 2022 for claims made on or after 28 May 2022, reducing the length of leave granted to 30 months renewable on a 10-year route to settlement, was challenged and not implemented.

Temporary leave to remain as a victim of trafficking or modern slavery

16.318

Art 14 of ECAT requires states to make provision for the issue of a residence permit to confirmed victims of trafficking in specified circumstances. The Secretary of State previously sought to give effect to this provision through the introduction of a policy on temporary permission to stay for those identified on conclusive grounds as a victim of trafficking. The policy was subject to significant number of challenges in terms of its compliance with Art 14 ECAT, including in R *(JP & BS) v Secretary of State for the Home Department*[299] where the court found it was unlawful for the Secretary of State to treat victims of trafficking with pending asylum claims differently from other victims and have a blanket requirement delaying the determination of their application for a residence permit under Art 14(1) ECAT before making a decision on the asylum application[300]. The circumstances in which victims with pending asylum applications qualified for trafficking leave under the policy have been further refined by litigation[301].

16.319

On 30 January 2023, the Home Office introduced Appendix Temporary Permission to Stay for Victims of Human Trafficking or Slavery into the Immigration Rules[302] to give effect to s 65 of NABA 2022 on leave to remain for victims of trafficking, which sought to place decision-making on a domestic footing rather than to give specific effect to Art 14 of ECAT. Although victims with pending asylum claims are not excluded from the new provisions, these are more restrictive in their scope. This is examined in **Chapter 4**.

Discretionary leave on medical grounds

16.320

Discretionary Leave is granted to applicants where there is a real risk that removal would breach Art 3 ECHR as a result of deterioration in health or the risk of suicide[303]. Discretionary Leave is normally granted for 30 months at a time. Subsequent period of leave may be granted if the applicant continues to meet the relevant criteria, becoming eligible for settlement after completing a continuous period of 10 years' limited leave to remain.

299 [2019] EWHC 3346 (Admin), [2020] 1 WLR 918 per Murray, J.
300 *Ibid*, paras 136–139, 150, 161–165.
301 *EOG & Anor, v SSHD* [2022] EWCA Civ 307 (17 March 2022); *R (KTT) v SSHD* [2021] EWHC 2722 (Admin) per Linden, J; *R (SSA (Ethiopia)) v SSHD*, JR-2021-LON-001894; *S & VLT* [2025] EWCA Civ 188.
302 Accompanied by new guidance, the most recent version of which is Home Office, *Temporary permission to stay: considerations for victims of human trafficking and slavery*, v.8.0 (11 August 2025).
303 Home Office, *Discretionary Leave*, v.11 (25 March 2025).

16.321

The SSHD also has a discretion to grant Indefinite Leave to Remain outside the immigration rules where the grounds are so exceptional that they warrant this[304]. The SSHD states that reasons to grant ILR early, are likely to be easily identifiable on their individual facts, for example, where it is considered that the precariousness of limited leave would create such serious distress as to have a disproportionately detrimental effect on the person's health or welfare that it would prevent recovery or development. The threshold is high and concerns the direct effect on the person concerned[305].

16.322

It is not open to the Tribunal to direct that the Home Office grant leave to remain for any particular period, or indefinitely[306]. However, the Home Office will need to lawfully implement an allowed appeal by the Tribunal, with the appropriate length of leave, where it is allowed on Art 3, or Art 4, or Art 8 ECHR grounds (inside or outside the rules).

16.323

Where a case warrants a grant of ILR, the previous mishandling of the case or some unreasonable or unlawful conduct by the Home Office, and the impact of that on a vulnerable victim of trafficking, may be a relevant factor[307]. This might include on the facts, any mishandling by the Home Office of its functions related to the case, eg asylum and human rights claim, age dispute, the NRM decision-making or safeguarding process (eg, a failure to correctly or promptly identify, protect, support, accommodate), or the mishandling of the case by another statutory agency, relevant to the Home Office decision-making which went unanswered or uncorrected, and requires reparation, or the correction of an injustice.

Part 5 Procedural issues in trafficking and modern slavery appeals

Vulnerable appellants and procedural safeguards in trafficking-related appeals

16.324

Where an appellant is a putative victim of trafficking or modern slavery, they are, by definition, a vulnerable party. **Chapter 8** addresses the application of special

304 Home Office, *Leave outside the Immigration Rules*, v.5.0 (5 August 2025).

305 Home Office, *Family life (as a partner or parent) and exceptional circumstances*, v.22 (17 July 2025).

306 *EK (Art 4 ECHR: Anti-Trafficking Convention) Tanzania* [2013] UKUT 313 (IAC) para 67.

307 *FT, R (on the application of) v Secretary of State for the Home Department ('rolling review'; challenging leave granted)* [2017] UKUT 331 (IAC) paras 62-63, 73-74.

measures in tribunal proceedings, and these should be actively considered in advance of any hearing. Appropriate special measures should be identified and sought to ensure the appellant's effective participation and protection.

16.325

Tribunal proceedings involving such individuals must be conducted in a manner consistent with the State's protective obligations under Art 4 ECHR. A failure to do so may amount to a breach of those obligations, particularly where the conduct of proceedings exacerbates trauma or undermines the appellant's ability to present their case.

Statutory provisions in trafficking related protection and human rights claims

The Nationality, Immigration and Asylum Act 2002

16.326

The Tribunal may allow an appeal on the grounds of the Refugee Convention, humanitarian protection or human rights grounds (inside or outside the rules under the ECHR) (s 84 of the NIAA 2002).

16.327

A breach of Refugee Convention or the ECHR also constitute exceptions to the automatic deportation of persons deemed to be a 'foreign criminal': s 33(2) UK Borders Act 2007[308]. A further exception to deportation is 'where the Secretary of State thinks that the application of s 32(4) and (5) would contravene the United Kingdom's obligations under ECAT' (s 33(6) of the 2007 Act).

The Human Rights Act 1998

16.328

Human rights are protected by our domestic law, interpreted and developed in accordance with the Human Rights Act 1998 ('HRA 1998')[309].

16.329

By s 2(1) HRA 1998 (interpretation of Convention rights) 'A court or tribunal determining a question which has arisen in connection with a Convention

308 Exception 1.

309 *A (A Child) (Withdrawal of Treatment: Legal Representation), Re* [2022] EWCA Civ 1221, *R Osborn v Parole Board* [2013] UKSC 61 [54-63].

right must take into account any: (a) judgment, decision, declaration or advisory opinion of the [ECtHR]' …if 'relevant to the proceedings in which that question has arisen.'

16.330

By s 3(1) HRA 1998 'So far as it is possible to do so, primary legislation and subordinate legislation must be read and given effect in a way which is compatible with the Convention rights'

16.331

By s 6(1) HRA 1998, 'It is unlawful for a public authority to act in a way which is incompatible with a Convention right.'

16.332

As such, any positive obligations in relation to trafficking arising under Arts 3, 4 or 8 (for example) are binding on public authorities as a matter of domestic law under s 6 of the HRA 1998[310]'

Evidentiary and procedural significance of positive NRM decisions

16.333

As outlined at the beginning of the chapter, a positive decision under the National Referral Mechanism (NRM), whether at the reasonable grounds or conclusive grounds stage, carries evidentiary weight in asylum and human rights appeals. It amounts to a formal recognition by the Competent Authority (the Home Office) that the individual is a victim of trafficking or other Art 4 abuse. As such, it may constitute a concession of fact, which the Tribunal should not disregard without good reason, even if not expressly referenced in the decision under appeal.

16.334

The Modern Slavery Statutory Guidance confirms that the consideration minute accompanying a positive decision is disclosable in Tribunal proceedings if directed.

310 Regarding Art 4 ECHR: TDT, *R (On the Application Of) v The Secretary of State for the Home Department* (Rev 1) [2018] EWCA Civ 1395 para 14, see further below.

16.335

Procedurally, the reasonable grounds decision aligns with the 'credible suspicion' threshold under Article 4. As confirmed in *Hoang Anh Minh*[311], this threshold triggers duties such as notification to the police. In *R (TDT)*[312], the Court of Appeal clarified that identification may occur even before a formal NRM decision, where prima facie evidence of trafficking is known or ought to be known to public authorities.

16.336

This significance is reinforced by the positive obligations under Art 4 ECHR. Any attempt by a public authority, including a tribunal, to go behind a positive identification without first ensuring compliance with protective and investigative duties risks breaching Art 4. This approach is supported by ECtHR case law, including *VCL and AN v United Kingdom* and *Chowdury v Greece*[313].

Section 120 notices and 'new matters' under s 85 of the Nationality, Immigration and Asylum Act 2002

The state's duty to identify victims of trafficking or modern slavery

16.337

The duty to identify victims is on the State, victims are not required to self-identify or declare exploitation or abuse[314]. This is because there are multiple good reasons why 'victims may be reluctant to, or unable to self-identify' as the Modern Slavery Statutory Guidance and caselaw accepts[315]. The Statutory Guidance also accepts that '[V]ictims may not be aware that they have been exploited or may be unwilling to self-identify for another reason[316].' Such reasons may include the trauma experienced, shame or fear[317]. The Statutory Guidance further accepts at para 13.18 that:

311 *Secretary of State for the Home Department v Hoang Anh Minh* [2016] EWCA Civ 565, [2016] Imm AR 1272.

312 *R (TDT) v The Secretary of State for the Home Department* [2018] EWCA Civ 1395, [2018] 1 WLR 4922.

313 *VCL and AN v United Kingdom* (2021) 73 EHRR 9; *Chowdury and others v Greece* App no 21884/15 (ECHR, 30 March 2017).

314 As analysed in **Chapter 4**, the Administrative Court in *R (ABW) v Secretary of State for the Home Department* [2025] EWHC 3280 (Admin) (Morris J, 17 December 2025) held that the Public Order Disqualification regime under s 63 of the NABA was unlawful in the form in which it had been implemented through the Modern Slavery Statutory Guidance. The Court's conclusions on the limited scope of the State's identification duty under Art 4 are, however, open to doubt for the reasons set out in that Chapter; and the subsequent reasoning of Sheldon J in *AYA v Secretary of State for the Home Department* [2026] EWHC 552 (Admin) reinforces that identification is integral to the practical discharge of Art 4's positive obligations, even if not recognised as a freestanding duty.

315 Home Office, *Modern Slavery Statutory Guidance*, [6.1-3 and 12.69] (criminal proceedings), Annex D 'Working with vulnerable people', para 13.10-13.24. *SM v Croatia* (2021) 72 EHRR 1 at [344]. See **Chapter 3**.

316 Modern Slavery Statutory Guidance, [6.2].

317 Modern Slavery Statutory Guidance, Annex D.

> 'A delay in disclosing facts should not be viewed as manipulative or taken to mean these facts are untrue. The late disclosure of these facts may be the result of an effective Recovery Period and the establishment of trust with the person to whom they disclose the information. Disclosures often come slowly and in a piecemeal way, sometimes over years.'

Procedural Implications of trafficking or modern slavery raised on appeal

16.338

Nevertheless, if trafficking or modern slavery is raised on appeal (and is not already contained in a s 120 notice or a ground of appeal under s 84) the procedural mechanisms to deal with this include that.

16.339

First, establish it if is 'new matter' within the meaning of s 85(6) of the NIAA 2002, ie, whether it 'constitutes a ground of appeal of a kind listed in s 84' (s 85(6)(a)), *and* the Secretary of State has not previously considered the matter in the context of the decision under appeal, or the appellant's response to the s 120 notice (s 85(6)(b))[318]. A new matter may be factually distinct, not simply further or better evidence of an existing matter. In *Hydar (s 120 response; s 85 'new matter': Birch)*[319], the Presidential Panel of the Upper Tribunal confirmed that where a new ground of appeal raised in response to a s 120 notice introduces a different legal basis upon which the appeal may be allowed, this constitutes a 'new matter' for the purposes of s 85. In such circumstances, the Tribunal lacks jurisdiction to consider the new matter unless the Secretary of State consents, as required by s 85(5). Section 85(6) defines a 'new matter' as one which both constitutes a ground of appeal under s 84 and has not previously been considered by the Secretary of State, either in the decision under appeal or in a prior s 120 statement. The determination of whether something constitutes a 'new matter' is fact-sensitive and turns on whether it introduces a distinct factual matrix and legal ground, rather than merely providing further evidence in support of an existing ground.

Art 4 ECHR obligations and tribunal jurisdiction: a rights-compatible interpretation

16.340

What may require further judicial scrutiny is the interaction between the State's positive obligations under Art 4 of the ECHR and the jurisdictional bar in s 85(5) of the NIAA 2002, particularly in the following scenarios:

318 *Hydar (s 120 response; s.85 'new matter'; Birch)* [2021] UKUT 00176 (IAC).
319 Ibid.

1. Where the factual matrix presented to the Home Office prior to its decision on international protection or human rights included *prima facie* evidence of trafficking or modern slavery, which the Home Office failed to engage with.

2. Where, prior to that decision, a referral had been made to the Home Office in its capacity as the Single Competent Authority.

3. Where, prior to the decision, a National Referral Mechanism (NRM) decision had already been made by the Home Office, in its capacity as Single Competent Authority.

16.341

In each of these scenarios, the facts arguably trigger the State's positive obligations under Art 4 ECHR (see the analysis of 'credible suspicion' in Part 1 of this chapter). These obligations include the duty to take operational protective measures. In light of *VCL and AN v United Kingdom*[320], such measures would likely encompass a requirement that the Home Office's consideration of the protection and human rights claims includes an assessment of trafficking and/or modern slavery.

16.342

In scenario (1) above, published guidance also requires the Home Office, as a First Responder, to refer an adult applicant to the NRM with their consent. Even absent consent, the protective obligation to consider trafficking or modern slavery within the protection claim remains engaged under Art 4 protective obligations.

Common law principles of statutory interpretation

16.343

Where there has been a breach of the Art 4 protective obligation, a question arises as to whether the Tribunal is precluded from considering the issue due to the interpretation of 'new matter' under s 85(6)(b). The Tribunal must first consider, applying common law principles of statutory interpretation, whether the Secretary of State's failure to engage with *prima facie* evidence of trafficking or modern slavery, despite its presence prior to the decision, renders the issue a 'new matter' simply because it was not addressed in the decision or in a s 120 statement.

320 *VCL and AN v United Kingdom* (2021) 73 EHRR 9.

16.344

It is arguable that s 85(6)(b) should not be construed so narrowly as to exclude Tribunal jurisdiction in such circumstances. The principle of legality requires that legislation be interpreted to protect fundamental rights unless Parliament has clearly indicated otherwise. Where relevant facts were already before the Secretary of State, construing them as 'new matters' would arguably unjustly oust Tribunal jurisdiction and risk breaching the UK's positive obligations under Art 4 ECHR. A purposive construction, aligned with access to justice and the protective aims of the NIAA 2002, may support the Tribunal's jurisdiction to consider such facts. Excluding them would arguably allow the Secretary of State to evade scrutiny and undermine the effective operation of human rights protections, contrary to the rule of law and fairness.

Human rights-compliant interpretation, s 3(1) of the HRA 1998

16.345

Alternatively, applying s 3(1) of the HRA 1998, the Tribunal must interpret s 85(6)(b) so far as possible in a manner compatible with the UK's obligations under Art 4 ECHR. This requires a three-step judicial process:

1. Determining the ordinary meaning of 'new matter' using standard interpretive principles.
2. Comparing that meaning with the requirements of Convention rights, in this case, the duty to take operational measures to protect against trafficking and modern slavery and the Tribunal's own procedural duty of effective justice[321].
3. If the ordinary meaning would prevent scrutiny of trafficking or modern slavery grounds (because the Secretary of State failed to consider them despite having the evidence), s 3(1) requires the Tribunal to adopt a rights-compatible interpretation, provided this is 'possible' and not fundamentally inconsistent with the legislative scheme.

16.346

This may entail construing 'new matter' as excluding facts that were before the Secretary of State but ignored, thereby preserving Tribunal jurisdiction and ensuring the claimant's Convention rights to effective protection and a fair hearing are upheld. Such an approach falls squarely within s 3's interpretative mandate, accords with Parliament's protective intent, and ensures compliance with the UK's human rights obligations.

321 *Chowdury and others v Greece* App no 21884/15 (ECHR, 30 March 2017).

Trafficking or modern slavery raised on appeal: constitutes a 'new matter' under s 85

16.347

Trafficking or modern slavery may be a matter arising after the date of the decision, or during an appeal before the FTT or UT. Where it is truly a 'new matter' the Tribunal may not consider it without the consent of the Home Office under s 85(5) of the NIAA 2002[322]. Therefore, it may be prudent to deal with this as soon as possible, for example, raising it in any s 120 notice, grounds or amended grounds under s 82, requesting confirmation of consent by the Home Office to it being treated as a new matter, and (possibly) dealing with it in any case management discussions, or requesting case management on the issue. This will ensure effective onward preparation and may avoid delay.

16.348

Where the evidence of trafficking or modern slavery meets the low threshold of *prima facie* evidence, the protective obligations under Art 4 ECHR should be central to the Secretary of State's decision on whether to consent to the new matter being considered by the Tribunal on appeal. These procedural obligations require careful consideration of the potential impact on the appellant's mental health and any other risks that may arise from delay in determining this aspect of the claim.

16.349

If consent is refused, that decision is amenable to challenge by way of judicial review. In any such challenge, regard should be had to the judgment of Chamberlain J in *KP v Secretary of State for Foreign, Commonwealth and Development Affairs* [323], where it was emphasised that the intensity of substantive judicial review varies according to the significance of the interests affected and the gravity of the potential consequences. Where a decision threatens interests of substantial moral or legal weight, such as the safety, dignity, or welfare of vulnerable individuals, a heightened standard of scrutiny is required. This is not contingent upon the existence of a formal legal right, but rather on the seriousness of what is at stake in the impugned decision.

Notice of withdrawal of decision under appeal or adjournments

16.350

In some appeals, including trafficking or modern slavery-related claims, a party may seek to withdraw the s 82 decision under appeal either by giving written

322 *Hydar (s 120 response; s85 'new matter'; Birch)* [2021] UKUT 00176 (IAC); see also Home Office guidance *Rights of appeal*, version 15.0, 11 December 2023.

323 *KP v Secretary of State for Foreign, Commonwealth and Development Affairs* [2025] EWHC 370.

notice of withdrawal of the appeal or oral withdrawal at a hearing (Rule 17(1) of the FTT Procedure Rules). In either case the reasons for that withdrawal 'must' be specified.

16.351

A notice of withdrawal in writing or orally does not automatically end the appeal.

16.352

The Tribunal should not treat the appeal as withdrawn 'save for good reason'[324]. A notice of withdrawal by the Home Office under rule 17 of the Tribunal Rules of Procedure, should be 'with a view to granting leave'[325]. Alternatively, the Home Office guidance states that, '[a]n adjournment should be sought [by the Home Office] where it is not reasonably clear that the new evidence or ground will lead to a grant of leave but where it needs to be considered in more detail.'

16.353

The appellant should have a fair opportunity to object or make representations in writing and/or orally on whether the Tribunal should allow the appeal to continue, or be heard, and give substantive consideration of the issues. Relevant factors in favour of substantive determination in a trafficking appeal may include eg the type of leave being considered, the appellant or dependents vulnerability, existing and further delay and the impact on the appellant and any children or dependents[326]. Judicial oversight may be required, in particular if the appellant not the respondent seeks to withdraw the appeal, and an issue arises as to whether the withdrawal was valid[327].

Practice direction and expert evidence

16.354

The overriding objective in the Tribunal is that asylum and human rights appeals are dealt with 'fairly and justly'[328]. The 'guiding principle' to further that objective, as set out in the Senior President of Tribunals, *Practice Direction of the Immigration and Asylum Chamber of the First-tier Tribunal*[329] is an 'issues based approach and procedural rigour'. In trafficking-related claims, the past account

324 The Tribunal Procedure (First-tier Tribunal) (Immigration and Asylum Chamber) Rules 2024, No. 2604, rule 17(2), Presidential Guide Note No.1 of 2014: The Tribunal Procedure (First-tier Tribunal) Immigration and Asylum Chamber) Rules 2014, paras16-20.

325 Home Office guidance, *Withdrawing decisions,* version 4.1, 9 December 2021, pages 5 and 6.

326 *ZEI and others (Decision withdrawn – FtT Rule 17 – considerations) Palestine* [2017] UKUT 00292 (IAC).

327 Anwar (rule 17(1): withdrawal of appeal) [2019] UKUT 00125 (IAC), [46].

328 The Tribunal Procedure (First-tier Tribunal) (Immigration and Asylum Chamber) Rules 2014, 2014 No.2604, rule 2.

329 1 November 2024.

of trafficking in whole or part, and/or the real risk on return may be issues in dispute between the parties. In such instances, the Tribunal may be required both to make factual findings on trafficking (or past persecutory acts) and the future risk of trafficking.

16.355

Expert evidence may assist on such issues, for example from trafficking, country, or medical expert or an independent social worker. Medical evidence is examined at length in **Chapter 3**.

16.356

A trafficking expert may provide an opinion on whether the victim's account meets the trafficking definition. A country expert may provide information on whether the account is plausible in light of his knowledge of that particular country and risks on return for that victim.

16.357

In addition, expert evidence can be used to comment on issues that the victim of trafficking is unable or unwilling to comment on. For example,

1. the modus operandi of the traffickers[330];
2. whether the victim of trafficking may still be under the control of the traffickers and therefore reluctant to provide full disclosure and/or be at risk of returning to them willingly;
3. the ability and/or willingness of the authorities in the country of origin to provide protection;
4. what support there is, if any, for victims of trafficking in the country of origin and the nature of that support;
5. whether the victim of trafficking would be able to access accommodation, employment, healthcare, etc in his country of origin[331].

16.358

This is not intended to be an exhaustive list, merely illustrative of the sorts of issues that an expert may be instructed to comment on.

16.359

Any expert report will need to comply with the Practice Direction (para 9). In particular, all experts will need to demonstrate that they have the requisite

330 An expert may be able to comment on whether the traffickers' modus operandi indicates that they are likely to have been operated as an organised crime network.

331 This is relevant in assessing whether they would be at risk of destitution/further exploitation in the country of origin. See Internal Relocation at [34].

expertise to comment on the matter that they are being instructed on. There are no set criteria to judge whether a person is qualified to be an expert witness. He should have particular expertise on the matters upon which he is being asked to comment, but that can have been obtained through study and qualifications or work experience. A trafficking expert may have gained expertise on trafficking through his work in specialist NGOs or the police force.

16.360

In *AA (unattended children) Afghanistan CG*[332], the Upper Tribunal rejected the Home Office's objection that an archaeologist did not qualify as a country expert 'as his professional expertise is as an archaeologist'. The tribunal observed that 'We accept that he is not one who has conventionally come to be described as a 'country expert'; but his considerable personal and recent experience of Afghanistan, and of the political situation within that country, together with the objectivity that is implicit in his professional qualifications and experience, give the authority to his evidence'.

16.361

In *AAW (expert evidence – weight) Somalia*[333] the Upper Tribunal found that it was able to attach little weight to the expert evidence of a journalist as an expert witness because it lacked objectivity. However, the Upper Tribunal acknowledged that the expert's evidence was not to be disregarded as it stood as 'the view of an experienced journalist with personal experience of the city from her regular visits.'

16.362

Expert evidence is regulated by guidance provided in case law, practice directions and procedure rules. In *MS (Trafficking – Tribunal's Powers – Art 4 ECHR) Pakistan*[334] the President of the Upper Tribunal considered that there was 'some force in the criticisms levelled' at the expert evidence in that case and highlighted the detailed treatment of the duties of expert witnesses in the decision of the Tribunal in *MOJ (Return to Mogadishu) Somalia*[335] (set out in detail below). The President directed that:

> 'those engaging expert witnesses should, in every case, ensure that the expert is provided with a copy of this section of the *MOJ* decision, as a matter of course, at the initial stage of receiving instructions. Each expert's report should, in turn, make clear that these passages have been received and read by the mechanism of a simple declaration to this effect'.

332 [2012] UKUT 00016 (IAC) at [116].
333 [2015] UKUT 00673 (IAC) at [46].
334 [2016] UKUT 00226 (IAC) at [69].
335 [2014] UKUT 00442 (IAC).

17 Human trafficking, terrorism and secret evidence

Dominic Lewis and Tony Vaughan KC

Introduction

17.1

There is an inevitable tension between, on the one hand, the interests of victims of trafficking – who may have been recruited using deception or coercion and then themselves exploited and forced into committing terrorism-related acts; and, on the other, the interests of the nation state to protect its populations, punish perpetrators of such acts, and pursue other measures in the public interest. The case of *Shamima Begum* is probably the most widely known case exemplifying these tensions. Begum travelled as a teenager from London to Syria (probably pursuant to grooming with a view to forced marriage), married an ISIL fighter and lived in ISIL-controlled territory, following which the UK Government deprived her of her citizenship on national security grounds, notwithstanding that it was accepted that there was a credible suspicion that she was a victim of trafficking. That decision was upheld by the courts[1] and is addressed further below.

17.2

Terrorist groups have engaged in human trafficking for several strategic purposes, including revenue generation, recruitment and control. Terrorist groups may also be related to organised criminal networks spanning several countries, working for mutual ends.

17.3

The multi-dimensional and multi-national nature of these phenomena pose difficult questions for national and international justice systems, which require evidence to prove wrongdoing. In the context of national security, the evidence against a person may be difficult to use in court because of its inherently confidential nature. For example, evidence may not be disclosable to the subject of the decision where it would identify informants or reveal the security services' intelligence gathering methods.

1 Most recently in *Shamima Begum v Home Secretary* [2024] EWCA Civ 152.

17.4

The UK has for some years operated procedural mechanisms for navigating these difficulties – Closed Material Procedures – which allow certain civil courts to consider secret evidence that is not shown to the subject of the decision, but which is scrutinised by Special Advocates acting in the affected person's interests. These mechanisms do constitute an encroachment on the principles of a fair trial – most importantly that a person should be able to see the case against them; however the English courts have upheld that encroachment, which is expressly authorised by Acts of Parliament.

17.5

This chapter will start by examining the connections between terrorism and trafficking; it will then go on to consider the UN Special Rapporteur's commentary on the way international legal frameworks are being applied by member states in this context; and will then look at UK practice on the tensions between trafficking victims and UK national security measures through the lens of immigration-related measures as scrutinised by the Special Immigration Appeals Commission, which has the power to hear secret evidence.

The connections between terrorism and trafficking

17.6

There are well documented links between organised criminal networks and terrorist groups. Terrorist groups often collaborate with organized crime networks who facilitate activities such as smuggling arms, drugs, and people. Organised crime can provide logistical support to terrorist groups, while terrorism can create environments of instability that organised crime exploits for profit[2]. This symbiotic relationship has been documented in various conflict zones[3].

17.7

The so-called Islamic State ('ISIL') is one of the most documented examples of a group engaging in systematic trafficking practices. These were characterised by formalised slave market infrastructure; there was an explicit ideological justification for trafficking (the existence and support of the 'caliphate'); there was systematic targeting of minority populations – particularly the Yazidis[4]; and

2 https://www.un.org/securitycouncil/ctc/sites/www.un.org.securitycouncil.ctc/files/2.-ms-delphine-schantz-cted.pdf (accessed 21 August 2025).

3 *Idem* (2018); https://rusi.org/publication/human-trafficking-sinews-crime-and-terror (2007) (accessed 21 August 2025).

4 *Identifying and exploring the nexus between human trafficking, terrorism and terrorism financing, UN* Counter-Terrorism Committee Executive Directorate (2021): https://www.un.org/securitycouncil/ctc/sites/www.un.org.securitycouncil.ctc/files/files/documents/2021/Jan/ht-terrorism-nexus-cted-report.pdf; https://giwps.georgetown.edu/resource/a-new-frontier/ (both sources accessed 21 August 2025).

they used technology as an integral part of their trafficking networks. ISIL used recruitment tactics of psychological manipulation, economic coercion, and ideological indoctrination. ISIL's direct trafficking revenue sources included slave markets, forced labour and sexual slavery economic models. Indirect financial strategies included taxation of trafficking routes, ransoms and extortion, and logistical infrastructure monetisation.

17.8

Another well-known example of sophisticated trafficking-terrorism integration is child soldier recruitment by the Boko Haram. That group engaged in the forcible recruitment of children; gender-based violence as a strategic tool; the destruction of community social structures; and long-term psychological warfare.

UN Special Rapporteur's views on international efforts to combat terrorists' use of trafficking

17.9

The main UN report that specifically addresses the intersection of trafficking and terrorism is A/76/263: *Report on the intersections between trafficking and terrorism* by Siobhán Mullally, the Special Rapporteur on trafficking in persons, especially women and children. This report, published in August 2021, examines the connections between trafficking by proscribed groups and terrorism, highlighting the failures in identifying and assisting victims and the need for effective protection measures. The key findings included:

- The ongoing failure to adequately identify and assist victims of trafficking, particularly in situations involving terrorism. Despite increased global attention to the issue, measures aimed at preventing trafficking remain limited and often ineffective. This oversight is concerning, as it leaves many individuals vulnerable to exploitation without access to necessary support or protection.
- Accountability for trafficking as a serious human rights violation is limited, leading to persistent impunity for those responsible. The Special Rapporteur underscores the need for concerted action by states and international organisations to address these gaps and ensure that perpetrators are held accountable for their crimes.
- The report stresses the importance of applying the principle of non-discrimination in combating human trafficking. This includes ensuring that individuals linked to proscribed groups are not wrongly criminalised but recognised as potential victims with corresponding rights. This approach is crucial in contexts where individuals may be coerced or manipulated into involvement with terrorist groups, and it highlights the need for nuanced policies that distinguish between victims and perpetrators.

- The report also draws attention to the heightened risks faced by children and displaced persons. Children are particularly vulnerable to trafficking, and the report notes that they are often targeted by proscribed groups. Similarly, forcibly displaced persons, including unaccompanied and separated children, face significant risks due to their precarious circumstances. These vulnerabilities are exacerbated in contexts of forced displacement, armed conflict, and terrorism, where the breakdown of social structures and institutions leaves individuals more susceptible to exploitation.
- In addition to these specific vulnerabilities, the report identifies structural discrimination, violence, poverty, and exclusion as root causes of trafficking. These factors are exacerbated in contexts of conflict and displacement, where the absence of effective governance and social services creates an environment conducive to exploitation.
- The Special Rapporteur calls for more effective international cooperation and adherence to legal frameworks, such as the Protocol to Prevent, Suppress and Punish Trafficking in Persons, to protect and assist victims of trafficking. This includes ensuring that states fulfil their obligations under international law to identify victims, provide assistance, and facilitate repatriation while ensuring non-discrimination and accountability for trafficking crimes.

17.10

The United Nations Security Council has also issued several key resolutions aimed at combating human trafficking, particularly when used by terrorist groups:

- UN Security Council Resolution 2388 (2017) specifically addresses human trafficking by terrorist groups, such as the Islamic State, and emphasises the importance of disrupting trafficking networks and providing support to victims. It also calls for enhanced international cooperation, information sharing and legal measures to combat trafficking.
- UN Security Council Resolution 2331 (2016) strongly condemns human trafficking in areas affected by armed conflicts, highlighting its role in undermining the rule of law and financing terrorism. It emphasises the need for international cooperation to combat trafficking and support victims, especially those targeted by terrorist groups like the Islamic State and Boko Haram.

17.11

The remainder of this Chapter will address how the UK has sought to balance the interests of victims with national security and the public interest in the context of cases in the Special Immigration Appeals Commission ('SIAC'). Although the High Court also has jurisdiction to hear secret evidence in civil proceedings by virtue of the Justice and Security Act 2013, the jurisprudence of SIAC is more developed, both in relation to closed procedures generally and in relation to victims of trafficking.

17.12

However, even in SIAC, the way that Art 4 ECHR and ECAT[5] apply to national security related decisions is evolving and contested. The principal case – or series of cases – on these issues is *Shamima Begum*. However, it is understood that her legal team seeks to apply to the Strasbourg court on the Art 4 issues arising which are discussed in detail below. In order to understand the courts' rulings on these cases it is first necessary to understand the procedural framework of SIAC and that of the Closed Material Procedure.

The origins of SIAC

17.13

SIAC was created to enable challenges to certain immigration-related decisions, which were based on national security concerns, to be determined by a court.

17.14

The primary purpose of creating SIAC, by the Special Immigration Appeals Commission Act 1997 ('the SIAC Act'), was to respond to the decision of the European Court of Human Rights ('ECtHR') in *Chahal v UK*[6]. That case concerned the detention pending deportation of an Indian citizen with indefinite leave to remain in the UK. The decision had been made on national security grounds which were not disclosed to Mr Chahal. At the time, there was no right of recourse to a court to review a decision taken on the basis of material which could not be disclosed to the affected individual. Instead, a process of review could take place before an advisory panel, typically including members of the senior judiciary, which would have access to the sensitive material. That panel could then give advice to the decision-maker. The advice would not be binding.

17.15

The ECtHR decided that the advisory system did not satisfy the requirements of Art 5(4) of the ECHR[7]. It described the inadequacies of the advisory system as follows:

---

5 Council of Europe Convention on Action Against Trafficking in Human Beings.

6 Application no. 22414/93, judgment 15 November 1996; (1997) 23 EHRR 413.

7 *'Everyone who is deprived of his liberty by arrest or detention shall be entitled to take proceedings by which the lawfulness of his detention shall be decided speedily by a court and his release ordered if the detention is not lawful.'*

> '130. Furthermore, although the procedure before the advisory panel undoubtedly provided some degree of control, bearing in mind that Mr Chahal was not entitled to legal representation before the panel, that he was only given an outline of the grounds for the notice of intention to deport, that the panel had no power of decision and that its advice to the Home Secretary was not binding and was not disclosed … the panel could not be considered as a 'court' within the meaning of Article 5 para. 4.'

17.16

Nor were the requirements of Art 13, which provides for the right to an effective remedy for breaches of Convention rights, satisfied. The advisory system was contrasted with what was said to be a model successfully operated in Canada, which was described in the following terms:

> '144. … [A] Federal Court judge holds an in camera hearing of all the evidence, at which the applicant is provided with a statement summarising, as far as possible, the case against him or her and has the right to be represented and to call evidence. The confidentiality of security material is maintained by requiring such evidence to be examined in the absence of both the applicant and his or her representative. However, in these circumstances, their place is taken by a security-cleared counsel instructed by the court, who cross-examines the witnesses and generally assists the court to test the strength of the State's case. A summary of the evidence obtained by this procedure, with necessary deletions, is given to the applicant.'

17.17

The response of the UK government to the decision of the ECtHR in *Chahal* was to establish SIAC as a court which was intended to conform to the model described above. That is, a court, assisted by security-cleared counsel, with the ability to review sensitive material, and to make binding rulings, including requiring the disclosure of a summary of the sensitive material to the affected individual.

Jurisdiction

17.18

The jurisdiction of SIAC extends to a number of categories of appeals and reviews against immigration decisions, including:

(a) Decisions on asylum and immigration related human rights matters, which would be the subject of an appeal under ss 82(1), 83(2) or 83A(2) of the Nationality, Immigration and Asylum Act 2002 but for the fact that they are subject to a certificate of the Secretary of State under s 97 of that Act: SIAC Act s 2

(b) Decisions concerning deprivation of citizenship made under s 40 of the British Nationality Act 1981, which would be the subject of an appeal under that Act but for the fact of a certificate under s 40A of that Act: SIAC Act s 2B

(c) Exclusion decisions made on the basis that they are conducive to the public good, which are not subject to a right of appeal, and which are certified as having been made wholly or partly in reliance on information which in the opinion of the Secretary of State should not be made public in the interests of national security, international relations, or some other aspect of the public interest: SIAC Act s 2C

(d) Refusals to grant naturalisation or registration as a British citizen under the British Nationality Act 1981 which are certified as per (c) above: SIAC Act s 2D

(e) Deportation decisions which are certified under s 97 or 97A(1) of the Nationality, Immigration and Asylum Act 2002: SIAC Act s 2E

(f) Other immigration decisions concerning the right to enter, reside in or remain in the UK, and those relating to removal, which are not otherwise subject to a right of appeal and are certified as per (c) above: SIAC Act s 2F

(g) Certain bail applications relating to persons detained on national security grounds under the Immigration Act 1971 or the Nationality, Immigration and Asylum Act 2002: SIAC Act s 3.

Test to be applied by SIAC

17.19

Where it is conducting a review under ss 2C, 2D, 2E, or 2F of the SIAC Act, the Commission is required to apply the principles which would be applicable in judicial review proceedings. However, when it is conducting an appeal under s 2 or (of particular relevance to this chapter) s 2B, SIAC is not confined to public law review principles. As Laing LJ explained in *U3 v SSHD*[8], an appeal under s 2B was fundamentally different from an application for judicial review, in that an appellant under s 2B would be able to challenge the merits of that

8 [2023] EWCA Civ 811, [2024] 2 WLR 319, at para. 170. U3 appealed to the Supreme Court. Her appeal was dismissed: [2025] UKSC 19. While the Supreme Court disagreed with some aspects of the judgment of the Court of Appeal in relation to SIAC treatment of 'pivotal facts', the passage referred to above was not criticised.

decision, unlike a judicial review claimant. Furthermore, where an issue arises as to whether one or more human rights have been breached by a decision, SIAC must decide for itself whether the impugned decision is lawful. However, particular restrictions apply to SIAC's ability to assess for itself the strength of the national security case, as explained further below.

Closed Material Procedures

17.20

In line with its original purpose, SIAC is typically charged with deciding cases in which the interests of national security are invoked by the decision-maker in support of the challenged immigration decision. Such proceedings will be conducted under a Closed Material Procedure ('CMP').

17.21

Closed material, for the purposes of SIAC, is defined as 'material which the Secretary of State would otherwise be required to disclose to the appellant or his representative … but which the Secretary of State objects to disclosing to the appellant or his representative'[9].

17.22

A full review of proceedings conducted under a CMP is beyond the scope of this chapter, which is primarily concerned with the recent Open jurisprudence in the area. However, the following features of a CMP are worth noting, in order to understand the context in which SIAC operates:

(i) In proceedings before SIAC, the individual who is challenging the relevant immigration decision will not be provided with the Closed material which underpins the decision under challenge. Nor will their legal representatives (commonly referred to as 'the Open Representatives').

(ii) One or more Special Advocates will be appointed to act on the individual's behalf[10]. The Secretary of State may not rely on Closed material unless a Special Advocate has been appointed[11].

(iii) Special Advocates are formally appointed to a case by the Attorney General, who administers a panel for these purposes. However, the Open Representatives may identify one or more Special Advocates from the panel as their preferred choice for the appointment.

---

9 Rule 37(1) of the Special Immigration Appeals Commission (Procedure) Rules 2003. ('the SIAC Rules). All subsequent references to Rules in this chapter are to the SIAC Rules unless expressly stated.

10 Under s.6 of the SIAC Act and r.34 of the SIAC Rules.

11 Rule 37(2).

(iv) Once they have viewed the Closed material, the Special Advocates are not permitted to communicate directly with the individual or their Open Representatives[12]. Prior to that point an Open conference may be held at which the Special Advocate is present and able to assist. As will be self-evident, at that stage they will have no greater knowledge of the Closed case than the Open Representatives. They will however be able to explain their particular role, advise on procedure, and gather information which may be of assistance to them in due course when they come to analyse the Closed material.

(v) The defined functions of the Special Advocate are to represent the interests of the appellant by (a) making submissions to the Commission at any hearings from which the appellant and his representatives are excluded; (b) adducing evidence and cross-examining witnesses at any such hearings; and (c) making written submissions to the Commission[13].

(vi) In substance, once they are 'in Closed', the role of the Special Advocate is twofold: first, to make submissions in support of further disclosure to the individual from the Closed material; second, to make submissions in the individual's interests on the substance of the Closed material, including at any final hearing.

(vii) At the conclusion of a hearing conducted under a CMP, there will typically be Open and Closed judgments handed down. Obviously enough, only the former are publicly available, and the information contained in this chapter is limited to the content of such Open judgments and other publicly available resources.

SIAC's approach to the national security assessment

17.23

There has been a considerable amount of litigation in recent years concerning the scope of SIAC's ability to form its own view as to an asserted risk of harm to national security which is pleaded in defence of a challenge to an immigration decision. The position now seems to be reasonably settled. In short, the ability of SIAC to depart from an assessment of the national security case which is relied upon by the decision-maker is restricted by considerations of institutional competence and democratic accountability. It cannot substitute its own view of the strength of the national security case for that of the expert decision-maker.

12 Rule 36(2).
13 Rule 35.

17.24

SIAC can, however, test the underlying evidence and make findings of fact for itself based on evidence which it has heard (including post-decision evidence, where appropriate). It is not restricted from making such findings of fact relating to the national security assessment, which it considers that, in its expert judgment, it is able to make, and which are appropriate in the appeal it is considering[14]. Its task is then:

> 'to see whether the SSHD's assessment can withstand its view of the evidence, provided that it remembers that the SSHD's assessment is frequently not solely or even primarily based on specific findings of fact made on the balance of probabilities but is an evaluation, based on a range of different types of material, many of which are not evidence for the purposes of litigation[15].'

17.25

The proper approach in SIAC to an assessment of national security is encapsulated in the judgment of Lady Carr LCJ in *Shamima Begum v SSHD*[16], a case concerned with an appeal under s 2B of the SIAC Act:

> '10. The relevant principles governing SIAC's jurisdiction and role on an appeal against a decision to deprive a person of citizenship under s 40(2) are now well established. In summary, those principles are:
>
> (i) SIAC is not the primary decision-maker. The exercise of the power conferred by s.40(2) must depend heavily on a consideration of relevant aspects of the public interest, which may include considerations of national security and public safety. The primary decision is entrusted to the Secretary of State who has the advantage of a wide range of advice, including from security specialists.
>
> (ii) SIAC's jurisdiction is appellate (and not supervisory). In general, SIAC's powers are restricted to considering whether the Secretary of State has acted in a way in which no reasonable decision-maker could have acted, or whether it has taken into account some irrelevant matter or has disregarded something to which it should have given weight, or has erred on a point of law (an issue which encompasses the consideration of factual questions). SIAC can consider whether the Secretary of State has made findings of fact which are unsupported by any evidence or based on a view of the evidence which could not reasonably be held.

14 *U3 v. SSHD* (CA), at para. 178.
15 Ibid, at para. 175.
16 [2024] EWCA Civ 152. As to which, see further below.

(iii) SIAC must have regard to the nature of the discretionary power in question, and the Secretary of State's statutory responsibility for deciding whether the deprivation of citizenship is conducive to the public good. It will bear in mind the serious nature of a deprivation of citizenship, and the severity of the consequences which can flow from such a decision.

(iv) In questions involving an evaluation of risk, SIAC allows a considerable margin, and real respect, to the Secretary of State's assessment. Some aspects of that assessment may not be justiciable; others will depend on an evaluative judgment. In matters of high policy, SIAC's deference may be effectively simple acceptance; at more granular levels, it is the function of SIAC to scrutinise all the evidence, open and closed, assisted by the invaluable contribution of the Special Advocates. It will apply a critical and expert intelligence – a 'powerful microscope' – to test the approach and the evidence bearing on the assessment, both for and against the conclusions of the Secretary of State, and then, applying due deference, decide whether the conclusions of the Secretary of State are sustainable.

(v) SIAC can make its own findings of fact which may be relevant to the assessment of national security, as long as it does not use those findings of fact as a platform for substituting its view of the risk to national security for that of the Secretary of State. Subject to that important limitation, it may make whatever findings of fact it considers it is able to on the evidence and which, in its expert judgment, it considers that it is appropriate to make.

(vi) SIAC can determine whether the Secretary of State has complied with s 40(4) (concerning statelessness) and must also determine for itself the compatibility of the decision with the obligations of the Secretary of State under the Human Rights Act 1998, where such a question arises[17]'.

17.26

The position has recently been authoritatively restated by the Supreme Court in *U3 v SSHD* [2025] UKSC 19 as follows:

17 The references cited by the LCJ for these propositions were: *Secretary of State for the Home Department v Rehman* [2001] UKHL 47; [2003] 1 AC 753 at [57] and [58]; *Begum v. SSHD* at [66] to [71] and [119]; *P3 v Secretary of State for the Home Department* [2021] EWCA Civ 1642, [2022] 1 WLR 2869 at [126]; *U3 v Secretary of State for the Home Department* [2023] EWCA Civ 811, [2024] 2 WLR 319 at [101], [169] and [176]. As noted above, while the approach identified by the Court of Appeal in U3 was the subject of some criticism when the case was considered by the Supreme Court, that does not affect the principles described by Lady Carr LCJ in the passage cited above.

> '… where the assessment of a risk to national security is based on an evaluation of a body of evidence, the issue SIAC has to decide is not whether the assessment is based on facts that have been established on a balance of probabilities. Rather, the central question is whether the evidence, viewed as a whole, provides a rational basis for the Secretary of State's decision, applying principles of administrative law …' [at para. 87]

17.27

Against that background, we turn to consider the way in which SIAC has recently approached the issue of trafficking in the case of *Shamima Begum*[18].

Begum v SSHD

The decision

17.28

On 19 February 2019, Shamima Begum, then aged 19, was deprived of her British citizenship by a decision under s 40(2) of the British Nationality Act 1981. As has been widely reported, back in 2015 Ms Begum had, together with others, travelled to Syria to join ISIL. She was 15 years old at the time of her travel. She subsequently married an ISIL fighter. As explained by Jay J when the matter came before SIAC in February 2023[19]:

> 'The self-styled caliphate effectively collapsed in January 2019 after a series of military defeats. Ms Begum, together with her husband, were in the last pockets of ISIL territory in Baghuz. They surrendered and were captured by members of the Syrian Democratic Forces ('the SDF'). Ms Begum was taken to the Al-Hawl camp in north-east Syria. In mid-February 2019, then nine months pregnant and subsequently even after she had just given birth, she gave a number of interviews to a reporter from The Times newspaper and to other print and TV journalists.'

17.29

The basis of the SSHD's decision was that deprivation was conducive to the public good due to the threat that she was assessed to pose to UK national

---

18 The majority of the references in this section are to the Open judgment of the Court of Appeal [2024] EWCA Civ 152, save where otherwise stated. For the avoidance of doubt, neither of the authors of this chapter have any knowledge of the Closed aspects of this case, either in SIAC or the Court of Appeal, including any Closed judgments.

19 At para. 9 of the Open judgment of SIAC dated 22 February 2023: SC/163/2019 ('the SIAC judgment').

security. The Ministerial Submission provided to the SSHD for the purpose of the decision contained the following[20]:

> 'The Security Service considers that any individual assessed to have travelled to Syria and to have aligned with ISIL poses a threat to national security. The basis for this assessment is set out [in the ISIL Statements]. The Security Service assesses that BEGUM travelled to Syria and aligned with ISIL, and has provided its assessment and national security case as included in the relevant annexes. SCU note that BEGUM travelled to Syria as a minor without informing her family [in Annex A, it is further pointed out that she used her sister's passport, suggesting that she had taken steps to plan her travel]. However BEGUM is assessed to have been in ISIL-controlled territory including after she turned 18 in August 2017. SCU therefore considers that the fact BEGUM travelled to Syria and aligned with ISIL as a minor does not alter the Security Service assessment of the risk she now poses to the UK. Recent media reporting indicates that she has also not sought to distance herself from ISIL and seeks to leave Syria as ISIL is losing its last remnants of territory there. … SCU have reflected on the interview given to The Times newspaper on 14 February 2019, and do not assess that the content undermines the Security Service assessment that BEGUM is aligned with ISIL and that she therefore poses a threat to UK national security.'

17.30

When taking the decision, the SSHD certified that the deprivation decision was taken wholly or partly in reliance on information which in his opinion should not be made public for reasons of national security[21]. As a result, Ms Begum's right of appeal lay to SIAC, and an appeal was duly brought under s 2B of the SIAC Act.

The appeal to SIAC

17.31

A number of grounds were raised in the appeal to SIAC, but two are of relevance for present purposes. On Ground 1 it was submitted that the Secretary of State had failed to take into account a relevant consideration, namely that Ms Begum may have been trafficked to Syria as a child in 2015. It was also said that he had failed to apply his own policy relating to minors assessed to have been radicalised[22]. On Ground 2, it was argued that the

20 Ibid, para. 128.
21 Under s.40A(2) of the British Nationality Act 1981.
22 The relevant policy is outlined at para. 130 of the SIAC judgment.

deprivation decision failed to respect Ms Begum's human rights under Art 4 of the European Convention on Human Rights because there was, at the very least, a credible suspicion that she was the victim of trafficking. It was submitted that the SSHD was in breach of Art 4 of the ECHR in terms of both the protective and the investigative duty.

Ground 2 – 'Deprivation decision was in violation of Art 4'

17.32

On 22 February 2023, SIAC, chaired by Mr. Justice Jay, dismissed Ms Begum's appeal. Dealing with Ground 2 first, the Commission concluded that there was a credible suspicion that Ms Begum had been the victim of trafficking in 2015. That was *'a low bar'*, which the Commission had *'little or no hesitation'* had been surpassed[23].

17.33

The Commission's view of this appears to have been fortified by a judgment of Hayden J sitting in the Family Division on 21 August 2015, which concerned an unrelated young female student who, like Ms Begum, had been planning to travel to Syria to join ISIS but had been taken off a plane bound for Istanbul at the last moment[24]. The Commission stated that the judgment of Hayden J *'merits close attention'*[25]. It quoted from the following passages of the judgment:

> '4. The case comes before me consecutively with a number of other cases within the Borough of Tower Hamlets, each of which involves intelligent young girls, highly motivated academically, each of whom has, to some and greatly varying degrees, been either radicalised or exposed to extreme ideology …
>
> 5. … In each of these cases … young women … have been captured, seduced, by a belief that travelling to Syria to become what is known as 'Jihadi brides' is somehow romantic and honourable both to them and their families. There is no doubt, to my mind, that young women have been specifically targeted, in addition to young men of course, but for different purposes. The reality is that the future for such girls as we know, holds only exploitation, degradation and risk of death; in other words these children with whose future I have been concerned, have been put at risk of really serious harm and as such the State is properly obligated to protect them. …'

23 Ibid, paras. 223 & 226.
24 [2015] EWHC 2491 (Fam).
25 SIAC judgment, para. 79.

17.34

Evidence specifically relating to the question of whether Ms Begum was trafficked appears at paras. 165 to 173 of the SIAC judgment. It was submitted on Ms Begum's behalf that it was difficult to avoid the inference that she was recruited etc. for the purpose of sexual exploitation. Under Art 4(c) of ECAT, *'the recruitment, transportation, transfer, harbouring or receipt of a child for the purpose of exploitation shall be considered 'trafficking in human beings"* regardless of the means[26].

17.35

However, the finding that there was a credible suspicion that Ms Begum had been trafficked to Syria as a minor in 2015 did not in and of itself mean that the deprivation decision amounted to a violation by the SSHD of Art 4 of the ECHR. In terms of the investigative duty, a violation of Art 4 would occur only if the SSHD were under an obligation to repatriate her for this purpose. In the view of the Commission, he was not. Nor did the recovery obligation to *'take appropriate measures within the scope of their powers to remove the individual'* from the situation or risk of their trafficking or exploitation bite in circumstances in which by the date of the decision Ms Begum was no longer in ISIL-controlled territory[27].

17.36

Turning to the protective duty, the Commission considered that 'the State may have failed in its duties to Ms Begum before she travelled to Syria, but she is now well beyond the scope of its protection[28].' The challenge, however, was to persuade the Commission that that any such violation was directly and necessarily relevant to the exercise of the s 40 power, to the extent that any exercise of that power pending any investigation would be unlawful. On behalf of Ms Begum, it was submitted that the link was provided by reliance on the 'non-punishment' principle found within Art 26 of ECAT:

> 'Each party shall, in accordance with the basic principles of its legal system, provide for the possibility of not imposing penalties on victims for their involvement in unlawful activities, to the extent that they have been compelled to do so.'

17.37

The Commission noted that the natural and ordinary meaning of Art 26 was that it was limited to criminal sanctions, or at least sanctions which are punitive in nature[29]. However, the opinion of the UN Special Rapporteur on trafficking

26 Ibid, para. 179.
27 Ibid, para. 236.
28 Ibid, para. 238.
29 Ibid, para. 241.

in persons, especially women and children, was relied upon by Ms Begum in support of a wider, purposive, interpretation of Art 26. In her opinion, the relevant range of punishments included, *inter alia*, non-repatriation and family separation[30].

17.38

The Commission considered that it was required to come to its own conclusion as to whether it would be a violation of Art 4 effectively to punish Ms Begum by exercising the section 40 deprivation power. It was being asked to determine a human rights point on *terra incognita*. The operative principle was, as had been explained by the Supreme Court in *AB v SSJ*[31], whether the Commission could be 'fully confident' that the ECtHR would conclude that the protections under Art 4 encompass the non-punishment principle as interpreted by the UN Special Rapporteur. The Commission could not be so confident. Accordingly, Ground 2 failed.

Ground 1 – mandatory relevant consideration

17.39

As explained by the Commission in relation to this ground of appeal[32]:

> 'The Secretary of State is required to consider and weigh in the balance all the known factors of Ms Begum's case which might militate against deprivation. In the Commission's judgment, he must do so in the context of this being one of the most potent powers conferred on Government against the individual, entailing the removal of one of the most fundamental rights in the international and domestic canon. This is a power to be exercised only where the national security of the United Kingdom requires it in the estimation of the Secretary of State.'

17.40

In addition to the above, it was submitted on Ms Begum's behalf that: (a) a finding that there is a credible suspicion that Ms Begum has been trafficked was obviously relevant to the exercise of the s 40 power; and (b) that:

> 'the panoply of assessments and protections bestowed by modern trafficking law have the status of being mandatory relevant considerations. They are so obviously relevant that they must be considered. They must be addressed before the deprivation power may be exercised[33]'.

30 Ibid, para. 242.
31 [2021] UKSC 28; [2022] AC 487.
32 At para. 248 of the SIAC judgment.
33 Ibid, para. 249.

17.41

As to the underlying facts upon which reliance was placed in support of this ground, the Commission explained:

> 'The Commission has already found that there is a credible suspicion that Ms Begum has been trafficked. Applying the principles in *Rantsev*, there is a credible suspicion that the State's protective duties were violated back in 2015. On the evidence, there is also a credible suspicion that Ms Begum was harboured by her traffickers until January 2019. How, then, can these factors not be mandatory relevant considerations?'[34]

17.42

The answer, in the view of the Commission, was that it was necessary to *'take stock and stand back'*. Its task in relation to Ground 1 was to review, applying public law principles, the policy of the SSHD. There was nothing in the applicable statute which suggested that the SSHD was required 'to make a formal judgment about trafficking with all the consequences that would flow from that; or, indeed, to take into account a credible suspicion that the individual may have been trafficked[35].' That being so, there was no obligation on the SSHD to view Ms Begum's case 'through the lens of trafficking'. Not being a mandatory relevant consideration, it was for the SSHD to decide what was in the public interest, and how much weight to give to certain factors, subject always to SIAC intervening on ordinary administrative law principles. The SSHD maintained that national security was a weighty factor and that it would take a very strong countervailing case to outweigh it. While reasonable people would profoundly disagree with the Secretary of State, that raised wider societal and political questions which it was not the role of SIAC to address. 'This is because questions of weight and balance are pre-eminently for the decision-maker and not for the Commission, subject always to *Wednesbury* review[36].'

17.43

Accordingly, this ground also failed, as did the remaining grounds of appeal advanced on behalf of Ms Begum.

The appeal to the Court of Appeal

17.44

Ms Begum then appealed to the Court of Appeal. In February 2024, the judgment of the court was handed down by Lady Carr, the Lady Chief Justice[37]. The Court of Appeal dismissed the appeal.

34 Ibid, para. 252.
35 Ibid, paras. 253-255.
36 Ibid, paras. 257-260.
37 [2024] EWCA Civ 152.

The Art 4 ground

17.45

In relation to the argument that the deprivation decision was in violation of Art 4, the court identified that the first stage of the assessment was met in Ms Begum's favour, in light of the Commission's finding that there was a credible suspicion that Ms Begum had been the victim of trafficking in 2015[38]. The second stage of the Art 4 assessment was to establish what duties and obligations flowed from that credible suspicion of trafficking. The operational and investigative duties were in issue in the present case[39].

The operational duty

17.46

From *Rantsev*, and *VCL*, the duty to take appropriate measures to protect victims or potential victims must be interpreted 'in a way which does not impose an impossible or disproportionate burden on the authorities'. The operational duty comprised protective and recovery aspects[40].

17.47

In terms of the protective duty, the court noted SIAC's conclusion that it was arguable that there were *'State failures, and possible violations of the corollary protective duty, between December 2014 and February 2015'*. However, the finding of arguable failures and violations only went so far. Furthermore, the court noted the passage of time between February 2015 and February 2019, and the lack of any causal link between the possible breaches of the protective duty in 2015 and the deprivation decision. Those obstacles were fatal to the argument that the UK authorities owed Ms Begum a protective duty under Art 4 at the time of the deprivation decision. More relevantly, it could not be said that the possibility of the existence of such a duty should have been taken into account: there was nothing to take into account, let alone anything obviously material[41].

17.48

Turning to the recovery duty, it was not argued that there was any obligation to repatriate Ms Begum, and as she was outside the jurisdiction there was no question of her now being provided with any support or treatment. Accordingly, the recovery duty did not assist: 'there was nothing arising as part of that duty

38 Judgment of the Court of Appeal, at para. 73. As a finding of fact made by SIAC, this was not appealable.
39 Ibid, para. 74.
40 Ibid, paras. 75–76.
41 Ibid, paras. 77–78.

which might have been material to the decision whether or not to deprive Ms Begum of her citizenship[42].' On the non-punishment principle and the interpretation of Art 26 ECAT, the court took the same view as SIAC[43].

The investigative obligation

17.49

There was no finding by SIAC of an actual breach in the investigative obligation. Accordingly, this submission was based on 'the asserted possibility of breach'[44].

17.50

While there would be cases in which it would be reasonable to expect the trafficked person to be in the UK to assist in the investigation, the court did not accept that there was any obligation on the SSHD to at least consider whether Ms Begum should be present in the UK to assist in any such investigation. That would be tantamount to an obligation to repatriate, which the court had already rejected in its consideration of the operational duty. It would also be inconsistent with the decision of the Supreme Court in *Begum v SSHD*[45] to the effect that the SSHD was not required to give Ms Begum leave to enter the UK in order to present her appeal to SIAC. Thirdly, the obligation on the State is only to take *reasonable* steps to investigate, and it was not arguable that reasonable steps extended to repatriating someone who is assessed to pose a threat to national security[46].

17.51

Any restitutionary duty would only arise where a breach was established. There was no established breach in this case. In any event, the asserted breach of the protective duty occurred four years prior to the deprivation decision. In the circumstances, the court concluded that there was no restitutionary duty owed to Ms Begum such as to trigger an obligation on the part of the Secretary of State to consider it[47].

17.52

The court explained its conclusion on the Art 4 ground as follows:

> 'Ms Begum was outside the jurisdiction and outside the control of the UK Government when the decision was made to deprive her of her

42 Ibid, para. 79.
43 Ibid, para. 82.
44 Ibid, para. 83.
45 [2021] UKSC 7; [2021] AC 765.
46 Judgment of the Court of Appeal, paras. 84–85.
47 Ibid, paras. 87–90.

citizenship. There was no obligation under the ECHR to repatriate her in 2015 or 2019 and there is none now. Further, the focus of a deprivation decision on the grounds of national security must be the assessment of risk. We do not accept that an individual who is assessed as presenting a risk to national security must be repatriated, or even that the Secretary of State is required to consider her repatriation, in order to meet obligations which might be owed under the protective duty, the recovery duty or the investigative duty (noting that any putative investigation would concern offences committed by other people, or State failures to protect her, four years earlier). Further, we do not accept that the non-punishment principle extends to a decision to deprive her of her citizenship on national security grounds or that a restitutionary duty exists even arguably on these facts[48].'

17.53

The court went on to hold that Art 4 gave rise to no obviously material consideration for the SSHD to consider in the context of the deprivation decision[49].

Mandatory relevant consideration

17.54

Turning to what had been Ground 1 before SIAC, the court agreed with a submission that the 'obviously material' test was context sensitive[50].

17.55

It noted that the ministerial submission did not discuss Art 4 ECHR, or ECAT, or the possibility that Ms Begum might have been trafficked for the purposes of sexual exploitation. However:

> '… the material before the Secretary of State included press articles referring to 'jihadi brides', a phrase much in use at the time, which incorporates the idea of young women being groomed by ISIL for the purpose of marriage and sexual exploitation. The material before the Secretary of State powerfully expressed the view that people who were children when they went to align with the ISIL caliphate should be considered first and foremost as victims.'

48 Ibid, para. 91.
49 Ibid, para. 92.
50 Ibid, para. 93.

17.56

But in any event, the court agreed with SIAC that:

> 'the Secretary of State was not obliged to view Ms Begum's case 'through the lens of trafficking'. By approving the ministerial submission, taken together with its annexes and the minors' policy, the Secretary of State accepted the view that Ms Begum's 'victimhood', to the extent that it was a point in her favour, was not of such weight as to affect his conclusion that she posed a threat to national security such that it would be conducive to the public good to deprive her of citizenship and thus the right to return to the UK[51].'

17.57

The assessment that Ms Begum was a risk to national security had been kept under review, and was maintained in a statement dated 17 October 2022. SIAC had been entitled 'as the specialist tribunal established by Parliament' to find that the issue of whether and to what extent Ms Begum's travel to Syria had been voluntary was within the expertise of the intelligence agencies advising the Secretary of State. Further, voluntariness was not a binary question, and 'the assessment of the national security risk was, as *Begum* UKSC made clear at [56]-[57], a question of evaluation and judgment entrusted by Parliament to the Secretary of State[52].'

17.58

In the circumstances, the court concluded that there was 'no material shortcoming on the part of the Secretary of State arising out of any failure to take account of the possibility that Ms Begum had been trafficked for the specific purpose of sexual exploitation[53].'

17.59

The appeal was dismissed.

Conclusion

17.60

Notwithstanding that Art 4 ECHR is absolute, the courts have ruled that potential victim status does not automatically preclude measures being taken against an individual on national security grounds. As noted above, the

51 Ibid, para. 94.
52 Ibid, paras. 95–98.
53 Ibid, para. 99.

UK Government was deemed to have accepted that Begum was a 'victim'; but concluded, lawfully, that this 'victimhood' was not weighty enough to affect the conclusion that she posed a threat to national security, and ought to be deprived of her citizenship.

17.61

This does not mean that the operational and investigative duties, which apply to a state in relation to a potential victim, may never have an impact in this context. In *Begum*, 'arguable' breaches by the state of the protective duty in 2015 were held not to affect the deprivation decision, made in 2019, given the absence of any 'causal link' between the possible breaches and the deprivation decision. In practical terms, the possible failure of the state to protect Begum from grooming and being lured out of the country in 2015 did not 'cause' the deprivation decision. The factual basis for this finding is unlikely ever to be publicly known. However, the reasoning suggests that, where the state failures to protect are sufficiently related to the national security decision, those failures may affect the lawfulness of the decision under Art 4 ECHR. A possible example might be a child who, owing to state failures, is groomed and forcibly recruited to a work as a suicide bomber, and the deprivation decision is made shortly thereafter when it is plain that the child remains coerced into doing so.

17.62

Begum illustrates the difficulty of asserting that coercion is operating on the person's will notwithstanding the passage of time. Indeed, where atrocities are committed many years after the initial recruitment, the 'causal' link may simply be a historical fact with little or no legal and moral relevance to the conduct in question. The case of *Dominic Ongwen* is such a case. Ongwen was forcibly recruited when he was nine years old by the Lord's Resistance Army (LRA) in Uganda. He later became a commander and was charged with war crimes, committed as an adult, by the International Criminal Court (ICC). The ICC rejected his defence that his status as a victim, as a child, was relevant to the question of whether his conduct as a commander was under threat or duress[54], although these matters were relevant to mitigation. This case is discussed further in **Chapter 18**.

17.63

The fact that Begum was outside the UK at the time of the deprivation decision meant that any failure of the investigative duty was thought to be immaterial; and there could be no duty to repatriate. Having said that, the Court's reasoning leaves open the possibility that, were Begum to have been in the UK at the date of the decision, the failure to investigate may well have precluded the decision

54 *The Prosecutor v Dominic Ongwen* (Trial Judgment) ICC-02/04-01/15 4 February 2021, §2592.

to deprive her of her citizenship, just as that failure rendered the decision to prosecute in violation of Art 4 ECHR in *VCL v United Kingdom*.

17.64

Ultimately, it was not possible for Begum to understand the precise allegations against her; and it was not possible for her to rebut them, given that they were not disclosed to her. It is not possible to understand why SIAC believed that there was no causal link between any failure to protect her and the conduct leading to her deprivation of citizenship, as that reasoning will be set out in a closed judgment. What is clear however is that the courts are very slow to trespass on the competence of democratically elected representatives to make assessments of what amounts to a threat to national security. They are also equally slow to question the specialist expertise of the UK security services on this issue. It follows that, where national security is in issue, Art 4 ECHR is unlikely to provide any basis to challenge the decision save, possibly, in very narrow and specific situations which have yet to be confirmed by the courts.

Editorial Note – Michelle Brewer

Begum v United Kingdom: Article 1 Jurisdiction and Article 4 Positive Obligations

17.65

The Strasbourg Court has framed four questions[55] which require careful consideration of the relationship between Art 1 jurisdiction and the positive obligations arising under Art 4. The first and third questions are central: whether the United Kingdom retained jurisdiction for the purposes of Art 4 where the alleged failures occurred while the applicant was a child within its territory, and whether Art 4 required the Secretary of State to consider her potential status as a trafficked child before depriving her of citizenship. The domestic tribunals accepted that there was, at minimum, a credible suspicion that the trafficking process had begun while she was in London, and the Supreme Court recognised that the development of the applicable Convention principles falls to Strasbourg. The Court must therefore determine whether obligations triggered at that earlier stage continued to have legal relevance when later decisions concerning her status were taken.

55 European Court of Human Rights, 'Communication to the Government of the United Kingdom in *Begum v United Kingdom* (App No 36427/24)' (ECtHR, 18 December 2025).

17.66

The first issue is whether Art 4 obligations, which are underpinned by rule of law principles[56], once engaged by domestic conduct, can be said to persist notwithstanding the individual's subsequent trafficking out of the jurisdiction. The principal penal instruments governing trafficking, the Palermo Protocol and ECAT, define trafficking as a sequence of acts beginning with recruitment, transfer etc (see **Chapter 1**) and culminating in exploitation, and apply without distinction to national and transnational cases. The ECAT Explanatory Report characterises trafficking as 'a modern form of the old worldwide slave trade' carried out by actors 'who do not respect boundaries', and its drafters extended the Convention's scope to 'all forms' of trafficking for the specific purpose of avoiding responsibility and impunity gaps of the kind historically associated with the slave trade[57]. Against that background, the proposal that Art 4 duties lapse or are significantly attenuated at the moment of departure sits uneasily with the structure of these instruments, which treat the domestic initiating phase as a legally significant point of responsibility, including criminal responsibility, that is not automatically extinguished by subsequent cross-border movement.

17.67

A second issue concerns the appropriate framework for determining jurisdiction under Art 1 where the alleged breach is anchored in antecedent domestic failures. In *Rantsev*[58] and *J v Austria*[59], the Court held that Art 4 duties may be anchored in the domestic stage of a trafficking process, and that the victim's later displacement does not extinguish investigative obligations already engaged. Stoyanova's analysis[60] proceeds from a straightforward proposition. Article 1 jurisdiction does not depend solely on physical control. It also reflects the legal relationship that arises when a person is within the State's own system of law and protection. That relationship is ordinarily created by territorial presence, but it may equally rest on the State's prior involvement in the events said to give rise to the duty. Where the complaint concerns failures occurring while the individual was within that system, the jurisdictional link derives from those earlier omissions rather than from the person's later location. Stoyanova distinguishes this threshold question from the separate issue of the scope of any consequent duty: jurisdiction is binary, whereas the content of the obligation may vary with the circumstances. She also makes clear that jurisdiction cannot be established simply because a domestic act has effects abroad. The question for the Court is therefore whether the UK's acknowledged failures during the domestic grooming and recruitment period constitute a sufficient and ongoing jurisdictional anchor for Art 1.

56 See **Chapters 4** and **10**.

57 ECAT Explanatory Report, https://rm.coe.int/16800d3812, paras 3, 36, 60–61.

58 App no 25965/04, 7 January 2010.

59 App no 58216/12, 17 January 2017.

60 Valdislava Stoyanova, *Positive Obligations under the European Convention on Human Rights: Within and Beyond Borders* (Oxford University Press 2023, Ch 8).

17.68

A further matter, raised squarely by the UN Special Rapporteur[61] and reflected in *VCL and AN*[62], concerns the potential characterisation of deprivation of citizenship as a 'penalty' in the trafficking context. The non-punishment principle, which the Special Rapporteur describes as a cornerstone of victim protection, is directed to the State's Art 4 positive obligation to secure recovery and reintegration, and the Court in *VCL and AN* held that prosecution of a trafficked child risks undermining those protective aims. The Special Rapporteur identifies deprivation of nationality as a form of punishment capable of violating the non-punishment principle and increasing risks of trafficking or re-trafficking. That approach reflects the ICC's treatment of children associated with armed groups, where the emphasis is on reintegration rather than penalisation. The Court must therefore consider whether, in the case of a child trafficked by a terrorist organisation engaged in armed conflict, deprivation of citizenship operates in substance as a penalty inconsistent with the protective purpose of Art 4.

17.69

Finally, this case does not require the Court to recognise an extraterritorial duty to protect the applicant in Syria. The issue is narrower: whether obligations that attached while the child was within the UK's jurisdiction persisted so as to require consideration in the decision to deprive her of citizenship. Trafficking is properly understood as a continuing wrong, and a jurisdictional analysis that ignores the initiating domestic phase would risk reopening the very responsibility gaps that ECAT was designed to eliminate. The Court must therefore determine whether the antecedent obligations continued to bear on the Secretary of State's decision in 2019, and whether their omission falls within the scope of the violations alleged.

61 Siobhán Mullally, *Implementation of the non-punishment principle*, Report of the Special Rapporteur on trafficking in persons, especially women and children, UN Doc A/HRC/47/34 (17 May 2021).

62 App nos 77587/12 and 74603/12.

18 Prosecuting and defending in the ICC

Jonathan Elystan Rees KC

Introduction

18.1

In the words of the ICC Prosecutor, 'Slavery and the slave trade are foundational crimes' which 'continue to entrap children, parents, migrants and civilians, causing incalculable harm'. In acknowledgment of the importance accorded to such crimes by international law, in December 2024 the Office of the Prosecutor ('OTP') issued the first policy by any international court or tribunal which specifically addresses slavery crimes[1].

18.2

The Policy on Slavery Crimes was developed to 'help discharge the Office's responsibility to fully and effectively investigate and prosecute slavery crimes' within the jurisdiction of the ICC, to present 'the principles underlying the Office's approach to slavery crimes', and to outline 'relevant aspects of its practice'.

18.3

The Policy provides *inter alia* a comprehensive review of the historical development of the approach towards slavery of international law, the key concepts and misconceptions, the specific offences relating to slavery set out in the Rome Statute and their relationship with other Rome Statute crimes, key principles such as following survivor-centred and trauma-informed approaches, and a guide to the application of these policy considerations to the planning and preparation of investigations, evidence gathering, witness interviews, witness protection and support, witness preparation, the selection of charges, witness examination and sentencing.

18.4

One disappointment is that the Policy avoids addressing directly the difficult questions that arise where a suspect/accused is also a victim of slavery. The

1 https://www.icc-cpi.int/sites/default/files/2024-12/policy-slavery-web-eng.pdf (accessed 21 August 2025).

recent decision of the Appeals Chamber in *Prosecutor v Ongwen*[2] sheds some light on that troubled ground (at least in the sense of narrowing the options) when it rejected the recommendation of the UN Special Rapporteur on Trafficking in Persons that the defence of duress should be interpreted more broadly where the specific context of slavery is present.

18.5

But clear guidance as to how the Prosecution and the Court should *positively* carry out the balancing act required by a survivor-centred approach when the survivor of slavery crimes is also the suspected perpetrator of crimes within the jurisdiction of the ICC, remains outstanding.

Survivor-centred and trauma-informed approaches

18.6

The OTP is guided by survivor-centred and trauma-informed approaches to slavery crimes[3].

18.7

The survivor-centred approach prioritises survivor's rights and orients all the OTP's actions and decision-making around treating survivors with dignity, compassion, empathy, respect and in a non-discriminatory manner.

18.8

In accordance with the trauma-informed approach, the OTP 'comprehends impacts on the physical, emotional, and mental-health, well-being, intra-personal and community relationships' of survivors, acknowledges 'that survivors differ in their responses to traumatisation over time' and 'recognises that survivors might experience traumatising bonds with their perpetrators, especially given the duration of some slavery situations'.

Approach of the Rome Statute to slavery and trafficking

18.9

The specific 'slavery crimes' provided for by the Rome Statute are:

- Enslavement; and
- Sexual Slavery.

2 *Prosecutor v Dominic Ongwen*, ICC-02/04-01/15A, *Public Redacted Judgment on the appeal of Mr Ongwen against the Decision of Trial Chamber XI of 4 February 2021 entitled 'Trial Judgment'*, ICC-02/04-01/15-2022-Red, 15 December 2022, Public.

3 The Policy at paragraph 84–86.

18.10

Enslavement and sexual slavery are both crimes against humanity, when committed as part of a widespread or systematic attack directed against any civilian population, with knowledge of the attack.

18.11

Sexual slavery is also a war crime when committed as part of a plan or policy or as part of a large-scale commission of such crimes during armed conflict.

18.12

Proof of slavery crimes focuses on the mental state and the acts or omissions of the enslaver, and not the consent, mental state, reactions, or actions of the victims/survivors. Slavery or enslavement does not require force, menace, compulsion, threat or lack of a victim's volition (although they may frequently be present)[4]. Similarly, proof of work, labour, sexual violence, reproductive harms, or establishment of any form of exploitation, or mental or physical harm are not required elements of slavery crimes (although they may frequently be present) – in fact, a person may be well-fed, clothed and housed, and still be enslaved[5]. The key to slavery crimes is the exercise of powers of ownership over a person or persons.

18.13

At the same time, the OTP recognises that contemporary slavery crimes are not always obvious, and do not always involve literal bondage, captivity or even clear nomenclature[6]. The OTP 'recognises slavery in all its subtle manifestations and references', the 'range of historical harms', including family separations, reproductive control, sexual harms, malnutrition, branding or corporal punishments for attempts to escape, and 'the euphemistic language that has often hidden slavery practices from view' such as references to 'fancy girls', 'comfort women', '*ting ting*' girls and 'bush wives'.

18.14

When the various indicators of enslavement are properly contextualised and seen through the lens of a survivor-centred and trauma-informed approach, it allows a comprehensive and accurate understanding of the complex and multi-faceted harm caused by slavery crimes[7].

---

4 The Policy at paragraph 47.

5 The Policy at paragraph 62, referring to *United States of America v Oswald Pohl et al,* Judgment, International Military Tribunal, 3 November 1947 at paragraph 15.

6 The Policy at paragraph 61.

7 The Policy at paragraph 71.

18.15

Trafficking in persons is proscribed, not by the Rome Statute, but by the Palermo Protocol[8] which in Art 3(a) thereof defines trafficking as the 'recruitment, transportation, transfer, harbouring or receipt of persons … for the purpose of exploitation' by means which include but are not limited to 'the threat or use of force or other forms of coercion'. It is sufficient that the means used include 'the abuse of power or of a position of vulnerability'. The definition of exploitation under Art 3(a) includes, but is not limited to, slavery.

18.16

Trafficking in persons is not itself a 'standalone' crime under the jurisdiction of the ICC, but when the conduct of trafficking, forced labour or servile status occurs with the exercise of powers attaching to the rights of ownership over a person, then it can amount to the crime of Enslavement (and where the necessary sexual element is present, Sexual Slavery).

Jurisdiction of the ICC

18.17

Article 5 of the Rome Statute of the International Criminal Court limits the jurisdiction of the Court to the most serious crimes of concern to the international community as a whole, and specifically the following crimes:

(a) the crime of genocide;

(b) crimes against humanity;

(c) war crimes;

(d) the crime of aggression.

18.18

Article 25(3) establishes individual criminal responsibility for the commission of the above offences within the jurisdiction of the ICC, but also for a range of inchoate types of conduct, including aiding, abetting or otherwise assisting in the commission of the offence, and contributing to the commission of the offence by a group of persons acting with a common purpose.

8 Protocol to Prevent, Suppress and Punish Trafficking in Persons, Especially Women and Children, supplementing the United Nations Convention against Transnational Organized Crime, supplementing the United Nations Convention against Transnational Organized Crime (adopted 15 November 2000, entered into force 25 December 2003) 2237 UNTS 319.

18.19

In addition to the four crimes set out in Art 5, Art 70(1) establishes that the Court also has jurisdiction over a series of offences against its administration of justice, including giving false testimony, presenting false evidence, and obstructing witnesses or otherwise tampering with evidence.

18.20

It is important to note that the criminal jurisdiction of the Court does not extend to any person who was under the age of 18 at the time of the alleged commission of a crime[9]. The ICC is concerned only with adult offenders.

Slavery crimes – crimes against humanity

18.21

Article 7(1) of the Rome Statute provides that, when committed as part of a widespread or systematic attack directed against any civilian population, with knowledge of the attack, 'Enslavement' and 'Sexual Slavery' are crimes against humanity.

> 'Article 7 – Crimes against humanity
>
> 1. For the purpose of this Statute, 'crime against humanity' means any of the following acts when committed as part of a widespread or systematic attack directed against any civilian population, with knowledge of the attack:
>
> …
>
> (c) Enslavement;
>
> …
>
> (g) sexual slavery, …;'

18.22

For the purpose of Art 7(1), an 'Attack directed against any civilian population' means a course of conduct involving the multiple commission of acts referred to in paragraph 1 against any civilian population, pursuant to or in furtherance of a State or organisational policy to commit such attack (Art 7(3)).

18.23

The Elements of Crimes publication[10], adopted to assist the Court in the interpretation and application of Arts 6, 7 and 8 of the Rome Statute, explains further at page 3:

---

9 Article 26 of the Rome Statute.

10 https://www.icc-cpi.int/sites/default/files/Publications/Elements-of-Crimes.pdf.

'2. The last two elements for each crime against humanity describe the context in which the conduct must take place. These elements clarify the requisite participation in and knowledge of a widespread or systematic attack against a civilian population. However, the last element should not be interpreted as requiring proof that the perpetrator had knowledge of all characteristics of the attack or the precise details of the plan or policy of the State or organization. In the case of an emerging widespread or systematic attack against a civilian population, the intent clause of the last element indicates that this mental element is satisfied if the perpetrator intended to further such an attack.

3. 'Attack directed against a civilian population' in these context elements is understood to mean a course of conduct involving the multiple commission of acts referred to in Article 7, paragraph 1, of the Statute against any civilian population, pursuant to or in furtherance of a State or organizational policy to commit such attack. The acts need not constitute a military attack. It is understood that 'policy to commit such attack' requires that the State or organization actively promote or encourage such an attack against a civilian population.'

18.24

Footnote 6 to the Elements of Crimes adds:

'A policy which has a civilian population as the object of the attack would be implemented by State or organizational action. Such a policy may, in exceptional circumstances, be implemented by a deliberate failure to take action, which is consciously aimed at encouraging such attack. The existence of such a policy cannot be inferred solely from the absence of governmental or organizational action.'

Slavery crimes – war crimes

18.25

Article 8 also makes Sexual Slavery a war crime if committed as part of a plan or policy or as part of a large-scale commission of such crimes during armed conflict:

'1. The Court shall have jurisdiction in respect of war crimes in particular when committed as part of a plan or policy or as part of a large-scale commission of such crimes.

2. For the purpose of this Statute, 'war crimes' means:

(a) …

(b) Other serious violations of the laws and customs applicable in international armed conflict, within the established framework of international law, namely, any of the following acts:

…

(xxii) … sexual slavery …

…

(e) Other serious violations of the laws and customs applicable in armed conflicts not of an international character, within the established framework of international law, namely, any of the following acts:

…

(vi) … sexual slavery …'

18.26

The Elements of Crimes provides that:

> 'the elements for war crimes under Article 8, paragraph 2, of the Statute shall be interpreted within the established framework of the international law of armed conflict including, as appropriate, the international law of armed conflict applicable to armed conflict at sea.
>
> With respect to the last two elements listed for each crime:
>
> (a) There is no requirement for a legal evaluation by the perpetrator as to the existence of an armed conflict or its character as international or non-international;
>
> (b) In that context there is no requirement for awareness by the perpetrator of the facts that established the character of the conflict as international or non-international;
>
> (c) There is only a requirement for the awareness of the factual circumstances that established the existence of an armed conflict that is implicit in the terms 'took place in the context of and was associated with'.'

Crime against humanity of enslavement

18.27

'Enslavement' is defined in Art 7(2) of the Rome Statute as:

> 'the exercise of any or all of the powers attaching to the right of ownership over a person and includes the exercise of such power in the course of trafficking in persons, in particular women and children'.

18.28

The Elements of Crimes lists the following elements of the offence:

1. The perpetrator exercised any or all of the powers attaching to the right of ownership over one or more persons, such as by purchasing, selling, lending or bartering such a person or persons, or by imposing on them a similar deprivation of liberty.
2. The conduct was committed as part of a widespread or systematic attack directed against a civilian population.
3. The perpetrator knew that the conduct was part of or intended the conduct to be part of a widespread or systematic attack directed against a civilian population.

18.29

While relevant where present, evidence of a commercial or financial transaction is not legally required[11]; there is no temporal or minimum duration requirement[12]; and evidence of formal imprisonment or detention is not necessary to establish the imposition of a similar deprivation of liberty – deprivation of liberty can take many forms[13]. Victims need not be physically confined, where there are other effective barriers which impede them from leaving[14].

Crime against humanity of sexual slavery

18.30

Sexual Slavery is not defined within the Rome Statute, but the Elements of Crimes set out the following elements:

---

11 The Policy at paragraph 69, referring to: *Prosecutor v Ongwen,* Trial Judgment, ICC-02/04-01/15-1762-RED, Trial Chamber IX, 4 February 2021 at paragraph 2713; *Prosecutor v Ntaganda,* Trial Judgment, ICC-01/04-02/06-2359, Trial Chamber VI, 8 July 2019 at paragraph 952; and *Prosecutor v Katanga,* Trial Judgment, ICC-01/04-01/07-3436-tENG, Trial Chamber II, 7 March 2014 at paragraph 976.

12 The Policy at paragraph 69, referring to: *Prosecutor v Ongwen,* Trial Judgment, ICC-02/04-01/15-1762-RED, Trial Chamber IX, 4 February 2021 at paragraph 2714; *Prosecutor v Taylor,* Judgement, SCSL-03-01-T, Trial Chamber II, 18 May 2012 at paragraph 447; *Prosecutor v Sesay,* Judgement, SCSL-04-15-T, Trial Chamber I, 2 March 2009 at paragraph 200; and *Prosecutor v Kunarac et al,* Judgement, IT-96-23-T& IT-96-23/1-T, Trial Chamber, 22 February 2001 at paragraph 121.

13 The Policy at paragraph 69, referring to: *Prosecutor v Ongwen,* Trial Judgment, ICC-02/04-01/15-1762-RED, Trial Chamber IX, 4 February 2021 at paragraph 2713; *Prosecutor v Ntaganda,* Trial Judgment, ICC-01/04-02/06-2359, Trial Chamber VI, 8 July 2019 at paragraph 952; *Prosecutor v Katanga,* Trial Judgment, ICC-01/04-01/07-3436-tENG, Trial Chamber II, 7 March 2014 at paragraph 977; and *Prosecutor v Taylor,* Judgement, SCSL-03-01-T, Trial Chamber II, 18 May 2012 at paragraph 420.

14 The Policy at paragraph 69, referring to: *Prosecutor v Ntaganda,* Trial Judgment, ICC-01/04-02/06-2359, Trial Chamber VI, 8 July 2019 at paragraph 952; and *Prosecutor v Ongwen,* Trial Judgment, ICC-02/04-01/15-1762-RED, Trial Chamber IX, 4 February 2021 at paragraph 2713.

1. The perpetrator exercised any or all of the powers attaching to the right of ownership over one or more persons, such as by purchasing, selling, lending or bartering such a person or persons, or by imposing on them a similar deprivation of liberty.
2. The perpetrator caused such person or persons to engage in one or more acts of a sexual nature.
3. The conduct was committed as part of a widespread or systematic attack directed against a civilian population.
4. The perpetrator knew that the conduct was part of or intended the conduct to be part of a widespread or systematic attack directed against a civilian population.

18.31

The OTP's Policy on Gender-Based Crimes: Crimes involving sexual, reproductive and other gender-based violence, December 2023 provides the following further assistance at paragraphs 32-33: An act can be 'sexual' even without physical contact, such as psychological violence that arises from threats of rape or genital mutilation. An act may be sexual regardless of whether sexual gratification was part of the intent or result. Sexual acts can be committed by and against any person regardless of sex or gender; it may also involve persons of the same sex. It should be noted that there is no single understanding of the term 'sexual', nor should one be imposed. Rather, the sexual nature and gravity of an act is determined by myriad factors such as age, gender, sex characteristics, culture, religion, historical precedents, ethnicity and indigenous status. Survivors may have diverse perspectives as to what constitutes an 'act of sexual nature'. Ultimately, as with other crimes, understanding acts of a sexual nature requires an intersectional approach[15]. Such an analysis can help discern whether an act was committed with sexual intent, had sexual impact or was perceived as sexual by affected persons. The Prosecution must, however, establish the sexual nature of the act in question in order to carry its burden of proof.

War crime of sexual slavery

18.32

The Elements of Crimes set out the following elements for the war crime of sexual slavery:

1. The perpetrator exercised any or all of the powers attaching to the right of ownership over one or more persons, such as by purchasing, selling,

15 'Intersectionality' refers to the way distinct forms of discrimination can combine and compound to result in consequences that differ from those resulting from any one of the individual forms of discrimination.

lending or bartering such a person or persons, or by imposing on them a similar deprivation of liberty.

2. The perpetrator caused such person or persons to engage in one or more acts of a sexual nature.
3. The conduct took place in the context of and was associated with an international armed conflict.
4. The perpetrator was aware of factual circumstances that established the existence of an armed conflict.

18.33

The Elements of Crimes explains that the elements for war crimes under Art 8, paragraph 2 (e), are subject to the limitations addressed in Art 8, paragraph 2 (f), which are not elements of crimes:

> 'Article 8(2)
>
> …
>
> (f) Paragraph 2 (e) applies to armed conflicts not of an international character and thus does not apply to situations of internal disturbances and tensions, such as riots, isolated and sporadic acts of violence or other acts of a similar nature. It applies to armed conflicts that take place in the territory of a State when there is protracted armed conflict between governmental authorities and organized armed groups or between such groups.'

'Deprivation of liberty' in relation to both enslavement and sexual slavery

18.34

In relation to both the crime against humanity of Enslavement and the crime against humanity of Sexual Slavery:

> 'such deprivation of liberty may, in some circumstances, include exacting forced labour or otherwise reducing a person to a servile status as defined in the Supplementary Convention on the Abolition of Slavery, the Slave Trade, and Institutions and Practices Similar to Slavery of 1956. It is also understood that the conduct described in this element includes trafficking in persons, in particular women and children[16].'

16 See footnotes 11, 18 and 53 to the Elements of Crimes.

18.35

In relation to Sexual Slavery, the Elements of Crimes acknowledges that: 'Given the complex nature of this crime, it is recognized that its commission could involve more than one perpetrator as a part of a common criminal purpose[17].'

Continuing offences

18.36

As the Policy observes:

> 'slavery crimes are not single, momentary acts. They are continuing crimes. They encompass the entire period from the commission of a slave trade through the entire time of enslavement in which the powers attaching to the rights of ownership are exercised over a person or persons.'

Awareness and consent is irrelevant

18.37

According to the Policy, 'awareness and consent are irrelevant' to the commission or otherwise of the crimes of Enslavement and Sexual Slavery:

> 'A survivor/victim is not required to be aware of their enslavement nor of the extent of the powers attaching to the right of ownership exercised over their person in order to establish the crime. Further, for slavery crimes, consent or lack thereof is neither an element to establish nor a defence to conviction. For sexual slavery, the element of 'caused to engage' in the act of a sexual nature does not require an examination of the survivor's consent at all.'

Other related offences

18.38

The Policy on Slavery Crimes provides a non-exhaustive list of factual indicators of slavery such as:

- use of child labour;
- use of child soldiers;

17 See footnote 17 and 52 to the Elements of Crimes.

- forms of force or control over workers;
- forced procreation;
- forced movement of people, especially children; and
- forced marriage.

18.39

Whilst proof of work, labour, sexual violence, reproductive harms, or establishment of any form of exploitation, or mental and physical harm are not required elements of the slavery crimes of Enslavement and Sexual Slavery, many examples of these *indicia* will amount to separate offences under the Rome Statute, such as:

(a) Crimes against Humanity:

- Deportation or forcible transfer of population (Art 7(2)(k))
- Enforced prostitution (Art 7(2)(n))
- Forced pregnancy (Art 7(2)(n))

(b) War Crimes:

- Compelling a prisoner of war or other protected person to serve in the forces of a hostile Power (Art 8(2)(a)(v))
- Unlawful deportation or transfer or unlawful confinement (Art 8(2)(a)(vii))
- The deportation or transfer of all or parts of the population of the occupied territory within or outside this territory (Art 8(2)(b)(viii))
- Enforced prostitution (Art 8(2)(b)(xxii); Art 8(2)(e)(vi))
- Forced pregnancy (Art 8(2)(b)(xxii); Art 8(2)(e)(vi))
- Conscripting or enlisting children under the age of fifteen years into the national armed forces or using them to participate actively in hostilities (Art 8(2)(b)(xxvi); Art 8(2)(e)(vii))
- Ordering the displacement of the civilian population for reasons related to the conflict, unless the security of the civilians involved or imperative military reasons so demand (Art 8(2)(e)(viii))

18.40

Additionally, the Policy observes that the offences of genocide (Art 6) and the crime against humanity of persecution (Art 7(1)(h)) may additionally be engaged:

> 'the acts and conduct underpinning slavery crimes (such as starvation, branding or family separation) could be characterised as various genocidal acts' such as 'causing serious bodily or mental harm (Article 6(b)), bringing about conditions of life calculated to destroy the group (Article 6(c)), or transferring children to a different group (Article 6(e)), if committed against members of a national, ethnic, racial or religious group with the intent to destroy that group in whole or in part'; and
>
> 'reducing a person to the status of a slave in and of itself amounts to a severe deprivation of a fundamental human right, an element of the crime against humanity of persecution under Article 7(1)(h)'.

18.41

The physical or mental harm caused by slavery crimes may bring into play the following offences:

- torture (Art 7(1)(f); Art 8(2)(a)(ii));
- cruel treatment (Art 8(2)(c)(i));
- inhumane acts (Art 7(1)(k));
- wilfully causing great suffering (Art 8(2)(a)(iii)); and
- committing outrages upon personal dignity (Art 8(2)(b)(xxi); Art 8(2)(c)(ii)).

Investigation and prosecution

18.42

The OTP has identified slavery crimes as crimes of priority, and as crimes amongst the gravest under the Rome Statute.

18.43

At the earliest stage, the OTP will identify patterns of targeting of particular victims or victim groups, to understand the background context of the situation and alleged crimes, and to recognise specific vulnerabilities affecting specific victims.

18.44

Where slavery crimes within the Court's jurisdiction have been identified, the OTP will consider admissibility by reference to gravity and complementarity. Complementarity assessments are fact-specific and are required where domestic proceedings may cover substantially the same underlying conduct. Various national barriers to genuine investigations and prosecutions may be relevant, such as discriminatory attitudes and stereotypes in substantive law, procedural rules limiting access to justice, the existence of amnesties or immunity laws, the absence of proper protective measures for victims, and the lack of political will.

18.45

The Policy on Slavery Crimes identifies multiple varied sources and types of evidence that are likely to be relevant, including:

- victim/survivor testimony;
- evidence of injuries such as branding/scarring and ligature injuries;
- digital and open-source evidence including Dark Web material;
- financial evidence of transactions relating to slave trading and trafficking;
- DNA evidence of paternity;
- psychological/psychiatric expert evidence on the impact of trauma, and long-term harm from slavery crimes, memory issues and child development;
- socio-political, historical or country experts;
- linguistic evidence as to the meaning of euphemisms; and
- military experts on the role and use of child soldiers.

18.46

Types of evidence relevant to establishing intent and knowledge will include the acts or statements of the direct perpetrators, legislation, policies or regulations promulgated by the perpetrator group or other authorities, the use of hate speech, slurs or discriminatory language, or public statements.

18.47

Pre-interview psychosocial assessment of victims of slavery are required to establish their capacity to be interviewed and may give a preliminary indication of the physical, psychological and social harms experienced. The psychosocial expert will make recommendations on the conduct of the interview, risks of re-traumatisation and any particular accommodations needed during the interview process.

18.48

Interviews with victims and survivors of slavery should be conducted only by teams who have undergone relevant training. Interviewers should take a survivor-centred, trauma-informed approach to all aspects of the interaction. Questioning should be appropriate and mitigate the risk of re-traumatisation.

Interviewers must be aware of how time and exposure to past traumatic events may affect a witness' memory or manner of recounting the past. A witness' credibility should not be judged solely on their capacity to recount events in a perfectly linear or comprehensive timeline.

18.49

The OTP will also conduct an individual assessment for each witness' security situation to determine potential risks arising from their cooperation with the OTP. In the pre-trial phase, the OTP will make 'deliberate, planned and empowering choices' on how most effectively to hear witnesses relevant to slavery crimes before the Trial Chamber, including the use of introducing previously recorded audio/video testimony, the use of audio-video links and/or screens, and seeking protective measures where appropriate, such as giving testimony in private session, through voice/image distortion, the use of pseudonyms and prohibiting disclosure to third parties.

18.50

Counsel conducting relevant witness examinations before the Trial Panel will also have undergone relevant training and must follow the survivor-centred, trauma-informed approach.

Victim-perpetrators

18.51

As observed above, the Policy on Slavery Crimes does not give any specific guidance as to how the OTP will approach 'victim-perpetrators' – those persons who are themselves victims of slavery crimes but find themselves suspected of having committed offences within the jurisdiction of the ICC.

18.52

Although the Policy does not directly address victim-perpetrators, there is no reason why those parts of the Policy which require the OTP to follow a survivor-centred and trauma-informed approach should not apply to those suspects/accused who are also victims of slavery.

18.53

For example, it is unlikely to be controversial to assert that the OTP ought to orient its actions and decision-making around treating all victims, including those who are also suspected of involvement in criminal offences within the jurisdiction of the Court, with dignity, compassion, empathy, respect and in a non-discriminatory way. Similarly, a trauma-informed approach would recognise that all survivors of slavery crimes, including victim-perpetrators, might experience traumatising bonds with their perpetrators, especially given the duration of some slavery situations. The OTP should recognise, in accordance with its child-competent approach, that victim-perpetrators who were enslaved at a young age are profoundly impacted by discrimination, stigma, economic disparities, societal rejection and long-term health and psychological consequences.

18.54

More difficult to discern from the Policy is how the OTP will approach the question whether to bring a prosecution against the victim-perpetrator for offences which are related to the perpetrator's enslavement. At the very least, the OTP might reasonably be required to give '… careful consideration … to whether public policy [calls] for a prosecution and punishment when a defendant was a trafficked victim and the crime had been committed when she was in some manner compelled, in the broad sense, to commit it[18].

18.55

Where the OTP determines that public policy does call for a prosecution and punishment, the only route to challenge that determination would seemingly be through an application to the Court to exercise its inherent jurisdiction to stay proceedings as an abuse of process.

18.56

The imposition of a permanent stay of proceedings by the ICC is an exceptional remedy to be applied as a last resort, but it is nevertheless available where 'it would be repugnant or odious to the administration of justice to allow the case to continue', even if the accused may otherwise have a fair trial[19].

18.57

It seems improbable that the balancing of interests required under this category of abuse of process (between the public interest in ensuring that those accused of crimes under the Rome Statute are prosecuted, and the competing public interest in ensuring that the treatment of victims of modern slavery and trafficking does not undermine confidence in the system and bring it into disrepute) would fall in favour of staying proceedings where the accused is alleged to have participated in the commission of the most serious international crimes.

---

18 *VCL and AN v UK, ECtHR, Applications No.74603/12 and No.77587/12*; (2021) 73 E.H.R.R. 9, Judgment, 16 February 2021 at paragraph 79, where the Court cited Hughes LJ's judgment of the Court of Appeal Criminal Division in *R v M(L)* [2010] EWCA Crim 2327 [2011] 1 Cr.App. R. 12, at [13].

19 *Prosecutor v Kenyatta,* ICC-01/09-02/11-868-Red, Trial Chamber V(B), *Public Redacted Version of Decision on Defence Application for a Permanent Stay of the Proceedings Due to Abuse of Process*, 5 December 2013 at paragraph 14.

18.58

The balance may be very different, however, where less serious matters within the jurisdiction of the Court are being investigated, such as allegations that the victim-perpetrator has participated in alleged offences against the administration of justice. It is not difficult to imagine circumstances where a decision to prosecute the victim of slavery for giving false testimony during the trial before the ICC of their enslaver might properly be described as repugnant or odious to the administration of justice[20].

Duress

18.59

If the prosecution of a victim-perpetrator proceeds to trial, the defence of duress may be available where the victim of slavery is compelled by threats of force to carry out the criminal offences alleged in the indictment.

18.60

Article 31(1) provides that a person shall not be criminally responsible if, at the time of that person's conduct:

'…

(d) The conduct which is alleged to constitute a crime within the jurisdiction of the Court has been caused by duress resulting from a threat of imminent death or of continuing or imminent serious bodily harm against that person or another person, and the person acts necessarily and reasonably to avoid this threat, provided that the person does not intend to cause a greater harm than the one sought to be avoided. Such a threat may either be:

(i) made by other persons; or

(ii) constituted by other circumstances beyond that person's control.'

The *Prosecutor v Dominic Ongwen*

18.61

In *Ongwen*, it was common ground that the Accused had been abducted by the Lord's Resistance Army (LRA) as a young child, integrated as a

20 'The punishment of victims of trafficking (for crimes that are caused or directly linked to their having been trafficked) constitutes a serious denial of justice' – 2013 Policy and Legislative Recommendations towards the Effective Implementation of the Non-Punishment Provision with regard to Victims of Trafficking published by the Organization for Security and Co-Operation in Europe ('the OSCE Recommendations') at Recommendation 10.2.

fighter into the LRA ranks, and thereafter spent his early years in the adverse and extremely violent environment of the LRA, bringing him great suffering[21]. He was nevertheless charged with a range of offences relating to his time as an adult within the LRA, including offences of Sexual Slavery, Enslavement and Conscription of Children under the age of 15 into an armed group.

18.62

The Appeals Chamber rejected arguments by the Accused and a number of *amici curiae* that, for the purposes of the defence of duress under Art 31(1)(d) of the Rome Statute, the court should take a broader approach to the question of a causal link between the 'modern slavery/human trafficking experience' and the crimes alleged to have been committed by the victim-perpetrator in the indictment[22].

18.63

For duress to exclude an accused's criminal responsibility, the Appeals Chamber maintained, only the threat of imminent death or of continuing or imminent serious bodily harm will suffice. The timing of the materialisation of the threat is linked to the terms 'imminent' and 'continuing'. For a person to be compelled to commit a crime under the jurisdiction of the Court, the threat must be 'present' and real at the time of the charged conduct:

> 'Any prior traumatic experiences of an accused person that may have an impact on him or her at the time relevant to the charges, which does not satisfy the threshold required for excluding the criminal responsibility of the accused pursuant to article 31(1)(d) of the Statute, may nonetheless be relevant for the purposes of sentencing'[23].

18.64

In short, the Appeals Chamber held, there is no special approach to *duress* where slavery or human trafficking is involved. Does it follow that there is no special pleading available to a victim of slavery/trafficking who appears before the ICC as an accused on trial?

---

21 *Prosecutor v Dominic Ongwen*, ICC-02/04-01/15A, *Public Redacted Judgment on the appeal of Mr Ongwen against the Decision of Trial Chamber XI of 4 February 2021 entitled 'Trial Judgment'*, ICC-02/04-01/15-2022-Red, 15 December 2022, Public at paragraph 35.

22 For example, *Prosecutor v Dominic Ongwen*, ICC-02/04/01/15A, *Amicus Curiae Observation*, ICC-02/04-01/15-1929, 21 December 2021, Public at paragraph 34.

23 *Prosecutor v Dominic Ongwen*, ICC-02/04-01/15A, *Public Redacted Judgment on the appeal of Mr Ongwen against the Decision of Trial Chamber XI of 4 February 2021 entitled "Trial Judgment"*, ICC-02/04-01/15-2022-Red, 15 December 2022, Public at paragraph 22.

Article 31(3) grounds for excluding criminal responsibility

18.65

As stated above, duress is specifically identified as a ground for excluding the criminal responsibility of an accused within Art 31(1)(d) of the Rome Statute. Art 31(1) also lists (a) mental disease or defect, (b) intoxication, and (c) necessary and reasonable self-defence as specific grounds for excluding criminal responsibility. Importantly, however, the list in Art 31(1) is not exclusive.

18.66

Article 31(3) of the Rome Statute provides:

> 'At trial, the Court may consider a ground for excluding criminal responsibility other than those referred to in paragraph 1 where such a ground is derived from applicable law as set forth in article 21.'

18.67

Article 21, in turn, states:

> '1. The Court shall apply:
>
> (a) In the first place, this Statute, Elements of Crimes and its Rules of Procedure and Evidence;
>
> (b) In the second place, where appropriate, applicable treaties and the principles and rules of international law, including the established principles of the international law of armed conflict;
>
> (c) Failing that, general principles of law derived by the Court from national laws of legal systems of the world, including, as appropriate, the national laws of States that would normally exercise jurisdiction over the crime, provided that those principles are not inconsistent with this Statute and with international law and internationally recognized norms and standards.
>
> …
>
> 3. The application and interpretation of law pursuant to this article must be consistent with internationally recognized human rights and be without any adverse distinction founded on grounds such as gender as defined in article 7, paragraph 3, age, race, colour, language, religion or belief, political or other opinion, national, ethnic or social origin, wealth, birth or other status.'

18.68

Can a ground for excluding criminal responsibility relating to modern slavery/trafficking be derived from the general principles and rules of international and/or national laws? If so, Arts 21 and 31(3) of the Rome Statute would enable the Court to consider it. What might such a ground look like?

18.69

On 1 January 2002, the UN Office of the High Commissioner issued its Recommended Principles and Guidelines on Human Rights and Human Trafficking ('OHCHR Principles and Guidelines')[24]. Guideline 5.5 thereof provides that states, intergovernmental and non-governmental organizations should guarantee that law enforcement does 'not place trafficked persons at risk of being punished for offences committed as a consequence of their situation'.

18.70

This principle of non-punishment 'has been solemnly affirmed' in commitments made since the turn of this century by a number of international organisations and their member constituents and is properly characterised as a general principle of law recognised by civilised nations[25].

18.71

UN human rights treaty bodies have repeatedly called upon States to implement this non-punishment principle. Several regional instruments also include references to, or encompass within their protections, the principle of non-punishment including:

- the Association of Southeast Asian Nations (ASEAN) Convention against Trafficking in Persons, Especially Women and Children 2015;
- the Organization of American States (OAS) Conclusions and Recommendations of the First Meeting of National Authorities on Trafficking in Persons 2006; and
- the Inter-American Convention on the Prevention, Punishment and Eradication of Violence against Women 1994[26].

18.72

The non-punishment principle is found in domestic legislation in several jurisdictions including Albania, Belgium, Cyprus, Ecuador, Egypt, Germany, Greece, Indonesia, Kosovo, the Lao People's Democratic Republic, Kenya,

24 For the purposes of the OHCHR Principles and Guidelines, conduct and offences related to trafficking includes slavery – see footnote 3 to the Principles and Guidelines.

25 Special Rapporteur 2021 Report at paragraph 20.

26 Special Rapporteur 2021 Report at paragraphs 22-23.

Malawi, Mexico, North Macedonia, Spain, Thailand, the United States of America, and Uruguay[27]. For a full exposition of the non-punishment measures adopted by the parties to the Council of Europe Convention on Action against Trafficking in Human Beings ('ECAT') see the Reports of the Group of Experts on Action against Trafficking in Human Beings ('GRETA'), the body appointed by the Committee of the Parties to the Council of Europe Convention to monitor the implementation of the Council of Europe Convention by the parties to it[28]. GRETA is discussed further at **18.80** below.

18.73

As observed by the Special Representative and Co-Ordinator for Combating Trafficking in Human Beings in her foreword to the OSCE Recommendations, the non-punishment principle is a legally binding obligation for all State parties to the Council of Europe Convention on Action against Trafficking in Human Beings and/or are members of the European Union[29].

18.74

The principle operates so that a person who has been trafficked should not be penalised for offences they have committed in the course, or as a consequence, of being trafficked[30]. This may include where a victim of trafficking has been manipulated by traffickers to assist in the exploitation of others, unless the trafficked person has acted independently and free from the operation of one or more of the means foreseen in Art 3(a) of the Palermo Protocol such as 'the abuse of power or of a position of vulnerability'[31].

18.75

Under this approach, a victim of the war crime of sexual slavery and who was used by her enslavers to assist in the exploitation of other sexual slaves (for example, by being required to manage a 'comfort house') should not face prosecution unless it can be said that she acted independently from any abuse of her position of vulnerability by her enslavers.

18.76

What might be the boundaries of such a ground for excluding criminal responsibility?

27 Special Rapporteur 2021 Report at paragraph 24; and the United Nations Office on Drugs and Crime Model Law against Trafficking in Persons 2009 at page 34.

28 GRETA Country Reports and Evaluation Rounds: https://www.coe.int/en/web/anti-human-trafficking/country-reports-and-evaluation-rounds (accessed 22 August 2025).

29 See also paragraph 2 of the OSCE Recommendations.

30 OSCE Recommendations at paragraph 50-51; see also the Report of the Special Rapporteur on Trafficking in Persons, Especially Women and Children on the Implementation of the Non-Punishment Principle to the UN General Assembly ('Special Rapporteur 2021 Report') A/HRC/47/34, 17 May 2021 at paragraph 18.

31 OSCE Recommendations at paragraphs 55 and 56.

18.77

According to the UN Special Rapporteur, the non-punishment principle should be applied 'whenever any of the means in the trafficking definition exist'. It would follow that if the means no longer exist, such that at the time of offending the former victim of trafficking was no longer subject *inter alia* to the abuse of power or of a position of vulnerability, then the non-punishment principle would not be involved.

18.78

Several states who have introduced specific provisions into domestic law on the non-punishment of victims of trafficking/slavery have qualified the application of those provisions by reference to the seriousness of the offences alleged to have been committed by the victim-perpetrator. For example:

> 'Armenia – exemption from liability for committing offences of 'insignificant' and 'medium' gravity while being in a trafficking or exploitative situation[32];
>
> Denmark – waiver of liability available provided that the alleged offence cannot be characterised as a 'serious crime'[33];
>
> Germany – dispensation available for a misdemeanour 'unless expiation is imperative because of the seriousness of the offence'[34];
>
> Slovak Republic – termination of a criminal prosecution available where the offence committed carries a maximum sentence of five years or less'[35].

18.79

Other states have limited the availability of any non-punishment provision by reference to specific offences. Art 20(1) of the Romanian Anti-Trafficking Law, for example, stipulates that: 'a person subject to trafficking who committed, as a result of his/her exploitation, the crime of unlawful crossing of a border of a state or donation of organs or tissues or cells of human origin…shall not be punished for these crimes'.

18.80

In England and Wales, the approach taken has been to create a general statutory defence for slavery or trafficking victims in s 45 of the Modern Slavery Act

32 Article 132(5) of the Criminal Code, Armenia.
33 Section 722(2) of the Administration of Justice Act, Denmark.
34 Article 154c, paragraph 2 of the Code of Criminal Procedure, Germany.
35 Article 215(2) of the Criminal Procedure Code, and Articles 10 and 40(1b) of the Criminal Code, Slovak Republic.

2015, but then disapply that defence for many serious offences specifically listed in Schedule 4 to the same Act. It is of particular note that Schedule 4 of the 2015 Act specifically provides that the statutory defence for slavery or trafficking victims created by s 45 does not apply to the offences of genocide, crimes against humanity and war crimes under the Rome Statute when prosecuted as domestic offences in the Crown Court. The statutory defence is available, however, where offences contrary to Art 70(1) (offences against the administration of justice in relation to the ICC) are dealt with in England and Wales under s 54 of the International Court Act 2001[36].

18.81

Each of the above states recognises the principle of non-punishment and is bound specifically by Art 26 of ECAT. As stressed by GRETA, Art 26 is not limited to specific offences, or gradations of seriousness, but appears to be of general application.

18.82

In compliance with Art 26, for example, Cyprus has simply stipulated that victims of trafficking are not to be prosecuted for their involvement in criminal activities if those were a direct consequence of the fact that the offender was a victim of trafficking[37]. Similarly, Moldova has provided that a victim of trafficking is exempted from criminal liability for crimes committed by them in connection with their status as a victim of trafficking[38].

18.83

Spain has taken a different approach again. Art 177bis, paragraph 11, of the Spanish Criminal Code provides that victims of trafficking will be exempted from punishment for criminal offences committed while being exploited, provided their involvement was the direct consequence of the abuse to which they were subjected, and 'provided there is an adequate proportionality between that situation and the criminal act perpetrated'.

18.84

Whereas proportionality is not specifically referred to in any of the international or regional instruments, it might properly be seen as a component of any nexus between the exploitation and the criminal conduct. In other words, where the criminal offence committed by the victim of trafficking is disproportionate in gravity to the abuse to which the offender was subjected by his trafficker,

36 Note that the protection from s 45 MSA 2015 works in conjunction with the non-prosecution provisions within the Crown Prosecution Service Guidance 'Modern Slavery and human trafficking: offences and defences, including the section 45 defence' see **Chapter 10**.

37 Article 29 of Law 60(I)/2014, Cyprus.

38 Article 165, paragraph 4 of the Criminal Code, Republic of Moldova.

that would indicate that the criminal conduct of the offender was in fact independent of the operation of one or more of the means foreseen in Art 3(a) of the Palermo Protocol such as 'the abuse of power or of a position of vulnerability'.

18.85

It is suggested, therefore, that the following elements of a ground for excluding criminal responsibility under Art 21 and 31(3) of the Rome Statute may be derived from the generally recognised principle of non-punishment of victims of trafficking:

> 'A person shall not be criminally responsible if, at the time of that person's conduct:
>
> (a) the person was a victim of trafficking as defined within Article 3(a) of the Palermo Protocol; and
>
> (b) the person continued to be subjected to one or more of the means foreseen in Article 3(a) of the Palermo Protocol such as 'the abuse of power or of a position of vulnerability' for the purposes of exploitation by another; and
>
> (c) the person committed the conduct which is alleged to constitute a crime as a consequence of being subjected to one or more of the means foreseen in Article 3(a) of the Palermo Protocol such as the abuse of power or of a position of vulnerability for the purposes of exploitation by another; and
>
> (d) the conduct which is alleged to constitute a crime was not disproportionate in gravity to the abuse to which the person was subjected by another for the purposes of exploitation.'

18.86

In accordance with the approach to all grounds for excluding criminal responsibility, it will be for the Accused to present evidence sufficient to raise reasonable doubt as to their criminal responsibility ('evidentiary burden') – it is not sufficient to merely give notice of an alleged ground for excluding criminal responsibility[39]. However, the Prosecution at all times retains the burden of proving to the criminal standard that the Accused is guilty[40].

---

39 *Prosecutor v Dominic Ongwen*, ICC-02/04-01/15A, *Public Redacted Judgment on the appeal of Mr Ongwen against the Decision of Trial Chamber XI of 4 February 2021 entitled 'Trial Judgment'*, ICC-02/04-01/15-2022-Red, 15 December 2022, Public at paragraphs 340, 341 and 343.

40 *Prosecutor v Dominic Ongwen*, ICC-02/04-01/15A, *Public Redacted Judgment on the appeal of Mr Ongwen against the Decision of Trial Chamber XI of 4 February 2021 entitled 'Trial Judgment'*, ICC-02/04-01/15-2022-Red, 15 December 2022, Public at paragraphs 340, 341 and 343.

18.87

It is suggested that this ground for exclusion of criminal liability should be available not only where offences against the administration are charged under Art 70(1) of the Rome Statute (as foreseen in England & Wales by the Modern Slavery Act 2015) but, in principle at least, to all offences under the Rome Statute. A proportionality element, embedded in the requirement of a nexus between the condition of slavery/trafficking and the alleged criminal conduct committed by the victim-perpetrator, ought to ensure that such ground of exclusion of criminal liability cannot become 'a loophole to commit serious international crimes with impunity'.

18.88

At the trial of *Ongwen*, there was a somewhat cursory submission made to the effect that 'Article 21(3) [of the Rome Statute] prohibits charging a victim of a crime with the same crime'[41], based on failures of the Uganda government to protect the Accused during and after his period of bondage. The Trial Chamber IX summarily rejected that submission on the basis that: 'a rule that would immunize persons who suffer human rights violations from responsibility for all similar human rights violations that they may themselves commit thereafter manifestly does not exist in international human rights law[42].' No specific consideration was given, however, to the more limited and specific principle of non-punishment for victims of trafficking for offences they have committed in the course, or as a consequence, of being trafficked.

18.89

Although many of the relevant features of a potential ground for exclusion of criminal liability under Art 21 and 31(3) related to slavery/trafficking were mentioned during the appeal in *Ongwen* (**18.60** et seq) the argument and the ruling of the Appeals Chamber was squarely framed within the scope of the defence of duress under Art 31(1)(d) of the Rome Statute. It is, perhaps, understandable that the Appeals Chamber was cautious to guard against any appearance that the strict requirements of duress might be diluted, in particular the imminence and severity of the threat requirement, when duress under Art 31(1)(d), is a general defence and may operate in a near-infinitely wide set of circumstances where threat, at some level or other, may be present.

18.90

The decision of the Appeals Chamber in *Ongwen* does not, therefore, close the door on the possibility of a distinct ground for excluding criminal responsibility

41 *Prosecutor v Ongwen*, Public Redacted Version of 'Corrected Version of 'Defence Closing Brief', ICC-02/04-01/15-1722-CORR-RED, Defence, 13 March 2020 at paragraphs 494-496.

42 *Prosecutor v Ongwen*, Trial Judgment, ICC-02/04-01/15-1762-RED, Trial Chamber IX at paragraph 2672.

under Art s21 and 31(3) of the Rome Statute, derived from the generally recognised principle of non-punishment of victims of slavery and human trafficking for offences they have committed in the course, or as a consequence, of being trafficked.

18.91

Instead, it will fall to a future Chamber to determine if such a ground for excluding criminal responsibility under Arts 21 and 31(3) of the Rome Statute can be recognised.

18.92

Such recognition, if forthcoming, would be consistent with the OTP's survivor-centred and trauma-informed approach.

18.93

Moreover, the recognition of such a ground by the ICC would be fully consistent with internationally recognised human rights in accordance with Art 21(3) of the Rome Statute: indeed, 'the principle of non-punishment of victims of trafficking is critical to the recognition of trafficking in persons as a serious human rights violation'[43].

43 Special Rapporteur 2021 Report at paragraph 18.

19 Tackling human trafficking and modern slavery in the global economy

Krishnendu Mukherjee, Geeta Koska and Michelle Brewer

Introduction and context

19.1

The presence of human trafficking and modern slavery across transnational corporations ('TNCs') and supply chains is now well recognised. In the 1990s, Nike was famously linked to child labour in their factories in Indonesia[1]. In the UK, Boohoo was accused of low pay and inadequate protection for workers in supplier garment factories in Leicester during the Covid-19 pandemic[2]. Globally, research by the International Labour Organization ('ILO') has estimated that nine out of ten instances of forced labour arise in the private economy; that is forced labour imposed by private individuals, groups, or companies in any branch of economic activity[3].

19.2

In light of this, the movement towards challenging trafficking and modern slavery in TNCs and supply chains has gained wider traction. However, effective measures to protect and remedy victims and survivors are in their infancy. Complex corporate group structures and fragmented multi-tiered supply chains obscure the responsibility of parent and lead companies, whilst gaps in legislation and enforcement mean that access to justice is often denied. Despite the challenges, there are emerging areas of intervention, regulation and opportunities to seek redress. This chapter provides an overview to assist affected people and communities, lawyers, campaigners, governments and businesses to navigate the landscape and work towards greater protection for those at risk.

1 'Disaster of the Day' (*Forbes,* 22 February 2001) <https://www.forbes.com/2001/02/22/0222disasternike.html> accessed 29 September 2025.

2 Archie Bland and Kalyeena Makortoff, 'Boohoo knew of Leicester factory failings' (*The Guardian,* 25 September 2020 <https://www.theguardian.com/business/2020/sep/25/boohoo-report-reveals-factory-fire-risk-among-supply-chain-failings> accessed 29 September 2025.

3 International Labour Organisation, 'Profits and poverty: The economics of forced labour' (2024) p.4.

19.3

The legal definitions of Slavery, Servitude, Forced or Compulsory Labour and Human Trafficking are set out at length in Chapter 1. In this chapter, the terms trafficking and modern slavery include broader phenomena of abuse and exploitation than the strict legal offences in the Modern Slavery Act ('MSA 2015'). Whilst the offences in the MSA 2015 and other legal instruments are crucial for enforcement; it is important to recognise the continuities between exploitative labour practices and forced labour. Further, in pursuing corporate accountability, alternative torts and modes of liability are relied upon. In the context of the climate crisis, the links between modern slavery, climate change and environmental degradation also need to be acknowledged and addressed[4]. Addressing modern slavery linked to the operations of TNCs and supply chains includes the broader task of dealing with labour practices, poor human rights and environmental standards in the global economy[5].

Legal and regulatory measures in the United Kingdom

19.4

In the UK, legislation mandating companies to identify, prevent and remedy human rights violations in their businesses and supply chains is limited. Rather, a patchwork of reporting requirements and subject-specific legislation is in place to promote transparency and governance, including within the MSA 2015, procurement rules, criminal law and environmental regulations.

Modern Slavery Act 2015 (s 54)

Transparency in Supply Chains

19.5

Section 54 of the MSA 2015 concerns transparency in supply chains. In their guidance, the Home Office describes the regime as intending to 'create a level

4 See Rogerson, M, Grosvold, J & Alves, K, *Climate change and modern slavery in public procurement: Research Report* (January 2024); Dr Michael Rogerson, Dr Johanne Grosvold, Dr Kyle Alves. *'Climate Change and modern slavery in public procurement'* (Modern Slavery and Human Rights Policy and Evidence Centre <https://www.modernslaverypec.org/resources/climate-change-modern-slavery-public-procurement> accessed 29 September 2025; D. Brown, D., Boyd, D., Brickell, K., Ives, C., Natarajan, N., & Parsons, L.' Modern slavery, environmental degradation and climate change: Fisheries, field, forests and factories' [2019]. Environment and Planning E: Nature and Space, 1-17.

5 In February 2026, the Anti-Trafficking and Labour Exploitation Unit (ATLEU) brought an Art 4 ECHR judicial review challenge to the structural features of the UK Seasonal Worker Scheme, arguing that its design creates conditions conducive to forced labour. This is the first Art 4 claim directed at the design of a government labour-migration scheme rather than at individual decisions or conduct, and the proceedings remained ongoing as of March 2026. If successful, the challenge would require structural reform of the Scheme and would establish that Art 4's positive obligations extend not only to the administration of such programmes but also to the way they are designed.

playing field'[6] and 'prevent modern slavery in organisations and their supply chains', with s 54 acting as conduit to 'increase transparency by ensuring the public, consumers, employees and investors know what steps an organisation is taking to tackle modern slavery'[7]. In July 2025, the Government published updated statutory guidance, *Transparency in Supply Chains: A Practical Guide*[8], which contains similar ambitions for s 54.

19.6

It is fair to acknowledge that when the MSA 2015 was first introduced, the reporting requirements under s 54 were considered as world leading. However, the measure has failed to fulfil the aims of preventing violations in supply chains or promoting transparency[9]. Furthermore, in this fast-paced area of the law, in the ten years since s 54 was enacted other jurisdictions have outrun the UK by introducing mandatory human rights and environmental due diligence obligations ('HREDD') and other targeted measures (see below).

19.7

The government has expressed its commitment to improving its response to modern slavery and is currently reviewing how to tackle forced labour in global supply chains most effectively[10]. Companies should therefore be proactive in anticipating how s 54 will be strengthened. If organisations do no more than comply with s 54 as it currently stands, they may be at risk of reputational damage, exposed to civil or criminal liability or face sanctions under alternative legislation.

---

6 Home Office, *Transparency in Supply Chains etc. A practical guide* (2022), para. 1.4 <https://assets.applytosupply.digitalmarketplace.service.gov.uk/g-cloud-13/documents/715396/modern-slavery-statement-2022-03-09-1519.pdf> accessed 1 October 2021.

7 Ibid., para. 1.5.

8 UK Home Office, *Transparency in Supply Chains: A Practical Guide* (updated 30 July 2025) <https://www.gov.uk/government/publications/transparency-in-supply-chains-a-practical-guide/transparency-in-supply-chains-a-practical-guide-accessible> accessed 26 August 2025 (Home Office, Transparency in Supply Chains Guide).

9 See Joint Committee on Human Rights, *Report on Human Rights and Business 2017: Promoting responsibility and ensuring accountability,* (HL PAPER 153/ HC 443); The Independent Review of the Modern Slavery Act 2015 conducted by Frank Field MP (chair), Maria Miller MP and Baroness Butler-Sloss (Final Report of May 2019); Home Affairs Committee, *Human Trafficking,* (HC 124); House of Lords Modern Slavery Act 2015 Committee, *The Modern Slavery Act 2015: becoming world leading again,* (HL Paper 8); Modern Slavery and Human Rights Policy and Evidence Centre, *Effectiveness of Section 54 of the Modern Slavery Act* (February 2021).

10 See Home Office, *Government response to House of Lords Modern Slavery Act 2015 Committee, Report of Session 2024-25 The Modern Slavery Act 2015: Becoming World-Leading Again,* (CP 1216) p.27 <https://assets.publishing.service.gov.uk/media/675b160b348e10a16975a419/E03257966_-_CP_1216_Gov_resp_world_leading_again_Web_Accessible.pdf> accessed 30 September 2025 (Government response to House of Lords Modern Slavery Act 2015 Committee); UK Government, *The UK's Trade Strategy,* (CP1339) <https://www.gov.uk/government/publications/uk-trade-strategy/the-uks-trade-strategy> accessed 29 September 2025.

Slavery and Human Trafficking Statement

19.8

Section 54 requires any commercial organisation in any sector supplying goods or services, which carries on a business or part of its business in the UK, and has over £36m turnover, to produce a Slavery and Human Trafficking Statement for each financial year of the organisation. The provision does not require that the organisation guarantees that the entire supply chain is slavery-free nor compels companies to identify and address forced labour in their supply chains.

19.9

The MSA 2015 is not prescriptive about the layout, content or level detail of a company's Slavery and Human Trafficking Statement ('the Statement'). Broadly, what is required is a 'Statement of the steps the organisation has taken during the financial year to ensure that slavery and human trafficking are not taking place in any of its supply chains and in any part of its own business'[11]. In line with the original aim of promoting transparency, if an organisation has not taken steps, they must publish a Statement stating this to be the case[12].

19.10

The current provision sets out the information that may be included in a statement[13], including:

- The organisation's structure, its business, and its supply chains;
- Its policies in relation to slavery and human trafficking;
- Its due diligence processes in relation to slavery and human trafficking in its business and supply chains;
- The parts of its business and supply chains where there is a risk of slavery and human trafficking taking place, and the steps it has taken to assess and manage that risk;
- Its effectiveness in ensuring that slavery and human trafficking is not taking place in its business or supply chains, measured against such performance indicators as it considers appropriate;
- The training and capacity building about slavery and human trafficking available to its staff.

11 MSA 2015, s 54 (4)(a).
12 MSA 2015, s 54 (4)(b).
13 MSA 2015, s 54 (5).

19.11

The content of the Statement must be approved and signed by a director, member, or partner of the organisation.

19.12

As of March 2021, there is now a central registry of Slavery and Human Trafficking Statements administered by the Home Office[14]. It is voluntary for an organisation to submit a Statement to the registry. Under s 54 as drafted, companies are only obliged to publish their Statement on the organisation's website. If the company does not have a website, a copy of the Statement is to be provided to anyone who makes a written request for one within 30 days of the request[15].

19.13

Amendments to the present reporting regime are anticipated. A House of Lords report published on 16 October 2024, *The Modern Slavery Act 2015: becoming world-leading again,* ('HL Committee Report') recommended, again, that the publication of statements on the registry be made compulsory[16]. In their response, the government indicated that the reporting requirements under the MSA 2015 would be improved; however, no details have been set out[17].

Organisations in scope

19.14

The obligations in s 54 apply to any organisation in any part of a group structure if they are a body corporate or a partnership, wherever incorporated, which carries on a business or part of its business supplying goods or services in the UK, with an annual turnover of £36m[18].

19.15

The key question is if an organisation 'carries on a business in the UK'[19]. This is to be given a common-sense approach and may capture charitable or

14 Home Office, *Modern slavery statement registry,* <https://modern-slavery-statement-registry.service.gov.uk/> accessed 30 September 2025.

15 MSA 2015, s 54.

16 House of Lords Select Committee on the Modern Slavery Act 2015, *Modern Slavery Act 2015: Independent Review*, vol II (HL 8, 2021) para. 189 <https://publications.parliament.uk/pa/ld5901/ldselect/ldmodslav/8/8.pdf> accessed 26 August 2025 (House of Lords Select Committee on the Modern Slavery Act 2015).

17 Government response to House of Lords Modern Slavery Act 2015 Committee, p.23.

18 MSA 2015, s 54(2)(b), read with the Modern Slavery Act 2015 (Transparency in Supply Chains) Regulations 2015, reg. 2.

19 MSA 2015, s 54(12)(a).

educational organisations, if they are engaged in commercial activities and have a total turnover of £36m. Whilst organisations incorporated or formed outside of the UK are technically within scope, a business must be carrying on a business in any part of the UK. The Home Office has issued guidance on how s 54 applies to franchises and parent and subsidiary organisations[20].

19.16

In 2019, the Independent Review recommended that the government should 'lead by example' and extend s 54 to the public sector[21]. In response, the previous government had proposed an amendment to the MSA 2015 to bring public sector bodies with a budget of £36m or above in scope, however, this was not legislated for. Currently, the Government publishes Slavery and Human Trafficking Statements on a voluntary basis.

Enforcement

19.17

Unfortunately, the present mechanisms in place to ensure compliance with the s 54 reporting requirement are weak and have undermined the overall effectiveness of the reporting requirement. Analysis by the Chartered Institute of Procurement and Supply, found that 29% of organisations which fall within the scope of s 54 had not submitted a statement in 2022. The Institute also found that in 2023, 46% fewer statements were recorded by the Registry of Modern Slavery Statements in 2023, compared to 2022, suggesting that businesses may be deprioritising the submission of a Modern Slavery Statement[22]. This is especially disappointing given the relatively minimal reporting requirements set out in s 54.

19.18

Under s 54, if an organisation fails to produce a Slavery and Human Trafficking Statement for a particular financial year, the Secretary of State may seek an injunction through the High Court requiring the organisation to comply. If the organisation fails to comply with the injunction, it will be in contempt of court, which is punishable by an unlimited fine. Despite there being provision to seek an injunction against non-compliant organisations, the power has never been used[23]. The government has sought to defend its poor record on the grounds of saving taxpayer's money and the challenges in assessing compliance with s 54[24].

---

20 Home Office, *Transparency in Supply Chains Guide.*

21 House of Lords Select Committee on the Modern Slavery Act 2015, para. 210.

22 House of Commons Home Affairs Committee, *Human Trafficking,* (HC 124, 2023–24) para. 71 <https://committees.parliament.uk/publications/42482/documents/211207/default/> accessed 26 August 2025 (Home Affairs Committee).

23 Ibid., para. 71.

24 Government response to House of Lords Modern Slavery Act 2015 Committee, p.24.

19.19

However, the initial design of the MSA 2015, which relied primarily on reputational damage and pressure from consumers, investors and NGOs to monitor enforcement, is going to evolve. Most recently, the Home Affairs Committee[25], the House of Lords[26] and the Joint Committee on Human Rights report on 'Forced Labour in UK Supply Chains' published on 24 July 2025 ('JCHR report')[27] have recommended that sanctions for non-compliance with s 54 be strengthened. The government has confirmed its intention to establish a 'proportionate enforcement regime' and is carrying out a review of how the penalties under the MSA 2015 can be strengthened[28]. It is therefore important for in-scope organisations to engage with the existing reporting requirements now to avoid serious penalties in the future, which could include director liability or financial penalties.

Human Rights and Environmental Due Diligence (HREDD)

19.20

HREDD is a tool to identify, prevent, mitigate and account for adverse human rights and environmental impacts a business may cause or contribute to through its operations. The concept is central to the United Nations Guiding Principles on Business and Human Rights, discussed in detail below, and requires companies to carry out an assessment of 'actual and potential human rights impacts, integrating and acting upon the findings, tracking responses, and communicating how impacts are addressed'[29]. Whilst internationally, mandatory due diligence laws are expanding[30], there is currently no legal requirement for an organisation to carry out a HREDD process under s 54. Instead, the government encourages voluntary due diligence, and companies are advised to conduct due diligence to comply with reporting legal requirements under s 54(5)[31].

25 Home Affairs Committee, para. 74–75.

26 House of Lords Select Committee on the Modern Slavery Act 2015, para. 192–197.

27 Joint Committee on Human Rights, *Forced Labour in UK Supply Chains,* (HC 633 / HL Paper 159) para.60 <https://publications.parliament.uk/pa/jt5901/jtselect/jtrights/633/report.html> accessed 28 September 2025 (Joint Committee on Human Rights Report on Forced Labour).

28 Government response to House of Lords Modern Slavery Act 2015, p.24.

29 United Nations Office of the High Commissioner for Human Rights, *Guiding Principles on Business and Human Rights: Implementing the United Nations 'Protect, Respect and Remedy Framework'* (2011) <https://www.ohchr.org/sites/default/files/documents/publications/guidingprinciplesbusinesshr_en.pdf> accessed 4 September 2025, Principle 17 (UN Guiding Principles on Business and Human Rights).

30 This is discussed further below.

31 Home Office, Transparency in Supply Chains Guide, para. 4.2. The Home Office guidance adopts the definition and guidance on due diligence set out in the UN Guiding Principles on Business and Human Rights and the Organisation for Economic Co-operation and Development Due Diligence Guidance for Responsible Business Conduct, discussed further below.

19.21

The updated Home Office Transparency in Supply Chains Guide provides detailed and practical guidance for companies to carry out a due diligence process and should be followed by organisations preparing a Slavery and Human Trafficking Statement. The Guide includes useful case studies and highlights particularly salient points to ensure an effective process, including:

- Assessing slavery and human trafficking risks across direct and in-direct suppliers, including those beyond tier one.
- Ensuring the integrity of investigations by engaging with independent experts, civil society and worker representatives instead of relying on internal or third-party audits to identify impacts.
- Addressing internal procedures that may influence and create modern slavery risks, for example, purchasing practices including aggressive pricing, short lead times and late high-volume orders.

19.22

Notwithstanding the legislative gap in the MSA 2015, it is advisable for organisations to carry out effective HREDD for their own risk management and to support their reporting obligations under s 54. Though HREDD remains voluntary at present, drawing on developments internationally, the JCHR[32] and HL[33] have recommended the introduction of mandatory due diligence legislation in the UK. In their response to the HL Committee Report, the government has indicated that it supports voluntary HREDD and will assess the effectiveness of due diligence rules going forward[34].

19.23

It is important to highlight that the absence of an effective due diligence framework could result in suppliers linked to modern slavery being excluded from participating in public procurement contracts[35]. Alternatively, it may leave an organisation vulnerable to proceedings brought under the Proceeds of Crime Act 2002 or the Economic Crime and Corporate Transparency Act 2023[36]. Additionally, due diligence laws in other jurisdictions may touch on some UK businesses and require them to carry out relevant due diligence in their operations and supply chains[37].

---

32 Joint Committee on Human Rights Report on Forced Labour, para.76.
33 House of Lords Select Committee on the Modern Slavery Act 2015, para. 227 and 231.
34 Government response to House of Lords Modern Slavery Act 2015 Committee, p.29.
35 This is discussed further below.
36 This is discussed further below.
37 This is discussed further below.

Corporate criminal offences

19.24

Section 54 has been the focus of large organisations. However, companies are persons by virtue of the Interpretation Act 1978. The existence of and compliance with s 54 does not prevent corporate criminal liability for persons who commit offences of Slavery, Servitude and Forced or Compulsory Labour (MSA 2015, s 1); Human Trafficking (MSA 2015, s 2) or another offence with intent to commit a Human Trafficking offence (MSA 2015, s 4).

19.25

Furthermore, prosecutors may consider charging companies, officers, and employees with inchoate offences under the Serious Crime Act 2007, ie:

- intentionally encouraging or assisting an offence (s 44);
- encouraging or assisting an offence believing it will be committed (s 45); or
- encouraging or assisting offences believing one or more will be committed (s 46).

19.26

Such inchoate offences are likely to be easier to prove than the substantive offences under ss 1, 2 and 4 of MSA 2015 and in the event of conviction would render the company or individual '… liable to any penalty for which he would be liable on conviction of the anticipated or reference offence' (Serious Crime Act 2007, s 58).

Proceeds of Crime Act 2002

Corporate criminal liability for money laundering risks in supply chains

19.27

The Proceeds of Crime Act 2002 ('POCA 2002') sets out the legislative scheme for the recovery of criminal assets through civil proceedings. The legislation has been used by NGOs as a mechanism to challenge the potential criminal offences connected to the importation of goods tainted by criminality, including the offences of Slavery, Servitude and Forced or Compulsory Labour under MSA 2015, s 1 that occur outside the UK[38].

38 POCA, s 340(2).

19.28

Under POCA 2002 there are three primary money laundering offences. First, the offence of acquiring, using, or possessing 'criminal property'[39]. Second, the offence of facilitating the acquisition, retention, use or control of 'criminal property' by or on behalf of another person[40]. Third, an offence against dealing with criminal property in various ways, including concealing it, disguising it, converting it, transferring it, or removing it from the UK[41]. Section 329(2)(c) provides an exemption, and a person will not commit an offence contrary to s 329(1), if they 'acquired or used or had possession of the property for adequate consideration'. There is no similar exception in s 327 or 328.

19.29

Whether property is 'criminal' is dealt with in the interpretation section under s 340(3), which states that 'property is criminal property if: (a) it constitutes a person's benefit from criminal conduct or it represents such a benefit (in whole or part and whether directly or indirectly); and (b) the alleged offender knows or suspects that it constitutes or represents such a benefit.'

19.30

Material to the definition of 'criminal property' is the concept of 'criminal conduct' defined at s 340(2)(a) and (b) as conduct which 'constitutes an offence in any part of the United Kingdom' or would constitute an offence in any part of the United Kingdom if it occurred there.'

19.31

In a landmark judicial review, *R (on the application of World Uyghur Congress) v National Crime Agency*[42], the Court of Appeal considered a challenge to the National Crime Agency's ('NCA') decision not to investigate the importation of goods from Xinjiang, China, despite evidence of forced labour and human rights abuses against the Uyghur population. In a unanimous judgment, the Court confirmed that goods produced through forced labour, and the proceeds from their sale, may constitute 'criminal property' and are 'recoverable property' within the meaning of Part 5 of the POCA 2002[43].

19.32

The full impact of the Court of Appeal's ruling is yet to be seen, however, the case clarified important principles regarding the application of POCA 2002 to modern slavery risks in supply chains. An importer who now suspects that

39 POCA, s 329.
40 POCA, s 328.
41 POCA, s 327.
42 [2024] EWCA Civ 715.
43 For further analysis see below.

goods are the product of forced labour may be caught by money laundering offences. As commented on by the Court of Appeal in at [31]:

> '…the concept of 'criminal property' is not only very broadly expressed, but it is a fluid one which depends on the state of mind of the alleged offender. The property in question must not only be or represent a benefit from someone's criminal conduct, but the alleged offender must know or suspect that to be the case at the time of carrying out one of the activities prohibited by sections 327 to 329.'

19.33

Coupled with ever expanding due diligence obligations that compel companies to carry out effective supply chain mapping and risk assessments, companies are likely to have the necessary state of mind and should be taking appropriate steps to limit their exposure to the risk of breaching money laundering offences.

Economic Crime and Corporate Transparency Act 2023

Failure to prevent fraud

19.34

The Economic Crime and Corporate Transparency Act 2023 ('ECCTA 2023') has established a new criminal offence of 'failing to prevent fraud'. As set out in the Home Office guidance, the aim is to hold companies to account for serious crimes and drive a shift in corporate culture to prevent fraud[44]. The offence came into force on 1 September 2025. At this stage it is not known how effective the legislation will be in addressing modern slavery and exploitation in supply chains, but NGOs are already starting to use the legislation to hold companies criminally liable for offences. The ECCTA 2023 strengthens company registration requirements, enabling NGOs to better scrutinise who controls a company and how corporate structures link to beneficial owners. As a result, NGOs will have greater opportunities to report suspected misconduct, challenge inaccurate filings, and leverage public data to drive campaigns for corporate accountability.

44 Home Office, *Economic Crime and Corporate Transparency Act 2023: Guidance to organisations on the offence of failure to prevent fraud* (November 2024) para.1.1 <https://assets.publishing.service.gov.uk/media/67f8ef1845705eb1a1513f35/Failure+to+Prevent+Fraud+Guidance+-+English+Language+v1.6.pdf> accessed 30 September 2025 (ECCTA Guidance).

19.35

Under the ECCTA 2023, large organisations[45] may be criminally liable where an employee, agent, subsidiary, or other 'associated person'[46], commits a fraud intending to benefit the organisation and the organisation did not have reasonable fraud prevention procedures in place[47]. The offence of failure to prevent fraud applies to a number of existing 'fraud offences' set out in Schedule 13 to the Act[48], which includes offences under the Fraud Act 2006, the Proceeds of Crime Act 2002, money laundering and cheating the public revenue. Aiding, abetting, counselling, or procuring the commission of any of the listed offences would also qualify as a relevant fraud offence[49].

19.36

The Act applies extraterritorially where a 'UK nexus' is established[50]. This means that one of the acts that forms part of the base fraud offence takes place in the UK, or that actual gain or loss occurs in the UK[51].

19.37

Crucially, to establish the offence, it is not necessary to establish that directors or senior managers ordered or knew about the fraud offence. Instead, the legislative regime is designed to change corporate culture, so that 'fraud is never acceptable, and [organisations] should reject profit based on, or assisted by, fraud'[52]. This is reflected in the defence available to corporations, which is focused on the steps to prevent fraud[53].

45 Under ECCTA, s 201, a large organisation is defined as corporates (including not-for-profit organisations and incorporated public bodies) and partnerships who meet two of the three following criteria in the year that proceeds the year of the fraud offence: more than 250 employees; more than £36 million turnover; and more than £18 million in total assets.

46 Under ECCTA, s 199(7), an associated person means a person who is an employee, agent or subsidiary undertaking of the relevant body, or a person who otherwise performs services for or on behalf of the body. However, the term does not include persons providing goods or individuals or entities providing services 'to' an organisation, such as external lawyers, valuers or accountants, see ECCTA Guidance, para. 2.3.

47 ECCTA, s 199-206 and Sch 13.

48 ECCTA, Sch 13.

49 ECCTA, s 199(6)(b).

50 Under the Criminal Justice Act 1993, ss 1 and 2 an offence is committed under sections 17 (false accounting) and 19 (false statements by company directors) of the Theft Act 1968; and ss 1 (fraud), 9 (participating in fraudulent business carried on by a sole trader) and 11 (obtaining services dishonestly) of the Fraud Act 2006, if a relevant event occurs in England and Wales.

51 ECCTA Guidance, para. 2.5.

52 ECCTA Guidance, para.3.1.

53 See below.

19.38

If convicted on indictment, an organisation can receive a fine[54]. As set out in sentencing guidelines, courts will take account of all the circumstances in deciding the appropriate level of fine for a particular case.

Supply chain liability

19.39

ECCTA adopts a broad definition of 'associated person', which includes not only employees and agents, but also subsidiary undertakings[55] and companies within the supply chain that perform services for or on behalf of the relevant body[56] even if they do not contract directly with the relevant organisation[57]. This expansive scope ensures that parent companies cannot insulate themselves from liability by operating through subsidiaries or outsourcing services to lower-tier entities. The provision reflects a legislative intent to hold large organisations accountable for fraudulent conduct occurring anywhere within their corporate or operational structures.

Defence: reasonable fraud prevention procedures

19.40

Under ECCTA 2023, s 199(4) and (5), organisations will have a defence to the offence if they have reasonable procedures in place to prevent fraud; or if they can demonstrate that it was not reasonable in all the circumstances to expect the organisation to have any prevention procedures in place. The question of reasonableness is a matter for the court to determine, considering the facts and circumstances of the case, and the level of control, proximity and supervision an organisation has over a person or entity[58].

19.41

The Home Office provides instructive examples of how the offence of failure to prevent fraud may arise in the context of corporate sustainability claims:

54 ECCTA, s 199(12).

55 ECCTA, s 199(7)(a). A subsidiary undertaking, as defined in section 1162 of the Companies Act 2006, refers to a company controlled by another, typically through majority voting rights or dominant influence over its affairs.

56 ECCTA, s 199(7)(b).

57 ECCTA, s 199(9); see also ECCTA Guidance, para. 2.3.2.

58 ECCTA Guidance, para.2.6.

'An investment fund provider promotes investment in a 'sustainable' timber company, knowing that, in fact, this company's environmental credentials are fabricated, and that the timber is harvested from protected forest. Investors are deceived into placing funds with the investment fund provider. The base fraud is fraud by false representation. The intent is to benefit the fund provider. The associated person is the relevant member of staff at the investment fund provider who knowingly used the false information in the investment fund's brochures for clients. The investment fund provider could be liable under section 199(1)(a) unless a court determines that it had reasonable procedures in place to prevent this fraud[59].'

Criminal liability for modern slavery in supply chains

19.42

In advance of the ECCTA 2023 coming into force[60], NGOs were serving dossiers of information to senior managers in companies with information and evidence of criminality in supply chains. The allegations concerned goods being produced in conditions that amount to offences under the MSA 2015, ss1, 2 and 4, and may be classified as 'criminal' property under POCA 2002. In consequence, the dossiers allege that the individual and the company may be committing money laundering under POCA 2002.

19.43

Under ECCTA 2023, s 196, the identification doctrine has been extended so that if a senior manager of a body corporate or partnership, acting within the actual or apparent scope of their authority, commits or attempts to commit certain offences, once the section came into force, the organisation is also guilty of the offence. The dossiers also serve to put companies on notice of the risk of economic crimes by 'associated persons' in their supply chain, which should trigger effective fraud prevention procedures in place.

Public procurement and supply chain regulation

19.44

The Covid-19 pandemic shed light on the vulnerability of supply chains, and the risk of public procurements being tainted by labour issues in supply chains. In the US, imports of rubber gloves by Supermax Corporation and its subsidiaries were banned in October 2021 based on information that reasonably indicated

59 Ibid., para.2.8.
60 The new offence of 'failure to prevent fraud' took effect on 1 September 2025.

the use of forced labour in manufacturing operations in Malaysia[61]. The high-profile action taken by the US had global consequences. Despite the US ban, the UK government continued to source gloves from the Supermax Healthcare Limited, the UK-based subsidiary of the Malaysian Supermax Corporation. As a result, judicial review proceedings were brought in 2022, challenging the decision to name Supermax Healthcare Limited as an approved supplier under the NHS Supply Chain's 'framework agreement' for the purchase of surgical gloves[62]. The claim settled, with the government undertaking that no orders would be placed with Supermax under the disputed agreement decision. Public procurement of goods and services linked to the systemic repression of the Uygur population in Xinjiang, China, has also been the focus amongst civil society organisation and Parliament. Concerned by allegations that products sold in the UK can be traced back to forced labour camps in China, the House of Commons Business, Energy and Industrial Strategy Committee carried out an inquiry, which was published in 2021[63].

19.45

In response, the government now aims to harness 'the public sector's spending power to ensure exploitative businesses do not take a share of the £400 billion that the public sector spends on goods and services each year[64].' Under new procurement rules, suppliers and downstream businesses are expected to map their supply chains and carry out human rights due diligence beyond the first tier to identify risks, and put in place measures to prevent modern slavery and remedy violations. Failure to do so now puts a company at real risk of being excluded from procurement processes. The Fair Work Agency (FWA) was launched on 7 April 2026, bringing together the functions of the GLAA, the Employment Agency Standards Inspectorate, and HMRC's National Minimum Wage enforcement team, and taking on certain enforcement responsibilities under the Modern Slavery Act 2015. Its creation consolidates labour-market and supply-chain enforcement in England and Wales. For businesses, the practical effect is that compliance engagement under s 54 of the MSA 2015, the

61 US Customs and Border Protection, *Agency will detain imports of disposable gloves produced using forced labor* (20 October 2021) <https://www.cbp.gov/newsroom/national-media-release/cbp-issues-withhold-release-order-supermax-corporation-bhd-and-its> accessed 30 September 2025.

62 See Wilson LLP, 'Written Evidence Submitted by Wilson LLP (MSA0072)', (House of Lords Modern Slavery Act 2015 Committee) <https://committees.parliament.uk/writtenevidence/129223/pdf/ accessed> 31 August 2025; Wilson LLP, 'Ground-breaking Legal Challenge Leads to Government Improving Due Diligence in Supply Chains', (Wilson LLP, 30 August 2023) <https://www.wilsonllp.co.uk/news/ground-breaking-legal-challenge-leads-to-government-improving-due-diligence-in-supply-chains accessed> 31 August 2025; Miranda Bryant, 'UK Faces Legal Action for Approving Firm Accused of Using Forced Labour as PPE Supplier', (*The Guardian*, 6 January 2022) <https://www.theguardian.com/global-development/2022/jan/06/uk-faces-legal-action-for-approving-firm-accused-of-using-forced-labour-as-ppe-supplier> accessed 31 August 2025.

63 Business, Energy and Industrial Strategy Committee, *Uyghur forced labour in Xinjiang and UK value chains,* (HC 1272, 2021) <https://committees.parliament.uk/publications/5095/documents/52855/default/> accessed 26 August 2025.

64 Government response to House of Lords Modern Slavery Act 2015 Committee, p. 26.

Procurement Act 2023, and the former GLAA licensing regime is now routed through a single regulator: the FWA.

The Procurement Act 2023

19.46

The new Procurement Act 2023 ('PA 2023'), which came into force on 24 February 2025, has simplified and strengthened the process and grounds for excluding or debarring suppliers from public procurement. Under the PA 2023, there are new obligations for suppliers submitting a tender or request to participate in a competitive tendering procedure. The Government has published guidance for transitional and saving arrangements; fundamentally, procurements commencing after 24 February 2025 is governed by the new regime, whereas procurements that commenced before are managed under the previous legislation[65]. The government has championed the PA 2023 and its application in tackling modern slavery in supply chains, highlighting that the Act has toughened 'the exclusion regime in relation to modern slavery, to prevent exploitative companies from securing government contracts[66].' It remains to be seen how the new measures will operate in practice, but the legislation provides a promising framework.

Mandatory or discretionary grounds for exclusion

19.47

Before allowing a supplier to participate in a competitive procurement procedure, a public authority must determine whether a mandatory or discretionary ground for exclusion applies. Mandatory exclusion grounds under the PA 2023, Schedule 6[67] now encompass both domestic and equivalent overseas convictions for offences relating to labour market exploitation, slavery, human trafficking, and tax offences. Specifically, the offences now captured include those under the MSA 2015, namely:

- **Section 1**: Slavery, Servitude, and Forced or Compulsory Labour;
- **Section 2**: Human Trafficking;

---

65 Cabinet Office, *Procurement Act 2023: Guidance on Transitional and Saving Arrangements* (updated 26 June 2025) <https://www.gov.uk/government/publications/procurement-act-2023-guidance-documents-plan-phase/guidance-transitional-and-saving-arrangements-html>accessed 26 August 2025.

66 Government response to House of Lords Modern Slavery Act 2015 Committee, p.25.

67 Including aiding, abetting, counselling or procuring the commission of the offence, inciting a person to commit the offence or attempting or conspiring to commit the offence: PA 2023 Schedule 6, Part 1, para.33.

- **Section 4**: Committing an offence with intent to commit a human trafficking offence;
- **Section 30**: Offences committed by bodies corporate.

19.48

Discretionary exclusion grounds under the PA 2023, Sch 7 cover a broader range of conduct, including conduct constituting an offence under s 1, 2, 4 or 30 of the MSA 2015, *even where this has not led to a conviction.* The Explanatory Notes to the Act state 'the intention behind this [discretionary] ground is to ensure that where there is sufficient evidence, suppliers involved in modern slavery can be excluded even if they operate in jurisdictions where conviction for these offences may be unlikely[68].' Other discretionary grounds include: a conviction involving significant harm to the environment or engaging in 'professional misconduct', such as where a serious breach of ethical standards is found. Similar standards apply not only to the supplier, but also to subcontractors down the supply chain[69]. The Act is accompanied by published guidance on exclusions[70].

Debarment list[71]

19.49

The Procurement Review Unit ('PRU') will have responsibility for oversight of the new regime under the PA 2023. The Debarment Review Service ('DRS') will manage debarment for all exclusion grounds, save for the national security exclusion grounds. Additionally, contracting authorities must notify the PRU of suppliers they have excluded, and the PRU may record the names of excluded or excludable suppliers on the list[72].

19.50

If a mandatory or discretionary ground for exclusion does apply, this could have a major impact on a business as it may be debarred from participating in future procurement procedures. A supplier may be an 'excluded supplier',

68 Explanatory Notes to the Modern Slavery Act 2015 (UK) <https://www.legislation.gov.uk/ukpga/2015/30/notes/contents accessed> 27 August 2025.

69 For further analysis of the scope of the PA 2023, see below.

70 Cabinet Office, *Procurement Act 2023: Guidance on Exclusions* (updated 29 July 2025) <https://www.gov.uk/government/publications/procurement-act-2023-guidance-documents-procure-phase/guidance-exclusions-html accessed> 27 August 2025 (Guidance on Exclusions).

71 The statutory provisions for Debarment are set out in PA 2023 ss 59–66. See also: Cabinet Office, *Procurement Act 2023: Guidance Documents – Procure Phase – Guidance on Debarment* (updated 29 July 2025) <https://www.gov.uk/government/publications/procurement-act-2023-guidance-documents-procure-phase/guidance-debarment-html accessed> 27 August 2025.

72 Cabinet Office, *Procurement Review Unit* (last updated 3 September 2025 <https://www.gov.uk/guidance/procurement-review-unit#debarment-services> accessed 1 October 2025.

meaning they are excluded from all future procurements automatically for a specified period of time if mandatory exclusion ground applies, or be listed as an 'excludable supplier', (if a discretionary ground applies), which means that authorities should be exercising their discretion as to whether to exclude a particular supplier in all future procurements. At the time of publication, no suppliers had been added to the debarment list[73].

Scope: Addressing modern slavery risks in the supply chain

19.51

An entire transnational supply chain can be scrutinised under the PA 2023 and mandatory and discretionary exclusion grounds can extend to persons and entities beyond the immediate supplier, down the supply chain. A contracting authority will consider whether the exclusion grounds apply to 'associated persons'[74], 'connected persons'[75] and sub-contractors. Contracting authorities must ask for details of all sub-contractors relied on by a supplier, extending to all sub-contractors (of all tiers) the supplier intends to subcontract the performance of all or part of the contract to[76]. A contracting authority must verify if any intended sub-contractor is on the debarment list[77], and has the discretion to consider whether all sub-contractors, or any category of sub-contractor, are excluded or excludable.

19.52

The Guidance on Exclusions advises contracting authorities to ask for further details in respect of a sub-contractor where particular supply chain risks are identified; regardless of where in the supply chain[78]. To assist organisations to identify and manage these risks an updated Procurement Policy Note (PPN) 009, *Guidance on Tackling Modern Slavery in Government Supply Chains* was issued by the Cabinet Office[79]. PPN 009 provides helpful guidance on assessing modern slavery risks in procurements and identifies particular industries as high

---

73 Procurement Review Unit, *Debarment List*, <https://assets.publishing.service.gov.uk/media/68595a94eaa6f6419fade63b/Debarment_List.pdf> accessed 29 September 2025.

74 Defined in the PA 2023, s 26(4) as a person the supplier is relying on in order to satisfy the conditions of participation. This could be an entity within the first tier of sub-contractors or further down the chain. See Guidance on Exclusions, para. 33-35.

75 Defined in the PA 2023, Sch 6, Part 3, para.45 and in summary includes persons and entities that are connected with a supplier, such as a director, subsidiary company or person with significant control.

76 PA 2023, s 28(1)(a); Guidance on Exclusions, para. 46.

77 PA 2023, s 28(1)(b).

78 Guidance on Exclusions, para. 49.

79 Cabinet Office, *PPN 009: Guidance on Tackling Modern Slavery in Government Supply Chains* (updated February 2025) <https://www.gov.uk/government/publications/ppn-009-tackling-modern-slavery-in-government-supply-chains/ppn-009-guidance-on-tackling-modern-slavery-in-government-supply-chains-html#identifying-and-managing-risks-in-new-procurements> accessed 30 September 2025 (Guidance on Tackling Modern Slavery in Government Supply Chains).

risk, including agriculture, mining, construction, manufacturing and electronics, textiles and health care[80]. The PPN 009 also identifies other key features that could indicate a higher risk procurement, including where a supplier relies on low-skilled or unskilled labour and has a complex supply chain, which obscures visibility and knowledge about the conditions of workers in the supply chain[81]. New strategies and approaches for addressing and remedying modern slavery risks in supply chains during the life of a contract are also provided for in the Guidance, including the use of contract conditions, ongoing monitoring of suppliers and developing action plans[82].

19.53

If applied correctly, the exclusion regime could be effective in identifying and addressing modern slavery risks across broad areas of procurement and government supply chains. However, the Joint Committee on Human Rights has raised concerns regarding the burden on procurement officers at the local level undertaking complex investigations to establish grounds for debarment[83]. As the new PA 2023 is rolled out, the operation of the debarment list will need to be scrutinised to ensure it is delivering on its aims.

Self-cleaning

19.54

The test for exclusion on a mandatory or discretionary ground takes into consideration whether the circumstances giving rise to a ground are 'continuing or likely to occur again'[84]. Before deciding whether a supplier is an excluded or an excludable supplier, the contracting authority must give the supplier a reasonable opportunity to submit evidence that the circumstances giving rise to exclusion are not continuing or likely to recur[85]; this is referred to as the 'self-cleaning' process. The factors relevant to assessing a supplier's 'self-cleaning' process include whether a supplier has taken the grounds of exclusion seriously, including through the payment of compensation, the steps taken to prevent

80 Ibid., para. 2.1.

81 Ibid., paras 2.3 – 2.4. The PPN refers to the United States' Bureau of International Labor Affairs ('ILAB') List of Goods Produced by Child Labor or Forced Labour as a source of information, which details of the source countries of major communities where there are risks of child or forced labour.

82 Ibid., para. 3.17 and 4.

83 Joint Committee on Human Rights Report on Forced Labour, para. 219-224.

84 PA 2023, s 58.

85 Guidance on Tackling Modern Slavery in Government Supply Chains, para. 54 describe the 'circumstances giving rise to the application of an exclusion ground' as including the underlying issues as well as the specific misconduct. The following examples are provided: 'a toxic office culture, due diligence failures, a lack of a compliance function or inappropriate governance mechanisms.'

the circumstances from reoccurring and monitoring[86]. As can be seen, these factors align with certain human rights due diligence standards, such that incorporating HREDD that effectively identifies modern slavery risks and provides a mechanism to remedy adverse impacts will be important to mitigate the risk of exclusion. Principles of responsible contracting[87], for example, which provide mechanisms to identify risks and abuses in supply chains and shared responsibility for addressing and remedying violations across supply chains can support human rights due diligence.

Health and Care Act 2022

19.55

The government has also taken action to address trafficking and modern slavery in the context of health care. In light of the risk of modern slavery in personal protective equipment supply chains, as highlighted by the Supermax case, and allegations of forced labour violations in the production of face masks in Xinjiang[88], the Health and Care Act 2022 ('HCA 2022') included specific provisions designed to address trafficking and modern slavery in NHS supply chains.

The National Health Service (Procurement, Slavery and Human Trafficking) Regulations 2024

19.56

The HCA 2022, s 81 inserted a new section 12ZC into the National Health Service Act 2006 ('NHS Act 2006') requiring the Secretary of State to make regulations 'with a view to eradicating the use in the health service in England of goods or services that are tainted by slavery and human trafficking'. In November 2024, the Department of Health and Social Care ('DHSC') and NHS England published draft regulations titled the *National Health Service (Procurement, Slavery and Human Trafficking) Regulations 2024*[89], with accompanying guidance, for

86 Procurement Act 2023, s 58(1); Guidance on Exclusions, para. 59 explains that self-cleaning evidence should include measures put in place to prevent misconduct by a connected person, associated person or sub-contractor, or 'more generally', which could include 'more robust training, due diligence and oversight arrangements for group companies'.

87 Responsible Contracting Project, <https://www.responsiblecontracting.org/> accessed 30 September 2025.

88 US Department of Labor, *Against Their Will: The Situation in Xinjiang* (2023) <https://www.dol.gov/agencies/ilab/against-their-will-the-situation-in-xinjiang> accessed 27 August 2025.

89 *National Health Service (Procurement, Slavery and Human Trafficking) Regulations 2024*, (draft, Department of Health and Social Care and NHS England, November 2024) <https://assets.publishing.service.gov.uk/media/673cbb659a48a5ab14acc402/draft-nhs-modern-slavery-regulations-2024.pdf> accessed 31 August 2025. Department of Health and Social Care, *Draft NHS Modern Slavery Regulations 2024* (2024).

public consultation. In June 2025[90], the government released the outcome of that consultation, providing an overview of the proposed regulatory framework. The National Health Service (Procurement, Slavery and Human Trafficking) Regulations 2025, SI 2025/1212 were made on 17 November 2025 and come into force on 17 May 2026. They require NHS bodies to carry out modern slavery risk assessments and to mandate supplier completion of the Modern Slavery Assessment Tool (MSAT). This is the first sector-specific mandatory modern slavery procurement duty in UK law, going beyond the voluntary reporting expectations in s 54 of the MSA 2015. The entry into force of these Regulations marks a clear shift in the UK's approach: unlike the PA 2023, which relies on exclusion grounds, these Regulations impose positive risk-assessment duties on NHS commissioners and establish the MSAT as the enforceable compliance mechanism.

19.57

The published guidance introduces a risk assessment tool developed by NHS England to assist in identifying modern slavery risks within procurement processes, which is aligned with the PA 2023. This tool evaluates risk based on six key characteristics:

1. Industry type
2. Nature of the workforce
3. Supplier location
4. Context in which the supplier operates
5. Commodity type
6. Business or supply chain model

19.58

The effectiveness of the new general procurement regime, and the specific rules that will apply to the health care sector, will require testing. As demonstrated by the Supermax judicial review challenge 2015, vigilance will be required to ensure that the PA 2023 is complied with and that mandatory or discretionary grounds for exclusion are robustly applied. However, this is an area that is ripe for further development and litigation.

90 Department of Health and Social Care, *Tackling Modern Slavery in NHS Procurement: Proposed Regulations and Guidance* (Consultation document, Updated 5 June 2025) <https://www.gov.uk/government/consultations/tackling-modern-slavery-in-nhs-procurement-proposed-regulations-and-guidance/tackling-modern-slavery-in-nhs-procurement-proposed-regulations-and-guidance> accessed 31 August 2025.

Great British Energy Act 2025

19.59

In line with the government's commitments to address modern slavery risks in the public sector, the new Great British Energy Act 2025 establishes a publicly-owned company with objectives that include 'measures for ensuring that slavery and human trafficking is not taking place in its business or supply chains[91].' The Act received Royal Assent on 15 May 2025, and as the company is still in its infancy, it is not yet clear how effective these provisions will be in eliminating slavery and human trafficking from its supply chains. However, companies intending to supply goods or services to Great British Energy will clearly require effective supply chain mapping and robust due diligence measures. Progress in implementing the company's objectives is expected to be monitored by relevant parliamentary committees, such as the Joint Committee on Human Rights[92].

Environmental law

Environment Act 2021

19.60

The Environment Act 2021 ('EA 2021'), Sch 17, introduced restrictions on the use of forest risk commodities and requirements relating to due diligence and reporting. The legislation is reflective of the global move towards HREDD, and the necessity of state regulation of trade. The overlap between communities and geographies at risk of modern slavery and environmental damage is increasingly recognised. Illegal logging and the associated agribusinesses are often coupled with instances of forced labour and child labour, an example being cattle ranching in Brazil[93].

Forest risk commodities – due diligence requirements

19.61

Schedule 17 introduces three new due diligence requirements on businesses:

91 Great British Energy Act 2025 3(2)(e).

92 Joint Committee on Human Rights Report on Forced Labour, para 238.

93 Bethany Jackson, *Modern Slavery as a Threat to Forests: Reviewing the Links between Modern Slavery, Deforestation, and Potential Solutions* (2021), in J. A. Daniels (Ed.), Advances in Environmental Research. Volume 84 <https://nottingham-repository.worktribe.com/output/6296966/modern-slavery-as-a-threat-to-forests-reviewing-the-links-between-modern-slavery-deforestation-and-potential-solutions> accessed 30 September 2025. In addition see: UN Human Rights Council, *Trafficking in Persons in the Agriculture Sector: Human Rights Due Diligence and Sustainable Development* (A/HRC/50/33, 28 March 2022) <https://www.ohchr.org/en/documents/thematic-reports/ahrc5033-trafficking-persons-agriculture-sector-human-rights-due accessed 31 August 2025> accessed 31 August 2025; E Brickell and K Shephard, *The Climate Change–Modern Slavery Nexus in Cambodia* (ESRC–DFID Research Impact, IDS and The Impact Initiative, 2018) <https://opendocs.ids.ac.uk/Arts/report/The_Climate_Change-Modern_Slavery_Nexus_in_Cambodia/26429350?file=48078190> accessed 31 August 2025.

- The prohibition on using illegally produced forest risk commodities, including both raw and derived products.
- Establishing a due diligence system for each regulated commodity.
- Annual reporting on their due diligence exercise, parts of which will be published to ensure transparency.

19.62

The implementation of the forest risk commodities regime in the UK, however, has stalled due to the general election in 2024 and secondary legislation that would bring the due diligence and reporting requirements of Sch 17 to EA 2021 into effect has not yet been laid before Parliament.

19.63

A consultation was carried out by the previous government, and on 12 December 2023 the then Secretary of State for Environment, Food and Rural Affairs issued a statement regarding the regime. At the time, it was explained that the regime would apply to businesses with a global annual turnover above £50 million, would target four commodities identified as key drivers of deforestation: cattle products (excluding dairy), cocoa, palm oil and soy and include a range of enforcement measures, including an unlimited monetary penalty[94]. As of July 2025, secondary legislation remains outstanding and the new government has been unable to provide a timetable, citing the need to consider 'their approach to addressing the impact of the use of forestry commodities' in supply chains[95]. Despite the urgent need for regulation in this area, however, the precise scope and design of the due diligence requirements that will apply to forest risk commodities remain unclear.

Remedies and enforcement mechanisms

Consumer protection law

19.64

Consumer protection law has increasingly been used to hold companies to account for 'greenwashing'. However, similar strategies could also be employed against companies involved in 'fairwashing' practices to deter businesses from

94 Secretary of State for Environment, Food and Rural Affairs, *Introduction of Forest Risk Commodities Regulations* (12 December 2023) (Statement UIN HCWS117) <https://questions-statements.parliament.uk/written-statements/detail/2023-12-12/hcws117> accessed 30 September 2025.

95 HC Deb 8 July 2025, Vol 847, col 1207<https://hansard.parliament.uk/lords/2025-07-08/debates/49ABE178-2471-4C1B-A308-4E71FE071179/ForestRiskCommodities> accessed 30 September 2025.

presenting their operations and supply chains as being ethical, whilst in fact being linked to labour violations.

19.65

The Digital Markets, Competition and Consumers Act 2024 ('DMCCA 2024') came into force on 6 April 2025 and replaces and updates the Consumer Protection from Unfair Trading Regulations 2008[96], subject to transitional provisions.

Prohibited conduct

19.66

The DMCCA 2024, Part 4 is concerned with the protection of consumers from unfair commercial practices, including misleading actions[97], misleading omissions[98] and certain banned practices[99]. The prohibitions apply to a 'commercial practice', which has a technical definition under the Act[100].

19.67

A misleading action arises where a commercial practice contains false or deceptive information; its overall presentation is deceptive and/or the commercial practice fails to comply with the requirements of a code of conduct[101]. The DMCCA 2024 will be engaged where such act is likely to cause the average consumer to take a different decision. In the updated guidance on unfair practices, the Competition Markets Authority ('CMA') offers an instructive example of a trader advertising a product as complying with a code of practice that promotes the sustainable use of wood, but in fact uses wood from endangered rainforests, as breaching the DMCCA 2024, s 226[102].

19.68

A commercial practice is misleading by omission where material information is omitted or unclear[103]. Material information is information that the average

---

96 Thereby implementing in the UK the Unfair Commercial Practices Directive 2005/29/EC (UCPD) following Brexit.

97 DMCCA 2024, s 226.

98 DMCCA 2024, s 227.

99 DMCCA 2024, s 227, Sch 20.

100 DMCCA 2024, s 225(3) defines 'commercial practice' as an act or omission by a trader relating to the promotion or supply of—(a) the trader's product to a consumer, (b) another trader's product to a consumer, or (c) a consumer's product to the trader or another person;

101 DMCCA 2024, s 226.

102 Competition and Markets Authority, *Unfair Commercial Practices: Guidance on the protection from unfair trading provisions in the Digital Markets, Competition and Consumers Act 2024* (4 April 2025), p.49 <https://assets.publishing.service.gov.uk/media/67eeac72e9c76fa33048c785/CMA207_Unfair_commercial_practices_guidance.pdf> accessed 30 September 2025.

103 DMCCA 2024, s 227.

consumer needs to take an informed transactional decision. Again, the prohibition will be engaged where such omissions are likely to cause the average consumer to take a different decision. In their recently updated guidance, the CMA suggests that the basis for a product's purported green credentials may be material and if this information is omitted or unclear, a trader may be in breach of s 227[104].

19.69

Under the DMCCA 2024, Sch 20, certain practices are banned entirely. This includes traders claiming to be a signatory to a code of conduct when they are not[105].

Enforcement

19.70

It is a criminal offence to breach certain prohibitions in the DMCC Act; which are largely strict liability offences[106]. Both the company and an individual can be prosecuted for a criminal offence[107]. Section 238 of the DMCCA 2024 makes provision for defences of due diligence and innocent publication. Penalties include a fine, on summary conviction, or a fine or imprisonment up to two years on conviction on indictment[108].

19.71

A consumer also has a right to redress for the prohibited practice for a misleading action or aggressive practice[109]. This includes a right to unwind a relevant contract or payment, a right to a discount in respect of a supply of a product under a relevant contract or damages in respect of financial loss, distress or physical inconvenience or discomfort.

19.72

Amendments in the DMCCA 2024 have strengthened the enforcement powers of the CMA, which is intended to strengthen the influence and effectiveness of the CMA in respect of breaches of consumer protection legislation. So far as relevant, the updated and amended powers of the CMA include:

- Issuing infringement notices and imposing fines for a breach of up to £300,000 or, if higher, 10% of the trader's turnover.

104 Ibid., p.51.
105 DMCCA 2024, s 227, Sch 20(1).
106 DMCCA 2024, s 237.
107 DMCCA 2024, s 239(5).
108 DMCCA 2024, s 240.
109 DMCCA 2024, ss 232, 234 and 235(2).

- Accepting undertakings and imposing penalties for non-compliance. The CMA can opt to accept undertakings from a trader instead of issuing an infringement notice and enforce any breach by imposing fines of up to £150,000 or, if higher, 5% of turnover. A daily penalty of up to £15,000 or, if higher, 5% of daily turnover can also be imposed.
- Requiring traders to compensate consumers and take other remedial steps.

Greenwashing and fairwashing

19.73

A strategic priority for the CMA in supporting the transition to low carbon growth and promoting competitive markets is sustainable products and services[110]. In line with this, the CMA has been active in addressing greenwashing across the market. In 2021, the CMA published a 'Green Claims Code' to ensure that environmental claims comply with the 2008 Regulations[111]. On 10 January 2022, the CMA launched a market study into environmental claims in the fashion retail sector[112]. Alongside these broader market studies, in July 2022, the CMA launched an investigation into the green claims made by ASOS, Boohoo and George at Asda. In March 2024, the investigation was concluded with the retailers signing broad and extensive formal undertakings. The undertakings agreed require the retailers to undertake supplier due diligence, including ensuring the accuracy of a product's composition or manufacturing process, mandating suppliers to provide relevant certificates of compliance and requiring retailers to carry out frequent spot checks of samples[113]. As can be seen, this goes some way toward HREDD, as retailers will need ensure they have a clear and transparent supply chain and effective mechanisms in place to ensure and verify how products are made. The CMA's action on greenwashing provides a useful blueprint, which could be used to successfully intervene to promote modern slavery due diligence across industries within the current legislative framework.

110 Competition and Markets Authority, *Annual Plan 2022 to 2023* (24 March 2022) <https://www.gov.uk/government/publications/competition-and-markets-authority-annual-plan-2022-to-2023/annual-plan-2022-to-2023> accessed 30 September 2025.

111 Competition and Markets Authority, *Green Claims Code: Making Environmental Claims* (20 September 2021) <https://www.gov.uk/government/publications/green-claims-code-making-environmental-claims> accessed 30 September 2025.

112 Competition and Markets Authority, *Misleading Environmental Claims* (26 January 2023) <https://www.gov.uk/government/collections/misleading-environmental-claims> accessed 30 September 2025.

113 Competition and Markets Authority, *Fashion greenwashing: investigation into ASOS, Boohoo and Asda* (updated 27 March 2024) <https://www.gov.uk/cma-cases/asos-boohoo-and-asda-greenwashing-investigation#undertakings-accepted-from-asos-boohoo-and-george-at-asda> accessed 30 September 2025.

Advertising Standards Authority

19.74

The Advertising Standards Authority ('ASA') also has a role in enforcing consumer rights. The ASA is the UK's independent regulator of advertising and rules on complaints in regard to non-compliance with the UK Code of Non-broadcast Advertising and Direct & Promotional Marketing ('the CAP Code'), which mirrors many of the prohibitions in the DMCC Act. Importantly, the CAP Code requires that advertisers hold documentary evidence to substantiate claims made in advertisements[114]. Claims may be considered misleading if a business fails to provide adequate evidence in the course of an investigation by the ASA.

19.75

The ASA has been used to target so-called fairwashing, and in 2018 the Authority upheld a complaint against Sainsbury's tea labelled as 'Fairly Traded' was misleading as it suggested a connection to the Fairtrade scheme[115].

19.76

As a system of self-regulation, however, the ASA has limited powers and can only recommend amending or withdrawing an advert found to be in breach of the CAP Code; with decisions being published on their website. Whilst a mechanism with little teeth, a complaint to the ASA provides a low-cost and low-risk tool to highlight unfair commercial practices in relation to a company's and product's links to modern slavery.

19.77

The preceding analysis highlights the divergent regulatory approaches taken across the private and public sector, industries and issues. Whilst encouraging due diligence, the regulatory framework lacks harmonisation and undermines the potential to tackle the over-reliance on modern slavery and labour exploitation across business operations and supply chains. Rather than introducing HREDD standards in a piecemeal manner, those subject to exploitation as well as businesses would clearly benefit from the certainty and clarity provided by a mandatory HREDD law in the UK, successful examples of which are discussed further below.

114 CAP Code s 3.7; *R (Actegy Ltd) v The Advertising Standards Authority Ltd & Anor* [2019] EWHC 2374 (Admin).

115 Advertising Standards Authority, *Ruling on J Sainsbury plc* (7 March 2018) <https://www.asa.org.uk/rulings/j-sainsbury-plc-a17-400992.html> accessed 31 August 2025.

Obtaining remedy against a UK domiciled company

19.78

As set out above, the mechanisms available to compel businesses to address trafficking and modern slavery in their operations in their supply chain are limited in scope. Crucially moreover, the tools discussed do not guarantee an effective remedy for those affected. In a recent report, the JCHR was critical of the difficulties survivors face in accessing a remedy from UK companies when they have been subject to forced labour in their operations or supply chains abroad[116]. The JCHR has recommended that the government introduce legislation establishing a 'duty to prevent' human rights abuses, requiring effective human rights due diligence, and enabling civil (and criminal) remedies against companies when abuses occur[117]. This proposal would create a clear route to establish a company's liability for modern slavery in their operations and supply chains, however, it has not received support from the government. In the lacuna, victims of human rights violations have turned to tort litigation against UK companies, and it is likely that this will remain an important vehicle for those affected to secure a remedy.

Tort litigation

19.79

In recent years claimants subject to modern slavery outside the UK have bought claims for damages in the UK, for *inter alia* the tort of unjust enrichment against UK-domiciled companies. They argue that the companies have breached their duty of care by materially benefiting from their gross and unlawful exploitation in their supply chains. Although small in number, the cases have highlighted the potential to use civil law to enhance accountability and secure remedies for victims. However, the litigation also exposes both the evidential difficulties in proving these claims, and the jurisdictional hurdle in establishing that the cases should be decided in the UK.

Evidential obstacles and jurisdiction

19.80

In *Josiya and others v British American Tobacco PLC*[118], over 7,000 Malawian claimants, including more than 3,000 children, alleged that British American Tobacco financially benefitted (unjust enrichment) from their unlawful exploitation

116 Joint Committee on Human Rights Report on Forced Labour, para.270.
117 Joint Committee on Human Rights Report on Forced Labour, para.266–269 and para.271.
118 [2021] EWHC 1743 (QB).

on tobacco farms and thereby facilitated, assisted, and/or encouraged it. The supply chain, as recorded in the judgment, involved contract farmers selling to state-regulated auction houses, referred to as 'leaf buyers', which were part of multinational groups headquartered in the US. These entities processed the tobacco and sold it on to the defendants.

19.81

A central issue in the claim was whether the defendants had purchased tobacco originating from farms worked on by the claimants, despite acquiring only a small share of Malawi's annual crop. The claimants had no direct contractual relationship with the defendants or their subsidiaries. Instead, they alleged that their tobacco entered the defendants' global supply chains via the intermediary leaf buyers. This 'nexus issue', at the heart of the defendants' strike-out applications, posed a significant evidential challenge, particularly in the absence of supply chain transparency.

19.82

The Court held that the claimants were not required to prove the nexus allegation at the pleading stage. It criticised the defendants for conflating the standard for pleading with that required at trial, affirming that a solicitor's justified belief in the allegation was sufficient. The Court declined to assess the statistical basis of the claim and found that the nexus allegation was not wholly speculative. It concluded that the Particulars of Claim were not an abuse of process and could proceed.

19.83

However, the case illustrates the evidentiary difficulties likely to arise at trial, particularly where claimants must trace goods through complex, multi-tiered supply chains without direct contractual links. These challenges are likely to persist in tort claims involving allegations of modern slavery arising within a supply chain.

19.84

Following the UK's withdrawal from the European Union, the Brussels I (Recast) Regulation ceased to apply to new claims against UK-domiciled defendants after 31 December 2020. Before Brexit, due to the mandatory jurisdictional rules under the Brussels regime, English-domiciled defendants were largely unable to invoke the common law doctrine of *forum non conveniens,* which requires the court to identify 'the forum in which the case can be suitably tried for the interests of all the parties and for the ends of justice'. As a result, cases pre-Brexit, such as *AAA v Unilever*[119], *Vedanta Resources plc v Lungowe*[120] *and*

119 [2018] EWCA Civ 1532.
120 [2019] UKSC 20, [2020] AC 1045.

Okpabi v Royal Dutch Shell plc[121] focused on challenging the substance of the parental duty of care claim rather than jurisdiction.

19.85

Post-Brexit, the reintroduction of common law principles has reopened the possibility for UK companies to argue that a foreign jurisdiction is more appropriate, even if they are domiciled in the UK. Jurisdictional questions are now governed by the common law, notably the test set out in *Spiliada Maritime Corporation v Cansulex Ltd*[122].

19.86

In *Limbu and Others v Dyson Technology Ltd and Others*[123], 24 claimants brought tort claims, including for unjust enrichment, alleging forced labour and exploitative conditions while employed by ATA Industrial (ATA), a Malaysian supplier to Dyson. The claimants argued that the UK-based Dyson companies exercised significant control over ATA's operations and working conditions and had implemented mandatory policies, such as the Dyson Ethical and Environmental Code of Conduct, explicitly addressing forced labour. These policies were central to the claimants' case, as they were said to impose obligations on suppliers and reflect Dyson's assumed responsibility for labour standards. The claimants further alleged that Dyson was aware of the risks through public reports, internal audits, and civil society notifications.

19.87

The defendants accepted that the claims had a real prospect of success. The central issue before the High Court was whether the claims should be heard in England or Malaysia. Applying the *Spiliada* test, the court considered: (1) which forum was more appropriate; and (2) whether substantial justice could be obtained in Malaysia. It concluded that Malaysia was the more suitable forum and that justice could be achieved there.

19.88

However, the Court of Appeal overturned this decision on 13 December 2024[124]. It held that the claims were primarily directed at the UK-based Dyson companies, particularly in relation to the promulgation of policies that arguably created a duty of care. The Court emphasised that these policies were not peripheral but formed the foundation of the claimants' case, linking corporate conduct in England to harm suffered abroad. This supported English jurisdiction.

121 [2021] UKSC 3, [2021] 1 WLR 1294.
122 [1986] UKHL 10, [1987] AC 460.
123 [2023] EWHC 2592 (KB).
124 *Limbu v Dyson Technology Ltd* [2024] 12 WLUK 213.

19.89

The Court found that the High Court had erred in treating Malaysia as the 'centre of gravity' of the dispute. While the alleged harm occurred in Malaysia, the claims focused on corporate responsibility and unjust enrichment arising from conduct in England. The Court concluded that the 'centre of gravity' was either England or neutral.

19.90

Another key factor was that the defence would be coordinated by UK-based Dyson personnel. The Court of Appeal also found the High Court was 'plainly wrong' to rely on undertakings by the defendants as a sufficient mechanism to ensure funding for disbursements in Malaysia. Considering all relevant factors: funding, party domicile, practical convenience, and equality of arms, observing the 'huge imbalance between the impoverished and vulnerable claimants and the well-resourced and commercially experienced defendants[125] 'the Court held that England was 'clearly and distinctly' the most appropriate forum. The Supreme Court subsequently refused the defendants' petition to appeal.

19.91

The *Spiliada* test has recently been applied in *Catarina Oliveira Da Silva and Others v Brazil Iron Limited and Another*[126] in which the court held that there was a real risk that substantial justice would not be obtained in Brazil, and as such was not the appropriate forum.

Certification and criminal proceedings

19.92

Certification schemes are increasingly used to give assurances that goods are not produced by modern slavery, such as child or forced labour. In the case of the Ali Enterprises Factory fire in Karachi on 11 September 2012, where 260 workers died (including child workers), the Italian company Rina Services S.p.A. had audited the factory and issued a certificate of compliance with social standards. An Organisation for Economic Co-operation and Development complaint filed on 11 September 2018[127] alleged that this certificate wrongfully implied the absence of child labour and other abuses.

125 Ibid at [39] and [59].

126 [2025] EWHC 606 (KB).

127 Ministero dello Sviluppo Economico, *Initial Assessment of the Specific Instance submitted by AEFFAA and others v RINA Services S.p.A.* (Italian National Contact Point for the OECD Guidelines, 8 April 2019) https://pcnitalia.mise.gov.it/attachments/Art/2035928/Case%20AEFFAA%20v.%20RINA%20-%20Initial%20Assessment%20DEF%20(5).pdf (accessed 3 September 2025).

19.93

The issue of whether an industry standards body can be held legally liable for the consequences of its accreditation or oversight activities is now being tested for the first time in court[128]. This landmark case concerns the London Bullion Market Association ('LBMA'), the principal authority for the global bullion market, which sets and enforces standards for gold and silver refineries through its Good Delivery List and Responsible Sourcing Programme. The families of two artisanal miners who died in Tanzania allege that LBMA acted negligently by accrediting gold from Barrick Gold's Tanzanian mine as 'responsibly sourced' under its Responsible Gold Certificate, despite the mine being the subject of multiple allegations of human rights abuses. The case is ongoing, and its outcome is expected to set an important precedent for the legal accountability of organisations that accredit or certify compliance with ethical sourcing standards.

19.94

During the Covid-19 pandemic, *The Sunday Times* reported allegations of modern slavery at Jaiswal Fashions, a garment factory in Leicester supplying the Manchester-based fast-fashion retailer Boohoo. These concerns were not unprecedented; reports of exploitative labour practices in Leicester's garment industry date back to at least 2017[129]. Notably, despite the identification of approximately 22,000 potential victims of exploitation[130], no criminal prosecutions have been brought, raising serious questions about the enforcement of labour and criminal law in this context.

The significance of R (World Uyghur Congress) v National Crime Agency

19.95

The Court of Appeal's decision in *R (World Uyghur Congress) v National Crime Agency*[131] represents a pivotal clarification of the 'adequate consideration' exemption under s 329(2)(c) of POCA 2002, particularly in the context of supply

128 Business & Human Rights Resource Centre, 'UK: Case over alleged wrongful gold classification from Tanzania to proceed to trial after LBMA drops jurisdictional challenge' (Business & Human Rights Resource Centre, 2 September 2025) https://www.business-humanrights.org/en/latest-news/uk-case-over-alleged-wrongful-gold-classification-from-tanzania-to-proceed-to-trial-after-lbma-drops-jurisdictional-challenge/ accessed 3 September 2025.

129 Andrew Busby, 'As Slavery Allegations Continue to Surround Boohoo, Why the Days of the £5 Dress Are Well and Truly Over' (*Forbes*, 7 July 2020) https://www.forbes.com/sites/andrewbusby/2020/07/07/as-slavery-allegations-continue-to-surround-boohoo-why-the-days-of-the-5-dress-are-well-and-truly-over/ accessed 3 September 2025.

130 Business & Human Rights Resource Centre, 'UK: Investigation Finds Garment Workers in Leicester Face Threats, Low Wages, Poor Conditions During the Pandemic' (*Business & Human Rights Resource Centre*, 6 July 2020) https://www.business-humanrights.org/en/latest-news/uk-investigation-finds-garment-workers-in-leicester-face-threats-low-wages-poor-conditions-during-the-pandemic/ accessed 3 September 2025.

131 [2024] EWCA Civ 715.

chains tainted by forced labour and other human rights abuses. In addition, the ruling imposed a stricter obligation on UK authorities to investigate potential breaches[132] of POCA 2002 proactively.

19.96

The appeal arose from the National Crime Agency's (NCA) refusal to investigate alleged offences under Part 7 of POCA 2002 or to initiate civil recovery under Part 5 of POCA 2002, despite detailed evidence that cotton goods imported from China's Xinjiang Uyghur Autonomous Region (XUAR) were produced through forced labour. It was common ground between the parties that there exists a substantial and growing body of evidence of serious human rights abuses in the XUAR cotton industry. Furthermore, it was accepted that products derived from forced labour occurring anywhere in the world can constitute 'criminal property' for the purposes of money laundering offences under Part 7, and 'recoverable property' under Part 5. Such conduct amounting to 'criminal conduct' under section 340 POCA 2002, by reference to offences under the Modern Slavery Act 2015 and the International Criminal Court Act 2001 (see section 340(2A) of POCA 2002).

Clarifying the Threshold for Investigation

19.97

The Court rejected that an investigation under POCA 2002 required prior identification of specific criminal property or conduct. It held that this interpretation was legally flawed and inconsistent with POCA 2002's purpose. The Court's reasoning significantly lowers the threshold for when UK authorities must consider using POCA powers in forced-labour supply chain contexts. The NCA conceded on appeal that:

- **An investigation into the proceeds of crime can lawfully begin even if specific criminal property or recoverable property has not yet been identified.** The investigative process itself is intended to uncover whether such property exists.
- **Generalised or high-level evidence of criminality is sufficient to justify the commencement of an investigation.** The absence of detailed or specific allegations does not preclude the use of POCA 2002 powers.
- **Money laundering can be proven at trial without establishing a specific underlying offence or identifying a particular offender.**

132 Section 327 criminalises dealing with criminal property, including concealing, disguising, converting, transferring, or removing it. Section 328 targets arrangements that facilitate the acquisition, retention, use, or control of criminal property by another. Section 329 makes it an offence to acquire, use, or possess criminal property, where the person knows or suspects its criminal origin.

It is sufficient either to demonstrate the general type of criminal conduct (eg fraud, forced labour), or to show that the way in which the property was dealt with gives rise to an irresistible inference that it represents the proceeds of crime.

- **The fact that property was acquired in exchange for payment, ie for adequate consideration, does not bar an investigation under POCA 2002.** The adequacy of consideration may be relevant to liability under s 329(1), but it does not prevent the property from being classified as criminal or recoverable, nor does it shield others in the supply chain from scrutiny.

19.98

The Court found that the NCA's decision conveyed a legally incorrect view that an investigation under POCA 2002 can only commence once there is evidence of criminal conduct or the existence of criminal property. This misdirection warranted quashing the decision and remitting the matter back to NCA for reconsideration.

Correct interpretation of s 329(2)(c) of POCA 2002

19.99

Under section 329(2)(c) of POCA 2002, a person does not commit an offence of acquiring, using, or possessing criminal property if they provide adequate consideration for it. This term refers to payment or value that is objectively reasonable in the circumstances, typically equating to market value or a fair commercial rate.The exemption is not contingent on the individual's knowledge or belief regarding the criminal origin of the property; it may apply even where the person knows or suspects the property is tainted, provided the consideration given is adequate.

19.100

The exemption is limited strictly to offences under s 329(1) and does not extend to offences under ss 327 or 328, which concern concealment, transfer, or facilitation of criminal property. Importantly, as the Court held, the exemption does not alter the status of the property itself, which remains criminal property regardless of the transaction. The Court clarified Irwin J's obiter comment in *Hogan v DPP*[133], which had suggested that adequate consideration removes criminal liability under POCA 2002. The Court held that this is true only in relation to s 329(1), and that the exemption does not 'cleanse' the property or prevent criminal liability under other provisions of the Act.

133 [2007] EWHC 978 (Admin).

19.101

The Court distinguished s 329(2)(c) from s 308, which provides a true bona fide purchaser exemption from criminal liability. Unlike s 329(2)(c), s 308(1) removes the property's recoverable status under Part 5, where the recipient acquires it in good faith, for value, and without notice of its criminal origin. Mere payment of market value is insufficient without these additional elements and remains recoverable under Part 5.

19.102

There has been no appeal against the judgment. The decision highlights the need for rigorous due diligence, particularly for businesses with complex supply chains. It confirms that money laundering offences can arise from commercial transactions linked to human rights abuses. Paying market value is no defence where there is reasonable suspicion of forced labour. It may give rise to companies considering whether to seek a Defence Against Money Laundering ('DAML') from the NCA if issues are identified in their own or target supply chains. The lack of specific official guidance from the NCA following this landmark decision appears to be a significant gap, particularly given the ruling's potential to fundamentally alter how POCA 2002 investigations are approached in supply chain contexts. At the time of writing, there is still no public, detailed NCA policy on POCA enforcement in supply chains.

Challenges to Stock Exchange Listings

19.103

Stop Uyghur Genocide ('SUG') launched a legal action against the Financial Conduct Authority ('FCA') to block the listing on the London Stock Exchange of Shein, a Singapore-based fast-fashion manufacturer. SUG claims that there are identifiable links between cotton production in the Chinese Uyghur region and forced labour, and that there is publicly available evidence to link Shein's supply chains to cotton produced in the Uyghur Region[134]. It is argued that Shein profits from criminal practices under POCA 2002 and consequently should not be allowed to raise capital on the London market. After failing to obtain Chinese regulatory approval for a London listing (despite FCA clearance), Shein altered its course and is now pursuing a Hong Kong IPO. Shein's strategy is to submit a confidential draft prospectus in Hong Kong and signals a desire

134 'Stop Uyghur Genocide threatens court challenge to Financial Conduct Authority over Shein bid to list on London Stock Exchange' (Leigh Day, 2025) <https://www.leighday.co.uk/news/news/2025-news/stop-uyghur-genocide-threatens-court-challenge-to-financial-conduct-authority-over-shein-bid-to-list-on-london-stock-exchange/ accessed 3 September 2025.

to limit public scrutiny of sensitive information, such as supply chain risks and forced labour allegations, until late in the process[135].

International, EU, and comparative approaches

Redefining responsibility: the EU's approach to forced labour and corporate due diligence

19.104

In a briefing paper published by the UK Trade Policy Observatory[136], Professor Erika Szyszczak analyses two pivotal EU instruments, the Forced Labour Regulation ('FLR') and the Corporate Sustainability Due Diligence Directive ('CSDDD'), finalised in April 2024. These measures mark a strategic shift in EU regulation, placing legal responsibility on private actors to uphold human rights and sustainability standards within global supply chains. Embedded within the EU's Open Strategic Autonomy framework, the FLR and CSDDD integrate trade policy with fundamental rights, introducing enforceable obligations, procedural safeguards, and avenues for redress. Notably, they empower individuals and stakeholders to initiate actions in national courts, even for violations occurring outside the EU. Szyszczak argues that, despite certain limitations, the move toward civil liability could significantly enhance corporate accountability and access to justice for victims of forced labour.

19.105

However, the durability of these reforms may be tested by the European Commission's Omnibus Simplification Package, proposed on 26 February 2025. This legislative initiative seeks to amend core sustainability instruments including the Corporate Sustainability Reporting Directive ('the CSRD') , CSDDD, EU Taxonomy Regulation, and CBAM under a consolidated framework. The proposal has drawn sharp criticism from civil society and legal experts, who argue that the consultation process lacked transparency and facilitated undue corporate influence, raising concerns about regulatory dilution and potential rollback of hard-won protections[137].

135 'China-founded fashion retailer Shein to file confidentially for Hong Kong IPO in rare move – sources' Reuters (27 June 2025) https://www.reuters.com/business/retail-consumer/china-fashion-retailer-shein-file-confidentially-hong-kong-ipo-rare-move-sources-2025-06-27/ accessed 3 September 2025.

136 Erika Szyszczak, *Trade and Illegal Labour: The EU's Forced Labour Regulation and Corporate Sustainability Due Diligence Directive* (UK Trade Policy Observatory Briefing Paper 84, December 2024) https://www.uktpo.org/wp-content/uploads/2024/12/BP84-TRADE-AND-ILLEGAL-LABOUR.pdf accessed 4 September 2025.

137 Action Aid, 'Legal Letter: Concerns About Inadequate Consultation Process – Omnibus' (2025) <https://actionaid.org/publications/2025/legal-letter-concerns-about-inadequate-consultation-process-omnibus> accessed 4 September 2025.

19.106

Following the European Union (Withdrawal) Act 2018, EU law is no longer part of UK domestic law (unless retained), but UK companies may still be caught by the EU laws which seek to mitigate modern slavery and trafficking in supply chains.

EU Corporate Sustainability Due Diligence Directive (CSDDD)

19.107

On the 25 July 2024, the Directive on Corporate Sustainability Due Diligence ('the Directive') entered into force. It is mandating legislation which requires Member States to bring in legislation requiring companies to comply with their stated obligations under the Directive. The stated aim of this Directive is to 'foster sustainable and responsible corporate behaviour in companies' operations and across global value chains. The new rules will ensure that companies in scope identify and address adverse human rights and environmental impacts of their actions inside and outside Europe[138].

19.108

The Directive applies to large EU limited liability companies and partnerships, where the number of employees is over 1000, and the net turnover is €450 million worldwide. The Directive also applies to non-EU companies, including UK-based companies, where the net turnover generated in the EU is €450 million. Small and medium enterprises ('SMEs') could also be indirectly affected as business partners in supply chains. The Centre for Research on Multinational Corporations ('SOMO') has compiled a datahub of EU and non-EU companies that would have to comply with the Directive[139]. EU Member States must transpose the Directive into national law and communicate the relevant texts to the Commission by 26 July 2026. The Directive will be introduced in phases, starting with the first group of companies in 2027, and will apply in full, from 26 July 2029, as follows[140]:

- Three years (26 July 2027): EU companies with more than 5000 employees and €1,500 million worldwide turnover, as well as non-EU companies with more than €1,500 million turnover generated in the EU.

138 European Commission, 'Corporate Sustainability Due Diligence' (European Commission, 25 July 2024) https://commission.europa.eu/business-economy-euro/doing-business-eu/sustainability-due-diligence-responsible-business/corporate-sustainability-due-diligence_en accessed 3 September 2025.

139 SOMO, 'CS3D Datahub' (SOMO) <https://www.somo.nl/csddd-datahub/ accessed 3 September 2025.

140 Directive (EU) 2024/1760 of the European Parliament and of the Council of 13 June 2024 on corporate sustainability due diligence and amending Directive (EU) 2019/1937 and Regulation (EU) 2023/2859 [2024] OJ L, art 37 <https://eur-lex.europa.eu/eli/dir/2024/1760/oj> accessed 3 September 2025.

- Four years (26 July 2028): EU companies with more than 3,000 employees and €900 million worldwide turnover, as well as non-EU companies with more than €900 million turnover generated in the EU.
- Five years (26 July 2029): All other companies in scope.

19.109

Two further points merit attention. Financial services provided in client relationships are excluded from the Directive's scope, though this may be reviewed within two years. Small and medium enterprises are not directly subject to the Directive and face no enforcement or liability, but they may be affected as business partners of in-scope companies. The Directive includes measures to support SMEs and prevent large companies from shifting compliance costs onto them. Larger companies may be required to adapt purchasing practices, invest in supply chains, and provide financial and non-financial support to SMEs under certain conditions[141]. Member States can also offer financial assistance to SMEs[142].

19.110

The Directive requires companies operating within the internal market to contribute to sustainable development by identifying, prioritising where necessary, and addressing actual or potential adverse human rights and environmental impacts linked to their own operations, subsidiaries, and business partners throughout their chains of activities. Companies must prevent, mitigate, and, where appropriate, remediate such impacts, while ensuring access to justice and effective remedies for those affected by non-compliance. These obligations are grounded in key international instruments[143], including the ILO Convention on the prohibition of the worst forms of child labour[144], forced or compulsory labour[145], the UN Convention on the Rights of the Child, and the Human Trafficking Convention[146] all listed in the Annex.

19.111

Due diligence under the Directive encompasses adverse human rights impacts arising from abuses of rights in the Annex, interpreted in line with international law, and extends to other foreseeable rights abuses. It also covers environmental harms resulting from breaches of listed prohibitions, such as soil degradation, water or air pollution, deforestation, and damage to ecosystem services that affect health, resources, or biodiversity[147]. Assessment considers factors such as scale,

141 Ibid, Art 11(3)(f).
142 Ibid, Art 20 (2).
143 See **Chapter 1** for a detailed analysis of these International Conventions.
144 Ibid, Paragraph 10, Annex.
145 Ibid, Paragraph 11, Annex.
146 Ibid, Paragraph 12, Annex.
147 Directive (EU) 2024/1760, Annex, Part II.

duration, and reversibility of harm. These measures aim to preserve biodiversity and improve environmental quality as part of the sustainability transition.

19.112

The Directive operates without prejudice to Member States' obligations under international law and to existing EU legislation on human rights, social rights, environmental protection, and climate change. Where conflicts arise, other Union acts with more specific or extensive obligations prevail, such as Regulation (EU) 2017/821, Regulation (EU) 2023/1542, and Regulation (EU) 2023/1115. The Commission may amend the Annex by delegated acts, for example, to include additional ILO conventions once ratified by all Member States.

19.113

Its scope extends across the 'chain of activities', covering upstream production and downstream distribution[148]. For example, a textile factory supplying fabric is an upstream partner, while a retail store selling finished goods is downstream. The Directive permits group-level[149] due diligence by parent companies for subsidiaries, provided compliance is effective, without limiting supervisory powers[150] or civil liability[151].

EU Due Diligence Framework: corporate obligations[152]

19.114

The EU Due Diligence Directive establishes a comprehensive framework requiring companies to implement risk-based human rights and environmental due diligence as an integrated corporate risk management tool. The framework comprises eight core obligations:

Core due diligence obligations

19.115

Companies must:

- Integrate due diligence into policies and risk management systems
- Identify and assess actual or potential adverse impacts, prioritising where necessary

148 Directive (EU) 2024/1760, Art 3 (g).
149 Ibid Art 6.
150 Ibid, Art 25.
151 Ibid, Art 29.
152 Ibid, Arts 7-16

- Prevent and mitigate potential adverse impacts, and end actual impacts
- Provide remediation for actual adverse impacts
- Engage meaningfully with stakeholders
- Establish notification mechanisms and complaints procedures
- Monitor due diligence effectiveness
- Communicate publicly on due diligence

Policy integration and risk management

19.116

Due diligence must be integrated into all relevant company policies and risk management systems. Companies must develop a due diligence policy following employee consultation, containing:

- The company's due diligence approach and long-term strategy
- A code of conduct for the company, subsidiaries, and business partners
- Implementation processes and compliance verification measures

Impact assessment and prioritisation

19.117

Companies must map operations across their value chains to identify where adverse impacts are most likely and severe. This requires in-depth assessment of high-risk areas within company operations, subsidiaries, and business partner activities. Where addressing all impacts simultaneously is unfeasible, companies must prioritise based on severity and likelihood, addressing the most severe impacts first within reasonable timeframes.

Prevention and mitigation

19.118

Companies must take appropriate measures to prevent potential adverse impacts or adequately mitigate where prevention is impossible. Measures depend on:

- Whether impacts are caused solely by the company, jointly with partners, or by partners alone
- Whether impacts occur in subsidiary or business partner operations
- The company's ability to influence the causing entity

19.119

Prevention measures include implementing action plans, securing contractual assurances, making necessary investments, modifying business plans, supporting SME partners, and collaborating with other entities.

Addressing actual impacts

19.120

For actual adverse impacts, companies must take appropriate measures to bring them to an end, considering the same factors as prevention. Required actions include neutralising impacts, implementing corrective plans, securing contractual assurances, making investments, and providing remediation.

Remediation requirements

19.121

Companies that cause or jointly cause actual adverse impacts must provide remediation. Where impacts are caused solely by business partners, companies may provide voluntary remediation or use their influence to ensure partner-provided remediation.

Stakeholder engagement

19.122

Effective stakeholder engagement requires providing comprehensive information and allowing reasoned requests for additional data. Consultation must occur when:

- Gathering impact information
- Developing action plans
- Deciding on business relationship changes
- Adopting remediation measures
- Developing monitoring indicators

19.123

Companies must identify engagement barriers and protect participants from retaliation through confidentiality measures.

Complaints and notification systems

19.124

Companies must enable complaints from affected persons, their representatives, trade unions, workers' representatives, and relevant civil society organisations. Procedures must be fair, transparent, and include measures preventing retaliation while maintaining complainant confidentiality.

Monitoring and communication

19.125

Companies must conduct periodic assessments of their operations, subsidiaries, and business partners to monitor due diligence effectiveness. Regular public reporting on due diligence matters is mandatory.

Responsible disengagement

19.126

The Directive permits responsible disengagement with appropriate safeguards to mitigate risks.

Enforcement framework

19.127

The Directive establishes a European Network of Supervisory Authorities with powers to impose sanctions, including fines. Claimants may seek injunctions for breaches, and non-compliance affects public procurement eligibility. Enforcement applies to both EU and non-EU companies.

Substantiated concerns

19.128

The Directive entitles natural and legal persons to submit substantiated concerns to supervisory authorities through easily accessible channels where they reasonably believe a company is failing to comply with national laws transposing the Directive. Crucially, supervisory authorities must, upon request, implement necessary measures to protect the identity and personal information of complainants where disclosure would cause harm to that person.

Civil liability

19.129

The Directive contains a civil liability regime for compensation for damage caused to a natural or legal person[153]. Compensation may be provided when companies intentionally or negligently fail to comply with their duty to prevent, mitigate, minimise or end adverse impacts, and this failure causes or contributes to damage.

19.130

Injured parties may authorise a trade union, a non-governmental human rights or environmental organisation or other non-governmental organisation based in a Member State to bring actions on their behalf, under the conditions set out in national law. A company will not be liable if only the business partner(s) in their chain of activities caused the damage.

The EU Omnibus Directive (Directive (EU) 2026/470): Amendments to the CSDDD

19.131

On 26 February 2025, the European Commission ('the Commission') proposed the Omnibus Directive, introducing substantive amendments to the Directive. Following an accelerated legislative process, the final text, Directive (EU) 2026/470 of the European Parliament and of the Council of 24 February 2026, was formally adopted by the Council of the EU on 24 February 2026 and published in the Official Journal on 26 February 2026. The Directive amends the CSDDD and the CSRD. Notably, the enacted text removes Art 29(7) which required Member States to treat civil liability provisions as overriding mandatory rules where the applicable law was not that of an EU Member State. This marks a departure from the Directive's original objective of establishing a harmonised EU-wide liability regime.

19.132

The Commission justified the change by invoking the subsidiarity principle and the need to reduce regulatory burdens, particularly for SMEs. However, this rationale has been criticised for undermining the legal basis of the Directive under Art 114 TFEU, which permits harmonisation to address fragmentation in national regimes affecting the internal market. Professor Geert van Calster

153 Ibid Art 29.

argues[154] that the removal of Art 29(7) increases legal uncertainty, as national courts may inconsistently apply overriding mandatory provisions under Art 16 of the Rome II Regulation. This could result in courts setting aside not only third-country laws but also those of other Member States, an outcome previously excluded under the Directive.

19.133

While the Omnibus removes the EU-wide liability framework, Member States must still ensure effective access to justice and full compensation under national law. However, this change would transform the Directive from a unified European standard into a framework where liability depends entirely on the vagaries of international conflict of law rules and potentially diverse national legal systems. The enacted text also eliminates the requirement to impose maximum penalties of at least 5% of global turnover, reducing the ceiling to 'not more than 3%' of net worldwide turnover, though national regimes may retain more stringent sanctions.

19.134

These substantive changes were adopted through an accelerated EU legislative process.The European Parliament approved the Omnibus I text on 16 December 2025, and the Council of the EU formally adopted Directive (EU) 2026/470 on 24 February 2026. The Directive was published in the Official Journal on 26 February 2026 and entered into force on 18 March 2026 (20 days after publication, applying standard EU legal-time computation). The Directive contains several transposition deadlines. Member States must transpose the CSDDD-related provisions by 26 July 2028, with companies required to comply from 26 July 2029. Other amendments, particularly those relating to the CSRD and general alignment measures, must be transposed earlier, by 19 March 2027. The Commission is required to review the effectiveness of the CSDDD, including whether an EU-level civil liability regime should be reinstated, by 26 July 2031[155]. The procedural path to adoption was contested. On 25–26 November 2025, the European Ombudswoman found that the Commission had committed maladministration in preparing the Omnibus I proposals, including by limiting inter-departmental consultation to less than 24 hours and by failing to conduct an impact assessment[156]. Legal experts have noted that these procedural defects could provide grounds for a challenge before the Court of Justice of the EU, although no such challenge had been filed at the date of this edition.

---

154 Geert van Calster, *Legal Opinion on the Conflict of Laws Aspects of the Corporate Sustainability Due Diligence Directive (CS3D)* (Business & Human Rights Resource Centre, June 2025) https://media.business-humanrights.org/media/documents/legal_opinion_gvc.pdf accessed 4 September 2025.

155 Generation Impact Global, *'Sustainability Reporting and Due Diligence in the EU after Directive (EU) 2026/470'* (26 February 2026) <https://www.generationimpact.global/> accessed 20 March 2026.

156 European Ombudsman, 'Ombudsman finds maladministration in how Commission prepared urgent legislative proposals' (Press Release 01/25, 26 November 2025).

The EU Forced Labour Regulation[157] (amending the Whistleblower Directive[158])

Legislative Framework and Timeline

19.135

On 19 November 2024, the Council of the European Union formally approved the Forced Labour Regulation, prohibiting products made with forced labour from the EU market[159]. The regulation entered into force on 13 December 2024 and will apply from 14 December 2027, providing a three-year implementation period. The regulation applies to all economic operators, including UK-based companies importing into or exporting from the EU[160].

Comprehensive scope and coverage

19.136

The Forced Labour Regulation's scope extends beyond traditional import controls to encompass the entire EU market ecosystem. Products sold online fall within its ambit where the sales offer targets EU consumers, reflecting the digital economy's realities[161]. Uniquely, the prohibition applies bidirectionally, covering both imports into the EU and exports from the EU, thereby extending the regulation's reach to global supply chains. The regulation applies universally to all economic operators regardless of size, from multinational corporations to small enterprises, though the latter's resources will be considered during enforcement proceedings.

19.137

Significantly, the prohibition applies to the entire life cycle of a product and its components, banning any item if forced labour was used at any stage of its production, manufacture, harvesting, extraction, or related processing, whether

157 Regulation (EU) 2024/3015 of the European Parliament and of the Council of 27 November 2024 on prohibiting products made with forced labour on the Union market and amending Directive (EU) 2019/1937 https://eur-lex.europa.eu/legal-content/EN/TXT/?uri=OJ:L_202403015, accessed 24 July 2026.

158 Directive (EU) 2019/1937 of the European Parliament and of the Council of 23 October 2019 on the protection of persons who report breaches of Union law [2019] OJ L305/17 https://eur-lex.europa.eu/legal-content/EN/TXT/PDF/?uri=CELEX:32019L1937 accessed 4 September 2025.

159 Art 3, Regulation (EU) 2024/3015 of the European Parliament and of the Council of 13 June 2024 establishing a framework for sustainable corporate governance [2024] OJ L https://eur-lex.europa.eu/eli/reg/2024/3015/oj/eng accessed 4 September 2025.

160 Ibid Art 39.

161 See White & Case, *EU Adopts Forced Labour Ban: 8 Things to Know* (White & Case LLP, 26 July 2024) https://www.whitecase.com/insight-alert/eu-adopts-forced-labour-ban-8-things-know accessed 4 September 2025.

in whole or in part. Transport services constitute the sole exception to this comprehensive coverage[162].

Regulatory objectives and definitional framework

19.138

The objective of the regulation is to contribute to the international efforts to eradicate forced labour[163]. Art 2 adopts the ILO Convention No. 29 definition of forced labour[164]. The Commission and Member State competent authorities bear responsibility for identifying violations, coordinating closely with labour inspection authorities and judicial bodies to avoid jeopardising parallel investigations, including those concerning human trafficking.

Investigation

19.139

Investigations under the regulation follow a two-phase structure: a preliminary investigation followed, where appropriate, by a formal investigation.

19.140

A formal investigation may only be initiated if the preliminary phase identifies a 'substantiated concern' regarding a potential breach of Art 3[165]. In such cases, the lead competent authority must notify the relevant economic operators of the scope and potential consequences of the investigation.

19.141

During the formal investigation, the authorities will prioritise economic operators closest to the suspected use of forced labour in the supply chain, considering factors such as company size, resources, product volume, and the severity of the alleged breach. Authorities bear the burden of proof, relying on all available evidence. Operators may submit exculpatory material, but unjustified failure to provide requested information may result in adverse findings. Field inspections may be conducted where necessary[166]. Authorities must establish non-compliance within nine months of initiating an investigation, employing

---

162 Recital (18), Regulation (EU) 2024/3015 of the European Parliament and of the Council of 13 June 2024 establishing a framework for sustainable corporate governance [2024] OJ L https://eur-lex.europa.eu/eli/reg/2024/3015/oj/eng accessed 4 September 2025.

163 Ibid, Recital (7), (13) and Art 1.

164 See Chapter 1

165 Ibid Art 17(5).

166 Ibid Art 19.

a risk-based assessment framework that considers the quantity and volume of products, the scale and severity of suspected forced labour, and the economic resources of the operators involved[167].

19.142

If the authority is unable to establish that the products in question were made using forced labour and unlawfully placed on the EU market, the investigation must be closed. However, the regulation permits the reopening of an investigation into the same product and economic operator if new, relevant information becomes available.

Enforcement measures and sanctions

19.143

Art 20 of the regulation provides that where the lead competent authority establishes a breach of the prohibition on products made with forced labour, it must promptly prohibit the placing, making available, and export of such products within and from the Union. Economic operators must withdraw affected products already on the market. Perishable goods should be donated to charitable or public interest causes, while non-perishable goods must be recycled or, if recycling is not feasible, destroyed, rendered inoperable, or otherwise disposed of in accordance with national law[168]. Authorities may also order products to be withheld for a defined period.

19.144

The lead competent authority must issue a decision identifying the product, setting out the findings and supporting evidence, and specifying a reasonable compliance deadline. These decisions must be made publicly available. Penalties apply where economic operators fail to comply[169]. To ensure consistent enforcement, decisions issued by one Member State must be recognised and enforced by other Member States in relation to products with the same identification and supply chain where forced labour has been found.

19.145

The regulation also provides for the establishment of a database identifying high-risk products and regions[170], and the creation of the EU Forced Labour Network[171] to facilitate structured coordination between competent authorities

167 Ibid Art 18.
168 Ibid Art 25.
169 Ibid Art 37.
170 Ibid Art 8.
171 Ibid Art 6.

and the Commission. The Commission will issue guidance to support companies, including on due diligence and identifying forced labour risks in supply chains[172]. Particular support will be provided to SMEs, with their size and resources taken into account during assessments and investigations[173].

The Corporate Sustainability Reporting Directive (CSRD)

19.146

On the 5 January 2023, the Corporate Sustainability Reporting Directive ('the CSRD') entered into force[174]. It modernises and strengthens the rules concerning the social and environmental information that companies must report.

19.147

Non-EU (third-country) companies must report if they generate over €150 million EU turnover for two consecutive years and have either a qualifying EU subsidiary or a large EU branch meeting listed thresholds. Such companies must publish sustainability reports either through an EU branch or subsidiary[175]. Certain SMEs, that are public-interest entities, will also be required to report[176]. The reporting is staged, with the first stage starting with the financial year beginning 1 January 2024[177].

19.148

The purpose of the rules is to ensure that investors and other stakeholders have access to the information they need to assess the impact of companies on people and the environment and for investors to assess financial risks and opportunities arising from climate change and other sustainability issues.

19.149

The content of the reporting is in accordance with sustainability reporting standards[178], and are different for SMEs which are proportionate and relevant to their capacities[179]. Companies subject to the CSRD will have to report according to European Sustainability Reporting Standards ('ESRS'). The first

172 Ibid Art 11.
173 Ibid Art 10.
174 Directive (EU) 2022/2464 of the European Parliament and of the Council of 14 December 2022 on corporate sustainability reporting [2022] OJ L322/15 https://eur-lex.europa.eu/legal-content/EN/TXT/?uri=CELEX:32022L2464 accessed 4 September 2025.
175 Ibid Art 40a.
176 Ibid Art 19a.
177 Ibid Art 5.
178 Ibid Art 29b
179 Ibid Art 29c

set of ESRS was published in the Official Journal on the 22 December 2023 under the form of a delegated regulation[180]. These standards apply to companies under the scope of the CSRD regardless of which sector they operate in. They are tailored to EU polices, while building on and contributing to international standardisation initiatives.

19.150

Companies must include sustainability information in their annual management reports in a dedicated section. Compliance with ESRS must be verified by independent assurance service providers or statutory auditors, who must be accredited. The assurance regime currently requires 'limited assurance,' but the scope may expand as sustainability audit standards develop at the EU level.

19.151

Member States are responsible for the provision and enforcement of penalties. Non-compliance will lead to national administrative and/or criminal penalties, depending on the Member State.

The EU Omnibus Directive (Directive (EU) 2026/470): Key Substantive Changes

19.152

On 26 February 2025, the European Commission published a comprehensive legislative package proposing fundamental changes to the CSRD and the CSDDD. The resulting amending legislation, Directive (EU) 2026/470, was adopted by the Council of the EU on 24 February 2026 and published in the Official Journal on 26 February 2026, enacting the following key changes The Directive makes two deliberate departures from the earlier CSDDD proposal. The first is the repeal of the requirement for companies to prepare and report a climate transition plan; the Directive removes the previous provisions entirely and leaves climate disclosures to the CSRD framework. The second is the removal of the harmonised EU civil liability regime, replacing it with reliance on national law and a review clause. These changes substantially alter the shape of the regime. They narrow the Directive's substantive obligations, reduce the degree of alignment between due diligence duties and the EU's climate objectives, and reintroduce material differences between Member States in

180 Commission Delegated Regulation (EU) 2023/2772 of 31 July 2023 supplementing Directive 2013/34/EU of the European Parliament and of the Council as regards sustainability reporting standards [2023] OJ L https://eur-lex.europa.eu/eli/reg_del/2023/2772/oj/eng accessed 4 September 2025.

standards of liability and enforcement. The result is a more limited and uneven framework than the one originally envisaged by the Commission[181].]

19.153

Reduction in Scope: The most significant reform enacted by Directive (EU) 2026/470 is a substantial narrowing of the scope of the CSRD, reducing the number of companies subject to reporting obligations by approximately 80%. For EU companies, the employee threshold would rise from 250 to 1,000, while financial thresholds would increase to either €50 million in turnover or €25 million in balance sheet total. For non-EU companies, the EU turnover threshold would increase from €150 million to €450 million, and the branch turnover threshold from €40 million to €50 million. While framed as a shift toward targeted regulation, critics warn this undermines the legal foundations of EU sustainability law. They argue the changes violate principles of legal certainty and non-regression, fragment the regulatory landscape, and expose companies to inconsistent national obligations and increased litigation risk. The revised scope may leave some Member States with fewer than ten companies covered, effectively rolling back sustainability standards to below those of the 2014 Non-Financial Reporting Directive[182].

19.154

Simplification of the ESRS: The Commission's enacted changes to the ESRS under Directive (EU) 2026/470 simplify the framework by removing sector-specific standards and focusing on quantitative data has sparked strong academic and legal criticism. In early 2024, 21 academics urged the Commission not to delay sector-specific standards[183], arguing they offer vital guidance, especially for first-time reporters and sector-specific risks. Legal experts also warned the move could slow meaningful progress. The shift toward numbers over narrative has also raised concerns: research shows that without standardisation, more data can lead to inconsistent Environmental, Social and Governance ('ESG') ratings.

181 European Coalition for Corporate Justice, *'PRESS RELEASE – EU's "Deregulation" agenda claims its first victim: Corporate Sustainability Due Diligence Directive gutted'* (16 December 2025) <https://corporatejustice.org/news/press-release-eus-deregulation-agenda-claims-its-first-victim-corporate-sustainability-due-diligence-directive-gutted/> accessed 20 March 2026.

182 See: Green Central Banking, 'EU Sustainability Omnibus Proposal Would Gut Corporate Reporting Rules' (26 February 2025) https://greencentralbanking.com/2025/02/26/eu-sustainability-omnibus-proposal/ accessed 4 September 2025; BIICL, 'More on the Omnibus Package and the Future of European Global Leadership on Sustainability' (BIICL Blog, 26 February 2025) https://www.biicl.org/blog/107/more-on-the-omnibus-package-and-the-future-of-european-global-leadership-on-sustainability?cookiesset=1&ts=1757006774 accessed 4 September 2025; Portfolio Adviser, 'Investors React as Omnibus Confirms Far-Reaching Changes to CSRD, CSDDD and Taxonomy' (Future, 26 February 2025) https://future.portfolio-adviser.com/investors-react-as-omnibus-confirms-far-reaching-changes-to-csrd-csddd-and-taxonomy/ accessed 4 September 2025.

183 Twenty-one European academics, 'Postponing Sector-Specific Standards: An Open Letter to the European Commission' (Climate & Company, February 2024) https://climateandcompany.org/wp-content/uploads/2024/02/Postponing-sector-specific-standards_Academic-Letter2.pdf accessed 4 September 2025.

Scholars caution that cutting narrative detail risks oversimplifying complex sustainability issues and losing essential context.

EU Deforestation Regulation (EUDR) and the Modern Slavery-Deforestation Nexus in Supply Chains

19.155

On 29 June 2023, the Regulation on deforestation-free products ('EUDR') entered into force[184]. The UK Forest Risk Commodities Regulations, to be introduced under Sch 17 to the Environment Act 2021, have been delayed following the general election but are expected to establish a due diligence framework broadly aligned with the EUDR, albeit the focus of Sch 17 is on preventing the use of commodities produced illegally[185]. Although the EUDR does not apply to UK companies operating solely outside the EU, businesses should anticipate similar obligations under forthcoming UK legislation.

19.156

Under the EUDR, operators and traders placing cattle, cocoa, coffee, oil palm, rubber, soya, and wood[186] on the EU market, or exporting them from it, must demonstrate that such products are not linked to recent deforestation or forest degradation[187]. This includes mandatory due diligence obligations prior to placing relevant products on the market, or prior to exporting them: (a) collection of relevant information, data and documentation[188]; (b) risk assessment measures[189]; and (c) risk mitigation measures[190]. Member States are required to establish competent authorities to oversee compliance, provide guidance, conduct checks, and impose penalties. The regulation also enables third parties

184 Regulation (EU) 2023/1115 of the European Parliament and of the Council of 31 May 2023 on the making available on the Union market and the export from the Union of certain commodities and products associated with deforestation and forest degradation and repealing Regulation (EU) No 995/2010 [2023] OJ L 150/206 https://eur-lex.europa.eu/eli/reg/2023/1115/oj/eng accessed 4 September 2025.

185 In 2024, the UK Parliament's Environmental Audit Committee (EAC) criticised its narrow focus on illegal deforestation, which leaves UK consumers exposed to goods linked to unsustainable forest loss where this is legalised by local governments in producer countries See Earthsight, 'Earth Day 2025: The Fight Against Deforestation and Corruption Continues' (22 April 2025) https://www.earthsight.org.uk/news/earth-day-2025 accessed 4 September 2025.

186 Art 2 (1) Regulation (EU) 2023/1115 of the European Parliament and of the Council of 31 May 2023 on the making available on the Union market and the export from the Union of certain commodities and products associated with deforestation and forest degradation and repealing Regulation (EU) No 995/2010 [2023] OJ L 150/206 https://eur-lex.europa.eu/eli/reg/2023/1115/oj/eng accessed 4 September 2025.

187 Ibid Art 3.

188 Ibid Art 9.

189 Ibid Art 10.

190 Ibid Art 11.

to submit substantiated concerns and mandates the European Commission to maintain a central information system for due diligence statements.

19.157

The importance of these measures is underscored by the growing recognition of the slavery-environment nexus. Frontier forestlands in tropical regions, particularly in Brazil, Ghana, Indonesia, Bangladesh[191] and Mozambique[192], are experiencing rapid deforestation driven by illegal logging, charcoal production, cattle ranching, and industrial agriculture. These activities frequently rely on exploitative labour practices, including debt bondage, forced labour, and trafficking.Vulnerable individuals, often recruited by intermediaries, are trapped in remote camps under inflated debts, with minimal oversight, entrenching impunity and isolation[193].

19.158

Empirical studies combining Global Slavery Index data with satellite-derived tree-loss metrics estimate that up to 15% of forced labour victims work in forestry-related sectors, clearing hundreds of thousands of hectares annually. In the Brazilian Amazon, cattle ranching and illegal timber harvesting are closely linked to debt-bonded labour, while in Southeast Asia, palm oil, cocoa, and rubber production often exploit migrant and child workers under coercive conditions[194]. Persistent enforcement gaps, due to under-resourced inspections and agribusiness influence, allow deforestation and modern slavery to reinforce one another.

19.159

This cyclical dynamic highlights the necessity of integrated due diligence frameworks, such as the EUDR and the forthcoming UK regulations, that address both forest-risk commodities and forced labour risks. By embedding environmental and human rights standards into trade regulation, these measures

191 D Brown, D Boyd, K Brickell, C Ives, N Natarajan and L Parsons, 'Modern Slavery, Environmental Degradation and Climate Change: Fisheries, Field, Forests and Factories' (2019) *Environment and Planning E: Nature and Space* 1–17. https://kclpure.kcl.ac.uk/ws/portalfiles/portal/125942902/2514848619887156.pdf accessed 4 September 2025

192 Jackson, '*Modern Slavery as a Threat to Forests: Reviewing the Links between Modern Slavery, Deforestation, and Potential Solutions*' in Justin A Daniels (ed), Advances in Environmental Research, vol 84 (Nova Science Publishers 2021) ch 1. https://nottingham-repository.worktribe.com/output/6296966/modern-slavery-as-a-threat-to-forests-reviewing-the-links-between-modern-slavery-deforestation-and-potential-solutions, accessed 4 September 2025.

193 Bethany Jackson et al, '*Understanding the Co-Occurrence of Tree Loss and Modern Slavery to Improve Efficacy of Conservation Actions and Policies*' (2020) 2 Conservation Science and Practice e183. https://conbio.onlinelibrary.wiley.com/doi/10.1111/csp2.183 accessed 4 September 2025.

194 Shannon Hobbs, '*From Chains to Chainsaws: Modern Slavery and Deforestation in the Brazilian Amazon*' (2024) Environment and Planning E: Nature and Space. https://journals.sagepub.com/doi/pdf/10.1177/25148486231187397 accessed 4 September 2025.

aim to disrupt the structural conditions that enable both deforestation and exploitation[195].

International soft law framework: UNGPs, OECD Guidelines

United Nations Guiding Principles on Business and Human Rights

19.160

On 16 June 2011, the UN Human Rights Council adopted Resolution 17/4, thereby unanimously endorsing the Guiding Principles on Business and Human Rights ('UNGPs')[196]. The UNGPs serve as the authoritative global normative framework for responsible business conduct and addressing human rights abuses in business operations and global supply chains. They do not create new international legal obligations but rather recognise existing State duties under international human rights law and articulate how both States and businesses should operationalise those duties. They provide a blueprint for action, outlining parameters within which States and businesses should develop policies, rules and processes to prevent and remedy human rights abuses. They constitute a global standard against which the conduct of both States and companies can be assessed.

19.161

The UNGPs comprise of 31 Principles and are organised under 3 pillars: Protect, Respect and Remedy.

Protect: Pillar 1 of the UN Guiding Principles sets out the State's duty to protect human rights by third parties, including business operations. This requires States to set clear expectations for companies by enacting effective policies, legislation, and regulations. In doing so, States establish that appropriate steps are in place to prevent, investigate, punish and redress human rights abuses or adverse impact on human rights[197].

Respect: Pillar 2 of the UN Guiding Principles articulates the corporate responsibility to respect human rights. Businesses are expected to identify any adverse human rights impacts they may cause or contribute to, and to

195 Bethany Jackson et al, 'Understanding the Co-Occurrence of Tree Loss and Modern Slavery to Improve Efficacy of Conservation Actions and Policies' (2020) 2 Conservation Science and Practice e183. https://conbio.onlinelibrary.wiley.com/doi/10.1111/csp2.183 accessed 4 September 2025.

196 United Nations Office of the High Commissioner for Human Rights, *Guiding Principles on Business and Human Rights: Implementing the United Nations 'Protect, Respect and Remedy' Framework* (2011) https://www.ohchr.org/sites/default/files/documents/publications/guidingprinciplesbusinesshr_en.pdf accessed 4 September 2025.

197 Ibid, Principles 1-10.

implement appropriate policies and procedures to address them. This includes making a clear commitment to respect human rights, conducting ongoing due diligence to prevent and mitigate harm, and ensuring access to remediation for those affected by their actions[198].

Remedy: Pillar 3 of the UN Guiding Principles affirms that victims of human rights violations must have access to effective remedies. These mechanisms, whether judicial or non-judicial, and implemented by States or businesses, must be legitimate, accessible, predictable, equitable, transparent, and compatible with human rights standards. Pillar 3 also emphasises that operational-level grievance mechanisms should be grounded in genuine engagement with affected stakeholders and designed to facilitate meaningful dialogue[199].

The Organisation for Economic Co-operation and Development (OECD)[200] Guidelines for Multinational Enterprises

19.162

The OECD Guidelines[201] ('the Guidelines') are the first international instrument to integrate respect for human rights as a corporate responsibility, thereby aligning with the UNGP. The Guidelines are also the first international corporate responsibility instrument to recommend incorporating risk-based due diligence. This due diligence expectation applies across workers' rights, human rights, environment, anti-bribery, consumers, and corporate governance wherever business activities intersect with society.

19.163

The OECD Due Diligence Guidance for Responsible Business Conduct[202] provides practical support to businesses on the implementation of the Guidelines by providing plain language explanations of its due diligence recommendations and associated provisions. Implementing these recommendations can help enterprises avoid and address adverse impacts related to workers, human rights, the environment, bribery, consumers and corporate governance that may be associated with their operations, supply chains and other business relationships.

---

198 Principles 11-24.

199 Principles 25-31.

200 The OECD is an intergovernmental international organisation established by the Convention on the Organisation for Economic Co-operation and Development, which entered into force on 30 September 1961. The OECD holds observer status at the United Nations.

201 OECD, *OECD Guidelines for Multinational Enterprises on Responsible Business Conduct* (2023) https://www.oecd.org/en/publications/2023/06/oecd-guidelines-for-multinational-enterprises-on-responsible-business-conduct_a0b49990.html accessed 4 September 2025.

202 OECD, *OECD Due Diligence Guidance for Responsible Business Conduct* (2018) https://www.oecd.org/en/publications/oecd-due-diligence-guidance-for-responsible-business-conduct_15f5f4b3-en.html accessed 4 September 2025.

19.164

National Contact Points for Responsible Business Conduct[203] ('NCPs') are a tool to promote respect for human rights in global supply chains. NCPs further the effectiveness of the Guidelines through promotional activities and by acting as mediation and conciliation platforms to help resolve 'specific instances' of alleged non-observance of the Guidelines. Any interested party may submit a case to an NCP, which can address matters involving companies operating in or from its jurisdiction. The NCP network offers a potential avenue for victims of corporate human rights abuse to seek remedy. NCP proceedings can result in remedy for victims and prompt changes to corporate policies, helping to prevent future violations.

19.165

The OECD Guidelines comprise 11 chapters, each of which may form the basis of a complaint. Whilst a detailed analysis is beyond the scope of this chapter, it is important to note that this responsibility should be exercised within the framework of internationally recognised human rights, the international obligations of the countries in which businesses operate, and relevant domestic laws and regulations. Enterprises are expected to avoid infringing on the rights of others and to address adverse impacts with which they are involved. This includes avoiding causing or contributing to harm through their own activities, seeking to prevent or mitigate impacts directly linked to their operations, products or services via business relationships, and establishing a public commitment to respect human rights. Businesses should also conduct human rights due diligence appropriate to their size, operational context, and the severity of potential risks, and provide for or cooperate in legitimate remediation processes where they have caused or contributed to harm[204].

19.166

The OECD NCP mechanism has delivered tangible remedies in forced-labour and modern-slavery cases: in the *European Center for Constitutional and Human Rights ('ECCHR')*[205]*, Sherpa & Uzbek German Forum ('UGF') v Paul Reinhart AG*, multiple cotton traders agreed through UK-led mediation to address allegations of forced child labour in Uzbekistan by implementing due diligence and compensation measures, marking the first settlement of

203 OECD, 'National Contact Points for Responsible Business Conduct' https://www.oecd.org/en/networks/national-contact-points-for-responsible-business-conduct.html accessed 4 September 2025.

204 The obligation to protect human rights through Human Rights and Environmental Due Diligence is reflected in both Chapter II ('General Policies') and Chapter IV ('Human Rights') of the OECD Guidelines.

205 ECCHR (the European Centre for Constitutional and Human Rights) is an independent, non-profit human-rights organization based in Berlin. It investigates and litigates cases of serious human-rights violations, with a focus on business and human-rights, migration, and war crimes.

its kind across four European NCPs[206]. In *Conectas Human Rights & ADERE MG vs. Nestlé*, the Brazilian NCP secured a 2023 agreement obliging Nestlé to conduct independent audits, establish worker consultation and social dialogue forums, and strengthen grievance mechanisms to address forced labour risks on its coffee farms in Minas Gerais. On 24 July 2025, the Brazilian NCP published a follow-up statement outlining progress since the agreement, identifying three key actions taken: a consultation between worker representatives and Nestlé in the São Sebastião do Paraíso region on labour and employment issues; eight Social Dialogue Forums involving workers, producers, and traders in the southern region of Minas Gerais; and the inclusion of the IPÊ whistleblowing channel on Nestlé Brazil's reporting posters. Additional commitments made during mediation, such as maintaining the fourth line of action in Nestlé's due diligence programme, consulting worker representatives on potential labour rights violations, and establishing a dedicated email address for reporting irregularities are currently being implemented. The parties have undertaken to keep the NCP informed of progress on these measures[207].

Complaints and Enforcement Mechanisms: UN Special Procedures, OECD NCPs

United Nations Complaints Mechanisms

19.167

The United Nations offers a range of complaints mechanisms that can be strategically employed to address violations beyond domestic remedies. These complaint mechanisms fall into three principal categories: the UN Human Rights Council Complaint Procedure, UN treaty bodies and the UN Special Procedures as established and mandated by the Human Rights Council.

The UN Human Rights Council's Confidential Complaint Procedure

19.168

The Human Rights Council's Confidential Complaint Procedure is the only universal mechanism within the UN system for addressing consistent patterns of gross and reliably attested violations of all human rights and fundamental freedoms. It applies to all 193 UN Member States, regardless of treaty ratification or reservations. Complaints may be submitted by individuals, groups, or non-

---

206 OECD Watch, 'ECCHR, Sherpa, UGF vs Paul Reinhart AG' https://www.oecdwatch.org/complaint/ecchr-sherpa-ugf-vs-paul-reinhart-ag/ accessed 4 September 2025.

207 OECD Watch, 'Conectas Human Rights & ADERE MG v Nestlé' https://www.oecdwatch.org/complaint/conectas-human-rights-adere-mg-v-nestle/ accessed 4 September 2025.

governmental organisations. Complainants are required to act in good faith. NGOs are required to have direct and reliable knowledge of the alleged violations and not to resort to politically motivated stands.

19.169

Submissions must be in writing, in one of the UN's official languages, and include detailed factual information such as names, dates, locations, and supporting evidence. Complaints must not be anonymous, abusive in tone, or based solely on media reports. Admissibility also requires exhaustion of domestic remedies unless they are demonstrably ineffective or unreasonably delayed, and complaints must not duplicate matters already under review by other UN mechanisms.

19.170

Once a complaint passes initial screening, it is reviewed by the Working Group on Communications, which assesses admissibility and may request further information. If deemed admissible, the complaint may be referred to the Working Group on Situations, composed of representatives of Human Rights Council Member States. This group evaluates whether the case reveals a consistent pattern of serious violations warranting further action. Final outcomes, communicated privately, may include discontinuation of the complaint, continued confidential review, public consideration by the Council, or recommendations for technical cooperation with the State concerned. The procedure is designed to be impartial, victim-oriented, and conducive to constructive engagement with States. However, it does not provide individual remedies, publish case summaries, or maintain a public docket. The only public record is the Council's annual report, which lists States under review and general recommendations without linking them to specific complaints. Exceptionally, if a case is moved to the Council's public agenda, its outcome may appear in session reports or resolutions, though the original communication remains confidential.

The UN Treaty Bodies

19.171

The UN treaty bodies, such as the Human Rights Committee (under the International Covenant on Civil and Political Rights ('ICCPR'), the Committee on the Elimination of Discrimination Against Women ('CEDAW'), and the Committee on the Rights of the Child ('CRC'), provide, through Optional Protocols, individual complaint and inquiry procedures[208] that allow individuals or groups to submit complaints alleging violations of rights protected by

208 Treaty bodies conduct 'inquiries' only in exceptional circumstances Most individual communications result in 'Views,' not inquiries.

specific treaties. These procedures are only available against States that have both ratified the relevant treaty and accepted the treaty body's competence to receive complaints, typically through an Optional Protocol or formal declaration[209].

19.172

The United Kingdom has ratified the ICCPR and the Convention on the Rights of the Child ('UNCRC'), but not the First Optional Protocol to the ICCPR ('OP-ICCPR') nor the Third Optional Protocol to the UNCRC ('OP-CRC-III'), both of which establish individual complaints mechanisms. The UK has ratified the Optional Protocol to CEDAW, thereby permitting individual complaints under CEDAW. Accordingly, individuals in the UK may submit complaints to the CEDAW Committee, but not under the ICCPR or UNCRC, as the UK has not accepted the competence of the respective treaty bodies to receive individual communications under those instruments.

19.173

Each treaty body has its own Secretariat within the Office of the High Commissioner for Human Rights ('OHCHR's') Treaty Body Branch, where complaints are lodged and undergo an initial admissibility screening. Complaints must meet strict admissibility criteria, including exhaustion of domestic remedies[210], non-anonymity, and relevance to the treaty's scope. If deemed admissible, they are registered and transmitted to the State party for response within a set timeframe. The complainant may then reply, and the case proceeds to consideration of admissibility and merits. The Human Rights Committee routinely merges admissibility and merits. Other bodies (eg, CEDAW Committee) normally rule on admissibility first and only then consider merits in a later session. Decisions are made by independent experts serving on the relevant treaty body, who assess whether a violation occurred and recommend remedies such as compensation, legislative changes, or guarantees of non-repetition. Each committee follows its own Rules of Procedure, though OHCHR provides a common portal and guidance.

19.174

While the Human Rights Committee routinely grants interim measures, not all treaty bodies have an explicit power to request them (CEDAW does, CRC-OP-III does, but the Committee on Economic, Social and Cultural Rights (CESCR) does not). Those committees who have the power to request interim measures, may do so to prevent irreparable harm during the process.

---

209 Both the Convention against Torture (CAT) and International Convention on the Elimination of All Forms of Racial Discrimination (CERD) establish individual communications procedures by a State 'declaration'.

210 Unless these are clearly ineffective or unreasonably delayed.

19.175

Follow-up procedures monitor State compliance, and CEDAW adopts a grading system to assess implementation. While decisions are not legally binding, they carry significant moral and political weight and contribute to the development of international human rights standards. States are expected to submit follow-up reports on implementation.

United Nations Special Procedures' Communications Mechanism

19.176

The United Nations Special Procedures of the Human Rights Council consist of independent mandate-holders, both individual experts (Special Rapporteurs and Independent Experts) and multi-member Working Groups, who receive and issue communications (also called 'cases') on alleged human rights violations, rather than operating a formal 'complaints procedure' like treaty bodies or the Human Rights Council's Confidential Complaint Procedure (formerly known as the 1503 procedure).

19.177

Mandate-holders report and advise on human rights issues from either a thematic or country-specific perspective. These procedures form a central component of the UN human rights framework and, collectively, address a broad range of civil, cultural, economic, political, and social[211]. Thematic mandates[212] include, inter alia, the Special Rapporteur on trafficking in persons, especially women and children; the Special Rapporteur on contemporary forms of slavery, including its causes and consequences; and the Working Group on the issue of human rights and transnational corporations and other business enterprises. These mandate-holders are particularly relevant in cases involving trafficking and modern slavery in the context of business-related human rights violations.

19.178

Communications are made via the OCHR 'communications submission portal'. Upon receipt, the relevant mandate-holder may issue a communication to the concerned State or other actor[213]. Communications may take the form

211 United Nations, Office of the Human Rights Council, Special Procedures of the Human Rights Council <https://www.ohchr.org/en/special-procedures-human-rights-council/special-procedures-human-rights-council> accessed 30 September 2025.

212 United Nations, Office of the Human Rights Council, Special Procedures of the Human Rights Council, Thematic Mandates <https://spinternet.ohchr.org/ViewAllCountryMandates.aspx?Type=TM> accessed 30 September 2025.

213 United Nations, Office of the Human Rights Council, < https://spsubmission.ohchr.org/> accessed 25 September 2025.

of urgent appeals, used in cases of imminent risk to life or serious harm, or allegation letters, which address past or ongoing violations. Unlike treaty-based mechanisms, Special Procedures do not require prior exhaustion of domestic remedies or ratification of specific human rights instruments, rendering them especially useful in urgent or life-threatening circumstances.

19.179

In cases where alleged human rights violations span multiple thematic areas, such as trafficking in persons associated with corporate activity, complainants may submit a single communication to more than one UN Special Procedures mandate holder. The system permits the selection of multiple relevant mandates on submission. While mandate holders may coordinate and issue a joint communication, it is more common for each to respond separately. In such instances, communications may be issued concurrently or with aligned messaging, depending on coordination between the respective secretariats and the nature of the subject matter.

19.180

A notable example occurred in 2019, when a submission was made to multiple mandate-holders concerning asbestos pollution in central India. Following the submission, separate but coordinated communications were issued not only to the companies directly implicated in the pollution but also to the governments of the countries where those companies are domiciled, as well as to the Indian authorities responsible for the affected region. This coordinated approach illustrates how Special Procedures can engage both corporate and state actors across jurisdictions in response to transnational human rights concerns[214].

Distinctions between special procedures communications and the confidential complaint procedure

19.181

Special Procedures mandate-holders, including individual experts (Special Rapporteurs and Independent Experts) and multi-member Working Groups, receive and issue communications (also called 'cases') on alleged human rights violations, acting independently of States. These communications are non-binding requests for information or action and may prompt States to reply, reassess policies, or engage with other UN mechanisms, but they do not themselves trigger formal inquiries or create legal obligations.

214 United Nations, Office of the Human Rights Council, https://spcommreports.ohchr.org/TMResultsBase/DownLoadPublicCommunicationFile?gId=24366, accessed 25 September 2025.

19.182

By contrast, the Human Rights Council's Confidential Complaint Procedure is a systemic mechanism administered by two Working Groups (on Communications and on Situations) under OHCHR's Treaty Body Branch. It addresses consistent patterns of serious human rights violations and operates entirely in confidence; individual cases are not taken up directly by the Council itself, and there is no public docket.

19.183

Special Procedures communications are generally the appropriate avenue for individual or urgent cases, such as trafficking or modern slavery, because they do not require exhaustion of domestic remedies and can be actioned quickly. The Confidential Complaint Procedure, by contrast, is intended to identify and address systemic abuses across one or more States.

Confidentiality safeguards

19.184

All Special Procedures communications processes are strictly confidential. Mandate-holders require submitters to secure informed consent from victims or their representatives, including consent to:

- Disclose personal and biographical details to the mandate-holder
- Share identifying information with the State or other relevant actors

19.185

Victims may request anonymity if there are credible risks of reprisals or threats. In such cases, mandate-holders will redact identifying details from both the communication and any publicly released materials. However, anonymity cannot eliminate all risk, and victims must be informed of any residual dangers. If reprisals occur, they may be reported to OHCHR[215].

19.186

Practitioners should conduct a thorough risk assessment with the victim prior to submission, considering the political context, the nature of the alleged violation, and any intersectional vulnerabilities. Use of secure communication channels, such as end-to-end encrypted messaging and password-protected documents, is strongly recommended.

215 They should be reported to reprisals@ohchr.org.

Cross-jurisdictional regulatory trends

19.187

Globally, states are taking increasing action to prevent trafficking and modern slavery across transnational business operations and supply chains and promote remediation where violations do occur. Initiatives include due diligence obligations and trade-based initiatives that restrict the importation of goods that may be tainted by modern slavery. The strategies discussed in this section provide examples of the diverse regulatory measures that are being engaged to promote accountability and secure access to remedies. For those advising and assisting affected groups, this section provides an overview of the tools available across different jurisdictions that could be engaged to pursue accountability.

Implications of foreign due diligence laws for UK-based companies

19.188

The evolution of mandatory due diligence regimes represents a significant development marking a shift from mere reporting requirements, such as those under s 54 of the MSA 2015, to binding obligations on companies to identify, prevent, and mitigate human rights harms.

19.189

At the EU level, the new Directive establishes a harmonised minimum standard of mandatory human rights and environmental due diligence across all Member States, while permitting stricter national measures. Before the Directive's adoption several countries including, France[216], the Netherlands[217], Germany[218] and Norway[219] had already enacted their own mandatory due diligence laws. On 1 January 2024, the Fighting Against Forced Labour and Child Labour in Supply Chains Act 2023 also came into force in Canada[220]. The scope, application, sanctions and remedies under the laws vary considerably

216 *Loi 2017-399 du 27 mars 2017 relative an devoir de vigilance des societes meres et des entreprises donneuses d'ordre* [Law 2017-399 of 27 March 2017] <https://www.legifrance.gouv.fr/jorf/id/JORFTEXT000034290626/> accessed 30 September 2025 (Duty of Vigilance Law).

217 *Wet Zorgplicht Kinderarbeid* van 24 oktober 2019, Stb. 2019 <https://zoek.officielebekendmakingen.nl/stb-2019-401.html> accessed 30 September 2025 (Dutch Child Labour Due Diligence Law).

218 Gesetz fiber unternehmerische Sorgfaltspflichten in Lieferketten 22 July, 2021, Elektronischer Bundesanzeiger [eBAnz] at 2959 2021 (Ger.) <https://www.gesetze-im-internet.de/lksg/index.html> accessed 30 September 2025 (German Supply Chain Due Diligence Act).

219 Lov om virksomheters åpenhet og arbeid med grunnleggende menneskerettigheter og anstendige arbeidsforhold, LOV-2021-06-18-99 https://lovdata.no/dokument/NLE/lov/2021-06-18-99 accessed 30 September 2025.

220 Fighting Against Forced Labour and Child Labour in Supply Chains Act 2023 <https://www.canlii.org/en/ca/laws/stat/sc-2023-c-9/latest/sc-2023-c-9.html?resultIndex=1 > accessed 30 September 2025.

by jurisdiction[221], and a detailed analysis of each falls outside this chapter's remit. Nonetheless, these developments constitute a marked shift in corporate responsibilities to investigate, and address forced labour and other human rights violations in global supply chains.

19.190

Notable cases under these laws underscore the enforcement potential of mandatory due diligence laws. Under France's Duty of Vigilance Law, a claim against Yves Rocher alleges failures in protecting workers' freedom of association, non-discrimination and health and safety in its Turkish subsidiary[222]. In Germany, a complaint was filed under the Supply Chain Due Diligence Act alleging VW, BMW and Mercedes Benz breached their obligations concerning possible forced labour in their supply chains in Xinjiang[223].

19.191

The emerging body of mandatory human rights and environmental due diligence legislation imposes new obligations on in-scope companies to establish and integrate due diligence procedures across their operations. These requirements inevitably extend to upstream suppliers and entire supply chains, creating indirect compliance obligations for entities beyond the immediate scope of the legislation. For certain rights holders, these laws also introduce new avenues for accessing remedy, whether through administrative, judicial, or non-judicial mechanisms. UK-based companies may be affected in several ways. A jurisdictional link may arise where a company is incorporated in a country with due diligence legislation (eg, Germany), sells products or services in that jurisdiction (eg, Norway), or meets specified turnover thresholds (eg, Canada). Additionally, UK-based suppliers, subcontractors, and business partners may be implicated through the substantive obligations imposed on in-scope companies, which must assess and address human rights risks throughout their supply chains.

Trade-based regimes

19.192

The EU Forced Labour Regulation establishes a common prohibition on imports tainted by forced labour, while permitting Member States to adopt

221 For fuller details see: Rachel Chambers & David Birchall, 'How European Human Rights Law Will Reshape US Business' (2024) 20 UC Law SF Business Journal and Fiona McGaughey, Rosie Rowe & Cora Lappel, 'Strengthening Australia's Response to Modern Slavery: Lessons from Comparative Human Rights Due Diligence Laws' (2023) 51 University of Western Australia Law Review.

222 Duty of Vigilance Radar, <https://vigilance-plan.org/cases-civil-lawsuits/> accessed 30 September 2025.

223 ECCHR, *German economic engine roars thanks to forced labor: Complaint filed against VW, BMW and Mercedes Benz*(21 June 2023) <https://www.ecchr.eu/en/press-release/deutscher-wirtschaftsmotor-brummt-dank-zwangsarbeit-beschwerde-gegen-vw-bmw-und-mercedes-benz-eingereicht/> accessed 30 September 2025.

more stringent national measures (Reg (EU) 2023/1115 Rec 9). The US Tariff Act 1930 prohibits imports produced with forced labour. The US Customs and Border Protection have 47 active Withhold Release Orders ('WROs')[224], including one issued against Supermax Corporation[225]. On 1 November 2024, CBP issued a WRO on frankincense imports from Somalia's Asli Maydi Exports & Imports Company, citing forced labour indicators such as deception, physical violence, abusive working conditions, intimidation and threats, and withholding wages[226].

19.193

The US Congress passed the so-called Uyghur Forced Labour Prevention Act ('UFLPA') in December 2021, which came into force in June 2022[227]. Congressional findings in the UFLPA's preamble explicitly cite 'credible information' that the PRC has orchestrated 'the systematic use of forced labour in Xinjiang'. The law creates a rebuttable presumption that goods produced or manufactured in Xinjiang, or by certain entities, are made with forced labour[228]. The presumption will apply unless and until the U.S Customs and Border Protection determines the presumption has been rebutted by the importers. As highlighted in guidance issued to importers, rebutting the presumption will require effective due diligence systems in place to map supply chains and identify and address forced labour[229]. According to CBP's publicly released UFLPA summary as of the latest update, 10,478 shipments have been denied entry into the US under the Act to date, predominantly from the Automotive and Aerospace sectors[230].

224 US Customs and Border Protection, *Withhold Release Orders and Findings Dashboard* (CBP, 2025) <https://www.cbp.gov/newsroom/stats/trade/withhold-release-orders-findings-dashboard> accessed 5 September 2025.

225 US Customs and Border Protection, *CBP Issues Withhold Release Order Against Supermax Corporation Bhd and Its Subsidiaries* (National Media Release, 20 October 2021) <https://www.cbp.gov/newsroom/national-media-release/cbp-issues-withhold-release-order-supermax-corporation-bhd-and-its accessed> 5 September 2025.

226 US Customs and Border Protection, *CBP Issues Withhold Release Order Against Asli Maydi* (National Media Release, 1 November 2024) <https://www.cbp.gov/newsroom/national-media-release/cbp-issues-withhold-release-order-against-asli-maydi> accessed 5 September 2025.

227 An act to ensure that goods made with forced labor in the Xinjiang Uyghur Autonomous Region of the People's Republic of China do not enter the United States market, and for other purposes, Public Law 117-78, <https://www.govinfo.gov/app/details/STATUTE-135/STATUTE-135-Pg1525> 30 September 2025.

228 UFLPA, s 3.

229 US Customs and Border Protection, *US Customs and Border Protection Operational Guidance for Importers* (13 June 2022), pp.13-15 <https://www.cbp.gov/sites/default/files/assets/documents/2022-Jun/CBP_Guidance_for_Importers_for_UFLPA_13_June_2022.pdf > accessed 30 September 2025.

230 US Customs and Border Protection, *Uyghur Forced Labor Prevention Act Statistics* (updated 19 September 2025) <https://www.cbp.gov/newsroom/stats/trade/uyghur-forced-labor-prevention-act-statistics accessed> 30 September 2025.

19.194

The United States–Mexico–Canada Agreement ('USMCA')[231], which entered into force on 1 July 2020, replacing NAFTA as a trilateral framework intended to benefit North American workers, farmers, and businesses, establishes a Facility-Specific Rapid Response Labour Mechanism ('RRLM')[232]. This mechanism represents a novel enforcement tool designed to address violations of workers' rights to freedom of association and collective bargaining at designated facilities. It enables the United States and Canada to request reviews of Mexican workplaces and, where warranted, to impose targeted trade sanctions.

19.195

Under Art 31-A.4, workers or their representatives may petition their national Interagency Labour Committee if freedom of association or collective bargaining is denied at a designated 'Covered Facility' in Mexico. Within 30 days, the Committee must decide whether to request that Mexico conduct a 45-day review. If Mexico does not review, rejects a finding of non-compliance, or fails to reach agreement on remediation, the requesting Party may convene an ad hoc Rapid Response Labor Panel to verify and determine if a denial of rights occurred. If the panel finds non-compliance, it may recommend facility-specific remedial measures, including suspension of preferential tariff treatment or suspension of liquidation of goods from that facility.

19.196

Despite its formal reciprocity, the mechanism operates asymmetrically. Mexico may only invoke the RRLM against US or Canadian facilities subject to a final domestic enforcement order, a threshold that significantly curtails its practical utility. Moreover, no RRLM exists between the US and Canada, reinforcing the one-sided nature of the mechanism. By mid-2024, 22 of 23 petitions had been filed by the US against Mexican facilities, predominantly in the automotive sector. Few cases proceeded to panel review; most were resolved through bilateral remediation, often without independent findings of non-compliance.

19.197

While the RRLM has prompted some improvements in Mexican labour practices, its deployment reflects broader trade priorities favouring US and Canadian interests. The mechanism's reliance on government cooperation, limited transparency, and exclusion of affected enterprises from remediation planning has raised concerns regarding its neutrality and effectiveness.

---

231 Office of the United States Trade Representative, *United States–Mexico–Canada Agreement* (USTR, 2020) <https://ustr.gov/trade-agreements/free-trade-agreements/united-states-mexico-canada-agreement> accessed 5 September 2025.

232 Ibid, Annexes 31-A and 31-B.

19.198

In sum, the RRLM offers a novel model for facility-level labour enforcement but remains constrained by structural asymmetries and its integration into a trade agenda that disproportionately benefits the US and Canada[233].

Procurement-based regimes

19.199

The UK's current focus on procurement-based regimes to drive due diligence in the private sector is mirrored in other jurisdictions. Again, these regimes support the effective implementation of due diligence mechanisms.

19.200

Under the Federal Acquisition Regulation ('FAR'), specifically the clause titled 'Prohibition of Acquisition of Products Produced by Forced or Indentured Child Labor,' contractors supplying goods to the US government must comply with enhanced anti-trafficking obligations. If a product appears on the Department of Labor's List of Goods Produced by Child Labor or Forced Labor, the contractor is required to certify that they have made a 'good faith effort' to determine that the goods they are providing were not produced with forced or indentured child labour. In addition, all federal contractors are required to comply with the mandatory provisions of the FAR, including certifying that neither they nor their employees have engaged in trafficking-related conduct. They must also implement risk-based due diligence, provide training, and establish reporting mechanisms to strengthen protections against trafficking in persons, particularly in the context of overseas procurement[234].

19.201

Brazil has maintained a *Cadastro de Empregadores*, a so-called 'Dirty List' since 2003, it publicly names companies and employers who have been found by government inspectors to be subjecting workers to 'conditions analogous to

233 See Kathleen Claussen, 'The Track Record of the USMCA Rapid Response Mechanism' (Brookings Institution, 6 March 2024) <https://www.brookings.edu/Arts/the-track-record-of-the-usmca-rapid-response-mechanism> accessed 5 September 2025 and Covington & Burling LLP, 'Four Years of the USMCA Rapid-Response Labor Mechanism' (Client Alert, 9 May 2024) <https://www.cov.com/en/news-and-insights/insights/2024/05/four-years-of-the-usmca-rapid-response-labor-mechanism accessed> 5 September 2025.

234 US Department of State, 'Strengthening Protections Against Trafficking in Persons in Public Procurement' (20 January 2025) https://www.state.gov/strengthening-protections-against-trafficking-in-persons-in-public-procurement/ accessed 5 September 2025.

slavery' and have undergone finalised administrative processes[235]. The legal regime itself does not include financial penalties, however, public and private institutions will generally refuse credit and other banking benefits to entities named on the list[236]. In 2023, the Brazilian brewery Kaiser, which is owned by Heineken, was added to the Dirty List[237]. The brewery was subsequently removed, and Heineken has stated that its inclusion was due to 'procedural irregularities'[238]. The mechanism is an important illustration of the role that countries in the economic-South can take to sanction companies, and bring to light the labour violations of the global supply chains of parent companies or lead companies situated in the economic-North.

Practical considerations for legal practitioners in business and human rights

19.202

Legal practitioners working in the field of business and human rights operate within a complex and often high-risk environment. The nature of transnational litigation, the vulnerability of affected communities, and the increasing use of strategic lawsuits against public participation ('SLAPPs') demand a careful, context-sensitive approach. Effective representation requires not only legal expertise but also ethical diligence, cultural awareness, and strategic foresight. This section outlines key considerations for lawyers engaging in this work, focusing on safeguarding clients, designing inclusive litigation strategies, responding to SLAPPs, and managing resource demands.

Protecting clients and communities

19.203

Advocacy and litigation in business and human rights have played a vital role in advancing protections for workers and affected communities. However, practitioners must remain alert to the personal risks faced by clients, impacted groups, and human rights defenders who seek accountability. These individuals

235 Agência Brasil, 'Slave Labor: 155 Employers Added to Dirty List' (20 April 2025) <https://agenciabrasil.ebc.com.br/en/economia/noticia/2025-04/slave-labor-155-employers-added-dirty-list accessed> 5 September 2025.

236 International Labour Office, *Fighting Forced Labour: The Example of Brazil*, (2009), para 5.2.3 <https://www.ilo.org/media/341631/download> accessed 30 September 2025.

237 Lisandra Paraguassu and Fabio Teixeira, 'Heineken-owned brewery added to Brazil 'slave labor' list' (*Reuters*, 6 October 2023) <https://www.reuters.com/business/retail-consumer/heineken-owned-brewery-added-brazil-slave-labor-list-2023-10-06/> accessed 30 September 2025.

238 Heineken, *HEINEKEN Brazil has addressed labour violations at Transportadora Sider* (2 April 2023) <https://www.theheinekencompany.com/newsroom/heineken-brazil-has-addressed-labour-violations-at-transportadora-sider/> accessed 30 September 2025.

may be subject to retaliation, intimidation, or other forms of harm, particularly in the Global South[239], where legal protections may be weaker and collusion between state and corporate actors more prevalent. Litigation strategies must therefore be designed with robust safeguards, including anonymisation of documents, secure communication protocols, and restricted access to sensitive information[240].

Designing inclusive and decolonial litigation strategies

19.204

To avoid reproducing colonial hierarchies, litigation must be grounded in the lived experiences, priorities, and cultural contexts of the communities represented[241]. This requires a bottom-up approach that centres affected communities as equal partners in defining legal objectives and success metrics. Practitioners should:

- Engage communities as co-strategists through participatory planning and decision-making.
- Incorporate local legal traditions, including customary and indigenous dispute-resolution mechanisms.
- Form multidisciplinary teams with anthropologists, sociologists, and regional experts to enrich contextual understanding.
- Embed capacity-building to equip local advocates with legal and advocacy skills, reducing dependency on external actors.
- Practise reflexive positionality, critically examining one's own assumptions and biases.

239 Business and Human Rights Resource Centre, 'Guardians at Risk: Confronting corporate abuse in Latin America and the Caribbean, accessed 27 September 2023 Latin America and the Caribbean saw the highest number of attacks in 2023: 41% of the global total (258 attacks). Almost a third (30% or 195 attacks) took place in Asia and the Pacific. The countries which saw the highest numbers of attacks on HRDs challenging corporate harm in 2023 were Brazil (68), India (59), Mexico (55), Honduras (44), the Philippines (36), USA (27), Iran (24), Colombia (22), Indonesia (18), Uganda (18), France (16) and the United Kingdom (15) <https://www.business-humanrights.org/en/from-us/briefings/hrds-2023/people-power-under-pressure-human-rights-defenders-business-in-2023/>.

240 Front Line Defenders provides resources and training to protect human rights defenders at risk, see <https://www.frontlinedefenders.org/en> accessed 1 October 2025.

241 Makau Mutua, 'Savages, Victims, and Saviors: The Metaphor of Human Rights' (2001) 42 *Harvard International Law Journal* 201; John Reynolds and Cynthia Cohen, 'Beyond the Courtroom: Integrating Social Science in Human Rights Litigation' (2018) 28 *Yale Human Rights and Development Law Journal* 45; María Amparo Ballivian, 'Capacity Building for Access to Justice: A Rights-Based Approach' (2012) 16 *International Journal of Human Rights* 89; Sari Kouvo, 'Reflexivity in Practice: Ethical Dimensions of Positionality in International Law' (2020) 10 *Transnational Law and Contemporary Problems* 117; Charmaine Chua, 'Reparative Justice in Post-Colonial Contexts: Lessons from Asia' (2019) 5 *Journal of Global Justice* 77.

- Facilitate South–South cooperation, enabling peer-to-peer exchanges and reducing reliance on Global North institutions.
- Pursue structural and reparative remedies, such as policy reform and community-led restitution, beyond conventional legal relief.

19.205

These approaches help dismantle colonial legacies in legal practice and ensure that outcomes are meaningful and sustainable for the communities involved.

Responding to Strategic Lawsuits Against Public Participation (SLAPPs)

19.206

SLAPPs are increasingly used by corporate actors to silence dissent and deter scrutiny. NGOs and individuals have faced defamation claims[242] for publishing reports on business-related harm, often as a punitive tactic. Legal practitioners must rigorously substantiate claims, assess litigation risks, and seek expert advice before proceeding.

19.207

Lawyers themselves may be targeted. The case of Steven Donziger[243], who faced contempt proceedings after successfully litigating against Chevron, illustrates the personal and professional risks involved. Regulatory bodies have responded: the Solicitors Regulation Authority ('SRA') has issued a warning against bringing unmeritorious claims or using intimidatory tactics, emphasising solicitors' duties to act with integrity and uphold the rule of law. The Bar Standards Board ('BSB') has similarly recognised its role in addressing SLAPP-related misconduct[244].

19.208

Legislative reform is emerging. The ECCTA 2023 marks the UK's first statutory recognition of SLAPPs, introducing early dismissal procedures and

242 Business and Human Rights Resource Centre, 17 May 2021 <https://www.business-humanrights.org/en/latest-news/edwar-lange-southern-africa-resource-watch-sarw/> accessed 25 September 2025 and Public Eye, 'Swiss Trader Kolmar AG claims 1.8 million US Dollars from Public Eye and TRIAL International <https://www.publiceye.ch/en/media-corner/press-releases/detail/the-swiss-trader-kolmar-group-ag-claims-18-million-us-dollars-from-public-eye-and-trial-international > accessed 25 September 2025.

243 Amnesty International, 'Environmental Lawyer Must be Pardoned' <(https://www.amnesty.org.uk/urgent-actions/environmental-lawyer-must-be-pardoned> accessed 25 September 2025.

244 Bar Standards Board, 'Response to the Solicitors Regulation Authority Consultation on Strategic Lawsuits Against Public Participation (SLAPPs)' (19 May 2022) <https://www.barstandardsboard.org.uk/static/76c909bc-7088-43ac-b9bf0a981576af1a/20220519-SLAPPs-consultation-BSB-response.pdf> accessed 5 September 2025.

cost protections for defendants. However, these measures are currently limited to economic crime. Broader protections are needed to safeguard public interest litigation and democratic participation[245].

Managing cost and resource demands

19.209

Transnational litigation in this field is resource intensive[246]. The risks to clients and defenders, combined with the threat of SLAPPs, demand careful planning and ethical diligence. Corporate defendants often have substantial financial and legal resources and may exploit procedural mechanisms to delay proceedings and escalate costs. As demonstrated in recent UK litigation, strategic foresight and resilience are essential to navigate these challenges effectively.

Best practice for businesses

19.210

Businesses must actively engage with the rapidly evolving international legal landscape that requires them to address trafficking and modern slavery. This demands not only expert guidance from legal and industry practitioners, but also a willingness to adopt new approaches in working with suppliers, workers and host states. Such proactive engagement is the most effective way to mitigate the risks of trafficking and modern slavery within supply chains, risks that include damage to brand reputation, exclusion from commercial opportunities, and exposure to litigation.

19.211

A range of resources is available to support businesses in this effort, including sector-specific best practice guides published by various organisations[247]. As the understanding of corporate responsibility for global human rights violations continues to evolve, so too do the opportunities for businesses to play a meaningful role in combating one of the most severe forms of abuse.

---

245 Hansard, 21 November 2024 <https://hansard.parliament.uk/Commons/2024-11-21/debates/DC2120EF-C6C9-4BC9-A263-507ACFC8FC08/StrategicLawsuitsAgainstPublicParticipation> accessed 25 September 2025.

246 *Limbu and others v Dyson Technology Ltd and others* [2024] EWCA Civ 1564.

247 OECD Guidance for Responsible Business Conduct, (1 February 2018), 'OECD Guidance for Responsible Business Conduct' https://www.oecd.org/en/publications/oecd-due-diligence-guidance-for-responsible-business-conduct_15f5f4b3-en.html accessed 25 September 2025. Business and Human Rights Resource Centre, ' Know the Chain Good Practice Guide 2024: Good Practice Guide' (13 August 2024) <https://www.business-humanrights.org/documents/40338/KTC_Good_Practice_Guide.pdf> accessed 25 September 2025.

20 Public funding for potential victims of exploitation

Steven Bird, Lindsay Cundall, Zubier Yazdani and Ben Douglas-Jones KC

20.1

Victims of trafficking will generally require public funding if they are to be able to benefit from legal advice in relation to the various legal issues that they encounter. Public funding is administered by the Legal Aid Agency ('LAA') and is commonly referred to as 'legal aid'. The nature and extent of the funding available depends on the type of legal problem under consideration. Eligibility for the relevant public funding is not uniform across the various legal aid schemes.

Advice on arrest for a criminal offence

20.2

The Police Station Advice and Assistance Scheme provides for free and independent legal advice to be available to any person arrested for a criminal offence in England and Wales regardless of his nationality or means. Advice under the scheme can only be provided by a firm of solicitors which holds a Standard Crime Contract 2025 ('SCC 2025')[1], and must be provided by a solicitor or accredited police station representative.

20.3

If the individual arrested does not know a solicitor to contact on arrest, he is entitled to advice from the duty solicitor. Most firms holding the SCC 2025 will have solicitors who are qualified as duty solicitors and who are allocated slots on the rota for the specific police stations local to their office. The LAA has to ensure that a solicitor is available at every police station at all times, and does so through the duty solicitor scheme.

1 The 2025 Standard Crime Contract started on 1 October 2025. For police station attendances prior to that date, the firm would have had to hold the SCC 2022. The 2025 Standard Crime Contract runs until 30 September 2035.

20.4

The scope of advice under the scheme can be limited and, in some circumstances, the advice will be provided not by the requested solicitor or the duty solicitor but by Criminal Defence Direct ('CDD'). The following matters fall within the scope of the CDD scheme[2]:

(i) an individual detained in relation to any non-imprisonable offence;

(ii) someone arrested on a bench warrant for failing to appear and being held for production before the court, except where the individual's solicitor has clear documentary evidence available that would result in him being released from custody, in which case attendance may be allowed provided that the reason is recorded on the solicitors' file;

(iii) anyone arrested on suspicion of:

- driving with excess alcohol, who is taken to the police station to give a specimen (Road Traffic Act 1988, s 5);
- failure to provide a specimen (Road Traffic Act 1988, ss 6, 7 and 7A); or
- driving whilst unfit/drunk in charge of a motor vehicle (Road Traffic Act 1988, s 4); or

(iv) anyone detained in relation to breach of police or court bail conditions.

20.5

The matter is removed from the CDD scheme if[3]:

- an interview or an identification procedure is going to take place;
- the person arrested is eligible for assistance from an appropriate adult under the PACE codes of practice;
- the individual is unable to communicate over the telephone;
- the individual complains of serious maltreatment by the police;
- the investigation includes another alleged offence which does not fall within the above restrictions;
- the solicitor is already at the same Police Station, albeit that the fee payable is limited to the Police Station Telephone Advice Fixed Fee;
- the advice relates to an indictable offence; or
- the request is a Special Request[4].

2 2025 Standard Crime Contract Specification ('SCC Specification'), para 9.3.

3 SCC Specification para 9.4.

4 A 'Special Request' is defined in SCC Specification para 1.2 as a request identified to the solicitor as such by the DSCC. Special Requests may include, for example: requests where CDD considers that, because of a conflict of interest, the request should be handled by the solicitor (instead of by a CDD Telephone Adviser); or considers that Advocacy Assistance is required or one of the other exceptions in section 9 applies.

20.6

When an individual is arrested, the custody officer at the police station will provide him with his rights and entitlements under the Police and Criminal Evidence Act 1984. One such entitlement is to speak to a solicitor free of charge[5]. The custody officer will notify a central agency called the Defence Solicitor Call Centre ('DSCC'), who will allocate the case a reference number without which no claim for fees will be paid. It is possible to receive instructions for an attendance by agreement or via a third party but the DSCC has to be informed within 48 hours of the attendance and a number allocated to the case[6].

20.7

If the case falls within the CDD scheme, advice will initially be provided by CDD, an agency contracted directly by the LAA to provide such advice. If CDD considers that the circumstances take the matter outside of the CDD scheme, the nominated solicitors will be called.

20.8

Those arrested who may be victims of trafficking will not always have been identified as victims of trafficking at this very early point after initial arrest. It is therefore possible that a victim of trafficking will be directed to CDD instead of his own (or the duty) solicitor in circumstances where advice from his solicitor would be appropriate and remunerable under the Police Station Advice and Assistance Scheme (for example the entitlement to an appropriate adult). It is equally likely that unless specifically trained to identify the potential signs of a victim of trafficking, the CDD adviser will not pick up the issue of trafficking at this stage.

20.9

Funding for legal advice under the Police Station Advice and Assistance scheme is not subject to a financial eligibility test. It is, however, subject to a form of merits test known as the Sufficient Benefit Test. For police station advice the Sufficient Benefit Test is deemed to be satisfied in circumstances where a person arrested has a right to legal advice, for example under PACE 1984 or the Terrorism Act 2000, at the police station and has requested such advice. The right to non-means tested legal advice arises where a suspect is to be interviewed either at a police station or another location and includes advice to a person detained under the Terrorism Act 2000, Sch 7 in accordance with Sch 8 thereof, either at a port or in a police station[7].

5 PACE 1984, s 58.
6 SCC Specification para 9.14.
7 SCC Specification para 9.8.

20.10

The SCC prescribes that the solicitor may provide further legal advice to the client immediately following charge. However, attendance upon the client thereafter, whilst fingerprints, photographs and swabs are taken, will not meet the Sufficient Benefit Test except where the client requires further assistance owing to his particular circumstances, in which case the relevant factors must be noted on the solicitor's file. The solicitor may remain at the police station if required to make representations about bail, provided that this justification is noted on the file[8]. It is likely that the particular vulnerabilities of a victim of trafficking will enable the solicitor to remain at the police station until all post-charge procedures have been completed.

20.11

Once a police station matter has been accepted from the DSCC by the solicitors, a telephone call should be made to the police station to provide initial advice and make contact with the police. Unless there are exceptional circumstances, the following is mandatory: attendance at the police station for all police interviews with the arrested person in connection with an offence, to attend any identification parade, group identification or confrontation, or in circumstances where there is a complaint of serious maltreatment by the police[9]. Attendance at video identification parades is discretionary[10].

20.12

Once instructed, the solicitors should conduct the matter throughout the investigation stage (ie. up to the point where a charging decision is made). There are restrictions on another firm taking over the case at the investigation stage and being entitled to claim a fee under the scheme. This may cause problems with victims of trafficking who are released on bail by police or released under investigation and then latterly come into contact with solicitors who have an expertise in this area (ie. trafficking expertise).

20.13

The solicitor must not make a claim under the SCC for Police Station Advice and Assistance given to a client who has received Police Station Advice and Assistance for the same matter from another firm within the six months except where:

- there is a gap in time and circumstances have changed materially between the first and second or subsequent occasions when the Police Station Advice and Assistance was sought;

8 SCC Specification para 9.10.
9 SCC Specification para 9.34.
10 SCC Specification para 9.36.

- the individual has reasonable cause to transfer from the first solicitor; or
- the first solicitor has confirmed that no claim for payment for the Police Station Advice and Assistance will be made[11].

20.14

The second firm should not take on the case and claim for a fee where:

- the client simply disagrees with the first advice and wants a second opinion;
- there is only a short time between the first and second occasions when the Police Station Advice and Assistance is sought and no material change of circumstances has occurred;
- the change requested is from a second to a third solicitor (unless exceptionally it is reasonable for a further change); or
- there is no reasonable explanation for the client seeking further Police Station Advice and Assistance from a new solicitor[12].

20.15

The most likely provision to apply in cases concerning victims of trafficking will be the victim of trafficking having reasonable cause to transfer from one firm to another based on the second firm's specialist knowledge of trafficking issues, especially in circumstances where the first firm has not identified that the individual may be a victim of trafficking. The second firm takes the risk of non-payment in these circumstances and should justify the change with a detailed file note of the client's concerns and reasons for transfer. There is no formal transfer process at this stage and the second firm can merely request the papers from the first firm who will then close and bill the case.

20.16

Remuneration for police station advice is on a fixed fee structure subject to a threshold at which hourly rate claims become available. There is a fixed fee for telephone only advice of £33 in London and £31.74 outside of London. The fee for providing advice at the police station is also fixed at £320 regardless of the location of the police station[13]. The telephone advice fee is not payable in addition, but forms part of the attendance fee.

11 SCC Specification para 9.64.

12 SCC Specification para 9.67.

13 Criminal Legal Aid (Remuneration) Regulations 2013, Sch 4 para 2 (4) as amended by Criminal Legal Aid (General and Remuneration) (Amendment) Regulations 2025, reg 4, Sch 2 in force for cases starting after 22/12/25. For cases starting prior to that date, fees depend on the location of the police station.

20.17

If the 'escape fee' threshold[14] is reached, a fixed fee is payable plus a fee based on hourly rates for work done beyond the threshold figure. The firm calculates the fee by reference to hourly rates and once that figure exceeds the stated threshold for the police station attended, further fees are paid – but only for the work done beyond the threshold.

20.18

The fixed fee is £320 and the threshold figure is £650, so the firm will be paid a fixed fee and then have to undertake further work unpaid until the threshold is reached. The unpaid portion (£330) is never recouped on an escape fee claim, which is also assessed for reasonableness by the LAA using a CRM18 form.

20.19

Only one fee is payable for the whole of the investigation stage of a case. This means that where an individual is released on bail or under investigation and subsequently re-interviewed, there is no further payment available for that attendance (unless it takes the case beyond the escape threshold).

20.20

It is possible to undertake work during the bail period or where someone is released under investigation but only if they are financially eligible for advice under the freestanding Advice and Assistance scheme[15]. This work is included in the calculation as to whether the case passes the escape threshold but, unless it takes the case beyond that threshold, no further fee is payable beyond the Police Station fixed fee. If work is required by way of the pre-charge engagement process in accordance with the Attorney-General's Guidelines on Disclosure, that work is not subject to the means test and is paid separately to the Police Station fixed fee[16].

20.21

The Police Station Advice and Assistance scheme applies to those attending the police station voluntarily to be interviewed under caution about criminal offences. The individual does not need to be under arrest to qualify for the funding.

14 The threshold limit is £650 on all claims which start after 22nd December 2025, Criminal Legal Aid (Remuneration) Regulations 2013, Sch 4 para 2(5) as amended by Criminal legal Aid (General and Remuneration) (Amendment) Regulations 2025, reg 4, Sch 2

15 See details below at paras **13.24–13.28** and **13.94** (re appeals and reviews), and SCC Specification paras 9.134–9.160.

16 SCC Specification 9.109 – 9.133.

20.22

Advice and Assistance is also available under the Advocacy Assistance provisions[17], where there is an application for a warrant of further detention, to vary police bail conditions or to extend police bail.

20.23

Each individual case is billed using a CRM11 form but the submission of bills to the LAA for payment is via the Legal Aid Agency online portal 'Submit a Bulk Claim' (SaBC). Files are audited and can be selected for review by the LAA at any time.

Work after release from police station but before charge

20.24

Once a client is released from the police station but where a decision on charge has not been made, legal advice is available under the Advice and Assistance scheme if the client is financially eligible. The eligibility limits are very low, but most clients who are potential victims of trafficking would usually meet the criteria. Work under the Pre-Charge Engagement scheme is not means tested but has to be limited to work under that scheme.

20.25

This funding requires the client to sign a CRM1 and CRM2 form and for the financial eligibility details to be provided and checked. The client will need to provide proof of his income even if he is being supported by a charity or friend. A letter from that person or organisation setting out what support they are providing will suffice, as long as it covers the date that the form was signed.

20.26

This funding will enable the solicitors to make representations to the Crown Prosecution Service against charging the client with criminal offences.

20.27

However, the reality of the situation for the solicitors is that this work will not add to the fee they are paid for representing the client at the investigation stage. The work done under this scheme will only be remunerated if it takes the work done in the investigation stage above the fixed fee threshold. If it does not, and in most cases it will not, no further fee is payable in addition to the fixed fee for

17 SCC Specification paras 9.161–9.173.

attending the police station. Work under the Pre-Charge Engagement scheme is paid in addition to the Police Station fixed fee.

20.28

The financial limit on the Advice and Assistance Scheme (see below)[18] applies and can be extended by application on the LAA Online Portal ('Sign in to Legal Aid Services' known as SiLAS) using the 'submit a crime form' option and then the link which is labelled 'Apply for extension to upper limits, formerly CRM5'. Disbursements for interpreters, experts, translators or any other necessary disbursement expense can be funded, subject to approval by the LAA. The disbursements will be funded additionally to the fixed fee.

Witnesses at risk of self-incrimination

20.29

On occasion a victim of trafficking may be requested to provide an account to police as a witness in a case, in particular where there is an investigation into that person's trafficked status and into the person allegedly responsible for the trafficking. This may be contemporaneous to a criminal investigation of the victim of trafficking or independent of it. These interviews are normally carried out under the Achieving Best Evidence video procedure.

20.30

In such interviews the victim of trafficking is likely to be in a position where he may potentially admit to having committed criminal offences, albeit under coercion. Consequently, there is a risk of self-incrimination and therefore a 'complicating factor'[19].

20.31

Advice and Assistance is available to a victim of trafficking in such circumstances under the SCC 2025[20] subject to a means test and passing the Sufficient Benefit Test.

20.32

The details of the Advice and Assistance Scheme are set out below[21]. The scheme is very strictly means tested, but potential victims of trafficking would normally expect to qualify for the funding subject to proof of their income.

---

18 See para **13.101**.

19 SCC Specification para 9.46.

20 SCC Specification paras 9.137.

21 See para **13.91** ff.

Advice during criminal court proceedings at first instance

20.33

If a victim of trafficking is charged with a criminal offence, legal aid from a firm of solicitors with an SCC 2025 may be available, subject to means and passing a merits test. An application is made online and the defendant has to sign a hard copy of a declaration form confirming that the information provided is correct.

20.34

The online application requires details of the defendant's income, outgoings and capital as well as details about the nature of the case being prosecuted against them. Most victims of trafficking will qualify for legal aid if the offence passes the merits test. The online application is on the combined CRM14 and CRM15 forms which is under the "Apply for criminal legal aid" option on the LAA Online Portal.

20.35

As a rough guide, anyone earning under £20,000 per annum is likely to qualify for legal aid for summary proceedings. For proceedings on indictment the financial limit is an annual disposable household income of £37,500. It should be noted that this is the disposable income after mortgage, rent and other expenses are deducted.

20.36

Legal aid is assessed on income initially, but it may be that in Crown Court cases a contribution from capital is ordered at the end of the case if the defendant is convicted and has assets in excess of £30,000. At this stage the LAA may request a contribution from capital.

20.37

If legal aid is granted, a representation order will be issued. This will cover the work indicated on the order.

Magistrates' court proceedings

20.38

If legal aid is granted for the magistrates' court in summary proceedings it will allow the solicitor to obtain experts' reports, interpreters and translations as necessary during the course of the case, as long as the work undertaken is reasonable. The funding regime for magistrates' court cases is set out in section 10 of the Specification to the SCC 2025 and a firm must have a contract to undertake the work.

20.39

It is advisable to make an application for prior authority from the LAA for any disbursement in excess of £100 using the CRM4 process on the LAA Online Portal SiLAS (under the 'Submit a crime form' option and the link). Apply for prior authority to incur expenses, formerly CRM4'). An estimate of the fees from three providers should be sought, although the LAA may not insist on this if the rates are within legal aid guidelines and the amount of time is reasonable. In cases of unusual expertise, it may be that higher rates might be agreed by the LAA and only one estimate may be possible in any event.

20.40

In most summary proceedings, the representation order will provide for representation by solicitors. Counsel can be instructed but would be paid by the solicitors rather than by the LAA. In these circumstances counsel is 'unassigned' and becomes an overhead of the firm. A fee will be agreed between the firm and chambers and the times worked by the advocate would be included in the solicitors' bill as if it were work undertaken by the firm.

20.41

In exceptional cases heard before the magistrates' court an advocate may be 'assigned' if the proceedings relate to an extradition hearing under the Extradition Act 2003 or an indictable offence (which in fact means an either way offence) and the relevant court determines that because there are circumstances which make the proceedings unusually grave or difficult, representation by an advocate would be desirable[22]. An advocate cannot be assigned on summary only offences.

20.42

Assigned counsel is paid directly by the LAA but the bill is submitted by the solicitors' firm on a CRM8 form to accompany the firm's CRM7 claim form (which is submitted online using SiLAS and the 'Submit a Crime Form' option).

20.43

The fees for magistrates' court cases are calculated on a fixed fee matrix but using underlying hourly rates excluding travel and waiting (except in certain (usually) rural areas). If the work done does not reach the 'lower limit', the lower fixed fee is payable. If the work done exceeds the lower limit but not the 'higher limit', the higher standard fee is claimed. If the work done exceeds the higher limit a non-standard fee is claimed whereby the work is claimed entirely at hourly rates and assessed for reasonableness by the LAA. There is a different fixed fee depending on whether the case is a trial (including a case that cracks

22 Criminal Legal Aid (Determinations by a Court and Choice of Representative) Regulations 2013, 2013/614, reg 16(2).

at the last minute) or a guilty plea (or equivalent) and whether on a guilty plea the case was summary only or either way[23].

20.44

Standard fees are claimed by using a CRM11 to calculate the bill and then submitted as part of the monthly bulk upload using the SaBC portal. All bills are potentially subject to audit by the LAA on request.

20.45

Non-standard fees are submitted online on SiLAS using the 'Submit a Crime Form' option and the CRM7 link. These are assessed on a case-by-case basis.

20.46

It is possible to claim enhanced hourly rates for all or part of the work undertaken and if such rates are claimed, the bill is submitted as a CRM7 for assessment. Enhanced rates should be claimed where it is considered, taking into account all the relevant circumstances of the case and compared to the generality of proceedings, that:

- the work was done with exceptional competence, skill or expertise; or
- the work was done with exceptional dispatch; or
- the case involved exceptional circumstances or complexity[24].

20.47

If the work or part of it attracts an uplift, the LAA will decide what rate to apply up to a maximum of 100% and having regard to the degree of responsibility accepted by the firm; the care, speed and economy with which the case was prepared; and the novelty, weight and complexity of the case[25]. Any assessment can be appealed to an Independent Funding Adjudicator (also known as an Independent Costs Assessor).

Crown Court proceedings

20.48

In the Crown Court, solicitors are paid via the Litigator Graduated Fee Scheme ('LGFS') and advocates by the Advocates Graduated Fee Scheme ('AGFS'). In the LGFS the fees for the work undertaken are fixed by a series of proxies, namely the nature of the charge (which will fall into one of eleven categories),

23 The full list of categories is set out at SCC Specification para 10.75.
24 SCC Specification para 10.82.
25 SCC Specification paras 10.84.

whether it is a guilty plea, cracked trial or trial (or equivalent outcome), the number of pages of prosecution evidence and the trial length. Under the AGFS scheme the advocate is paid a basic fee according to the offence banding and level of advocate and a daily attendance fee for each day of the trial. Standard appearances attract separate payments. Guilty pleas are paid on the basic fee alone. Cracked trial fees depend on the stage at which the trial cracked after the PTPH and before trial. There may be additional payments for 'special preparation'[26].

20.49

The fee payable is not related to the amount of work undertaken. Disbursements are paid in addition to the lawyers' fees via the solicitors who include them in their fee submission.

20.50

The number of pages of prosecution evidence in a LGFS claim is capped at 10,000 pages and any work above that is paid on an hourly rate (not subject to enhancement) and assessed on submission of the bill for reasonableness.

20.51

Work on unused material is remunerated separately under both schemes by way of a small fixed fee to cover work up to three hours and then on an hourly rate. No additional fee is paid under either scheme for a case which is claimed as a guilty plea.

Prior authority for disbursements

20.52

Experts, such as trafficking and country experts, as well as psychiatric and psychological experts may need to be instructed on human trafficking cases. As stated above, if a disbursement expense is to be incurred, an application for prior authority should be made to the LAA if the amount involved exceeds £100. This application is made on the LAA Online SiLAS Portal using the 'Submit a Crime Form' option and the CRM4 link. The LAA may require three estimates from experts but this is not always essential. There are prescribed rates for experts of different types and it is occasionally possible to exceed those rates if no suitable expert can be found for the usual legal aid rate, or if the case requires a specific expert who will not undertake the work at those rates. Refusals to grant the prior authority requested can be appealed to an Independent Costs Assessor.

26 See the Criminal Legal Aid (Remuneration) Regulations 2013, as amended, particularly by the Criminal Legal Aid (Remuneration) (Amendment) Regulations 2022 (SI 2022/848).

20.53

Once prior authority has been granted and the work undertaken, an interim claim can be made for the disbursement if the case is in the Crown Court under the LGFS. No such claim can be made in magistrates' court cases unless the payment claimed is likely to exceed the value of the next monthly payment[27]. In effect this means that such payments are very rarely made in magistrates' court proceedings.

20.54

Any work in excess of the prior authorised figure cannot be guaranteed payment and would have to be justified to the LAA at the conclusion of the case. Experts must therefore know that their fees are fixed by their estimates and the solicitor will not make up any shortfall if the final bill exceeds the estimate and is not reimbursed by the LAA. A provision to this effect should be put into the solicitors' letter of instruction to the expert.

Defendant intermediaries

20.55

An intermediary acts as a facilitator for a witness or defendant to ensure complete, accurate and coherent communication between the vulnerable individual and the legal professionals concerned. The core concept is to ensure the individual's general understanding of the process and an ability to provide coherent instructions to his legal team.

20.56

If the solicitor or advocate instructed considers that the individual client requires the assistance of an intermediary, the court must be notified so that the issues can be further explored and a timetable set to accommodate assessments.

20.57

A psychologist (with specific experience of adults or children) will have to be instructed in order to carry out specific communication assessments. Funding for this assessment is obtained via the LAA by making an online CRM4 application to cover the assessment and report fee.

20.58

Should the psychologist conclude that an intermediary ought to be appointed, a specific intermediary report should be obtained. This will require a further

27 SCC Specification para 10.90.

assessment of the individual by an intermediary to determine the individual's difficulties, specific needs and proposed requirements. The intermediary should be provided with information about the case prior to assessment, in addition to any medical records and reports previously obtained. Again, funding can be obtained via the CRM4 procedure, although the report may be funded by the court if the application for an intermediary is granted.

20.59

The intermediary report once prepared shall provide specific recommendations as to language, breaks and general approach which must be adopted to ensure the most effective participation and understanding of the vulnerable individual in the case. Such issues shall be considered by the court in determining the application.

20.60

Once an intermediary report has been prepared, it must be sent to the relevant court. There is no statutory power to appoint an intermediary for a defendant and the court must be expressly invited to exercise its inherent power to appoint an intermediary.

20.61

The application shall be determined by the allocated judge and if the criteria are met, an intermediary shall be appointed by the court. The fees are then met by the court and do not come from the defendant's legal aid.

Extension of legal aid to King's Counsel or two advocates

20.62

Legal aid in the Crown Court automatically includes representation by solicitors and an advocate. It can be extended to include representation by King's Counsel, either alone or with a junior advocate by application to the Crown Court[28]. Very exceptionally King's Counsel or two advocates can be instructed in the magistrates' court in extradition proceedings where the court determines that the defendant could not otherwise be adequately represented[29].

20.63

In Crown Court proceedings legal aid can be extended to include King's Counsel alone if the case involves substantial novel or complex issues of law or

28 Criminal Legal Aid (Determinations by a Court and Choice of Representative) Regulations 2013, SI 2013/614, reg 18.

29 Criminal Legal Aid (Determinations by a Court and Choice of Representative) Regulations 2013, reg 17.

fact which could not be adequately presented except by a King's Counsel, and either the 'exceptional condition' is met or the 'counsel condition' is met.

20.64

The 'counsel condition' means that a King's Counsel or senior Treasury Counsel has been instructed on behalf of the prosecution. The 'exceptional condition' means that the case is exceptional compared with the generality of cases involving similar offences.

20.65

Legal aid can be extended to two junior advocates if the case involves substantial novel or complex issues of law or fact which could not be adequately presented by a single advocate, including a King's Counsel alone, and either the 'exceptional condition' is met or the 'prosecution condition' is met.

20.66

The 'prosecution condition' means either two or more advocates have been instructed on behalf of the prosecution and the relevant court is satisfied that the individual will be, or will be likely to be, prejudiced if they too are not represented by two or more advocates; or the number of prosecution witnesses exceeds 80; or the number of pages of prosecution evidence exceeds 1,000.

20.67

Legal aid can be extended to include a King's Counsel and a junior advocate if the case involves substantial novel or complex issues of law or fact which could not be adequately presented except by a King's Counsel assisted by a junior advocate, and either the exceptional condition is met, or the counsel condition and the prosecution condition are met.

Transfers of legal aid

20.68

If a defendant is not happy with his solicitors, he may apply to the court to transfer the legal aid to another firm. This is not always a straightforward process and courts are often unwilling to transfer representation orders where they fear that the system is being manipulated by the defendant or where significant additional costs will be incurred. In fact, in most cases the extra costs incurred to the legal aid fund are not large, especially if the application is made at an early stage in proceedings and before any papers have been served or prior to the Plea and Trial Preparation Hearing.

20.69

The application is made by the defendant completing a form (available on the Justice website)[30] setting out his reasons for requiring a transfer of representation. This is then sent to the proposed new solicitor to complete and then to the currently instructed solicitor. The form is then submitted to the court for a decision by a judge at the Crown Court.

20.70

The transfer application is more likely to succeed if the incumbent firm does not object. In seeking a transfer, clients may be critical of their current solicitors. In trafficking cases, it may be justified by the client being a potential victim of trafficking, and this not having been identified by the solicitor, or due to the solicitors having failed to make representations about the case continuing as a result of the State's non-prosecution obligations or not having advised on an NRM referral or defence under MSA 2015, s 45. Even in these circumstances, the incumbent firm may object to the transfer request.

20.71

In order for legal aid to be transferred, the defendant has to demonstrate that[31]:

- there has been a breakdown in the relationship between the individual and the original solicitor such that effective representation can no longer be provided by the original solicitor; or
- there is some other compelling reason why effective representation can no longer be provided by the original solicitor.

20.72

Alternatively legal aid may be transferred if the original solicitor considers there to be a duty to withdraw from the case in accordance with his professional rules of conduct or is no longer able to represent the individual through circumstances outside the solicitor's control. In such circumstances the original solicitor has to supply the relevant court with details as to the nature of any such duty to withdraw from the case or the particular circumstances that renders him unable to represent the individual.

20.73

There will be issues of privilege involved and the form contains a box to tick if privilege is to be waived for the purposes of considering this application. In

30 See https://www.gov.uk/government/publications/application-by-person-with-legal-aid-to-change-solicitor, last accessed 22 August 2025.

31 Criminal Legal Aid (Determinations by a Court and Choice of Representative) Regulations 2013, reg 14 and Criminal Procedure Rules 46.3 and 46.4.

effect, where there are criticisms of the current solicitor, privilege will have to be waived so that the solicitors can deal with the issue.

20.74

It is helpful for the proposed new solicitors to set out a reasoned argument as to why legal aid should be transferred, bringing the client's own reasons within the regulation. Where solicitors object to transfer requests and the court refuses to grant the application, this leaves a vulnerable defendant with a firm that he does not want to be represented by, and this firm is aware that he has made complaints about their conduct of the case. This does not make for effective representation, particularly given the importance of building the trust of a potential victim of trafficking.

20.75

If the defendant chooses to revoke legal aid, it is unlikely that a fresh application for legal aid will be granted and there is a significant risk that he will be unrepresented. In a potential victim of trafficking case, that situation could give rise to significant injustice.

20.76

It may be that the incumbent firm, while not accepting any overt criticism, would nonetheless agree that the transfer should take place in order that the defendant has a functional working relationship with his solicitors to prepare the case for trial. Even if they are not objecting in principle on the basis that the client should be able to trust his legal representative implicitly, especially when the defendant is particularly vulnerable, will not guarantee a transfer of legal aid.

Billing time limits

20.77

Bills should be submitted within three months of the conclusion of the part of the case to which they relate.

Advice on appeal against conviction and/or sentence

Appeals from the magistrates' court to the Crown Court

20.78

Legal aid granted for the magistrates' court includes advice on appeal to the Crown Court. If the advice is positive and an appeal is lodged, a new legal aid application has to be made to the LAA via the online SiLAS portal.

20.79

Appeals against conviction and sentence in the Crown Court attract a fixed fee for advocates and litigators regardless of the nature of the case or its complexity. The fee payable is generally considered to be derisory, not providing adequate remuneration.

20.80

The Law Society has provided guidance to solicitors that they are not obliged to take on legal aid cases if the fee is not economic. This guidance is particularly apt for appeals to the Crown Court.

Appeals from the Crown Court to the Court of Appeal

20.81

Legal aid in the Crown Court includes advice on appeal to the Court of Appeal (Criminal Division). If the advice to appeal from the Crown Court is negative, there is no additional fee to the LGFS or AGFS trial fee.

20.82

If the advice is positive, a claim for the work done by solicitors in considering the advice, advising the client and preparing and submitting the appeal can be made to the Court of Appeal once the decision on leave has been made. The fee is paid on an hourly rate basis and per item for telephone calls and out-going correspondence.

Funding in the Court of Appeal (Criminal Division)

20.83

If leave is granted, legal aid will also be granted but this would normally be for the advocate only as long as the box indicating that legal aid was required was ticked on the form NG. Legal aid is not means tested at this stage and there are no forms to complete or submit to the court or the LAA. The Court may in due course require a means form to be completed, as costs may be an issue should the appeal fail.

20.84

Legal aid can be extended to include representation by solicitors as well as counsel and/or for two counsel. If the advocate considers that the assistance of a solicitor in preparing and presenting the appeal is required or that the case is suitable for representation by two advocates, a written application should be sent to the Registrar for an extension of the representation order. There is no prescribed form for such an application.

20.85

The Court of Appeal frequently limits representation orders granted to solicitors to include only specific work. This may not include all the work that the solicitor might wish to undertake to prepare a case for the appeal. Any work outside the limitations will not be remunerated.

20.86

It should be noted that the Advice and Assistance Scheme cannot be used to bridge any gap in funding and ceases once the appeal is lodged. If work has been undertaken by solicitors after the lodging of the appeal, it is possible to request at the final hearing of the appeal that the Court allows funding under legal aid for that work[32]. It may be possible to ask the Court of Appeal to allow funding post lodging and pre-leave where work is required and requested of the solicitors by the Court. Although it is rarely granted, the Court has the ability to grant a representation order in these circumstances as illustrated by the decision to allow funding retrospectively in *R v JXP*.

20.87

If the Single Judge refuses leave, any advice and representation thereafter is on a pro bono basis unless the client is willing and able to pay privately. The client is entitled to advice as to whether to renew the application for leave to the full court and the potential consequences if such an application is unsuccessfully made. This would normally be by way of advice from the advocate or letter from the solicitor and should be included in the bill to the court. It would not cover a meeting with the client unless specifically agreed with the court in advance.

20.88

For litigators it is possible to claim enhanced rates on the work undertaken up to 100% on the same basis as for work in the magistrates' court (see para **20.46**).

20.89

It is also possible to instruct experts if the representation order allows for their instruction. There are no prior authority provisions at this stage, but the court will sometimes pay in advance on specific request. Such payment will be subject to recoupment at the final assessment of the bill at the end of the case. Given that no agreement on rates or hours is given, the solicitors remain at risk if payment is made in this way.

32 *R v JXP* [2019] EWCA Crim 1280.

20.90

Bills should be submitted within three months of the conclusion of the case to the Costs Department at the Court of Appeal.

Applications to the Court of Appeal out of time and CCRC applications

20.91

In many cases the individual may not be identified as a victim of trafficking until after his conviction. In such circumstances it may be possible to appeal to the Court of Appeal or indeed the Crown Court out of time. Usually this will mean the instruction of a firm that did not represent the victim of trafficking at trial, there being at least an implication that the trial firm should have identified the issue earlier.

20.92

Public funding is available under the Advice and Assistance Scheme for work within the Appeals and Reviews class[33]. The client will need to sign and complete a CRM1 and CRM2 form.

Sufficient Benefit Test

20.93

In order to receive Advice and Assistance under the scheme the case must meet the Sufficient Benefit Test:

> 'Advice and Assistance may only be provided on legal issues concerning English (or Welsh) law and where there is sufficient benefit to the Client, having regard to the circumstances of the matter, including the personal circumstances of the Client, to justify work or further work being carried out'[34].

20.94

This is an ongoing test throughout the life of the case, and must be considered at all times. As soon as it ceases to apply, no more work should be done on the case.

33 See SCC Specification at section 11.
34 SCC Specification para 3.10.

Financial test

20.95

In order to obtain advice under this scheme the potential client also has to meet the financial criteria. There is both an income and a capital limit so on occasions even people in prison will not qualify for advice under the scheme if they have too much capital. The limits are very low and have not changed for over a decade, currently set at £99 per week disposable income (only deducting tax and not items such as rent). There is a fixed deduction to take into account for dependants of £48.50 for a partner and £77.78 for each child.

20.96

Insofar as capital is concerned the limits depend on whether the client has any dependants. The limit is £1,000 if there are no dependants, £1,335 if one, £1,535 if two and an extra £100 is added for each extra dependant. The income and capital of any partner of the victim of trafficking is included, even if the victim of trafficking is in prison, if he had been living as a couple prior to the incarceration. It may be possible to argue that it would be inequitable or impractical to include the partner's resources[35] in certain circumstances, but the solicitor takes a risk that the claim will be disallowed on audit (if selected for audit) if the LAA takes a contrary view. It would be advisable to seek a determination on this from the LAA before undertaking any work and keeping a note of any positive decision on file.

20.97

Victims of trafficking, who are foreign nationals, are often in the position whereby they cannot work legitimately or claim benefits. They are often supported by friends or by a charity. It will be essential for the solicitor to obtain documentary proof of the support that the victim of trafficking is getting to ensure that he is below the threshold.

20.98

A letter from the person providing the support setting out how much he provides will be sufficient and it must cover the time at which the legal advice and assistance forms (CRM1 and CRM2) are signed by the victim of trafficking. However, particularly relevant to trafficking cases are the 'Mandatory Disregards' in relation to income and capital. Any payment under any Modern Slavery Victim Care Contract (MSVCC) or equivalent payment or any payment of compensation for a Miscarriage of Justice made under section 133 of the Criminal Justice Act 1988 is not included in the eligibility calculation. In addition, there are two 'Discretionary Disregards', namely any compensation

35 Criminal Legal Aid (Financial Resources) Regulations 2013, SI 2013/471, reg 9.

payments made to victims of Grenfell Tower and any compensation payments made under the Victims of Overseas Terrorism Compensation Scheme 2012[36].

20.99

If the client does not pass both parts of the financial assessment, advice under the scheme is not available to them. There is no contribution-based system and no other public funding for this advice.

Previous advice

20.100

If the victim of trafficking has received an adverse opinion on appeal and wishes to obtain a further opinion, the scheme is not automatically available as the solicitor must consider how long it was since the first opinion was given. If it was recent and it appears that all issues have been considered, no further work should normally be undertaken[37].

20.101

However, where there is further evidence or the solicitor believes there may be some defect in the opinion or the proceedings, then further work may be justified for a further opinion, regardless of when the first opinion was obtained[38]. In relation to victims of trafficking cases, it is often the case that the fact that the defendant was a victim of trafficking was not identified at trial and therefore any advice given will automatically be flawed. This is rarely a bar to advice on these cases.

Financial limits and applications to extend

20.102

The scheme has an initial financial limit of £346.29 (approximately 6 hours' work) for out of time appeals and £577.16 for CCRC applications (approximately 10 hours' work). Up to the point that the limit of work has been reached, an application can be made to the LAA to extend it. If the limit is exceeded before an extension application is made, the work undertaken above the limit will not be funded.

36 Civil and Criminal Legal Aid (Financial Resources and Contribution Orders) (Amendment) Regulations 2024, reg 3.

37 SCC Specification para 11.5.

38 SCC Specification para 11.6.

20.103

An application for authority to exceed the upper limit must be made to the LAA Online Portal on the CRM5 option which should explain what work has been done, what needs to be done and the amount of any disbursements required or already incurred within the limit.

20.104

Advice and Assistance includes the solicitors' fees at the contracted hourly rate (not subject to any uplift) and any disbursements, including an advocate's fees which are properly incurred by the solicitor in connection with the giving of Advice and Assistance (VAT is not included within the limit calculations). Disbursements will include experts, interpreters, transcripts, and translation of documents.

20.105

Once a limit has been granted, it can be further extended, but at no point will work be remunerated if it exceeds the limit as then granted. It is important to note that extensions cannot be granted retrospectively and do not operate retrospectively.

20.106

If the LAA refuses to grant an extension to the upper limit, a right of review arises to the Independent Funding Adjudicator.

CCRC applications

20.107

Applications to the Criminal Cases Review Commission are funded under this scheme and come about where the victim of trafficking has already unsuccessfully appealed his conviction but something new has materialised since the time of the appeal which was not known about at the time of trial or appeal. It may be that a victim of trafficking is identified as such after an appeal has been lodged.

20.108

In addition, in cases where there has been a conviction in a magistrates' court on a guilty plea but it then transpires that the person is a victim of trafficking, the only recourse is to the CCRC under exceptional circumstances and this funding is available for such applications.

Postal application

20.109

In terms of the practical aspects of this funding, it may be more cost effective to send application forms for signature in the post. This is allowed 'where there is good reason to do so'[39] and the reason must be noted on the file[40].

20.110

In appellate work, the client may be in custody. It would be reasonable in those circumstances to send the client the CRM1 and CRM2 forms in the post, as this will be more cost effective than a visit, especially when the case is at such an early stage that a visit may not be necessary.

Telephone advice

20.111

Although unusual with victims of trafficking, the solicitor may claim payment for advice given to a client over the telephone before that client has signed the application form where the client cannot for good reason attend the office and the client meets the qualifying criteria and has subsequently signed the application form[41]. The solicitor would have to consider that in all the circumstances it was appropriate to provide the advice in this way and the reasons relied upon should always be noted and kept on the file[42].

20.112

The client does not have to attend the office to sign the application form after having been given the telephone advice. Instead, the solicitor may send the form to the client, after having given the advice, for signature and return.

Outward travel

20.113

The solicitor may claim for the mileage or cost of public transport for outward travel but not travelling time to visit a client away from the office before the application form is signed where the visit is justified for good reason (and noted

39 SCC Specification para 11.11.
40 SCC Specification para 11.12.
41 SCC Specification para 11.13.
42 SCC Specification paras 11.14 and 11.15.

on file) and the client meets the qualifying criteria and has subsequently signed the application form[43].

20.114

It is sometimes advisable to see victims of trafficking away from the solicitor's office, even if the individual is not in custody, where he is particularly vulnerable or needs the assistance of other parties to communicate effectively.

20.115

If the individual is in detention, prison or hospital a claim may also be made for the travelling time at the appropriate rate[44]. Costs must be reasonably incurred taking account of all the circumstances[45] including, for example, the distances involved as against the availability of advice from a more local firm and the justification for travelling to attend on the client at all, bearing in mind that telephone advice can be given and applications accepted by post.

20.116

With victims of trafficking it may not be possible for them to find firms more local to their place of detention with sufficient expertise to advise in trafficking-related matters, and travel may be more justifiable over a longer distance. The use of interpreters will mean that telephone advice will be of limited use and indeed even the use of video links to the prison can be problematic with extremely vulnerable individuals who do not speak English.

Previous advice under the Legal Advice and Assistance Scheme

20.117

In some cases, the victim of trafficking may have received previous advice under this scheme. The solicitor must not claim for Advice and Assistance provided to a client who has received Advice and Assistance for the same matter from another solicitor within the six months preceding the application, except where:

- there is a gap in time and circumstances have changed materially between the first and second occasions when the Advice and Assistance was sought; or
- the client has reasonable cause to transfer from the first solicitor; or
- the first solicitor has confirmed to the new solicitor that they will not be making a claim for payment for the Advice and Assistance[46].

43 SCC Specification para 11.16.
44 SCC Specification para 11.17.
45 SCC Specification para 11.18.
46 SCC Specification para 11.27.

20.118

If the solicitor provides Advice and Assistance in these circumstances, he must record the justification for so doing on the file.

20.119

Where a client is requesting further advice from a new firm under the Advice and Assistance scheme, there should be no claim under that scheme by the second solicitor where:

- the client simply disagrees with the first advice and wants a second opinion;
- there is only a short time between the first and second occasions when the Advice and Assistance is sought and no material change of circumstances has occurred;
- the change requested is from a second to a third solicitor (unless exceptionally it is reasonable for a further change); or
- there is no reasonable explanation for the client seeking further Advice and Assistance from a new solicitor[47].

20.120

Where the work is nonetheless justifiable, the solicitor must make a note on the file to confirm that Advice and Assistance has been given previously by another solicitor and the client must complete a fresh application form and must meet the qualifying criteria.

Counsel's fees

20.121

There is no fixed rate for counsel in the Contract. The LAA therefore relies on its own Guidance[48] to fix an appropriate rate. The Guidance applies to all Advice and Assistance matters (not just appellate work) and states that counsel often provides advice for a fixed fee of £200–£400. Where higher sums are requested a full breakdown of times should be submitted.

20.122

However, it would be an extremely rare appeal case upon which counsel could advise for a fixed fee as low as those set out in the now very outdated Guidance.

47 SCC Specification para 11.30.
48 https://assets.publishing.service.gov.uk/media/682db395a599d03a16bff37b/Lord_Chancellor_s_guide_to_determining_financial_eligibility_Certificated_.pdf (last accessed 3 July 2026).

It may be possible on other Advice and Assistance matters but is extremely unlikely on appeal cases. The Guidance recognises this, as it states that 'it should be noted that in Appeals cases, as the issues are likely to be more complex, it is more likely that the fixed fee will not be appropriate and that hourly rates and a full breakdown will be required'.

20.123

The Guidance seeks to fix an hourly rate for counsel, which it says should not exceed £80 per hour (unless a reasonable fixed fee is charged). However, if solicitors provide sufficient and detailed justification as to why a case may be considered to be exceptional, a higher rate can be authorised. Since the Guidance was drafted there have been changes in legal aid rates generally and this rate was uplifted by 15% to £96 for cases started after September 2022 and should be further uplifted by another 10% to £105.60 for cases starting after 22 December 2025. A higher rate may be agreed in exceptional cases and certainly where the case merits instruction of King's Counsel. In the past King's Counsel have been funded at £120 per hour so with the uplift of 15% from September 2022 that rate would be £144 and a further 10% would take it to £158.40 for cases started after 22 December 2025. These rates are not set out at all in any regulations and are based entirely on unpublished LAA guidance which it is suggested should be uplifted as legal aid rates have been increased since September 2022. Cases involving victims of trafficking may well be considered complex or involving novel or complex points of law. If the case is exceptional, a higher fee should be sought. The LAA have become more entrenched in not allowing fees for counsel above £96 per hour (now £105.60) but their own guidance allows it in exceptional cases. Any refusal can be appealed to an Independent Financial Adjudicator.

Applications to re-open the case in the magistrates' court

20.124

In some cases where a client has pleaded guilty in the magistrates' court and it transpires he should not have been prosecuted, it may be possible to apply to the magistrates' court to re-open the case[49] instead of applying to the CCRC to refer the case to the Crown Court by way of appeal.

20.125

In such circumstances, initial work on the case to establish how the case should be dealt with and to gather the evidence that the client is a victim of trafficking, and should not have been prosecuted should be undertaken under the Advice and Assistance Scheme.

49 Magistrates Court Act 1980, s 142.

20.126

However, if the application is to be made to reconsider the case at the magistrates' court, a fresh application for legal aid should be made by the LAA online SiLAS portal using the 'Apply for legal aid' option as if the matter were a new case in the magistrates' court.

20.127

If the LAA refuses to grant a representation order on the basis that one already exists for that case, an application for a transfer of legal aid will have to be made.

Applications for compensation under s 133

20.128

Applications for compensation for being the victim of a miscarriage of justice are made to the Ministry of Justice. The initial work involved in preparing representations to the Ministry of Justice as to whether the applicant qualifies for compensation can be funded by way of Legal Help. It is necessary for the firm to have a Civil Contract to use this funding scheme as it is not included within the definition of Associated Civil Work in the SCC 2025.

20.129

If the claim is accepted, the work is undertaken effectively as a privately-funded case and the legal fees are part of the claimant's damages. The firm will have to obtain permission from the Ministry of Justice to incur any disbursement such as experts or to instruct counsel.

20.130

The rates payable are legal help rates unless the firm can justify higher rates due to the circumstances of the case. In fact, the Ministry of Justice has for the most part allowed rates at the equivalent of private rates as this work is unusual and specialised, usually using the SCCO Guideline rates. However, the newly appointed Independent Assessor is reviewing the use of SCCO/private rates and may take a more robust line than that of his predecessors.

20.131

The firm will also have to agree with its client how to deal with the situation where legal fees are requested but not paid in full as part of the compensation by the Ministry of Justice. The shortfall may come from the balance of the compensation, the firm could write it off or a compromise could be reached. Such agreement should be set out in writing in advance with the client.

Legal aid for potential trafficking victims in immigration matters and judicial review

Availability

Legal Aid, Sentencing and Punishment of Offenders Act 2012

20.132

The Legal Aid, Sentencing and Punishment of Offenders Act (LASPO) 2012 removed many categories of immigration law from the scope of legal aid. Providers should refer to LASPO 2012, Sch 1 for the full list of matters which remain in scope, as there are some discrete categories which – although not commonly relevant to potential victim of exploitation claims – may be relevant to a case, such as representation for victims of domestic violence. However, subject to the individual satisfying the financial means and merits test, the civil legal aid categories which remain in scope and that are most relevant to such cases are as follows:

(i) Immigration and Public Law **Legal Help**

- rights to enter or remain in the UK arising from the Refugee Convention 1951 or ECHR, Arts 2 and 3 (asylum/international protection claims)[50];
- representation on any immigration claim where an individual has been granted a positive reasonable grounds decision or conclusive grounds decision[51];
- if a potential victim of trafficking is detained in an Immigration Removal Centre ('IRC'), they can receive Legal Help for advice and assistance on detention and bail[52]; and
- restrictions of asylum seekers or pending deportation on residence, such as a challenge to a requirement for a potential victim of trafficking to report to the Home Office or police on a regular basis, or a curfew[53];
- representation on any immigration/nationality claim where the individual is a separated child[54];
- challenging a failure to refer a person into the National Referral Mechanism ('the NRM')[55];
- challenging a negative reasonable or conclusive grounds decision[56];

50 LASPO 2012, Sch 1, Part 1, para 30(1).
51 LASPO 2012, Sch 1, Part 1, para 32(1).
52 LASPO 2012, Sch 1, Part 1, paras 25–26.
53 LASPO 2012, Sch 1, Part 1, para 27.
54 LASPO 2012, Sch 1, Part 1, para 31A.
55 LASPO 2012, Sch 1, Part 1, para 19(1).
56 Ibid.

- challenging a decision to apply the public order or bad faith disqualification[57];
- challenging the NRM support (or lack of/suitability) received by a potential victim of trafficking[58]; and
- challenging failures or decisions not to grant temporary permission to stay to victims of trafficking[59].

The above list is not exhaustive and public law cases on behalf of victims of exploitation can also include challenges to State failures to protect victims, decisions of the Home Office to detain or remove victims, etc. Community care challenges and damages claims on behalf of victims are outside of the scope of this chapter.

(ii) **Controlled Legal Representation (Help at Court; CLR)**

- representation at a First-tier Tribunal or Upper Tribunal statutory appeal in relation to rights to enter or remain in the UK arising from the Refugee Convention 1951 or ECHR, Arts 2 and 3 (asylum/international protection claims)[60];
- representation at a First-tier Tribunal to appeal a refusal of any type of immigration claim where an individual has been granted a positive reasonable grounds decision or conclusive grounds decision[61];
- if a potential victim of exploitation is detained, representation at a tribunal to represent them at a bail hearing[62];
- representation on any immigration/nationality claim where the individual is a separated child[63];

(iii) **Civil Legal Aid**

- civil legal services provided in relation to judicial review of an enactment, decision, act or omission, subject to the exclusions set out in LASPO 2012 (discussed below)[64] or an Upper Tribunal statutory appeal.

20.133

It should be noted that where an individual has a positive reasonable grounds or conclusive grounds decision, this opens up the possibility of legal aid

57 Ibid.
58 Ibid.
59 LASPO 2012, Sch1, Part 1, para 32(1), 32A(1).
60 LASPO 2012, Sch 1, Part 1, para 30(1).
61 LASPO 2012, Sch 1, Part 1, para 32(1).
62 LASPO 2012, Sch 1, Part 1, paras 25–26.
63 LASPO 2012, Sch 1, Part 1, para 31A.
64 LASPO 2012, Sch 1, Part 1, para 19.

representation for that individual in immigration matters which are normally out of scope for legal aid[65].

20.134

The most common relevant claims for (potential) victims of exploitation are claims based on ECHR, Art 8 (family and private life), claims for EEA nationals and/or their family members relying on residual rights under the Withdrawal Agreement and representations made to request a grant of discretionary leave to remain ('VTS leave') as a victim of exploitation in the UK.

20.135

For legal aid cases, there is a time restriction of 12 months from the date of the grant of the conclusive grounds decision that the individual is a victim of exploitation or before the end of any leave outside the rules granted to the victim[66]. There is no similar time restriction for Legal Help cases.

20.136

Further, whilst many areas of immigration law are out of scope for Legal Help and CLR, an individual can potentially later secure legal aid under paragraph 19 of Sch 1 to LASPO 2012 to fund a judicial review challenge of a decision, act or omission of a public body taken in respect of an out of scope area of law.

The gap in legal aid provision for victims of exploitation

20.137

Notwithstanding this advantage for potential victims of exploitation, LASPO 2012 created a gap in the legal aid available for such persons who have not received a positive reasonable grounds decision or who have a negative reasonable/conclusive grounds decision (in Legal Help/CLR matters). This lacuna is concerning, particularly given that potential victims of exploitation can be at their most vulnerable before receiving a positive reasonable grounds decision or after receiving a negative reasonable or conclusive grounds decision. Legal intervention is often critical at these stages.

20.138

There are some practical solutions available in these circumstances. Firstly, it is possible to provide advice and assistance to a potential victim of exploitation where the exploitation claim is inextricably linked to a matter that is within

65 LASPO Sch 1 Part 1 paras 32(1)(a) and (b), and 32A(1)(a) and (b).
66 Civil Legal Aid (Procedure) (Amendment) Regulations 2012 reg 31(8).

scope under LASPO 2012. A common example is a potential victim of exploitation who also has an international protection claim.

20.139

For example, if a potential victim of trafficking fears return to his country of origin because he fears his traffickers, or if he is at risk of re-trafficking on return and faces conditions of destitution, this is likely to be so intertwined with his protection claim that the provider is justified in advising and making representations in relation to the trafficking claim, as the asylum claim cannot be properly determined without first considering the trafficking claim.

20.140

Secondly, another common scenario arises where advice on a potential/refused trafficking claim is linked to advice and assistance on detention and immigration bail (which is within scope under LASPO 2012).

20.141

It is advisable to set out in a detailed attendance note justification for providing advice and representation specific to the trafficking claim by detailing how the trafficking claim is linked to the 'in scope' aspects of the case.

20.142

An alternative approach is to open a Legal Help file for pre-action work only. This may be suitable if the potential victim of exploitation already has a negative reasonable grounds or conclusive grounds decision at the point of instruction, or there is an issue in a pre-reasonable grounds case which may be challenged by way of judicial review. A pre-action Legal Help file is funded as an hourly-rate matter with a limit of £500 for profit costs and £400 for disbursements (immigration contract matters)[67] or a graduated fee public law Legal Help case with a limit of £277 profit costs and reasonable disbursements[68].

20.143

It is also possible to open a Legal Help matter as a public law file to draft representations on an exploitation case after the grant of a reasonable grounds decision, where the conclusive grounds decision is delayed and/or there are concerns that the Home Office will not make a lawful conclusive grounds decision because they have either not made enquiries with the potential victim of exploitation and/or the NRM subcontractor is not providing adequate support to the potential victim. Practitioners should always make sure they

67 2024 Standard Civil Contract Specification, section 8.
68 The Civil Legal Aid (Remuneration) Regulations 2013.

draft a careful attendance note before starting work on a public law case setting out why the work is in scope under paragraph 19 of Sch 1 to LASPO 2012.

Exceptional case funding

20.144

When LASPO 2012 removed large swathes of legal aid assistance for the general population, provision for legal aid funding to be granted in exceptional cases on any out of scope matter was provided for through the possibility of a grant of Exceptional Case Funding ('ECF'). The aim of ECF is to provide a mechanism by which to avoid a breach of the ECHR.

20.145

If funding is granted under ECF the individual can access legal aid representation. An ECF team within LAA deals with such applications and cases. To qualify for ECF, the person must meet the ECF criteria as set out in LASPO 2012 and described in the Lord Chancellor's funding guidance[69]; they must be financially eligible for legal aid and his case must meet the merits criteria. Form CIV ECF1 should be completed and signed by the potential victim of exploitation. The application should be sent with a copy of the CW1 (Legal Help form) or CW2 (controlled legal representation) (depending on the type of matter), along with the relevant evidence to meet the ECF criteria and submitted by e-mail to the ECF team e-mail address at contactECC@legalaid.gsi.gov.uk. At present the LAA aims to process claims within 25 working days (10 days if urgent) and if funding is granted, it will be backdated to the date the CIV ECF1 was signed. If a decision is required urgently, this should be flagged up with the ECF team. If a provider is applying for civil legal aid in a non-judicial review matter which is out of scope, exceptional case funding can be applied for online via the Client and Cost Management System (see para **20.164** below).

20.146

An ECF grant of funding can apply to part of a case, if only part of the case is in scope for legal aid funding. For example, the provider may be providing Legal Help advice on a protection claim and a trafficking claim; however, there may be an additional element of the case, such as a claim under Art 8 ECHR, which will require a grant of exceptional case funding. If the potential victim of exploitation is then granted a positive reasonable or conclusive grounds decision, all immigration legal work is then in scope. Conversely, providers may also need to be alert to potentially having to apply for exceptional case funding

69 Legal Aid: Exceptional Cases Funding: Provider Pack, 2 September 2022, available at, https://assets.publishing.service.gov.uk/media/635ab670e90e070bc2faa806/ECF_Provider_Pack_September_2022_Amendments.pdf last accessed 31 March 2025.

part way through a case, for example, if Legal Help was initially provided on the basis of a positive reasonable grounds decision, but subsequently the potential victim of exploitation is given a negative conclusive grounds decision and there is no other way of justifying representation.

20.147

In the case of *HJK and Ors v the Director of Legal Aid Casework*[70], the High Court declared that denial of ECF to four victims of trafficking to access legal advice, to prepare an application for criminal injuries compensation, breached their rights under Article 6 of the ECHR.

Legal aid for potential victims of exploitation in immigration detention

20.148

It is common to encounter potential victims of trafficking or exploitation who are detained in an Immigration Removal Centre. All detainees are able to sign up to receive 30 minutes free legal advice from the duty solicitor at advice surgeries that are held regularly (normally a few times per week) at all the detention centres around the UK. The detainees should put their name on the list for legal advice at the library or the welfare office within the detention centre. The 30 minutes advice can be in relation to any immigration/detention matter, even if it is outside the scope. However, if the detainee is signed up for legal aid, the detainee must be financially eligible for legal aid and the legal matter must be a matter that is within scope under LASPO 2012, otherwise ECF must be applied for.

20.149

At present only specific legal aid providers who have an exclusive schedule agreement with the LAA can attend the duty advice surgeries. The exclusive schedule agreement providers are contractually obliged to take on all cases which meet the financial means and merits eligibility requirements. These providers are also allocated the cases of detainees whose asylum claims are being processed in the detained asylum casework process through a rota.

20.150

Only exclusive schedule agreement providers can take on cases for Legal Help and Controlled Legal Representation through the rota or the detention advice

70 [2025] EWHC 774 (Admin).

surgeries[71]. Other than via the detention advice surgeries, detainees can only be represented by a legal aid provider without an exclusive schedule agreement if: (i) the provider has already carried out at least five hours of work on the case; (ii) they already represent a close family member and it is in the detainee's best interests to continue to be represented by that legal aid provider instead of an exclusive schedule agreement provider; or (iii) where there are no exclusive schedule agreements where the person is detained[72]. If the provider has a public law legal aid contract, a detainee could be represented on a Legal Help matter or on a civil certificate (immigration or public law legal aid contract).

Practical steps needed to represent a potential victim of exploitation under legal aid in immigration and public law matters

Legal Help

20.151

In order for an immigration legal representative to begin assisting a potential victim of trafficking, the common starting point is by opening a Legal Help matter so that the legal representative can take initial instructions and give initial advice. The legal aid provider will complete a CW1 form[73] with the client, and once the declaration has been fully understood and signed by the client, the practitioner can open a file and begin work.

Evidence of means

20.152

Detailed guidance as to what evidence of means (evidence of a client's income and savings showing his financial eligibility for legal aid) is required is set out in the Lord Chancellor's guidance on determining financial eligibility for Controlled Work and Family Mediation (May 2025). All practitioners should comply with this guidance[74].

71 2024 Standard Civil Contract Specification: Immigration and Asylum, section 8, para 8.5, available at https://assets.publishing.service.gov.uk/media/682c7be838753e5f0ce8ecfa/8_2024_Immigration_and_Asylum_Category_Specific_Rules_Clean.pdf , last accessed 29 September 2025.

72 2024 Civil Contract Specification: Immigration and Asylum chrome-https://assets.publishing.service.gov.uk/media/66a9ff2d0808eaf43b50da63/4_8_2024_Immigration_and_Asylum_Category_Specific_Rules.pdf last accessed 31 March 2025.

73 CW1 form, available at https://assets.publishing.service.gov.uk/media/679d0312c496e5d3ddafb69e/CW1_form__Version_32_February_2025.pdf, last accessed 22 August 2025.

74 Available at: https://assets.publishing.service.gov.uk/media/682db395a599d03a16bff37b/Lord_Chancellor_s_guide_to_determining_financial_eligibility__Certificated_.pdf (last accessed 3 July 2026).

20.153

Certain individuals are 'passported' and do not require evidence of income (capital must still be assessed) other than evidence that they are in receipt of the passported benefit. The relevant individuals are those directly or indirectly in receipt of Income Support, Income-based Jobseeker's Allowance, Income-related Employment and Support Allowance, Guarantee Credit or Universal Credit. In relation to immigration and asylum category work only, an individual is 'passported' for both income and capital if they are in receipt of S.4 or S.95 Asylum Support[75]. In all other cases, evidence of the potential exploitation victim's income (and their partner's income if necessary) which was received during the exact month prior to the client signing the form (the computation period) is required. For example, bank statements, pay slips and a tenancy agreement. If a potential victim of exploitation has no income and is supported by friends or a third party, a letter of support from the person/third party supporting them should be provided, confirming what support is provided and from when.

20.154

In practice many potential victims of trafficking are destitute or have a very low income, and are likely to be eligible for legal aid. In order to be eligible, after deducting income needed for outgoings for dependants, housing costs and other specified expenses, the individual qualifies if they have £733 per calendar month or less in disposable income and £8,000 or less in capital[76].

20.155

In some cases, a potential victim of exploitation may state that they have no access to any income or capital, and they have no documentary evidence showing this. It would be for the provider to decide and make a detailed note on the file whether such a statement was credible and whether or not it was therefore impracticable to obtain evidence of means.

20.156

A common scenario is for a potential victim of trafficking to instruct his legal representative whilst in prison or detention where they have been detained for the computation period, and the only income received by the client is a small amount of pocket money provided to all those detained/incarcerated. It is not necessary to provide evidence of the income from this pocket money in such cases and an explanation should be provided on the file/legal aid form.

75 Support provided under the Immigration and Asylum Act 1999, s 4 and s 95.

76 Civil Eligibility Key Card, https://www.gov.uk/government/news/civil-legal-aid-eligibility-keycard, last accessed 1 May 2025

20.157

A further common scenario is where a potential victim of trafficking has recently escaped a trafficking situation and it is not practical or safe for them to obtain evidence of any past income. Again, a detailed explanation should be provided on file.

20.158

From 20 November 2024 Modern Slavery Victim Care Contract payments are disregarded when assessing means[77].

Merits

20.159

To open a Legal Help file the provider should be satisfied that there is likely to be sufficient benefit to the individual, having regard to all the circumstances of the case, including the circumstances of the individual, to justify the cost of provision of Legal Help. The test for sufficient benefit is whether a reasonable private paying individual of moderate means would pay for the legal advice and assistance[78].

20.160

The guidance recognises that even in a matter with poor prospects of success, it may well be considered worthwhile for an individual to pay for initial advice, including the advice that the case is not worth pursuing further. The low threshold of the Sufficient Benefit test allows practitioners to open a Legal Help file in most cases in the first instance. However, the Sufficient Benefit test should be continually reviewed as the case continues, as the more Legal Help is provided, the more that the benefits deriving from the costs incurred will need to be taken into account[79].

Controlled Legal Representation

20.161

Controlled Legal Representation ('CLR' or 'Help at Court') may be granted by a legal aid provider to represent a client at the First-tier Tribunal if the

77 The Civil and Criminal Legal Aid (Financial Resources and Contribution Orders) (Amendment) Regulations 2024 https://www.legislation.gov.uk/uksi/2024/1074/made last accessed 31 March 2025

78 Lord Chancellor's Guidance, para 4.2.13, available at https://assets.publishing.service.gov.uk/media/682db395a599d03a16bff37b/Lord_Chancellor_s_guide_to_determining_financial_eligibility__Certificated_.pdf (last accessed 3 July 2026).

79 Lord Chancellor's Guidance, para 4.2.14.

matter is either in scope for legal aid or ECF funding has been granted. There is no statutory right of appeal in the event of negative reasonable grounds or conclusive grounds decision. However, as explained above, the potential victim of exploitation may also have an international protection claim which is inextricably linked to his trafficking claim; and therefore it is common for providers to grant CLR to represent clients at the Tribunal in relation to their protection claim and trafficking claim on this basis.

20.162

Further, although an NRM decision is not an immigration decision, in *MS (Pakistan) v Secretary of State for the Home Department*[80], the Supreme Court held that: the Tribunal is not bound by a previous negative NRM decision; it is not necessary to find public law errors in that decision; and the Tribunal does have jurisdiction to make its own decision on whether an appellant was a victim of trafficking or whether the respondent failed to follow its published policy in making an NRM decision. The proper consideration and weight to be given to a previous NRM competent authority's decision will depend on the nature of that decision and its relevance to the issue before the tribunal.

20.163

The Civil Legal Aid (Remuneration) Regulations 2013[81] and the LAA guidance provide detailed information as to which matters are funded by hourly rates for the work carried out, and which cases are paid by the graduated fixed fee scheme, in addition to how much is payable for profit costs and disbursements. However, the profit costs and disbursements limits for CLR are higher than for Legal Help[82].

20.164

For graduated fixed fee matters in CLR matters, payment is divided into cases that do not use the online procedure: stage 2A (where CLR is granted to prepare an appeal but the matter concludes prior to the substantive hearing) and stage 2B (where a substantive hearing takes place)[83] or cases that do use the online procedure: stage 2C (if the case was opened on or before 6 October 2020), 2D (where case is opened on or after 1 April 2023 and CLR is granted to prepare an appeal but the matter concludes prior to the substantive hearing) and 2E (where case is opened on or after 1 April 2023 and CLR is granted

80 [2020] UKSC 9.

81 https://www.legislation.gov.uk/uksi/2013/422/contents, last accessed on 31 March 2025.

82 Civil Legal Aid (Remuneration) Regulations 2013, Sch 1; 2024 Standard Civil Contract Specification: Immigration and Asylum, section 8, para 8.5, available at https://assets.publishing.service.gov.uk/media/682c7be838753e5f0ce8ecfa/8_2024_Immigration_and_Asylum_Category_Specific_Rules_Clean.pdf, last accessed 22 August 2025.

83 2024 Standard Civil Contract Specification: Immigration and Asylum, section 8, para 8.79, available at https://assets.publishing.service.gov.uk/media/682c7be838753e5f0ce8ecfa/8_2024_Immigration_and_Asylum_Category_Specific_Rules_Clean.pdf, last accessed 22 August 2025.

to prepare an appeal and there is a substantive hearing). CLR can also be granted to represent a detainee at a First-tier Tribunal bail hearing, which is an hourly-rates matter with a limit of £500, including disbursements. The legal aid provider will complete a CW2 IMM form[84] with the potential victim of trafficking, and once the declaration is fully understood and signed by the client, the practitioner can open a file and begin work.

Evidence of means

20.165

The evidence of means required is the same as set out for Legal Help (see paras **20.141–20.143**). Note, however, that for a grant of CLR, the capital savings limit is £3,000, rather than £8,000. The computation period is also one month prior to signing the CW2 IMM form.

Merits

20.166

CLR can only be granted where there is likely to be sufficient benefit to the individual, having regard to all the circumstances of the case, including the circumstances of the individual, to justify the cost of provision of help at court. The nature and circumstances of: (i) the proceedings; (ii) the particular hearing; and (iii) the individual, must be such that advocacy is appropriate and will be of real benefit to that individual[85]. The provider should be satisfied that there is more than a 50-50 chance of success. If a provider deems there is insufficient merit, the provider must advise the client of a right of review to the LAA of the provider's decision and assist him in completing a CW4 form[86].

Legal Help and CLR: extensions, costs limits and experts

20.167

The Civil Legal Aid (Remuneration) Regulations 2013 and the LAA guidance provide detailed information as to which matters are funded by hourly rates for the work carried out and which cases are paid by the graduated fixed fee

84 Available at https://www.gov.uk/government/publications/immigration-clr-disbursement-limit-extension-review-of-refusal, (last accessed 3 July 2026).
85 Civil Legal Aid (Merits Criteria) Regulations 2013, SI 2013/104, reg 33.
86 Available at https://assets.publishing.service.gov.uk/media/679d044360059d127f7adf78/cw4-form.pdf, last accessed 22 August 2025.

scheme, in addition to how much is payable for profit costs and disbursements[87]. A provider will only be paid the fixed fee for a case, even if he has carried out more work than the fixed fee value, unless the work carried out has reached three times the value of the fixed fee, when it will then become payable by hourly rates, subject to being assessed and accepted as the same by the LAA as an 'Escape Fee Case' before payment is approved. In practice, given that many trafficking cases are complex, the clients are vulnerable and it may be necessary to instruct experts, it is common to reach the escape fee threshold.

20.168

Instructing experts to assess potential victims of exploitation and produce expert reports can be crucial to the prospects of success of a case and case planning should always consider whether an expert should be instructed to address any material issue. When representing victims of exploitation, experts that are commonly instructed include psychologists, psychiatrists, scarring experts, country experts and trafficking / exploitation experts. Providers should refer to the detailed LAA guidance on requesting funding for experts before applying for funding for experts on Legal Help and CLR cases[88]. Funding for expert reports in a pre-decision Legal Help case can be difficult to secure, therefore it may be preferable to consider whether funding can be obtained for expert reports after the grant of a legal aid certificate or for a CLR appeal matter.

20.169

Extensions for disbursements in graduated fixed fee cases are applied for via form CW3C, and hourly rates cases via form CW3B. A paper form can be completed and scanned; however, it is envisaged that eventually extensions will only be submitted via the electronic online form. At present, both can be submitted via email to cw3@justice.gov.uk.

Civil legal aid for judicial review

20.170

As there is no right of appeal against a negative reasonable or conclusive grounds decision, providers have to apply for a civil legal aid certificate to fund potential judicial review proceedings to challenge such negative decisions. In addition, there may be many other issues that affect potential victims of exploitation

87 Civil Legal Aid (Remuneration) Regulations 2013, Sch 1; 2018 Standard Civil Contract Specification: Immigration and Asylum, section 8, Part D, available at The Civil Legal Aid (Remuneration) Regulations 2013, last accessed on 6 April 2025.

88 Legal Aid Agency, *Escape Cases Electronic Handbook, Controlled Work* (updated 1 December 2024), available at Escape Case Electronic Handbook V3, last accessed 31 March 2025.

which can be challenged by way of judicial review, as set out in para **20.130**, above.

Evidence of means

20.171

The evidence of means required for an application for a civil legal aid certificate is similar to controlled representation, although providers should refer to the guidance specific to certificated legal aid[89]. Evidence of income and savings for the three months prior to instruction is required, rather than one month. In practice many potential victims of exploitation are destitute or have a very low income, and are likely to be eligible for legal aid. The maximum income threshold per calendar month is still £733; however, if a client earns between £316 and £733 per calendar month, or has capital savings over £3,000, a monthly contribution is payable[90]. The maximum capital savings limit is £8,000.

Merits

20.172

The provider must firstly be satisfied of the standard criteria for determinations of legal representation: that the client could not pay for his legal case by any other means, that the client has exhausted other remedies and that there is a need for legal representation, considering the complexity, the interests of the parties and existence of other proceedings[91]. As many potential victims of exploitation have limited resources, there is no statutory right of appeal against a negative exploitation decision and a judicial review challenge is likely to be complex, the standard criteria for civil legal aid is likely to be met in most cases.

20.173

When the representative has considered the merits of the case, the representative must then decide whether to apply for investigative representation or full representation.

Investigative representation

20.174

Investigative representation is defined as:

89 Legal Aid Agency, *Means Assessment Guidance* (November 2024), available at Means Assessment Guidance, last accessed 31 March 2025.
90 Ibid.
91 Civil Legal Aid (Merits Criteria) Regulations 2013, reg 39.

'legal representation which is limited to the investigation of the strength of the contemplated proceedings and includes the issuing and conducting of proceedings but only so far as necessary:

(a) to obtain disclosure of information relevant to the prospects of success of the proceedings;

(b) to protect the position of the individual or legal person applying for investigative representation in relation to an urgent hearing; or

(c) to protect the position of the individual or legal person applying for investigative representation in relation to the time limit for the issue of the proceedings'[92].

20.175

A legal aid certificate for investigative representation is appropriate in cases where:

(i) the prospects of success of the case are 'unclear' and substantial investigative work is required before those prospects can be determined; and

(ii) there are reasonable grounds for believing that, once the investigative work is completed, the case will satisfy the criteria for full representation (discussed below)[93].

20.176

For a potential judicial review, funding under investigative help would only be granted if the LAA accepts that:

(a) the act, omission or other matter complained of in the proposed proceedings appears to be susceptible to challenge; and

(b) the individual exhausted all administrative appeals and other alternative procedures which are available to challenge the act, omission or other matter before bringing a public law claim[94].

20.177

Before applying for investigative representation, the representative has to notify the proposed defendant of the individual's potential challenge, which can be done by way of a simple early notification letter to the proposed defendant. If this is not done, the representative must provide the LAA with evidence as to why doing so would be impracticable[95].

---

92 Civil Legal Aid (Merits Criteria) Regulations 2013, reg 18(3).
93 Ibid reg 40.
94 Ibid reg 53.
95 Ibid reg 54.

Full representation

20.178

As noted above, it is not possible to issue judicial review proceedings on an investigative representation certificate if the issue under challenge is solely an exploitation matter[96], therefore a full representation legal aid certificate is almost always more appropriate. To meet the merits test for full representation the prospects of success at a final hearing should be:

- 'very good' (80% or more chance of obtaining a successful outcome);
- 'good' (60% or more chance, but less than 80%); or
- 'moderate' (at least 50%, but less than 60%)[97].

20.179

When the prospects of success are borderline (at least 50% chance of success) or poor (20% to 49% chance of success), funding can be granted if it is either:

- necessary to prevent a breach of the individual's Convention rights or their enforceable EU rights to legal services; or
- appropriate to approve funding due to the risk that failing to do so would lead to such a breach.

20.180

When the prospects of success are unclear, funding can be provided if the case meets one of the following criteria:

- it is of significant wider public interest;
- it holds overwhelming importance for the individual involved; or
- the core issue of the case pertains to a breach of Convention rights[98].

20.181

Note the important distinction between 'unclear' merits as opposed to 'borderline' or 'poor' merits. In 'unclear' prospect cases, there must be identifiable preliminary investigations that can be undertaken, after which it should be possible to assess prospects as within one of the other categories. By contrast,

96 Ibid reg 22.

97 Ibid reg 60(3)(a), amended by the Civil Legal Aid (Merits Criteria) (Amendment No 2) Regulations 2015, SI 2015/1571.

98 Ibid reg 60(3)(b), amended by the Civil Legal Aid (Merits Criteria) (Amendment No 2) Regulations 2015.

the prospects of success of a case assessed as borderline may remain uncertain up to a final hearing itself[99].

20.182

The cost benefit criteria must also be met. In many cases, challenging a negative exploitation decision where the claim is not primarily for damages is likely to meet the test of 'overwhelming importance to the individual', and accordingly, the cost benefit criteria is met if the Director of Legal Aid Casework is satisfied that a reasonably private paying individual would pay for the legal services[100]. For damages claims, the specific cost benefit ratio should be satisfied, which is set out in the regulations[101].

Application process

20.183

An application for investigative or full civil legal aid representation is done online via the LAA online portal, Client and Cost Management System ('CCMS')[102]. To complete the application, the client (and their partner, if relevant) would need to attend the representative's office with their evidence relating to their financial eligibility and the merits of his case. At the appointment, the legal representative then uploads all the relevant information and evidence to CCMS with the client, the declarations relating to means and merits must be read to the client and, if they agree, the application is submitted, printed and signed by the client (and their partner, if relevant) at the same appointment.

Emergency certificate

20.184

It is often necessary to apply for an emergency legal aid certificate due to urgency. For example, if a client is detained, if a client has received a notice of a scheduled removal/deportation from the UK (with or without notice), or the limitation period is due to expire. In such circumstances an emergency certificate can be applied for.

20.185

If an urgent decision is required from the LAA within 48 hours then the representative must call the LAA to have the application expedited.

99 Lord Chancellor's Guidance, para 4.1.3
100 Civil Legal Aid (Merits Criteria) Regulations 2013, reg 42(3).
101 Ibid reg 42(2).
102 See https://portal.legalservices.gov.uk, last accessed 22 August 2025.

20.186

Although the judicial review pre-action protocol requires 14 days for the defendant's response it expressly provides that the pre-action protocol will be inappropriate in (genuinely) very urgent cases such as a challenge to removal directions[103]. In such cases, a truncated time for a response would be appropriate if possible.

20.187

If the emergency certificate is granted, it will be to cover all steps up to the decision on permission on the papers, to the value of £2,250. The emergency certificate expires eight weeks after the grant and the representative must ensure that they apply to amend the emergency certificate to a substantive certificate within seven calendar days of the grant of the emergency certificate.

20.188

It should be noted that it is also possible to request that an emergency certificate is backdated, so that a provider can begin working on an urgent matter straight away if it is in the interests of justice to do so. Justification for backdating should be submitted on the CCMS application; however, the legal aid provider should be alive to the financial risks of this, given that the LAA could still refuse to grant the emergency certificate and any work carried out until the provider receives the decision on the emergency certificate is at risk.

Substantive certificate

20.189

A substantive certificate can be applied for either by amending an emergency certificate within seven calendar days of the grant of the emergency certificate, or by applying for a substantive certificate in the first instance. At present, it takes between one week and three weeks to wait for a grant of a substantive certificate. If granted, funding is granted for all steps and all costs (including counsel's fees, disbursements and expert's fees) until a decision on permission on the papers to a value of £5,000.

Declaration against instructions

20.190

As above, a legal aid practitioner representing a potential victim of exploitation should be ready for a potential judicial review from the point of instruction,

103 See https://www.justice.gov.uk/courts/procedure-rules/civil/protocol/prot_jrv, paragraph 6.

and potentially to do so on an emergency basis. For this reason, in addition to completing the relevant legal aid forms with the client at the first interview to enable the representative to assist the client under Legal Help or controlled legal representation, it is also prudent to take the necessary instructions/evidence needed to complete and sign the 'declaration against instructions' form[104]. This is in case it is necessary to apply for investigative or full representation on an emergency or substantive application and the client (or their partner, if relevant) is unable to attend the office for a good reason (for example, if they are hospitalised, imprisoned or detained).

20.191

Before the client (and their partner, if necessary) signs the declaration against instructions, the representative should either have first completed the CCMS means and merits declarations, or have drafted their own attendance note to record the client's information about their means and the merits of their case. This information will be inputted onto CCMS once instructions have been obtained. The signed declaration against instructions will then replace the signature that would usually be obtained on the Application Summary screen on CCMS. In order to ensure the client retains the protection awarded by the existing process, the Application Summary must be sent by the provider to the client, and the client is given 14 days to advise if any of the information is incorrect. If any of the information is incorrect, a further signed declaration should be obtained. The provider should give the required warnings and information as stated in the means and merits declarations to the client. Providers must comply with the full process as set out by the LAA in its guidance[105].

The permission decision, amending scope

20.192

After proceedings are issued and a permission decision on the papers is received, if permission is granted, the provider must pay the continuation fee to the Court and also apply to amend the scope of the legal aid certificate to cover all steps up to and including the full trial. If permission is refused, if the provider is instructed to apply for permission to be heard at an oral renewal hearing, the provider must seek counsel's opinion on prospects of success at an oral renewal hearing. If there are sufficient merits, the provider must apply to amend the scope of the certificate to cover the costs of an oral renewal hearing. Amendments to the scope and costs limit are done on CCMS.

104 See https://cloud-platform-e218f50a4812967ba1215eaecede923f.s3.amazonaws.com/uploads/sites/47/2024/09/CCMS_Client-Declaration-Against-Instructions.pdf, last accessed 22 August 2025.
105 See https://assets.publishing.service.gov.uk/media/69b7eaedba47c264e6c8cfb7/Civil_Finance_Electronic_Handbook_V4.1.pdf.

Experts and extensions of cost limits

20.193

Instructing experts to assess potential victims of exploitation and produce expert reports can be crucial to the prospects of success of a case and case planning should always consider whether an expert should be instructed to address any material issue in the case. The LAA Guidance on the Remuneration of Expert Witnesses[106] introduced new rates for most types of expert, instructed since 2 December 2013. The rates are set out in Annex 1 of the Guidance. The LAA cannot pay fees or rates in excess of those listed in the guidance or the Civil Legal Aid (Remuneration) (Amendment) Regulations 2013 unless the LAA has granted prior authority to exceed the fees or rates. If an expert can be instructed within the existing costs limit on the certificate, it should be within the codified rates at Annex 1 in the guidance and there should be clear justification on the file as to why an expert is needed. If the type of expert is not listed in Annex 1 and/or there are insufficient funds to pay for the expert within the existing cost limit, prior authority should be applied for before instructing the expert. The application to request prior authority or increase the cost limit should be done on CCMS.

Civil legal aid: financial risks

20.194

Unfortunately, the legal aid provider bears a disproportionate financial risk in terms of payment for judicial review cases and all providers should be fully alive to the financial risks they are undertaking by applying for certificated legal aid on behalf of the client. The Civil Legal Aid (Remuneration) Regulations 2013[107] provide that the representative is only paid for the work carried out if:

- the court gives permission to bring judicial review proceedings;
- the court neither gives nor refuses permission, and the LAA considers payment is reasonable in the circumstances: a 'discretionary payment';
- the defendant withdraws the decision to which the application for judicial review relates and the withdrawal results in the court: (a) refusing permission to bring judicial review proceedings; or (b) neither refusing nor giving permission;

106 https://assets.publishing.service.gov.uk/media/67ecea97632d0f88e8248b83/Guidance_on_Remuneration_of_Expert_Witnesses_v11__April_2025_.pdf last accessed 31 March 2025.

107 Regulation 5A, as inserted by the Civil Legal Aid (Remuneration) (Amendment) Regulations 2015, SI 2015/898. The position now generally reflects the previous position, as set out by the Civil Legal Aid (Remuneration) (Amendment) (No 3) Regulations 2014, SI 2014/607, while additionally taking into account the findings of the High Court in *R (on the application of Ben Hoare Bell Solicitors) v The Lord Chancellor* [2015] EWHC 523 (Admin).

- the court orders an oral hearing to consider whether to give permission to bring judicial review proceedings;
- the court orders a rolled-up hearing.

20.195

The financial risk to providers is particularly acute in this area of law where the representative may have to deal with unforeseen circumstances such as a potential victim of exploitation who goes missing/is potentially re-trafficked before judicial review proceedings are concluded. Whether permission is granted in a case or not, particularly with a decision made on the papers, is not necessarily an indication of the merits of the case. In cases where a potential victim of exploitation has gone missing, it may be advisable to seek a stay in proceedings to protect the client's position. However, this creates a difficult financial burden for the representative who has a refusal of permission on papers and is awaiting an oral permission hearing. In such circumstances, the provider cannot expect payment unless the client is encountered and their claim is continued and thereafter a positive permission decision is made. However, if no decision has been made on the papers, it is possible to apply for a discretionary payment (as above). It should also be noted that the provider will be paid for work carried out in relation to applications for interim relief and some disbursements, even if the rest of the work is not paid for under the Civil Legal Aid (Remuneration) Regulations 2013[108].

108 As amended by the Civil Legal Aid (Remuneration) (Amendment) Regulations 2015, regs 2(2) and (3).

21 Professional ethics in legal representation of victims of trafficking and modern slavery

Silvia Nicolaou Garcia and Basmah Sahib

Introduction

21.1

Ethical challenges in human trafficking and modern slavery cases are complex, particularly around the duties of confidentiality, legal professional privilege, and safeguarding when representing potential victims, especially children. Legal practitioners are required to balance the best interests of their clients with obligations to the court and public authorities. Legal practitioners must ensure legal professional privilege (LPP) is not waived without consent. The absolute nature of LPP extends, where applicable, to communications with instructed third parties such as medical experts in legal proceedings.

Legal professional privilege and confidentiality

Definitions and scope of privilege

21.2

Legal advice privilege protects confidential communication between client and lawyer relating to advice, while litigation privilege covers documents and communications produced for litigation. LPP may extend to non-lawyer third parties (eg, medical experts, interpreters, accountants) instructed as part of legal proceedings, if their involvement is necessary for rendering legal advice or conducting litigation. Privilege ensures clients can fully confide in lawyers, maintaining the integrity of justice.

Privilege against self-incrimination

21.3

Clients may refuse to answer questions or produce documents if there is a 'real and appreciable' danger of exposing themselves (or spouses/partners) to prosecution or penalty. Practitioners must advise clients and relevant third parties of this right during interviews and legal processes.

Waiver of privilege and informed consent

21.4

Privilege is generally absolute and can only be waived by the client or overridden by statute. If a third party (such as a medical expert) obtains privileged information under instruction for legal proceedings, they are bound by the same rules; disclosure to external parties is only possible via client waiver or statutory exception, regardless of any personal or professional ethical obligations they may owe.

Communications with third parties

21.5

Not all third-party communications are privileged. The key test is whether the third party (such as a medical expert) is instructed for the dominant purpose of legal advice or litigation. If so, their work and communications regarding the case are privileged and strictly protected. If the third party is providing support or acting independently (eg, as a treating doctor or NGO advocate), privilege generally does not apply; communication is only confidential, not privileged.

- **Instructed expert:** Where a medical expert is commissioned by the legal team to produce a report for use in litigation, and during assessment the child client discloses ongoing abuse or being under control of a trafficker, LPP attaches. The expert cannot disclose such information to authorities (eg, social services, police) absent a client waiver, even in face of serious safeguarding concerns, unless a statutory duty overrides privilege.
- **Other third parties:** Communications with NGOs, interpreters or support workers may be confidential but usually do not meet the criteria for privilege unless strictly within the legal team's litigation/advice preparation remit.

Privilege in multi-jurisdictional proceedings

21.6

Privilege may not always transfer seamlessly between jurisdictions (criminal, immigration, family, civil). Sharing information or documents across these proceedings requires examining whether privilege applies to communication, especially if prepared with third party input. Non-privileged third-party reports may be disclosable unless protected as confidential by other rules.

Risks of unauthorised disclosure

21.7

Unauthorised disclosure of privileged material, including third party expert reports, can constitute contempt of court, professional misconduct, and breach of client's rights. All parties, including non-lawyers who are instructed, must act with care, and practitioners should ensure robust protection is in place when sharing materials, especially with other solicitors and external experts or collaborators.

Child victims and legal professional privilege

Distinguishing privileged vs confidential information

21.8

Communications made for the purpose of obtaining advice for a legal case, including those involving third parties such as instructed medical experts, are protected by legal professional privilege (LPP). Other information imparted to practitioners or support workers that isn't for legal advice or litigation preparation may simply be confidential. Practitioners must clarify and record which category applies to each communication and act accordingly.

Ethical dilemmas in: non-disclosure and missing clients

21.9

A child victim may disclose ongoing abuse/control by traffickers during forensic examination with a medico-legal expert instructed for proceedings but refuses to report this to authorities. If LPP applies, the expert and the legal team cannot report the abuse to authorities unless the client provides consent or statute compels such disclosure. This restriction applies even where the expert's professional code (eg, GMC) encourages or requires reporting suspected ongoing abuse to protect a child at risk. If information is confidential only (not privileged), a balancing exercise can allow disclosure if necessary to prevent 'real, immediate and serious' harm. The Law Society guidance note for solicitors working with victims of modern slavery notes that although there are no specific obligations to the duty of confidentiality, a conflict may sometimes arise between the duty of confidentiality and the ability of a practitioner to act with integrity[1]. The note makes clear that practitioners should consider whether any threat to a child or vulnerable adult's life or health is serious

1 https://www.lawsociety.org.uk/topics/immigration/victims-of-modern-slavery-guidance-for-solicitors.

enough to justify a breach of the duty of confidentiality, not the case for privileged communication, which is absolute.

21.10

The note also recommends that practitioners, as a matter of good practice, should make sure that their retainer with their trafficked client remains effective even in the event that their client goes missing or loses touch with them. They can do this by seeking their client's instructions on what to do in those circumstances, and record this in an attendance note or a witness statement from the client. The case of *TDT v SSHD*[2] was able to proceed in the client's absence.

Capacity and consent in child clients

21.11

This section should be read with **Chapter 3**[3].

21.12

Even when a young person is asked to consider disclosure for the sake of their own safety, the principles of capacity and informed consent remain essential. If a child is *Gillick* competent, or has litigation capacity, they may refuse to disclose to the relevant public authorities, this refusal will bind all parties, including third party experts, where privilege applies. Assessments of competence or capacity should be thoroughly recorded, especially if the child's decision may place them at risk or conflict with safeguarding.

21.13

Practitioners should be familiar with two key concepts when assessing clients who are aged 16 or older: first, that of 'fluctuating capacity', as recognised by the Mental Capacity Act 2005. Second, the possibility that their decision-making capacity is being influenced, not by a mental health condition, but rather by the threat of further trafficking and potential coercion.

Fluctuating capacity

21.14

Looking first at fluctuating mental capacity: post-traumatic stress disorder, and the symptoms associated with this mental health condition, can affect a person's mental capacity. This is examined in detail in **Chapter 3**.

2 [2018] EWCA Civ 1395.

3 Chapter 3: Modern Slavery and Human Trafficking: Trauma-Informed Practice for Legal, Public Authorities and Support Professionals.

21.15

PTSD is the most common mental health condition in this client group (unaccompanied asylum-seeking minors, and victims of trafficking). During a discussion about reporting their traffickers to the police, it is the threat of being re-trafficked that is activating their hypervigilance (which is a symptom of PTSD). Hypervigilance is related to being constantly watchful and misinterpreting signs of threats, such as people who may resemble the traffickers, or indeed are the traffickers. This is why victims avoid talking to others, going out and experience sleepless nights (they are hyper-alert to any noise that could indicate the traffickers have found them). This is especially the case for young people who had little sense of safety growing up in situations of abuse, destitution, war or insurgence, with little access to any structured support, in the form of education for example. It is immediately apparent how this hypervigilance could temporarily interfere with a young person's decision-making capacity (for example, perceiving their traffickers as a greater, insurmountable threat than they in fact are) in the specific context of consenting to disclosure.

21.16

Other symptoms associated with PTSD, like hyperarousal and dissociation, interfere with young people's ability to concentrate and remember, which is why they may not retain information to make informed decisions leading to a finding that capacity is impaired or fluctuates depending on how rested the young person is.

21.17

If a legal representative encounters difficulty in assessing a client's litigation capacity, they may seek assistance from expert witnesses to help determine it. As outlined in Chapter 3, professional conduct issues may arise where a client does not have capacity to provide instructions.

Presence of coercion and control

21.18

As for the presence of coercion and control, practitioners should bear in mind the role of the High Court, which retains its inherent jurisdiction to make a broad range of decisions (including, in theory, consenting to third party disclosure) in circumstances where a child is unable to make that decision themselves; or where a capacitous adult is rendered vulnerable and unable to make the decision due to the impact of coercion and control by their traffickers (see Munby J's ruling in *Re SA (Vulnerable Adult with capacity: Marriage)*[4]).

4 [2005] EWHC 2942 (Fam), at [77].

21.19

Such applications to the High Court should be a remedy of last resort, due to the inevitable distress of disclosure without the otherwise capacitous young person's consent, which is why practitioners should rely on trauma-informed techniques to obtain consent in the first instance (see Chapter 3).

21.20

Second, such an application would be novel. Case law containing examples of instances where the High Court's inherent jurisdiction has been used relates predominantly to contact (as opposed to disclosure) decisions made by High Court judges on behalf of vulnerable victims of domestic abuse. As such, an application concerning a victim of trafficking, and the need for disclosure, would, at the time of writing, be the first of its kind, and it is consequently unclear how the High Court would deal with it. This is examined further below.

21.21

Given the risks that can arise for minors who have been trafficked, held in slavery or subjected to related harms, legal representatives should be proactive in securing an Independent Child Trafficking Guardian for a young person (see **Chapter 5**). This measure can significantly reduce the risk of a young person going missing or being subjected to further trafficking, slavery or related harms. An Independent Child Trafficking Guardian can act as a Litigation Friend.

Children, trafficking, modern slavery[5] and the protective obligations under Art 4 ECHR

21.22

It is arguable that the protective obligations arising under Art 4 ECHR require consistent and effective safeguards for children across legal jurisdictions, particularly where there is *prima facie* evidence of trafficking or other abuses within the scope of Art 4. The recurring pattern of trafficked children going missing further underscores the need for these obligations to be actively engaged. The positive duties imposed by Art 4 are examined in detail in **Chapters 4, 5, 14,** and **16**.

Litigation friend and the role of the Independent Child Trafficking Guardian

21.23

In cases involving children who may have been trafficked, held in slavery or related harms, early referral to an Independent Child Trafficking Guardian

5 This encompasses slavery, servitude and forced or compulsory labour (see **Chapter 1**).

(ICTG) is essential. Such a referral ensures that decisions concerning the child's protection, recovery, and safety are made with their best interests at the forefront. It may also facilitate disclosure by helping the child feel sufficiently safe and supported (see **Chapters 3** and **5**). Notably, an ICTG may act as a litigation friend and, where necessary, provide instructions on a best interests' basis, within the limits of statutory and safeguarding frameworks.

21.24

As discussed in **Chapter 8**, the appointment of a litigation friend involves granting broad authority to act on behalf of a party, including the power to initiate or settle proceedings, or to influence their conduct. As Lord Justice Underhill observed in *AM (Afghanistan)*[6], this authority enables the litigation friend to 'dispose of a party's legal rights, either directly by bringing and/or compromising proceedings, or indirectly by the way in which he or she conducts those proceedings.'

21.25

Such an appointment should be seen in the context that in civil proceedings, the default position is that a litigation friend must conduct proceedings on behalf of a child. In family proceedings, unless the court directs otherwise, children are similarly required to have a litigation friend to act on their behalf.

21.26

Where a referral to an ICTG is refused, consideration should be given to whether that decision is amenable to judicial review. It is likely that the judicial review would be against the Secretary of State for the Home Department in light of the statutory duties to make arrangements for ICTG (see section 48 of the Modern Slavery Act 2015. This may require representations to be made to the Secretary of State for the Home Department requesting that the refusal be reconsidered and request that specific arrangements be made for the appointment of an ICTG, particularly where such an appointment would enable the ICTG to act as litigation friend. If relevant and material the facts of the case, it may require confirming to the SSHD that this measure is required under the UK's Art 4 protective obligations. A refusal to make such arrangements may itself be subject to judicial review. It may be necessary to identify and explain why that role or responsibilities of an ICTG cannot be met by another public authority (ie local authority under their statutory duties).

21.27

In any such challenge, regard should be had to the judgment of Chamberlain J in *KP v Secretary of State for Foreign, Commonwealth and Development Affairs*[7],

6 *AM (Afghanistan) v SSHD* [2017] EWCA Civ 1123.
7 [2025] EWHC 370 (Admin).

where it was emphasised that the intensity of substantive judicial review depends on the significance of the interests at stake and the gravity of the potential consequences. Where a decision threatens interests of substantial moral or legal weight, such as the safety, dignity, or welfare of vulnerable individuals, a heightened standard of scrutiny is required. This is not contingent upon the existence of a formal legal right, but rather on the seriousness of the harm potentially caused by the impugned decision.

21.28

In circumstances where no ICTG is available and no alternative mechanism exists to secure a litigation friend, consideration may be given, as a measure of last resort, to an application to the High Court to exercise its inherent jurisdiction to ensure the child's protection and welfare. In such cases, the relief sought may mirror the functions of an ICTG, particularly where it can be demonstrated that the necessary functions fall outside the scope of the Children Act 1989.

21.29

An application to invoke the High Court's inherent jurisdiction would be made under Practice Direction 12D. The court may, in exercising this jurisdiction, make any order or determine any issue in respect of a child, unless expressly limited by statute or binding authority. However, such proceedings should not be commenced unless the issues concerning the child's welfare cannot be adequately addressed under the Children Act 1989. The Court of Appeal has confirmed that it is possible to make a child a ward of court even where they are accommodated under s 20 of the Children Act 1989.

21.30

A frequently cited articulation of the inherent jurisdiction is found in the judgment of Lord Denning MR in *re L (An Infant)*[8] where he said:

> 'It derives from the right and duty of the Crown as parens patriae to take care of those who are not able to take care of themselves. The Crown delegated this power to the Lord Chancellor, who exercised it in his Court of Chancery. … the Court of Chancery had power to interfere for the protection of the infant by making whatever order might be appropriate. … This wide jurisdiction of the old Court of Chancery is now vested in the High Court of Justice and can be exercised by any judge of the High Court.'

21.31

Lord Eldon LC in *Wellesley v Duke of Beaufort* (1827) 2 Russ 1, p 18 said this:

8 [1968] P 119, at 156.

'… it has always been the principle of this Court, not to risk the incurring of damage to children which it cannot repair, but rather to prevent the damage being done.'

21.32

As Lady Black observed in the matter of *T (A Child) (Appellant)*[9] at [67]–[68]:

> 'The inherent jurisdiction has had to rise to the challenge of some of the most extreme human and moral dilemmas imaginable, a notable example of this in relatively recent times being In re A (Children) (Conjoined Twins: Surgical Separation) [2001] Fam 147. As Lord Donaldson of Lymington MR said in *re F (Mental Patient: Sterilisation)* [1990] 2 AC 1, p 13 (in a passage approved by the House of Lords on appeal):
>
>> 'the common law is the great safety net which lies behind all statute law and is capable of filling gaps left by that law, if and in so far as those gaps have to be filled in the interests of society as a whole. This process of using the common law to fill gaps is one of the most important duties of the judges.'
>
> The route by which the assistance of the High Court, acting under its inherent jurisdiction, was commonly sought (including by local authorities) used to be by means of wardship proceedings. This no doubt explains the heading to section 100, which can be found set out in the next paragraph below. However, this was, as Lord Denning succinctly put it in In re L, 'only machinery', and the court could exercise its inherent jurisdiction without the child being made a ward.

Professional duties and withdrawal

21.33

Conflicts between legal professional privilege and a third party's regulatory obligations, such as a doctor's safeguarding duties under GMC guidance, can present significant ethical dilemmas. Where privilege prohibits disclosure, professionals must uphold its absolute nature and consider whether to withdraw from the case or seek guidance (for example, from the Solicitors Regulation Authority's Professional Ethics Helpline or the Bar Council's Ethical Enquiries line). In respect of children, the steps identified above should be contemplated first, to ensure that the best interests of the child are central to decision making.

9 *In the matter of T (A Child) (Appellant)* [2021] UKSC 35.

21.34

Nonetheless, practitioners are not precluded from discussing with a capacitous (or competent) client the potential benefits of voluntary disclosure to a third party. For instance, if a young person expresses concerns about their safety following a police disclosure, particularly in relation to protection from traffickers or abusers, an informal, pre-interview meeting with the police, or a multi-agency meeting involving the police and local authority, may help to reassure them. There is nothing preventing the solicitor from proposing and facilitating such a meeting, with the client's informed consent, at their own offices (which the young person may perceive as a safe, neutral space). This preliminary step may reduce the apprehension associated with making a formal police complaint.

21.35

Practitioners should carefully document the nature of the conflict, seek appropriate guidance, and record their reasoning, while maintaining privilege unless it is expressly waived by the client or overridden by statute.

Practical steps

21.36

Practical points for practitioners and the instructed third parties:

- **Determine privilege:** Clarify whether communications with third parties in a legal matter are privileged or merely confidential.
- **Seek consent:** Strive to obtain informed client consent for necessary disclosures, explaining risks and benefits to the client.
- **Assess mental capacity, or *Gillick* competence:** While the assessment for *Gillick* competence in children aged 15 or younger is less formal, practitioners should familiarise themselves with the requirements of litigation capacity assessments as outlined in the Mental Capacity Act 2005 for clients aged 16 and older (see Chapters 3 and 8). Attendance notes should be kept which reference concepts such as the presumption of capacity, as well as the responses given by the young person to specific questions raised as part of the capacity assessment.
- **Either make a decision in their best interests or consider the role of the High Court:** For those clients lacking litigation capacity, a decision should be made in accordance with their best interests and with the involvement of their litigation friend and/or guardian. For capacitous adults who are vulnerable due to coercion and control, an application to the High Court should be considered as a last resort.

- **Limit disclosure:** Where disclosure is ethically justified (in relation to confidential, non-privileged information), restrict to what is strictly necessary and only inform appropriate authorities.
- **Record keeping:** Meticulously document all steps, including discussions with child clients, experts' decisions, and advice sought from senior colleagues or regulatory bodies.
- **Withdrawal:** If irreconcilable conflict arises between privilege and other duties, consider withdrawal from the matter by both the legal team and the expert, maintaining confidentiality and privilege.

Advising clients on referrals to the national referral mechanism: ethical and procedural considerations

21.37

Chapter 4 of this book examines the legal framework and operational processes of the National Referral Mechanism (NRM), the UK's system for identifying potential victims of human trafficking and modern slavery. For the purposes of this chapter, the focus is on the ethical and professional considerations that may arise when advising a client about a potential referral into the NRM.

21.38

A number of overarching points should be noted:

- First, as explained in **Chapter 4**, legal representatives do not have standing to refer clients directly into the NRM. Only designated First Responders are authorised to make such referrals. However, legal representatives may approach a First Responder on behalf of a potential victim to initiate the referral process.
- Secondly, informed consent is central to any referral. Ensuring that the client can give informed consent is essential, and a trauma-informed approach should be adopted throughout (see Chapter 3). In some cases, the client may still be in a situation of exploitation, and disclosures made during instructions may be protected by legal professional privilege (see above).
- Thirdly, the position is more complex in relation to child clients. A First Responder does not require a child's informed consent to make a referral into the NRM, as the process is primarily a safeguarding measure. Nonetheless, it remains important that legal representatives seek the child's views and explain the process in an age-appropriate and trauma-informed manner.

21.39

Misunderstandings frequently arise regarding consent and NRM referrals. While adult victims must provide informed consent before a referral can be made, it is good practice for legal representatives to obtain consent from both adult and child clients before approaching a First Responder. Disclosing information to a First Responder without such consent may breach the duty of confidentiality owed to the client[10].

Clients facing criminal proceedings: balancing protection and risk

21.40

Where a potential victim of trafficking or modern slavery is also facing criminal charges, the decision to initiate an NRM referral raises additional ethical considerations. Practitioners should be aware that all information disclosed during the NRM process, including confession evidence, is disclosed to the police[11] and may be admissible in subsequent criminal proceedings. For example, statements made in NRM forms or during the referral process may be relied upon in court. This underscores the importance of advising clients carefully and ensuring that any referral is made with full awareness of the potential legal consequences.

21.41

Disclosure of information about traffickers may expose the client to significant risk, and this must be carefully assessed. The client's age is a critical factor: consent is required for referrals involving individuals over 18, but not for those under 18. Where age is uncertain, it is generally appropriate to accept the client's stated age unless there is a clear reason to question it. If an age assessment later determines that the client is an adult, the issue may need to be revisited (see Chapter 6).

21.42

While a defence under the Modern Slavery Act 2015 does not require an NRM referral, such a referral may provide supporting evidence for the defence or prompt a review of a decision to prosecute[12]. This is particularly relevant where evidence of trafficking exists in the form of intelligence about

10 See para 6.3 of Code of Conduct for Solicitors.

11 Modern Slavery: statutory guidance for England and Wales (under s49 of the Modern Slavery Act 2015) and non-statutory guidance for Scotland and Northern Ireland (accessible version) – GOV.UK, last accessed on 15 October 2025 at Annex B.

12 See **Chapter 10**, *VCL and AN v UK* and CPS guidance, Crown Prosecution Service, *Modern Slavery and Human Trafficking: Offences and Defences, including the section 45 defence* (Legal Guidance, updated 22 July 2025) <https://www.cps.gov.uk/legal-guidance/modern-slavery-and-human-trafficking-offences-and-defences-including-section-45-defence> accessed 15 October 2025.

organised criminal networks. Given the challenges defence practitioners may face in gathering such evidence independently, the balance may favour making a referral. Where there are different strands of litigation it is important to act in a co-ordinated way, albeit ensuring that this is done with the client's consent.

Police interviews and ethical considerations

21.43

This should be read alongside **Chapters 3** and **11**.

21.44

Ethical issues arise where there is evidence, information, or client instructions indicating that the individual may have been trafficked. This includes situations where the client may have been both a victim and a perpetrator, such as being compelled to traffic others within a criminal network.

21.45

Guidance issued by the National College of Policing on 28 July 2015[13], following the implementation of the Modern Slavery Act 2015, addresses this complex victim/perpetrator paradigm. It states:

> 'If a person is arrested and so enters the criminal justice system as a perpetrator, and officers discover through the police interview under caution that the person committed a modern slavery offence through coercion and may also be a victim, the interview should continue and evidence should be obtained. On conclusion of the interview the person should be referred through the NRM if they consent.'

21.46

The guidance further recognises that the roles of victim, witness, and suspect may be interchangeable in the context of modern slavery and human trafficking[14]. Legal representatives must therefore be alert to the possibility that a client's involvement in criminal conduct may have occurred under coercion or exploitation.

21.47

In such cases, legal representatives must carefully consider whether disclosure of coercion in the commission of a trafficking offence could influence the decision

13 Modern Slavery, National College on Policing (2015), available at: Modern slavery | College of Policing, last accessed on 31 March 2025.

14 P Ahluwalia, 'Poacher Turned Gamekeeper' (2015) 3 *CBQ* 5.

to charge. This requires a nuanced understanding of the client's legal position, the potential for a s 45 defence under the Modern Slavery Act 2015, and the implications of any referral to the National Referral Mechanism (NRM).

21.48

For further discussion of ethical considerations at the police station stage, see **Chapter 11**.

21.49

The role and responsibilities of the police and prosecution under Arts. 4 and 6 of the ECHR, where a person discloses that they are a victim of trafficking, slavery or related harms for criminal exploitation is examined in **Chapter 10**. In short, the police may not have discharged their obligations under Art 4 ECHR if they refer the suspect to the NRM and take no further steps to investigate the Art 4 allegation.

Conclusion

21.50

In human trafficking and modern slavery cases, obligations of confidentiality and legal professional privilege must be strictly observed for all parties, including third party experts instructed for proceedings. Practitioners must exercise vigilance, clearly distinguishing between privileged and confidential information in relation to third parties and act accordingly. Where privilege conflicts with external professional duties (for example, a doctor's safeguarding obligations), the law maintains the primacy of privilege, and professionals must adhere to these standards, seeking consent or statutory authority before disclosure.

Index

[all references are to paragraph number]